At B&W, music is our very reason for being. In our search for the perfect music reproduction, the B&W Nautilus, has pioneered technologies such as the hollow pole magnet drivers and the transmission pipe principle, which will shape the direction of the audio industry well into the next millennium.

It symbolises all the innovation, dedication and love of music which have inspired B&W engineers ever since the company was established 30 years ago.

In the search for transparency of sound, the Nautilus represents a true audio miracle. It can only be limited or coloured by the source, amplifiers and cables, without any colouration of its own.

Hailed as 'the best loudspeaker that money can buy', the Nautilus enables the listener to hear nuances and subtle dynamics hitherto unattainable, offering a level of sonic accuracy unmatched by any other speaker.

The Nautilus offers a unique chance to hear music exactly as recorded – detailed, vibrantly alive, full of power and unhindered by driver distortion or cabinet diffraction.

Listen and you'll see!

*The B&W Nautilus is absolutely the most ideal speaker I have ever heard. It can be limited or coloured by the sources, amplifiers and cables, without any coloration of its own. This is the best loud-speaker that money can buy – Hi-Fi Review Japan*

*Special award for component of the year – Stereo Sound Japan*

*Special award for Grand Prix component of the year– Radio Gijutsu Japan*

### DM601
The 601s sound like
the voice coils of God.

### CDM1
For a domestic loud-
speaker that knows how
to groove, our European
Award is an honestly-
bestowed plaudit.

### P4
These classy British
boxes leave you in
no doubt either physi-
cally or sonically about
how your money's
being spent.

B&W's patented method
of using Kevlar for loud-
speaker cones, has been
a major factor in reduc-
ing unwanted standing
waves. Kevlar's unique
woven fibres along with
further 'doping' by B&W
provide a remarkably
near perfect solution
to this problem.

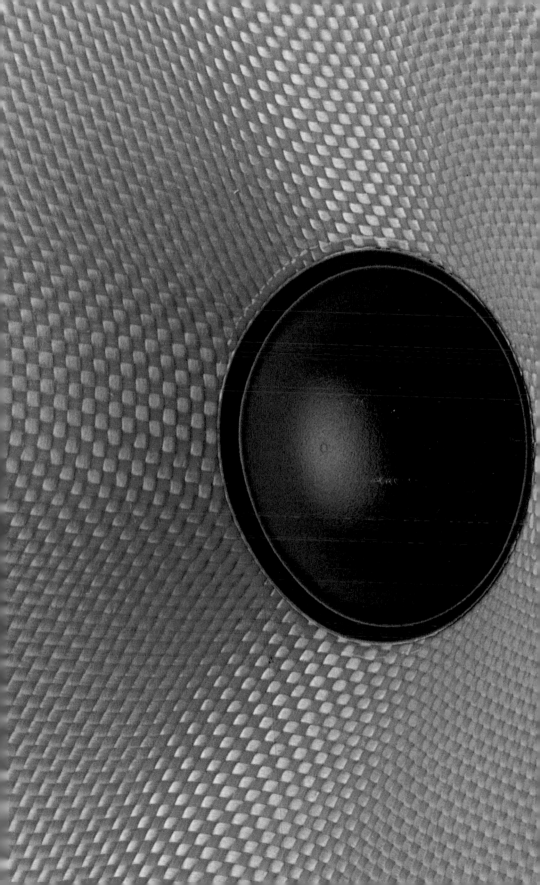

The result for the problem of resonances inside budget speaker cabinets is B&W's Prism construction. The solution involves a series of tapered wedges on the rear panel. Sound waves reflect off these wedges in a random fashion, reducing the build up of resonances and so contributes to clearer, uncoloured sound.

prism system®

B&W

DM302

European loudspeaker
of the year 1996/97

WHAT HI·FI?

This is a hard-nut
speaker, but it's edu-
cated and decisive too.
Dynamic and controlled
– there's not a lot to
touch it at the price.

# *Listen and you'll see*

For more information please contact:-
B&W Loudspeakers (UK) Ltd +44(0)1903 750 750
B&W Loudspeakers of America (508) 664 2870
http://www.bwspeakers.com.

# Gramophone

# JAZZ

## GOOD CD GUIDE

*Gramophone* magazine, founded by the novelist and writer Compton Mackenzie and the broadcaster Christopher Stone, has been published monthly since 1923. As one of the first magazines devoted to the discussion of recorded music, *Gramophone* has maintained its position as the most informed and influential publication of its kind. Calling on the wealth of talent of a panel of the world's leading writers on music, *Gramophone* is the record collector's bible and it is from these writers and in the tradition of *Gramophone* that this book is published. Each month the magazine carries over 200 reviews of music across a wide spectrum and talks to the leading performers of the day. We are delighted to be publishing the *Jazz Good CD Guide* in association with a fellow British company, B&W Loudspeakers, whose dedication to producing fine loudspeakers closely matches the ideals of *Gramophone* itself: expertise drawing on experience, consistency and an awareness of the requirements of the consumer.

Published by

**Gramophone Publications Limited,
135 Greenford Road,
Sudbury Hill, Harrow,
Middlesex HA1 3YD, Great Britain.**

| | |
|---|---|
| Editor | **Keith Shadwick** |
| Production | **Dermot Jones** |
| Design | **Dinah Lone** |
| Contributors | **Ronald Atkins** |
| | **Chuck Berg** |
| | **Bob Blumenthal** |
| | **Linton Chiswick** |
| | **Francis Davis** |
| | **Dave Gelly** |
| | **Mark Gilbert** |
| | **Simon Hopkins** |
| | **Miles Kington** |
| | **Art Lange** |
| | **Graham Lock** |
| | **Barry McRae** |
| | **Alun Morgan** |
| | **Chris Parker** |
| | **Brian Priestley** |
| | **Ben Ratliff** |
| | **Tony Russell** |
| | **Keith Shadwick** |
| | **Alyn Shipton** |
| | **Steve Voce** |
| | **Kevin Whitehead** |
| Editorial Director | **Christopher Pollard** |

© **Gramophone Publications Limited 1997**

UK ISBN 0 902470 79 5

USA ISBN 0 902470 80 9

## Sales and distribution

North America

**Music Sales Corporation**
257 Park Avenue South,
New York, NY 10010, USA.
**Telephone** (212) 254 2100
**Fax** (212) 254 2013

UK and Rest of World Record trade

**Gramophone Publications Limited**
135 Greenford Road, Sudbury Hill, Harrow,
Middlesex HA1 3YD, Great Britain.
**Telephone** +44 (0)181-422 4562
**Fax** +44 (0)181-869 8404

UK and Rest of World Book trade

**Music Sales**
8/9 Frith Street,
London W1V 5TZ
**Telephone** +44 (0)171-434 0066
**Fax** +44 (0)171-734 2246

Cover illustration **Zia Hall**
Printed in England by **William Clowes Limited**,
Beccles, Suffolk, NR34 9QE.

# Contents

# Introduction

**Keith Shadwick**

Although the first acknowledged jazz recording was not made until 1917, over a decade after Enrico Caruso began his spectacular recording career and over two decades after Edison's cylinders began the era of recorded sound, the music itself is not far off its centenary. That makes it a good time to be compiling a reference book such as the one you are holding in your hands; the perspective gained is inevitably more long-term, the judgement more dispassionate and less amateur the further the music being discussed is from our own times.

But this book does not just deal with music over 50 years old, either in deed or spirit: the jazz of every age and style is discussed on the ensuing pages. The team chosen to make the recommendations is a carefully balanced one, with writers allowed to choose the artists they are interested in writing about, from the Original Dixieland Jazz Band to recent CD débutees such as Jeremy Davenport and Jacqui Dankworth. One aspect of the team's composition about which I am particularly pleased is that I am gratified that so many of the authors from both sides of the Atlantic whose writing I personally admire consented to be involved in this project.

## Aims of the Guide

The basic premise of this Guide is that the average person interested in jazz doesn't have a kaleidoscopic knowledge of – or even an interest in – every current jazz release worldwide. They have their firm favourites they'd like to follow up on some more; they also have players they are getting interested in and would like some guidance on. That's where the Guide steps in, because in the majority of cases we recommend a single title made by that artist as being a good summation of their output. There are cases where the current selection of CDs by a given player is not very strong, so the critic concerned has graded accordingly. In some instances he has also suggested a currently unavailable album to look out for when it finally makes it onto CD. With players who have had a more widespread effect on the music, the Guide has multiple entries which give an accurate and balanced perspective on each particular career as it is currently reflected on CD. A good example is Duke Ellington, who has 12 entries here. So that the reader gets a multi-faceted outlook on these artists, rather than the same point of view – however favourable – no critic writes more than one entry about any given artist. This gives us (to take the Ellington example) the following writers giving their insights and opinions on different Ellington achievements: Chuck Berg, Bob Blumenthal, Francis Davis, Dave Gelly, Graham Lock, Barry McRae, Alun Morgan, Brian Priestley, Ben Ratliff, Alyn Shipton, Steve Voce, Kevin Whitehead and me. This diversity of opinion can only be a good thing in building up an accurate picture of what is the best currently available on the Duke Ellington front.

## A word about scope

In a reference book such as this, one of the most fundamental issues to be grappled with is: where are the lines which, once transgressed, declare us to be in non-jazz territory? All solutions to this question, however they are couched, are finally going to be subjective and based on a private set of criteria. The rule of thumb applied by me to this book is: does it feel like jazz? Does the performer have an interpretation of the material to hand which has roots in the basic tenets of the jazz tradition? A positive reply to these questions has given this book an exceptionally wide scope, applied to each of this century's jazz decades, and allowed a number of perhaps marginal performers to be included (many critics would argue that Glenn Miller, for example, has no place in this Guide). If your eyebrows are raised by any of the names you come across, I can only suggest that you have a close listen to the disc being reviewed, and perhaps the reason for its inclusion will then become clear.

## New releases, deletions and title availability

One of the problems which lies beyond our control in the compiling of this book is the availability of titles on an international basis. Many titles, especially those owned by the major multi-national companies, are available in some territories and not in others. Thus an album can be released in, say, France, but never released in the UK or the USA. This doesn't necessarily mean that it is completely unavailable in those countries, but that it is available only as an import and therefore invariably it will be harder to find and more expensive when you do find it. The other problem brought about specifically by the larger companies is one of deletions: while an album can be available in, say, the USA for a number of years after its initial release, it could well be deleted by the domestic UK company (and vice versa).

When it comes to the smaller independents, the problems are simpler, but no less frustrating: with albums released by these companies, availability is usually sustained for much greater lengths of time, but it is unconscionably difficult to find a copy of the desired title outside of the specialist shops and mail order firms, due to local distribution deals and the reluctance of the larger retailers to carry constant stocks of slower-moving back-catalogue items from small companies.

All of this lies outside our control, but I can at least affirm that at the time of going to press, every item in this book was currently domestically available either in the USA or in Europe (or, most happily, both). For precisely the availability problems mentioned above, Japanese releases have not been included unless they have been made available domestically in the USA or Europe. Conversely, if there is an artist missing from this Guide (and I am aware of many), the most common (although not only) reason is the simple non-availability of their work on CD, however many LPs or MCs may still be around.

It may strike some readers as unrealistic highmindedness, but I have also ruled out all CDs which are self-evident 'pirate releases': albums or performances stolen from other companies or owners and released in a country with vague or non-existent copyright laws, then exported elsewhere. As the artists and their heirs benefit not one jot from such releases, and have never sanctioned the release of such material, it will not be brought to your attention here. Should you want to buy such discs, then I am sure you will seek them out anyway, without our help.

### Acknowledgements

In a book of this nature, the editor invariably relies on the goodwill and co-operation of a great many people. In this imperfect world it has come as a genuinely pleasant surprise that so many people connected with the music and recording industries have been so helpful during the gestation period. There is not room enough to thank everyone, but those below have helped more than their jobs called upon them to:

Record companies/distributors: Steve Sanderson and Kerstan Mackness at New Note Distribution; Amadu Sowe and Gaylene Martin at Coalition; Wendy Furness and Jo Pratt at EMI (UK); Trevor Mainwaring at Harmonia Mundi; Phil Knox-Roberts and Andrea Gibbs at Warners; Adam Sieff and Sharon Kelly at Sony/Columbia (UK); Amanda England at EFZ; Mike Cox at Discovery Imports (UK), Becky Stevenson and Michael Lang at PolyGram (UK and US); Grainne Devine at BMG/Conifer (UK); Tony Williams at Spotlite; Terri Hinte at Fantasy Group; Don Lucoff at DL Media/Blue Note (US); Monique Walker at GRP/Impulse! (US); Laurie Staff at Topic/Direct; Noreen Allen at Sequel; Helen Moore and Jeremy Elliott at Complete Record Co; John Jack at Cadillac; Amjad Ali at Stash; Jennifer Dirkes at Delmark; Peter Jacobsen at VSOP Records; Alistair Robertson at Hep; Joe Fields at Muse; John Steadman at JSP.

Interested and disinterested parties: Sid Whelan and Jay Hoffman (New York), who were as helpful, courteous and painstaking as they were when the first edition of the Guide was compiled; Peter Fincham at Mole Jazz, London, for his knowledge, resourcefulness and unflappable good humour in many last-minute situations; Steve Voce for his always fair and careful opinions on a whole range of matters, plus his generous help beyond the call of duty on the editorial front; Barry McRae for ingenious solutions to many intractable problems; Alun Morgan and Art Lange for unfailing help and courtesy; Dermot Jones, Ivor Humphreys, Emma Roach, Mairé Taylor, Mark Walker and Dinah Lone at *Gramophone* for their sheer professionalism.

# Using the guide

I have endeavoured to keep the terminology and symbols as simple as possible, so that there are no artificial barriers erected between the reader and the text. Being someone who has extreme difficulty with anything not intended to be interpreted literally in a reference book, I have kept closely to the notion that simple = good, complex = bad. Therefore, in a normal entry, there will be a typical amount of basic information which the reader can expect. The leader, album title, record company and catalogue number, personnel and recording date are invariably given, but I have also included the following: the number of discs (where there is more than one); running time; performance and recording quality rating (from one to ten); a symbol to indicate membership of the Basic Jazz Library (most don't have this, because most aren't essential purchases if you are starting a jazz collection); price guide (budget, mid and full price are the three most common categories used here). I give an example here in elucidation:

## John Coltrane
1926-1967

---

**A Love Supreme** Coltrane (ts); **McCoy Tyner** (p); **Jimmy Garrison** (b); **Elvin Jones** (d).
MCA/Impulse! Ⓜ GRD 155 (33 minutes). Recorded 1964.

Thereafter follows the critique. Every entry is initialled, so that the reader can quickly establish just who is giving these pithy opinions.

Considering the dangers of grading anything, from ball bearings to olive oil, a few words about the gradings applied here may not go astray:

- ⑩ a well-nigh perfect representation of what the artist concerned is on about. In the vast majority of cases, the artist also has something significant to say.
- ⑨ a highly satisfying and significant album which though not perhaps the best-ever example of the artist-in-question's work. There may be a drawback in the recording which prevents it from being included in the above category.

⑧ a fine example of the artist's output, and a superior effort all round. Can be purchased with confidence.

⑦ a very good album of its kind, although it is probable that the average album in this category is not particularly ambitious in conception.

⑥ a good album with nothing much wrong with it at all, but probably lacking that extra spark which pushes you to the edge of your seat in excited anticipation as the bars tick by.

⑤ a fair album with good points to it, but with weaknesses or periods of mediocrity within its playing time.

④ a passingly fair album, but one with obvious problems. It will probably fail to give much satisfaction to the uninitiated. One for the curious or the faithful only.

③ a poor album, incompetently executed and thoughtlessly assembled.

② an unworthy effort which should be avoided.

① or less: beware! You could be in for a serious waste of money.

Considering that this is a guide to the best CDs currently available, the incidence of albums under ⑥ is relatively low, and there is nothing here which rates a zero (although there are a handful with a reference to the text below), but the categories are explained for completeness's sake.

There is a mirror grading which applies to recording quality as well, and I think the general comments above can also happily apply to this aspect. At all times, critics have graded the recording quality with a mind to the fact that a great deal of the music was recorded in less than DDD sound in the first place. What we have attempted to do is grade according to the original sound quality and (where applicable) the relative success (or lack of it) of the digital transfers to the new medium.

## Recording dates

A brief explanation of date usage. Where a CD is compiled from music recorded in more than one year, a glance at the form of separation used between the dates quoted will reveal some date information. For example, 1934/38 means that there are performances from those two years on the disc in question. A marking of 1934-38 means that there are performances from those two years, plus other years in between these dates.

## The price guide

It is as well to point out at this stage that, although we have attempted accuracy in all aspects of this Guide, pricing can vary dramatically from one country to another, and often even within the same country, state or town. Sometimes even the same shop will have two copies of the same album at two different price levels. Our pricing indicators are based on information passed on to us either by the record companies themselves or their official representatives in Britain or America.

Ⓕ Full price
Ⓜ Medium price
Ⓑ Budget price

## Appendices

Apart from the review section, this book also includes reference sections designed to help the reader to locate discs in which they become interested. Hence we have a list of labels and their distributors, addresses of the main UK jazz distributors, a list of recommended specialist UK dealers, an index and a Basic Jazz Library, which is explained below.

## Basic jazz library

✔ There are albums (and before them, shellac discs) in the history of this music which undoubtedly stand as cornerstones in its evolution; some of them because they were the high-water marks of a particular artist or epoch of significance, others because they signal the beginning of something new and exciting. To help the user of this Guide build a balanced and comprehensive selection of jazz on CD with the fewest number of titles, I have built into this book a designation: Basic Jazz Library. This library was chosen by the critics who wrote the reviews as they wrote those reviews, and so the titles in the Library chose themselves. Each designated title has a Basic Jazz Library moniker by it, but for quick reference purposes I have extrapolated all such entries into a separate list which appears overleaf. Of course, no two people will agree on what should constitute such a library, but this list reflects the informed opinion of 21 jazz writers.

## The Mosaic question

Mosaic is a US mail-order company which, over the past decade or so, has made available some great jazz treasures of the past. However, all their boxed sets are collectors' editions of a range of jazz artists and only available in limited editions specifically designed only to be ordered direct from the record company itself. That makes them pretty hard to find in record shops, and when they do find their way there, they are at a very high price, as the retailers have had to pay the normal mail-order rate for them, then add something on top to cover their own costs and give themselves some sort of margin.

Given such a complicated situation, it seemed counter-productive to recommend such releases in the general run of the Guide. The label is very much for serious collectors only, most of whom will already be familiar with their activities. Thus, for example, when it comes to tenorist Ike Quebec, this guide recommends a very fine one-disc Blue Note compilation of his later work, widely available at mid price, rather than either of the two Mosaic boxes which detail at length his Blue Note years. If anyone should feel moved to enquire into any of the releases on the Mosaic label they will not be disappointed by the high levels of research, documentation and remastering which are the standard fare for the company. Anyone wanting further information can write to Mosaic Records at 35 Melrose Place, Stamford, CT 06902 USA.

# Abbreviations

| | | | | | |
|---|---|---|---|---|---|
| acc | accordion | el | electric/electronic | pic | piccolo |
| af | alto flute | elb | electric bass | pic cl | piccolo clarinet |
| ah | alto horn | elg | electric guitar | pic t | piccolo trumpet |
| arr | arranger | elp | electric piano | pkt t | pocket trumpet |
| as | alto saxophone | elvn | electric violin | pp | pan pipes |
| b | double bass | euph | euphonium | prog | programming |
| bb | brass bass | EWI | electronic wind | pw | penny whistle |
| bcl | bass clarinet | | instrument | rec | recorder |
| bf | bass flute | f | flute | seq | sequencer |
| bg | bass guitar | flh | flügelhorn | snino s | sopranino saxophone |
| bgo | bongo | frh | french horn | sr | sitar |
| bhn | baritone horn | g | guitar | ss | soprano saxophone |
| bj | banjo | gfs | goofus | ssph | sousaphone |
| bmba | bass marimba | gspiel | glockenspiel | st | slide trumpet |
| bn | bassoon | gsyn | guitar synthesizer | str | stritch |
| bph | brötzophone | h | harpsichord | syn | synthesizer |
| bs | baritone saxophone | hca | harmonica | t | trumpet |
| bss | bass saxophone | hfp | hot fountain pen | ta | tabla |
| bt | bass trumpet | hmn | harmonium | tb | trombone |
| btb | bass trombone | hp | harp | tba | tuba |
| c | cornet | kba | kalimba | tg | tarogato |
| cbcl | contrabass clarinet | kbds | keyboards | thn | tenor horn |
| cbs | contrabass saxophone | kz | kazoo | tim | timpani |
| cel | celeste | ldr | leader | tbra | tamboura |
| cga | conga | mand | mandolin | ts | tenor saxophone |
| cl | clarinet | mba | marimba | tt | turntable(s) |
| clav | clavinet | mph | mellophone | v | vocal |
| c-ms | c-melody saxophone | mzo | manzello | va | viola |
| comp | composer | oas | only available separately | vb | vibraphone |
| cond | conductor | ob | oboe | vc | violoncello |
| cym | cymbals | orch | orchestra | vn | violin |
| d | drums | org | organ | vtb | valve trombone |
| dir | director | p | piano | wshbd | washboard |
| d-prog | drum-programming | perc | percussion | xyl | xylophone |
| ehn | english horn | p-hn | peck-horn | z | zither |

# Basic jazz library

**Muhal Richard Abrams**
 The Hearinga Suite
 Black Saint 120103-2
**Julian 'Cannonball' Adderley**
 Somethin' Else
 Blue Note B21Y-49338
 Mercy Mercy Mercy!
 Capitol CDP8 29915-2
**Louis Armstrong**
 Portrait of the Artist as a Young Man
 Columbia/Legacy 57176
 The Complete Recordings of Louis Armstrong and the Blues Singers

Affinity AFS1018-6
 Highlights from The American Decca Years
 MCA/Decca GRP26382
 Hot Fives and Sevens, Volumes 1-4
 JSP CD312/3/4/5
 Satchmo at Symphony Hall
 MCA/Decca GRP16612
 Satchmo: A Musical Autobiography
 Jazz Unlimited JUCD2003-05
 The California Concerts
 MCA/Decca GRP46132

**Art Ensemble of Chicago**
 The Art Ensemble 1967-68
 Nessa NCD-2500A-E
**Albert Ayler**
 Spiritual Unity
 ESP-Disk 1002-2
**Mildred Bailey**
 The Rockin' Chair lady
 MCA/Decca GRP16442
**Chet Baker**
 The Legacy
 Enja ENJ9021-2
**Count Basie**
 Count Basie: The Original American Decca Recordings
 MCA/Decca GRD3-6112

**The Essential Count Basie,**
**Volume 1**
Columbia 460061-2
**The Complete Atomic Mr Basie**
Roulette 8 28635 2

**Sidney Bechet**
**The Ledgendary Sidney Bechet**
RCA Bluebird ND86590
**Jazz Classics, Volumes 1 and 2**
Blue Note 789384/85 2

**Bix Beiderbecke**
**Volume 1: Singin' the Blues**
Columbia 466309-2

**Art Blakey**
**The History of Art Blakey and**
**the Jazz Messengers**
Blue Note CDP7 97190-2
**Free For All**
Blue Note CDP7 84170-2
**Album of the Year**
Timeless SJP155

**Carla Bley**
**Escalator over the Hill**
JCOA 839-310-2

**Paul Bley**
**Open, to Love**
ECM 1023 (827 751-2)

**Anthony Braxton**
**Willisau (Quartet) 1991**
hatART4 61001/04

**The Brecker Brothers**
**Collection, Volumes 1 & 2**
RCA Novus ND90442/83076

**Peter Brötzmann**
**Machine Gun**
FMP CD24

**Clifford Brown**
**The Complete Paris Sessions,**
**Volumes 1-3**
Vogue 15461/63-2
**Complete Blue Note and Pacific**
**Jazz Recordings**
Blue Note CDP8 34195-2

**Don Byron**
**Tuskegee Experiments**
Elektra Nonesuch 979280-2

**Benny Carter**
**Central City Sketches**
MusicMaster CIJD60126X

**Oscar 'Papa' Celestin**
**New Orleans Classics**
Azure AZ-CD-12

**Charlie Christian**
**Genius of the Electric Guitar**
Columbia CK40846
**Solo Flight**
Vintage Jazz Classics VJC1021-2

**Cozy Cole**
**1944**
Classics 819

**Nat King Cole**
**Big Band Cole**
Capitol CDP7 96259-2

**Ornette Coleman**
**The Shape of Jazz to Come**
Atlantic Jazz 781317-2
**Free Jazz**
Atlantic Jazz 781364-2
**Virgin Beauty**
Columbia Portrait RK44301

**Steve Coleman**
**The Tao of Mad Phat**
RCA Novus 63160 2

**John Coltrane**
**Blue Train**
Blue Note CDP7 46095-2
**Soultrane**
Prestige OJCCD 021-2
**Giant Steps**
Atlantic Jazz 781337-2
**My Favorite Things**
Atlantic Jazz 782346-2
**Coltrane's Sound**
Atlantic Jazz 781419-2
**Crescent**
Impulse! IMPD12002
**A Love Supreme**
Impulse! GRD155
**Meditations**
Impulse! IMP11992

**Chick Corea**
**Now He Sings, Now He Sobs**
Blue Note CDP7 90055-2

**Tadd Dameron**
**Fontainebleau**
Prestige OJCCD055-2

**Miles Davis**
**Birth of the Cool**
Capitol CDP7 92862-2
**Chronicle**
Prestige 8PCD012-2
**Round About Midnight**
Columbia 460605-2
**Miles Ahead**
Columbia CK65121
**Porgy and Bess**
Columbia CK65141
**Kind of Blue**
Columbia 460603-2
**Miles Smiles**
Columbia 471004-2
**A Tribute to Jack Johnson**
Columbia CK47036

**Wild Bill Davison**
**The Commodore Master Takes**
Commodore CMD14052

**Paul Desmond**
**Two of a Mind**
RCA Victor 68513-2

**Eric Dolphy**
**Out to Lunch**
Blue Note CDP7 46524-2

**Billy Eckstine**
**No Cover, No Minimum**
Blue Note B21S98583

**Roy Eldridge**
**After You've Gone**
MCA/Decca GRP16052
**Little Jazz: Best of the**
**Verve Years**
Verve 523 338-2

**Duke Ellington**
**Early Ellington (1926/31)**
MCA/GRP36402
**The Duke's Men – Small Groups**
**Volumes 1 & 2**
Columbia CK46995/48835
**Braggin' in Brass**
Columbia/Legacy R2K44395
**Fargo, North Dakota**
**November 7, 1940**
Vintage Jazz Classics 1019/20-2
**The Blanton-Webster Band**
RCA Bluebird ND 85659
**Black, Brown & Beige**
RCA Bluebird 6641-2-RB

**The Great Ellington Units**
RCA Bluebird ND86751
**Ellington at Newport**
Columbia 472385 2
**The Far East Suite – Special Mix**
RCA Bluebird 366551 2

**Bill Evans**
**At the Village Vanguard**
Riverside FCD60017
**Conversations with Myself**
Verve 821 984-2
**At Town Hall, Volume 1**
Verve 831 271-2

**Gil Evans**
**Out of the Cool**
Impulse! IMP11862
**The Individualism of Gil Evans**
Verve 833 804-2

**Art Farmer**
**Portrait of Art Farmer**
Contemporary OJCCD166-2

**Ella Fitzgerald**
**The Original American**
**Decca Recordings**
MCA/Decca GRP26192
**The Best of the Song Books**
Verve 519 804-2
**At the Opera House**
Verve 831 269-2

**Erroll Garner**
**Concert by the Sea**
Columbia 451042-2
**Solitaire**
Mercury 518 279-2

**Kenny Garrett**
**Black Hope**
Warner Bros. 945017-2

**Stan Getz**
**Stan Getz & J.J. Johnson**
**at the Opera House**
Verve 831 272-2
**Focus**
Verve 821 982-2
**Sweet Rain**
Verve 815 054-2
**Anniversary**
EmArcy 838 769-2

**Dizzy Gillespie**
**The Complete RCA Victor**
**Recordings**
RCA Bluebird 66528 2
**Shaw 'Nuff**
Musicraft MVSCD-53
**Dizzy Gillespie's Big 4**
Pablo OJC443-2

**Egberto Gismonti**
**Danca das Cabecas**
ECM1089 (827 750-2)

**Benny Goodman**
**The Birth of Swing**
RCA Bluebird ND90601/3

**Henry Grimes**
**The Call**
ESP-Disk 1026-2

**Charlie Haden**
**Liberation Music Orchestra**
Impulse! IMP11882

**Lionel Hampton**
**1937-8, 1938-9, 1939-40**
Classics 524, 534, 562
**Flying Home**
MCA/Decca MCAD-42349

**Herbie Hancock**
Maiden Voyage
Blue Note CDPB21Y46339-2
Headhunters
Columbia/Legacy 471239 2

**Coleman Hawkins**
1943-4
Classics 807
Hollywood Stampede
Capitol CDP7 92596-2
Encounters Ben Webster
Verve 823 120-2

**Fletcher Henderson**
A Study in Frustration
Columbia/Legacy 57596

**Woody Herman**
Keeper of the Flame
Capitol CDP7 98453-2

**Andrew Hill**
Point of Departure
Blue Note CDP8 4167-2

**Earl Hines**
Grand Reunion
Verve/Limelight 528 137-2
Plays Duke Ellington
New World 361/62-2

**Johnny Hodges**
Passion Flower
RCA Bluebird 66616-2

**Billie Holiday**
Love Songs
Columbia 483878-2
The Quintessential
Billie Holiday, Volume 9
Columbia CK47031
The Complete Original
American Decca Recordings
MCA/Decca GRP26012
Lady in Satin
Columbia CK65144

**Wayne Horvitz**
Miracle Mile
Elektra Nonesuch 79278-2

**Bobby Hutcherson**
Cruisin' the Bird
Landmark LCD1517-2

**Abdullah Ibrahim**
African River
Enja ENJ6018-2

**Willis Jackson**
Bar Wars
Muse MCD6011

**Keith Jarrett**
Belonging
ECM 1050 (829 115-2)
The Köln Concert
ECM 1064/65 (810 067-2)

**Bunk Johnson**
1944
American Music AMDC3

**J.J. Johnson**
The Eminent Jay Jay Johnson,
Volumes 1 & 2
Blue Note CDP7 81505/6-2

**Louis Jordan**
Five Guys Named Moe
MCA DMCL1718

**Stan Kenton**
Stan Kenton in Hi-Fi
Capitol Jazz CDP7 98451-2

**Rahsaan Roland Kirk**
We Free Kings
Mercury 826 455-2

Rip, Rig & Panic/Now Please
Don't Cry, Beautiful Edith
EmArcy 832 164-2

**Lee Konitz**
Subconscious Lee
Prestige OJC186-2
Live at the Half Note
Verve 521 659-2

**Steve Lacy**
Vespers
Soul Note 121260-2

**Yusef Lateef**
The Centaur and the Phoenix
Riverside OJCCD721

**Meade Lux Lewis**
1927-1939/1939-1941
Classics 722, 743

**McKinney's Cotton Pickers**
The Band Don Redman Built
RCA Bluebird ND90517

**John McLaughlin**
Extrapolation
Polydor 841598-2
Inner Mounting Flame
Columbia CK31067

**Jackie McLean**
Destination Out!
Blue Note CDP8 32087-2

**Carmen McRae**
The Great American Song Book
Atlantic Jazz 7-81323-2

**Wynton Marsalis**
Citi Movement
Columbia CK53324

**Helen Merrill**
Collaboration
EmArcy 834 205-2

**Charles Mingus**
Pithecanthropus Erectus
Atlantic Jazz 781456-2
Mingus Ah Um
Columbia 450436-2
Blues & Roots
Atlantic Jazz 781336-2
Charles Mingus Presents
Charles Mingus
Candid CD9005
The Black Saint and the
Sinner Lady
Impulse! IMP11742
Let My Children Hear Music
Columbia/Legacy CK48910

**Hank Mobley**
Soul Station
Blue Note CDP7 46528-2

**The Modern Jazz Quartet**
Odds Against Tomorrow
UA/Blue Note CDP7 93415-2

**Grachan Moncur III**
Some Other Stuff
Blue Note CDP8 32092-2

**Thelonious Monk**
Complete Blue Note Recordings
Blue Note CDP8 30363-2
The Unique Thelonious Monk
Riverside OJCCD064-2
Brilliant Corners
Riverside OJCCD026-2
Monk's Music
Riverside OJCCD084-2
The Thelonious Monk
Orchestra at Town Hall
Riverside OJCCD206-2
It's Monk's Time
Columbia 468405-2

**Wes Montgomery**
The Incredible Jazz Guitar
Riverside OJCCD036-2
Impressions: The Verve
Jazz Sides
Verve 521 690-2

**Lee Morgan**
The Best of Lee Morgan
Blue Note CDP7 91138-2

**Jelly Roll Morton**
The Pearls
RCA Bluebird ND86588
His Complete Victor Recordings
RCA Bluebird ND82361

**Bennie Moton**
Kansas City Orchestra
1923-1927/1930-32
Classics 518, 519

**Gerry Mulligan**
Best of Gerry Mulligan with
Chet Baker
Pacific Jazz CDP7 95481-2

**David Murray**
Hope Scope
Black Saint 120 139-2

**Fats Navarro**
Complete Blue Note and Capitol
Recordings of Navarro/Dameron
Blue Note CDP8 33373-2

**Oliver Nelson**
Blues and the Abstract Truth
Impulse! IMP11542

**New Orleans Rhythm**
N.O.R.K. and Jelly Roll Morton
Milestone MCD 47020-2

**Jimmie Noone**
New Orleans Jazz Giants
1936-40
JSP JSPCD336

**Greg Osby**
Art Forum
Blue Note CDP8 37319-2

**King Oliver**
King Oliver's Jazz Band 1923
Jazz Archives 15746-2

**Charlie Parker**
The Immortal Charlie Parker
Denon/Savoy SV-0102
The Charlie Parker Story
Denon/Savoy SV-0105
Charlie Parker On Dial:
The Complete Sessions
Spotlite/Dial SPJCD4-101
Jazz at the Philharmonic, 1946
Verve 513 756-2
The Quintet: Jazz at Massey Hall
Debut OJCCD044-2

**Jaco Pastorius**
Jaco Pastorius
Epic CDEPC81453

**Art Pepper**
Art Pepper Meets the
Rhythm Section
Contemporary OJCCD5338
Art Pepper + Eleven:
Modern Jazz Classics
Contemporary OJCCD341-2

**Oscar Peterson**
The Song Is You
Verve 531 558-2
Night Train
Verve 821 724-2

**King Pleasure (Clarence Beeks)**
King Pleasure Sings/Annie
Ross Sings
Prestige OJCCD217-2

**Bud Powell**
The Complete Blue Note and
Roost Recordings
Blue Note CDP8 30083-2
The Complete Bud Powell
on Verve
Verve 521 669-2

**Don Pullen**
New Beginnings
Blue Note CDP7 91785-2

**Freddie Redd**
Music from the Connection
Blue Note CDP8 89392-2

**Don Redman**
Don Redman and his
Orchestra 1931-3
Classics 543

**Django Reinhardt**
Chronological Volume 1
JSP CD341
Swing in Paris, 1939-40
Affinity CDAFS1003-5

**Emily Remler**
Transitions
Concord CCD4236

**Max Roach**
We Insist! – Freedom Now Suite
Candid CCD9002

**Sonny Rollins**
Saxophone Colossus
Prestige OJCCD291-2
A Night at the Village Vanguard,
Volumes 1 & 2
Blue Note CDP7 46517/8-2
Freedom Suite
Riverside OJCCD067-2
The Bridge
RCA Victor 68518-2
Alfie
Impulse! IMP12242

**Jimmy Rushing**
The You and Me That Used to Be
RCA Novus 6460-2

**George Russell**
Ezz-Thetics
Riverside OJCCD070-2
The Outer View
Riverside OJCCD616-2

**David Sanborn**
Close Up
Reprise 925715-2

**John Scofield**
Still Warm
Gramavision 18-8508-2

**Artie Shaw**
Begin the Beguine
RCA Bluebird ND86274

**Archie Shepp**
Four For Trane
Impulse! IMP12182

**Horace Silver**
Horace Silver and the
Jazz Messengers
Blue Note CDP7 46140-2
Song For My Father
Blue Note CDP7 84185-2

**Frank Sinatra**
Come Dance With Me!
Capitol CDP7 48470-2

**Bessie Smith**
1925-33
Hermes HRM6003

**Jimmy Smith**
Open House
Blue Note CDP7 84269-2

**Willie 'The Lion' Smith**
Willie 'The Lion' Smith
and His Cubs
Timeless CBC1-012

**Eddie South**
Eddie South 1923-37
Classics 707

**Muggsy Spanier**
The 'Ragtime Band' Sessions
RCA Bluebird 366550-2

**Maxine Sullivan**
Swingin' Sweet
Concord CCD4351

**Sun Ra**
The Heliocentric Worlds of Sun
Ra, Volumes 1 and 2
ESP-Disk 1014/17-2

**John Surman**
Such Winters of Memory
ECM810 621-2

**Ralph Sutton**
Last of the Whorehouse Piano
Players (The Original Sessions)
Chiaroscuro CR(D)206

**Art Tatum**
The Complete Capitol
Recordings, Volumes 1 and 2
Capitol CDP7 92866/7-2
The Complete Pablo Solo
Masterpieces
Pablo 7PACD4404-2
The Complete Pablo Group
Masterpieces
Pablo 6PACD4401-2

**Cecil Taylor**
Jumpin' Punkins
Candid CD9013
Unit Structures
Blue Note CDP7 84237-2
Conquistador!
Blue Note CDP7 84260-2

**Frank Teschemacher**
Muggsy, Tesch and the
Chicagoans
Village VILCD001-2

**Ralph Towner**
Solstice
ECM (825 458-2)

**Lennie Tristano**
Lennie Tristano/The New
Tristano
Rhino/Atlantic 271595-2

**'Big' Joe Turner**
The Boss of the Blues
Atlantic 781459-2

**Sarah Vaughan**
Sarah Vaughan with
Clifford Brown
EmArcy 814 641-2
Swingin' Easy
EmArcy 514 072-2
Crazy and Mixed Up
Pablo PACD2312 137-2

**Joe Venuti**
Violin Jazz
Yazoo 1062

**Mal Waldron**
The Quest
Prestige New Jazz OJC082-2

**Fats Waller**
The Middle Years, Volume 1
RCA Bluebird 66083-2
The Last Years (1940-3)
RCA Bluebird ND90411

**Dinah Washington**
For Those in Love
EmArcy 514 073-2

**Ernie Watts**
The Long Road Home
JVC2059-2

**Weather Report**
I Sing the Body Electric
Columbia 468207-2
This is Jazz
Columbia CK64627

**Chick Webb**
Rhythm Man
Hep HEPCD1023

**Eberhard Weber**
The Colours of Chloë
ECM (833 331-2)

**Ben Webster**
Soulville
Verve 833 551-2
Ben Webster Meets
Oscar Peterson
Verve 829 167-2

**Dicky Wells**
Swingin' in Paris
Charly LeJazz CD20

**Randy Weston**
The Spirit Of Our Ancestors
Antilles 511 896-2

**Lee Wiley**
Night in Manhattan
Columbia SRS75010

**Teddy Wilson**
Teddy Wilson and
His Orchestra 1939-41
Classics 620

**Jimmy Witherspoon**
Rockin' with Spoon
Charly CDBM25

**Lester Young**
A Lester Young Story
Jazz Archives 157342
Lester-Amadeus!
Phontastic CD7639
The Complete Lester Young
Mercury 830 920-2
Lester Young Trio
Verve 521 650-2
The President Plays with
the Oscar Peterson Trio
Verve 831 670-2

**Joe Zawinul**
Zawinul
Atlantic Jazz 781579-2

**John Zorn**
Spy vs. Spy
Elektra Nonesuch 960844-2

# The reviews

# Greg Abate

**Dr Jekyll and Mr Hyde**  Abate (ss, as, ts, bs, f); **Richie Cole** (as); **Chris Neville** (p); **Paul Del Nero**
  (b); **Artie Cabral** (d). Candid Ⓕ CCD79715 (77 minutes). Recorded 1994.

⑥ ❽

If Abate is Dr Jekyll, then unreconstructed bebopper Richie Cole is Mr Hyde in this straight-ahead
session, captured live in a Providence, Rhode Island, club. Both saxophonists have served their time
in the bands of the great and the good, and here they prove their claims as soloists, Cole winning by
a short head for passion and power. Abate's previous albums have pitched him against better known
rhythm sections, but this one does him proud, notably pianist Neville, a Benny Carter alumnus who
turns in several gripping solos, but few better than on Abate's *C.C.A.* This isn't earth shattering jazz,
but it's more than workmanlike and captures both saxophonists after several months of working
together and clearly still enjoying the experience.                                          **AS**

# Kaoru Abé                                                                          1949-78

**Mokuyobi No Yoru**  Abé (as). PSF Ⓕ PSFD66 (51 minutes). Recorded 1972.

⑧ ❼

While true in earlier times, the extent of plagiarism in the Japanese jazz scene is probably exaggerated.
Never more so than in the work of Kaoru Abé, a multi-instrumentalist and alto specialist who, in a
musical career that lasted barely ten years, put his own personal brand on free improvisation. He recorded
with guitarists Masayuki Takayanagi and Derek Bailey, drummer Milford Graves and percussion and
guitar major Keiji Haino. Kaoru was self-taught; he was something of an anarchist and this was reflected
in his music. He did not avoid working with fellow musicians but he practised alone and these practice
sessions formed the basis of his improvised performances. His discography boasts 14 items and they show
him as a player of unbridled passion, his tone stridently demanding at the top of his range and full of
plummy warmth lower down. His technique is impressive and is all that is required to accommodate his
musical thinking process. Albums such as **Trio 1970** (PSFD56) give exciting evidence of his group
awareness, but this solo CD provides a clearer indication of his daunting creativity. Two of the selections
show how effectively he builds from a simple motif or an open-ended stance, achieving a distinctive
formality, yet one tempered by a sense of drama. The remaining title uses *Fly Me to the Moon* as its
starting point and Abé's headlong demolition takes it into a musical free fall that never completely deserts
the parent theme. For the conservative, his music may prove to be unrelentingly ugly. For those prepared
to search it out, there is, however, a wild inner beauty. His solos are rarely arrested by barren moments
and his death, at the age of 29, robbed Japan of one of its most original jazz voices.          **BMcR**

# John Abercrombie                                                                    1944

**Timeless**  Abercrombie (g, elg); **Jan Hammer** (p, org, syn); **Jack DeJohnette** (d). ECM
  Ⓕ 829 114-2 (44 minutes). Recorded 1974.

⑥ ❽

Although there have been recent vigorous exceptions, Abercrombie's work over the last decade or so has
generally reflected his admiration for the pastel-toned Jim Hall school of guitar playing. However, this
untypically energetic début for ECM shows that in the heady seventies even the apparently deferential
Abercrombie was not immune to the allure of high octane fusion. Keyboardist Jan Hammer was only six
months out of John McLaughlin's Mahavishnu Orchestra, and the influence of that group looms large in
much of this music. Hammer's frenetically paced opener quickly sets the scene, inspiring eight-bar
exchanges between his galloping Hammond and Abercrombie's uncommonly aggressive *staccato* guitar
(shades of the type of guitar work to come many years later on Abercrombie's recent **Speak of the Devil**),
complete with the overdrive and phase-shift effects typical of McLaughlin's sound at the time.
  Other tracks, such as the limpid piano and acoustic guitar duets of *Love Song* and *Remembering*,
announce Abercrombie's more meditative inclinations, as well as being redolent of Mahavishnu's
quieter moments. There isn't much of the unmodified changes playing that Abercrombie has latterly
developed, but the record is seductively atmospheric, dynamically varied, and incidentally shows that
the organ trio had places to go after Jimmy Smith. It was recorded in the LP era, so the playing time
is average, but there's no lack of breadth in the music.                                     **MG**

# Rabih Abou-Khalil

**Blue Camel**  Abou-Khalil (oud); **Kenny Wheeler** (t, flh); **Charlie Mariano** (as); **Steve Swallow** (b);
  **Milton Cardona** (cgas); **Nabil Khaiat** (frame d); **Ramesh Shotham** (Indian d, perc).
  Enja Ⓕ ENJ7053-2 (61 minutes). Recorded 1992.

⑧ ❽

As Rabih Abou-Khalil himself points out, "the music of the first world is much less foreign to the Third World than vice versa", and **Blue Camel**, its participants coming from India, North and South America, goes some distance towards proving this point. Rabih Abou-Khalil is a virtuoso player, and his eight pieces on this album employ the classical rhythms and modes of his traditional music, yet they are arranged in such a way as to accommodate improvisation from jazz musicians Kenny Wheeler, Charlie Mariano and Steve Swallow, and their interaction with the percussion of Milton Cardona, Nabil Khaiat and Ramesh Shotham. The main problem bedevilling such an accommodation lies in the fact that the pieces rely for their power more on rhythmic than harmonic development, so Kenny Wheeler, for instance, who is virtually peerless in the jazz world for his ability to breeze inventively through changes, has to adapt to an entirely novel approach, and take his cues from the percussion players. It must be said that Charlie Mariano adapts to this process more easily than the Canadian. Likewise Steve Swallow, although the contributions of each player are never less than cogent, but overall, it is difficult to see quite what Abou-Khalil's exhilarating and beautifully contemplative music gains from the presence of jazz musicians within it. All the most satisfying passages on **Blue Camel** feature the rich and resonant oud, improvising at the prompting of percussionists. The experiment must thus be put down as a failure, but a consistently intriguing and occasionally deeply enjoyable one.          **CP**

# Muhal Richard Abrams                                                    1930

**Levels and Degrees of Light** Abrams (cl, p); **Anthony Braxton** (as); **Maurice McIntyre** (ts); **Leroy Jenkins** (vn); **Charles Clark**, **Leonard Jones** (b); **Gordon Emmanuel** (vb); **Thurman Barker** (d); **Penelope Taylor** (v); **David Moore** (poet). Delmark Ⓕ DD413 (43 minutes). Recorded 1967.
⑧ ❼

**Levels and Degrees of Light** was the third record from Chicago's AACM organization, the first under the leadership of their *éminence grise*, Muhal Richard Abrams. Though it does not have the shock value of Roscoe Mitchell's **Sound** (the initial AACM release), the album is not short on fascination. The title track is a striking exploration of higher registers, Abrams's clarinet and Penelope Taylor's wordless soprano soaring over a swirl of vibes and cymbals to create a sound-world of crystalline beauty. Although Abrams used the voice again on his later **Rejoicing with the Light**, this facet of his work has since remained largely undocumented.

The CD's centrepiece is *The Bird Song*, which begins with David Moore declaiming vivid images of apocalypse, moves through a quiet passage of violin, chimes and birdsong, then climaxes with an intense ensemble free-for-all. The closing *My Thoughts are My Future – Now and Forever* is a more conventional sequence of solos, Abrams's fast, skipping piano lines carrying just a hint of his stride and bebop roots.

The disc's variety of forms and unusual timbral palettes set out a radical programme that Abrams's subsequent music has continued to explore. His later records often show greater assurance, but **Levels and Degrees of Light** has a spark of invention that still excites. The CD version removes the heavy artificial reverberation in which the original vinyl release was bathed.          **GL**

**The Hearinga Suite** Abrams (p, syn, cond); **Ron Tooley**, **Jack Walrath**, **Cecil Bridgewater**, **Frank Gordon** (t); **Clifton Anderson**, **Dick Griffin** (tb); **Jack Jeffers**, **Bill Lowe**, (btb); **John Purcell** (f, cl, ts); **Marty Ehrlich** (pic, f, cl, as); **Patience Higgins** (bcl, ts); **Courtnay Wynter** (bn, bcl, ts); **Charles Davis** (bs, ss); **Deidre Murray** (vc); **Fred Hopkins** (b); **Warren Smith** (vb, gspiel, perc); **Andrew Cyrille** (d). Black Saint Ⓕ 120103-2 (42 minutes). Recorded 1989.
✓                                                                    ⑨ ❽

Abrams's writing for medium to larger groups in the eighties had been ambitious but **The Hearinga Suite** of 1989 used a much larger aggregation and posed problems commensurate with the numerical increase. This CD shows that, although Abrams handled the task with some skill, his diversity of approach created some elements of disunity. On the credit side, internal contrapuntal dialogues as well as solos by the likes of Ehrlich, Gordon, Hopkins, Murray and Walrath are ideally cushioned and there is not a jarring moment. But while every title has individual merit, the suite as a whole lacks stylistic consistency. It rightly shuns sequential ambitions but the band's actual identity is often confused in a catalogue of unusual ensemble voicings and cute instrumental devices.

*Seesall* teams conversational voice-overs with an Ellingtonian ensemble sound. *Oldfotalk* has a Kollektief-style lift that never explodes into the threatened Breckerish climax, while the title track has a Gil Evans-ish lightness of texture. *Aura Of Thought* boasts a simulated string section while Wynter's stately swing-era tenor ushers *Bermix* into tone-poem territory. It must qualify as a fine recording project but it does suggest that it is a blueprint for four or five more integrated works.          **BMcR**

**Blu Blu Blu** Abrams (p, syn, bells, cond); **Jack Walrath** (t); **Alfred Patterson** (tb); **Mark Taylor** (frh); **Joe Daley** (tba); **John Purcell** (as, f, cl); **Robert De Bellis** (as, cl, bcl); **Eugene Ghee** (ts, cl, bcl); **Patience Higgins** (bs, f, cl); **Warren Smith** (vb, timp); **David Fiuczynski** (g); **Brad Jones**, **Lindsey Horner** (b); **Thurman Barker** (d); **Joel Brandon** (whistler). Black Saint Ⓕ 120117-2 (77 minutes). Recorded 1990.
⑨ ❽

Abrams's masterpiece is **The Hearinga Suite**, reviewed above. Although lacking **Hearinga**'s thematic unity and lyrical rapture, this compensates with a greater breadth that confirms Abrams's stature as

Duke Ellington's and Charles Mingus's greatest living heir. The title track is an earthy tribute to Muddy Waters sparked by Abrams's sly piano and Fiuczynski's boomeranging guitar (more evocative of B.B. King than Waters, though it hardly matters). Among the other highlights is a stirring reprise of *Bloodline*, a modernistic salute to the big bands originally recorded by Abrams in 1983, on **Rejoicing with the Light**. The slightly quieter, more speculative pieces here convey something of the urgent intellectual activity that one associates with pre-**Pithecanthropus Erectus** Mingus, although Abrams's pieces are generally more angular in design and more successful in interweaving composition and improvisation. The presence of a whistler shouldn't send up a red flag; Brandon is an ex-flautist who adds just the right amount of shrillness to the ensembles, and whose unique gift Abrams exploits to telling advantage on a section of *One for the Whistler* in 5/4. Even so, the standout soloist throughout the programme is trumpeter Walrath, and the standout on this particular piece is Ghee, an unsung tenor saxophonist whose yearning solo is what one tends to remember afterwards. **FD**

# George Adams

1942-92

**Adams/Pullen Quartet Live at The Village Vanguard** Adams (ts); **Pullen** (p); **Cameron Brown** (b); **Dannie Richmond** (d). Soul Note Ⓕ SN1094CD (56 minutes). Recorded 1983.

⑧ ❻

A pupil of jazz flute pioneer Wayman Carver, Adams's early musical experience was in the r&b field. Throughout the seventies he worked with Art Blakey, Charles Mingus and Gil Evans, and in 1979 he formed a quartet with Pullen. This became the above line-up when Cameron joined the group in the early eighties, and it was still making public appearances, with a replacement for the late Dannie Richmond, until shortly before Adams's own demise. This CD finds the quartet in prime form and gives the listener a clear picture of Adams's various musical personalities. On *Intentions* and *Diana* he is a staggeringly inventive soloist, strictly from the John Coltrane generation but steeped in high-proof bluesy spirit, totally at home with the turbulent buoyancy provided by the explosive trio at his back. Both his opening cadenza and coda on *Solitude* display a Garneresque detachment from the theme, but the main body of the piece offers for comparison two more facets of his playing. He treats the theme statement to a romantic stroll, maintaining an almost mainstream gait, with the odd irascible aside tossed in our direction. In contrast, his solo takes him into Albert Ayler territory, the statements stark, the passion naked and with thoughtful improvisation kept to a minimum. Adams may have worn different hats, but here they all suit his highly personal musical outfit. **BMcR**

# Johnny Adams

1932

**New review**
**The Verdict** Adams (v); with a collective personnel including: **Tony Dagradi** (ss); **Houston Person** (ts); **Harry Connick Jr**, **David Torkanowsky** (p); **Carl LeBlanc**, **Steve Masakowski** (g); **James Singleton** (b); **Shannon Powell** (d). Rounder Ⓕ CD2135 (57 minutes). Recorded 1994.

⑦ ❾

New Orleans native Adams is a relative newcomer to the jazz scene, but has had a long and successful r&b career. His rich baritone voice is equally at ease with New Orleans funk and the most classically perfect jazz balladry, and a long-time love of jazz has led him in recent years to make two albums given over exclusively to jazz standards, of which this is the second. Adams has a fine combination of tone and phrasing, and an innate ability to deliver the emotional core of a lyric (he has long been a successful songster himself), and with the all-star line-up he and producer Scott Billington mustered for this effort, high quality is in abundance on all fronts. A rewarding effort for any fan of good jazz vocalizing. **KS**

# Pepper Adams

1930-86

**New review**
**Pepper Adams** Adams (bs); **Walter Norris** (p); **George Mraz** (b); **Makaya Ntshoko** (d) on four titles. **Adams** (bs) featured with the **Denny Christianson Big Band** on two titles. Enja Ⓕ ENJ9079-2 (48 minutes). Recorded 1975/86.

⑧ ❽

To describe a player as "in demand" is a typical journalist's ploy but in the case of Pepper Adams it was most accurate. From his early days in his native Detroit right up to his death, from lung cancer in September 1986, he could place his unmistakable stamp on bands large and small. Like Serge Chaloff, he refused to accept that his chosen instrument was in any way unwieldy or inflexible. The four quartet tracks here originally comprised one of two Enja LPs recorded at Munich's Domicile jazz club three weeks after Pepper, Norris and Mraz had all played on a Thad Jones-Mel Lewis album. They were joined on the Munich gig by African drummer Ntshoko to make a compact and exciting quartet (with the proviso that material recorded live at clubs tends to suffer from the apparent need to give everyone a solo on every tune). There is a fine blues, *Twelfth and Pingree,* with some unexpected bitonality in one chorus, a moving *Child is Bor*n and a *Well You Needn't* which would surely have earned a nod of approval from Monk. Two big band tracks by the Canadian Denny Christianson orchestra have been added to expand the original LP (although the playing time is still not generous) and showcase Pepper in marvellous form, driving through *Osage Autumn* (based on the chords of *Indian Summer*) and, best of all, a heart-wrenching *My Funny Valentine*. These big-band titles are among the last Adams recorded and have been licensed by Enja from Justin Time Records. On the strength of these alone the complete Denny Christianson albums must be worth hearing.                                                                                                       **AM**

## Steve Adams

**In Out Side** Adams (pic, f, ss, as, ts, bs); **Ken Filiano** (b, chimes). 9 Winds Ⓕ NWCD0156
  (57 minutes). Recorded 1991-2.

⑥ ❽

It is sometimes damning a project with faint praise to call it interesting, but this time I mean it with no hidden agenda. This is a creative and engaging use of a recording studio's capacity for double-tracking and going back over pieces of work to create multiple layers of conversation between two imaginative instrumentalists. Both men exhibit a fine capacity for humour as well as contemplative stillness or fiery, brazen playing. Adams tends to lead the way, his 'angle' on the music more proactive than Filiano's, who enjoys embellishment and counterpoint and is content to supply it in many forms.

  The album is given a great deal of variety through the sheer number of instruments Adams plays, but there is more to the versatility of the music than that: these two have worked at making small definitive statements and know when to stop: an art not all musicians manage to master in their careers. Some of the pieces here are as short as 40 seconds: one track (a walking blues) is five minutes, another (a slowish ballad) just over seven. Nothing outwears its welcome, and as Adams comments in the CD booklet about four so-called *Haiku*s, "The Haiku pieces are something we have always done – pieces that are only one thought long. No rambling or association." Freedom through discipline and hard work, then. Not a bad idea ...                                                                              **KS**

## Julian 'Cannonball' Adderley                                                        1928-75

New review
**Sophisticated Swing: The EmArcy Small Group Sessions** Adderley (as); **Nat Adderley** (c);
  **Junior Mance** (p); **Sam Jones**, **Al McKibbon** (b); **Specs Wright**, **Jimmy Cobb** (d). Verve/Mercury
  Ⓜ 528 408 2 (two discs: 158 minutes). Recorded 1956-8.

⑧ ❽

Adderley was fortunate in that his eloquent bebop style was tailor-made to be popular and he rose quickly to prominence after his first recordings in 1955. Here is the first quintet at its finest: the leader was always able to draw in the best musicians to play for him and there were many, particularly pianists, before and after these sessions. But the compact quality of the group and its lean music are as well demonstrated on these EmArcy tracks as they were on the later Riverside ones. Despite the quality of Mance and Nat Adderley there is only one star; Cannon's articulation and musical expressiveness puts the alto saxophone in total command. Adderley was one of the brightest stars to come along after Parker and, while his playing is not completely without fault (he sometimes resorts to hackneyed phrases), he stood head and shoulders above the many Parker imitators of the mid-fifties who collectively had not an ounce of Cannonball's originality.                                          **SV**

**Somethin' Else** Adderley (as), **Miles Davis** (t); **Hank Jones** (p); **Sam Jones** (b); **Art Blakey** (d).
  Blue Note Ⓜ B21Y 49338 (41 minutes). Recorded 1958.

⑧ ❽

✔ Cannonball Adderley still stands as one of jazzdom's most passionate and lyrical saxophone voices. His boppishly swinging style and wailing gospel-inflected tone, one of the few readily recognizable signature sounds in jazz, was appreciated by musicians and the public alike. An exponent of the overlapping hard-bop and soul schools of the sixties, the altoist first gained prominence in 1955 with Oscar Pettiford. In 1957, pressed by financial exigencies when his own group foundered, Adderley joined Miles Davis in what would prove a profitable association for both men. Indeed, in his ensuing two years with the trumpeter, Adderley played a large role in catapulting Davis, and himself, to the jazz world's front ranks, thus paving the way for Adderley's later successes as a leader.

  In this deceptively relaxed but often edgy 1958 date, Adderley shares the spotlight with Davis, then his employer. It is a meeting of co-equals where the menu includes such familiar fare as *Autumn Leaves* (using the Ahmad Jamal-penned introduction), *Love for Sale* and *Dancing in the Dark*. And while we hear Davis moving closer to the shrouded intensities of **Kind of Blue** (1959), we also hear the melismatic and bluesy Parker-inflected declamations that would inform so much of Adderley's later work. But though Parker was his touchstone (along with a large dose of Benny Carter), Adderley evolved a singular approach at once sophisticated and primal, and passionately lyrical. The CD version of this classic has an extra track, *Alison's Uncle*.                                             **CB**

**In San Francisco**  Adderley (as); **Nat Adderley** (c); **Bobby Timmons** (p); **Sam Jones** (b); **Louis Hayes** (d). Riverside Ⓜ OJCCD03-2 (61 minutes). Recorded 1959.

⑧ ❻

Cannonball Adderley never sounded quite at one with the Miles Davis set-up. His alto soared happily, with a lighter-than-air feel, and that didn't wholly suit the sombre Davis ambience. When Adderley made this record – one of the first he made with a group of his own – he had just emerged from his years with Miles, and his choice of sidemen, including his cornet-playing brother Nat and the funky pianist Bobby Timmons, late of the hard-bop Jazz Messengers, created a sophisticated modern version of a good-time group. At a time in jazz when live club recordings were a rare occurrence, his new company Riverside (Cannonball had just left Mercury) ventured into the Jazz Workshop in San Francisco and came away with this hour's worth of in-person, audience-sparked jazz.

The occasional funky cliché aside, the group generates considerable excitement. Cannonball is on wonderful form and the rhythm section, one of this period's great unsung teams, is spot-on. The album spawned a number of what were to become Adderley staples, but one of the best tracks is *Hi-Fly*, which Adderley announces as being by "the young composer and pianist, Randy Weston". The 11 minutes of *Straight, No Chaser* is a bonus, as the track was not on the original LP.      **MK**

---

**New review**

**Mercy Mercy Mercy!**  Adderley (as, ldr); **Nat Adderley** (c); **Joe Zawinul** (p); **Victor Gaskin** (b); **Roy McCurdy** (d). Capitol Jazz Ⓜ CDP8 29915-2 (41 minutes). Recorded 1966.

✔  ⑨ ❽

By 1966 Adderley's particular groove was firmly established, both in a musical and audience sense. He was, along with Getz and Brubeck, a jazz artist in the vanguard of popular appreciation and one with much to offer on an artistic level. His own brand of soul-jazz, a genre also successfully exploited by luminaries such as Horace Silver and Gene Ammons, as well as his genial and all-embracing stage presence, had given him a standing well in advance of his old boss, Miles Davis, and a head start in terms of being a style leader to a large international white audience, let alone an understanding of what the urban blacks of the mid sixties wanted to hear when they were not listening to Tamla Motown and James Brown. It was no coincidence that Miles subsequently used both Zawinul and his compositions on his own breakthrough albums, **In a Silent Way** and **Bitches Brew**.

**Mercy Mercy Mercy!** was Cannonball's own breakthrough record with the wider non-jazz audience, giving him a chart-topping single and album (both derived from the title track) while allowing him the rare luxury for a jazz musician of not needing to diverge substantially from his established musical style. Recorded three months after the Japanese tour marked by the now-deleted album included in the previous Guide, and also made in front of an audience (this time in Chicago), it generates tremendous atmosphere. There is an argument to be made for this being Cannonball's most attractive period, for he was truly centred in his music; he was leading a dynamic but tightly disciplined unit of outstanding talents, and his own playing was charged with a commanding authority. The combination of straight-ahead neo-bop compositions (usually from his own hand) and more catchy, funk-based tunes (from his brother Nat, Zawinul, and earlier in his career from group pianist Bobby Timmons) gave the music a compelling variety and freshness which was easy to embrace as a fan and impossible to be sniffy about as a critic. As the sixties wore on, his group's standards would become corroded by the constant touring and the pressure to play his 'hits' every night, and only in the next decade would he take corrective action and aim for new artistic targets. Meanwhile, if you were a casual listener looking for just one album which would neatly summarize just why so many casual listeners of the sixties found Cannonball Adderley quite irresistible, then this record will happily suffice.      **KS**

---

**New review**

**Inside Straight**  Adderley (as); **Nat Adderley** (c); **Hal Galper** (elp); **Walter Booker** (b); **Roy McCurdy** (d); **King Errisson** (perc). Fantasy Ⓜ OJCCD750-2 (40 minutes). Recorded 1973.

⑦ ❽

Cut live in the studio, as he so often preferred, this is one of the few latter-day Adderley Quintet recordings available on CD and points to a spirited, more intense ensemble direction sadly never fulfilled. Together with the nucleus of his road band, which had recorded the impressive **Black Messiah** double set in 1970, the decision to add pianist Hal Galper, who had previously worked with Sam Rivers and Tony Williams, was a smart move. Not only is he a fluid, inventive player, but his sharp writing skills provide a fresher, more contemporary platform for Adderley, avoiding the need for endless re-workings of his trademark soul-jazz classics.

Ironically, the brief opening title track is the closest to Adderley's typical good-humoured vamps. But it's the rest of the date, particularly Galper's probing *Inner Journey* and *Second Skin*, that warrants the attention. The ebb and flow of Galper's restless electric piano waves, peppered by the street grit of Errisson's chattering congas, provide a splashy undercurrent for Adderley, who applies himself with customary big-hearted warmth, if not with the full gusto of earlier years. It's brother Nat, however, who most impresses, soaring and stabbing in the upper register as the rhythm section pile on the coals with muscular ease on the furnace-hot groove of *Snakin' the Grass*. Its belching, angular funk direction was one that Herbie Hancock would subsequently explore with considerable crossover success a few years later.      **JN**

# Nat Adderley

**Mercy, Mercy, Mercy** Adderley (c, v); **Antonio Hart** (as, ss); **Rob Bargad** (p); **Walter Booker** (b); **Jimmy Cobb** (d). Alfa Jazz Ⓕ ALCB3904 (54 minutes). Recorded 1995.

⑧ ❿

Thanks to the presence of Antonio Hart, Adderley is able to make a jubilant return to the formula that he originally established with his brother Cannonball. The result is a hard-swinging celebration which could have suffered built-in obsolescence, but which, in the hands of the ageing Adderley and his young (Hart, Bargad) and old (Booker, Cobb) men, matures instead into a contemporary re-evaluation of what was a great era. Adderley is one of a distinguished group of men of diminutive physical stature who chose to play the cornet (Hackett, Braff, Berry and Nance were a few of the others). While this gives him a mellow sound, it decreases the range available to him and keeps him from entering the Clark Terry/Miles Davis league. That accepted, he remains a convincing player who bubbles with charisma – apart from his cornet work he is a hilarious raconteur – and his singing of *Sunny Side of the Street* and *Trouble in Mind* is both righteous and good humoured. Bargad, like Hart, masterful throughout the album, evokes early piano blues convincingly on *Trouble in Mind,* while Hart is most eloquent in his front-line partnership. His poignant Hodges tribute, *Rabbit*, is a good song movingly played. The rest of the material is a mixture of standards and originals from the Adderley brothers. They *do* make records like this any more! **SV**

# Air

**Live Air** Henry Threadgill (as, f, perc); **Fred Hopkins** (b); **Steve McCall** (d). Black Saint Ⓕ 0034 (40 minutes). Recorded 1976-7.

⑥ ❻

A second generation ensemble from Chicago's Association for the Advancement of Creative Musicians (though drummer Steve McCall was one of the AACM's founding members in 1964), Air first came together in the early seventies to provide arrangements of Scott Joplin rags for a theatrical production. Their subsequent 1979 recording of Joplin and Jelly Roll Morton tunes, *Air Lore*, is one of their best, but not currently available on CD. Their fine early LPs have yet to be reissued on CD, and **Live Air**, recorded about the time of their third studio LP but not released until 1980, is (despite short playing time and uneven sound quality) at least representative of the group in its heyday. The compositions by Henry Threadgill reflect a few of their many personal influences and stylistic concerns, ranging from Japanese to Latin musics and dynamically interwoven free improvisations. *Eulogy for Charles Clark* (dedicated to an AACM friend and bassist who died tragically young) is an especially evocative piece, beginning and ending with the quiet, sparse, delicate sounds of shakuhachi-like flute, *arco* bass, and bells, framing a broad alto sax and bass theme played over a funereal drum cadence. *Keep Right On Playing Thru the Mirror Over the Water* is another noteworthy performance, where a melody line that floats, dips, and pivots like a bird in flight gives way to McCall's extended mallet solo; on the return of alto sax and bass the music gradually builds in levels of intensity, culminating in the kind of three-part interaction that defined Air's group improvising. The band's ultimate break-up, after more than a decade of outstanding music, was mourned by many listeners. **AL**

# Kei Akagi

**Mirror Puzzle** Akagi (p); **Rick Margitza** (ts); **Charles Fambrough** (b); **Willie Jones III** (d). AudioQuest Ⓕ AQCD 1028 (65 minutes). Recorded 1994.

⑦ ❽

Pianist Akagi is no household name, but he's played with his fair share of them – Miles Davis (for two years), Stanley Turrentine and Airto Moreira for starters. Akagi's family moved from Japan to Cleveland in the US when he was five and the naturally musical child gradually became a professional after completing his studies. Based in L.A., he has paid the price of not being in New York, but his peers on this record are no local yokels – Margitza was in the same Miles band as Akagi, while Fambrough and Jones are two of the most in-demand people on their instruments. The group on this date actually gig together from time to time, so there is none of the tentativeness of so many studio-made line-ups, all the players sounding familiar and comfortable with not only the material (all of which, apart from Wayne Shorter's *Lester Left Town*, comes from Akagi) but with each other's approach to the music. So it all fits together intelligently and with a rare cohesion. The album starts ambitiously with Shorter's famous tune, a five-minute introduction of considerable elaboration masking the direction the band will finally take after the theme is finally stated. This type of intelligent deflection of the listener's casual expectations continues throughout a superior recording session. Of the players, Margitza still has some way to escape Coltrane's shadow but plays sensitively throughout, Akagi has constantly interesting voicings for the progressions he invents and is a fine technician, and the rhythm team quietly steal the album. **KS**

# Toshiko Akiyoshi

1929

---

**Carnegie Hall Concert** Akiyoshi (p, leader); **Mike Ponella, John Eckert, Greg Gisbert** (t); **Joe Magnarelli, Herb Besson, Conrad Herwig, Larry Farrell** (tb); **Matt Finders** (btb); **Frank Wess** (fl, as); **Jim Snidero** (pic, f, cl, as, ts); **Lew Tabackin** (f, ss, ts); **Walt Weiskopf** (f, cl, ss, ts); **Scott Robinson** (bs, bcl); **Peter Washington** (b); **Terry Clarke** (d). Guest trumpet: **Freddie Hubbard**. Columbia Ⓕ 48805-2 (77 minutes). Recorded 1991.

⑧ ❽

Akiyoshi has been living in the US for over 30 years and for a goodly amount of that time she has been giving vigorous new life to the old pre-avant big-band formulas. The band she co-led with her husband, flautist/saxophonist Lew Tabackin (who is featured on this new album) in the seventies was vital in its own time for keeping the idea alive that an acoustic band which swung did not have to sound like a Quincy Jones or Count Basie re-hash. That band is documented on an RCA Novus reissue which is worth having, but this new album is something special. There is a wonderful balance between both the compositions and their arrangements in this concert. Impeccably played throughout, they display Akiyoshi's incredible ear for instrumental blends, and this is nowhere more evident than in the Akiyoshi arrangement for the only piece on the album not written by her, Frank Wess's *Your Beauty is a Song of Love*. There are passing reflections of other large-group leaders and composers, including Mingus and Ellington, but what comes over most strongly is that Akiyoshi has almost single-handedly wrought something contemporary and worthwhile from the advances made by people such as Gary McFarland, Oliver Nelson and Gil Evans 25 years ago and more. Like these men, Akiyoshi proves repeatedly that formal structures and symmetry in compositions do not preclude imagination and flair. She also does not need to parody other styles to make her points. By turns absorbing, exciting and evocative, this album should be sought out. Excellent recorded sound, too, considering it's a live date and few people know how to record a big band anymore.   **KS**

---

**New review**
**At Maybeck** Akiyoshi (p). Concord Ⓕ CCD4635 (61 minutes). Recorded 1995.

⑧ ❽

Akiyoshi is a powerful player who generates much excitement. Her tumbling improvisations are filled with good ideas and bright devices. Her thinking processes are remarkable and in her own composition *The Village* she can be heard following three lines at once. She is an original composer, but *The Village* is one of only two originals in her Maybeck recital. No matter, for the other material she uses is unhackneyed or, in the case of *Sophisticated Lady* or *That Old Devil Moon* treated with refreshingly new settings. The latter employs left-hand work that would have pleased Art Tatum, and Toshiko's rhythmic power with the left is also a vital prop for *The Village. Polka Dots and Moonbeams* shows a good set of ballad credentials but it is the fireworks of her treatment of Powell's *Tempus Fugit* that causes the sudden intake of breath from the listener, reminding us of her deep attachment to Powell's music (she made a Powell tribute album some years ago). Her treatment of *Come Sunday* is exquisite, confirming this as another jewel in the series, now at number 36.   **SV**

# Joe Albany

1924-88

---

**The Right Combination** Albany (p); **Warne Marsh** (ts); **Bob Whitlock** (bs); **Ralph Garretson** (d). Riverside Ⓜ OJCCD1749-2 (43 minutes). Recorded 1957.

⑧ ❻

Albany was one of the more shadowy figures of the post-war jazz years, a man with a great 'inside' reputation as Charlie Parker's favourite pianist but whose appearance on record was limited to just four sides with Lester Young and two with Georgie Auld. Although he made several trio and solo albums, principally in Europe, during the seventies and eighties, none of them has the magic of **The Right Combination**. Never intended for issue, it emanates from a rehearsal in Garretson's apartment and has the boxiness of an amateur recording, although at no time is the playing of Marsh or Albany indistinct. There are many occasions when Albany overcomes the mechanical qualities of his instrument by producing single-note lines which slither across the chords like a saxophone. Warne Marsh, one of the greatest pure improvisers jazz has ever heard, responds with solos of remarkable invention. Their version of *Body and Soul* is a stunning example of empathy while Clifford Brown's intriguing tune, *Daahoud*, provides a challenge to which Joe and Warne respond admirably. Gary Hobish's remastering has given the instruments greater clarity than was present on the LP, making this CD of even greater value.   **AM**

# Howard Alden

1963

---

**The Howard Alden Trio Plus Special Guests Ren Peplowski & Warren Vaché** Alden (g); **Vaché** (c); **Peplowski** (cl, ts); **Lynn Seaton** (b); **Mel Lewis** (d). Concord Ⓕ CCD4378 (49 minutes). Recorded 1989.

⑧ ❽

Alden is that rarity of rarities – a young musician whose basic affinities lie with pre-bop styles, yet who is not averse to bop and post-bop material; a latter-day Dick Wellstood of the guitar. He has recorded in various formats, including a quintet co-led with trombonist Dan Barrett, a two-guitar combo with George Van Eps and his own trio. This album is looser than the sets with Barrett, yet allows Alden to show his comping sensitivity by adding either Vaché or Peplowski on most of the 11 tracks. Tune choices are typically astute – a pair each from Ellington and Reinhardt; some Bird, Monk, Waller and Van Eps; and a few choice warhorses, rarely of the overplayed variety. The guitarist has picked two horn soloists with an intimate, deferential approach to the classic material, and paired them with a rhythm section that lets enough of its more abstract inclinations out to provide the necessary jolt. Through it all, Alden remains relaxed and engaged, avoiding both easy choices and grandstanding, and blurring distinctions between the mouldy and the modern.　　**BB**

# Monty Alexander
1944

**New review**

**At Maybeck**  Alexander (p). Concord Ⓕ CCD-4658 (59 minutes). Recorded 1994.

⑧ ❾

Alexander is hardly an under-recorded artist and while there is a high level of technical consistency to his playing the buyer should be circumspect in his choice of Monty's albums. This one may be purchased with no qualms; it places Alexander in the most exposed position, with nowhere to hide. Concord's Maybeck Hall series (this is volume 40) has produced some wonderful music, all of it played on the Yamaha S-400B piano lovingly maintained in the Maybeck Recital Room, Richmond, California. The sound of the piano, the actual acoustic qualities and recording balance are above reproach. Monty rises to the occasion to produce 11 flawless solos commencing with a rollicking version of *When the Saints*. His touch is brittle and precise, producing an individual tone from the instrument and making him an ideal concert performer (although he has, of course, turned in very efficient work backing Milt Jackson). There is a wide range of material here, from Johnny Mandel's *Close Enough for Love* to Charlie Chaplin's *Smile* by way of the hypnotic *Estate*. And what Monty Alexander programme would be complete without a reference to his native Jamaica? On this occasion it is a revitalized treatment of *Island in the Sun*.　　**AM**

# Lorez Alexandria
1929

**The Great/More of the Great** Alexandria (v); with various groups including: **Bud Shank** (f); **Paul Horn** (as, f); **Ray Crawford** (g); **Wynton Kelly** (p); **Al McKibbon** (b); **Jimmy Cobb** (d). Impulse! Ⓜ MCAD33116 (69 minutes). Recorded 1964-5.

⑥ ❻

There are no definitive versions among these 20 songs, but no disasters either. At the time when these two albums were recorded Lorez Alexandria had a growing reputation as the hipsters' vocalist, largely as a result of her excellent taste in material and accompanists. Essentially, she comes across as a very good cabaret artiste, a bit on the breathless side at times and with a tendency to overdo the meaningful pauses, but musical rather than theatrical (more Lena Horne than Eartha Kitt, if you take my meaning). She certainly did not shy away from challenges. Among the songs here are *Angel Eyes*, *No More*, *My One and Only Love* and *But Beautiful*, each a little minefield in its way and efficiently negotiated.　　**DG**

# Hasaan Ibn Ali

**The Max Roach Trio Featuring the Legendary Hasaan** Ali (p); **Art Davis** (b); **Max Roach** (d). Atlantic Jazz Ⓜ 782273-2 (41 minutes). Recorded 1964.

⑦ ❺

Hasaan falls into that select group of unfortunates (other fully paid-up members include Elmo Hope, Herbie Nichols, Von Freeman and Cal Massey) who have both an outsize dose of talent and an original musical vision, and spend their professional careers suffering for it. This is the only record he has ever made, and it is his date in all but name (clearly, Atlantic records didn't think that his name alone on the cover would be enough to get sales out of double figures, and they were probably right). All credit then to Roach who, alone among his peers, went past just talking to his friends about this Philadelphia legend and organized a record date for him.

The big drawback on this session is a chronically sick piano: somebody must have spent days getting it to sound so bad. That Hasaan overcomes this obstacle sufficiently to deliver his special pianistic brew (all seven tracks are Hasaan originals) and make the listener concentrate through the instrument's shortcomings speaks volumes for his talent and his perseverence. A self-professed fan of Elmo Hope (a musician Hasaan sees as giving the lead to both Monk and Powell in the forties), he displays a similar angularity, rhythmic asymmetry and combination of the traditional and the revolutionary. There is little of the bebop pianistic vocabulary in Hasaan's playing: like Monk, Nichols and the young Cecil Taylor, he has a very heavy touch and a decidedly firm, measured rhythmic pulse. His music can be equally as dissonant, surprising and intriguing as any of the above players. Roach and Davis provide detailed and greatly sympathetic support to Hasaan, giving him the attention and commitment he deserves. This is an album for the specialist listener, but it rewards close and careful study. **KS**

# Eddie Allen

**New review**
**R 'n' B** Allen (t); **Donald Harrison** (as); **Anthony Wonsey** (p); **Christian McBride** (b); **Marvin 'Smitty' Smith** (d). Enja Ⓕ ENJ9033-2 (55 minutes). Recorded 1995.

⑦ ❽

Despite the title, this album, by the experienced ex-Lester Bowie Brass Fantasy trumpeter, is straight-ahead post-bop jazz, with some innovative polyrhythmic overtones, and a set of pleasant original compositions. Allen's hard-hitting trumpet contrasts well with Harrison at his most laid back, nowhere better than on *Frick and Frack* where Allen's lines are underpinned by bleary saxophone phrases, lazily floating over the very impressive rhythm section. Twenty-four-year-old Wonsey, a one-time pupil of veteran trumpeter Zilner Randolph, more than holds his own against two of the strongest session rhythm players around. Allen's idea was to integrate various different rhythmic ideas into a broad jazz and blues palette, and he succeeds admirably in an entertaining album with no weak links in the playing and a genuine sense of ensemble collaboration. Here and there are moments of real inspiration: the challenging opening to *As Quiet As It's Kept* with some free-range drumming from Smith, and the loosely Caribbean feel of *Clairvoyant*. Both Allen and Harrison have an instinctive and intellectual interest in jazz heritage, and this gives the album depth while avoiding the pitfalls of repertory playing on the one hand and dulling their spontaneity on the other. **AS**

# Geri Allen

1933

**New review**
**Twenty One** Allen (p); **Ron Carter** (b); **Tony Williams** (d). Blue Note Ⓕ CDP830028-2 (78 minutes). Recorded 1994.

❽ ❾

A graduate of Brooklyn's M-Base school of further education, Allen has made her reputation in especially good company. She successfully led a trio with Charlie Haden and Paul Motian and, after joining Blue Note, fronted larger units with equal aplomb. This CD finds her leading a trio as testing as any she had previously fronted. Carter, one of the finest and most prolific string bassists, is ideal for her. He supports infallibly but there are always little challenges to suggest alternatives to the pianist. Williams, of the fast hands and ineluctable energy, serves equally well and, like Carter, does so with a faint hint of confrontation. Allen's response is to match the assertiveness of her colleagues with her own self-assurance. Her choice of material certainly accommodates such an approach. Her own *Drummers Song* is a reminder that the piano is itself a percussion instrument and she shows her understanding of 'Monkery' by a respectful re-evaluation of *Introspection/Thelonious*. She also shows her versatility as she contrasts the drive of *Beautiful Friendship* or *Tea for Two* with the graceful strength of *If I Should Lose You* or *Old Folks*. Allen is now the artist to be fazed by nobody and, in fact, has here made an outstanding recording by dint of that artistic resilience. **BMcR**

# Harry Allen

1966

**New review**
**Blue Skies** Allen (ts); **John Bunch** (p); **Dennis Irwin** (b); **Duffy Jackson** (d). John Marks Records Ⓕ JMR 9 (67 minutes). Recorded 1994.

❽ ❽

The album is subtitled **Jazz Ballads from the 1930s to Today**, but the bounds of Allen's eclectic style are cast so far out that many of his ballads receive punching, swinging performances that recall nothing so much as the genial good humour and swing of the late Zoot Sims or Al Cohn. Allen's personal frontier is at Rollins, Coltrane and Shorter, whose work he, at least currently, chooses to eschew. Sims and Cohn left a huge hole in the premier league of tenor playing, and Allen, still young, shows every sign of being able to fill a good part of it. He is one of the still-young mainstream virtuosos like Howard Alden and Ken Peplowski who suddenly emerged from the woodwork without explanation. He is a more sophisticated player than Scott Hamilton, with whom he is bound to be compared, and any preference must be personal. His albums are getting better (there is a good one on Nagel Heyer CD011 recorded a fortnight later than this one by the same group). Although he doesn't reach the phenomenal bar rate of the classic Stan Getz version, he sails through a very fast *Shine* while another Getz standby, *Nobody Else But Me*, gets a severe thumping considering it is meant to be a ballad. Bunch and Jackson are experienced quarteteers and Jackson too confirms his burgeoning talent. Allen is God's gift to those who have decided not to venture forth from their record collections of the fifties and sixties. **SV**

# Henry 'Red' Allen

1908-67

**Henry Allen and his New York Orchestra 1929-30, Volumes 1 and 2** Allen (t, v); Otis Johnson (t); J.C. Higginbotham, Jimmy Archey (tb); Albert Nicholas, Charlie Holmes, Teddy Hill, Thornton Blue, Greely Walton (reeds); Luis Russell (p); Will Johnson (bj, g, v); Pops Foster (b); Ernest Hill (bb); Paul Barbarin (d, vb); Victoria Spivey, Sweet Peas (Addie Spivey), The Four Wanderers, Dick Robertson, Vic Dickenson (v). JSP Ⓕ JSPCD332/33 (two discs, oas: 138 minutes). Recorded 1929-30.

⑧ ❿

Often unjustly overlooked as a transitional figure in the history of jazz trumpet, Allen worked briefly with hometown heroes King Oliver and Jelly Roll Morton, but his main sideman associations were with the early swing outfits of Fletcher Henderson and Mills Blue Rhythm Band, plus the Luis Russell group whose members contribute to these first recordings under his own name. Naturally impressed by the then-current work of Armstrong (for whom Russell worked at this period and again later), Allen lacked Satchmo's power but capitalized on his freely rhythmic fantasias. 'Red''s unique rubbery tone sounded equally appropriate playing obliquely-phrased lead parts or backing the Spivey sisters, who sing separately on several tracks of each volume. Common to all except a few items is the excellent New Orleans bass-and-drums team of Foster and Barbarin (incidentally, the excellent remastering makes it clear that Foster plays bowed bass rather than tuba on *Telephoning the Blues*). JSP's disposition of the alternate takes between these two different chronological programmes requires both of them to be recommended. If a choice has to be made, the guest vocals by Robertson and Vic Dickenson on Volume 2 pale beside Allen's own singing on the Volume 1-only *Patrol Wagon Blues*. **BP**

**Original 1933-41 Recordings** Allen (t, v); with various personnel, including: Dickie Wells, J.C. Higginbotham (tb); Buster Bailey, Cecil Scott, Edmond Hall (cl); Hilton Jefferson, Tab Smith (as); Chu Berry, Joe Garland (ts); Horace Henderson, Fletcher Henderson, Edgar Hayes, Clyde Hart, Billy Kyle, Ken Kersey (p); Danny Barker (g); John Kirby (b); Paul Barbarin, Kaiser Marshall, Cozy Cole (d). Tax Ⓕ S32 (70 minutes). Recorded 1933-41.

⑦ ❻

By the time these recordings were made, 'Red' Allen was an established and (as far as it was possible under the all-embracing influence of the seminal Louis Armstrong) original stylist, both as a vocalist and trumpeter. Even the most cursory listen will establish key identifying traits such as Allen's wonderfully throwaway sense of time over a metric pulse, his love of large intervallic leaps and contrasting low-down gutbucket slurs and growls. In this last sense, if not in others, he continues the King Oliver tradition, rather than Armstrong's; he was an inspired distorter of the trumpet's open tone, as well as someone who could play with commanding authority and astonishing technical ease. His natural sound was lighter and rather thinner than Armstrong's. This Tax disc covers a period when Allen led the sections of a number of bands, those of Fletcher Henderson, Lucky Millinder and Luis Russell included, and also occasionally led his own studio groups. The transfers are clean and true, the track selection serviceable and one gets a good helping of both Allen the vocalist and Allen the trumpeter. He is often in the company of top-drawer talent, with the rhythm sections in particular contributing some serious swinging. There has recently been a release on the Topaz label (1929-35) which covers much of the material found on this and the Robert Parker record. **KS**

# Eric Allison

1951

New review

**Mean Streets Beat** Allison (ts, cl); Melton Mustafa (t); Turk Mauro (ts, bs); Dr Lonnie Smith, Billy Marcus, Vince Maggio (p); Jeff Grubbs, Phil Flanagan, Dennis Marks (b); Danny Burger (d). Contemporary Ⓕ CCD 14080-2 (69 minutes). Recorded 1996.

⑥ ❾

Allison has been a mainstay of the Florida scene since the mid seventies and plays virtually every night of the week in virtually every style of jazz. This album uses local Floridan talent and is produced by the original owner of Prestige, Bob Weinstock, now a Floridan resident. No prizes for guessing, then, that it is a session of swinging music with the emphasis on blues-tinged, funky repertoire and some hefty blowing from the two saxophonists (Mauro is present on the first five tracks). There is little here which hasn't been covered on countless Weinstock sessions of the past, although the clarinet/baritone evocation of Ellington's *Creole Love Call* on Allison's *Lonely Avenue* is fetching, as is Smith's spare piano solo, and the unaccompanied sax duet *Improvisation* is great fun, like Gene Ammons meeting Bob Crosby. The last five tracks have James Martin on drums with a number of different pianists and bassists, but the groove remains modern mainstream whoever's providing the backing. Trumpeter Mustafa appears on two tracks and plays competently. **KS** 21

# Mose Allison

1927

**Back Country Suite** Allison (p, v); **Taylor La Fargue** (b); **Frank Isola** (d). Prestige Ⓜ
OJCCD075-2 (35 minutes). Recorded 1957.

⑦ ❽

Born in Mississippi and weaned on the boogie and blues music of the area, Allison came to bebop via
swing-era piano stylists such as Nat King Cole. In the mid fifties he worked in New York as a sideman
with the likes of Zoot Sims and Stan Getz, but since that time has performed mainly as a cabaret artist
with his own trio. This CD highlights the range of moods that he puts into his piano work. The longer
pieces take on a special character, with *I Thought about You* treated as straight-ahead bebop,
*Blueberry Hill* featured as only Thelonious Monk might attempt it and *You Won't Let Me Know*
delivered with a Ray Bryant-like nonchalance. The excellent *Back Country Suite* is appropriately
bucolic, offering orthodox bop on *Scamper* and *Highway 49* but elsewhere showing how best to
broach the subject of musical description. *New Ground* is a rolling blues, *Train* avoids the simulated
locomotive clichés but still makes the journey, while *January* has an almost contrived sense of apathy.
The Baptist church creeps into *The Promised Land,* while *Spring Song* shows that even the Back
Country has cocktail lounges. Allison's laconic post-Hoagy Carmichael drawl mixes no-hope
pessimism with hip self-realization on *One-Room Country Shack,* but for more obvious vocal mayhem
there is the brother CD, **Local Colour** (Prestige OJCCD457-2), plus three early-sixties discs from the
Columbia vaults which have recently been given a dust-down once more. **BMcR**

# Karrin Allyson

1962

New review

**Collage** Allyson (v, p); **Bob Bowman** (b); **Todd Strait** (d); **Paul Smith**, **Laura Caviani** (p); **Rod
Fleeman**, **Danny Embrey** (g); **Kim Park** (as); **Mike Metheny** (flh); **Randy Weinstein** (h); **Claude
'Fiddler' Williams** (vn); **Carter Brey** (vc). Concord Ⓕ CCD4709 (67 minutes). Recorded 1996.

⑦ ❾

In her fourth release for Concord, Kansas City jazz diva Karrin Allyson strikes a variety of comely poses
with an all-star cast of Kansas City's "best and brightest". A gifted young singer whose scrapbook of raves
continues to grow, Allyson is also a *bona fide* musician (and an excellent pianist). Like Ella Fitzgerald,
Allyson conjoins evocative sophistication with girlish glee in a beguiling style sizzling with sensual as well
as musical allure. When she waxes lyrical on *Joy Spring* or warns that *It Could Happen to You*, you believe
her. And, happily, as she takes us into the palm of her hand, she does so *sans* histrionic plays to the
balcony. Allyson's supporting players are perfect. On the brooding balladic treatment of Monk's *Ask Me
Now*, Laura Caviani's piano weaves spells. So, too, does Claude 'Fiddler' Williams's violin on *Autumn
Leaves*. As for barn-burners, Kim Park's alto run-down of *Cherokee* is torrid, and a perfect foil for
Allyson's scat-magic. For home cooking, the singer's pungent take on Bonnie Raitt's finger-lickin' *Give It
Up or Let Me Go* pays fitting tribute to K.C.'s tradition of barbecue-smothered jazz-cum-blues. **CB**

# Herb Alpert

1935

New review

**Second Wind** Alpert (t, kbds); **Jeff Lorber** (kbds); **Nathaniel Phillips** (elb); **John 'J.R.' Robinson**
(d); **Paul Pesco** (elg). Almo Sounds Ⓕ ALMCD010 (53 minutes). Recorded 1996.

⑦ ❾

Herb Alpert's work in the Tijuana Brass left no doubt that he could play the trumpet, but his recent
output has added a degree of good taste to his accomplishments. In the eighties there were recordings that
seemed to take their pitch from the Miles Davis of **Decoy**. Here, in a suitably titled comeback on a new
label, his conversion from pop to jazz goes a few steps further, thanks in large part to a fruitful
partnership with the exceptional writer and arranger Jeff Lorber. Lorber's input is crucial to the success
of the record, his deceptively intricate and powerful funk backdrops an absolute joy. On the open horn,
Alpert's brassy tone is dominant, but when, as on *Flirtation,* he plays little chromatic licks through the
mute, Miles is instantly recalled. His lines are effective if unambitious and, like Miles, the technique is a
little shaky at times, but in the context of Lorber's skilful arrangements his playing fits the bill very well.
Things do become rather limp half way through when Herb's predilection for romantic ballads takes hold,
and there are disappointingly weak funk readings of *Flamingo* and *My Funny Valentine,* but the record is
worth hearing for the more vigorous early stuff, not least the hip *So What* paraphrase, *Sneakin' In.* **MG**

# Barry Altschul

1943

New review

**For Stu** Altschul (d); **Ray Anderson** (tb); **Anthony Davis** (p); **Rick Rozie** (b). Soul Note Ⓕ 121015-2
(42 minutes). Recorded 1979.

⑦ ❽

Altschul's empirical attitude toward jazz has led to his becoming one of the truly versatile drummers. A Charlie Persip student in his teens, he worked with Paul Bley in his formative years and was also associated with the Jazz Composers' Orchestra. He was a member of the influential group Circle with Chick Corea and Anthony Braxton and became a prominent figure in the seventies 'loft movement' in New York. From 1978 he taught drumming and, for a brief period, led this quartet. **For Stu** is an album dedicated to drummer Stu Martin and was made after the quartet had enjoyed a mutual introductory gig at New York's Sweet Basil Club. It shows that Altschul is not only a fine time-keeper but also an adroit controller of dynamics. The solo *Drum Role* confirms that he is essentially a musical drummer; it shows his mastery of tempo changes and parades his skill as a climax-builder. It also keeps him in touch with being creative; the drum line breathes and confirms his comfort with tricky, tacet areas. In a very different manner, Altschul's brushes provide an aptly somnambulistic element on *Sleepwalker*, in the process complementing Anderson's superbly quarrelsome trombone solo. Throughout, Altschul's tidy cymbal work rounds off his all-kit control. *Orange Was the Color of Her Dress* caps the performance. It offers total quartet integration and, by means of different responses to his sidemen's solos, demonstrates his sympathy for their individual needs. **BMcR**

## Flavio Ambrosetti

1919

**New review**

**Anniversary** Ambrosetti (ss, as), with collective personnel: **Hazy Osterwald, Raymond Court, Franco Ambrosetti** (t, flh); **Ernst Hîllerhagen** (cl); **Barney Wilen, Sal Nistico, Alan Skidmore** (ts); **Lars Gullin** (bs); **Toots Thielemans, Franco Cerri** (g); **Francis Cuppieters, Francis Burger, George Gruntz, Joe Zawinul** (p, elp, syn); **Sonny Lang, Franco Cerri, K.T. Geier, Eric Peter, George Joyner, Sam Jones, Gilbert Roväre, Guy Pedersen, Henri Texier, J. Franáois Jenny-Clark, Ron Mathewson** (b); **Gil Cuppini, Rodolfo Bonetto, Pierre Favre, Buster Smith, Kenny Clarke, Louis Hayes, Daniel Humair** (d). Enja ⓔ ENJ9027-2 (two discs: 140 minutes). Recorded 1949-76.

⑦ ❼

Born in Lugano, Switzerland, in 1919, Flavio Ambrosetti is the perfect age to straddle all styles of jazz from swing through bop to modern, and a representative sample of his efforts in all these areas can be heard on these two CDs. Like his trumpeter son, Franco, Ambrosetti *père* commutes between the business world and jazz, but has nevertheless managed to carve out a considerable niche for himself in European jazz history, often appearing both with his son and pianist/bandleader George Gruntz, most frequently in the small groups to whose music the bulk of the second CD is dedicated. The elder Ambrosetti began on tenor but switched to alto on hearing Benny Carter, his early swing-based playing retaining a hint of the smooth elegance of his influence until it is overlain with the more *staccato* bop mannerisms which he was among the first European players to assimilate. The first CD covers Ambrosetti's pre-seventies playing, embracing Ellington (*Perdido, It Don't Mean a Thing ...*) through Charlie Parker (*Anthropology*) to Thelonious Monk (*Straight, No Chaser*), and showcases his thoughtful, agile alto sound; the second features his seventies band (with Gruntz frequently resorting to that most dating of instruments, the electric piano), spearheaded by an altogether tarter, more astringent alto tone and culminating with a brief excursion into funk in stellar company. Although chiefly notable for its documentary importance – dealing as it does with a neglected period of jazz history: the importation of bop into Europe and its adoption by indigenous players in the fifties – this album also provides a welcome record of a fine pioneering career. **CP**

## Franco Ambrosetti

1941

**Gin and Pentatonic** Ambrosetti (t, flh); **Lew Soloff, Michael Mossman** (t); **Alex Brophy, John Clark** (frh); **Steve Coleman** (as); **Michael Brecker** (ts); **Howard Johnson** (bs, tba); **Kenny Kirkland, Tommy Flanagan** (p); **Buster Williams, Dave Holland** (b); **Daniel Humair** (d). Enja ⓔ ENJ4096-2 (68 minutes). Recorded 1983-5.

⑧ ❽

Compiled from his much-acclaimed 1983 sextet recording **Wings** and the later **Tentets**, **Gin and Pentatonic** provides an excellent introduction to the work of jazz-playing business executive Franco Ambrosetti. Although his neo-bop style has been compared with that of Freddie Hubbard, Ambrosetti's purity of tone (particularly on flügelhorn), his flawless balance and control at high tempos, enabling him to rip through a tune's changes without apparent effort, also bring Kenny Wheeler to mind. Ambrosetti's compositions are, however, utterly individual, and provide the meat of this compilation, being excellent platforms not only for Ambrosetti himself, but for his all-star **Wings** band. Michael Brecker, always burly and sinewy, sounding more engaged in an unalloyed jazz setting than he frequently does in more fusion-based fare, is a perfect front-line foil, John Clark's french horn provides valuable extra tone and texture, Kenny Kirkland is exhilarating throughout and Buster Williams's sonorous, full-bodied bass drone is an excellent anchor. Long-time associate Daniel Humair is the powerhouse behind each band and is particularly effective on the George Gruntz material – unsurprisingly, given the three Europeans' long association in

Gruntz's concert band. The tentet recordings conjure up less immediate excitement than the sextet material, but are nevertheless faultlessly – if unspectacularly – arranged, and are particularly notable for providing an intriguing glimpse of altoist Steve Coleman in his pre-M-Base, Mel Lewis/Thad Jones band period. Overall, a highly enjoyable, exuberant but tasteful collection from a European master.                                                        **CP**

# AMM

**The Nameless Uncarved Block** Lou Gare (ts, vn); **Keith Rowe** (g, electronics); **John Tilbury** (p); **Eddie Prévost** (d). Matchless Ⓕ MR20 (74 minutes). Recorded 1990.

⑧ ❽

AMM will soon be celebrating three decades together, although the personnel has altered somewhat over the years, as has the direction and possibly the intent of their music. Even though totally improvised, it is somewhat distinct from free jazz, although that is the way they started out in the sixties when Prévost, Gare and Rowe began exploring instinctual methods of structuring sound. After years of experimentation they are now able to create not just a language (as do most new musics) but an environment; a way of defining space and filling it with meaningful sounds. The *idea* of jazz may create a subtle tension in the listener's mind; the saxophone and piano produce tones which we may identify with jazz (although Tilbury, particularly, is trained and experienced in 'classical' New Music), but the context is unfamiliar. In fact, they desire to create new contexts, intentionally confusing their own contributions and our responses: each instrument might be used percussively *or* melodically, or in a way so as to make it unrecognizable, as individual details mesh into a complex fabric free of conventional form (which is why they work in such large time-frames: the three pieces here clock in at 29, 37, and seven minutes). The album's title is apt; the gradually exposed sounds are frequently layered like the grain in rock. Sometimes the musicians seem to be excavating unformed sounds from a bottomless quarry, other times they are sculpting them into abstract shapes. This is music not of virtuosity, but concentration and risk, and AMM has reached a point of success where, regardless of its newness, the sounds have a feeling of inevitability – not of compositional precision, but of Nature.                                              **AL**

# Albert Ammons                                                                       1907-49

**The First Day** Ammons, **Meade Lux Lewis** (p). Blue Note Ⓜ CDP7 98450-2 (74 minutes). Recorded 1939.

⑧ ❼

Ammons shares this record with his boogie-woogie contemporary Meade Lux Lewis, and the difference in their approaches is at once obvious: whereas Lewis's slow blues appear to be largely improvised, Ammons's creations seem to have been thought through, planned in detail – and there is a great deal of detail in pieces like *Boogie Woogie Stomp* or the superb *Bass Goin' Crazy*, where the left hand launches a series of bold invasions into the right hand's home ground. The contrast of steady pulse and flamboyant adventure, so characteristic of the idiom, is for Ammons a particularly rich source of ideas. Some of them are almost visual in their effect; without too much effort the listener can see a stocky, good-humoured man strolling amiably but purposefully along, say, Lenox Avenue, joyfully rattling the money in his pockets.

Ammons also evinces an interest in reshaping traditional themes and earlier compositions, such as *Easy Rider Blues*, *Backwater Blues* and *Suitcase Blues*, and in later years he had some success with boogie-woogie translations of more *outré* material, as in *Swanee River Boogie*. Although more conventional in design, Ammons's 1941 duets with Pete Johnson are classics of their kind; they can be found on **Barrelhouse Boogie** (RCA Bluebird ND88334), together with recordings by Lewis and Jimmy Yancey.                                                                              **TR**

# Gene Ammons                                                                        1925-74

**Young Jug** Ammons (ts); **Billy Massey** (t); **Matthew Gee, J.J. Johnson** (tb); **Sonny Stitt** (bs); prob. **Willie Jones, Christine Chatman, Junior Mance, John Houston** (p); **Leo Blevins** (g); **Leroy Jackson, Lowell Pointer, Gene Wright, Ernie Shepherd** (b); **Wesley Landers, Ike Day, Teddy Stewart, Rob Wilson** (d); **Tom Archaia** (ts). Chess Ⓜ GRP18012 (60 minutes). Recorded 1948-52.

⑧ ❻

Ammons, son of pianist Albert, is sometimes dismissed as a forerunner of populist players such as Lou Donaldson and Grover Washington, but for the black audience who appreciated his soulful tenor he personified the boundary of jazz and r&b. As a teenage star of the Billy Eckstine big band, he partnered Dexter Gordon (later, like Dexter, spending nearly a decade out of circulation) and for some years toured with Sonny Stitt. The equal of Gordon in combining Parker's influence with a strong allegience to Lester Young, he was famous for ballads in a simplified version of the style established by Hawkins and Chu Berry.

This material, some of the first under Ammons's own name (though he also recorded prolifically for Mercury and Prestige during the same period), shows his great qualities applied to a number of current ballads (*My Foolish Heart, Somewhere Along the Way* ) as well as standards already long in the tooth. But these were almost all issued on 78rpm singles with a more up-tempo B-side such as *Jug Head Ramble* (a title incorporating Ammons's nickname) or *More Moon* (remaking a hit from his brief stay with Woody Herman). Inferior production mars the first four tracks, including the witty *Swingin' for Xmas*, but these can be programmed out or could, indeed, have been put at the end of the programme by the producer.                                                                                      **BP**

**New review**

**Jug**  Ammons (ts); **Richard Wyands** (p); **Clarence 'Sleepy' Anderson** (p, org); **Doug Watkins** (b); **J. C. Heard** (d); **Ray Barretto** (cga). Prestige Ⓜ OJCCD701 (37 minutes). Recorded 1961.

⑧ ❼

For much of his career, Gene Ammons attracted the record-buying public and won the respect, if little more, of reviewers. There was nothing extreme about what he played. Skirting r&b, he rarely produced the shattering honks of a Jacquet. His warm, breathy tone would rate midway on some hypothetical Ben Webster-Lester Young scale and his phrases occasionally remind one of Dexter Gordon but come over with less of a swagger. The format of this album fits him like a glove. For a start, the balance between Heard and Barretto, who between them could so easily have come up with quasi-Latin stodge, is perfect, adding a rhythmic ripple that reflects great credit on both. Apart from a couple of blues and a ballad by Anderson, the tunes are standard songs that give Ammons plenty to chew on without putting him under pressure, since no track lasts more than six minutes. The whole adds up to stimulating, soulful tenor playing, with the blues and *Easy to Love* being especially recommended. One gripe about these OJC reissues relates to the way petty errors survive: in this case Doug Watkins still appears as "Dough", 30 years later.                                                                          **RA**

# David Amram                                                                                          1930

**New review**

**Havana/New York**  Amram (frh, g, p, f, whistle, claves, xyl, perc); **Thad Jones** (t, flh); **Arturo Sandoval** (t); **Jerry Dodgion, Paquito De Rivera** (as); **Billy Mitchell** (ts); **Pepper Adams, George Barrow** (bs); **Eddie Gomez, John Ore** (b); **Billy Hart** (d); **Alfredo De La Fe** (vn, perc); **Candido, Oscar Valdes** (cga); **Ray Mantilla, Johnny Rodriguez, Los Papines** (perc). Flying Fish Ⓕ FF70057 (39 minutes). Recorded 1977.

⑥ ❻

Born in Philadelphia, Amram became a world traveller and a multi-culturalist before that status became *de rigueur* in jazz circles. He attended Oberlin Conservatory and was later to compose over 100 orchestral and chamber works as well as writing two operas. He did his national service in Europe and later returned to Paris, where he became involved in the local jazz scene and made his recording début in 1955. His instrumental skills are many and varied. He is best known as a French horn player but also plays composer's piano and is impressive in his use of wooden flutes and whistles. This CD presents all of these skills, but it is also of historical importance in that it documents the US/Cuban musical exchange of 1977. No US citizen had legally visited since 1961 and there was considerable excitement at the time; the party included Dizzy Gillespie, Stan Getz and Earl Hines, although none of these musicians are on *En Memoria de Chano Pozo*, the track recorded in Cuba on the trip. The other titles were recorded in New York but they successfully recapture the spirit of the event and feature fine solos by Jones, Adams and De La Fe. Amram remains involved in jazz and his recently reissued 1988/9 album **Pull My Daisy** (Premier PRCD1046) confirms no diminution of skills in any of his instrumental departments.                                                                                  **BMcR**

# Cat Anderson                                                                                          1916-81

**Cat Anderson Plays W.C. Handy**  Anderson (t, v); **Booty Wood** (tb); **Norris Turney** (as); **Harold Ashby, Gerald Badini** (ts); **André Persiany, Raymond Fol, Philippe Baudoin** (p); **Aaron Bell, Michel Gaudry** (b); **Sam Woodyard** (d). Black & Blue Ⓕ 59163-2 (55 minutes). Recorded 1978-9.

⑧ ❽

The razor blade-like notes of Cat Anderson were part of Duke Ellington's imprimatur for the best part of three decades. Usually Ellingtonians did not sound as good away from the Ellington band as they did within it; Anderson was an exception, and this wonderfully flourishing album makes one wonder what might have been. The excellent material – Handy collected the best tunes – lets Cat and his associates play comfortably within their limits, the outbursts of stratospheric notes husbanded in a miserly fashion. Much use is made of mutes and Anderson reveals himself to be both dextrous and tasteful. He is generously supported by his sidemen – Booty Wood's muted solos on *Careless Love* and *Beale Street Blues* are masterful. Ashby preaches on *St Louis Blues* and sings on his horn in *Hesitating Blues*, no doubt inspired by the spanking but rather repetitive drumming of Sam Woodyard. Persiany's piano is also most effective. But Anderson predictably towers over the proceedings with a dazzling display of trumpet expertise and good taste. The influence he took from Armstrong is much in evidence and this sterling album is indeed a worthy match for Armstrong's similar essay on Handy's tunes.   **SV**

# Ernestine Anderson                                                    1928

**Hello Like Before**  Anderson (v); **Hank Jones** (p); **Ray Brown** (b); **Jimmie Smith** (d). Concord
Ⓕ CCD4031 (38 minutes). Recorded 1976.

⑦ ❽

Anderson has been a professional singer now for 50 years, having started in the early forties with Russell Jacquet and progressed to singing with Lionel Hampton and Johnny Otis, among others. By the mid fifties she had developed away from her r&b roots, spending time in Europe and evolving a modern approach to standard repertoire which jazz-based audiences found pleasing. This new career withered with the onset of the sixties, and she spent more than a decade in England before landing in Los Angeles. After a few gigs around and about, she was invited to appear at the 1975 Concord Jazz Festival. Her set there effectively re-launched her Stateside career and led directly to **Hello Like Before**, her first album for Concord and still arguably her best, though there have been many since.

A large part of the reason for this success is the superbly sympathetic and imaginative support she receives from Hank Jones, one of the greatest jazz accompanists of any era. There is not a moment on this disc when Jones is not supplying delightful instrumental commentary and subtle shadings of his own to Anderson's supple and winning ways with a lyric or a melody. The singer herself avoids bombast or interpretative clichés, chooses her standards with care (even *'Tain't Nobody's Business* sounds fresh here), and manages to sustain that magical intimacy between singer and audience which is the essence of good vocalizing.   **KS**

# Fred Anderson                                                         1929

**Destiny**  Anderson (ts); **Marilyn Crispell** (p); **Hamid Drake** (perc). Okkadisc Ⓕ OD12003
(67 minutes). Recorded 1994.

⑧ ❽

Now an elder statesman of the Chicago scene, Fred Anderson was among the AACM's prime movers in the mid sixties. His later groups, often co-led with trumpeter Billy Brimfield, provided a valuable testing-ground for a rising generation of players: notable alumni have included reedsmen Douglas Ewart and Chico Freeman and trombonist George Lewis. Anderson's fluent, big-toned sound seems to encompass the tenor tradition, although he has named Gene Ammons, Chu Berry, Don Byas and Lester Young as particular favourites and reported too that he sharpened his technique by constantly practising Charlie Parker tunes. Those influences were woven into a distinctive, personal style that one writer has suggested is the 'missing link' between late-fifties Ornette Coleman and early AACM saxophonists such as Roscoe Mitchell and Joseph Jarman (on whose 1967 **Song For** Anderson guested).

Unfortunately, discs by Anderson himself have been extremely rare: even this CD, his first new recording in nearly 15 years, comes from a concert that was nominally under Crispell's leadership. Yet Anderson's is often the dominant voice, simply through the magnificent authority of his playing. The disc's six improvisations run the gamut from vigorous excitement to reflective calm, with Anderson's sudden foray into Trane-like balladry on *Destiny 5* leading to the most inspired sequence of this absorbing trio encounter.   **GL**

# Ivie Anderson                                                         1905-49

**With Duke Ellington and his Famous Orchestra**  Anderson (v) with collective personnel
   including: **Ellington** (p); **Arthur Whetsol**, **Cootie Williams** (t); **Rex Stewart** (c); **Lawrence Brown**,
   **Tricky Sam Nanton**, **Juan Tizol** (tb); **Johnny Hodges**, **Otto Hardwicke** (as); **Barney Bigard** (cl, ts);
   **Ben Webster** (ts); **Harry Carney** (bs); **Wellman Braud**, **Billy Taylor**, **Jimmy Blanton** (b); **Sonny
   Greer** (d). Jazz Archives Ⓑ 157352 (65 minutes). Recorded 1932-40.

⑧ ❻

Ivie Anderson was the best singer that Duke Ellington ever had. It is curious that Ellington, whose flair for choosing players is legendary, saddled himself for the most part with a series of dire vocalists. But in Ivie he found a true Ellingtonian voice. It is a strange, matter-of-fact kind of voice, not at all conventionally beautiful but fragile and oddly touching. Her very first record (and the first number on this CD) was the famous *It Don't Mean a Thing If It Ain't Got That Swing*, a piece whose cheery message is surrounded by a weird, faintly menacing orchestral aura, in the midst of which Ivie pops up like a not entirely well-intentioned elf. There is a coolness about Ivie's voice that gives an ironic edge to her love-songs and a watchful reserve to the good-time numbers. She was unique and inimitable and might have become a jazz diva, had her life not been blighted by asthma. This collection of 22 songs represents her reasonably well, although I cannot understand why it leaves out *I Got It Bad*, one of her best performances. But it does have *All God's Chillun, I'm Checkin' Out – Go'om Bye* and *Truckin'*.   **DG**

# Ray Anderson

**Azurety** Anderson (tb, tba); **Christy Doran** (g); **Han Bennink** (d). hatART Ⓕ CD6155 (56 minutes). Recorded 1994.

⑧ ❽

Like his fellow-trombonist Roswell Rudd, Anderson is able to work convincingly in an impressive number of musical situations. This dynamic trio is just one of them, but it allows Anderson tremendous scope for his ideas. This is not to downplay the contributions of either Bennink or Doran, who emerge as equal partners here. It is just that Anderson's voice on his instrument is so developed and clear that his eloquence is often mesmerizing. The ease with which he and Bennink deliver an easy-swinging statement of the theme to Ellington's *Just Squeeze Me*, Anderson by the means of passing tones suggesting by sure touches what the rest of the band would be doing if they were there, is breathtaking. He is equally persuasive on the tuba, as his introduction to *The Waters/Dixon Line* demonstrates, and although he is not the type of player to ignore the comic possibilities in the lower-pitched instrument, he brings it a plasticity and expressiveness only perhaps Howard Johnson could approach. Doran seems to be having a lot of fun on *Waters/Dixon* as well, apeing Hendrix, Buddy Guy and others, but his adaptability is also on display across this disc, from absolutely free to the most subtle chording. Bennink, as ever, does not disappoint. A trio which fits happily together and a programme which entertains. **KS**

New review

**Alligatory Band: Heads and Tails** Anderson (tb, v); **Lew Soloff** (t); **Jerome Harris** (g); **Gregory Jones** (b); **Tommy Campbell** (d); **Frank Colón** (perc). Enja Ⓕ 9055-2 (56 minutes). Recorded 1995.

⑦ ❾

The prolific Ray Anderson shows signs of being the trombone equivalent of David Murray: a catalyst on recordings by other leaders and responsible for a steady stream of his own material, both in terms of composition and performance. In the few months between August 1994 and May 1995 he returned to the studios with Dutch percussionist Bennink and Irish-Swiss guitarist Doran (see the review of **Azurety**), recorded with an unaccompanied trombone quartet, and cut this first-rate session with the Alligatory Band. Like Steve Turré, Anderson has the ability to combine in his playing an innovative and original strand of soloing with an eclectic respect for earlier styles and approaches to jazz trombone. Teamed with a versatile rhythm section, trumpeter Soloff and a set of original charts (plus one arrangement of an Irving Berlin song) Anderson displays his full stylistic and tonal range on this disc, a joyous, infectious album with outstanding playing from all participants, living up to the definition of *alligatory* as : "swamp-infested rug-cutters from the bayous of the mind with allegorical twists and an aleatoric *joie de vivre*". **AS**

# Krister Andersson

**About Time** Andersson (ts, cl); **Ion Baciu** (p); **Torbjorn Hultcrantz, Markus Wikstrom** (b); **Leif Wennerstrom, Jan Robertson** (d); **Malando Gassama** (perc). Flash Music Ⓕ FLCD1 (50 minutes). Recorded 1993.

⑧ ❽

Although small in terms of overall population, the Scandinavian countries continue to produce a wealth of high-quality jazz players and Krister Andersson is one of the most accomplished soloists to emerge from the Swedish jazz scene. He plays tenor throughout the six tracks on this CD, adding an extra clarinet line to strengthen the theme statements on *About Time*. His powerful, expressive sound is reminiscent of both Lucky Thompson and Sonny Rollins; like them he has enormous stamina. On *How High The Moon* he opens with an astonishing seven minutes of sustained invention which has all the confidence and imagination of a true jazz master. *Markus' Blues* (by Wikstrom) shows that the 12-bar format can still provide jazz soloists with a stimulating basis for improvisation. The disc closes with an arresting tenor and drums duet, *All Of A Sudden*, the kind of thing which takes great nerve and confidence, but Andersson and Leif Wennerstrom are equal to the task. **AM**

# Ernie Andrews

**No Regrets** Andrews (v); **Houston Person** (ts); **Junior Mance** (p); **Jimmy Ponder** (g); **Ray Drummond** (b); **Michael Carvin** (d). Muse Ⓕ MCD 5484 (51 minutes). Recorded 1992.

⑥ ❼

This album, produced by Houston Person, brings back Ernie Andrews after a long time away from the recording studio and settles him in the musical milieu for which his voice was created: a small-group mainstream jazz setting redolent in blues feeling. In that sense, his most obvious antecedent might well be Jimmy Witherspoon, except that he has been around almost as long as Spoon and has always been closer to the jazz tradition than the latter, having started his career at Birdland and recorded with, among others, Harry James, Cannonball Adderley and Benny Carter.

The music here is made up of standards (*Sweet Lorraine, Until The Real Thing Comes Along*), with a couple of less obvious choices (a Lucky Millinder ditty, *Sweet Slumber*, for example) thrown in to keep it interesting, and Andrews works closely with his backing group to make sure that it is not merely a singer-plus-band date but a properly collaborative effort. The sidemen respond with spirited work, and both Mance and Person excel in a way which does not detract from the confident but curiously vulnerable light baritone which Andrews possesses.　　　　**KS**

## Peter Apfelbaum　　　　1960

**New review**
**Luminous Charms** Apfelbaum (ts, p, org); **Jeff Cressman** (tb, elb); **Will Bernard** (g); **John Shiflett** (b); **Deszon X. Claiborne** (d); **Josh Jones** (perc); on one track **Jai Uttal** (hmn). Gramavision Ⓕ GCD79511 (47 minutes). Recorded 1996.

⑦ ❽

Apfelbaum started winning awards while still in his mid-teens and by his seventeenth year had formed his big band, Hieroglyphics Ensemble. This group continued on and off through years of moving between New York and hometown Berkeley, California, and when Apfelbaum began musical associations with musicians like Don Cherry, they would appear with the ensemble. Cherry also asked Apfelbaum to perform with his own MultiKulti group, and as the nineties progressed Apfelbaum proceeded to play with a wide range of *avant* talents. The group on **Luminous Charms** often performs together, and shows a goodly range of Apfelbaum's interests and activities. His fascination with unusual metres and interesting rhythmic displacements and emphases gives extra life to music which often touches the M-Base as well as the thoughts of bands like Kamikaze Ground Crew. This music is more carefully structured and serious-minded than the Kamikazes, and Apfelbaum also has better and more engaging soloists in his sextet, but the sound is quite contemporary. This is music to admire rather than to luxuriate in.　　　　**KS**

## Julian Argüelles　　　　1966

**New review**
**Home Truths** Argüelles (ss, ts, bcl); **Mike Walker** (g); **Steve Swallow** (elb); **Martin France** (d). Babel Ⓕ BDV9503 (61 minutes). Recorded 1995.

⑧ ❽

Although Julian Argüelles's previous album, **Phaedrus**, marked him out as one of the UK's more interesting new saxophone talents, this album, crackling with energy and vitality as it does, firmly establishes him not only as a passionately virtuosic soloist but also as a fine composer and leader. Like a growing number of nineties bands – John Scofield's with Joe Lovano, Paul Motian's trio with Lovano and Bill Frisell, the UK's Julian Siegel/Phil Robson Quartet – it utilizes a front line of saxophone and electric guitar to great effect, fully exploiting the textural possibilities granted by the combination of Argüelles's warm, breathy keening with Mike Walker's electronic blizzard of sound. The material – all pieces, bar one, by the leader – ranges from swooningly lovely ballads, on which Argüelles's plangent, warbling tone is genuinely affecting, through hectic, folkish skirls, to gloriously rowdy free-for-alls. Walker, a vital member of Manchester's excellent Creative Jazz Orchestra and recently heard in the big bands of Mike Gibbs and George Russell, is cogently inventive throughout, whether his guitar is howling and screaming over Martin France's tumbling drums or chiming delicately behind a softly wafting tenor solo. Swallow is his customary impeccable self, imperturbably anchoring even the wildest jams over repeated changes with his rock-solid bass; France is rumbustious and discreet as required, but always tight. In all, one of the most exciting UK recordings in recent years.　　　　**CP**

## Steve Argüelles　　　　1963

**New review**
**Busy Listening** Argüelles (d); **Julian Argüelles** (as); **Stuart Hall** (g, vn); **Huw Warren** (acc); **Mick Hutton** (b). Babel Ⓕ BDV9406 (61 minutes). Recorded 1993.

⑥ ❼

The slightly laddish eclecticism of his formative band, the 21-piece Loose Tubes, is still to the fore in Steve Argüelles's music, though the disquieting heterogeneousness of this band's previous eponymous recording on AhUm has been replaced here by a more considered approach. The original material still ranges from wheezy tangos to skew-whiff ballads, taking in most points in between, and the cover versions are drawn from composers as diverse as John Scofield, Charles Mingus and Herbie Nichols, with the odd wry standard thrown in, but the band seems closer-knit than before, and Julian Argüelles's dignified alto in particular commands attention throughout. Where the formula works, as in the bustling, compressed title track or in the gracefully eccentric version of Bill Frisell's *Rag*, there are hints that Argüelles might have carved out an original niche for himself in the music. Where it fails, though, as in the hectic scramble of Nichols's *The Gig*, or in Mingus's *Jelly Roll* (all its overblown menace converted into ingenuous jokiness in a version fatally lacking the *gravitas* of the original), the album, like its predecessor, veers uncomfortably close to pastiche. As a live act, particularly in an intimate late-night jazz club setting, the band comes over splendidly; on CD, its breezy informality is somewhat less attractive.                                                                                    **CP**

# Tim Armacost

**New review**

**Fire** **Armacost** (ts, ss); **Kenny Barron** (p); **Gerald Cannon** (b); **Billy Hart**, **Shingo Okudaira** (d). Concord Ⓕ CDD4697 (68 minutes). Recorded 1995.

⑥ ❽

It takes enormous technical ability (or slightly less ability and a lot of money) for a young musician to make it to a first album under his own name these days. In earlier eras a Wardell Gray, a Coleman Hawkins or a Stan Getz had such palpable talent that it was a much easier job to detect the emergent star. The task is harder because today 'jazz musicians' pour from the colleges stuffed to the gills with musical education at the highest levels. The problem is not finding the good players, but the potentially great ones. On the evidence here Armacost, perhaps on the mature side of 'young', has already risen well above the thundering herd of his fellows. But is he good enough to merit backing from Stan Getz's musical partner Kenny Barron? Predictably the two don't have a vestige of the empathy which existed between Getz and the pianist, but that's not Armacost's fault, for this is not his regular group. *Pennies from Heaven* which, like the other tracks, contains vintage solo Barron, is a good point to begin an evaluation. After a surprisingly orthodox melody statement Armacost slants his improvisation in an original angle which is yet never far from the theme. There's much more freedom in the leader's *The Tabla Master*, which opens with keening soprano into a rhythm of 15 beats – eight for a bar and then seven – generated by a year studying Hindustani rhythms in India. The soprano playing is most articulate at the high tempo that follows. It's wielded again for a searing version of Barron's *Voyage*, originally made a classic by the Barron/Getz pairing.                                                       **SV**

# Lil Hardin Armstrong                                                                    1898-1971

**New review**

**And Her Swing Orchestra** **Hardin Armstrong** (p, v); **Joe Thomas, Shirley Clay, Reunald Jones, Jonah Jones** (t); **Al Philburn, J.C. Higginbotham** (tb); **Chu Berry, Robert Carroll, Prince Robinson, Russell Johns** (ts); **Buster Bailey** (c); **Tony Zimmers** (c, ts); **Don Stovall** (as); **Teddy Coleman, James Sherman, Frank Froeba** (p); **Huey Long, Arnold Adams, Dave Barbour** (g); **John Frazier, Wellman Braud, Haig Stephens** (b); **George Foster, Manzie Johnson, Sam Weiss, O'Neil Spencer** (d); **Midge Williams, Hilda Rogers** (v). Classics Ⓜ 564 (76 minutes). Recorded 1936-40.

⑦ ❼

For a woman who, with King Oliver and one time husband Louis Armstrong, made some of the most important records in jazz history, Lil was a limited pianist. She seemed unable to rid herself of the formality stemming from her early training at Fisk University and she never fully mastered the art of improvisation. She did, however, successfully lead both all-girl and all-male bands in the thirties and this CD offers the cream of that crop. It is also an excellent example of the small swing bands that, for many years, received less than their due in critical circles. Much of the material here is dominated by Armstrong's singing and, although there are inept vocal items such as *Or Leave Me Alone* and *Knockin' at the Cabin Door*, she otherwise sings engagingly in a jazz-tinged manner. The canvas backing is better than the musical paint put on it, however, and it is solos by accompanists Thomas, Bailey, Berry, Higginbotham and the two trumpeters named Jones that earn the above points rating. Armstrong did take part in the 'revival' and her 1961 session on Riverside (OJCCD1823-2) featured a band and arrangements that suggest an atavistic return to the earlier days in Chicago. The Classic CD may have only eight titles with her on the piano stool, but it provides music-making of an altogether higher quality.                                                                                **BMcR**

# Louis Armstrong                                                                         1901-71

**Portrait of the Artist as a Young Man, 1923-1934** **Armstrong** (c, t, v); with a collective personnel including: **Joe Oliver, Elmer Chambers, Howard Scott, Elmer Chambers, Joe Smith, James Tate, Bill Wilson, Homer Hobson, Henry 'Red' Allen, Otis Johnson, Leon Elkins, George Orendorff, Harold Scott, Zilner Randolph, Ellis Whitlock, Jack Hamilton, Leslie Thompson** (c, t); **Honore Dutrey, Charlie Irvis, Aaron Thompson, Charlie Green, Edward 'Kid' Ory, Eddie Atkins, Roy Palmer, Johnny Thomas, Fred Robinson, Jack Teagarden, J.C. Higginbotham, Tommy Dorsey, Lawrence Brown, Luther Graven, Preston Jackson, Keg Johnson, Lionel Guimaraes** (tb); **Johnny Dodds, Jimmy Dorsey, Albert Nicholas, Jimmy Noone, Buster Bailey** (cl); **Sidney Bechet, Don Redman, Angelo Fernandez, Stump Evans, Boyd Atkins, Joe Walker, Jimmy Strong, Charlie Holmes, Bert Curry, Crawford Wethington, Leon Herriford, Willie Stark, Les Hite, Marvin Johnson, Lester Boone, George James, Scoville Brown, George Oldham, Pete DuConge, Henry**

**Tyree** (cl, as, ss, bs); **Coleman Hawkins, Norvai Morton, Albert Washington, Happy Caldwell, Teddy Hill, William Franz, Charlie Jones, Albert 'Budd' Johnson, Alfred Pratt** (ts, cl, c-ms, bss); **Lil Armstrong, Clarence Williams, Fletcher Henderson, Fred Longshaw, Richard M. Jones, Hersal Thomas, Teddy Weatherford, Earl Hines, Joe Sullivan, Luis Russell, Justin Ring, Gene Anderson, Buck Washington, L.Z. Cooper, Harvey Brooks, Henry Prince, Charlie Alexander, Teddy Wilson, Herman Chittison** (p); **Bill Johnson, Bud Scott, Johnny St Cyr, Buddy Christian, Charlie Dixon, Frank Etheridge, Mike McKendrick** (bj); **Rip Basset, Lonnie Johnson, Mancy Carr, Dave Wilborn, Eddie Lang, Lonnie Johnson, Will Johnson, Jimmie Rodgers, Ceele Burke, Bill Perkins, Maceo Jefferson** (g); **John Hare, Pops Foster, Joe Bailey, John Lindsay, John Oldham, German Arago** (b); **Charlie Jackson, Ralph Excudero, Pete Briggs, Reggie Jones** (tba); **Baby Dodds, Kaiser Marshall, Jimmy Bertrand, Tubby Hall, Zutty Singleton, Paul Barbarin, Stan King, Lionel Hampton, Yank Porter, Oliver Tines** (d); **Harry Hoffman, Carroll Dickerson** (vn); **Eva Taylor, Margaret Johnson, Maggie Jones, Bessie Smith, Bertha 'Chippie' Hill, Hociel Thomas, Mau Alix, Clarence Babcock, Lillie Delk Christian, Seger Ellis, Jimmie Rodgers** (v). Columbia/Legacy Ⓜ 57176 (four discs: 248 minutes). Recorded 1923-34.

✔                                                                    ⑩ ⑧

This extraordinary four-disc boxed set reveals a ripe but still maturing Louis Armstrong during a singularly significant phase when he consolidated and coined jazzdom's basic grammar and syntax virtually single-handedly. It duplicates a good deal of the repertoire to be found on some of the other sets below, but it is an extremely handy way to obtain a quick overview of this crucial period in Armstrong's career. It is an 11-year odyssey during which we glimpse such Armstrong ports-of-call as King Oliver and Fletcher Henderson, and collaborations with such fellow legends as Bessie Smith, Maggie Jones, Clarence Williams, Sidney Bechet, Johnny Dodds, Lonnie Johnson, Earl 'Fatha' Hines and Lionel Hampton. The discographic survey commences in 1923 with King Oliver's Creole Jazz Band and *Chimes Blues*, the first Armstrong solo committed to wax, wrapping up in 1934 with *Song of the Vipers*, recorded in Paris with a European cast.

Along the way, Armstrong's seemingly innate capacity to swing, his penchant for dividing quarter-notes into eights, and his inimitable 'vocalized' instrumental style and 'instrumentalized' vocals are all present and accounted for. So, too, is the trumpeter's contagious *joie de vivre*. For Louis, as well as his cohorts and audiences, music was a means of joyful transcendence. Trips to the summit abound – there's the zesty *Struttin' with Some Barbecue* (1927) with his Hot Five in Chicago; the hand-in-glove Armstrong-Hines duet on *Weather Bird* (1928); the landmark *Ain't Misbehavin'* (1929) from **Hot Chocolates**, the Andy Razaf/Fats Waller revue whose broad appeal helped make Armstrong a pop as well as jazz star; the deeply felt *Knockin' a Jug* (1929), the first important inter-racial jazz date featuring Jack Teagarden, Eddie Lang and Kaiser Marshall; a rollicking *I'm a Ding Dong Daddy* with Lionel Hampton's exuberant drumming; and an upbeat *I've Got the World on a String* (1933) where Teddy Wilson's sprightly break sets up the maestro's warm, gravelly vocal, and stentorian trumpeting. In all, it is a priceless time capsule of one of the era's great personalities and jazz's most seminal stylists. Sound quality, which beats any previous Columbia issues of Armstrong's material, ranges from good to excellent.                                                                    **CB**

---

### The Complete Recordings of Louis Armstrong and the Blues Singers **Armstrong**
(c, t, v); **Charlie Green** (tb); **Buster Bailey** (cl, ss); **Charles Irvis** (tb); **Sidney Bechet** (cl, ss); **Aaron Thompson** (tb); **Lil Armstrong** (p); **Fred Longshaw** (hmn, p); **Don Redman** (cl, as) **Coleman Hawkins** (ts); **James P. Johnson, Hersal Thomas, Richard M. Jones** (p); **Artie Starks** (cl); **Jimmy Noone** (cl); **Earl Hines** (p); **Tommy Dorsey** (tb); **Jimmy Dorsey** (cl); **Fred Robinson** (tb); **Jimmy Strong** (cl); **Joe Venuti** (vn); **Arthur Schutt** (p); **Eddie Lang** (g); **Clarence Williams Blue Five; Red Onion Jazz Babies; Bill Jones' Southern Serenaders; Fletcher Henderson Orchestra; Perry Bradford's Jazz Phools; Armstrong's Hot 5**. Affinity Ⓜ CDAFS1018-6 (six discs: 366 minutes). Recorded 1924-30.

✔                                                                    ⑩ ❹

By the time Armstrong joined Fletcher Henderson in 1924 he was jazz music's most avant-garde figure. He had also undertaken what were meant to be backroom duties as an accompanist to singers, but as this boxed set of six CDs shows he almost always stole the show. The Clarence Williams Blue Five and its related Red Onion Jazz Babies were fertile ground for him. Behind or around the likes of the jaunty Eva Taylor or the more bluesy Alberta Hunter he waged a running musical battle with Sidney Bechet or Buster Bailey and, on titles such as *Mandy Make Up Your Mind* and *Cake Walkin' Babies*, gave masterful trumpet recitals that pre-date the Hot Five records by almost a year. He also enhanced the work of impressive blues artists such as Sippie Wallace and Victoria Spivey as well as lending stature to lesser talents such as Maggie Jones, Trixie Smith, Hociel Thomas and Margaret Johnson. With poorer singers like Nolan Welsh, he produced solos that turned routine performances into essential listening. He deflected attention from the poor intonation of Virginia Liston, the eccentric timing of Blanche Calloway and even the 'little-girl-lost' bathos of Lillie Delk Christian.

Where his true majesty is most evident, however, is with artists of equal stature. His preaching cornet behind Ma Rainey on *Countin' the Blues*, his dramatic response to the superbly strident Chippie Hill on *Low Land Blues* or *Pleadin' for the Blues*, or his sensitivity in matching the inherent sadness of Clara Smith on *Shipwrecked Blues* all bear the mark of genius. These are masterpieces of blues collaboration, but there are nine titles with Bessie Smith that represent the pinnacle of art. There is the definitive *St Louis Blues*, the impossibly moving *Reckless Blues* and even the bravura rivalry of *Cold in Hand Blues*. All save *Second Fiddle* are incomparable.

Colour is added with novelties from Grant and Wilson, a badly recorded Perry Bradford, a Hot Five-inspired *Butterbeans and Susie*, and the incongruous Jimmy Rodgers. In spite of major contributions from Armstrong, the Billy Jones, Baby Mack and Seger Ellis items are of rarity value only and it must be pointed out that, had the transfer/recording assessment been based on the Columbia or Okeh items only, the sound quality rating would have been upped to seven.　　**BMcR**

---

**Highlights from His American Decca Years** Armstrong (c, t); Howard Scott, Elmer Chambers, Leonard Davis, Gus Aiken, Louis Bacon, George Thow, Toots Camarata, Shelton Hemphill, Red Allen, Otis Johnson, Bernard Flood, Frank Galbraith, Gene Prince, Billy Butterfield, Bernie Privin, Aaron Izenhall, Carl Poole, Yank Lawson, Melvin Solomon, Paul Webster, Andy Ferretti (t); Roy Palmer, Kid Ory, Charlie Green, Harry White, Jimmy Archey, Bobby Byrne, Joe Yukl, Don Mattison, George Matthews, George Washington, J.C. Higginbotham, Wilbur De Paris, Claude Jones, Norman Green, Henderson Chambers, James Whitney, Jack Teagarden, Will Bradley, Morton Bullman, Lou McGarity, Cutty Cutshall, Phil Giardiana, Jack Satterfield, Trummy Young (tb); Ralph Escudero (tba); Johnny Dodds, Buster Bailey, Hank D'Amico, Edmond Hall (cl); Barney Bigard, Bingie Madison, Jimmy Dorsey, Albert Nicholas, George Koenig, Jack Greenberg, Art Drellinger, Milton Chatz (cl, ts); Sidney Bechet (ss); Don Redman, Charlie Holmes, Henry Jones, Jack Stacey, Pete Clark, Rupert Cole, Sid Stoneburn, Jules Rubin, Sid Cooper, Johnny Mince, Milt Yaner, Hymie Schertzer, George Dorsey, Hilton Jefferson (as); Coleman Hawkins, Greely Walton, Fud Livingston, Skeets Herfurt, Joe Garland, Carl Frye, Prince Robinson, Bill Stegmeyer, Art Rollini, Josh Jackson, Bill Holcombe, Al Klink, Lucky Thompson (ts); Paul Ricci, Dave McRae (bs); Earl Hines, Lil Armstrong, Fletcher Henderson, Luis Russell, Bobby Van Eps, Dick Cary, Dave Bowman, Joe Bushkin, Billy Kyle, Bill Doggett, Bernie Leighton (p); Bud Scott, Johnny St Cyr, Charlie Dixon, Lee Blair (bj); Roscoe Hillman, Bernard Addison, Lawrence Lucie, Carl Kress, Norman Brown, Danny Perri, Everett Barksdale, Carmen Mastren, George Barnes (g); Pops Foster, Jim Taft, Wellman Braud, Hayes Alvis, John Simmons, Bob Haggart, Arvell Shaw, Trigger Alpert, Joe Benjamin, Bob Bushnell, Jack Lesberg, George Duvivier, Sandy Clock, Squire Gersh (b); Baby Dodds, Kaiser Marshall, Paul Barbarin, Ray McKinley, Sidney Catlett, Zutty Singleton, Johnny Blowers, Cozy Cole, Jimmy Crawford, Joe Morris, Ed Grady, Barrett Deems (d); The Mills Brothers, Ella Fitzgerald, Billie Holiday, Louis Jordan, Bing Crosby, Velma Middleton (v); Sy Oliver Choir, Gordon Jenkins Choir. GRP Ⓜ 26382 (two discs: 124 minutes). Recorded 1924-57.

✓　　　　　　　　　　　　　　　　　　　　　　　　　　　　　　　　⑧ ⑧

Spanning the whole of Armstrong's career from the Fletcher Henderson big band in 1924 to his **Musical Autobiography** in the late fifties, this is an essential selection of his best work. The anthology is produced by Orrin Keepnews, whose knowledge of his subject, sure hand in juxtaposing the material, and access to first-rate source material make this one of the essential jazz collections. The Hot Five and Seven are best represented elsewhere (see below), and sensibly this release does not seek to duplicate other groupings of Armstrong's earliest work. The core of the collection, and the major section of Armstrong's life represented on these two CDs, is the big band he led (in effect Luis Russell's band fronted by Armstrong) from the early thirties until the mid forties. The majority of the first disc is taken up with highlights of their most memorable sessions, from the trumpet fireworks of *Struttin' with Some Barbecue* to examples of their successful formula for Louis's vocals (band intro, trumpet statement, vocal and soaring trumpet out-chorus) like *I'm Confessin'* and *I'm in the Mood for Love*. The second disc combines Armstrong's move back to small-group jazz and the birth of the All -Stars with many of his collaborations with other singers and entertainers. Few Dixieland revivalists could compete with the heat and energy of *Muskrat Ramble* from Boston Symphony Hall, and the only dubious selection is the final hokum of *King of the Zulus*, which might have been better replaced by one of the more musical highlights from the **Autobiography**.　　**AS**

---

**Hot Fives And Sevens, Volumes 1-4** Armstrong (c, t, v); with a collective personnel including: Bill Wilson (c); Homer Hobson, Henry 'Red' Allen (t); Kid Ory, Hy Clark, Honore Dutrey, Jack Teagarden, J.C. Higginbotham, Fred Robinson (tb); Johnny Dodds, Don Redman, Albert Nicholas, Charlie Holmes (cl, as); Boyd Atkins (cl, ss, as); Joe Walker (as, bs); Albert Washington, Happy Cauldwell, Bert Curry, Teddy Hill (ts); Jimmy Strong (cl, ts); Lil Armstrong (p, v); Earl Hines, Joe Sullivan, Luis Russell, Gene Anderson (p); Johnny St. Cyr, Rip Bassett, Mancy Cara, Eddie Condon (bj, g); Lonnie Johnson, Eddie Lang (g); Peter Briggs (tba); Pops Foster (b); Baby Dodds, Tubby Hall, Zutty Singleton, Kaiser Marshall (d); Paul Barbarin (d, vb); Hoagy Carmichael, Joe Edwards, Susie Edwards, May Alix (v); Carroll Dickerson (vn, dir). JSP Ⓟ CD312/3/4/5 (four discs, oas: 72, 67, 70 and 68 minutes). Recorded 1925-31.

✓　　　　　　　　　　　　　　　　　　　　　　　　　　　　　　　　⑩ ⑧

These four CDs contain what is undoubtedly one of the most important bodies of recorded work in the entire history of jazz. The first three volumes cover the two-and-a-half years during which all the Hot Fives and Sevens titles were recorded in Chicago, the city to which Armstrong returned after his year with Fletcher Henderson. There are priceless masterpieces to be heard here: the perfect *West End Blues* of course, but also gems such as *Potato Head Blues, Fireworks, Wild Man*

*Blues* and the slightly later Armstrong-Hines duet *Weather Bird*. The Hot Five was essentially a recording band (it only appeared in public twice) but it represented the important period when Louis stepped outside the traditional New Orleans ensemble, focusing attention on the soloist. Strictly speaking, and despite the album titles, half of Vol. 3 and the whole of Vol. 4 are not by the Hot Five and Seven but by later bands put together by Carroll Dickerson, Luis Russell and others to back Armstrong. But no matter; the chronology and the continuing magic is complete. The third volume ends with the splendid *Knockin' A Jug* by a racially mixed group (and marks the first time Louis and Jack Teagarden recorded together) while Vol. 4 has two very rare takes of *Rockin' Chair* and *I Can't Give You Anything But Love* in addition to the originals. The remastering throughout has been done by John R.T. Davies and must be rated as a high point even by his own superior standards in the field of record restoration. There is no doubt that these issues (and two further JSP CDs by Armstrong which continue the chronology) are the best available collections of these important recordings. **AM**

---

**New review**

### Satchmo at Symphony Hall Armstrong (t, v); Jack Teagarden (tb, v); Barney Bigard (cl); Dick Carey (p); Arvell Shaw (b); Sid Catlett (d); Velma Middleton (v). GRP Ⓜ GRP16612 (70 minutes). Recorded 1947.

✔ ⑩ ⑧

Both Armstrong and Teagarden had folded their big bands six months earlier in order to form the All-Stars and were still experiencing the first flush of relief and enjoyment at this Boston concert in November 1947. The programme had not yet begun to harden into any kind of routine. According to the original album notes by promoter Ernie Anderson (reproduced here), the band would start each show with only the first couple of numbers decided, Louis calling the tunes as they went along. The result is a wonderfully relaxed and good-humoured set by some of the best jazz musicians ever to set foot on a bandstand. The programme itself is a gloriously mixed affair, ranging from Ory's *Muskrat Ramble* (in the key of A flat, just to settle an ancient argument) to Hawkins's neo-bop riff tune *Boff-Boff* (a drum feature for Catlett). Teagarden sings a memorable *Stars Fell on Alabama*, Bigard delivers an elegant *Body and Soul* and Armstrong delightedly grabs every solo opportunity that presents itself. The whole 70 minutes is an inspiring experience. Recording balance is remarkably good, catching the live atmosphere to perfection. The only items missing from the original two 12-inch albums are a couple of Velma Middleton vocals and a bass feature. **DG**

---

### Satchmo: A Musical Autobiography Armstrong (t, v); Edmond Hall, Barney Bigard (cl); Jack Teagarden, Trummy Young (tb); Bud Freeman (ts); Billy Kyle (p); Arvell Shaw, Squire Gersh (b); Sid Catlett, Barrett Deems (d); Velma Middleton (v); Sy Oliver (arr, cond) and others. Jazz Unlimited Ⓔ JUCD2003-5 (three discs: 209 minutes). Recorded 1947-57.

✔ ⑧ ⑥

The idea of re-creating a large number of Armstrong's earlier hits came to fruition in 1956, and it paid off, because, unexpectedly, Armstrong plays even better on numbers like *Cornet Chop Suey* than he did on the original versions. The mass of this music gives a better idea of his imagination, humour and majesty than any other collection of CDs which come to mind. Along with the W.C. Handy and Waller sets on CBS, this music makes up the very finest collection of latter-day Armstrong. The best tracks are the ones by a version of his All Stars (Hall, Young and Kyle) augmented by a saxophone section. These recreate such hits of the thirties as *Lazy River*, *That's My Home* and *Sunny Side of the Street*. The Hot Fives and Sevens of the twenties are well reinterpreted (not copied) with Edmund Hall on particularly fine form. Velma Middleton does a fair job of recalling some of the classic blues singers who Louis accompanied, although her work is best regarded as a foil for Armstrong's obbligatos rather than for its own merit. Most of these tracks were studio recorded in 1956-7 and it is only a handful (the ones featuring Teagarden and Bigard) which come from the earlier period. The earlier tracks were often truncated by Decca, who made the original issues, but here they are restored to their full lengths. *Froggie Moore* was not in the original set and has been taken from the only copies located, both of which suffered from added reverberation. This is the only track which defied the rejuvenating recording techniques of sound engineer Dave Bennett, who has otherwise been able to do an excellent job. **SV**

---

### The California Concerts Armstrong (t, v) with, in 1951: Jack Teagarden (tb, v); Barney Bigard (cl); Earl Hines (p); Arvell Shaw (b); Cozy Cole (d); Velma Middleton (v); in 1955: Trummy Young (tb, v); Barney Bigard (cl, v); Billy Kyle (p); Arvell Shaw (b); Barrett Deems (d); Velma Middleton (v). MCA/GRP Ⓜ 46132 (four discs: 184 minutes). Recorded 1951/5.

✔ ⑨ ⑥

The fifties are generally regarded as a time of revived fortunes for Armstrong and these remarkable live recordings do nothing at all to gainsay such received opinions. Both sets of performances were famous in their own right as single LP releases, but this newly-remastered four-CD collection gives us the full story of the 1951 L.A. Civic Auditorium concert as part of a Gene Norman *Just Jazz* package, and also fills out the picture on a remarkable night's music at the Crescendo Club in early 1955.

The Civic concert features the original All-Stars line-up and shows the full extent of its fire and panache prior to the disaffection and subsequent departure of Hines and Teagarden. While Louis is clearly the leader, there is a sense of the co-operative give-and-take about this ensemble's performances which had been replaced by a carefully guided spotlight on Armstrong by the time of the 1955 performances. Hines is a busy pianist, whether comping or soloing, and pushes the trumpeter all the way. Teagarden does such glorious things to the trombone that he's worth the price of the set by himself and at no stage does he sound like Armstrong's sideman. This is not to denigrate the 1955 sets at the Crescendo, because they have different plus points. But the people playing with Louis there – and I would include Bigard, who is present on both dates – know that they are his sidemen, and adapt their roles accordingly.

There is a wonderful sense of spontaneity (even though all the routines were well-grooved, and solos rehearsed) which the presence of an audience always evoked in Armstrong. His great fifties studio sessions may be more momentous events (and amongst those I would include the long-unavailable **Satchmo Plays King Oliver** on Audio Fidelity), but these concerts, familiar repertoire and all, tell us the real story.                                                                                    **KS**

**Satch Plays Fats** Armstrong (t, v); **Trummy Young** (tb); **Barney Bigard** (cl); **Billy Kyle** (p); **Arvell Shaw** (b); **Barrett Deems** (d); **Velma Middleton** (v). Columbia Ⓜ 450980-2 (38 minutes). Recorded 1955.

⑥ ❽

This version of the All-Stars, in which Trummy Young's broad and sometimes vulgar gestures acted as both counterweight and goad to the maestro, was actually a much more balanced band than its predecessor with Jack Teagarden (it is a pity that there is no satisfactory album available from the period when clarinettist Edmund Hall had replaced Bigard). Many of these Fats Waller standards had been featured by Armstrong in years gone by, but few were in his active repertoire at the time of this recording. There are, of course, vocals on every track (Middleton appears on three, and has *Squeeze Me* to herself) and Louis's are better than average for this period, but it is the distilled majesty of the trumpet that compels attention. These latter-day versions of *Ain't Misbehavin'* and *Black and Blue* compare with his 1929 originals as the wisdom of middle age to the impetuosity of youth.

Humphrey Lyttelton's accompanying notes, clearly *not* "taken from the original analogue release", detail exactly how that release differed from the present version, which omits Armstrong's overdubbed trumpet behind his voice, and replaces several previously edited takes. Despite this and the short playing time, the representation of Louis at a late peak is unbeatable.                                    **BP**

# Thomas Arnesen

New review
**Backwater Blues** Arnesen (g); **Anders Widmark** (p); **Hans Beckenroth** (b); **Egil Johansen** (d); on four tracks **Anders Johansson** (g) or **John Högman** (bs). Sittel Ⓕ SITCD 9227. Recorded 1995.

⑥ ❽

Arnesen is regarded by many in Sweden as that country's most outstanding guitarist. The evidence here is of an immensely capable but rather introverted player, capable of beautiful touches (*Softly as in a Morning Sunrise*) or the odd touch of raunch (*Backwater Blues*), but he mishandles *Goodbye Porpie Hat* quite appallingly, having perhaps never got over Jeff Beck's version of it in his youth. On other self-penned tracks he veers close to MOR (a constant danger when guitarists occasionally go acoustic), but the ballads like *With All Due Respect* and *Stella by Starlight* bring out the best of him, giving the listener an elusive intensity which is too often absent elsewhere.                        **KS**

# Art Ensemble of Chicago

**The Art Ensemble 1967-8** Lester Bowie (t, perc); **Roscoe Mitchell, Joseph Jarman** (reeds, perc); **Malachi Favors Maghostut** (b, perc); **Philip Wilson, Thurman Barker, Robert Crowder** (d); **Charles Clark** (b). Nessa NCD-2500A-E. (five discs: 304 minutes). Recorded 1967-8.

✔                                                                                          ⑧ ❽

Throughout the seventies and eighties, the Art Ensemble of Chicago was one of jazz's (or as they prefer, Great Black Music's) most innovative and exhilarating ensembles; their importance in the evolution of the music certainly ranks them with such groups as Jelly Roll Morton's Red Hot Peppers, Louis Armstrong's Hot Fives and Sevens, the classic quartets of John Coltrane and Ornette Coleman, and Miles Davis's quintets of the fifties and sixties. Their first works were in many ways their most iconoclastic, and much of the shocking experimentalism that subsequently influenced so many musicians came from the original concepts of Roscoe Mitchell. Until recently we have only had sketchy documentation of the group's crucial formative period, but thanks to the efforts of Chuck Nessa, a long-time supporter of the Art Ensemble, we now have a more complete picture of their amazing discoveries. Some of the previously unreleased material from this five-CD collection comes from rehearsal tapes (the sound quality is remarkably fine considering the source) where the original quartet – Mitchell, Lester Bowie, Malachi Favors and Philip Wilson, Joseph Jarman not yet having joined – are in the very process of creating a truly new music from Mitchell's ideas. In questioning every conceivable musical parameter, they are forming a new language with its own inherent drama, humour and form.

The quartet's colours and dynamics are stunning, the ensemble relationship always coherent regardless of the broad range of individual emotions and unconventional instrumental voices. Listening to the newly released versions of *Number 1* and *Number 2* alongside those issued on LP, it is obvious that the four achieved an amazing unity of purpose. Multi-sectional, intricate and still flowing in design, the group improvisations cohere around quickness and appropriateness of response, as incongruous sounds and extremes of timbres blend subtly or clash vehemently, suggesting layers of irony and dramatic immediacy. By the last recordings here, issued on LP as **Congliptious**, the Art Ensemble (plus Jarman) was intact, sure in their methods and message, and ready to conquer Europe. This music remains as shocking and satisfying today as when it was initially created, and these recordings are essential to anyone wishing to understand one of the great post-bebop revolutions in jazz.                                    **AL**

**Full Force**  **Lester Bowie** (t); **Joseph Jarman** (af, f, cl, bcl, snino s, ss, as, ts, bs, bss, pic, bn, whistle, conch shell, cel, vb, gongs, cgas); **Roscoe Mitchell** (f, cl, ss, as, ts, bs, bss, pic, gspiel, gongs, cga); **Malachi Favors Maghostus** (melodica, b, perc, v); **Famoudou Don Moye** (whistles, conch shells, bikehorns, d, perc, bells, gongs, etc.). ECM Ⓕ 829 197-2 (43 minutes). Recorded 1980.

⑧ ❿

After a spell of prolific music-making in France (many of which sessions are currently out of the catalogue), the Art Ensemble returned to the US in 1972. Recording opportunities at home remained sporadic, but finally an agreement with the Munich-based ECM label brought a series of new releases that appeared between 1979 and 1985. **Nice Guys**, **Full Force**, the live **Urban Bushmen** and **The Third Decade** were typically erratic works, with passages of brilliant ensemble interplay (*Dreaming of the Master*) interspersed with longueurs and occasional, ill-judged stabs at populism (*JA, Funky AECO*). **Full Force**, free of these latter traits, is the most consistent of the ECM albums and makes an attractive introduction to the group's versatile polystylism.

*Full Force* itself is a collective improvisation, all fast colours and humorous asides, while *Magg Zelma* is a more structured excursion into similar territory, its gentle array of 'little instruments' the prelude to a series of stately, then agitated, horn passages. Other tracks hew closer to conventional form: *Charlie M*, Lester Bowie's Mingus tribute, is a smouldering ensemble prowl; Joseph Jarman's cheery *Old Time Southside Street Dance* is lit by volatile saxophones. Despite the later increase in their output, **Full Force** remains one of the Art Ensemble's more engaging sets.                **GL**

# Georges Arvanitas                                      1931

**Arvanitas Trio with Francis Darizcuren**  **Arvanitas** (p); **Francis Darizcuren** (vn); **Jacky Samson** (b); **Charles Saudrais** (d). EPM Ⓕ 982252 (60 minutes). Recorded 1992.

⑥ ⑧

Marseilles-born Arvanitas is one of the many fine post-war French pianists. He has worked with a variety of Americans, from Albert Nicholas to David Murray, by way of Chet Baker and Ben Webster. A valuable accompanist, his trio has worked together since the late sixties and here they provide Basque violinist Darizcuren with exemplary support, sensing with accuracy the need to increase or decrease the tension. The violinist is an excellent technician (not always the case with all jazz violinists) who can double-stop with accuracy, notably in the theme statement of the 12-bar *Ça Alors*. He receives a written accolade from Stephane Grappelli in the accompanying booklet and there is a careful version of Reinhardt's *Nuages* in the 15-tune programme. *Digital Dream* is an unaccompanied violin solo making use of electronic delay devices and, although credited to Darizcuren, the entire theme of Bud Powell's *Parisian Thoroughfare* crops up in the middle. In fact something seems to have gone slightly awry with the composer listing in places; *Cute, You're So Cute* is actually Neal Hefti's tune *Cute* and not a Darizcuren original while *To Big Mike* turns out to be a medley of known songs. Arvanitas briefly switches to electric piano but he comes into his own on *Claude et Catherine*, a fine piano solo full of the post-Bud Powell and Hank Jones feeling that we associate with this excellent pianist.                  **AM**

# Dorothy Ashby                                         1932-86

New review
**In a Minor Groove**  Ashby (hp); **Frank Wess** (f); **Herman Wright** (b); **Arthur Taylor**, **Roy Haynes** (d). Prestige Ⓜ PCD24120-2 (76 minutes). Recorded 1958.

⑦ ⑥

This CD is a reissue of two chamber jazz albums recorded in 1958 at the height of the hard-bop orthodoxy. Its motivations are somewhat different; bebop is its chosen language but it essays understatement and favours subtlety rather than extravagance. Ashby was initially a pianist and lists keyboard men such as Oscar Peterson and George Shearing as her greatest influences but, as she shows here, she realizes her solos with distinctly guitar-like lines. She is at her best with more propulsive challenges but her improvisational skills are evident throughout. The gentleness of a title such as *Moonlight in Vermont* very nearly defeats her but there is certainly no lack of backbone in blues originals like *Pawky* and *Back Talk*. She is well supported by the fluent and creative Wess on flute but it is significant that she is both more aggressive and more swinging with Haynes's drumming at her back. Swopping fours with Taylor on *Charmaine* simply does not work in terms of sound contrasts and it perhaps highlights the fact that even the normally infallible Rudy Van Gelder has some difficulty in engineering the balance. Later in her career Ashby moved to California and spent time in the studios there before her untimely death at the age of 54. **BMcR**

## Harold Ashby 1925

**The Viking**  Ashby (ts); **Norman Simmons** (p); **Paul West** (b); **Gerryck King** (d).
  Gemini ℗ GMCD60 (49 minutes). Recorded 1988.

Ashby deputized for various members of the Duke Ellington sax section over a period of years before he gained a permanent place, taking over from the departed Jimmy Hamilton at the 1968 Newport Jazz Festival. He makes no secret of his admiration for the late Ben Webster; the two recorded together and, for a time, shared an apartment. Inevitably Ashby sounds like Ben at times, especially when producing his ravishing version of *I Got It Bad* (included here amongst the eight tracks, four of them being Ashby originals). The music is uncomplicated, enjoyable at various levels and is, in many ways, the epitome of contemporary mainstream jazz. Ashby was attending the Oslo Jazz Festival when this recording was made and he is supported by a fine rhythm team, then working as accompanists to singer Joe Williams. The session took place in Oslo's Rainbow Studio, a location which has been the venue for many other well recorded jazz albums put out by Gemini. The power of Harold's playing has been expertly captured, together with that breathy approach to ballads which is an ever-present legacy of his continuing admiration for Webster.  **AM**

## Arne Astrup

**Seven Brothers**  Astrup (ts); **Paul Hindberg** (cl); **Louis Hjulmand** (vb); **Mogens Petersen** (p);  **Frits von Bulow** (g);  **Jorgen Johnbeck** (b); **Hans Sorensen** (d). Olufsen ℗ DOCD5126 (61 minutes).
  Recorded 1989-90.

Tenor player Astrup is best known internationally for his exemplary discographical work on such major figures as Gerry Mulligan and Stan Getz. As is often the case, however, his own abilities on the saxophone have gone largely unrecognized outside his native Denmark. This is a shame, because not only does his career span close on 50 years of playing, but he is a well-schooled and warm player in the progressive tradition of the post-war years. This album features his Septet and at times it sounds more like the late-forties Goodman small-groups than a post-bop band. Still, this fact should hinder no one's enjoyment of a smoothly swinging and urbane collection of arrangements. The great majority of pieces here are originals, though Parker's *Scrapple from the Apple* gets a reappraisal, courtesy of Paul Hindberg's arrangement. Hindberg's own playing is very much in the shadow of Goodman, while Astrup's has a friendly personality of its own.  **KS**

## Eden Atwood 1969

**There Again**  Atwood (v); **Dave Berkman** (p); **Michael Moore** (b); **Ron Vincent** (d); with **Marian McPartland** (p) on two tracks; **Chris Potter** (ts) on four tracks. Concord ℗ CCD4645
  (56 minutes). Recorded 1994/5.

This, Atwood's third album for Concord (the fourth, the 'live' **A Night in the Life**, marks a return to some of the glibness which was her greatest weakness on her first two records), remains her most mature. Her first two showed her to have a clean, acceptably versatile, technically competent voice which shone most brightly on medium tempo swingers. She showed no particular aptitude for the slower ballads also attempted on those discs. On **There Again** she still sounds most comfortable on these swingers, with *You're My Thrill* having a nicely balanced combination of flirtatiousness and sheer enjoyment of the situation, and *In Love in Vain* showing her ability to inject irony into a situation. But progress has been made with the ballads: *The Nearness of You* succeeds quite acceptably, as does *Music That Makes Me Dance*. *It Never Entered My Mind*, quite frankly, still has a "danger – deep water" sign in front of it for her, although she makes an honest attempt at rendering it. She just does not yet have the inner intensity to make songs such as this burn. Yet there is much to enjoy in her singing, and the more straightforward songs of love, lust and life are delivered with nothing less than panache. Atwood has come a long way, has a long way still to go, and it will be interesting for we listeners to trace her journey on the albums undoubtedly still to come.  **KS**

# Lovie Austin
1887-1972

**1924-6** Austin (p); **Tommy Ladnier, Natty Dominique** (c); **Kid Ory** (tb); **Johnny Dodds, Jimmy O'Bryant** (cl); **Eustern Woodfork** (bj); **W.E. Burton** (d, perc); **Edmonia Henderson, Ford & Ford, Priscilla Stewart, Viola Bartlette, Henry Williams** (v). Classics Ⓜ 756 (73 minutes). Recorded 1924-6.

⑧ ❷

Although active on the vaudeville circuit, Austin and her fine groups were frequent visitors to the Paramount recording studios. She made outstanding sides with the major blues singers, but the two years covered by this CD present her at her finest, in the company of her Blues Serenaders and playing many of her own compositions. Austin was that rarity among piano leaders in that she took no solos. She was a cajoler rather than a challenger and she was happiest in her ensemble role, calibrating each selection and guaranteeing that neither tuba nor string bass were missed. Her arrangements were rudimentary but effective and the likes of *Steppin' On The Blues* and *Mojo Blues* were models of concision. Sound balances varied even on the original recordings and, if she is too dominant on *Too Sweet*, the contrast occurs when Woodfork's banjo backs her on the final session. When the piano is favoured, as behind Dodds and Ory on *Jackass Blues*, she is more able to present her 'solo' piano voice.

Later in her life she became a musical director in Chicago theatres, worked as an accompanist in a dancing school and, in 1961, actually recorded again (Prestige/Bluesville OBCCD510). Nevertheless, it was the Serenaders's titles, in the company of masters like Ladnier, Dodds and Ory, for which she will be remembered. **BMcR**

# Teodross Avery
1973

New review

**My Generation** Avery (ts); **John Scofield, Mark Whitfield, Peter Bernstein** (g); **Charles Craig** (p); **Rodeny Whitaker** (b); **Greg Hutchinson** (d); **Andrew Daniels** (perc); **Black Thought of the Roots** (rap). Impulse! Ⓔ IMP11812 (69 minutes). Recorded 1995.

⑥ ❾

It seemed from Avery's first release in 1994 (**In Other Words**, GRP97982) that despite his youth, a new and mature saxophone voice had arrived. He was then just 21 and in the interplay with Craig and the melodic interpretation of his own and others' compositions he had something unique to say and a personal voice in which to say it. This album suggests that Avery has now experienced some growing pains. On four tracks, the interplay with Charles is as vibrant as ever, though the Coltrane influence is harsher and less melodic than before. Elsewhere, the chordal interest is provided by guitarists, among whom Scofield stands out, though partly because in the context of Avery's clean sound Scofield's echoey tone sounds anachronistic – a throwback to late-seventies/early-eighties jazz that Avery seemed to be well beyond in his earlier album. By contrast, the cleaner sound of Whitfield, both on a sumptuous duet opening to *Lover Man* and on two of Avery's own compositions, seems to hit exactly the right timbre to move Avery's playing up a notch and to show a development forward from his early work with Craig. Full marks to Avery for trying to extend his range and to vary his accompaniments. In keeping with such an experiment, the album is less even than before, and not everything works (the rap vocal on the title track is less than brilliant) but where it does, there is genuine evidence of Avery's development as a new solo voice. **AS**

# Roy Ayers
1940

New review

**Ubiquity: Live at the Montreux Jazz Festival** Ayers (vb, perc, v); **Harry Whitaker** (elp, v); **Clint Houston** (b); **David Lee** (d). Verve Ⓜ 531 641-2 (67 minutes). Recorded 1972.

⑦ ⑧

Some of Ayers's recent albums are little more than monologues delivered over a funk beat and it's hard to understand from them just what all the fuss was about when he was at the forefront of fusion. This set from Montreux was one of his first international festival appearances, catching him in innovative and energetic mode turning in a set of the kind that has subsequently been enthusiastically sampled as a backdrop to the hip-hop or acid jazz scene. For the most part he operated at medium tempo, building a series of mini-climaxes over a repetitive funk beat and relying on Houston and Lee's power and Whitaker's sympathetic shadowing of the vibes and vocals to create the necessary tension. *Moove to Groove* is faster and more representative of some of his later work, while *Raindrops Keep Fallin' on My Head* is proof that a then-current hit song from the movies could be purloined and subjected to the funk treatment. The festival audience catches the mood, even joining in the spirit of a slow-paced *Thoughts*, and as a single Ayers collection, this live set in its entirety is probably as good an example as the double-CD **Chronicles** (Polydor 527 054-2), not least because it includes some outstanding examples of Ayers's ability to meld his solo lines seamlessly with Whitaker's electric piano. **AS**

# Albert Ayler

**Spiritual Unity**  Ayler (ts); **Gary Peacock** (b); **Sunny Murray** (d). ESP-Disk Ⓜ ESP1002-2
(30 minutes). Recorded 1964.

✔  ⑩ ❻

Ayler had experience with the r&b field before spending almost three years with military bands in
Europe. On release, he decided not to return to America and for some time worked in Sweden,
where he made his first somewhat inchoate recordings, wrestling unsuccessfully with bebop. A
period with Cecil Taylor and a return to the US helped to clear his mind and to formulate a style
that was to make him one of jazz's outstanding innovators on the tenor saxophone. *Spiritual Unity*
was Ayler's **Saxophone Colossus** and **Giant Steps** and it provides an ideal example of his style. It uses
very basic, almost folk-like tunes and shows how each slender thematic starting point projects his
solos on their path. There are inevitable variations and, whereas *The Wizard's* development circles
back to a simple paraphrase of the original, the *Spirits* solo is departmentalized into thematic sub-
areas, each using the same harmonic base, yet all exploring different levels of melodic density and
emotional power. *Ghosts II* is the better of the two takes that offer further examples of Ayler's
improvisational method, although it is *Ghosts I* that perhaps emphasizes the aptness of his primitive
sound and unique phrase shapes. On all he is superbly complemented by Peacock, who shoulders
most of the responsibility for rhythmic and harmonic movement, and Murray, who provides the
textural stratum while swinging in a detached, almost subliminal manner. The three men make this
a very important jazz CD.                                                                **BMcR**

**Spirits Rejoice**  Ayler (ts); **Donald Ayler** (t); **Charles Tyler** (as); **Henry Grimes**, **Gary Peacock** (b);
**Sunny Murray** (d); **Call Cobbs** (h). ESP-Disk Ⓜ ESP1020-2 (33 minutes). Recorded 1965.

⑩ ❹

As was true during his brief career, critical discourse on Ayler still tends to emphasize the intensity
and dark spirituality of his music, with little attention paid to the the humour of which he was capable
when playing with other horns (though it must be acknowledged that listening to Ayler has always
been a guessing game, inasmuch as no one can be certain of what was intended as irony and what was
evidence of madness). Along with *Bells* from the same year, *Spirits Rejoice* is where Ayler's humour
first came to the fore, showing up not only in the allusions to *Le Marseillaise* on the title track and
the echoes of Salvation Army bands throughout, but also in the way that Ayler's solos vacillate
between ecstasy and what could be interpreted as self-mockery. Then still in Ayler's thrall, Tyler is
often virtually indistinguishable from him, a similarity compounded by the poor recording quality
(the sound here is better than on the original LP, however) and the tendency of both saxophonists to
pitch their solos in the *altissimo* register. The bassists are practically inaudible except during their
solos, but Murray's drum interjections are strongly felt, as are Donald Ayler's fractured trumpet solos,
which have a hint of Booker Little to them, although delivered at twice the speed. Cobbs's silent-film
harpsichord is present only on *Angels*, a rubato ballad on which Ayler – exiled from the jazz canon
by those who prefer to pretend that the sixties never happened – recalls no one so much as Sidney
Bechet, with his oversized vibrato and the operatic scale of his emotion. You cannot get more 'in the
tradition' than that.                                                                **FD**

**Love Cry**  Ayler (as, ts); **Don Ayler** (t); **Call Cobbs** (h); **Alan Silva** (b); **Milford Graves** (d). Impulse!
Ⓜ GRP11082 (54 minutes). Recorded 1967-8.

⑧ ⑩

This is the last good album Ayler made before his precipitous decline. In an odd sense, it is a little
like a 'greatest hits' package, with six of the eight tunes being straightforward unison statements of
the main theme, plus a little sprinkling of trumpet obbligato thrown in for good luck. On the original
LP issue of **Love Cry** this impression was all the more intense, because that album carried only
*Universal Indians* as a track containing any significant degree of improvisation by Ayler or his
brother. The rest of it we could all presumably sing along with. And good clean fun it all was, too.
     This CD reissue redresses this balance by including another edit of *Universal Indians* (same take, just
more of it), plus a previously unissued track, *Love Cry 11* (not to be confused with *Love Cry*, to which
it bears no resemblance). Both get quite wild enough, thereby demonstrating what a superbly apposite
drummer for the Aylers Graves really was. This new material puts the bite back into the overall message
and puts this album in a position much more central to the Ayler tradition. A fitting *vale* to a major
artist, even if he did not see it that way himself at the time. Compared to the dire low-fi to be found on
earlier, non-Impulse! Aylers, this one sounds like it was recorded in Paradise.                 **KS**

# Azimuth

**Azimuth '85**  **John Taylor** (p, org); **Kenny Wheeler** (t, flh); **Norma Winstone** (v).
ECM Ⓟ 827 520-2 (44 minutes). Recorded 1985.

⑥ ⑩

Azimuth is one of those groups which so closely defines the ECM ethos. Just like Eberhard Weber's
early efforts, or Terje Rypdal's continuing odyssey of sound, it creates both the intellectual and sonic

environment for that Cathedral-like ECM resonance to emerge in all its glory. The space the music naturally has enhances this quality to the point that every note in each chord, every melodic filament of the greater whole, is etched unerringly across your mental palette.

It is possible that all this was once challenging to the listener; now it seems comforting, or comfortable, like a well-worn jacket which fits perfectly; a quality product which serves you well. No mood or emotion becomes overpowering; nothing seems ill thought out, or the subject of an irresistible impulse. If you like musical understatement, wistfulness and elliptical melodic shapes conveying faintly other-worldly notions and sentiments, then this album will strongly appeal. It is not New Age music, because it has bucketloads more musical ideas in one minute than a whole New Age album uses up in 60, and three superbly talented improvising musicians. However, if one was not careful, the end result could superficially be confused with New Age, Wheeler's eloquence notwithstanding.                                          **KS**

# Alice Babs                                                    1924

**Far Away Star** Babs (v); **Duke Ellington Orchestra**; **Nils Lindberg Orchestra**. Bluebell
Ⓕ ABCD005 (36 minutes). Recorded 1973/6.

④ ⑧

No one has ever accounted for Ellington's Achilles' heel – the ability to select what appeared to be totally unsuitable singers for his orchestra. Babs was the shining example of the exception to the rule. Her extraordinary voice enables her to be equally at home with pop music, Mozart or Ellington, and she has a feeling for jazz which never lets her down. Even when she has scat exchanges with the trumpets in the band on *Spacemen* her jazz sense never falters, and she has all the abilities of the more established Ellingtonian soloists.

Babs's voice is truly unique and in the four numbers with the 1973 Ellington band her voice highlights the fabric of the orchestral ensembles behind her. This effect is particularly evident on the beautiful *Far Away Star* and on *Jeep's Blues* she is as lyrical as the normal incumbent of that work, Johnny Hodges, used to be. The tracks with Lindberg use mostly Ellington material and include his best ballad, *Warm Valley* and a second version (the first is with Ellington) of the beautiful *Serenade to Sweden*, a fortuitous tribute to Miss Babs's native land.                **SV**

# Benny Bailey                                                  1925

**For Heaven's Sake** Bailey (t); **Tony Coe** (ts, ss, cl); **Horace Parlan** (p); **Jimmy Woode** (b); **Idris Mohammad** (d). Hot House Ⓕ HHCD1006 (53 minutes). Recorded 1988.

⑧ ⑧

Born in Cleveland, Ohio, Benny Bailey worked with Jay McShann, Dizzy Gillespie and Lionel Hampton before settling in Europe in 1953 to become one of the most sought-after session trumpet players on the entire continent. He is a faultless section leader and a hugely inventive soloist. Curiously, the reputation of being a successful man at the top of his profession has caused him to become invisible to jazz commentators; if he had been in and out of jail for a series of lurid offences the press would have beaten a path to his door.

Although he has spent his life in recording studios, this album is one of the few to be issued under his own name. For an example of Benny Bailey's exceptional jazz talent you need only to hear the first number, Roy Eldridge's *Little Jazz*; swinging, resourceful, witty, without a trace of vulgarity or empty show. Everyone on the date plays superbly and there is a great feeling of relaxed enjoyment about the proceedings. If this had been recorded in New York and issued on Blue Note it would have had five-star reviews everywhere. Since it was made in London and issued by a small British company it was largely overlooked. Fortunately for us it is still available.                    **DG**

# Derek Bailey                                                  1931

**Figuring** Bailey (g); **Barre Phillips** (b). Incus Ⓕ CD05 (58 minutes). Recorded 1987-8.

⑩ ⑧

Bailey is one of the very few British-born jazz musicians who has been an influence on his peers world-wide. His career began in the most commercial circles, and he even played in the pit at the London Palladium. Having decided that he wanted to take a more creative path, he became involved with the Spontaneous Music Ensemble and other members of London's free improvisation movement. This CD, a culture shock for newcomers, takes the listener to the heart of his style. There is no episodic continuity but his essentially chromatic music is played with scrupulous accuracy. Ideas are thrown up, flourish briefly and then end abruptly as these musicians move to the next exposition. As a duo, Bailey and Phillips play together superbly: they listen to each other yet never completely tailor their lines to those of their team-mate. Bailey's work has been described as "avant-garde bottleneck" and, following his convoluted, slurring path through a solo, it is not difficult to see why this should be so. An essential avant-garde purchase.                                         **BMcR**

# Mildred Bailey

1907-51

**The Rockin' Chair Lady** Bailey (v) with **The Casa Loma Orchestra**; **Her Alley Cats** (Bunny Berigan, t; Johnny Hodges, as; Teddy Wilson, p; Grachan Moncur, b); **The Delta Rhythm Boys**; small group with **Herman Chittison** (p); **Dave Barbour** (g); **Frenchy Covetti** (b); **Jimmy Hoskins** (d); **Harry Sosnick and His Orchestra** (Billy Butterfield, t; Jack Jenney, tb; Jimmy Lytell, cl; Sal Franzella, bcl; Billy Kyle, p; Carmen Mastren, g; Charlie Barbour, b; O'Neil Spencer, d); **Vic Schoen and His Orchestra** (John Best, t; Murray McEachern, Ed Kusby, Hoyt Bohannon, Sy Zenter, tb; Wilbur Schwartz, Ted Nash, as; Johnny Rotella, ts; Rudy Herman, bs; Willy Usher, p; Al Hendrickson, g; Joe Mondragon, Irv Cottler, d). MCA Ⓜ GRP16442 (63 minutes). Recorded 1931-50.

✔                                                                          ⑩ ❽

If it had not been for Billie Holiday, there is little doubt that Mildred Bailey would now be regarded as *the* jazz voice of the thirties, the young Ella notwithstanding. Her voice was light and sensual, her sense of rhythm remarkably supple, her diction clear. This collection not only bears out the opening sentiment, but also produces a handy snapshot guide to the majority of her entire recording career. She first made a name as featured vocalist with The Paul Whiteman Orchestra (she was with him from 1929-34); the earliest recording in this set, from 1931 and using the Casa Loma Orchestra as backing, is cast in the Whiteman style of the day and shows Bailey's singing to be deeply rooted in the declamatory, emotive style then in vogue on Broadway. By 1935 her jazz phrasing is fully evolved, her use of blues-inflected swoops and glides idiomatic: the only left-over from Broadway is an occasional broad vibrato or shake at the finish of a note (she was certainly not alone in using this technique). By 1941, such decoration has been judged superfluous and discarded, and the sessions from that year reveal an artistry which is perfect and an interpretative depth which is completely fulfilling. Indeed, the versions of *Rockin' Chair* (her one big hit, back in 1930) and *Georgia on My Mind* have rarely been bettered, such is their sense of ease and their remarkable quiet eloquence. In all, there are nine tracks from 1941 on this collection, and every one deserves the status of a classic.

Finally, a note of commendation to transfer engineers Steven Lasker and Erick Labson at MCA Studios, who have done an exceptional job in giving us such a clear, full sound. **KS**

# Chet Baker

1929-88

**The Pacific Jazz Years** Baker (t, v); with various personnels including: **Don Fagerquist** (t); **Frank Rosolino** (tb); **Bob Brookmeyer** (vtb); **Art Pepper**, **Bud Shank**, **Herb Geller** (as); **Stan Getz**, **Phil Urso**, **Herb Geller**, **Jack Montrose**, **Bill Holman**, **Bill Perkins** (ts); **Gerry Mulligan** (bs); **Russ Freeman**, **Pete Jolly**, **Bobby Timmons** (p); **Carson Smith**, **Red Mitchell**, **Leroy Vinnegar**, **Monty Budwig** (b); **Chico Hamilton**, **Larry Bunker**, **Bob Neel**, **Shelly Manne**, **Mel Lewis** (d); **Jack Montrose**, **Bill Holman**, **Bob Zieff** (arr); **Annie Ross** (v). Pacific Jazz Ⓜ CDP7 89292-2 (four discs: 226 minutes). Recorded 1952-7.

                                                                          ⑧ ❼

Baker hit musical highs all through his career, but there is little doubt that they arrived most consistently during the fifties. The trumpeter made his deepest impact during his initial stay in the Gerry Mulligan Quartet, and that group's initial recordings propelled Baker into the international spotlight. The famous *My Funny Valentine* (made for Fantasy at the instigation of Dave Brubeck and recently reissued on CD) is not included here, although you get an excellent live version, almost twice as long as the studio one, which is every bit as intense. Much of the material in this compilation has been available on CD in various forms in the past few years, but this is a very handy way to gather together a representative sampling of the trumpeter at his best or near-best, amongst musicians sympathetic to his art and stimulating to his soul.

Baker's association with Mulligan lasted less than 12 months; his more long-term partnership with Russ Freeman gets a healthy representation here, as well as the dates with Stan Getz, Art Pepper, Phil Urso and Herb Geller. The larger ensembles, used mostly as a foil for Baker's melodicism, function cleanly and with appropriate spirit, while the much-lauded 1957 reunion with Mulligan is given three tracks (for a review of the complete session, see below). Baker had a unique gift and many of the recordings sampled here find that gift displayed to its fullest advantage. That, plus the useful booklet and sturdy packaging of the four discs, suffering less than usual from the EMI art department's idea of meaningful design, makes this a convenient summary of Baker's art. **KS**

**The Italian Sessions** Baker (t); **Bobby Jaspar** (ts, f); **Amadeo Tommasi** (p); **René Thomas** (g); **Benoit Querson** (b); **Daniel Humair** (d). RCA Victor Ⓜ 68590-2 (55 minutes). Recorded 1962.

                                                                          ⑧ ❹

By 1962, Baker was living in Italy, where he was reunited with two players from his 1955 Paris dates in an international sextet boasting a great Belgian guitarist, Swiss drummer and Belgian tenor saxophonist. Baker is in exceptionally good lip; the heavy Miles Davis influence often imputed to him is virtually nowhere in evidence. Instead, he sounds indebted (like Miles) to Dizzy Gillespie, judging by his crackling up-tempo work on Monk's *Well, You Needn't*, his aggressive attack and singing vibrato on Tommasi's *Ballata in forma di blues*, his fat brass timbre on Pettiford's up-tempo *Blues in the Closet*. Even on the slow ballads *These Foolish Things* and *Over the Rainbow*, Baker's introspective playing has substantial body.

Fellow soloists Jaspar, Thomas and Tommasi set the hard-bop tone, different from the laid-back groupings Baker habitually appeared in. Bird's calypso *Barbados* even has a shout chorus at the end. Many jazz fans, Americans especially, think fluent European jazz musicians are a recent phenomenon, but this crew speaks the language with no awkward accent. They challenge Baker, who rises to the task. About the only thing wrong with this session is the tinny, echo-ridden recorded sound. Chet doesn't even get to sing ...                                                                                  **KW**

---

**Chet Baker and Paul Desmond Together: The Complete Studio Recordings** Baker (t, v); **Paul Desmond** (as); **Jim Hall** (g); **Bob James**, **Kenny Barron**, **Roland Hanna** (p); **Ron Carter** (b); **Steve Gadd**, **Tony Williams** (d). Epic ⓜ 472984-2 (56 minutes). Recorded 1974-7.

⑥ ❽

Baker and Desmond did not record much together, and were not the most obvious of partners, being too much like each other for comfort, so one imagines that the reason for this CD – a compilation from three other Epic records – is mostly nostalgic. Baker and Desmond are both comparatively recently dead, so there is a kind of wispy logic in teaming them retrospectively. Baker was always seen as a tough survivor who played fragile, dreamy trumpet, while Paul Desmond had more the corporate image – Mr Nice Guy in the Brubeck set-up – but against expectations it is Baker who comes across as the stronger soloist here, more forceful and more memorable. Nearly 20 minutes of the 60 is devoted to one piece, Rodrigo's *Concierto de Aranjuez* – strange, the appeal this piece has had for jazz musicians.        **MK**

---

**The Touch of Your Lips** Baker (t, v); **Doug Raney** (g); **Niels-Henning Ørsted Pederson** (b). SteepleChase ⓕ SCCD31122 (43 minutes). Recorded 1979.

❽ ⑥

Baker's restless life-style was clearly an expensive road to ultimate self-destruction, causing him to be ever-ready to make records, especially during his years in Europe. For that reason one has to be circumspect in one's choice from the dozens of albums which continue to appear under his name, but this one may be purchased with safety. Recorded in Copenhagen, it is one of the warmest and most intimate examples of Baker's craft on one of his very good days. Doug Raney (son of Jimmy) is ideal in this context, with a warm sound and expert knowledge of chords, while NHØP is a tower of strength and dependability. When one considers that there is no fixed-pitch instrument in this trio, there are no intonation problems, nor do Raney and NHØP experience any harmonic clashes. Chet's trumpet sound is fragile on the ballads, and one immediately warms to his work; even the very occasional cracked note evokes a feeling of sympathy in the listener; this is great trumpet playing in the tradition of Bix, Bobby Hackett and Miles Davis. Baker sings on the title track and on *But Not for Me*, indulging in a chorus of scat on the latter. The vocals neither add to nor diminish the value of a CD on which the clarity of the recording adds to the intimacy of the music.        **AM**

---

**New review**
**The Legacy** Baker, Lennart Axelson, Heinz Habermann, Manfred Moch, Paul Kubatsch (t); Wolfgang Ahlers, Hermann Plato, Manfred Grossmann, Egon Christmann (tb); Herb Geller, Jochen Ment (as), Stan Sulzman, Harald Ende (ts); Werner Ronfeldt (bs); Wolfgang Schluter (vb); Walter Norris (p); John Schroder (g); Lucas Lindholm (b); Alex Riel (d). Enja ⓕ ENJ9021-2 (53 minutes) Recorded 1987.

✓                                                                                                      ⑨ ❾

It is often claimed that Chet Baker's final years betrayed his youthful promise. This set, released for the first time in 1995, triumphantly and conclusively refutes that gloomy view. Recorded at a Hamburg concert with the big band of Norddeutscher Rundfunk, it is not merely as good as anything he ever did, but probably better. His tone is full and warm, his technique virtually faultless and he consistently bubbles over with invention. Naturally, there is a great deal of the whispy, winsome elegance at which he was a master, but the boldness and confidence which so often eluded him is here too, and that is what makes this disc so impressive. The material consists of American songs and jazz standards, including Miles Davis's *All Blues* and Herbie Hancock's *Dolphin Dance,* neither of which seem to have been part of his regular repertoire, and he brings a soft, lyrical quality to them which casts them in a new light. A large measure of the disc's success is due to the arrangements, dark and glowing in the Gil Evans manner (the work of three writers – Jorg Keller, Horst Muhlbradt and someone credited only as 'Gorzel') and the exceptional playing of the orchestra        **DG**

# Ginger Baker                                                                                           1937

---

**Going Back Home** Baker (d); **Bill Frisell** (g); **Charlie Haden** (b). Atlantic ⓕ 782652-2 (45 minutes). Recorded 1994.

❽ ❾

What's going on? Is this really the man who played in Cream all those years ago? Yes, it is. Baker was a jazzer long before he stumbled into r&b and, later, rock. His personal odyssey has since seen him deeply involved in many musical styles, including the African beat a good 15 years before it was hip.

Here he closes the circle and plays rinky-tink variations like someone who never went away. This is another power trio, but of a very different ilk to the Baker-Bruce-Clapton one who would deliver high-volume jams on *Spoonful* for 15 minutes. Here the irresistible momentum of Baker's stroll is matched by the deep hue of Haden's beautiful tone and powerful rhythm. Frisell, meanwhile, remains a light and agile performer, content to react to the directions fed him by the other two members of the trio. This relationship works admirably because all three players have the imagination and empathy to investigate unusual angles in mutually enhancing ways, especially when it comes to such latter-day jazz standards as *Straight*, *No Chaser* and *Ramblin'*. An impressive showing for all three musicians.　　　**KS**

# Kenny Baker　　　　　　　　　　　　　　　　　　　　　　　　　　　1921

**The Boss is Home**　Baker, Derek Healey, Bruce Adams, Simon Gardner (t); Don Lusher, Bill
　Geldard, Richard Edwards (tb); Roy Willox, Alan Barnes, Vic Ash, Dave Willis, Eddie Mordue
　(reeds); **Brian Dee** (p); **Dave Green** (b); **Ralph Salmins** (d). Big Bear Ⓕ ESSCD224 (70 minutes).
　Recorded 1993.

⑧　❻

The weekly broadcasts by Kenny Baker's Dozen during the fifties brought succour to beleaguered European jazz fans who were, by union restrictions, denied live American jazz. This re-creation of the days of the Dozen, recorded live at Ronnie Scott's in Birmingham, builds nicely on the original and manages to be contemporary while holding on to the nostalgic spirit.

　These spirited performances blow away the usual 'show band' *ennui* of what have become known as graveyard groups. Baker always chose his material well and here it varies from *Street of Dreams*, *Stumbling* (with its startling explosion of trumpet from Bruce Adams) and *When Sunny Gets Blue* to an unhackneyed clutch of Ellingtonia which includes the little-heard *Golden Cress*, arranged by Baker for the trombone of Don Lusher, to the shouting *In a Jam*, which includes one of several solos on the album by Richard Edwards, an emergent trombone great. Baker is liberal with solo space and his team of soloists, youngsters and veterans alike, respond magnificently to produce a triumph of melodic, swinging mainstream jazz.　　　**SV**

# Shorty Baker　　　　　　　　　　　　　　　　　　　　　　　　　1913-66

New review
**And Doc Cheatham**　Baker, Cheatham (t); **Walter Bishop Jr.** (p); **Wendell Marshall** (b); **J. C.**
　**Heard** (d). Prestige Swingville Ⓜ OJCCD839-2 (43 minutes). Recorded 1961.

⑦　❽

Undoubtedly at his best with Ellington (the Columbia **Ellington Indigos** album was a triumph) Baker was also heard to great advantage in Johnny Hodges small groups. However, like many Ellingtonians his character diminished when away from home ground. By the time of this session what had been one of the world's most beautiful trumpet sounds was inhibited; some of his ballad artistry remains on his solo version of *I Didn't Know What Time It Was*, but there is about his and Doc Cheatham's playing on this album a somewhat perfunctory approach which is not helped by the absence of a saxophone in the line-up. Not surprisingly, given the personnel, there is a lack of imagination in the programming. Whereas Baker at his best was the equal of either Buck Clayton or Clark Terry he couldn't hold a candle to them here. The worthy Cheatham, a remarkable 90-year-old and still playing effectively at the time of writing, was never (despite the great romance of his jazz life) one of the great soloists. Bishop and the rhythm section do all that is required of them, but they can't breathe fire into a passionless front line.　**SV**

# Jon Balke

New review
**Nonsentration**　Balke (kbds, comp, arr); **Per Jørgensen, Nils Petter Molvær** (t); **Torbjørn Sunde**
　(tb); **Morten Halle** (as); **Tore Brunborg, Arne Frang** (ts); **Audun Kleive** (d); **Jon Christensen**
　(d, perc); **Finn Sletten, Miki N'Doye** (perc). ECM Ⓕ 849 653-2 (43 minutes). Recorded 1990.

⑦　❽

With their crisp, non-vibratoed phrasing and cool demeanour, Oslo 13 may initially create an aura of emotional detachment but first impressions can be deceptive. Swing is not what they do best; fortunately composer/arranger Jon Balke seldom calls on them to attempt it. Rather than integrating theme and accompaniment and blending the instruments, he prefers to isolate and layer the contrasting departments – frequently the percussion section will instigate a flurry of activity over which the horns and brass punch chords and hover calm, folk-sounding melodies in open space. Balke's compositions tend to build slowly, present their points gradually, find a climax and end suddenly. His pieces inevitably make a statement but seldom *go* anywhere. Harmonies are often static and the melodic content is stark – at its best they convey a fetching wistfulness. The use of electric keyboards reveals a surprising seventies fusion influence, especially when combined with the percussion in Miles-like proportions on *Nord* and *Blic*. The soloists are decent and comfortable in the open air, though they aren't intended to be exposed for long. If Balke's approach seems more calculated than spontaneous, it's nevertheless an intriguing alternative to the usual big band boisterousness.   **AL**

# Kenny Ball

1930

**Strictly Jazz**  Ball (t); **John Bennett** (tb); **Dave Jones** (cl); **Colin Bates**, **Ron Weatherburn** (p); **Diz Disley**, **Tony Pitt**, **Paddy Lightfoot** (bj); **Vic Pit** (b); **Ron Bowden** (d). Kaz Ⓜ CD19 (75 minutes). Recorded 1960-2.

⑤ ❻

Some listeners might quibble with the title, but Ball is synonymous with the Dixieland end of the 'trad' phenomenon in sixties Britain, and this album collates much of his best work from the dawn of that period. The sleeve-note contains no personnel or recording details, but most of this material dates from Ball's recordings for Pye or Enja, including one live concert from Liverpool's Empire Theatre.

The banjo is relentless and dominant, but Jones plays a full and accomplished clarinet, while Ball and Bennett supply energetic and full-ranged brass work, consistent with Ball's background in larger bands with great demands on iron-lipped trumpeters. Weatherburn is the star pianist, and Bowden relaxes from the straitjacket of the fifties Chris Barber band which he had joined at its inception. Missing are Ball's great hits, *Samantha* and *Midnight in Moscow*, but the album has a full sweep of the early Dixieland repertoire from *Ole Miss* to *Ostrich Walk*. *High Society* has Ball's party piece of shadowing the classic clarinet choruses on trumpet.   **AS**

# Iain Ballamy

1964

**All Men Amen**  Ballamy (ss, as); **Django Bates** (p, kbds, frh); **Steve Watts** (b); **Martin France** (d, perc). B&W Music Ⓕ BW065 (45 minutes). Recorded 1994.

⑧ ❽

Although somewhat under-recorded as a leader (his previous album, **Balloon Man**, featuring the same personnel as above, was released in 1989), Iain Ballamy has established himself as a highly individual voice since the demise of Loose Tubes. His is a light-toned, breathily intimate saxophone sound more overtly beholden to, say, Warne Marsh or even Paul Desmond than to the more usual model for eighties UK players, John Coltrane; his romantic, deeply contemplative style often brings Charles Lloyd to mind. His playing on this album, however, like that on the US-made **Meeting in Brooklyn**, is immediately recognizable as quintessential Ballamy, whether he is contributing keening soprano over Django Bates's luminous, rippling piano, or warbling alto, delicately propelled by Martin France's skittering drums and Steve Watt's rock-solid bass. Although Ballamy is a fine interpreter of standards – particularly ballads – all the material here is original, and there are signs on pieces such as *Meadow* (given great textural depth by the use of Bates's horn and embellished with hunting noises for atmosphere) that he is developing into a considerable composer, especially adept at writing tender, at times wistfully plaintive, vehicles for his alternatively rhapsodic and meditative saxophones.   **CP**

# Gabe Baltazar

1929

**Back in Action**  Baltazar (as); **Tom Ranier** (p); **Richard Simon** (b); **Steve Houghton** (d). VSOP Ⓕ #85 CD (MODE201) (64 minutes). Recorded 1992.

⑥ ❽

A Hawaiian native, Baltazar had early experience with Howard Rumsey. He was Stan Kenton's lead alto for five years from 1960, and in the sixties worked with Terry Gibbs, Gil Fuller and Oliver Nelson. A return to Hawaii took him out of the recording limelight but this CD marks a reasonably auspicious return from the wilderness. The programme, with three of his pleasingly melodic originals, is imaginative and Baltazar shoulders most of the solo responsibility. Time has lent a greater opulence to his tone but his improvisations remain as logical and melodically sensitive as ever. There is evidence of the occasional faulty note production but he never seems to lose his direction. His most challenging work is on *Ruby, My Dear*, where his unpredictable line and adroit tempo changes add genuine colour, or on *Dream Dancing*, where an inventive outing also emphasizes the warmth and relaxation of his style. The three little-known men who comprise the rhythm section do a good job and seem to have the needs of the alto saxophonist uppermost in their minds. Baltazar could be said to be back.   **BMcR**

# Billy Bang

1947

New review
**Spirits Gathering**  Bang (vn); **Brett Allen** (g); **Akira Ando** (b); **Denis Charles** (d). Creative Improvised Music Projects Ⓕ CIMP109 (66 minutes). Recorded 1996.

⑧ ❾

Bang's ebullient playing draws on the hard-driving style of Stuff Smith and the new microtonal sound worlds first explored by Ornette Coleman and AACM innovator Leroy Jenkins. The result is a potent mix of swing, blues and free-form abstraction, further spiced by Bang's often acerbic tone – he loves to hit the spaces between notes. A member of the String Trio of New York in the seventies, he also headed a wide range of projects, from solo concerts to writing for large string ensemble (Outline 12). In the mid-eighties his group featured an attractive and unusual front line of violin/trumpet/ marimba (**The Fire Within**; **Live at Carlos I**). **Spirits Gathering** is by his latest quartet, three strings deftly propelled by veteran drummer Charles. Bang's playing here attains an extraordinary intensity at times. Perhaps being evicted from his apartment the previous day had fired him up, because he lights into *Know Your Enemy* with almost manic fervour and is hardly less ferocious on the cathartic *Blues in E*. *My Funny Valentine* elicits an impassioned display in a more romantic vein, while other tracks settle into calmer grooves, the violin a sinuous thread through fluent group interplay. As Bang says, this is music of "real gut feelings", rendered faithfully by CIMP's pin-sharp recording. **GL**

# Paul Barbarin

1899-1969

**Paul Barbarin and His New Orleans Jazz** Barbarin (d); John Brunious (t); Bob Thomas (tb); Willie Humphrey (cl); Lester Santiago (p); Danny Barker (bj); Milt Hinton (b). Atlantic Ⓜ 790977-2 (48 minutes). Recorded 1955.

⑦ ❻

Already a professional by 1915, Barbarin arrived in Chicago in 1917. He worked with King Oliver and Jimmie Noone and earned a considerable reputation for his uncomplicated but propulsive drum style. In 1928 he joined Luis Russell and became part of one of the most dynamic rhythm sections of its day. The band was ultimately taken over by Louis Armstrong, but Barbarin remained very much its heartbeat. In the late forties he returned to New Orleans to lead his own bands and this CD presents a typically professional 1955 edition. Swing era inflections are discernible in Brunious's accomplished style, but he is a highly effective ensemble leader. Thomas's forthright trombone adds the tailgate muscle and Humphrey's flowing solos and coherent contrapuntal skills complete a fine front line. Despite being a drummer's band, the four-man rhythm section is strategically understated. Barker and Hinton apply a light touch, but it is the leader's jaunty two-beat drum style at its core that most imparts the feeling of good-humoured buoyancy. The list of drummers influenced by Barbarin would be short, but as groups grew in size in the twenties he played an important part in providing a workable vernacular for the new jazz language. **BMcR**

# Chris Barber

1930

New review

**The Chris Barber Concerts** Barber (tb, v); Pat Halcox (t); Monty Sunshine (cl); Johnny Duncan (g); Eddie Smith (bj); Dick Smith (b); Ron Bowden, Graham Burbidge (d); Ottillie Patterson (v, p). Lake Ⓜ LACDD/5556 (two discs: 143 minutes). Recorded 1956/8.

⑧ ❽

This Lake two-CD set virtually replaces the two separate Barber concert issues on Dormouse (now deleted) covered in the previous edition of the book. All of the music comes from three concerts which took place at the Royal Festival Hall, Birmingham Town Hall and the Dome in Brighton (this set contains a version of *Indiana* from the Brighton concert which may well be making its first appearance anywhere; it certainly wasn't on the Dormouse CDs). The music is very well played with a precision which was not always to be found in other trad bands of the period. Chris has succeeded in leading his hugely successful unit since 1954 and all of the material here appeared first on the Pye-Nixa label. The net has been spread wide and the material includes songs by Duke Ellington, Wilber De Paris, Stephen Foster and Bill Broonzy as well as Kid Ory and Paul Barbarin, although there is a glossy sheen superimposed which tends towards the formulaic. A single budget-priced CD called **The Essential Chris Barber** (Kaz) comprises 21 tracks by the same band and from the same period but duplicates only six on the double-CD issue. There are a couple of attractive trio/quartet titles featuring Monty Sunshine's sub-tone clarinet and, of course, the surprisingly virile singing of Ottillie Patterson is featured with the band. **AM**

**Concert for the BBC** Barber (tb, v); Pat Halcox (t); Ian Wheeler (cl, as); John Crocker (cl, as, ts); Roger Hill (g); Johnny McCallum (bj, g); Vic Pitt (b); Norman Emberson (d). Timeless Ⓕ CDTTD509/10 (62 minutes). Recorded 1982.

⑥ ❻

The piano-less banjo-propelled rhythm section of the Barber band has become more sophisticated over the years, but it is in the front line that fundamental change has taken place. *Perdido Street Blues* is an interesting case of metamorphosis because it retains the clarion clarinet solo from the Johnny Dodds original while adding a booting contemporary tenor solo from John Crocker. The two reed players Crocker and Ian Wheeler are versatile in their various roles, and the employment of a guitar soloist (Roger Hill) adds yet another colour to the solo strength. Barber himself seems to sing more than play on this occasion, but when he does sing the obbligato playing of Pat Halcox is sensitive and creative. This is the Barber band caught at its very best. It represents what is probably the most potent and imaginative latter-day use of a traditional jazz line-up. **SV**

## Gato Barbieri                                                            1934

**In Search of the Mystery** **Barbieri** (ts); **Carlo Scott** (vc); **Sirone** (Norris Jones) (b); **Bobby Kapp** (d). ESP-Disk Ⓜ ESP1049-2 (40 minutes). Recorded 1967.

⑦ ❽

Barbieri's increasing determination to use his Argentinian musical heritage led to a progressive dilution of jazz content as his career progressed. With Don Cherry in Europe and on records in the sixties he had given notice of becoming a major talent. This 1967 album, while still not the finished article, shows him as an exciting saxophonist with a brilliant grasp of multiphonics and with the technique to project them. Initially a John Coltrane devotee, Barbieri had already charted his own course and titles like *In Search of the Mystery* and *Obsession No. 2*, while not always exploiting the rhythmic freedom made available, demonstrate an array of tonal colours as he takes his tenor into ranges normally associated with high-note trumpet men. The motif-based brick-building tradition of the free formers may not be greatly developed here, but Barbieri tends to evoke the feeling of solo evolution by repeating phrases in which either minute timbral adjustments or more violent changes of pitch occur. Rather than being the album that might have opened the door for a musical giant, it now appears as something of a pinnacle from which a very good player retreated. **BMcR**

## Guy Barker                                                              1957

**Isn't It?** **Barker** (t, flh); with a collective personnel of: **Jamie Talbot** (ss); **Peter King** (as); **Nigel Hitchcock** (as, ts); **Julian Joseph**, **Stan Tracey** (p); **Jim Mullen** (g); **Alec Dankworth** (b); **Clark Tracey** (d). Spotlite Ⓕ SPJ-CD545 (68 minutes). Recorded 1991.

⑧ ❽

In the light of his considerable expertise as a trumpet player and his obvious accomplishments as a jazz soloist it is surprising that until 1995 it was left to the independent labels (Spotlite and Miles Music) to record Barker as a group leader. A great deal of care went into the production of this album and Spotlite's Tony Williams was clearly anxious to give Barker the settings and the musical colleagues to bring out the best in this world-class player. Almost every track sees a change in instrumentation; *Goodspeed*, for example, puts Barker with Peter King and Nigel Hitchcock (both playing altos) while Hoagy Carmichael's lovely *I Get Along Without You Very Well*, like *Amandanita*, is just trumpet and rhythm section. Two of the most startling performances are duets. The breadth of Barker's knowledge of jazz tradition comes to the fore on *In a Mist*, a transcription of a Bix Beiderbecke piano piece for just trumpet and bass. Guy's accuracy in pitching here is complete while the burnished tone, one of his strongest features, is well in evidence. *Lament for the Black Tower* is the second duet, this time Barker with Stan Tracey, who composed the tune (this is Tracey's only appearance on the CD). *Black Tower* is music-making of the highest quality, but the entire album is a credit to all concerned, musicians and producer. Barker's move to a major company notwithstanding, this remains his best effort to date. **AM**

## Alan Barnes                                                             1959

New review
**Alan Barnes Plays Harold Arlen** **Barnes** (cl, as); **Brian Lemon** (p). Zephyr Records Ⓕ ZECD7 (67 minutes). Recorded 1995.

⑩ ⑩

The Zephyr label was invented by John Bune because he thought that Brian Lemon was under-represented on disc. Bune has rapidly become an English version of Norman Granz and, although Lemon features on 98 per cent of his sessions, young Barnes is coming up on the outside, having made several albums in various combinations with Lemon and others. Barnes is one of the finest all-round jazz musicians that Britain has produced. Fortunately he doesn't know this and so he keeps trying harder, with beneficial results for all his listeners. He is a virtuoso player on baritone as well as on the two horns he confines himself to here and his world class has been confirmed in duets he recorded for Bune with Ken Peplowski – as yet unreleased.

Bune's musicians are melodists to a man (they include Ruby Braff and Roy Williams) and there is probably not a bad tune in the whole catalogue. Harold Arlen is a composer who has been wrongly placed second to the Berlins and Gershwins of this world. He is, as the 13 songs here confirm, as great as any of them. Lemon is a pianist who doesn't need a bass to prop up his playing, the purity of his left-hand work being something to wonder at. This is not to denigrate his long-time partner, bassist Dave Green, who is another giant, but it is simply a fresh change to hear Lemon exposed. *My Shining*

*Hour* encapsulates Barnes's talents, for it opens with a Websterian grandeur (on alto) before sweeping into a Parkeresque series of embellishments which have the bounce from Pete Brown added. The album is clever, original, imaginative and deeply satisfying. Will that do?  **SV**

# Emile Barnes

1892-1970

**New review**

**The Louisiana Joymakers** Barnes (cl); **Joseph 'DeDe' LaCroix Pierce**, **Lawrence Toca** (t); **Harrison Brazley** (tb); **Billie Pierce** (p); **Albert Glenny** (b); **Josiah 'Cié' Frazier** (d). American Music Ⓕ AMCD13 (57 minutes). Recorded 1951.

⑥ ❻

Brother of fellow clarinettist Paul Barnes, Emile's career spanned almost 60 years. He began as a teenager in 1908, enjoyed two golden periods, one in the twenties with the likes of Chris Kelly and Buddy Petit and another in the sixties, when he became something of a cult figure at the newly opened Preservation Hall. The session covered by this CD comes from a period between those dates and is highly regarded by New Orleans's revivalist followers. Its authenticity and the emotional commitment of the players cannot be faulted, although listeners making more stringent musical demands might find wanting the contributions made by Brazley and Toca. Barnes's work is exemplary throughout. His highly personal vibrato adds warmth to a naturally assuaging style, his flair for ensemble playing is demonstrated throughout and his rich chalumeau behind the Pierce vocals is perfect. He takes a particularly propitious stance in certain passages and it is illuminating to hear him lend continuity to Brazley's pedestrian solo on *Lonesome Road* and rescue the ensemble incoherence of *Panama*. Barnes may not stand beside New Orleans giants Dodds, Nicholas, Noone or Simeon but he shows here that he can be ranked at the top of the second division with Lewis, Burbank and brother Paul.  **BMcR**

# George Barnes

1921-77

**Carl Kress and George Barnes – Two Guitars** Carl Kress, George Barnes (g); **Bud Freeman** (ts). Jass Ⓕ JCD636 (71 minutes). Recorded 1962/3.

⑥ ❻

When it came to guitarists, Kress and Barnes believed there was safety in numbers. Both recorded with other guitarists in tandem (Barnes with Earl Backus, Kress with Tony Mottola) and George actually made an LP for Mercury on which he was joined by no less than ten other guitarists. Most of the tracks here were recorded at a New York club called Chuck's Composite and were closely miked to catch every nuance, including the squeaking of a stool! There is never any doubt about the identities of the guitarists, for it is Barnes who plays the single-note lines and Kress who keeps the rhythm going, often sounding like a bass. The notes refer to the parallel with the Eddie Lang/Lonnie Johnson duets (Kress also made some duet recordings with Lang), but there is a slickness here which, after a time, leads to a certain sameness of approach. There is not a note out of place, and the way the two work together on a harmonically complex song such as *Gone with the Wind* is perfection itself, but in the final analysis this is music for guitarists. Even the addition of Bud Freeman's tenor on five titles does little to change the overall sound or concept. (The Freeman titles may well be from Bud's own United Artists studio album with Kress and Barnes.)  **AM**

# Charlie Barnet

1913-91

**New review**

**Skyliner** Barnet (ss, as, ts) with various personnel, including: **Bob Burnet, Charlie Shavers, Billy May, Peanuts Holland, Al Killian, Roy Eldridge** (t); **Eddie Bert, Ed Fromm, Porky Cohen, Tommy Pederson** (tb); **Kurt Bloom, James Lamare, Buddy de Franco, Mike Goldberg, Danny Bank** (reeds); **Nat Jaffe, Bill Miller, Dodo Marmarosa, Al Haig** (p); **Bus Etri, Turk Van Lake, Barney Kessel** (g); **Phil Stevens, Jack Jarvis, Howard Rumsey, Harry Babasin** (b); **Jackie Mills, Harold Hahn, Wesley Dean** (d); **Andy Gibson, Jimmy Mundy, Ralph Burns, Billy May, Ralph Flanagan** (arr). Topaz Ⓕ TPZ1041 (71 minutes). Recorded 1939-45.

⑦ ❽

This recent release has twice as many tracks as the RCA title recommended in the last issue of the Guide and has a span of four more years. Avid's method of cleaning up the sound has produced interesting results. Barnet was able to live an unusually good life because he had one big asset which we could all use – inherited money. He was able to indulge the wine and women bit, but when it came to the song he went the whole way and bought himself a band. He was an outstandingly good saxophone player with superb taste in music and thus his bands were always at the top of the second rank (after Ellington, Basie, Herman, Kenton, Goodman and Shaw in the first). His soloists and arrangers were so good that his music was invariably good and often as exciting as that of the first-rank bands. There was more Ellington influence than was usual in Barnet's music and some of the later tracks arranged by Howard McGhee, Ralph Burns and Andy Gibson show that he didn't simply recreate bygone eras. Barnet lived the kind of life we might all have coveted, but he was also very much a creative artist with an honourable place in the history of jazz. **SV**

**Drop Me Off in Harlem** Barnet (ss, as, ts, ldr); with a collective personnel of: **Peanuts Holland, Irving Berger, Joe Ferrante, Chuck Zimmerman, Al Killian, Jimmy Pupa, Lyman Vunk, Art House, Roy Eldridge, Johnny Martel, Jack Mootz, Holland Killian, Everett McDonald, George Seaberg, Ed Stress, Paul Webster, Art Robey, Dennis Sandole** (t); **Russ Brown, Kahn Keene, Wally Baron, Bill Robertson, Eddie Bert, Ed Fromm, Spud Murphy, Bob Swift, Porky Cohen, Tommy Pederson, Ben Pickering, Charles Coolidge, Gerald Foster, Dave Hallett, Burt Johnson, Bill Haller, Frank Bradley, Lawrence Brown** (tb); **George Bone, Conn Humphries, Murray Williams, Buddy DeFranco, Ray De Geer, Harold Herzon, Joe Meisner, Les Robinson** (as); **Kurt Bloom, James Lamare, Mike Goldberg, Andy Pinot, Ed Pripps, Denny Dehlin, Dave Mathews** (ts); **Danny Bank, Bob Polland, Bob Dawes** (bs); **Bill Miller, Dodo Marmarosa, Al Haig, Sheldon Smith** (p); **Tommy Moore, Turk Van Lake, Barney Kessel** (g); **Jack Jarvis, Bob Elden, Russ Wagner, Andy Riccardi, Howard Rumsey, Morris Rayman, Irv Lang** (b); **Cliff Leeman, Harold Hahn, Mickey Scrima** (d); **Frances Wayne, Peanuts Holland, Art Robey, Kay Starr** (v). MCA/Decca Ⓜ GRD612 (57 minutes). Recorded 1942-6.

⑧ **❽**

Saxophonist and big band leader Charlie Barnet catapulted to the front ranks of the swing era with hits such as *Cherokee* (1939) and *Old Black Magic* (1942), the latter heard here with Frances Wayne's soulful vocal, and the still sleek *Skyliner* (1944). Barnet, like Benny Goodman, also deserves credit for featuring black jazz stars as early as 1937 when trumpeter Frankie Newton joined the band. On this disc we hear such prominent Afro-American jazz players as trumpeters Roy Eldridge, Al Killian and trombonist Lawrence Brown. In 1942 Barnet, who had just finished a successful tenure with Bluebird, signed with American Decca for a productive stint that was to see some of the band's best work. A generous leader who allowed his men plenty of elbow-room to strut their stuff, Barnet was also a first-rate soloist whose robust tenor, Hodges-inflected alto and pioneering work on soprano still impress. Indeed, the Decca sessions reveal an inspired, no-nonsense band which had discipline and élan aplenty. The title track, Ellington's *Drop Me Off in Harlem*, propelled by pianist Dodo Marmarosa, guitarist Barney Kessel and drummer Harold Hahn plus Eldridge's wailing trumpet, is a gem, as is the exotic Ralph Flanagan arrangement of the insinuating *Gulf Coast Blues*. In all, a poignant reminder of one of the great jazz swing bands. **CB**

# Joey Baron

**Raised Pleasure Dot** Baron (d); **Steve Swell** (tb); **Ellery Eskelin** (ts). New World Ⓕ 80449-2 (77 minutes). Recorded 1993.

⑥ **❽**

Joey Baron is best known for his work with John Zorn's various projects, but he occasionally strikes out on his own as a leader. This is one such excursion. Some of Zorn's own obsessions flow over into this record, especially the one of two melody instruments interchanging snippets of a theme while playing at around 1,000 mph. This makes for some good clean fun and keeps everyone on their toes, musicians and listeners alike. It also points perhaps to the ultimate source of much of this music – Ornette Coleman. So this is from the tradition, then, whatever Baron does with the beat.

It is impossible to approach this music on a level playing field without a sense of humour, so do not play **Raised Pleasure Dot** if you're in a bad mood: it will only make you feel worse. However, if you have more than an hour to spare to listen to three guys having a whale (and wail) of a time going from what sound like carefully prepared pieces to clearly unpremeditated rants, then this is for you. It is not the most essential of releases for modern music followers, but it is more than mildly diverting, if only for its humour, which on occasion rises to Zappa-esque heights. **KS**

# Sweet Emma Barrett
1897-1983

New review

**And Her Dixieland Boys** Barrett (p, v); **Percy Humphrey** (t); **Jim Robinson** (tb); **Willie Humphrey** (cl); **Emanuel Sayles** (g, bj); **McNeal Breaux** (b); **Josiah 'Cié' Frazier** (d). Riverside Ⓜ OJCCD1832-2 (55 minutes). Recorded 1961.

⑧ **❽**

In her dotage, Sweet Emma was a pathetic wheelchair-bound figure, carried several nights a week into Preservation Hall, where she played one-handed piano and sang in a plaintive moan. Only her red cap and the bells strapped to her lifeless legs hinted at her past. Yet 20 years before her death she led one of the most energetic and authentic of all the New Orleans revival bands and her own strong forthright character, complete with robust vocals and barrelhouse piano, was a vital ingredient in the band's sound. In 1961 Percy Humphrey still had all the fire in his playing that ignited his work with the Eureka Brass band. His playing, with Robinson's tailgate trombone and Frazier's magisterial drumming, conjures up the impression of a riotous second line, bobbing and weaving around the beat on *Just a Little While to*

*Stay Here*. Willie Humphrey's nimble clarinet and the subtle guitar chords of Manny Sayles all go to make this one of the best of the Riverside "Living Legends" series: the stately *St Louis Blues* with Willie's extended clarinet solo is a paradigm for revivalists everywhere. The real strength of this album is in the hard-edged blues vocals from the diminutive leader and the iron discipline she exerted over her musicians to create such a consistent example of first rate revivalism.  **AS**

# Bill Barron
1927-89

**The Next Plateau**  Barron (ts, ss); Kenny Barron (p); Ray Drummond (b); Ben Riley (d). Muse
Ⓟ 5368 (43 minutes). Recorded 1987.

⑧ ❽

Kenny Barron's older brother was always an underrated player, perhaps to some degree because he never fell under Coltrane's critically accepted sway. He first received some recognition in the late fifties with stylistically opposed leaders Philly Joe Jones and Cecil Taylor and within a few years was co-leading an exciting band with trumpeter Ted Curson, proving his linear approach (similar to that of, say, Joe Henderson, a decade younger) was adaptable inside and outside chord changes. By the time of this, his final album, his tone had deepened, reaffirming his roots in Coleman Hawkins's muscularity, and his linearity was modified to emphasize intervals rather than chords, the results approaching the feel of early Ornette. But this date is solidly in the mainstream, aided by a sturdy rhythm section. Barron had long been a writer of interesting tunes; here, *This One's For Monk* acknowledges one of his compositional influences, alluding to several Monk themes including *Misterioso* and *We See* (a.k.a. *Manganese*). In fact, Barron's writing and playing are so rich in allusions (a tad of Rouse here, a dash of Dexter there) as to reinforce the breadth of his conception. A remarkably consistent player of invention and integrity, Barron fortunately left behind a few – too few – recordings like this one to treasure.  **AL**

# Kenny Barron
1943

**The Only One**  Barron (p); Ray Drummond (b); Ben Riley (d). Reservoir Ⓟ 115 (66 minutes).
Recorded 1990.

⑧ ❹

Barron is one of those jazz pianists who is too good for their own good: too tasteful, too devoted to the needs of the leaders he has worked for to call attention to himself. Those employers have included Bill Barron, Dizzy Gillespie, Yusef Lateef, Ron Carter, Freddie Hubbard and Stan Getz. His style is distinguished less by flash than by exquisite touch, absence of wasted motion, authentic lyricism and a strong feel for the blues with little recourse to hard-bop funk licks (which he does in fact trot out for the Latinized head of *Love for Sale*). The title track is an affectionate counterfeit of a romping Monk tune. Taste is the hallmark of Riley's drumming too, and his animated and animating touch with wire brushes is quietly displayed. Riley is so discreet on *Sunny Side of the Street* that he is more felt than heard. Drummond is one of the most reliable, supportive and swinging bassists around, a huge man who handles the bull fiddle as effortlessly as a ukulele. Alas, as with most modern sessions done at Rudy van Gelder's legendary New Jersey studio, the bass was recorded using a pickup instead of a microphone, and has an ugly, unnatural sound.  **KW**

# Gary Bartz
1940

New review
**The Blues Chronicles: Tales of Life**  Bartz (ss, as); Tom Williams (t); George Colligan (p);
Cyrus Chestnut (p, org); Russell Malone (g); James King (b); Greg Bandy, Dennis Chambers (d);
Jon Hendricks (v); Nezkar Keith, Ransom (rap); Maatkara Ali (street holler). Atlantic Ⓟ 82893-2
(69 minutes). Recorded 1995.

⑧ ❾

Slowly but surely, Gary Bartz is getting his recording career back on track. Where recent albums like **Episode One: Children of Harlem** (Challenge CHR70001) nodded in passing to the social concerns that characterized Bartz's NTU Troop period of the early seventies, his latest recording reverts to political truth-telling over often populist rhythms as the musical focus, and results in one of the best-produced and infectious efforts of the saxophonist's career. As the title indicates, the blues provides the musical matter, often in surprising form (*Makes Me Wanna Moan* being an unusual five-bar version, for example). Bebop, rock, swing and reggae rhythms figure into the mix, with the influence of John Coltrane keeping all of the music within the post-bop aesthetic realm. Bartz's horns (primarily alto) are at their tart and impassioned best, and if the album has a drawback it is the brevity of the tracks which stop the leader's solos at a point where inspiration is hardly exhausted. Young pianist George Colligan is the most impressive member of the core quintet, and the various vocal/rap interludes are well placed. The album's message is often provocative, as Bartz continues to call white society to task, although the affirmative spirit of the music does much to cut the vitriol. **The Blues Chronicles** is that rarity, a successful concept album worth hearing from beginning to end.  **BB**

# Paul Bascomb

1910-86

**Bad Bascomb** Bascomb (ts), Eddie Lewis (t); Frank Porter, Tommy Waters (as); Harold Wallace (bs); Duke Jordan (p); James McCrary (b); George DeHart (d) Bascomb, Porter (v). Delmark Ⓕ DD431 (49 minutes). Recorded 1952.

⑦ **7**

Paul, tenor-playing brother of trumpeter Dud Bascomb, shared sideman duties with him in the Erskine Hawkins band when it was at its zenith in the early forties, and successfully ran his own small groups for the next 30 years, mostly in and around Chicago and Detroit. Bascomb recorded intermittently for the United label, both as a leader and as a sideman, and it is a measure of his musicianship and dedication that he sticks to his stylistic guns all through these sides. His roots are in the swing era, just as Louis Jordan's were, and so the occasional jump-style touch is no mere lip-service to the then-burgeoning r&b scene, but more a harking back to Jordan's own golden era. All the playing is polished and well rehearsed, and there is no hint of bad taste: indeed, as a self-confessed Coleman Hawkins fan, Bascomb on *Body and Soul* tries an interesting re-working of the Hawk's classic by going medium-tempo, dispensing with the melody and jamming on the chords. Oddly enough, in the process he sounds like Jack McVea on the 1944 JATP sides.

Of course this type of playing was dreadfully recherché by 1952, as even greats like Webster and Hawkins themselves discovered, so Bascomb's name has not endured as it might have. These sides demonstrate the unfairness of this neglect, no more so than on tracks like *More Blues-More Beat*, where Ellington's *Jam with Sam* receives a jump-style rewrite. For the quite astonishing fluency of his improvising ideas, try his solo on the previously unissued *Nona*: this is the equal of what Jacquet was doing for Norman Granz at this time. Bascomb is well worth hunting down in your specialist shop. **KS**

# Count Basie

1904-84

**The Essential Count Basie, Volume 1** Basie (p, ldr) with: Carl Smith, Buck Clayton, Shad Collins, Ed Lewis, Harry Edison (t); Dan Minor, Dickie Wells, Benny Morton (tb); Earl Warren (as); Jack Washington (as, bs); Lester Young, Buddy Tate (ts, cl); Freddie Green (b); Walter Page (b); Jo Jones (d); Jimmy Rushing, Helen Humes (v). Columbia Ⓜ 460061-2 (47 minutes). Recorded 1936/9.

✓ ⑩ **7**

Apart from the very first, all 16 tracks here date from 1939, one of the peak years for the first Basie band. With the world's finest rhythm section and an unrivalled cast of soloists this was the band which defined the meaning of 'swing'. There are several famous classics here, including the Lester Young feature *Taxi War Dance*, the double-length *Miss Thing* and the archetypal Jimmy Rushing up-tempo blues, *Baby Don't Tell On Me*. The first track is the even more famous (and classic) *Lady Be Good* from the 1936 Jones-Smith Inc. quintet date, Lester Young's first recording session and one of the finest things he ever did. With music of this unquestioned stature the important point is the quality of the edition. This one seems to have been compiled on the basis of taking something from every Basie session recorded by Columbia in 1939 (between 1936 and 1939 Basie was contracted to Decca), and the job is well done. Nothing vital is missing, except perhaps for *Shoe Shine Boy* from 1936. Moreover, the transfers are good and the notes comprehensive. Of course this only represents a tiny part of Basie's 60-year recording career. **DG**

**Count Basie: The Original American Decca Recordings** Basie (p); Buck Clayton, Carl Smith, Harry 'Sweets' Edison, Ed Lewis, Bobby Moore, Shad Collins (t); George Hunt, Dan Minor, Benny Morton, Dicky Wells (tb); Eddie Durham, (tb, g); Lester Young, Herschel Evans (cl, ts); Chu Berry (ts); Caughey Roberts, Earl Warren (as); Jack Washington (as, bs); Freddie Green (g); Walter Page (d); Jo Jones (d); Jimmy Rushing, Helen Humes (v). MCA/Decca Ⓜ GRD3 6112 (three discs: 186 minutes). Recorded 1937-9.

✓ ⑨ **9**

This superbly remastered collection of classics from the first editions of the legendary Basie Band, recorded during its 1937-9 Decca contract, provides a dynamic snapshot of the rumbunctious juggernaut that in terms of its insinuating rhythms and bluesy, riff-based arrangements captured the essence of big band swing more persuasively than the plusher, more polished dynamics of either Ellington or Lunceford.

In the course of the three discs (one each for 1937, 1938 and 1939), we witness the band's growing maturity, the addition of key personnel like guitarist Freddie Green, and the rounding of its initial rough edges; by 1939, ensembles had clicked and everyone played consistently in tune. Throughout, the band kept swinging and having fun. Indeed, a sense of *joie de vivre* is everywhere evident, a tribute to Basie's loose, relaxed leadership. We also hear such stalwarts of the blues-inflected Kansas City style as singers Jimmy Rushing and Helen Humes, saxmen Lester Young, Herschel Evans, Earl Warren and Chu Berry, and trumpeters Buck Clayton and Harry 'Sweets' Edison. That group of soloists is still close to unrivalled in big band history. In pianist Basie, guitarist Green, bassist Walter Page and drummer Jo Jones, we also savour one of the great rhythm sections of jazz. Additionally, we get to hear such staples of the big band tradition as *One O'Clock Jump* and *Jumpin' at the Woodside*.

The package is accompanied by Steven Lasker's expert sleeve-notes, a generous sampling of photos, and comprehensive discographical information.                                    **CB**

---

**Verve Jazz Masters 2**  Basie (p, org); **Paul Campbell, Wendell Culley, Joe Newman, Charlie Shavers, Reunald Jones, Thad Jones, Snooky Young, Fip Ricard, Al Aarons, Sonny Cohn, Don Rader** (t); **Henry Coker, Benny Powell, Jimmy Wilkins, Bill Hughes, Grover Mitchell, Urbie Green** (tb); **Marshall Royal** (as, cl); **Bill Graham** (as); **Ernie Wilkins, Eric Dixon** (as, ts); **Frank Wess** (as, ts, f); **Paul Quinichette, Floyd Johnson, 'Lockjaw' Davis, Frank Foster** (ts); **Charlie Fowlkes** (bs); **Freddie Green** (g); **Jimmy Lewis, Gene Ramey, Eddie Jones, Buddy Catlett** (b); **Gus Johnson, Sonny Payne** (d); **Eddie Durham, Buster Harding, Neal Hefti, Wilkins, Foster, Quincy Jones** (arr); featured guests:  **Roy Eldridge** (t); **Lester Young, Illinois Jacquet** (ts); **Jo Jones** (d); **Jimmy Rushing, Joe Williams** (v). Verve Ⓜ 519 819-2 (66 minutes). Recorded 1952-63.

⑧ ❽

One could argue that most of Basie's worthwhile achievements reflect the profound influence of the blues. The excellent **Plays the Blues** (Verve 513 630-2) compilation only overlaps the present selection by three titles (and only one in the same version), but nine of these 16 items adhere to the 12-bar format. With only one sixties track, the whole album dates from the period when the blues expression was still central to the band's output. This was the band which Basie formed in 1952 after a couple of years working with a small group, and its personnel rapidly developed into a superbly cohesive unit, less loose than the thirties band but more punchy. The four sextet tracks here are drawn from the big-band, including three rare items with Basie on organ and tenorman Quinichette, who is heard in remakes of *Every Tub* and *Blue and Sentimental*; the other 1952 tenor, 'Lockjaw' Davis, is also backed by organ on *Paradise Squat* (a remake of *Mr Roberts' Roost* from the forties).

Later arrivals Foster and Wess join trumpeter Newman as most prolific soloists, and the band proves its continuity with the thirties by its spontaneous head arrangements on the closing Newport Jazz Festival tracks from 1957 with Jones and Young.                                    **BP**

---

**At Newport**  Basie (p, ldr); **Wendell Culley, Joe Newman, Reunald Jones, Thad Jones** (t); **Henry Coker, Benny Powell, Bill Hughes** (tb); **Marshall Royal, Bill Graham, Frank Foster, Frank Wess, Charlie Fowlkes** (s); **Freddie Green** (g); **Ed Jones** (b); **Sonny Greer** (d); with featured guests: **Roy Eldridge** (t); **Lester Young, Illinois Jacquet** (ts); **Jo Jones** (d); **Jimmy Rushing, Joe Williams** (v). Verve Ⓜ 833 776-2 (57 minutes). Recorded 1957.

⑨ ❼

Norman Granz, the founder and original owner of Verve, recorded close to the entire 1957 Newport Jazz Festival, and a goodly amount of it was eventually released on Verve, including such oddities as an LP with the young Cecil Taylor's Quartet on one side and the Gigi Gryce/Donald Byrd Jazz Lab on the other. This Basie CD has been a long time in the making, but is worth the wait, because it finally reunites nearly all the material played by the Basie band in their set at the festival (there is still a fugitive track, featuring Joe Williams joined by Sarah Vaughan, which has never been issued) originally released over one-and-a-half vinyl albums. Thus we have as an added delight the songs crooned by Joe Williams with the band, as well as a rip-roaring Basie outfit charging through *Blee Blop Blues* like an express train.

But the real treasures are the guest stars, with Lester Young making a rare return to form very late in his creative life on three tracks, Roy Eldridge shining on his features, and Illinois Jacquet bringing it all back home on a stirring *One O'Clock Jump*. Jimmy Rushing and Jo Jones also make worthy contributions and the atmosphere throughout is electric. This is a band which really revelled in playing, and it is also fascinating to hear such a well-drilled group playing tight arrangements but also making room for such stellar solo talent. The sound is adequate: everyone is audible, in roughly the right amounts.  **KS**

---

**The Complete Atomic Mr Basie**  Basie (p); **Joe Newman, Thad Jones, Wendell Culley, Snooky Young** (t); **Benny Powell, Henry Coker, Al Grey** (tb); **Marshall Royal** (cl, as); **Frank Wess** (as, ts); **Frank Foster, Eddie 'Lockjaw' Davis** (ts); **Charlie Fowlkes** (bs); **Freddie Green** (g); **Eddie Jones** (b); **Sonny Payne** (d); **Neal Hefti** (arr); on one track **Joe Williams** (v). Roulette Ⓜ 828635-2 (57 minutes). Recorded 1957.

✓                                                                                          ⑩ ❽

A change of record company often signals an alteration in style, policy and recorded sound. Such was the case when Basie left Norman Granz's label and signed with the new Roulette concern. This remains a most important album, the first for Roulette and also the first time an entire Basie record had been devoted to the compositions and arrangements of one man. The very album title became an identifying term for a vital period of Count's post-war musical history. Packed with soloists (but with the greatest of them seated at the piano) this was one of the finest swing bands the world has ever known. Neal Hefti's writing captures all the special nuances for which this Basie orchestra was famous; the unparalleled ability to swing, irrespective of tempo, the splendid internal balance and a *non-pareil* reed section under the leadership of Royal. *Li'l Darlin'* remains an object lesson in dynamics and on how to swing at just 18 bars to the minute. This is the edition to collect, for it contains five additional tracks to the original LP (although it must be said that the original 11 titles are still the most impressive) and, more importantly, has been remixed back to the original gorgeous mono, restoring the opening bars of *Kid from Red Bank*, invariably missing from the unsatisfactory stereo tapes.                          **AM**

# Django Bates

1960

**New review**

**Winter Truce (and Homes Blaze)** Bates (kbds, p, p-hn, comp, arr); **Chris Batchelor**, **Sid Gauld** (t); **Roland Bates** (tb); **Richard Henry** (btb); **Dave Laurence** (frh); **Sarah Waterhouse** (tba); **Iain Ballamy**, **Steve Buckley**, **Mark Lockheart**, **Barak Schmool**, **Julian Argüelles** (reeds); **Sarah Homer** (cl, bcl); **Eddie Parker** (f, bf); **Stuart Hall** (g, bj,vn); **Michael Mondesir** (b); **Martin France** (d, perc); **Christine Tobin** (v). JMT ℗ 514 023-2 (67 minutes). Recorded 1995.

⑦ ❽

The keyboardist/composer's third JMT album continues his perambulation through the seasons, following **Summer Fruits (and Unrest)** and the solo **Autumn Fire (and Green Shoots)**. Prior to these he was already well known, of course, as a driving force behind both Loose Tubes and Human Chain, and as with **Summer ...** the latter group is responsible for a couple of tracks, with the rest by Bates's Delightful Precipice big band. The composer's bizarre humour shows not only in his track-titles and programme notes but in the music itself, examples being the feature dedicated to Martin France and the choral anthem *You Can't Have Everything*, which opens and closes the album. The one non-original, the film theme *New York, New York* (programme note: "So good ... yet so bad!"), is worthy of a latter-day Spike Jones, with singer Christine Tobin in the Red Ingle role. The ultimate interest, however, lies in the musical detail. Bates's discreetly used harmonic sense and feel for combining electric and acoustic textures have relatively few antecedents. Also typical are the cross-references between different pieces, the *Loneliness of Being Right* motif recurring in disguise on *Fox across the Road*. I don't know why, but meanwhile why not ponder the spoken comment of the album's closing seconds: "I believe fundamentalism is fundamentally wrong but I could be mistaken." **BP**

# Alvin Batiste

1937

**New review**

**Late** Batiste (cl); **Wes Anderson** (as); **Kenny Barron**, **Fred Sanders** (p); **Elton Heron**, **Rufus Reid** (b); **Herman Jackson** (d); **Donald Edwards** (cga). Columbia ℗ CK 53314 (65 minutes). Recorded 1993.

⑨ ❾

Nicknamed 'Mozart', Batiste has long been a clarinet virtuoso and composer in both the jazz and classical fields. In the fifties he played with Ed Blackwell and Ornette Coleman and toured with Ray Charles, but he has spent most of the last 35 years teaching in New Orleans and at Southern University in Baton Rouge. Not until the eighties did he begin to record regularly, playing with Clarinet Summit and the American Jazz Quintet and releasing two discs as leader – 1984's **Musique d'Afrique Nouvelle Orléans** and 1988's **Bayou Magic** (both on India Navigation). Batiste's jazz roots are in bebop but his eclectic approach and brilliant technique disdain stylistic barriers. **Late** is a relatively mainstream date, a beautiful example of small-group blues and ballads topped by some exquisite clarinet playing. Batiste is a master of the instrument's entire tonal range, negotiating subtle, timbral inflections or abrupt intervallic leaps with equal facility. Backed on most tracks by Reid, Jackson and a superbly on-song Kenny Barron, he offers a varied and largely original set that begins with *Late*'s seductive blues and closes with the irresistible groove of *Kinshasa*, extracted from Batiste's first clarinet concerto and certainly played here *con brio*. **GL**

# Mario Bauzá

1911-93

**944 Columbus** Bauzá (ldr); **Victor Páz**, **Michael Mossman**, **Daniel Colette** (t); **Manny Durán** (t, flh); **Gerry Chamberlain**, **Bruce Eidem**, **Don Hayward** (tb); **Rolando Briceno** (as, ss); **Pete Yellin** (as, cl); **Enrique Fernadez** (ts, f); **Dioris Rivera** (ts, f); **Pablo Calogero** (bs, bcl); **Marcus Persiani** (p); **Joe Santiago** (b); **Bobby Sanabria** (d); **José Mangual Jr**, **Carlos 'Patato' Valdes**, **Joe Gonzales**, **José Alexis Diaz** (perc); **Graciela**, **Rudy Calzado** (v). Messidor ℗ 15828-2 (48 minutes). Recorded 1993.

⑦ ❽

Bauzá assumed an important role in the most successful of all jazz fusions. He played for and led Afro-Cuban jazz bands, using the best elements of each idiom and detracting from none. He initially studied clarinet in Havana and recorded in New York with Antonio Maria Romeu in 1926. He moved to America in 1930, switched to trumpet and worked with, amongst others, Chick Webb, Fletcher Henderson and Cab Calloway. In 1941 he joined Machito as lead trumpet, became musical director and ushered the band along the Afro-Cuban jazz trial.

Cubop is what is heard on **944 Columbus**. The powerful trumpet of the ageing leader is absent but the celebration of his music permeates every title. Mossman is the pick of the arrangers; the driving mambo of *Cubauzá* contrasting with the almost Ellingtonian bolero of *Lourdes Lullaby*. Irving Berlin's *Heatwave* assumes a Latin cloak and Chico O'Farrill's excellent reed writing elevates *Congratulations to Someone* to the seriously good category. Bauzá left Machito in 1976, led his own band through the eighties and added salsa to his musical menu. The solos on **944 Columbus** aren't spectacular but the band epitomizes the thriving spirit of the Afro-Cuban movement. **BMcR**

# Jim Beard

**Lost at the Carnival** Beard (p, syn, perc); **Jon Herington** (elg, hca, perc); **Bill Evans** (ts, ss); **Stan Harrison** (cl, bcl, f, af); **Ron Jenkins** (elb); **Steve Rodby** (b); **Scooter Warner, Mike Mecham, Billy Ward** (d). Lipstick ⑤ LIP89027-2 (55 minutes). Recorded 1994.

⑥ ⑧

Jim Beard is best known for his straight-ahead funk and fusion work with John McLaughlin, John Scofield, Bob Berg, The Brecker Brothers, Pat Metheny and others. Here, while he retains the funky agenda, he adopts something of a concept album approach, using the textures, moods and styles of the carnival both to flavour and unify his programme. To this end, several tracks are prefaced or closed with fairground organ, *Chunks and Chairknobs* being a whimsical march-like piece dominated by woodwinds, while *Holiday* is reminiscent of a fifties palais band.

If this seems a recipe for banality, the discordant aural assault of the carnival actually gives Beard a licence to create all manner of harmonic and stylistic colourations, much as Charles Ives used the collision of contrasting ensembles to create polytonal effects. For example, although *Poke* is in essence a four-chord Latin vamp, the insertion of flattened thirds and fifths quickly undermines its superficial innocuity. The set is dotted with jazz solos from Beard's piano and Evans's saxes, but the main attraction for jazz listeners is likely to be in the subversive totality of Beard's concept. **MG**

# Sidney Bechet

1897-1959

**The Legendary Sidney Bechet** Bechet (ss, cl); with a collective personnel of **Tommy Ladnier, Sidney de Paris, 'Red' Allen, Charlie Shavers** (t); **Rex Stewart** (c); **Mezz Mezzrow, Albert Nicholas** (cl); **Happy Cauldwell, Lem Johnson** (ts); **Teddy Nixon, Sandy Williams, J.C. Higginbotham, Claude Jones** (tb); **Hank Duncan, Cliff Jackson, Jelly Roll Morton, Sonny White, Earl Hines, James Tolliver, Willie 'The Lion' Smith** (p); **Teddy Bunn, Lawrence Lucie, Charlie Howard, Bernard Addison, Everett Barksdale** (g); **Wilson Myers, Elmer James, Wellman Braud, John Lindsay** (b); **Morris Morland, Manzie Johnson, Zutty Singleton, Kenny Clarke, Big Sid Catlett, Baby Dodds, J.C. Heard, Arthur Herbert** (d). RCA Bluebird Ⓜ ND86590 (86 minutes). Recorded 1932-41.

✓ ⑧ ⑧

On the first number in this collection, *Maple Leaf Rag*, Sidney Bechet never once stops playing. This is a fair indication of his personality, both musical and personal. A forceful and truculent individual, Bechet never willingly shared the limelight, even with Louis Armstrong, and this trait of character is reflected in the unstoppable flow of his playing. It probably explains, too, why he took up the soprano saxophone quite early in his career, relegating the clarinet to second place; the soprano is louder.

In the period covered by these 22 tracks Bechet's playing was at its best – bravura, florid, headlong and unfailingly inventive. The solo breaks in the aforementioned *Maple Leaf* would defeat most players today, even after much practice – but Bechet made them up on the spur of the moment. *High Society*, from Jelly Roll Morton's 1939 Victor session, is a famous performance in which the traditional clarinet solo is taken first by Bechet (on soprano) and then by Albert Nicholas (on clarinet) – a contest which ends in a dead heat. Equally praised as a classic of the genre is the recording session which featured Earl Hines, Baby Dodds and Rex Stewart and produced *Blues in Thirds, Ain't Misbehavin'* and two versions of *Blue for You, Johnny*. The band billed as "Sidney Bechet and his New Orleans Feetwarmers" had a somewhat transient personnel but produced many authentic jazz classics, including *Shake It and Break It, Wild Man Blues* and *Stompy Jones*, all included in this anthology. The CD transfers are in mono and perfectly satisfactory, bearing in mind the variable quality of the originals. Anyone wanting the entire Bechet RCA output is strongly urged to locate for themselves a copy of the five-CD boxed set **Complete Bluebird Sessions** (ND90317). **DG**

**Sidney Bechet In New York 1937-40** Bechet (cl, ss); **Louis Armstrong** (t, v); **Charlie Shavers** (t); **Claude Jones** (tb); **Sammy Price, Luis Russell** (p); **Teddy Bunn, Bernard Addison** (g); **Richard Fulbright, Wellman Braud** (b); **Zutty Singleton** (d); **O'Neil Spencer** (d, v); **Trixie Smith, Coot Grant, Kid Wesley Wilson** (v). JSP ⑤ CD338 (69 minutes). Recorded 1937-40.

⑧ ⑧

Bechet bought his first straight soprano saxophone in London in 1919 during his first visit to Europe. Almost singlehandedly he put the instrument on the jazz map, frequently using it on record with various Clarence Williams recording units. He worked with Noble Sissle's band for a number of years and the opening tracks here come from his closing period with the band. In fact there is probably more of Bechet's clarinet to be heard here than soprano; on both instruments he manifested a biting, attacking tone and had a tendency to dominate other front-line players, even trumpeters. Here he has to allow Shavers and Armstrong pride of place in the ensembles, although it must be said that all the musicians play with considerable sensitivity on the date with Trixie Smith and the other singers. The 1940 date with Louis Armstrong achieved classic status, even though Bechet said later that he was disappointed with the date because Louis ignored the previously agreed arrangements. *Perdido Street Blues* has superb work from Sidney and Louis, but the whole session is a memorable achievement. The CD has been lovingly remastered by John R.T. Davies who has achieved the best possible sound. In addition, the disc includes both original and alternative takes of Sissle's *Characteristic Blues* and Armstrong's *Down in Honky Tonk Town*. **AM**

---

**Jazz Classics, Volumes 1 and 2** Bechet (cl, ss); with collective personnel including: **Sidney De Paris, Max Kaminsky, Bunk Johnson, Frankie Newton** (t); **Vic Dickenson, George Lugg, Sandy Williams, J.C. Higginbotham, Jimmy Archey** (tb); **Albert Nicholas** (cl) **Art Hodes, Meade Lux Lewis, Cliff Jackson, Don Kirkpatrick** (p); **Teddy Bunn** (g); **Pops Foster, John Williams** (b); **Manzie Johnson, Big Sid Catlett, Danny Alvin** (d); **Fred Moore** (d, v). Blue Note Ⓜ 789384/5-2 (two discs, oas: 39 and 43 minutes). Recorded 1939-51.

✅ ⑩ ⑧

It is a shame that the running time here is a couple of minutes more than a single CD can cope with, because combining these two famous, separate volumes on to one disc would have made a great deal of sense. As it is, the old LP order (disorder?) has been preserved across the two discs, so the listener hops from date to date and constantly refers to the reproduced LP sleeve-notes to find out what is going on. Not that this should detract one jot from the enjoyment of some of the most exhilarating jazz ever committed to wax (these all date from the pre-tape era). Bechet was rarely below peak form anyway, but the combination of above-average recorded sound and considerably above-average fellow musicians makes the magic come tumbling out on virtually every track. Just to look at the track listing on Volume 1 is enough to gladden the heart – an imperiously swinging *Muskrat Ramble* featuring De Paris, Dickenson and Art Hodes, followed by the deep blues cry of *Blue Horizon* with the same band, then *Weary Blues* with Max Kaminsky followed by the immortal 1939 recording of *Summertime* with Teddy Bunn, Meade Lux Lewis and Big Sid. This really is one version of musical paradise.

One of the most striking musical factors consistently on display here is just how disciplined and swinging Bechet's rhythm sections were. Even when Bunk Johnson is fluffing notes on the lead line in 1945, Cliff Jackson, Pops Foster and Manzie Johnson are registering levels of rockin' rhythm which border on the ecstatic. This is simply not typical for New Orleans bands, but is rarely absent from a Bechet session anywhere in his career. One can only conclude that it is his own vitality which translates itself to his sidemen when they are of the calibre mentioned above. But above all it is the ever-persuasive voices of Bechet's soprano and clarinet which dominate, and rightly too. A personality so strong as to be overwhelming, he was often at his best with musicians not quite his equal (only a handful could get close anyway) but strong enough to stick to what they do best and not get in his way, and this is what the majority of tracks here contain. Bechet is an inspired and bewitching presence throughout these two records, and they should be a part of every jazz collection. **KS**

---

**The King Jazz Story, Volume 1** Bechet (ss, cl); **Mezz Mezzrow** (cl); **Hot Lips Page** (t, v); **Sammy Price, Fitz Weston** (p); **Pops Foster, Wellman Braud** (b); **Big Sid Catlett, Baby Dodds, Kaiser Marshall** (d); **Pleasant Joe, Coot Grant, Douglas Daniels** (v). Storyville Ⓜ STCD8212 (77 minutes). Recorded 1945-7.

⑧ ⑧

Some of Bechet's most majestic playing was recorded for Mezzrow's King Jazz label. His most notable compositions here are *Delta Mood*, a heart-breaking and lyrical slow blues, and *Where Am I?*, a similarly melancholy and delicate theme. Bechet soars above the simple ensembles with an authority reminiscent of some of Armstrong's finest blues performances of the late twenties. "I'm a genius," Mezzrow claimed at one point in his comments on these sessions, "and Sidney Bechet helps me prove it". The reverse is palpably the case and Bechet takes full advantage of one of the most bountiful recording opportunities of his career. It is hard to overestimate the importance of these tracks (the ones on the four companion volumes, STCD8213, 8214, 8215 and 4104 are just as good) in the traditional mainstream field. **SV**

---

**Jazz at Storyville** Bechet (ss); **Vic Dickenson** (tb); **George Wein** (p); **Jimmy Woode** (b); **Buzzy Drootin** (d). Black Lion Ⓜ BLCD76090-2 (57 minutes). Recorded 1953.

⑧ ⑥

By this period of his career, Bechet had finally achieved the kind of lasting fame that Armstrong was enjoying, though not in Bechet's case while remaining based in the US. For the last decade of his life he was based in France, where he was viewed as a sort of musical Merlin and where his well-meaning backing bands were several stages less competent than the worst of Armstrong's big bands. Back home his reputation was seriously diminished, like that of most of the classic and mainstream players at the time, and Bechet's last US visit is documented here through the then Boston-based promoter George Wein's invitation to appear at his club and on his Storyville record label. Contrary to current discographies, the CD combines all of the two 10-inch LPs, with *Ole Miss* occupying the second half of *Bugle Blues*.

The local rhythm section is competent but rather ill-served by the recording, whereas the still imperious Bechet – although probably sharing a single microphone with Dickenson – is better registered than on many of the French albums. There is scarcely any division between Bechet's ensemble leads and his solos, but the stimulating inclusion of Dickenson provides a challenge and a counterweight to the saxophonist's sweeping style. **BP**

# Gordon Beck

**For Evans' Sake** Beck (p); **Jack DeJohnette** (d); **Dave Holland** (b); **Didier Lockwood** (vn). JMS Ⓔ 059-2 (59 minutes). Recorded 1991.

⑥ ❽

Gordon Beck was a familiar figure on the modern British scene in the sixties, playing with Tubby Hayes and for a time leading the house trio at Ronnie Scott's. However, work with Phil Woods's European Rhythm Machine brought him valuable European exposure, and since the late seventies he has forged many continental connections. It is from such an association – with French record producer Jean-Marie Salhani – that this recording emanates. The title is every bit as revealing of the contents as it might seem. Beck's informative sleeve-notes make no secret of its author's admiration for Bill Evans and neither does the music, most of it composed by Beck. However, although Evans might be a cornerstone of Beck's style, other pianists who absorbed Evans have had an effect on his playing. Thus the album's two most dramatic tracks – the splintered, occasionally Monkish *Try This* and the taut, virtuosic *Trio Type Tune Two* – carry strong echoes of Chick Corea's trio work from the sixties and eighties. Another vigorous outing, *Not the Last Waltz*, honours McCoy Tyner, an influence from the other end of the modern piano spectrum. The set has its routine moments, but Beck's most spirited performances speak eloquently of his talent. DeJohnette and Holland are muscular and flawless, and Didier Lockwood adds rococo flourish to a reworked *All the Things You Are*. **MG**

# Harry Beckett

**All Four One** Beckett, **Chris Batchelor, Jon Corbett, Claude Deppa** (flh); **Alastair Gavin** (p); **Fred T. Baker** (b); **Tony Marsh** (d); **Jan Ponsford** (v). Spotlite Jazz Ⓔ SPJCD547 (53 minutes). Recorded 1991.

⑧ ❼

An early fan of Miles and Dizzy, Harry Beckett came to London from his native Barbados in 1954, first making his mark working with Charles Mingus on the 1961 film *All Night Long*. In the subsequent three decades he has played with many of the UK's leading ensembles, including small groups led by Graham Collier and Stan Tracey, plus big bands such as the Brotherhood of Breath, the London Jazz Composers Orchestra and the Jazz Warriors. He has also led several groups of his own, notably Joy Unlimited, and currently co-leads the Anglo-Italian Quartet, but little of his best work is available on CD.

**All Four One** features a recent Beckett project, the Flügelhorn 4+3. Although a versatile player, adept at free jazz, bebop, even West African Highlife, Beckett's own music has a graceful romanticism at its core which is well suited to the soft tones of the flügelhorn. His playing typically mixes this with darting excursions into a more abstract language of gruff expostulation and avuncular chuckles. He is also known as a composer of attractive tunes, and **All Four One** underlines the point, with the bright *Time of Day* and a musing *The Shadowy Light* being outstanding. Singer Jan Ponsford adds a powerful vocal to the ballad *Enchanted* and Beckett closes an amiable set with a rousing flourish on Mingus's *Better Get it in Your Soul*. **GL**

# Bix Beiderbecke

**Bix Beiderbecke and the Chicago Cornets** Beiderbecke (c); with a collective personnel of: **Jimmy McPartland, Muggsy Spanier** (c); **Al Gande, George Brunies, Miff Mole, Tommy Dorsey, Guy Carey** (tb); **Don Murray, Volly DeFaut** (cl); **Jimmy Hartwell** (cl, as); **Frank Trumbauer** (c-ms); **George Johnson** (ts); **Rube Bloom, Paul Mertz, Mel Stitzel, Dick Voynow** (p); **Bob Gillette** (bj); **Marvin Saxbe** (bj, g, cym); **Min Leibrooke** (tba); **Vic Moore, Vic Berton, Tommy Gargano** (d). Milestone Ⓜ MCD47019-2 (76 minutes). Recorded 1924.

⑧ ❹

Nineteen of these 28 tracks are the first recordings Bix made, 15 of them by the Wolverines, the dedicated band of young white musicians who had been captivated by the work of the Original Dixieland Jazz Band. All the titles were made for the Gennett company under primitive recording conditions in the 'pre-electric' days, so we miss the magic, shimmering Beiderbecke cornet sound of the later Okeh discs. Nevertheless it is apparent that Bix stands head and shoulders, musically speaking, above his colleagues, always ready with an apt turn of phrase and playing with an assurance which belies his age. By the end of 1924 he had left the Wolverines. This CD includes two titles featuring his replacement Jimmy McPartland, who has clearly learned Bix's solos but who at the time lacked the singular qualities which highlighted Beiderbecke's work. The disc also contains seven titles by the Bucktown Five, a lusty little band fronted by the then 17-year-old Muggsy Spanier. The CD is virtually the equivalent of a two-LP set Milestone issued in 1974 (the Bucktown Five's *Someday Sweetheart* replaces an alternative take of *Buddy's Habits*). The sound seems to have been improved, although some of the titles have a built-in swish from the 78s used for dubbing. **AM**

**Volume 1: Singin' the Blues** **Beiderbecke** (c, p) with **Frank Trumbauer and his Orchestra**:
**Sylvester Ahola** (t); **Miff Mole, Bill Rank** (tb); **Jimmy Dorsey** (cl); **Don Murray** (cl, ts, bs); **Frank Trumbauer** (c-ms); **Adrian Rollini** (bs); **Paul Metz, Frank Signorelli** (p); **Eddie Lang** (g); **Joe Venuti** (vn); **Howdy Quicksell** (bj); **Chauncey Moorhouse, Vic Burton** (d); Columbia Ⓜ 466309-2 (61 minutes). Recorded 1927.

✓ ⑩ ❽

Of all the current Beiderbecke reissues this is undoubtedly the best collection on a single CD. At the age of 24 Bix was at the height of his powers and on these sessions he was working with some of his finest contemporaries. Unimpeded by ornate arrangements or fumbling sidemen, he was able to relax into that bright, clipped eloquence which has been captivating listeners ever since.

Bix Beiderbecke's cornet is one of the authentic voices of jazz. It has become a cliché to describe his tone and articulation as 'bell-like', but in this case the cliché is exact. His improvised line has the same kind of brisk confidence as that of the young Armstrong (his near-contemporary) and listening to it brings the same feeling of satisfaction, of following an unerring and elegant mind. There are many classics among these 20 pieces, including *Singin' the Blues*, *I'm Coming Virginia*, *Riverboat Shuffle*, and *Way Down Yonder in New Orleans*. The high point is always the cornet solo, but another unique voice can also be heard – the floating C-melody saxophone of Frank Trumbauer, Lester Young's first idol. The disc also contains a few examples of Bix's piano playing, including his best-known keyboard piece, *In a Mist*. **DG**

# Beijbom Kroner Big Band

New review

**Live in Copenhagen** **Bjorn Ringkjobing, Knud Norgaard, Thomas Fryland, Jesper Sveidahl** (t); **Erling Kroner, Calle Linderg** (tb); **Niels Gerhardt** (btb, tba); **Flemmin Lund** (f); **Per Backer** (as, f, cl); **Claus Laidtlow** (as, ss, f); **Cennett Jonsson** (ts, ss, bcl); **Henrik Frisk** (ts, f); **Ed Epstein** (bs); **Rolf Nisson** (g); **Jacob Karlzon** (p); **Hans Andersson** (b); **Lars Beijbom** (d) Four Leaf Clover Ⓕ FLCCD143 (78 minutes). Recorded 1995.

⑦ ❽

This excellent Swedish-Danish band is jointly run by Beijbom and Kroner along similar lines to the old Thad Jones-Mel Lewis Orchestra. The leaders are the principal arrangers and the overall sound of the band is modern, with a wide range of orchestral colour and first-rate soloists. An enterprise like this can only be undertaken for love these days, and the amount of work that must have gone into creating an ensemble as unified as this, even with such seasoned professional players, must have been phenomenal. I would strongly recommend this live recording to anyone with a taste for contemporary orchestral jazz. **DG**

# Richie Beirach                                                                                  1947

New review

**The Snow Leopard** **Beirach** (p); **George Mraz** (b); **Billy Hart** (d); on three tracks **Gregor Huebner** (vn). Alfa Jazz Ⓕ ALCB3908 (68 minutes). Recorded 1996.

⑦ ❾

Richie Beirach, admirer of such twentieth-century composers as Bartók, Scriabin and Webern, has made explorations of the outer reaches of tonality his speciality (perhaps most obviously in his largely impromptu CMP solo album **Self Portrait**), but here, in the company of a rhythm team steeped in post-bop swing, he works mostly in a straight-ahead vein, something which probably shouldn't be surprising now that he has entered Concord's Maybeck Hall of Fame. His own pieces, *The Snow Leopard* and *Citizen Code*, swing in a largely uncomplicated way and *Naima* is easily recognizable as the Coltrane standard, the form, harmonic rhythm and phrasing all fully intact, the touch light like Herbie Hancock's. There's also David Mann's *In the Wee Small Hours*, a tune which, unadorned, might be seen as the epitome of orthodoxy. However, paradoxically, this track points up Beirach's singularity. Through subtle harmonic colorations and asides he stamps this and any other standard material he approaches with his own personality. There are darker, more abstract moments, most chillingly so in the piano and violin reading of Bartók's *Bagatelle, Op. 6 No. 1*, but Beirach's chief preoccupation, jazzing the modern classicists, is well served by this record, and connoisseurs of the post-bop piano tradition embodied by Tyner, Hancock and Corea should feel at home. **MG**

# Louie Bellson                                                                                  1924

New review

**Their Time Was the Greatest** **Bellson** (d); **Conte Candoli, Pete Candoli, Walt Johnson, Frank Szabo, Snooky Young** (t); **Thurman Green, Andy Martin, Mike Wimberly,**

**Jimmy Zito** (tb); **Sal Lozano, Ray Reed** (as); **Tommy Newsom, Pete Christlieb** (ts); **Bill Green** (bs); **Frank Strazzeri** (p); **Dave Carpenter** (b); **Jack Arnold** (perc). Concord Ⓔ CCD4683 (60 minutes). Recorded 1995.

⑧ ❿

Listening to drummers on record can be a tiresome experience. On the other hand watching one like Buddy Rich or Jo Jones in action can be a most instructive as well as an enjoyable experience for the listener. Bellson, who is, like Rich and Jones, one of the handful of the greatest, is also fascinating to listen to because, like Rich, his playing is so clear and precise that one can almost visualize it. Rated as a textbook this would easily merit maximum points and it is so recommended to drummers. Bellson is an astonishing rhythm section player and he's able to be creative without being intrusive. This is drumming with its hair combed in the form of a wonderful series of tributes to drummers from Gene Krupa and Chick Webb to Tony Williams and Steve Gadd. The excellent arrangements are played by a typically good Bellson big band and leave room for creative improvisations from the underrated Conte Candoli, Andy Martin, Christlieb and Strazzeri, amongst others. Bellson has never settled for less than the best in his musical life and his team of arrangers includes Nat Pierce, Bob Florence, Thad Jones, Tommy Newsom as well as himself; it was he who also wrote the tributes to Sid Catlett, Art Blakey, Tony Williams and Steve Gadd. **SV**

# Tex Beneke
1914

**Jukebox Saturday Night: The 1946 Glenn Miller Orchestra Live at the Hollywood Palladium** Beneke (ts, ldr); **Bobby Nichols, Graham Young, Steve Steck, Whitey Thomas** (t); **Jimmy Priddy, Paul Tanner, John Halliburton, Bobby Pring** (tb); **John Graas** (frh); **Sol Livero, Freddy Guera** (cl, as); **Manny Thaler** (as, bss); **Stanley Aaronson, Vince Carbonne** (ts); **Gene Bergen, Gene Shepherd, Phil Cogliano, Earl Cornwall, Stan Harris, Jasper Hornyak, Joseph Kowalewski, Stan Kraft, Richard Motylinski, Norman Forrest, Michael Violooky, Carl Ottobrino** (vn); **Henry Mancini** (p, arr); **Bobby Joe Gibbons** (g); **Rollie Bundock** (b); **Jack Sperling** (d); **Artie Malvin, Lillian Lane, Murray Kane, Gene Steck, Steve Steck, 'The Crew Chiefs'** (v); **Bill Finegan, Jerry Gray, Norman Leyden** (arr). Vintage Jazz Classics Ⓔ VJC1039 (73 minutes). Recorded 1946.

⑤ ❹

'Ghost' bands are a major area of controversy among jazz lovers. How could anyone fill the shoes of the great leaders of the past, like Ellington or Basie? And how does the attempt to keep a living commercially based band on the road square with the jazz repertory movement that tries faithfully to recreate the classic performances of the long-gone? At least Tex Beneke's leadership of Miller's band had some advantages. It was set up immediately after the war by the Miller estate and re-employed many of Miller's sidemen as they re-entered civvy street from the Army/Air Force Band. Composer/arranger Henry Mancini added new charts based on popular songs to the book, but Beneke was employed by Helen Miller to play the old arrangements from both the pre-war band and the AAF group. The results are unspectacular but swinging, with the amiable Beneke hooting through tenor solos that sound jazzy in this context, but which are isolated from contemporaneous jazz events. Apparently Beneke was keen to invoke some bop charts, but there's little sign of this as the band swan through Miller favourites like *Moonlight Serenade* and *Sun Valley Jump*. **AS**

# Don Bennett
1941

New review

**Chicago Calling!** Bennett (p); **Arthur Hoyle, Steve Smith** (t); **Art Porter** (as, ss); **Eddie Peterson** (ts); **Eric Hochberg** (b); **Paul Wertico, Darryl Ervin** (d). Candid Ⓔ CCD79713 (75 minutes). Recorded 1990.

⑦ ❽

Brisk, invigorating post-bop from a sextet of Chicagoans led by pianist Don Bennett, who also wrote five of the nine tunes. Most of these tracks were originally issued by Southport, a Chicago label with a fairly limited circulation. Some names will be familiar; Arthur Hoyle played trumpet on several early Sun Ra records while Art Porter was given the hype treatment by Verve a couple of years after this session took place. There is a surprisingly good tenor player to be heard and I imagine Eddie Peterson is content to carry on with his job as head of the music department at Chicago's University of Illinois rather than immerse himself in the competitive world of full-time jazz playing. There is nothing startlingly new here but it is very worthwhile jazz-making and Bennett's two trio tracks, *Makin' Whoopee* and *Prayer for Sean*, certainly warranted Candid giving him the opportunity of making an all-trio album (**Solar**; Candid CCD79723) in 1994. He has an expressive touch and a clarity of expression which I find very attractive. His opening chorus on the lengthy *All the Things You Are* manages to eschew any of the clichés normally associated with this overworked Kern tune. **AM**

# Tony Bennett

1926

**Sings the Rodgers and Hart Songbook** Bennett (v); **Ruby Braff** (c); **George Barnes**, **Wayne Wright** (g); **John Guiffrida** (b). Horatio Nelson Ⓕ CDSIV1129 (56 minutes). Recorded 1973.

⑧ ❼

Tony Bennett loves jazz and has recorded with accompaniments ranging from the solo piano of Bill Evans to the full Count Basie orchestra. They are all worth hearing, but this collaboration with the Ruby Braff-George Barnes Quartet is the best of the lot. Like Bennett, Braff feels great affinity with the classic American song repertoire and no trumpeter, not even the great Hackett himself, ever provided more discreetly apt obbligatos to a vocalist. The light texture of the quartet provides Bennett with all the rhythmic support he needs while restraining his occasional tendency to overact a song. At the age of 47 his voice had attained that brief plateau which Italian-American singers seem to reach at around this time of life – in which a slight gravelly undertone can be detected beneath the *bel canto* smoothness. As for the band, it has the worn-in ease and comfort of a regularly working group, which it was, despite strained relations between its co-leaders. The 20 tracks on this CD, including such classics as *Lover*, *Manhattan* and *My Romance*, were originally contained on two vinyl LPs. **DG**

# Han Bennink

1942

**Clusone 3** Bennink (d); **Michael Moore** (as, cl); **Ernst Reijseger** (vc). Ramboy Ⓕ 01 (66 minutes). Recorded 1990-1.

⑧ ❹

Dutch jazz is notorious for its irreverent humour, and no Dutch improviser is nuttier than Bennink, who may hurl his cymbals like frisbees or build a small fire inside his hi-hat. But Bennink – who has recorded with Eric Dolphy, Major Holley, Peter Brotzmann and (often) with *alter ego* Misha Mengelberg – doesn't let his antics disrupt the music's flow. He is one of the most powerfully swinging jazz drummers, even (or especially) using wire brushes, as on Herbie Nichols's tunes *117th St* and *Sunday Stroll* here. A musician of uncommon presence, Bennink evokes big-beat masters like Sid Catlett and gets a beautiful, tough sound from his drum kit.

The Clusone trio is his hand-picked band. Moore, an American living in Amsterdam, has a clean, sleek clarinet sound, feisty alto sax style and a passion for fetching tunes, like Neal Hefti's lovely *Girl Talk* or his own plaintive *Debbie Warden*. Reijseger, perhaps the most technically adept jazz cellist, can sound like a drunken blues guitarist or a jazz bassist on amphetamines. Sometimes this CD sounds like a tenor/bass/drums LP on 45rpm. The music ranges from the lyrical to the bopping to the outward-bound; virtually all of it swings like crazy. **KW**

# George Benson

1943

**Compact Jazz** Benson (elg, v); **Clark Terry, Ernie Royal, Snooky Young** (t); **Jimmy Owens** (t, flh); **Garnett Brown** (tb); **Alan Raph** (btb); **Arthur Clarke, George Marge** (ts); **Pepper Adams** (bs); **Eric Gale** (elg); **Herbie Hancock, Paul Griffin** (p); **Jimmy Smith** (org); **Buddy Lucas** (hca); **Ron Carter, Bob Cranshaw** (b); **Chuck Rainey** (elb); **Billy Cobham, Jimmy Johnson Jr, Leo Morris, Donald Bailey** (d); **Jack Jennings** (cga, vb); **Johnny Pacheco** (cga). Verve Ⓜ 833 929-2 (55 minutes). Recorded 1967-9.

⑥ ❻

The opening *Billie's Bounce*, by a quintet featuring Ron Carter and Herbie Hancock, is a model example of Benson's straight-ahead jazz playing, and sufficient inducement alone to buy this CD. The ensemble is supple and responsive, Benson has a vigorous and strongly focused solo, and Hancock catches the fire, his excursion forming the perfect complement to Benson's. Things deteriorate later, but not before another three tracks by the same group from the 1967 **Giblet Gravy** album have passed. None of these cook with the bristling invention of the opener, but none suffer from the incipient mass-market strategies of *That Lucky Old Sun*, the first of four tracks from the 1968 **Goodies** album. There, in contrast to the democratic setting of the small group, Benson's guitar and vocals are rigidly framed by shrill big-band r&b textures. The small-group *Doobie Doobie Blues* and a wild card, a live *Tuxedo Junction* with Jimmy Smith, are exceptions, but the string-shrouded *I Remember Wes* leaves no doubt about the way things were going. Within a year Benson had been adopted by Creed Taylor to fill the shoes of the late Wes Montgomery. Soul-jazz celebrity was just around the corner. **MG**

**Breezin'** Benson (g, v); **Phil Upchurch** (g); **Ronnie Foster** (elp, moog); **Jorge Dalto** (p, clav); **Stanley Banks** (b); **Harvey Mason** (d); **Ralph MacDonald** (perc); unidentified orchestra. Warner Bros Ⓜ 27334-2 (39 minutes). Recorded 1976.

⑥ ❻

This is often claimed to be the biggest-selling jazz album of all time. It may well be, but a more accurate description would perhaps be the biggest-selling jazz-inflected album. There is no way of doubting Benson's jazz pedigree (he even appeared as a sideman on a Benny Goodman small-group date), and he still contributes some very tasty solos to this record (*Six to Four* is especially effective), but there is also no doubting the fact that Benson took what Wes Montgomery was doing a few steps further. He plays largely within the then contemporary popular styles, stating the melodies in a quite unadorned way, then moves on to some easeful improvisation, letting the rhythm section do most of the cooking. In doing so he set the pattern for thousands of imitators in the years to come, and a close listen to the original here (for this is the original, significantly different from what Montgomery did before) reveals a good deal more toughness and bite in Benson's guitar work than what could be found in that of his followers. In that sense at least, Benson has often been given short shrift for what he did. But then the material weighs against him here, being largely lightweight and arranged to stay that way, whatever interest he can generate after the themes are dispensed with. **KS**

## Bob Berg

1951

**Riddles** Berg (ts, ss, rec); **Gil Goldstein** (acc); **Jim Beard** (kbds, org, p, elp); **Jon Herington** (g, elg, mand); **Victor Bailey**, **John Patitucci** (elb); **Steve Gadd** (d); **Arto Tuncboyaciyan** (v, perc). Stretch Ⓕ GRS00112 (50 minutes). Recorded 1994.

⑧ ❽

At a time when his peers were almost universally embracing fusion, Berg's unfailingly melodic soloing on Sam Jones's 1978 **Visitation** was one of the delights of seventies hard bop. In due course he turned to fusion, first with Miles Davis and then in several albums with the Denon label. The first of these, **Short Stories**, spawned a minor fusion classic in *Friday Night at the Cadillac Club*, but sadly this early promise was not fulfilled on later Denon issues.

However, signing with Stretch has marked an artistic renaissance for Berg, and although his first Stretch album, in which he revisited hard bop, didn't match his seventies work, **Riddles**, his second, is his most satisfying since **Short Stories**. In an appealingly varied programme which offers an impressively integrated fusion of folk, funk, world music and jazz, Berg's sound and melodic creativity seem fully restored, the new settings providing the ideal foil for his bristling, raw-toned inventions. A good deal of thanks for the success of the date are due to the compositions and arrangements (notably by Berg, Chick Corea and Jim Beard) from which Berg's solos emerge as perfectly placed organic elements. **MG**

## Karl Berger

1935

**Conversations** Berger (p, vb); **Ray Anderson** (tb); **Carlos Ward** (as, f); **Mark Feldman** (vn); **James 'Blood' Ulmer** (g); **Dave Holland** (b); **Ingrid Sertso** (v). In & Out Ⓕ IOR77027-2 (72 minutes). Recorded 1994.

⑥ ❽

Initially a bop pianist in his home town of Heidelberg, Berger adopted the vibraphone and followed free pioneers Ornette Coleman and Don Cherry to Paris. His next stop was America and he worked briefly with both of these luminaries. He became involved in education and is currently in a major musical post in Frankfurt.

As this CD demonstrates, he is still very much a practising musican and composer, with the piano rejoining the vibes in his performance equation. This excellent series of duo *Conversations* shows that he uses whatever best suits the job. Both piano and vibes are effective in the gentle dialogues he has with Ward but crisp vibraphone lines seem more appropriate to the tête-à-tête that unites him with Sertso's voice on *Why is It*. His piano on *Bemsha Swing* is a model of good design and execution while the musical badinage he has with Anderson proclaims that unforced humour favours neither instrument. *North* takes calm piano into polemic territory with Ulmer's quarrelsome guitar, while Berger's reflective piano on *Lover Man* shows his genuine sympathy for Feldman's romantic violin recitation and for Ramirez's original theme. Long gone are the free-form aspirations but, in their place, there is a maturity and depth that transcends the choice of instrument. **BMcR**

## Borah Bergman

New review

**The Fire Tale** Bergman (p); **Evan Parker** (ss). Soul Note Ⓕ 121252-2 (57 minutes). Recorded 1990.

⑦ ❼

Borah Bergman has one of the most highly developed keyboard techniques in all music, a total independence of thought and limb that enables him to play unrelated ideas in each hand, articulate multi-voiced counterpoint at incredible speeds and devise near-orchestral textural and harmonic complexities. In this regard his music is reminiscent of Lennie Tristano's fifties experiments with overdubbing or Conlon Nancarrow's constructions for player piano. But, as with Jascha Heifetz and Art Tatum, virtuosity is sometimes suspect – justifiably or not – as insubstantial, calculated, without soul. There are times when technical considerations influence the emotional content of Bergman's music. **The Fire Tale** exemplifies both the compelling and confusing aspects of his approach. The fact that Evan Parker restricts himself to the soprano saxophone – his most volatile instrument – suggests that he senses a challenge, or at least an environment conducive to his pattern-weaving circular-breathing heroics. In any event, he meets Bergman's relentless attack head-on. Their three long improvisations surge forward in a dense wave of details – pitches reduced to the smallest conceivable note value at the fastest tempo possible, a blur of energy and motion. At this level of intensity the musicians are primarily concerned with shaping melodic contours; Parker locates small shifts in the line's emphasis or design while Bergman holds his position with jagged clusters or angular counter-melodies. Furiously kinetic, the music's obsessive urgency makes specific details difficult or impossible to grasp – much of its exhilaration results from balancing on the brink of incomprehension. In the brief *Helixian Steps* the texture thins out to a point where one may discern hints of stride and bebop phrasing that suggest a historical context for Bergman's elaborations, and *Red Shadows* contains tantalizing moments of calm, quiet improvising. But these are exceptions to a programme that is as demanding to listen to as it must have been to play. **AL**

## Jerry Bergonzi                                                      1947

**Vertical Reality** Bergonzi (ts); on four tracks **Andy LaVerne** (p); on five tracks **Mike Stern** (g); **George Mraz** (b); **Billy Hart** (d). Musidisc Ⓔ 50064-2 (55 minutes). Recorded 1994.

⑤ ❾

This may be Bergonzi's album, but for five of the eight tracks Mike Stern steals it from him. Why? Because Bergonzi is a supremely competent saxophonist who can play up a storm but who possesses few distinguishing traits. He has a muscular post-Coltrane tone, a style which is Coltrane and Brecker entwined (with perhaps some Joe Henderson thrown in for ballast), and a relentless swing. He is one of those players for whom the word 'brisk' – or perhaps even brusque – could have been coined. So he does not invite the listener's affection; rather, his respect. Stern is more ready to insinuate himself into your consciousness, more able to pause in a solo and take off in a different direction or on a different phrase. His touch is commendably varied, so he is capable of rhythmic emphases which escape Bergonzi in their subtlety. The tracks with LaVerne are more conventional in execution, but hardly lessen the problem. LaVerne is the more interesting soloist, especially on *Lover Man* where Bergonzi abandons all attempts to retain some form of continuity with the theme's message and opts for a punchy workout on familiar ideas. A less than scintillating album, then. **KS**

## Bunny Berigan                                                      1908-42

**Portrait of Bunny Berigan** Berigan (t) with **Eddie Miller, Bud Freeman, Forrest Crawford** (ts); **Claude Thornhill, Cliff Jackson, Joe Bushkin** (p); **Grachan Moncur, Mort Stulmaker** (b); **Edgar Sampson** (cl, as); **Dave Barbour, Eddie Condon** (g); **Dave Tough, Cozy Cole, Ray Bauduc** (d); **Connee Boswell** with **The Dorsey Brothers Orchestra**; **Paul Hamilton and his Orchestra**; **Frankie Trumbauer and his Orchestra**; **Glenn Miller and his Orchestra**; **Gene Gifford and his Orchestra**; **Benny Goodman and his Orchestra**; **Bud Freeman and his Windy City Five**; **Tommy Dorsey and his Orchestra**; **Bunny Berigan and his Blues Boys**; **Bunny Berigan and his Boys**; **Bunny Berigan and his Orchestra**. ASV Living Era Ⓜ AJACD5060 (69 minutes). Recorded 1932-7.

⑧ ❻

Throughout his short life Berigan was inspired by the trumpet playing of Louis Armstrong; he added a special kind of poetry of his own and the result was a style which fitted bands large and small. His unbreakable attachment to alcohol was ultimately his downfall and this excellent and representative selection from his extensive discography gives a good idea of what jazz lost when he was cut down at the age of only 36. With either muted or open trumpet, he could enhance the work of vocalists, but a fine example of his power and bottled-up excitement with a big band is included here in the shape of Benny Goodman's classic, *King Porter Stomp*. His own small recording units produced little masterpieces; the four titles with his Blue Boys in 1935 have marvellous solos by pianist Cliff Jackson and tenor saxist Eddie Miller as well as Bunny himself. His service with Tommy Dorsey produced the masterly *Marie* included here, but for many it was his own version of *I Can't Get Started* which epitomized his best work, as a trumpeter and a vocalist. Fittingly, it is the closing track on a collection in which the transfers are good, although some surface noise remains from the original 78rpm sources. **AM**

New review
**The Pied Piper 1934-40** Berigan (t); as above plus: **Charlie Spivak** (t); **Jack Teagarden** (tb); **Matty Matlock** (cl); **Artie Shaw** (cl, as); **Hymie Schertzer** (as); **Dick McDonough, Carman Mastren** (g); **Bob Haggart** (b). Bluebird Ⓜ 66615-2 (74 minutes). Recorded 1934-40.

⑧ ❻

**The Pied Piper** is an ideal companion issue to the above. It duplicates only five performances, poses further questions and fills in several vital pieces of Berigan history. It again shows that, in the almost self-satisfied mood of the Dorsey Orchestra, he sounded like an inspired amateur. The need for inspiration on jam session items like *Honeysuckle Rose* and *Blues* made this a virtue and an inevitable outcome for a player whose range of expression was broad. Further evidence of this is found in the smouldering intensity he achieves on *Jelly Roll Blues*, a trumpet outing that is in stark contrast to his lyrical reading of *Candlelights*. On the 1939 *Blue Lou* he throws down the gauntlet and exposes Spivak's bluster. *Trees* brings out an understated, almost sombre improvisation, while his superb note-choice puts backbone into the mannered contours of *Wearing of the Green*. One might question the wisdom of doing the title tune, but the way in which Berigan shows his mastery amidst the self-conscious jive of Ruth Gaylor's vocals perhaps provides the key to the man's native talent.   **BMcR**

# Tim Berne                                                                1954

**Fractured Fairy Tales**  Berne (as, v); **Herb Robertson** (t, c); **Mark Feldman** (vn, bar vn); **Hank Roberts** (vc, v, electronics); **Mark Dresser** (b); **Joey Baron** (d, electronics). JMT Ⓕ 834 431-2 (55 minutes). Recorded 1989.

⑦ ❼

Starting in 1979 from a loosely adapted Braxton/Hemphill/John Carter base, Berne's recordings have grown steadily more unpredictable. With several of his crucial early albums unavailable on CD, attention falls on this promising band. Unlike many *ad hoc* aggregations, this one has the advantage of familiarity; it is an enhancement of the trio Miniature (Berne, Roberts, Baron) and the same personnel that made Berne's second CBS disc, **Sanctified Dreams**, with the addition of the galvanic violinist Feldman (Feldman, Roberts, and Dresser, by the way, have their own string trio, Arcado). Such common experience allows for the concise, intuitive group activity of *Now Then*, stretching a free-bop line into new parameters without breaking the thread. Nothing stays the same for too long here, the arrangements are constantly broken apart for various instrumental re-groupings. Thus *Hong Kong Sad Song/More Coffee* begins with three separate layers of activity – wah-wah brass, *col legno* percussion, and a mournful Ornette-ish theme – before expanding into a taut Berne solo, a staggered string trio, and so on. *SEP* is a smoky blues with unusual twists and a duo between stinging Feldman and sputtering Robertson. Not all of this is imaginative; a couple of the tunes meander a bit. But this is a band with bite, still under development, as the later two JMT albums, **Paris Concerts**, reveal. **AL**

# Peter Bernstein                                                          1969

**New review**
**Signs of Life**  Bernstein (g); **Brad Mehldau** (p); **Christian McBride** (b); **Gregory Hutchinson** (d). Criss Cross Ⓕ 1095CD (72 minutes). Recorded 1994.

⑤ ❽

A blindfold test subject would understandably mistake this for an album made in the late fifties, such are the minutiae of that period's guitar small-group albums imitated. The recording quality gives Hutchinson's drums a pleasantly flat, splashy sound, such as that achieved by Art Taylor and Philly Joe Jones on countless Prestige and Riverside recordings, McBride's deep tone and loping rhythmic gait strongly suggests Paul Chambers (he even gives us an *arco* solo *à la* Chambers on Bernstein's own *Jet Stream*), while Bernstein and Mehldau, competent and even assured players, for all the world could be Montgomery and Wynton Kelly stretching out on a late-night date.

It may be that all this is some sort of accident, but such an accident would seem hard to sustain for over 70 minutes of music, so my guess is that the comparison was looked for. Even Bernstein's take on *Tea for Two*, transferred to 5/4 metre and re-named *Jive Coffee*, is the sort of light-hearted, hip jazz slant on old chestnuts which was regularly indulged in during that period. Does this make it good or bad music? Well, it makes it little more than a pleasant outing along familiar lanes, rather than a more invigorating ride through open country, but if that's OK by you, then this guitar-led quartet album will not disappoint.                                                                    **KS**

# Bill Berry                                                               1930

**Bill Berry's L.A. Big Band**  Berry (c); **Cat Anderson, Gene Goe, Blue Mitchell** (t); **Jack Sheldon** (t, v); **Britt Woodman, Jimmy Cleveland, Benny Powell, Tricky Lofton** (tb); **Marshall Royal, Lanny Morgan** (as); **Richie Kamuca, Don Menza** (ts); **Jack Nimitz** (bs); **Dave Frishberg** (p); **Monty Budwig** (b); **Frank Capp** (d). Concord Ⓕ CCD4027 (49 minutes). Recorded 1976.

⑧ ❽

Berry is a bop cornettist who first formed a rehearsal band in New York in the fifties. Like many musicians in that pre-synthesizer era he migrated to California because that was where studio work then abounded. He reformed his band there and drew into it a glittering assembly of jazz stars. The musicians played, as Jack Sheldon said "for fun and $30". Berry's talents as an arranger and a leader enabled him to shape the band into one of the best in the country. His experience in Duke Ellington's trumpet section and the presence of other ex-Ellington men in his band (Anderson and Woodman) enabled him to re-create Ellington's music more convincingly than any other band (better even than the Ellington ghost band led by Duke's son Mercer). Like Juggernaut, a similar L.A. band led by Frankie Capp and Nat Pierce, he had the benefit of the playing of Marshall Royal, one of the finest lead alto players in the business. Berry knows that the way to keep musicians happy is to give them plenty of solos, and there are rewarding features here for Anderson (*Boy Meets Horn*) and Sheldon (*Tulip or Turnip*) as well as a plethora of good solos all round on the rest of the tracks.     **SV** 59

# Chu Berry

1910-41

**Berry Story** Berry (ts); Roy Eldridge, Irving Randolph (t); Hot Lips Page, Wingy Manone (t, v); George Matthews, Keg Johnson (tb); Benny Goodman, Buster Bailey (cl); Joe Marsala (cl, as); Doc Rando (as); Lionel Hampton (vb, p, v); Jess Stacy, Horace Henderson, Benny Payne, Conrad Lanoue, Clyde Hart (p); Allen Reuss, Lawrence Lucie, Dave Barbour, Jack Lemaire, Danny Barker, Zeb Julian (g); Israel Crosby, Milt Hinton, Artie Shapiro, Jules Cassard (b); Gene Krupa, Cozy Cole, Leroy Maxey, Danny Alvin, Sid Catlett (d). EPM/Jazz Archives ® ZET738 (68 minutes). Recorded 1936-9.

⑧ ❽

During the absence in the thirties of Coleman Hawkins in Europe, musicians who had worked with both the great man and Berry hailed the latter as the reigning champion of the Hawkins school of tenor. Like most of his contemporaries, he ignored the challenge of Lester Young and instead mastered Hawkins's fluency and power, falling short only occasionally in terms of imagination.

The selection covers many of his small-group recordings while a sideman with Fletcher Henderson and Cab Calloway (he was still with Calloway at the time of a fatal road accident). It omits alternate takes and the 1941 Commodore session (currently only in a Mosaic box) and includes such cherished favourites as Wingy Manone's *Jumpy Nerves* and the Lionel Hampton date that produced *Sweethearts On Parade* and *Shufflin' at the Hollywood*. His partnership with Eldridge, fellow Henderson and Calloway sideman, was continued in much after-hours jamming, which is celebrated in *Sittin' In'* (a *Tiger Rag* variant) and a two-tempo version of *Body and Soul*, whose success provoked Hawkins's subsequent masterpiece. A highly rhythmic player (and author of the popular *Christopher Columbus* riff), Berry's originals here include *Maelstrom*, which was later vocalized by Calloway as *Jive*. A reminder that Berry's neglect is unjust, this album deserves a follow-up volume.
**BP**

# Eddie Bert

1922

**Encore** Bert (tb) with a collective personnel of **J.R. Monterose** (ts); **Joe Puma** (g); **Hank Jones** (p); **Clyde Lombardi** (b); **Kenny Clarke** (d). Denon/Savoy Ⓜ SV0229 (35 minutes). Recorded 1955.

⑩ ❾

J.J. Johnson's speed on the trombone eventually led him to compromise the tone of the instrument, and the 'pea-shooter' sound persevered for some years. Eddie Bert, already a veteran, was the first to combine the new style with the proper tonal values of the horn. No doubt his studies with Benny Morton and Trummy Young helped him in this. He is the ultimate veteran, having been a stalwart section man and soloist in the big bands of Norvo, Barnet, Herman, Goodman, Monk, Hampton, Elliott Lawrence, Thad Jones-Mel Lewis and just about everyone but Duke Ellington. At the time of the current CD he was effective in the Mingus quintet, and working with such tasteful musicians as Puma and Jones was obviously a great delight to him. He is an eloquent player who today still (though now in his seventies) plays with great power and imagination. Everybody knows his name, but not enough people make a fuss about him. This is as good a collection of trombone solos as you will find anywhere with Bert showing himself to be very much a match for his pals Jay and Kai. He is credited on the insert-note as composer of *Conversation* (a track with a boisterous Rollins-like solo from Monterose). When Pete Rugolo recorded the tune with Shorty Rogers and Milt Bernhart he took composer credit. Bert has a lovely open tone and is also an excellent player with the mutes. Don't worry about the playing time; feel the quality of the material.
**SV**

# Ed Bickert

1932

**Third Floor Richard** Bickert (g); **Neil Swainson** (b); **Terry Clarke** (d); **Dave McKenna** (p). Concord Jazz Ⓕ CCD4380 (53 minutes). Recorded 1989.

⑧ ❽

Bickert's apparent preference for spending most of his time in his native Canada probably accounts for his modest international reputation. He made important contributions to some fine Paul Desmond albums, but **Third Floor Richard** is a wide-ranging, comprehensive picture of his talents. On the basis of a few tracks, one might be excused for thinking he was a somewhat introvert soloist with a penchant for dreamy, wistful ballads. That is only part of the story. When the tempo is up and with guest Dave McKenna laying down a percussive keyboard backing, Bickert turns into a hard-driving soloist capable of producing long and interesting lines with no loose musical ends. The 11 tracks contain some beautiful and unhackneyed material including a tune which even its composer, Duke Ellington, seems to have forgotten, for he seldom recorded it: *Tonight I Shall Sleep (With a Smile On My Face)*. Harry Warren's *I Know Why (And So Do You)* is a duet by McKenna and Bickert; on all the other tracks Swainson and Clarke provide ideal support. Concord may have many guitarists in their catalogue but none better than Ed Bickert.
**AM**

# Barney Bigard

**New review**

**Barney Bigard Story** Bigard (cl, ts); Bubber Miley, Arthur Whetsol, Freddie Jenkins, Cootie Williams, Wallace Jones, Ray Nance, Louis Bacon (t); Rex Stewart (c); Joe 'Tricky Sam' Nanton, Juan Tizol, Lawrence Brown, Jack Teagarden, Benny Morton (tb); Johnny Hodges (as, ss); Otto Hardwicke (as, bss); Harry Carney (bs, as, cl); Ben Webster (ts); Duke Ellington, Billy Strayhorn, Jelly Roll Morton, Billy Kyle, Freddie Washington, Sammy Benskin (p); Fred Guy (bj, g); Django Reinhardt, Brick Fleagle (g); Wellman Braud, Hayes Alvis, Jimmy Blanton, Billy Taylor, Israel Crosby (b); Sonny Greer, Zutty Singleton, Dave Tough, Eddie Dougherty (d); Charlie Barnet (chimes). Jazz Archives Ⓕ 158502 (74 minutes). Recorded 1929-45.

**⑨ ❼**

Listening to Bigard's often inauspicious work with the Louis Armstrong All Stars in the latter part of his career is to hear a man less than totally at ease with his musical environment. New Orleans-born Bigard was a Duke Ellington man! He originally studied clarinet with Lorenzo Tio Jr and, although always identifiable as a product of his hometown, he had a highly personal style. He had played tenor with the bands of Albert Nicholas and King Oliver but, after joining Ellington in 1927, specialized almost exclusively on his beloved Albert system clarinet. This CD could hardly be bettered as a catalogue of his finest work. It ignores the period after 1945 but includes his finest moments with Ellington-based music, undoubtedly the genre which most inspired him. The extent of his backstage musical liaison with his leader, before the arrival of co-composer Billy Strayhorn in 1939, is continually apparent; as is the way in which the sinuous grace of his clarinet helped to balance the brass domination of the late twenties band. Titles such as *Tiger Rag* and *Wall Street Wail* show how his spectacularly flowing New Orleans style fitted the band's (then) avant-garde aspirations. There are magnificent blues choruses on *Saturday Night Function* and *Across the Track Blues*, while *Slippery Horn* suggests there was a didactic quality in the shape and design of his clarinet solo that influenced some saxophonists. Bonuses are a delightful journey back to the roots with Jelly Roll Morton, a precious chamber jazz exercise with Stewart, Reinhardt and Taylor and items with Stewart's Big Seven, Teagarden's Big Eight and (Benny) Morton's All Stars. All these show that, even away from Ellington, he remained a jam session master. Almost the equal of this release is **The Introduction to Bigard** (Best of Jazz 4028) which, with only five duplications, complements this issue ideally. **BMcR**

# Acker Bilk

**Acker and Humph** Humphrey Lyttelton (t, cl); Acker Bilk (cl, v); Dave Cliff (g); Dave Green (b); Bobby Worth (d). Calligraph Ⓕ CLGCD027 (68 minutes). Recorded 1992.

**⑧ ❽**

Outgrowing the hype and publicity which pushed him to fame in the fifties and sixties, Bilk has surreptitiously metamorphozed from being an icon of the trad boom into a hard swinging mainstream clarinettist and jazz vocalist. Traces of his early influence from George Lewis remain, and his vocals are Armstrong-inspired, but he yet contrives to have his own sound, as did that other British original Sandy Brown. Bilk has made several good albums with musicians ranging from Al Fairweather and Bruce Turner to Stan Tracey, but this one with Lyttelton stands out amongst them. Lyttelton has always had an affinity for clarinet and alto saxophone players and the ensembles he creates with Bilk call to mind the best of the 'jump' sessions of the thirties.

The sometimes delicate moods created, as on *When You and I Were Young, Maggie,* are much aided by the replacement of a piano by guitarist Cliff, most sophisticated in both solo and accompaniment. Green leads as a bass player should and provides a resounding mattress for the two horns to bounce their ideas on. Amongst the fresh and appropriate material chosen, Bilk fashions a delicate version of Bechet's poignant *Southern Sunset*, a tune unknown to him until Lyttelton played him the original record shortly before the session. **SV**

# Walter Bishop Jr

**What's New** Bishop (p); Peter Washington (b); Kenny Washington (d). DIW Ⓕ 605 (46 minutes). Recorded 1990.

**⑥ ❽**

Bishop is of the same generation as Bud Powell and Al Haig, being just three years younger than both men, and a stylist with his roots deep in bop. He was Charlie Parker's preferred pianist for much of the last five years of the saxophonist's life. His own solo career, however, has never been high-profile, and he has usually appeared in other people's bands.

This lively trio album, made in New York five years ago, will help redress the balance a little. Although the *un poco loco* tempo of the opening *I'll Remember April*, an obvious Powell tribute, is a little beyond Bishop in terms of finding him creating new ideas and patterns at that sort of pace, the rest of this pleasingly varied programme enchants and impresses. Certainly, the treatment of Wayne Shorter's *Speak No Evil* is enterprising, with all three musicians swinging in unison and finding a light-as-air feel to glide on. That and Kenny Dorham's *Una Mas* are perhaps the stand-outs. *Crazy She Calls Me*, a solo feature, finds Bishop in Tatum territory and coping quite well, but the world was not waiting for another flat and uninspired version of the old Ellington warhorse, *Things Ain't What They Used To Be*. **KS**

## Cindy Blackman

1959

**Telepathy** Blackman (d); **Antoine Roney** (ss, ts); **Jacky Terrasson** (p); **Clarence Seay** (b). Muse Ⓔ MCD5437 (51 minutes). Recorded 1992.

⑧ ❽

A busy, bustling drummer in the Tony Williams mode, Cindy Blackman proved on the stellar hard-bop session **Code Red** that she was not only a tastefully rumbustious musician but also a fine composer. On this later session (there has since been a similar small-group session, **The Oracle**), featuring a working band rather than an *ad hoc* studio grouping, she again demonstrates both skills in abundance, but there is a maturity about her work present only sporadically in previous recordings. Where **Code Red** was something of an assault on the ears – albeit a surprisingly subtle one at times – **Telepathy** bears all the hallmarks of a more considered piece of work. The drum performance still bristles with press rolls, sudden felicitous side drum interventions and delicate cymbal work, but there are signs that, instead of favouring the headlong charge, Blackman has now recognized the virtues of a carefully planned campaign. Thus up-tempo material driven by tumbling drums and fleshed out by Antoine Roney's grainy, long-spun lines and Jacky Terrasson's spiky, delightfully unpredictable playing is tellingly juxtaposed with whisper-soft material; percussive originals with an intelligent version of Monk's *Well, You Needn't* and a wonderfully hectic romp through Miles Davis's *Tune Up*. Where previous albums have tended to be enjoyable showcases for individual virtuosity, **Telepathy**, as its name suggests, is all about communication within the quartet, and although not as immediately accessible as some of Blackman's earlier work, richly rewards repeated listenings. **CP**

## Dave Blackmore

1966

**New review**
**Fields of Fire** Blackmore (ss, as, bcl); **Phil Robson** (g); **Tim Wells** (b); **Paul Clarvis** (d). FMR Records Ⓔ CD30-E0596 (54 minutes). Recorded 1996.

⑦ ❽

Although he began his jazz career with the Sheffield-based hard-bop quintet Big Sun, Dave Blackmore's music now betrays his love of both European jazz and classical music and his interest in English folk. The sound produced by Fields of Fire on this, their eponymous début album, locates the band somewhere between the jazz/folk fusion of Lammas and the understated chamber-jazz of Perfect Houseplants: softly propulsive and warmly intimate, it is considerably more robust than might be expected from such composition titles as *Still Green Way* or *Painting the Colour of the Wind*. Blackmore himself sets the tone both with his gently insistent originals and his lively, plangent arrangement of the traditional tune *Rufford Park Poachers*; his pleasantly breathy alto, strident soprano and agile bass-clarinet mark him out as among the most accomplished and versatile of the UK's current crop of younger players. Guitarist Phil Robson, too, is a neat, logically inventive soloist and particularly adept at providing softly chiming accompaniment, and with bassist Tim Wells and drummer Paul Clarvis providing their customary discreet, supple support throughout, this is a highly enjoyable album from a band promising much for the future. **CP**

## Ed Blackwell

1929-92

**What It Is?** Blackwell (d); **Graham Haynes** (c); **Carlos Ward** (f, as); **Mark Helias** (b). Enja Ⓔ ENJ7089 2 (63 minutes). Recorded 1992.

⑨ ❾

Ed Blackwell was an exceptionally versatile, melodic drummer who graced every record he played on. Though best known for his early sixties recordings with Ornette Coleman, he stayed close to the music's cutting edge, his discography in the seventies and eighties including dates with players such as Anthony Braxton, Joe Lovano, David Murray and the Coleman alumni group, Old and New Dreams. **What It Is?**, taped live in California just two months before his death from kidney failure, is a rare excursion as leader for Blackwell and features his Ed Blackwell Project. The date brings the best from the players; bassist Mark Helias is rock-steady and also takes several bravura solos, as does the impressive Haynes on cornet, notably on *Pettiford Bridge*. Carlos Ward plays eloquently and contributes four of the disc's six compositions. Blackwell shines on *The Mallet Song*, a ceremonial exchange of drum solos and brief ensemble unisons. His drumming throughout is wonderfully alert and buoyant, a dancing pulse that he threads through the music with a master's deftness of touch. **What It be Like?**, a second disc from the same concert, is also highly recommended. **GL**

# Eubie Blake 1883-1983

**Memories of You**  Blake (piano rolls); **Gertrude Baum**, **Steve Williams** (one piano roll each).
  Biograph Ⓕ BCD112 (50 minutes). Recorded 1915-73.

⑥ ❽

A professional ragtime pianist at 15, Blake first recorded in 1917. He had a long association with singer Noble Sissle and together they took the first Negro musical to Broadway in 1921. Most of their recordings in the twenties concentrated on the cabaret side of their music, but after a lengthy period of retirement from public playing Blake emerged to launch a second recording career. Naturally the latter-day records were the real thing, but Blake was now 86 and time had taken its toll. Most of the rolls on this CD present Blake from the 1917 to 1921 period and make a fine job of documenting the more youthful end of his musical life. As with many ragtime rolls, the timing is somewhat regimented and (as *Dangerous Blues* demonstrates) the odd difficult phrase is negotiated rather stiffly. Blake was an accomplished player however, and a more legato feeling is engendered on *Memphis Blues* and *Good Fellow Blues*. This stride element in his style was to become more significant as his career progressed and is more evident on the final two tracks that took him back to a roll-recording piano for the first time in 52 years. They show that this great musical figure still knew how to present *Wild About Harry* and *Memories of You*, his two great compositional hits, to maximum advantage.  **BMcR**

# Ran Blake 1935

**The Short Life of Barbara Monk**  Blake (p); **Ricky Ford** (ts); **Ed Felson** (b); **Jon Hazilla** (d).
  Soul Note Ⓕ 1127 (42 minutes). Recorded 1986.

⑧ ❽

Blake's music, usually so intricate, individual and insular, is allowed to interact with a sensitive rhythm section and a forthright tenor saxophonist. The result is, quite naturally, unlike his highly charged solo discs, but still evocative and satisfying. A harmonically and structurally original artist, he sacrifices a measure of freedom to blend with the others but maintains the unorthodox voicings that prove him to be a movement of one, and his oblique solos are balanced by Ford's more direct statements. The programme reflects the leader's Third Stream idealism and eclecticism, with two versions of a brief Sephardic melody, a mournful Greek folk-song by Mikis Theodorakis, a lightly Latin swinger (where his Monkish interjections come to the fore) and Stan Kenton's theme song. But there is a consistent emotional undercurrent too, a leitmotiv of death, specifically in the tender waltz dedicated to Thelonious's daughter, a quizzical meditation on a friend's suicide (*Pourquoi, Laurent?*), and the brooding *Impresario of Death*. Still, the mood is never bleak, optimism being registered in the lush Strayhornesque ballad *In Between* and a clash of keys on *I've Got You Under My Skin*. As always, Blake's music is both subtle and richly rewarding.  **AL**

# Rob Blakeslee 1952

New review

**Long Narrows**  Blakeslee (c, t, flh); **Vinny Golia** (cl, bcl, ss); **Tad Weed** (p); **Michael Bisio** (b); **Bob Myer** (d). Nine Winds Ⓕ NWCD0167 (73 minutes). Recorded 1994.

⑥ ❼

Since Blakeslee's playing career began on the West Coast in 1970, it is not surprising that his music should steer a course between the tangible freedoms of the free-form revolution and the well-defined tonalities of fifties Cool jazz. He is a widely experienced trumpeter, has included Europe in his touring programme and has performed with such diverse stylists as Andrew Hill, Oliver Lake, Elton Dean and Anthony Braxton. He met Golia in 1989 and, despite now being based in Portland, Oregon, has worked with him ever since. The strength of their musical coalition is a considerable factor in the success of this CD. They are helped considerably by the tense, pushy feeling generated by the rhythm section, as well as by the mixture of piano directives and Cecil Taylor-like abstractions provided by Weeds. As the title track shows, Blakeslee is not reluctant to progress from free cadenza to more orthodox solo reading when the occasion demands. He is a positive and imaginative soloist, he has a fine brassy tone and he plays with an urgent diction that is well suited to his thought patterns. On themes like *Candlelight Liberation* and *White Cigars* he exploits the melodic shapes at his disposal and his long-lined development allows no time for showboating. Most of his work has been for the Nine Winds label but, in a list nearing 20, there are issues by Black Saint and Music & Arts.  **BMcR**

# Art Blakey 1919-90

**The History of Art Blakey and the Jazz Messengers**  Blakey (d); Kenny Dorham, Clifford Brown, Bill Hardman, Lee Morgan, Freddie Hubbard, Woody Shaw, Valery Ponomarev, Wynton Marsalis (t); Howard Bowe, Curtis Fuller, Robin Eubanks (tb); Sahib Shihab, Lou Donaldson, Jackie McLean, Bobby Watson (as); Musa Kaleem, Hank Mobley, Benny Golson, Wayne Shorter, Carter

**Jefferson, Dave Schnitter, Bill Pierce** (ts); **Ernie Thompson, Branford Marsalis** (bs); **Walter Bishop, Horace Silver, Sam Dockery, Bobby Timmons, Cedar Walton, Walter Davis, James Williams** (p); **Laverne Barker, Curley Russell, Doug Watkins, Spanky DeBrest, Jymie Merritt, Reggie Workman, Mickey Bass, Dennis Irwin, Charles Fambrough** (b); **Kevin Eubanks** (g); **John Ramsey** (d); **Tony Waters** (cga). Blue Note Ⓜ CDP7 97190-2 (three discs: 202 minutes). Recorded 1947-81.

⑧ ⑧

This is the best survey of Blakey's Messengers, spread over 34 years and taken principally from his Blue Note albums (some of the later tracks have been leased from Prestige, Timeless and Roulette). A glance at the collective personnel listed above gives a good idea of the important young musicians who benefited from their experience with the Messengers. Two of the earliest tracks in this chronological survey were taped one night at Birdland in New York by an ephemeral quintet containing both Clifford Brown and Horace Silver. The next tracks are by one of the first and best-known Blakey units, a co-operative quintet containing Kenny Dorham and Hank Mobley. This is classic hard bop, with great interaction between Art and the front line men. Inevitably over the years there were changes, and the arrival of Lee Morgan and Benny Golson gave the band a new character with tunes such as *Blues March* and *Moanin'* (both included here), but it was the sixties units with the three-piece front line and Wayne Shorter contributing eminently suitable arrangements which shifted Art's group on to a new plane of excellence. The third disc introduces Bobby Watson and Wynton Marsalis, but it also reminds us of the fine band with trumpeter Ponomarev and tenor saxist David Schnitter. Throughout this well-compiled set Blakey steers his various bands like a true leader and the bright sound and good transfers help to give the music maximum presence.　**AM**

**Art Blakey's Jazz Messengers with Thelonious Monk** Blakey (d); Monk (p); **Bill Hardman** (t); **Johnny Griffin** (ts); **Spanky DeBrest** (b). Atlantic Ⓜ 781332-2 (44 minutes). Recorded 1957.

⑧ ⑥

Few drummers could relax when they played with Monk. Blakey could and the bond between him and the pianist meant, in the early days at least, that when Monk really hit his stride, Blakey was on drums. Griffin also had more than a grasp of the music and the coming together of the three men on this date meant that it was set fair to succeed. It did beyond expectation, and it would be hard to find a better monument to both Monk and to the hard-bop era. Monk's tunes are built like Rome, and he and Blakey set up a continual onslaught of inspired creation. Griffin's solos have a life of their own and it is only the young trumpeter to whom Blakey feels the need to give the occasional supercharging from the drums.

Many of the groups in which Monk played were flawed for various reasons – often because the musicians were intimidated by the music. This one is as nearly without flaw as makes no matter. It also confirms that the sparse and concise early versions of the Messengers were far better than the sprawling later bands. Unfortunately the recording quality is not as good as the music.　**SV**

**Free for All** Blakey (d); **Freddie Hubbard** (t); **Wayne Shorter** (ts); **Curtis Fuller** (tb); **Cedar Walton** (p); **Reggie Workman** (b). Blue Note Ⓜ CDP7 84170-2 (37 minutes). Recorded 1964.

⑩ ⑩

I don't know what was bugging Blakey the day this album was made, but boy does he beat the stuffing out of both his drum kit and the band on the title track! Things get to such a pitch of passion that Shorter, the first soloist, sounds like a drowning man during the last verse of his solo, and hands over to Curtis Fuller in the manner of someone who has just gone the distance with the then-Cassius Clay. Fuller simply cannot cope with the barrage, and while Hubbard skips joyfully over the worst that Blakey can do to him (including a 6/8 snare roll that lasts for five bars and blots everyone else out), the only possible way out of all this is a drum solo. When it comes, it has the manic exultation of a man just escaped from prison. Or hell. The rest of the date, the Latin-based *Pensativa* aside, lowers the emotional temperature only by degrees, so that *Hammer Head*, a Shorter line cast in the mould of so many Messengers two-beat anthems, sounds distinctly threatening, and *Hubbard's Core*, a fast-ish, scalar composition, comes across as a speedboat in choppy seas as Blakey thrashes away underneath the soloists, creating a tricky polyrhythmic base for them to slither on. This may not be a typical Messengers date but it's one of the great Blakey albums, with only Riverside's **Caravan** able to get anywhere near it for emotional intensity.　**KS**

New review

**Child's Dance** (Volume 1) and **Mission Eternal** (Volume 2) Blakey (d); with, on Volume 1: **Woody Shaw** (t); **Manny Boyd** (f); **Buddy Terry** (ss); **Ramon Morris** (f, ts); **Carter Jefferson** (ts); **George Cables, Cedar Walton** (p, kbds); **Walter Davis, John Hicks** (kbds); **Essien Nkrumah** (g); **Mickey Bass, Stanley Clarke** (b); **Nathaniel, Pablo Landrum, Sonny Morgan** (perc); **Ray Mantilla, Emmanuel Rahim, Tony Waters** (cga); on Volume 2: **Woody Shaw, Carter Jefferson, Cedar Walton, Mickey Bass, Tony Waters** plus **Steve Turre** (tb); **Michael Howell** (g); **Jon Hendricks** (v). Prestige Ⓜ PRCD21430/24159-2 (two discs, oas: 72 and 74 minutes). Recorded 1972-3

⑥ ⑦

Measured by audience appeal and critical acclaim, the seventies was not a good decade for the Jazz Messengers. The old formula had slipped out of fashion. Jazz-rock and electric pianos were in and one suspects Cedar Walton might today regret having spent quite so much time here with the Fender Rhodes. These two albums combine four Prestige LPs and include a couple of unissued tracks. A member of the greatest of all Messengers, Walton would undoubtedly be hailed by Blakey as the Prodigal Son Returned. As for the New Star on the modern jazz horizon, Carter Jefferson probably got the nod even if, apart from a nicely structured solo on the tune *Mission Eternal*, he overdoes the Coltrane effects. Woody Shaw, a Messenger when the 1972 tracks were recorded and later a guest, is suitably inspired by the traditional trumpet feature *I Can't Get Started* on Volume 1 and plays consistently throughout. Former hits *Moanin'* and *Along Came Betty* (now with vocals by Jon Hendricks) are revived and it's fun to hear Shaw sounding like Lee Morgan. Volume 2 has the edge and the final track is the best: *Walton's Fantasy in D* imparts a satisfying crackle that would not have been out of place on **Mosaic** or **Ugetsu** and he even plays steam piano. **RA**

---

**Album of the Year** Blakey (d); **Wynton Marsalis** (t); **Bobby Watson** (as); **Billy Pierce** (ts); **James Williams** (p); **Charles Fambrough** (b). Timeless Ⓕ SJP155 (43 minutes). Recorded 1981.

✔ ⑧ ⑥

Yes, the title is presumptuous, but the Jazz Messengers did produce an excellent set when they cut this date in a Paris studio shortly before a wholesale turnover in personnel. The balance toward new material (originals by Watson and his wife, Williams and Fambrough) plus the inclusion of jazz classics (by Parker and Shorter) not previously identified with Blakey, underscore this edition of the Messengers' distance from a fixation in the past. Marsalis is vivid and technically impeccable, but only one of a group of strong soloists, and the charged contribution of the others drives home the point that they (especially Watson and Williams) were the real architects of Blakey's resurgence in the last decade of his life. For the leader's part, the expected energy is present, plus substantially more shading than he could manage as his hearing loss progressed. Fambrough's big-enough bass is too far forward in the mix, which is not the comment one generally makes about Blakey albums and a tribute of sorts to Fambrough's muscular attack. That caveat aside, it is hard to fault this definitive snap-shot of why the Jazz Messengers remained important well into their fourth decade. **BB**

# Terence Blanchard

1962

**New review**

**The Heart Speaks** Blanchard (t); **Ivan Lins** (p, v); **Oscar Castro-Neves** (g); **Edward Simon** (p); **David Bohanivich**, **Fred Zlotkin** (vc); **David Pulpus** (b); **Troy Davis** (d); **Paulinho Da Costa** (perc). Columbia Ⓕ 483638-2 (64 minutes). Recorded 1995.

⑧ ⑩

Thirty years ago this would have been called a bossa nova album. At times the vocal similarity between the Brazilian Ivan Lins and João Gilberto is quite spooky, while the atmosphere of the whole proceedings is strongly reminiscent of the Getz-Gilberto Verve sessions. In these surroundings Blanchard's trumpet tone takes on an especially warm glow and his lines fall in soft folds around the rhythm. Always a romantic at heart, he is obviously captivated by both the idiom and the songs, which are all Lins's compositions. Simon and Castro-Neves approach the music with just the right degree of delicacy and the occasional discreet touches of cello work very well. A delightful set in all respects. **DG**

# Carla Bley

1938

**Escalator Over the Hill** Bley (p, org, cel, ch, v); **Enrico Rava**, **Michael Snow** (t); **Don Cherry** (t, v); **Michael Mantler** (t, vtb, kbds, perc); **Sam Burtis**, **Jimmy Knepper**, **Roswell Rudd** (tb); **Jack Jeffers** (btb); **Bob Carlisle**, **Sharon Freeman** (frh); **Jack Buckingham**, **Howard Johnson** (tba); **Souren Baronian**, **Peggy Imig**, **Perry Robinson** (cl); **Jimmy Lyons** (as); **Gato Barbieri** (ts); **Chris Woods** (bs); **Don Preston** (syn, v); **Karl Berger** (vb); **Sam Brown**, **John McLaughlin** (g); **Leroy Jenkins** (vn); **Nancy Newton** (va); **Calo Scott** (vc, v); **Charlie Haden**, **Ron McClure**, **Richard Youngstein** (b); **Jack Bruce** (elb, v); **Paul Motian** (d, perc); **Roger Dawson** (cgas); **Bill Morimando** (orch bells, cel); **Paul Jones**, **Sheila Jordan**, **Jeanne Lee**, **Linda Ronstadt**, **Viva** (v). JCOA Ⓜ 839-310-2 (two discs: 121 minutes). Recorded 1968-71.

✔ ⑩ ⑧

Given Bley's description of her *Genuine Tong Funeral* (recorded by an augmented Gary Burton band in 1968) as a "dark opera without words", **Escalator Over the Hill** qualifies as her dark opera with words – libretto courtesy of Paul Haines, whose poetry frequently suggests Paul Bowles overtaken by whimsy. 'Opera' literally means story, but the story told by Haines amounts to little more than existential posturing. Even so, the principal singers – Jack Bruce, the unlikely Paul Jones, late of the Manfred Mann Band, and the perhaps even less likely Ronstadt – make surprising sense of it all, though the real story is Bley's flair in casting according to type a variety of emotive improvisers, including the garrulous Rudd, the solemn Haden and the fire-breathing Barbieri. Until this and **Funeral**, Bley was prized as a gifted miniaturist, having made her mark with compositions for her ex-husband Paul's piano trio. *Escalator* suggested the full size of Bley's talents as a composer and orchestrator. Some of the most beguiling moments are provided by a 'Desert Band' featuring Cherry and Lee; these can be listened to as a preview of Cherry's adventures in

World Music. One complaint: shrunk to fit a jewel-case, the facsimile of the original LP booklet reduces the libretto to a squint and the lavish session photography to a series of meaningless blurs.                                                                                                          **FD**

---

**Carla Bley Live**  Bley (p, org, gspiel); **Michael Mantler** (t); **Steve Slagle** (ss, as, f); **Tony Dagradi** (ts); **Gary Valente** (tb); **Vincent Chancey** (frh); **Earl McIntyre** (tba, btb); **Arturo O-Farrill** (p, org); **Steve Swallow** (b); **D. Sharpe** (d). Watt ⓕ 815 730-2 (41 minutes). Recorded 1981.

⑧ ⑥

As it gradually becomes apparent that Carla Bley's band may be the best sounding band led by any pianist-composer since Duke Ellington died, it makes more sense to search out records like this. More than a dozen years old now, but sounding as fresh as a shower of rain, and with all the characteristics you come to expect from Carla Bley – great slabs of sound, sudden blasts of exotic air, odd interludes on organ, bits that sound like circus music, bits of gospel, bits of Gary Valente's force-ten trombone (always sounding a bit similar, but nobody cared that Tricky Sam Nanton always played more or less the same solo for Duke), bits of parody, jokes ... but all joined together by something more basic than logic. And only ten people producing such a grand sound!                                **MK**

---

**Fleur Carnivore**  Bley (p); **Lew Soloff, Jens Winther** (t); **Frank Lacy** (frh, flh); **Gary Valente** (tb); **Bob Steward** (bb); **Daniel Beaussier** (ob, f); **Wolfgang Puschnig** (as, f); **Andy Sheppard** (cl, ts); **Chistof Lauer** (ss, ts); **Roberto Ottini** (ss, bs); **Karen Mantler** (h, org, vb, ch); **Steve Swallow** (b); **Buddy Williams** (d); **Don Alias** (perc). Watt ⓕ 839 662-2 (56 minutes). Recorded 1988.

⑧ ⑧

One came to expect Carla Bley to be touring and recording with small to medium-sized groups during the eighties. This CD, recorded live at the Montmartre in Copenhagen, returned her to the fruitful area of the bigger band. This 15-piece group, equipped with excellent original Bley material, takes her back into pure jazz territory. Her arrangements are imaginative, with the four-man rhythm section sounding much larger and with Valente's trombone voice smearing across the lower reaches of the ensemble almost as a trade mark. The trumpet/horn section also achieves a remarkable depth, matching the reeds with its dancing lilt. *Fleur Carnivore* was written to commemorate the tenth anniversary of Duke Ellington's death and something of the great man's approach to leading permeates the whole session. Each soloist is accommodated in a way that suits him. Puschnig chooses the title track to show his ease with an attractive tune, and even becomes Hodges-like in his theme statement in the third movement of *The Girl Who Cried Champagne*. Valente shines in the same piece, and also in *Song of the Eternal Waiting of Canute*, where the horns pace his throaty utterings. Soloff is his usually confident solo self and Lauer deals several heavy tenor hands in a score that demands such treatment. Although too little is heard of Bley's quirky piano, her talent as composer, arranger and leader has rarely been so effectively displayed.                                              **BMcR**

# Paul Bley                                                                                      1932

---

**Ramblin'**  Bley (p); **Marc Levinson** (b); **Barry Altschul** (d). Red ⓕ 123117-2 (44 minutes). Recorded 1966.

⑧ ⑥

Canadian-born Bley has had a long and occasionally influential career. He has been in the habit of being around when important things were happening – making an album for Mingus's Debut label when in his early twenties; forming a band for a club date in late-fifties L.A. which turned out to be the entire Ornette Coleman Quartet plus himself on piano; being one of the formative members of the Jazz Composers' Guild in mid-sixties New York; making a crazy album for avant-garde label ESP (titled **Barrage**) which none the less was one of the first New Wave records and holds up quite well today; marrying such talents as Carla Bley and Annette Peacock, and premièring their early work on his records; and getting involved in the electronic rush of the early seventies before, like Keith Jarrett, beating a hasty retreat to his former acoustic style.

This album is quintessential mid-sixties Bley; all the major stylistic traits are in place, including a tendency to lose his accompanists at ultra-slow tempos. Recorded in the RCA Roma studios and released on a variety of labels (and under a variety of titles) over the years, it contains playing from the extremes of Bley's natural stylistic ambit, from the ebullience of his reworking of Ornette's *Ramblin'* to the harsh drama of *Both* and the almost unbearable intensity of Annette Peacock's *Albert's Love Theme*, a tune covered often by Bley at this time but never better than on this occasion. There is also a rapturous reading of *Ida Lupino*. A definitive set.                                    **KS**

---

**Open, To Love**  Bley (p). ECM ⓕ 827 751-2 (43 minutes). Recorded 1972.

✓                                                                                              ⑨ ⑨

Paul Bley has the rare distinction of being one of jazz's most recorded and, at the same time, most underrated pianists. Crucially influential but seldom credited as such, his music over the past four decades has addressed and altered our perception of rhythm and harmony. This solo disc, which is really an extension of many of the concepts he explored in sixties trios, frees him from jazz conventions of form and phrasing to expand possibilities of expression. It also marked his rediscovery of the acoustic piano after a long period of working with electronics. Thus his tone and subtle pedal effects are lovely (and captured marvellously by the excellent engineering). The thematically unified programme, consisting of moody, atmospheric pieces by Bley and two former wives, Carla Bley and Annette Peacock, is a mirror of Bley's introspective nature and commitment to absolute spontaneity. The sparse textures throughout are a reflection of the material (whether the poignancy of Carla's *Closer*, the fragility and exposed vulnerability of Annette's *Open, To Love*, or his own abstracted view of *I Can't Get Started* ) and an indirect homage to the laconism of Monk and Count Basie in an entirely different context. Bley's remarkable lyricism, chromaticism, modulations, and rubato combine in a uniquely moving voice. **AL**

**Solo Piano** Bley (p). SteepleChase Ⓕ SCCD31236 (68 minutes). Recorded 1988.

⑩ ❾

From the tumble of notes that opens *If I Loved You*, it is clear that this is top-form Bley; a sure touch and a precision of thought that has become ever-sharper over the years. Every note is 'just so'. **Tears**, a 1983 solo album for the French label Owl, was similarly exact, but implacable in mood, fraught with desolation. There is a hint of that here in a mournful *Tin Tin Deo*, but overall **Solo Piano** is a far friendlier record, its abstractions spiced with blues, romance and a touch of dry wit.

One of Bley's great talents is succinctness. His improvisation is so well-focused that each track becomes a reverie almost from the first note. Moods and styles flit through his playing in playful profusion: *Gladys* is rolling boogie; *If I Should Lose You*, subtle rumination; *Slipping*, abstract fun. He alters *You Go to My Head* beyond recognition, yet his own *Mariona* turns out to be *Fools Rush In*. There are one or two excursions inside the piano, notably the collage of twangs that leads into *And Now the Queen*. Mostly, though, his radicalism is diffident; a slight shift of tempo, a new harmonic twist – but all shaped with the loving care that comes from 40 years' experience. **GL**

# Jane Ira Bloom

1953

New review

**The Nearness** Bloom (ss); **Kenny Wheeler** (t, flh); **Julian Priester** (tb); **Fred Hersch** (p); **Rufus Reid** (b); **Bobby Previte** (d). Arabesque Ⓕ AJ0120 (68 minutes). Recorded 1995.

⑧ ❽

Like Steve Lacy, Jane Ira Bloom has forged an impressive career by focusing her considerable talents on the soprano saxophone. It is a decision that has paid handsome dividends. So, too, has her decision to concentrate on a repertory centred largely on her own work. A genuinely contemporary composer-performer as much influenced by Charles Ives as Charles Mingus, she is one of very few saxophonists to have successfully incorporated live electronics as an artistic rather than commercial adjunct.

In a departure from previous projects, Bloom's poignant soprano is heard without electronic enhancement. There are striking originals such as the puckishly titled *It's a Corrugated World* and *The All-Diesel Kitchen of Tomorrow*. Also, there are bracing takes on standards such as *Summertime* and the haunting title track, *The Nearness of You*. And by expanding her usual duo/trio format to a sextet, Bloom's impressive arranging skills are more fully displayed. In her startling *Midnight Round!'Round Midnight*, Bloom achieves paradoxically stark yet sonorous textures, revealing yet new aspects of the Monk classic. Throughout, the soprano saxophonist's purplish lines are given exquisite support by the warm brass of Kenny Wheeler and Julian Priester, and the lithe rhythms of Fred Hersch, Rufus Reid and Bobby Previte. **CB**

# The Blue Notes

New review

**Live in South Africa 1964** Mongezi Feza (t); Nick Moyake (ts); Dudu Pukwana (as); **Chris McGregor** (p); **Johnny Dyani** (b); **Louis Moholo** (d). Ogun Ⓕ OGCD007 (73 minutes). Recorded 1964.

⑥ ❺

Under the leadership of Chris McGregor, The Blue Notes were formed in South Africa in 1963. This CD was recorded live in Durban just prior to their departure to Europe the following year and documents their approach to jazz at the time. It shows their inspiration as coming from American models such as the Jazz Messengers and the Miles Davis Quintet, but what makes the group distinctive is the added South African element; a touch of High Life *élan* that permeates everything they do. With just one exception the material is by members of the band; Pukwana is the major soloist and his blustering confidence meets each challenge head on. Feza's work embraces unexpected musical turns while the more conservative Moyake looks back to a slightly earlier era. The rhythm section is well integrated: Dyani is already an accomplished bassist, Moholo a self-assured drummer and McGregor – at this stage – the calming hand on piano. All were to become better players and the stimulation that they gave to the British scene in the sixties and early seventies can't be overestimated. Their approach became more free as they became more accomplished and they formed the nucleus of Brotherhood of Breath, a joyous big band that lit a further beacon of inspiration. **BMcR**

## Hamiet Bluiett
1940

**Nali Kola** Bluiett (bs, f); **Hugh Masekela** (t, flh); **James 'Plunky' Branch** (ss); **Donald Smith** (p); **Billy 'Spaceman' Patterson** (g); **Okeryema Asante** (d); **Chief Bey** (d); **Tito Sompa** (d); **Seku Tonge** (d); **Quincy Troupe** (author and poet). Soul Note Ⓔ 121 188-2 (48 minutes). Recorded 1987.

⑦ ❽

Bluiett had experience with St Louis's Black Artists Group before moving to New York in 1969. There he played a prominent part in the eighties loft movement. He established himself as the marauding samurai of his instrument, vocalizing his passion on the baritone sax, dredging honks from his very soul and using overtones with superb control. The eighties found him to be a cornerstone of the World Saxophone Quartet and leader of the Telepathic Arkestra, Rainshout and the Clarinet Family. His open mind made him amenable to most musical situations and this CD is a typical challenge. The absence of a bass player ensures a free harmonic plain over which he can roam and the driving drum barrage becomes a buoyancy factor. This is never more evident than on *Enum*, a piece with changing time signatures and with Bluiett ranging freely across them. His switch to flute on *Ganza* offers a different response to the same situation as he wheezes an extremely creative path over the hot coals of the drum bed. The presence of three horns does change the emphasis on *Nali Kola*, perhaps bringing the music back from the pan-tonal sound canvas so adeptly provided by the drummers. The master drummers do set the tone of the whole session, however, and in so doing, they help Bluiett to show yet another facet of his multi-talented approach to jazz. **BMcR**

## Arthur Blythe
1940

New review
**Calling Card** Blythe (as); **John Hicks** (p); **Cecil McBee** (b); **Bobby Battle** (d). Enja Ⓔ 9051-2 (73 minutes). Recorded 1993.

⑦ ❽

A stalwart of the West Cost avant-garde, Blythe joined the New York loft movement in 1974. This was mutually successful, but in some ways it was a marriage of convenience. The more graceful contours of his style sometimes seemed at odds with the more angular elements and perhaps finally led to the conservatives seeing him as their link with loft extravagances. On the credit side, this resulted in his involvement with a major record company, although often with projects that compromised his talent. In the eighties he led a superb group containing cellist Abdul Wadud and brass bass specialist Bob Stewart, as well as working as a sideman in the controlled atmosphere of the Gil Evans band. No such restraints occur here. With McBee and Battle providing assertive punctuation and Hicks showing his flexibility, Blythe flourishes. He is a natural alto player with no interest in multi-instrumental challenges and it would be difficult to imagine his mode of improvisation on another horn. Appropriately, he achieves an almost Hodges-like cadence on *Odessa*, steers a plaintive route through *Naima's Love Song*, shows his inventive wiles on *Elaborations* and demonstrates his total control with the gut wrenching reality of *Blue Blues*. It all makes for a fine example of Blythe in the work place. **BMcR**

## Jimmy Blythe
1901-31

**Johnny Dodds and Jimmy Blythe 1926–8** Blythe (p); prob. **Freddie Keppard, Punch Miller, Louis Armstrong, Natty Dominique** (c); **Roy Palmer** (tb); **Junie Cobb** (cl); **Johnny Dodds** (cl, as); **Bud Scott** (bj); **Jimmy Bertrand, Baby Dodds, Buddy Burton** (wbd); **Jasper Taylor** (d, wbd). Timeless Ⓜ CBC1-015 (66 minutes). Recorded 1926-8.

⑧ ❽

Kentucky-born Blythe moved to Chicago in his teens, studied with Clarence Jones and became one of the most ubiquitous figures on the South Side scene. Early solo recordings suggest the proxy influence of the Harlem stride piano school, but at heart he was very much a blues player. His technique was adequate for the tasks he set himself and his sense of timing was suited to the rolling gait proposed by his style. Arhythmic passages confirmed his confidence and his two-handed method ideally accommodated his unpretentious creative process.

This CD sets his barrelhouse piano in various combo situations and lusty solos on *Poutin' Paper* and *Idle Hour Special* can be seen as vital parts of the ensemble fabric. Their natural momentum is in itself a stimulant but the way in which he drives the entire ensemble on *Adam's Apple* gives a clearer indication of his inspirational skills. His sympathy for vocalists is found on *Messin' Around*, but it is his relaxed interaction with Dodds on *Buddy Burton's Jazz* that draws attention to his more subtle contrapuntal talents. He died when he was 30 but the rhythmic basis of his style seems to have lived on, firstly through Chicago's hard boppers and then beyond. **BMcR**

# Peter Bocage

**Peter Bocage** Bocage (t, vn); **Charlie Love** (t); **Homer Eugene, Albert Warner** (tb); **Louis Cottrell, Paul Barnes** (cl); **Benjamin Turner** (p); **Sidney Pflueger** (g); **Emanuel Sayles** (bj); **McNeal Breaux, Auguste Lanoix** (b); **Alfred Williams, Albert Jiles** (d). Riverside Ⓜ OJCCD1835-2 (48 minutes). Recorded 1960/1.

⑤ ❻

Bocage's playing typifies the more gentle Creole approach to jazz. He began his professional career at 19 and worked in his hometown, New Orleans, with the Superior Orchestra, Original Texedo Orchestra and the Onward Brass Band. He played the riverboats during World War I then joined A.J. Piron for a lengthy stay. His contribution on trumpet is acknowledged in the Piron entry but Bocage played many instruments, as well as composing and arranging for the band. This CD, under his own name, inevitably features more of his solos on both trumpet and violin. He was, however, well into his seventies when its two sessions took place and allowances must be made. A poor quality piano was used on one date and several players experience intonation problems. On the credit side, Bocage was a deft ensemble leader on trumpet and, although the collective sound suggests a perambulation on eggshells, there is a genuine Crescent City bounce at all tempos. Age had dealt more kindly with his violin playing and, although the 'original ragtime' titles require little in the way of improvisational investigation, it is a specialist music that the 1960-1 Bocage turns to good account. **BMcR**

# Bohuslän Big Band

**The Blue Pearl** Lars Lindgren, Lennart Grahn, Hildegunn Oiseth, January Eliasson, Frederik Norén (t); Bengt Åke Anderson, Christer Olofsson, Ralph Soovik, Niclas Rydh (tb); Niklas Robertson, Claes Lidqvist Erik Norstrom, Ove Ingmarsson, Mikael Karlsson, January Forslund (reeds); **Lars Jansson** (p); **Ulf Wakenius** (g); **Yasuhito Mori** (b); **Anders Kjellberg** (d); **Jacob Anderson** (perc). Phono Suecia Ⓟ PSCD97 (65 minutes). Recorded 1996.

⑥ ❽

How should this band be categorized? It's the sort of band that became both workshop and clinic for the likes of Bob Brookmeyer or Thad Jones. But with one enormous difference. All the music was composed and arranged by the pianist Lars Jansson who, at the time when he was invited to work with the band for a year, had only ever written one arrangement. He had, in 1981, played with a radio group led by Brookmeyer which had included Red Mitchell and Mel Lewis, the mere thought of which had given him four days of sweaty palms and sleepless nights. He's come on since then and these ten arrangements show he has attained a remarkably swift mastery of his craft. He writes with great feeling for melody and also knows how to score for the sections. In this he is helped by this perfectly-rehearsed and quite magnificent band. The tenor saxist Erik Norstrom solos with great warmth on *White Cliff* whilst guitarist Ulf Wakenius was brought in to feature on *A Cup of Mintzer-Tea*, a tribute to another influence of Jansson's. Jansson takes some good piano solos but there is a noticeable absence of trombone solo in the ten pieces. What happened to the Åke Persson tradition? **SV**

# Claude Bolling

**Vintage Bolling** Bolling (p); **Jean-Pierre Rampal** (f); **Pinchas Zukerman, Patrice Fontanarosa** (vn); **Renaud Fontanarosa** (vc); **Alexandre Lagoya, Eric Franceries** (g); **Max Hediguer, Michel Gaudry, Pierre-Yves Sorin** (b); **Marcel Sabiani, Vincent Cordelette** (d). Milan Ⓜ 35735-2 (63 minutes) Recorded 1975-93.

⑥ ❽

The integration of classical music and jazz seems to have a peculiar fascination for French musicians: Jacques Loussier, Jean-Loup Lognon and Martial Solal have all experimented with such fusions. Among them, however, Claude Bolling is paramount: a former child prodigy, whose impeccable jazz credentials include backing many US visitors to France, most notably on Albert Nicholas's best European trio recordings. In the popular French imagination, Bolling is not familiar so much as an impeccable swing pianist but as the composer and co-performer of such pieces as his *Suite for Flute and Jazz Piano Trio* and similar works for other instruments. Unlike many of his French counterparts, he successfully broke through to the US public; his flute suite spent over ten years on the classical charts there, two of them in the Top 40. This selection of highlights from 'the Father of Crossover' has movements from his flute, guitar and violin suites as well as his more recent *Crossover USA*, which gives quasi-baroque treatments to jazz standards. Most of it's pretty saccharine stuff, and the rating above is strictly how much the album is "a representation of what the artist is on about". Jazz content is more like thirty per cent, and enthusiasts would do better to seek out Bolling's more overtly jazz work, such as his outstanding and deeply-felt big-band 1990 Grand Prix Du Disque version of Ellington's full-length tone parallel, *Black, Brown and Beige*, also available on Milan. **AS**

# Sharkey Bonano

1904-72

**Sharkey Bonano**  Bonano (c, t, v); Julian Lane, Santo Pecora, Moe Zudecoff, George Brunies (tb); Meyer Weinberg (cl, as); Irving Fazola, Joe Marsala (cl); Dave Winstein (ts); Armand Hug, Clyde Hart, Joe Bushkin (p); Bill Bourjois (bj, g); Frank Frederico, Eddie Condon (g); Ray Bonitas, Thurman Teague, Artie Shapiro, Hank Wayland (b); Augie Schellange, Ben Pollack, George Wettling, Al Sidell (d); Johnnie Miller's New Orleans Frolickers; Monk Hazel and His Bienville Roof Orchestra; Santo Pecora And His Back Room Boys. Timeless Jazz Ⓕ CBC1-001 (70 minutes). Recorded 1928-37.

⑥ ➏

Although Bonano's musical career centred on New Orleans, he was one of jazz's nomads. This CD documents his career in the twenties and thirties, a time when he also worked with Jean Goldkette, Larry Shields and Ben Pollack. He was a lyrical trumpeter; he had an ample, warm tone, a discreet vibrato and he built his solos with taste and logic. Suspect intonation did not help his singing, but he had a colourful way with a vocal. He was happiest in a Dixieland set-up and it is significant that this issue has him working with tailgate specialists Pecora and Brunies and clarinettists Sidney Arodin, Fazola and Marsala, who knew their way around a New Orleans ensemble. His way of combating the arrival of the swing era was to pretend it was not happening. His fine solo on the 1928 *High Society* could be easily transplanted into the 1936 version and, with Fazola and Marsala reneging and his rhythm team accepting the new stylistic rules, he was forced to make some concessions on the Sharks of Rhythm titles in the thirties. After World War II the revivalist movement allowed him to return to his first love, and his last musical days were spent entertaining tourists in the Crescent City. **BMcR**

# Joe Bonner

1948

New review

**Impressions of Copenhagen**  Bonner (p, chimes); Paul Warburton (b); J. Thomas Tilton (d); with Carol Michalowski, Peggy Sullivan (vn); Carol Garrett (va); Beverly Woolery (vc); Holly Hofmann (f); Eddie Shu (t); Gary Olson (tb). Evidence Ⓕ ECD22024-2 (44 minutes). Recorded 1992.

⑧ ➑

On a previous recording, the consistently impressive **Suite for Chocolate**, Bonner lends an attractive chiming quality to his piano work by sharing front-line duties with vibes player Khan Jamal; on this album, mainly consisting of a suite inspired by his extended stay in Copenhagen in the late seventies, Bonner goes one better by overdubbing real chimes where appropriate. The resultant overall sound not only elegantly evokes the church-graced, seafront atmosphere of the Danish capital, but also brings to mind the textural variety so crucial to the work of Bonner's most famous erstwhile employer, Pharoah Sanders. Soloing is undertaken only by the leader himself and his bassist, Paul Warburton, but Bonner's imagination is so fertile, his embellishments of his own airy themes so cogent – sweetly rippling and vigorously percussive by turns – and the latter's contributions so lyrical, that other solo voices are not missed. Bonner's compositions range from the accessible title track, through the sonorous waltz, *The North Star*, and the lightly latinate *I'll Say No*, to a plaintive theme, *Why Am I Here?*, set to a gently rocking rhythm that suddenly launches out into a wonderfully lively straight-ahead piano solo set against tight but fleet rhythm-section work. Given depth and subtlety by the intelligent use of both the string and brass/woodwind sections, and rounded off by a suitably brooding pianistic exploration of Billy Strayhorn's *Lush Life* over *arco* bass, this is another fine album. **CP**

# Earl Bostic

1913-65

New review

**Jazz Time**  Bostic (as); Richard 'Groove' Holmes (org); Joe Pass (g); James Bond, Herb Gordy (b); Charles Blackwell, Shelly Manne (d); Buddy Collette (arr). Charly/Le Jazz Ⓑ CD52 (33 minutes). Recorded 1963.

⑥ ➑

Some may still view Bostic's fifties r&b best-sellers as undemanding forerunners of Kenny G, but (in terms of style if not sales) Maceo Parker would be a better comparison. However, the altoist was into his thirties with much playing and arranging experience behind him before recording under his own name and did not record his first hit (*Temptation*) until 1948. It's perhaps understandable that he then refined and stuck to its winning formula for the next 15 years, before making the present album, originally titled **Jazz As I Feel It**. Eschewing his usual backing of vibes and a few ensemble horns, he opted for the newly fashionable sound of Hammond organ and guitar and reverted to a swing rather than r&b feel from the bass and drums. Rather than his simplified (some would say vulgarized) melodic approach, the vast technique that impressed Coltrane and others came to the fore, as in the high harmonics at the end of *Don't Do It Please*. There is little genuine improvisation from the altoist and, although Holmes and Pass do get a look-in, he does dominate proceedings. But even if the end result is a little like Willie Smith on speed, it is an impressive contrast to most of Bostic's output. **BP**

# Boswell Sisters

**It's the Girls!** Connee and Helvetia Boswell (v); Martha Boswell (v, p) with various accompaniment, including: Manny Klein (t); Tommy Dorsey (tb); Jimmy Dorsey (cl, as); Arthur Schutt, Martha Boswell (p); Eddie Lang (g); Joe Venuti (vn); Joe Tarto (b); Stan King (d). ASV Living Era Ⓜ CDAJA5014 (62 minutes). Recorded 1925-31.

**⑥ ❺**

The American popular music factory of the twenties and early thirties, while offering only a back-door entrée to Bessie Smith and her black sisters, boasted a flourishing department of white women whom it would describe as blues singers – apparently meaning that they lent their material, whether formally blues or not, a blue tone and often a Southern accent. The best of this group were the New Orleans-born Boswell Sisters. Connee shared with Bing Crosby (whom she would occasionally partner on record) a deep warm voice, a way with languorous sliding notes and great rhythmic assurance. She recorded a number of solos, some included here, such as *Time On My Hands* with the Victor Young Orchestra. But the Boswells's *métier* was their vivacious and elaborate harmonizing, often deployed through several changes of tempo, as on *Heebie Jeebies, Shout, Sister, Shout!* and the bravura *Roll On, Mississippi, Roll On.* Such numbers, which make up about a third of this collection, were accompanied with matching verve by a contingent from the Dorsey Brothers Orchestra, and ever since they were first issued these performances have been admired for the pointed contributions of Klein, Jimmy Dorsey, Venuti and Lang. Others have more staid orchestral settings, or employ Martha's piano, as on their 1925 début *I'm Gonna Cry (Cryin' Blues)*. This quaint performance, with its mock-instrument effects in the manner of the Mills Brothers, has a funny-hat air that gives no hint of the thoroughly modern millinery they would strut in just five years later. **TR**

# Jean-Paul Bourelly

**Tribute to Jimi** Bourelly (g, v); T.M. Stevens (b); Alfredo Alias (d); Kevin Johnson, Irene Datcher (v). DIW Ⓕ DIW893 (73 minutes). Recorded 1994.

**⑧ ❿**

This album is decidedly not for jazz purists. On it, Jean-Paul Bourelly comes closer to re-creating the sound and passion of Jimi Hendrix's music than anyone else since the master died in 1970. It is uncanny: Bourelly is not only able to reconstruct Hendrix's sound, he can also get frighteningly close approximations of his phrasing, precise rhythms, his little hesitancies, his searing intensity, his audaciousness. What has all this got to do with jazz? Well, Hendrix was one of the supreme improvisers of his generation, his music was thoroughly based in the blues and his music profoundly influenced subsequent jazz musicians as much as rock, funk or fusion. Bourelly, a guitarist with impeccable jazz credentials and a string of associations with top-flight jazz musicians, brings his wide knowledge and abilities to this project and breathes new life into an important musical legacy. His version of Hendrix's *Machine Gun* here is spine-tingling, almost savage, and it takes on a *doppelgänger* relationship to the famous 'live' Hendrix original at Fillmore East.

This is certainly one way to reinvigorate the jazz tradition, and if you want to see how inventive it can get without resorting to rap and sampling, try Bourelly's version of *Power of Soul*, where he uses just fragments of Hendrix's original composition to create a mesmerizing and wildly catchy, utterly new piece of music. This is a CD to revive your faith in both the past and the future. **KS**

# Lester Bowie

1941

**Lester Bowie's Brass Fantasy: The Fire This Time** Bowie, E.J. Allen, Gerald Brazel, Tony Barrero (t); Vincent Chancey (frh); Frank Lacy, Louis Bonilla (tb); Bob Stewart (tba); Vinnie Johnson (d); Famoudou Don Moye (perc). In & Out Ⓕ IOR7019-2 (75 minutes). Recorded 1992.

**⑧ ❽**

Lester Bowie has been the one member of the Art Ensemble of Chicago to create a public persona large (and popular) enough away from the group to be perceived as Lester Bowie, trumpeter and showman, rather than "that guy from the Art Ensemble". The records and concerts given under his name, or that of his Brass Fantasy, have a distinct personality, and freely indulge his rollicking sense of fun and irony. The Brass Fantasy has, of course, got more than half-a-decade's experience behind it now, and inevitably the personnel has experienced change. From the evidence of this, its latest record, made live in concert in Switzerland, the band's enthusiasm and verve continues to grow apace rather than diminish.

Bowie is still very much the focal point and the band's repertoire remains as eclectic as ever (Michael Jackson and Jimmie Lunceford rub shoulders on this disc), but there is no dissipation of spirit and no fossilizing of the structures through which the wholly brass-bound music is created. This means that the arrangements (from a multitude of pens) really work and continue to challenge the players in useful ways. E.J. Allen's ten-minute piece *Journey Towards Freedom* may well be the standout composition and performance here, but there is plenty more to enjoy. The sound, especially for a live recording, is vivid and full. **KS**

# Ronnie Boykins

1935-80

**Ronnie Boykins**  Boykins (b, bb); **Joe Ferguson** (ss, ts, f); **Monty Waters** (as, ss); **James Vass** (as, ss, f); **Daoud Haroom** (tb); **Art Lewis, George Avaloz** (perc). ESP-Disk Ⓜ 3026-2 (44 minutes). Recorded 1975.

Associated for many years with Sun Ra, Boykins latterly worked with Roland Kirk, Sarah Vaughan and Steve Lacy. He was a very effective servant for the Arkestra and his superbly rounded tone, accurate pitching and seemingly effortless pizzicato mobility stamped him as one of jazz's most outstanding bassists. His *arco* tone was pleasingly clean and, as *The Will Come, Is Now* and *Starlight at the Wonder Inn* on this CD show, he builds solos that have the legato feeling of a saxophone line. This release also provides the opportunity to judge him as a composer and demonstrates that he works in a style that would not immediately suggest a bass player. His arrangements are functional rather than detailed, but he knows how to turn unison saxophone and solo bass into balanced counterpoint. The solo strength at his disposal is something of a limiting factor and, not surprisingly, the emphasis is centred on the leader's bass. His sousaphone is heard on *The Third*, but it is rather pedestrian and poorly recorded. Fortunately there is enough here to confirm Boykins as a brilliant bassist, as well as a man who makes the most of the troops at his disposal.  **BMcR**

# Charles Brackeen

1940

**Worshippers Come Nigh**  Brackeen (ts); **Olu Dara** (c); **Fred Hopkins** (b); **Andrew Cyrille** (d, perc); **Dennis Gonzalez** (perc). Silkheart Ⓕ SHCD111 (56 minutes). Recorded 1987.

Initially a pianist and violinist, Brackeen moved to California in 1956 and worked as a tenor saxophonist with Dave Pike and Joe Gordon. He moved to New York in 1966, married pianist JoAnne Grogan and worked alongside Don Cherry and Ed Blackwell before becoming involved with the loft movement and the likes of Dara, Frank Lowe and with his own Melodic Art-tet. This CD, with a title from the Attainment session added to the original LP, is an excellent introduction to Brackeen's comprehensive, musical talents. He wrote all of these consistently strong themes, as well as fashioning arrangements to give the impression of a larger unit. The illusion of size is further fuelled by the fullness of Hopkins's generously-toned bass lines and Cyrille's kicking, group-conscious drumming. Both play for the soloists and the horn men respond well. Brackeen is a successful escapee from the mighty influence of John Coltrane, his dry-toned and economical approach especially evident on *Bannar* and *Cing Kong*. Dara is a talent that blossomed in the eighties and his fiery horn really ignites *News Stand* and the title track. Fine solos apart, the clear aarchitecture of the arrangements makes one of the freer jazz forms accessible to the sceptics.  **BMcR**

# Joanne Brackeen

1938

**New review**

**Turnaround**  Brackeen (p); **Donald Harrison** (as); **Cecil McBee** (b); **Marvin 'Smitty' Smith** (d). Evidence Ⓕ ECD22123-2 (66 minutes). Recorded 1992.

Alongside Harold Land, Dexter Gordon and Charles Lloyd, Brackeen was part of the West Coast's largely unsung late-fifties scene. She moved to New York in 1965 and worked with the Jazz Messengers, Joe Henderson and Stan Getz as well as a string of small groups delighted to feature her mature piano style. Leading her own combos came naturally and sidemen such as Eddie Gomez, Sam Jones, Billy Hart and Jack DeJohnette have graced her bands. This CD finds her in the ideal company of McBee and Smith. It showcases her structural awareness as well as her instrumental fluency, but it also confirms the way in which adroitly chosen tonalities distance her from romanticism. She has a good knowledge of the American song book but shows on *No Greater Love* and *Bewitched, Bothered and Bewildered* that she is not about to let respect inhibit her creative investigations. The title track is a reminder of the regard she holds for Ornette Coleman, while three original compositions confirm her own considerable talents. The excellent Harrison completes the full hand, one that uses hearts as its chief suit but keeps improvisational trumps available to spring the quality surprises.  **BMcR**

# Don Braden

1964

**After Dark**  Braden (f, ts); **Scott Wendholt** (t, flh); **Noah Bless** (tb); **Steve Wilson** (as); **Darrell Grant** (p); **Christian McBride** (b); **Carl Allen** (d). Criss Cross Ⓕ 1081CD (65 minutes). Recorded 1993.

This is not Braden's latest album (he has a 1994 quartet date on Landmark and a subsequent CD, **Organic**, on Columbia) but it is still his most varied and resourceful effort. Part of the reason for this is that the expanded front line gives him so many more options, and on the five originals he takes appropriate advantage. Braden, a graduate of the Betty Carter, Wynton Marsalis and Tony Williams groups, is a skilled soloist, but more importantly to his long-term career he writes tunes with a clear personality and his arrangements nicely illuminate the interesting corners of each song's harmonic structure. Which puts me in mind just a little of Wayne Shorter, and although there is a deal of difference between the two saxophonists, stylistically and otherwise, the implication is clear for his future development.

Meanwhile, there is this album, and there is little here to fault. Everything is tastefully and intelligently done, and Braden is skilfully supported by Wendholt, Bless and Wilson, while the rhythm section has such a nice groove to it (McBride, a particular delight, is very sweetly recorded) that it is possible to listen through each track taking them in alone and not get bored. If you're concerned over the viability of the young jazz mainstream, try this for size. **KS**

# Bobby Bradford                                                                     1934

**Comin' On** Bradford (c); **John Carter** (cl); **Don Preston** (p, syn); **Richard Davis** (b); **Andrew Cyrille** (d). hatART Ⓕ CD6016 (75 minutes). Recorded 1988.

⑧ ❽

In the mid sixties cornettist/trumpeter Bobby Bradford joined forces with reedsman John Carter to co-lead the New Art Ensemble, a West Coast-based quartet that further explored the free jazz territory first opened up by their mutual acquaintance Ornette Coleman. That group broke up in 1974 but Bradford and Carter continued to work together, often playing support on each other's projects. **Comin' On** captures one of their final collaborations before Carter's death in 1991, a Hollywood club performance on which they front a rhythm section well-versed in the more lyrical areas of free jazz.

Compared to the New Art Ensemble, this music has more colours, more textures (thanks in part to Preston's dashing swathes of synthesizer), while the two leaders are now so attuned that their every exchange is a mercurial delight. Carter, who by this time was playing clarinet exclusively, is arguably the more adventurous of the pair, but Bradford is the more graceful player, his lines spun with a melodic logic and rythmic flexibility that hint at his bop roots. His poise on the title track, the elegance he brings to *Ode to the Flower Maiden*, the fire and urgency he displays throughout, together with his distinctive, blues-inflected tone, all reaffirm his status as a master stylist of contemporary jazz. **GL**

# Ruby Braff                                                                        1927

**Hi-Fi Salute to Bunny** Braff (c); **Benny Morton** (tb); **Pee Wee Russell** (cl); **Dick Hafer** (ts); **Nat Pierce** (p); **Steve Jordan** (g); **Walter Page** (b); **Buzzy Drootin** (d). RCA Victor Ⓜ 118520 2 (53 minutes). Recorded 1957.

⑧ ❼

This record, an early attempt at a 'concept' album, quite neatly sums up the hybrid nature of Braff's talent and appeal. He has an instrumental style which forges together elements of Armstrong, Beiderbecke and others, but his phrasing fits very comfortably over the free-flowing common time which is at the root of swing, plus he has a sufficiently sophisticated technique and harmonic imagination to incorporate elements of later jazz styles with which to add colour and drama to his playing. In making this album a tribute to a technically and lyrically gifted trumpeter from an earlier age, Braff has given himself the room to roam freely through repertoires and styles as it suits him. This is very much to the music's advantage, giving it a Basie-ish rhythmic drive, a modified Dixieland-cum-mainstream ensemble, and (for the most part) swing-style solos. If nothing else, this means that men as disparate as Hafer and Russell sound equally at home, and each element gels convincingly. Russell is particularly persuasive at slower tempos (his spot on *I Can't Get Started* being a highlight), but Braff excels at all tempos and plays with great conversational poise, as well as an attractively burnished brass tone. That he is also a fine ensemble leader is amply demonstrated.

The only drawback discernible on this album is the decision by RCA Victor's producer on the session to bathe Braff in excessive reverb, spoiling the otherwise commendably clean, sharp and balanced recording quality. If that can be ignored, then some fine music-making will come your way. The CD reissue has an extra track from the session, *Did I Remember*, originally released on LPM 1644 due to lack of space on the original LP. **KS**

**New review**

**Inside and Out** Braff (c); **Roger Kellaway** (p). Concord Jazz Ⓕ CCD4691 (60 minutes). Recorded 1995.

⑩ ❿

Some years ago Ruby Braff became one of the great giants of jazz. It is incredible that, despite problems with his health, he continues to play ever more beautifully: whenever one thinks that he has achieved perfection he comes up with something better. The something better under consideration is perfection. He has always been a master of the duet form of horn and piano (and of the trio with piano and drums) and his work in this medium, going back to the early session with Mel Powell in the fifties, is unique. One can only wonder how he would have reacted if he had been teamed with Art Tatum. Hearing him with Kellaway goes some way to telling us. Kellaway must be one of the most accomplished and inspired pianists playing today and he drives Braff to reach for previously unscaled heights of melody and invention. The listener is privileged to eavesdrop as each man creates while listening to the other. As mentioned in the last Guide, Braff's *forte* is melodic improvisation and Kellaway is happy to meet him on his own ground. Braff admires composers above all and his honest treatment of these standards, even *Basin Street Blues* and *I Got Rhythm*, gives them a new life.    **SV**

# Leandro Braga

**E Por Que Nao? (And Why Not?)** Braga (p); Bob Mintzer (f, ts); Steve Nelson (vb); Romero Lubambo (g); David Finck, Jose Pienasola (b); Ignacio Berroa (d); Giovanni Hidalgo (perc). Arabesque Jazz Ⓕ AJ104 (47 minutes). Recorded 1991.

⑥ ❽

Braga is one of the newer generation of musicians who are equally at home in Latin and jazz-based music, rhythms and forms. The resultant mix is potent and bodes well for the future. He is an assured technician and has clearly picked his cohorts carefully. Mintzer and Nelson have jazz credentials from any number of sources, and David Finck shows himself to be a thoroughly modern bass player in both technique and in thought. A ballad like *My Little One* displays Braga's touch and poise and gives a clear pointer towards Bill Evans as one of his sources of inspiration, while both the title tune and *Not a Chance* are exciting because the mix of jazz and Latin is so adept and fluid that it is not a case of them co-existing but melding into a new musical language. Which is just possibly a new phase for the broad church of jazz, some 50 years after Dizzy's first recorded efforts to explore the dialogue between the two musics. Braga has some way to go to find the perfect balance, but he and his musicians here exude an easy familiarity with the two cultures which is the perfect building block for the future. **KS**

# George Braith                                                                    1939

**Double Your Pleasure** Braith (braith-horn, ts); Ronnie Mathews (p); Tarik Shah (b); Mark Johnson (d); Jimmy Lovelace (d). King Ⓕ KI-CJ114 (66 minutes). Recorded 1992.

⑥ ❽

Circus tricksters simultaneously playing three trumpets have never much impressed the jazz world, but the impact of Roland Kirk and his one-man saxophone section was widely felt. Players on both sides of the Atlantic began concomitantly playing different saxophones simultaneously. One such player was Braith, who also played the stritch, Kirk's alto variant, as well as the ancient c-melody sax. During the sixties he was featured on several Blue Note and Prestige sessions, mainly in the company of organists such as Billy Gardner and John Patton. Little has been heard of him on record since that time, but this CD has him in good company and showing undiminished enthusiasm. His self-designed Braith-horn has two bodies but only one bell, and the effect is similar to Kirk's two-horn excursions. Moreover, Braith is a practised jazzman; he knows how to swing and he builds uncomplicated solos that accept the limitations of the instrument while showing genuine inventive flair. His approach to the tenor confirms that he doesn't need gimmicks to get his message across, and he is buoyed by sparkling support from Mathews, Shah and Johnson.    **BMcR**

# Anthony Braxton                                                              1945

New review

**3 Compositions of New Jazz** Braxton (ss, as, cl, f, mus, acc, bells, d, etc.); Leroy Jenkins (vn, va, hca, d, rec, cym, etc.); Leo Smith (t, mph, xyl, bottles, etc.); Muhal Richard Abrams (p, vc, cl). Delmark Ⓕ 415 (43 minutes). Recorded 1968.

⑧ ❽.

History, of course, is not always a case of what happened but rather who's noticing. This, for example, was Braxton's recording début as a 'leader' (he'd appeared a year earlier on Muhal Richard Abrams's **Levels and Degrees of Light**) though in fact the core trio of Braxton, Jenkins, and Smith was really a co-operative band formed to develop ideas which all three musicians shared. During the group's three-year existence (which included a residency in France) they recorded three more albums (all of which have resurfaced under Braxton's name alone) in addition to the two LPs of their 1971 farewell concert (with guests) which were released under the group's actual name, the Creative Construction Company. Thus the music here represents only one small area of Braxton's interests, and is quite misleading as to the multi-dimensional breadth of his composing even at this early stage of his career. What this preliminary document illustrates is how all three musicians contributed equally to the invention and evolution of the music – chiefly, extending the palette of available sounds through multi-instrumentalism and emphasizing their dramatic placement in open space, as can be gauged from two of the pieces here, Braxton's *Composition 6E (840M ... Realize)* and Smith's *The Bell*. Within such an indeterminate setting, the musicians' poise and commitment contribute greatly to the unique flavour of this short-lived ensemble. Braxton variously describing aspects of their approach as "collage form," "multiple-generated rhythmic dynamics," and "improvisational theatre," radical attitudes derived from the AACM environment of the time. Braxton's determination to open up the sound-field includes vocalization and secondary instruments like harmonica, kazoo and percussion, continuously introducing and juxtaposing new sonorities in an Alice in Wonderland fantasy, though his own alto sax outing is anticipatory of things to come. Smith's *The Bell*, more classically proportioned, slowly reveals new aspects of the plot like a Japanese scroll painting. (Smith was the only one of the three who continued to work with such spacious, synergistic principles.) The remaining piece, Braxton's *Composition 6D (N ... M488)* involves expressionistic solos in a more recognizably jazzy manner, with Abrams's piano as bubbling undercurrent replacing the conventional rhythm section. As an example of stylistic concepts he seldom returned to with such clarity and purity, **3 Compositions of New Jazz** is a valuable document, but as other samples of Braxton's music from this period appear, they reveal that it is only one piece of a much larger puzzle. **AL**

---

**Eight (+3) Tristano Compositions 1989 – For Warne Marsh** Braxton (as, sps, f); John
   Raskin (bs); Dred Scott (p); Cecil McBee (b); Andrew Cyrille (d). hatART Ⓕ CD6052
   (75 minutes). Recorded 1989.

Ⓑ Ⓨ

Throughout the eighties Braxton concentrated mainly on his compositions with their attendant pulse tracks; his excursions into jazz standards had been rewarding but rare. This CD represents his first investigation into the music of Lennie Tristano. Being essentially a free player, his solos produced on his own material tended to be organic parts of the whole work. Here he is a far more orthodox improviser. There are starting points and climaxes, his solos have balance and a consistent inner logic and his improvisations take place not because he is obliged to, but because the tune offers options that he is prepared to pursue. There are some very testing tempos here and where it would be easier to parade favourite phrases as you coast through changes, Braxton thinks at speed on *Two Not One*, *Lennie's Pennies* and *Victory Ball*, building well-articulated solos, free from clichés and invested with a rich strain of musical ideas. His readings of *How Deep is the Ocean* and *Time On My Hands* are fine examples of cogent development and they project an emotional involvement not always transmittable on flute. Raskin is solid in support, Scott makes an impressive recording début and McBee and Cyrille play as well as their reputations suggest they should. **BMcR**

---

**Willisau (Quartet) 1991** Braxton (f, cl, cbcl, ss, as); Marilyn Crispell (p); Mark Dresser (b);
   Gerry Hemingway (d, mba). hatART Ⓕ 4 61001/04 (four discs: 259 minutes). Recorded 1991.
✓
⑩ ⑩

The late eighties have brought a rich harvest of Braxton's music on record. As well as the Tristano tribute (see above), outstanding discs included a trio date with Tony Oxley and Adelhard Roidinger, three quartet concerts from his 1985 UK tour and an excellent big-band CD, **Eugene (1989)**. The jewel in the crown was this four-CD set from his regular quartet, which was released by Hat Hut Records to celebrate his first 25 years in creative music. The two studio CDs offer a broad spectrum of Braxton's quartet writing. They include four newer pieces plus several examples from the earlier *23* and *40* series of quartet compositions. *40M* and *40B* (the latter graced here with an alto solo that rides on a slipstream of happiness) both show Braxton's love for twisting, speedy bebop-derived lines, while the feinting *23M* recalls the unpredictable phrasing of Warne Marsh, one of his several saxophone heroes. Of the newer pieces, *161* stands out as a lovely example of ensemble lyricism, here gathered around the creaking sonorities of a contrabass clarinet. The use of 'pulse tracks' and 'collage forms' has been a major factor in Braxton's music since the early eighties. The two live CDs show just how much these structural innovations have changed the shape of his quartet concerts, where the main compositions are now played at the same time as various kinds of improvisation and/or extracts from other Braxton works, which the members of the quartet are free to quote from almost at will. The result is a brilliant flow of colours, dramas and flashing interplay; loving tangles that alternate with outbursts of fiery intensity or dreamy solos or droll exchanges. However complex the ground-plan, the quartet are so well attuned to it and to each other that the music remains gloriously alive as it dances through its maze of choices. **Willisau (Quartet) 1991** places the Braxton quartet in a small-group lineage which includes the Armstrong Hot Fives and The Ornette Coleman Quartet and in which jazz is recast anew and the tradition carried forward. **GL**

# Joshua Breakstone

---

New review
**9 By 3** Breakstone (g); Dennis Irwin (b); Kenny Washington (d). Contemporary Ⓜ CCD14062-2
   (52 minutes). Recorded 1990.

⑥ Ⓨ

Despite the dateline and the label name, Joshua Breakstone has little truck with the modern world. Apparently unmoved by the notion of climbing new mountains, he prefers to scale extinct volcanoes. The one in question is sixties guitar giant Grant Green and few would take issue with such an exemplary model. However, while Breakstone evidently has the commitment, the mellow tone, the right bag of notes and the general drift, he does not have Green's unerringly funky drive, flawless articulation and architectural sense of form. Furthermore, where the homogeneity of sound in the jazz guitar trio did not diminish Green's expressive potency, in Breakstone's case it serves to accentuate the sameness of this diet of bop, blues, Latin and ballad. The quality rhythm team of Washington and Irwin motor efficiently (perhaps on autopilot) and the listener tends to switch on to the same facility, although in the dancing *All Alone* there is a small fire warning. Fifties guitar fanciers may well be overjoyed at yet another example of their favourite music arriving in their local shop. They won't find anything new here, but then they probably wouldn't want to. **MG**

## The Brecker Brothers

**Collection, Volumes 1 and 2** Randy Brecker (t, flh); **Michael Brecker** (ts); **David Sanborn** (as); **Don Grolnick, Doug Riley, Mark Gray, Paul Schaeffer** (kbds); **Steve Khan, Hiram Bullock, Barry Finnerty, Bob Mann, Jeff Mironov, David Spinozza** (elg); **Will Lee, Neil Jason, Marcus Miller** (elb); **Harvey Mason, Steve Gadd, Chris Parker, Terry Bozzio, Richie Morales, Alan Schwartzberg, Steve Jordan** (d); **Ralph McDonald, Sammy Figueroa, Rafael Cruz, Manolo Badrena, Airto** (perc); **George Duke** (syn); **Victoria** (tamb); **Kash Monet** (perc, v); **Jeff Schoen, Roy Herring** (v). RCA Novus Ⓜ ND90442/83076 (two discs, oas: 71 and 69 minutes). Recorded 1975-81.

✔ ⑧ ⑧

There are surely few listeners who can recall such Brecker Brothers abominations as *Finger Lickin' Good* and *Lovely Lady* without head-shaking disbelief, but it seems that once some critics got hold of a good angle they refused to let go. As a result, the brothers' pioneering and intelligent jazz-rock has often been thrown out with the bathwater. Luckily, populist concessions are absent from this valuable retrospective on the first edition of the siblings' band (1975-81).

Although one could argue with the amount of space given to the rather pallid George Duke-produced items from the early eighties, the 22 selections in these two volumes offer a good representation of the group's strikingly individual and influential fusion of the rhythm and soul of Sly Stone, Stevie Wonder, Cream, Hendrix and others with the harmonic and improvisatory richness of post-bop jazz. Perhaps the set's strongest suit is the inclusion of the whole of the legendary 1978 album **Heavy Metal Bebop**, with its rough but detailed live renditions of such classics as *Some Skunk Funk* and *Squids*. The studio originals are here too, for comparison, and so is the splenetic *Rocks*, with some tough jockeying between Michael Brecker and David Sanborn. Digitally remastered and offered at mid price, these discs of long-unavailable material offer a long overdue opportunity for critical revision. **MG**

## Michael Brecker 1949

**New review**

**Tales from the Hudson** Brecker (ts); **Pat Metheny** (elg, gsyn); **Joey Calderazzo, McCoy Tyner** (p); **Dave Holland** (b); **Jack DeJohnette** (d). Impulse! Ⓕ IMP11912 (60 minutes). Recorded 1996.

⑧ ⑨

Though they were well received in some quarters, Brecker's first two efforts for Impulse!, **Michael Brecker** and **Don't Try This at Home**, tried to introduce some of his noted electric and vernacular voices into a serious jazz context with uneven results. No such compromise afflicts **Tales from the Hudson**, a fine collection of straight-ahead playing which draws together all the strands of Brecker's recent involvements in that idiom, both in terms of material and personnel. Just as Brecker guested on McCoy Tyner's 1995 trio record on Impulse!, so Tyner turns up here in two tracks, but the piano stool is chiefly occupied by Joey Calderazzo, a young player who has often featured in Brecker's latter-day non-electric bands. He skilfully updates and augments Tyner's rich polytonal lexicon and provides a superb composition in *Midnight Voyage*, a stealthy, bluesy swinger with a strong suggestion of backbeat which elicits an uncharacteristically relaxed, strolling solo from the leader. Pat Metheny also makes outstanding contributions throughout the record, with strong solos on guitar and one on guitar synth on his own rollicking *Song for Bilbao*. There are duller stretches, but the muscular moments and the leader's brilliant soloing tip the balance emphatically in the right direction. **MG**

## Willem Breuker 1944

**De Onderste Steen** Breuker (cl, bcl, ss, as, ts, rec, v); **Andy Altenfelder, Kees Klaver, Boy Raaymakers, Gerard V.D. Vlist** (t); **Gregg Moore** (tb); **Bernard Hunnekink** (tb, tba); **Willem de Manen** (tb, v); **Iman Soeteman, Jan Wolff** (frh); **Dil Engelhardt, Lien de Wit** (f); **Andre Goudbeek, Bob Driessen** (as); **Maarten van Norden** (ts); **Peter Barkeman** (ts, bs); **Hank de Wit** (bsn); **Bert van Dijk, Emil Keijzer, Reinbert de Leeuw** (p); **Leo Cuypers** (p, melodica); **Henk de Jonge** (p, acc, syn); **Louis Andriessen** (p, org, h); **Michel Waisvisz** (hca, syn); **Johnny Meyer** (acc); **Sytze Smit** (vn);

**Maarten van Regteren Altena**, **Arjen Gorter** (b); **Han Bennink**, **Martin van Duynhoven**, **Rod Verdurmen** (perc); **Frits Lambrechts**, **Olga Zuiderhoek** (gamelan); **Mondrian Strings**; **Ernö Ola String Quartet**; **Daniël Otten String Group**; **Amsterdam Philharmonic Orchestra / Anton Kersjes**. Entr'acte Ⓕ CD2 (69 minutes). Recorded 1972-91.

⑨ ❽

Dutchman Willem Breuker's early influences were Arnold Schoenberg, marching bands and free jazz. In 1967 he co-founded Holland's ICP (Instant Composers' Pool) with Han Bennink and Misha Mengelberg, but later found its bias towards free improvisation too restricting. In 1974 he set up his own label, BVHaast, and formed his long-standing big band, the Kollektief, whose repertoire takes in the history of jazz, plus waltzes, marches, film scores, theatre music, folk tunes, pop hits and occasional forays into the classical canon – all of which the band may play straight or tongue-in-cheek or ruthlessly satirize, their madcap air balanced by precisely drilled ensembles. This band recorded for MPS on a number of occasions, with their performance at the 1975 Donauschingen Festival recently being reissued on a mid-priced CD and well worth seeking out.

**De Onderste Steen**, a collection of mostly unreleased material from the last 20 years, makes a marvellous entrée to Breuker's eclectic creativity. It may not all be jazz – few of his records are – but two of the best tracks fit the description. *Besame*, a Breuker clarinet solo, is an hilarious fantasia that mixes free jazz squalls and duck quacks with abrupt snatches of popular classics; *Duke Edward Misère*, a sombre threnody for Ellington with growling solo trumpet, demonstrates (as does *Hawa-Hawa*) Breuker's gift for successfully integrating large string ensembles into big band jazz. Other tracks feature tangos, TV themes, gamelan, accordion, comic rhythm and blues and, in most instances, Breuker thumbing his nose at bourgeois notions of culture.          **GL**

# Dee Dee Bridgewater

1950

`New review`

**Love and Peace**  Bridgewater (v); **Stephane Belmondo** (t); **Lionel Belmondo** (ts); **Thierry Eliez**, **Horace Silver** (p); **Jimmy Smith** (org); **Hein Van De Geyn** (b); **Andre 'Dede' Caccarelli** (d). Verve Ⓕ 527 470-2 (64 minutes: DDD). Recorded 1994.

⑧ ❾

This CD is subtitled **A Tribute to Horace Silver** and, although he plays on only two numbers, his good-natured presence can be felt throughout. All the compositions are his, both words and music, and the trumpet-tenor-rhythm sound is archetypal Silver. Dee Dee Bridgewater has always been an exceptional jazz singer, one who can swing and remould melodies in the grand manner and still treat songs as songs, not raw material. In the case of Silver's tunes, they were written as jazz vehicles in the first place and therefore suit her to perfection. Quite a few of them are very old favourites indeed – *Nica's Dream*, *Tokyo Blues*, *Song for My Father* – and they take to lyrics very well. There are times, especially when Silver himself is on piano, when the band could be one of the classic Quintets; Stephane and Lionel Belmondo are both splendid soloists. In all respects, this is one of the most convincing jazz vocal records of the past few years.          **DG**

# Arthur Briggs

1899-1991

`New review`

**Hot Trumpet in Europe**  Briggs, George Hirst, Bobby Jones, Theodore Brock (t); **Jean Naudin**, **Isidore Bassart**, **Billy Burns** (tb); **Georges Jacquemont-Brown** (as, ts, cl); **Mario Scanavino** (ts, bs, cl); **Franz Feith**, **Billy Barton** (as, cl); **J. Mario** (ts, cl); **C.B. Hilliom** (bs, bss); **Charlie Vidal** (cl, bs); **Francis Giulieri** (ts, bs); **Peter Ducong** (cl, as); **Frank 'Big Boy' Goudie** (cl, ts); **Alcide Castellanos** (as); **Freddy Johnson**, **Egide Van Gils**, **Georg Haentzchel**, **Stephane Mougin** (p); **Sterling Conaway** (g); **Harold M. Kirchstein**, **Mike Danzi**, **Maceo Jefferson** (bj); **Hans Holdt** (b, bb); **Arthur Brosche** (bb); **Juan Fernandez** (b); **Chappy Orlay**, **Dick Stauff**, **Jean Taylor**, **Billy Taylor** (d); **Al Bowlly** (v). Jazz Archives Ⓕ 158472 (74 minutes). Recorded 1923-33.

⑤ ❻

This CD looks back to the time when jazz readily co-existed with popular music. The chequered career of Arthur Briggs was living proof. He was alleged to have been born in Charleston, South Carolina in 1899 but there is some doubt about this. He made his recording début with Wilbur Sweatman in 1919 and toured Europe, alongside Sydney Bechet, with the Revue Négre. He made sporadic returns to America but spent the majority of his years in Europe. Cornet legend Crickett Smith was his uncle and he played in a style that suggested the Joe Smith and Ed Allen school. He was very much an individualist, however, and his briefly explosive solo on *Then Came the Dawn* sports the Jabbo Smith brand of excitement before that worthy actually recorded. There is even a slightly Bixish lilt to his solo work on *Miss Annabelle Lee* and *Yale Blues* but his relaxed, flowing style was rarely without the odd Armstrong mannerism. Throughout his long career he was involved with dance bands, cabaret, radio shows and studio work; here he is heard behind and in support of Bowlly's singing. But whatever the musical challenge, he remained a jazz musician. *Foxy and Grapesy* is an ideal illustration of his quality ensemble lead and it also emphasizes the fact that, throughout his life, bands were frequently built around him. For his last 20 years he taught music in Paris and finally retired at the age of 84 when his sight began to fail. **BMcR**

# Ronnell Bright                                                                      1930

**Bright's Spot** Bright (p); **Leonard Gaskin** (b); **Kenny Burrell** (g). Denon/Savoy Ⓜ SV-0220 (31 minutes). Recorded 1956.

⑧ ❽

Bright worked as Sarah Vaughan's accompanist for a time during the fifties and made a handful of albums under his own name. He later played piano with the California-based Supersax unit (a group dedicated to playing transcriptions of Charlie Parker's recorded solos) and more recently has turned to acting. The stage's gain has been jazz's loss, for although not an innovator he was nevertheless a very fine pianist in the long tradition of 'utility' players, from Teddy Wilson to Hank Jones. He has a light, graceful touch and the ability to make the notes stand out with clarity. Although this was not a regular working trio the three men function so well together that the unit is as compact as almost any of the better-known established piano-guitar-bass triumvirates (such as the Clarence Profit Trio of the early forties). Three of the eight tunes are originals, the other five good-quality standards including a sensitive reading of *If I'm Lucky*. Kenny Burrell fits into the group sound very well and takes some melodic solos. The playing time is ludicrously short, only marginally justified by the price range. **AM**

# Nick Brignola                                                                      1936

**It's Time** Brignola (ss, as, ts, bs, cl, acl, bcl, f, pic); **Kenny Barron** (p); **Dave Holland** (b). Reservoir RSR Ⓕ CD123 (64 minutes). Recorded 1991.

⑥ ❽

Since leaving Berklee College of Music, Brignola has been something of a stylistic nomad. He has worked with Herb Pomeroy and Woody Herman's Big Band as well as with Latinesque Cal Tjader and Sal Salvador. He also took up the more modern challenge of Ted Curson and for some time led his own rock/jazz fusion band. He has been back in the bop world for some time now and this CD is typical of his current work. It does, however, have an important extra dimension. With overdubbing, Brignola plays all the horn parts in a one-man reed section that has tonal depth, is clearly articulated and is imbued with a naturally buoyant swing. To omit a drummer was a conscious decision by the leader, but it was a strategic omission. Barron and Holland are a powerhouse team and some of the horn parts come over as if deliberately designed to sound like a snare fill or a ride cymbal substitute. Brignola also displays his solo versatility with excellent soprano on *Walkabout*, graceful clarinet on *I Thought About You* and boppish alto on *How Tasteful of You*. Unsurprisingly, it is on his first-choice baritone that he is most prominent, his gruff, faintly edgy sound lending urgency to all he plays and, in particular, dominating *'Round Midnight* in a one-man, five-horn contrapuntal tone-poem. **BMcR**

# Alan Broadbent                                                                    1947

**Live at Maybeck Hall** Broadbent (p). Concord Jazz Ⓕ CCD4488 (57 minutes). Recorded 1991.

⑨ ❾

New Zealand-born Alan Broadbent is a consummate jazz pianist whose immense talent can perhaps be seen as a logical extension of a line tracing Art Tatum, Bud Powell, Lennie Tristano and Bill Evans. Although classically trained, Broadbent came under the sway of Bill Evans and sojourned in the US, studying at Berklee College of Music. Coming to prominence as Woody Herman's pianist/arranger in the late sixties, Broadbent settled in Los Angeles to become a top jazz studio player/writer whose continuing associations include Charlie Haden's Quartet West and singer Natalie Cole. As a leader, Broadbent's trio sessions with bassist Buster Smith and drummer Frank Gibson Jr, for example, **Another Time** (Trend), or **Everything I Love** (Discovery), are passionate, thoughtful and exquisitely wrought. But on this intimate solo set recorded live in Berkeley, California, Broadbent makes his piano a veritable orchestra without sacrificing either rhythmic momentum or shifting textural densities. While the set incorporates his virtuoso technique and sophisticated architectonics, it is Broadbent's sinewy lyricism that emerges as the ultimate authorial seal. Superb playing and sound. **CB**

# Bosse Broberg

New review

**Regni** Broberg, **Jan Allan** (t); **Peter Asplund**, **Magnus Broo**, **Thomas Driving**, **Hans Dyvik** (t, flh); **Nils Landgren** (tb); **Olle Holmquist** (tb, tba, euph); **Sven Larsson** (btb, tba, didjeridu); **Bertil Strandberg** (tb); **Krister Andersson** (as, ts, cl); **John Högman** (bs); **Dave Wilczewski** (ss, ts); **Lennart Aberg** (as, ts); **Gosta Rundqvist** (p); **Dan Berglund** (b); **Martin Lofgren** (d). Phono Suecia Ⓕ PSCD93 (64 minutes). Recorded 1995.

Here are eight compositions by trumpeter-arranger Broberg who, for 25 years, has been head of the Swedish Radio's jazz department. His handling of the ensemble is masterly and the interpretation by the orchestra is first class, for this is challenging – though logical – music. The opening track, playfully titled *Sir Gil Ahead*, is what you might expect, a tribute to Gil Evans with trumpeter Jan Allan as the featured soloist. Broberg can call on several fine soloists, men who have established their reputations with small groups, notably Krister Andersson, Lennart Aberg, John Högman and, of course, Allan. The longest (and perhaps most exciting) track is *Monkey Serenade*, which is based (if you listen closely) on the harmonies of *Gone With the Wind*. But there is a considerable amount to be enjoyed throughout the CD, such as Aberg's beautifully controlled tenor over just drums at the beginning of *Portrait of Uriah*, the whole thing acting as a prelude to some excellent muted trumpet from Broberg. The most ingenious writing, and certainly the most challenging for the trumpets, is the final *Double Steps and Track Fragments* which is a thorough reworking of Coltrane's *Giant Steps* capped by a ferocious tenor solo from Krister Andersson. **AM**

## Bob Brookmeyer
1929

**New review**
**The Dual Role of Bob Brookmeyer**  Brookmeyer (vtb, p); **Teddy Charles** (vb); **Jimmy Raney** (elg); **Teddy Kotick** (b); **Mel Lewis**, **Ed Shaughnessy** (d); **Nancy Overton** (v). Prestige Ⓜ OJCCD1729-2 (40 minutes AAD). Recorded 1954/5.

Brookmeyer fulfills the dual role of valve trombonist and pianist on these early sessions. The general tone is cool and subdued but there is plenty of swing in Brookmeyer's trombone solos. In fact, his playing at this stage was more sprightly and waggish than it later became, with a lively attack and much variety. The best number here is Gerry Mulligan's piece *Revelation*, featuring both valve trombone and piano solos. In the latter Brookmeyer reveals a crisp and fluid technique far removed from the prodding 'arranger's piano' which is all that most horn players aspire to. The other soloists of note are Jimmy Raney, whose improvised line is as pithy and concise as ever, and the almost-forgotten Teddy Charles, a more than adequate devotee of Milt Jackson. **DG**

**New review**
**Gloomy Sunday and Other Bright Moments/How to Succeed in Business Without Actually Trying**  Clark Terry, Doc Severinsen, Bernie Glow, Herb Pomeroy Joe Newman (t); **Brookmeyer** (vtb); **Willie Dennis**, **Billy Byers**, **Wayne Andre**, **Bill Elton** (tb); **Eddie Caine**, **Phil Bodner**, **Ed Wasserman**, **Phil Woods**, **Gene Quill**, **Al Cohn**, **Oliver Nelson**, **Sol Schlinger**, **Gene Allen**, **Wally Caine** (reeds); **Hank Jones** (p); **Gary McFarland**, **Eddie Costa** (vb); **Jim Hall**, **Kenny Burrell** (g); **George Duvivier**, **Joe Benjamin** (b); **Mel Lewis**, **Osie Johnson** (d). Verve Ⓜ 527 658-2 (75 minutes). Recorded 1961.

These are two separate LPs rolled onto one CD. **How to Succeed** is arranged and conducted by Gary McFarland, while the same band appears under Bob Brookmeyer's name for **Gloomy Sunday**. The music Frank Loesser composed for the show *How to Succeed* was not Broadway's greatest, and this is the only imperfection in this collection. The flaw is not enough to detract from the maximum marks for artistry, for the Bob Brookmeyer sides are so good that they defy description. The eight tracks under his name rank with the best of Ellington and Gil Evans. Four were arranged by Brookmeyer, the awesome *Gloomy Sunday* by Eddie Sauter, with others from Ralph Burns, Al Cohn and McFarland. Brookmeyer is appropriately the most potent soloist but the standard is high, with good work from Terry, Cohn, Woods, Newman, Quill and Costa. The eight McFarland sides rise triumphantly above their material to provide in *Brotherhood of Man* perhaps Clark Terry's greatest *tour de force*. Hank Jones and Kenny Burrell share the medals and all the sessions are pinned by the inspired drumming of Mel Lewis. Brookmeyer is a giant amongst jazz musicians, a triple threat as soloist, composer and arranger. McFarland might have been, too, if he hadn't died in 1971 after playing Russian roulette with drinks, one of which (the one he chose) was poisoned. It is remarkable that Verve have chosen not to issue this album in Europe. **SV**

## Cecil Brooks III
1961

**New review**
**Smokin' Jazz**  Brooks (d); **Jack Walrath** (t); **Ravi Coltrane** (ts); **Antonio Hart** (as); **Stephen Scott** (p); **Lonnie Plaxico** (b). Muse Ⓕ MCD5521 (58 minutes). Recorded 1993.

America's neo-classical jazz movement takes as its inspiration the hard-bop pioneers of the fifties and sixties. An academic background ensures accurate intonation and clean-lined improvisational methods; while musical workshops have taught communication, audience awareness and other aspects of stage craft. The pure perfectionism of such an outlook could be a formula for the vapidly unexciting and it takes CDs such as this to re-establish the more vital qualities of animation, spontaneity and Brooks's own special 'swing with simplicity'. His aggressive drumming at the heart of his sparky rhythm section guarantees the right foundation and he has taken the further precaution of blending brat-pack aspirants like Hart and Coltrane with proven stalwarts Walrath and Plaxico. The trumpeter, tightly muted and swinging on *2am in the Village*, relates his most telling story on *Everything Happens to Me*. Hart has the technique with which to boast but settles for more sober comment, while Coltrane, in a style some distance from that of his father, rides the changes with aplomb and only rarely moves into the realms of verbosity. The negative contention that such recordings do not extend jazz bounderies is true, but this is mainstream jazz, played with flair and imagination, by musicians whose creative processes demand a clear and tangible base. **BMcR**

# David 'Bubba' Brooks                                                    1923

**New review**
**The Big Sound of** Brooks (ts); **Bross Townsend** (p); **Bob Cunningham** (b); **Grady Tate** (d). Claves Jazz Ⓕ 50-1395 (55 minutes). Recorded 1995.

⑥ ❽

Brooks, brother of the Harold 'Tina' Brooks who recorded for Blue Note in the early sixties, was 72 years old when he made this, his first headlining album. A product of the Hawkins/Herschel Evans school of tenors, Evans worked in and around Baltimore in his youth, and after War service he went into the burgeoning r&b scene, playing for leaders like Sonny Thompson, Wynonie Harris and Lula Reed. By the sixties he was working with Bill Doggett, where he stayed for two decades. Brooks is still active in New York, playing now in a style shaped by that long experience in r&b and with Doggett, so that the sound and phrasing of players like Arnett Cobb and Joe Thomas, as well as Don Byas, is clearly discernible. He can use his huge sound to caress a ballad as well as Lockjaw Davis, Cobb or Ammons could, or he can set a medium tempo for the blues and make it wail. Not much else happens here, with the backing group nailed down to doing little else but back discreetly, but that's enough for the listener to get by on. **KS**

# Harold 'Tina' Brooks                                                  1932-74

**True Blue** Brooks (ts); **Freddie Hubbard** (t); **Duke Jordan** (p); **Sam Jones** (b); **Art Taylor** (d). Blue Note Ⓜ CDP8 28975-2 (50 minutes). Recorded 1960.

⑦ ❽

Brooks (his nickname 'Tina' being a corruption of the childhood soubriquet 'Tiny', and thus pronounced in the manner of McCoy Tyner's surname) had a brief recording career in the early sixties, with just one album, this one, being released during his lifetime (all of his sessions as a leader for Blue Note are now available in a Mosaic boxed set). His style is not dissimilar to Hank Mobley's, with a pleasing combination of what was then called 'soul' in jazz circles and a hard-bop harmonic tilt, but his lines are more convoluted, more wide-ranging than Mobley's. Brooks can easily deceive you into thinking not much is going on (most of the songs here are relatively pedestrian reworkings of standard changes), but if a decent degree of concentration is levelled at it, this music is rewarding for head, heart and feet. Of the others around for this session, Hubbard plays cleanly and with taste, his attractive tone and good intonation a constant pleasure, and while Jordan keeps to a supportive role, that big, woody tone and driving rhythm of Sam Jones's bass cannot be suppressed.

Music like this got rapidly lost in the quick-fire evolution of jazz at the beginning of the sixties. While not being earth-shattering, it is worth rediscovering. The CD has alternative takes of two tracks to take the playing time up to an acceptable level. **KS**

# Peter Brötzmann                                                        1941

**Machine Gun** Brötzmann (ts, bs); **Willem Breuker** (ts, bcl); **Evan Parker** (ts); **Fred Van Hove** (p); **Peter Kowald** (b); **Buschi Niebergall** (b); **Han Bennick** (d); **Sven-Ake Johansson** (d). FMP Ⓕ CD24 (62 minutes). Recorded 1968.

✔ ❽ ❹

This CD was a musical landmark. It followed John Coltrane's **Ascension**, Ornette Coleman's **Free Jazz** and Albert Ayler's **New York Eye and Ear Control** but was unlike any of them. Brötzmann, a former Dixielander, was making a statement for European Free Music that was utterly dramatic, faintly unsure of its direction and ear-shatteringly loud. Brötzmann, Parker, Van Hove, Kowald and Bennink have all played better elsewhere but the real impact here is by the entire ensemble, clamouring their collective anti-establishment discord. There are solos from a young Parker at his most discursive, Van Hove in combat with the rhythm team and Breuker using raw emotion as his calling card. It is Brötzmann, however, who has the most to say; his typical solos on both takes of *Machine Gun* are frenetic to the brink of hysteria, inchoate to order, and are delivered with a power and a bombast that suggests the demented rather than the abandoned. His seventies trio with bassist Harry Miller and drummer Louis Moholo may well have contained work by a more creative saxophonist, but Brötzmann was a harbinger of musical anger, confrontation and the consciously ugly long before the world had heard of punk. In the process, **Machine Gun** provided ground rules for much of the wildest of the music to follow. **BMcR**

---

**New review**

**No Nothing** Brötzmann (as, ts, bss, cl, bcl, tg, bph). FMP Ⓕ 32 (73 minutes). Recorded 1990.

⑧ ❽

Brötzmann's reputation for aggression and noise may have been forged in the fires of free jazz, but over the years this has proved to be only one aspect of an evolving musical aesthetic. Working with variously permutated groups, his playing has grown to embrace a private, sometimes bitter lyricism, as well a folk-like songfulness and an expansive timbral repertoire. Some of his best playing may be heard in a 1971 quartet alongside Albert Mangelsdorff, Fred Van Hove, and Han Bennink on an FMP double-CD set. Other important sessions have not yet been reissued. **No Nothing** not only displays the full range of his instrumental prowess but isolates the key components of Brötzmann's individual style – carefully modulated degrees of tonal production, shades of pitch, short choppy motifs, bursts of energy, a harsh cry of pain. Perhaps to balance the 'optimism' of his 1984 solo LP **14 Love Poems**, the titles of this programme lean towards the bleak and inhuman: *Man is to Man a Beast*, *Gloating Minotaur*, *The Stallions of Blood*, and *All Art is Quite Useless* among them. But the music is not as nihilistic as all that. The tunes featuring the Hungarian tarogato have a folkish flavour, and if his playing on bass clarinet produces his most strangulated effects, the Eb clarinet puts him in a lyrical state of mind. His characteristic growl and bite emerge on alto and tenor, along with his most effective use of overblowing and phantom pitches. There are moments of rumination and respite amid the craggy, chiselled gestures. It's impossible to say Brötzmann has mellowed, but his range of expression has certainly matured. It may not always be pleasant to listen to, but this naked, vulnerable music is impossible, on hearing, to remain unaffected by. **AL**

# Cleo Brown

1909

**New review**

**The Legendary Cleo Brown** Brown (p, v); **Perry Botkin, Mike McKendrick, Bobby Sherwood** (g); **Artie Bernstein, Leonard Bibbs, Manny Stein** (b); **Gene Krupa, Tubby Hall, Vic Berton** (d) President Ⓜ PLCD548 (46 minutes). Recorded 1935-6.

⑨ ❼

Cleo Brown played stomping piano and sang with the voice of a rather smutty-minded angel. She was five years younger than Fats Waller and took over his CBS radio show in 1935, when he left for the Coast. She was the model and inspiration for a whole school of girl singer-pianists – Rose Murphy, Hadda Brooks, Nellie Lutcher – and quite possibly influenced men like Nat King Cole, too. Ill-health was partly to blame for the later stalling of her career, but being a woman and black probably didn't help. These 17 pieces come from her Decca recordings of the mid thirties and sound remarkably modern for that time, with their smooth swing and hip understatement. It's a mystery to me how she got away with songs like *The Stuff is Here and It's Mellow* on a mainstream label, but good for her. Listening to these sweet, mischievous pieces from so long ago raises once again the reflection that the art of jazz singing has not necessarily improved in the past 60 years. **DG**

# Clifford Brown

1930-56

**The Complete Paris Sessions, Volumes 1-3** Brown (t); with the following collective personnel: **Art Farmer, Quincy Jones, Walter Williams, Fernard Verstraete, Fred Gerard** (t); **Al Hayes, Jimmy Cleveland, Bill Tamper, Benny Vasseur** (tb); **Gigi Gryce, Anthony Ortega, Clifford Solomon, Henry Bernard, Henry Jouot, Andre Dabonneville, William Boucaya** (reeds): **Henri Renaud** (p); **Jimmy Gourley** (g); **Pierre Michelot** (b); **Alan Dawson, Jean-Louis Viale, Benny Bennett** (d). Vogue Ⓜ 15461/3-2 (three discs, oas: 65, 68 and 59 minutes). Recorded 1953.

✅ ⑧ ❽

The band Lionel Hampton brought to Europe in the autumn of 1953 had a very high proportion of young, comparatively unknown musicians, men such as Quincy Jones, Art Farmer, Alan Dawson, Gigi Gryce and, of course, Clifford Brown. Thanks to the perspicacity of French pianist Henri Renaud, then acting as a consultant to the Vogue label, arrangements were hastily made to record this burgeoning talent in all manner of sessions, from large Franco-American big bands to quartets. These three CDs (available separately) comprise all the titles from the period on which Brown solos, a remarkable body of work completed in just over two weeks, all of it carried out without Hampton's knowledge or permission. A lot of the writing is by Gryce, a composer and arranger of considerable skill and originality as well as being a very capable alto soloist. But it is Brown whose rich, warm-toned trumpet attracts the ear, from the two takes of the opening big band *Brown Skins* (a twotempoed excursion over the *Cherokee* chords) on Volume 1 to the 13 titles by a quartet on Volume 3. There are fine sextet and octet pieces too, with Renaud playing his distinctive understated piano on nearly every performance on the three CDs. On the second volume you can hear Brownie actually learning a tune (*Venez Donc Chez Moi*) which appears in completed form on Volume 3. These are essential records, especially for those who recognize Brown as one of the greatest of all jazz trumpeters. **AM**

---

**New review**

**The Complete Blue Note and Pacific Jazz Recordings** Brown (t); J.J. Johnson (tb); Stu Williamson (vtb); Lou Donaldson (as); Gigi Gryce (as, f); Charlie Rouse, Zoot Sims (ts); Jimmy Heath (ts, bs); Bob Gordon (bs); Elmo Hope, John Lewis, Russ Freeman, Horace Silver (p); Percy Heath, Joe Mondragon, Curly Russell (b); Philly Joe Jones, Art Blakey, Kenny Clarke, Shelly Manne (d); Jack Montrose (arr – one session only). Blue Note/Pacific Jazz Ⓜ CDP 8 34195-2 (four discs: 245 minutes). Recorded 1953-4.

✓ ⑧ ⑧

The release of this material on CD simultaneously with Blue Note's Fats Navarro reissue affords the inevitable comparison. Their parallel premature demise (Brown at 25, Navarro at 26) renders speculation risky, but it does seem that even at 22 – his age for the first 110 minutes here – Clifford was a more thoroughgoing improviser than Fats and, in his studio work, more willing to take chances. Despite his brassy tone, Brown was more interested in light and shade (an extraordinary moment on *Bones for Jones* has him prolonging a phrase with unexpected breath and tone control, just like a great vocalist). Light and shade, and variation of note values, are also fundamental to Clifford's spacing and construction of phrases, and his use of the trumpet's extremities of range.

This set has the same contents as the deleted Mosaic five-LP set, but with new (unsigned) notes. The first disc is, with the addition of two additional takes, identical to Blue Note's **Memorial Album** (a single-CD release recommended in the last *Jazz Good CD Guide*), with the famous *Brownie Eyes* and Brown's first recording of *Cherokee*. The second disc's J.J. Johnson session and the likewise recommended **Jazz Immortal** date (with the début versions of Clifford's *Daahoud* and *Joy Spring*) lead to the jewel in the crown of the live **A Night at Birdland**, reuniting Brown with Lou Donaldson and Art Blakey plus Horace Silver. Although the trumpeter's command and poise increased during his remaining two years with Max Roach (documented by EmArcy), this could well be the best single recording that Brown was involved in. **BP**

---

**The Complete EmArcy Recordings** Brown (t); with a collective personnel including: Maynard Ferguson (t); Joe Maini, Herb Geller (as); Sonny Rollins, Walter Benton, Harold Land, Paul Quinichette (ts); Herbie Mann (f); Richie Powell, Kenny Drew, Jimmy Jones, Junior Mance (p); Keter Betts, George Morrow, Joe Benjamin, Curtis Counce (b); Max Roach, Roy Haynes (d); Dinah Washington, Sarah Vaughan (v); Quincy Jones (arr, cond). Featured albums: **Clifford Brown/Max Roach Quintet with Harold Land**; **Helen Merrill with Strings**; **Clifford Brown All-Stars / Herb Geller**; **All-Star Live Jam Session / Clark Terry**; **Clifford Brown with Strings**. EmArcy Ⓜ 838 306-2 (ten discs: 604 minutes) . Recorded 1954-6.

⑩ ❼

This set is not the perfect introduction to Clifford Brown, yet it is every bit as important a body of music as the Verve Billie Holiday collection, the RCA Jelly Roll Morton set, or the Verve Charlie Parker box. The reason is simple: Brown carved a new and brilliant trumpet style out of the old bones of bebop, created a challenging body of work in just four years of recording, and substantially influenced every jazz trumpet player to come after him. Without him, people as significant in the music as Lee Morgan, Booker Little, Freddie Hubbard, Blue Mitchell, Woody Shaw and Wynton Marsalis would never have got past first base, for it was his fallen mantle they, in turn, picked up.

The sessions so lovingly and thoughtfully packaged here span just 19 months, and come at the end of his playing life (he died in a car crash in June 1956, four months after the last session here). Undoubtedly the perfect vehicle for his artistry was the quintet he co-led with Roach, regardless of whether Land or Rollins was the tenor player. In Max Roach he had a drummer-partner with the musical intelligence to develop each rhythmic area, punctuate each newly-minted phrase, and generally shape the music with an eye to its overall form. Richie Powell (Bud's younger brother) was a prodigiously talented pianist with a real gift for accompaniment and an arranger's ear. These players, with Brown's rich, optimistic sound and fresh melodies, made a unique combination which has not suffered through endless imitation. The group in many ways was the soul of mid-fifties modern jazz.

The other sessions included here range from great fun (the two discs with Dinah Washington) to intriguing cocktails (Clifford as featured soloist with Sarah Vaughan and Helen Merrill) to timeless interpretative beauty (Clifford with strings). All of this material (*sans* alternative takes) has been available on single CDs as originally issued on vinyl, and the Vaughan and Washington dates have recently been reissued, but the **With Strings** album and all the original LP compilations of Brown-Roach are not currently available separately on CD. This boxed set is itself a limited edition, so if you are a Clifford Brown fan, get it while it lasts. Annotation and transfer standards are exemplary. **KS**

**Jazz Masters 44**  Brown (t); collective personnel, including: **Harold Land, Sonny Rollins** (ts); **Barry Galbraith** (g); **George Morrow** (b); **Max Roach** (d); **Helen Merrill** (v); unknown strings; **Neal Hefti** (cond). Verve Ⓜ 520 109-2 (64 minutes). Recorded 1954-6.

⑧ ❼

Despite his tragically short career, Brown's recorded legacy on Verve extends to ten CDs, so any single-disc is a compilation, bound to have its contentious inclusions and omissions. The previous **Compact Jazz** selection offered a generous 74 minutes of playing time yet still left off two of the trumpeter's more coruscating performances – a dashing *Cherokee* and the exquisite ballad *It Might As Well Be Spring*. This **Jazz Masters** set is a case of one step forward, two steps back: *Cherokee* and *Spring* are included but three other classic Brown tracks have disappeared (*Parisian Thoroughfare*, *Daahoud* and *I'll Remember April*) and ten minutes have been lopped from the playing time. One could also raise an eyebrow at the inclusion of Helen Merrill's breathy *What's New* while Brown's celebrated date with Sarah Vaughan is not represented. Still, we shouldn't be too churlish. Nearly everything Brown recorded is of interest and much is miraculously good. His best work came in the quintet he co-led with Max Roach and this features on eight of the disc's 12 tracks. The trumpeter excels on the slinky *Jordu* and his own, aptly-titled *Joy Spring*; his solos on these tracks are models of the melodic finesse and vivacious elegance with which, all too briefly, he held the world enthralled.                                      **GL**

**The Beginning and the End**  Brown (t) with, on two tracks (1952): **Chris Powell** (v, perc); **Vance Wilson** (as, ts); **Duke Wells** (p); **Eddie Lambert** (g); **James Johnson** (b); **Osie Johnson** (d). On remaining tracks (1956): **Ziggy Vines**, **Billy Root** (ts); **Sam Dockery** (p); **Ace Tisone** (b); **Ellis Tollin** (d). Columbia Ⓜ 477737-2 (35 minutes). Recorded 1952/6.

⑧ ❻

Brown's career on record lasted for four years and three months. Fortunately for us his unique talents were always recognized and he packed an abnormal amount of recordings into that period. His death at the age of 26 was a hammer blow to jazz. Perhaps unusually for such a virtuoso he was a simple, outgoing man, very modest and liked by all who came into contact with him. He was, after Gillespie, one of the most influential modern trumpet players and, had he not died, his life could very well have assumed Armstrong proportions. The fact that his wellspring was in the playing of Fats Navarro and Gillespie is almost irrelevant, for he moved so far away from those two.

   The first pair of tracks here, done in Chicago with Chris Powell's Blue Flames (Powell was a Jamaican singer at the bottom of the Cab Calloway league) are of little musical interest, being two sides of a calypso-styled 45rpm single with less than a minute of Brown's solo work between them. However, the substance of the album is in *Walkin'*, *Night in Tunisia* and *Donna Lee*. These come from a jam session at a musical instrument shop in Philadelphia called Music City on June 25th, 1956. Brown plays luminous trumpet solos with the local musicians. Nobody approaches his aura but the two tenor players, Billy Root and the legendary Ziggy Vines, are of interest. Brown left the club after the session to go back out on the road. A couple of hours later he and fellow-travellers, pianist Richie Powell and Powell's wife, Nancy, were killed when their car skidded off the Pennsylvania Turnpike.                         **SV**

# Donald Brown                                      1954

**Cartunes**  Brown (p); **Bill Mobley** (flh, t); **Don Braden** (f, ts); **Steve Wilson** (ss, as); **Steve Nelson** (vb); **Essiet Essiet** (b); **Carl Allen** (d); **Rudy Bird** (perc); on one track add **Harold Mabern** (v). Muse ⓕ MCD5522 (58 minutes). Recorded 1993.

⑥ ❾

Brown first came to prominence with Art Blakey and went on to give sterling service in the bands of such like-minded musicians as Freddie Hubbard, Donald Byrd and Milt Jackson. On his previous release reviewed in the last issue of this guide, I noted a tendency to cover many stylstic bases. **Cartunes** has not resolved Brown's impulses in this direction, though it reconfirms his stature as a composer and arranger, using the small and varied resources he calls upon here from track to track to deliver finely-judged and colourful readings of his own tunes, plus an engaging reworking of the standard *I Didn't Know What Time It Was* (which develops an urban soul). Brown's music is always intelligently paced and given characteristic twists, thereby giving his soloists an optimum platform upon which to improvise, while the music's air of affable expertise makes it eminently approachable. If he were able to harness his undoubted abilities to a more clear-cut keyboard personality of his own, then he may just make the popular breakthrough he has yet to achieve. Of the others here, Braden and Nelson make the most distinctive contributions as soloists, though drummer Carl Allen is also having a very good day in the studio.                 **KS**

# Jeri Brown

**Fresh Start**  Brown (v); **Cyrus Chestnut** (p); **Avery Sharpe** (b); **Wali Muhammad** (d); on one track
add **Greg Carter** (ss). Justin Time Ⓕ JUST78-2 (68 minutes). Recorded 1995.

⑦ ⑧

Although having a bass solo on each of the opening two tracks is hardly the most auspicious of
starts, this, Brown's third album for Justin Time, is confidently her best to date. Her own
performances continue to mature and become more clearly focused as she takes a firmer grip on
her own strengths, and the group she employs here gives her consistent and sympathetic support.
Brown has shed most of the archness in her stylings which occasionally gave her previous albums
a brittle and unappealing edge, and concentrated on the actual shape of her lines, both when
relaying the songsmith's original melody and when improvising her own inventions and variations.
For the most part the material is written by band members, with Greg Carter and Avery Sharpe
supplying the music to which Brown has set the lyrics. The majority of tunes are convincingly
constructed and attractive in manner and style, with a strong penchant for rhythms taken from
other popular music forms. Brown has a wide range and rich, burnished timbre, and her intonation
is unusually good (although not infallible), especially when she is improvising a line both long and
complex. Here and there the music lurches towards easy listening (*Nothing Else But You* sounds
like updated Nancy Wilson), but with the superb Cyrus Chestnut at the keyboards, there is always
something of interest to be found in the backgrounds for Brown's vocals. His work on a sprightly
version of *Bohemia After Dark* is especially noteworthy. **Fresh Start** is a satisfying step forward in
a career which promises much.                                                                           **KS**

# Lawrence Brown

**Everybody Knows Johnny Hodges/Inspired Abandon**  Brown (tb); **Hodges** (as); **Ray Nance**,
**Cat Anderson**, **Rolf Ericson**, **Herbie Jones** (t); **Buster Cooper**, **Britt Woodman** (tb); **Russell Procope**
(as, cl); **Paul Gonsalves**, **Jimmy Hamilton**, **Harold Ashby** (ts); **Harry Carney** (bs); **Jimmy Jones** (p);
**Ernie Shepard**, **Richard Davis** (b); **Grady Tate**, **Gus Johnson**, **Johnny Hodges Jr** (d). Impulse!
Ⓜ GRP1162 (69 minutes). Recorded 1964-5.

⑥ ⑧

Brown was one of the most distinctive trombone stylists ever, and his total of nearly 30 years in the
Ellington band capitalized on both his swing phrasing and his sensuous, cello-like ballad work. By
the time of the above recordings he had also shouldered the role of plunger-mute specialist created
by Joe Nanton.

The above issue combines two mid-sixties LPs, the second of which, **Inspired Abandon**, was issued
under Brown's name; the key organizational figures, though, are Hodges with his original material
and the absent Duke, whose tunes are re-created on both albums. Only four tracks employ a 15-piece
band, the rest being by either a scarcely less full 12-piece or an octet which recalls Hodges's earlier
small-group recordings (Brown was never accorded this treatment, and only ever made one other
album in his own right). The trombonist is well featured on both albums, while also heard on four
tracks (including *Main Stem*, not indicated in the otherwise comprehensive notes) is his egregious
section-mate Buster Cooper, who points up the uniqueness of Brown. Replacements in the rhythm-
section give it a rather insensitive feel, while Richard Davis's bass on the second album is mixed so
forward that the graphic equalizer is essential to enjoyment.                                           **BP**

# Marion Brown

**Afternoon of a Georgia Faun**  Brown (as, zomari, perc); **Anthony Braxton** (f, ss, as, cl, cbcl, mus,
perc); **Bennie Maupin** (af, f, ts, bcl, perc); **Chick Corea** (p, bells, gong, perc); **Jack Gregg** (b, perc);
**Andrew Cyrille**, **Larry Curtis** (perc); **William Green** (top o'lin, perc); **Billy Malone** (African d);
**Jeanne Lee** (v, perc); **Gayle Palmoré** (v, p, perc). ECM Ⓕ 527 710-2 (35 minutes). Recorded 1970.

⑦ ⑧

In the sixties Brown was inspired by Ornette Coleman, worked with Sun Ra and recorded with Archie
Shepp (**Fire Music**) and John Coltrane (**Ascension**). Yet his playing retained a light-toned melodic
fluency that perhaps points back to Johnny Hodges, with whom he played briefly in the late fifties.
Brown was also influenced by the AACM's use of 'little instruments' and he began to construct such
instruments himself. A painter and a student of African musics too, his work has been characterized
by a willingness to experiment in a variety of musical contexts. Much of Brown's best work from the
seventies and eighties is not yet on CD, but 1970's **Afternoon of a Georgia Faun** is the most striking of
his early experiments. The title track is, he says, "a tone poem" depicting nature in his home state of
Georgia. A collage of percussion, flutes, piano and voices, it conjures a forest, raindrops and sunlight
in moments of fleeting beauty and delicate interplay. Less successful is **Djinji's Corner**, which
demonstrates Brown's concept of "interchangeable discourse", a form of collective improvisation in

which the players keep swapping instruments to create a continuous, densely-textured swirl of sounds. The brief playing time and ECM's failure to reprint Brown's original LP notes are drawbacks. **GL**

# Ray Brown                                                      1926

**Some of My Best Friends Are ... the Sax Players** Brown (b) with the following collective personnel: **Benny Carter, Jesse Davis** (as); **Joe Lovano, Ralph Moore, Joshua Redman, Stanley Turrentine** (ts); **Benny Green** (p); **Gregory Hutchinson** (d). Telarc Jazz Ⓕ CD83388 (72 minutes). Recorded 1995.

⑥ ❿

This continues the format introduced on **Some of My Best Friends Are the Piano Players** (Telarc Jazz CD83373). On this occasion six saxophonists perform two numbers apiece with Ray's excellent trio and their ages range from 88 (Benny Carter) to 25 (Joshua Redman). All the chosen tunes are standards or well-known jazz works such as *Moose the Mooche* and *Crazeology*. The latter is the Benny Harris tune incorrectly credited here to Bud Freeman who wrote an entirely different tune with the same title. The playing throughout is near perfect and it is interesting to hear relative newcomer Jesse Davis, who has a warm tone on alto and a good jazz conception. The difficulty in arriving at an assessment of the music lies in the fact that it is fairly predictable and, dare one say it, a little cozy. Everyone does what you expect of them and the supporting rhythm team provides ideal support from start to finish. It would have been more successful to have featured fewer 'guests' playing more extended performances and perhaps striking sparks off each other in a few wars of attrition. As it is, this sounds almost like a continuous ballad medley. The playing time includes a total of four minutes conversation between Ray and his six guests. **AM**

# Rob Brown                                                      1962

**Youniverse** Brown (as); **Joe Morris** (g); **Whit Dickey** (d). Riti Ⓕ CD3 (65 minutes). Recorded 1992.

⑧ ❽

As an alto saxophonist coming of age in the eighties, Brown was drawn to the music of Ornette Coleman, Eric Dolphy and Roscoe Mitchell, and is now using their innovations to develop his own voice. Thinking intervallically rather than harmonically, he has the ability to sustain phrases along unusual melodic contours, and the equally unorthodox guitarist Morris is a good match, providing ambiguous chordal clusters and complementary lines that tangle with Brown's in attractively complex ways. The lack of a bass or piano opens the trio textures considerably and they reply with pungent implied harmonies and loose polyrhythms. The music flirts with freedom but maintains a firm grasp on ensemble principles, and they are not afraid of varied dynamics or delicacy (thanks largely to Whit Dickey's perceptive drumming); sheer energy seldom threatens to get the best of them. Brown supplies the finely etched tunes, although the improvisations are liable to wander far afield. Some pieces use this to their advantage: *Sonic Film*, for example, teeters on the fulcrum balancing melody and indistinct pitch, ending only after the brief, tender theme finally arrives; *Svengali* toys with a hypnotic four-note motif. Others, like the title song, reflect a more direct Ornette flavour. Either way, **Youniverse** offers an auspicious beginning for these talented, thoughtful players. **AL**

# Sandy Brown                                                    1929-75

**McJazz and Friends** Brown (cl); **Al Fairweather** (t); **Jeremy French** (tb); **Dick Heckstall-Smith** (ss); **Ian Armit, Dave Stephens, Dill Jones, Harry Smith** (p); **Diz Disley** (g, bj); **Cedric West, Bill Bramwell** (g); **Tim Mahn, Major Holley, Brian Brocklehurst, Arthur Watts** (b); **Graham Burbidge, Stan Grieg, Don Lawson, Eddie Taylor** (d). Lake Ⓕ LACD58 (72 minutes). Recorded 1956-8.

⑦ ❼

With the same dedication he has brought to the reissuing of material by Ken Colyer, Bruce Turner and Alex Welsh, Lake's Paul Adams here turns his attention to the work of Sandy Brown, an outstanding jazz talent. The core of this CD is an album, originally issued for Pye as **McJazz**, which spawned a whole series of follow-up discs. Those will wait for a subsequent issue, but the 11 additional tracks here are made up from EPs and singles recorded under Brown, Fairweather or Heckstall-Smith's leadership. Like the Lyttelton band of the period (with whom there were to be some personnel in common) Brown used a high proportion of compositions by members of the band, often incorporating African High-life and similar rhythms, giving the group an unusual texture in comparison with most British bands of the period. Pared down to a quartet with just Disley and Holley, it is clear how much rhythmic drive came from Brown and Fairweather, especially on a track like the New Orleans standard *Chinatown*. The most unusual tracks are the pairing of Brown and Heckstall-Smith, where the Mezzrow-Bechet sound is adapted to the idiosyncrasies of both reed players. Within a broadly revivalist context this is some of the most refreshing and invigorating British jazz of the fifties, presenting Brown at the high water mark of his career. **AS**

# Ted Brown
1927

**Free Wheeling** Brown (ts); **Art Pepper** (as); **Warne Marsh** (ts); **Ronnie Ball** (p); **Ben Tucker** (b); **Jeff Morton** (d). Vanguard Ⓜ 662089 (41 minutes). Recorded 1956.

⑧ ❽

Playing in Warne Marsh's shadow must have been a difficult experience for Ted Brown; after their short-lived two-tenor quintet broke up in 1957 he moved to New York, took a day job, and all but retired from the music scene. He recorded only once in the seventies (an excellent date with Lee Konitz, **Figure and Spirit**, on Progressive) and twice in the eighties (under his own name for the Dutch label Criss Cross). His playing has always been of high quality, with a similar taste for long bar-stretching lines and circuitous imagery but lacking Marsh's capricious melodic and rhythmic genius, as if never willing to take that dangerous next step. This was Brown's first session as a leader, and what distinguishes it is the company he keeps. The rhythm section, adhering closely to Tristano's principles, is a rather stodgy affair, but the horns are exhilarating. Recorded less than a month after Pepper and Marsh's underrated Contemporary date, the addition of Pepper to Brown and Marsh's working band is a welcome spice. Three of the tunes (two of Ball's and Marsh's *Long Gone*) reflect Tristano's stamp of intricacy, the others are from Tin Pan Alley. The horns' unison chorus on *Broadway* is an act of homage to Lester Young. The fact that Brown can hold his own with two of the most individualistic post-war saxophonists is a recommendation in itself. **AL**

# Tom Browne
1955

New review

**Another Shade of Browne** Browne (t); **Javon Jackson** (ts); **Larry Goldings** (p); **Ron Carter** (b); **Idris Muhammad** (d). Hip Bop Essence Ⓕ HIBD8011 (50 minutes). Recorded 1996.

⑦ ❾

Browne is ever associated in the public mind with one of the hippest singles of the late seventies, *Funkin' for Jamaica*, which for a brief few years made him a major instrumental star. By the mid eighties the steam had run out of his musical career and he literally took to the skies, qualifying as a commercial pilot. For his second go at a musical career (still balanced between scheduled flights) Browne has returned to his true musical roots, that of the hard-bop style which was in vogue as he grew up in New York City, and which he played before his popular success. This new disc is performed wholly within the genre espoused by Blakey, Silver and their acolytes, as the name-checks on the songs played reveals, with songs by Lee Morgan, Freddie Hubbard and Kenny Dorham rubbing shoulders with those of Ron Carter (the pretty, funk-based *Eighty-One* recorded by Miles when Carter was in his quintet), Booker Little and Duke Ellington. Browne has always possessed a fine, full open tone and a persuasive edge to his muted sound, and here he exploits it imaginatively and with great author-ity, much in the manner of the mature Lee Morgan. His instrument's range is as wide as it was in the early eighties, his technique outstanding and his concept considerably augmented; he is the standout soloist here, his ideas constantly commanding attention. As for the others, Jackson is competent but not as impressive as on his own records for Blue Note, Goldings relatively faceless during solos but excellent as an accompanist, while Carter and Muhammad work well together. The whole project was produced by Bob Belden, well known for similar projects on the Blue Note/EMI-Toshiba labels, and I can only add that this is at least as good as anything he has so far done for them. **KS**

# Darius Brubeck
1947

New review

**Afro Cool Concept** Brubeck (p, syn); **Victor Ntoni** (b); **Barney Rachabane** (ss, as); **Lulu Gontsana** (d). B&W Ⓕ BW024 (52 minutes). Recorded 1990.

⑦ ❽

Amid several recent Darius Brubeck releases on B&W this live set from the New Orleans Jazz and Heritage Festival stands out. Brubeck runs the jazz studies course in Durban, South Africa, and his abiding interest is the interaction of indigenous African music and jazz (more recently adding Indian music to the mix). Here he achieves his aims splendidly, with a tight rhythm section anchored by Ntoni and Gontsana, who play as one. Brubeck, for the most part on piano, plays his heart out, and a mixture of the heady excitement of playing for the festival crowd, the intoxicating atmosphere of New Orleans and the plangent, passionate alto of Rachabane makes this an unusually satisfying album. There are plenty of high points, particularly the gentle slide back into the swaying head arrangement after Brubeck's solo on his own *Daveyton Special*, and the low key swagger of the ballad *Lakutshon 'Ilanga*. Gontsana is outstanding on *Mokotedi* (a Rachabane composition), pouring cross rhythms into a mêlée that nevertheless remains simple, owing to his persistent backbeat. In contrast with some of Brubeck's more complex and ambitious projects, this gains from being straightforward and unpretentious. **AS**

# Dave Brubeck

1920

**Octet** Brubeck (p); **Dick Collins** (t); **Bill Smith** (cl); **Paul Desmond** (as); **David van Kriedt** (ts); **Bob Collins** (bs); **Jack Weeks** (b); **Cal Tjader** (d); **Jimmy Lyons** (narr). Fantasy ⑩ OJCCD0101-2 (48 minutes). Recorded c1946-50.

⑧ ❻

The Cool jazz that swept California in the fifties is traditionally heard as stemming from Miles Davis's **Birth of the Cool** sessions. The Brubeck Octet apparently anticipated Cool as well – apparently, as the dates of their recordings are uncertain. But at least some charts date from 1946. Most octet members, Brubeck included, were composer Darius Milhaud's students at Mills College near San Francisco in the mid forties. Brubeck's arrangement of *The Way You Look Tonight* employs counterpoint and the pastel harmonies West Coast Cool would soon adopt; Smith's *Ipca* could easily fit into the Miles Nonet's repertoire. Some of the music is more self-consciously arty. *How High the Moon*, performed in various jazz styles and fatuously narrated, comes off sophomoric. But on Smith's *Schizophrenic Scherzo*, no matter how formal the voice leading or forward-looking the frequent textural shifts, the phrasing swings. Even van Kriedt's *Fugue on Bop Themes*, which is not very boppish, floats on Cool's light, driving pulse. Brubeck's own playing is less heavy than it became later, though hints of his mature style are evident. Prescient though this music was, Cool musicians rarely cite them as an inspiration. Nevertheless, these sides give evidence that in jazz – as in other fields – good ideas often arise simultaneously from different quarters. **KW**

**Jazz at Oberlin** Brubeck (p); **Paul Desmond** (as); **Ron Crotty** (b); **Lloyd Davis** (d). Fantasy ⑩ CDR1VM007 (38 minutes). Recorded 1953.

⑦ ❻

This live recording was made early in the quartet's life and legend has it that it was a troubled session; Brubeck and Desmond are alleged to have quarrelled, Crotty was working out his notice and Davis had a fever. Ironically the outcome was better than might have been expected. The tightly-knit formula was breached possibly because of this atmosphere, and there is little doubt that it was the element of internal warfare that gingered up all four players. The gifted Desmond was particularly inspired and his light-toned and lilting improvisations on *These Foolish Things* and *The Way You Look Tonight* are as inventive as anything he ever did. On the latter title there are even examples of ill-formed, thin notes as excitement seems to take over. Brubeck is his normal self; controlled and exploratory at first but too often allowing his solos to run into a cliché-laden barrage with little trace of swing. Davis's brushes do their best to give shape to these tirades but, with Crotty content to stick to the script rather than direct from the back, it is difficult to avoid the odd static moment. The days of Joe Benjamin, Eugene Wright and Joe Morello were still some time off, but this CD documents the music of the quartet of the period and must always be rated amongst its very best. **BMcR**

**Dave Digs Disney** Brubeck (p); **Paul Desmond** (as); **Norman Bates** (b); **Joe Morello** (d). Columbia ⑩ 471250-2 (51 minutes). Recorded 1957.

⑧ ❻

When this album was recorded Brubeck's quartet was just reaching its ultimate maturity. It is often thought that it finally did this when bassist Eugene Wright joined, but this is to undervalue Bates, who made up what he lacked in Wright's technical abilities with good jazz sense and feeling. Brubeck depended mightily on Desmond's unflagging improvisations and beautiful tone. If ever there was authority without the big fist, then it was in the alto player's deceptively limpid-sounding solos. Here they are almost without flaw. The Disney songs (made up from *Give a Little Whistle*, *Some Day My Prince Will Come* and others of the genre) work surprisingly well and Brubeck adapts them skilfully to his rhythmic methods. Perhaps, appropriately to Disney, there is just that little touch too much polish. Brubeck's earlier **Jazz Goes to College** for the same label had, along with a couple of other concert recordings, offered more warts but also more challenges to the four players, challenges rumbustiously taken up. For those who prefer their Brubeck compiled, the luxury version (with the music, from the Fantasy, Columbia and Brubeck archives, chosen by Brubeck himself) is available on the four-CD set **Time Signatures** (Columbia 472776-2), while the economy route is available for the price of the two-CD set, **Jazz Collection** (Columbia 480463-2). **SV**

**Jazz Impressions of Eurasia** Brubeck (p); **Paul Desmond** (as); **Gene Wright** (b); **Joe Morello** (d). Columbia ⑩ 47129-2 (40 minutes). Recorded 1958.

⑧ ❼

This album was recorded and released just prior to the explosion of popularity Brubeck enjoyed through the unprecedented success of **Time Out**. Being one of Brubeck's first themed albums, the concept was still quite fresh and the group's response to the ideas mapped out by Brubeck relaxed, sensitive and imaginative (one of the pieces originally written for this album, *Blue Rondo à la Turk*, eventually turned up on **Time Out**). The pianist's own playing has his by-now familiar vices and felicities on unembarrassed display and there seems to be a greater intensity of vision and unity of purpose to many of his solos. An often busy player (although he always accompanied Desmond with wonderful empathy), he uses space and sustained tones to great dramatic effect, especially in *The Golden Horn* and *Calcutta Blues* (which anticipates Keith Jarrett's explorations of Near Eastern scales by a good 15 years). Many people would find his obsessive reiterating of a rhythmic and harmonic motif for an entire chorus in *The Golden Horn* simply too much, but it is an exciting idea, and if it had been an early Cecil Taylor solo, everyone would still be cheering. Poor old Dave just isn't hip, so he gets the sackcloth and ashes.

There are many good things to be heard here, not least the compositions themselves (Brubeck didn't only write *The Duke* and *In Your Own Sweet Way*), and for once nobody could accuse Desmond of carrying the date. **Eurasia** is a quiet triumph for Brubeck.          **KS**

---

**Time Out** Brubeck (p); **Paul Desmond** (as); **Gene Wright** (b); **Joe Morello** (d). Columbia
Ⓜ 460611-2 (39 minutes). Recorded 1959.

⑧ ❼

It was Stan Kenton who opened up the colleges and high schools as places receptive to jazz, and by the fifties Brubeck was spear-heading the follow-up wave. His working quartet with the late Paul Desmond became immensely popular as a result (and, such is the perverse way of the world, largely unpopular with 'true' jazz enthusiasts). **Time Out** was an honest attempt to explore time signatures other than 4/4 for use in jazz extemporization and, thanks to the inclusion of Desmond's tune *Take Five*, the original LP issue became one of Brubeck's biggest and most durable sellers. Musically it remains of interest, and not just for curiosity value. Signatures such as 9/8 (for *Blue Rondo à la Turk*) and 6/4 (for *Pick Up Sticks* ) are still unusual in jazz, but it must be pointed out that Brubeck cheated slightly; although theme statements observe the unexpected meters, the quartet often reverts to common time for the solo choruses. Nevertheless, **Time Out** is a praiseworthy attempt to push the boundaries of jazz outwards, and in the charming *Strange Meadow Lark* we have a most attractive Brubeck composition (to which words were subsequently added by Brubeck and Carmen McRae for the **Tonight Only!** album).          **AM**

# Bill Bruford                                                        1948

---

**Feels Good to Me** Bruford (d, perc, tuned perc); **Kenny Wheeler** (flh); **Dave Stewart** (kbds, syn, p); **Allan Holdsworth**, **John Goodsall** (elg); **Jeff Berlin** (elb); **Annette Peacock** (v). Editions EG/Virgin Japan Ⓜ VJD-28051 (48 minutes). Recorded 1977.

⑧ ⑧

Given the predominant rhythmic tilt and the background of the players, it is tempting to file this session under art-rock. By 1977 Bill Bruford had made a splash as a member of Yes and King Crimson, and he protests that he approached this as a rock session. Yet the evidence of the disc suggests that that description needs qualifying. For one thing, **Feels Good to Me** is replete with improvisations as satisfying as any in post-bop jazz. Allan Holdsworth, one of the most original but undervalued guitarists of his generation, has an extraordinary impact on several tracks, playing densely chromatic lines with an inspiration and creativity he has rarely bettered. Kenny Wheeler also has a number of lyrical solos.

The disc's not inconsiderable appeal to jazz lovers might end there, but it has other strengths. In such suite-like forms as *Adios à la Pasada* there is a level of textural, metric and dynamic contrast often absent from jazz, and themes like *Beelzebub* and *If You Can't Stand the Heat* ... have all the harmonic and rhythmic sophistication and velocity of bebop without the idiomatic clichés. The whispered passion and coiled menace of Annette Peacock's vocals and the thoroughly musical bass-playing of Jeff Berlin are no less attractive parts of the package. The analogue recording sounds as well in digital as the music does in the nineties.          **MG**

# Rainer Brüninghaus                                                 1949

---

**Continuum** Brüninghaus (p, syn); **Markus Stockhausen** (t, picc t, flh); **Fredy Studer** (d). ECM
Ⓕ 815 679-2 (45 minutes). Recorded 1983.

⑦ ❿

Brüninghaus first came to international attention on Eberhard Weber's epochal **Colours of Chloë**, and played with the bassist on and off for most of the seventies. **Continuum** remains his best and most cohesive effort to date as a leader and is a remarkable document, in its own unassuming way. The rather eccentric instrumentation has its own logic, and one is not aware, while listening, of the lack of any one sound or texture. This is largely due to Brüninghaus's rhythmic and colouristic dexterity on his various keyboards, plus his meticulous organization of both the music and the musicians within it. On *Strahlenspur*, for example, the keyboards, piccolo trumpet and drums all occupy separate registers as well as having their own clear sonic and timbral differences. This would all be to no avail if the music itself was vacuous, but this is thankfully not the case. Brüninghaus's melodies are catchy and hummable, his keyboard work wide-ranging and always exquisitely tasteful, while Stockhausen

(Karlheinz's son) has both technique to burn and a wonderful combination of rhythmic freedom and melodic expressivity, in the same way that Booker Little did in a different musical context. Some of the tracks are a little long. The recording quality is stunning.                                                    **KS**

# Jimmy Bruno

New review

**Like That** Bruno (elg); **Joey DeFrancesco** (org, t); **Craig Thomas** (b, elb); **Steve Holloway** (d). Concord Jazz Ⓕ CCD4698 (61 minutes). Recorded 1995.

⑧ ❾

In as far as he solos over swinging changes, Jimmy Bruno conforms well with the Concord house style. This approach is epitomized by the gently pulsing *There is No Greater Love* (with superb muted trumpet from DeFrancesco) and the guitar-trumpet duet of *Stars Fell on Alabama*. On the other hand he frequently pushes the modern mainstream boundaries to the limit, both by playing (like his guest Joey DeFrancesco) with great fire and technique and by edging into dark modal regions not normally associated with Concord. A good example of this is his own *Razer's Edge*, where a sinister chromatic bass riff reminiscent of *The Pink Panther Theme* is the excuse for some edgy outside playing. In fact, this well-constructed tune is like a reduction of Bruno's whole style, the tense ostinato juxtaposed and contrasted with a section of traditionally swinging functional harmony. The booklet-note is by Pat Martino, and in terms of both style and excitement, Bruno often comes close to his endorser's class, especially on the Martino dedication, *Pat's House*. He produces consistently creative, well-formed solos with a tone which is rounded and mellow without being muffled. A well-varied session of post-1960 mainstream, full of good taste and thoughtful musicality, although DeFrancesco might benefit from allowing his organ solos to breathe like those of his on trumpet.                                                                                                           **MG**

# Ray Bryant                                                                         1931

New review

**All Blues** Bryant (p); **Sam Jones** (b); **Grady Tate** (d). Pablo Ⓜ OJCCD863-2 (47 minutes). Recorded 1978.

⑧ ⑧

A blues feeling is never far away when Ray Bryant plays and his fourth album for Norman Granz's Pablo label was based around the 12-bar format. His second album for Prestige, made 20 years before this one, was based on the same premise and was equally successful but the Pablo release contains more different approaches. The opening *Stick With It* is the blues at its most attractive, in terms of melodic beauty; this is a memorable ballad by Ray worthy of a lyric. The version of *Blues Changes* is as good as they get, an exercise in how to breathe new life into the form by altering the chords in bars one to four of the chorus. Bryant also picked Miles Davis's haunting tune *All Blues*, a superficially simple theme using a repeated three-note riff played over a 3/4 rhythm, but the outcome is light years away from Bessie Smith. Ray's fleet fingering and beautifully resolved ideas give his playing a very personal sound and the work of the two other members of the trio is simply above reproach. Bryant seemed to mature early (his first records date from 1955) and over the years he has maintained a high and consistent level of creativity which must be the envy of many fellow musicians. Recommended without reservation.                                                                                              **AM**

# Willie Bryant                                                                     1908–64

**Willie Bryant and His Orchestra** Bryant (ldr, v); **Edgar Battle** (t, vtb); **Benny Carter**, **Otis Johnson**, **Taft Jordan**, **Jack Butler** (t); **George Matthews**, **Eddie Durham** (tb); **Glyn Paque** (cl, as); **Johnny Russell**, **Ben Webster** (ts); **Charles Frazier** (ts, f); **Teddy Wilson**, **Roger 'Ram' Ramirez** (p); **Arnold Adams** (g); **Ernest 'Bass' Hill** (b); **Cozy Cole** (d). Jazz Archives Ⓑ 157682 (68 minutes). Recorded 1935-6.

⑤ ❼

As a musician Bryant was a useful song and dance man. A failed trumpeter, his musical input into his own band was negligible and his sentimental speaking and vocal style had little to do with jazz. Fortunately for music, he did need to keep faith with audiences at Negro dancehalls like the Apollo. As a result, he employed a string of outstanding soloists and used skilled arrangers such as Benny Carter, Edgar Battle and Teddy Wilson to give style and credibility to his bands. These he led from 1934 to 1938 and from 1945 to 1948; the first was the better and all of the titles here are from that period. The CD offers love songs and comedy numbers as well as straight instrumentals, but more significantly it allows a good look at most of the soloists. Wilson's sparkling piano, Webster's fast maturing tenor and Paque's clarinet and alto all impress. Matthews's trombone is authoritative rather than inspired but Jordan's trumpet and Louis Armstrong-ish vocal style are well captured on *All My Life*. When Bryant quit the band-leading business he worked as a disc jockey and actor and actually served as master of ceremonies at the Apollo. It was for his first band, however, that he is best remembered.                                                                                                    **BMcR**

## Jeanie Bryson

New review
**Some Cats Know (Songs of Peggy Lee)** Bryson (v); **Ronnie Buttacavoli** (t, flh); **Paquito D'Rivera** (cl); **Red Holloway** (ts); **John Chiodini** (g); **Terry Trotter** (p); **Jim Hughart** (b); **Harold Jones** (d); **Mayra Casales** (perc). Telarc Jazz Ⓕ 83391 (59 minutes). Recorded 1995.

⑧ ❾

Both Bryson's previous Telarc albums had accompanying groups packed with stellar guests, which made them interesting but uneven. Here she sings with the same rhythm section throughout and usually one horn as a counterfoil for her voice, which continues to improve. Red Holloway has always been a master of subtle accompaniment and interplay on the tenor, and his duets with Bryson (including the Lieber/Stoller title track) are among the best moments on a remarkably consistent and entertaining album of vocal jazz. Peggy Lee's influence extends little further than the choice of repertoire, as Bryson's inflexions are increasingly her own, and her subtle, middle-range medium tempo vocals burn with a passionate intensity that even infuses the old Harlem Hamfats song *Why Don't You Do Right* with a smouldering sensuality a million miles removed from the original jumping jive of Herb Morand and Joe McCoy. On *Fever* Ronnie Buttacavoli produces one of the cameo appearances that are becoming his stock in trade, and the other duettist is Paquito D'Rivera, a veteran of Bryson's earlier albums, but here playing clarinet with great aplomb rather than his usual bustling alto. There's a slight over-dependence on slow tempos, but where Bryson opts for an up-tempo treatment, as on *'Deed I Do*, she also shows how much she's matured and developed as a singer since her Telarc début in 1993.                                                                   **AS**

## Milt Buckner                                                                              1915–77

New review
**Masterpieces** Buckner (p, org); **Jimmy Woode** (b); **Kenny Clare**, **Jo Jones** (d). MPS Ⓜ 529 094-2 (77 minutes). Recorded 1966-9.

⑥ ❽

The compass of Buckner's music is narrow but its concentrated energy is considerable. He is not given to extravagant exercises in improvisation but he has a good turn of phrase, supported by a strong rhythmic undertow that gives his playing a churning insistence. A multi-instrumentalist, he began his professional career in 1932 with the Don Cox band. He enjoyed several influential spells with Lionel Hampton, where he was a potent force in a demanding rhythm section and, from the mid fifties, he has functioned mainly as a leader of his own small groups. His main claim to fame was his 'block-chord' or 'lock-hands' (as opposed to 'lock-jaw') piano method; the playing of patterned parallel chords in a way that gave his style tremendous power and colour. This is well in evidence on this disc and compelling interpretations of *Pennies from Heaven*, *Four Brothers* and *Robbins' Nest*, in particular, are ideal illustrations. If this style is to maintain buoyancy it is important that it is supported by players sympathetic to its special needs. This it has here, with Woode carrying the bare bones of each tune superbly and both Clare and Jones keeping it clean of line and insistently swinging. It is a style that also translates comfortably to the organ and Buckner is heard to good effect on *Sunny* and *Jitterbug Waltz*.                                                                             **BMcR**

## Jane Bunnett                                                                              1955

New review
**New York Duets** Bunnett (ss, f, pan f); **Don Pullen** (p). Denon Ⓕ CAN-9008 (61 minutes). Recorded 1989.

⑦ ❼

Canadian Bunnett has been a srong presence in the music for a decade or more. She leads her own band and has spent a good deal of the present decade in Europe, playing and recording with a wide selection of modern and *avant* musicians. This duet disc is typical of the intense partnerships she is capable of forming with other musicians, where her special combination of lyricism and carefully thought-through improvisatory patterns, often with a clearly astringent edge, settles perfectly with Pullen's own strong rhythmicality and harmonic resourcefulness. Both players here have no problem crossing the Rubicon between respect for conventional forms and gleeful kicking over of the traces. They also both have in common a deep love of Latin rhythm structures and the colour which a wide variety of Latin music habitually covers. The classical music of Argentina is evoked on Bunnett's *Ginastera* just as surely as Cuban patterns are worked through on *For Merceditas*. The occasional bout of wild-eyed frenzy aside (plenty of that on Pullen's cheeky *Double Arc Jake*), most of this music is as immediate as one would like, and the two Monk reinventions, of

*Bye-Ya* and *Little Rootie Tootie* (two of his happiest themes) reveal tough and uplifting examinations. **KS**

# Dave Burrell
1940

**Plays Ellington and Monk** Burrell (p); Takashi Mizihashi (b). Denon Ⓕ DC-8550 (47 minutes). Recorded 1978.

⑧ ❽

Although an adept player of freer jazz (his past credits include stints with Archie Shepp, Pharoah Sanders, Beaver Harris and Sunny Murray) Dave Burrell here concentrates (like latter-day Shepp) on reinterpretations of the work of two masters, Duke Ellington and Thelonious Monk. 'Ellington' actually refers to material played, not necessarily composed, by the great band leader, since Burrell's set not only includes Billy Strayhorn's *Lush Life* but also his tender Johnny Hodges feature *A Flower is a Lovesome Thing*. There are stately, near-reverential treatments of *In a Sentimental Mood* and *'Round Midnight* and an occasionally over-dramatic bass feature on *Come Sunday*, where Burrell restricts himself to an accompanying role, but it is on the Monk staples *Straight, No Chaser* and *Blue Monk* that the pianist's virtuosity is truly allowed free rein. On the majority of the other tracks, which rarely stray far from the melody, the listener's chief pleasure derives from discovering just how much individual idiosyncrasy Burrell can display within the tight limits he has set for himself; in the aforementioned Monk standards, operating with fewer restrictions, he employs splashes of dissonance, hypnotic repetition, sly allusions and all-round Monkish quirkiness to superb effect, bringing great harmonic and dynamic variety to a highly accomplished session. **CP**

# Kenny Burrell
1931

**Guitar Forms** Burrell (g, elg); Gil Evans (arr, cond); Roger Kellaway (p); Ron Carter, Joe Benjamin (b); Grady Tate, Elvin Jones, Charlie Persip (d); Willie Rodriguez (cga); Johnny Coles, Louis Mucci (t); Jimmy Cleveland, Jimmy Knepper (tb); Andy Fitzgerald (f, engh); Ray Beckenstein (af, f, bcl); George Marge (engh, f); Richie Kamuca (ts, ob); Lee Konitz (as); Steve Lacy (ss); Bob Tricarico (ts, bsn, f); Ray Alonge, Julius Watkins (frh); John 'Bill' Barber (tba). Verve Ⓜ 825 576-2 (39 minutes). Recorded 1964-5.

⑥ ❽

As its title suggests, **Guitar Forms** sets out to explore the stylistic scope of the guitar. Its range of idiom actually tends to be rather selective – there is no representation for atonality or the new guitar sonorities rock had introduced by the mid sixties – and its moods tend to blandness, but within its limitations the programme is attractively varied. The brevity of many of the nine tracks – most last three or four minutes – enhances the sense of contrast between the pieces. The music falls into two broad categories, reflecting the dualism of Burrell's guitar style: on the one hand lie his small group jazz talents, showcased by the country blues of *Downstairs*, the urban blues of *Terrace Theme* and the brisk swing of *Breadwinner*, and on the other lie his classical finger-style skills, displayed in a transcription for solo guitar of part of Gershwin's Prelude No. 2 and in five concerto-like settings by Gil Evans. Evans can't resist the temptation to recall **Sketches of Spain**, and *Lotus Land* shimmers in an Iberian heat haze, but he also fleshes out a bossa nova (*Moon and Sand* ), a couple of ballads that show Burrell's pretty lyricism, and a jaunty reading of *Greensleeves*. At times the latter has the lubricity of shopping mall music, but like many other items here it also features excellent jazz. **MG**

New review
**Ellington à la Carte** Burrell (g); Rufus Reid (b). Muse Ⓕ MCD5435 (44 minutes). Recorded 1983.

⑥ ❼

The Village West was a New York club that presented small groups (mainly duos and trios) throughout the early eighties with considerable success. It was the regular home for some seasons of the Ron Carter/Jim Hall bass/guitar duo (reviewed under Carter's name), and this is a good example of another such duo, recorded *in situ* at the club. Many of Burrell's more recent recordings have veered towards the bland, notably his three-CD set for Concord (CCD4045, CCD4121 and CCD4668), where the playing is never less than exemplary, but there's a lack of vitality. He has always been highly regarded as a catalyst by his fellow musicians, however, and there's plenty of life in his appearances on other people's discs, for example his compositions and playing on Frank Morgan's **Listen to the Dawn**. This 1983 session catches Burrell adding a little competitive spice to a characteristically accomplished set under his own name, alongside jazz educator and equally well-known catalyst Rufus Reid. Clearly they are having fun, and pieces like *Mellow Tone* and Burrell's *Blues for Duke* fairly jump out of the gentle swing of the duo into something altogether more powerful. The recording doesn't flatter the tone of Reid's bass, but it does catch the unique atmosphere of a club that is sorely missed by its regular devotees for presenting exactly this kind of chamber jazz. **AS**

# Don Burrows

**The First Fifty Years** Burrows (f, alto f, cl, ss, as, bs, ldr); various groups, collective personnel
including: **Wally Norman, Ken Brentnall, James Morrison, Bob Barnard** (t); **John Bamford** (tb,
vb); **Bob McIvor** (tb); **Rolf Pommer, Frank Smith, Charlie Munro, Bernie McGann** (as); **Errol
Buddle** (f, cl, ts, ob, bn); **Graeme Lyall, Bob Bertles, Lee Hutchings, Dale Barlow** (ts); **John
Sangster** (vb, d); **Tony Ansell** (kbds); **Jack Allan, Billy Walker, Terry Wilkinson, Judy Bailey,
Roger Frampton, Julian Lee, Paul Grabowski, Kenny Powell** (p); **George Golla** (g); **Ron Hogan,
Ed Gaston, Jack Thorncroft, Craig Scott, Doug De Vries** (b); **Paul Baker** (elb); **Joe Singer, Jack
Dougan, Alan Turnbull, Laurie Thompson, David Jones** (d); **Norman Erskine** (v); on two tracks
**Luiz Bonfa** (g); on one track each **Stephane Grappelli** (vn); **Chris Hinze** (af). ABC Jazz Ⓜ 514
295-2 (five discs: 371 minutes). Recorded 1944-92.

⑥ ⑧

Burrows is to Australian jazz what Sidney Nolan was to Australian fine art: he is the one everyone
overseas has heard of. As such, he has been a worthy ambassador, for he has always combined high levels
of professionalism and technical competence with unfailing good taste. With the clarinet as his first
instrument his own stylistic predilections have never wandered very far away from updated variations on
the West Coast music of the fifties, although his first models were clarinet-wielding big band leaders such
as Goodman and Herman. Probably due to the lack of recording opportunities, the first 20 years of
Burrows's career is served by the first disc, while the following 28 are spread across discs two to five. His
achievements are many and varied, and he has dabbled in a range of ventures which have brought
different cultural colours to the basic jazz vein of his output (hence the appearance of Luiz Bonfa): he
has even moved successfully into the deploying of electronics in his music. But the byword with Burrows
is 'taste', and this is exemplified by his use, for over 30 years, of the guitarist George Golla, a massively
skilful musician whose playing makes Jim Hall's sound impassioned. Burrows's own emotional
temperature, by the evidence of this set, comes across as 'moderate', and this approach is emphasized in
his work after the mid sixties by his increasing preference for the flute. There is fire to be found in this
collection, but it usually emanates from one of the sidemen, such as James Morrison on *The Flintstones
Theme*. Which leads me to wonder rather uncharitably whether the set as a whole might have made more
of an impact if there had been less music in it, making the focus tighter. Burrows is rarely at his best in
a jam session, and some of those could have been dropped without loss.

Incidentally, the work of the mercurial John Sangster is scattered liberally through this set. Presently
not represented as a leader on CD, he is one of the most venturesome and original of all Australian
musicians of any generation, often utilizing an extensive range of ethnic musics in any given project,
and his work in the Burrows groups of the sixties is worth seeking out. **KS**

# Abraham Burton

1972

**New review**

**The Magician** Burton (as); **Marc Cary** (p); **Billy Johnson** (b); **Eric McPherson** (d). Enja
Ⓕ ENJ9037-2 (63 minutes). Recorded 1995.

⑦ ⑧

Burton was a member of Art Taylor's wailers prior to that leader's recent death, and has been leading
his current quartet for over a year now, interspersing live work involving his own band with gigs as
sideman or co-leader with a number of younger players. The line-up on this, his second album as a
leader, is identical to the first, with the difference being that this latter disc is recorded live, at
Visione's, thus capturing what Burton feels is an essential part of his music, the live, burning
experience of a quartet sweating it out over a bunch of songs in front of an involved audience and
driving each other to new levels of creativity together. Burton brings great passion and fire to his
playing, sometimes building up a head of steam worthy of Coltrane (*Little Melonae*), sometimes
packing a heavy emotional punch into an over-used standard (*I Can't Get Started*). *Melonae* gives a
hint at where some of this power may have originated, its composer Jackie McLean managing a pretty
fierce emotional commitment in much of his own sax work. The band sound is admirably integrated,
also coming across as a unit committed to working through the music together and bringing it to a
point of newness. Burton's stylistic references are to be found in the first wave of musical freedom-
seekers of the sixties rather than the second wave, his energy and work method smacking of McLean,
Coltrane and Dolphy rather than Ayler and Shepp. He turns Satie's *Gnossiene* No. 1 into an *a capella*
Coltrane soul-rinsing. He is an admirably accomplished player, and his commitment is quite clearly
total. The second album, then, continues the progress, though as ever some tracks which would have
been fine live come across as a tad long on disc. **KS**

# Gary Burton

1943

**Hello Hotel** Burton (vb, mba, org); **Steve Swallow** (b, p). ECM Ⓕ 835 586-2 (36 minutes).
Recorded 1974.

⑧ ⑨

Vibraphonist Gary Burton was a teenage prodigy who made his first recordings with country guitarist Hank Garland. After studies at the Berklee College of Music he toured with George Shearing and recorded under his own name for RCA. A two-year tenure with Stan Getz expanded his reputation, enabling him to organize the notable 1967 quartet with Larry Coryell, Steve Swallow and Bob Moses. Other Burton albums include Pat Metheny, John Scofield and Makoto Ozone. The intimate small-group settings have allowed Burton to establish a distinctively open-ended style that contrasts with the more percussive mallet pioneers Lionel Hampton and Milt Jackson; Burton has also succeeded in incorporating the seemingly contradictory influences of European classical and American country and folk music. Here, in a cosy and consistently satisfying disc from 1974 released under the co-leadership of Burton and bassist Steve Swallow, we find Burton the inspired conversationalist. We also hear him on organ and marimba and Swallow on piano, in rare but happily felicitous departures from their usual roles. Throughout, moods and textures shift with kaleidoscopic abandon. There are ethereal moments as in the poignant *Chelsea Bells* (*For Hern*) and *Impromptu*. But there are tracks like *Hello Hotel* and *Sweet Henry* where the effectively overdubbed mixes dance with dashes of rock and country. Pity about the playing time, however. **CB**

---

**New review**

**Dreams So Real** Burton (vb); **Mick Goodrick** (g); **Pat Metheny** (elg); **Steve Swall** (b); **Bob Moses** (d). ECM Ⓟ 833 329-2 (39 minutes). Recorded 1975.

⑦ ⑧

For Burton, even more than for his peers, being a Flower Power role model was a hard act to follow. His 1967 quartet with Larry Coryell had set a performance pattern and for some time he used similar groups with guitarists in support. John Scofield was one, while Goodrick and Metheny recorded with him individually and, as here, as a pair. It is certainly a formula that works: ensemble cohesion is achieved and, by choosing an entire programme by Carla Bley, it encourages a single mindedness of purpose. Unfortunately, it brings out the studied architect in Burton; it portrays a gifted vibraphonist, seemingly disinclined to dismantle pieces that have been lovingly assembled by the composer. Burton caresses where Hampton, Jackson and Hutcherson attack and, on titles like *Intermission Music* he fashions phrase shapes that favour easy contours rather than dramatic peaks. His rhythmic propulsion remains positive and, if *Vox Humana* is overtly reverential, it shows him as a romantic who can swing at even the most testing, slow tempo. This musical situation worked more potently than the Chick Corea piano/vibes duo with which he toured extensively at the time, and marginally better than his musical partnership with excellent pianist Makoto Ozone that survives into the nineties. **BMcR**

---

**New review**

**Reunion** Burton (vb, mba); **Pat Metheny** (g); **Mitchel Forman** (p, kbds); **Will Lee** (b); **Peter Erskine** (d). GRP Ⓟ 9598-2 (59 minutes). Recorded 1989.

⑦ ⑧

Although he produced some very rugged straight-ahead playing in the sixties, Burton is perhaps most often associated with the pastel-toned, folk-inflected style he developed on the ECM label in the seventies. Lyricism has been his method ever since, but on this disc, as on others he has made for Dave Grusin's easy-listening jazz label GRP (including the bluesy album, **Six Pack**, with guest B.B. King) he operates once again in a relatively forthright setting – albeit of a type which contrasts with his work with, say, Stan Getz. The swing is replaced here by firmly stated mid-tempo Latin rhythms and, on Vince Mendoza's *Will You Say You Will*, by undiluted funk. This and its companion albums may represent a compromise between Burton's aestheticism and GRP's shrewd commercialism, but the artistic balance sheet is in good order too: Burton lacks the drive that his fellow vibist Mike Mainieri would bring to such material, and often his light, gossamer tone and smooth, inside playing slip by unnoticed, but the tunes (all by others – as usual Burton shies away from writing himself) are strong, and the heavyweight company – Metheny thick-toned, Will Lee resonant and funky, and Forman tastefully orchestrating from the synth – provide a useful contrast to the leader's flyaway vibes. **MG**

# Joe Bushkin
1916

---

**The Road to Oslo and Play It Again, Joe** Bushkin (p,v, flh); on 11 tracks: **Johnny Smith** (g); **Milt Hinton** (b); **Jake Hanna** (d); **Jack Parnell Orchestra**; **Bing Crosby** (v on two tracks); on nine tracks: **Warren Vache** (t); **Al Grey**, **Dan Barrett** (tb); **Phil Bodner** (cl); **Howard Alden** (g); **Major Holley** (b); **Butch Miles** (d); string section arranged by **Glenn Osser**. DRG Ⓟ 8490 (69 minutes). Recorded 1977/86.

⑤ ⑥

The CD title uses the names of the two original LPs, one on United Artists and one on RCA Victor, which have been combined for this reissue. Bushkin's jazz credentials are impeccable; he worked with the bands of Bunny Berigan, Joe Marsala, Muggsy Spanier, Tommy Dorsey and Benny Goodman as well as leading his own trio and writing some successful songs. In 1977 he was Bing Crosby's musical director on a tour which took in Norway and Britain (and culminated in Crosby's death on a Madrid golf course); the first 11 tracks were made during the tour, topped and tailed by short appearances by Bing. Bushkin talks engagingly and plays a lot of attractive piano, albeit aiming his work at a showbiz rather than an outright jazz audience. Johnny Smith is featured on a so-called Norwegian song titled *Sunday of the Shepherdess* which turns out to be the same tune as *Ack Varmeland Du Skona*, or *Dear Old Stockholm*. The remaining tracks were made in a studio nine years later and repeat four of the songs including, inevitably, *Oh Look at Me Now*, Bushkin's perennial hit. Occasionally the brilliant keyboard work which marked his work with Berigan and Marsala (and his own Commodore sessions) bursts through and even less occasionally the small band is featured (Vaché on *What's New?*, Bodner on *It Had to Be You*, and so on) but much of the music is pleasant rather than profound. **AM**

# John Butcher

New review

**Concert Moves** Butcher (ss, ts); **John Russell** (g); **Phil Durrant** (vn). Random Acoustics Ⓕ 011 (54 minutes). Recorded 1991-2.

⑧ ❽

It is quite an achievement to carve out a niche in the intimidating mountain of post-Coltrane saxophonists, but John Butcher has succeeded by ignoring prevalent trends. One of an impressive second generation of British free improvisers, Butcher has devised a palette of unorthodox sonorities and a personal approach to 'narrative' (melodic) playing. Subtle and subdued, this involves a host of unpitched sounds, microtones and rarefied effects which emphasize texture over harmony within the music's formal design. In fact, this trio – a spin-off from the quintet News From the Shed – focuses on texture and timbre as primary musical impulses, achieving through this a radical coherency. Theirs is a devoutly ensemble approach, based on acute dynamics, quick response, and locating the overall shape of the musical form by exposing its smallest details. (Many years of experience in John Stevens's Spontaneous Music Ensemble no doubt attuned Butcher to this sensibility.) Typically employing prickly guitar, violin harmonics, and wispy horn motifs, this is intricate, tightly improvised music built upon complementary or contrasting gestures and sounds in a rhythmically ambiguous environment. The results are frequently breathtaking. **AL**

# Jaki Byard

1922

**Phantasies II** Byard (p, ldr); **Roger Parrett, Graham Haynes, Jim White** (t); **Carl Rienlieb, Steve Swell, Rick Davies, Steve Calial** (tb); **Bob Torrence, Susan Terry** (as); **Jed Levy, Bruce Revels** (ts); **Don Slatoff** (bs); **Peter Leitch** (g); **Ralph Hamperian** (b); **Richard Allen** (d); **Vincent Lewis, Diane Byard** (v). Soul Note Ⓕ 121175-2 (42 minutes). Recorded 1988.

⑥ ❻

Byard has been a respected figure in the music world since at least the early fifties, when he was a Boston legend and, due at least in part to his reluctance to hit the road, something of a well-kept Boston secret as far as the wider jazz public went. His move to New York and subsequent appearance on a string of albums on the Prestige label in the early sixties established an international profile which his role as a sideman with Charles Mingus during the early part of that decade rapidly developed. His own albums were somewhat hit-and-miss affairs, although none is without interest or musical ambitions, and some – notably **Out Front** (Prestige, 1963, recently reissued on CD) and the 1968 **Jaki Byard Experience** with Roland Kirk (Prestige LP – nla) – are not far short of classic status. Yet his best playing was invariably found on other people's albums, and for a long time he failed to record under his own name. Soul Note have made strenuous efforts to put that right over the past decade, and this quite typical Byard album reveals the breadth of his ambitions and the problems inherent in realizing them.

One of his most basic quandaries is that he is both one of the world's great eclectics and a musician of genuine originality. Hence, many of his compositions flick from a pastiche of an earlier style to a profound reflection from deep within his soul. On this album his arrangements of other people's works (as well as his approach to his own) show a driving need to switch from style to style, often more than once within the same piece. His band respond admirably to his direction, and much passionate music-making is the result. Countless references to previous jazz landmarks are also there to be uncovered by the diligent, although at times one longs for an undiluted shot of pure Byard. But then perhaps eclecticism is the core of his achievement, making the tribute to B.B. King, electric guitar blues and all, as much pure Byard as is his own *Concerto Grosso* or the decidedly off-centre version of Sondheim's *Send in the Clowns*, with off-pitch vocals to boot. **KS**

# Don Byas

1910-72

New review

**Savoy Jam Party** Byas (ts); **Charlie Shavers, Emmett Berry, Benny Harris** (t); **Rudy Williams** (as); **Clyde Hart, Dave Rivera, Jimmy Jones, Teddy Brannon, Sanford Gold** (p); **Slam Stewart, Milt**

**Hinton**, **John Levy**, **Frank Skeete**, **Leonard Gaskin** (b); **Jack 'The Bear' Parker**, **J.C. Heard**, **Fred Radcliffe**, **Max Roach** (d). Savoy Ⓜ SV0268 (74 minutes). Recorded 1944-6.

⑧ ❼

Under-appreciated today, Byas was by the mid forties one of the four leading tenor players, along with Hawkins, Young and Ben Webster, and for a brief moment the most popular of the four. His achievement was to extend Hawkins's harmonic explorations, and to do so with an improbably chunky Chu Berry-like tone. The impact of his early records after leaving Count Basie was as dramatic as those of Parker, whom he had probably influenced as he certainly did Coltrane. Unlike some of the scandalously short-playing transfers from LP in Denon's Savoy series, the present release contains most of what was a mid seventies double-LP set of the same title, and its 25 tracks give a good idea of the tenorman's commanding presence at this period.

Heard mainly in quartets or quintets, Byas is the centre of attention at all times. Classic forties repertoire such as *How High the Moon*, *Cherokee* or the *Stompin' at the Savoy*-based line here called *Byas-a-Drink* find the leader sounding simultaneously terse and prolix, in a way that carries over to his ballads such as *Candy* and *Old Folks*. Whoever pruned the track-listing of the LP set dispensed with a couple of alternate takes, but made a considerable error in dropping the egregious version of *Danny Boy* (originally issued as *London-Donnie*), for which Byas is still remembered. However, reproduction is markedly improved over the previous issue. **BP**

# Charlie Byrd

1925

**Moments Like This** Byrd (g); **Ken Peplowski** (cl); **Bill Douglass** (b); **Chuck Redd** (d, vb). Concord Jazz Ⓔ CCD4627 (61 minutes). Recorded 1994.

⑧ ❽

Byrd has never been rated in most critical circles as a profound jazzman, but his finger-style work has appealed to many. He shot to international fame with the first of Stan Getz's bossa nova albums but later LPs in the genre showed that his playing lacked the easy fluidity of the true Brazilian guitarists. Nevertheless his semi-jazz approach is a valid part of our music and this entirely pleasant album has many virtues, commencing with a good choice of material which takes in *Wang Wang Blues*, *Rose of the Rio Grande* and numbers by Ellington and Bechet. A considerable asset is the fine, warm-toned clarinet playing of Peplowski, who goes from strength to strength in all manner of contexts; he is certainly a more individual soloist on clarinet than on tenor. Chuck Redd makes his recording début as a vibraphonist on six tracks and there is an air of quiet professionalism about the whole disc. Byrd, it would seem, is at his most impressive when the jazz is not too demanding. **AM**

# Donald Byrd

1932

**Free Form** Byrd (t); **Wayne Shorter** (ts); **Herbie Hancock** (p); **Butch Warren** (b); **Billy Higgins** (d). Blue Note Ⓜ CDP7 84118-2 (38 minutes). Recorded 1961.

⑧ ❼

Byrd's career has been long and varied, and a goodly proportion of its latter-day output falls outside the scope of this guide, being buried deep in the musical vocabulary of seventies funk and soul. No such demarcation disputes here: this is classic Blue Note jazz of the period and an unusually thoughtful album at that. Byrd, one of the most well-rounded players on the New York scene at the time (he later gained a doctorate of music and ran his own music courses), demonstrates a keen interest in a variety of musical styles and disciplines here. He ranges from the Baptist beat of the opener, *Pentacostal Feelin'*, to the delicacy of pianist Hancock's ballad *Night Flower* and the disciplined, stimulating experimentation of the title track, where the basic framework for the 11-minute piece is a tone-row which can be – and is – interpreted in any number of ways. Shorter and Hancock, impressive elsewhere on the date, excel in such an environment and contribute some of their strongest playing. Byrd shows himself willing to take chances, bending notes and accelerating in and out of rhythm at will, although his musical language remains firmly based in Clifford Brown. A stimulating and intelligently-prepared album, with good sound for the period. **KS**

New review
**Street Lady** Byrd (t, flh, v); **Roger Glenn** (f); **Fonce Mizell** (clav, t); **Jerry Peters** (p, elp); **Fred Perren** (syn); **Chuck Raney** (elb); **Harvey Mason** (d); **Stephane Spruill**, **King Ericson** (perc). Blue Note Ⓜ CDP8 53923-2 (42 minutes). Recorded 1973.

⑦ ❽

Few jazz writers derive much pleasure from Byrd's seventies electric funk forays, but it is undeniable that Byrd and the group he fathered, the Blackbyrds, had an uncommonly large influence on the instrumental music of the time. Whether that influence was for the good or not is neither here nor there (and it's worth remembering Earth, Wind and Fire before judgement is passed), for Byrd managed a number of good-quality funk-jazz records as well as more than a few musical duds before he returned to acoustic jazz in the late eighties. **Street Lady**, part of the largely inglorious reissue, Blue Note **Rare Groove** programme (who *needs* all those third-rate latter-day organists and souled-out jazzers when the good stuff is still relatively easy to find?), is one of his better crossover efforts, with sprightly arrangements, effective soloing (mostly from the leader himself) and a decided lack of contemporary clichés which usually date such efforts quicker than a loaf of sliced white. Byrd's tone is intact and his ability to carry a melody unimpaired, so even the most recalcitrant of purists will find things to admire here. In these days of retro everything, it's reassuring to remember that not even the hard boppers themselves played hard bop for their entire careers. **SV**

## Donna Byrne

New review

**It Was Me** Byrne (v); Herb Pomeroy (t, flh); Ken Peplowski (ts, cl); Bill Cunliffe (p); Gary Sargent (g); Marshall Wood (b); Artie Cabral (d). Daring Records Ⓕ CD3022 (51 minutes). Recorded 1995

⑧ ➑

An informed glance at the personnel will tell you that this is a Boston affair, and Boston is a focal point for that school of musicians known as the 'New England Songhounds'. This is where jazz and classic American song are cultivated side by side, with serious regard to artistry and expression. Songhounds set high standards and it is not easy for a singer to meet with their approval. Tony Bennett does, and Carol Sloane – and so does Donna Byrne. Her first CD, **Let's Face the Music and Dance** (Daring, 1992), came as a delightful surprise to everyone outside her immediate circle and this new release confirms the fact that she is superb – not only as a straight interpreter of good songs, but as a scat singer, too. Listen to her adaptation of Lester Young's *Lady Be Good* solo for proof of that. And when she swings a melody, she does it with the minimum of fuss, as witness this version of *Lullaby of the Leaves*. Peplowski and Pomeroy play beautifully and the rhythm section is just fine. **DG**

## Don Byron

**Tuskegee Experiments** Byron (cl, bcl); Edsel Gomez, Joe Berkovitz (p); Richie Schwanz (m); Greta Buck (vn); Bill Frisell (g); Lonnie Plaxico, Reggie Workman (b); Kenny Davis (elb); Ralph Peterson Jr, Phereoan akLaff (d); Sadiq (poet). Elektra Nonesuch Ⓕ 979280-2 (62 minutes). Recorded 1990-01.

✅ ⑧ ➑

Initially marked out for his classical background, Byron paints on a very broad canvas. His New York upbringing avails him many choices and tapping into the town's Klezmer tradition was only one. On this CD, that aspect is clearly evident and the way that it interacts with Frisell's raw freedoms and with inescapable jazz undertones completes the package. Jewish romanticism is most evident when percussionists are not involved, but when Peterson and akLaff appear to discourage flowing rhetoric, Byron responds to their goading by applying his own rules. He challenges each tune on his own terms, uses slurs and note distortions and juggles the points of emphasis. The spirit of the material affects him in different ways; his irreverent treatment of *Main Stem* cuts a jagged swathe across Ellington's flowing jam session sward while his dedication to Diego Rivera suggests an affinity with the artist's powerful style. Fortunately, Byron seems as much at home with the pathos of Buck's violin as he is with Frisell's carousing guitar and subsequent albums such as **Music for Six Musicians** (Nonesuch 59354-2) point to **Tuskegee** as providing a working pattern for development. If in the process jazz becomes a more potent factor, this musical maverick seems less than prepared to discount the kosher element entirely. **BMcR**

## George Cables

1944

New review

**Quiet Fire** Cables (p); Ron McClure (b); Billy Hart (d). SteepleChase Ⓕ SCCD31357 (58 minutes). Recorded 1994.

⑧ ➑

Much of Cables's work in the nineties has found him as a leader and albums such as the 1991 **Night and Day** (DIW) distanced him to some extent from the compliant skills that had made him a stalwart sideman with leaders such as Art Blakey, Sonny Rollins, Cannonball Adderley, Joe Henderson and Dexter Gordon. Through such sessions he has become established as a front man in his own right and, most especially, as a controller of the piano trio. This CD endorses Cables as a master of his own destiny and shows his unerring ability either to select or to write material ideal for himself, as well as for the musicians with whom he chooses to record.

Initially influenced by Thelonious Monk and Herbie Hancock, it is Monk who is invoked on *Uncle Bubba*. The rippling title track shows the natural affiliation between Cables's writing and his improvising *My Ship* has its challenging changes fully respected, while *You Stepped Out of a Dream* takes him on a stylistic trip from the Caribbean to 52nd Street. This performance in particular suggests how he views each harmonic structure. When soloing, his story-telling right hand darts above and between each imaginatively-built new outline and is never a separate entity. In the process it provides its own logic, although he does hang his most extravagant extempore comments on the modal frame provided by Freddie Hubbard's *The Decrepit Fox*. In all of his guises Cables is sympathetically and dramatically supported by McClure and Hart, confirming the music-making here as a genuine two-way process. **BMcR**

## Uri Caine

New review

**Toys** Caine (p); **Don Byron** (bcl); **Gary Thomas** (f, ts); **Dave Douglas** (t); **Joshua Roseman** (tb); **Dave Holland** (b); **Ralph Peterson** (d); **Don Alias** (pc). JMT Ⓔ 514 022-2 (70 minutes). Recorded 1995.

⑦ ❾

In these retrospective days, another record grounded in the hard bop and avant-garde of the sixties might seem like the last thing we need, but Caine is not another of today's earnest re-creators. It has to be admitted that his mastery of the sixties piano lexicon, especially of McCoy Tyner and Chick Corea (witness his prodigious soloing on *Woodpecker*), is conventionally exhilarating, but beyond that he finds fresh and engaging perspectives on the old styles, as evidenced by the spicily skewed salsa of the opening track. Even when his band follows the letter of the originals it covers, there's always the feeling that some new twist lies around the corner. As the title suggests, *Toys* tips its hat to Herbie Hancock, but there is no slavish imitation – four of the numbers are Hancock's but in *Dolphin Dance* and *Cantaloupe Island* the interpretations are extremely liberal. Caine is aided by an excellent crew, including the fantastic Gary Thomas, but in keeping with his creative approach none of them is over-exposed; although several soloists queue up for their say on *Toys,* the group's on-the-hoof arranging and tasteful sense of dynamics rules out the sense of anything as banal as a string of solos. **MG**

## Joey Calderazzo                                              1965

New review

**Secrets** Calderazzo (p); **James Genus** (b); **Clarence Penn** (d). A five-piece horn section and **Fareed Haque** (g) appear on six tracks; **Tomas Ulrich** (vc) arranged by **Bob Belden**. AudioQuest Ⓔ AQCD1036 (47 minutes). Recorded 1995.

⑦ ❿

This is a very grown-up album indeed, the young pianist's nineties equivalent to Herbie Hancock's **Speak Like a Child**. Calderazzo makes the comparison himself when quoted in the detailed booklet-notes. On previous albums for Blue Note, Calderazzo has been content to burn up the keyboard at a frightening speed, spurring various small groups playing with him to white-hot improvisation generally cast in the style of Tyner and Hancock. This date stretches him a good deal farther because Belden has been brought in to write some intriguing arrangements to Calderazzo originals (both ballads and medium-tempos) as well as a melancholy Vince Mendoza piece called *Scriabin*, which carries distinct echoes of the Russian composer, and a version of Miles Davis's *Filles de Kilimanjaro* which Calderazzo himself declares the album's centrepiece. The pianist responds with his most varied and intriguing playing so far on record, allowing himself the luxury of space and time in theme statements where he would usually rush them out of the way to get to the solos. Belden has deliberately echoed the arrangements for Hancock's classic, although he has used a larger small ensemble to do it. The whole thing is finely judged and, though it may well be accused of looking backwards rather than forwards, there is much to admire here. **KS**

## Cab Calloway                                              1907-94

New review

**The King Of Hi-De-Ho!** Calloway (v) with a collective personnel including: **Lammar Wright, Shad Collins, Doc Cheatham, Dizzy Gillespie** (t); **Claude Jones, Keg Johnson, Quentin Jackson** (tb); **Tyree Glenn** (tb, vib); **Eddie Barefield, Walter Thomas, Ben Webster, Chu Berry, Jerry Blake, Hilton Jefferson** (reeds); **Benny Payne** (p); **Danny Barker** (g); **Al Morgan, Milt Hinton** (b); **Leroy Maxey, Cozy Cole** (d). Conifer Ⓜ CDHD260 (77 minutes). Recorded 1931-41.

⑧ ❽

Since Calloway's death there have been several releases of his recordings from what was probably his most important period, so in a fairly competitive field this is highly recommended. It comprises 27 tracks and only duplicates two on Topaz TPZ1010. The remastering was done by Ted Kendal and gives the music a brilliance, allowing us to savour the splendid ensemble work. Not all of Calloway's musicians were happy with the leader's cavorting and nonsense vocals but there was no denying the power of the band or, for that matter, its solo strengths. The final track here is Hilton Jefferson's gorgeous feature *Willow Weep for Me* and there are also Gillespie solos of note. Dizzy composed and arranged *Pickin' the Cabbage* (March, 1940) and is also to be heard on Benny Carter's arrangement of the Leonard Feather tune *Calling All Bars*. Good insert-notes and complete personnels and dates are further inducements to purchase this bargain-price example of Calloway in his prime. **AM**

# Gary Campbell

New review
**Intersection**  Campbell (ts, ss); **Mike Orta** (p); **Nicky Orta** (elb); **Ignacio Beroa** (d); **Rafael Solano** (perc). Milestone Ⓕ CDMCD9236-2 (42 minutes). Recorded 1993.

⑦ ❾

A saxophonist with a clear, open style and an original, highly melodic turn of phrase, Campbell has evolved a synthesis of contemporary jazz and Latin-American music which has a genuinely fresh sound. Instead of the customary Coltrane-and-water over a driving but inflexible Latin beat, his method is to loosen the improvised line by basing it upon a two-beat rather than a four-beat pulse. At the same time the rhythm section works more in the jazz manner, with shifting accents, punctuations and comments. The result is both enjoyable and stimulating.                                    **DG**

# Roy Campbell                                                                      1952

**New Kingdom**  Campbell (t); **Ricardo Strobert** (as, f); **Zane Massey** (ts); **Bryan Carrott** (vb); **William Parker** (b); **Zen Matsuura** (d). Delmark Ⓕ DE456 (65 minutes). Recorded 1991.

⑤ ❻

Campbell was taught by Lee Morgan and shows many elements of Morgan's exciting yet audience-oriented style. The timbre of this group is unusual, with vibes taking the conventional piano or guitar role of supplying chords, and, through Carrott's comping on tracks like *Thanks to the Creator,* bringing a light airy quality to the sound. Where Campbell plays open horn, he has a full tone and a strong personal presence. On three tracks he works with just bass and drums, his delicate muted playing on bassist Parker's composition *Angel* showing an introspective side to his character, nodding in the direction of Miles Davis, but clearly showing Campbell's originality. Strobert, who plays impassioned alto, particularly on *Thanks to the Creator*, is a schoolteacher. His playing is more alert and arresting than Massey's, although Massey contributes a solo feature, *Peace,* with just Parker and Matsuura's feathery brushwork that almost steals the album.                     **AS**

# Conte Candoli                                                                    1927

**Lighthouse All-Stars: Jazz Invention**  Candoli (t); **Bob Enevoldsen** (tb); **Bob Cooper** (ts); **Bud Shank** (as); **Claude Williamson** (p); **Monty Budwig** (b); **John Guerin** (d). Contemporary Ⓜ CCD14051-2 (53 minutes). Recorded 1989.

⑦ ❽

Candoli's credentials go back through the big bands of Woody Herman, Stan Kenton, Terry Gibbs and Charlie Barnet. He was in Doc Severinsen's 'Tonight Show' band and has worked continually in film and television studios. As such a record suggests, he is an extremely versatile trumpeter and this CD places him amongst his West Coast peers. Musical director Cooper provides loose arrangements that allow players to relax into their solos rather than compete with each other and, although the concept of 'cool' oversees this live concert, there is an element of latent passion lurking beneath the surface. The record is published under the collective title of the Lighthouse All-Stars, but Candoli in particular is the man to add the cutting edge, which he does most effectively through his adroitly re-worked *Topsy* solo. This, therefore, is an appropriate disc to select as a showcase for his talents. *Woody'n You* is very much his tribute to his mentor Dizzy Gillespie and he ensures that there is no showboating. He does take *Broadway* somewhat by storm but he employs his own special brand of good judgement to make the hackneyed *Bernie's Tune* a model of creative discretion. 'Good taste' when applied to Candoli's trumpet is never a euphemism for mediocrity.                **BMcR**

# Frankie Capp                                                                     1931

**Juggernaut**  Capp (d, ldr); **Bill Berry, Gary Grant, Blue Mitchell, Bobby Shew** (t); **Buster Cooper, Alan Caplan, Britt Woodman** (tb); **Marshall Royal, Bill Green** (as); **Richie Kamuca, Plas Johnson** (ts); **Quinn Davis** (bs); **Nat Pierce** (p); **Chuck Berghofer** (b); **Al Hendrickson** (g). Concord Jazz Ⓕ CCD4040 (50 minutes). Recorded 1977.

⑧ ❽

Motivated by the example of the Ellington-inspired Bill Berry's L.A. Big Band, Pierce and Capp drew on the same pool of Hollywood studio musicians to create a band which was designed to follow the Basie philosophy. Juggernaut immediately became better than the contemporary Basie band and, despite the fact that it was not recorded as often as it should have been, it put considerable heart into the West Coast jazz scene. Most of the library was chosen and arranged by pianist Nat Pierce, a man who literally lived for jazz. Enlivened even more by the skilful drumming of Capp and by a team of soloists who, apart from being as strong as any which could have been put together anywhere, simply wanted to play jazz, it is not surprising that Juggernaut became one of the most consistently invigorating big bands of the seventies and eighties. The album bubbles over with exuberant solos from Buster Cooper, Blue Mitchell and, notably on Pierce's arrangement of *Dickie's Dream* where they follow each other one by one, soloists from all the sections. Pierce's brilliant ability to mirror the heart and soul of any other pianist – in this case Basie – is the catalyst to a live album which captures the concert presence to perfection. **SV**

## Una Mae Carlisle
1915-56

**1944** Carlisle (p, v); with a collective personnel including: **Ray Nance** (t); **Budd Johnson** (ts); **Snags Allen** (g); **Basie Robinson** (b) **Shadow Wilson** (d) (on eight tracks); **Billy Butterfield** (t); **Vernon Brown** (tb); **Bill Stegmeyer** (cl); **Bob Haggart** (b); **George Wettling** (d) (on four tracks); **Doc Cheatham** (t); **Trummy Young** (tb); **Walter Thomas** (ts); **Cedric Hardwick** (b); **Wallace Bishop** (d) (on three tracks). Two tracks have **Maxine Sullivan** (v) with three violinists; **Ken Billings** (p); **Everett Barksdale** (g); **Cedric Wallace** (b). Final four tracks are **Savannah Churchill** (v); **Russ Case** (t); **Will Bradley** (tb); **Jimmy Lytell** (cl); **Frank Signorelli** (p); **Carmen Mastren** (g); **Haig Stevens** (b); **Chauncey Morehouse** (d). Harlequin Ⓕ HQCD19 (61 minutes). Recorded 1942-4.

⑦ ❼

Carlisle's early career thrived under the auspices of Fats Waller, and it was Waller who, when she returned from an ill-fated stay in Europe, relaunched her Stateside career by duetting with her on his hit *I Can't Give You Anything But Love*. After that, she was ready to go out as a solo act again, and the forties saw a string of respectable hits on the Beacon label, allied with her own shows on radio and TV, and regular appearances in films. By the mid fifties persistent ill-health led to retirement, and soon after came her premature death.

Carlisle's vocal style owes less to Billie Holiday than often thought; her delivery is measured, her voice lighter in timbre, while her characteristic sound is one with a smile on its face. Today her most famous session is one from 1941 with Lester Young guesting, but the standard of material on that date is very poor indeed, and the songs chosen for her work with Beacon in 1944 give her infinitely more opportunities to shine. Naturally, a more balanced picture of her talent emerges, especially her ability to give apt delivery to any half-decent set of lyrics.

The two Sullivan tracks would be unbearable were it not for the singer's sweet voice. The songs are as bad as the string arrangements. Savannah Churchill is a different matter. Her Dixieland backing is appropriate to her half-jazz, half-showbiz delivery. Her discs were big sellers in their day, with the mildly risqué *Fat Meat* (the last track here) selling over 200,000, and while the material sometimes borders on corn, the band swings well enough, in its own clumsy sort of way. **KS**

## Janusz Carmello
1994

**Portrait** Carmello (pkt t); **Keith Hutton** (tb); **Jimmy Woods** (as); **Phil Bancroft** (ts); **Gordon Cruickshank** (bs); **Brian Kellock** (p); **John Hartley** (b); **Tony McLennan** (d); **Jimmy Deuchar** (arr). Hep Ⓕ CD2044 (54 minutes). Recorded 1989.

⑥ ❻

The full personnel only appears on one track, Jimmy Deuchar's version of the Ellington/Strayhorn *Daydream*. For the rest of the album, Carmello displays his very considerable talent as a pocket trumpet soloist, either with rhythm or just with Brian Kellock's eloquent piano.

When Carmello first arrived in Britain in 1973, with a reputation acquired in his native Poland and previous port-of-call – Italy, he struggled hard for every gig he could find, playing in pick-up bands in pubs one minute and opening supermarkets with New Orleans marching bands the next. As he garnered experience (and friends) everywhere he went, he grew in stature as a musician. This is a joyous showcase for his mature style. His affinity for (and technical mastery of) Clifford Brown's style shines through on *Tiny Capers* and *Joy Spring*. He includes two of his own compositions but is at his most original when deconstructing standards from the inside. No one could find a hint of a tired trad warhorse in his *Saints* and his delicate exploration of Neal Hefti's *Lil' Darlin'* evokes the ghost of Basie's whole band in its carefully-chosen open spaces. **AS**

## Mike Carr
1937

New review
**Bebop from the East Coast 1960/1962** Carr (p, org) with the following collective personnel: **Ian Carr** (t); **Gary Cox** (ts); **John McLaughlin** (g); **John O'Carroll**, **Spike Heatley**, **Midge Pike**, **Malcolm Cecil** (b); **Ronnie Stephenson**, **Johnny Butts**, **Jackie Dougan** (d). Birdland Ⓕ MC596 (61 minutes). Recorded 1961/7.

⑨ ❼

There may still be some who believe that the only significant British jazz events take place in London. This welcome reissue on CD of a superb LP (extra tracks have been added for the new release) gives the lie to such a mistaken belief. A dozen of the 14 tracks are by a quintet with Mike Carr on piano, his brother Ian on trumpet, tenor saxist Gary Cox and bass and drums producing marvellous music very much in the Horace Silver or Roach-Brown style. All of this came into being, and flourished, in Newcastle in the early sixties and I know there was no better band of this type anywhere in Britain at the time. The quintet's success was its eventual undoing: Ian joined the Don Rendell group, Cox signed up with the Northern Dance Orchestra, drummer Ronnie Stephenson came to London to join the Dankworth band and Mike Carr became one of the best jazz organists. But this is not simply a record of nostalgia; the music retains its vitality for it was produced by young men who had total commitment to their art and the CD deserves a place alongside the Silver Quintet output of the day. Some of the tracks have been taken from rare demo discs and one, *Bell's Blues*, features guitarist McLaughlin and Cox after Ian Carr had left the band, but most of the music is by the EmCee Five, a 'territory' band of real and lasting quality.                                                                    **AM**

# Baikida Carroll                                                                    1947

New review
**Door of the Cage**  Carroll (t, flh); **Erica Lindsay** (ts); **Steve Adegoke Colson** (p); **Santi Debriano**
   (b); **Pheeroan akLaff** (d). Soul Note Ⓕ 121123-2 (62 minutes). Recorded 1994.
                                                                    ⑦ **❾**

Carroll's experience stretches from backing r&b singers to working in the testing ground of St Louis's Black Artists Group. He conducted the BAG Orchestra and was also involved in the educational side of the organization. His own playing showed a man who was no stranger to the freer areas of the jazz spectrum and his writing, arranging and group leading reflects this awareness. He spent much of the mid seventies in Paris but, after returning to New York in 1975, wrote for films and for other specialized musical productions. He proved to be a versatile and gifted composer and several albums issued in the eighties attest to that fact. This CD makes it clear that various influences are instrumental in reaching the 1994 product. The freer aspects are surrendered to the hard-bop core of his music but examination of apparently orthodox pieces reveals highly imaginative rule bending. The title track simultaneously employs more than one time signature, *King* has a deliciously abstract opening, while *At Roi* throws down the gauntlet of choice with its challenging harmonic options. In contrast, beautifully crafted ballads make nonsense of the contention that jazzmen should feature fewer of their own tunes. The melodic strength of *Legacies* and *I Thought You Knew* display Carroll's compositional flair as well as promoting his logical solo skills.                                                **BMcR**

# Barbara Carroll                                                                    1925

New review
**Everything I Love**  Carroll (p, v); **Randy Sandke** (t); **Bucky Pizzarelli, Jay Berliner** (g); **Jay**
   **Leonhart** (b); **Joe Cocuzzo** (d); **Jim Saporito** (perc). DRG Ⓕ 91438 (52 minutes). Recorded 1995.
                                                                    ⑦ **❼**
Carroll's career began back in the forties when she led a bop trio in New York and invited the likes of Charlie Parker and Stan Getz to share her stage. A family-raising sabbatical interrupted her musical activities but she returned to the jazz scene in the mid seventies with no artistic damage done. The years had mellowed her approach and albums such as **This Heart of Mine** (DRG) with Art Farmer and Jerome Richardson showed her to be very much at home with horn-playing guests. This CD finds her permutating the talents of two guitarists and a trumpeter and deploying each in the manner best suited to them. As a soloist she shows similar adaptability, with *Now's the Time* explaining why she was known as "the first girl to play bebop". In contrast, she nurtures themes such as *Heavenly* and *Chelsea Bridge* with the romantic's mastery of the well-turned phrase and, one suspects in the case of the latter, to pay homage to composer Billy Strayhorn. *Ace in the Whole* provides a glimpse of her idiosyncratic out-of-tempo piano, while her supper club sing/speak vocals on *As Long as I Live* and *100 Years from Today* show how she guards her shallow range and suspect intonation while at the same time making each lyric her own property. Like the Carroll of her 1949 record début, however, this talented woman is primarily a jazz pianist and her best work is done at the keyboard.                    **BMcR**

# Benny Carter                                                                    1907

**Complete Recordings 1930-40, Volume 1**  Carter (as, ts, cl, t, p, v, arr); playing with and
   leading various groups, including **The Chocolate Dandies; McKinney's Cotton Pickers; The**
   **Ramblers**. Charly Ⓜ CDAFS1022-3 (three discs: 213 minutes). Recorded 1930-7.
                                                                    ⑧ **❻**

The very first number gives a good indication of what is to come: Carter composed the tune, wrote the arrangement, sings the vocal and plays the alto solo. On the ensuing 69 tracks he also plays trumpet, tenor, clarinet and piano – sometimes several in the course of one three-minute piece. For sheer all-round brilliance nobody in jazz has ever been able to top Benny Carter. The groups to be heard on this hugely entertaining collection vary from full-blown big bands to quartets, almost always with Carter as leader, arranger and principal soloist. His alto playing grows more delectable with the passing years, so that you begin to get irritated with his constant and determined displays of versatility, astounding though they are. This is particularly true of the big-band numbers recorded during his period in London during 1936-7, where he plays three instruments per tune as a matter of routine. On the other hand, there is a little throw-away performance of *When Lights Are Low* (composer Benny Carter, with an enchanting vocal chorus by Elisabeth Welch) in which Benny Carter the alto saxophonist delivers a stunning demonstration in the art of playing a straight melody and making it swing. At moments like this you hear him speaking in his own voice, forgetting the virtuosity for the moment, and it is irresistible. In later years he wisely concentrated his playing on the alto and came to be regarded as one of the great alto triumvirate – Hodges, Carter, Parker – an eminence he would never have achieved if he had continued to present himself as the man who could do everything. That is why I cannot rate this set as part of an essential jazz collection, although it is so enjoyable that it is worth having in any case. **DG**

**Cosmopolite** Carter (as); **Bill Harris** (tb); **Oscar Peterson** (p); **Herb Ellis, Barney Kessel** (g); **Ray Brown** (b); **J.C. Heard, Buddy Rich, Bobby White** (d). Verve Ⓜ 521 673-2 (78 minutes). Recorded 1952/4.

⑩ ❻

This album comprises all the Verve Carter material which features Oscar Peterson in a supporting role. On four 1954 tracks Bill Harris is added to the basic quartet format. It complements – and supplements – the previous Norgran/Clef/Verve compilation, **3, 4, 5 – The Small Group Sessions**, which found Carter on superb form and accompanied by, among others, Teddy Wilson, Jo Jones and Louie Bellson. The Peterson trio were Carter's accompanists on the last three tracks of that collation, and this CD picks up where that finished. A subsequent album, **New Jazz Sounds – The Urbane Sessions**, which squeezes three old LPs on to two CDs and covers Carter's sessions with strings, Dizzy Gillespie and Roy Eldridge, is also worth seeking out, although it is not central to his output. That there is empathy here is hardly to be doubted. On ballads, Peterson's group act as the softest and plushest of musical suspensions for Carter's rich tone and elegant phrasing to glide upon, while medium and faster tempos find Carter being driven harder than usual. Happily, he responds with alacrity, showing that he could swing as hard as Hodges when he needed to. His powers of paraphrase are as sharp as ever here, and his ability to deliver miraculously balanced phrases over the course of an entire solo is fully exploited. This may not be spectacular jazz, but if you are looking for that, then Carter is the wrong place to start anyway. What you get is beautifully crafted, sophisticated music played with complete commitment by a born communicator. What you get is sheer pleasure. **KS**

**Jazz Giant** Carter (as, t); **Frank Rosolino** (tb); **Ben Webster** (ts); **André Previn, Jimmy Rowles** (p); **Barney Kessel** (g); **Leroy Vinnegar** (b); **Shelly Manne** (d). Contemporary Ⓜ OJCCD167-2 (39 minutes). Recorded 1957.

⑧ ❽

From the forties Carter established himself as the first important black composer of Hollywood background music, initially (for 20 years, that is) 'ghosting' for white writers but paving the way for such as Quincy Jones, Oliver Nelson and J.J. Johnson. In the meantime jazz saxophone became largely a sideline for him, although you would scarcely know it from his recordings of the fifties onwards. His mellifluous alto is surprisingly urgent when pushed by Manne's trio and Kessel's rhythm-guitar, while his trumpet on two tracks exhibits a similar broad tone reminiscent of Charlie Shavers but with more direct phrasing. The repertoire consists of well-worn tunes from the twenties, with the exception of Edgar Sampson's *Blue Lou* and two delightfully simple Carter originals which bridge the gap between the genuine old material and the then current backward-looking Horace Silver approach. The additional horns on most tracks give them a suitably timeless feel and, although there is a difference of dialect between Webster and the punchy, mobile Rosolino, you are unaware of the actual generation gap. Fellow film composer Previn (relieved on two numbers by the understated Rowles) contents himself with Petersonisms, but hardly detracts from this beautifully relaxed date. **BP**

**Further Definitions/Additions to Further Definitions** Carter (as, arr), with, on Definitions: **Phil Woods** (as); **Coleman Hawkins, Charlie Rouse** (ts); **Dick Katz** (p); **John Collins** (g); **Jimmy Garrison** (b); **Jo Jones** (d). On Additions: **Bud Shank** (as); **Buddy Collette, Bill Perkins, Teddy Edwards** (ts); **Bill Hood** (bs); **Don Abney** (p); **Barney Kessel, Mudell Lowe** (g); **Ray Brown** (b); **Alvin Stoller** (d). Impulse! 12292 (71 minutes). Recorded 1961/66.

⑧ ❽

The original idea for the former session was to reinterpret some of the music which Carter and Hawkins had recorded in Paris with Django Reinhardt before the war. Because of Carter's outstanding arrangements the group had moved beyond that concept before a note had been blown. In the event only lip-service was paid to the earlier occasion and the new originals which Carter had written for the date stand out as some of the best mainstream of the period. Carter's ballad *Blue Star* is a beautiful example of his writing with the four saxes knitting into a most impressive section – perhaps one would not have expected such individuals to be able to suborn themselves so well to a common cause. The rhythm section is ideal, and Katz shows himself to be a versatile accompanist and soloist. The match between scoring of the highest quality and similarly first-division sax solos is quite outstanding, with the unlikely matching of Hawkins and Woods seeming to inspire both players. It is interesting to hear *The Midnight Sun Will Never Set*, normally a feature for Woods with the Quincy Jones band, scored by Carter to feature himself and Hawkins. The music is near perfect. **Additions**, using a similar saxophone-dominated line-up, assumes much the same air, and while Hawkins was not present, certainly the three tenor sax players on call are no slouches. **SV**

---

**Central City Sketches** Carter (as, t, arr); with **American Jazz Orchestra**; **John Eckert**, **Virgil Jones**, **Bob Milikan**, **Marvin Stamm** (t); **Eddie Bert**, **Jack Jeffers**, **Jimmy Knepper**, **Britt Woodman** (tb); **Bill Easley**, **John Purcell** (as, f); **Loren Schoenberg** (ts); **Lew Tabackin** (ts, f); **Danny Bank** (bs, bcl); **Dick Katz** (p); **Remo Palmieri** (g); **Ron Carter** (b); **Mel Lewis** (d); **John Lewis** (p). MusicMasters Ⓕ CIJD60126X (72 minutes). Recorded 1987.

✔  ⑩ ⑩

Recorded a few months before his eightieth birthday, this was Carter's first big band album in two decades and the first in at least that long to show him off to full advantage as both a soloist and composer. His blues choruses on *Easy Money*, to cite one example among many, show that Carter remains one of jazz's most dazzling improvisers – still in full possession of the roseate, almost Marcel Mule-like tone that has been his signature for over half a century, but surprisingly modern in his harmonic values and rhythmic placements. The programme offers a Carter retrospective, with material ranging from *Lonesome Nights*, *When Lights Are Low*, *Symphony in Riffs* and *Blues in My Heart* (unaccountably burdened with a doubled-up and dated-sounded 'contemporary' beat – Carter's only injudicious revision) from the thirties, to the varied six-piece title suite finished just in time for the recording session (the melodic accelerations of the section subtitled *Promenade* are especially winning). The set is also a reminder of the key role played by the now-defunct AJO in the jazz repertory movement of the eighties, with music director Lewis spelling Katz on four numbers, including Carter's no-doze arrangement of the Fred Waring warhorse, *Sleep*. **FD**

# Betty Carter                                                                          1930

**'Round Midnight** Carter (v); **Norman Simmons** (p); **Lisle Atkinson** (b); **Al Harewood** (d). Roulette Ⓜ CDP7 95999-2 (42 minutes). Recorded 1969.

⑦ ⑥

Betty Carter sang with Charlie Parker as a teenager, was dubbed Betty Bebop by Lionel Hampton and toured with Ray Charles during the sixties. She began leading her own trio in 1969 and today (1995) still works in that manner. The trio heard on this CD was her first group, and this recording, live from Judson Hall in New York, is typical of her work at the time. She successfully breathes bebop into everything she sings, an easy task with the likes of *'Round Midnight* and a good scat vehicle like *Surrey With a Fringe On Top*, but not quite so simple with *Ev'ry Time We Say Goodbye* or *My Shining Hour*. A considerable amount of preparation goes into her arrangements, she makes no concessions to popularity and, when she succeeds, she produces brilliant pieces of bop improvisation. Little attempt is made to dignify the lyrics; if Carter needs to override them for creative purposes, she literally ignores their meaning – in Carter we have a jazz musician first and a singer second. She has chosen her rhythm section with skill; Simmons was previously with Carmen McRae for nine years and he is an accompanist *par excellence*. **BMcR**

---

**The Audience With Betty Carter** Carter (v); **John Hicks** (p); **Curtis Lundy** (b); **Kenneth Washington** (d). Verve Ⓕ 835 684-2 (two discs: 93 minutes). Recorded 1979.

⑨ ⑨

Ten years to the night after the Judson Hall concert that produced the **'Round Midnight** and **Finally** CDs, Betty Carter recorded a second live date for what many people now regard as her masterpiece. **Audience** is certainly one of the finest live jazz vocal performances on disc and confirms her feeling that "an audience makes me think, makes me reach for things I'd never even try for in a studio". She is backed, as before, by a trio of super-alert young talents; but, ten years the wiser, her singing now has an extra degree of sophistication and daring. The extremes of tempo she likes have become almost surreal – she tears up a manic *My Favorite Things*, yet sinks beautifully into a lugubrious *Everything I Have Is Yours*. Her intervallic swoops are so dramatic, so startling, those low, gruff notes dragged across the syllables are like an erotic caress. She can also inhabit a song as never before, time virtually suspended as she delves into *Spring Can Really Hang You Up the Most*. Her scatting runs like a grain through the music, from rapid-fire delivery to lullaby coo. The totally improvised *Sounds (Moving On)* is a *tour de force*, perhaps the most brilliant scat on record, although its 25-minute length could be considered indulgent. Carter continues to record excellent new albums, her latest being **I'm Yours, You're Mine** (Verve), but this remains outstanding. **GL**

# James Carter                                                                         1969

**New review**

**Conversin' with the Elders** Carter (as, ts, bs, bcl); **Craig Taborn** (p); **Jaribu Shahid** (b); **Tani Tabbal** (d); with, on two tracks each: **Lester Bowie**, **Harry Edison** (t); **Buddy Tate** (ts); **Hamiet**

**Bluiett** (bs); on one track: **Larry Smith** (as). Atlantic Ⓕ 782908-2 (62 minutes). Recorded 1995-6.

⑧ ❾

Carter's career is currently in fast-forward, and this, his fourth album in three years, shows the distance he has travelled since **J.C. on the Set** (DIW). On his previous disc, **The Real Quietstorm** (Atlantic), Carter demonstrated the romanticism he is capable of, leavened with the occasional bluesy ramble. On this latest effort he has chosen to duet with a number of richly talented elders, one of whom, Lester Bowie, is also a previous employer. Each pairing has a very distinctive flavour, although Carter himself no more subsumes his distinctively dynamic style than did Eric Dolphy when paired with Roy Eldridge or John Coltrane. Carter clearly enjoys the rumbustious approach of Bluiett on the two twin-baritone sorties, with *Composition 400* at times becoming overtly slapstick. His conversations with Lester Bowie accentuate the trumpeter's sly humour and oblique phraseology, while Carter and Larry Smith dig deep into Charlie Parker's blues backyard on their twin-alto workout on *Parker's Mood*. On two brightly-paced numbers 'Sweets' Edison imperturbably plays what he always has, while Carter generates terrific excitement with him on *Lester Leaps In*. With Tate, things are not quite so equal, for the older man is clearly not the force he once was, his tone wavery, his once immaculate rhythm at times faltering, and here it is the twin ghosts of Rollins and Hawkins, *c*1963, which hover closest, although that particular pairing was considerably more equal, the older man there still able to deliver at something like full strength. Carter has a similar angle of approach to Rollins, even though his style is considerably removed from the older master's: he is able to toy with fragments, smears and rhythmic figures (as well as his session mates), creating a crazy dance around the more conventional patterns of others in a manner which is both subversive and exciting. Like Rollins, Carter possesses the abundance of technique to pull this off, just as he also has a cart-load of his own ideas to wow us with. On this evidence, Carter will remain one of the key reed men in jazz as we move into the next century. **KS**

# John Carter

1929-91

**Castles of Ghana  Carter** (cl, v); **Bobby Bradford** (c); **Baikida Carroll** (t,v); **Benny Powell** (tb); **Marty Ehrlich** (bcl, perc); **Terry Jenoure** (vn, v); **Richard Davis** (b); **Andrew Cyrille** (d, perc). Gramavision Ⓕ R2 79423 (49 minutes). Recorded 1985.

⑨ ❾

John Carter's five-suite magnum opus, *Roots and Folklore: Episodes in the Development of American Folk Music*, displays a breadth of vision rare in modern jazz. Over the course of five CDs, Carter and his octet trace the evolution of African-American music from its origins in the ancient kingdoms of West Africa (**Dauwhe**), along the bloody passage of the transatlantic slave routes (**Castles of Ghana, Dance of the Love Ghosts**), to the rural communities of the American South (**Fields**) and the later black migrations to the cities of the North (**Shadows on a Wall**). Elements of country blues, rhythm and blues, gospel and other 'roots' musics are woven into this narrative, but Carter does not attempt to re-create these styles. Rather he uses the manifold possibilities of freedom-based music to evoke a series of moods, scenes and incidents that tell the story of his people's travails.

**Castles of Ghana** – the reference is to the fortified trading posts that were used as "holding stations for captives awaiting shipment"– is a particularly moving work that conjures up crepuscular feelings of pensiveness and desolation. The ensemble playing is superb – disconsolate reeds, growling brass, a throb of African percussion – whilst Carter's clarinet is masterful (he gave up his other reeds in the early seventies to concentrate on the clarinet and became its leading modern jazz virtuoso). His exquisite work on this album embraces the floating lines of *Evening Prayer*, the restless flutters of *Conversations* and, on *Capture*, an *a cappella* solo of truly breathtaking facility. **GL**

# Regina Carter

New review

**Regina Carter  Carter** (v); **Steve Turre** (tb); **David Lee Jones** (as); **Rachel Z (Nicolazzso)** (p, syn); **Lonnie Plaxico** (b); **Victor Bailey** (b, syn, d-prog, v); **Damen Duewhite** (d); **Andrew Daniels** (pc); **Abdoulaye Epizo Bangoura** (djembe); **Carla Cook, Mark 'Led' Ledford** (v). Atlantic Jazz Ⓕ 82750 2 (46 minutes). Recorded 1995.

⑦ ⑧

Violinist Carter's varied background has produced an adaptable and confident performer. As a teenager, she toured with pop-funk group Brainstorm; at the New England Conservatory she studied with Fred Hirsch and was in class with Najee and Nelson Rangell. She worked with the all-girl Straight Ahead group in Detroit in the eighties and in 1992 took the challenging violin chair in the String Trio of New York (Black Saint 120131-2). This CD provides a summation of all of these activities and goes some distance in returning jazz fiddle to the swinging, soulful temper of Stuff Smith. It presents a very different Carter to that heard with STONK and takes her through various stylistic settings. No attempt is made to stay loyal to the pure jazz ethic but she displays genuine jazz qualities as well as commensurate creative skills. Her playing has substance, her solos are well designed and she swings in any circumstance. Her cello-like sweeps on *Last Time* are in total contrast to her romantic flippancy on *Sticks and Stones* or to her slashing bowing on *Beau Regard*. At times her tone adopts a woody, autumnal hue, while at others it has a flautist's spring-like lightness of touch. Her reading of *Don't Explain* carries almost Billie Holiday-like conviction and helps to explain why, in the nineties, she is prominent on the festival tours. **BMcR**

# Ron Carter
1937

**Telephone** Carter (b); **Jim Hall** (g). Concord Jazz Ⓕ CCD4270 (46 minutes). Recorded 1984.
⑦ ❽

Carter's curriculum vitae would fill this entry without reference to the details of the music. Stalwart of more than a thousand albums in various fields of music, he remains one of jazz's finest string bassists. Work with Chico Hamilton, Thelonious Monk, Miles Davis, The New York Jazz Quartet and V.S.O.P. barely scratches the surface, but his duo recordings with Jim Hall and Cedar Walton give perhaps the most positive exposure to his personal style. This CD with Hall affords him room to breathe while at the same time testing his concomitant skills. It is one of his most successful duos because his brilliant ability as an accompanist does not overshadow his solo exploits and his desire to stretch out is suitably accommodated. The ductile *Indian Summer* is an ideal vehicle for him: it shows how cunning re-routing can take a pretty tune into fertile new territory while retaining the spirit of the original. His aptitude for contrapuntal playing is emphasized on *Alone Together* and *Choral and Dance*, non-gladiatorial confrontations which reflect well on both men, while *Telephone* gives evidence of Carter's facility in unison passages. The richness of his full tone is never better demonstrated than on his journey through the range on *Stardust*. He remains the complete jazz bassist. **BMcR**

# Michael Carvin
1945

**New review**
**Each One Teach One** Carvin (d); **Claudio Roditi** (t); **Antoine Roney**, **Houston Person** (ts); **Carlton Holmes** (p); **David Williams** (b). Muse Ⓕ MCD5485 (47 minutes). Recorded 1992.
⑥ ❼

Considering that Carvin worked for a year on the music of this album before recording it, it is not surprising to find it highly polished and confidently played by his impressive band. A professional since the seventies, Carvin has worked with illustrious names such as Hampton Hawes, Gillespie, McLean, Jacquet and Cecil Taylor. Naturally he is a very good drummer, but he has a drummer's outlook and not unnaturally wants to hear drums. This is hard on people who don't like drum solos or, much more irritating, the dominance of an ensemble by drums. The line-up is more controlled than, say, the Blakey Jazz Messengers were, consequently giving a detached feel to the music where individuals shine rather than the band spirit. Roditi is the best of them, both in ballads and up-tempos, his playing notable on *Waltz for Gina* and *Smoke Gets In Your Eyes*. There are welcome touches of Shorter in Roney's tenor whilst a sumptuous *Ghost of a Chance* is given over to the fat sound of the album's producer, Houston Person, making his only appearance. The pianist and bassist play adequately, with Holmes having some good solos. Carvin is a teacher with 25 private students. They should each have tattooed on their wrists "Too much damn' drums." **SV**

# Marc Cary
1967

**Cary On** Cary (p); **Roy Hargrove** (t); **Yarborough Charles Laws** (f); **Ron Blake** (ts); **Dwayne Burno** (b); **Dion Parson** (d); **Charlene Fitzpatrick** (v). Enja Ⓕ ENJ9023-2 (44 minutes). Recorded 1994.
⑦ ❽

Cary is one of the string of remarkably talented pianists that have been recruited over the last few years to back singer Betty Carter (Cyrus Chestnut, who succeeded him, is another notable example). He has also put in a deal of time behind Abbey Lincoln, whom he regards as both mentor and friend. Cary's playing is particularly impressive when backing his guest soloists Hargrove, Laws and Blake (some tracks are with just bass and drums) but his propulsive soloing is attractive, and he has an unusual way of accenting the rhythms in his right-hand figures which is appealing. The album also shows that Cary is no slouch as a composer, his efforts standing up well in comparison to the two tracks by Sonny Clark and Roy Hargrove. There's special empathy between Cary and Hargrove (they worked together for some time) and Hargrove's sombre ballad *The Trial* produces some of the best playing on the album. Cary has some native American forebears and this influence is also included in the rhythms of *He Who Hops Around*, a tune that suggests Cary's writing will benefit from further exploration of contrasting tempos and time signatures. The most accomplished composition is the song *So Gracefully*, which includes some dramatic passages for unison saxophone and voice as well as featuring (all too briefly) Laws's flute. As a début album, this is an impressive start: his follow-up, **Listen** (Arabesque, 1996) is worth getting as well – it shows admirable growth in his accomplishments and, while it lacks a guest soloist of the stature of Hargrove, is ambitious in scope. **AS**

# Casa Loma Orchestra

**New review**

**Maniac's Ball** Glen Gray (as, dir); Joe Hostetter, Dub Shoffner, Bobby Jones, Grady Watts, Sonny Durham, Frank Zullo (t); Pee Wee Hunt, Billy Rauch, Fritz Hummel (tb); Clarence Hutchinrider (cl, as); Kenny Sargent (as, v); Pat Davis (ts); Art Ralston (as, ob); Joe 'Horse' Hall (p); Gene Gifford (bj, g, arr); Jack Blanchette (g); Mel Jenssen (vn); Stanley Davis (bb, b); Tony Briglia (d); Jack Richmond (v). Hep Ⓔ CD1051 (77 minutes). Recorded 1931-7.

⑥ ❼

The Casa Loma Orchestra occupies an important place in jazz history. Named after a club that failed, the band was formed in 1930 when the members of the Orange Blossoms split with manager Jean Goldkette and became masters of their own destiny. The musical brains behind the band was banjoist/guitarist Gene Gifford, whose arrangements gave the band a personal identity and ultimately made them the standard-bearers for the white swing bands that emerged in the latter half of the decade. At the time, the cynical view was that they played jazz for people who didn't like jazz. The truth was somewhat more complicated. Their book did include many jazz standards from the previous era and Gifford's new arrangements called for a high degree of precision, resulting in the inevitable need for extensive rehearsal. As this CD illustrates, riffs were often the basis of the music and some items were played at fast tempos that obstructed the band's ability to swing naturally. Nevertheless, the white campus audiences saw it as modern jazz rather than dance music and *White Jazz*, *Maniac's Ball* and *Clarinet Marmalade* represented the non-jazz audience's idea of jazz excitement. The outspoken trombone solos by Hunt and the facile clarinet interludes by Hutchinrider made a large impression and the band's desire to capture the element of swing gradually came with performances such as *Black Jazz*, *Lady from St Paul* and *Royal Garden Blues*. The latter-day bands of Benny Goodman, Tommy Dorsey and Glenn Miller had their model and, if the quality of the Casa Loma's musical output was less than commensurate with their historical importance, they certainly deserve more than the tarnished honour that was theirs. **BMcR**

# Al Casey

1915

**Buck Jumpin'** Casey (g); Rudy Powell (cl, as); Herman Foster (p); Jimmy Lewis (b); Belton Evans (d). Swingville Ⓜ OJCCD675-2 (48 minutes). Recorded 1960.

⑥ ❻

Casey was still attending high school when he started working with Fats Waller in 1934, but his allegiance to Waller's music remains strong. This is a reissue of an LP made at a time when Casey and the rhythm section were all working with tenor saxophonist King Curtis's band, a unit in which Al was called upon to play electric guitar. For this Prestige-Swingville date he went back to unamplified guitar and it is a pleasure to hear the instrument throughout all nine tracks. The opening *Buck Jumpin'* revives memories of Waller (this was one of Casey's features with Fats) and the presence of another ex-Wallerite, Rudy Powell, helps to give the music period charm. On *Casey's Blues* Powell comes on like a reedy Pete Brown, but elsewhere his tone is sweeter and on *Ain't Misbehavin'* his clarinet sound is mellow. Casey relishes the up-tempos and the ballads (*Body and Soul* is a gem) so while the music may not be too significant, it happily conjures up a past era. The CD has two previously unissued titles: *Gut Soul* is a blues which may have been previously rejected due to some unsteady tempos and a chopped-off ending. **AM**

# Mario Castronari

1954

**New review**

**Roadside Picnic – la famille** Castronari (b, comp, arr); Matt Watts (as); Graham Harvey (kbds); Ivor Goldberg (g); Winston Clifford (d, v); plus, on three tracks: Steve Waterman (t); Bosco De Oliveira (perc); on two tracks: Mornington Lockett (ts); on one track: Dinesh Pandit (tabla). B&W Ⓔ BW067 (59 minutes). Recorded 1994.

⑦ ❿

Castronari has been leading differing line-ups under the name Roadside Picnic for some ten years now; the first band under that name, which featured Dave O'Higgins on sax, made two albums for RCA in the eighties. Quite apart from his resourceful and propulsive bass playing and the singing tone he achieves on his instrument, Castronari has from the outset been a gifted composer and a visionary of sorts, always possessing a view on where he wanted his own music to go. This third album for the group brings with it a considerable change in direction, a great lightening of tone and a general loosening of structures which has upped the improvisation quotient and the general freedom of expression within the band. This is not meant to suggest a loss of structure: Castronari's music always carries a very clear blueprint and tells its own story. On this album there are new stories for him to tell. In the booklet-notes to the album he puts this down to being recently introduced to the joys of fatherhood (hence the album's title); whatever the actual combination of reasons, his band here is breathing fresh musical air and benefiting from the experience. There is no sign of past tendencies to over-arrange and occasionally lapse into bombast, nor is there any remnant of the need to be so specific about the programme behind the music, where a programme is to be found. Here the music comes first, it comes unforced and for the most part ideally balanced, and the contributing musicians get a large say in how the overall ambience of the music is defined. Of the soloists, Castronari and Goldberg strike the listener as the most characterful and completely personalized, even more so than guests Lockett and Waterman. This well-thought-through and invigorating collection of compositions, ranging across a great deal of the largely acoustic contemporary tradition (no drum tracks and samples here), whether it be jazz, rock, fusion or the occasional ethnic touch, has to be put down as a successful return to recording by Castronari and his re-constituted group; hopefully he will be given the chance to develop further on subsequent albums by B&W.          **KS**

## Philip Catherine                                                    1942

**Moods Volumes 1 and 2** **Catherine** (g); **Tom Harrell** (t, flh); **Michel Herr** (kbds); **Hein Van De Geyn** (b). Criss Cross Ⓕ 1061/2 (two discs: 60 and 62 minutes). Recorded 1992.

⑧ ❽

These two volumes are separate CDs, but they stem from the same date and are clearly meant to be heard in tandem: indeed, anyone who enjoys one album will certainly enjoy the other. Catherine's career has seen him gradually move away from a wild and woolly musical youth at the opening of the seventies with such people as Jean-Luc Ponty and Charlie Mariano, and into the arms of musical conservatism. Yet this is not necessarily a process we need mourn, because his playing is as expressive and rewarding today as it ever was. He is just a lot more subtle in the way he goes about it. The absence of a drummer on this date should be a giveaway, and may even put some people off without so much as a cursory listen, but the fascinating dialogue between Harrell and Catherine should by itself be enough to satisfy anyone, let alone the lyrical beauty which both men continually exhibit on both volumes. Van De Geyn's bass offers exemplary support, which is as it should be, given the extra weight his role assumes in the absence of a drummer, while Herr, who appears on five tracks in all, fulfils his discreetly colouristic function sensitively. Harrell's idea organization in his solos is a thing to treasure, while Catherine manages to wring so many contrasting moods and nuances from the simplest melodic line or the most casual harmonic substitution that these discs will continue to give satisfaction for years to come. Both Harrell and Catherine, by the way, contribute a number of highly evocative original themes.          **KS**

## Oscar 'Papa' Celestin                                              1884-1954

**New Orleans Classics** **Celestin, 'Kid Shots' Madison, Guy Kelly, Ricard Alexis** (c); **William Ridgley, August Rousseau, Ernest Kelly** (tb); **Willard Thoumy** (cl, as, ts); **Manual Manetta, Jeanette Salvant** (p); **John Marrera** (bj); **Simon Marrera** (b); **Abby Foster** (d, w); **Paul Barnes** (cl, as); **Earl Pierson** (ts); **Charles Gills, Ferdinand Joseph** (v); **Sid Carriere** (ss, ts); **William Matthews** (tb); **Clarence Hall** (cl, ss, as); **Oliver Alcorn** (cl, ts); **Josiah Frazier** (d); **Narvin Kimball** (bj); **Sam Morgan's Jazz Band**. Azure Ⓕ AZCD12 (73 minutes). Recorded 1925-8.

✔                                                                    ⑦ ❽

Celestin founded the Original Tuxedo Orchestra in 1910 and worked in and around New Orleans for more than 20 years. He excelled as a leader, although as a soloist he was something of an artisan. His plunger solo on the 1926 *My Josephine* is perhaps most typical, showing him as a good but comparatively straight player, a tweaker of melodies rather than an improviser. Since most of the records made when he returned to jazz in 1946 are feeble revivalist fare, this CD offers his very best work. The personality of the excellent 1925 band is obvious, but it was certainly influenced by King Oliver, using Oliver-style two-cornet breaks on *Original Tuxedo Rag* as well as *Mable's Dream*-style trumpet conversations and a swannee-whistle obbligato on *Careless Love*. The introduction of brass bass and a larger personnel took the 1927 band further along the Oliver path, this time capturing much of the Savannah Syncopators' gambolling mobility. The solo work by Alexis, Celestin and Hall make *It's Jam Up* one of the best titles, but a further lightening of the band's rhythmic approach in the 1928 session took the Tuxedos to greater sophistication. Sadly, no further records were seen for 19 years.          **BMcR**

## Eugene Chadbourne                                                  1954

New review
**In Memory of Nikki Arane** **Chadbourne** (dobro, g, hand-held contact microphones, electric rake); **John Zorn** (c, ss, as). Incus Ⓕ CD23 (62 minutes). Recorded 1980.

⑥ ❽

Although referring to his musical instrument, the electric rake, a man with 'The Rake' as an adjunct to his autograph is likely to be something of a musical maverick. Chadbourne does not disappoint. Although born in New York, he was raised in Colorado and came to jazz and improvised music via rock. For this free improvisation recital he is joined by Zorn in a partnership that had already survived three years. All means are used by these players to make sounds. Electronic guitar distortion, strangled sounds from the throat, contorted saxophone multiphonics, random percussion, indiscriminate scrapings, wayward harmonics or anything else available from the *musique concrète* arsenal. The way in which sound is produced is immaterial; it is music that calls for player and listener interaction. The rapport between the two is tangible and, as this CD shows, sound sensations freely offered can be readily shared. What is required is a listening technique built on the principle of 'beauty' being in the ear of the listener.                                      **BMcR**

# Dennis Chambers

**New review**

**Getting Even**  Chambers (d); Bob Berg (ts); John Scofield, Jimi Tunnell (elg); Jim Beard (syn); Gary Grainger, Anthony Jackson (elb); Victor Williams (perc). 101 South 101 Ⓔ 87 7079 (50 minutes). Recorded 1991.

⑥ ❾

Dennis Chambers came to fame in John Scofield's ground-breaking fusion quartet of the mid eighties and since then the new vitality and intensity he introduced to both funk and swing drumming has made him first choice for numerous major bandleaders, among them The Brecker Brothers and John McLaughlin. Without in any way diminishing his abilities as a rhythmist, it can be observed that in this 1991 début as leader (mysteriously not issued in the UK until 1996) the old joke about three musicians and a drummer probably applies. All eight pieces here are by others, among them Jon Herington and Adam Holzmann, and the arrangements and musical direction are by Jim Beard. However, the writing is good, even if the style is now familiar, and gives Chambers plenty of scope to flex his slamming drum muscles in the manner typified by his performance on *Widow's Peak,* where he appears in tandem with his old mate Gary Grainger. The other sidemen are no slouches either, Tunnell and Scofield both doing their respective takes on bluesy, outside guitar playing, while Bob Berg is effective if mawkish. The record might not say anything new about the idiom or Chambers's drumming, but it's certainly far more musical than many albums led from the trap set.          **MG**

# Joe Chambers                                                                              1942

**Phantom of the City**  Chambers (d); Philip Harper (t); Bob Berg (ts); George Cables (p); Santi DeBriano (b). Candid Ⓔ 79517 (59 minutes). Recorded 1991.

⑦ ⑧

Despite being one of the most active and impressive drummers of the sixties, Chambers's visibility has dropped considerably over the past decades. Except for his role in Max Roach's Mboom, he has been something of a phantom; this is in fact his first recording as a leader in the US since the seventies. Given the challenging musical environment he inhabited earlier in his career, the mainstream nature of this return is a disappointment. For one thing, his work as a composer is slighted. He contributed a number of evocative, engagingly constructed compositions to albums by Bobby Hutcherson, for example, and on his own dates took advantage of a wider timbral palette, including piano/organ duets and pieces for multiple percussion. In his two tunes here, a tender ballad (*For Miles*) and the genial *Nuevo Mundo*, there is none of the 'free counterpoint' or expansive harmonic profile of his best work. Berg, the featured soloist, is solid in the mid-period Coltrane mode and sets off sparks on Joe Henderson's *In and Out*. Philip Harper, although of a younger generation, has most of the proper moves down. Cables, with whom Chambers recorded as far back as 1971 for Muse, is fluid throughout. But even though this is a pleasant, occasionally potent date, it does not reflect the breadth of Chambers's experiences or the depth of his talents.                     **AL**

# Paul Chambers                                                                        1935-69

**New review**

**The Whims of Chambers**  Chambers (b); Donald Byrd (t); John Coltrane (ts); Horace Silver (p); Kenny Burrell (g); Philly Joe Jones (d). Blue Note Ⓜ CDP 837647-2 (38 minutes). Recorded 1956.

⑦ ⑧

Chambers was just 21 when this record was made, but his evolution had been so quick and so successful that he sounds entirely mature and complete as an artist here, either as an accompanist or as a soloist. His tone, note-choice and rhythm is unerringly satisfying, his awareness of the music happening around him comprehensive. Chambers is an essential link in the bass-playing chain from Jimmy Blanton to the present day, applying the musicality and technical assuredness of Blanton to bop and post-bop patterns and forms. He was also one of the few jazz bassists (leaving aside the swing players such as Slam Stewart, who were pursuing different goals) to further the practice of *arco* bass solos after Blanton. On this record most of *Nita* (a Coltrane composition based on *I Want to Be Happy*) is given over to Chambers's *arco* playing, while *We Six* spotlights his plucking technique.

This is one of a couple of fine albums Chambers made for Blue Note in the fifties, and when you look at the line-up you wonder how anything could go wrong. Well, not much does: Coltrane is in fine early form, playing as he does on the famous Miles Davis Quintet sides of this period; Chambers and Philly-Joe – both in Miles's band at this time, along with Coltrane – combine effortlessly to push and stretch the soloists; while Silver is inspired, his accompanying wonderfully poised and inventive, his soloing constantly surprising and inventive. Burrell is consistency and taste personified. Byrd is the disappointment; it was simply an off-day for him, his lip not in the best of shape and his ideas consequently somewhat fractured. The disc was recorded in mono and sounds fine that way.     **KS**

## Thomas Chapin

**Safari Notebook** Chapin (f, ss, as); **Tom Harrell** (t, flh); **Peter Madsen** (p); **Kiyoto Fujiwara** (b); **Reggie Nicholson** (d). Arabesque Ⓕ AJ0115 (63 minutes). Recorded 1994.
⑥ ❽

This is Chapin's second album as a leader for Arabesque, although he has appeared on numerous albums in a sideman role. A veteran of many nights at the Knitting Factory, but just as comfortable stretching the sonic boom at CBGB's, Chapin held down a job with the Lionel Hampton band for six years before moving on to an equally rewarding sojourn with Chico Hamilton. From that list it is clear he is nothing if not versatile, and although both this and the previous Arabesque album tend to suggest his natural niche is at the more exotic end of modern mainstream, this is not meant to portray him as a player without vision or imagination. **Safari Notebook** is a loosely-connected series of tunes which give little pictures of places in Africa. As such it is not a borrowing of native music but more a musician's impressions of the people, the landscapes and the cityscapes he was moving through.

As with many albums being made by players who have arrived on the scene in the past decade, this is one which could conceivably have been made any time in the past 20 years, although the giveaway on its contemporaneity is the control and crafting which is evident is everyone's playing. Chapin solos with plenty of fire, but avoids long, self-indulgent solos and formless raves: each piece has a pleasant sense of forward motion. Harrell plays with engagement, while pianist Madsen also impresses with his measured support. A good, thoughtful and at times exciting album. By the way, this, to my ears, sounds like it is mastered in mono, not stereo. Strange ...     **KS**

## Bill Charlap

New review
**Souvenir** Charlap (p); **Scott Colley** (b); **Dennis Mackrel** (d). Criss Cross Ⓕ Criss1108CD (62 minutes). Recorded 1995.
⑨ ❾

As there is no shortage of good jazz pianists in the world today one looks for character as much as jazz ability. Charlap has both in unusual abundance. Currently with Phil Woods's quartet, he first distinguished himself during his two years with Gerry Mulligan's four-piece on the latter's **Lonesome Boulevard** album. But then both Woods and Mulligan have always been good at picking new sidemen. This is Charlap's first trio album and shows him as a hard-swinging player who comes closer to the Eddie Costa tradition than anyone else has come since that unique pianist died in 1962. This side of him is particularly on display in the opening Ornette Coleman blues *Turnaround*. *Alone Together* starts gently but swiftly becomes a 12-minute *tour de force*. *Godchild* is a homage to Mulligan's **Birth of the Cool** days and Charlap keeps in with his current boss by closing with an emotional version of Woods's tribute, *Goodbye Mr Evans*. One looks forward with relish to Charlap's future albums.     **SV**

## Ray Charles                                                                              1930

**Soul Brothers/Soul Meeting** Charles (p, as); **Billy Mitchell** (ts); **Milt Jackson** (p, vb, g); **Skeeter Best** (g); **Oscar Pettiford** (b); **Connie Kay** (d): on five tracks **Charles** (p, as); **Jackson** (p, vb); **Kenny Burrell** (g); **Percy Heath** (b); **Art Taylor** (d). Atlantic Jazz Ⓜ 781951-2 (two discs: 94 minutes). Recorded 1957/8.
⑧ ❻

A famous pairing (and originally one which had Jackson's name first) and two justly prized albums from it, recorded almost exactly a year apart. The first session is steeped in the blues from beginning to end, but the ghosts of Charlie Parker and Kansas City also hover, each performance sharing that familiar loping beat and the phraseology of bop which was Parker's most immediate musical legacy. Jackson is of course a peerless blues improviser on the vibes, but also exhibits considerable dexterity as a pianist, while Charles gets some uniquely persuasive solos out of his alto in a style somewhere between Parker and Pete Brown. Billy Mitchell, then known for his work with Dizzy's big band, is meaty and alert in his solos. What is most memorable about the first date in particular, however, is the atmosphere of relaxed co-operation. This really does sound like an after-hours session where everything is mellow, everyone inspired. Even Jackson's guitar playing (on *Bags' Guitar Blues*) has an earthy conviction about it.

The second session is a little smoother, partly because Kenny Burrell is a smooth guitarist and takes some of the themes with Jackson and Charles, but mostly because Mitchell is absent and Charles only gets his alto out of the case on one track (on *X-Ray Blues*). Still, there is much to admire, not least Jackson and his unstinting inventiveness across a blues sequence.

This is probably Charles's best jazz work. However, if you want to combine the two sides of his genius in one set, Rhino/Atlantic have a superb two-CD compilation, **Blues+Jazz**, currently available. It includes two tracks from the sessions reviewed here. The CD booklet with my copy of **Soul Brothers/Soul Meeting** has the two sets of booklet-notes mixed up because the page sequence has been muddled. Read with care! **KS**

## Teddy Charles 1928

**The Teddy Charles Tentet** Charles (vb); **Art Farmer** (t); **Eddie Bert** (tb); **Jim Buffington** (frh); **Don Butterfield** (tba); **Gigi Gryce**, **Hal Stein** (as); **Robert Newman**, **J.R. Monterose** (ts); **George Barrow**, **Sol Schlinger** (bs); **Hall Overton**, **Mal Waldron** (p); **Jimmy Raney** (g); **Addison Farmer**, **Teddy Kotick**, **Charles Mingus** (b); **Joe Harris**, **Ed Shaughnessy** (d). Atlantic Ⓜ 790983-2 (68 minutes). Recorded 1956-9.

⑧ 🎱

A reasonably fluent, although not innovative vibist, Charles was nevertheless an important instigator and focal point for the fifties modernist movement, straddling the West Coast (Shorty Rogers, Jimmy Giuffre, Charles Mingus) and East Coast (Teo Macero, George Russell, Charles Mingus) scenes. This tentet (different recording sessions account for the collective personnel above) was an outgrowth not only of the famous Miles Davis nonet, but also lesser-known groups like Mingus's Composers Workshop and Charles's own New Directions quartet. It was a vehicle for some of the period's most progressive composer/arrangers, attempting to integrate improvisation with classically-influenced writing and greater juxtaposition of material and mood. The most inventive and convincing charts are George Russell's brisk and exciting *Lydian M-l* (an early exercise in his new harmonic concept) and Mal Waldron's confrontational *Vibrations*. Gil Evans, Jimmy Giuffre and Bob Brookmeyer each contribute a chart exploring harmonic movement or formal reorganization in a jazz setting. Charles's own *Word from Bird* is rather ponderous; his *The Emperor* at least offers altered chords from *Sweet Georgia Brown* for the soloists' familiarity. Much of this music remains fresh and feisty today; and all of it is of historical interest. **AL**

## Allan Chase 1956

New review
**Dark Clouds with Silver Linings** Chase (ss, as); **Ron Horton** (t, flh); **Tony Scherr** (b); **Matt Wilson** (d, perc). Accurate Ⓕ AC5013 (61 minutes). Recorded 1994.

⑧ 🎱

Chase has featured on a variety of recordings in the eighties and nineties, including CDs by Your Neighborhood Saxophone Quartet, Prima Materia (with Rashied Ali) and Gunther Schuller, but **Dark Clouds with Silver Linings** marks his début as a leader. He says the music here "plays with tension between opposites", such as spontaneous improvisations pitched against tight arrangements, and he also points to the fact that his pianoless quartet plays "music associated with pianists" on this CD. (There are pieces by Bud Powell, Sun Ra, Horace Silver.) Chase cites the two-horn quartets led by Sonny Rollins and Gerry Mulligan as his models, naming the former for their "melodic imagination and humor", the latter for their use of counterpoint and "clear, concise form". This is a pretty accurate account of a music that sounds fresh and alert without ever straying too far from its sources. Chase and Horton are graceful, incisive soloists, Scherr and Wilson provide a spare yet flexible rhythmic underpinning and ensemble passages are smartly executed. What gives the disc its distinctive edge is the intriguing choice of repertoire, which balances decidedly quirky items (Powell's *Comin' Up* and *Borderick*, Dominique Eade's *Routine*) with affectionate versions of standards like *Close Your Eyes* and *Of Thee I Sing*. **GL**

## Doc Cheatham 1905

**At the Bern Jazz Festival** Cheatham (t); **Roy Williams** (tb); **Jim Galloway** (ss); **Ian Bargh** (p); **Neil Swainson** (b); **Terry Clarke** (d). Sackville Ⓕ CD2-3045 (58 minutes). Recorded 1983-5.

⑧ 🎱

Doc Cheatham is one of the most experienced jazz musicians still playing. He has worked with innumerable bands, including six years with Cab Calloway during the thirties. An immensely popular figure internationally, he appeared at the Bern Festival in Switzerland with a Scot, a Canadian rhythm section and England's fine trombonist Roy Williams. The six titles from that concert are supreme examples of mainstream jazz with everyone not only on top form but determined to work as a group. Doc inevitably takes on the role of leader when it is called for, but this is very much a combined effort. Galloway's piping soprano weaves through the ensembles, never once sounding like a Bechet clone, and the 'unknown' Ian Bargh (unknown, that is, to non-Canadian jazz lovers) is a two-handed revelation. Roy Williams demonstrates his class and the two choruses he plays on *Polka Dots and Moonbeams* are perfect in conception and execution, while he displays an apt turn of phrase and Ellingtonian effects on *Creole Love Call*. But it is Doc who, at the age of 78, is the star, a position reinforced on the final three tracks recorded in Toronto some time later. *My Buddy*, from the Toronto dates, is an immensely satisfying performance. The Bern concert was digitally recorded, the Toronto dates analogue; in all cases the sound is excellent. **AM**

# Jeannie Cheatham

**Gud Nuz Blues** Cheatham (p, v); **Jimmy Cheatham** (btb); **Snooky Young** (t); **Nolan Smith** (t, flh); **Louis Taylor** (as, ss); **Rickey Woodard** (ts, ss); **Plas Johnson** (ts); **Charles Owen** (bs, bcl); **Richard Reid** (b); **John Harris** (d). Concord Ⓕ CCD4690 (57 minutes). Recorded 1995.

⑧ ❾

When the late Carl Jefferson gave up his car dealership to start the Concord label in the early seventies some were quick to criticize his product for the musical blandness and the squeaky-clean image. Over the years Jefferson broadened the scope of his catalogue and one of his most attractive signings was the husband and wife team, the Cheathams. Their credentials are impressive (both have taught jazz at universities: she has worked with Dinah Washington and Jimmy Witherspoon; he has played with Ellington, Thad Jones and Ornette Coleman); even more impressive is their ability to generate a most engaging blues atmosphere, rather like a Harlem jump band. This is their eighth album for Concord and, like the earlier issues, it features a guest, in this case the fine blues tenor saxist Plas Johnson. But the band is a good one, anyway, with fine solos from Rickey Woodard, Snooky Young and Jimmy Cheatham. This is good-time music laced with some fine blues performances such as the extended *Coal Yard* and *Ice House Blues* and a surprisingly effective *Careless Love* taken at up tempo. But it is Jeannie who adds the deepest blues aura with her excellent singing and piano playing. There's nothing in the least bland about this music. **AM**

# Don Cherry                                                                1936-95

**The Avant-Garde** Cherry (t); **John Coltrane** (ts, ss); **Charlie Haden**, **Percy Heath** (b); **Edward Blackwell** (d). Rhino/Atlantic Ⓜ 790041-2 (36 minutes). Recorded 1960.

⑩ ❽

In 1967, when this session was first released, its title was even less accurate than when it was recorded. By 1960, Cherry was thoroughly conversant with the free-bop method of his usual partner Ornette Coleman, whose influence here is paramount – he wrote three of the five tunes – so the music sounds comfortably lyrical, not radical. Despite the co-billing, this was obviously Cherry's date. All of the players save Coltrane had recorded with Don under Coleman's leadership; Cherry wrote one tune (Coltrane none), and usually solos first. The trumpeter's lines loosely imply chord changes, but never as systematically as harmony-obsessive Coltrane's do. The rhythm section, with either bassist, has a light, springy feel.

The Avant-Garde was the first album recorded (but not first released) on which Coltrane plays soprano – not that you would know it, his sinewy playing is so assured. The album also contains some uncommonly splendid Cherry. He has always been more intuitive than chops-oriented, with a raw, raspy, airy brass sound, but his harmon-muted improvisation on *The Blessing* is one of his loveliest, most limber and inspired on record. Cherry obviously had fond memories of the date; he revived its *The Blessing* and *Bemsha Swing* (by Thelonious Monk) and much of its feel for 1989's **Art Deco**. A shame two alternative live takes were not included, especially when the playing time is taken into account. **KW**

**Symphony for Improvisers** Cherry (c); **Gato Barbieri** (ts); **Pharoah Sanders** (ts, pic); **Karl Berger** (vb, p); **Henry Grimes**, **J.F. Jenny-Clark** (b); **Ed Blackwell** (d). Blue Note Ⓜ CDP8 28976-2 (39 minutes). Recorded 1966.

⑦ ❽

Cherry made three of his best and most consistent records for Blue Note in the mid-sixties; this is the only one of them currently on CD. Remarkably similar personnel share them. As is the way of the world, the first (**Complete Communion**) was probably the best, the second (this one) almost as good, the third (**Where is Brooklyn?**) somewhat lagging behind, the format by then getting a little frayed at the edges. Cherry is often best when having a strong central personality to bounce delightedly off, and here that role is played (in more than one sense) by Barbieri, who is still revelling in what was an early creative peaking of his powers. In this he is duplicating the role he inhabited on **Complete Communion**, but the space is shared with Sanders, although on side one Pharoah sticks to piccolo, thus clearing the centre ground a little, while on side two Barbieri plays on the first two tunes, Sanders on the latter two. The music is in the form of two suites (suiting the two sides of the old LP format), the themes only very loosely associated, the cues mostly quite blatantly signalled by Berger or Cherry himself blurting out a snippet of the next piece as a rallying cry. In a typically thoughtful piece of programming, Blue Note have given us just two index points to the whole CD.

Still, the music is there for all to hear, and on *Manhattan Cry*, the piece which starts side two (or Movement Two, according to the CD running order), Cherry makes one of his most convincing and technically secure ballad statements, with not a saxophone or piccolo within earshot. Barbieri also solos strongly. The concluding two pieces with Pharoah on board find the band sounding a deal more hesitant, with the tenor player unable or unwilling to shift his ground to accommodate Cherry's concepts.                                                                                          **KS**

**New review**

**Dona Nostra**  Cherry (t); **Lennart Aberg** (ts, ss, f); **Bobo Stenson** (p); **Anders Kjellberg** (d); **Okay Temiz** (perc). ECM Ⓕ 521 727-2 (57 minutes). Recorded 1993.

⑥ ❾

His involvement with less rewarding projects dogged Cherry's latter years. The World Music carrot was pursued but rarely overtaken and indifferent concert, club and record performances somehow diminished this extrovert free form jazz pioneer. This CD finds him with good material in useful company and in the mood to accept the challenge. Unfortunately, his confidence does not always match his enthusiasm. He is at his most diffident on *M'Bizo*, *Race Face* and *Vienna*, although he never takes the soft option. When the odd fluff occurs it is often in his search for new and valid directions and there are times when such transgressions genuinely provide new inspiration. This becomes more apparent in his better moments and *Fort Cherry*, *What Reason Could I Give* and *Prayer*, while not up to his highest standards, are fine jazz. Compared with the peerless works of his earlier days, too much here is speculative. To its credit it offers little to the listener concerned with complacency; rather it presents Cherry indulging in imaginative brinkmanship and putting spontaneity and excitement before demure sobriety. Alas, Cherry was never destined to inherit the Earth.                                          **BMcR**

# Ed Cherry                                                                                                1954

**First Take**  Cherry, **Jon Faddis** (t); **Paquito D'Rivera** (cl); **David Jensen** (ts); **Kenny Barron** (p); **Peter Washington** (b); **Marvin 'Smitty' Smith** (d). Groovin' High Ⓕ 519 942-2 (67 minutes). Recorded 1993.

⑦ ❾

Cherry played guitar in Dizzy Gillespie's touring band for what seemed like decades, although in fact it was a mere 14 years. For this, his first album as leader, he chose Peter Washington and Marvin 'Smitty' Smith as the rhythm section and a cast of four guests: Kenny Barron, Paquito D'Rivera, Jon Faddis and David Jensen. Together they make an enjoyable and varied programme, with D'Rivera's clarinet solo on his own composition *Lorenzo's Wings* the outstanding item, closely followed by Ed's own interpretation of Duke Ellington's *In a Sentimental Mood.* Altogether an excellent début, well worth hearing. I urge you to read Cherry's little reminiscence of Gillespie in the booklet. The man is a natural born writer.   **DG**

# Cyrus Chestnut                                                                                          1962

**Another Direction**  Chestnut (p); **Christian McBride** (b); **Carl Allen** (d). Alfa Jazz Ⓕ ALCR317 (48 minutes). Recorded 1993.

⑦ ❽

Chestnut has in recent years become one of that select group of pianists who are first-choice for virtually anybody's recording session. Like Kenny Barron, Hank Jones and Tommy Flanagan, Chestnut has spent time giving miraculous support to some of the best singers in jazz (in Chestnut's case, the most regular employer has been Betty Carter) while at the same time being ubiquitous in the recording studios. Also like them, he is the younger generation's answer to that well-known producer's problem: how do we make this new horn player sound even better? Hire Cyrus. On the other hand, the CD market is not exactly overflowing with releases headlined by him, this being his first and recorded in spring 1993 for the Japanese company, Alfa Jazz (although there has since been another for Atlantic), a label with reasonable overseas distribution.

When it comes to his own session, Chestnut has opted for the best in terms of fellow-players, with McBride in particular making his own imperious mark on the music. The programme is heavily loaded in favour of standards – some of them dating back to the twenties. Chestnut impresses in the way Peterson in his prime did – he just has so much time to do what he does, whatever the tempo. Nothing is forced; it is beautifully placed and impeccably played. The other bonus is that he doesn't overplay and distort a song's proportions. All of which makes this an impressive and very pleasant outing in the post-war modern-mainstream tradition. Chestnut has released a new album on Atlantic, a solo piano collection of hymns, spirituals and carols called **Blessed Quietness**, but this trio date remains a better jazz yardstick for now.                                                      **KS**

# Herman Chittison

1909-67

**Herman Chittison 1933-41** Chittison (p, v); **Ikey Robinson** (g, v); **Arita Day** (v). Classics Ⓜ 690 (63 minutes). Recorded 1933-41.

⑤ ❻

Chittison was of the generation which grew up in the shadow of the great stride pianists and came to honour Art Tatum. He had a wide and varied experience, working with comedian Stepin' Fetchit, accompanying Louis Armstrong and making some fine sides with Willie Lewis's orchestra. He spent the years 1934-40 in Europe, and the majority of this 'classics' volume was recorded in Paris. The first two tracks here, where a rather distant-sounding Chittison accompanies the dully derivative vocalizing of Ikey Robinson and his equally uninspiring guitar, can safely be given a miss, but the real thing can be found in a sprightly solo workout on Waller's *Honeysuckle Rose*. While Chittison here is by no means as technically secure as Tatum or even Waller himself, he is a superior craftsman with more than a hint of Jelly Roll in his left hand, which is rhythmically closer to ragtime in its emphasis and weightings than Waller and his ilk were by the early thirties. Some of these tracks are taken at ill-advised tempos, and Chittison is a lot more impressive when he slows down and allows himself a little more time to direct his fingers rather than let them fall into pre-conceived patterns. An example of this is *You'll Be My Lover*, where the tempo is hardly slow (it bounces along nicely at the sort of speed Teddy Wilson was most comfortable at: 'sprightly' is the best way to put it), but Chittison can for once think more subtly than usual.

The two tracks where he accompanies Arita Day find him virtually overwhelming a small-voiced and none-too-confident chanteuse: the lure of Tatumesque arabesques are, for Chittison, irresistible. Things improve by the 1938 solo sessions, where a fully mature and more finely-balanced Chittison style has emerged, and although it may owe too much to Tatum to be of more than historical interest, it is mighty prettily executed, for all that.                                                                    **KS**

# Charlie Christian

1916-42

**The Genius of the Electric Guitar** Christian (g); with a collective personnel of **Benny Goodman** (cl, ldr); **Alec Fila, Irving Goodman, Jimmy Maxwell, Cootie Williams** (t); **Cutty Cutshall, Lou McGarity** (tb); **Gus Bivona, Skippy Martin** (as); **Georgie Auld, Pete Mandello** (ts); **Bob Snyder** (bs); **Lionel Hampton** (vb); **Fletcher Henderson, Count Basie, Johnny Guarnieri, Dudley Brooks** (p); **Artie Bernstein** (b); **Nick Fatool, Harry Jaeger, Jo Jones, Dave Tough** (d). Columbia Ⓜ CK40846 (49 minutes). Recorded 1939-41.

✓                                                                             ⑨ ❼

Initially recorded and released under Benny Goodman's name, these classic sessions now stand at the centre of the abbreviated but prophetic canon of jazz guitar pioneer Charlie Christian. Born in Dallas but raised in Oklahoma City, Christian got his professional start with Alphonso Trent's sextet. On a tip from Mary Lou Williams, entrepreneur John Hammond 'auditioned' the youngster, lining him up for the Goodman juggernaut on the spot. The simpatico with Goodman was immediate and profound. Indeed, on each of these BG tracks the clarinettist made sure that his new 'discovery' had ample room to stretch out.

Christian was the right guitarist at the right time to take advantage of the possibilities of the technologically evolving electric guitar. Thanks to amplification, Christian could be heard above the band. Technology, though, was only part of the story. Influenced by the flowing lyricism of Lester Young and the riff-style blues of the American Southwest, Christian gave the guitar a jazz persona. On *Rose Room*, his insinuating single-note lines swing with bluesy looseness and disciplined panache. The more brightly paced *Seven Come Eleven* shows off Christian's swinging virtuosity, and like the 1941 take on *Air Mail Special*, antecedents of boppish things-to-come. The guitarist brought a new edge to Goodman's already stellar, small-group forays, inspiring Goodman anew: on all these selections the clarinettist sounds terrific. The one big-band track, *Solo Flight*, is an ebullient feature for Christian. Thanks to well-executed digital remastering, sound quality is excellent.          **CB**

**Solo Flight** Christian (g); **Buck Clayton, Cootie Williams** (t); **Benny Goodman** (cl); **Lester Young, Georgie Auld** (ts); **Lionel Hampton** (vb); **Fletcher Henderson, Johnny Guarnieri, Count Basie** (p); **Freddie Green** (g); **Artie Bernstein, Walter Page, Walter Iooss** (b); **Nick Fatool, Jo Jones, Harry Jaeger, Gene Krupa, Dave Tough** (d); **Benny Goodman Orchestra**. Vintage Jazz Classics Ⓜ VJC1021-2 (76 minutes). Recorded 1939-41.

✓                                                                             ⑧ ❻

The influence of Christian on jazz and way beyond is quite incalculable and it was affected by a career of less than two years in the national spotlight before he was hospitalized with terminal tuberculosis. His CV is almost identical to that of bassist Jimmy Blanton, who likewise catapulted his instrument into the second half of the century before dying in 1942.

Two months before Blanton hooked up with Ellington, Christian joined Benny Goodman, with whom all his formal appearances and recordings were made. While sporadic jazz use had been made of the amplified guitar in the preceding few years, it was Charlie who saw that it could be a major voice rivalling the saxophone and, while having little in common stylistically with Lester Young, his 'new sound' was at the time as revolutionary as Young's. Christian's slender output has been reissued in a more cavalier fashion than that of almost any other major figure, so it is a pleasure to turn to these broadcast versions of the studio material recorded with Goodman, plus one originally unreleased Goodman studio rehearsal set (with the added bonus of glorious playing from Young, Clayton and the Basie rhythm-section) which first appeared on Jazz Archives JA6 and JA42. **BP**

**Live Sessions at Minton's Playhouse** Christian (g); with, on four tracks: **Joe Guy** (t); **Thelonious Monk** (p); **Nick Fenton** (b); **Kenny Clarke** (d); on one track: unknown (t); **Don Byas** (ts); **Monk** (p); **Fenton** (b); **Clarke** (d); on three tracks: **Dizzy Gillespie** (t); **Don Dyas** (ts); **Kenny Kersey** (p); **Fenton** (b); **Clarke** (d). Jazz Anthology ℗ 550012 (38 minutes). Recorded 1941.

⑧ ❻

Charlie Christian was the man who invented modern jazz guitar and whose work with the Benny Goodman Sextet was a revelation to musicians and jazz lovers. He was a frequent habitué of the New York 'after hours' clubs with the young Turks of the day and we are fortunate that a college student, Jerry Newman, took his primitive disc recorder along to locations such as Clark Monroe's Uptown House and Minton's Playhouse to record the events. The tracks here enable us to hear Christian's improvisations at considerably greater length than he was allowed on the Goodman records, and *Swing to Bop* (based on *Topsy*) opens this fine collection with a superb guitar solo. The personnel listed above, taken from the insert card, is somewhat tentative; for example, there are a number of other horns to be heard playing the final notes behind Don Byas's rich-toned *Stardust*. But the sound generally is clear and jazz owes Newman a lot for his work in documenting events (other items from his archives featuring Art Tatum, Billie Holiday, Lips Page and many others have been released on Xanadu and Onyx but are not currently available on CD). This release also enables us to study the work of the Minton's 'house' band containing Thelonious Monk and Kenny Clarke plus a notable guest, Dizzy Gillespie, who plays well on two versions of *Stardust*, open on the first, muted on the second, and a thinly disguised *Take the 'A' Train*, re-labelled *Kerouac*. **AM**

# Jodie Christian

1932

**Experience** Christian (p); **Larry Gray** (b); **Vincent Davis** (d). Delmark ℗ DD454 (59 minutes). Recorded 1991-2.

⑧ ❽

This album is a delight. Christian has been a musician to reckon with since the fifties and has had an international reputation since the early sixties, but this record is, quite incredibly, his first as a leader. Equally comfortable with the likes of Coleman Hawkins, Eddie Harris, Roscoe Mitchell, Dizzy Gillespie and Stan Getz, his sheer adaptability, plus a desire to stay put in Chicago rather than spend his life touring, has kept him from a more high-profile career. If nothing else, **Experience** should win him some of the attention he has deserved and not received for far too long.

Six of the ten tracks are solo piano performances, and the pianist who springs to mind – not because of any stylistic overlap, but rather because of a similarly robust touch and imaginative harmonic approach – is Jaki Byard. Christian is much less intent on covering the entire history of the music on one album, but his playing reveals an equal knowledge of the history of each selection, be it a standard (*They Can't Take That Away from Me*), a Goodman signature tune (*Goodbye*) or a bop anthem (*All the Things You Are*). An accomplished and invigorating record. Four of the compositions are Christian originals, with the sensuous ballad *Reminiscing* probably the pick of them. **KS**

# Christie Brothers Stompers

**Christie Brothers Stompers** Collective personnel: **Ken Colyer** (c); **Dickie Hawdon** (t); **Keith Christie** (tb); **Ian Christie** (cl); **Pat Hawes, Charlie Smith** (p); **Ben Marshall** (bj); **Nevil Skrimshire** (g); **Micky Ashman, Denny Coffee** (b); **George Hopkinson, Bernard Saward, Pete Appleby** (d); **Bill Colyer** (wshbd); **Neva Raphaello** (v). Cadillac ℗ SGC/MELCD20/1 (68 minutes). Recorded 1951-3.

⑧ ❻

The Christie Brothers – Keith (1931-80) and Ian (born 1927) – formed their band in the early part of 1951 to make records for the Esquire label using men from the Humphrey Lyttelton and Crane River groups. The records were successful and the Christie Brothers Stompers became a regular unit. All their subsequent recordings were for the now-defunct Melodisc label and this 23-track CD comprises all the Melodisc sides, including two that were withdrawn quickly (for technical reasons) and *Old Grey Bonnet*, originally rejected. In addition there are four privately recorded titles, one with Neva Raphaello singing the vocal. Ken Colyer played cornet with the Christies until he left on his much-publicized trip to New Orleans. Colyer is present here on nine of the tracks, his place taken on the others by Dickie Hawdon. The years have dealt kindly with the music of the Stompers simply because it was created by dedicated young men who also believed that jazz was something to be enjoyed. Kid Ory was perhaps the band's principal hero (and Keith Christie plays some of his best solos on record here; his subsequent move into the 'modern' field with John Dankworth and Ted Heath diminishing his importance as a soloist) but there is a high degree of originality within the general constraints of the New Orleans format. Pat Hawes, who plays piano on all but four of the tracks, has written the most informative notes, Charlie Crump has remastered the original Melodisc 78s and the attractive gate-fold packaging contains facsimiles of historic posters and photographs. Recommended.     **AM**

# June Christy                                                          1925-90

**Something Cool** Christy (v); **Orchestras / Pete Rugolo** (arr). Capitol Ⓜ CDP7 96329-2 (69 minutes). Recorded 1953-8.

⑧ ❽

June Christy's voice, bright and clear but with a slight haze at the edges, could have been made for her time. It fits the American fifties to perfection: outwardly happy and contented but clouded with a vague sense of unease. She began her career as a vocalist with Stan Kenton's Orchestra in the late forties and, although she gave it up as a permanent job in 1948, most of her best subsequent work was done with ex-Kenton players and arrangers, such as Pete Rugolo and Bill Holman.

This background determined the general tone of her work, which brings to the classic American song a certain detachment and deliberation. The accompaniments on this and other recordings tend to be far more dissonant than was usual at the period, and sometimes her interpretations seem on the verge of turning popular song into a species of art song. A case in point here is the title piece of this CD, a touching dramatic monologue with overtones of Tennessee Williams. These 24 tracks include the whole original **Something Cool** album, about half of **This is June Christy** and numerous previously unreleased singles. The sound is excellent. For those interested in the June Christy of an earlier vintage, **Day Dreams** (Capitol) documents the 1947-50 period where, as a member of the Kenton band, she made a series of solo recordings using often quite adventurous arrangements from Rugolo and many of Kenton's star musicians. A further compilation, **The Best of** (Capitol), covers the period after Christy's success with **Something Cool**.     **DG**

# Gioconda Cilio

New review
**Sounds of My Soul** Cilio (v); **Stefano Maltese** (ts, cl); **Alberto Alibrandi** (p); **Nello Toscano** (b); **Antonio Moncada** (d). IREC Ⓕ 128016-2 (65 minutes). Recorded 1995.

⑤ ❻

I should imagine that Gioconda Cilio takes her inspiration from Billie Holiday in her later, torch-singer years. The mere list of songs suggests that much – *Don't Explain, Loverman, Lush Life*. Singers whose first language is not English face a dilemma when dealing with this material: either they try hard to sound American or they make a virtue out of singing with a foreign accent. The first of these usually fails and the second sometimes works (e.g. Marlene Dietrich, Astrud Gilberto) but unpredictably. Gioconda Cilio attempts to steer a path mid-way between these two approaches and comes unstuck. Her pronunciation gets in the way of the song. If you can ignore this, there is a lot to enjoy in these performances. The playing is excellent, exactly right in mood and style, and the smoky timbre of Gioconda Cilio's voice suits the material very well. I hope that the details given here are helpful; there is no obvious label name on the CD box or disc other than a tiny 'IREC Milano' tucked away in a corner. One wonders sometimes whether people actually want to sell their products.     **DG**

# Mino Cinelu

New review
**Swamp Sally** Cinelu (mand, bj, g, syn, d, perc, special effects, v); .**Kenny Barron** (p, kbds, syn, b). Verve Ⓕ 532 268-2 (66 minutes). Recorded 1995.

⑨ ❾

The opening track of this consistently surprising album sets the tone for the rest. Documenting the results of the duo's first musical encounter on the bluesy territory that constitutes the most familiar of the common ground between them, it demonstrates just how extraordinary was their instant rapport. Cinelu plays mandolin, banjo and assorted percussion instruments, Barron electronic keyboards, and the result is a gloriously multi-textured confection positively dripping with country blues, to which the only proper response is the delighted laughter with which both participants greet its conclusion. From here, their dialogue – in which each is clearly genuinely inspired to reach for rare heights of imagination by the presence of the other – explores a great range of musical styles, from bluesy shuffles spearheaded by Cinelu's evocative guitar work, through straight-ahead jazz sparked by Barron's fluent acoustic piano, and gentle ballads embellished by an astonishing variety of percussive sounds, to freely improvised pieces in which their mutual understanding is near telepathic. For those who have heard either player only in his more accustomed settings – Cinelu in Miles Davis's eighties band, or even in trios with the likes of Kevin Eubanks and Dave Holland; Barron providing tasteful but vigorous accompaniment to

Stan Getz or Gary Bartz, or leading his own poised mainstream-bebop sessions – this superb, wonderfully rich album will be something of an eye-opener. **CP**

# Sonny Clark

1931-63

**Sonny Clark Trio**  Clark (p); **Paul Chambers** (b); **Philly Joe Jones** (d). Blue Note Ⓜ B21Y 46547 (49 minutes). Recorded 1957.

⑧ ❻

In his relatively brief recording career from February 1953 (with Teddy Charles) to October 1962, Clark established himself as probably the most fluent of the post-Bud Powell pianists: this CD is the best example of his work in trio context. He is in fast company here, with Jones keeping up the pressure especially on the faster-paced numbers such as *Bebop*, but Clark is the master of the situation. He had a brittle sense of touch and a way of slithering from one phrase into the next with the easy facility of a saxophonist. He was the progenitor of a keyboard style in which the left hand made the most telling stabs at the relevant chords while allowing the right to trace out long, serpentine lines. The original LP has been fleshed out with extra takes of *I Didn't Know What Time It Was*, *Two Bass Hit* and the attractive Tadd Dameron tune, *Tadd's Delight*. Clark recorded with all of the great drummers of the fifties – Art Blakey, Max Roach, Louis Hayes, Dannie Richmond, Art Taylor and Elvin Jones amongst them – but in the final analysis the interplay between Sonny and Philly Joe Jones on sessions such as this achieved a close and very special cohesion. **AM**

# Kenny Clarke

1914-85

**Clarke-Boland Big Band en concert avec Europe 1**  Clarke (d); **Francy Boland** (p); **Benny Bailey**; **Art Farmer**, **Derek Watkins**, **Idrees Sulieman** (t); **Aake Persson**, **Nat Peck**, **Erik Van Lier** (tb); **Derek Humble**, **Johnny Griffin**, **Sahib Shihab**, **Tony Coe**, **Kenny Clarke** (saxes); **Jimmy Woode** (b); **Kenny Clare** (d). Trema Ⓔ 710413/14 (two discs: 101 minutes). Recorded 1969.

⑧ ❽

The brainchild of jazz promoter Gigi Campi, who decided in 1960 to programme a big band for mardi gras in Germany as an antidote to "traditional junk carnival music", the Clarke-Boland big band is notable chiefly for the ease with which the US and European musicians gel within it. Their début recording, indeed, was entitled **Jazz is Universal**, but this live recording documents their sound almost a decade later, in concert in Paris, the band comprising eight Americans, five British players, a Swede, a Dutchman and a Belgian, Francy Boland himself. Their overall sound and approach are celebratory rather than innovative, their material chiefly straightforward platforms for the roaring bustle and thunderous attack in which the band specialized, but it is the quality of the soloists which grabs and holds the attention. Benny Bailey and Art Farmer, and – more eccentrically – Tony Coe, who provides a startlingly original interpretation of *Gloria*, are all outstanding, as are Johnny Griffin and the self-effacing co-leader himself, Francy Boland. No new ground is broken on either disc of this high-energy set, but most of the old ground is covered with some panache, and the masterful way Kenny Clarke – always a genius at discreetly fitting into any group context – adapts his drumming to a big-band context is worth the price of admission alone. **CP**

# Stanley Clarke

1951

**Journey to Love**  Clarke (elb, perc); **Chick Corea** (p); **George Duke** (kbds); **David Sancious**, **Jeff Beck**, **John McLaughlin** (g); **Lenny White**, **Steve Gadd** (d); **Jon Faddis**, **Lew Soloff**, **David Taylor**, **Peter Gordon**, **Allen Rubin**, **Thomas Malone**, **John Clark**, **Earl Chapin**, **Wilmer Wise** (brass). Epic Ⓜ 468221-2 (39 minutes). Recorded 1975.

⑧ ❽

Being, along with Miles Davis and Sly Stone, one of the seminal jazz-rock figures of the seventies, Stanley Clarke consolidated an already precociously substantial reputation made with Chick Corea's Return to Forever with a series of commercially successful fusion albums throughout that decade. **Journey to Love** in many ways encapsulates both the strengths and weaknesses of the jazz-rock form in particular and the decade's music in general. So-called progressive rock at the time was somewhat burdened by an over-concentration on the spuriously 'cosmic', both in theme and electronic effects; jazz was prone to tender the commercial strengths of rock – its immediacy and punch, its accessible, unsophisticated approach to harmony – an exaggerated respect. Thus Clarke's considerable strengths such as his virtuosic pioneering of the 'hammered' electric bass, producing a strangulated, percussive sound that would reverberate throughout the eighties; his ability to lay down a fearsomely taut rhythm for the brass to punctuate and wailing guitars to soar over, are too frequently diluted by dreamy vocals (another seventies affliction) and an over-reliance on rock's unsubtle, inflexible beat. The bass guitar playing of Clarke himself and the lead guitar playing of his featured soloists Jeff Beck and John McLaughlin is always vital and exciting, and Chick Corea's acoustic piano brings a touch of class to a two-part John Coltrane tribute, but overall **Journey to Love** is perhaps better viewed as a wildly above-average rock album rather than a jazz recording. **CP**

# James Clay
1935

**A Double Dose of Soul** Clay (f, ts); **Nat Adderley** (c); **Vic Feldman** (vb); **Gene Harris** (p); **Sam Jones** (b); **Louis Hayes** (d). Riverside Ⓜ OJCCD1790-2 (53 minutes). Recorded 1960.

⑥ ❻

Clay is from Texas and has the big tenor sound associated with others from that state, men such as Buddy Tate, Herschel Evans, Arnett Cobb and Budd Johnson. He created enough of an impact on his first visit to Los Angeles in 1956 to get Miles Davis interested in employing him (for non-musical reasons the job never materialized). It is his tenor sound which is immediately impressive, big and soulful as it is, but his improvisations do not always live up to that initial imprint as he allows time to pass while he assembles his ideas. The occasional reed squeaks are also disturbing. On flute he is much more assured, creating long, flowing lines with ease and a fine delivery. Nat Adderley plays cornet on the tenor tracks and produces two splendid choruses in the middle of his solo on the blues *Pockets*; tightly muted, he is supported by just Sam Jones's purposeful bass line. The rhythm section is an inspiration with fine Gene Harris piano. Vic Feldman plays vibes on the flute tracks, two of the tunes being his compositions. **AM**

# Buck Clayton
1911-91

**Jam Sessions from the Vaults** Clayton, Billy Butterfield, Ruby Braff, Joe Newman (t); J.C. Higginbotham, Urbie Green, Henderson Chambers, Bennie Green, Dicky Harris (tb); Tyree Glenn (tb, vb); **Lem Davis** (as); **Coleman Hawkins, Buddy Tate, Julian Dash** (ts); **Charlie Fowlkes** (bs); **Kenny Kersey, Sir Charles Thompson, Al Waslohn** (p); **Steve Jordan, Freddie Green** (g); **Walter Page, Milt Hinton** (b); **Bobby Donaldson, Jo Jones** (d); **Jimmy Rushing** (v). Columbia Ⓜ 463336 2 (52 minutes). Recorded 1953-6.

⑥ ❻

Clayton was one of the most individual and important trumpeters from the swing era, and his solos and arrangements greatly enhanced the reputation of the Count Basie Band. A key figure in the establishment of mainstream jazz as an identifiable sub-category, he was the titular head of many star-studded studio jam session groups, of which those for Columbia, produced by George Avakian and John Hammond, are the most important. This release is a reissue of an LP called **All the Cats Join In**, with the important difference that all five titles are alternative takes to those used previously and the playing time is boosted by *After Hours*, which Columbia had not previously put out. Clayton plays a vital part in organizing the music, devising background riffs for soloists, setting the most suitable tempos but never hogging the solo microphone. The level of solos is sometimes uneven and there are examples of uncertainties which would have been duly edited out of these takes, had they been issued previously, but all that is of minor importance to the overall enjoyment and impact of the music. Coleman Hawkins, Ruby Braff and Urbie Green in particular are in fine form and it is to be regretted that, at the time of writing, Sony/Columbia have yet to transfer to the compact disc format any of the other five **Buck Clayton Jam Session** originally issued on LP. That, it seems, has been left to Mosaic. **AM**

**Ben and Buck** Clayton (t); **Ben Webster** (ts); **Henri Chaix** (p); **Alain Du Bois** (g); **Isla Eckinger** (b); **Romano Cavicchiolo** (d). Sackville Ⓕ SKCD2-2037 (65 minutes). Recorded 1967.

⑧ ❻

This was virtually the last occasion on which Clayton played at the height of his powers. Immediately after this concert he suffered a medical collapse with the result that he never played effectively again.

He and Webster play so well here that it is to be regretted that more privately-recorded concert performances like this have not surfaced on CD. Delicate and incisive are words which it is hard not to use when writing about Clayton and he was the leading mainstream trumpeter of the two decades before this Baden concert. He plays beautifully throughout and, as always, manages to make *I Want a Little Girl* sound as though he was playing it for the first time. Webster is similarly on good form, bustling through *In a Mellotone* and playing exquisitely on *My Romance*.

Henri Chaix's group is world-class and the pianist probably deserves inclusion in this Guide with his trio. But there is enough of him here, sandwiched between the masters, for the listener to assess his proficiency. **SV**

# Jay Clayton
1941

**Live at Jazz Alley** Clayton (v); **Julian Priester** (tb); **Stanley Cowell** (p); **Gary Peacock** (b); **Jerry Granelli** (d). ITM Pacific Ⓕ ITMP970065 (61 minutes). Recorded 1987.

⑥ ❽

Jay Clayton is best known as an abstract and experimental vocalist, but this set, recorded live at a Seattle club, finds her singing mainly standard material. In scat numbers, such as Gillespie's *Birks' Works*, her phrasing and almost vibrato-less voice are often reminiscent of Miles Davis in his **Kind of**

Blue period, and free from the self-conscious hipness that overtakes most jazz vocalists in these circumstances. But the best things here are the ballads, especially *My Foolish Heart*, in which she sings the melody with great restraint, alongside a wonderfully sensitive obbligato by Priester, and *But Beautiful*, with lovely piano from Cowell. The recording is particularly good, discreetly capturing the live atmosphere and maintaining perfect balance throughout.                                    **DG**

## Clementine

**Mes nuits, mes jours**  Clementine (v); André Villeger (ss, ts); Kenny Drew (p); Niels-Henning
   Ørsted Pedersen (b); Alex Riel (d). Orange Blue Ⓕ OB007 (54 minutes). Recorded 1990.

⑥ ❽

Clementine is a young Parisienne singing in the tradition of intimate, small-voiced French singers of the fifties and sixties. She chooses her material with care, not pushing her voice too hard and using its natural charm to beguile the listener into the moods she is projecting. She also has excellent taste in her choice of accompanists (previous albums have found her in the company of Ben Sidran and Johnny Griffin), and all four players here provide sympathetic and insightful support. The repertoire is a combination of old standards like *Everything Happens to Me, Makin' Whoopee* and *When Sunny Gets Blue* and more obviously jazz-derived pieces such as Coltrane's *Naima* with lyrics by Mimi Perrin, or Ben Sidran's *It Didn't All Come True*. It is fascinating to listen to records like this because there is simply no tradition for this type of singing in Britain, and a patchy one at best in America. The majority of the record is sung in English, and there is no doubt that it is a jazz date. It has a unique charm and should be sampled at least once by those with an ear for the unusual.                                    **KS**

## Dave Cliff                                                                                      1944

**New review**
**Sippin' at Bells**  Cliff (elg); Geoff Simkins (as); Simon Woolf (b); Mark Taylor (d). Spotlite Ⓕ
   SPJCD553 (68 minutes). Recorded 1994.

⑧ ❾

Dave Cliff is a hugely adaptable guitarist who can fit convincingly into almost any jazz environment, but he has a distinct style of his own. It shows the influence of Lee Konitz, Warne Marsh and the Tristano school, but the contours are rounder and the general approach more lyrical. Here he is joined by alto saxophonist Geoff Simkins, a scandalously under-appreciated player whose warm sound and limpid delivery are a sheer joy to listen to. Four of the 14 pieces here are played by just the two of them and the remainder by the full quartet, a superb group which would soon develop into something quite exceptional if it could only work regularly as a unit for a while. As we go to press Spotlite have released a new Dave Cliff album, this time in tandem with a Geoff Simkins co-led quintet, where the music of Tadd Dameron is given a new and invigorating reinvestigation.                                    **DG**

## Rosemary Clooney                                                                                1928

**Blue Rose**  Clooney (v); The Duke Ellington Orchestra (Clark Terry, Willie Cook, Cat Anderson, t;
   Ray Nance, t, vn; Quentin Jackson, Britt Woodman, John Sanders, tb; Jimmy Hamilton, cl, ts;
   Russell Procope, as, cl; Johnny Hodges, as; Paul Gonsalves, ts; Harry Carney, bs, cl, bcl;
   Ellington, p, ldr; Jimmy Woode, b; Sam Woodyard, d). CBS Ⓜ 466444 (39 minutes). Recorded
   1956.

⑧ ❽

Although not a jazz singer *per se*, Rosemary Clooney not only knows what jazz is about but has made some very successful latter-day albums with the Concord stable (Scott Hamilton, Warren Vaché, Dave McKenna *et al* – see below) and the full Woody Herman band. But **Blue Rose** occupies a special place in her discography and the sympathy she shows for the music and the magnificent Ellington orchestra is manifest. A lot of play was made at the time of the initial issue over the fact that the band recorded its parts in Chicago, leaving Rosie to dub in her vocals a few weeks later in New York. In fact this has nothing to do with the success of the album (particularly in the light of the tape surgery which today is standard practice in every studio). Miss Clooney's voice has a warmth which is immediately appealing, while her pitching and diction are exemplary. Her version of *Sophisticated Lady* here must rank as one of the finest interpretations of this ballad. But the programme does not depend only on the expected Ducal war-horses; there are excellent readings of fairly obscure songs such as *I'm Checkin' Out, Goom Bye, Hey Baby* and *Me and You*. Duke wrote a song especially for the occasion, which gives the album its title: it provides a wordless vehicle for the singer. Rosemary is absent from one title, a magnificent reading of Billy Strayhorn's *Passion Flower* by Johnny Hodges, surely one of his most intense and involving showcases on record.                                    **AM**

**Tribute to Billie Holiday** Clooney (v); **Warren Vaché** (c); **Scott Hamilton** (ts); **Cal Collins** (g); **Nat Pierce** (p); **Monty Budwig** (b); **Jake Hanna** (d). Concord Ⓕ CCD4081 (42 minutes). Recorded 1978.

⑧ ⑧

Rosemary Clooney is one of the great generation of American singers which served its apprenticeship with bands during the swing era, and she always showed great affinity with the jazz side of classic American song. Had she been contracted in the fifties to a label such as Capitol we might now have a string of superb albums from her, made when her voice was in its prime. Unfortunately, her label was Columbia, where she suffered under the régime of trivia-king Mitch Miller. It was not until her late middle age that Miss Clooney was able to begin recording consistently good material in the congenial surroundings of the Concord repertory company – Scott Hamilton, Warren Vaché and pals.

This disc is one of the best of many, a sparkling set of ten numbers associated with Billie Holiday, but with no hint of pastiche. In particular, she sings *Ev'rything Happens to Me* with wonderful simplicity and control of ironic tone. The playing is excellent throughout, especially from Nat Pierce, whose piano introductions alone could be used as object lessons in how to be an accompanist. **DG**

# Clusone Trio

New review

**Soft Lights and Sweet Music** **Michael Moore** (as, cl, bcl, vc, melodica); **Ernst Reijseger** (vc); **Han Bennink** (d, perc). hatART Ⓕ CD6153 (62 minutes). Recorded 1993.

⑧ ⑨

The Clusone Trio first came together in 1978, split up in 1981, then reformed in 1988. One third expatriate American, two thirds Dutch, the trio represent an intriguing musical blend. The California-born Moore is the melody man, his clarinets inspired by 1961-vintage Jimmy Giuffre; Bennink is the legendary drum-master of Dutch anarchy; Reijseger, from a younger generation of improvisers, spikes his virtuoso technique with deadpan drolleries. **Soft Lights**, the trio's third CD, is devoted to the music of Irving Berlin. The inauspicious opening – predictably abstract and noisy – is misleading: these guys appreciate a good tune and they treat Berlin's music with respect, with only the occasional act of comic vandalism. Bowed cello and creaking bass clarinet create lovely dark sonorities on *What'll I Do* and *Let's Face the Music and Dance*, while a wistful *The Song Is Ended* and the simple charm of *White Christmas* show the trio can be most effective when most restrained. Of course they can also put the boot in to hilarious effect, no one more adroitly than Bennink, who runs his usual gamut from inspired clatter to genteel brushwork. But it's the romantic frisson between Berlin's tunes and Moore's gorgeous clarinets that is **Soft Lights**'s main attraction. **GL**

# Arnett Cobb                                                                                     1918-89

**Blow Arnett, Blow** Cobb, **Eddie 'Lockjaw' Davis** (ts); **Strethen Davis** (org); **George Duvivier** (b); **Arthur Edgehill** (d). Prestige Ⓜ OJC794-2 (37 minutes). Recorded 1959.

⑩ ⑥

It has been a long wait, but at last some of the best Arnett Cobb has crept onto CD. Cobb was maligned in the same way that Illinois Jacquet still is, and for much the same reasons. A Texas tenor (from Houston), he was Jacquet's replacement in Lionel Hampton's roaring big-band after the two of them had previously been section mates in the Milton Larkins band. While with Hampton Cobb had a hit with *Flying Home No. 2* (Jacquet, of course, had recorded *No. 1* with Hamp) and by the late forties he was leading his own rip-snorting small group. Between them, he and Jacquet had launched the honking tenors school, garnering the critical damnation that went along with it.

But Cobb was not a johnny-one-honk. He had a massive, caressing tone on ballads, a fierce attack on swingers, and endless inventiveness (of the pre-bop variety) when it came to constructing an orderly and melodically interesting solo. Yet his calling card remained his unique ability to send shivers down the listener's spine when he opened a solo with a searing tenor moan, signalling his readiness for some heavyweight action. On this album, the first long-playing disc he made (a bad car accident had put him out of action for part of the fifties), the action comes thick and fast: in fact, on both *Go Power* and *Go Red, Go*, things get so heated that both tenor men start excitedly yelling to each other during their respective solos. In a no-holds-barred session, 'Lockjaw' Davis keeps pace with the older man on the screamers, while both saxophonists play with big-toned sensitivity on their ballad features. The backing group is adequate for the job and the recording quality perfectly acceptable. If you are a fan of the tenor sax, then this is definitely one to treasure. **KS**

# Junie Cobb                                                                                     1896-c1970

**The Junie Cobb Collection 1926-9** Cobb (cl, ts, ss, vn, v); **Jimmy Cobb** (c, t); **Johnny Dodds**, **Angelo Fernandez** (cl); **George James** (as, bar); **Tiny Parham**, **Jimmy Blythe**, **Alex Hill**, **Earl Frazier** (p); **Bill Johnson** (b); **Walter Wright** (bb); **Eustern Woodfork** (bj); **Clifford Jones** (d, kz);

**Jimmy Bertrand** (d, xyl, wshbd); **Harry Dial** (d); **W.E. Burton**, **Thomas A. Dorsey** (v). Plus four titles by **Kansas City Stompers** (without Cobb). Collectors Classics Ⓜ COCD14 (74 minutes). Recorded 1926-9.

⑥ ❹

Arkansas-born multi-instrumentalist Junius C. Cobb had his musical awakenings in New Orleans. His next move took him to Chicago where he became a central figure on the South Side and in the free-wheeling jazz scene that blossomed there in the late twenties. He enjoyed prestigious stints with King Oliver and Jimmie Noone, but in the main it was his casual, on-the-spot recordings that earned him his quiet corner in jazz history.

His best instrument was clarinet; on this CD, he is heard playing excellent straight man to the creatively devious Johnny Dodds on *Chicago Buzz*, crafting more shapely solos on *Barrell House Stomp* (sic) and *Shake That Jelly Roll* and wringing true blues feeling from *South African Blues*. His spikey soprano seeps into *Panama Blues*, his good-time violin scrapes to good effect on *Shake That Jelly Roll* and his bar-room vocals fit the mood ideally. His slap-tongue effects on tenor are mercifully brief but the simple lyricism of his style made him an ideal blues player on the horn. With trumpet-playing brother Jimmy he was among the rough diamonds of the twenties recording scene. Their mutually homespun music was without artifice but it had an ingenuous quality that was instantly appealing to the audiences that filled Chicago's dance clubs and speakeasys. **BMcR**

# Billy Cobham
1944

**The Best of Billy Cobham** Cobham (d); **Randy Brecker** (t); **Garnett Brown**, **Glenn Ferris** (tb); **Michael Brecker** (ts); **Tommy Bolin**, **John Abercrombie**, **John Scofield**, **Cornell Dupree** (g); **Jan Hammer**, **George Duke**, **Milcho Leviev** (kbds); **John Williams**, **Lee Sklar**, **Alex Blake** (b). Atlantic Ⓜ 781558-2 (45 minutes). Recorded 1973-6.

⑥ ❽

Although Billy Cobham's seventies brand of bustling fusion was extraordinarily important, particularly for drummers, for whom he became (and remains) a super-hero, from a nineties perspective it is not immediately apparent what all the fuss was about. The up-tempo material showcases Cobham's unique technique and sheer physical stamina, but is less interesting either for its melodic content or for the quality of the soloing it inspires. The medium-tempo numbers settle quickly into solid, attractive grooves, but lack direction and punch, despite the usually inspirational presence of players such as George Duke, the Brecker brothers and John Abercrombie. It would be tempting to dismiss Cobham's output as unremarkable music played remarkably fast, or in impressively tricky time-signatures, were it not for its undeniable visceral impact when experienced live. Perhaps more importantly, the all-pervasive nature of its influence in the eighties, accustoming the ear to virtuoso fusion music of its type, has retrospectively (and unfairly) lessened its impact. Certainly Billy Cobham is one of contemporary jazz-fusion's great drummers, but perhaps his most sympathetic recording environment remains the Mahavishnu Orchestra. **CP**

# Michael Cochrane

New review

**Impressions** Cochrane (p); **Calvin Hill** (b); **Yoron Israel** (d). Landmark Ⓕ LCD1548-2 (50 minutes). Recorded 1996.

⑧ ❾

Cochrane is a Berklee graduate who has paid his dues with, among others, Sonny Fortune, Chico Freeman and Hannibal Marvin Peterson. A mature and imaginative pianist with a delicate touch and deep harmonic resources, he is the kind of player that jazz needs far more than it needs the one-shot wonders. This delightful set consists mainly of Cochrane originals and pieces by other pianists – Tyner, Corea, Barron – plus a remarkable and very tricky version of *There Will Never Be Another You*, in 3/4 (or possibly 6/8) time. Cochrane's rapport with the excellent rhythm team of Calvin Hall and Yoron Israel is quite exceptional. **DG**

# Tony Coe
1934

**Nutty** Coe (cl, ss, ts); **Chris Laurence** (b); **Tony Oxley** (d). Hat Hut Records Ⓕ hatARTCD6046 (73 minutes). Recorded 1983.

⑧ ❽

A virtuoso player on several reeds, Tony Coe's remarkably catholic range of activities has included working with Humphrey Lyttelton, Count Basie, Derek Bailey and Franz Koglmann; recording film scores with Henry Mancini; and a little crooning with the Melody Four, a madcap trio he runs with Lol Coxhill and Steve Beresford. No one disc can be described as representative of such a versatile talent, but **Nutty**, recorded live at the Willisau Jazz Festival (and officially credited to Coe, Oxley and co.), offers a wonderful display of instrumental bravura in the challenging context of extended improvisation.

Coe transforms *Body and Soul* into a tide of barbed tenor fragments, makes a witty extract of Monk's *Nutty* and winds a skein of supple clarinet lines through Bill Evans's *Re: Person I Knew*. Laurence engages the leader in some daunting exchanges and takes a couple of characterful solos, while Oxley's subtle, pitter-patter scurries of percussion dart intrepidly to the thick of the action. **Nutty** shows three players using freedom and invention to re-fire the tradition with a new sense of adventure. Hat Hut have generously squeezed the original double album onto a single CD, though at the cost of losing one track (*Gabriellissima*). **GL**

# Al Cohn 1925-88

**Nonpareil** Cohn (ts); **Lou Levy** (p); **Monty Budwig** (b); **Jake Hanna** (d).Concord Ⓕ CCD4155 (43 minutes). Recorded 1981.

⑧ ❽

Had he not given up so much of his time to writing, Cohn could have become the most powerful of the group of saxophonists to which he belonged. Indeed, the leaders of that group, Zoot Sims and Stan Getz, each insisted that Cohn was their favourite tenor soloist. Cohn's wide-ranging blues-based style is shown at its best here with a truly *simpatico* West Coast rhythm section that could not have been bettered. He swings, grunts and roars through a well-chosen repertoire which includes two of his own numbers, two by Johnny Mandel and one each by Billy Strayhorn and Gary McFarland. Cohn's firm treatment of Mandel's beautiful *Unless It's You* also inspires a fine solo from Lou Levy, and Al's unusual treatment of Weill's *This is New* must have been the inspiration for the version which Getz added to his repertoire a few months later. There was never anything flashy in Cohn's playing and his are invariably trenchant improvisations which, when called for, swing with great fire. His ballad performances have the same qualities and are totally devoid of superfluous embellishment or sentiment. **SV**

# Cozy Cole 1906-81

**1944** Cole (d); with a collective personnel of: **Joe Thomas, Lamar Wright, Emmett Berry, Frankie Newton, Shad Collins** (t); **Trummy Young, Ray Conniff, Tyree Glenn** (tb); **Eddie Barefield, Earl Bostic** (as); **Coleman Hawkins, Ben Webster, Walter 'Foots' Thomas, Budd Johnson, Don Byas** (ts); **Earl Hines, Johnny Guarnieri, Teddy Wilson** (p); **Teddy Walters, Remo Palmieri** (g); **Billy Taylor, Slam Stewart** (b). Classics Ⓜ 819 (69 minutes). Recorded 1944.

✔ ⑩ ❻

The list above looks like a roll-call of swing small-group greats, and it is a tribute to Cole's talents as a drummer and organizer of men that he could get them all into a studio and get them to play so well. Cole made his name in the late twenties in New York and recorded with Jelly Roll Morton before playing in Blanche Calloway's band. After success in other groups, he returned in 1938 to the Calloway aggregation, now very famous and run by Blanche's brother, Cab. He stayed there until war broke out, and after a later spell with Louis Armstrong's All-Stars he freelanced as a leader, working in film studios as well as straight jazz situations.

Cole was ever the immaculate swing-style drummer who could hold down a swinging beat and drive on the most leaden-footed soloist. In the company he keeps here, there is no need for that, and all is sweetness and light. These sessions, all in the year before bop started to get widely recorded, is almost a swan-song from the Indian summer of small-group swing. That does not make these tired performances, or in any way corny. But there is an added touch of poignancy that all this perfection would soon be swept away in the post-war flood. **KS**

# Holly Cole

**New review**
**It Happened One Night** Cole (v); **Aaron Davies** (p); **Kevin Breir** (g); **David Piltch** (b); **Dougie Bowne** (d). Metro Blue Ⓕ CDP 852699 (39 minutes). Recorded 1996.

⑥ ❽

Cole may be on the long slow journey away from jazz to a more commercially viable musical lifestyle (the set I saw at London's Jazz Café with the same group was notably more electrified), but this is her best and most in-the-tradition album for a couple of years. Recorded live in Montreal, it is dominated by the creative frisson between Cole and her pianist, Davies. There is real soul in the music they make here, and Cole Porter's *Get Out of Town* has rarely sounded so much like a threat as well as a promise. There are world-music type things here as well, but nothing that Cassandra Wilson fans would find too problematic, and nothing that is overproduced in an attempt to intellectualize such music into another (usually more pretentious) sphere. Cole is adept at stepping between musical styles, sometimes sounding like a singer-songwriter, sometimes like a chantreuse. Her passion for Tom Waits's songs resurfaces here with a sexy version of *Train Song*, but in terms of raunch, *Que Sera Sera* takes some beating: nothing like this has been heard live since Annette Peacock took her family to task on **X-Dreams** back in the seventies. At 38 minutes, this is a short serving, but the quality's there. **KS**

# Nat King Cole

**New review**
**The Vocal Classics (1942-6)** Cole (p, v); **Oscar Moore** (g); **Johnny Miller** (b). Capitol Jazz Ⓜ
CDP8 33571-2 (66 minutes). Recorded 1942-6.

⑧ ❼

Nat King Cole's reputation as a pianist has never been in dispute, while even the more hidebound fans should by now have come to terms with his singing. During the forties these talents co-existed on record, so that most tracks here include at least 16 bars of piano improvisations. Cole was able to blend the rhythmic dash of Earl Hines with the cooler approach of Teddy Wilson, occasionally sprinkled with unusual chord patterns (which he displays on *Embraceable You*) that beboppers would learn to appreciate. Oscar Moore's solos, in the Christian style but with some of Django Reinhardt's unorthodox touches, also deserve a positive mention. The trio's considerable impact on jazz, from Oscar Peterson to Ray Charles, extended of course to the vocals. Cole's deceptively off-hand and conversational style, lyrics delivered with the acute sense of time one would expect from a top musician, may have owed something to Billie Holiday; he transforms the opening *All for You* very much in the Holiday manner. Ballads such as *For Sentimental Reasons* eventually took over but one remembers the trio best for the novelty swingers: *Straighten Up and Fly Right*, *The Frim Fram Sauce* and the catchy and much-emulated *Route 66* (note the happy coincidence of the playing time!). A follow-up CD, **The Vocal Classics 1947-50** (Capitol), has recently appeared and is equally agreeable for fans of small-group Cole. **RA**

**Jazz Encounters** Cole (p, v); **Dizzy Gillespie**, **Bill Coleman**, **Ernie Royal** (t); **Bill Harris** (tb); **Buddy DeFranco**, **Benny Bailey** (cl); **Benny Carter** (as, arr); **Flip Phillips**, **Coleman Hawkins**, **Charlie Barnet** (ts); **Billy Bauer**, **Oscar Moore**, **Irving Ashby**, **Johnny Moore** (g); **Eddie Safranski**, **John Kirby**, **Art Shapiro**, **Joe Comfort** (b); **Buddy Rich**, **Shelly Manne**, **Max Roach**, **Nick Fatool** (d); **Pete Rugolo**, **Paul Weston** (arr); **Kay Starr**, **Jo Stafford**, **Nellie Lutcher**, **Woody Herman**, **Johnny Mercer** (v). Capitol Ⓜ 96693-2 (61 minutes). Recorded 1945-50.

⑥ ❻

Cole is heard here in varied jazz and pop settings. He plays on all 21 tracks; his trio with bass and guitar is the core band on most of them. It is a grab-bag, but suggests Cole's range as pianist, crooner and comic. As accompanist, he feeds the Metronome All-Stars soloists' bop chords in taut rhythm, and lays down frilly arpeggios for pop singer Jo Stafford on *I'll Be with You in Apple Blossom Time*. The influence of Earl Hines's creative irrationality is evident in Nat's solo on the Metronomes' *Leap Here* (alternate take) and in the left-hand runs that conclude his spot on the Capitol International Jazzmen's *Riffamarole* (alternate).
A third of the cuts feature Cole's singing (maybe bantering is a better word) with guests including singer Nellie Lutcher. His sense of humour was as light as his voice, and devoid of eye-rolling degradation, no matter how vaudevillean the material. There is a bizarre, hipster's *Mule Train* sung with Woody Herman, where the special-effects mule sounds like a robot dog barking in a sewer pipe. With ever-jocular Johnny Mercer he travesties Burke and van Heusen's *Harmony*, hammering out clinkers on a tack-piano. Not a great record, but an entertaining one. **KW**

**Big Band Cole** Cole (v); **John Anderson**, **Joe Newman**, **Wendell Culley**, **Thad Jones**, **Snooky Young**, **Henry Coker**, **Al Grey**, **Benny Powell** (t); **Marshall Royal**, **Frank Wess** (as); **Frank Foster**, **Billy Mitchell** (ts); **Charlie Fowlkes** (b); **Gerald Wiggins** (p); **Freddie Green** (g); **Eddie Jones** (b); **Sonny Payne** (d); **Dave Cavanagh** (arr, cond); **King Cole Trio** (Cole, Irving Ashby, g, Joe Comfort, b); **Stan Kenton Orchestra**; **Pete Rugolo**, **Shorty Rogers** (arr). Capitol Ⓜ CDP7 96259-2 (45 minutes). Recorded 1950/8.

✅ ⑧ ❽

It has often been suggested that Nat King Cole turned into an entirely different person when he stopped playing piano and became a stand-up ballad singer, but this is absurd. All the musicality that went into making him the finest jazz pianist of his generation was still there, and can be heard in every vocal performance he ever recorded. For jazz lovers, this is the one to get. Originally issued under the title **Welcome to the Club**, it features Nat with the Count Basie Orchestra (minus Basie himself, for contractual reasons). There is always drama inherent in the combination of solo voice and orchestra, and the contrast between Nat's warm, unhurried tones and the purring ferocity of the great swing machine brings it out magnificently. **DG**

# Richie Cole

**Side By Side** Cole (as, v); **Phil Woods** (as); **Eddie 'Lockjaw' Davis** (ts); **John Hicks** (p); **Walter Booker** (b); **Jimmy Cobb** (d). Muse Ⓕ MCD6016 (52 minutes). Recorded 1980.

⑥ ❽

This is an ideal CD through which to discover Cole because, while still at school, the young saxophonist studied with his partner here, Woods. After Berklee, he worked with Buddy Rich and Lionel Hampton and since the mid-seventies has led combos of his own. As a player he has always come over better on live dates. His Woods-like style has its wayward as well as its humorous moments; his search for the correct improvisational route sometimes takes him into musical forests from which he is pressed to extricate himself. He could have sounded a trifle lightweight alongside Woods (and the heavyweight Davis, who appears on just one track), but their presence does mean that he can neither coast or showboat. His tough, swaggering tone is distinctive and, if Woods sounds cleaner, more controlled and more obviously creative, it is not the one-sided contest it might have been. Cole is certainly not overawed; *Naugahyde Reality* is his brief free jazz send-up, while it is his alto that winds up the tension on *Scrapple from the Apple*, produces the tastefully concise reading of *Polka Dots and Moonbeams* and in the juxtaposed *Eddie's Mood* and *Side By Side* proves that, when the chops are up, he can match even the likes of Woods.     **BMcR**

# Bill Coleman                                                                1904-81

**New review**
**Hangin' Around** Coleman (t, v) with **Luis Russell Orchestra** (on one track); **Willie Lewis Orchestra** (two tracks); **Joe Marsala** (cl); **Pete Brown** (as); **Carmen Mastren** (g); **Gene Traxler** (b) (three tracks); **Coleman Hawkins** (ts); **Andy Fitzgerald** (cl); **Ellis Larkins** (p); **Al Casey** (g); **Oscar Pettiford** (b); **Shelly Manne** (d) (two tracks); and the following collective personnel on 15 tracks: **Bill Dillard, Shad Collins** (t); **Dicky Wells** (tb); **Edgar Courance** (cl, ts); **George Johnson** (cl, as); **Garnett Clark, Herman Chittison, Stephen Grappelli** (p); **Django Reinhardt, Oscar Aleman, John Mitchell** (g); **Eugene d'Hellemmes, Richard Fulbright, Wilson Myers, June Cole** (b); **William Diemer, Bill Beason, Ted Fields, Tommy Benford** (d). Topaz Ⓕ TPZ1040 (71 minutes). Recorded 1929-43.

⑧ ❼

Coleman, one of the most elegant of all trumpet soloists, spent many years in France, giving the lie to the story that American jazzmen away from home failed to reach their peak. No less than 17 of the tracks here were made in Paris before the war, halcyon days for jazz in the French capital, and for Bill too. There are gems here, *Rosetta* and *Star Dust* with Garnett Clark at the piano, the memorable *Mood for Love* played as a trumpet-piano duet with Herman Chittison, but perhaps best of all are the tracks made in the summer of 1937 when the Teddy Hill band was in Paris. The French Swing label was quick to put Bill in the studio with such distinguished visitors as Bill Dillard, Shad Collins and Dicky Wells for timeless tracks such as *Devil and The Deep Blue Sea*, *Hangin' Around Boudon* and the three-trumpet feature *I Got Rhythm*. Teddy Hill's third trumpeter on the tour was Dizzy Gillespie, who was ignored by record producer Hugues Panassie when these dates were set up. The final five tracks mark Bill's return to the US, three by an intimate-sounding band under Joe Marsala's leadership and two with a more forthright septet placing Bill alongside Coleman Hawkins to very good effect. The Coleman choice in the previous edition (**Bill Coleman 1929-40** on Jazz Archives 157 822) duplicates six of the tracks on the Topaz set.     **AM**

# Earl Coleman                                                               1925-95

**New review**
**Earl Coleman Returns** Coleman (v); **Art Farmer, Nat Howard, Nat Woodward** (t); **Henderson Chambers, Edwin Moore** (tb); **Gigi Gryce** (as), **Gene Ammons** (ts); **Gene Easton, Cecil Payne** (bs); **Hank Jones, John Houston, Lawrence Wheatley** (p); **Wendell Marshall, Oscar Pettiford, Ben Stuberville, Ernie Shephard** (b); **Wilbert Hogan, George Brown, Shadow Wilson** (d). Prestige Ⓜ OJCCD187-2 (46 minutes). Recorded 1955/6.

⑦ ❽

A romantic baritone in the general manner of Billy Eskstine and Arthur Prysock, Earl Coleman received a curiously mixed blessing in 1947. Charlie Parker admired his singing and promised to include him in one of his recording sessions. He was as good as his word and, in the teeth of opposition from Dial Records boss, Ross Russell, Coleman sang two numbers – *This is Always* and *Dark Shadows* – on Parker's **Cool Blues** session of February 19th. The first of these songs became a juke-box hit and Dial's biggest-selling record ever. However, posterity saw fit to regard Earl Coleman as an interloper on a classic session and no further breaks came his way. This is a shame, since he was a pleasant and intelligent singer, albeit in a style which is now deeply unfashionable. Accompanied by a series of excellent small bands made up from the above personnel, Coleman sings ten numbers here, including particularly good versions of *Say It Isn't So* and *Ghost of a Chance*. Art Farmer and Gene Ammons are outstanding among the soloists.     **DG**

# George Coleman                                                            1935

**My Horns of Plenty** Coleman (ss, as, ts); **Harold Mabern** (p); **Ray Drummond** (b); **Billy Higgins** (d). Birdology Ⓕ 511 922-2 (63 minutes). Recorded 1991.

⑥ ❽

Coleman is indissolubly linked with two great mid-sixties recordings, Herbie Hancock's **Maiden**

**Voyage** and Miles Davis's **My Funny Valentine**. Yet it is odd that this fine player is rarely given his fair share of the credit for the success of those ventures. Coleman, born in Memphis, is of the same generation as Booker Little and Frank Strozier, and in the late fifties played with Little in the Max Roach Quintet. By the time he graduated to the Miles Davis Quintet, replacing Hank Mobley, his was a highly personal style combining elements of Coltrane, Getz, Young and perhaps Jacquet, using a sophisticated harmonic and rhythmic palette to create a great deal of understated lyrical beauty. From that point on he played mostly with leaders like Elvin Jones or with his own groups, and has carved a solid if unspectacular career.

This present set is good but not at the same level as his work on the above-mentioned albums, where his impassioned lyricism is at times transcendent. The shadow of Coltrane hovers a little closer than in the past, not helped by a decidedly toppy recorded sound which imparts less than the usual warmth to his tenor tone (he plays tenor on the majority of tracks here). Mabern is very busy throughout, and is perhaps not the ideal partner. However, a Coleman disc is always full of thoughtful, uncompromising improvisation with little reliance on cliché, so those who like their sax to be modern mainstream with a touch of flair will be satisfied by this one.

A new live album recorded at Ronnie Scott's Club and featuring Peter King and Julian Joseph may be more recent, but is no better. **KS**

# Ornette Coleman

1930

**Beauty is a Rare Thing** Coleman (as, ts); **Eric Dolphy** (as, f, bcl); **Don Cherry** (c, pkt t); **Freddie Hubbard** (t); **Charlie Haden, Scott LaFaro, Jimmy Garrison** (b); **Billy Higgins, Ed Blackwell** (d); **Bill Evans** (p); **Contemporary String Quartet**. Rhino/Atlantic Jazz Ⓜ R2-71410 (six discs: 427 minutes). Recorded 1959-61.

⑩ ❽

Listening to this music today, it is hard to hear it as revolutionary, not because its value or profundity has lessened (it hasn't), but because what was shocking once is now so familiar, what was called by some 'anti-jazz' has become a pervasive influence on so much contemporary music. In retrospect it is easier to hear how with such simple means Ornette extended the hyper-reality of Charlie Parker into a new formal consideration, redesigning, as one album cover aptly put it, the *shape* of the music to come by erasing barlines, loosening rhythms and reducing harmony to an incidental by-product of the creation of pure melody. And as a melodist, Coleman is a master storyteller – *à la* Lester Young.

Each of the individual Atlantic LPs may be available singly, but among the advantages of this collection (other than the six previously unreleased numbers, the Japanese-only **To Whom Who Keeps a Record**, and the so far unreissued Gunther Schuller-composed pieces from **Jazz Abstraction**, all included here) is the opportunity to experience classic performances in a fresh, revealing context. One point that jumps out is that, for all the freedom Ornette's procedures supposedly granted each player, this is an amazingly interdependent *ensemble*. In the booklet-notes Don Cherry reminds us of how thoroughly prepared the musicians were in order to deal with this freedom, and how organized the music was, although the details and – the truly revolutionary aspect – the form was spontaneously improvised. Yet another is the brilliant and absolutely crucial contribution of Charlie Haden, who was literally inventing the role of 'free' bassist on the spur of the moment. But it is Ornette's vision and courage which comes through the strongest. That it ultimately and forever changed how and what we hear as jazz is secondary; separately or together, it is the music for its own sake – imaginative, joyful, bluesy, funny, ecstatic and essential – that must be heard. **AL**

**The Shape of Jazz to Come** Coleman (as); **Don Cherry** (c); **Charlie Haden** (b); **Billy Higgins** (d). Atlantic Ⓜ 781317-2 (38 minutes). Recorded 1959.

❼ ⑩ ❽

Today this music sounds so clear and flowing it is hard to believe people at the time thought it cacophonous. They did so because Ornette Coleman's new conception of jazz simply bypassed bebop's predetermined patterns of chord changes and bar lengths and left each player (in Coleman's words) "free to contribute what he feels in the music at any given moment". The result was not the anarchy that some feared but, on Coleman's classic Atlantic recordings, a new kind of spontaneous group rapport plus improvisation that, based on melody, roamed freely.

**The Shape of Jazz to Come** was Coleman's début recording for Atlantic and the first to feature his regular quartet (for various reasons, they had not all played on his two previous albums for Contemporary). This was a vital plus. Coleman and Cherry's then near-telepathic understanding is complemented here by the group's ability to hang together even when horns, bass and drums are playing independent lines. A striking example is *Lonely Woman*, one of Coleman's best-known compositions, where the horns announce the dirge-like theme over racing drums and a separate accented bass line. Coleman's brief solo here, with its vocalized cry and asymmetrical phrases, typifies his breakdown of conventional form to give voice more directly to feeling.

The ultimate introduction to Ornette from this period is the boxed set **Beauty is a Rare Thing** (reviewed above), but if that is too daunting, then this is a perfect beginning. **GL**

**Free Jazz** Coleman (as); **Freddie Hubbard** (t); **Don Cherry** (pkt t); **Eric Dolphy** (bcl); **Scott LaFaro**, **Charlie Haden** (b); **Billy Higgins**, **Ed Blackwell** (d). Atlantic Ⓜ 781364-2 (54 minutes). Recorded 1960.

✓                                                                              ⑨ ⑧

You needed to be a special kind of visionary to conceive this in 1960. John Coltrane's **Ascension** and Peter Brötzmann's **Machine Gun** are probably the two most celebrated sons of **Free Jazz**. In the longer term, Ornette Coleman's idea of the interactive double quartet may have planted the seed that led him to harmolodics and Prime Time. His scheme of things, in which a round of free solos, supported by the other musicians as they thought fit, were connected by pre-set melodies and chords, still has implications for anyone tackling extended forms. When first reviewing the album many years ago I didn't realize there was a stereo version! The acquisition of same, together with the shorter *First Take* (literally the first recorded effort at the same composition, made the same day), opened my ears particularly to Eric Dolphy, whose solo had previously been mixed almost out of earshot. Now one can also appreciate the value of his bass clarinet as chief noise-maker in the ensembles. Hubbard's attempt to phrase melodiously was clearly what Coleman wanted: accompanying fanfares grow more relaxed until, during Coleman's extraordinary alto passage, the others are given plenty of space to interject. After Cherry's flourishes comes the haunting bass duet (speedy LaFaro intertwined with soulful Haden) and the final contrast between Blackwell's drums and Higgins's cymbals. What stands out as much as ever is the lyrical strength of *Free Jazz*, far removed from clichés of energy music. I would still quibble about this and that, and would prefer some occasional relief from the relentless percussion. However, Coleman didn't get where he is by taking advice from other people. **RA**

**At the Golden Circle, Volumes 1 and 2** Coleman (as, t, vn); **David Izenzon** (b); **Charles Moffett** (d). Blue Note Ⓜ CDP7 84224/5-2 (two discs, oas: 39 and 44 minutes). Recorded 1965.

⑨ ⑥

Sometimes jazz history and some people's perception of it is affected by the sequence in which recordings are issued. Coleman's Town Hall concert had given the jazz world a brief glimpse of his trumpet and violin work. For those who did not hear him on his European tour, the **Golden Circle** issue was their first exposure to these new elements. Coleman had re-assembled his pre-sabbatical trio for the tour and united the classically devoted Izenzon and the propulsive Moffett into an ideal team. His own alto skills remain undiminished. He makes *The Riddle* a melodic 'free fall', he builds *Faces and Places* from scantily related melodic statements, while on *Antiques* he shows how he moves away from his strong parent themes, elaborating on each idea before moving to the next. On *Dawn* we are treated to another superb Coleman dirge, full of bluesy implications and Texas rhythm & blues know-how. Both violin and trumpet appear on *Snowflakes and Sunshine* and confirm that they are 'like his alto' in a way that his formal (non jazz) compositions are not. The violin hints at a more radical departure in style and shows that a theme taken on the instrument is not so much rebuilt as given a new state. The trumpet parts are rhythmically more similar to the alto; they adopt the same chromatic stance but do not aspire to the same controlled methods of execution. Both are important aspects of Coleman's art and these two CDs occupy a significant place in his portfolio. **BMcR**

**Virgin Beauty** Coleman (as, vn, t); **Charles Ellerbe**, **Bern Nix**, **Jerry Garcia** (g); **Al MacDowell**, **Chris Walker** (elb); **Calvin Weston** (d); **Denardo Coleman** (d, kbds, perc). Columbia Portrait Ⓕ RK44301 (45 minutes). Recorded 1987-8.

✓                                                                              ⑧ ⑧

Perhaps Coleman's most accessible recording, although oddly one of his most overlooked. If the synthesis of funk and free jazz that he achieved in the name of harmolodics on 1975's **Dancing in Your Head** was the freshest thing some of us had ever heard, this item from 12 years later sounded to many like the freshest thing they had ever heard before. A closer listen to **Virgin Beauty** reveals delightful new wrinkles. The synthesized, playfully static backdrop to Coleman's rolling alto on *Healing the Feeling* is an example of his son Denardo's increased production savvy, as is the double-tracking that allows Ornette to play trumpet and alto duets with himself here and there. Spread over the stingy length of this disc are tempos and rhythms new to jazz, or at least uncommon to it: the camel lope on *Three Wishes*, the hoedown feeling on the irresistible *Happy Hour* and the lick borrowed from Wilson Pickett on *Bourgeois Boogie*. Coleman's shapely, unaccompanied introduction to *Unknown Artist* ranks as one of his most lyrical solos on record. The Grateful Dead's Jerry Garcia guest stars on three tracks and blends in so nicely with Prime Time regulars Ellerbee and Nix that you do not even notice him. **FD**

**Tone Dialing** Coleman (as, vn); **Ken Wessel**, **Chris Rosenberg** (g); **Al MacDowell**, **Bradley Jones**, **Chris Walker** (b); **Denardo Coleman** (d); **Badal Roy** (perc); **Avenda 'Khadijah' Ali**, **Moishe Naim** (v). Harmolodic/Verve Ⓕ 527 483-2 (67 minutes). Recorded 1995.

⑦ ⑨

Issued by Verve under Ornette Coleman's Harmolodic imprint, this streetwise implosion of funk, 'found' sounds and free jazz is a celebration of international accents and the cultures from which they derive. In the album's sleeve-notes Coleman welcomes his listeners: "Enter **Tone Dialing**, a sound experience of music in the present perception of society as it becomes an ethnical (sic) civilization of all world citizens." In piecing together his polyglot collage, Coleman appropriates elements from the U.S. (*Street Blues*), Mexico (*Guadalupe*), India (*Badal*), China (*Ying Yang*) and more. A *Bach Prelude*, at first ethereal, then funky, serves as a historical/musical reference point; it also demonstrates the power of stylistic pastiche as a means of making us re-think and re-evaluate basic assumptions.

Drilling through densely compacted striations combining the inspired playing of Prime Time with an array of sounds plucked from life itself, Coleman soars like a prophet. Not since Charles Ives has an American sketched in tones so brash and contradictory. In tracks like *Sound is Everywhere*, the leader's alto dances atop an urban soundscape spiked by literal city sounds and edgy rhythmic backdrops, a set of bold juxtapositions corroborating John Cage's liberating insight on the cosmic immensity of the envelope containing 'music'. As evidenced here, Coleman remains, to paraphrase media guru Marshall McLuhan, "an antenna of the race" reporting on the ethnic-technological mega-trends sweeping us toward the millennium. **CB**

## Steve Coleman 1956

**The Tao of Mad Phat** Coleman (as, p); **Andy Milne** (p, kbds); **David Gilmore** (g, gsyn); **Reggie Washington** (elb); **Oliver Gene Lake Jr** (d, perc); **Roy Hargrove** (t); **Josh Roseman** (tb); **Kenny Davis** (b); **Matthew Garrison** (elb); **Junior 'Gabu' Wederburn** (perc). RCA Novus Ⓕ 63160 2 (76 minutes). Recorded 1993.

✔ ⑧ ❽

The principles that fuel the M-Base ethic are more consistent with the inspirational sources that motivated Jelly Roll Morton, Louis Armstrong and Charlie Parker than are the academic ground rules nurturing the neo-classical boppers or any other revivalist movement. The Five Elements heard here are part of Brooklyn's M-Base world and they take as their starting point the rhythms of their own black youth. By their very circumstances, this means the pulsating and often unsubtle heartbeat of soul and funk as much as it does the jazz tradition of Ornette Coleman and John Coltrane. The outcome can be heard clearly on this CD as Coleman's men, recorded live before a studio audience, show how they have synthesized both extremes to produce a 1993 music that is their own. The acoustic *Incantation* presents their jazz basics, but it is items such as *Laid Back Schematics* and the title track that best demonstrate Coleman's outstanding improvisational skills in a style born of namesake Ornette's free jazz, but painted on a soulful canvas. Steve Coleman's moments of greatest inspiration may be found in the acoustic fabric of Dave Holland's small groups, but the altoist is very much at home in the different rhythmic environment on offer here. He has continued to prosper in this style, with his latest simultaneous releases for Novus, the live **The Way of the Cipher** (with Metrics) and **Curves of Life** (with Five Elements) keeping the heat well and truly turned up. **BMcR**

**Def Trance Beat (Modalities of Rhythm)** Coleman (as); **The Five Elements** (Andy Milne, p, kbds; Reggie Washington, b; Gene Lake, d, perc); on three tracks, add **Ravi Coltrane** (ts). RCA Novus Ⓕ 63181 2 (69 minutes). Recorded 1994.

⑨ ❿

Coleman has always been a rigorous theorist, unafraid to investigate the musical application of his ideas. This has led him into some notable cul-de-sacs, some of which have been sheer hard work for the listener with no concomitant pay-off of pleasure. This album is different: his ideas spontaneously combust into a compelling tapestry of technique, passion and plain old excitement. The title is an apt one, for the whole basis of the music is profoundly rooted in the swirling matrix of rhythm created by the intricately plotted intersections of drum, piano, bass and saxophone. This is not, as has been suffered in the past, some warmed-over cod-funk workout; this is genuinely challenging music, with a wild excitement about the resultant melding together of timbre, tone and punctuation. When tenor player Ravi Coltrane is added to the chemistry, the effect can be close to overwhelming, the richness of the scoring and the solos like a Fauvist painting. This challenging album is an important step forward for Coleman, and is a fascinating synthesis of many contemporary musical developments. Essential contemporary listening. **KS**

## Johnny Coles 1926

New review
**Little Johnny C** Coles (t); **Leo Wright** (as, f); **Joe Henderson** (ts); **Duke Pearson** (p); **Bob Cranshaw** (b); **Walter Perkins, Pete LaRoca** (d). Blue Note Ⓜ CDP 832129-2 (40 minutes). Recorded 1963.

⑦ ❽

This was the first album Coles made under his own name. It has always been highly regarded since its initial release in 1964, and has previously been reissued only in Japan. Now it is returned to general release in the Blue Note Connoisseur series. Coles came to prominence with the late-fifties Gil Evans orchestra before transferring to James Moody's quintet. Prior to that he had done time with a number of bands inhabiting the borderland between jazz and r&b. By the time this album was in the shops Coles was touring Europe with a famous Mingus septet featuring Dolphy and Clifford Jordan. Having said all that, this is Duke Pearson's record in all but name. Five of the six tunes (including the title number) were penned by him and he hired the talent who recorded with Coles. This guarantees that the record doesn't stray far from Blue Note groove-land, that the arrangements are tidy and that no one solos to the point of exhaustion. It's a swinging, conversational, convivial set of music, unprepossessing but of uniformly high quality. Coles has a distinctively warm, full tone and a very personal lyricism (it was for these reasons that Evans used him so often, to fill Miles's shoes on albums like **Great Jazz Standards** and **Out of the Cool**). Coles's understated charm has often left him in the shade of other more boisterous talents, but he is still capable today of producing the goods, as the latter-day **New Morning** (Criss Cross, 1982) will attest, should you seek it out. **KS**

# Buddy Collette

1921

**New review**

**Nice Day with Buddy Collette** Collette (cl, as, ts, f); **Don Friedman, Dick Shrieve, Calvin Jackson** (p); **John Goodman, Leroy Vinnegar** (b); **Bill Dolney, Shelly Manne** (d). Contemporary Ⓜ OJCCD747-2 (43 minutes). Recorded 1956-7.

⑥ ❽

When this record was made, Collette was a high-profile front-line man with Chico Hamilton's chamber-jazz group and had already amassed more than two decades of professional music-making. Collette's cool and immaculate playing perfectly fitted Hamilton's low-flame intricacies, and although the group is largely forgotten today, it was one of the true popularizers of cool West Coast jazz during the fifties, enjoying a substantial popular audience. Collette chose a line-up for his second album as a leader which eschewed the cello and guitar to be found in his employer's band, and the resultant overall sound of the groups here is considerably more conventional. As a showcase for Collette's instrumental talents this is an attractive and well-balanced session, allowing all the players considerably more room for expression than the featherweight **Jazz Loves Paris** (Speciality) from 1958, the only other Collette-led date from this decade currently available. Of the three featured pianists Friedman is the most immediately impressive, giving exquisite backing to Collette's flute on *Over the Rainbow* in particular, while Jackson adds a more ebullient touch to his three featured tracks. Collette himself plays with perfect tone and intonation throughout, chooses his phrases well and manages a genial expressiveness which is unerring in its reflection of the album's title. On that basis, have a nice day, y'all! **KS**

# Graham Collier

**New review**

**Charles River Fragments** Collier (dir); **Art Themen, Chris Biscoe, Mark Lockheart, Geoff Warren** (reeds); **Henry Lowther, Steve Waterman, Patrick Whit** (t); **Hugh Fraser, Bell Mee** (tb); **Andy Grappy** (tba); **Pete Saberton** (p); **Dudley Phillips** (b); **John Marshall** (d). Boathouse Ⓕ BHR004 (66 minutes). Recorded 1994.

⑦ ❽

Based in London, Graham Collier's 14-strong Jazz Ensemble is "an improvising big band" inspired by such free-wheeling collectives as those led by Charles Mingus and Gil Evans (in his later days) and the Globe Unity Orchestra. In his notes, Collier indicates that the two extended tracks include a considerable amount of writing and preplanning. They do, and that undoubtedly helps give the variegated segments of the 56-minute long *Charles River Fragments* a sense of over-arching structure. As a colourist, Collier favours the lower end of the big band tessitura. His adroit couplings of bass trombone and baritone saxophone are downright ominous. Dedicated to Mingus and Herb Pomeroy (Collier's guru at Boston's Berklee College where the Charles River flows), *Fragments* and the smaller scale *Hackney Five* are both within and beyond the traditional big band pocket. Commissioned by BBC Radio 3, Collier conjures up sounds at once abstract and accessible. **CB**

# Alice Coltrane

1937

**New review**

**Ptah, the El Daoud** Coltrane (p, h); **Pharoah Sanders, Joe Henderson** (ts, af); **Ron Carter** (b); **Ben Riley** (d). Impulse! Ⓜ IMP 12012 (46 minutes). Recorded 1970.

⑥ ❻

With the death of John Coltrane in 1967 the Impulse! label looked to his close musical companions to provide the way to the music of the coming decade. Both his wife Alice (formerly Alice McLeod, pianist wth Terry Gibbs's small group) and Pharoah Sanders were signed and began producing a steady stream of records. While Sanders concentrated on one aspect of Coltrane's legacy, the music Alice created bore little relation to her late husband's. As a pianist she was particularly comfortable with blues phrasing and the joys of repetition, contrasting long arpeggios with small repeated motifs mostly based on the blues. As a harpist she gave herself completely to the wash of sound the instrument could deliver, relying on the ostinatos of her bass player and the steady metric pulse of the drummer to give the music forward momentum. This meant her albums could get rather monochrome, and one solution to this problem was to bring in other soloists. Here there are two, Sanders himself and Joe Henderson (Joe returned the favour by having Alice on one of his dates for Milestone). The title track pitches both men into a minor mode, and the two solo interestingly, although at 14 minutes the track runs out of steam. Alice's trio rendition of the very bluesy ballad *Turiya and Ramakrishna* follows peaceably enough, then the horn players return, this time both on alto flute (with Alice on harp), for *Blue Nile*. Neither the theme nor their flute techniques are strong enough to sustain interest, even over six minutes. The last track, *Mantra*, brings us full circle to a piano/sax/sax line-up, and the saxes solo strongly. All in all, then, an uneven album, as were all of them, as interesting in its own way as **Journey in Satchidananda**, but without its beauty. The recorded sound (the album was recorded in the Coltranes' house studio) is greatly improved from the chronic inadequacies of the original vinyl release.                                    **KS**

# John Coltrane                                                        1926-67

---

**Blue Train**  Coltrane (ts); **Lee Morgan** (t); **Curtis Fuller** (tb); **Kenny Drew** (p); **Paul Chambers** (b); **Philly Joe Jones** (d). Blue Note Ⓜ CDP7 46095-2 (43 minutes). Recorded 1957.

✅                                                                      ⑧ ❽

Coltrane made his professional début at 19 and spent much of his early career in the rhythm & blues bands of Cleanhead Vinson and Earl Bostic. Spells with Dizzy Gillespie and Johnny Hodges honed his big-band disciplines until, in 1955, he joined Miles Davis. The implications of that partnership are well documented in this CD, made while he was briefly with Thelonious Monk. The triumphs of **Giant Steps** (reviewed below) are nearly two years ahead, but this is one of the first sessions to hint at the awesome authority that would attend his later work. Playing with Monk placed moderately strict harmonic restrictions on him and it is as if, on this album in particular, he sees leadership of his own session as a licence to extend the melodic aspect of his style. His detailed horizontal progress can still sound like three men playing in a telephone booth but there is an excitement and power in the music that transcends all other issues. His improvisations have already broken free of standard structures, but fortunately Miles Davis's colleagues, Chambers and Jones, know what is expected of them. The presence of the outstanding Morgan and journeyman Fuller is of little significance on a session that is increasingly being acknowledged as the first landmark in Coltrane's group-leading exploits.                           **BMcR**

---

**Soultrane**  Coltrane (ts); **Red Garland** (p); **Paul Chambers** (b); **Arthur Taylor** (d). Prestige Ⓜ OJCCD021 (40 minutes). Recorded 1958.

✔                                                                      ⑧ ❽

The conservative listener is more likely to find pre-1961 Coltrane preferable to the later work where his tendency to prolixity was so often given its head. The intense and precise nature of his inventions on albums such as this one and on the contemporary ones he made with Miles Davis (see below) brought a succinct and powerful new manner of improvising into jazz. Most of Coltrane's important innovations had become apparent by the time of this session, made with two thirds of the Davis rhythm section (for some reason Taylor replaced Philly Joe Jones). The intensity of Coltrane's feeling is offset by the elegant piano playing of Red Garland, sounding much more relaxed playing for Coltrane than he did for Davis, who was apt to be more proscriptive about how his pianists played.

Having said that Coltrane is succinct, so he is, but some of the tracks are quite long, with *Good Bait* running for 12 minutes. *I Want to Talk About You* lasts for 11 minutes and is the earliest recording of a tune that Coltrane was later to play almost nightly. It is a beautiful blues ballad composed by Billy Eckstine and is particularly suitable for the keening melodicism with which the tenorist imbues it. This is arguably Coltrane's best work before the **Giant Steps** album which opened another phase of his career a year or so later.                                                   **SV**

---

**Giant Steps**  Coltrane (ts); **Cedar Walton, Tommy Flanagan, Wynton Kelly** (p); **Paul Chambers** (b); **Lex Humphries, Art Taylor, Jimmy Cobb** (d). Atlantic Jazz Ⓜ 781337-2 (63 minutes). Recorded 1959.

✔                                                                      ⑩ ❽

When Coltrane's contract with Prestige expired at the end of 1958 he moved to Atlantic, an organization which had resources to allow him to spend more time on the production of albums. **Giant Steps** is arguably one of the three most important LPs Coltrane ever made. All seven tunes were not only written by Coltrane but all were highly original and each has become part of the larger jazz repertoire. Here at last he was able to present his music in a considered and comprehensive manner. He was ridding himself of the overpowering obligation of a repeated chord progression; instead the music uses scales, allowing the soloist more options, more possibilities to branch out into a fresh direction. Throughout **Giant Steps** his enormous instrumental technique (he could cruise comfortably through more than three octaves on a tenor) is allied to a most fertile imagination to produce music of supreme quality. Not only are there headlong assaults at fast tempo (*Giant Steps* itself is a perfect example) but there is the tender, moving ballad approach of *Naima*. The LP has been lovingly transferred to CD and adds alternative versions of five of the tunes, three of them actually recorded at an earlier session with a different rhythm section, all of which makes for fascinating listening.                                                                                       **AM**

---

**New review**

## The Heavyweight Champion: The Complete Atlantic Recordings  Coltrane (ts, ss); **Hank Jones**, **Cedar Walton**, **Tommy Flanagan**, **Wynton Kelly**, **McCoy Tyner** (p); **Milt Jackson** (vb); **Paul Chambers**, **Steve Davis**, **Art Davis**, **Reggie Workman**, **Charlie Haden** (b); **Connie Kay**, **Lex Humphries**, **Art Taylor**, **Jimmy Cobb**, **Elvin Jones**, **Ed Blackwell** (d); **Don Cherry**, **Freddie Hubbard** (t); **Eric Dolphy** (as, f). Rhino/Atlantic Jazz Gallery Ⓜ R2 71984 (seven discs: 480 minutes). Recorded 1959-61.

⑩ ❽

In this masterfully assembled seven-disc package, reissue producer Joel Dorn has taken Coltrane's pivotal Atlantic material and presented it chronologically rather than album by album. Dorn's decision allows us to track Coltrane's evolution through the chordal complexities of *Giant Steps* and a tentative foray into free jazz with Ornette Coleman's rhythm section to the stripped-down harmonic maps that launched the saxophonist's Mid-Eastern inflected modal flights. Spanning sessions running from January 15th, 1959 to May 25th, 1961, arguably Coltrane's most focused and productive period, these meticulously remastered sides put us into the eye of an aesthetic storm whose fallout is still being examined and incorporated into improvisational forms embracing rock and pop as well as jazz.

What is most fascinating about the 1959-61 period is the juxtaposition of Coltrane's capstone efforts to push the harmonic logic of bebop to its ultimate conclusions while at the same time deconstructing those very same conclusions. Thus, while taking Parker to the wall via the chordal overlays of his *Giant Steps* approach, Coltrane was simultaneously paring standard harmonic schemes to skeletal outlines as in the pivotal reframing of Rodgers and Hammerstein's *My Favorite Things*, whose landmark status was redoubled by Coltrane's Mid-Eastern atmospherics and influential use of soprano saxophone. Both tactics combined to make him the most emulated jazz player of his era.

Underpinning each foray is Coltrane's constant search for new frontiers. It was a search informed by the saxophonist's extensive musicological researches and obsessive practice routines. Also palpable is Coltrane's great heart. A reformed alcoholic and drug addict, Coltrane sought a purification in his art and life that unified his spiritual and musical quests. In the process, he became a sixties icon of truth-seeking and integrity, qualities that speak as clearly today as they did during the height of America's civil rights movement. Rhino's handsomely packaged boxed set includes all of Coltrane's Atlantic releases (**Giant Steps**, **Coltrane Jazz**, **My Favorite Things**, **Bags & Trane**, **Olé**, **Coltrane Plays the Blues**, **Coltrane's Sound**, **The Avant-Garde**, **The Coltrane Legacy** and **Alternate Takes**). The seventh disc comprises 75 minutes of never-before-released outtakes from the *Giant Steps* session of March 1959 in which we hear the false starts and studio chatter leading up to the definitive versions of *Giant Steps*, *Naima* and *Like Sonny*. The 72-page hard-cover booklet includes an incisive Lewis Porter essay as well as loving tributes from Charles Lloyd, McCoy Tyner, Elvin Jones, Jimmy Heath, Yusef Lateef, producer Nesuhi Ertegun and engineer Tom Dowd. There are 29 evocative photos, reproductions of the Coltrane LP jackets, and a warm interview with Coltrane's cousin and childhood companion, Mary Alexander, whom Coltrane immortalized with *Cousin Mary*. For vinyl fetishists, **The Heavyweight Champion** is available in a 12-LP version.                                                                                      **CB**

---

## Coltrane's Sound  Coltrane (ss, ts); **McCoy Tyner** (p); **Steve Davis** (b); **Elvin Jones** (d). Atlantic Jazz Ⓜ 781419-2 (50 minutes). Recorded 1960.

✅                                                                                      ⑧ ❻

There is a lot of exceptional Coltrane in the mass of pre-Impulse! material, including **Traneing In**, **Settin' the Pace**, **Coltrane Jazz** and especially the present set. This album is hardly unknown, containing as it does the ballad *Central Park West*, the mysterious blues *Equinox* and Coltrane's afro-vamp arrangement of *Body and Soul* which manages the impossible task of moving this classic out from under the looming shadow of Coleman Hawkins's version. While the above compositions/arrangements have entered the realm of jazz standards, the tracks that give us Coltrane's take on bebop are equally valuable. *Liberia* is his reworking of *Night in Tunisia*, *Satellite* his *How High the Moon*, and bonus-track *26-2* his theme on the chords of *Confirmation*. There is also a blistering *The Night Has a Thousand Eyes* with an exultant Elvin Jones, plus an alternative take of *Body and Soul*. McCoy Tyner was still developing, and could have used a better studio piano, but it is otherwise hard to fault this view of Coltrane from the sessions that also produced **My Favorite Things** and **Coltrane Plays the Blues**.                                                                                      **BB**

---

## My Favorite Things  Coltrane (ss, ts); **McCoy Tyner** (p); **Steve Davis** (b); **Elvin Jones** (d). Atlantic Jazz Ⓜ 782346-2 (41 minutes). Recorded 1960.

✅                                                                                      ⑧ ❼

Coltrane's first issued workout on soprano sax (**The Avant-Garde** with Don Cherry was recorded earlier, released later), *My Favorite Things* remained a staple of Coltrane's live performances thereafter. As a popular song with graceful modal chord changes and an insinuating, incantatory melody, it was perfect for his gifts, although one should note that the 14-minute version here is less expansive than renditions he would play on the bandstand in future years. The influence of nasal-sounding Asian and Mid-Eastern reed instruments on Coltrane's soprano is often noted, but the similarities in tone and range between soprano and trumpet suggest the valve instrument's influence also; indeed, the soprano ballad feature *Ev'ry Time We Say Goodbye* betrays Miles Davis's stamp (later it was to become associated with Chet Baker).

An up-tempo swing through Gershwin's *Summertime*, with Trane on tenor, is in the splashy style of his emerging classic quartet, which at this point lacked only bassist Jimmy Garrison. Jones's polyrhythmia and Tyner's billowing extended chords, both designed to restrict a soloist as little as possible, were already developing. Coltrane's art was often about process; **My Favorite Things** finds him poised at the beginning of a key phase of his development. **KW**

---

**New review**

**The Complete Africa/Brass Sessions** Coltrane (ss, ts); **Booker Little**, **Freddie Hubbard** (t); **Britt Woodman** (tb); **Carl Bowman, Charles Greenlee, Julian Priester** (euph); **Jimmy Buffington, Donald Corrado, Bob Northern, Robert Swisshelm, Julius Watkins** (frh); **Bill Barber** (tba); **Eric Dolphy** (f, as, bcl, cond); **Garvin Bushell** (pic, reeds); **Pat Patrick** (bs); **McCoy Tyner** (p); **Yaul Chambers, Art Davis, Reggie Workman** (b); **Elvin Jones** (d). Impulse! Ⓜ IMP21682 (two discs: 89 minutes). Recorded 1961.

⑧ ❼

John Coltrane's first recording sessions for his new label saw his quartet (with Workman on bass) augmented by a large ensemble of mostly brass pieces. The original **Africa/Brass** LP comprised three tracks (*Africa, Greensleeves, Blues Minor*). In the mid seventies three more tracks (*Song of the Underground Railroad* and alternative takes of *Africa* and *Greensleeves*) were released on the **Africa/Brass Volume Two** album, then a further two (*The Damned Don't Cry* and a second alternative take of *Africa*) appeared on the double-LP compilation **Trane's Modes**. Thanks are due to GRP, current custodians of the Impulse! label, for releasing these sessions in their entirety for the first time and for correcting errors in the previous personnel listings. The music itself is fascinating and boasts what was at the time some of Coltrane's strongest tenor playing. The large ensemble is used sparingly and the arrangements – by Coltrane, Dolphy and Tyner – are minimal, although there are moments of tremendous excitement as Coltrane's tenor soars and screams above the stabbing brass lines. *Africa* is the most adventurous track, its semi-improvised ensembles making it, as Brian Priestley has noted, "far more expressionist and collectivist" than nearly all previous jazz. *Greensleeves*, a modal setting in 6/8, is the first of several unlikely tunes to follow *My Favorite Things* as a feature for Coltrane's bewitching soprano. *Blues Minor* is a bright swinger with exultant tenor; *The Damned Don't Cry*, a complex chart by Cal Massey, has fine trumpet from Booker Little, but sounds under-rehearsed. *Song of the Underground Railroad*, with its tenor-and-drums axis, anticipates the frenetic *Chasin' the Trane* of six months later. **GL**

---

**New review**

**Ballads** Coltrane (ts); **McCoy Tyner** (p); **Reggie Workman, Jimmy Garrison** (b); **Elvin Jones** (d). Impulse! Ⓜ IMP11562 (32 minutes). Recorded 1962.

⑨ ❽

Made at producer Bob Thiele's instigation, to counter critics' claims that John Coltrane's music was "windy, flat and needed editing", **Ballads** features eight standards, only one of which, *It's Easy to Remember*, had been played by the quartet before. This CD reissue is indistinguishable from the LP release: not only does it faithfully reproduce the complete channel separation of the music, so that Coltrane appears in one speaker, Elvin Jones in the other, but it also appears in a smaller but otherwise identical sleeve, with Gene Lees's original booklet-notes. Coltrane was reportedly experiencing intonation problems at up-tempo at the time due to unwise DIY refinements to his favourite mouthpiece, but negotiates this selection of plangent ballads with enviable assurance, whether charging *I Wish I Knew* with tender, yearning melancholy, shuffling languorously through *What's New* or decorating *You Don't Know What Love Is* with his characteristic, almost querulously interrogative, throaty clusters of notes.

McCoy Tyner provides near perfect settings for Coltrane's tenor meditations, his playing either lushly romantic or subtly dramatic as appropriate; Elvin Jones is all whispering brushes, judiciously applied mallets and breathing cymbals; Jimmy Garrison (and Reggie Workman on *It's Easy to Remember*) underpins the music with faultless, sonorous poise. Although the whole album is taken at an almost uniformly stately pace (only *All or Nothing at All* approaches mid tempo, Coltrane having marked it with "Arabic feeling"), this very uniformity of mood renders it a classic and deeply affecting recording. **CP**

---

**New review**

**Crescent** Coltrane (ts); **McCoy Tyner** (p); **Jimmy Garrison** (b); **Elvin Jones** (d). Impulse! Ⓜ IMP 12002 (41 minutes). Recorded 1964.

✔ ⑩ ⑩

The latest record in Coltrane's discography I'd unqualifiedly recommend to a person who feels queasy in the face of religious conviction or bored in the face of energy playing. It is also one of his absolute best. **Crescent** is soaked in regret; its mood isn't just the blues, it's understanding. It's not anger or joy, but quiet compassion, and Coltrane scales back his own playing to a distilled presence. His solos, full of patient, rotating three-note phrases on a single chord while the band moves on beyond him, like a man leaving the mainstream of life to understand fully one sure thing – are some of the great dramatic moments in jazz. *Lonnie's Lament* is surely one of the finest modern jazz ballads, with a nearly foolproof 32-bar theme. And Elvin Jones's *The Drum Thing* gently explores the melodic values of a trap set; rarely do drum solos contain such serenity. The last stop before **A Love Supreme**, these were charmed sessions. Impulse!'s digital remastering is surprisingly warm – a big improvement over the initial MCA CD issue. **BR**

---

**A Love Supreme** Coltrane (ts); **McCoy Tyner** (p); **Jimmy Garrison** (b); **Elvin Jones** (d). Impulse!
Ⓜ GRD155 (33 minutes). Recorded 1964.
✓                                                                                              ⑩ ⑧

With **Giant Steps** in 1959 and *Chasin' the Trane* two years later, Coltrane redefined the standards by which a musician would be judged a master on his horn. But with *A Love Supreme* – a turbulently lovely four-part work ending with what Coltrane explicitly intended to be heard as a prayer – he altered public perception of the jazz musician from hipster's hipster to seeker of higher truths. In a paradox central to Coltrane's mystique, this was both his most intensely personal album and the one which most struck a chord with audiences. With the possible exception of **Kind of Blue** (to which Coltrane was, of course, a significant contributor), **A Love Supreme** is the one jazz album most likely to be found in the collections of people only casually interested in jazz. As an indication of **A Love Supreme**'s musical staying power, it continues to yield new insights after hundreds or even thousands of hearings. Has anyone ever pointed out, for example, that the eight-bar theme subtitled *Pursuance*, the springboard for one of Coltrane's most vocalized and furious solos, borrows its intervals from Miles Davis's *Nardis*, much as *Impressions* borrowed from Davis's *So What*?

Insofar as the religious reawakening that Coltrane describes in his sleeve-note can be likened to that of an evangelical Christian, **A Love Supreme** can be taken to be his public testimony. Usually hailed as a culmination of sorts (it does represent an apex for this quartet, although Tyner's piano was becoming increasingly superfluous), the album might also be regarded as the beginning of a new chapter, its truncated and/or elementary song forms suggesting Coltrane was attempting to simplify his approach even as his solos took on greater complexity. Perceived this way – as a masterpiece disassembled into a work-in-progress – **A Love Supreme** renders inevitable everything that followed in the not-quite-three years that Coltrane had to live.

This latest reissue, the first along with **Ballads** (GRD156) and **And Johnny Hartman** (GRD157) from the revitalized Impulse! label, comes with appropriately lavish packaging, plus a 20-bit remastering process direct from the two-track master which finally makes a decent stab at aural exactitude after many half-hearted attempts on previous MCA reissues. **FD**

---

**The Major Works of John Coltrane** Coltrane (ts); **Freddie Hubbard**, **Dewey Johnson** (t); **John Tchicai**, **Marion Brown** (as); **Archie Shepp**, **Pharoah Sanders** (ts); **Donald Garrett** (bcl, b, perc); **McCoy Tyner** (p); **Jimmy Garrison**, **Art Davis** (b); **Elvin Jones**, **Frank Butler** (d, perc); **Juno Lewis** (perc, v); **Joe Brazil** (f). Impulse! Ⓜ GRP 21132 (two discs: 142 minutes). Recorded 1965.
                                                                                               ⑧ ⑥

The 11-piece group on *Ascension* remains a unique entry in Coltrane's discography, and an achievement that in the succeeding years inspired much emulation but considerably less success. Unlike his 1961 **Africa/Brass** sessions (reviewed above) which were akin to conventional soloist-with-big-band albums, Trane here developed the approach of Coleman's **Free Jazz** but, where the latter's horn ensembles were head-arranged in "harmolodic unison", *Ascension*'s soloists are separated by ferocious passages of collective improvisation from seven horns. These include both Shepp, then at his most far-reaching, and Coltrane's partner in live appearances from this date onwards, Pharoah Sanders.

Two versions of *Ascension* were issued, the first being withdrawn and replaced at Trane's request by *"Edition II"* – and Marion Brown has confirmed that this better-focused recording was the second performance, contrary to speculation. Both are included, occupying somewhat more than half the playing time, which is completed by three sextet and octet pieces originally issued as album title tracks: *Om, Kulu Sé Mama* and *Selflessness*. These are anti-climactic, compared to the intense yet channelled energy of *Ascension*, but historically they are significant for introducing African percussion into a free-jazz context. Tyner, who left Coltrane two months later, has a fine swan-song on *Kulu*. **BP**

---

**Meditations** Coltrane (ts, bcl); **Pharoah Sanders** (ts); **McCoy Tyner** (p); **Jimmy Garrison** (b); **Elvin Jones**, **Rashied Ali** (d). Impulse! Ⓜ IMP11992 (37 minutes). Recorded 1965.
✓                                                                                              ⑩ ⑧

1965 was, for Coltrane, a year of turbulent change which ended in the dissolution of the classic early-sixties quartet. It was also a year of a few triumphs and a number of near-misses. This album is definitely one of the triumphs. It remains the only instance of Jones and Ali recording together, and the resultant rhythmic maelstrom on *The Father and the Son and the Holy Ghost* makes for some of the most intoxicating listening in the history of recorded jazz. Add to this Coltrane in the frame of mind to contribute some of his most highly-disciplined playing to what is a concept album which takes **A Love Supreme** another step further, plus Pharoah Sanders in two solos of mind-bending ferocity, and you have a highly coherent and overwhelmingly powerful record.

As with **A Love Supreme**, the music is organized as a suite of contrasting parts (this one has five movements) which leads from the turbulence and chaos of *The Father* to the hard-won musical and emotional resolutions to be found in the last piece, *Serenity*. In between, all manner of things are displayed, including one of the most gorgeously sensual ballad readings of Coltrane's career on *Love*, a volcanic Tyner solo on *Compassion*, and a wistful, disturbing five-minute reading of the final theme by Coltrane which suggests not so much serenity as an unconfined yearning. This is Coltrane's most carefully-prepared and completely satisfying latter-day recorded statement.　　**KS**

---

**Expression**  Coltrane (ts, f); **Pharoah Sanders** (pic, f, tamb); **Alice Coltrane** (p); **Jimmy Garrison**
　　(b); **Rashied Ali** (d). Impulse! Ⓜ IMP 11312 (51 minutes). Recorded 1967.

⑧ ❽

By 1967 the devotional preoccupations which Coltrane had announced in such early sixties pieces as **Spiritual** and 1964's **A Love Supreme** (see above) had become all-consuming. It might have seemed that the unbridled energy of the 1965 **Ascension** was a final cathartic exorcism of his search for higher things, but the pursuit continued into his final months and, in **Expression**, was often surprisingly sanguine.

Although on a rhythmic level the music is uniformly rubato and harmonically often threatens to break free of its loose modal basis, there are moments of relative serenity, such as on the short, elegaic *Ogunde*, or in the opening minutes before Coltrane builds up a fervent heard of steam, and also throughout *To Be*, where his use of flute dictates a lower volume and more lyrical aesthetic. But even when the pressure builds the music is rarely entirely free, acquiring form through variations of tone and texture and, when Coltrane's tenor is dominant, always shaped by his virtuosic command of phrasing and dynamics. The rewards of this music may not be immediately apparent, but as the final chapter in one of the most ceaselessly progressive careers in modern jazz it will be of interest to all who have relished Coltrane's earlier, more readily accessible work. Impulse! have recently revisited the sessions from whence **Expression** came and issued **Stellar Regions**, a high-quality set of ultra-late Coltrane which incidentally includes one track where the leader plays alto sax (a subtlety overlooked by the CD's compilers and annotators).　　**MG**

# Ravi Coltrane　　1965

---

**Grand Central: Tenor Titans**  Coltrane (ss, ts); **Antoine Roney** (ts); **Jacky Terrasson** (p); **Jeff**
　　**Chambers** (b); **Ralph Penland**. Alfa Jazz Ⓔ ALCD313 (59 minutes). Recorded 1993.

⑦ ❿

This is fun. Ravi, son of John and Alice, co-leads this studio group with Antoine Roney, brother of Wallace, and as his name comes first on both albums the band has made, the album is entered under him in this book. Roney has already débuted under his own name (see below), but Ravi Coltrane is still biding his time, despite extensive appearances on others' records. There is little doubt that this and its 1992 predecessor, **Sax Storm** (also on Alfa), give us his best recorded playing to date, and the presence of both Roney and a fiercely swinging rhythm section led from the front by piano *enfant terrible* Jacky Terrasson helps enormously. So: does he sound like the famous one? Yes and no. He has the slightly vulnerable tone of the mid-fifties Trane, but his phrasing is closer to the Joshua Redman version of Rollins. He has a firm grasp of harmony, pushing through the changes and substitutions at a terrific rate even on a harmonically simple piece such as Victor Feldman's *Joshua*. Roney shows himself to be no slouch either, bringing a slightly more bustling, harder-edged personality to the music, creating a finely-balanced foil for the other horn man.

Both of them acquit themselves well at slow tempos, with Larry Clinton's *My Reverie* and Victor Young's *Stella By Starlight* coming in for some sumptuously rapturous playing, with both Roney and Coltrane avoiding the temptation to double-time and destroy the moods created. The album closes with a re-creation of *The Chase*, the old Dexter Gordon-Wardell Gray warhorse, and as noted at the beginning, much fun is had. This is good modern mainstream music with no strings attached.　　**KS**

# Ken Colyer　　1928-88

---

**Marching Back to New Orleans: The Decca Years, Volume 7**  Colyer (t, v); **Bob Wallis,**
　　**Sonny Morris** (t); **Mac Duncan, Mick Clift** (tb); **Ian Wheeler** (cl); **Dave Keir** (as); **Derek Eastern**
　　(ts); **Johnny Bastable** (bj); **Dick Smith** (b); **Mo Benn** (tba); **Stan Greig, Colin Bowden, Neil Millet**
　　(d). Lake Ⓔ LACD21 (59 minutes). Recorded 1955/7.

⑥ ❹

Sincerity was the watchword for 'The Guvnor', as Colyer was known to fans of the British New Orleans revival. He found it in the music of Mutt Carey and George Lewis, and jumped ship in New Orleans in 1952 to meet and play with some of the surviving pioneers of their style of jazz. This album catches Ken in his heyday, during the mid-fifties. Seven tracks are by his influential small band with Duncan and Wheeler, oozing sincerity and displaying a cross-section of his repertoire from *Hiawatha*

*Rag* to a storming *Red Wing*. Remastered from none-too-hi-fi Decca originals by Paul Adams, the set is dominated by a stately *Dallas Blues* that goes a long way to prove that Great Yarmouth could produce a heartfelt blues style.

The balance of the disc is by Ken's Omega Brass Band, the first European attempt to recreate the marching bands of New Orleans. It comes close in its ragged excitement to the spirit of the original, although modelled on Bunk Johnson's somewhat old and staid approach rather than the looser Eureka or Young Tuxedo bands. The album is a good introduction to Colyer, avoiding both the clinical precision of his first band with Chris Barber and the stodgy decline of his later years.  **AS**

# Eddie Condon
1905-73

**New review**

**Chicago Style**  Condon (bj, g); **Jimmy McPartland, Muggsy Spanier, Bobby Hackett** (c); **Leonard Davis, Charlie Gaines, Red Allen Max Kaminsky, Marty Marsala** (t); **Jack Teagarden** (tb, v); **Charlie Irvis, Floyd O'Brien, George Brunis, Brad Gowans, Miff Mole** (tb); **Bud Freeman** (ts, cl); **Mezz Mezzrow** (ts, c-ms, pc); **Frank Teschemacher** (cl, as); **Arville Harris** (cl, ts, as); **Pee Wee Russell** (cl, ts); **Joe Marsala** (cl); **Happy Cauldwell** (ts); **Adele Girard** (h); **Ray Biondi** (vn); **Joe Sullivan, Fats Waller, Alex Hill, Joe Bushkin, Jess Stacy, Dave Bowman, Joe Bushkin** (p); **Jim Lanigan** (b, bb); **Al Morgan, Artie Bernstein, Artie Shapiro** (b); **Jack Bland**(g); **Gene Krupa, Zutty Singleton, Big Sid Catlett, George Wettling, Danny Alvin** (d); **Red McKenzie** (v). ASV Ⓜ CDAJA5192 (78 minutes). Recorded 1927-40.

⑦ **6**

Condon was an unspectacular guitarist, club owner, author, band leader, irresistable raconteur and enthusiastic drinker. He infiltrated the Austin High School Gang in the late twenties and, without making a massive musical contribution, became one of the leading lights in what confusingly became known as the "Chicago jazz movement". The original Austins had set out to emulate the outstanding black players in Chicago and, in the process, stumbled into a unique style of classic jazz. Initially, Condon played banjo in a discreet but lightly propulsive manner and, as this CD shows, could be an excellent foil for drummer Krupa. Condon had a flair for rhythmic conformity and later dates show him musically cohabiting with such vastly different percussionists as Singleton, Catlett and the man who became something of a rhythmic soul brother, Wettling. His reaction to pianists was perhaps less discernible but Condon was as comfortable with powerhouse men like Waller or Sullivan as he was with Bushkin and Stacy. He switched entirely from banjo to guitar in the mid-thirties with little significant effect on his style,. although the shuffle rhythms on *Minor Drag* give the impression of a guitar before the switch was made. *Easy to Get* suggests a familiarity with Basie's 'All American' Freddie Green. Although this CD contains outstanding solo work by Hackett, Allen, Teschemacher, Freeman and O'Brien, Condon's major contributions were still to be made.  **BMcR**

---

**The Original Decca Recordings**  Condon (g); **Max Kaminsky, Billy Butterfield, Yank Lawson** (t); **Bobby Hackett, Wild Bill Davison** (c); **Jack Teagarden** (tb, v); **Lou McGarity** (tb); **Brad Gowans** (vtb); **Pee Wee Russell, Edmond Hall, Tony Parenti** (cl); **Bud Freeman** (ts); **Ernie Caceres** (bs); **Joe Dixon** (cl, bs); **Joe Sullivan, Gene Schroeder, Joe Bushkin** (p); **Clyde Newcombe, Bob Haggart, Sid Weiss, Jack Lesberg** (b); **George Wettling, Dave Tough, Johnny Blowers** (d); **Lee Wiley** (v). MCA/Decca Ⓜ GRD637 (61 minutes). Recorded 1939-46.

⑧ **6**

This album includes the four tracks originally recorded in 1939 as an album called **Chicago Jazz**, plus a further 16 titles done between 1944 and 1946. Unfortunately the set is not as complete as the album implies. One classic, *Aunt Hagar's Blues*, is omitted without reason, and some lesser titles which featured James P. Johnson and Ralph Sutton are also overlooked.

The earlier quartet have spiky solos from Russell and powerfully-fisted piano from Joe Sullivan, but it is the later tracks which really displayed that Condon's music was not by any means all hell-raising. The ballads here are without exception quite outstanding in the jazz of the forties. They include Wiley's beautiful version of *Someone to Watch Over Me* and Condon's unlikely composition *Wherever There's Love* with its fine Teagarden solo. Teagarden, Hackett and Butterfield share the superlative instrumental *When Your Lover Has Gone*, Hackett has *My One and Only,* Bushkin, at his most delicate, takes the first half of *The Man I Love* whilst Butterfield glories in the rest. There are plenty of very hot numbers, notably the pair with Wild Bill Davison and the previously unissued take of *I'll Build a Stairway to Paradise* which features Hall and Lawson. Thanks to the good quality of the clean-up job, Condon's rhythm guitar can actually be heard (most often it could not). He had a faultless feel for time, which no doubt was a major factor in the success of many of his recordings.  **SV**

# Harry Connick Jr
1968

**When Harry Met Sally ...**  Connick (v, p); **Benjamin Jonah Wolfe** (b); **Jeff 'Tain' Watts** (d); **Frank Wess** (ts); **Jay Berliner** (g), **Marc Shaiman** (arr, p). Columbia Ⓔ CK 45319 (38 minutes). Recorded 1989.

⑥ **8**

The Harry Connick Jr phenomenon raises a number of thorny issues. Is he really a jazz singer? Is he really a jazz pianist? And since so many jazz commentators have answered such queries with a resounding "no", just where should the blue-eyed Crescent City crooner be classified?

The Sinatra comparison is an obvious starting point. Indeed, in his singing and playing, Connick has affected Sinatra's nonchalant cool and blasé world-weariness with obvious success, at least for the general public. He has also surrounded himself with jazz players and big band charts cut from the same cloth as the post-war hits of the Basie Band. Not insignificantly, Connick has helped re-popularize a batch of venerable tunes from the catalogue of the classical American song. Indeed, his soundtrack album for **When Harry Met Sally**, the romantic comedy starring Billy Crystal and Meg Ryan, includes *It Had to Be You, Our Love is Here to Stay, But Not for Me, Stompin' at the Savoy, Autumn in New York, Don't Get Around Much Anymore, I Could Write a Book, Let's Call the Whole Thing Off* and *Where or When*. It is not surprising then that many musicians feel grateful to Connick for having once more made the world safe for standards, at least some of the time.

The album, while launching Connick's star, reveals an attractive if somewhat cloying voice. Settings range from solo piano and trio to big band. Finally, whatever his shortcomings, it is useful to keep in mind that Connick is still a very young man. The question is whether a matinée idol can also become a *bona fide* artist. We shall see. **CB**

# Chris Connor                                                              1927

**New review**

**Two's Company: Maynard Ferguson and Chris Connor** Connor (v); Ferguson (t, tb, frh); **Chet Ferretti, Rolf Ericson, Rick Keifer, Bill Berry** (t); **Ray Winslow, Kenny Rupp** (tb); **Lanny Morgan** (as, f); **Willie Maiden** (ts, cl); **Joe Farrell** (ts, ss, f); **Frank Hittner** (bs, bcl); **Jaki Byard** (p); **Charlie Saunders, John Neves** (b); **Rufus Jones** (d). Roulette Ⓜ CDP8 37201-2 (39 minutes). Recorded 1960-1.

⑧ ❽

Although she was better than many of the singers with whom she has been categorized, and arguably the best of the ones who sang with the Stan Kenton band, Miss Connor seems never to have been accorded her due by historians. Here she is backed by an on-form Ferguson band, full of nascent stars and with its leader happily slotting into the section an octave or more above where any normal horn man would be. The voice is very flexible and confident, the material superbly chosen and including such beautiful but under-used pieces as Russ Freeman's *The Wind*, Arlen's *When the Sun Comes Out* (where the brass ensemble roars an introduction), Jenkins's *New York's My Home* and Alec Wilder's *Where Do You Go?* All these are beautifully arranged and it is irritating that none of the arrangers are acknowledged in the booklet. The band chart for *Love is a Barren Land* is exquisite. The shouters, with the singer pushed by Ferguson's vibrant brass section, are *I Feel a Song Coming On, Can't Get Out of This Mood* with Ferguson knocking the tiles off the roof and a brief but good solo from Farrell, and a basic swinging blues called *Send for Me*. **SV**

**New review**

**Blue Moon** Connor (v); **Lew Soloff** (t); **Frank Vicari** (ts, ss), **Michael Abene** (p, arr); **Dom Chicchetti** (kbds); **Chip Jackson** (b); **Danny Gottlieb** (d). Alfa Jazz Ⓕ ALCB 39021995 (50 minutes). Recorded 1995.

⑦ ❾

In her sixties, Chris Connor's voice has dropped quite markedly in pitch – although not as markedly as Sarah Vaughan's had at a similar age. She sings more simply than she did in her early prime, and with a kind of detachment which, paradoxically, calls attention to the meaning of lyrics more effectively than any amount of emotional 'interpretation'. This CD is much more of a jazz event than her superb 1991 Enja CD, **As Time Goes By**, made with the Hank Jones Trio. This time she has a quintet of seasoned New York veterans and some quite challenging arrangements to deal with. She manages very well, but I cannot help suspecting that Abene's charts were originally written as band numbers and adapted. They sound like instrumental numbers 'with vocal refrain', not vocal numbers with instrumental setting, nor yet informal pieces incorporating the singer as an equal. It is noticeable that Connor sounds happier on songs like *All the Way*, when she can relax with just rhythm section and discreet, synthesized strings, than in the band numbers – even such comfortably familiar ones as *The Days of Wine and Roses*. Even so, this is an excellent demonstration of what a sensitive and intelligent singer she is, and of the eternal freshness of these great songs. **DG**

# Bill Connors                                                             1949

**Of Mist and Melting** Connors (g); **Jan Garbarek** (ss, ts); **Gary Peacock** (b); **Jack DeJohnette** (d). ECM Ⓕ 847 324-2 (48 minutes). Recorded 1977.

⑦ ❽

Connors first came to international notice in Return to Forever, and spent most of the seventies swapping between acoustic and electric guitars. On this album he favoured the former, and this helps distance him from any pervasive Forever influence; not that such a thing could be expected with Peacock and DeJohnette down in the boiler room.

The guitarist is hardly a soloist of the first order; although a superb technician, able to bring a wide degree of nuance from his instrument, he does not have the presence or ideas of a McLaughlin or Abercrombie. Perhaps that is what Garbarek was there for; if that is the case, then he does what is asked of him, and keeps the dialogue with a decidedly hot rhythm section bubbling away. Connors seems happiest when supplying textures for Garbarek to solo across, or for him to declaim Connors's melodies. Whatever, there is plenty of room for DeJohnette to get his rocks off, and on the opening track, *Melting*, he does so in thrilling style.

Not essential listening – all the sidemen have reached greater heights elsewhere – but a pleasant and absorbing collection, and very much of a piece with ECM's then-philosophy of atmospherics and muscle seamlessly combined. That still doesn't explain, though, why we have to pay full price for the CD reissue of a 19-year-old album.                                                                                                     **KS**

## Norman Connors                                                                               1947

**New review**

**Dance of Magic/Dark of Light**  Connors (d); Herbie Hancock, Alan Gumbs, Elmer Gibson (p, elp); Carlos Garnett (ss, ts); Gary Bartz (ss, as); Eddie Henderson (t); Art Webb (f); Alfred Williams (af, bn); Cecil McBee, Stanley Clarke, Buster Williams (b); Nat Bettis, Tony Wiles, Babafemi, Al Mouzon, Billy Hart, Airto Moreira, Lawrence Killian, Warren Smith, Henry Palmer, Gerald Roberts (pc); The U.H.F. Singers, Dee Dee Bridgewater, Ellen DeLeston, Michael Brown (v); Ted Dunbar (g, elg); Gail Dixon, Pat Dixon, Jerry Litte (strings). Sequel Records Ⓜ NEMCD683 (76 minutes). Recorded 1975/76.

⑦ ❼

In the seventies, drummer Norman Connors specialized in translating Coltrane's spiritualism into more populist soul-oriented contexts, and the result was, in the main, hypnotic grooves in which the focus of development was textural variation. On that basis alone, there mightn't be much jazz appeal, but he employed top drawer jazz players, and it's in their contributions that the chief jazz interest in this two-LP CD resides. The trouble is there's often a fair bit of none-too-polished psychedelic waffling before the solos appear. The 21-minute title track *Dance of Magic* is typical in this respect, eventually offering good breaks from Carlos Garnett, Eddie Henderson, Gary Bartz and Herbie Hancock. The 12-minute *Dark of Light* is similar, though there's an extra challenge here for the listener in the distinctly indifferent vocals which front the piece. About four and a half minutes in, Eddie Henderson starts to solo and is followed by Bartz, Hancock and Dunbar. The soloists acquit themselves well here and throughout, but this is not perhaps the best place to encounter them. So, a record of mixed and mainly historical interest which will probably have most appeal to the faddish denizens of retro raves and discos. They'll probably relish the period atmosphere created by the mediocre sound quality too.                                          **MG**

## Junior Cook                                                                                1934-92

**On a Misty Night**  Cook (ts); Mickey Tucker (p); Walter Boker (b); Leroy Williams (d). SteepleChase Ⓔ SCCD31266 (65 minutes). Recorded 1989.

⑧ ❽

Florida-born Cook spent several years in the Horace Silver Quintet, where he was always in danger of being overlooked due to the strong solo work of the leader and trumpeter Blue Mitchell. But Junior was always a highly skilled player and a soloist whose lines had great continuity. These aspects are highlighted here on what is certainly his best album under his own name. Cook responds well to strong thematic material and makes telling use of the Tadd Dameron title tune which, although strongly associated with John Coltrane through the **Mating Call** album on Prestige, soon becomes Cook's own property. He also resurrects a forgotten but very attractive Cannonball Adderley tune, *Wabash* (from the **Cannonball in Chicago** Mercury release), and turns it into one of the strongest performances on the CD. But the programme is full of delights, especially for those of us who cherish unhackneyed show tunes; Cook plays two superb Arthur Schwartz songs here, *By Myself* and *Make the Girl Love Me*, the latter from **A Tree Grows in Brooklyn** (a fact not mentioned anywhere on the package, which contains no programme notes whatsoever). An excellent rhythm section (Tucker is a most helpful accompanist) and splendid engineering by Jim Anderson make this a truly memorable release.                                        **AM**

## Al Cooper                                                                                  1911-81

**Al Cooper and The Savoy Sultans 1938-41**  Cooper (cl, as, bs); Pat Jenkins (t); Sam Massenberg (t); Rudy Williams (as); Ed McNeil, Sam Simmons, Irving 'Skinny' Brown (ts); George Kelly (ts, v); Paul Chapman (g, v); Oliver Richardson, Cyril Haynes (p); Grachan Moncur (b); Alex 'Razz' Mitchell (d); Helen Proctor, Evelyn White (v). Classics Ⓜ 728 (72 minutes). Recorded 1938-41.

⑧ ❻

Talent-spotted by John Hammond when leading a band in upstate New York, Al Cooper auditioned for the Savoy Ballroom and made an immediate impression. The name Savoy Sultans was adopted and a residency was begun in 1937; there were few changes in personnel and the band stayed at 'The Track' for many years. This CD nicely represents their most productive period and presents them as the ideal dance band for the Harlem crowd. They were, however, very much more than that. The rhythm section (with Cooper's half-brother Moncur on bass) was outstanding, leading the whole band to swing incessantly. The simple arrangements were ideal for the band and Dizzy Gillespie, who occasionally guested, once described them as the "most exciting band ever". Williams was the outstanding soloist, happy with the Johnny Hodges testimony on *Jeep's Blues* but singularly driving on *Jumpin' the Blues* and *Stitches*. The band, which finally broke up in 1946, will be remembered as a great dance band that also played for listeners and it is no coincidence that six titles on this issue include the word 'jump'.                                                    **BMcR**

# Bob Cooper                                                                    1925-93

**Tenor Sax Jazz Impressions**  Cooper (ts); **Michael Fahn** (vtb); **Ross Tompkins, Carl Schroeder** (p); **Chuck Berghofer**, **Bob Magnusson** (b); **John Guerin, Jimmie Smith** (d). Trend Ⓕ TRCD543 (55 minutes). Recorded 1979/86.

⑧ ❽

The fact that it took seven years to accumulate enough tracks under his own name to compile a Bob Cooper CD is a reflection on one of jazz's more serious oversights. Because Cooper persistently graced the bands of other leaders (Shorty Rogers, Capp-Pierce Juggernaut and others) he was not accorded his correct ranking in the tenor hierarchy. He comes somewhere between Zoot Sims, Stan Getz and Al Cohn. His playing is characterized by technical fluency, a Sims-like swing and a penchant for blues phrases which all four men share.

Cooper was one of those consistent players who never recorded a bad solo, and this was his best album since his 1954 **Kenton Presents** session for Capitol (not yet issued on CD). Strayhorn's *Kissing Bug* draws out his best blues playing and gives Michael Fahn a chance to shine and make one wonder if he is to be the next Brookmeyer – he is that good.                                          **SV**

# Jim Cooper                                                                    1949

**Nutville**  Cooper (vb, belaphon); **Ira Sullivan** (t, ts, ss); **Bob Dogan** (p); **Dan DeLorenzo** (b); **Charlie Braugham** (d); **Alejo Poveda** (perc). Delmark Ⓕ DD457 (63 minutes). Recorded 1991.

⑦ ❼

Chicago has always had its own strangely personal jazz scene. This CD presents the virtually unknown Cooper with the superb multi-instrumentalist Sullivan and even has Paul Serrano, one of the city's unsung trumpet heroes, as its engineer. Cooper is from the Gary Burton generation but with his own way of approaching the improvising process. He responds in a way that is appropriate to the material, taking the gentle Latin route on *Cantor Da Noite*, a strong attack to *Bemsha Swing* and on *Nutville* giving his fine solo a distinctive edge by the use of the belaphon, an African xylophone. Pianist Dogan solos well and leads a useful rhythm section but it is Sullivan who makes the biggest impression. As always, he switches horns throughout a session with no detrimental effect to his playing of them. The difference between his approach to his two saxophones on *Autumn Nocturne* is typical, with his soprano soulfully reverential and his tenor assertively matter-of-fact. In contrast, the breathy tonal quality of his tenor is emphasized on *Mallethead*, while he selects the oddly changing time signatures of *Sui Fumi* to provide the stimulant for a really authoritative soprano outing. His stylish trumpet playing is captured on *Tanga* and on the title track, displaying a mode of improvising some distance from his saxophone work. The session belongs to the admirable Cooper but Sullivan does tend to steal his thunder.                                                    **BMcR**

# Marc Copland

**Ilg/Copland/Hirschfield: What's Goin' On**  Dieter Ilg (b); Copland (p); Jeff Hirschfield (d). Jazzline Ⓕ JL11138-2 (63 minutes). Recorded 1993.

⑧ ❽

The most striking aspect of this excellent trio's work   the installation of rock beats underneath a jazzy harmonic conception – is, of course, not essentially new, but by retaining acoustic instruments, especially acoustic bass, they have developed an attractively fresh perspective on piano jazz. In its original form the Marvin Gaye title track was hardly a model of harmonic sophistication, but before the first minute of the trio's version is out, Copland's cheeky sideslips and polytonalisms prick up the ears of the jazz-minded and scupper any possibility of the track leaping into the Soul 100. *Scrapple from the Apple* suffers similarly glorious indignities at the hands of an ostinato vamp, a tart reharmonization and piano figures which suggest Richie Beirach, and two originals in a similar vein, *Bigfoot* and *Take it to the Bridge*, are further examples of the delights awaiting the jazz piano trio which escapes the tyranny of the Broadway song form and triplet bass lines. However, it is not all pranks and japes. Pleasure is balanced by the pain of limpid, Jarrett-esque readings of *Young and Foolish*, *In the Wee Small Hours of the Morning* and Dori Caymmi's poignant *Photograph*.                                                                                                    **MG**

# Chick Corea                                                                                                        1941

---

New review
**Music Forever and Beyond – The Selected Works of Chick Corea 1964-96**  Corea (p, kbds); solo, duets and with various groups comprising: **Miles Davis**, **Woody Shaw** (t); **Michael Brecker, Bob Berg** (ts); **Eric Marienthal** (ts, as); **Joe Farrell** (ts, ss, f); **Bill Connors, Al DiMeola, Frank Gambale, John McLaughlin** (g); **Steve Swallow, Dave Holland, Eddie Gomez** (b); **Stanley Clarke, John Patitucci** (b, elb); **Roy Haynes, Lenny White, Steve Gadd, Dave Weckl, Gary Novak** (d). GRP Ⓕ 5-9819 (five discs: 328 minutes).

⑧  ❾

Inevitably, Chick Corea gets awarded the jazz equivalent of the MBE – the multi-CD box set and glossy retrospective booklet. Not always the critics' favourite, it's easy to forget however that he's been in the vanguard of every new jazz movement of the past 30 years, as well as racking up more than a small shelf of classic and influential albums. Spanning virtually his entire career, this crisply produced package nails each twist and turn with an eye for the rare and unusual as well as the more obvious items. Early highlights include *Chick's Tune* from Blue Mitchell's 1964 Blue Note date **The Thing to Do**, *Windows* from a previously unreleased Stan Getz session in 1967 and *Litha* from his much sought-after Atlantic début album **Tones for Jones Bones**. Unfortunately, due to clearance problems, his ECM period is not represented here, but alongside standout cuts from his trailblazing, electric **Return to Forever** line-ups, there's a bunch of tracks from his somewhat overlooked late seventies Polydor years covering albums like **The Leprechaun**, **My Spanish Heart** and **The Mad Hatter**.
    Corea's technology-laden Elektric Band divided critics and fans alike with guillotine-like efficiency during the mid 1980s, but none the less acted as a tough finishing school for an endless pack of new young gunslingers. Disc three chronicles their better moments together with two unreleased live scorchers, *Rumble* and *Ished*. Elsewhere, highlights include previously unreleased duets with John McLaughlin from Montreux in 1982 and Miles Davis in Antibes in 1969, while the final disc is a brand new recording from his latest straight-ahead acoustic quartet, featuring the highly charged skills of Bob Berg, John Patitucci and Gary Novak. Fastidious it may be, but among the polished renditions of standards like *Stella by Starlight*, *Straight No Chaser* and *Monk's Mood*, there's one stunning new Corea tune, *Story*, featuring bold, blistering, edge-of-the-seat improvisation that does plenty to suggest it's his finest band in years.                                                                                   **JN**

---

**Now He Sings, Now He Sobs**  Corea (p); **Miroslav Vitous** (b); **Roy Haynes** (d). Blue Note Ⓜ CDP7 90055-2 (70 minutes). Recorded 1968.
✔                                                                                                                ⑩  ❻
This was one of the most welcome reissues of the late eighties. It presents Corea at the height of his powers and, thanks to the diligent Michael Cuscuna, brings together his trio's entire March 1968 session in one digitally remastered package. Previously it was available only as two LP issues divided by a decade.
    The impeccable production and presentation is the perfect complement to the music: if Corea has fallen into mannerism in recent years, he is captured here in his first prime, and the results are unselfconscious, impassioned and devoid of contrivance. His influences are clearly apparent, but so is his incipient individualism. Thus *My One and Only Love*, *Windows* and *Pannonica* are infused with the poetry of Bill Evans, while *Matrix* and the first section of *Steps – What Was* are exhilarating rollercoasters in the manner of McCoy Tyner; *Steps'* second section illustrates Corea's proto-Hispanicism and suggests a sketch for the later standard *Spain*, and the abstractions of *Fragments* and *Gemini* prefigure his work in the seventies improvising group Circle (see below). The musicianship is first class throughout, Vitous and Haynes enjoying an uncommon empathy with Corea and shadowing his lithe, agile lines with wit and vigour. Their pushing and pulling of the time on the title track is just one in a seemingly endless variety of excitements.                                                      **MG**

---

**Piano Improvisations, Volumes 1 and 2**  Corea (p). ECM Ⓕ 811 979/829 190-2 (two discs, oas: 42 and 40 minutes). Recorded 1971.

⑧  ⑩

There is a feeling of joy running through much of the music on these two CDs, products of the same recording session in April 1971. Whatever Corea's personal circumstances at the time, there is no doubt that these albums represented something akin to a liberation. To understand why, it may be worth recalling that in 1971 solo piano recitals were a rarity, rather than the norm. Corea, being one of the few modern pianists of the time fully equipped to take full advantage of being solo (Jarrett had just done the same thing for ECM, and Paul Bley did so shortly after), plays through a programme of his own music (plus one Monk piece, *Trinkle Tinkle*, on Volume 2) and simply revels in the interpretative freedom he finds for himself.

It is salutary to compare his solo piano version of *Sometime Ago*, a composition also covered on the group album **Return to Forever** shortly after. With the latter, the piece is rushed, as if the group cannot wait to get to the major-key groove of the main theme, which Flora Purim delivers with panache. Here, Corea paces the work beautifully, and returns repeatedly to the central section of the piece, the minor, Spanish-feel refrain. The major chorus is used only as relief. It is eight minutes of real magic, with no punches pulled.

Both discs contain plenty of uncompromising, gritty playing across a large range of subjects and styles, with the focus held sharp throughout.                                                             **KS**

New review

**Remembering Bud Powell**  Corea (p); **Wallace Roney** (t); **Kenny Garrett** (as); **Joshua Redman** (ts); **Christian McBride** (b); **Roy Haynes** (d). Stretch/Concord Ⓕ SCD9012-2 (74 minutes). Recorded 1996.

⑩ ❾

Corea has had his detractors over the years, but even his fiercest critics would have to be confounded by this, one of the most sumptuous tributes from one jazz musician to another in the history of the music. Corea has not merely gathered together a collection of Powell compositions and thrashed through a bunch of performances for the benefit of a microphone: this band toured with this concept after Corea had spent many hours checking and re-checking the source material to make sure that he both chose the best-suited and most challenging material and that he was scrupulously accurate in his transcriptions. Of course it helped (as Corea generously acknowledges in his booklet-notes) that the drummer on the project was Roy Haynes, a man who spent many nights in the early fifties playing with Powell at various venues. Corea has not gone for the soft options, just as he avoided such things when he made his Monk tributes with Trio Music back in the eighties. We find here not only *Willow Grove* and *Tempus Fugit*, but new and beautiful versions of *I'll Keep Loving You* (with just Corea, McBride and Redman), a more rehearsed version of *Glass Enclosure* than Powell ever managed to record (using the full band), a trio version of *Dusk in Sandi* (also known as *Dusky 'n Sandy*) and a moving re-thinking of the chaotic but shatteringly intense *Mediocre*, which Corea guesses was recorded before Powell had rehearsed it fully with his trio. All the musicians respond to this project with immense verve and imagination, the music sounds wonderfully fresh and Corea himself plays as well as he has in years. A very good record indeed, for all the right reasons.  **SV**

# Jayne Cortez

New review

**Taking the Blues Back Home**  Cortez (v); with a collective personnel including: **Al MacDowell** (b); **Carl Weathersby**, **Bern Nix** (g); **Talib Kibwe** (as); **Frank Lowe** (ts); **Billy Branch** (hca); **Nakoyo Suso** (v); **Sarjo Kuyateh**, **Salieu Suso** (kora); **Abdoulaye Epizo Bangoura** (djimbe d); **Denardo Coleman** (d). Harmolodic/Verve Ⓕ 531 918-2 (46 minutes). Recorded 1996.

⑤ ❻

Harmolodic/Verve is a relatively new partnership between the Polygram-owned Verve jazz label and the Harmolodic coalition, run by Ornette and Denardo Coleman and committed to recording music that follows the polyphonic, improvised 'harmolodic' system they pioneered in the Prime Time band. Poet Jane Cortez's backing band The Firespitters features a hefty number of Prime Time players. It's a challenging record. Playing versions of the blues, The Firespitters do harmolodic imitations of a Mississippi blues band, r&b shuffle-rockers, an African band, a wailing Chicago electric band and a bebop small group. But the music ultimately lacks variety and too many tracks merge into a vaguely insurgent, rock-rooted blast over the 12-bar structure. Cortez herself, a well-known and respected poet on the contemporary American scene, tends to challenge with repetition, while elsewhere she gives the impression her work would be appreciated best perhaps isolated from the music. The better moments have a kind of fearsome energy. The title track, for instance – a black reclamation of the blues and its history, set against a fast polyrhythmic background – combines political content and music skilfully. *I Have Been Searching*, with its pretty African harp backing, is a painful story about the search amongst the nameless bodies of an African massacre. But too much of the text is either old-fashioned and already covered by Gil Scott-Heron, or just painfully clichéd.  **LC**

# Larry Coryell                                                                                  1943

New review

**Introducing the Eleventh House with Larry Coryell**  Coryell (g); **Randy Brecker** (t); **Mike Mandel** (elp, syn); **Danny Trifan** (elb); **Alphonse Mouzon** (d, perc). Vanguard Ⓕ VMD79342 (45 minutes). Recorded 1974.

⑦ ❼

It's easy to forget but Larry Coryell was in at the earliest birth pangs of jazz-rock with Free Spirits, a 1966 experimental group with Bob Moses and Jim Pepper. "I felt it was only a matter of time before somebody who liked Elvin Jones could also like George Harrison," he earnestly ventured, and in 1970 he embarked on his Hendrix phase recording **Spaces** with Billy Cobham, John McLaughlin and Miroslav Vitous, which laid foundations for the emergent electric *Zeitgeist*. But it was not until 1974 however and **Eleventh House** that Coryell finally built a jazz-rock group that achieved any sizeable recognition. Maybe Coryell didn't possess the blinding, genius edge of McLaughlin but his undoubted virtuosity, and not inconsiderable writing skills, made sure that **Introducing the Eleventh House** had a good roof and solid walls.

The scope, unlike many jazz-rock albums from this period, pitches wider, moving from the fierce Mahavishnu-like onslaught of the opener *Birdfingers*, where Mouzon immediately announces the album's intentions with a withering pressed roll and bass-drum blitz, via atmospheric acoustic interludes to the salty, jagged sway of *Funky Waltz*. Mandel is the least interesting soloist with an irritating, dinky synthesizer tone that has not aged well, but Brecker is on sharp, early form, despite the occasional lapse into Herb Alpert territory. His breezy, wah-wah-etched squeals push and probe, squaring off against Coryell's Concorde fast runs with a Miles-like intensity, especially on the album's standout track *Yin*. But it's the dark, worrying angular lines and arpeggios that Coryell so brilliantly conjures up on *Low Lee Tah* that make you wish he'd followed a similar, more challenging path for future releases. **JN**

# Eddie Costa                                                                     1930-62

**Eddie Costa Quintet** Costa (p, vb); **Art Farmer** (t); **Phil Woods** (as, p); **Teddy Kotick** (b); **Paul Motian** (d). VSOP Ⓕ #7CD (31 minutes). Recorded 1957.

⑧ ❻

At the time of his death in a tragic road accident, Costa was recognized as one of the most individual keyboard players of his day. He favoured a hard, driving two-handed style, making full use of the lower half of the piano as much as the top half, unlike a number of his contemporaries who relied on bass players to fill out the roots of the chords. Of the comparatively few records under his own name his Jubilee trio set (with Vinnie Burke and Nick Stabulas) is overdue for translation to CD, but this album, recorded for the Mode label originally, is welcome. It features Costa leading an efficient, well-rehearsed quintet with some searing alto solos from Phil Woods and carefully considered statements from Art Farmer. Costa lays down a propulsive backing on piano which would stir the most recalcitrant of soloists into action. Like Horace Silver and Dave McKenna he seemed capable of playing the complete rhythm section's part on the piano keyboard. He plays vibes on two tracks, a finely-etched version of Brubeck's *In Your Own Sweet Way* and a delicately sketched out *I Didn't Know What Time It Was*. On both titles Phil Woods plays very capable piano support. Motian is recorded a little too prominently in places but generally the balance and the transfers are acceptable. The playing time of the original LP (and this CD) is so meagre that the Top Rank label once issued it in the UK as a ten-inch album without any loss of tracks. **AM**

# Tom Coster

New review
**The Forbidden Zone** Coster (kbds); **Bob Berg** (ts); **Scott Henderson** (g); **Alphonso Johnson** (elb); **Dennis Chambers** (d); **Raul Rekow, Karl Perazzo** (perc). JVC Ⓕ JVC2040 (60 minutes). Recorded 1994.

⑧ ❿

First noticed with the jazz-slanted version of Santana's latin-rock fusion in 1972, it comes as little surprise to find that Coster initially cut his teeth with gipsy guitarist Gabor Szazbo, one of Carlos Santana's major influences. Coster's colourful, latin-flavoured Rhodes piano and striking synthesizer squeals, as well as his mainstay Hammond organ, helped drive the Santana band through its most imaginative phase and kicked off what should have been a promising solo career in the early eighties. Two ineffectual albums for Fantasy, however, followed by a radio-play targeted horror for JVC did little to suggest Coster had much left to say. But his renaissance came with 1993's knowingly titled **Let's Set the Record Straight**, a blistering, contemporary jazz-rock onslaught that first saw him working with top-flight ball breakers like Berg, Chambers and Johnson.

Happily this follow-up has proved to be one of the nineties' most devastating fusion efforts so far. Coster's sharp, edgy compositions hover around a chrome-plated Weather Report/Mahavishnu soundscape with plenty of space for Berg and guitarist Scott Henderson, on loan from Tribal Tech, to slash and burn with tough, muscular ease. Coster's dense, multi-layered keyboard textures are a league away from the gooey, soporific mush that nearly drowned fusion in the eighties, while his crisp piano flurries pile on the pressure with all the gusto of a mid-period McCoy Tyner. And with a ticking bomb rhythm section like Chambers and Johnson primed and ready to blow, Coster makes doubly sure **The Forbidden Zone** is decidedly off limits to those who prefer their music in a less explosive vein. **JN**

# Curtis Counce                                                                   1926-63

**You Get More Bounce with Curtis Counce!** Counce (b); **Jack Sheldon** (t); **Harold Land** (ts); **Carl Perkins** (p); **Frank Butler** (d). Contemporary Ⓜ OJCCD159-2 (51 minutes). Recorded 1956-7.

⑧ ❽

To refute the notion that all fifties California jazz was cool and creamy, critics cite Counce's hard-bop quintet, which swung aggressively *à la* New York's Art Blakey and Horace Silver. The Clifford Brown/Max Roach quintet is even more of a role model (as a fast, mildly intricate *Mean to Me* and the underrated Butler's attentive drumming make clear), although that East Coast band was founded in California. But it's important not to oversimplify; *Complete*'s jaunty walking and open latticework arrangement suggest quintessential West Coaster Shorty Rogers's *Martian* pieces more than Blakey's Messengers.

Born in Kansas City, Counce retained that city's taste for relaxed, unfettered swing. A key player on the L.A. scene in the fifties (he died prematurely of a heart attack), Counce epitomizes the decade's exemplary pre-amplification bass stylings, when players were expected to have a plump, robust tone and propulsive approach. Brown/Roach veteran Land, who had a long, productive subsequent career, and Perkins, who had a tragically short one (dying at 29, in 1958), lack nothing in blues authority or soul. Trumpeter Sheldon brings a warm, full tone to ballads (like *Stranger in Paradise*), but crackles hot as well. This facsimile edition's tacky cheesecake cover is a period classic.                    **KW**

# Stanley Cowell                                                                     1941

**We Three**  Cowell (p); **Buster Williams** (b); **Freddie Waits** (d). DIW Ⓕ 807 (66 minutes). Recorded 1987.

⑧ ❽

Cowell has been deeply involved with projects such as  Music Inc., the seven-piece Piano Choir and the CBA Ensemble. A University of Michigan graduate, he has worked with Marion Brown, Max Roach and the Heath Brothers and is currently himself a teacher. He is a fine composer and arranger and both of these talents are evident on this trio session. It is as a pianist in the intimacy of this group, however, that he makes his mark and, in choosing Williams and Waits, he has given himself the best possible opportunity. All of the tunes were written by members of the trio and they maintain a high standard. This trio really succeeds because all three men are virtuosi. Williams swings as do few bassists, his solos have shape and purpose and in the ensemble he never hesitates to re-direct. Waits is one of that rare breed of drummers, a percussionist that can play not only the tune but also his own version of it. In spite of this, Cowell remains the star in this stellar company. He plays sparklingly daring runs yet still manages to remain relaxed, even at the most daunting up-tempos. In addition he still manages to rock gently with the medium tempo *Sienna* and to play with genuine sensitivity in his two fine readings of his own *Winter Reflections*. A later release on DIW, **Close to You Alone**, is equally affecting.                **BMcR**

# Ida Cox                                                                            1889-67

**I Can't Quit My Man**  Cox (v); **Hot Lips Page, Henry 'Red' Allen** (t); **J.C. Higginbotham** (tb); **Edmond Hall** (cl); **James P. Johnson, Fletcher Henderson, Cliff Jackson** (p); **Charlie Christian** (g); **Artie Bernstein, Billy Taylor** (b); **Lionel Hampton, Jimmy Hoskins** (d). Affinity Ⓜ CDAFS1015 (55 minutes). Recorded 1939-40.

⑥ ❻

This album offers a rare chance to hear a leading blues singer of the twenties who retained her abilities long enough to give an accurate account of her style in relatively good recording conditions. On the 1939 sessions Cox's deliberate, unornamented delivery is faithful to her past and her accompanists play with the accents of the day, yet there is nothing uncomfortable about the collaboration; indeed, *Death Letter Blues* matches anything in Cox's discography. There was little of nostalgia in these sessions: *Pink Slip Blues* and *Hard Time Blues* allude to contemporary events, while in the sprightly *One Hour Mama* the singer forsakes the measured pace typical of the songs of her heyday. The 1940 session, which has 'Red' Allen rather than Page, and a different rhythm section, has a decidedly modern flavour, especially in *You Got to Swing and Sway*, which has attractive solos by all the front line.

The 11 tracks produced at these three dates are supplemented by rejected takes (eight in all) of six of them, different only in detail. These may be valuable only to specialists, but the core material is music of ready appeal and enduring value.                          **TR**

# Lol Coxhill                                                                        1932

**The Dunois Solos**  Coxhill (ss). Nato Ⓕ 95 (42 minutes). Recorded 1981.

⑧ ❽

Over the years the idiosyncratic Coxhill has recorded with birds, bagpipes, a loose floorboard, punk rockers and a curious nostalgic trio called The Melody Four. Obviously, there is more than a trace of Dada in his blood, but as a serious improviser he has developed a personal vocabulary quite unbeholden to Steve Lacy, Wayne Shorter, Evan Parker or any other soprano saxist you care to name. For pure, undiluted Coxhill, this solo album is hard to beat, consisting of two low-key, sustained improvisations, aptly titled *Distorted Reminiscences* and *Further Developments*. Like a hazy memory, this music has no prearranged beginning or ending; Lol's elusive logic allows free association, a wide range of references, connections and diversions. It is fascinating to stroll with him along these winding melodic paths, which twist and climb or dip at unexpected intervals, widen or narrow as notes pinch or broaden with vibrato. He gets a lovely, singing quality from the horn as, despite the occasional pitch bending and smear, he is a lyrical improviser above all, often with a touch of the pastoral or melancholy. Given his comedic talents, he is not always taken seriously, and so in mixed groups somewhat resembles Pee Wee Russell among the Condon gang. In fact he admits an affinity to Pee Wee, crediting the quixotic clarinettist with his awareness of the "spaces between the notes". And like Russell, he is a vastly underrated nonconformist of marvellous artistry. **AL**

## Hank Crawford                                    1934

**Midnight Ramble** Crawford (as, elp); **Charlie Miller**, **Waymon Reed** (t); **Dick Griffin** (tb); **David 'Fathead' Newman** (ts); **Howard Johnson** (bs); **Dr. John** (p, org); **Calvin Newborn** (g); **Charles 'Flip' Green** (b); **Bernard Purdie** (d). Milestone Ⓜ MCD9112-2 (39 minutes). Recorded 1982.

⑧ ❽

The former music director of Ray Charles's big band, Crawford is among the most consistent of performers. Any of the half-dozen or so similar albums he has made for Milestone in the last ten years would do just as nicely as this one, which is the choice here mainly because it was the prototype. Even then, it follows the pattern set on the r&b-influenced albums that Crawford made for Atlantic in the sixties, when he was still with Charles. Nothing wrong with that. If not exactly essential jazz library items, those albums were classics of their unpretentious genre. So is **Midnight Ramble**, if only for testifying to Crawford's knack for making four or five horns roar like a dozen – a trick arrangers used to learn on the road with jump bands forced by circumstances to play the same venues as the big swing bands. This album and those which have followed also show off Crawford's singing tone and straightforward but lusty approach to improvisation. He is an especially winning ballad player, as demonstrated here by *Street of Dreams* and Gamble and Huff's pretty *Forever Mine*. Crawford is a soul man from the old school: like Charles himself, he knows that the way to make it *really* funky is to make it *s-l-o-w*. **FD**

## Ray Crawford                                    1924

**Smooth Groove** Crawford (g); **Johnny Coles** (t); **Cecil Payne** (bs); **Junior Mance** (p); **Ben Tucker** (b); **Frankie Dunlop** (d). Candid Ⓜ 79028 (43 minutes). Recorded 1961.

⑦ ❻

Crawford, a consistently interesting and intelligent guitarist, has never really had the chance to establish himself in the limelight. Originally trained as a saxophonist, he played back in the early forties with Fletcher Henderson, but ended up in hospital with tuberculosis and after his recovery switched to the guitar. As the fifties began he joined Ahmad Jamal, playing with him for six years, only to leave the trio not long before Jamal's big break with his Pershing Lounge album. After that, Crawford moved on to New York and gravitated towards the Gil Evans circle, playing on and off for him for a number of years. It was his outstanding work on Evans's **Out of the Cool** (see below) which led Candid proprietor Nat Hentoff to invite him to record this album. Like Cal Massey and others, Crawford was to see the original Candid label go broke before his album was released. This, then, is its first issue.

The music is tightly organized, each player contributing a clearly defined personality to a role created for them by Crawford. This is no mere blowing session. Crawford himself has a pleasing edge to his sound, and a willingness to dig in and groove which justifies the album's title. Coles, another under-recorded alumnus of the Evans band, plays exquisitely throughout, while Payne alternates winningly between warmth and bustle. Dunlop is outstanding in the rhythm section. All five tunes are Crawford originals, and all are carefully crafted pieces. This is a very worthy effort which certainly did not deserve to dwell in darkness for nearly 30 years. **KS**

## Marilyn Crispell                                 1947

New review

**Spring Tour** Crispell (p); **Anders Jormin** (tb); **Raymond Strid** (d). Alice Ⓟ ALCD013 (75 minutes). Recorded 1994.

⑧ ❽

Crispell is a musician whose playing conclusively proves that academic studies and jazz can mix. A graduate of the New England Conservatory, she was won over to jazz by listening to John Coltrane and Cecil Taylor. Since that process of conversion she has become one of the most outstanding of all free jazz pianists, one whose concept of improvisation is realized in her own mind as instant composition. Her early albums featured chamber-style units, third stream experiments, work with fellow jazz marauders and her own solo piano. Some of the smaller units emphasized the aggressive elements rather too much, but this CD follows a well-balanced approach and takes her from the gentle explorations of *Tune for Charlie* and *Night Light Beach* to the headlong improvisational momentum of *Spring Flood*. As is normal with Crispell units, the members of the group make up a partnership of equals. Jormin's well-crafted bass lines and Strid's astutely arhythmic drum patterns share the dialogue with the piano, rather than merely support it. It is a process that allows the listener clear access and, although Crispell's piano is the dominant voice, it is not so by virtue of misplaced loudness or hostile sustaining pedal use. She has proved herself to be an imaginative player with 'changes', at home in a modal context and entirely adventurous on the free perimeter.

**BMcR**

## Sonny Criss
1927-77

**Portrait of Sonny Criss** Criss (as); **Walter Davis** (p); **Paul Chambers** (b); **Alan Dawson** (d). Prestige Ⓜ OJCCD655-2 (32 minutes). Recorded 1967.

⑧ ❻

As a teenager Criss grew up in Los Angeles, playing with bands led by men such as Howard McGhee and Billy Eckstine. The visit of Charlie Parker to the city at the end of 1945 gave Criss a new hero to worship and his earliest recordings have the strained, urgent sound of Parker before his nervous breakdown. After a period of residency in Europe in the early sixties, Criss returned to the US where Prestige's Don Schlitten set up a number of recording sessions; this New York date is certainly one of the best, despite the miserly playing time. Criss's tone is big and expressive, especially so on ballads where an admiration for Benny Carter seems to have overtaken the Parker mantle. There is a memorable reading of *God Bless the Child* and a suitably wistful air on pianist Walter Davis's tune *A Million More Times*. But the spirit of Parker still looms large on the up-tempo numbers, especially the hectic *Wee* (or *Allen's Alley*) where the occasional slight reed-squeak adds to the "you are there" sense of excitement. Walter Davis is a most helpful pianist and Alan Dawson's drumming simply cannot be faulted. Strongly recommended.

**AM**

## Bing Crosby
1904-77

**Bing Crosby and Some Jazz Friends** Crosby (v); featured with: **Louis Jordan and His Tympany Five**; **Connee Boswell**; **Bob Crosby's Bob Cats**; **Georgie Stoll Orchestra**; **Joe Sullivan**; **Louis Armstrong**; **Tommy Dorsey Orchestra**; **Jack Teagarden Orchestra**; **Eddie Condon Orchestra**; **Lionel Hampton Orchestra**; **Lee Wiley**; **Victor Young Orchestra**; **Woody Herman's Woodchoppers**; **John Scott Trotter Orchestra**. MCA/Decca Ⓜ GRP6032 (60 minutes). Recorded 1934-51

⑦ ❽

A giant of popular music, Crosby was also a good-natured comedian and an extremely successful film actor. His involvement in jazz began when he was a member of the Rhythm Boys with Paul Whiteman in the twenties and his association with players such as Bix Beiderbecke, Frankie Trumbauer and Eddie Lang began then, resulting in his lifelong enthusiasm for the music. He was not a jazz singer in the true sense, but when in the right company and with the right material he fitted well into the jazz milieu. The more maudlin aspects of his style are exposed here on 'square' performances such as *Someday Sweetheart* and *Pennies from Heaven* but on *Yes, Indeed!* and *When My Dreamboat Comes Home*, with brother Bob's Bob Cats, or *After You've Gone*, with the Condon mob, he demonstrates plenty of jazz virtues in a rollicking Dixieland atmosphere. His timing could never be said to give his music the cutting edge of true jazz singing, but his relaxed, richly legato style had a rhythmic strength of its own. If nothing else, *The Waiter and the Porter and the Upstairs Maid, I Ain't Got Nobody* and *Gone Fishing* are classics from the jazz fringe and they stamp him as probably the most jazz-inspired one-handicap golfer.

**BMcR**

## Bob Crosby
1913-93

**South Rampart Street Parade** Crosby (ldr); with a collective personnel of: **Yank Lawson, Shorty Sherock, Phil Hart, Max Herman, Zeke Zarchy, Lyman Vunk, Andy Feretti, Billy Butterfield, Charlie Spivak, Sterling Bose** (t); **Ward Silloway, Buddy Morrow, Artie Foster, Warren Smith, Elmer Smithers, Mark Bennett, Jim Emert, Ray Conniff, Floyd O'Brien** (tb); **Gil Rodin** (cl, as, ts); **Matty Matlock** (cl, as); **Irving Fazola** (cl); **Noni Bernardi, Bill Stegmeyer, Joe Kearns, George Koenig, Art Mendelsohn, Art Rando** (as); **Eddie Miller** (ts, cl); **Dean Kincaide** (ts); **Gil Bowers, Bob Zurke, Joe Sullivan, Jess Stacy** (p); **Nappy Lamare** (g, v); **Bob Haggart** (b, arr); **Ray Bauduc** (d). MCA/Decca Ⓜ GRP16152 (62 minutes). Recorded 1936-42.

⑧ ❻

Bing's younger brother Bob was invited to front a band formed of musicians who had all left the Ben Pollack orchestra. His pleasant although innocuous singing is not heard here, but he was nevertheless an important figure in the undoubted success of this unique band, unique because it played an orchestral form of Dixieland at a time when nearly every other big band was producing swing music.

All but one of the 20 tracks here are by the Crosby Orchestra as opposed to the Bob Cats small group (the only non-orchestral track is the Haggart-Bauduc duet *Big Noise from Winnetka*). Seldom has a band produced such zestful music, bouncing along on the steady beat laid down by Bauduc's fine drumming. A lot of the success is due to the consistently excellent arangements of Haggart and the outstanding solos from Eddie Miller, Irving Fazola and a wealth of memorable trumpeters. The underrated Sterling Bose, plunger-muted, is superb on *I'm Prayin' Humble*, for example. Pianists Bob Zurke and Jess Stacy are strongly featured on *Little Rock Getaway* and *Complainin'* respectively. The transfers are generally good, although they are evidently taken from a variety of sources.     **AM**

## Pat Crumly                                                                                   1942

**Flamingo**  Crumly (ss, as, ts, f); **Guy Barker** (t); **Richard Edwards** (tb); **John Pearce** (p); **Alec Dankworth, Simon Woolf** (b); **Simon Morton** (d); **Bosco DeOliveira** (perc). Spotlite Ⓕ SPJCD550 (74 minutes). Recorded 1993.

⑧ ❽

Like his earlier Spotlite album **Behind the Mask**, **Flamingo** is a showcase for a somewhat neglected talent. Pat Crumly is equally at home in rock, r&b and jazz, having decorated the albums of Eric Burden, Alan Price and Jimmy Witherspoon while developing a jazz sound rooted in bop and the blues. He is inspired by, but by no means slavishly imitative of, Cannonball Adderley and Phil Woods. Like the latter, on his favoured horn – alto – Crumly produces freewheeling, uninhibited solos laced with tart astringency, but he also plays driving if slightly querulous tenor, agile soprano and (on one track, *It Might as Well be Spring*) pure-toned, sure-footed flute. The material on this, as on **Behind the Mask**, consists of carefully selected standards from the likes of Rodgers and Hart (*Bewitched*), Kern and Fields (a storming version of *The Way You Look Tonight*) and Henry Mancini (a lithe alto treatment of *The Days of Wine and Roses,* packed with felicitous touches), interspersed with attractive Crumly originals. The album's centrepiece is its title track, in Crumly's words "a pleasing update of the Mingus chart" first heard on the bassist's 1957 album **Tijuana Moods**. His core quartet is augmented on this, his own bustling *Eucalypso* and the sinewy opener for tenor, *Nightwalk*, by the classy, bright sophistication of Guy Barker and the warm but gutsy trombone of Richard Edwards. Crumly demonstrates on this album just how strong the current UK jazz scene is.     **CP**

## Ronnie Cuber                                                                                1941

**Cubism**  Cuber (bs, ts); **Joe Locke** (vb); **Michael Formanek** (b); **Bobby Broom** (g); **Ben Perowsky** (d); **Potato Valdez** (cga). Fresh Sounds Ⓕ FSRCD188 (49 minutes). Recorded 1991.

⑧ ❽

Was a man ever blessed with a more appropriate surname? Cuber is perhaps best-known as a funk and pop session player, but his masterly treatments of the Latin style comfortably earn him the right to exploit the punning Caribbean potential of his name. His versatility should not be a surprise, since eclecticism has long been his stock-in-trade: before tackling the bespoke demands of the New York studios in the seventies, he played in big bands with Maynard Ferguson and others, and in organ combos with George Benson.

Cuber's Blue-Note-inspired Latin, bop and rhythm & blues tunes make no major stylistic departures, but it is hard to imagine such familiar idioms being delivered with more spirit, authenticity and polish. The period material and robust delivery combine to create the atmosphere of a sixties club somewhere on the wrong side of the tracks, the scene set perfectly by the sophisticated yet unpretentious opener, *Arroz Con Pollo*. The use of vibes and guitar in place of piano adds exotic tonal colour, and there are fine solos all round – from Cuber's chesty Coltrane-through-Pepper Adams bari, Joe Locke's urbane but earthy vibes and the perpetually inspired Bobby Broom, still improving on the style George Benson abandoned in the late sixties.     **MG**

## Laurent Cugny

New review
**Reminiscing/In Tempo**  Cugny (kbds, arr, cond); The Orchestre National de Jazz: **Claude Egea, Claus Stotter, Flavio Boltro** (t, flh); **Bernard Francois** (frh); **Phil Abraham** (tb); **Christian Laisne** or **Philippe Legris** (tba); **Denis Barbier, Pierre-Olivier Govin, Stefano Di Battista, Stephane Guillaume** (reeds); **Benoit De Mesmay** (kbds); **Lionel Benhamou** (g); **Frederic Monino** (bg); **Stephane Huchard** (d). (**Marc Richard** (comp, arr) – two tracks on **Reminiscing**; **Lucky Peterson** (org, vc); **Brent Nance** (perc) – two tracks on **In Tempo**). Verve Ⓜ 532 437-2/532 438-2 (two discs: oas: 67 and 57 minutes). Recorded 1994-5.

⑦ ❽

Whether a permanent national big band is a good idea, or the best possible use of the generous subsidy available for jazz in France, is for the French to decide. Certainly, the frequently changing personnel has achieved some memorable work, under a series of musical directors including François

Jeanneau, Denis Badault and now Laurent Cugny. Cugny's previously issued work included a collaboration with the latter-day Gil Evans, and several of Gil's trade marks have carried over. The use of funk rhythms and one-chord vamps, with rocky guitar and lots of unison writing for the horns, is offset by subtle harmonies, unusual tonal voicings and unexpected rhythmic shifts. With these attributes goes the ability to structure slender materials into longish pieces (such as the title track of the first record) and, though no one soloist stands out, they do more than merely decorate the space allotted to them.

**Reminiscing** begins and ends with two very different short tracks written by mainstream multi-instrumentalist Marc Richard and inspired by the twenties Fletcher Henderson band, whereas Lucky Peterson takes the Jimmy Smith role on *Theme From Joy House* and sings a Howlin' Wolf number on **In Tempo**. The fact that much of the latter is live, including a storming *Right Off* (by Miles), perhaps gives it the edge but both albums are impressive.                                                                  **BP**

# Bill Cunliffe

**A Rare Connection**  Cunliffe (p) with the following collective personnel: **Clay Jenkins** (t, flh); **Bruce Paulson** (tb); **Bob Sheppard** (ts, bcl); **Dave Carpenter** (b); **Peter Erskine** (d); **Kurt Rasmussen** (perc). Discovery ⓕ 77007 (55 minutes). Recorded 1993.

⑧ ❽

Cunliffe won the 1989 Thelonious Monk Jazz Piano Award around the time he was working with the Clayton-Hamilton Jazz Orchestra (which also included trumpeter Clay Jenkins). In the notes to this CD he is reported as saying "my intention was to take the language of traditional bebop jazz and bring it into the nineties." He has a delicate, expressive touch and a post-Bill Evans approach. Despite some Coltrane-inspired tenor from Sheppard this is not hard-bop music; in fact, it sounds like a logical extension of the jazz associated with the West Coast movement of the fifties. A considerable asset is the presence of Peter Erskine, one of the most tasteful, intelligent and musical drummers since the late Shelly Manne. The music flows evenly with no awkward breaks in the mood. Cunliffe wrote seven of the tunes but his approach to the standards, *Stella by Starlight* and the latter-day Jerome Kern song *Nobody Else But Me*, is very personal. *A Rare Connection* is a piano trio number of great charm (aided by some subdued synthesizer) and is a clear indication of Cunliffe's considerable keyboard control.                **AM**

# Ted Curson                                                                                                                                    1935

**Plenty of Horn**  Curson (t); **Bill Barron** (ts); **Kenny Drew** (p); **Jimmy Garrison** (b); **Roy Haynes**, **Danny Richmond, Pete LaRoca** (d). On two tracks **Eric Dolphy** (f) replaces Barron. Old Town/Boplicity Ⓜ CDBOP018 (40 minutes). Recorded 1961.

⑦ ❼

Curson first gained attention in 1960 as a member of Charles Mingus's Jazz Workshop at New York's Showplace. He, along with Eric Dolphy and Booker Ervin, was to become a permanent part of Mingus's front line for close on a year. Since then he has led his own bands and over the years has enjoyed a close working relationship with tenorist Bill Barron, brother of pianist Kenny. Curson made a number of albums in the sixties, and their value ranges from excellent to more-or-less interesting. The present album was his leadership début, and is certainly his freshest, brightest recording of the sixties. There is surprisingly little evidence here of his stay with Mingus (although drummer Richmond and Dolphy, present on two and three tracks respectively, are physical traces of the link), and Curson sticks for the most part to a style not that far removed from early Lee Morgan, although his brighter tone occasionally hints at Don Cherry.

Bill Barron, here like Dolphy to provide support rather than compete for time at the mike, contributes effectively to the more harmonically adventurous themes, but tends to drift through the blues-based numbers. Curson's *Ahma (See Ya)* has an opening arpeggio which uncannily combines elements of John Coltrane's 1959 *Giant Steps* and Wayne Shorter's *E.S.P.* of six years later, and Barron's solo on this track could even be Shorter himself. The album does not have the emotional depth of Curson's 1964 **Tears for Dolphy**, but does have a clear identity, a firm creative focus, and plenty to interest the curious.          **KS**

# King Curtis                                                                                                                               1934-71

New review

**Soul Meeting**  Curtis (ts); **Nat Adderley** (c); **Wynton Kelly** (p); **Paul Chambers, Sam Jones** (b); **Oliver Jackson, Belton Evans** (d). Prestige Ⓜ PRCD24033-2 (79 minutes). Recorded 1960.

⑧ ❽

As the generous playing time suggests, this CD contains all the tracks from two vinyl albums, **The New Scene of King Curtis** and **Soul Meeting**. Curtis (real name Curtis Ousley) had a talent bordering on genius for producing bursts of high-octane r&b saxophone on pop records, such as the Coasters' *Yaketty-Yak*, *The Locomotion* by Little Eva and Chubby Checker's *Let's Twist Again*. These reveal an unfailing instinct for tersely dramatic utterance and the ability to conjure an atmosphere with half a dozen well-timed notes.

In the context of a 'blowing session', however, these strengths count for much less. His long solos here are really a series of short solos stuck together, end-to-end, and he tends to skate rather inelegantly over chromatic changes, such as occur in the modern blues sequence. He was obviously much happier with the down-home, three-chord blues. But he remained a marvellously expressive player in the Texas tradition, with its typical heavy tone and rolling delivery, and a fountain of musical good humour.          **DG**

## Andrew Cyrille                                                                          1939

**My Friend Louis**  Cyrille (d); **Hannibal** (t); **Oliver Lake** (ss, as); **Adegoke Steve Colson** (p);
   Reginald Workman (b). DIW Ⓔ DIW858 (63 minutes). Recorded 1991.

⑧ ❽

Master percussionist Andrew Cyrille is best known for his 11-year (1965-75) stint with Cecil Taylor, a role that established him as a pioneering influence on free-jazz drumming. In recent years he has played across the spectrum of modern jazz, an in-demand figure who has graced records by (for instance) Muhal Richard Abrams, Anthony Braxton, John Carter and David Murray. He has also worked as a solo percussionist, in duos with improvisers such as Jimmy Lyons and Vladimir Tarasov, and has led his own group Maono (a Swahili word for 'feelings'), whose late-seventies-early-eighties albums for Soul Note (notably the fine **The Navigator**) are worth checking out.
   This CD's dedicatee is South African drummer Louis Moholo. Its music is relatively 'inside' with a loose, friendly feel, although the quintet are razor-sharp when they need to be, as on Cyrille's convoluted *Shell*. Hannibal's trumpet, all fire and quicksilver, is a good foil for Lake's acerbic reeds, and Colson's gentle pianism complements Workman's firm, melodic pulse. Cyrille himself brings a stream of felicitous touches, fierce and playful by turn, fringed with a stinging patter of cymbal cross-rhythms. Whether he is brushing ballads with a delicate lustre or rapping out the township bop of *My Friend Louis*, he has the gift to make his drum kit sing and dance.          **GL**

## Meredith d'Ambrosio                                                                     1941

**South to a Warmer Place**  d'Ambrosio (v); **Eddie Higgins** (p); **Don Coffman** (b); **Danny Burger**
   (d); **Lou Colombo** (t). Sunnyside Ⓕ SSC1039D (65 minutes). Recorded 1989.

⑦ ❼

John Coltrane so liked d'Ambrosio's voice that in 1963 he invited her to tour with his quartet. She declined the offer so we can only speculate as to how her intimate singing style would have fitted with the saxophonist's pyrotechnics. It was more than 20 years later (motherhood intervened) before d'Ambrosio finally made her mark in the jazz world with a series of intriguing, erratic records for the Sunnyside Label. **South to a Warmer Place** is the best of these. Her love of wincingly cute lyrics is held in check on a set that comprises mostly high-class romantic standards such as *The Touch of Your Lips, Dream Dancing* and *More Than You Know*. After trying several instrumental settings on previous albums with varying degrees of success, d'Ambrosio sounds completely at home with this lightly-swinging trio. Coffman and Burger (plus Colombo, who guests on four of the 17 tracks) offer discreet support, while husband Higgins threads bright piano lines through the songs, his slashes of colour a perfect foil for her low voice and quietly compelling style.          **GL**

## Tadd Dameron                                                                            1917-65

**Fontainebleau**  Dameron (p, comp); **Kenny Dorham** (t); **Henry Coker** (tb); **Sahib Shihab** (as); **Joe
   Alexander** (ts); **Cecil Payne** (bs); **John Simmons** (b); **Shadow Wilson** (d). Prestige Ⓜ OJCCD055-2
   (31 minutes). Recorded 1956.

✔                                                                              ⑧ ❻

Tadd Dameron is the least well known of the great jazz composers. Many of his themes became jazz standards during the bebop era (*Ladybird, Our Delight*, etc.) and his small-group recordings with bands including Fats Navarro, Wardell Gray and Alan Eager are among the finest of their period. He also provided some superb arrangements for the young Sarah Vaughan. But Dameron found few opportunities to develop his talent for composition, in particular for orchestration.
   The title piece of this disc is the most substantial work he succeeded in completing. Typically, it is scored for the smallest possible line-up and the shortage of rehearsal time is sometimes painfully obvious, but a distinct atmosphere comes through nonetheless. The effect is not unlike that of Monk's early Blue Note sessions, produced under similar circumstances, although the melodies and harmonic structures are unmistakably Dameronian. *Fontainebleau* is that rare thing, a completely through-written jazz composition (like Ellington's *Harlem*). It is in three linked sections – *Le Forêt, Les Cygnes, L'Adieu* – and Dameron was inspired to write it after visiting Fontainebleau while he was in Paris for the 1949 jazz festival. Although there are no improvised solos, it could only ever be performed by jazz musicians. Interestingly, Dameron recorded *Fontainebleau* again in 1962, with a full band and proper rehearsal, but the result has nothing like the personality and depth of the 1956 original. The remaining five tracks are rather sketchy performances, presumably because time was running out, but the title piece is a classic.

The original recording quality was far from brilliant, but the CD transfer has improved matters somewhat. **DG**

# Dameronia

**Live at the Theatre Boulogne – Billancourt, Paris** Don Sickler (t, cond); Virgil Jones (t); Benny Powell (tb); Clifford Jordan (ts); Cecil Payne (bs); Walter Davis Jr (p); Larry Ridley (b); Kenny Washington (d). Soul Note Ⓕ 121202-2 (67 minutes). Recorded 1989.

**⑥ ❽**

Drummer Philly Joe Jones struck on the idea of having a band dedicated to the music of the late Tadd Dameron, a pianist and composer whose multi-dimensional music had fitted most circumstances and had served the bebop pioneers ideally. The problem was that most of the scores had been lost and it was not until 1982 that Jones, together with transcribers Don Sickler and John Oddo, set about producing a 'book'. The result was Dameronia, an excellent band and a triumphant celebration of Dameron's music.

Sadly, Jones died in 1985, but this new manifestation of the band came about in 1989, using seven players involved in the early eighties. This CD pays tribute to Dameron's memory and, at the same time, produces music of immediate appeal. The choices of tempo are sympathetic, the themes get a chance to breathe and the mood of the composer is never shattered. The reeds as a team are especially effective but solo interludes, provided by Jordan's tenor on *Philly J.J.*, Wess's almost Hodges-like alto on *Soultrane* and Powell's shapely trombone on *Gnid* and *Good Bait*, lend further substance to music that makes it difficult to believe that Dameron has been gone for 30 years. **BMcR**

# Cedric Dandaré

**New review**
**Rhythmical Nature** Dandaré (g) with a large collective personnel featuring: Joey Rivera (t); Philip Kolb (as); Denise Jannah (v). Columbia Ⓕ 483719-2 (49 minutes). Recorded 1993-5.

**⑥ ❼**

Dandaré hails from Curacao, which is part of the Dutch Antilles, and for some time has been a resident in Holland, where he has made a considerable impact with his Caribbean-based jazz. He currently leads his own big band in Holland and teaches in Dutch conservatories. This album has the bright colours and big rhythms one would associate with his musical heritage, and also contains the occasional burst of scorching guitar work from the leader. It being a big band, the tracks tend to be chart-heavy, and by the time the solos arrive one is occasionally gasping for musical air. Still, it's no doubt perfect for summer parties. **KS**

# Eddie Daniels                                                                      1941

**To Bird With Love** Daniels (cl); Fred Hersch (p, elp); Roger Kellaway (p); John Patitucci (b); Al Foster (d); Steve Thornton (perc). GRP Ⓕ 95442 (53 minutes). Recorded 1987.

**⑥ ❾**

Initially a saxophonist, Daniels was six years with the Thad Jones-Mel Lewis Orchestra. In more recent times, he has concentrated on clarinet and has been featured in the Benny Rides Again group with Gary Burton. This CD takes him on an entirely different route. He plays tunes associated with Charlie Parker and does so with consummate artistry. He has a superb technique, a pure tone and he swings effortlessly. He is creative at all tempos but does move into double time when not always appropriate and his tempo choices for *East of the Sun* and *Just Friends* are suspect. More significantly, his style is not entirely suitable for Parker's music. His phrase shapes do not sit naturally with bebop and, not surprisingly, it is his respectful *Old Folks* reading and the loping perambulations of *Repetition* that show him at his best. In a duet with Kellaway, he takes *Why Do I Love You?* to the brink of contemporary chamber music. Daniels remains a gifted player whose technical accomplishments sometimes cloud his creative vision. **BMcR**

# Lars Danielsson

**... Continuation** Danielsson (b); John Abercrombie (g); Adam Nussbaum (d). L+R Records Ⓕ CDLR45085 (58 minutes). Recorded 1993.

**⑦ ❽**

Continuation is both the name of this début album from the young Swedish bass player and also the name of the trio which plays on it. Danielsson has an exceptionally wide list of career credits, having played with Herbie Hancock, John Scofield, Michael Brecker, Mike Stern, Bob Berg, Bill Evans, Muhal Richard Abrams, Flora Purim and Victor Lewis, among others. His technique is in the tradition of Scott LaFaro, his sense of time a cross between the late bassist and Dave Holland, while his sound is clear and resonant.

Abercrombie enjoys the space this set-up allows him, producing solos and interplay which come across as utterly involved. His overall contribution shows him to be listening closely to what is going on around him, and he gets plenty of bite into his tone and execution. Nussbaum is his usual sensitive and immaculate self. If you intend purchasing this, then be warned that you will have to be someone who enjoys bass solos. Although Danielsson doesn't take many, there is the occasional one. All such things are made up for by the wonderful way he can walk that bass; just try the middle section of *Flykt* for a demonstration of this fine, fine art. **KS**

# Harold Danko
1947

**New review**
**After the Rain** Danko (p). SteepleChase Ⓕ SCCD31356 (69 minutes). Recorded 1994.

⑩ ❾

This lengthy recital of the works of John Coltrane shows the touch of a master. Danko is a skilled veteran who sounds more appropriate to the concert hall than to his real background of coming up through the big bands – notably those of Woody Herman and Thad Jones-Mel Lewis. Coltrane's compositions are beautifully elucidated in a way which leaves them newly revealed to the listener. The harmonies and lines of the themes prove them well suited for solo piano interpretation and, coming together in abundance as they do here, one is made aware of a Coltrane 'songbook'. Danko's touch is masterful and his manifest technique is complemented by an extraordinarily good instrument. Danko has been an enthusiast for and student of Coltrane's work for over 30 years and, while these titles may largely be familiar to the listener only as they fly past at the beginning of a complex tenor rearrangement by the master, the butterfly of the beauty of his melodies is pinned down by Danko, who has the music in his blood. Coltrane would undoubtedly have been very moved by this set of interpretations and the listener should be warned that having bought this CD he will want to give up a lot of his time to listening to it. **SV**

# Jacqui Dankworth

**New review**
**Housman Settings** Dankworth (v); **Dick Pearce** (t, flh); **Mike Revell, Lynn Bottomley** (fhn); **Andy Panayi** (cl, as); **Julie Robinson** (ob, ehn); **John Williams** (cbcl, bs, dir); **Peter Hurt** (bcl, ts); **Gabrielle Byam-Grounds** (f, pic); **Elizabeth Elliott** (bn); **Phil Lee** (g); **Jeff Clyne** (b); **Trevor Tomkins** (d). Spotlite Ⓕ SPJ-CD559 (58 minutes). Recorded 1996.

⑧ ❾

One may be forgiven for making the more obvious connections here: Dankworth is the daughter of John Dankworth and Cleo Laine and possesses a voice not unrelated to her mother's. The type of project this album entails is similar to the type of project the Dankworths were ready to tackle 30 years ago (*Wordsongs*, for example), and the approach, although taken by a number of different composer/arrangers including Andrea Vicari, Dick Walter and Patrick Gowers, hints of the chamber-jazz attitude which reaped such artistic dividends for the earlier generation those years ago. That is not to say there is a problem with this record: it is superbly crafted and scintillatingly executed by a group of musicians exhibiting real cameraderie, and the vocalist is a model of artistry and exactitude, making a much more impressive entry in every way than on the rather diffuse and indulgent **First Cry** on EFZ. The lack of piano allows lines to flow better here, and each writer takes advantage of this: it also helps to link these new Housman settings with the English pastoral tradition of close to a hundred years ago, when a then-new group of British composers discovered the intoxicating versifications of this Shropshire poet and wrote an impressive body of songs. In that sense, this is a very British album, with a clear ancestry, and it is true to that ancestry. It is for the most part a gentle effort and takes a while to make its points to the listener: not always the best approach in this day of fast-forward and instant gratification. But if you take your time, much will please here, including the makeweight but excellent arrangements of a few jazz standards such as *Green Dolphin Street* and a couple of Ellington classics. Dick Pearce is particularly pleasing in all his solo work. **KS**

# James Dapogny
1940

**Original Jelly Roll Blues** Dapogny (p); **Jon-Erik Kellso, Paul Klinger** (c); **Bob Smith** (tb); **Mike Walbridge** (tba); **Kim Cusack** (cl, as); **Peter Ferran** (cl, ss, as); **Russ Whitman** (cl, ts); **Rod McDonald** (bj, g); **Wayne Jones** (d). Discovery Ⓕ 74008 (61 minutes). Recorded 1993.

⑥ ❻

Dapogny's Chicago Jazz Band is one of the leading traditional bands in the US, with a long history and recordings for Jazzology dating from the early eighties. It is also, most importantly, a repertory band, and its unique strengths stem from the personal and scholarly interests of its leader. Jim Dapogny, as well as having edited the monumental Smithsonian edition of Jelly Roll Morton's piano music, is a fervent advocate of the live performance of Morton's oeuvre, bringing his considerable keyboard, arranging and bandleading skills to bear in playing this music sympathetically and well. Here his band is a model of revivalism, with none of the stilted rhythm often found in this type of group. The beat is laid back and relaxed, not least due to Dapogny's own keyboard work. He is a far more subtle and expert player of Morton's piano style than virtually anyone else playing today, with the possible exception of Butch Thompson. But his real achievement was to apply his musicological skills to create new arrangements in the style of various sizes of Morton bands for pieces that only survive in piano versions, like *Seattle Hunch* and *Chicago Breakdown*.                                                                        **AS**

# Carlo Actis Dato

**Ankara Twist** Actis Dato (ts, bs, bcl); **Piero Ponzo** (as, bs, bcl, f); **Enrico Fazio** (b); **Fiorenzo Sordini** (d, perc). Splasc(h) Ⓕ 302-2 (72 minutes). Recorded 1989.

⑧ ❽

Tarantellas, saltarellos and istampitas may mean nothing to most jazz listeners, but they're the life blood of Carlo Actis Dato. One of a generation or more of Italian (that includes Sicilian and Sardinian) musicians who look to their roots music for inspiration, Actis Dato has arranged original material based on various dance forms – some dating back to medieval times – using ostinatos, repetition and cyclical themes. The rhythms are infectiously buoyant and reflect the intermingling of different cultures in historical Italy, with Greek and Balkan influences as well as an audible Moorish presence. In a vivid sense, Actis Dato and cohorts draw on folk traditions rather than those of jazz (that is, in their fluent improvising the details are less important than heightening the moment, extending the spirit of the tune. Invention takes a back-seat to intensity) and Actis Dato is an intense soloist, especially on baritone saxophone, where he is liable to erupt *à la* Mount Vesuvius. Fellow reedman Ponzo is an apt, engaging foil, and together the saxes twist lines around the bass and drums with an almost satiric abandon. There is nothing in this music that you could call profound, but taken in small doses, it is intoxicating.                                                                        **AL**

# Wolfgang Dauner                                                                        1935

**Up and Dauner: Masterpieces** Dauner (p); with a collective personnel including: **Jean-Luc Ponty** (elvn); **Zbigniew Seifert** (vn, as); **Hans Koller** (ss, ts); **Gerd Dudeck** (ts); **Jasper van't Hof** (elp, org); **Pierre Cavalli** (g); **Eberhard Weber** (vc, b); **Götz Wendland**, **NHØP** (b); **Daniel Humair**, **Alphonse Mouzon** (d); **Kurt Bong** (bgo); **Mani Neumeier** (ta). MPS Ⓜ 533 548-2 (71 minutes). Recorded 1962-75.

⑥ ❽

Auto-dictat Dauner has been a strong influence on modern jazz in Germany since the early sixties and has led a number of important European groups as well as occasionally dabbled in the more *avant* areas of music and art. One of his major achievements was the establishment of the United Jazz and Rock Ensemble in 1975, a band which led the way for many other serious-minded musicians looking for points of contact. As the years have gone on Dauner has increased the scope of his musical activities, embracing classical and world music as well as his jazz legacy. This collection focuses on his jazz work for the German MPS label, and is a pretty fair series of snapshots. It certainly pinpoints Dauner's wandering attention, reflecting an interest in music from many lands and multiple styles, and while much of this sounds so of-its-time to be little more than cute these days, the seeds of later accomplishments are there to be heard. Dauner's own playing is always full of interest, and some of his colleagues, especialy a young Ponty full of fire and jazz, are well worth a close listen. Hit-and-miss, then, but a fair enough reflection of what was going on at the time.                                                                        **KS**

# Jeremy Davenport

Davenport (t, v); **Peter Martin**, **Glenn Patscha** (p); **Neal Caine** (b); **Shannon Powell**, **Martin Butler** (d). Telarc Jazz Ⓕ CD83376 (56 minutes). Recorded 1995.

⑧ ❾

I can tell you very little about Jeremy Davenport, except that he plays trumpet and sings in a style not unadjacent to that of the late Chet Baker, that he looks about 20 years old and that, judging by the huge 'thank you' list in the CD booklet, he must have a wide circle of friends and acquaintances. The rest of the booklet is taken up with pictures, stuff about microphones and the lyrics of the songs. Since Davenport's diction is perfectly clear, these are quite unnecessary. On the other hand, I find the music itself quite charming. It is a curious fact that instrumentalists, when they sing, often do far better justice to a song than full-time singers. This applied to Chet Baker and it also applies to Jeremy Davenport. He sings a standard like *I'm Old Fashioned* with the plain gravity which it deserves, and his own songs are pleasant little pieces sprinkled with wit, both verbal and musical. He is not a Superman trumpet player, but we've got enough of those already. Davenport's strong points are a sweet, gentle tone and a melting turn of phrase, both qualities in short supply these days. **DG**

## Kenny Davern

1935

**Dick Wellstood and His All-Star Orchestra Featuring Kenny Davern** Davern (ss, cl); **Dick Wellstood** (p); **Bobby Rosengarden** (d). Chiaroscuro Ⓕ 129 (78 minutes). Recorded 1973/81.

⑧ ❼

Do not be confused by the billing. The 'orchestra' consists solely of Wellstood's 88s, and he and Davern are equal partners. Half the disc is a reissue of a Chiaroscuro LP of the same name, Wellstood duetting with Davern's soprano sax; the other half is a Chaz Jazz LP by the Blue Three, with Davern on clarinet and adding Rosengarden's drum patter. The repertoire is heavy on Jelly Roll, as might be expected, with singular excursions into the ODJB, Tin Pan Alley, and even Monk. The latter's *Blue Monk* is one of two informal homages to Pee Wee Russell (Russell having performed this with Monk at Newport), with Davern's clarinet essaying Pee Wee-like pitch bending, unpredictable swoops and groans. On the second, *Oh Peter* from the 1933 Rhythmakers date, Davern growls *à la* Pee Wee while Wellstood evokes Joe Sullivan's flash. Together with Rosengarden, the three stalk each other like bloodhounds. Other trio highlights include a leisurely stroll through *Indiana*; a *Tiger Rag* that begins as a rag and ends as a stop, without the cornball dixie-isms; and *Please Don't Talk About Me...* with a passage so evanescent the tune nearly evaporates. Without the drummer, the duo is more intimate, despite the brassier tone of the soprano and Wellstood's rolling orchestral chords. Davern does a terrific job approximating Armstrong's power on *Wild Man Blues*, elsewhere offering fluid commentaries without overt Bechet-isms, with Wellstood *Wallering* in and out of stride. Of course, Davern's playing in Soprano Summit was marvellous, but this disc is special too. **AL**

## Lowell Davidson

1941-90

**Lowell Davidson Trio** Davison (p); **Gary Peacock** (b); **Milford Graves** (d). ESP-Disk Ⓜ ESP1012-2 (45 minutes). Recorded 1965.

⑥ ❺

This is Davidson's only record as a leader, and although it was announced as part of the initial ESP programme back in the mid-sixties, it was in fact never released. So 1993 marked its first appearance, three years after the pianist's death. It certainly did not deserve so harsh a fate, being absorbing music balanced stylistically around halfway between Paul Bley and Cecil Taylor. Davidson quite clearly had considerable technical facility, a formed compositional sense, and an awful lot of bad luck.

His partners on this disc, both considerably more celebrated than him and both still successfully pursuing their careers, give Davidson strong support. Peacock plays in the manner still associated with him today, although he is understandably a little more free with his phrasing here than with Jarrett and Co. Graves, ubiquitous on early ESP-Disk albums and a fine free drummer, makes a lively and not altogether inappropriate contribution, although I feel that a player such as Barry Altschul or Tony Williams would have helped Davidson a little more. **KS**

## Matthew Davidson

1964

New review
**Voodoo Queen** Davidson (p). Mastersound Ⓕ DFCDI-220 (64 minutes). Recorded 1995.

⑤ ❽

Davidson is an experienced, well-trained and highly educated pianist who, in addition to performing the conventional classical concert repertoire, has a penchant for promoting new music and the kind of piano jazz that sits somewhere between classic ragtime and stride. As a ragtimer he favours a bravura approach and his timing and touch are a robust alternative to Joshua Rifkin's classic Nonesuch recordings. As a jazz player he works mainly from transcriptions, and it is in this area that the present album is less than successful – a transcription of Tatum's *Sweet Lorraine* showing how inimitable Tatum was. The most interesting area of music presented here is the work of the Eastern ragtimers like Eubie Blake, whose 1962 *Kitchen Tom* gets a rather startlingly *staccato* reading somewhat at odds with the way the old man himself used to play. Davidson deserves credit for unearthing this and other unusual repertoire, as well as for playing more recent rags, both his own and those of other writers including the late Donald Ashwander. On the other hand his playing lacks the jazz spark so obviously present in the work of other musicians like James Dapogny or Butch Thompson who have recorded similar works, and for those with a serious interest in this music, little surpasses Thompson's three-volume series for Daring (CD3001/3), collecting the music from the interstices of rags and stride from New Orleans, New York and Chicago.  **AS**

# Anthony Davis

1951

**Hemispheres**  Davis (p); **Leo Smith** (t, perc); **George Lewis** (tb); **Dwight Andrews** (f, pic, cl, ss, cond); **J.D. Parran** (cl, cbcl); **Shem Guibbory** (vn); **Eugene Friesen** (vc); **Rick Rozie** (bn); **David Samuels** (vb, mba); **Pheeroan akLaff** (d, perc). Gramavision Ⓕ R2 79428 (39 minutes). Recorded 1983.

⑨ ❽

The remarkable breadth of Anthony Davis's music is rare for one ostensibly identified as a jazz artist, which shows how confining such labels can be. From the critical and public success of his opera, *X*, to chamber trio improvisations, a violin concerto, programmatic tone poems for mixed ensembles, impressionistic solo piano recitals, and appearances as sideman on jazz dates, it is apparent Davis draws on multiple sources for inspiration. On the surface, **Hemispheres** would seem to have little connection to jazz. Composed to a commission from the modern choreographer Molissa Fenley, the suite's five movements speak with a harmonic language more familiar to classical than jazz listeners, and the intricate rhythmic emphasis (structured around contrasting complex metres and layers of heavily accented rhythms) reflect Davis's interest in Stravinsky as well as music from Africa, Bali and Java. But there are precedents in the music of Mingus and Ellington – in fact, one can hear the fourth movement as an extended Ducal meditation on an exotic theme, with intimations of Ray Nance's violin, Lawrence Brown's trombone, and Duke's piano; or Leo Smith's solo entrance in the second movement atop a suggestion of big band riffing, echoes of New Orleans polyphony resonating within the classical counterpoint. The fluidity of Davis's scoring is masterful, the music accomplished and highly evocative, regardless of how you categorize it.  **AL**

# Charles Davis

1933

**Reflections**  Davis (ts); **Barry Harris** (p); **Peter Washington** (d). Red Ⓕ RR123247 (48 minutes). Recorded 1990.

⑥ ❽

Despite his lack of prominence Charles Davis is a veteran and gifted baritone saxophonist who has spent most of his career as a key sideman with people as diverse and Billie Holiday, Dinah Washington, Kenny Dorham, Sun Ra, Steve Lacy and the Thad Jones-Mel Lewis Jazz Orchestra. He is also a distinctive exponent of the soprano, but here restricts himself to tenor. His association with Barry Harris has persisted for some years and the latter's ascendancy in interpreting the music of Thelonious Monk is reflected in Davis's composition, *Monking*. There seems to be as much of Monk and Bud Powell about Harris's playing of his own composition *To Duke With Love* as there is Ellington. The rest of the pieces, all substantial, are composed by Davis. *Miriam's Delight* evokes Monk even more strongly since there is much of Monk's tenor player Charlie Rouse in Davis's own work here. The influence of Coltrane (with whom Davis once worked) is minimal, and indeed Davis's softer tone is more out of Hawkins via Hank Mobley.

Barry Harris's piano playing is something to savour on every track; he must surely be one of the most gifted of the bop pianists. Like those of Davis, his solos are both strongly constructed and unfailingly imaginative.  **SV**

# Eddie 'Lockjaw' Davis

1921-86

**The Eddie 'Lockjaw' Davis Cookbook, Volume 1**  Davis (ts); **Jerome Richardson** (f, ts); **Shirley Scott** (org); **George Duvivier** (b); **Arthur Edgehill** (d). Prestige Ⓜ OJCCD652-2 (41 minutes). Recorded 1958.

⑥ ❽

'Lockjaw' was, like several of his contemporaries such as Gene Ammons, a living bridge between the tenor tradition of the thirties and the post-rhythm & blues of the fifties. Temperamentally, rhythmically and sometimes tonally close to Illinois Jacquet, Davis seemed more complex; yet, despite his stylistic link with the tortuous phrasing of Paul Gonsalves, his choppy terseness gave him a direct line to the populace. Appropriately, he was the virtual founder of the tenor-and-organ trio, using players such as Bill Doggett on record as early as 1949 and fronting a regular trio from 1954 onwards. The five years in which the keyboardist was Shirley Scott represented Lockjaw's popular peak, and her relatively subdued approach and awareness of dynamics providing a suitable contrast to his brusque attack. Although his up-tempo playing is most immediately compelling, the heart of his work is the ballads (here *But Beautiful*) and slow blues (*In the Kitchen*, themeless but mistakenly credited to Johnny Hodges). On most tracks guest Richardson is restricted to flute, played as it was before Lateef and Kirk showed everyone how. Davis's preceding album, where the guests were Count Basie and Joe Newman, might be more desirable if transferred to CD, but meanwhile this will do nicely, especially as Fantasy have now seen fit to reissue Volumes 2 and 3 in the **Cookbook** series.  **BP**

# Jesse Davis

New review
**From Within** Davis (as); **Nicholas Payton** (t); **Hank Jones** (p); **Ron Carter** (b); **Lewis Nash** (d). Concord Ⓕ CCD4727 (60 minutes). Recorded 1996.

⑧ ❽

Don't let the ghastly cover fool you: this, Davis's fourth album for Concord, is a very good record indeed. Cast in the post-bop mainstream style which is prevalent at many record labels at present, it is a superior example of that genre because Davis gives the music his all, and is very successful at communicating his undoubted emotions through a raft of original compositions (there are just two standards thrown in here for ballast) and a daringly human alto sound. Davis's rhythm team could be different, but hardly better, with Jones and Carter giving near-telepathic support and Nash establishing an easy, quietly intense feel to the session. Davis's front-line partner, Payton, is one of the most gifted of his young generation, and plays with great understanding of Davis's goals. Davis himself has an unusual warmth and persuasiveness, a real sense of emotional and intellectual honesty about his playing and compositions, making this no empty exercise over stale musical territory. Records like this remind one why such musical styles were so persuasive in the first place.      **KS**

# Miles Davis                                                                1926-91

**Birth of the Cool** Davis (t); **Kai Winding, J.J. Johnson** (tb); **Junior Collins, Sandy Siegelstein, Gunther Schuller** (frh); **John Barber** (tba); **Lee Konitz** (as); **Gerry Mulligan** (bs); **Al Haig, John Lewis** (p); **Joe Shulman, Nelson Boyd, Al McKibbon** (b); **Max Roach, Kenny Clarke** (d); **Kenny Hagood** (v). Capitol Ⓜ CDP7 92862-2 (36 minutes). Recorded 1949/50.

✓                                                                           ⑩ ❼

This is the nine-piece band which lasted two weeks in public, made a total of a dozen 78rpm sides and has had an influence on jazz lasting more than four decades. So much has been written about the music and the circumstances which brought this particular grouping of musicians and arrangers together that further comment now is largely superfluous. This CD brings together all 12 titles (inexplicably not in chronological order of sessions, let alone individual titles) and, while the transfers have not magically added anything that was not on the Dutch Capitol LP – the best previous manifestation of the music – then it has not taken anything away either. There is still so much to study, understand and enjoy here that, like the best in any art form, it has proved to be timeless. Johnny Carisi's handling of the traditional blues form in *Israel* is an object lesson in ingenuity; Davis's *Boplicity* (a collaboration with Gil Evans) is musical poetry while Mulligan's handling of *Darn That Dream* makes Kenny Hagood's accurate singing all the more remarkable. No self-respecting jazz collection can claim to be complete without this important music and, despite the meagre playing time, the CD is strongly recommended.      **AM**

**Chronicle** Davis (t); with a collective personnel of: **J.J. Johnson, Benny Green** (tb); **Lee Konitz, Jackie McLean, Dave Schildkraut** (as); **John Coltrane, Sonny Rollins, Lucky Thompson, Charlie Parker, Zoot Sims, Al Cohn** (ts); **Milt Jackson** (vb); **Thelonious Monk, Red Garland, Horace Silver, John Lewis, Walter Bishop Jr, Tommy Flanagan, Ray Bryant, Sal Mosca** (p); **Billy Bauer** (g); **Percy Heath, Paul Chambers, Charles Mingus, Oscar Pettiford** (b); **Kenny Clarke, Philly Joe Jones, Art Taylor, Art Blakey, Max Roach, Roy Haynes** (d). Prestige Ⓕ 8PCD012-2 (eight discs: 522 minutes). Recorded 1951-6.

✓                                                                           ⑧ ❻

This set contains the complete recordings in 17 sessions which Davis made for Prestige. It also chronicles the first major movement in jazz after the bebop and cool periods. When the first recordings were made Davis had suffered a setback in his playing, brought on by the euphemistic "personal problems". The opening session, with Sonny Rollins on tenor and John Lewis on piano, has one flawed masterpiece in *Blue Room*. An early session under Lee Konitz's name had cool music more typical of the altoist, and was followed by more sessions with Sonny Rollins. On the second of these Charlie Parker also played tenor, and although Bird was not on his normal inspired form, these tracks are not nearly as bad as has sometimes been suggested. A session with Cohn and Sims was more interesting for Cohn's compositions and arrangements than for the solos, and it was not until the subsequent sessions that Davis is heard playing with the command and confidence which were to be with him for the rest of his career. There are some stark but appealing quartet blues in the early sessions, and indeed blues pieces abound until the emergence of the classic quartet with Coltrane.

The recordings with Milt Jackson and Monk are amongst the best examples of a post-swing jam session and the inclusion of long alternate takes of *The Man I Love* and *Bags' Groove* is totally justified by the excellence of the music. The final three discs are given over to the quintet with Coltrane and Red Garland – a virtual jazz crucible and one of the most influential small groups since Louis Armstrong's Hot Five. The intensity of invention produced in the reworking of such a host of good and unhackneyed standards is breath-taking and the high standards rarely falter. While appreciating the quintet as a unit, the piano playing of Red Garland should be especially noted as some of the best in a career which often took him away from the limelight.

And the fuse was by this time well alight on the bomb that John Coltrane was carrying.      **SV**

**'Round About Midnight** Davis (t); **John Coltrane** (ts); **Red Garland** (p); **Paul Chambers** (b); **Philly Joe Jones** (d). Columbia Ⓜ 460605-2 (39 minutes). Recorded 1955-6.

✓                                                       ⑩ ❽

For anyone seeking a single representative album of the classic Miles Davis Quintet of the mid-fifties, this is it. All the individual strengths and stylistic innovations which made this one of the most influential bands in jazz history are summed up in these six numbers.

The poignant, lost quality of Miles's trumpet sound, indispensable background music to fashionable life in the late fifties, commands the attention, even when surrounded by such strong musical personalities as Coltrane and Philly Joe. This effect is particularly striking when he plays through a harmon mute directly into the microphone, as he does here in *'Round Midnight*, *All of You* and *Bye Bye Blackbird*. His phrases are simple in outline but generate an extraordinary feeling of tension because of the way he poises them over the light, springy beat. This in itself was a complete departure from the clenched, nervous rhythms of bebop. Everything about this record sounds as fresh today as when it first appeared, even though endless imitation has reduced some of its most original strokes to clichés.

This is the original Columbia mono LP transferred to CD and the playing time is short, although there are several more pieces from the same sessions which might also have been included. The digital transfers are very effective.                                **DG**

**New review**

**The Complete Miles Davis/Gil Evans Columbia Studio Recordings** On *Miles Ahead*: Davis (flh); Evans (arr, cond); Ernie Royal, Bernie Glow, Louis Mucci, Taft Jordan, Johnny Carisi (t); Frank Rehak, Jimmy Cleveland, Joe Bennett (tb); Tom Mitchell (btb); Willie Ruff, Tony Miranda (frh); Bill Barber (tba); Romeo Penque (f, cl, bcl, ob); Sid Cooper (f, cl); Lee Konitz (as); Danny Bank (bcl); Paul Chambers (b); Arthur Taylor (d). Add Eddie Caine (f, cl) and Wynton Kelly (p) on some tracks. On *Porgy and Bess*: Davis, Evans; Ernie Royal, Bernic Glow, Johnny Coles, Louis Mucci (t); Dick Hixon, Frank Rehak, Jimmy Cleveland, Joe Bennett (tb); Willie Ruff, Julius Watkins, Gunther Schuller (frh); Bill Barber (tba); Phil Bodner, Romeo Penque (f, alto f, cl); Cannonball Adderley (as); Danny Bank (af, bcl); Paul Chambers (b); Philly Joe Jones (d). Add Jimmy Cobb (d) and Jerome Richardson (f, af, cl) on some tracks. On *Sketches of Spain*: Davis, Evans; Ernie Royal, Bernie Glow, Louis Mucci, Taft Jordan (t); Dick Hixon, Frank Rehak (tb); Jimmy Buffington, John Barrows, Earl Chapin (frh); Jimmy McAllister (tba); Al Block, Eddie Caine (f); Romeo Penque (ob); Harold Feldman (cl, ob); Danny Bank (af); Jack Knitzer (bn); Janet Putnam (h); Paul Chambers (b); Jimmy Cobb (d); Elvin Jones, Jose Mangual (perc). On *Quiet Nights*: Davis, Evans, Royal, Glow, Mucci, Harold Baker (t); J. J. Johnson, Frank Rehak (tb); Ray Alonge, Julius Watkins, Don Corrado (frh); Bill Barber (tba); Steve Lacy (ss); Al Block (f); Jerome Richardson, Ray Beckenstein (f, reeds); Bob Tricarico (bn); Garvin Bushell (bn, contra-bn); Janet Putnam (h); Paul Chambers (b); Jimmy Cobb (d); Willie Bobo (bgo); Elvin Jones (perc). Others included on various tracks originally from *Jingle Bell Jazz*, *Sorcerer* and *The Giants of Jazz*. Columbia Ⓔ 67397 (six discs, nas: 449 minutes). Recorded 1957-68.

                                                             ⑩ ⑩

A mighty obelisk in the field of jazz CD reissues, this set chronicles the entire studio collaboration of Davis and Evans – an intense and fruitful partnership for a few years in the late fifties and then a drifting period for about a decade, with the occasional compromised project. Their music is a strange beast: if you're repudiating Kenton, as Evans was, why would you pair tubas and french horns? Why a "jazz chamber orchestra with guts," as Bill Kirchner calls his idea in one of the set's sleeve-notes – why not a smaller group? Why run the risk of burying a great soloist? Perhaps the answer can be found in Jack Chambers's Miles biography, when he discusses the impact of the 1949 Evans/Davis **Birth of the Cool** sessions. That music was both alien and celebrated; it may not have reached a mass audience when finally released on LP in 1954, but it made a great impact on musicians and critics. Certainly, it was responsible for West-Coast cool. Davis had a unique situation with Columbia from 1955 to 1957: the company kept him on salary while he finished up the final two years of his contract with Prestige. It made it much easier for him to finance a working band, the classic quintet with Coltrane; he also snuck in on a couple of Columbia projects, one being the **Music for Brass** album, the purest third-stream album there was and one that would fire Davis's imagination for more work with an orchestra. It led to his second great collaboration with Evans, in 1957, a moment when Davis was at his peak as an improviser. Evans worked with meticulous care; each musician received his part in the mail well in advance of the sessions. The music was mostly steered by Evans and yet **Miles Ahead** sounds like a love letter to Miles: the orchestra became a giant cushion for the trumpeter's crabby, forlorn signature. In what represents the greatest accomplishment yet of the jazz archivist and reissue producer Phil Schaap, the set restores the album in its original stereo and elsewhere separates the tracks, cutting away the connective passages Evans wrote to make it a continuous suite; there are also numerous overdubbed solos and studio discussions contained on the sixth disc. (The chatter isn't all worthless: you hear Evans singing a line to trombonist Joe Bennett before a *Blues for Pablo* take, adding "that kind of sound. Like you're in misery.")

The reissue history of **Porgy and Bess**, **Sketches of Spain** and the other material in the box is a good deal less complex, but this set contains the original issues with extreme frequencies restored (certain instruments in Evans's orchestra were nearly inaudible on recent reissues), as well as added treats like a Miles-less *Concierto de Aranjuez*, a take when Miles was simply listening. A 1963 collaboration, *The Time of the Barracudas*, written for a stage play but possibly never used as such, is included, and several takes of Gil Evans's 1968 *Falling Water*. Not all the material is essential, and most listeners will confine their listening to the first four discs, before the analytical work starts again from the beginning of the collaboration. But the set represents a complicated behemoth done right, with absolutely gorgeous sound. **BR**

**Miles Ahead** Davis (f); **Gil Evans** (arr); **Bernie Glow, Ernie Royal, Taft Jordan, Louis Mucci, John Carisi** (t); **Willie Ruff, Tony Miranda, Jimmy Buffington** (frh); **Frank Rehak, Jimmy Cleveland, Joe Bennett** (tb); **Tom Mitchell** (btb); **Bill Barber** (tba); **Lee Konitz** (as); **Danny Bank** (bcl); **Romeo Penque, Sid Cooper, Eddie Caine** (f, cl); **Wynton Kelly** (p); **Paul Chambers** (b); **Art Taylor** (d). Columbia Ⓜ CK65121 (37 minutes). Recorded 1957.
✓ ⑩ ⑧

According to George Avakian this was recorded on a two-track machine which Columbia had acquired just days before the 1957 recording date, thus capturing binaurally something which couldn't come out in stereo then. The stereo mix was débuted in the early nineties, and this freshly remastered effort takes advantage of the overhaul given the masters when the recent boxed set was researched. All this work merely confirms what you always knew – that if it is not the finest jazz big-band record ever made, then nobody ever made a better. Three odd things emerge. One is that there were no saxophones among the 19, except for Lee Konitz. Another is that, at less than 40 minutes, it was pretty short even for an LP. The third is that the star of the record is not Miles Davis, but Gil Evans, whose writing is the wonderful river that carries Davis's frail boat towards the sea. Davis's fragile, poignant sound is really just a foil for the ever-changing colour of the Evans sound, which moves faster and more flexibly than Miles ever does. This is the **Birth of the Cool** in its maturity. One other odd thing: even on his greatest record, jazz composer Gil Evans wrote none of the tunes. For those of you who want the warts-and-all viewpoint on this masterpiece, then the boxed set of all Miles-Gil studio collaborations (reviewed above) contains all the extant takes of each selection. For others who want to stick with what the two principals eventually decided on as their best efforts on each piece, then this single issue is still the one to own. Both this and **Porgy and Bess** now benefit from newly pristine sound taken from the two-track masters. **MK**

**Porgy and Bess** Davis (t, flh); **Ernie Royal, Bernie Glow, Johnny Coles, Louis Mucci** (t); **Dick Hixon, Frank Rehak, Jimmy Cleveland, Joe Bennett** (tb); **Willie Ruff, Julius Watkins, Gunther Schuller** (frh); **John 'Bill' Barber** (tba); **Phil Bodner, Romeo Penque, Jerome Richardson** (f); **Julian 'Cannonball' Adderley** (as); **Danny Bank** (bs, bcl); **Paul Chambers** (b); **Philly Joe Jones, Jimmy Cobb** (d). Columbia Ⓜ CK65141 (51 minutes). Recorded 1958.
✓ ⑧ ⑧

This, the second orchestral collaboration between Miles Davis and Gil Evans on Columbia, re-emerged as a digitally remastered CD in 1991, and this latest (1997) incarnation offers a significant improvement in clarity over both the analogue issue and the previous CD. Mercifully, it also escapes the idle meddling accorded the original digital reissue of **Miles Ahead**, where several of the originally issued takes were supplanted by alternatives. This **Porgy** finally corrects the niggling problems previous reissues have been bedevilled by. Charles Smith's retained original note illuminates the chief business of the record, namely the singularity and sensitivity of Evans's orchestral conceptions, and the aptness of his adaptations of themes from Gershwin's folk-opera for Miles Davis's style. By this time Miles had devised an unassailable rationale for his circumscribed technique and cool aesthetic, and the settings here suit it well. He is able to exercise his lyric intensity on such as *Prayer*, or swing lightly at a sympathetic medium tempo over simple, sometimes modal harmonies of the sort heard on *It Ain't Necessarily So* without fear of meeting a *Donna Lee* or an *Ornithology*. If you want **Porgy** by Miles and Gil, this new reissue is the one to seek out. **MG**

**Kind of Blue** Davis (t); **Julian 'Cannonball' Adderley** (as); **John Coltrane** (ts); **Bill Evans, Wynton Kelly** (p); **Paul Chambers** (b); **Jimmy Cobb** (d). Columbia Ⓜ 460603-2 (45 minutes). Recorded 1959.
✓ ⑩ ⑧

Few albums have been granted the destiny this one received. Recorded when each of its participants was at a personal peak of one kind or another, it is both a celebration of what has gone before in their careers and a door opening on the next ten years of small-group modern jazz.

Davis, with the help of pianist Bill Evans (and the input of arranger Gil Evans), prepared a set of charts for the recording sessions which, for the most part, abandoned the conventional song structures and bop changes, substituting instead a series of interrelated scales, or modes. This allowed the soloist the freedom to develop any improvisational angle he chose, and it is fascinating to hear the quite different approaches taken by the four main soloists to music they had not had a chance to get accustomed to before the sessions. Miles revels in the new space he finds for himself, becoming even more rhythmically daring than before, using pauses and sudden ringing notes to great effect. Adderley is stimulated to some remarkably fresh invention. His usual busy style is modified somewhat and his choice of notes more judicious than before. Coltrane, especially on the medium-tempo *So What* and *Freddie Freeloader*, invents complications for himself, but also relies heavily on thematic improvisation – a comparative rarity in his work.

Bill Evans sounds like a man reborn, and gives a perfect performance, whether as accompanist or as soloist. His playing, more than any others', dictates the extraordinary mood of the album (Wynton Kelly is present on *Freddie Freeloader* and generally sticks to the Evans approach, albeit with a touch more funk), and it is no accident that Miles chose him as collaborator.

There is little need to enumerate the many felicities of this unique record, although I would mention one personal favourite – Coltrane's heartstopping entrance to, and exquisite lyricism during, his *Flamenco Sketches* solo.                                                                                    **KS**

**The Complete Concert: 1964**  Davis (t); **George Coleman** (ts); **Herbie Hancock** (p); **Ron Carter** (b); **Tony Williams** (d). Columbia Ⓜ 471246-2 (two discs: 120 minutes). Recorded 1964.

⑨ ❽

Originally marketed as two separate releases, the landmark **My Funny Valentine** and **Four and More**, this new compilation of the entire 1964 Carnegie Hall concert is almost pure pleasure. The one caveat is Columbia's decision not to re-sequence the tracks in accordance with their placement in the original programme; as a result, the second disc (the original **Four**) is one up-tempo tune after another. Even more spurious is the repetition of Mort Fega's 're-introduction' of the group in the middle of each disc, a deceptive dodge suggesting that the original concert consisted of four parts!

Otherwise, this is one of Davis's great straight-ahead acoustic bands at the apex of its powers. There is the justly celebrated rhythm section of Hancock, Carter and Williams. Equally significant is the incandescent and yet lyrical tenor saxophone of George Coleman, inexplicably one of the least appreciated of prominent ex-Davis sidemen. Indeed, there is an argument to be made that it is Coleman who gives this particular Davis group its transcendent and distinctive sound. The repertory of timeless standards, in spite of the sequencing, includes *All of You, Stella by Starlight, All Blues, Walkin'* and *So What.* There is also a brilliant extended exploration of the poignant *My Funny Valentine,* with Coleman's *non-pareil* solo, and the dashing *Four.*                                    **CB**

**The Complete Live at the Plugged Nickel, 1965**  Davis (t); **Wayne Shorter** (ts); **Herbie Hancock** (p); **Ron Carter** (b); **Tony Williams** (d). Columbia Ⓜ CXK66955 (seven discs: 454 minutes). Recorded 1965.

⑧ ❻

Over two nights at Chicago's Plugged Nickel Club, just before Christmas in 1965, Columbia's microphones picked up every nuance and every shade of every set by one of the best Miles Davis quintets, hovering on the cusp between hard-swinging conventional jazz, the opening up of time and form that constituted Miles's flirtation with freer music, plus some presaging of jazz-rock. Not issued at the time, highlights were released in the form of two LPs nigh on two decades later. Now, as we become eager to understand more about Miles, how he worked, what he did and his role in the development of the music, it is fitting to follow on the 1992 release of the bulk of this material on Japanese Columbia with a US issue of every remaining scrap. As a document, this is as comprehensive and useful as the GRP release of Louis Armstrong's **California Concerts**, an equally warts-and-all presentation of a master at work.

Musically, despite the formulaic repetition of the set-list from one house to the next, the variety and invention of the quintet makes listening through the several hours of material a valuable exercise. There is a trap in the study of recorded jazz that makes one view a particular performance as definitive. This album debunks that view, with radically different readings of standards like *My Funny Valentine,* neither of them conforming to the studio or earlier live versions, but both showing an inventive and ever-changing approach. Here, as on *Stella by Starlight,* the melody itself often counts for little, Davis and Shorter's own melodic gifts substituting paraphrase and fragmentation for the coherence of the original. Carter's bass proves to be the lynch-pin of the band, anchoring harmony and time with understated confidence. Williams adds flamboyant and complex textures on drums, particularly apparent in the two takes of *Agitation,* the first marked by Miles's rapid-fire phrases running all over the horn in parallel with the shifting drum rhythms. Hancock frequently lays out, leaving just bass and drums to carry the soloist. His own solos are understated, too, if masterly, and he adds just the right level of support for Miles in transition and Shorter (on the verge of becoming a major soloist).                                                                              **AS**

**Miles Smiles**  Davis (t); **Wayne Shorter** (ts); **Herbie Hancock** (p); **Ron Carter** (b); **Tony Williams** (d). Columbia Ⓜ 471004 2 (42 minutes). Recorded 1966.

✔                                                                                                ⑩ ⑩

Hancock and Williams came into the band in 1963 and Shorter joined in 1964. These changes presaged a considerable shift in the way that Davis approached his music. He seemed willing for the dynamic Williams to assume the emotional reins and for Shorter and Hancock to have a greater say in the choice of material and in writing duties. Commencing with **E.S.P.** (Columbia 467899-2), his recording sessions concentrated on a new book and a new freedom. Davis, hospitalized during the period, had been able to re-assemble his group without loss when he returned to the scene and this CD endorses the kind of unity that the new line-up had established. The programme includes three originals by Shorter and one by Davis, and finds both horn players reacting in their own way to the rhythmic challenges thrown down by Williams. Eddie Harris's *Freedom Jazz Dance* is typical, with Davis taking an economical, open solo, using space as a vital element and allowing Williams front-line status in a virtual trumpet/drum duo. Shorter makes a similar impact, both as a player and composer, and *Footprints*, with its adroit use of a five-note vamp in the *So What* manner, was perhaps his most memorable contribution. The same title also elicited from Davis a timeless performance, confirming that the trumpeter had again moved on as a creative force. **BMcR**

---

**A Tribute to Jack Johnson** Davis (t); **Steve Grossman** (ss); **Herbie Hancock** (kbds); **John McLaughlin** (g); **Michael Henderson** (elb); **Billy Cobham** (d). Columbia Ⓜ CK47036 (53 minutes). Recorded 1970.

⊘ ⑧ ⑥

The personnel given above is that listed on some pressings of the original LP and on the CD reissue. Yet Sonny Sharrock has confirmed that the echoplex guitar solo toward the end of *Yesternow* is indeed his, and several other musicians are suspected to have participated in the recording sessions. Exact personnel is just one of the mysteries surrounding this television film documentary tribute to a boxer who dabbled in music by a trumpeter who dabbled in the ring. *Right Off*, the first of the two lengthy performances here, has the crunch of a studio jam, yet producer Teo Macero, probably pieced it together from several different sessions, just as he did the spacy *Yesternow*, which more obviously betrays signs of such after-the-fact editing.

Jack Johnson avoids the bombast of **Bitches Brew** and **Live Evil**, the empty noodling of **On the Corner** and (save for parts of *Yesternow*) the pleasant tinkering of **In a Silent Way**. Yet it is not completely satisfying as jazz *or* rock; if you wanted to explain to someone why fusion is not rock & roll, all you would need to do is play this and tell him to concentrate on Billy Cobham's tight drumming. For all of that, the album has its electrifying moments, most of them coming either from the superb McLaughlin or when Davis aims for his upper register on *Right Off*. **FD**

---

**On the Corner** Davis (t, org?); **Dave Liebman, Carlos Garnett** (ss, ts); **Teo Macero?** (sax); **Bennie Maupin** (bcl); **Chick Corea** (elp); **Herbie Hancock, Harold I. Williams** (elp, syn); **David Creamer, John McLaughlin** (g); **Colin Walcott** (sitar); **Michael Henderson** (b); **Jack DeJohnette, Billy Hart** (d); **Badal Roy, Don Alias, James Mtume Foreman** (perc). Columbia Ⓜ CK 53579 (55 minutes). Recorded 1972.

⑥ ⑥

On first release, **On the Corner** was greeted with open hostility by critics and musicians, and indifference on the part of record buyers. In retrospect, it is apparent they were all listening for things that were not there: harmonic motion, prominent trumpet, clear demarcation between soloist and rhythm section. Miles said in his autobiography that in the seventies he wanted his music to be more African, less European. This loud electric band – strings, keyboards, percussion and trumpet played (like the guitars) through a wah-wah pedal – functions more like an African drum choir than a jazz group, with each player adding another layer to the polyrhythmic weave. With vamps that go on forever, these pieces appear to be about stasis rather than progress, but that is an illusion; it is just that the rate of change tends to be slow. Soloists bubble up to and then slip back under the fluid surface.

If that description suggests an unlikely kinship between this street funk and the emerging minimalism of such composers as Steve Reich, who are also indebted to African percussion ensembles, give Miles the last word (from his autobiography): "I got further and further into the idea of performance as process … I never end songs, they just keep going on." (The question-marks over some of the personnel and instrumentation are a result of them never being adequately identified, either by Miles or the record company.) **KW**

---

New review

**Agharta. Pangea** Davis (t, org); **Sonny Fortune** (as, ss, f); **Pete Cosey** (g, syn, perc); **Reggie Lucas** (g); **Michael Henderson** (elb); **Al Foster** (d); **Mtume** (perc). Columbia Ⓜ 467897/467087 (two two-disc sets, oas: 97 and 89 minutes). Recorded 1975.

⑧ ⑨

"The devil's not as black as he's painted." At the original time of release in 1975 **Agharta** represented a Bosch-like vision of hell to the majority of jazz critics. Yet, despite the unwarranted loathing, these two live double albums – **Pangea** wasn't released in the UK until 1992 – have come to represent some of Miles's most enjoyable and important electric jazz dates, as well as becoming highly influential amongst the next generation of young, jazz-rock lions. They were the last recordings Miles made before his six-year lay-off and closed the chapter on the first half-decade of jazz-rock experimentation with barely concealed resentment. Both were tracked at Japan's Osaka Festival Hall on January 1st, 1975. **Agharta** is the afternoon show and **Pangea** the evening slot.

All Miles's major influences of the previous five years – Hendrix, Sly Stone, James Brown and Stockhausen – are distilled here into a thick, churning electric soup: the nearest he came on record to nailing his vision of a deep, African-American groove. Both sets feature continuous performances that ebb and flow on an intense, loping funk undercurrent, dense with percussion and Miles's occasional organ layers. **Agharta** draws on *Maiysha* and *Theme from Jack Johnson* with Fortune proving an able foil and Cosey and Lucas adding the Electric Ladyland sonics. Miles, as ever, is at the centre, cueing, glaring and growling while shifting from piercing upper register assaults and wah-wah stabs to lethal, cool moodiness. Of the two sets, though, **Pangea** gets the edge: a creeping masterwork with Davis in sombre mood echoing **Sketches of Spain**'s mournful cries, particularly on *Gondwana*, where Fortune also impresses with a remarkable, trance-like flute improvisation. Buy both, but look out for the recent Sony Japanese Master Sound versions which include an extra ten minutes of music on **Agharta**: a spooky, freeform electronic coda that would have gained Stockhausen's hefty nod of approval. **JN**

---

**Decoy** Davis (t, syn); **Branford Marsalis**, **Bill Evans** (ss); **John Scofield** (g); **Robert Irving lll** (syn, prog); **Darryl Jones** (b); **Al Foster** (d); **Mino Cinelu** (perc). Columbia Ⓜ 468702-2 (40 minutes). Recorded 1984.

⑧ ❻

The penultimate Columbia Miles Davis album, featuring two tracks recorded live in Montreal with one of his strongest electric bands, **Decoy** is one of the trumpeter's most straightforwardly accessible recordings. Although his relaunched career really took off with the (arguably inferior but more wine-bar-friendly) **You're Under Arrest** album of the following year, **Decoy** firmly established Davis as the most widely influential jazz figure of the eighties. Many have argued that his whole-hearted embracing of popular music's synthesized sound, hammered bass and unsubtle beats had stifled his creativity, but **Decoy** provides one of the best counter-arguments to this viewpoint. As in another underrated Davis album, **Agharta**, the leader's genius is manifest in subtle dynamic and textural shifts rather than, as previously, in flaring improvisational brilliance or an affecting poignancy of tone. In John Scofield he has his most sympathetic guitar foil since John McLaughlin, both Bill Evans and Branford Marsalis are supremely competent without being remarkable, and Robert Irving's synthesizer and programming work sets off the front line to perfection. The rhythm section is taut and dependable without ever lapsing into the robotic monotony frequently characterizing music of this sort. **Decoy** is a late peak in a protean career which is perhaps only paralleled in jazz by that of Ellington's. **CP**

---

**Amandla** Davis (t); **Kenny Garrett** (as, ss); **Rick Margitza** (ts); **Joe Sample** (p); **George Duke** (kbds, arr); **Joey DeFrancesco** (kbds); **John Bigham** (kbds, g, prog arr); **Michael Landau**, **Foley McCreary**, **Jean-Paul Bourelly**, **Steve Khan**, **Billy Patterson** (g); **Marcus Miller** (b, kbds, g, ss, bcl, d, arr); **Ricky Wellman**, **Omar Hakim**, **Al Foster** (d); **Don Alias**, **Mino Cinelu**, **Paulinho Da Costa**, **Bashiri Johnson** (perc); **Jason Miles** (prog). Warner Bros Ⓕ 925 873-2 (43 minutes). Recorded 1989.

⑧ ❿

Becoming bored with Miles's latest usually meant one was bored with life, or that one was merely nostalgic for his earlier work. Different listeners had different sticking-points, but even some who had gone along with him right up to the mid eighties jumped off when he began adopting pre-recorded backgrounds. Despite their occasional use in **Jack Johnson** and **Get up with It**, Miles almost invariably worked with a live band in the studio, even when less creative and less forward-looking souls had all but abandoned the interactive approach.

All the backings on **Amandla**, with the exception of the bass and drums of the Gil Evans-like *Mr Pastorius*, were prepared in advance and masterminded (apart from two tracks) by the ubiquitous Marcus Miller. His melodic hooks are often simplistic but, as in *Jo-Jo* (very reminiscent of the slightly earlier **Tutu** album), his textures are less blatant than Miles's later touring bands, and the drums are often played with brushes. Many of the other musicians listed play on only one or two items – fortunately, in the case of the bland Joe Sample – but Kenny Garrett distinguishes himself throughout and Davis, taking it easy and mostly muted, still creates the old magic. **BP**

# Richard Davis

1930

---

**One for Frederick** Davis (b); **Cecil Bridgewater** (t); **Ricky Ford** (ts); **Roland Hanna** (p); **Frederick Waits** (d). Hep Ⓕ CD2047 (74 minutes). Recorded 1989.

⑧ ❽

In the front rank of jazz bass players since the late fifties and equally at home in classical and rock settings (his contribution to Van Morrison's **Astral Weeks**, in particular, is a stunning piece of virtuosity), Richard Davis assembled this group of like-minded individuals for a tour of Japan in 1989. It brings its considerable collective musical experience to bear on a repertoire broadly representative of small-group jazz from the sixties to the present – Waits's previous collaborations range from stints with Johnny Hodges to Cecil Taylor, Hanna's from Benny Goodman to James Newton. The quintet thus moves from Benny Golson, Horace Silver and Kenny Dorham tunes to Monkish Davis originals and a relaxed Bridgewater vehicle with all the ease and confidence born of technical mastery and familiarity with the material. Hanna is sly and delightfully eccentric without ever sliding into gratuitous idiosyncrasy; the front line performs with controlled gusto and acerbic bite; Davis – as ever – is lithe, supple and simply one of the great bass soloists in the music (although a slow, bowed *Ev'ry Time We Say Goodbye* reveals occasional pitch problems). The album's dedicatee, Freddie Waits, who died shortly before its release, is faultless; sensitive to nuance but always propulsive. Recorded at New York's Sweet Basil the album showcases a great band swinging and relaxed in a congenial setting. **CP**

## Sammy Davis Jr

1925-90

**The Wham of Sam** Davis Jr (v); with **The Marty Paich Dek-tette**: **Jack Sheldon**, **Al Porcino** or **John Audino** (t); **Stu Williamson** (tb); **Vince DeRosa** (frh); **William Hood**, **Bud Shank**, **Bill Perkins** (reeds); **Red Callender** (tba); **Joe Mondragon** (b); **Mel Lewis** (d); **Marty Paich** (arr, cond). Warner Bros Ⓜ 245637-2 (37 minutes). Recorded 1963.

⑥ ⑧

Sammy Davis Jr as a jazz singer? For the vast majority of his career, frankly, no. But the jazz basis of his style would surface from time to time, no doubt guided by Sinatra's lead, and on this, his first session for Reprise, he opted for arrangements and accompaniment from Paich and his unit which are not just jazz-drenched, they are jazz from go to whoa. With such tight, sophisticated and insightful arrangements of standards like *My Romance*, *Thou Swell*, *Can't We Be Friends?* and *Blame It on My Youth*, Davis Jr has firmly embraced the sort of territory often explored by Mel Tormé, and carries the whole thing off with no little panache. His way with lyrics remains essentially superficial, preferring mostly to skate elegantly across the rhythm patterns they present to him, but his phrasing and his habit of paraphrase owe everything to jazz stalwarts such as Armstrong, Lester Young, Billie and Ella. Obviously scared to death about their new star's intentions, Reprise never issued these tracks as a single LP, but scattered them through Davis Jr's first batch of albums for them, leavening them with his more usual fare. This, then, is the first release of the Dek-Tette material as originally intended. **KS**

## Walter Davis Jr

1932-90

New review

**Davis Cup** Davis (p); **Donald Byrd** (t); **Jackie McLean** (as); **Sam Jones** (b); **Art Taylor** (d). Blue Note Ⓜ CDP832098-2 (38 minutes). Recorded 1959.

Davis first came to attention playing in the bands of Charlie Parker, Max Roach and Dizzy in the early to mid fifties. At home in the hard-bop style which took hold as the fifties came to a close, Davis made a considerable impression in the Jazz Messengers of that period and became a close associate of Jackie McLean, who appears on this date. The session's trumpeter, Byrd, was also one of Davis's erstwhile employers. **Davis Cup** is a hard-bop date typical of so many from that time, with a loosely swinging rhythm section and bright but essentially conservative soloing from the two horns. Davis was a talented composer, and all six tracks here stemmed from his pen, with the memorably brooding ballad *Sweetness* being a standout and also an indication of the depth of the impression Bud Powell (and through him, Thelonious Monk) made on this session's leader. An interesting album, then, caught as it is between the nervous angularity of the pure bop style and the funkier mannerisms of the hard-bop movement which followed on from it. Davis moved in and out of the music scene through the sixties and came back to full-time playing in the seventies, but albums under his leadership remained rare events. This is possibly the pick of them. **KS**

## Wild Bill Davison

1906-89

New review

**The Commodore Master Takes** Davison (t); with the following collective personnel: **George Brunies**, **Lou McGarity**, **Vernon Brown**, **George Lugg** (tb); **Pee Wee Russell**, **Edmond Hall**, **Joe Marsala** (cl); **Bill Miles** (bs); **Gene Schroeder**, **Dick Cary** (p); **Eddie Condon** (g); **Bob Casey**, **Jack Lesberg** (b); **George Wetling**, **Danny Alvin**, **Dave Tough** (d). Commodore Ⓜ CMD14052 (74 minutes). Recorded 1943-6.

✓ ⑩ ⑧

Davison followed Bix Beiderbecke into the Wolverines but he quickly moved away from the elegance and clarity of the cornettist and struck out towards his mature style. By the time he made these sides with the Condon gang for Commodore all the elements of his exciting, honest approach to music had long been in place. Inevitably, when someone is closely associated with such a colourful bunch of characters there is a temptation to linger over the rosy glow of anecdote and personality, but when the music itself is taken on its own terms it hardly needs the false props of sentiment and special pleading: this is superb, hard-driving jazz in a style which by 1943 was already a relic and by the end of these sessions was positively antediluvian, but you wouldn't be able to tell from listening. These guys are enjoying themselves, they know what they're doing, and they swing like hell. This is music for when you're feeling no pain and want to stay that way. It is also classic jazz of a persuasion which is impossible to resurrect in all its innocence and youthful flush of excitement and anti-establishmentarianism, just like Charlie Parker's is today. **KS**

## Doris Day

1922

**Doris Day With Les Brown** Day (v); **Les Brown Orchestra**. CBS Ⓜ 466958 (52 minutes). Recorded 1945-6.

The Les Brown band was always immaculate and tasteful with a good helping of jazz feeling. While it may seem unlikely on the strength of some rather cloying film roles ("I knew her before she was a virgin," said Oscar Levant), the same description applies to Miss Day.

Day is typical of the superb talents who were the big-band girl vocalists of the forties (Jo Stafford, Frances Wayne and June Christie were others). This well-chosen collection omits her biggest hit with Brown, *Sentimental Journey*, but splendid collaborations with the band like *Aren't You Glad You're You?* and *Come to Baby Do* show Day's impressive musicality and sense of time in combination with powerful work from the band, spiced with good instrumental solos. None of the soloists is identified, but the expressive tenor on a typically fine ballad like *We'll Be Together Again* is probably Ted Nash.

Apart from making the case for Day to be treated seriously as an excellent singer, the album is a fine showcase for one of the most immaculate and impressive of the big bands. Because of the skills involved all round, the music has hardly dated.                                                     **SV**

## Elton Dean                                                                                       1945

**New review**
**All the Tradition**  Dean (saxello, as); **Howard Riley** (p); **Paul Rogers** (b); **Mark Sanders** (d).
   Slam Ⓕ CD201 (54 minutes). Recorded 1990.

⑧ ❽

Dean began his career in a variety of trad, soul and showbands. In 1967 he joined Bluesology, fronted by Long John Baldry; in 1968 he began a long association with improvising pianist Keith Tippett, playing in the latter's sextet; and from 1969 to 1972 he was a member of Soft Machine, then in their jazz-rock phase. He has subsequently played with the London Jazz Composers Orchestra and the Carla Bley Band, led or co-led a number of groups, including EDQ, Ninesense and El Skid, and established a reputation as a fiery, free-jazz player who is also comfortable in more conventional settings, where he often brings a lyrical tenderness to the proceedings. **All the Tradition** shows Dean in both of these contexts on a set that features three jazz standards (*Darn That Dream*, Coltrane's *Crescent*, Benny Golson's *I Remember Clifford*) interspersed with two long, rather claustrophobic collective improvisations. Dean's slightly sour-toned saxello (a variant of the soprano saxophone) adds a nicely keening edge to *Darn That Dream* and his up-front, emotive alto on *I Remember Clifford* is no less affecting. *Crescent*, however, is the standout track, a fine display of sustained intensity and group rapport topped by Dean's blistering solo. Co-leader Riley is in excellent form throughout. **GL**

## Blossom Dearie                                                                                  1926

**Once Upon a Summertime**  Dearie (v, p); **Mundell Lowe** (g); **Ray Brown** (b); **Ed Thigpen** (d).
   Verve Ⓜ 517 223-2 (36 minutes). Recorded 1958.

⑧ ❽

It is hard to be anything but subjective when it comes to Blossom Dearie. One either likes what she does or hates it. Whatever your stance, this reissue is the best possible case for the defence, because it is probably her best album and is certainly from her best period, the late fifties. Her voice is small, and she makes little attempt to sing out with it, choosing instead to go for a special intimacy with the listener. At times this can result in performances which can sound a little too cutesy (*Doop-Doo-De-Doop (a Doodlin' Song)* definitely fits into this category). But then again, that intimacy makes her renditions of *Tea for Two* and *It Amazes Me* extraordinary in the way she persuades the listener that she is engaged in a one-to-one monologue with no one else in the world but them. These are genuinely moving performances. Her backing musicians are models of discretion and support, the recording balance and ambience is perfect for her, and one couldn't wish for a better representation of her art. For those wanting more, Verve have reissued both **Blossom Dearie** and a **Jazz Masters** volume which, although it duplicates five of the titles here, has 11 further tracks otherwise unavailable on CD. **KS**

## Dedication Orchestra

**New review**
**Ixesha (Time)**  Harry Beckett, Claude Deppa, Ian Hamer, Pat Higgs, Henry Lowther, Kenny Wheeler (t); **Jim Dvorak** (t, v); **Mark Charig** (c, thn); **Dave Amis, Roland Bates, Malcolm Griffiths, Paul Rutherford** (tb); **Andy Grappy, Dave Powell** (tba); **Neil Metcalfe** (f); **Lol Coxhill** (ss, ts); **Elton Dean, Mike Williams** (as); **Sean Bergin** (as, ts); **Evan Parker** (ts); **Chris Biscoe** (bs); **Keith Tippett** (p); **John Law** (p, v); **Paul Rogers** (b); **Louis Moholo** (d); **Maggie Nicols, David Serame, Julie Tippetts** (v). Ogun Ⓕ OGCD102/103 (two discs: 89 minutes). Recorded 1994.

⑦ ❽

London in the early sixties saw an influx of South African musicians fleeing the horrors of apartheid. These self-exiles included bassist Harry Miller and the Blue Notes group, with Johnny Dyani, Mongezi Feza, Chris McGregor, Louis Moholo and Dudu Pukwana. Their infectious township swing and explosive free-form later galvanized the capital's modern jazz scene and in 1970 they provided the core of McGregor's Brotherhood of Breath, one of the finest of the free-jazz big bands. **Ixesha (Time)**, like its predecessor **Spirits Rejoice**, was co-organized by Moholo, now the soul surviving Blue Note, as a tribute to his colleagues. It features a selection of their compositions, specially arranged for this large orchestra of leading UK improvisers and played by them with tremendous élan and passion. The horns in particular fire up the music, punching home the scintillating cross-rhythms (*Mofolo*, *The Serpent's Kindly Eye*, *MRA*) and adding rich timbral colour to the poignancy of *Sondela* and *Lost Opportunities*. The title track seems a mite indulgent (it has Moholo thanking all the participants by name several times over), but elsewhere **Ixesha (Time)** splendidly evokes the musical power and exuberance of its dedicatees. However, the playing time for two discs is less than generous.      **GL**

# Joey DeFrancesco

1971

**New review**

**Street of Dreams**  DeFrancesco (org, p, t, v); **Paul Bollenbeck** (g); **Byron Walndham** (d); on two tracks add **Keeter Betts** (b); six-piece brass section arr. by **Horrace Ott**. Big Mo Ⓕ 20252E (55 minutes). Recorded 1995.

⑦ ⑧

Since being let go by industry giant Columbia, DeFrancesco has joined the majority practice of the jazz community in moves from one independent label to another. His last two albums as leader have been with the Big Mo label, both demonstrating that this man has a great deal to offer, **Street of Dreams** being his most diverse record yet. Diverse doesn't always equal good, but in DeFrancesco's case what he attempts he generally pulls off. For a start, he sings on four tracks, débuting a light baritone with the Sinatra approach all over it but managing to stay swinging and in tune; something a good many vocal specialists can't manage. His piano playing is taut and finely judged, with ample touch to demonstrate that he's not just an organ grinder. DeFrancesco never strays from the mainstream approach, but he makes this a virtue by giving his heart and soul to each performance and he has also intelligently paced and varied this set with aggregations of differing sizes and make-ups. In another life he would have been the perfect match for producer Creed Taylor during his Verve years. As it is we'd be short-sighted indeed to spurn the unadventurous but highly satisfying fare DeFrancesco has to offer us in the nineties.      **KS**

# Buddy Defranco

1923

**Chip Off the Old Bop**  DeFranco (cl); **Larry Novak** (p, syn); **Joe Cohn** (g); **Keter Betts** (b); **Jimmy Cobb** (d). Concord Ⓕ CCD4527 (58 minutes). Recorded 1992.

⑧ ⑩

From being an icon of the swing era, the clarinet has declined almost to the status of an oddity in contemporary jazz. And yet the leading players form a wonderfully varied and individual bunch, from the darkly lyrical Kenny Davern to the mercurial Eddie Daniels. But of all the jazz clarinettists living none is more brilliant than Buddy DeFranco. This is the latest in a long line of recordings stretching back to the late forties, and it is as good as any of them.

With his tone of polished glass and his impeccable technique, DeFranco makes every solo an object of wonder and fascination for the listener and of despair for aspiring clarinet players. It used to be said that his playing was 'cold', which was never true, although there is a kind of icy deliberation in the way he constructs his phrases. But listen to these versions of the ballads *If You Could See Me Now* and *You're Blasé* and hear how warm his tone can be. DeFranco is joined on this disc by the guitarist Joe Cohn, a partnership which shows great promise for the future.      **DG**

# Jack DeJohnette

1942

**New review**

**New Directions in Europe**  DeJohnette (d, p); **Lester Bowie** (t); **John Abercrombie** (g, mandolin guitar); **Eddie Gomez** (b). ECM Ⓕ 829 158-2 (57 minutes). Recorded 1979.

⑧ ⑦

On paper, this record should not have been the success that it is. DeJohnette's themes (three are his; the fourth is probably a group improvisation) are rather slight affairs – a brisk Latin vamp (*Salsa for Eddie G.*), a slower Latin vamp (*Bayou Fever*, introduced by a display of DeJohnette's accomplished piano playing) and a loose chordal skeleton given variety by metric shifts (*Where or Wayne*) – but in true jazz style, the music is what is played rather than what is written, and when the musicians have the skill and empathy that these do, the quality is guaranteed. There is brilliance throughout, from DeJohnette's opening five-minute drum solo to Abercrombie's masterful playing over the fierce, changeless swing of the closing track, but the rawest excitement and greatest creativity is evident on the visceral *Salsa for Eddie G.* The atmosphere is electric with possibilities (thanks partly to a partisan audience), and most of them are realized by Lester Bowie, whose exuberant, bawdy soloing is more than enough to dispel the occasional suspicion that with the Art Ensemble of Chicago his trumpet becomes a stage prop in a comedy act. There's plenty of humour in this solo, but it is clearly just one aspect of his style rather than a primary objective. **MG**

---

**Album Album** DeJohnette (d, p, kbds); **John Purcell** (ss, as); **David Murray** (ts); **Howard Johnson** (tba, bs); **Rufus Reid** (b). ECM Ⓕ 823 467-2 (43 minutes). Recorded 1984.

⑧ ❿

By 1984 drummer-keyboardist Jack DeJohnette, an important member of the jazz-rock and fusion revolution due to his tenures with Charles Lloyd and the electrified Miles Davis, had expanded his acoustic horizons through vital collaborations with Keith Jarrett, John Abercrombie and Stan Getz. In the mid seventies, DeJohnette originated his band Special Edition to explore the implications of his varied musical associations in a context where the leader's compositional designs often played as important a part in the music's substance as improvisation.

In this evocative date dedicated to his mother (who had just passed away), DeJohnette creates dazzling spells. On *New Orleans Strut*, for example, there's a rolling Cajun-influenced beat backdropped with the leader's concertina-like atmospherics and simmering drums. The Crescent City mood also extends to *Festival,* where tumultuous group fireworks evoke traditional New Orleans music's collective approach to improvisation. Here, in contrast to later configurations of Special Edition, DeJohnette is among players who are his musical equals. Bassist Reid is the veritable anchor mooring DeJohnette's overdubbed drum and keyboard tracks. The vibrant horn section of Purcell, Murray and Johnson is simply magnificent. DeJohnette's meticulously crafted compositions are full of fascinating detail (which the group articulates brilliantly), yet they are also expansive and exuberant in outlook. Instead of referring back to Miles, DeJohnette's rich ensemble sonorities and bracing harmonies use Ellington and Mingus as their touchstones. In all, a highly satisfying session. **CB**

---

New review
**Dancing with Nature Spirits** DeJohnette (d, perc); **Steve Gorn** (f, ss, cl); **Michael Cain** (p, kbds). ECM Ⓕ 531 024-2 (72 minutes). Recorded 1995.

⑦ ⑨

If **Album Album** demonstrates DeJohnette's music at its most concise and structured, this album shows him to be equally at ease in compositions leaving ample room for the most ruminative extemporizations. The start of the title track here is as casual (perhaps incidental is closer to the process) as you are likely to find on record, the music slowly issuing out of silence, before a long, gradual *crescendo* brings us all, logically, to the end of a 20-minute long piece. *Anatolia* explores more esoteric combinations of background from piano and percussion while Gorn's clarinet sticks to Middle-Eastern scales. There is a myriad of detail to be picked out on each track here, and the listener with a mind to do it will enjoy the spontaneous combinations being discovered. **KS**

---

# Peter Delano

1976

---

**Bite of the Apple** Delano (p); with the following collective personnel: **Tim Hagans** (t); **Dick Oatts, Chuck Wilson** (f); **Gary Bartz** (as); **Chris Potter, Craig Handy** (ts); **Richard Locker, Tomas Ulrich** (vc); **Joe Locke** (vb); **Eddie Gomez, Marc Johnson, Gary Peacock, Peter Washington** (b); **Joe Chambers, Jeff Hirshfield, Victor Lewis, Adam Nussbaum, Bill Stewart** (d); **Ray Mantilla** (cga). Verve 521 869-2 (72 minutes). Recorded 1994.

⑥ ❽

This is pianist Delano's second CD for the Verve label, featuring various groupings of instrumentalists including several well-known younger players from the New York recording scene. The music is very efficiently played but the listener's enthusiasm may be tempered by those occasions when pure technique takes over and the music takes on a relentlessness which sometimes sounds superficial. The most impressive titles are the ones taken at slower pace or with more intimate instrumentation. *Heartfelt* has the pleasing sound of two cellos behind Chuck Wilson (playing alto and flute) while *Sunrise Remembered* is a beauty, played by just Delano and Joe Locke on vibes. **AM**

---

# Barbara Dennerlein

1961

---

**That's Me** Dennerlein (org, syn); **Ray Anderson** (tb); **Bob Berg** (ts); **Mitch Watkins** (g); **Dennis Chambers** (d). Enja Ⓕ ENJ7043-2 (64 minutes). Recorded 1992.

⑧ ❿

This really is an organ record for people who hate Hammond B3 organs. It demonstrates quite convincingly that organs can be fun, and that they do not all have to sound like Jimmy Smith the morning after. Dennerlein has a number of things going for her, prime among them real taste in the choice of sidemen on her records: this is by no means the first time either Ray Anderson or Mitch Watkins, both very superior musicians, have recorded with her, and the results have never been less than stimulating.

She also composes most of her own material, and is sufficiently adept at it to bring an unusual breadth of outlook to her repertoire. She plays with enormous drive and enthusiasm: all her albums have that energy and it emanates from her outward to the other musicians, rather than the other way around. Her bass lines, all created on the pedals, invariably swing like crazy. On this, her last album for Enja, Dennerlein's normal group is joined by saxophonist Berg, and he does not waste time getting acquainted. His solos bristle with ideas and his section playing helps keep the whole thing moving along at a bright clip. Although she has moved to Verve and has released her début album, **Take Off!** there, this remains her best record to date. Recording quality is first-rate.                **KS**

# John Dennis

New review

**New Piano Expressions**  Dennis (p); **Charles Mingus** (b); **Max Roach** (d). Debut
Ⓜ OJCCD1843-2 (56 minutes). Recorded 1955.

⑧ ❻

Dennis was a discovery of Charles Mingus and Max Roach, joint proprietors of Debut records. Apart from a session the previous year, as pianist on Thad Jones's first album, this was his first and, apparently, only recording. The notes, while lavish in their praise, are almost devoid of useful information. One appreciates the helpful gesture and the kudos involved, but it might have been better if Mingus and Roach had not played. The solo tracks are by far the best, and reveal Dennis as an impressive solo pianist, posed midway between the fulsomeness of Erroll Garner and the delicate impressionism of Bill Evans. In his compositions *Chartreuse* and *Variegations* he explores each of these territories in turn and both are uncommonly attractive pieces.                **DG**

# Paul Desmond                                                                     1924-77

**East of the Sun**  Paul Desmond (as); **Jim Hall** (g); **Percy Heath** (b); **Connie Kay** (d). Discovery
Ⓜ DSCD840 (43 minutes). Recorded 1959.

⑧ ❽

The fact that Desmond spent most of his career trapped within the Dave Brubeck Quartet has tended to obscure his proper eminence in jazz. He should be ranked with Stan Getz, Lee Konitz, Al Cohn and Phil Woods. His cool veneer diverted attention from the passion and exhilaration of his best work. This quartet was in fact a late development from the by-then defunct cool school, and its music was played with a light touch and delicacy which easily upstaged the contemporary music of Brubeck's group. Desmond and Hall rarely played better than in their five recording sessions together and this, the first of them, was the best. The exquisite *For All We Know* is flanked by a pastoral *Greensleeves*, an eloquent reading of John Lewis's fine blues *Two Degrees East, Three Degrees West*, and a bouncing *I Get a Kick Out of You* which is as near to muscle as this team gets. Percy Heath and Connie Kay from the Modern Jazz Quartet, well versed in such intimate surroundings, make a perfect rhythm team.                **SV**

**Two of a Mind**  Desmond (as); **Gerry Mulligan** (bs); **John Beal**, **Wendell Marshall**, **Joe Benjamin** (b), **Connie Kay**, **Mel Lewis** (d). RCA Victor Ⓜ 68513-2 (41 minutes). Recorded 1962.

✔                ⑩ ❼

I originally intended giving this a slightly less than perfect rating, as my memory of it was that it had some outstanding tracks but somehow didn't quite sustain itself to the end. I was wrong. On re-hearing it I am happy to declare it perfect. By that, I don't mean that every note is perfectly articulated and each phrase is the best possible phrase in its context; I just mean that there is a perfect fusion of intentions and the realization of them. Desmond and Mulligan make a beautiful ensemble sound together and find exciting and different routes to that sound in each selection. They both also play inventively and resourcefully, inspiring each other to reach for more in each solo. Their interplay is uncanny, the contrast between their instrumental approaches keeping the record continually on the boil.

Why does this album work better than Desmond's other RCA dates of the same period? And why is it also better than the Verve album these two made together in 1957? Firstly, this date has neither piano nor guitar, and the resulting clarity of texture leaves the listener with ample room to follow the two lead men in every detail. It also brings an intimacy to their efforts which would have been hard to sustain with a harmony instrument added. As for the second question, it may be that both players are better at creating something new out of a group of old standards than they are at playing the blues, and the first album had its fair share of blues-based numbers. It also wasn't very well recorded. Summation: this is a classic, and bears not just repeated listening, but years of familiarity. The tender, rapt, eight-minute version of *Stardust* included here is as good a thing as either player has ever done, separately or together.                **KS**

New review

**Pure Desmond**  Desmond (as); **Ed Bickert** (g); **Ron Carter** (b); **Connie Kay** (d). Epic Ⓔ ZK64767
(46 minutes). Recorded 1974.

⑧ ❾

Having spent most of his working life in the Dave Brubeck Quartet, it is hardly surprising that Paul Desmond, when left to his own devices, should have avoided the company of pianists. His preference was for guitarists, in particular Jim Hall and Ed Bickert, the delicacy of whose touch provided the ideal harmonic foil for his own ethereal tone. Asked once how he came by his remarkable sound, he replied, "I think I had it at the back of my mind that I wanted to sound like a dry martini" – which is as good a description as anyone has ever come up with. This collection of ten old and newish tunes, from *Squeeze Me* to the *Theme from M\*A\*S\*H*, is at once stimulating and relaxing. Not unlike a dry martini, in fact. **DG**

# Laurent DeWilde

New review
**The Back Burner** DeWilde (p); **Eddie Henderson** (t); **Antonio Hart** (as); **Ira Coleman** (b); **Billy Drummond** (d). Columbia Ⓕ 480784-2 (49 minutes). Recorded 1995.

⑦ ⑨

DeWilde's previous three records have all been with his trio, the only exception being Eddie Henderson added to his very first, **Off The Boat** (Ida, 1987). Coleman has been a fixture since then, with Drummond coming on board on the third date, **Open Changes** (Ida, 1992). DeWilde was born to French parents in the US and has zig-zagged across the Atlantic a number of times during his relatively short life. Presently he is based in Paris. He is a thoughtful pianist, doesn't normally waste notes or over-elaborate harmonically, but is astute in everything he does. His tidy arrangements of well-known songs (*Besame Mucho*, for example) betray an acute ear for fresh angles on jaded territory, and he incidentally stimulates his sidemen through this approach to unclichéd playing and intelligent responses. This is modern mainstream and the decibel level remains fairly low apart from the occasional Hart flurry, but nothing is wasted and no one overplays. A slow burner, indeed. **KS**

# Vic Dickenson                                                           1906-84

**Gentleman of the Trombone** Dickenson (tb, v); **Johnny Guarneri** (p); **Bill Pemberton** (b); **Oliver Jackson** (d). Storyville Ⓕ STCD5008 (58 minutes). Recorded 1975.

⑧ ⑧

The trombone seems to be one of those instruments in jazz which attract individualists. Dickenson can certainly be numbered in those ranks. He made a late start to soloing after spending most of the thirties in big-band trombone sections, but his work with Lester Young for Commodore and Aladdin, amongst other dates, certainly launched his highly vocalized and good-humoured style. He has been leading his own small groups since the late forties and this group is typical of his favoured environment. Guarneri is a pianist capable of emulating any pre-bop style you care to name, always soloing with wit and drive, while the bass and drums have been around plenty of top-grade swing outfits.

Dickenson is in typically relaxed form here, using his mutes to snake and angle his line through the chord changes with the maximum of sly ease. His swing, like Teagarden's, is seemingly lazy but highly infectious. He sings on a couple of tracks, which I guess is extra value for money, but his trombone playing, with its charming twists and exhortations, is the main event for every pair of ears here. The CD reissue, by the way, has three extra tracks not released on the original vinyl version. **KS**

# Walt Dickerson                                                          1931

New review
**Relativity** Dickerson (vb); **Austin Crowe** (p); **Ahmed Abdul-Malik** (b); **Andrew Cyrille** (d). Prestige New Jazz Ⓜ OJCCD1867-2 (35 minutes). Recorded 1962.

⑧ ⑨

In the last edition of the Guide I lamented the lack of Dickerson CD reissues by the Fantasy group, especially that of the classic **To My Queen**, which featured Andrew Hill at the piano. Well, something has at last stirred in Berkeley, and we now have three of Dickerson's early-sixties records on CD, all at mid-price; but, alas, still no sign of **To My Queen**. Yet this is not to denigrate **Relativity**, which is a fine album in its own right and a considerably more varied and enticing proposition to the casual listener than the SteepleChase duet CD, **Divine Gemini**, which had to suffice last time around. Dickerson on this disc displays his thrillingly varied touch, his supple and limitless rhythmic command on top of a pellucid sound which, although discernibly contemporary, cannot easily be confused with any other vibist. The programme is the typical Prestige fare of the time for a new and adventurous musician – a selection of the leader's own distinctive pieces, leavened with a couple of timeless standards which are meant to demonstrate that the cats really can play the changes like everybody else when they have to. To this end, *It Ain't Necessarily So* and *I Can't Get Started* are given fresh and respectful interpretations. Dickerson in particular seems stimulated by *Started*, and comes up with lines as newly formed and exciting here as he does anywhere else on the disc. On that basis, then, it is fair to say that this is a remarkably consistent effort, helped considerably by sympathetic and finely wrought backing from Malik, a pre-Cecil Taylor Cyrille, and the obscure but accomplished pianist Austin Crowe. Everybody is listening intently and playing with real élan, and I can do no more than recommend you to do the decent thing and listen intently too. **KS**

# Al Di Meola 1954

**New review**

**Orange and Blue** Di Meola (g, p, syn, pic, d); **Mike Pinella** (t); **Andres Boyarsky** (s); **Conrad Herwig** (tb); **Simon Shaheen** (vn); **Hernan Romero** (v, g, p, syn, pic), **George Dallas**, Noa (v); **Mario Parmisano** (p, syn); **Marc Johnson** (b); **Pino Palladino** (elb); **Peter Erskine**, **Manu Katché**, **Steve Gadd** (d); **Gumbi Ortiz** (perc). Verve Ⓕ 523 724-2 (59 minutes). Recorded 1994.

⑦ ❾

In his seventies incarnation as guitarist with Chick Corea's Return to Forever and then as a solo artist on Columbia, Al Di Meola got a rather poor press for his empty parades of technique, his impressive speed and articulation failing to disguise a rather monochrome harmonic sense. This, the first of a new deal with Verve, finds him pursuing a broader, more restrained and more jazzy policy, the aesthetic shift well illustrated by a soft focus reading of the old RTF tune, *Theme of the Mother Ship*. While the sound of Spain became intrinsic to his seventies style, titles here like *Paradisio*, *Chilean Pipe Song* and *Ta'alina Chant* explore the world beyond Andalusia. It's not, however, an untrodden path. The mellow sound of his Gibson Di Meola model, the delicate, cymbal-driven Latin rhythms, the synth string washes and wordless vocals often bring to mind Pat Metheny's jazzing of Milton Nascimento's Brazilian pop style. However, Di Meola does bring his own variations to bear, often shading the Metheny sound with a few darker tones. The sense of emotional shortfall remains, as if the rocking bombast of earlier years has been replaced by ethno-soundbites that would fit well in the travelogue files of an incidental music library. Still, there's good jazz guitar sprinkled throughout, and the new course may yet bring him to more interesting destinations. **MG**

# Gene DiNovi 1928

**New review**

**Live at the Montreal Bistro, Toronto** DiNovi (p); **Dave Young** (b); **Terry Clarke** (d). Candid Ⓕ CCD79726 (64 minutes). Recorded 1993.

⑥ ❾

DiNovi was born in Brooklyn and is of the generation which came to maturity with the heady sounds of bop swirling in their heads. His self-professed early influences include George Wallington, Dodo Marmarosa, Ellington and Basie at the piano, with Charlie Parker asserting an overall hegemony on his musical thinking. Later influences include Nat Cole, Tatum and Teddy Wilson. All this allowed him to record with both Goodman and Fats Navarro and gradually become recognized as one of the outstanding accompanists to vocal stars such as Peggy Lee, Lena Horne and Anita O'Day. A move to Toronto in the seventies after a number of years in the California studios took him out of the mainstream but ironically gave him the opportunity to record under his own name for the first time. This is his second album for Candid and something like his fourth as a leader. It carries the same personnel as its predecessor and the same overall musical message, but this time we have a live audience geeing the trio up a little. The sense of it being George Shearing we're hearing still occasionally overpowers the listener, but whoever DiNovi reminds us of, his playing is superior and utterly free of the unnecessary. In other words, worth listening to. **KS**

# Joe Diorio 1936

**Rare Birds** Diorio, **Mick Goodrick** (g). Ram Records Ⓕ RMCD4505 (75 minutes). Recorded 1993.

⑧ ❽

Recordings from Joe Diorio seem to come along like buses – none for a decade then three in a row. **Rare Birds** is one of three recordings Diorio made during visits to Italy in 1992 and 1993, but where the other two – one solo, one with bass – are rather subdued, this one, in duo with a like-minded fellow guitarist, is a hot one. Although he played in earlier years with Getz, Freddie Hubbard, Eddie Harris and others, Diorio is perhaps best known to guitarists around the world for his *Intervallic Designs* guitar manual, and those whose interest was aroused by that volume now have a fresh opportunity to hear the theory in practice. Indeed, the duo's treatments of such standards as *Green Dolphin Street*, *Out of Nowhere*, *Well, You Needn't* and *Blue in Green* are rich in quartal harmony and abstruse chord substitution, and this is one element which helps distinguish this date from so many routine jazz guitar duets. But the session also thrives on imaginative use of texture and arrangement, exploiting the contrasts between block chords and walking bass, between chord and solo and two-voice counterpoint, between functional harmony and pointillistic free improvisation;

and by doing it all in an adversarial but co-operative spirit, the duo are able to sustain interest in a format that otherwise often induces polite boredom in its audiences.          **MG**

## Dirty Dozen Brass Band

**Live: Mardi Gras at Montreux**  Gregory Davis (t); Efrem Towns (tb); Kevin Harris (ts); Roger Lewis (bs, ss); Kirk Joseph (bb); Jenell Marshall (snare, v); Lionel Batiste (bass d). Rounder Ⓟ CD2052 (47 minutes). Recorded 1985.

⑥ ❻

Initially little more than a skiffle group, the Dirty Dozen arrived at their present size and shape in 1975. Their New Orleans origins are obvious in every note they play and they are as ideally suited to march amongst their concert audiences as they once did around the streets of the Crescent City. As this CD shows, their music is a wonderfully homogenized mixture of traditional, New Orleans jazz, r&b, hard bop and swing era riffs. Their ineluctable bounce is superbly captured on Mardi Gras in New Orleans, *It Ain't What You Think* and *Lickity Split*, but it is the way they boogie through *Night Train* or take a quasi-serious look at a tune like *Blue Monk* that draws attention to a wider stylistic range than is at first apparent. Little profundity is intended or achieved from the band's soloists but, like Marshall's occasional vocal, they are often used as a means to stir the audience. In addition a liberal seasoning of humour adds to their vivacity and the response from the audience at this 1985 Montreux Festival is typical. Whether the Dozen should be considered a jazz band is immaterial. They are a permanent fixture on the jazz tour and a large number of serious jazz musicians stand at the side of the stage to listen and stomp.          **BMcR**

## Dixieland Jug Blowers

New review

**Louisville Stomp**  Johnny Dodds (cl); Lockwood Lewis (as, v); George Allen (as, ss); Hense Grundy (tb); Clifford Hayes (vn); Johnny Gatewood (p); Cal Smith, Curtis Hayes, Freddie Smith (bj); Earl McDonald, Henry Clifford (jug, v); Elizabeth Washington, Prince La Vaughn (v). Frog Ⓟ DGF6 (77 minutes). Recorded 1926/7.

⑦ ❼

The jug as used on this CD was an empty stone jar. It acted as a resonator from which the manipulators, using double-lip blowing techniques, produced flatulent sounds. This simulated the melody line of the tenor, the tailgate shapes of the trombone or the support patterns of the tuba. It was certainly not an activity peculiar to the United States. Comparable musical forms are known in Asia, Africa and Australia, but there did seem to be a tradition of such bands in Kentucky and in Louisville, in particular. The name of the Dixieland Jug Blowers was coined by the RCA Victor company that recorded them, but they were actually made up of Earl McDonald's Louisville Jug Band, plus guest violinist Hayes and 'bass' jug man Clifford. Horn players were used but this was speciality music. Certainly Hayes's strident country fiddle was a more appropriate instrumental voice than Lewis's alto, even if his phraseology did suggest a reed player. Much more significant was Victor's introduction of Dodds for one session. This elevated all four titles made that day to the serious jazz category. It is unlikely that Dodds himself took them seriously, but his dancing clarinet on *Carpet Alley Breakdown* and his two blues-drenched choruses on *Hen Party Blues* bring unlooked-for dignity to the music. Predictably, musical inaccuracies abound, the vocals have little blues or jazz feeling and Grundy's rustic trombone has few creative pretensions. A typical title such as *Southern Shout*, however, is good-natured hokum and this is, after all, music to put a smile on the face.          **BMcR**

## Bill Dixon                                                                                      1925

**Son of Sisyphus**  Dixon (t, p); John Buckingham (tba); Mario Pavone (b); Laurence Cook (d). Soul Note Ⓟ 121138-2 (39 minutes). Recorded 1988.

⑩ ❽

Trumpeter, composer, educator and a painter of international repute, Bill Dixon's tiny discography is a poor indication of his talent. A major figure in the sixties avant-garde, he worked with Cecil Taylor and Archie Shepp, co-founded the New York Contemporary Five and recorded, in **Intents and Purposes**, one of the decade's most original and beautiful albums. Neither that LP nor his two fine seventies records for the Italian Fore label are currently available, but thanks to a later association with Soul Note at least two Dixon masterworks are now on CD; the live **November 1981** and the later **Son of Sisyphus**.

Dixon's music has been described as painterly, although its attention to the details of form, line, texture and colour are as much the mark of a composer (and testament to a rigorous instrumental technique). Like his paintings, his music is abstract; titles such as *Thoughts* and *Considerations* indicate its reflective quality, an impression reinforced by his liking for darker sonorities (tuba and bass here). Much of **Son of Sisyphus** sounds deep in thought, notably tracks such as *Fusama Codex*, *Mandela per*

*Mandala* and *Negoro Codex*, where his elegiac trumpet wanders through shadowy thickets of low-register support. In contrast, *Vecctor* is skittering group empathy; *Schema VI-88* a delve into brass timbres, all gargles and leonine growls. Dixon also plays telling piano on two brief duos with bass, *Sumi-E* and the valedictory *Silences for Jack Moore*, its grief imbued with the dignity of the blues.　　**GL**

# Johnny Dodds                                    1882-1940

**Johnny Dodds 1926-40, Volume 1**　Johnny Dodds (cl); **Louis Armstrong**, **George Mitchell**,
　Natty Dominique (c); **Kid Ory**, **Roy Palmer** (tb); **Jelly Roll Morton**, **Earl Hines**, **Jimmy Blythe**, Lil
　Armstrong (p); **Johnny St Cyr**, **Bud Scott** (bj); **Baby Dodds**. **Jimmy Bertrand** (d, wshbd). Affinity
　Ⓜ CDAFS1023-3 (three discs: 193 minutes). Recorded 1926/7.

⑧ ❻

There were better technicians and more sophisticated exponents of the clarinet, but Dodds was the best all-rounder and set much of the method of ensemble playing for the instrument. His abilities within a group are best displayed on four tracks by Jimmy Bertrand's Washboard Wizards where he and Armstrong form the front line. It is interesting to hear Armstrong trying to change his style on six tracks by Dodds's Black Bottom Stompers because he was under contract to another record company and was trying to avoid being recognized – as a consequence his playing is inhibited on these tracks when compared to his magnificent work on *I'm Going Hunting* with Blythe. Dodds flowers with chalumeau performances of great beauty on *Wild Man Blues* and *Melancholy*.

Eight tracks by the New Orleans Wanderers/Bootblacks feature the estimable George Mitchell, while Dodds's performance on *Perdido Street Blues* is one of the finest of his career. Coming from obscure sources, some of this material has had to be taken from worn recordings, but where the source is good the transfers are excellent.　　**SV**

# Klaus Doldinger                                    1936

New review
**Doldinger's Best**　Doldinger (ts, ss, kbds); with various groups including: **Ingfried Hoffman** (org);
　Peter Trunk (b); **Attila Zoller**, **Philip Catherin** (g); **Cees See**, **Pete York** (d); **David Newman** (ss);
　Johnny Griffin (ts); **Les McCann** (p, v); **Etta James** (v). ACT Ⓕ 9224-2 (71 minutes). Recorded
　1963-77.

⑥ ❼

Berlin-born Doldinger has had a more varied career than almost any other active jazz musician, commencing with the leadership of the Feetwarmers, a very successful trad band which played down in New Orleans and in New York's 'Birdland' on the same 1960 US tour. He led a hard-bop quintet for a time, worked extensively with an outstanding organist, Ingfried Hoffman, and later formed a jazz-rock band called Passport. This 14-track selection from his fairly extensive discography commences with a powerful blues from the only Doldinger LP that I recall being issued in the UK. *Blues for George* has marvellous tenor choruses and powerful organ from Hoffman. There's also a track featuring Klaus with the NDR Jazz Workshop band, a stellar unit containing men such as Donald Byrd, Benny Bailey, Idrees Sulieman, Johnny Griffin and Ake Persson. *Stormy Monday Blues* was taped at the 1977 Montreux Festival and finds Doldinger as the star of the show both in solo and playing obbligato behind Etta James. Other tracks use the bossa nova format and elements of Indian music. I suppose one could criticize Klaus for dabbling in too many styles but the fact remains that he is a truly commanding soloist on tenor, especially when playing the blues.　　**AM**

# Niels Lan Doky                                    1963

**Misty Dawn**　Doky (p); **Niels-Henning Ørsted Pedersen** (b); **Alex Riel** (d). Columbia Ⓕ 477460-2
　(54 minutes). Recorded 1993-4.

⑦ ❽

Doky, a native of Denmark, spent most of the eighties in New York, where he got to play with a wide selection of the music's front-runners, including John Scofield, Joe Henderson, Woody Shaw, Charlie Haden and Ray Brown. He now spends his professional career swapping between the two sides of the Atlantic, and has to his credit over 14 albums under his own name. This is the latest, and is typical. Although these three have not made a trio album before, they are old colleagues, and their playing sits together seamlessly. NHØP hardly needs any introduction, although it is worth remembering that he was playing in a trio with Bud Powell when he was just 16, while Alex Riel is probably best known internationally for being the drummer on Eric Dolphy's **Last Date**.

The music here is very much in the tradition of modern piano trios such as Bill Evans, Chick Corea and Herbie Hancock, although a partiality to quasi-classical music effects in his own compositions suggests the more pronounced duality of his musical experience and origins. NHØP plays beautifully throughout, eschewing the impulse to overplay and fill in too many gaps, while Riel is the soul of sensitive drive. Hardly music to change the world, but no less enjoyable for that. Doky's later Blue

Note album, which features his brother Chris Minh Doky on bass, shows other aspects of his talent, but hardly puts this album in the shade. **KS**

# Eric Dolphy

1928-64

**The Complete Prestige Recordings** Dolphy (f, as, cl, bcl); with a collective personnel: **Booker Little, Freddie Hubbard, Richard Williams** (t); **Ken McIntyre, Oliver Nelson** (as); **Booker Ervin** (ts); **Jaki Byard, Mal Waldron, Richard Wyands, Water Bishop Jr, Bent Axen** (p); **Ron Carter** (vc, b); **George Tucker, George Duvivier, Sam Jones, Richard Davis, Chuck Israels** (b); **Roy Haynes, Ed Blackwell, Art Taylor, Charlie Persip, Jørn Elniff** (d); **The Latin Jazz Quintet**. Prestige Ⓕ 9PRCD4418-2 (nine discs: 640 minutes). Recorded 1960-1.

⑧ ❾

Dolphy recorded for Prestige's New Jazz label for just 15 months, cutting three studio albums for them as a leader and six as featured soloist. On top of this, his last official Prestige date was as co-leader (with Booker Little) of a quintet recorded live one evening at the Five Spot, from which more than three LPs were eked, some appearing only after Dolphy's demise. A further live session, recorded by Stockholm Radio in September 1961, was subsequently released on Prestige and titled **Eric Dolphy in Europe**. Again, more than three LPs finally made their way on to the market. In addition to this, Dolphy appeared as a non-soloist on an Eddie 'Lockjaw' Davis big-band session, which is also included here for the sake of completeness. The material at the core of Dolphy's achievement in these years remains the titles originally made under Dolphy's name – **Outward Bound, Out There, Far Cry** and the three **Five Spot** albums. These present his artistic credo in uncompromised and undiluted terms and also reveal him to have been a superb and provocative jazz composer. Of the three studio albums, **Outward Bound** is a careful and coherent presentation of Dolphy's early ideas on how to extend bebop's legacy through the means of a standard quintet, while **Out There** returns to the Chico Hamilton format of horn-with-strings (cello and double-bass) and features strong Dolphy compositions mixed with some uneven playing, especially from Ron Carter, who was apparently quite ill during the session. **Far Cry** again addresses bebop, but from a more distant viewpoint, achieving a wonderful balance between compositional and harmonic advances and the desire to achieve these within a conventional instrumental format. Booker Little and Jaki Byard are outstanding on this disc. The live recordings from the Five Spot eight months later feature Dolphy and Little in extended performances with Mal Waldron, Richard Davis and Ed Blackwell and find the music stretched to the limit of what is possible within older jazz forms. This in itself is half the fascination of this adventurous and imaginative music. In comparison, the live selections from Europe break no new ground as far as Dolphy is concerned, although *In the Blues* is an otherwise unrecorded original, *Laura* is a sensational reading of an old favourite, and *Hi-Fly* a perfectly balanced duet with Chuck Israels, while *God Bless the Child* is the best version of an *a cappella* reading Dolphy often gave during the summer and fall of 1961.

As far as the sideman material goes, the two albums with Oliver Nelson are great fun while never capturing the special ambience of Nelson's famous **Blues & the Abstract Truth** (recorded for Impulse), the Ken McIntyre album is an only partial success and the date with the Latin Jazz Quintet is frankly a waste of time unless you're a Dolphy completist. Ron Carter's album **Where?** has its moments but not enough of them, but the Mal Waldron session **The Quest** is a *bona fide* classic. Featuring Dolphy with Booker Ervin alongside, as well as a set of challenging Waldron compositions, it deserves a place in any jazz collection. It is worth pointing out that each and every one of these records is available separately on CD, with alternative takes added where appropriate, so those who may blanch at the idea of a nine-disc set of Dolphy can cherry-pick the best, one at a time. If that idea appeals, start with **Far Cry** or the Five Spot sessions. **KS**

**Vintage Dolphy** Dolphy (as, cl, bc, f); **John Oberbrunner** (f); **Phil Woods** (as); **Benny Golson** (ts); **Edward Armour, Don Ellis, Nick Travis** (t); **James Knepper** (tb); **Lalo Schifrin, Eddie Costa** (p); **Warren Chiasson, Eddie Costa** (vb); **Jim Hall, Barry Galbraith** (g); **Richard Davis, Chuck Israels, Art Davis, Barre Phillips** (b); **J.C. Moses, "Sticks" Evans, Charles Persip** (d); **Gloria Agostini** (hp); **Louis Krasner, Adrienne Galmier, Matthew Raimondi, Lewis Kaplan** (vn); **Joan Mulfinger, Samuel Rhodes** (va); **George Mulfinger, Jr, Michael Rudiakov** (vc). GM Ⓕ GM3005CD (68 minutes). Recorded 1962-3.

⑦ ❻

Produced by Gunther Schuller, this second edition of **Vintage Dolphy** offers a greatly improved remastering job and a previously unreleased Dolphy performance of Schuller's *Variants on a Theme by Thelonious Monk*. Reflecting Dolphy's interest in employing free improvisation with contemporary compositional procedures and unusual (for jazz) instrumental formats, this stunning collection, while further solidifying Dolphy's avant-garde credentials, demonstrates why the multi-instrumentalist never connected with a larger audience. In Schuller's poignant *Densities*, for example, Dolphy's clarinet paints pointillistic blips over a serrated harp/bass/vibraphone backdrop that demands a Gestalt-like connecting-of-the-dots response from the audience. Dolphy's music was never easy.

It was, though, influential. Coltrane's playing became increasingly radical after collaborating with Dolphy. And in contrast to a number of sixties pretenders who camouflaged ineptitude with 'new-thing' honks and squeals, Dolphy could run changes with the best, a fact demonstrated in an extended jam on Parker's *Donna Lee* where Dolphy soars with Woods, Golson, Knepper and Hall. In fact, Dolphy's alto solo exemplifies the side-slipping that, though 'out' when first heard, is now a bedrock of the contemporary mainstream. The grand triumph is Schuller's five-part *opus de Monk*, a provocative set of atonal études whose emotional and musical depths speak as forcefully today as they first did in 1962.                                                                       **CB**

---

**Conversations** **Dolphy** (as, bcl, f); **Woody Shaw** (t); **Clifford Jordan** (ss); **Sonny Simmons** (as); **Prince Lasha** (f); **Bobby Hutcherson** (vb); **Richard Davis**, **Eddie Kahn** (b); **Charles Moffett, J.C. Moses** (d). Celluloid Ⓜ CELD5014 (34 minutes). Recorded 1963.

⑩ ❷

Along with its companion volume from the same sessions, **Iron Man**, **Conversations** is rivalled only by **Out to Lunch** as Dolphy's most mature statement as a leader. It's also the most varied: each of four selections features different line-ups.

**Conversations** includes a couple of his most charming performances; the merry mariachi-cum-calypso *Music Matador* by Lasha (later Lawsha), for three reeds, flute, bass and drums, and a lilting, definitive take on Fats Waller's *Jitterbug Waltz*, for quintet. Featuring Dolphy on flute, it showcases Hutcherson, who has never sounded better than with Dolphy, while *Music Matador* affords an excellent example of Eric's goose-cry bass clarinet and his knack for making spectacular dramatic/comic entrances. On an intense and slowly unfolding *Alone Together*, for bass clarinet and double-bass, Dolphy's and Davis's joint attention to silence and open space comments on the title. The leaping *staccato* intro and outro to a solo alto version of the standard *Love Me* look ahead to Anthony Braxton's and Roscoe Mitchell's angular styles, and to the late-sixties Chicago vanguard's penchant for solo-horn recitals in general. There are severe problems with this reissue: the remastered sound is tinny and distant; **Iron Man** would easily have fitted onto the same CD, where it belongs. The disc seems to be withdrawn in the US but available in Europe, where part of these sessions, at least, is also available on the budget Charly Le Jazz label (CD14) (with even worse sound reproduction)! Even so, this is essential music.                                                    **KW**

---

**Out to Lunch** **Dolphy** (f, bcl, as); **Freddie Hubbard** (t); **Bobby Hutcherson** (vb); **Richard Davis** (b); **Tony Williams** (d). Blue Note Ⓜ CDP7 46524-2 (43 minutes). Recorded 1964.

✓                                                                       ⑩ ❽

Dolphy's last studio recording as leader is now widely regarded as his masterpiece. **Out to Lunch** has taken its place alongside titles such as **Free Jazz** and **Unit Structures** as a landmark of early modern jazz. It is Dolphy's most advanced set, notable particularly for its radical experiments with rhythm. The catalyst here was the young Tony Williams, then marking out a path between the polyrhythmic complexities of Elvin Jones and Sunny Murray's total freedom. What little regular pulse there is on **Out to Lunch** tends to be carried by Richard Davis's roaming bass, while Williams disrupts and dislocates the beat with counter-rhythms, abetted by sudden percussive flurries from Hutcherson's vibes.

Dolphy and Hubbard both negotiate this tricky new terrain surefootedly, although it is the leader who more often grabs the attention: the quizzical bass clarinet expostulations on *Hat and Beard*; the rapid, feisty flute on *Gazzelloni*; the alto's collage of fragmentary phrases on the title track, or its wildly humorous slurs on *Straight Up and Down*. Solos, though, are all succinct, facets here of a brilliantly integrated group music. Dolphy's growing sophistication as a composer (most evident on the lovely *Something Sweet, Something Tender*) plays its part, but it is the group interaction – the way they hold the music together even as they take it apart – that makes **Out to Lunch** so contemporary and so compelling.                                                          **GL**

---

**Last Date** **Dolphy** (f, bcl, as); **Misja Mengelberg** (p); **Jacques Schols** (b); **Han Bennink** (d). EmArcy/Limelight Ⓜ 510 124-2 (46 minutes). Recorded 1964.

⑧ ❻

Eric Dolphy is generally agreed to have been one of the major talents in modern jazz, yet somehow he is not much talked about these days, perhaps because he was overshadowed by his contemporary John Coltrane. Perhaps, too, Coltrane was the sort of talent that could influence people, whereas Dolphy's style did not incite imitation (certainly, it is hard to think of anyone who could be said to be a Dolphy stylist). His passionate improvising on all three of his main instruments, harmonically shrewd and rhythmically daring though it was, also tended to have a slightly gurgling quality which was not immediately beautiful. The best track on this album (not his last date, incidentally, but a transcription from a Dutch television programme), recorded with a Dutch rhythm section, is his long flute feature *You Don't Know What Love Is*, which is still quite striking; it is hard to gurgle on a flute and he does not. But the music as a whole is quite spacious and thoughtful and if you had to have a record called **Last Date** (he died only a month later), then this isn't a bad way to be remembered. You can hear Dolphy's voice at the end, extracted from an interview in the programme, saying: "When you hear music, after it's over, it's gone in the air. You can never capture it again." An odd inclusion, perhaps, when you can hear records like this again and again, but then only a jazz musician is aware of quite how much stuff does go into the walls of jazz clubs and never re-emerges. **MK**

## Lou Donaldson                                                                     1926

**Sentimental Journey**  Donaldson (as); **Dr Lonnie Smith** (org); **Peter Bernstein** (g); **Fukushi Tainaka** (d); **Ray Mantilla** (perc). Columbia Ⓕ 478177-2 (55 minutes). Recorded 1994.

⑧ **❽**

When Donaldson erupted onto the New York scene, hailed inevitably as the 'new' Charlie Parker (with the 'old' one still playing ...) he appeared on Blue Note sessions in the heavyweight company of men such as Horace Silver, Thelonious Monk, Milt Jackson and Clifford Brown. Although he clearly acknowledged the blanket influence of Bird, his tone was fuller with a tinge of sweetness in place of the sour sound produced by some other Parker devotees. Over the years he has worked consistently, although his many records on Blue Note, Argo/Cadet, Timeless and Milestone have varied from uncompromising jazz to funk by way of the blues. This is his first album for a major label and Columbia must be given credit for allowing Lou to come up with an uncompromising set using his regular group and orthodox material. On the title track (the old Les Brown signature tune) he has a very attractive broad sound, while on *Messin' Around With C.P.* he takes off like a bebop rocket (the C.P. of the title is Charlie Parker). *Midnight Creeper* uses an attractive broken rhythm similar to that of Lee Morgan's *Sidewinder* and Bird's *My Little Suede Shoes* showcases his fine guitarist Peter Bernstein. Lonnie Smith (not to be confused with keyboard player Lonnie Liston Smith) has been with Donaldson for years and his Hammond work is exactly in context. An additional star for musical quality may be added by those with fond memories of albums featuring sax and B3. **AM**

## Dorothy Donegan                                                                   1924

**Live at the 1991 Floating Jazz Festival**  Donegan (v); **Dizzy Gillespie** (t); **Jon Burr** (b); **Ray Mosca** (d). Chiaroscuro Ⓕ CRD318 (73 minutes). Recorded 1991.

⑥ **❻**

Initially a church organist, Donegan graduated to the night club circuit. She appeared in the *Sensations of 1945* film and worked in Broadway plays. She was an attraction at the Embers in the forties as her style developed from its early boogie influences, felt the impact of bebop and embraced the Art Tatum message. Summarily dismissed by the Jepsen discography as a fringe player, she has consistently made her presence felt in the jazz world. It is true that some of her appeal is based on her extravagant actions on stage but her antics cannot conceal her musical talent. This CD offers the full range of her style, with her singing mercifully restricted to one title. Her classical aspirations are humorously paraded in a *Warsaw Concerto* that leads her into *Secret Love*, *Just In Love* and finally *Lover*. Her ability as an orthodox stride pianist is captured on *Things Ain't What They Used to Be* and the presence of Tatum is felt throughout, most especially on *Tea for Two* and *Lover*, where her clean articulation and strong left hand give her access to the master's powerful swing. Gillespie guests on *Sweet Lorraine*, and a reminder of her roots is provided by *Bumble Bee Boogie*. She is not a jazz major but she has created her own specialist niche in the jazz world. **BMcR**

## Pierre Dørge                                                                      1946

**Even the Moon is Dancing**  Dørge (g, balafon, v); **Harry Beckett** (t, flh); **Kenneth Agerholm**, **Niels Neergaard** (tb, african hn); **Soren Eriksen**, **Doudou Gouirand** (ss, as); **Jesper Zeuthen** (as); **John Tchicai** (ts, v); **Morten Carlsen** (ts, ney, taragot, bs, cl, zurna); **Irene Becker** (p, syn); **Bent Clausen** (vb, perc); **Hugo Rasmussen** (b); **Johnny Dyani** (b, p, v); **Marilyn Mazur** (d, perc, kalimba); **Ahmadu Jarr** (f, perc). SteepleChase Ⓕ 31208 (69 minutes). Recorded 1985.

⑨ **❽**

The eighties were an explosive period for mid-sized ensembles led by composers rethinking the jazz tradition. Many of the most adventurous outfits sprang up in Europe, and the New Jungle Orchestra from Denmark created their own niche by highlighting relevant aspects of world music. Leader Pierre Dørge had studied African and Asian musics first-hand in Gambia and Nepal; his guitar serves a similar role to that in Nigerian juju music, as commentator and, often, as conductor. The New Jungle Orchestra's unique sound is partially due to its instrumentation (which includes African horns, balafon – a wooden/gourd xylophone – and thumb piano, Turkish oboe and flute and the Hungarian clarinet-like taragato), and to key musicians such as 'talking bassist' Johnny Dyani, tenor saxist John Tchicai and trumpeter Harry Beckett, all of whom are fluent in a variety of folk styles. But primarily the NJO is a groove band; Dørge's arrangements feature loose textures, vibrant solos over pervasive percussive vamps, and infectious, buoyant rhythms – such as the 14-beat melody on *Mirjam's Dadadance* or the intertwining African and Caribbean motifs on *Even the*

*Moon is Dancing.* The choice of *The Mooche* as the opening track on this, their début album, was a symbolic one, not only paying homage to Dørge's predecessor in exotica, Duke Ellington, but reminding us of jazz's roots in the extended instrumental timbres and ensemble polyphony of non-American, non-European musics. **AL**

# Kenny Dorham

1924-72

**New review**

**Round About Midnight at the Cafe Bohemia** Dorham (t); J.R. Monterose (ts); Kenny Burrell (elg); Bobby Timmins (p); Sam Jones (b); Arthur Edgehill (d). Blue Note Ⓜ CDP8 335762-8 (two discs: 123 minutes). Recorded 1956.

⑩ ❽

A brilliant and expressive trumpeter, Dorham never received the public recognition he deserved. He was, however, held in high esteem by his fellow musicians and played on equal terms alongside the greatest of his contemporaries, including Charlie Parker. Chronologically, this set comes between his tenure as a founder-member of the Jazz Messengers and his joining the Max Roach Quintet, following the death of Clifford Brown. The band is his regular group of the time, the Jazz Prophets, with Kenny Burrell added. The Café Bohemia was a jazz club in Greenwich Village. No better extended example of Dorham's playing exists, especially since this CD reissue contains a great deal more material than the original vinyl edition. His tone is light, dry and almost devoid of vibrato, perfectly suited to his long, agile phrases. There is a purposeful briskness about his whole approach which commands attention the way a good story-teller does. His solo on the minor-key *Mexico City* (credited as an original but perilously close to Bud Powell's *Tempus Fugit*) is a little masterpiece, as good as anything that Miles Davis was doing at the time. J.R. Monterose, whose breathless style is slightly reminiscent of Jimmy Heath, acts as an excellent partner, while Burrell plays with his customary suavity. Among the rhythm section mention must be made of Arthur Edgehill, a superb and infinitely tasteful drummer whose name is almost totally unknown to the jazz public. It seems incredible today that it was once possible to drop into a small club and hear music of this quality for the price of a drink and a modest cover-charge. **DG**

# Jimmy Dorsey

1904-57

**Contrasts** Dorsey (cl, as); with the following collective personnel: George Thow, Toots Camarata, Joe Meyer, Shorty Sherock, W.C. Clark, Ralph Munzillo, Nate Kazebier, Johnny Napton, Shorty Solomson, Jimmy Campbell, Paul McCoy, Bill Oblak, Ray Linn, Bob Alexy, Phil Napoleon, Marky Markowitz (t); Bobby Byrne, Don Mattinson, Joe Yukle, Bruce Squires, Sonny Lee, Jerry Rosa, Nat Lobovsky, Al Jordan, Phil Washburn, Andy Russo, Billy Pritchard, Nick DiMaio (tb); Dave Matthews, Rud Livingstone, Skeets Herfurt, Jack Stacy, Leonard Whitney, Charlie Frazier, Non Bernardi, Milt Yaner, Herbie Haymer, Sam Rubinwich, Frank Langone, Don Hammond, Babe Russin, Chuck Gentry, Bill Covey, Bob Lawson (reeds); Bobby Van Eps, Freddy Slack, Joe Lippman, Johnny Guarnieri, Dave Mann (p); Roc Hillman, Guy Smith, Allen Reuss, Tommy Kay (g); Slim Taft, Jack Ryan, Bill Miller (b); Ray McKinley, Buddy Schutz (d); June Richmond, Helen O'Connell, Bob Eberly (v). MCA/Decca Ⓜ GRP16262 (63 minutes). Recorded 1936-43.

⑧ ❽

Jimmy was the less rumbustious of the battling Dorseys and the bands he led never seemed to attract the same attention as Tommy's. But in many ways his bands were more adventurous; he commissioned arrangements from Dizzy Gillespie and in the forties had jazzmen such as Serge Chaloff, Stan Getz, Al Haig, Johnny Mandel and Herb Ellis on the payroll. This CD dates from a slightly earlier period and while the music is clearly intended for the dancing public there is much to recommend. Jimmy broke new ground by bringing in a coloured singer (June Richmond, prior to her term of service with Andy Kirk's band), heard here on a couple of tracks, including her success, *Darktown Strutters' Ball.* But Dorsey suffered from his record company's desire to produce cover versions of Benny Goodman hits during the late thirties. The policy seems to have changed at the end of 1940 and this issue makes it clear that from the recording of *Dolomite* onwards, Jimmy seemed determined to go his own way. The brass hits hard and with fine soloists such as tenor saxist Herbie Haymer and trumpeter Nate Kazebier Dorsey's output improves. In fact the closing *King Porter Stomp,* with its flaring trumpet solo from Ray Linn and big-toned tenor from Babe Russin, would do credit to any swing band of the period. **AM**

# Tommy Dorsey

1905-56

**And His Clambake Seven: The Music Goes Round and Round** Dorsey (tb); with a collective personnel of: Sterling Bose, Max Kaminsky, Pee Wee Irwin, Yank Lawson, Jimmy Blake, Charlie Shavers, Ziggy Elman (t); Joe Dixon, Johnny Mince, Buddy DeFranco (cl); Sid Block, Bud Freeman, Skeets Hurfurt, Babe Russin, Boomie Richman (ts); Dick Jones, Howard

**Smith, John Potoker, Teddy Wilson** (p); **Bill Schaeffer, Carmen Mastren, Sam Herman** (g); **Gene Traxler, Sid Block, Billy Bauer** (b); **Dave Tough, Maurice Purtill, Graham Stevenson, Cliff Leeman, Alvin Stoller** (d); **Edythe Wright, Hughie Prince, Hanna Williams** (v). RCA Bluebird Ⓜ ND83140 (64 minutes). Recorded 1935-47.

⑦ ❻

One thing Dorsey's bands always had was an identity, and this is as true of his small groups as of the big bands. The Clambake Seven was formed in 1935 to allow Dorsey an outlet for his high spirits, and it would be a very basic mistake indeed to assume that in forming this band Dorsey was attempting the same sort of innovation and serious music-making Goodman managed with his trios and quartets of the same period. This band was a good-time outfit full of excellent jazz musicians playing in a Dixie style which was already slightly behind the times, but not that far to be perceived as a bad joke. It was a good joke in which both the band and the listener can join. The Clambake Seven was strong on vocals and on clearly stated melodies where the trombone combined fruitily with the trumpet and tenor, and the clarinet wove driving, rhythmic embellishments. Dorsey may have had a retro approach to making music and little inclination to take his own improvisation too seriously, but his ability to carry a melody rivalled Teagarden's and Armstrong's, and his fabled discipline made for superbly tailored band performances.

The vocalist on most of these tracks, Edythe Wright, was not the most technically assured of the period, but her full voice has its own charm, and she at least manages to phrase in line with the rest of the band. She left Dorsey in late 1939. Hanna Williams, present on the last two tracks from 1947, is a thorough professional and sings deliciously on *But I Do Mind If Ya Don't*, which also has a tasty eight bars from Wilson. The four late-forties tracks chosen here show a different style of small-group music, quite similar to that being played at the time by Lips Page, Jonah Jones and their ilk, but it is the earlier material which most will regard as typical. **KS**

---

**The All-Time Hit Parade Rehearsals** **Dorsey, Walter Benson, Nelson Riddle, Tex Satterwhite** (tb); **Sal La Perche, Mickey Mangano, Dale Pearce, George Seaburg** (t); **Buddy De Franco** (cl, as); **Gail Curtis, Mickey Sabol** (ts); **Bruce Branson** (bs); **Dodo Marmarosa** (p); **Bob Bain** (g); **Sid Block** (b); **Joe Park** (tba); **Buddy Rich** (d); **Bobby Allen, Bonny Lou Williams, The Sentimentalists, Judy Garland, Frank Sinatra** (v). Hep Ⓜ HEPCD39 (68 minutes). Recorded 1944.

⑧ ❽

During World War II Tommy Dorsey led one of the most successful (and expensive) dance orchestras. In the summer of 1944 he was in Los Angeles for a series of engagements including the weekly NBC radio show "The Lucky Strike All-Time Hit Parade". This CD comprises 24 titles taken from previously unavailable dress rehearsals for eight of the shows, well recorded and remastered and featuring guest singers Judy Garland (on *I May Be Wrong*) and Frank Sinatra (on *I'll Walk Alone* and *If You Are But a Dream*) as well as Dorsey's regular vocalists. The CD is particularly valuable for it comes from a period when a recording ban was in force in the US; here are the earliest recordings by the band with Buddy Rich back on drums, after his discharge from the Marines. Heard on a number of tracks is the brilliant clarinet of Buddy De Franco, and Dorsey features his unique ballad trombone style on songs such as *Dancing in the Dark* and *Embraceable You*. There are some fine arrangements by Sy Oliver, Bill Finegan and Axel Stordahl and Bonny Lou Williams sings the seldom-heard verse to *I Can't Give You Anything But Love*. Dodo Marmarosa is heard on Dean Kincaide's arrangement of *Boogie Woogie*, introduced by Jose Iturbi. With the Bluebird Dorsey Archive currently in confusion on disc, this is a good summary of his band's strengths. **AM**

# Double Six of Paris

**Les Double Six** **Mimi Perrin** (v); on all tracks, with collective personnel of: **Monique Guerin, Louis Adelbert, Jean-Claude Briodin, Claude Germain, Eddy Louiss, Ward Swingle, Jean-Louis Conrozier, Roger Guerin, Christiane Legrand, Jacques Denjean** (v); various piano trio accompaniments, featuring: **Rene Urtreger, Georges Arvanitas** (p); **Art Simmons, Pierre Michelot** (b); **Daniel Humair** (d). Open/OMD Ⓕ CD1518 (68 minutes). Recorded 1959-62.

⑦ ❼

The Double Six was the brainchild of Mimi Perrin, an effervescent musical personality with great stage presence but, more crucially for the CD listener, a highly sophisticated arranger's ear. The group was formed in 1959 and first recorded that same year. The fruits of those sessions, and the follow-up disc featuring Quincy Jones compositions, are all contained on this generous CD reissue, overseen by Mimi Perrin herself.

The group, which was never more than six in number, used to double-up in the studio via double-tracking, thus allowing extremely rich voice arrangements: their style may have grown out of the King Pleasure/Eddie Jefferson/Lambert-Hendrick-Ross tradition of vocalizing previously instrumental jazz performances, but their music reached a degree of formal sophistication much in advance of any of their models. In a genre which was mostly given over to happy-go-lucky, fun-time entertainments, the diversity of moods, the ambition of the project and the sheer charm of the vocal blend were elements which remained virtually unique to this group. On this disc, a listen to *Naima* (ironically, a solo Perrin vocal) will illustrate the unusual emotional range of the group, while *Scrapple from the Apple* shows not only their extraordinary versatility and scrupulous accuracy, but also their ability to capture the real flavour of the original. OK – it's all in French, but non-French speakers can still enjoy the glories of the vocals, unaffected by literal meaning. **KS**

## Boots Douglas
1908

**Boots and His Buddies, 1935-37** Douglas (d, ldr); **Theodore Gilders, Percy Bush, Douglas Byers, Charles Anderson** (t); **Johnny Shields** (tb); **Alva Brooks, Wee Demry** (as); **Baker Millian, David Ellis** (ts); **A.J. Johnson** (p); **Jeff Vant** (g); **Walter McHenry** (b); **Celeste Allen, Israel Wicks,** anon. vocal trio (v). JSP Ⓕ CD327 (70 minutes). Recorded 1935-7.

④ ❻

The world of the territory bands during the twenties and thirties is shadowy. Many bands, like 'T' Holder's, did not record, and others are only spottily represented on record and in oral histories. There were two great bands from San Antonio, Texas. One was led by Don Albert from New Orleans, an urbane trumpeter who imported talent from his home town, cut some good discs, and survived as a working musician into the international festivals of the seventies. The other was led by Boots Douglas, and is more obscure. Apart from its regular recordings in the mid thirties, little else survives, none of its star players having gone on to fame elsewhere. The performances are propulsively driven by the leader's straight-ahead drumming, giving a sense of the sound of a working band. Some arrangements are stocks (thinly disguised with new names, like *San Antonio Tamales* for *Angry*) and some section playing, such as on *Jealous*, is ragged. Singer Celeste Allen (a man) lacks Jimmy Rushing's strength, but there is an earthy, honest quality about the band that makes it compulsive listening. As you hear the musicians shouting encouragement to trumpeter Charles Anderson, or as they storm through *Riffs* or *The Vamp*, your mind's eye conjures up the long-dead dancers and a little light is shed on a dark corner of jazz history. **AS**

## Dave Douglas

**New review**
**Five** Douglas (t); **Mark Feldman** (vn); **Erick Friedlander** (vc); **Drew Gress** (b); **Michael Sarin** (d). Soul Note Ⓕ 121276-2 (61 minutes). Recorded 1995

⑧ ❽

Douglas is a trumpeter who has not allowed academics to overpower either his own personality or his empirical motivations. A Berklee old boy, he graduated from N.Y.U.'s Gallatin Division in 1986. In the following year he toured with Horace Silver, came to Britain with Vincent Herring and has since spread his talents over a wide range of the musical landscape. His easy lyricism was an ideal photo-fit for Don Byron's klezmer group, his comfort with microtones and his rhythmic flexibility made him a natural for the music of Tim Berne and his triumph with John Zorn's **Masada** series added the finishing touch. **Five** is an ambitious performance by his 'string' splinter group which has been together since 1992. All save two of the compositions are by him, but it is the arrangements (and the way in which they acknowledge his colleague's strengths and motivations) that matter most. Dedicatees are nominated and saluted. *Mirrors* is for the quizzical side of Steve Lacy, *Going Going* moves into Wayne Shorter's freer zones, while Gress's *arco* bass points *Seven* toward Mark Dresser. Roland Kirk's *Inflated Tear* demands Douglas's most emotional commitment and *Mogador* looks at Zorn's Colemanesque persona. Albums such as **In Our Lifetime** (New World 80471-2) perhaps present Douglas in a more orthodox jazz environment but this is a challenging musical exercise which showcases his meticulously crafted trumpet work, his expansive improvisational skills and the individuality of his writing and arranging talents. **BMcR**

## Mark Dresser
1952

**New review**
**Force Green** Dresser (b); **Dave Douglas** (t); **Denman Maroney** (p); **Phil Haynes** (d); **Theo Bleckmann** (v). Soul Note Ⓕ 121273-2 (59 minutes). Recorded 1994.

④ ❽

Classically trained, a regular colleague of the avant-garde and those who inhabit the land between free jazz, improvised music and experimental composition, Dresser's affiliations with Anthony Braxton and David Murray make him a talent to be taken seriously. His playing involves numerous techniques of treating the bass as a percussion instrument, or using both sides of the bow, but mastery of these and other effects sometimes dominates over content. Unfortunately **Force Green** bears this out in great detail, some genuinely inspired moments such as *For Miles* giving way to a 23-minute *Castles for Carter* that is a model of vapid noodling for much of its tedious length. The most compelling interplay is between Dave Douglas and Dresser. Other moments, many of them involving the falsetto voice of Bleckmann and prepared piano noises of Maroney, suggest that an alternative title for the album could be "The Emperor's New Clothes". **AS**

# Kenny Drew

**This is New**  Drew (p); **Donald Byrd** (t); **Hank Mobley** (ts); **Wilbur Ware** (b); **G.T. Hogan** (d).
  Riverside Ⓜ OJCCD483-2 (43 minutes). Recorded 1957.

Kenny Drew's classical training was apparent in his very obvious understanding of the keyboard and his careful approach to slow tunes. He worked with several important leaders, including Lester Young, Charlie Parker, Coleman Hawkins and Buddy De Franco. He was with Art Blakey when this session took place and it may have been Riverside's idea to create in the studio a Jazz Messengers-type of group. The music is well played but lacks the explosive excitement which a few of Blakey's gigantic press-rolls behind the soloists might have created. Drew himself is very much in control of the keyboard, even at the fastest of tempos; his playing has an easy fluidity and continuity not always found in the playing of bebop pianists. Byrd has several praiseworthy solos and the music actually sounds better now than it did to me when it was first released; at that time it was judged against a monthly barrage of new hard-bop issues.  **AM**

# Kenny Drew Jr

**Portraits of Charles Mingus and Thelonious Monk**  Drew (p); **Lynn Seaton** (b); **Marvin
  'Smitty' Smith** (d). Claves Jazz Ⓕ CD50-1194 (61 minutes). Recorded 1994.

Drew is the son of the late Kenny Drew (see above), an excellent and wholly reliable pianist who worked with men such as Lester Young and Buddy De Franco. Drew Jr is classically trained and came to jazz via rhythm and blues, pop music and his father's records. Actually he does not sound like Kenny Sr and is, in some ways, a more impressive player. This is certainly his best album, beautifully recorded with two excellent rhythm men in support on eight of the ten tunes, five each by Monk and Mingus. *Light Blue* and *Weird Nightmare* are unaccompanied solos; the notes incorrectly state that *Trinkle Tinkle* is also a solo. The formal training comes out in Kenny's superb digital control and acute gradation of touch. Yet he also appreciates the humour which lurks just beneath the surface of Monk and Mingus's work and is not above bringing in a bit of two-handed stride-style playing. But it is the care which has gone into both the selection and the interpretation of the music which is impressive. Not many would tackle Monk's *Skippy* or dig out comparative Mingus rarities such as *Eclipse*, *Farewell, Farewell* or *Weird Nightmare*, the latter played as a thoughtful ballad. Drew has also worked with the exciting Mingus Big Band on and off record which helps to add authenticity to his interpretations of Charles's music. Recommended to all interested in contemporary jazz piano.  **AM**

# Paquito D'Rivera

**Havana Café**  D'Rivera, (cl, as, ss); **Fareed Haque**, **Ed Cherry** (g); **Danilo Perez** (p); **David Finck**
  (b); **Jorge Rossy** (d); **Sammy Figueroa** (p). Chesky Ⓕ JD60 (58 minutes). Recorded 1991.

Paquito D'Rivera is a fiery saxophonist-clarinettist whose uniquely exciting style reflects the combined influences of bebop, the music of Latin and South America, and the brio of his hometown of Havana. The precocious son of one of Cuba's finest reed players, the conservatory-trained D'Rivera, while working in theatre and radio orchestras as a teenager, 'studied' jazz by listening to Willis Conover's "Jazz Hour" on Voice of America. He also played in Orquesta Cubana de Musica Moderna out of which Irakere, Cuba's foremost modern jazz band, was formed. In 1980 D'Rivera defected to the US to pursue his muse free from Castro's constraints.

On this consistently satisfying 1991 date D'Rivera is surrounded by some of New York's best young Latin players, and in the tradition of Art Blakey and his often youthful Jazz Messengers, the open exchange of ideas between two generations of inspired players works wonders. Guitarist Fareed Haque's *The Return*, a gear-shifting power glide for Paquito's soaring soprano, and pianist Danilo Perez's percolating *Havana Café*, a showcase for the leader's caffeinated alto, are among several charts contributed by D'Rivera's young colleagues. Also striking are the intimate clarinet features, Claudio Roditi's charming *Bossa do Brooklyn*, and Paquito's own solo piece, *Contradanza*.  **CB**

# Billy Drummond

New review
**The Gift**  Drummond (d); **Seamus Blake** (ss, ts); **Renee Rosnes** (p); **Peter Washington** (b). Criss
  Cross Ⓕ 1083 (61 minutes). Recorded 1993.

Drummond is a young veteran from an area of Virginia that has nurtured several recent arrivals on the jazz scene, including James Genus, Sam Newsome and Steve Wilson. The band Out of the Blue gave Drummond and his soon-to-be-wife Renee Rosnes important early exposure and the pair went on to work together in the quintets of Buster Williams and J. J. Johnson as well as in the co-operative quartet Native Colors. Drummond has also been heard with Steve Kuhn's trio and Sonny Rollins's band. This invaluable experience is reflected in his second album, a warm-up of sorts for Native Colors that reflects Drummond's spirit, taste and flexibility. As with his other recordings, the programme displays great taste and historic knowledge, with worthy new music from Rosnes, Donald Brown, Jonny King and Walt Weiskopf as well as cover versions of lesser-known tunes by Harold Land, Charles Lloyd, Clifford Jordan and Bob Dorough. Saxophonist Blake (like Rosnes a Vancouver native) displays admirable momentum and slices his phrases in the Joe Henderson manner without sounding overtly derivative, while Rosnes adds her usual fresh ideas as both soloist and composer and bassist Washington turns in another estimable performance. Nice pacing from track to track, and the inclusion of such gems as Jordan's *Dear Old Chicago* and Dorough's *Devil May Care* make this a fine effort from a drummer whose reputation continues on its upward spiral.     **BB**

# Ray Drummond

**New review**
**Vignette** Drummond (b); **Gary Bartz** (as, ss); **Chris Potter** (ts); **Renee Rosnes** (p); **Billy Hart** (d); add
**John Richmond**, **Joe Lovano** (ts) on one track. Arabesque Ⓕ AJ0122 (62 minutes). Recorded 1995.
⑧ ❾

Drummond's three albums for Arabesque (this is the third) all display different aspects of his talents. Here the playing has a free quality, but never free in the sense of the lunatic fringe of the avant-garde. There are, for example, two entirely different versions of his *Ballade Poétique*, both played by a trio of Drummond, Rosnes and Hart. "No chords, no bar lines, just phrases strung together" sounds like a recipe for musical anarchy but what emerges has the unexpected cohesion of, say, Tristano's *Intuitions*. *Dance to the Lady* uses *accelerando* and *rallentando* passages in the solo choruses which could easily have been a disaster but all five musicians are completely in accord and the result is very attractive. Two additional horns are added for the Lennon/McCartney tune *Eleanor Rigby*, a 6/8 recasting of the melody which, as Fred Bouchard points out in his notes, "sounds like 'Trane meets *We Free Kings*'". In fact the opening chorus, with the saxes playing the song at slow tempo over Drummond's *arco* pedal point, all but obscures the well-known tune. This is probably Ray's best album yet as leader and he must be given further praise for choosing such excellent soloists. Rosnes in particular plays the leader's music with great sensitivity.     **AM**

# George Duke                                                                                              1946

**Brazilian Love Affair** Duke (kbds, syn, v); **Byron Miller**, **Jamil Joanes** (elb); **Ricky Lawson** (d);
**Roberto Silva** (d, perc); **Airto**, **Chico Batera**, **Sheila Escovedo** (perc); **Roland Bautista** (elg); **Toninho
Horta** (g, elg); **Milton Nascimento** (g, v); **Jerry Hey** (t, flh); **William Reichenbach**, **Raul De Souza** (tb);
**Larry Williams** (ts, as, f); **Flora Purim**, **Josie James**, **Lynn Davis**, **Zéluiz**, **Flavio Faria**, **Lucia Turnbull**,
**Lucinha Lins**, **Simone** (v). Columbia Legacy Ⓜ 471283-2 (49 minutes). Recorded 1979/80.
⑧ ❽

George Duke had an early and close involvement with jazz, playing in the late sixties and early seventies with Don Ellis, Jean-Luc Ponty, Frank Zappa and Cannonball Adderley, but he fell sharply from grace in the eyes of critics, if not the general public, when he joined the disco gravy train in the mid seventies. Thus this frequently creative session came as a surprise and went a good way to restoring his stock with the jazz crowd.

For one thing it features a generous allowance of Duke's well-structured, highly musical solo work on Fender Rhodes (especially effective on *Sugar Loaf Mountain*) and Moog synth, and some resonant, melodic trombone from Raul De Souza. In addition, with the exception of a couple of dirges by Milton Nascimento, the arrangements are crisp, intelligent and colourful, and generally infused with the rhythmic verve associated with Brazilian music. Furthermore, although Brazil provided the stimulus for the record, this is no mere exercise in cultural colonialism: perhaps as a result of his disco experience, Duke was able to conceive a spirited and individual fusion of funk and Brazilian impulses. The result is hardly profound, but it can be very exciting. The set appears in digitally remastered form as part of Columbia's Contemporary Masters series.     **MG**

# Hans Dulfer

**New review**
**Express Delayed** Dulfer (ts); **Herbert Noord** (org); **Joop Scholten** (g); **Johnny Engels** (d). Limetree
Ⓕ MCD0041 (50 minutes). Recorded 1978.
⑥ ❼

In the late sixties Dulfer and Noord formed a group based on the tenor-and-organ concept. Eventually they went their different ways but came back together in 1977 at the instigation of Joop Scholten and this CD dates from that period. The music has never previously appeared on record and

I suspect that insufficient was recorded at the time; of the seven tracks on the CD *A Home is Not a House* and *The Troubleshooter* each appear in two takes. Despite these shortcomings the group plays in the idiom with remarkable authority, sounding as if this is a completely natural way for them to express themselves. Noord uses the Hammond B3 as if to the manner born and Dulfer cruises through the high harmonics of the tenor with great skill and control (he doesn't play on one tune, incidentally). Gene Ammons is credited with one of the numbers and drummer Engels, who scales his volume down to the right level, was a first choice for both Chet Baker and Ben Webster.          **AM**

# Paul Dunmall                                                                     1953

**New review**

**Quartet and Sextet/Babu Trio** Dunmall (ss, c-ms, ts, bs); **Jon Corbett** (c); **Simon Picard** (ts);
   **John Adams** (g); **Paul Rogers** (b); **Tony Levin** (d). Slam Ⓕ SLAMCD207 (two discs: 110 minutes).
   Recorded 1993.

⑧ ⑧

A volatile improviser, Dunmall's chief inspiration was John Coltrane: he has described listening to **A Love Supreme** as "like a religious experience". After playing rock initially, he went to America in 1973, where he worked with Alice Coltrane and Johnny 'Guitar' Watson. Returning to England, he went on to co-found Spirit Level in 1979 and in the eighties played with Tenor Tonic, the London Jazz Musicians Orchestra, Danny Thompson's Whatever and Musician, as well as leading his own quartet. **Soliloquy**, a versatile solo disc, was recorded in 1986 and has been followed by several impressive duo CDs: **If DuBois Only Knew** with Elton Dean, **Spiritual Empathy** with Tony Levin and the rootsy celebration, **Folks**, with Paul Rogers. Rogers and Levin partner Dunmall throughout this double-CD, which has one disc by their Babu Trio and one that comprises five short(ish) quartet tracks with Picard plus a 25-minute sextet improvisation. The latter is a typically well-executed free-form soundscape. The quartet tracks are brief bursts of intensity, the Babu disc a chance for more expansive playing – it's here the trio best display their fluent exchange of ideas and Dunmall shows his barn-storming capabilities on all four horns.          **GL**

# Cornell Dupree

**New review**

**Bop 'n' Blues** Dupree (g); **Terrell Stafford** (t); **Bobby Watson** (as); **Ronnie Cuber** (bs); **Leon Pendarvis** (p, org); **Chuck Rainey** (b); **Ricky Sebastian** (d); **Sammy Figueroa** (perc). Kokopelli
   Ⓕ KOKO1302 (50 minutes). Recorded 1994-5.

⑦ ⑦

Dupree hails from Fort Worth and has a solid background in the blues world of Southern Texas. His musical outlook has always been more expansive, however, and he has proved to be as much at home with the sparky drive of the Gadd Gang as he is with a down-home blues unit. In more recent times he has been prominent on the touring circuit, in the nineties working with the cosmopolitan mix of Herbie Mann and Cissy Houston. The two most consistent features of his work are that he has always been a superbly supple and swinging guitarist and that he is an unfailing scene stealer on other people's dates. This CD exposes him to the reverse possibility, but although it is set in a potentially alien area and features bop saxophonists Watson and Cuber, it finds Dupree equal to the challenge. The idea behind it was to see how the subtleties of bebop could be stacked up alongside the raw edge of a blues guitarist. The outcome is perhaps predictably successful. His unforced blues feel makes him a natural for *Bags' Groove* and *Walkin'*, he floats with the Latin tide of *Manteca* and he knowledgeably fuses *Hucklebuck* and *Now's the Time*. *Little Suede Shoes* is some-what glib, but if one single item portrays his emotional involvement with the project it is *'Round Midnight*.          **BMcR**

# Dutch Swing College Band

**New review**

**Swinging Studio Sessions** Peter Schilperoort (cl, bs, ss); **Oscar Klein, Bert De Kort** (c); **Ray Kaart** (t); **Dick Kaart** (tb, bhn); **Jan Morks, Bob Kaper** (cl); **Arie Ligthart** (bj, g); **Bob Van Oven, Chris Smildiger** (b); **Martin Beenen, Jan Morks, Louis De Lussanet, Huub Janssen** (d). Philips Ⓜ
   824 256-2 (62 minutes). Recorded 1959-69.

⑥ ⑦

Formed in 1945 by Schilperoort and pianist Fred Vink, the DSCB was born in the Dutch Swing College, a school that had been founded the previous year. The music they played has always been open-minded Dixieland with mainstream affiliations and they recorded with the likes of Sidney Bechet and Joe Venuti. Most of this CD was recorded when the band was taking a more traditional stance, displaying a good control of dynamics and faithfully reproducing the New Orleans ensemble pattern. Klein provided a good lead and, although Kaart was a limited soloist, he was the earth father of the tailgate role. The clarinet parts were mainly shared by Morks and Schilperoort with the latter sometimes introducing his special brand of rustic baritone. Playing with the likes of Jimmy

Witherspoon, Billy Butterfield, Hot Lips Page and Albert Nicholas did broaden their outlook: much later, items such as *Green Dolphin Street* crept into the repertoire. Nevertheless, the DSCB did not embrace more modern jazz with quite the same conviction and, in retrospect, will probably earn more plaudits for their fine collective approach to earlier forms. **BMcR**

## John Eardley 1928-91

**From Hollywood to New York** Eardley (t); J.R. Monterose (ts); Pete Jolly, George Syran (p); Red Mitchell, Teddy Kotick (b); Larry Bunker, Nick Stabulas (d). NewJazz/Prestige Ⓜ OJCCD1746-2 (41 minutes). Recorded 1954/5.

⑧ ❽

Having joined Gerry Mulligan's quartet in 1954, Eardley is often compared with his predecessor Chet Baker, but Eardley had his own distinctive crackling attack and fatter, sassier tone, and he wasn't nearly so enamoured of slow ballads. He's closer to Clifford Brown than to the other C.B. Despite the presence of Mulligan stalwarts Mitchell and Bunker on the 1954 Hollywood session, the music throughout is closer to emerging East Coast hard bop than West Coast cool.

Most of the tunes from these two sessions move at medium-to-fast tempos – an exception being Tadd Dameron's lovely *If You Could See Me Now*. *Demanton* is Eardley's romp on *Sweet Georgia Brown*'s chords; on *Hey There*, he carefully balances rests and jaunty lines, deftly structuring his solo without aiming toward an explosive climax. Like the rest of the New York session, the tune features the little-recorded, throaty tenorist J.R. Monterose, whose presence is a plus.

In recent years Eardley has lived in Germany and Belgium, and been associated with the WDR Big Band in Cologne. Of late he has testified to the subtle influence on his playing of Bix Beiderbecke (who sat beside Jon's father in Paul Whiteman's trumpet section), but that influence is undetectable here. Fantasy have recently reissued another Eardley date from this period, **John Eardley Seven**. **KW**

## Charles Earland 1941

**Unforgettable** Earland (org); Kenny Rampton (t); Clifford Adams (tb); Eric Anderson (ss, ts); Houston Person (ts); Oliver Nevels (g); Gregory Williams, Buddy Williams (d); Laurence Killian (perc). Muse Ⓕ MCD5455 (46 minutes). Recorded 1991.

⑦ ❽

Earland has been working the same musical area for most of his career, hitting the chitlin circuit in the sixties and having commercial success at the end of that decade. This latest offering from him does not break with tradition, sticking with loping, easy feels and blues-drenched phrases. Producer Houston Person appears on tenor on three numbers; otherwise, the excellent saxophonist with Earland's working band, Eric Alexander, dominates solo space along with the organist.

This album is a cut above the average, if only for the reason that it was recorded a couple of months after Earland had suffered a near-fatal heart attack and been nursed back to health by his wife, Sheila, the album's dedicatee. The music is lovingly coaxed along by the organist throughout; there is also a happy absence of crass, fabricated climaxes as well as long, aimless jams where everyone gets a solo because there is no other way to fill the album up. There is one 12-minute piece, Carlos Santana's *Europa*, but this is at a bright, happy tempo and none of the solos sound too long. A fine, tasteful organ-and-sax disc, not generous on playing time, but it's all meat and no potatoes. **KS**

## Madeline Eastman

New review

**Art Attack** Eastman (v); Kenny Barron, Marcos Silver, Pablo Perez (p); Jeff Buenz (g); Peter Barhsay, David Belove (b); Tony Williams (d); Michael Spiro (perc); Turtle Island String Quartet. Mad Kat Ⓕ MKCD10005 (54 minutes). Recorded 1994.

⑤ ❽

Eastman is based in the Bay Area on the West Coast and her three records to date (all for Mad Kat) show her to be an adventurous and stylish interpreter within the modern jazz tradition. She can improvise tidily, scat competently and paraphrase astutely. Her vocal sound is not particularly attractive, being rather hard-edged and throwaway, and her intonation is sometimes vague, hinting perhaps at a lack of formal training, although this is just guessing on my part. Yet she hires top-rate players here (most tracks have fine trio support, with Barron and Williams outstanding) and is comfortable with them at all times. She works very hard for the results and ventures far beyond the repertoire associated with the first two tracks, *The Thrill is Gone* and *Gypsy in my Soul*. Monk's *Evidence* is rarely included in vocalists' repertoires, and the same can be said for Wayne Shorter's *Nefertiti*. The Latinesque pieces with the alternative line-ups tend to be bland, their Latin flavour being diluted by the muzak-inspired course the group adopt, although the Turtle Islanders improve things a little on the aforementioned Monk piece. The quartet alone back Eastman on *Nefertiti*, and everyone benefits from it, not least the listener. **KS**

# Billy Eckstine

**Imagination**   Eckstine (v); with a big band including: **Pete Candoli**, **Don Fagerquist** (t); **Bud Shank** (f, as); **Gerry Wiggins** (p); **Red Callender** (b); **Larry Bunker** (d); **Pete Rugolo** (ldr, arr); remainder unidentified. EmArcy Ⓜ 848 162-2 (40 minutes). Recorded 1958.

⑦ ❽

Back in the mid forties Eckstine led the first big bebop band, employing such Young Turks as Charlie Parker, Fats Navarro, Dexter Gordon and Art Blakey. Although he joined the 'establishment' later to become one of the most popular (and most imitated) baritones of his day, he never lost touch with his jazz background. While this album consists of a dozen good standards, his approach is clearly that of a man who knows how to phrase correctly and, moreover, how to keep that powerful vibrato under control. Occasionally arranger Rugolo allows Billy to take off with just a small group behind him, as on *What a Little Moonlight Can Do* for example, but much of the time it is Eckstine pitching his wares at the wider audience. *Gigi*, from a different session, has been added to the 11 tracks which comprised the original LP, but EmArcy have failed to discover any more personnel details. There is a good trombonist to be heard and a guitarist who might well be the late Howard Roberts. Kiyoshi Tokiwa has remastered the original tapes with skill.   **AM**

**No Cover, No Minimum**   Eckstine (v, t); with big band including: **Charlie Walp** (t); **Bucky Manieri** (tb); **Charlie McLean**, **Buddy Balboa** (saxes); **Buddy Grievey** (d); **Bobby Tucker** (p, arr). Blue Note Ⓜ B21S 98583 (65 minutes). Recorded 1960.

✔   ⑩ ❽

This was Eckstine's first and best live album, and arguably his greatest album ever. He is forever associated with the revolutionary big band he put together in the mid forties after leaving Earl Hines, but in fact the support he gets here is much more sympathetic and far less distracting. Here, we have Eckstine in prime voice in front of a (thankfully inaudible) Las Vegas audience, cossetted in perfect little-big-band arrangements penned by long-term associate Bobby Tucker. His repertoire is a judicious mix of pieces long identified with him and newly covered songs, some of them at that stage still fresh from Broadway (*I've Grown Accustomed to Her Face*, for instance). All through, that oft-imitated and never-matched voice, deep and sensual in a way Nat King Cole never attempted to be, handles every challenge effortlessly. This is a stunning display of sustained vocalizing, the intimacy of the Tucker arrangements only throwing it into further relief. Eckstine is often omitted when it comes to lists of Great Jazz Singers. He should not be, and this album is living proof of it.

   This entirely remixed CD reissue (originally available on Roulette, now only on the US Blue Note issue) is an enormous improvement over the old vinyl set, both in terms of recording balance and sound quality and in terms of playing time. We have no less than 13 extra tracks here. Now that's value for money. A further Roulette classic has recently reappeared, the studio date **Basie/Eckstine Inc**. Equally cleaned-up for CD; it makes a fine companion to this release.   **KS**

# Harry Edison

**Jawbreakers**   Edison (t); **Eddie 'Lockjaw' Davis** (ts); **Hugh Lawson** (p); Ike Isaac (b); **Clarence Johnston** (d). Riverside Ⓜ OJCCD487-2 (42 minutes). Recorded 1962.

⑧ ❻

Over the years the music created by these two ex-Basie stars tended to be predictable but nevertheless enjoyable. This is a well-transferred reissue of their first album together, and it retains the freshness of that early meeting. This was Edison's regular quintet, with Davis taking tenor saxist Jimmy Forrest's place for the day; the rhythm section performs with the assurance of a regular trio. There can have been few major jazz soloists with more immediately recognizable sounds than Edison and Davis, each in his own way making telling use of a fairly limited vocabulary. Harry's tightly muted opening statement on his blues *Moolah* is a case in point, for this is in effect a compendium of his favourite phrases, yet he creates a sense of tension which is riveting for the listener. The eight tunes hold a few surprises, such as the way the two produce the theme statement on Miles Davis's tune *Four*. All in all, a fine example of mainstream jazz played by experts of the genre.   **AM**

# Teddy Edwards

**Together Again!**   Edwards (ts); **Howard McGhee** (t); **Phineas Newborn Jr** (p); **Ray Brown** (b); **Ed Thigpen** (d). Contemporary Ⓜ OJCCD424-2 (40 minutes). Recorded 1961.

⑦ ❽

An extremely well-equipped player, Edwards had to wait unfairly long to be recognized. He figured in the West Coast bebop scene of the mid to late forties, which is when he first worked with McGhee. The trumpeter went on to sudden fame, prestigious bookings and a long spell out of action through drug addiction; Edwards stayed in California, healthy and obscure. But by 1961 he was building a name, and when McGhee dropped into Los Angeles for an engagement, their reunion was unquestionably a meeting of equals. It proved a wonderfully relaxed affair, although something more than the amiable blow through well-worn standards that such meetings often turn into. Edwards is an excellent blues player, but he had already demonstrated that on **Teddy's Ready** (also available on CD). Here, apart from Charlie Parker's *Perhaps*, he chooses other structures, bustling through the boppish changes of *Up There* and bringing a dry, unsentimental sensitivity to *Misty*. McGhee plays dextrously throughout, usually muted, developing the ballad *You Stepped Out of a Dream* and his own *Sandy* with taste and imagination, qualities shared by the rhythm section. The album's undimmed vitality stems less from the players' individual achievements than from its air of fellowship and mutual appreciation.          **TR**

# Mark Egan                                                                          1951

**Beyond Words**  Egan (b); **Toninho Horta**, **Steve Khan** (g); **Bill Evans** (ss); **Clifford Carter** (syn); **Danny Gottlieb** (d); **Don Alias**, **Manolo Badrena**, **Gordon Gottlieb** (perc). Blue Moon Ⓕ R279171 (50 minutes). Recorded 1991.

⑥ ❾

Bassist Mark Egan is an important member of the first generation of jazz-oriented musicians who have devoted the majority of their efforts to the so-called fusion school. Indeed, Egan has been a central part of groups led by such popular and varied performers as guitarist Pat Metheny, saxophonist David Sanborn, and the Brazilians Airto Moreira and Flora Purim.

Here, as in the work of his previous units South Dade and Elements, Egan has evolved an attractive electronic palette through the use of such custom-instruments as the Pedulla double-neck 4 and 8 string bass guitar. Like Metheny, he is a lyrical player whose pieces unfold with kaleidoscopic swirls of genuine improvisation, gentle but no less dynamic Latin-rock rhythms, plus an often poignant ethnic music ambience that have made his efforts popular with world-music and New-Age as well as jazz audiences.

As suggested by the tune titles such as *Campfire Stories*, *Swept Away* and *The Bamboo Forest*, there is a strongly picaresque dimension to Egan's broadly stroked sketches. His soundscapes are largely confined to a narrow range of postcard-pretty pastels; still, there is a palpable element of sincerity – Egan's music is heartfelt. So, although deviating from the usual criteria associated with jazz, Egan (as well as Metheny, *et al*) is again raising the question, "what is jazz?"          **CB**

# Marty Ehrlich                                                                      1955

**The Traveller's Tale**  Ehrlich (ss, as, cl, bcl); **Stan Strickland** (ss, ts, v); **Linsday Horner** (b); **Bobby Previte** (d). Enja Ⓕ 6024-20 (54 minutes). Recorded 1989.

⑧ ❽

A graduate of the New England Conservatory of Music, Ehrlich has worked in the testing musical workshops of George Russell, Gunther Schuller and Ran Blake. He is a young veteran of nearly 50 recording dates and his name has not altogether inappropriately been linked with the Knitting Factory, New York's own cosmopolitan music academy. Five of the eight compositions and all of the functional arrangements here are by Ehrlich and they serve the quartet well. *Alice's Wonderland* is especially imaginative and yet, like the remainder, it never obstructs the individual contributions. For their part, the rhythm duo are consciously obtrusive. Both behind the written unisons and the most detailed solos their fractured progress provides the kind of accent displacement to stimulate the horns. Ehrlich and Strickland respond well. Ehrlich's solos are imaginatively varied; they do not take a wildly convoluted route but, like the plaintive alto on the title track, use the freer harmonies of the avant-garde in a way that colours and enhances them. No attempt is made to shock and there are sequences where simplicity becomes its own virtue. Behind Strickland's idiosyncratic vocal on *The Reconsidered Blues*, Ehrlich's clarinet pulls on its Pee Wee-ish cloak to warm the agonizingly vulnerable voice. It is typical of the way in which Ehrlich chooses whatever approach or whatever of his many horns suits the situation.          **BMcR**

# 8 Bold Souls

**Sideshow**  Robert Griffin (t, flh); **Isaiah Jackson** (tb); **Aaron Dodd** (tba); **Mwata Bowden** (cl, bs); **Edward Wilkerson Jr** (ts, arr); **Naomi Millender** (vc); **Harrison Bankhead** (b); **Dushun Mosley** (d). Arabesque Jazz Ⓕ AJO103 (66 minutes). Recorded 1991.

⑧ ❽

A third generation AACM member, Edward Wilkerson Jr may be best known for his involvement in the three-piece Ethnic Heritage Ensemble, but his gargantuan orchestra Shadow Vignettes and this flexible octet are the primary outlets for his distinctive compositions. In terms of length and compositional breadth, his pieces could be considered tone-poems; they frequently evolve through contrasting episodes and integrate solos within the dramatic atmospheres Wilkerson strives to create. *Black Herman* is a case in point, with a calm, dark, moving dirge framing a surprisingly upbeat boppish line that houses his tenor solo. The arrangement of Ornette Coleman's *Lonely Woman* creates its own ebb and flow, growing out of a striking cello and bass introduction. *Glass Breakers* reveals the main source of his inspiration – the trombone theme and assisting horn harmonics, especially the trumpet and clarinet voicings, are lessons learned from Ellington. A tenor saxist of brawn and swagger, Wilkerson is out of the Hawkins/Webster/Shepp lineage, and each of the other Bold Souls have their own noteworthy talents. In writing for the ensemble he favours deep, rich velvet sonorities; as the arrangements drift from scene to scene, textures, the timbres, and colours are sure to shift as well. These pieces seldom shout, but you may find yourself seduced by their unexpected curves and noir-ish moods.                                                                                          **AL**

# Roy Eldridge                                                                                          1911-89

**Heckler's Hop**  Eldridge (t, v); with a collective personnel including: **Robert Williams, Eli Robinson** (tb); **Benny Goodman** (cl); **Scoops Carey** (as); **Joe Eldridge** (as, arr); **Chu Berry, Dave Young, Prince Robinson, Franz Jackson** (ts); **Jess Stacy, Teddy Cole, Clyde Hart, Kenny Kersey** (p); **John Collins, Danny Barker** (g); **Israel Crosby, Truck Parham, Artie Shapiro, Ted Sturgis** (b); **Gene Krupa, Zutty Singleton, Sid Catlett, Panama Francis** (d); **Helen Ward, Gladys Palmer, Laurel Watson** (v). Hep Ⓜ HEPCD1030 (66 minutes). Recorded 1936-9.

⑧ ❻

Eldridge was not alone in providing hints of the bebop to come, for the same might be said of 'Red' Allen, the undervalued (especially on CD) Charlie Shavers, and even Ellington's Rex Stewart. But Roy was the idol of young Dizzy Gillespie who, during the period of the above recordings, was busy succeeding to what had been Eldridge's chair in the Teddy Hill band.

While not the most complete trumpeter of the thirties, he was certainly the most fiery and, by this time, the most aware of his debt and implicit challenge to Louis Armstrong. Much of his phraseology was Armstrong played faster, while the coda of his famous *After You've Gone* (later re-made with Gene Krupa's band) refers explicitly to the Armstrong/Hines *Weather Bird* duo.

This collection usefully collects his early small-group work, if his Chicago-based eight-to-ten-piece band may be described this way. Some dubious vocals (easily overshadowed by Roy's own on *You're a Lucky Guy*) are intermingled with impressive trumpet features. The standouts are eight tracks with Chu Berry, the first four under Krupa's leadership; the five duplicated on Berry's own album have less surface noise there, but the instrumental sound is more faithful here.                                                                **BP**

**After You've Gone**  Eldridge (t, v); with a collective personnel including: **Sidney De Paris, Yank Lawson, Elmon Wright** (t); **Ted Kelly, Sandy Williams, Gerald Wilson, Vic Dickenson, Wilber De Paris** (tb); **Buster Bailey** (cl), **Joe Eldridge, Andrew Gardner, Porter Kilbert, Sahib Shihab** (as); **Chu Berry, Hal Singer, Franz Jackson, Tom Archia, Ike Quebec,** (ts); **Cecil Payne, Ernie Caceres** (bs); **Teddy Cole, Ted Brannon, Dave Bowman, Buster Harding, Duke Jordan, Rozelle Gayle** (p); **John Collins** (g), **John Kirby, Ted Sturgis, Billy Taylor, Rodney Richardson** (b); **Harold West, Cozy Cole, Lee Abrams, Sid Catlett** (d). MCA/Decca Ⓜ GRP16052 (64 minutes). Recorded 1936-46.

✅                                                                                          ⑩ ❻

After Gene Krupa broke up his band in the spring of 1943, Roy Eldridge fronted various small groups, then joined Artie Shaw. After leaving Shaw he formed his own big band which failed, not for musical reasons but simply because the climate was not right for a new big band. This recommended CD covers that period, opening with seven titles from a November 1943 Chicago date (three of the tracks are previously unissued) which contain some of Roy's most exciting solos, including the exceptional *The Gasser* which builds and builds. Ike Quebec is on tenor, making his record début on this session. The big-band titles are designed principally as showcases for Eldridge, who rises to the occasion, as always. The Armstrong influence is strong at times but the heated tone is uniquely Eldridge, especially on numbers such as *St Louis Blues* and *After You've Gone*. *Embraceable You* is by Roy and a big-but-efficient studio band. The final track is a version of *Christopher Columbus*, the only number to appear from Roy's first date as leader (in 1936) by what is, in fact, a small group taken from the Fletcher Henderson band. The transfers to CD are good, with the instrumentalists clearly defined. Strongly recommended.                                                                                          **AM**

**Roy and Diz**  Eldridge, **Dizzy Gillespie** (t); **Oscar Peterson** (p); **Herb Ellis** (g); **Ray Brown** (b); **Louis Bellson** (d). Verve Ⓜ 521 647-2 (76 minutes). Recorded 1954.

⑩ ❻

The two LPs which made up the original release of this material back in the fifties have been subject to many fluctuations of critical standing: presently, this late-autumn 1954 L.A. session is generally seen as an OK date where neither trumpeter really takes off and delivers a sermon from the Olympus of trumpet playing. But perhaps that view is too coloured by the idea of challenge, of contest and of the need to have an ultimate victor. For all Eldridge's fabled competitiveness, and Gillespie's ability to cut other trumpeters, there is a great deal of playing here distinguished by a clear desire to create a performance which is more coherent than mere endless choruses trying to top the other guy. A track like *Trumpet Blues*, basically an idea rather than a tune (the idea is to give the two horns a chance to trade choruses and bounce off each other's lines), shows both men slowly warming to the task, creating balanced statements, mindful of light and shade, and also creating background riffs from time to time.

Similarly, the *Ballad Medley* features some truly outstanding and sensitive interpretations of quality material. Eldridge's naked emotionalism brings out the most sincere side of Gillespie's balladry and curbs his tendency to mug, while Gillespie's wonderful technical control pushes Eldridge to form his notes and phrases with especial care. This is not to say that both players have too much respect for each other not to ruffle a few feathers, but no one is out for blood, even on a warhorse such as *I've Found a New Baby*, and the listener benefits from the friendly rivalry and exploration of each trumpeter's limits. It is a co-operative, and one by which the listener benefits dramatically. Don't be put off by those who always know better: this is the real thing, down to the last note.  **KS**

**Little Jazz: The Best of the Verve Years** Eldridge (t, flh, v); Joe Ferrante, Bernie Glow, Ernie Royal, Nick Travis (t); Jimmy Cleveland, J.J. Johnson, Fred Ohms, Kai Winding, Benny Morton, Vic Dickinson (tb); Eddie Barefield (cl); Sam Marowitz, Hal McKusick, Benny Carter, Johnny Hodges, Sonny Stitt (as); Aaron Sachs, Eddie Shu, Coleman Hawkins, Ben Webster (ts); Danny Bank (bs); Oscar Peterson, Dave McKenna, Dick Wellstood, Billy Strayhorn, Bruce Macdonald, Hank Jones, Ronnie Ball (p); Oscar Peterson (org); Barney Kessel, Barry Galbraith, Herb Ellis (g); Ray Brown, John Drew, Walter Page, John Simmons, Jimmy Woode, Benny Moten, George Duvivier (b); Jo Jones, J.C. Heard, Gene Krupa, Alvin Stoller, Buddy Rich, Sam Woodyard, Eddie Locke, Mickey Sheen (d); Anita O'Day (v); The Orchestras of Gene Krupa, George Williams, Russell Garcia and Johnny Hodges. Verve Ⓜ 523 338-2 (77 minutes). Recorded 1952-60.

✔ ⑨ ❽

If anyone deserved the nickname 'Little Jazz', it was trumpeter extraordinaire Roy Eldridge. Although often pegged as the link between Louis Armstrong and Dizzy Gillespie, Eldridge should be recognized as their co-equal, the prime innovator of the swing trumpet tradition and an indefatigable spirit whose rhythmic finesse, melodic inventiveness and *joie de vivre* always lifted the bandstand. In this splendid collection culled from his varied projects for Norman Granz's Verve label between 1952 and 1960, we catch 'Little Jazz' in an array of settings. There is a 1956 reprise of Eldridge's first big hit as a member of the 1941 Gene Krupa Band, *Let Me Off Uptown*, featuring Roy's snappy vocal exchange with a sassy Anita O'Day and a cooking Krupa-led studio band. There are tips-of-the-hat to the Armstrong tradition where Roy and his Central Plaza Dixielanders elevate *Bugle Call Rag* and *Ja-Da*. Although string dates are not everyone's cup of tea, Roy's heart-on-sleeve limning of *How Long Has This Been Going On?* is a show-stopper embellished by Russ Garcia's Orchestra. The quintet date with Eldridge confrère Coleman Hawkins is another grabber. For barn-burners, the romp through *Allen's Alley* with Sonny Stitt, Oscar Peterson's trio and Jo Jones shows that Roy could bop with the best. With 19 great tracks, many with star colleagues from Granz's Jazz at the Philharmonic, Eldridge jumps with poignant joy whatever the tempo or format.  **CB**

# Eliane Elias
1960

**Cross Currents** Elias (p); Barry Finnery (g); Eddie Gomez (b); Jack DeJohnette, Peter Erskine (d); Café (perc). Denon Ⓕ CY2180 (62 minutes). Recorded 1987.

⑧ ❽

Elias has no fewer than six albums on the market at present, with the later ones on Blue Note and Manhattan for the most part emphasizing her Brazilian heritage rather than her strong jazz credentials. This earlier Denon date, her second for the label, shows why we should be excited about her talent and rather concerned that, for the time being, she has put the jazz side of her playing more or less under wraps. To open with a flawless rendition of Bud Powell's *Hallucinations* at the sort of tempo Bud himself would use to scare other pianists off with is pretty impressive. To follow it up with an attractively funky, riff-based title song with plenty of meaty improvisation to boot means that this album is not about potential, but about already realized talent. Elias has the ability to send her improvised lines in any direction at any moment, has a highly developed dynamic sense so that any phrase she plays carries many meanings, and has a tidy elegance which may be a leftover of the inevitable Bill Evans influence, but more truly indicates the high quality of her musical thought. To enjoy the sheer confidence of her playing, go no further than her version of Mingus's *Peggy's Blue Skylight*. Let's hope she comes back onto this course on future albums.  **KS**

# Kurt Elling
1967

**Close Your Eyes** Elling (v); Edward Peterson, Von Freeman (ts); Laurence Hobgood (p, syn); Dave Onderonk (g); Eric Hochberg, Rob Amster (b); Paul Wertico (d). Blue Note Ⓕ CDP8 30645-2 (64 minutes). Recorded 1994.

⑥ ❾

Young Chicagoan Elling takes the opportunity, during his list of dedicatees, to mention Eddie Jefferson, Jon Hendricks and Mark Murphy "who taught me how to sing Jazz", and indeed it is difficult to envisage this album existing without the prior example laid out by that triumvirate, although the ghost of Sinatra also hovers. Elling has a voice with plenty of texture, and he uses its limitations to his own advantage, pushing it, bending it, growling with it, straining it, using an expressive falsetto, so you get a clear impression that he has done a lot of homework to get this far. He has taken a leaf out of Hendricks's book by adding lyrics to previously instrumental works (Wayne Shorter's *Dolores* becomes *Dolores' Dream*, a delirious and funny recounting of a romantic interlude) as well as singing pieces with lyrics already intact (the title song, *Wait 'Til You See Her* and *Ballad of the Sad Young Men*). He can scat and slur with the best of them but his diction is mostly excellent.

The supporting players stick very much to the background, with the tenors appearing on just three tracks between them. It is not too important, because there is plenty going on out front. **KS**

## Duke Ellington
1899-1974

**Early Ellington: The Complete Brunswick and Vocalion Recordings of Duke Ellington 1926-31** Ellington (p); **Bubber Miley, Louis Metcalf, June Clark, Arthur Whetsol, Freddie Jenkins, Cootie Williams** (t); **Joe Nanton** (tb); **Juan Tizol** (vtb); **Prince Robinson, Otto Hardwick, Rudy Jackson, Harry Carney, Barney Bigard, Johnny Hodges** (cl, ss, as, ts, bs); **Fred Guy** (bj); **Teddy Bunn** (g, bj); **Bennie Payne** (p, v); **Mack Shaw** (tba); **Wellman Braud** (b); **Sonny Greer** (d, v); **Bruce Johnson** (wshbd); **Harold Randolph** (kz); **Joe Cornell** (acc); **Bill Robinson** (v, speech, tap); **Dick Robertson** (v). MCA Ⓜ GRP36402 (three discs: 204 minutes). Recorded 1926-31.

✓ ⑧ ❻

This issue demonstrates simultaneously the strengths and weaknesses of a single label reissue policy for as prolific a recording artist as Ellington. Only passing references in Stephen Lasker's admirably detailed notes make clear that during the same period Ellington recorded for Okeh, Victor, Columbia and a handful of lesser labels. For this reason, despite the formidable span of material included here, and the opportunity to hear the orchestra coalesce from near chaos to slick professionalism, great chunks of the story are missing, and Jabbo Smith's alternative vision of *Black and Tan Fantasy* (for example) or Adelaide Hall's glowing, wordless *Creole Love Call* need to be sought elsewhere.

If incompleteness is a weakness in the set, the benefits (as compared to the comprehensive but technically flawed reissues on Classics 39, 542, 550, 559, 569, 577 and 586) are the uniformly high quality of the originals (many from Jerry Valburn's unique collection, or from original metal masters) and excellent (if slightly 'toppy') re-mastering. Lasker's painstaking and occasionally over-pedantic research, adhering to the spelling "Whetsel", for instance, makes the whole document remarkably illuminating. During the course of the five years spanned by this set, Braud and Greer redefined the rhythm section to something akin to Luis Russell's New Orleans beat, and Bigard and Miley recorded much of their finest work. The high points are too many to list, but this set is indispensable as the best-produced cross section of Ellington's work as his genius emerged. **AS**

**The Duke's Men – Small Groups, Volumes 1 and 2** Selected collective personnel under leaderships: **Rex Stewart, Ellington, Johnny Hodges, Barney Bigard, Cootie Williams, The Gotham Stompers**; including: **Rex Stewart** (c); **Cootie Williams, Freddie Jenkins** (t); **Lawrence Brown, Joe 'Tricky Sam' Nanton** (tb); **Juan Tizol** (vtb); **Barney Bigard** (cl); **Johnny Hodges** (ss, as); **Otto Hardwick** (as, bss); **Harry Carney** (bs); **Duke Ellington, Tommy Fulford** (p); **Bernard Addison, Fred Guy, Brick Fleagle** (g); **Wellman Braud, Billy Taylor, Hayes Alvis** (b); **Sonny Greer** (d); **Mary McHugh, Jean Eldridge** (v). Columbia Ⓜ CK46995/48835 (two two-disc sets, oas: 128 and 119 minutes). Recorded 1934-9.

✓ ⑩ ❻

While all the major developments and monumental achievements in Duke Ellington's career were reached through the vehicle of his Orchestra, some of the most sublimely happy episodes took place within his various small group aggregations. These recording groups took on different names during the thirties and forties, but all operated under the Duke's aegis and relied on him to give the numbers their distinctive aura. Although not always based on blues changes, most of the numbers had blues phrasings grafted onto them by the soloists, and the minor voicings gave Ellington a chance to display his endless variety. The smaller numbers of musicians present also meant that the limited recording facilities could do the rhythm sections more justice, and the added drive evident here is welcome.

Many of these tracks are classics of long standing (Volume 2 favours Hodges, while the earlier title shows off the trumpeters more), but there are felicities in most performances, and we are given delicious draughts of Hodges soprano on the early sides in particular. Cootie Williams growling his way through Juan Tizol's *Caravan*, Rex Stewart returning the compliment on *The Back Room Romp* plus Hodges making joyful noises on *Tea and Trumpets* and soulful sounds on *Jeep's Blues* and the famous *Wanderlust* are joys not be missed, but then these sides are one of the great miniature collections in jazz. Sony/Columbia US, often rightly criticized for their slap-dash approach to their jazz reissue programme, got it right here, from the improved sound through to the good playing times and the excellent notes by Helen Oakley Dance, who presided over many of these sessions. **KS**

**New review**
**Braggin' in Brass** Ellington (p, tom-tom); **Harold Baker, Wallace Jones, Cootie Williams** (t); **Rex Stewart** (c); **Lawrence Brown, Joe Nanton** (tb); **Juan Tizol** (vtb); **Barney Bigard, Johnny Hodges,**

Harry Carney, Otto Hardwicke (reeds); Fred Guy (g); Hayes Alvis, Billy Taylor (b); Sonny Greer (d); Ivie Anderson, 'Scat' Powell (v). Columbia/Legacy Ⓜ R2K44395 (two discs: 96 minutes). Recorded 1938.

✓                                                                                          ⑩ ❹

In the late seventies the Smithsonian Collection and Columbia issued two-record Ellington sets for each of the years 1938-41, representing the annual output of the orchestra in chronological order. Only the first of these has made it to CD, minus the extensive Gunther Schuller commentary and with the inferior sound that marred many of Columbia's first wave of CD reissues. Still, the music contained here is exceptional, refuting the notion that Ellington was in a slump during the height of the swing craze. He would go beyond this rarefied level once Strayhorn, Blanton and Webster were aboard, but any 12-month period that produces *The New Black and Tan Fantasy*, *Riding on a Blue Note*, *Lost in Meditation*, *I Let a Song Go Out of My Heart*, *Pyramid*, *A Gypsy Without a Song*, *Prelude to a Kiss*, *Boy Meets Horn* and other gems is hardly an off year. Two takes of *Rose of the Rio Grande* and *Blue Light* have been included, to illustrate how Ellington fine-tuned his music. If only Columbia/Legacy would return all four of the Smithsonian sets to the catalogue, with production values commensurate with the original LPs: is that too much to ask?          **BB**

**Fargo, North Dakota November 7, 1940** Ellington (p, arr); Rex Stewart (c); Wallace Jones (t); Ray Nance (t, v); Joe 'Tricky Sam' Nanton, Juan Tizol, Lawrence Brown (tb); Johnny Hodges (as); Otto Hardwick (cl, as); Ben Webster (ts); Harry Carney (bs); Freddie Guy (g); Jimmy Blanton (b); Sonny Greer (d); Billy Strayhorn (arr); Ivie Anderson, Herb Jeffries (v). Vintage Jazz Classics Ⓜ 1019/20-2 (two discs: 155 minutes). Recorded 1940.

✓                                                                                          ⑩ ❽

Ellington was on the road as usual – Winnipeg the night before, Duluth the night after – when the band stopped in Fargo for a typical evening playing five sets for dancing. Typical except that two fans brought a borrowed disc-cutter, and with Duke's permission recorded as much of the show as possible, breaking away only to change discs. The Fargo recordings are justly prized for vividly documenting a good night by a great band – by common consent Duke's best – in which bassist Blanton and tenorist Webster temporarily took their places among the orchestra's long-time stars. Some players listened to playbacks on their breaks, and were delighted by the good sound the amateur engineers got, off-microphone vocals aside. The hectic ambience of a night at a local ballroom comes across, replete with great solos, missed cues, a local radio announcer talking in the background during one set, and Duke's everyday but astoundingly rich mix of pop tunes, ballads, concertos and flag-wavers, all featuring breathtaking reed and brass voicings. Incidentally, one of the recordists was Jack Towers, who later went on to become an expert at cleaning up valuable but noisy old recordings like this.          **KW**

**The Blanton-Webster Band** Ellington (p, cond); Wallace Jones, Cootie Williams (t); Ray Nance (t, v); Rex Stewart (c); Joe 'Tricky Sam' Nanton, Lawrence Brown (tb); Juan Tizol (vtb); Johnny Hodges (as, ss, cl); Otto Hardwick (as, bs); Barney Bigard, Chauncey Haughton (cl, ts); Ben Webster (ts); Harry Carney (bs, as, cl); Billy Strayhorn (p); Fred Guy (g); Jimmy Blanton, Junior Raglan (b); Sonny Greer (d); Ivie Anderson (v). RCA Bluebird Ⓜ ND85659 (three discs: 209 minutes). Recorded 1940-2.

✓                                                                                          ⑩ ❻

Towards the end of 1939 the 21-year-old bass virtuoso Jimmy Blanton joined Duke Ellington and his Famous Orchestra; in January 1940 Ellington added a fifth saxophone to the band in the substantial form of Ben Webster. Thus was completed the band which, over the following two years, produced some of the finest work Ellington ever recorded and thus, by definition, some of the greatest masterpieces in the history not only of orchestral jazz but of twentieth-century music. This set contains 66 numbers from those years, including all the great works such as *Ko-Ko*, *Bojangles*, *Harlem Airshaft*, *Concerto for Cootie*, *Cottontail*, etc. It is astonishing to recall that these hugely sophisticated pieces were written, rehearsed and recorded in the midst of a full schedule, during which Ellington and the band worked long hours every night in ballrooms, hotels and amusement parks, often travelling hundreds of miles between engagements.

Whole books of scholarly exegesis have been written around Ellington the composer, his musicians and his manner of working, and there is no room here to begin a summary. The one quality which emerges from all his work, and especially from these pieces, is a kind of breathing humanity. The sound of this Ellington orchestra is the sound of a huge, many-tongued human voice. It is not a thing of pinpoint accuracy or snappy effects, but of depth, warmth and endless invention. The music fully merits a comprehensive CD package such as this, it being essential to any jazz collection.          **DG**

**Black, Brown & Beige** Ellington (p); Cat Anderson, Harold 'Shorty' Baker, Shelton Hemphill, Taft Jordan, Rex Stewart, Francis Williams (t); Ray Nance (c, vn, v); Lawrence Brown, Wilbur DeParis, Tommy Dorsey, Claude Jones, Joe 'Tricky Sam' Nanton (tb); Jimmy Hamilton (cl, ts); Johnny Hodges, Russell Procope (as); Al Sears (ts); Harry Carney (bs, bcl); Billy Strayhorn (p, arr); Freddie Guy (g); Bob Haggart, Al Lucas, Oscar Pettiford, Alvin 'Junior' Raglin, Sid Weiss (b); Sid Catlett, Sonny Greer (d); Marian Cox, Kay Davis, Marie Ellington, Al Hibbler, Joya Sherrill (v). RCA Bluebird Ⓜ 6641-2-RB (three discs: 181minutes). Recorded 1944-6.

✓                                                                                ⑩ ❼

Picking up where **The Blanton-Webster Band** left off, this surveys the orchestra's output through 1946, beginning with studio recordings of portions of *BB&B*, "the tone parallel to the American Negro" débuted at Ellington's first Carnegie Hall concert, in 1943. (The entire concert is available on Prestige PCD34004-2 and there is an almost-complete studio version of *BB&B* from the mid sixties on Volume 10 of The Private Concerts, Saja 91234-2.) *BB&B* was initially greeted less than enthusiastically, the problem being (as Ellington himself might have put it) that it was neither tulip nor turnip – neither a full-blown, organic symphonic work nor conventional jazz, even by Ellington's standards. Yet *BB&B* fully deserves the reputation it has subsequently acquired as not merely the most ambitious of Ellington's extended works, but perhaps the most majestic. It hardly suffers from the trimmings it receives here. The fanfare that announces the section called *Work Song* is one of the most stirring passages in modern music, and there are few passages even in the rest of Ellington's work as haunting or as finely measured as the guitar-and-bass tremolos behind Hodges on *Come Sunday*. This set also presents the complete *The Perfume Suite*, as much Billy Strayhorn's work as Ellington's and one of several numbers here illustrating the influence Strayhorn was beginning to exert on his mentor, especially in terms of the melodic use of dissonance. The three-minute masterpieces include *Blue Cellophane* and *Transblucency*, the latter spawned from Ellington's earlier *Blue Light* and featuring Hamilton and Kay Davis in an incredible duet between clarinet and coloratura. What else? Generous samples of irresistible jive such as (*Otto, Make That*) *Riff Staccato*, the maestro's own updatings of ten of his classic pieces from the thirties, a handsome showcase for fellow bandleader Dorsey on *Tonight I Shall Sleep* and inimitable solos by Hodges, Nanton, Carney, Stewart, Brown and the rest – ample evidence of Ellington's ability to weather wartime shortages, union recording bans and the deaths or defections of several key sidemen. The digital remastering is a little boxy, although better than on **The Blanton-Webster Band**. **FD**

---

**The Great Ellington Units**  Ellington (p, ldr); with collective personnel including: **Rex Stewart** (c); **Cootie Williams**, **Ray Nance** (t); **Lawrence Brown** (tb); **Juan Tizol** (vtb); **Barney Bigard** (cl); **Johnny Hodges** (ss, as); **Ben Webster** (ts); **Harry Carney** (bs); **Jimmy Blanton** (b); **Sonny Greer** (d). RCA Bluebird Ⓜ ND86751 (69 minutes). Recorded 1940-1.

The short duration of the 78rpm record left Ellington no alternative but to become the master of the three-minute form. It is arguable that his subsequent lengthier works never matched his superbly concentrated recordings of 1940, but it is indisputable that his genius spilled from the big band recordings to those of the small groups of that outstanding period. Earlier Ellington small groups had passion, fire and *joie de vivre*, but the 1940 ones achieved those qualities and added a greater degree of subtlety and sophistication.

The casual perfection of Johnny Hodges's alto playing on *Good Queen Bess* and *Squaty Roo* is the epitome of swing or 'jump' music, while the lush exotica of *Day Dream* offers an early example of the potent new element brought to Ellingtonia by composer Billy Strayhorn. Barney Bigard's ripe clarinet is at its best on six tracks under his name, and the eccentric cornettist Rex Stewart, already undervalued as a horn player, reveals himself as an original and memorable jazz composer with his *Menelik (The Lion of Judah)*, which includes a turbulent display of his freak abilities on cornet, and *Poor Bubber*, the wistfully melancholic tribute to his forebear in the Ellington band, Bubber Miley.

It is difficult to find a weak point amongst the 22 tracks on offer here, although it is a point of some irritation that two of the eight Barney Bigard tracks recorded for RCA at this time were omitted from this disc, although CD technology would certainly have allowed a further six minutes' worth of music. **SV**

---

**Ellington at Newport**  Ellington (p); **Willie Cook**, **Clark Terry**, **Cat Anderson** (t); **Ray Nance** (c); **Britt Woodman**, **Quentin Jackson**, **John Sanders** (tb); **Russell Procope** (as, cl); **Johnny Hodges** (as); **Paul Gonsalves** (ts); **Jimmy Hamilton** (ts, cl); **Harry Carney** (bs); **Jimmy Woode** (b); **Sam Woodyard** (d). Columbia Ⓜ 472385 2 (44 minutes). Recorded 1956.

Things looked somewhat bleak for big bands in the early fifties, but in 1953 Woody Herman assembled the Third Herd, by 1955 the 'Atomic' Basie band line-up was in place and in 1956 Johnny Hodges returned to Ellington to begin a period of personnel stability for the Duke. On this CD, Hodges gives a superb reading of his beloved *Jeep's Blues* but it was Gonsalves whose one single performance really changed the band's fortunes. His 27 electrifying choruses on *Diminuendo and Crescendo in Blue* sent the 1956 Newport Jazz Festival audience into a state of near delirium and re-established the Ellington Orchestra in the eyes and ears of the world. The incredible atmosphere is genuinely captured on this CD, as some 7000 fans stood on their seats, cheered and whistled and seemed almost mesmerized as Anderson added his killer touch at the end of the performance. Ellington's *Newport Jazz Festival Suite* had earlier warmed up the audience with characteristic contributions from the likes of Hamilton, Nance, Procope, Terry and the band's masterful pianist. It had all been a normally immaculate Ducal presentation until that fateful moment when, at around midnight on July 7th 1956, Gonsalves stood up to solo. An act that somehow re-directed the band, it also sparked Ellington's compositional enthusiasm and led the band into a new and highly successful phase. It is rumoured that a remastered Columbia reissue due late in 1997 will contain (for the first time ever) all the music Ellington's band played that night. One can only wait and see. **BMcR**

**Such Sweet Thunder** Ellington (p, ldr); **Cat Anderson, Clark Terry, Willie Cook** (t); **Ray Nance** (c, vn); **John Sanders, Britt Woodman, Quentin Jackson** (tb); **Johnny Hodges, Russell Procope, Paul Gonsalves, Jimmy Hamilton, Harry Carney** (reeds); **Jimmy Woode** (b); **Sam Woodyard** (d); **Billy Strayhorn** (arr). Columbia Ⓜ 469140-2 (36 minutes). Recorded 1956-7.

⑧ ❼

Ellington consolidated his orchestra's return to favour at the 1956 Newport Festival with two new suites: *A Drum is a Woman*, his bizarre re-telling of jazz history, and the Shakespeare-inspired *Such Sweet Thunder*, which has the more attractive music. Some critics have complained that the suite's links with Shakespeare are pretty tenuous. More to the point is Ralph Gleason's comment that "*Such Sweet Thunder* runs the Ellington gamut ... Every single moment of it is well done." One novel outcome of the Duke's encounter with the Bard was a new 14-line musical form written in imitation of the sonnet. The four examples on *Such Sweet Thunder* work well, with *Sonnet for Caesar*, which features beautiful, rapt clarinet from Jimmy Hamilton, among the disc's highlights. The remaining music, although more conventional in form, shows plenty of felicitous Ducal touches (check the horns' funky prowl on the title track), while nearly every piece has a showcase solo from a leading player. Johnny Hodges's languorous alto has made *The Star-Crossed Lovers* (a Billy Strayhorn tune) the suite's best-known track, but Harry Carney's baritone stroll through *The Telecasters* is hardly less sensual. **Such Sweet Thunder** is well crafted, consistently charming and lifted at times by real inspiration. A "concord of sweet sounds" for all but the most strategem-minded. **GL**

**New review**

**Blues in Orbit** Ellington (p, ldr); **Billy Strayhorn** (p); **Cat Anderson, Shorty Baker, Clark Terry** (t); **Ray Nance** (t, v); **Quentin Jackson, Britt Woodman, Booty Wood, John Sanders** (tb); **Matthew Gee** (tb, bhn); **Jimmy Hamilton** (cl); **Bill Graham, Russell Procope** (as, cl); **Paul Gonsalves** (ts); **Harry Carney** (bs); **Jimmy Woode** (b); **Sam Woodyard, Jimmy Johnson** (d). Columbia Ⓔ CK44051 (46 minutes). Recorded 1958-9.

⑦ ❽

It was recorded in two bursts, after two different European tours, and Ellington didn't come armed with a concept. Made at the height of Ellington's and Strayhorn's involvement with suites (and recorded during the period that he made the soundtracks to **Anatomy of a Murder** and **Paris Blues**), this album of stand-alone pieces contains wide pockets of open space in the arrangements, majestic projection, and superior group energy on a mixed-bag programme. Some of it you've heard to death (*C-Jam Blues, In a Mellotone*), other bits are new tricks (*Track 360*, with its buzzing dissonant clusters, the pitter-patter mambo *Blues in Blueprint*). *Sweet and Pungent* features Booty Wood on a ripe, expressive plunger-trombone solo that apparently even Wood didn't believe he was well suited to, before being leaned on to play it. But the star of the record is Johnny Hodges, who winds through a good number of spotlighted solos with his pure, gorgeous, rising and falling steam-valve emanations. Easygoing but high-quality Ellington from one of his great periods. **BR**

**Money Jungle** Ellington (p); **Charles Mingus** (b); **Max Roach** (d). Blue Note Ⓜ CDP7 46398-2 (57 minutes). Recorded 1962.

⑧ ❻

**Money Jungle** is a Summit Meeting which almost foundered. Mingus walked out of the session, refusing to play with "that drummer" (Roach, in fact, was an old comrade and friend) and it was Ellington who cajoled him into returning to the studio. Almost any recording session with Mingus had its moments of tension and this on-edge feeling is present here. This time it actually works to the advantage of the resultant music. The CD version contains the complete programme of music (13 tracks) and plays for more than twice the duration of the original United Artists LP. There are three established Ellington works (*Caravan, Solitude* [two takes] and *Warm Valley*) which are, by comparison with the rest of the material, 'safe'. It is on numbers such as the explosive title track (where Mingus, attacking his instrument with something close to violence, goads Ellington into some unusually fiery and searching playing), the blues *Switch Blade* and the beautiful *Fleurette Africaine* that the interaction between these three instrumental masters is heard at its best and most dynamic. Roach senses the shape and direction of Duke's music to perfection (the two had recorded once before, in 1950) while Mingus's playing, despite some coloratura passages, is magnificent. *REM Blues* turns out to be a familiar riff, sometimes known as *Blues for Blanton*. The remix engineer has improved the sound from the original muddy LP production. The only drawback is that the original (and very successful) LP track sequence has been abandoned on the CD reissue. Those readers who have kept their turntables in good condition may prefer to hunt down a copy of the now-deleted contemporaneous vinyl reissue, which has most of the added music and a closer approximation of the original track order. **AM**

**The Far East Suite – Special Mix** Ellington (p, arr, ldr); **Cat Anderson, Herbie Jones, Mercer Ellington, Cootie Williams** (t); **Lawrence Brown, Chuck Connors, Buster Cooper** (tb); **Johnny Hodges** (as); **Russell Procope** (cl, as); **Jimmy Hamilton** (cl, ts); **Paul Gonsalves** (ts); **Harry Carney** (bs, bcl); **John Lamb** (b); **Rufus Jones** (d); **Billy Strayhorn** (arr). RCA Bluebird Ⓜ 366551-2 (61 minutes). Recorded 1966.

⑩ ❽

One of the last great Ellington albums, and the last to be issued before the final great edition of his band began to disperse. However, drummer Sam Woodyard (who played on earlier, then-unissued recordings of parts of the suite) was unavailable and it was left to Rufus Jones, a newcomer to Duke, to add his personal touch to this 'exotic' repertoire.

Titled after Ellington's first Middle East and Japanese tours, material was written during a two-year period, and equates the inspiration of foreign climes with sixties modal jazz (which could be described as descending from *Caravan*, written in 1936!). As always, Duke and co-writer Billy Strayhorn managed to absorb outside influences in a way that spiced up the Ellington sounds yet remained faithful to its own traditions. And, as usual, it is the relative freedom afforded to the players that both complicates and facilitates the balancing act. Gonsalves's features on *Tourist Point of View* and *Mount Harissa* could be pronounced typical, while *Blue Pepper* and *Isfahan* have typical Hodges solos (despite the thematic link between *Isfahan* and *Harissa*). But they are also highly individualized, as are Duke's piano contributions to *Harissa*, *Depk*, *Amad* and *Ad-Lib On Nippon*.

The reason for the so-called "special mix" is explained in the sleeve-notes by reissue producer Orrin Keepnews: the two-track tape machine used to create a stereo master from the four-track session tapes had not been aligned properly, creating a slight but noticeable tonal distortion. Keepnews located the original session tapes, thankfully clear of all distortion, and remixed from them. During this process he discovered the four alternative takes included here, which are a considerable bonus. The remix has also subtly but markedly improved what was always a rather brittle sound on previous LPs and CD reissues, thus helping the various elements in the Ellington tonal palette to blend more sweetly. A masterpiece for the 21st century. **BP**

**New Orleans Suite** Ellington (p); **Cootie Williams, Money Johnson, Cat Anderson, Mercer Ellington, Al Rubin, Fred Stone** (t, flh); **Booty Wood, Julian Priester** (tb); **Dave Taylor, Chuck Connors** (btb); **Russell Procope** (cl, as); **Johnny Hodges** (as); **Norris Turney** (cl, as, f); **Harold Ashby** (cl, ts); **Paul Gonsalves** (ts); **Harry Carney** (cl, bcl, bs); **Wild Bill Davis** (org); **Joe Benjamin** (b); **Rufus Jones** (d). Atlantic Jazz Ⓜ 781376-2 (43 minutes). Recorded 1970.

⑧ ➑

The five-part *New Orleans Suite* was commissioned by George Wein for performance at the 1970 New Orleans Jazz Festival. At first glance, Wein's choice of the Washington DC-born/New York-honed Ellington may seem odd. However, as Stanley Dance notes in the informative sleeve-note, Ellington had been entranced and subsequently open to and influenced by Crescent City players since first hearing Sidney Bechet in 1921 declaim *I'm Coming, Virginia*. When Ellington's Washingtonians moved to New York, the gutsy swingingness of Louis Armstrong made its impact. So, too, did the hiring of clarinetist Barney Bigard and bassist Wellman Braud in late 1927, two New Orleans masters with credentials including Armstrong, King Oliver and Jelly Roll Morton.

For this wonderful 1970 studio recording made just after the *Suite*'s successful première in New Orleans, Ellington interspersed four additional but related *Portrait* segments saluting Louis Armstong, Mahalia Jackson, Sidney Bechet and ex-Ellingtonian Wellman Braud (still no place for Jelly Roll, though, even at this late stage). Among the Suite's gems are the rollicking *Second Line* and the frothy *Aristrocracy à la Jean LaFitte*, where Harry Carney's dainty baritone saxophone (yes, dainty!) waltzes gracefully with Fred Stone's lithe flügelhorn. The opening *Blues for New Orleans* showcases Wild Bill Davis's wailing Hammond B-3 organ and the bluesy alto saxophone of Johnny Hodges, who died on May 11th, 1970, and to whom the album is dedicated. **CB**

# Don Ellis
1934-79

**Autumn** Ellis (t, ldr); **Glenn Stuart, Stu Blumberg, John Rosenberg, Bob Harmon** (t); **Ernie Carlson, Glenn Ferris, Don Switzer** (tb); **Ira Schulman, Frank Strozier** (as); **Sam Falzone, John Klemmer** (ts); **John Magruder** (bs); **Pete Robinson** (kbds); **Ray Neapolitan, Dave Parlato** (b); **Ralph Humphrey** (d); **Gene Strimling, Lee Pastora** (perc); on three tracks add **Ron Starr** (as, f); **Terry Woodson** (tb); **Doug Bixby** (tba); on two tracks add **Mike Lang** (kbds); **Roger Bobo** (tba). Columbia Ⓜ 472622-2 (58 minutes). Recorded 1968.

⑦ ➏

From the mid sixties to the early seventies, Don Ellis's big bands combined post-Kenton extended charts and experimental forms with complex rhythms, rock energy, electricity, high-voltage soloists and, toward the end, a string section, achieving a fair amount of popularity in so doing. **Autumn** is the only one of the representative albums from that period available on CD, and gives a good idea of what all the shouting, pro and con, was about. Ellis loved bombastic arrangements and some of the effects and affectations (especially his electronically modified trumpet) do not wear well today, but his ambition and talent was such that a banal passage was likely to be followed by something quite remarkable. An extreme example is the six-part *Variations for Trumpet*, which includes plush themes far beyond anything Claude Thornhill might have envisioned, as well as a swinging 7/4 Latin section with four polyrhythmic percussionists. Most impressive here are *K.C. Blues*, a straight-ahead bash with an excellent Frank Strozier introduction and a transcribed Charlie Parker episode that anticipates Supersax, and *Indian Lady*, which whips up a firestorm of excitement. As their titles indicate, *Scratt and Fluggs* and *Pussy Willow Stomp* are intended as comic relief, and *Child of Ecstasy* is a brief, atmospheric showpiece with a 12-tone row or two hidden in the arrangement and enough trumpet pyrotechnics by Glenn Stuart to chill the blood of even Maynard Ferguson. Other outstanding soloists in the band at this time were altoist Strozier, tenorman John Klemmer (fresh from his days in Chicago, when he was breathing fire and not the thinner New Age air), trombonist Glenn Ferris, adventurous keyboardist Pete Robinson and tuba virtuoso Roger Bobo. History should not forget that Ellis himself was a trumpeter of enormous facility, if extremely uneven taste, best when he could scatter bright, penetrating variations of swing phrasing upon the band's contrapuntal sections. At those moments, the Don Ellis Orchestra was truly exciting.                                    **AL**

# Herb Ellis                                                                                              1921

**Nothin' But the Blues**  Ellis (g); **Roy Eldridge, Dizzy Gillespie** (t); **Stan Getz, Coleman Hawkins** (ts); **Oscar Peterson** (p); **Ray Brown** (b); **Stan Levey, Gus Johnson** (d). Verve Ⓜ 521 674-2 (58 minutes). Recorded 1957/8.

⑧ ❽

The first eight tracks of the album are by a piano-less quintet made up of Ellis, Eldridge, Getz, Brown and Levey. Years after the session the musicians involved talked about it with pleasure, and it remains one of Ellis's favourites of his own recordings. So it should. This is an unpretentious collection of swinging mainstream, powered by the leader's abiding love of the blues. Everyone lets his hair down and the music flows and flows. Solos from Getz and Eldridge, moving into the centre for the occasion, are invariably inspired, but not as much as Ellis, a modest man who for once lets his aura pervade the whole session. There is much harking back to the classic Goodman sextet, with *Big Red's Boogie Woogie* notable both for a good drenching of Charlie Christian and for the punching Goodman-like riffs. Brown, a great stalwart on the session, opens *Tin Roof Blues* with an almost inaudible bass intro and later in the piece Stan Getz, who often made a virtue of blowing blues into a ballad, turns *Tin Roof* itself into a ballad for his solo.

Four interesting fragments have been added to make up the weight of the CD. These were recorded for the French film *Les Tricheurs* and feature individual performances from Eldridge and Getz (again), Gillespie and Hawkins.                                                                        **SV**

# Pee Wee Ellis

**Twelve and More Blues**  Ellis (ts, bs); **Dwayne Dolphin** (b); **Bruce Cox** (d). Minor Music Ⓕ MM801034 (72 minutes). Recorded 1993.

⑦ ❽

Ellis is one more of the excellent hornmen to have emerged from the James Brown band over recent years to begin carving a career under his own banner, and while Maceo Parker may have made the greater public impact, this album demonstrates a deeper grounding in the bop tradition than anything Parker may have come up with to date.

For a start, the album, recorded live in Cologne last year, features the same trio line-up favoured by Sonny Rollins on his epochal **Live at the Village Vanguard** (see below), and the first two tracks (*There is No Greater Love* and *Doxy*) are actually taken from the Rollins performing book. Ellis's tenor sound is a likeable amalgam of Rollins and early Archie Shepp, while his phrasing has the rhythmic regularity of 'Lockjaw' Davis plus a number of enjoyable twists from more contemporary concepts. *Doxy* may be a pedestrian effort compared with the manic genius of Rollins's classic 1961 live version with Don Cherry, but the pedestrian strolls with admirable humour and takes the listener with him every step of the way. No little part of the reason for this stems from the supple rhythms and emphases of the bass-drums team of Dolphin and Cox, who are commendably supportive of Ellis throughout. The sax player, by the way, sticks mostly to tenor on this album, essaying the larger horn just once, on the walking blues *In the Middle*, where he offers a sensible sonic variation in quite a long programme. This is a good-humoured and engaging album with little of the humdrum about it and plenty of well-directed improvisational energy, and as such it deserves your attention.   **KS**

# Sidsel Endresen

**Exile**  Endresen (v); **Hans Petter Molvaer** (t); **Django Bates** (p); **Jens Bugge Wesseltoft** (kbds); **David Darling** (vc); **Jon Christensen** (d). ECM Ⓕ 521 721-2 (56 minutes). Recorded 1993.

⑦ ❿

Endresen is like fifties Helen Merrill translated into the bleak and harsh realities of the fin-de-siècle nineties, except that she also touches on borderline figures of folk and pop like Mary Travers, Nico and Buffy Sainte-Marie. The compositions here are mostly shared between herself and Jon Eberson, with Django Bates contributing the music to one of the most complex and fully-fleshed piece, *Stages I, II, III*. The music is spare, with long stretches of *pianissimo*, and Jon Christensen has certainly been much busier on other days in the studio. This is a borderline entry for this guide, but then often it is the music on the edge of a style which has the widest resonance, because it constantly hints at other dimensions. By this I am not endorsing 'crossover' but suggesting that strong talents with a clear idea of what they are at can sail close to the wind in any form. Whichever way she is coming from, Endresen can sail closer than most. Her key talent is the quiet distillation of experience as if it was already past experience when in fact it is still happening. That is a special talent, a special intensity and an acquired taste. It will be worth your while to acquire the taste for this record.     **KS**

## Lena Ericsson

**Doodlin'** Ericsson (v); **Arne Domnerus** (as, cl); **Ulf Johansson** (p); **Rune Gustafsson** (g); **Bo Stief** (b); **Aage Tanggaard** (d). Phontastic Ⓕ NCD8808 (63 minutes). Recorded 1990.

⑧ ❽

From the opening notes of the first track *Days of Wine and Roses*, which she sings gently over Gustafsson's guitar, it is obvious that Miss Ericsson is going to cause a lot of re-thinking of the vocal stakes. She takes her place as a worthy companion to Domnerus and the other Swedes, indisputably at the head of European jazz musicians and, in Miss Ericsson's case, able to see off many of the Americans.

Her voice is full and her confident control of it remarkable. She has a good range and an imposing skill with dynamics. She can hit hard on the blues and fine-tune nuances in her ballads with the skill of a Vaughan or a Fitzgerald, and yet she is very much an original. She seems little troubled by the difficulties Scandinavians often have with lyrics in English and her histrionics on *Doodlin'* are not as intrusive as they are in others' versions. The flying version of *Love for Sale* with only drum accompaniment is more spectacular than moving, and one has to go to the next track, the Laine-Dankworth *It's Not Easy*, for one of her superb ballad performances.

She would be good even without the fine accompanists, but it should be noted that Domnerus, Gustafsson and Johansson take powerful and potent solos throughout.     **SV**

## Peter Erskine                                                                                          1954

**Sweet Soul** Erskine (d); **Randy Brecker** (t); **Joe Lovano** (ts, ss); **Bob Mintzer** (ts); **Kenny Werner** (p, org, syn); **John Scofield** (elg); **Marc Johnson** (b). BMG Novus Ⓕ PD90616 (75 minutes). Recorded 1991.

⑧ ❽

Erskine's work with Weather Report and Steps Ahead in the late seventies and early eighties could hardly have prepared his listeners for the directions he has taken in recent years. For one thing he has returned to the swinging, often standard material of his apprenticeship; but he has also ventured into experimental areas that were circumscribed by the Weather Report he served, including an involvement with theatre music.

This richly varied session touches all his favourite musical bases without overbalancing, as some of his earlier efforts did, in favour of composition. The programming covers a wide and satisfying emotional range, from the poignant, tiptoeing balladry of William Walton's *Touch Her Soft Lips and Part* through the tart abstractions of three Vince Mendoza pieces to the slow-burning gospel funk of the title track and the surprisingly authentic-sounding Shorterisms of *To Be or Not to Be*. Erskine's talents as a percussionist have long been evident, but *Sweet Soul* proves him a composer of exceptional ability. Kenny Werner stands out from a group of top-drawer soloists for his treatments, thrilling and witty respectively, of his own *Press Enter* and Brubeck's *In Your Own Sweet Way*. The direct to two-track digital sound is irreproachable.     **MG**

## Lars Erstrand

New review

**The Lars Erstrand Sessions** Erstrand (vb); with a collective personnel of: **Bob Barnard** (t); **Roy Williams** (tb); **Danny Moss** (ts); **Kjell Ohman, Jan Lundgren** (p); **Tommy Johnson, Arne Wihelmsson** (b); **Leif Dahlberg, Ronnie Gardiner** (d). Opus 3 Ⓕ CD19405 (73 minutes). Recorded 1994/5.

⑧ ❽

Sweden's Erstrand has never made any secret of his admiration for the playing of Lionel Hampton and the three sessions represented here were Lars's attempts to rekindle the spirit of those marvellous 1939/40 Hampton sessions for RCA Victor. The difference is that only one horn is present at any one time; there are four titles with Roy Williams, vibes and rhythm, four with Australian cornet player Barnard taking Roy's place and a final five with Danny Moss taking over. With a programme of tunes including *One Morning in May, Stuffy, Lester Leaps in* and *Struttin' with Some Barbecue* perhaps the results are a little predictable, but who cares? These men are masters of the great middle period of jazz playing and Erstrand is one of the mightiest swingers to take up vibes mallets since Hampton first placed the instrument on the jazz platform. Roy Williams's titles are a little disappointing due to the weaker of the two rhythm sections and a balance which gives us too much of Leif Dahlberg's cymbals for comfort. But that smooth articulation and singing phrases place Roy at the top of the trombone tree. Bob Barnard is strongly influenced by Armstrong and pulls out the stops for some marvellous solos, notably on *Jubilee*. Danny Moss is one of the finest mainstream tenor players anywhere in the world and some of the classiest moments occur when he and Erstrand lovingly caress *Talk of the Town*. As an extra bonus Jan Lundgren plays perfect piano on nine tracks.                           **AM**

## Booker Ervin                                                                      1930-70

**New review**
**The Freedom Book**  Ervin (ts); **Jaki Byard** (p); **Richard Davis** (b); **Alan Dawson** (d). Prestige
  Ⓜ OJCCD845-2 (42 minutes). Recorded 1963.

⑩  ⑩

A latter-day Texas tenor, Ervin made his first impact in New York with the Charles Mingus band which included John Handy, shortly afterwards becoming a charter member of the Mingus group which evolved from a residency at the Showplace and which eventually included Eric Dolphy and Ted Curson. His style and tone was sufficiently original and individual, his artistic stance sufficiently uncompromising, for him to have a difficult time trying to sustain a career as a leader, and it is typical of his station in the jazz échelon that this magical group only ever convened in recording studios. They managed a number of classics around this time, but **The Freedom Book** is perhaps the highest pinnacle they scaled, the whole group burning with the same intensity and unpretentious directness of expression which encapsulated Ervin's musical credo. What constantly hits the listener is the unbroken polyphony to be enjoyed as each of the four men spin continually stimulating musical lines which not only engage your ear in their own right but instantly dovetail with the work of the other three men around them. Dawson doesn't just keep time; he embroiders it and fits his patterns to the group around him; Davis doesn't just walk, or take off into free-time space; he constantly varies his accompaniment, interspersing countless little attractive ideas beneath piano and sax, colouring what the drummer is doing. Byard plays sparingly as ever, but his note-choice and rhythmic displacement is Ellingtonian in its degree of interest, and his solos are full of élan. Ervin bears down on the music like an express train on the swingers, and wails like a man possessed on the slower numbers (*Cry Me Not*; *A Day to Mourn*), making it impossible for the listener to remain unmoved. No one here is merely trying to impress; everyone is making truly inspired music.                          **KS**

**Setting the Pace**  Ervin (ts); **Dexter Gordon** (ts); **Jaki Byard** (p); **Reggie Workman** (b); **Alan Dawson** (d). Prestige Ⓜ OJC24123-2 (77 minutes). Recorded 1965.

⑨  ⑧

Ervin's early death quieted a horn of great authority and power. A celebrated stint with Mingus and a cache of excellent albums on his own, most assisted by the impeccably creative rhythm team of Byard, Richard Davis and Dawson, had preceded this remarkable evening's (actually early morning's) work, as chronicled by David Himmelstein's surrealistic sleeve-notes and initially released on two LPs (intact here bar one track), **Setting the Pace** and **The Trance**. Suffice to say, extreme conditions and near-exhaustion sometimes lead to exceptional results, as they do here. On a pair of marathon excursions, Ervin locks horns with Gordon, the tenor duellist *par excellence*, and both are inspired to breathtaking heights. On *Setting the Pace* Booker's harsh cry swells to a wail at climactic points, or he envelops chords with sheets-of-sound after Dexter elaborates on his original 1947 solo; Booker is impressive on *Dexter's Deck* but Gordon owns the tune, taking a full nine minutes to weave a patchwork quilt of quotes and oblique ideas. On *The Trance* and *Speak Low* Ervin seems relieved that Dexter's not around, and the latter receives a fascinatingly uncharacteristic reading, in two tempos simultaneously with the rhythm pulled like taffy. Workman and Dawson do yeoman's service and Byard is a hero; his solos are full of unexpected delights and it is nearly as rewarding to follow his comping (echoes of Ellington and Monk), with splashed chords, punched notes, huge rolling tremolos, broken and rebuilt rhythm schemes. Two LPs of awesome performances on a single CD make for rare value.                          **AL**

## Ron Escheté                                                                      1948

**New review**
**Soft Winds**  Escheté (elg); **Todd Johnson** (elb); **Paul Humphrey** (d). Concord Ⓕ CCD4737
  (64 minutes). Recorded 1996.

⑧  ⑨

Those who bought Ron Escheté's last trio record, **Rain or Shine**, hoping to find more of the hot, bluesy playing he brought to Gene Harris's many Concord recordings might have been disappointed by its preoccupation with low key chord-melody solos. This rather more vigorous programme fits the bill better, and shows that the man who declined to tour with Harris because he preferred his home life has not gone soft. There are a few slow moments – the virtually catatonic *Because of You* and *But Beautiful* and a cosy *Sweet and Lovely* are perfect for swish hotel lobbies – but even slow, Harris can be earthy, as he shows on the creeping 12-bar *I-5 Blues*. On top form, as in a sprightly *Soft Winds*, he should impress the most discriminating mainstream guitar fan, and in his own *Rumpled Silk Skin*, after a routine start, he suggests an awareness of a more modern, even Scofieldian vernacular. Electric bassist Johnson has a better time of it too. While his ensemble work, including fluent chords as well as single lines, seems consistently impeccable, he was over-exposed without good reason as a soloist on **Rain or Shine**. Here, he takes the spotlight less often but far more effectively, developing an especially good solo on *Sleepwalk*.                                                               **MG**

# Ellery Eskelin                                                                              1959

**Forms**  Eskelin (ts); **Drew Gress** (b); **Phil Haynes** (d). Open Minds ℗ 2403 (62 minutes). Recorded 1990.

⑧ ❽

Eskelin's adventurous outlook separates him from the great majority of saxists of his generation. Unwilling to recycle the encyclopaedia of post-bop licks, he is working hard on an individual voice, exploring extreme chromaticism and unruly rhythmic accents within a still recognizable song form. It is an approach reminiscent of Sonny Rollins in his most open period. Although a gutsy, unfettered album of solo sax gave his sense of fantasy free rein, he works best with the support of long-time collaborators Gress and Haynes (together with trumpeter Paul Smoker, they have recorded as a co-operative band named Joint Venture). The bassist and drummer are remarkably attuned to the music's flow no matter where it goes, and are equally adept at subtle pressure to redirect the action. There is plenty of irony in this programme; the titles (*Blues*, *In Three*, *Ballad*, *Latin*) may be generic but the forms are deceptively re-cast and the playing has real personality. *Blues* shows off Eskelin's alternately melismatic and fragmented phrasing and a fountain of ideas, one after the next; Dizzy's *Bebop* features un-boppish phrasing and a free middle, while Ellington's *African Flower* receives a lean, fragrant reading (especially Haynes's hypnotic drumming). A good introduction to musicians worth watching in the future.                                                                          **AL**

# Ethnic Heritage Ensemble

**Ancestral Song**  Kahil El'Zabar (sansa, d, perc, v); **Joseph Bowie** (tb, mba, perc); **Edward Wilkerson** (cl, ts, perc). Silkheart ℗ 108 (63 minutes). Recorded 1987.

⑧ ❽

A second-wave AACM group, the Ethnic Heritage Ensemble has since the mid seventies reflected the purer strains of African influence on jazz. Led from its inception by the talented multi-percussionist Kahil El'Zabar, the trio's evocative instrumentation and open, flowing compositions allow them to explore the relationship between the folk sources of African music and those of American urban experience. A good example of this is *Loose Pocket*, which begins with Wilkerson's bluesy tenor inflections and an El'Zabar vocal; when the percussionist shifts to the drum set the laid-back theme becomes a hard-bop riff and Bowie's trombone rips off a hot solo. El'Zabar is an excellent conga player as well as trap drummer, but the focus here is the sansa (or mbira, an African thumb piano). Its buzzing, bell-like sonorities introduce and unify the various phrases which serve as loose thematic structures. Bowie, who is also leader of the avant-funk dance band Defunkt, has been a member since 1986; he adds percussion, including a moving marimba part to *Papa's Bounce*, to his trombone contributions. Reedman Wilkerson supplies most of the fireworks. A formidable tenor saxist with a narrative style, his playing throughout is notable for its slippery tonal manoeuvres and melodic ingenuity. Wilkerson's own groups, 8 Bold Souls and Shadow Vignettes, are also recommended.                                                                           **AL**

# Kevin Eubanks                                                                              1957

**Spirit Talk**  Eubanks (g, elg); **Robin Eubanks** (tb); **Kent Jordan** (f); **Dave Holland** (b); **Marvin 'Smitty' Smith** (d, perc, v); **Mark Mondesir** (d). Blue Note ℗ CDP7 89286-2 (53 minutes). Recorded 1993.

⑦ ❽

Eubanks's musical career began with rock; he recorded in Europe with Chris Hinze but in the early eighties found himself comfortable in the jazz company of men such as Ronnie Matthews, Sam Rivers, Chico Freeman and Wynton Marsalis. More recently he has been involved in several M-Base sessions, although he is guarded about any permanent commitment to them. His 1991 **Turning Point** (Blue Note CDP7 98170-2) marked his début as a leader of a pure jazz date and seemed to shut the door on the fuzak gloss of his distant past. This fine CD enlarges on that project and uses the accomplished trombone of brother Robin on five titles. Despite the use made of the horns, it is Kevin Eubanks who dominates. His ease of execution, his relaxed rhythmic application and his ability to construct coherent solos is demonstrated throughout. On the acoustic instrument he allows himself a degree of romanticism, but if his electric guitar is marginally more dramatic, there is no real diversity of style. Sparing use is made of multi-tracking but most of the best musical conversations that take place are between guitar and trombone on *Union* or guitar and flute on *Going Outside*. If anything, Kevin Eubanks sounds more comfortable in a pure jazz setting and in the company of long-term working colleague Holland.                                                 **BMcR**

# Robin Eubanks

**Karma**  Eubanks (tb, etb, rap); **Earl Gardner** (t); **Greg Osby** (as); **Kevln Eubanks** (elg); **Renee Rosnes**, **Kenny Werner** (kbds); **Lonnie Plaxico** (elb); **Marvin 'Smitty' Smith** (d); **Kimson Albert** (rap); **Mino Cinelu** (perc); **Dave Holland** (b); **Branford Marsalis** (ts); **Cassandra Wilson** (v). JMT Ⓕ 834 446-2 (63 minutes). Recorded 1990.

⑦ ⑧

An important aspect of the M-Base ethic of the eighties was its promotion of rap. Eubanks, a man of instrumental experience with Sun Ra, McCoy Tyner's Big Band, Abdullah Ibrahim and Geri Allen as well as Patti LaBelle and Talking Heads, was one of the best M-Base rappers. As this CD shows, his rap oratory swings, but also reminds the listener that while bad rap is self-indulgent space-filling, a piece such as *Karma* is poetic and meaningful. Eubanks is also an outstanding trombone player who has moved some distance from the clean-lined articulation of the bop masters. His vocalized tone has a throat-clearing quality that adds depth to his playing and his solos move from the rich legato ease of *Maybe Next Time* to the busy declamatory rebuilding of Monk's *Evidence* or his own *Pentacourse*. His natural flair for shapely improvisation is matched by his good taste as a composer and he is a frequent guest on the recording dates of his M-Base colleagues.                                    **BMcR**

# Bill Evans

**At the Village Vanguard**  Evans (p); **Scott LaFaro** (b); **Paul Motian** (d). Riverside Ⓜ FCD60017 (65 minutes). Recorded 1961.

✓                                                                                          ⑩ ⑩

This CD contains nearly all the material originally released on two separate LPs, **Sunday at the Village Vanguard** and **Waltz for Debby**. In addition to this, alternative takes of the same songs have been released on later compilations. To my ears, this composite CD is still better value for money than buying the CD equivalents (also currently available, with alternative takes added) of those two original releases.

For many people, the Evans trio with LaFaro and Motian reached a peak which the pianist never scaled again. The reason why this may be the case is a simple one: this trio has all the freshness and intensity of youth – there is a palpable delight in discovery going on all the time here, shared between the three players. Whatever the later Evans oufits had, that freshness had gone. Perhaps it went with the death of LaFaro. Perhaps something else happened. Luckily for us, these recordings catch the trio at their best. The dialogue between the three players is extraordinary, the depth of interpretation always surprising, no matter how many times you play these selections. Evans is famed for his harmonic sophistication and LaFaro for his virtuosity, but what impresses most from all three men here is their ability to make their instruments truly *sing*. Any track will show this, but *All of You* perhaps best of all.                                                              **KS**

**Conversations With Myself**  Evans (multi-tracked p). Verve Ⓜ 821 984-2 (44 minutes). Recorded 1963.

✓                                                                                          ⑧ ⑥

Strange that the two most convincing early examples of overdubbing in jazz should have been started in the same month. Unlike its serendipitous use in Mingus's **Black Saint and the Sinner Lady**, it was clearly integral to the conception of this Evans album produced by Creed Taylor. Two tracks tucked away at the end of the original album seem to represent an early phase of the project, before the problem of getting the parallel piano tracks absolutely in tune was solved, but they include the desolate modal improvisation *N.Y.C.'s No Lark* (dedicated to the late Sonny Clark, of whose name the title is an anagram) and are now followed by two bonus items.

Both pianist and producer worked hard to achieve an orchestral texture in which the 'lead' piano sounds are mixed up-front while the more accompanimental parts are suitably backgrounded. Some of the tinkly bits seem in retrospect to be errors of judgement but, rather than being oppressive, on the whole the combination of up to three keyboard tracks enhances both the material and what Evans does with it. This is certainly superior to his later overdubbed albums and, although ultimately less typical than his trio or even solo work, **Conversations** is essential Evans.                                                                         **BP**

**Empathy/A Simple Matter of Conviction**  Evans (p); **Monty Budwig, Eddie Gomez** (b); **Shelly Manne** (d). Verve Ⓜ 837 757-2 (73 minutes). Recorded 1962/6.

⑧ ⑧

Manne built his early reputation as a powerful big-band drummer (Kenton, Herman, Shorty Rogers) but after taking up residence in California his true value as an imaginative, sensitive painter of rhythmic sounds in small groups emerged. He was particularly adept at working with pianists (notably Russ Freeman and André Previn), and the two LPs he did with Bill Evans can only make the listener wish they had made more records together. Both LPs are combined here, a feast of sensitive playing by two masters of their instruments. The first date produced half a dozen standards (although one would be hard-pressed to find any other version of Berlin's *The*

*Washington Twist* or *Let's Go Back to the Waltz*) and **Empathy** is certainly a most apt title. The way Manne and Evans interlock on *With a Song in My Heart* is nothing short of brilliant (coincidentally Manne made a fine duet version of this same tune with Russ Freeman) but the clever 'stop-start' approach to Frank Loesser's *I Believe in You* is the highlight in a consistently fine programme. The second session was actually the first time Evans and Gomez had recorded together, but the magic is repeated. No other drummer Evans recorded with had such an acute appreciation of the variety of sounds capable of being produced from his kit, and this obviously inspired the pianist. The clear recording balance allows us to hear all the subtle nuances of the music-making.                                                                                            **AM**

---

**Bill Evans at Town Hall, Volume 1** Evans (p); **Chuck Israels** (b); **Arnold Wise** (d). Verve Ⓜ 831
   271-2 (53 minutes). Recorded 1966.

✅                                                                                                       ⑧ ❽

At the centre of this absorbing concert is the unaccompanied 13-minute tribute Evans dedicated to the memory of his father who had died two weeks before the date of the concert. In keeping with the cerebral nature of much of Evans's playing, this is not overtly emotional, but its compositional depth repays repeated listening. The central section of the piece is built around two song themes, but they are almost irrelevant in the tissue of finely crafted lines that Evans runs together into his solo. In the piece, the boundaries between improvisation and composition become blurred, and the listener is caught up in Evans's ever-deeper dissection of his ideas. In sharp contrast, the rest of the concert is stimulating ensemble playing, containing some of Chuck Israels's best work, less brittle than LaFaro, who had preceded him, and less technically perfect than Gomez, who was to follow. The trio romps through a mixture of Broadway show tunes and standards, the CD carrying three tracks in addition to the original LP release, one of which is the previously unreleased tribute to his manager Helen Keane, Evans's own *for Helen*. In an original note to part of this session, Leonard Feather wrote of Evans's "almost mystical ability for drawing even more out of a song than the composer put into it". This album is the perfect exemplar of that observation. A point of clarification: Volume 2 (presumably meant to be the Evans Trio with Orchestra which made up the other half of the concert) has never been issued.                                                                                       **AS**

---

New review
**But Beautiful** Evans (p); **Stan Getz** (ts); **Eddie Gomez** (b); **Marty Morell** (d). Milestone
   Ⓜ MCD9249-2 (70 minutes). Recorded 1974.

                                                                                                        ⑩ ❽

The bulk of this music appeared, unauthorized and briefly, on Jazz Door a few years ago, but this is the definitive edition. It consists of eight numbers with Getz and two by the trio alone, recorded live in Holland and Belgium for broadcasts by Dutch and Belgian radio. The results are superb. They more than make up for the studio session ten years before which turned out to be a complete disaster. The rapport between Getz and Evans is quite amazing, even though one number has virtually no piano on it because Stan changed the programme without telling Bill and he went on strike. If you want to hear what perfect saxophone control sounds like, listen to the long unaccompanied introduction to *You and the Night and the Music*, and for a demonstration of perfect, smooth swing, listen to the way the trio picks up the tempo afterwards. As for *But Beautiful* itself, rarely can either Getz or Evans have played with greater delicacy of feeling. This is an important addition to the discographies of both artists.                                                                                    **DG**

# Bill Evans                                                                              1958

---

**Push** Evans (ss, as, ts, kbds); **Keith O'Quinn, Conrad Herwig, Gary Smulyan, Barry Bryson, Dave
   Stahl, Michael Davis, Chris Botti** (brass); **Chuck Loeb, Jeff Golub, Nick Moroch, Max
   Risenhoover** (g); **Clifford Carter, Bruce Hornsby, Philippe Saisse, Bob James, Chris Ming
   Doky, Victor Bailey, Marcus Miller, Mark Egan** (b); **Billy Ward** (d); **Evans, Clifford Carter, Max
   Risenhoover, K.C. Flight, Jimmy Bralower, Michael Colina** (programming). Lipstick
   Ⓟ LIP89022-2 (61 minutes). Recorded 1993.

                                                                                                        ⑥ ❽

While never quite matching the expressive range and harmonic sophistication of such other post-1980 Miles Davis reedmen as Bob Berg, Gary Thomas and Kenny Garrett, Bill Evans did make a number of striking contributions to Miles's late bands, among them several memorably fine solos on **We Want Miles.** There followed a couple of patchily successful fusion dates recorded live in Japan, but it was not until 1993, and **Push**, that his early promise was realized.

   In the fashion of the day, **Push** has Evans teamed up with an assortment of acid jazz, rap, hip-hop and techno specialists. The album was studio-produced, which allowed for close attention to detailed arrangement, and it is in large part this aspect which occasions the record's success. The clarity of the sound and the imaginative and precise interplay between synths, variously toned electric guitars and horns on the Sanborn-ish *Road to Ruin*, for example, is more significant than the melodic or harmonic content of the tune. Having said that, the more focused setting does draw out the best of Bill Evans, as his feverish soprano on *London House* illustrates.                                                                **MG**

# Ceri Evans

**Hidden Treasure** Evans (p); **Gerard Presencer** (t); **Tim Garland** (ts, ss); **John Miles** (ts); **Arnie Somogyi** (b); **Tristan Maillot** (d). Big Life Jazz Ⓕ BLJCD001 (66 minutes). Recorded 1995.

⑥ ⑧

Evans is a keyboardist, arranger and pop record producer whose reputation was earned with the Brand New Heavies, a band who, despite the name, achieved some expertise in re-creating the sub-funk soul-jazz that emerged 25 years ago. Now, for reasons which are presumably motivated by personal taste, he has branched out into old-fashioned post-bop featuring acoustic piano. His original material conjures up images of Thelonious Monk and various Art Blakey groups, while his own playing often recalls McCoy Tyner. While none of the compositions has the instant down-market memorability of his earlier work, they have a well-defined melodic streak as well as harmonic and rhythmic subtlety to spare. The performance of his studio colleagues – particularly Presencer and Garland – is crucial in the success of this album. Certainly, if Evans decides to continue on this path, it will be interesting to see where his muse leads him. **BP**

# Gil Evans
1912-88

**Gil Evans and Ten** Evans (p, arr); **Louis Mucci, Jake Koven, John Carisi** (t); **Jimmy Cleveland** (tb); **Willie Ruff** (frh); **Bart Varsalona** (btb); **Steve Lacy** (ss); **Lee Konitz** (as); **Dave Kurtzer** (bs); **Paul Chambers** (b); **Nick Stabulas, Jo Jones** (d). Prestige Ⓜ OJCCD346-2 (33 minutes). Recorded 1957.

⑩ ⑧

Evans already had close on two decades in the music business under his belt when he came to make this, his first album as a leader, just four months after completing the sessions on his first album in collaboration with Miles Davis, **Miles Ahead** (the **Birth of the Cool** sessions were never conceived as an album, and Evans, while still the guiding spirit, was only one of a number of arrangers there). This record has its own character, quite distinct from **Miles Ahead**, and Evans makes judicious use of a number of soloists, himself included, with Steve Lacy and Jimmy Cleveland being the most persuasive in that role. The man Gerry Mulligan termed Svengali chose here a diverse set of tunes and gave them all the gift of his unique soundscapes. With Evans, at least in this phase of his career, it is always the choice of instruments balanced off against each other, and the inner voicings of the harmonic paths they follow, which gives the music its often startling identity. His added ability to home in on the part of a tune which will give the most dramatic re-working of its essence is starkly etched on *Just One of Those Things*, taken at a moderately brisk tempo, where the melody is virtually ignored throughout. It is the descending chords behind the theme which attract Evans, and he brings them to the fore. In jazz, only Ellington had a comparable orchestral imagination and love of subtle sonorities. **KS**

**Out of the Cool** Evans (p, arr, cond); **Johnny Coles, Phil Sunkel** (t); **Jimmy Knepper, Keg Johnson, Tony Studd** (tb); **Bill Barber** (tba); **Ray Beckenstein, Eddie Caine, Budd Johnson, Bob Tricarico** (reeds); **Ray Crawford** (g); **Ron Carter** (b); **Charlie Persip, Elvin Jones** (d, perc). Impulse! Ⓜ IMP 11862 (38 minutes). Recorded 1960.

✪ ⑩ ⑧

Evans believed in giving as much creative freedom as was practical to his musicians, and as a consequence the quality of his work depended to some extent on the quality of his soloists. Recorded at a time when he was working for another company with Miles Davis, he was well served by the men on this session. Like Ellington, Evans often reworked chunks of previous composition. *La Nevada*, which runs for 15 minutes, is a simple four-bar theme which Evans had used before. Its use for the development of a string of solos makes it a text book for arrangers as Evans places the soloists under pressure at certain points and raises and then relaxes tension. Some of the filigree figures scored (for example for bassoon) behind the soloists are supreme examples of the orchestrator's art. At the time Evans used Coles as a Davis clone with enormous success. Bewildered at first when Evans gave him no direction as to how to play his feature role on *Sunken Treasure*, Coles nevertheless produced a classic improvisation – one could not sense that he was at the outer limits of his perception of Evans's music and was shortly to give it up. In Knepper Evans had the services of the most creative trombonist of the time; his poised and eloquent variations on *Where Flamingos Fly* make this one of the most outstanding statements on the instrument. In a decided improvement over the slipshod reissue noted in the previous guide, this latest Impulse! reinvention not only includes the extra track from this session, Horace Silver's composition *Sister Sadie*, which first saw the light of day on a mid-seventies vinyl reissue of this music, but reproduces the original LP notes in a legible size and format. **SV**

**The Individualism of Gil Evans** Evans (p, arr, cond); **Johnny Coles, Thad Jones** (t); **Jimmy Cleveland** (tb); **Al Block** (f); **Phil Woods** (as); **Wayne Shorter** (ts); **Kenny Burrell** (g); **Paul Chambers, Richard Davis, Milt Hinton** (b); **Elvin Jones, Osie Johnson** (d). Verve Ⓜ 833 804-2 (68 minutes). Recorded 1964.

✪ ⑩ ⑧

Nowhere else, not even in the music he wrote and conducted for Miles Davis, does the genius of Gil Evans come over more strongly than it does on this disc. Like Duke Ellington, he created a unique and instantly recognizable sound from an orchestra and could write parts for soloists with such understanding of their style that it is often impossible to tell where the written part ends and the improvisation begins. That is the case here with his reworking of Kurt Weill's *Barbara Song*, in which Wayne Shorter's tenor saxophone gradually emerges from a kind of orchestral mist, delivers a meditative solo and sinks back again. Throughout the piece the instrumental textures change like cloud formations, slowly altering their patterns of light and shade. His mastery of orchestration was astounding: like Debussy, he could voice a phrase for piccolo and tuba in such a way that you are convinced you can hear the ghostly harmonies between. At the same time his music is full of rhythmic energy. Harmonically, *Las Vegas Tango* shimmers like a desert mirage but it is lifted and kept airborne by the drumming of Elvin Jones, doing exactly what he always did for John Coltrane.

This CD release is virtually twice as long as the original vinyl issue, with five previously unissued pieces included, some of them in newly restored mixes and removing previous edits, all of which work was done expertly and under the supervision of Evans himself. **DG**

**Svengali** Evans (p, elp, arr); **Tex Allan**, **Marvin Peterson**, **Richard Williams** (t); **Sharon Freeman**, **Peter Levin** (frh); **Joseph Daley** (tb, tba); **Howard Johnson** (tba, flh, bs); **Dave Sanborn** (as); **Billy Harper** (ts, f); **Trevor Koehler** (ss, bs, f); **David Horowitz** (syn); **Ted Dunbar** (g); **Herb Bushler** (elb); **Bruce Ditmas** (d); **Susan Evans** (perc). ACT Ⓜ 9207-2 (41 minutes). Recorded 1973.

⑧ ➑

When Evans began leading a live band, which he had seldom done before the seventies, the distillation of textures and careful plotting of structure was substantially loosened. Fortunately, he used creative players who, rather than splitting the seams of his scores, on the whole enhanced his original conception. The above album, recorded live at two concerts but with little audience noise, shows the process at work. For instance *Zee Zee*, perhaps the simplest composition of the lot, becomes a soaring improvisation by Peterson, but probably neither would stand up without the other. The same applies to *Cry of Hunger*, written by and featuring Harper, which is not only arranged by Evans but reorganized by him at the editing stage, as the new liner note by Howard Johnson points out.

The other four pieces are remakes in one way or another. Both Gershwin's *Summertime* and Evans's *Eleven* (a.k.a. *Petits Machins*) distantly resemble the versions arranged by Gil for Miles Davis, but turning them over to Dunbar and Williams respectively makes them very different, and the backgrounds are changed accordingly. Harper's *Thoroughbred* and George Russell's *Blues in Orbit* are closer to the Evans recordings of a couple of years earlier (reissued on Enja 3069-2), but these versions have a sharper edge. **BP**

# Don Ewell
1916-83

**New review**

**Man Here Plays Fine Piano** Ewell (p); **Darnell Howard** (cl); **Pops Foster** (b); **Minor Hall** (d). Good Time Jazz Ⓜ GTJCD100043-2 (40 minutes). Recorded 1957.

⑦ ➑

Mild, bespectacled Don Ewell from Baltimore looked more like a bank clerk than a stride pianist, but behind his meek manner was a musical tiger, a scholar of the works of Jelly Roll Morton and Fats Waller and creator of his own virile brand of stride piano. His solo on *Blue Turning Grey Over You* takes Waller's original and pushes out the boundaries of phrasing and harmony, just as his own *Frisco Rider,* with its chromatically descending second strain, extends the line of compositional thought begun by James P. Johnson and Eubie Blake. Fascinating as the solo tracks are, the quartet tracks are more of an acquired taste. Ewell co-opted fellow sidemen from Kid Ory's band, so the rhythm has the stark four-square feel of Ory's revivalist groups with no trombone to break it up. Nevertheless Foster swings hard within his own limits, moving the beat around in *Everybody Loves My Baby*. The idiosyncratic star is clarinettist Howard, no longer the innocuous sideman he had once been with King Oliver and Earl Hines, but a player with a tone as wide as Bechet's, prone to wild, higher register swirls and throbbing chalumeau melodies, like his own *Green Swamp* or Morton's *My Home is in a Southern Town*. The miserly playing time is the result of the direct transfer of an original LP to CD with no bonus material, and it might have been a better policy to conjoin this with Ewell's other GTJ session from the same period as a single issue by a pianist who deserves more recognition. **AS**

# Jon Faddis
1953

**Legacy** Faddis (t); **Harold Land** (ts); **Kenny Barron** (p); **Ray Brown** (b); **Mel Lewis** (d). Concord Ⓕ CCD4291-2 (42 minutes). Recorded 1985.

⑧ ➑

Trumpeter Jon Faddis was a precocious 18-year-old 'young lion' when he moved to New York from his hometown of Oakland, California, to join Lionel Hampton's band in New York City in 1971. Once in the Big Apple, his powerful high-register, keen reading skills and Gillespie-derived solo style led to important tenures with the Thad Jones-Mel Lewis Orchestra, Gil Evans and Charles Mingus. Faddis's most significant association, though, was with Gillespie himself. Indeed, Gillespie included his virtuosic protégé in any number of concert, club and recording engagements.

On this sterling 1985 date, Faddis deploys his clarion sound, stratospheric probes and fleet technique in heartfelt salutes to some of the greats of jazz's trumpet 'legacy'. On *West End Blues* we sense the presence of Louis Armstrong, whereas on *Little Jazz* it is Roy Eldridge who 'appears'. With *A Child is Born*, Faddis pays poignant tribute to former colleague Thad Jones. For *Night in Tunisia* and *Things to Come*, Faddis honours mentor Dizzy Gillespie with dazzingly boppish flights. Throughout, Faddis is ably supported by the superb rhythmic team of Kenny Barron, Ray Brown and Mel Lewis, while Harold Land's smouldering tenor provides an apt front-line foil on lines such as *Li'l Darlin'* and *Whisper Not*. In the booklet-notes, Dizzy Gillespie writes that "this new album of Jon's is terrifying!" Amen! **CB**

## Don Fagerquist
1927-74

**Eight By Eight**  Fagerquist, **Ed Leddy** (t); **Bob Enevoldsen** (vtb); **Vince DeRosa** (frh); **Herb Geller** (as); **Ronnie Lang** (bs); **Marty Paich** (p); **Buddy Clark** (b); **Mel Lewis** (d). VSOP Ⓕ #4CD (34 minutes). Recorded 1957.

⑧ ❽

This is an example of West Coast jazz at its best. All its finest qualities – technical skill, lyricism and passionate improvising – are here in abundance. Fagerquist's playing, although here in a small 34 minute bottle, is amongst the finest of jazz wines, and this collection of ballads and standards is the noblest part of his legacy, for although he was much in demand as a sideman, notably with Les Brown, he recorded shamefully little in relation to the size of his talent. His work is essentially mellow, reminding one very much of Clifford Brown without the fireworks. The eminent West Coast personality Marty Paich was responsible for all the arrangements; consequently they are stamped with his seal of excellence. His piano soloing and accompanying is both fiery and immaculate.

Herb Geller, here not far behind Art Pepper, is a potent alto soloist who works predictably well as a foil to the trumpet, whilst Enevoldsen is a consistently inspired and original voice on valve trombone. An elementary finger calculation reveals that the album should be titled **Eight By Nine**. **SV**

## Peter Fairclough
1956

New review
**Wild Silk**  Fairclough (d, perc); **Keith Tippett** (p, plastic pp, z). ASC Records Ⓕ ASCCD8 (56 minutes). Recorded 1995.

⑥ ❽

A graduate of Leeds College of Music in 1981, Fairclough has since been a prominent figure on the Bristol jazz scene. He has occupied the demanding drum chair in the Mike Westbrook Orchestra since 1986 and has demonstrated his flexible and astylistic approach to percussion by freelancing with the diverse talents of Kenny Davern, Don Weller, Billy Jenkins and Steve Berry's Foolish Hearts. His compositional talents on **Shepherd Wheel** (ASCCD1) were much acclaimed, but as an opportunity to assess his varied percussion skills this CD is ideal. There was no rehearsal and the first sound on the album is the first thing they played. Fairclough makes no attempt to 'play tunes' and, by comparing title with performance, the listener is taken into his descriptive world. *The Woodstone Bird* evokes the mood of the forest, *Humble* adopts a Uriah Heep-like gait, while *Recurring Dream* is described by insistent riff figures. *Casting the Net* perhaps tries too hard to capture the turmoil of life on a fishing smack but *Through the Gate* has overtones of cattle counting and *Under Thunder* earns an obvious response.

As a tasteful musical exercise, it is strangely efficacious and, although the success of descriptive music finally rests with the listener, the musical imagery here invites the listener's imagination. **BMcR**

## Richard Fairhurst

New review
**The Hungry Ants**  Fairhurst (p); **Iain Ballamy, Osian Roberts** (ss, ts), **Steve Watts** (b); **Tim Giles** (d). Babel Ⓕ BDV9504 (50 minutes). Recorded 1995.

⑥ ❼

Fairhurst is an impressive new pianist on the British scene who has made an impact so early in his career that he looks set to become a very considerable presence. On this album he is joined by two teenage contemporaries, Giles and Roberts, as well as two hoary veterans half a generation older, but until recently identified as young turks themselves, Ballamy and Watts. All the tracks on the disc are saxophone-plus-piano-trio quartets, Ballamy and Roberts sharing the solo duties between them. Almost all the playing is of a high order, Ballamy's originality, as ever, standing out. The weak link at present is the writing. A high proportion of the pieces are by Fairhurst and they are lacking in variety, but suggest an original compositional imagination is developing which may now advance rapidly on the strength of Fairhurst's subsequent studies in the USA. The quartet comes into its own on Mingus's *Self-Portrait in 3 Colours*, where Roberts asserts himself on saxophone and, given a substantial composition to get to work on, so do his colleagues. **AS**

## Maffy Falay                                                                    1930

New review

**Hank's Tune**  Falay (t); **Elvan Araqci** (tb); **Bernt Rosengren** (ts); **Åke Johansson** (p); **Per-Ola Gadd** (b); **Ronnie Gardiner** (d). Liphone Ⓕ LiCD3157 (55 minutes). Recorded 1993.

⑥ ❼

By now well-stricken in years, Maffy Falay is a Turk who settled in Sweden in 1965. He is a veteran of bands led there by Quincy Jones, Harry Arnold and the Swedish Radio Jazz Group. He also worked with Gillespie and George Russell. His rather pungent trumpet is much in the style of fifties bop and the opening *Hank's Tune*, written by Hank Mobley for Silver's quintet, is symptomatic of the music which is to be found here. Going back to Lars Gullin (with whom Mafay worked over a 16-year period) and Åke Persson, there is a tradition of gifted bebop musicians in Sweden (they headed to Europe for many years during the fifties and sixties) and Falay and his associates here are very fine examples of it. Trombonist Elvan Araqci (a much younger Turk) is an energetic trombonist and Bernt Rosengren a convincing tenor soloist. Johansson is another of the accomplished Swedish pianists. You won't find many innovations here but there is plenty of strenuous hard-bop blowing. Those who like the idiom won't find this music dated. **SV**

## Charles Famborough

New review

**Keeper of the Spirit**  Famborough (bs); **John Swana** (t, EWI); **Grover Washington Jr** (ss); **Joel Levine** (ss, as); **Ralph Bowen** (ts, ss, f); **Art Webb** (f); **Edward Simon** (p); **Adam Holzman**, **Jason Shatill** (kbds); **Lenny White** (d); **Marlon Simon**, **Joe Gonzalez** (perc). AudioQuest Ⓕ AQ 1033 (54 minutes). Recorded 1994.

⑤ ❽

Famborough came up in the version of Art Blakey's Jazz Messengers which had Marsalis brothers the way other people have mice. He was Blakey's right-hand man and might therefore have been expected to have Blakey's philosophy of the jazz bludgeon. Not a bit of it, for Famborough is all things to all men, with the bulk of this album consisting of gentle and poignant themes which he has composed himself and only the occasional tip of the hat, notably via the excellent tenor saxophone of Ralph Bowen on *Descarga*, to the less genteel side of life. Bowen also plays good flute in a front line usually comprising flute, soprano sax or recorder. Swana's EWI is a new horror, a kind of electrified trumpet, but let's pass by it quickly. Washington is good at urbane soprano, but the best jazz soloist here is undoubtedly pianist Edward Simon. It would have been better if Famborough had stuck to the Blakey line and left the soggy feel of funk and disco to others. **SV**

## Georgie Fame                                                                  1943

New review

**The Two Faces of Fame**  Fame (v, org, g); **Eddie Thornton**, **Greg Bowen**, **Derek Watkins**, **Ian Hamer**, **Kenny Wheeler**, **Les Condon** (t); **Derek Wadsworth**, **Keith Christie**, **Johnny Marshall**, **Chris Smith**, **Gib Wallace** (tb); **Alan Branscombe** (as); **Tubby Hayes** (as, ts); **Ronnie Scott**, **Dick Morrissey**, **Lynn Dobson** (ts); **Harry Klein**, **Johnny Marshall** (bs); **Gordon Beck** (p); **Rik Brown**, **Phil Bates**, **Jeff Clyne** (b); **Hughie Flint**, **Bill Eyden**, **Tony Oxley** (d); **Harry South** (arr). Columbia Rewind Ⓜ 477850-2 (40 minutes). Recorded 1967.

⑧ ❽

This was the record, after **Rhythm & Blues from the Marquee**, that every dedicated Fame fan absolutely had to possess. When the rest of the world was floating about enveloped in psychedelia, kaftans and bells, Georgie constituted a one-man resistance movement. And now, 30 years later, the music that he was playing and singing then still sounds good. In fact, he is still doing virtually the same thing today – and thriving on it. He has a genuine style of his own, not just a collection of mannerisms, and he is comfortable with it. The live concert at the Royal Festival Hall which makes up the bulk of this programme was something of a milestone in his career. It proved, to himself as much as to the public, that he could work effectively over a broad expanse of jazz. It also showed that he had impeccable taste in his choice of musicians and collaborators. The personnel of the Harry South Big Band is quite amazing – Ronnie Scott, Tubby Hayes and Dick Morrissey, all in the same saxophone section, not to mention the trumpets! Even though its playing time is short, this is certainly one to have. **DG**

# Tal Farlow
1921

**A Sign of the Times** Farlow (g); **Hank Jones** (p); **Ray Brown** (b). Concord Ⓕ CCD4026 (40 minutes). Recorded 1977.

⑥ ❽

Tal Farlow emerged in the late forties to deify guitar technique, bebop and otherwise, and his digital dexterity earned him the nickname 'The Octopus'. In the late fifties, after a few busy years, he withdrew from full-time performance and worked as a signwriter, but he returned in the mid seventies, and this recording was evidence of that renascence. By then, the years had perhaps taken their toll on the celebrated technique, since his timing is often wayward, his articulation imprecise. However, the guitaristic tricks remain intact. Most of these are commonplace now, and outnumbered by the catalogue of electric guitar techniques that grew from rock, but his production of a bongo drum effect on the damped strings of the guitar – heard here on *Stompin' at the Savoy* – is still intriguing. More routine is his skilful use of harmonics on *You Don't Know What Love Is* and often stuttering bebop fluency. The programme is mostly standards, but several are imaginatively arranged: *You Don't Know What Love Is* is the most striking, opening with a lugubrious two-bar ostinato divided into alternating bars of 5/8 and 3/8. It is completely out of character with the rest of the tune, which swings in a conventional way, but it adds welcome drama to an otherwise rather bland set. The modest playing time reflects the recording's analogue origins. **MG**

# Art Farmer
1928

**Portrait of Art Farmer** Farmer (t); **Hank Jones** (p); **Addison Farmer** (b); **Roy Haynes** (d). Contemporary Ⓜ OJCCD166-2 (42 minutes). Recorded 1958.

✔

⑩ ❽

Despite a commendably consistent and high-level career (or perhaps because of it), Farmer has always been underrated. By the time of this album he had worked for Lionel Hampton and Horace Silver and was currently with Gerry Mulligan, as seen in *Jazz on a Summer's Day*. Possessing an individual tone and a manner often compared to early Miles, his choice of notes was markedly different even by the time of his first major recordings with Wardell Gray.

This is one of the great quartet albums irrespective of artist and, like Farmer's later **Sing Me Softly of the Blues** (which has sadly yet to be reissued on CD), it is highly representative of the trumpeter's work during the period in question. Everyone plays at the top of their game, with a puckish but sensitive Jones contrasting pleasantly with the ebullient Haynes, who was on the point of joining Thelonious Monk. The session includes a couple of ballads that are gentler than Miles's (and more interesting than anything by Chet Baker), alongside more challenging material by George Russell and Benny Golson. Blues and rhythm changes are attacked without pre-set themes and, from the opening *a cappella* Farmer solo, here is an album to treasure. **BP**

**Live at the Half Note** Farmer (flh); **Jim Hall** (g); **Steve Swallow** (b); **Walter Perkins** (d). Atlantic Jazz Ⓜ 790666-2 (38 minutes). Recorded 1963.

⑧ ❼

Farmer is one of those players beloved of other musicians and of critics for his impeccable musicianship, taste and invention, but never fully appreciated by the wider world because his music is unspectacular, almost diffident, to the casual listener. First heard from in the late forties, by the time of this recording Farmer had fully mastered every aspect of his art. The Jazztet, an excellent group he co-led with Benny Golson, was in the recent past, and his band with Jim Hall is currently one of the most intriguing in modern jazz. The live context here allows all four musicians to stretch out, and they respond enthusiastically. Hall, sometimes a rather remote player, sounds fully engaged with the rest of the group and comes up with some stupendous ideas, both while soloing and while backing Farmer. The flügelhornist delivers well-constructed solos, playing with great warmth and enthusiasm (his solo on the up-tempo *Swing Sping* must be one of his most spirited), and in this he also receives superb backing from Swallow and Perkins. A memorable engagement at the Half Note, then. **KS**

New review
**The Meaning of Art** Farmer (t, flh); **Slide Hampton** (tb); **Ron Blake** (ts, ss); **Geoff Keezer** (p); **Kenny Davis** (b); **Carl Allen** (d). Arabesque Recordings Ⓕ AJO118 (50 minutes). Recorded 1995.

⑧ ❽

Farmer has all the technical attributes of a great trumpeter, to which he adds unfailing good taste and imagination. Keezer, one of the best of the younger pianists, has become the older man's constant musical companion and Farmer's last few albums have been very potent as a result. On this one the partnership is diluted by the presence of lesser beings in the form of Hampton, a fine trombonist, arranger and composer but not a brass man of Farmer's class, and the intelligent but rather prosaic Ron Blake. Like Farmer, Hampton lives in Europe and the two men work together there often.

Ballads are the trumpeter's *forte* and a lovely *Just the Way You Look Tonight* is transcended by a ravishing performance of Benny Golson's *One Day Forever*. The former has a generously melodic solo from Keezer, who has voiced his own rather sombre *Free Verse* to give it a most unusual ensemble sound. Hampton demonstrates some fleet trombone tonguing on his composition *Lift Your Spirits High*, but once again it is the fast valve work of Farmer which impresses most. **SV**

## Allen Farnham

New review

**At Maybeck** Farnham (p). Concord Ⓕ CCD4686 (63 minutes). Recorded 1994.

⑧ ❽

As Thelonious Monk proved, you don't have to be a virtuoso in the usual sense to survive an unaccompanied piano recital. It helps, though, and Allen Farnham's comprehensive pianistic technique is such that he rarely seems to strain during this, the forty-first Maybeck issue. He comes up with various devices to keep the beat going, including a walking bass on part of *I Hear a Rhapsody* and some boogie on the blues, but is equally effective when just improvising and letting the beat take care of itself. Now in his mid-thirties, Farnham doesn't have a high profile, probably because the public has yet to identify him with any group of musicians. By including *Waltz for Debbie*, he underlines a leaning towards Bill Evans, a popular influence but one whose appealing lyricism can too readily be used as a substitute for anything else. While Farnham doesn't completely avoid this trap, he tends to hit the keys harder than Evans and cheerfully throws in Tatum-like flourishes and, as on *Lover*, the parallel runs associated with Phineas Newborn. **RA**

## Joe Farrell                                                                 1937-86

**Vim 'n' Vigour** Farrell (ts, ss, f); **Rob Van Den Broeck** (p); **Harry Emmery** (b); **Louis Hayes** (d). Timeless Ⓕ CDSJP197 (45 minutes). Recorded 1983.

⑧ ❽

Saxophonist/flautist Joe Farrell was one of the most accomplished and versatile players of the seventies and eighties. Although he had absorbed the basics of bebop, his fascination with the more melodic side of the modal approach of Miles Davis and John Coltrane led him to a distinctly lyrical yet steely style. Farrell also possessed a remarkable versatility that allowed him to productively mesh in settings as varied as the big bands of Maynard Ferguson and Thad Jones-Mel Lewis, the fusion of Chick Corea's original Return to Forever and the dynamic small group of drummer Elvin Jones. Farrell also achieved a degree of commercial success with a series of albums in the early seventies for CTI including **Outback** and **Moon Germs**.

Here, in a highly satisfying straight-ahead date recorded in Holland in 1983, Farrell's swinging modal approach soars. There is a throbbing tip-of-the-hat to Sonny Rollins, *Three Little Words*, in which Farrell's tenor skips in tandem with co-leader Louis Hayes's 'dialoguing' drums. There are impressive soprano forays, Farrell's serpentine *Arab Arab* and Coltrane's aptly tagged *Miles' Mode*. Farrell's fleet flute work is spotlighted on the Latin-inflected *Besame Mucho*. On the exuberant title track, his smoking tenor stamps out a dazzling set of modern blues choruses that jump with stylish modern jazz élan. **CB**

## Pierre Favre                                                               1937

**Singing Drums** Favre, **Paul Motian**, **Fredy Studer** (d, perc); **Nana Vasconcelos** (perc, v). ECM Ⓕ 823 639-2 (42 minutes). Recorded 1984.

⑧ ❽

Wholly self-taught, Swiss drummer and percussionist Favre has drawn together each of his successive influences into a non-idiomatic, almost contemporary classical style which is entirely his own. Initially going down the mainstream path alongside the likes of Philly Joe Jones and Bud Powell, in the mid sixties Favre went on to join all the European noisemakers busy offering their own version of urban America's New Thing: Evan Parker, Peter Brötzmann, Irene Schweizer and Manfred Schoof and so on (especially of note: Favre's contribution to the latter's seminal, blistering **European Echoes**). But where other European free-jazz drummers, most remarkably Han Bennink, have continued to explore the endless possibilities offered by (and the endless problems encountered in) spontaneous music-making, Favre has instead looked to non-Western cultures for inspiration. Mastering a myriad of esoteric instruments, he allows tuned gongs, bowed cymbals and crotales to get a look in on *Singing Drums*, his 1984 paean to the joys of banging things to make music. He is joined on seven of his own compositions by three other master drummers: the American Paul Motian, ex-Bill Evans sideman and one of the finest drummer-composer bandleaders in jazz history, the underrated Fredy Studer, one-time sideman of Stockhausen's trumpeter son Markus, and the Brazilian Nana Vasconcelos, whose berimbau soloing in particular is known to jazz audiences worldwide for its contribution to the music of Pat Metheny, Jan Garbarek and Andy Sheppard. The music they make together ranges from tone-poem to pan-global swing; its diversity and beauty will shock anyone who has ever groaned at the words 'drum solo'. A glimpse of his more formal Europeanized sense of music is obtainable on 1995's **Window Steps** (ECM), which features Kenny Wheeler, David Darling and Roberto Ottaviano. **SH**

# Victor Feldman

1934-87

**The Artful Dodger** Feldman (p); **Chuck Domanico, Monty Budwig** (b); **Colin Bailey** (d); **Jack Sheldon** (t, v). Concord Ⓕ CCD4038 (40 minutes). Recorded 1977.

⑧ ❻

Britain lost one of its most talented jazz musicians when Feldman decided to work in the US in 1955. His achievements there were numerous in both the popular music and jazz fields: he played piano with the Cannonball Adderley Quintet, worked as an accompanist to Peggy Lee, wrote and played for Miles Davis, to name a few. Although he confines himself to the keyboard on this CD, the extent of his musicianship is overwhelming. He wrote four of the tunes and leads a most exciting trio which contains another British-born immigrant in Colin Bailey whose fast hands and feet contribute so much to the drive and accuracy of the music. *A Walk on the Heath* is a beautiful Feldman waltz and the treatment of Stevie Wonder's *Isn't She Lovely?* is jazz from start to finish. On two tracks Feldman switches to Fender Rhodes piano, one being the closing version of his *Haunted Ballroom*, which ends eerily with the sound of a ten-year-old Feldman taking a drum solo with the Glenn Miller Band in October 1944 at a London concert. This CD is a well-transferred copy of what was a splendid LP. **AM**

# Eric Felten

**T-Bop** Felten, **Jimmy Knepper** (tb); **Joshua Redman** (ts); **Jonny King** (p); **Paul LaDuca** (b); **Jorge Rossy** (d). **Tom Everett, Evan Dobbins** (tb); **Paul Henry** (b). Soul Note Ⓕ 121196-2 (75 minutes). Recorded 1992.

⑦ ❽

Eric Felten is young, but he was brought up steeped in the jazz tradition, having a grandfather who played with the territory bands in the twenties and an aunt who graced Ina Ray Hutton's outfit, while his father is still a music teacher. All of which gave him the great commonsense to contact Jimmy Knepper when he had this album to make. Knepper, one of the instrument's great individuals and most neglected voices, adds his inimitable magic to the whole date, although he only solos on five of the ten cuts. His velvety tone and oddly phrased, bleary, arpeggiated style comes across like an old friend in unfamiliar company here, although Felten himself has a very cleanly phrased and visceral style, showing not only the technical assurance of a J.J. Johnson fan but the love of a big, open, brass tone which doubtless comes from an appreciation of the opposite tradition, that of Bill Harris and Roswell Rudd.

Redman makes a worthy contribution, as does the admirable rhythm section, but the spotlight rightly falls on the two slide trombonists. Felten takes two duets with bass only, in which he demonstrates admirable maturity, but one of the most beautiful moments on the disc occurs when Knepper's singing tone comes floating out of the simple two-part harmony ensemble vamp of *Hold Back the Dawn*. Knepper's highly vocalized approach is one which he has held intact for over 30 years, and although this album is not his show, he steals it more than once. It is a tribute to the younger player's generosity of spirit that he is prepared to let the old stager be there to do it in the first place. **KS**

# Maynard Ferguson

1928

**New review**
**One More Trip to Birdland** Ferguson (t, flh); **Scott Englebright, Carl Fischer, Larry Foyen** (t); **Tom Garling** (tb, g); **Matt Wallace** (ts, as, v); **Chris Farr** (ts, ss); **Dan Zank** (p, kbds); **Phil Palombi** (b); **Mark Marcinko** (d, perc). Concord Ⓕ CCD4729 (53 minutes). Recorded 1996.

⑧ ❾

Ferguson's Big Bop Nouveau is big in sound but small in numbers. Maynard has found that by employing just nine men (ensuring they are all capable of responding to the exacting challenges of the scores and the leader's own amazing technical abilities) he can produce music as exciting as many of the greatest big bands. Obviously this makes economic sense but it should not be forgotten that this is a fine band on its own terms. A lot of the writing for Ferguson's orchestras has come from within the ranks of the band and this one is no exception. Trombonist Tom Garling scored four of the nine pieces here, crafted for this specific line-up, which accounts for their success. There is a brilliance and vitality with solo spaces shared out fairly evenly. Even trumpeters Englebright and Fischer are given choruses (I don't think this kind of thing happened very often in Harry James's band!) and both tenor players produce effective solos. Matt Wallace also sings on *She Was too Good to Me*, which perhaps was a mistake. The band's hectic version of *Milestones* is a tribute to Miles Davis, but none of Miles's bands ever sounded like this. Good, energetic music, sometimes a little frantic but never lacking in excitement or high-class musicianship. **AM**

# Rachelle Ferrell

**First Instrument** Ferrell (v) with: on six tracks **Eddie Green** (p); **Tyrone Brown** (b); **Doug Nally** (d); on one track add **Alex Foster** (ss); on one track **Terence Blanchard** (t); **Gil Goldstein** (p); **Kenny Davis** (b); **Lenny White** (d); on one track **Wayne Shorter** (ts); **Michel Petrucciani** (p);

**Stanley Clarke** (b); **Lenny White** (d); **Pete Levin**, **Gil Goldstein** (syn). Blue Note Ⓔ CDP8 27820-2 (57 minutes). Recorded 1989/90.

⑥ ❽

As a great deal of jazz makes use of the popular song as its basis for improvisation, singers often find themselves restricted by the original lyrics in their attempts to find the freedom enjoyed by instrumentalists. I would not say that Rachelle Ferrell has completely solved the problem but she comes much closer to a satisfactory resolution than most. Of course she could have based her entire programme on originals, but instead of that she shows what can be achieved by using the words and music of writers such as Cole Porter, Frank Loesser, Richard Rodgers, Gene DePaul, etc., as well as two pieces of her own. The results are sometimes startling for she has the vocal equipment to soar up through the octaves with great accuracy. On *What is This Thing Called Love?* she cuts down the supporting group to just Doug Nally's drums, stays in tune, skates around the melody with ease and even manages to insert a quotation from *Hot House*. At rest, so to speak, she reveals the warm, sensuous voice and extracts great feeling from ballads such as *My Funny Valentine* and Cy Coleman's *With Every Breath I Take*. She is at her most self-indulgent, and least successful, on the live performance of *Autumn Leaves* where her shrieks and yodels delight the groundlings just as Flip Phillips and Illinois Jacquet did with JATP.　　**KS**

# Barry Finnerty

**Straight Ahead** Finnerty (g); **David Kikoski** (p); **Mike Richmond** (b); **Victor Lewis** (d); **Chuggy Carter** (perc). Arabesque Ⓕ AJ0116 (62 minutes). Recorded 1994.

⑦ ❿

Finnerty is no spring chicken, and his début comes after 20 years of professional music-making, but that does not mean that this album should be ignored. Suffering the fate of many jobbing guitarists, he has made money playing music away from jazz and been discounted when he has come to companies with jazz ideas for albums or songs. His style of playing is not that far removed from Emily Remler, and he swings every bit as fluently as the late and gifted mainstream player. His range is quite broad within the ambit mentioned above, and he is not afraid of beefing up, cranking up and going for broke on, say, *Carnaval*, or Joe Henderson's old stormer, *Inner Urge*. He also improvises fluently on *Count Up*, his own version of Coltrane's ferocious set of changes, *Countdown*.

The supporting musicians do well, although poor David Kikoski has to labour with a piano that has an octave of its range in a distinctly *desafinado* shape. Victor Lewis is, as usual, immaculate but busy enough for you to know he is there.　　**KS**

# Firehouse Five Plus Two

**New review**
**Twenty Years Later** Ward Kimball (tb, ldr, duck noises); **Danny Alguire** (c); **Don Kinch** (t, birdcalls); **George Probert**, **Tom Kubis**, **John Smith** (ss); **K.O. Eckland** (p); **Bill Newman** (bj); **George Bruns** (tba); **Eddie Forrest** (d). Good Time Jazz Ⓜ 10054-2 (42 minutes). Recorded 1969.

⑥ ❽

If you're going to go in for the funny hats and comedy side of dixieland jazz, you may as well go so far over the top that what you do becomes an art-form in its own right. No band in the history of jazz has gone further in this direction than the motley collection of Disney animators, scriptwriters and studio alumni who made up the Firehouse Five (usually an eight-piece band, as here). Spike Jones and the Temperance Seven pushed the boundaries of comedy and jazz in the direction of chaos and British eccentricity, respectively. This band, taking its cue from a number written to celebrate the vintage comic character *Barney Google*, adds duck noises, bird-song and dog effects to raucous, energetic dixieland, where everyone plays fit to bust and with considerable panache. The Five made several albums between their inception in 1949 and this 20-year anniversary celebration, all of them consistent in humour, music and, for the most part, personnel. The recording quality here is excellent, and the inclusion of non-standard material, from show songs to US reworkings of hits by Ball and Bilk, is imaginative. In general, a Firehouse Five record requires the mind's eye to add a gaudily animated cartoon to its ready-made soundtrack. The moments on this disc that call up the best images are the dog and train effects on *Yellow Dog Blues* ("We thought it was a tune for dogs ... then we found out it was actually about a shortline railroad" said leader Kimball) and the wildly over-enthusiastic soprano sax trio belting through Alphonse Picou's classic solo on *High Society*.　　**AS**

# Clare Fischer

1928

**New review**
**Just Me** Fischer (p). Concord Ⓔ CCD4679 (62 minutes). Recorded 1995.

⑦ ❼

Fischer's has always been a special talent. He first came to wide attention through his arrangements for Dizzy Gillespie's **Portrait of Duke Ellington**, but even before this his love of Latin music had been established. This interest gave rise to one of his most popular compositions, *Pensativa*, which was even given a treatment in the sixties by the Jazz Messengers.. In a long and eventful career since then Fischer has been active on many fronts, though never to the extent that his name has been box-office. Some of his most stimulating latter-day work was for the Prince album **Parade**, where his arrangements add much to the exoticism of the music. His current CD representations are mostly solo piano (comparisons with Bill Evans are appropriate), with this being the latest and quite representative. Fischer's arranger's mind gives him a head start over most pianists who plough their way through chestnuts like *Autumn Leaves* and *'Round Midnight*, and his improvisation hews closely to the character of every piece he plays, whether it is a Brazilian-flavoured original (*Pra Baden*) or a moody ballad such as *Ill Wind*. This is a quiet, understated disc, but Fischer warns in his notes "This is not background music!" I agree.                                                                **KS**

# Ella Fitzgerald                                                                    1918-96

**The Original American Decca Recordings** Fitzgerald (v); with her **Savoy Eight**, her **Famous Orchestra**, **Louis Armstrong**, **Louis Jordan**, **The Chick Webb Orchestra**, **The Sy Oliver Orchestra**, **The Bob Haggart Orchestra**, **The Ink Spots**, **The Delta Rhythm Boys**; **Billy Kyle**, **Ellis Larkins**, **Hank Jones** (p); **Ray Brown** (b). MCA/Decca Ⓜ GRP26192 (two discs: 119 minutes). Recorded 1938-55.

✅                                                                                   ⑧ ❽

This is a sensible overview of Ella's recordings during the years indicated above. The Decca sessions were much hotter than her later famous sessions for Verve and some of the contrived alliances, notably with Armstrong and her boy-friend Louis Jordan, worked very well. The many tasteful ballads, a rare form during the forties, are sung with great brio and Ella's scat workouts, including *Flying Home*, *Lady Be Good* and others included here, are the original benchmarks for the style. Although a good number of the songs, from *A Tisket, A Tasket* (1938) to *Hard Hearted Hannah* (1955) were popular hits, all the 39 tracks are high in jazz interest and consistency. "Man, woman and child," said Bing Crosby, "Ella's the greatest." On this showing that is a reasonable motion for debate. The tracks included from the fifties demonstrate Fitzgerald's ability to overcome any musical obstacle or constriction imposed upon her by an increasingly distant record company management. She imparts something special to every performance. Erudite essays by Dan Morganstern and a comprehensive discography grace the lavish but rather clumsy book which contains the discs.   **SV**

**New review**

**Ella and Friends** Fitzgerald, **Louis Armstrong**, **The Ink Spots**, **Louis Jordan**, **The Delta Rhythm Boys**, **The Mills Bros** (v); accompaniment by **Bob Haggard and his Orchestra**, **Sy Oliver and his Orchestra**, **Dave Barbour and his Orchestra**, **Louis Jordan's Tympany Five** (Eddie Johnson, ts; Dallas Bartley, b; Chris Columbus, d; Aaron Izenhall, t; Jordan, as; Carl Hogan, g; on one track Josh Jackson, t; Jesse Simpkins, b; Eddie Byrd, d). Accompaniment to **Delta Rhythm Boys** (Rene Knight, p; Hy White, g; Haig Stephens, b; George Wettling, d); on two tracks replace with **Jimmy Shirley** (g); **Lamont Moten** (b); **Eddie Bourne** (d). GRP Ⓜ 16632 (60 minutes). Recorded 1946-51.

                                                                                     ⑨ ❾

All these vocal pairings are from the Decca years, which means that they are preludes to greater accomplishments. These records were all attempts at hits and of course don't have the expanse of the Norman Granz album-length projects on Verve. Ella started scatting on record in 1947, though there is none of that here; this is mostly a record of light ballads and humour. The five collaborations with Louis Jordan and a real band have the most kick, the five cuts with Louis Armstrong, including the lovely *Would You Like to Take a Walk?* have the best unscripted kidding. (*In Can Anyone Explain*, Ella asks primly, "have you ever been in love?" The response is a great cackle, a pause, and then an answer: "I've been in love four times.") The material is mostly all on Decca as the two-CD set **The War Years** (1941-7), and in part on **The Original American Decca Recordings**. But for lovers of duet routines – and of vocal harmony groups, to which Fitzgerald is really added as a guest voice – this does the job in one, with crisp sound.                                                                    **BR**

**New review**

**The Concert Years** Fitzgerald (v); accompanied by **Duke Ellington and his Orchestra**, **The Count Basie Orchestra**; plus the following small-group musicians: **Roy Eldridge**, **Charlie Shavers**, **Harry 'Sweets' Edison**, **Clark Terry** (t); **Bill Harris**, **Al Grey**, **J.J. Johnson** (tb); **Benny Carter**, **Willie Smith** (as); **Ben Webster**, **Flip Phillips**, **Stan Getz**, **Eddie 'Lockjaw' Davis**, **Zoot Sims** (ts); **Raymond Tunia**, **Oscar Peterson**, **Tommy Flanagan**, **Jimmy Jones**, **Count Basie**, **Paul Smith** (p); **Herb Ellis**, **Freddie Green**, **Joe Pass** (g); **Ray Brown**, **Bob Cranshaw**, **Frank De La Rosa**, **Keter Betts**, **Nils-Henning Ørsted Pedersen** (b); **J.C. Heard**, **Sam Woodyard**, **Ed Thigpen**, **Bobby Durham**, **Louie Bellson** (d). Pablo Ⓜ 4PACD4414-2 (four discs: 310 minutes). Recorded 1953-83.

                                                                                     ⑨ ❽

As well as deftly managing Ella Fitzgerald's studio recording career from the mid fifties onwards, Norman Granz supervised the way in which she appeared on the international concert circuit. This

well-presented boxed set packages the singer as adroitly as Granz presented her in concert, covering the main 30-year span of Ella's live appearances for Granz: her own trio integrated with JATP touring groups, with Ellington and Basie's orchestras, or going it alone on stage or at clubs like Ronnie Scott's. The variety of settings and the ups and downs of what amounts to ten separate sessions give this set a marginally lower rating than Ella's studio recordings of the Song Books, but overall her consistency is remarkable. This is the Ella that thousands of people the world over who attended her live concerts felt was singing just for them and the generally excellent standard of live recording captures the intimacy of her ballads with the trio (like *Spring Can Really Hang You Up the Most*, or *I Ain't Got Nothing but the Blues*), the excitement of the JATP chases (a pulse-quickening *C-Jam* with Basie alumni plus Stan Getz and Clark Terry) and the sheer grandeur of her concert collaborations with jazz's two best-known orchestras. Ella's voice is slightly below par on a 1974 session from Ronnie Scott's, but otherwise her bell like clarity is as remarkable in 1983 as it was 30 years before. Most of this material originally came out in separate Pablo LPs of each individual event, and those seeking the complete presentation of a Fitzgerald concert might prefer the **Berlin** or **Opera House** sets reviewed below. Nevertheless, the unique feature of this anthology is the careful selection of tracks to avoid almost entirely duplication of material. **AS**

---

**Ella and Louis** Fitzgerald (v); **Louis Armstrong** (t, v); **Oscar Peterson** (p); **Herb Ellis** (g); **Ray Brown** (b); **Buddy Rich** (d). Verve Ⓜ 825 373-2 (54 minutes). Recorded 1956.

⑦ ⑧

While it would be impossible to deny the professionalism and sheer class of these performances, it must be said that the setting and the material favours Ella rather than Louis. Of the 11 songs making up this first Verve collaboration, Armstrong had never previously recorded nine of them and (perhaps significantly) was never to record them again. Louis, like Billie Holiday, actually seemed to thrive on the trite and the banal; the sophisticated melodies and lyrics of Berlin, the Gershwins, etc., seem to defeat him at times, and *Tenderly* is pitched in a key which may have suited Miss Fitzgerald but is frankly beyond Louis's comfortable range. Having said all that, the music is ideal for those mellow moments when the listener wants to hear some of the greatest jazz personalities at their most relaxed. Louis's occasional trumpet solos and obbligatos are never less than apt while the conjunction of the Oscar Peterson Trio and Buddy Rich makes for the most flawless platform. Ella, of course, is superb (was she ever otherwise at this time?) and makes a passable imitation of Louis himself at the end of *Tenderly*. Just less than a year later Norman Granz assembled virtually the same group (with the substitution of Louie Bellson for Rich) in the same studio with equally memorable results. **AM**

---

**The Best of the Song Books** Fitzgerald (v); with orchestras of: **Nelson Riddle**, **Billy May**, **Duke Ellington**, **Buddy Bregman**, **Paul Weston**; and various small groups including: **Ben Webster** (ts); **Stuff Smith** (vn); **Paul Smith** (p); **Barney Kesel** (g); **Joe Mondragon** (b); **Alvin Stoller** (d). Verve Ⓜ 519 804-2 (63 minutes). Recorded 1956-64.

✅ ⑩ ⑧

No two people will ever agree on which 16 numbers constitute the 'best' of a gigantic undertaking like Ella Fitzgerald's **Song Book** albums, but this is as good and varied a selection as any so far attempted. Included are the obligatory *Ev'ry Time We Say Goodbye* and *Our Love is Here to Stay*, two songs which now exist for most people solely in Ella's versions, and the complete *Bewitched, Bothered and Bewildered*, restoring some of Lorenz Hart's mildly risqué sallies ("Horizontally speaking, he's at his very best ...") and running to just over seven minutes. Over the years the song books have acquired the reputation of presenting 'definitive' versions of songs by the great American songwriters, but if 'definitive' means a straight and undeviating reliance on the songsheet this is not the case. Ella brings to the songs the elasticity of time and melody that only a superb jazz singer can manage. For a prime example, hear *Between the Devil and the Deep Blue Sea*, in a setting by Billy May, or *Hooray for Love* – or, indeed, any of the pieces included here. **DG**

---

**The Complete Song Books** Fitzgerald (v); accompanied by: **Duke Ellington and his Orchestra**, **The Nelson Riddle Orchestra**, **The Billy May Orchestra**, **The Buddy Bregman Orchestra**, **The Paul Weston Orchestra**; plus the following small-group musicians: **Ben Webster** (ts); **Stuff Smith** (vn); **Paul Smith**, **Oscar Peterson** (p); **Barney Kessel**, **Herb Ellis** (g); **Joe Mondragon**, **Ray Brown** (b); **Alvin Stoller** (d). Verve Ⓕ 519 832-2 (16 discs: 932 minutes). Recorded 1956-64.

⑩ ⑧

First things first: it is certain that Norman Granz had clear ideas on how Ella Fitzgerald's recording career should develop when he wrested her from Decca and started this series with the **Cole Porter** project in 1956, but it is doubtful that even he realized what the eventual size of one of popular music's most comprehensive and enduring achievements would be. It boggles the mind even today, and the most remarkable aspect of the whole thing is its consistency. There is simply nothing here which is not top quality or, as Ellington noted, "beyond category". The arrangers, the musicians, the conductors; all involved gave of their best and exerted restraint, flair and good taste at every turn. But not even the best-intentioned project can succeed without a central object worthy of the care and attention. In Ella, Granz had an artist who simply never let him down, and who responded creatively to every situation he constructed for her. Considering the track record of many other popular and jazz singers when it came to consistently giving of their best in the studio, this alone is a remarkable feat.

Of course a lot of the arrangements are couched in the commercial pop rather than jazz idiom, with string sections and Latin percussionists, so it is at least arguable that many of the **Song Books'** sides fall outside the scope of this Guide. That is to reckon without Ella, for everything she does as a singer – her phrasing, her attack, her expression, her moulding of notes, her humour – is thoroughly imbued with jazz feeling. She is taking these songs and giving them a definitve interpretation, rather than using them as a vehicle for self-promotion.

All the Song Books have their own highlights and utilize great musicians (Benny Carter is featured, for example, during the **Harold Arlen Song Book**), but one is slightly different from the rest. The **Duke Ellington** project had Duke and his orchestra on hand, plus extra sessions with a small-group which remain some of the brightest treasures in Ella's recording career. Feelings remain mixed about the sides with Duke's orchestra, but too much has been made of the suggestion that Duke and Strayhorn didn't make new arrangements of the songs chosen. A close listen suggests this to be not entirely true, and anyway, the old ones sound beautiful behind her and the band plays with great spirit.

It is worth noting that, for those prospective purchasers who are understandably nervous about investing a substantial amount of money in such a large set as this, the **Song Books** remain available as separate entities, although they don't come with the dazzling packing and information granted the boxed set. **KS**

---

**At the Opera House** Fitzgerald (v); Oscar Peterson (p); Herb Ellis (g); Ray Brown (b); Jo Jones (d); plus on three tracks: Roy Eldridge (t); J.J. Johnson (tb); Sonny Stitt (as); Stan Getz, Coleman Hawkins, Illinois Jacquet, Flip Phillips, Lester Young (ts); Connie Kay (d). Verve Ⓜ 831 269-2 (59 minutes). Recorded 1957.

✔ ⑩ ❽

Ella Fitzgerald's long association with promoter, producer and manager Norman Granz resulted in a string of classic recordings for Verve, plus frequent Jazz at the Philharmonic tours. The short sets she sang on Granz's star-crammed road-shows allowed her to pull out all the stops on stage; she and Peterson's quartet attack *Goody Goody*, Benny Goodman's 1936 novelty hit (which she had recorded in 1952), with some of the raw exuberance of Elvis Presley's 1954 Sun Sessions (the comparison may strike some as odd, but Fitzgerald's jazz roots were in the raucous dancehall variety, not supper-club fare).

This CD documents two concerts, recorded a week apart (one in stereo, one mono), on which she performed almost identical programmes. It is an ideal situation for observing the creative leeway she took within relatively fixed arrangements. Selections include rhythm tunes where she scats magnificently (an *Oh, Lady Be Good!* with riffing guest horns), relaxed up-tempo romps (*It's All Right with Me*) and classic ballads (*Moonlight in Vermont*, Arlen's *Ill Wind*). Too much of Fitzgerald's pre- or non-song-book work is dismissed as frivolous, but only by those who underestimate the ecstatic mode in jazz. On these concerts, she is in gorgeous voice and high spirits. **KW**

---

**Mack the Knife – The Complete Ella in Berlin** Fitzgerald (v); Paul Smith (p); Jim Hall, Barney Kessel (g); Wilfred Middlebrooks, Joe Mondragon (b); Gus Johnson, Alvin Stoller (d). Verve Ⓜ 519 564-2 (50 minutes). Recorded 1960.

❽ ❼

The **Song Books** were vital to her career portfolio but Fitzgerald was very much a working singer. She was on the Norman Granz circuit and live performances provided an alternative example of her artistry. **Ella in Berlin (Mack the Knife)**, performed in the Deutschlandhalle in front of 12,000 people, is a perfect example. The basics do not change; her faultless intonation is a source of constant wonder, her control of vibrato is exemplary and her ability to swing is never in doubt. The challenge of a live date gives her a keening edge, however, and on this CD she really entertains.

She does a Sinatra-style massacre of *Lady is a Tramp*, she mugs through the forgotten lyrics of *Mack the Knife* and her supremely confident readings of *Misty* and *The Man I Love* show how effortlessly she stamps her own personality on other people's material. Her subtle Jimmy Rushing-type reconstruction of *Just One of Those Things* improves on the original, while her unforced humour throughout provides alternatives, not desecrations. Her scat singing has always been a tad perfunctory but the ease with which she discriminates between the bop lines of Charlie Parker and Dizzy Gillespie on *How High the Moon* is masterful. In 1960, Fitzgerald was up and singing. More was to come. **BMcR**

# Flanagan-Ingham Quartet

---

New review

**Zanzibar** Kevin Flanagan (ts); Chris Ingham (p, v); Andrew Brown (b); Russ Morgan (d). Gray Brothers Ⓕ CD2 (47 minutes). Recorded 1995.

⑥ ❽

This tight-knit group is well known on the British club circuit, featuring US-born tenorist Flanagan with three UK counterparts. Several of the tracks are originals by the leaders, and the balance is a mixture of instrumental standards and songs for Ingham's pleasant middle-range voice. The star soloist is Flanagan, whose playing has some overtones of Sonny Rollins, but an altogether warmer and more welcoming tone. Flanagan was a member of Tommy Chase's quartet for some time, but like other ex-members his playing has lost the relentless pressure one associates with Chase and become more reflective and contemplative. A good example is Rollins's *Pent-up House*, where Flanagan is always in control, but creates enough space for his ideas to have some room to breathe. This is the group's début album, and suggests a bright future for them. **AS**

# Tommy Flanagan
1930

**New review**

**Sea Changes** Flanagan (p); **Peter Washington** (b); **Lewis Nash** (d). Alfa Jazz ℗ ALCB3907 (63 minutes). Recorded 1996.

⑨ ❾

The poise and subtlety of Flanagan's work is best appreciated in this context and this must rank as one of his finest trios. Tommy's major strength lies in his impeccable sense of touch; all too often jazz pianists press the keys down with little regard for the actual sound they produce. Flanagan shares with masters such as Teddy Wilson and Hank Jones the knowledge that a personal sense of touch immediately gives their playing individuality. But there is much more to Tommy's playing; there is nothing discursive in his improvisations. All the ideas are worked out to logical resolutions, the kind of approach which hallmarked the work of another piano giant, Al Haig. At up-tempo there is a crisp, whip-cracking feel to the music and Lewis Nash senses when to increase the tension. This ranks as one of Flanagan's very best trio recordings but as the notes are in Japanese I'm not sure if there was any intended significance in the fact that five of the 11 tunes, viz *Verdandi, Dalarna, Eclypso, Beat's Up* and *Relaxin' at Camarillo*, are 1996 versions of numbers he recorded back in 1957 with a trio (completed by Wilber Little and Elvin Jones) when he was in Sweden with Jay Jay Johnson's group. I suspect it was deliberate, as the final number here is *Dear Old Stockholm*. **AM**

# Reinhard Flatischler

**New review**

**Layers of Time** Flatischler, **Zakir Hussain, Airto Moreira, Valerie Naranjo, Glen Velez, Milton Cardona** (perc); **Wolfgang Puschnig** (f, ts). Intuition Music ℗ INT3173-2 (48 minutes). Recorded 1995.

⑧ ❾

Both for his erudition concerning the place and significance of the drum and related percussive instruments in cultures from South America through the Caribbean to Asia and Africa, and for his decade-long leadership of the world-percussion projects known as MegaDrums, Austrian composer Reinhard Flatischler is justifiably known as the "Ambassador of World Language Rhythm". The personnel of his projects varies over the years but on this latest offering, recorded on the group's fifth European tour, Flatischler is joined by a stellar band of like-minded percussionists, the depth and variety of whose experience – ranging from work with Indo-jazz fusion projects like Shakti through the electric jazz of Return to Forever and the minimalism of Reich and Glass to collaborations with rock musicians such as the Grateful Dead's Mickey Hart and world-avant-pop darling David Byrne – gives this album a richness and breadth of cultural reference that raises it far above the spontaneous percussive jams it superficially resembles. The standout tracks from a jazz perspective are those on which Wolfgang Puschnig is allowed to float his keening, almost Garbarek-like tenor, or his surprisingly robust flute, over an intriguingly multi-textured brew of percussion utilizing everything from marimba through waterphones and gongs to berimbau and tabla. The success of the Puschnig-less pieces, even the short *Olua*, which features oddly affecting antiphonal chanting, depends on individual listeners' willingness to forgo the comforts of conventional thematic progression and settle for the more spiritual joys available from the slow-building, hypnotic trances conjured up by the repeated drummed rhythms in which this deeply felt album abounds. **CP**

# Fleurine

**New review**

**Meant To Be!** Fleurine (v); **Tom Harrell, Don Sickler** (flh); **Bobby Porcelli** (f, as); **Ralph Moore** (ts); **Renee Rosnes** (p); **Jesse Van Fuller** (g); **Christian McBride** (b); **Billy Drummond** (d). Blue Music ℗ BM1001 (63 minutes). Recorded 1996.

⑥ ❾

Fleurine is a young Dutch singer (the booklet-notes by producer Don Sickler mention that she's "in her twenties") with a sunny vocal outlook and a penchant for what the other booklet-note writer, Jon Hendricks, calls "vocalese". Her preferred working method is to take an instrumental jazz composition and write lyrics to it, occasionally incorporating parts of a recorded improvisation into her work, occasionally simply extemporizing in her own right. The stellar support group (replacing her regular European quintet) sounds interested and alert, concerned to give the performances life and character. Fleurine herself has a clear, clean alto voice with a natural flexibility and freshness. She occasionally pitches above the note, quickly scooping down to the correct pitch, but this habit is not too distracting. What she lacks in interpretative depth she makes up for in her sheer zest for the music she is making. This is one happy session, with fetching new workings of songs by Monk, Tom Harrell, Joshua Redman, Ray Bryant and Kenny Dorham, among others. She's one to watch. **KS**

## Bob Florence                                                                1932

**The Limited Edition – State of the Art**  Florence (ldr, kbds, arr); **George Graham, Charley Davis, Warren Luening, Steve Huffsteter, Larry Ford** (t, flh); **Chauncey Welsch, Rick Culver, Charlie Loper, Herbie Harper** (tb); **Don Waldrop** (btb); **Lanny Morgan, Kim Richmond** (ss, as, f, cl); **Dick Mitchell, Bob Cooper** (ts, f, cl); **Bob Efford** (f, bcl); **John Lowe** (bs, cl); **Tom Warrington** (b); **Peter Donald** (d); **Alex Acuna** (perc). BBC/Prestige Ⓜ CDPC797 (56 minutes). Recorded 1989.

⑥ ❽

Although Florence is one of the hardest working arrangers active in the Los Angeles area, his name is seldom found in jazz reference books. Yet his big studio bands invariably play exciting music, featuring solos by men such as Pete Christlieb, Nick Ceroli, Bill Perkins, Bob Cooper, etc. He also earned himself a Grammy nomination in 1982 for his album **Westlake**. This CD is a typically efficient Florence release, this time making use of five standards as well as four original compositions. *Moonlight Serenade* is turned into a samba, while *Stella by Starlight* is a swirling showcase for the altos of Morgan and Richmond. Steve Huffsteter is featured playing flügelhorn throughout *Silky* and Bob Efford's baritone adds dignity to *Auld Lang Syne*, which also benefits from a most sympathetic Florence arrangement. The band may lack an instantly recognizable style, but it packs an impressive punch, well captured in the recording; Nimbus are credited with the mastering. **AM**

## Marty Fogel

**Many Bobbing Heads, At Last**  Fogel (cl, ss, ts); **David Torn** (g); **Dean Johnson** (b); **Michael Shrieve** (d, perc). CMP Ⓕ CD37 (47 minutes). Recorded 1989.

⑥ ❽

Fogel and guitarist David Torn had been playing together for nearly 20 years, primarily in the Upstate New York Everyman Band, at the time of this recording, which is the kind of avant/world/fusion one might expect from players who count Lou Reed and Don Cherry among their past associates. Most tracks are either by the saxophonist (heard mostly on tenor) or are collective creations by the band, and are frequently enhanced by the studio soundplay of engineer/co-producer Walter Quintus, who provides the typically excellent and appropriately overheated CMP sound to this high-energy date. While one might wish for a bit less eclecticism at times, Fogel and Torn are always pushing, never simply lolling in the exotic moods; and the one cover, *Cherry's Guinea*, is a bashing beauty. Michael Shrieve, best known for his work with Santana, also gives a good accounting of his more creative impulses. The electric trappings of this music should not scare away acoustic music fans, particularly those who lean toward the more exploratory end of the jazz spectrum. **BB**

## Ricky Ford                                                                1954

New review
**Tenor Madness Too!**  Ford, Antoine Roney (ts); **Donald Brown** (p); **Peter Washington** (b); **Louis Hayes** (d). Muse Ⓕ MCD5478 (51 minutes). Recorded 1992.

⑦ ❽

Tenor saxophonist Ricky Ford is a 42-year-old veteran whose diverse credits include big-band traditionalists Duke Ellington and Lionel Hampton as well as modernists Charles Mingus, Danny Richmond and Abdullah Ibrahim. A scholar as well as practitioner, the Boston-bred native also teaches at Brandeis University. An intensely robust player, Ford employs a passionate neo-modern approach suggesting the spirit and eclecticism of Sonny Rollins. On his rollicking *Rollin' and Strollin'*, one hears echoes of Rollins's puckish push-pull rhythmatics as well as a rich, reedy sound redolent of the majesterial Dexter Gordon. Indeed, the date's two-tenor line-up and title refer to Rollins's classic 1956 *Tenor Madness* date (and the now standard jazz tune) in which Rollins and John Coltrane locked horns. Here, Ford is joined by Antoine Roney, a bright young Coltrane-inflected player. Instead of slashing with over-the-top, cutting-session frenzy, the two horns mesh with a front-line panache recalling the best of Blakey. Subtle yet forceful support is supplied by pianist Donald Brown, bassist Peter Washington and drummer Louis Hayes. Burners like the leader's *Summer Summit* sizzle. Equally impressive is Ford's impassioned balladry on Mal Waldron's *Soul Eyes* and Ellington's *I Got It Bad and That Ain't Good*. **CB**

# Michael Formanek

**Low Profile** Formanek (b); **Dave Douglas** (t); **Ku-Umba Frank Lacy** (tb); **Marty Ehrlich** (cl, bcl, as, ss); **Tim Berne** (as); **Salvatore Bonafede** (p); **Marvin 'Smitty' Smith** (d). Enja Ⓔ ENJ8050-2 (77 minutes). Recorded 1993.

⑦ ❽

Californian bassist Formanek paid his dues in the seventies with Joe Henderson, Dave Liebman and Herbie Mann. He worked in Europe during the eighties and has since established himself as a first call player in New York. The bonus is that the nineties have seen him emerge as a successful leader in his own right. His arrangements show an awareness of his soloist's requirements and their presentation needs.

This CD is a perfect example. He has a stylistically varied team and he showcases them with genuine style. He wrote and arranged every title and the way in which he encourages the flow of Ehrlich's bass clarinet on *Rivers* is in total contrast to the jocular mood of the Lacy-driven *Groogly* or to the subtle stimulation he provides for Berne's alto on *Great Plains*. The trumpet and trombone team bask in the latitude available on *Paradise Revisited* and the manner in which the horns alternate the lead in the all-ins on *Shuddawuddacudda* shows that the implications of John Coltrane's **Ascension** and Ornette Coleman's **Free Jazz** have been fully grasped. He has a superb *pizzicato* solo on *Great Plains* but it is the adroit way in which his varied charts unite the band that establishes his real status. **BMcR**

# Jimmy Forrest

**Most Much!** Forrest (ts); **Hugh Lawson** (p); **Tommy Potter** (b); **Clarendon Johnson** (d); **Ray Barretto** (cga). Prestige Ⓜ OJCCD350-2 (50 minutes). Recorded 1961.

⑥ ❻

Born in St Louis, Missouri and apprenticed in bands such as those of Andy Kirk and Jay McShann, it was inevitable that Forrest would emerge as one of those powerful, big-toned tenors. He worked in the Duke Ellington orchestra for seven months (1949-50) and succeeded in turning parts of a couple of Ducal tunes (*Happy-Go-Lucky-Local* and *That's the Blues, Old Man*) into a best-selling 'original' which he called *Night Train*. **Most Much!** is certainly the best album he did for Prestige, and the CD version adds two tracks to the original LP programme which were previously only issued on a separate album. Forrest, like Charlie Parker, had a way of infusing every tune he played with deep blues inflections. The opening *Matilda* is a somewhat repetitive calypso, but the rest of the nine-tune programme is nicely varied. The title tune is a powerful blues by Forrest in which time passes all too quickly; even the potentially lachrymose *I Love You* emerges as a fine jazz performance after the theme has been disposed of. A special mention must be made of the helpful, tasteful conga drumming of Barretto throughout the session. **AM**

# Sonny Fortune

**Monk's Mood** Fortune (as); **Kirk Lightsey** (p); **David Williams** (b); **Joe Chambers** (d). Konnex Ⓕ KCD5048 (58 minutes). Recorded 1993.

⑩ ❿

In the past I have often found Fortune a hard player to warm to, his brilliant tone and fleet technique somehow bypassing my emotions. This date, however, is something special. Maybe it was the repertoire, or the personnel, or good planning, or just plain luck. Whatever it was, this has such a positive focus and is so full of humour, commitment and inspired twists that it makes you hear Monk's songs as if they were new once again. Not that Fortune and Co. wilfully pull them about and generally shred their original forms; that they most decidedly do not do. But they sound utterly at home with not only the changes and the rhythms, but also the attitude – what Bill Evans once described as Monk's "angle" – which is essential in keeping to the spirit of the work. Too many Monk covers obey the letter and lose the spirit. This one gets it just right, and the interplay between Fortune and Lightsey is worthy of Monk and his most distinguished horn men.

Fortune has gone on to make a further Monk album, **Four in One**, for Blue Note, again in tandem with the admirable Lightsey. Make no mistake: this Konnex date is the one to get. It has the extra-special glow. Fortune's subsequent Blue Note album, **A Better Understanding** (1995), where he occasionally experiments with double-tracking, is a curiously lacklustre affair. **KS**

# Frank Foster

**No 'Count** Foster (ts); **Frank Wess** (ts, f); **Benny Powell, Henry Coker** (tb); **Kenny Burrell** (g); **Eddie Jones** (b); **Kenny Clarke** (d). Denon/Savoy Ⓜ SV0114 (36 minutes). Recorded 1956.

⑥ ❽

Foster had a cutting edge to his sound which later became fashionable with the hard-bop saxophone players. This distinguishes him from the equally inventive Wess, who has a slightly softer, more mainstream attack. Foster must be regarded as a product of the Dexter Gordon school of thought, whilst Wess came from Hawkins and Byas. Foster is an inventive musician who has also distinguished himself as an arranger. All the horns in the front line were part of the fine Count Basie band of the time, and it was their contemporary thinking (and in Foster's and Wess's case, writing) which, grafted on to the Basie rhythm style, gave that band its powerful character.

But Foster and his band were of the second bebop generation and although there is a leavening here of Basie-type blues, the more stimulating numbers are Foster's originals. These are good themes beautifully voiced and, thanks to the quality of Rudy Van Gelder's recording, Foster's playing crackles with a fire not normally captured on his early Basie records. The trombones, released from Basie's section, show how well they could solo. Kenny Burrell was an ideal guitar choice, for he is a player possessed of natural jazz feeling, and his presence in the rhythm section in lieu of a pianist adds freshness to the band's sound.                                                                                  **SV**

# Ronnie Foster

New review

**Two-Headed Freap**  Foster (org); **George Devens** (vb); **Gene Bertoncini** (g); **Gene Bianco** (h); **George Duvivier** (elb); **Jimmy Johnson** (d); **Arthur Jenkins** (cga). Blue Note Ⓜ CDP830282-2 (37 minutes). Recorded 1972.

⑥ ❽

Wherein Jimmy Smith meets George Shearing in a funky inner-city alley on a dark winter night early in the seventies. Meanwhile Sun Ra, in the shape of ex-Ra percussionist Johnson, looks on benignly, we hope. For a time in the early seventies Foster was a popular back-beat funk merchant who made a series of albums for Blue Note. They are no better (and certainly no worse) than anyone else's efforts of the time, Charles Earland, Jack McDuff, Jimmy McGriff, Les McCann and even Jimmy Smith himself included. The album may start off with a perfectly dreadful fuzz guitar-Fender bass riff (*Chunky*), but it is uphill, rather than down the drain, all the way from there. Foster is a fine technician who knows his instrument and coaxes tasteful sounds from it at all times (the allusion to Shearing is not an unconsidered one). This is limited and extremely unadventurous music (no improvisation lasts more than around two minutes and most of that time is taken up with licks borrowed from other players), but taken on its own terms it is successful. Foster's popularity was short-lived and he currently rates no mention in any jazz encyclopaedia or guide I've seen.                       **KS**

# Pete Fountain                                                                                        1930

New review

**Do You Know What It Means to Miss New Orleans**  Fountain (cl); **Manny Klein, Conrad Gozzo, Shorty Sherock, Al Hirt, Charlie Teagarden, Jack Coon** (t); **Abe Lincoln, Moe Schneider, Lew McCreary, Bill Schaeffer, George Roberts, Dick Noel, Bob Havens** (tb); **Mattly Matlock, Wilbur Schwartz, Eddie Miller, Babe Russin, Chuck Gentry** (reeds); **Phil Stephens** (bb); **Godfrey Hirsch** (vb); **Stan Wrightsman, Merle Koch, John Propst, Earl Vuiovich** (p); **Bobby Gibson, Paul Guma** (g); **Morty Corb, Don Bagley, Oliver Felix** (b); **Jack Sperling, Ray Bauduc, Nick Fatool, Paul Barbarin, Paul Edwards** (d); **Charles 'Bud' Dant** (cond). GRP Ⓜ 26582 (two discs: 133 minutes). Recorded 1956-65.

⑤ ❻

Since making his recording début as a leader in 1954, Fountain has been a mainstay of tourist Dixieland in New Orleans. At times a club owner, he has worked copiously with Tony Almerico and Al Hirt and he gained nationwide popularity on the Lawrence Welk Show. Fountain has a good tone in all registers and is a natural swinger in a style that falls between Benny Goodman and Irving Fazola. This CD offers the best of his work for the Coral label and rather like his live performances, offers proof that he loves people. His solos are inoffensive, softly contoured, melodic translations rather than in-depth improvisations and would seem to be aimed at the middle ground of the cursory listener. In the circumstances, he is equally at home with the cushion of Dant's orchestra or parading his technical facility alongside Hirsch's vibes or Koch's Teddy Wilsonish piano. Instead of the fervour demanded by *Just a Closer Walk*, he gives an amiable rendering, full of cosy assurance. His best moments here include a surprisingly modern arrangement of *Da Da Strain*, a fine Teagarden driven *Struttin' with Some Barbecue* and King Oliver's *Dippermouth* solo on clarinet. It is 'good time' jazz with little content and even less emotional involvement, but it is well done.                                                                **BMcR**

# Fourth Way

New review

**The Sun and the Moon Have Come Together**  **Micheal White** (vn); **Mike Nock** (elp); **Ron Mclure** (b); **Eddie Marshall** (d). Jazz View Ⓜ COD022. Recorded 1968.

⑦ ❺

Predating Weather Report by a good three years, and even Miles's nascent electric whispers by several months, Fourth Way have ended up a mere footnote in the evolution of jazz-rock fusion. A footnote though with size 12 boots. Formed by Mike Nock and Micheal White from John Handy's mid-sixties quintet, together with Ron Mclure from the Charles Lloyd Quartet and Bay Area drum demon Eddie Marshall, Fourth Way took Handy's groundbreaking jazz concepts and plugged then directly into the mains. They managed three albums in their all too brief stay. This, the most notable, was cut live at the New Orleans House, Berkeley in 1968 but not released by Capitol's US Harvest imprint until 1970. The material is typically hippie eclectic for the period, moving from the gripping neo-boppish thrust of *Blues My Mind*, where White's scratchy, amped-up fiddle and Nock's distorted Rhodes piano figures rage noisily over the punchy rhythm section, to short, messy half-baked thumb-piano and recorder doodles more suited to the likes of The Fugs. But on the best cuts Fourth Way probe territories then uncharted. The modal intensity of the title track, where White's aggressive agility and Marshall's propulsive clout forerun Mahavishnu Orchestra's vertiginous attack, and the dark, edgy impressionism of *Strange Love*, reveal an inventive fire and passion they were sadly unable to ignite further. **JN**

# Fourth World

New review
**Encounters of the Fourth World**  Jovino Santos (f, kbds); **José Neto** (g), **Gary Brown** (b, v); **Airto Moirera** (d, perc); **Flora Purim** (v). B&W Ⓕ BW045 (57 minutes). Recorded 1995.

⑦ ❼

Moirera and Purim, the Dankworths of Brazil, are the core of this exhilarating world-music flavoured band. The disc was recorded live at Ronnie Scott's and in Amsterdam. Some of the tracks suffer from the extended flavour of a live session and might have been shorter and more focussed in studio versions. Nevertheless, playing live is what the band is about and it's easy to forgive some over-extended guitar solos when there are equally lengthy percusssion solos by Moirera that justify their presence by showing his simultaneous mastery of dynamics, timbre and milking an audience, as on the opening *Burning Money*. Purim shows why she is viewed as a major influence by so many singers: scatting one minute, deftly negotiating rapid close harmony passages with Moirera and Brown (in Portuguese) the next, before delivering the English lyrics to *What You See* and other songs with aplomb. Her voice blends well with the other singers and the joint vocals, together with Santos's sensitive keyboard settings, give the band a unique tonal palette.

Above all this is a vibrant and lively album with no signs of the tiring rigours of the lengthy world tour that preceded the recording. **AS**

# Karen Francis

New review
**Where Is Love?**  Francis (v); **George Colligan** (p); **James King** (b); **Aaron Walker** (d). SteepleChase Ⓕ SCCD31393 (63 minutes). Recorded 1996.

⑥ ❽

This is largely a ballad album, with only a few mid-tempo pieces and one bossa nova to break up the generally tranquil mood. Karen Francis has a bright, clear voice and an admirably thoughtful approach to a song. Her reading here of *Guess I'll Hang My Tears Out to Dry* is one of the most sympathetic I have heard, and everything she does is distinguished by taste and great musicality. The accompanying trio is excellent, in particular Colligan, who plays with great sympathy while retaining his individuality. His own début album was released on SteepleChase in 1996. Altogether, this is an excellent, if somewhat subdued, set. **DG**

# Panama Francis

1918

**Gettin' in the Groove**  Francis (d); **Francis Williams**, **Irvin Stokes** (t); **Norris Turney** (as, cl); **Howard Johnson** (as); **George Kelly** (ts, arr); **Red Richards** (p); **John Smith** (g); **Bill Pemberton** (b). Black & Blue Ⓕ 233320 (66 minutes). Recorded 1979.

⑥ ❻

Francis worked with the Lucky Millinder band in the early forties, spending plenty of time at the Savoy in Harlem. This medium-sized band sets out to create the kind of music that Millinder, Al Cooper's Savoy Sultans, Erskine Hawkins and dozens of other bands provided for dancers during that period. Under Francis's careful hands (and feet) the band bounces along and produces an infectious beat suitable for dancing, but also potent as a tapestry against which soloists can perform. Nearly everyone solos here (it is unfortunate that we do not hear a solo from John Smith, the guitarist who replaced Al Casey with Fats Waller years ago); Norris Turney turns in a fine tribute to Johnny Hodges on his own *Checkered Hat* and Francis Williams takes the trumpet role once played by Taft Jordan on the exciting *Harlem Conga*, a tune associated with Chick Webb. Panama calls the band his Savoy

Sultans and pays tribute to the original Sultans by including such Al Cooper tunes as *Stitches*, *Rhythm Doctor Man*, *Frenzy* and *Second Balcony Jump*. The music may be eclectic but it is all played with verve. **AM**

# Aretha Franklin
1942

**Aretha's Jazz** Franklin (v, p); 1968 tracks with orchestras arranged and conducted by **Quincy Jones; Ernie Royal, Snooky Young, Bernie Glow, Richard Williams, Joe Newman** (t); **Jimmy Cleveland, Benny Powell, Urbie Green, Thomas Mitchell** (tb); **George Dorsey, Frank Wess** (as); **Seldon Powell, King Curtis** (ts); **David 'Fathead' Newman** (f, ts); **Pepper Adams** (bs); **Spooner Oldham** (org); **Junior Mance** (p); **Joe Zawinul** (elp, org); **Kenny Burrell, Jimmy Johnson** (g); **Ron Carter** (b); **Tommy Coghill, Jerry Jemmott** (elb); **Bruno Carr, Roger Hawkins** (d); 1972 tracks with unidentified ensembles, soloists including: **Phil Woods** (as); **Billy Preston** (p). Atlantic Jazz Ⓜ 781230-2 (35 minutes). Recorded 1968/72.

⑥ ❼

Franklin, from Memphis, Tennessee, had a Baptist church background and as a teenager featured in her father's gospel troupe. In something of a career turnaround, she signed for Columbia records in 1960 and made a string of jazz-based albums with remarkably inappropriate arrangements and song selections. It took a move to Atlantic and an astute return to her natural musical habitat for her to register her first popular success. Since then her career has rarely faltered, though in recent years she has veered in style more towards the popular mainstream.

This disc takes selections first released on two different albums, **Aretha Franklin: Soul '69** and **Hey Now Hey (The Other Side of the Sky)**. The former record features thoroughly Basie-inspired charts from Quincy Jones and concentrates squarely on the blues. Franklin, utterly at home with the idiom, responds with some blues shouting the like of which had not been heard in a jazz context since the death five years previously of Dinah Washington. It may not be supper club jazz, but Jimmy Rushing would recognize a kindred spirit. Of the three 1972 tracks, *Somewhere* veers more towards the type of pop arrangement singers from Andy Williams to Diana Ross were then experimenting with, probably with the success of Roberta Flack in mind. However, all is retrieved in a swinging double-tracked vocal workout with a jazz big band on *Moody's Mood* before the date is wrapped up with a long, slow blues, *Just Right Tonight*, on which Billy Preston excels with a long, mood-setting opening solo. **KS**

# Nnenna Freelon

New review
**Shaking Free** Freelon (v); **Bill Anschell** (p); **John Brown** (b); **Woody Williams** (d); also appearing: **Rickey Woodard** (ts); **Scott Sawyer** (g); **Alex Acuña** (perc). Concord Ⓕ CCD4714 (58 minutes). Recorded 1996.

⑤ ❽

After three relatively commercial efforts on Columbia, Freelon has experienced something of a creative rebirth on her first album for Concord, recording it with her working trio of some two years' standing and allowing herself prodigious elbow-room within which to rephrase and variously reinvent songs such as *Out of This World*, *Birks' Works* and *Nature Boy*. Her voice still tends to be jammed on full volume much of the time, blotting out the possibilities inherent in light and shade, and the naturally garrulous quality this approach spawns tends to wear thin on the more reflective songs (*I Thought about You* with unaccompanied intro; *My Shining Hour* with piano alone), where archness can creep in uninvited. On sensitive pieces such as *Black Is the Colour* and Stevie Wonder's *Visions*, her upbeat interpretations are disastrously misplaced. The better-judged delivery and arrangement on *What Am I Here For?* suggests better things next time. **KS**

# Bud Freeman
1906-91

**Great Original Performances 1927-40** Freeman (ts, cl); **Jimmy McPartland, Bobby Hackett** (c); **Max Kaminsky, Bunny Berigan** (t); **Floyd O'Brien, Jack Teagarden, Tommy Dorsey** (tb); **Brad Gowans** (vtb); **Joe Venuti** (vn); **Pee Wee Russell, Benny Goodman; Frank Teschemacher** (cl); **Dave Matthews** (as); **Adrian Rollini** (bs, s); **Dave Bowman, Joe Sullivan, Jess Stacy, Claude Thornhill** (p); **Eddie Condon, Dick McDonough** (g, bj); **Jim Lannigan, Artie Bernstein, Artie Shapiro** (b); **Gene Krupa, Cozy Cole, Big Sid Catlett, Dave Tough** (d). Jazz Classics In Digital Stereo Ⓕ RPCD604 (63 minutes). Recorded 1927-40.

⑧ ❻

Robert Parker's techniques for turning old 78s into stereo have produced some turkeys, but this is not one of them. His successful rejuvenation of these tracks is fortuitous, for he has made a remarkably good choice from Freeman's best work. Freeman was the next major tenor sax innovator after Coleman Hawkins. His playing was lighter than Hawk's and probably had a considerable sway on the development of Lester Young's 'cool' style (Freeman plays 'cool' here on Ray Noble's 1935 *Dinah*, which has weathered the years surprisingly well). The McKenzie-Condon Chicagoans of 1927 are represented by *China Boy*, there is some nice Freeman clarinet in his quintet with Bunny Berigan, polished big-band things with Noble and Dorsey, a couple of tracks by Bud's Summa Cum Laude Orchestra, and all eight classics from the 1940 Famous Chicagoans' session which included both Jack Teagarden and Pee Wee Russell, as well as some of the finest collective ensemble playing on record. Also included is the 1933 version of *The Eel*, a performance which confirmed that Freeman was an important and progressive soloist in the thirties. Some people have unkindly suggested that Freeman spent the rest of his life re-working *The Eel*; be that as it may, Freeman made a substantial contribution to jazz, and it is well illustrated here. **SV**

---

**Chicago/Austin High School Jazz in Hi-Fi** Freeman (ts); with, on four tracks: **Jimmy McPartland** (t); **Pee Wee Russell** (cl); **Dick Cary** (p); **Al Casamenti** (g); **Milt Hinton** (b); **George Wettling** (d); on two further tracks sub: **Billy Butterfield** for **McPartland** (t); add **Tyree Glenn** (tb); on five tracks: **Billy Butterfield** (t); **Jack Teagarden** (tb, v); **Peanuts Hucko** (cl); **Gene Schroeder** (p); **Leonard Gaskin** (b); **George Wettling** (d). RCA Victor ⓜ 113031-2 (44 minutes). Recorded 1957.

⑥ ❽

Another worthy release in the fine RCA Germany reissue programme of fifties LPs which rarely these days get the chance to reappear as originally conceived. This stereo workout, from three different 1957 sessions, uses Freeman's soubriquet Summa Cum Laude Orchestra to cover the disparate personnel, but really just a re-convening of jam sessions from the past with old mates. Everybody knows what their role is and goes on to fulfil it, with the two trumpeters sounding particularly at ease. Freeman is content to add the second or third line to the ensemble passages, but usually takes the first solo on a piece, and his full, instantly recognizable tone is captured superbly. Even Russell's acrid sound, often punished harshly by unsympathetic engineers, has a properly balanced body behind the edge it undoubtedly possesses.

The lessening of energy which comes with middle-age is quite noticeable here, but that is largely compensated for by unselfish ensemble joys and a general glow of warm happiness from every player. McPartland in particular keeps his tone ringing and bright, his rhythm sharp as a tack. On the five tracks featuring Teagarden, the crisp ensemble work is supplemented by the trombonist's wonderfully graceful solo work, while on Freeman's anthem, *Prince of Wails*, Butterfield gets in a spirited chorus. And if Schroeder does not have Cary's sensitivity as an accompanist, then two Teagarden vocals make up any deficiency. **KS**

# Chico Freeman

1949

---

**Spirit Sensitive** Freeman (ss, ts); **Jay Hoggard** (vb); **John Hicks** (p); **Cecil McBee** (b); **Billy Hart**, **Don Moye** (d). India Navigation ⓔ IN1045CD (64 minutes). Recorded 1979.

⑧ ❽

Son of Chicago tenorman Von Freeman and a seventies member of the AACM, Chico Freeman's career has been rather erratic, the promise of his brighter moments never quite flowering into sustained achievement. A relatively conservative player, he is a good stylist, happy in most areas of the tradition, yet seemingly disinclined to forge a strong music of his own. He does excel at playing ballads, however, as the ten that comprise **Spirit Sensitive** make clear.

Freeman plays with great restraint and tenderness, his phrasing eloquent, his tone incorporating the barest hint of breathy vibrato. He gets sensitive support too, especially from the responsive McBee. Their duo track, a haunting *Autumn in New York*, is among the disc's high spots, as are the gentle reveries *A Child is Born* and *Carnival* (the latter featuring vibes and wistful soprano).

This CD has four more tracks than the original LP, including *Lonnie's Lament* and *Wise One*, where the Coltrane influence in Freeman's playing is to the fore. Regrettably, this generosity does not extend to the documentation, which omits recording details and composer credits. **GL**

---

**New review**

**Focus** Freeman (ts); **Arthur Blythe** (as); **George Cables** (p); **Santi Debriano** (b); **Yoron Israel** (d). Contemporary ⓔ CCD14073-2 (61 minutes). Recorded 1994.

⑧ ❽

Chico Freeman suffers a slight identity crisis among some fans, the result of earlier connections to what in the loosest sense can be called the avant-garde. Since then his best work has been realized in a fairly conservative context (though his electric Brainstorm group has its moments) and usually when playing the tenor. Far from reviving memories of what used to be called energy music, his solos exude the kind of calm that, linked to a warm and well-rounded tone, one associates with Yusef Lateef. The impact of later Stan Getz can also be heard, noticeably during the stop-start passages of *Blackfoot*, a stimulating tune by pianist Cables, and in parts of the ballad *To Hear a Tear, Drop in the Rain*. A long-time partner in various groups, Arthur Blythe makes the perfect foil, his unique shrill-singing sound generally allied to more agitated phrasing. Freeman exploits this contrast tellingly on *Peacemaker* by (as he points out) letting each of them interpret the tune in his own way. A faultless rhythm section, with Cables and Debriano taking fine solos, ties things up nicely. **RA**

# Von Freeman                                                    1922

**Walkin' Tuff**  Freeman (ts); **Jon Logan**, **Kenny Prince** (p); **Carroll Crouch**, **Dennis Carroll** (b); **Wilbur Campbell**, **Mike Raynor** (d). Southport Ⓕ 0010 (69 minutes). Recorded 1989.

⑧ ❼

Von Freeman is a great saxophonist and a Chicago legend; that his reputation has seldom escaped the Windy City's borders is due to sheer neglect on the part of the recording industry. A contemporary and peer of Illinois Jacquet, Dexter Gordon and Gene Ammons, he was not recorded as a leader until he was 50, and there have been precious few discs since then. This is a casual date, split between two competent rhythm sections (energized only by the presence of Campbell, another of the unsung legends of Chicago's post-bop community), that captures Freeman's unpredictability and peculiarities in a congenial setting. His tone is full of vigour and vinegar, in fact his playful idiosyncrasies of pitch are part of his charm and individuality, and he is unafraid to honk, squawk, or squeal expressively. *Bruz, George and Chico* (dedicated to his musician brothers and son) displays the convoluted logic of his lines, and the extreme chromaticism and jittery multi-noted phrases of *Blues for Sunnyland* lead to Dolphy. But *Every Tub* reveals his true roots in Herschel Evans and Lester Young, while the unaccompanied *How Deep is the Ocean* rivals Rollins for melodic intimations and ingenuity. The interest level drops dramatically when Von stops playing – the pianists are self-effacing and the bass solos tedious – but fortunately he is well featured, and should be heard.                **AL**

# Paolo Fresu

**New review**

**Mythscapes**  Fresu (t, flh, electronics); **Jon Balke** (p); **Furio DiCastri** (b, elb, electronics); **Pierre Favre** (d). Soul Note Ⓕ 121257-2 (73 minutes). Recorded 1995.

⑥ ❾

In one sense allocating this album to Fresu's leadership is misleading (the cover names all four musicians as co-leaders, as do the players themselves in the booklet-notes). In another, it seems apt. Fresu's is the dominant voice, even though each musician contributes at least one composition, and Blake's persuasive piano is ever-present. Fresu strikes the tone of the record and also contributes five tunes. His use of electronics to occasionally double and split his trumpet lines, either in union, octave, thirds or other intervals, is enhancing and at times startling, his Miles-based approach sufficiently abstracted to make it individual. If there is anything so much as a fault in this music, it could be that too much of the same mood of pensive creativity prevails, but if enough close listening is indulged in, then there are endless details of execution to delight and distract.                **KS**

# Don Friedman                                                    1935

**At Maybeck**  Friedman (p). Concord Ⓕ CCD4608 (63 minutes). Recorded 1993.

⑧ ❿

Friedman has worked, and sometimes recorded, with a number of important leaders including Dexter Gordon, Jimmy Giuffre, Shorty Rogers, Booker Little and Joe Henderson but his most fully realized work has always been as the leader of his own trio or, as here, as a true soloist. He has always worked closely to the manner of expression exemplified by Bill Evans (his earliest trio recordings for the Riverside label were remarkably similar in concept to Evans's albums which were appearing on the same label at the same time). This is probably his best solo album to date and he seems to have been inspired by the Maybeck piano (a Yamaha S-400B) and the attentive, appreciative audience. Unlike some of his other solo albums, there is a very positive approach here and a lack of self-indulgence. From the opening notes of *In Your Own Sweet Way* the listener knows he is in for a memorable musical experience. Friedman's careful gradation of touch and accurate digital work makes it easy to understand why he has worked for some time as a teacher. At the same time his classical training manifests itself too, notably on his thoughtful, original *Memory for Scotty*. But it is the manner in which he works out his musical ideas, developing them into a logical whole, which makes this such an important album of contemporary keyboard jazz. For those after a representative Friedman trio date, **Red Sky Waltz** (Alfa Jazz) is an up-to-date example.                **AM**

# David Friesen                                                    1942

**New review**

**Two for the Show**  Friesen (b); **Michael Brecker** (ts); **Uwe Kropinski** (g); **John Scofield** (elg); **Bud Shank** (as); **Clark Terry** (t, flh); **Denny Zeitlin** (p). ITM Pacific Ⓕ ITMP 970079 (66 minutes). Recorded 1992-3.

⑦ ❽

Friesen's 1987 album **Remember the Moment** was recorded live at The Hobbit, a club in Portland, and it provided the jazz world with a fine snap-shot of the local Oregon scene. More significantly it marked out the bassist as a player with considerable technical command, immediate creative flair and a genuine sympathy for the musicians around him. Since then, Friesen's horizons have broadened considerably and this CD confirms that he now belongs on the world stage. It also proposes that duos are a rewarding challenge, for here he has chosen partners on widely different instruments and representing distinctly varied stylistic areas. He manages several outstanding solos and takes part in fine chase passages but it is the way in which he responds to the two-man interactions that are of special interest. Each guest gets two titles and, in their way, all are well used. In Brecker's case the effect is virtually conversational, with the tenor predictably authoritative, inventive and fast-fingered. Scofield's full guitar sound makes for an ideal string duet, with the solo elements matched by beautifully balanced counterpoint. The belt is loosened a tad for Terry, where Friesen is happy to play second (bass) fiddle to the trumpeter's swing-drenched bebop. Zeitlin is the man to provide wave-clipping melody lines and allows Friesen to apply the undertow, while both Shank and Friesen deftly exploit the gulf between the alto's strident challenge and the bassist's relaxed walking gait. No such confrontation occurs with Kropinski, where emotional as well as creative acquiescence attend a fine partnership. Friesen can be judged by the company he keeps here. **BMcR**

## Johnny Frigo 1916

**New review**
**Début of a Legend** Frigo (vn); **Bob Kindred** (ts, cl); **Gene Bertoncini** (g); **Joe Vito** (p); **Michael Moore** (b); **Bill Goodwin** (d). Chesky Ⓕ JD119 (60 minutes). Recorded 1994.

⑦ ❾

Violinist Johnny Frigo plays with a warmth and facility comparable to those of his French peer, Stephane Grappelli. Why then, at the age of 79, does Frigo fall under the category "talent deserving wider recognition"? First, he spent the bulk of a productive career in Chicago as the Windy City's first-call studio bassist. In that capacity, he backed such diverse performers as Billie Holiday, Barbra Streisand, Lenny Bruce and Woody Allen. He also composed the official song of baseball's Chicago Cubs, *Hey, Hey, Holy Mackerel*, as well as the jazz standard *Detour Ahead*. It was only in the mid eighties when Frigo put aside his bass to focus on violin that his star began to shine widely.

Armed with a sheaf of glowing reviews and prominent TV guest shots, Frigo had a second recording 'début' (there had been a leader date on Mercury back in the fifties) in 1994 at the age of 77. It is an inspiring date brimming with lithe readings of evergreens such as Fats Waller's twirling *Jitterbug Waltz*, Django Reinhardt's haunting *Nuages*, Billy Strayhorn's poignant *Lush Life* and a punny original, *Bow Jest*. Frigo's soulful balladry is displayed in a lovely medley of two unlikely 'jazz' tunes, *Heather on the Hill* and *How Are Things in Glocca Morra?*. Abetted by Chicago crony, pianist Joe Vito, and a crew of swinging New Yorkers, the young-at-heart Frigo proves that experience (and grey hair) count! **CB**

## The Fringe

**It's Time for the Fringe** George Garzone (ts, ss); **John Lockwood** (b); **Bob Gullotti** (d). Soul Note Ⓕ 121205-2 (66 minutes). Recorded 1992.

⑦ ❽

Formed in Boston in the early seventies, this group has enjoyed an underground following for more than 20 years. This, their sixth album, explains why. The trio's musical outlook is free and all of the pieces at this concert were conceived on the spot. Appropriately all composer credits are given as by The Fringe, and in the main they are simple melodic hooks on which the players hang their personal statements. Garzone is both an inventive and lyrical player, able to put the right tonal flavour into his tenor and soprano work; his tenor on *Peace for L.A.* shows him also capable of subtlety, strength and an in-built sense of time. Circular breathing and the other contemporary saxophone tools are in his performance kitbag but there is no gratuitous showboating. Lockwood has a singing tone and a fine melodic flair, while the busy Gullotti gets his ride cymbal ringing with Billy Higgins-like intensity. He is a drummer who thinks ahead, both for himself and his colleagues, and his deliberately out-of-tempo passages greatly add to the rhythmic intensity. There is a strong feeling of relaxation, even in the more passionate moments, and this, allied to the freely melodic aspect of Fringe jazz, could make it more accessible to those suspicious of the more incontinent free players. **BMcR**

## Bill Frisell 1951

**Lookout for Hope** Frisell (g, elg, bj); **Hank Roberts** (vc, v); **Kermit Driscoll** (b); **Joey Baron** (d). ECM Ⓕ 833 495-2 (45 minutes). Recorded 1987.

⑦ ❿

Frisell was always destined to be an unconventional player. His early interests were varied and he tapped into Jimi Hendrix and the creative side of pop. He studied under Mike Gibbs at Berklee College and came to Europe with the trombonist's big band. There he met Eberhard Weber and in the late seventies and early eighties became something of a house guitarist at ECM. As this CD shows, he has managed to produce a personal synthesis of influences, never forgetting Wes Montgomery, but using the implied power of rock, as well as the texture-conscious sound production of the ECM ethic. In fact the title track demonstrates Frisell nursing rich tonal fluctuations with considerable artistry and showing how he is prepared to get his results by any means available. Performances like *Little Brother Bobby* and *Lonesome* have charm rather than depth and in his more clinical moments there is a certain New Age preciousness about his work. He is at his best, as on Remedio's *The Beauty* or *Hackensack*, when he rakes the thematic entrails and reminds the listener of the music's dirt road origins. The most important aspect of his playing is that he is now an original; he has made available new techniques and provided ground-rules to promote another generation of guitarists.     **BMcR**

---

**Have a Little Faith**   Frisell (g); **Don Byron** (cl, bcl); **Guy Klucevsek** (acc); **Kermit Driscoll** (b); **Joey Baron** (d). Elektra Nonesuch Ⓕ 79301-2 (61 minutes). Recorded 1993.

④ ❿

Frisell's eclecticism continues to become more all-embracing as his career broadens. Here we have some rather dicey re-arrangements of Aaron Copland's suite from his ballet, *Billy the Kid*, a crazy-mixed-up elaboration of Charles Ives's "Col. Shaw" from his *Three Places in New England*, plus retreads of songs by Bob Dylan, Madonna, Sonny Rollins, Stephen Foster and Muddy Waters.

Eclecticism is fine, just as long as it contributes something fresh to the original subject – even if that is merely a good-humoured send-up. To these ears, the Copland and Ives adaptations add little if anything to the original works (just as piano transductions of symphonies often have you longing for the full colour of the real thing), and it is only among the popular song rewrites, inconsistent as they are, that things get going. *Just Like a Woman* is not strong enough to stand on its own two musical feet, judging by this instrumental version, badly missing the emotion of Dylan's words, but Muddy's *I Can't Be Satisfied* receives a wonderful arrangement here, utterly different in instrumentation, but similar in intent to Muddy's own. Madonna escapes censure, while Rollins inspires a similarly quirky sense of humour to his own. A long programme, and one to dip into, rather than digest at one sitting. Frisell's later albums for Nonesuch, including the current **Quartet**, have diverged ever more widely from what could be described as a jazz format and content, so this session from 1993 remains the most potent of his recent jazz work.     **KS**

# Dave Frishberg                                                                     1933

---

**Can't Take You Nowhere**   Frishberg (p, v). Fantasy Ⓕ 9651-2 (54 minutes). Recorded 1986.

⑧ ❽

Frishberg is the most talented of the several jazz singer/songwriter/instrumentalists currently active. An accomplished pianist, (early in his career he had accompanied Carmen McRae and recorded with Bud Freeman and Jimmy Rushing, among others) Frishberg sometimes bases his songs on tunes by other musicians (the barrelhouse title track's melody comes from two blues by Tiny Kahn and Al Cohn). On this concert recording from San Francisco, he does a medley of songs by his hero Frank Loesser, plays compositions by Ellington, Berlin and Porter *sans* vocals, and showcases some of his own best melodies and lyrics, including *My Attorney Bernie* and a touching evocation of homesickness, *Sweet Kentucky Ham*, which demonstrate his verbal facility, wit, and eye (or ear) for telling detail (he studied journalism in college).

As a singer, Frishberg is an acquired taste, with a narrow range, adenoidal timbre, and a conversational delivery indebted to his early champion Blossom Dearie (she had a minor hit with his *I'm Hip*, co-written with Bob Dorough, which Frishberg hams up here). But his confidential delivery enhances the quiet humour of his lyrics – which is why he interprets his songs better than technically superior singers such as Rosemary Clooney or Susannah McCorkle.     **KW**

# Fred Frith                                                                        1949

---

**Step Across the Border**   Frith (g, b, vn, d, perc, v, kbds, home-made instr); **Tim Hodgkinson** (bcl); **Jean Derome**, **John Zorn** (as); **Haco** (p, v); **Bob Ostertag** (syn, sampler, tapes); **Lasse Hollmer** (kbds); **Zeena Parkins** (kbds, v, d); **Eino Haapala** (g); **Pavel Fajt** (g, v, perc); **Iva Bittova** (vn, v); **Tom Cora** (cel, d, v); **Tina Curran**, **Bill Laswell**, **Rene Lussier** (b); **Hans Bruniusson**, **Eitetsu Hayashi**, **Fred Maher**, **Kevin Norton** (d). East Side Digital Ⓕ 80462/RecRec30 (74 minutes). Recorded 1979-89.

⑧ ❻

Frith works mostly in the fields of art rock and non-idiomatic (i.e. non-jazz) improvisation, but there are good reasons to consider him a fellow-traveller with jazz. He has helped shape modern electric guitar concepts, notably by attaching alligator clips to the strings directly over the pickups – 'preparing' the guitar to get ringing doubled overtones and to warp the distance between intervals, creating artificial scales. He has also been allied with key figures on the New York and Amsterdam jazz scenes, such as John Zorn (as bassist in Zorn's loud thrash band, Naked City) and Han Bennink, with whom he plays duo.

A true internationalist, Frith, born and raised in England, has lived in New York and Munich, and his bands often reflect a conscientious ethnic/gender mix. This soundtrack from a documentary portrait finds him in more than a dozen settings: solo, duos with Zorn, Cora, Hodgkinson and others; with Skeleton Crews (Frith, Cora, Parkins); playing a few rock songs, improvising with collaborators from England, the US, Quebec, Sweden, Japan and the Czech Republic, occasionally using home-made mutant guitars. Always a resourceful, sound-conscious guitarist, Frith has a flair for appealing but not too simple melodies, some relying on East European scales, and is an original, tuneful electric bassist and good fiddler. **KW**

## Curtis Fuller                                                        1934

**Blues-ette** Fuller (tb); **Benny Golson** (ts); **Tommy Flanagan** (p); **Jimmy Garrison** (b); **Al Harewood** (d). Denon/Savoy Ⓜ SV0127 (37 minutes). Recorded 1959.

⑥ ❽

Fuller is to the post-bop era what J.J. Johnson was to early bop; in other words, he ignored the fact that the trombone should have appeared clumsy and inappropriate, and made it work alongside the fleet and flowing trumpeters and saxophonists who defined these styles. Naturally, Fuller was as influenced by Johnson as almost every other player of his generation, but he also aimed for the simplicity and obliquity of Miles Davis – perhaps more successfully in his early work than the later. Displaying a most attractive tone, often aided by a felt mute, he aims straight for the melodic core while the rhythm-section opens each piece by loping along in the two-to-the-bar style which Miles had recently reintroduced. Meanwhile Golson, lately graduated from the Jazz Messengers, offers the piquant contrast of a multi-noted style influenced equally by Don Byas/Lucky Thompson and his teenage colleague, John Coltrane. The material has a suitable modern-mainstream feel for the period, with the début recording of Golson's B-minor blues, *Five Spot After Dark* (a.k.a. *Nightlife*), being followed by Charlie Shavers's *Undecided*. It is, of course, reprehensible that Denon have failed to include on a single CD another of Fuller's equally short-running LPs for the same label, although, as part of their new recordings programme, they recently issued a CD called **Bluesette Part 2**. **BP**

## Slim Gaillard                                                       1916-91

**Laughing in Rhythm: The Best of the Verve Years** Gaillard (v, g, p); with a collective personnel of: **Taft Jordan** (t); **Bennie Green** (tb); **Buddy Tate**, **Ben Webster** (ts); **Dodo Marmarosa**, **Dick Hyman**, **Maceo Williams**, **Cyril Haynes** (p); **Pepe Benque** (bj); **Bam Brown**, **Ernie Sheppard**, **Clyde Lombardi**, **Ray Brown** (b); **Herbie Lovelle**, **Charlie Smith**, **Milt Jackson** (d); **Jim Hawthorne** (barks). Verve Ⓜ 521 651-2 (65 minutes). Recorded 1946-53.

⑥ ❺

As half of the twosome Slim & Slam (with Slam Stewart), Gaillard had a major hit in the late thirties with *Flat Foot Floogie*. Such giddy commercial heights were never reached again, but he did enjoy some ten years of wide popularity, and the period covered by this disc seems to represent something of a peak in terms of his overall musical activities. Certainly the live 'suite', later titled *Opera in Vout*, which comes from a spring 1946 JATP concert, shows both Gaillard and his partner Bam Brown working at comic white-heat in 12 minutes of inspired mayhem, much of which revolves around either verbal gymnastics or sly take-offs of then-popular jazz musicians and singers. It also confirms his largely neglected talents as a guitar improviser (also to be found at length on the out-of-print **Slim Gaillard at Birdland** (Hep), taken from radio airshots in the early fifties). Studio-bound moments of comic anarchy on this disc include the almost Dadaist *Chicken Rhythm* and *Serenade to a Poodle*, with their animal imitations and deliberately idiotic lyrics. At moments like these, Gaillard was jazz's equivalent of The Goons. Other performances find the formulas wearing a trifle thin, but Gaillard's good humour usually wins through on even the most mundane material. Two tracks here, by the way, see their long-delayed début: *Genius* and *Federation Blues*. The latter is a heartfelt moan directed at the Musician's Union as controlled at that time by James C. Petrillo (a good enough reason for its quick suppression), while *Genius*, an altogether more remarkable piece featuring Gaillard multiple-tracked on all instruments (including tap-dancing), was damned by association, being another number from the same withdrawn EP. Hopefully that will have piqued your interest enough to take the time to explore this fascinating period-piece. For those intent on Slim with Slam, Columbia have recently reissued 20 tracks from 1938-42 and called the disc **The Groove Juice Special**. **KS**

## Jim Galloway                                                        1936

**Jim Galloway and Art Hodes: Recorded Live at Café des Copains** Galloway (saxes); **Art Hodes** (p). Music & Arts Ⓔ CD610 (69 minutes). Recorded 1988.

⑧ ❽

This is a little gem of a record. By emigrating from Scotland to Canada, Jim Galloway has ensured that his soprano playing has never been in the centre of things, but he has recorded over the years with some mighty fine pianists such as Dick Wellstood, Jay McShann and Ralph Sutton, and it is reasonable to assume that such men would not have entered the cruel spotlight of a duo relationship if they were not sure of their partner. With this partnership, you could assume that the nerves were on Galloway's side. Not only was Hodes a living legend, but his technique is not exactly flamboyant; when all you have as a safety net is Hodes's rather sparse keyboard playing, you have to fly right. Galloway does fly right; his soloing throughout is fluent and ear-catching, while Hodes's backing is immensely satisfying – like all pianists who do not have technique to fall back on (Stan Tracey is another example), he has to think more than most, and a lot of the textures and patterns he supplies are not ones that would occur to more facile pianists. They enjoyed playing this date; the audience enjoyed it, and the players respond to the audience. The tunes are mostly standards (*I Would Do Most Anything*, *Some of These Days*, etc.) although Hodes's two solos are both more modern (*The Preacher*) and more ancient (*Tomorrow's Blues*). **MK**

# Hal Galper                                                            1938

New review

**Rebop**  Galper (p); **Jerry Bergonzi** (ts); **Jeff Johnson** (b); **Steve Ellington** (d). Enja Ⓕ ENJ9029-2 (59 minutes). Recorded 1994.

⑧ ❽

Initiated in what he now refers to as the "straight-ahead rhythm section" of 'Cannonball' Adderley, taught "drama and restraint" by his experience with Chet Baker, and his talent finally honed and polished by his decade-long stint with the chamber jazz group *par excellence*, the Phil Woods quintet, Hal Galper is now close to being the complete pianist, and this is his finest album since 1986's **Dreamsville** (Enja), a wonderfully subtle, elegant trio album featuring Wood's rhythm section. Galper is joined on this live outing by Dave Brubeck alumnus Jerry Bergonzi, long-time associate Steve Ellington, and a fresh but totally dependable bassist, Jeff Johnson. The saxophonist's sinewy, gruff tone provides a pleasing contrast to the leader's alternately burnished and chunkily percussive playing on an intelligent selection of standards and jazz originals ranging from a rhythmically ambitious version of Monk's *Jackie-ing*, through a spacy, contemplative *It's Magic*, to a clipped, slightly acerbic *Laura*. The title is defined on the CD's cover and neatly summarizes the band's approach: "[Post-bebop] jazz improvising ... that embodies the traditions of bebop but includes the musical advances since that time, i.e., group improvisation, medalism, free, pentatonic and intervallic improvising, as well as incorporating contemporary and historic rhythmic concepts." **CP**

# Frank Gambale                                                        1958

New review

**Thinking Out Loud**  Gambale (g); **Otmaro Ruiz**, **David Goldblatt** (kbds); **Brian Auger** (org); **Alphonso Johnson**, **Tim Landers** (b); **Dave Weckl** (d); **Walfredo Reyes** (perc). JVC Ⓕ 2045-2 (61 minutes). Recorded 1995.

⑥ ❾

Australian-born Gambale has been an influential performer and teacher of guitar on the West Coast of the USA since the early eighties and he is also the author of several books on guitar playing. His own music involves high-speed picking and a fluent assimilation of the semi-acoustic jazz guitar into the rock-fusion idiom. This is a balanced but ultimately rather samey set in a jazz-rock groove, enlivened on a couple of tracks by some passionate Hammond B3 organ playing from Brian Auger, recalling his pioneering group Trinity and his later work with John McLaughlin. There's no doubting Gambale's ability, but the diet is not sufficiently varied here to make a satisfying meal, nor are Gambale's claims to be inspired by a group of surrealist painters obvious enough to have any musical significance. More variety in tempo and perhaps a broader change in the line-up from one configuration to another would help put Gambale's own playing in a wider context, as well as offer more differentiation between his sidemen. Some of these are obviously noteworthy, and in particular some impressive piano flurries in the two-part *Avengers Suite* suggest that Ruiz possesses much of the mercurial talent of his namesake Hilton. **AS**

# Ganelin Trio

**Poco-A-Poco**  Vyacheslav Ganelin (p, basset); **Vladimir Chekasin** (reeds); **Vladimir Tarasov** (d). Leo Ⓕ CDLR101 (61 minutes). Recorded 1978.

⑦ ❼

The Ganelin Trio was formed in Russia in 1971, a mixture of American avant-garde, Willem Breuker laugh-in and European free improvisation. To this potent brew they added their own Russophian folk extras and an indomitable spirit as they faced sceptics, both home and abroad. This CD is from a session that took place before any other Ganelin issues appeared in the West. The music is equally dramatic, however, with Chekasin at his most potent, demonstrating throughout his impressive range, control of the false upper register and ability to build detailed solos from the most meagre of thematic germs. Tarasov is a comparable powerhouse, a muscular drummer who reads his colleagues well while balancing his work from whisper to shout with both taste and rhythmic subtlety. Ganelin himself is a comparative conservative, seemingly happier when harmonically positive themes are on the table. The trio is best judged as a whole, however, and it is then that the contrast between the group's surface fury and its more formal approach to structure becomes apparent. The projection of individual passion is undeniable but it cannot disguise the fact that the Ganelin's music is well prepared, even if only in outline form, and that the jazz world suffered a considerable loss when Ganelin emigrated to Israel and the group folded in 1987. **BMcR**

# Jan Garbarek

1947

**Afric Pepperbird** Garbarek (ts, bss, cl, f, perc); **Terje Rypdal** (g, bugle); **Arild Andersen** (b, thumb p); **Jon Christensen** (perc). ECM 843 475-2 (41 minutes). Recorded 1970.

⑦ ⑨

Born in Norway and influenced by John Coltrane at an early age, Garbarek was discovered by and later worked with George Russell. This CD offers the result of his first session for a major label and, as with Archie Shepp (another of his influences), it starts a recording career at a 'way out' point from which he later retreated. It shows an eclectic interest in the American scene of the time and takes him from the Chicagoan 'little instruments' soundscape of *Skarabee* to the headlong, freely improvised tirades of *Beast of Kommodo*, *Blow Away Zone* and the title track. He interacts consistently with his powerful group and, although inevitably the focal point, does not insist on total domination. On *Skarabee* he meets the need to be controlled in the false upper register superbly, on *Afric Pepperbird* he uses the bass saxophone like a subtle bludgeon, while on *Kommodo* his tenor strokes his personal conflagration from spark to free-ranging blaze, with an abrasive Shepp-like tone sounding the fire warning. Creativity was already a high priority and, although at this stage he was a player looking for a personal direction, he was already a very impressive jazz musician. **BMcR**

**Paths, Prints** Garbarek (ss, ts, wood f, perc); **Bill Frisell** (g); **Eberhard Weber** (b); **Jon Christensen** (d, perc). ECM Ⓕ 829 377-2 (51 minutes). Recorded 1981.

⑧ ⑩

**Path, Prints** is one of Jan Garbarek's most meditative and discreetly eloquent recordings. More abstract than much of his later, deeply folk-rooted anthemic work, its considerable power derives more from the variety of textures and moods created by the free interplay of the four musicians involved than from melody or rhythm. As the titles suggest – *Kite Dance*, *Considering the Snail*, *Still*, etc. – **Paths, Prints** is largely impressionistic, evoking subtle effects through nuance, quiet shifts of mood and hypnotically insistent repetition, rather than through unambiguous melodic statement. Garbarek mostly plays soprano saxophone – although he does contribute an affecting introduction to *Footprints* on wooden flute and a deceptively simple four-note tenor figure to *Ar* – and the combination of this pure-toned, plangent instrument with Bill Frisell's absorbed, deeply ruminative electric guitar sound is one of the album's chief attractions. Eberhard Weber is a superb anchor, his singing bass often carrying the pieces' closest approximation to the melodic line, allowing Garbarek, Frisell and the uniformly excellent Jon Christensen a freedom to embellish of which they take full and telling advantage. Not Garbarek's best work but very close to it, and an album of some importance in defining the ECM sound. **CP**

**Twelve Moons** Garbarek (saxes); **Rainer Bruninghaus** (kbds); **Eberhard Weber** (b); **Manu Katche** (d); **Marilyn Mazur** (perc); **Agnes Buen Garnas**, **Mari Boine** (v). ECM Ⓕ 519 500-2 (76 minutes). Recorded 1992.

⑤ ⑩

Garbarek has come a long way from the high-energy approach he adopted at the beginning of his solo career, over 25 years ago. In between, he has skirted the bottomless pit of twee-ness associated with ECM's more atmospherics-oriented musicians, but has never really fallen. Part of the reason for this is his continuing interest in folk music, both from his own and from other lands. **Twelve Moons**' title track is derived quite considerably from this interest; the knotty rhythms derived from these sources, plus the unpredictable melodic leaps, allow the musical associations to resonate rather than implode into fey pastiche.

Elsewhere, though, this album is much softer than its predecessor, **I Took Up the Runes**, and I'm not sure that's a good thing. Garbarek can be an incendiary soloist when the mood takes him, and the mood took him sufficiently to light up most of **Runes**. Here his concerns seem to lie with the overall sound and shape of his compositions and the way the group conjures this. When the drums are absent, things congeal rather quickly for lack of forward propulsion. They are what make *Twelve Moons* and the other long track, *Gautes-Margjit*, such enjoyable listening, giving a decided splash of sensuality to Garbarek's often severely ascetic vision, and spurring him to his most distinguished playing of the date. Garbarek's musical concerns (including the surprise hit **Officium** (ECM), with the Hilliard ensemble) have been moving him further from his jazz interests of late, and no subsequent release has yet mustered the impact to dislodge **Twelve Moons** from this guide. **KS**

# Paula Gardiner

**Tales of Inclination** Gardiner (b, f, g); **John Parricelli** (elg); **Mark Edwards** (p, kbds); **Ron Parry** (d). Sain Ⓕ SCDC2103 (55 minutes). Recorded 1995.

⑦ ❾

On the surface, this excellent début album by bassist and composer Paula Gardiner is a winsome, poetic affair, reflecting in large part her fascination with the rural calm of Wales, her adopted homeland. At its most literal, this effect is evident in the mystical impressionism of *Breathing,* but even at fast tempos, as on the soft textured, guitar-led samba of the opening track, a relaxedly expansive mood is generated. However, while delicacy and lyricism are surely keywords in Gardiner's musical vocabulary, her writing is deceptively muscular (sometimes explicitly so, as in the Tynerish bridge of the title track), and the presence of John Parricelli, one of Britain's finest young guitarists, as lead voice and chief soloist (sample his blistering work on *One Day!*) considerably thickens the mixture. Above all, although it contains many fine individual moments, **Tales** is to be savoured as a totality; apart from being a very competent bassist and an effective flautist, Gardiner loves to compose, and it is in that department that the record's greatest strengths lie, the imaginative writing combining with thoughtful programming to produce a work of suite-like integrity. Reduced to essentials, Gardiner's tunes fall into the usual categories – swing, Latin and ballad – but she offers rather more than mere essentials. **MG**

# Red Garland

**A Garland of Red** Garland (p); **Paul Chambers** (b); **Art Taylor** (d). Prestige Ⓜ OJCCD126-2 (42 minutes). Recorded 1956.

⑧ ❽

Texas-born Red Garland received his first musical training on clarinet and alto saxophone. Though he studied alto with Prof. Buster Smith, Charlie Parker's early mentor, a three-year boxing career provided a sabbatical that eventually led to piano. In the decade following the Second World War Garland worked with a host of stylistically varied players, including Billy Eckstine, Charlie Parker, Fats Navarro, Coleman Hawkins, Flip Phillips and Miles Davis. When he joined the latter's quintet in 1955, he soon won international recognition for his spare yet harmonically and rhythmically supple playing.

While influenced by fellow pianists Count Basie, Nat King Cole, Art Tatum, Erroll Garner, Ahmad Jamal and Bud Powell, Garland synthesized these and other contrasting sources into a uniquely individual style which was lean without being austere, sprightly (especially at medium tempos) and always swinging. A player of impeccable taste, Garland is an exemplar of Buckminster Fuller's "dymaxium principle" of doing more with less. Here, with poignant and self-effacing support from bassist Paul Chambers and drummer Art Taylor, Garland fashions exquisite medium-up interpretations of standards such as *A Foggy Day* and *September in the Rain*. There is a flag-waver, Parker's *Constellation*, where the boppish influence of Powell is evident, and there are thoughtful ballads like *Little Girl Blue* where the effect is like that of a subdued and meditative Garner. In all, a superb demonstration of the timeless talents of one of the jazz piano giants. **CB**

# Tim Garland

**Tales from the Sun** Garland (ts, ss, f, syn); **Anthony Kerr** (vb, mba); **Huw Warren** (p); **Tim Wells** (b); **Mark Fletcher** (d); **Bosco De Oliveira** (perc). EFZ Ⓕ 1014 (59 minutes). Recorded 1995.

⑥ ❽

A background that includes working with Ronnie Scott and performing in Lammas, a folk/jazz group formed with guitarist and poet Don Paterson, has provided Garland with a cosmopolitan outlook. He speaks of his early admiration for pianist Bill Evans rather than of the saxophone giants and he plugs into the same musical internet in terms of organization. His compositions have melodic grace and there are five on this, his début album as a leader. It is a quality that translates readily to his tenor, soprano and flute work and assists in solos that are well assembled and happy to retain the original themes as inspiration. His full-toned tenor is used to rebuild *All That's Left*, *Re: Person I Knew* and the title track, his soprano evokes thoughts of the thoroughfare on *Bebé* and the chill of winter on *Season of Faith*, while his flute flutters effectively on *Dawn Bird*. It could be argued that Garland places too much emphasis on restraint but, whatever the horn, there is a sense of conviction in all he plays. There are tasteful interludes for Kerr's vibraphone and marimba, Warren's piano roams from the gentle to the more obviously outspoken and the rhythm section assist in guaranteeing this promising newcomer a sympathetic hearing. **BMcR**

# Erroll Garner

**New review**

**This is Jazz** Garner, John Simmons, Wyatt Ruther, Al Hall (b); Specs Powell, Eugene Heard, Shadow Wilson (d). Columbia Ⓜ CK64968 (54 minutes). Recorded 1950-6

⑥ ❼

Garner was the first primitive produced by 'modern' jazz and remained the hottest bebop player of his time. His playing is as infectious as Armstrong's or Waller's and anyone who becomes blasé about his work is truly tired of jazz. He didn't read music and had his own way with its rudiments and rhythms. Nat Pierce was hired on one occasion to teach Garner new songs. The two sat at separate pianos and Pierce never lost the intense image of playing the tune and then suddenly having it power back at him in a musical tidal wave as Garner took hold of it. Garner's is a vivid music which had steady standards and consequently was rarely under par. This collection has him in varied moods and is well up to his standards, with *Easy to Love* and *Birdland* matching the form of his best album, **Concert by the Sea**. **SV**

**Concert by the Sea** Garner (p); Eddie Calhoun (b); Denzil Best (d). Columbia Ⓜ 451042-2 (44 minutes). Recorded 1955.

✔ ⑧ ❻

This is one of the very few jazz albums to get into the 'Billboard' pop charts (No. 12 in 1958) and is a strong candidate for the best-selling jazz piano record ever. It sold in its millions and could be found, along with Brubeck and Sinatra, on the shelves of people who would never have called themselves jazz fans.

All this is very easy to understand. Garner's style is tuneful, dramatic, by turns witty and swooningly romantic, full of virtuosity smilingly presented. It is also unique; even the most unpractised ear can recognize Erroll Garner after a few bars. All his trade marks are on display in this live recording; the chugging left hand (like rhythm guitar), the bouncing right-hand fingers, the filigree treble. There are also several examples of his speciality, the 'keep-'em-guessing introduction'. These can go on for several minutes, with great, portentous chords, meaningful pauses and misleading hints until, at the least expected moment, the tune comes blithely tripping out. It never failed to raise a storm of applause, as it duly does here.

It is almost impossible to deliver a judgement on Erroll Garner's music because there is nothing else remotely like it. Even his technique was so unorthodox that classically trained pianists declare it to be impossible. Along with all his other gifts he was completely ambidextrous; this, plus his intuitive grasp of the most complex harmonies, made it impossible for him to be precisely duplicated. **DG**

**Solitaire** Garner (p). Mercury Ⓜ 518 279-2 (72 minutes). Recorded 1955.

✔ ⑩ ❼

This and its companion piece **Afternoon of an Elf**, which has already been and gone on CD, are the product of one spring day's work in the studio when Garner was not only nursing an injury to one hand (he had a finger in a splint), but was also uncommonly inspired. And for once, the sound quality is pretty good, too. It has often been said that Garner hardly needed a rhythm section because his left hand was one in itself. Here there is no rhythm section, and although **Solitaire** concentrates for the most part on the reflective side of his playing (**Elf** highlighted the more dynamic aspects), not once do you wonder where the bass and drums got to.

As usual, Garner re-casts his choice of standards to the point where he virtually reinvents them, and with *Over the Rainbow* he launches into over ten minutes of incredibly rich pianistic embroidery and fantasy. Garner may have been a player who by and large stuck to a particular form in his performances – intro, theme, extemporization, theme and cadenza – but then most jazzmen don't even think as far about form as Garner did, and although his model in this may have been Tatum, he was a great deal more imaginative in the way he applied this form to his own performances. His imagination is at its peak when he plays solo, and this collection is Garner on top solo form. His *A Cottage for Sale* is a good illustration of this, where the stages of his treatment of the song flow seamlessly into each other, sounding for all the world like an intimate conversation between the pianist and his listener. An apt way to describe the song's lyrics. There are four extra tracks here, originally released on the LP **Erroll!** (the **Afternoon of an Elf** CD has the rest of the **Erroll!** solo pieces on it). None of the performances fall below a formidably high standard. **KS**

# Carlos Garnett

**New review**

**Resurgence** Garnett (ts); Carlton Holmes (p); Brad Jones, Steve Neil (b); Taru Alexander, Shingo Okudaira (d); Neil Clarke (perc). Muse Ⓕ MCD5544 (58 minutes). Recorded 1995.

⑥ ❽

A musical soldier of fortune, Garnett paid his dues, dropped out due to personal problems and returned, retaining the best of his music and jettisoning the surface gloss. Born in Panama, he settled in New York in 1962. He served a year in Blakey's academy of Jazz Messengers and worked with

Andrew Hill, Charles Mingus and Miles Davis. **Black Love** (Muse 5040), his recording début as a leader in 1974, has recently returned to the catalogue, but as something of a confusion of fusion it did little for his reputation. This CD gives a picture of Garnett today. The appropriately named *Resurgence* establishes Coltrane as his mentor by proxy and presents Garnett at his most swaggeringly extrovert. He applies a discreet samba touch and flowing logic to *Maiden Voyage* but it is the soulful intensity found on *Panamoon, Part 1* and *Soul Eyes* that most impresses. His flirtation with fusion probably exerted as much evolutionary pressure as did his days with Blakey and Mingus but this album presents a musician who has put that episode in the past and is reconciled to his place in the present scheme of things.                                           **BMcR**

# Kenny Garrett

**Black Hope**  Garrett (as, ss); **Joe Henderson** (ts); **Kenny Kirkland** (p, syn); **Donald Brown** (syn); **Charnett Moffet** (b); **Brian Blade** (d); **Don Alias** (perc). Warner Bros. Ⓕ 945017-2 (66 minutes). Recorded 1992.

✓                                                                                                    ⑦ ❽

Another messenger from the Art Blakey finishing school, Garrett was the saxophonist in Miles Davis's last group and, with the trumpet giant's health failing, was the group's most creative spokesman. His duties with Davis put some emphasis on the blues but Garrett's own recording dates have presented a more cosmopolitan face, using material from various jazz strains with the emphasis on the bop vernacular rather than the rarefied Davis dialect. This CD is typically non-specific and shows that he fits easily into most of his contemporary stances. *Jackie and the Bean Stalk* and *Books and Toys* have him driving an orthodox hard-bop quartet; on *Tacit Dance Computer G* and the gladiatorial *Bye Bye Blackbird* he jousts with the eloquent Henderson, while on three titles he enjoys the comfort of a percussion-assisted Latinesque ride. The recently left Davis-world is conjured up on *Two Step* and *Bone Bop*, in particular, and he closes the album with a brief but heartfelt alto solo. The various line-ups used throughout make a nonsense of stylistic wars, and if you were to leave a CD in a time capsule to be opened in the year 2300, this would be as honest an example of jazz from 1992 as you could find.                                                                                        **BMcR**

# Michael Garrick                                                                              1933

New review

**Parting is Such**  Garrick (p); with the following collective personnel: **Dave Green** (b); **Alan Jackson** (d); **Don Rendell** (ss); **Chris Garrick** (vn). Jazz Academy Ⓕ JAZA3 (76 minutes). Recorded 1994/95.

⑧ ❾

Garrick's second trio CD for Jazz Academy (his first was **Lady in Waiting**, JAZA1) is an impressive example of his playing and compositional abilities. There are moments of introspection but plenty of extrovert swinging plus, on *Premises Blues*, a 'disciplined' piece of free playing. The apparent contradiction is explained by the fact that this comprises 12-bar choruses which don't use the blues harmonies and form the basis for some amazing interlocking of piano, bass and drums lines. The opening *Bailero* is played as a solo by Michael and is an interpretation of a fairly obscure piece by the French composer Joseph Canteloube. Garrick rotates the theme through all 12 keys, each modulation giving the musical fragment a new and intriguing persona. There are two tributes by Garrick to other musicians, *3/4 for Bill* for Bill Evans and *Goodbye Dad* dedicated to the late Bruce Turner. Don Rendell makes just one appearance, playing soprano on *Song of the Elms* to such good effect that one wishes he had been more prominently featured on the CD. The surprise is Paul McCartney's *Here, There and Everywhere* played by Garrick's violinist son Chris as a tribute to his teacher, the late Johnny Van Derrick; hopefully Chris will be heard again on later Garrick CDs.                                                                                          **AM**

# George Garzone

New review

**Fours and Twos**  Garzone (ts, ss); **Joe Lovano** (ts); **Joey Calderazzo** (p); **John Lockwood** (p); **Bill Stewart** (d). NYC Ⓕ 6024-2 (61 minutes). Recorded 1996.

⑦ ❾

Garzone casts a fresh hue over post-bop exercises. He's an intellectual player and an occasionally stunning one. Long, unbroken lines spilling over the expected stopping places recall Warne Marsh; his writing quickly shifts between moods, and he uses Lovano, of a heavier tone, as a timbral foil. *Have You Met Miss Jones* uses a weird eighth-note spin-off of the Rodgers and Hart melody played in unison by Garzone and Calderazzo, with Lovano heavy-breathing the melody below it: these are solid arranging ideas, somewhere between eccentric and perfectionist. Lovano's role was likely to be secondary since the record is under Garzone's name, but to hear the two saxophonists circle around the chord changes, creating odd intervals on the fly, is to wish that there could have been more dialogue on this level – convoluted, heady, searching.                                                    **BR**

# Giorgio Gaslini                                                                                    1929

**Multipli**  Gaslini (p); **Roberto Ottaviano** (ss, as, bcl); **Claudio Fasoli** (ss, ts); **Bruno Tommaso** (b); **Giampiero Prina** (d). Soul Note Ⓕ 121220-2 (45 minutes). Recorded 1987.

⑧ ❽

Gaslini is more than just the best-known, most accomplished jazzman in Italy; he is a world-class artist who has toured extensively and recorded over 50 albums with his own groups and musicians like Anthony Braxton, Roswell Rudd, Jean-Luc Ponty and Steve Lacy. A thoughtful, fluent pianist, his individual approach is that of a conceptualist, as his challenging programmes of music by Monk, Robert Schumann and Albert Ayler prove. On the aptly titled **Multipli** he explores the variety of voicings, textures and moods available to the quintet *à la* Andrew Hill or Stan Tracey. His airy arrangements make excellent use of Ottaviano and Fasoli, a matched pair of blithe spirits. The title tune offers them space and open harmonies, and they use the freedom with great restraint. Gaslini's classical touch and quizzical demeanour is evident on *Interni,* and there is an echo of *Harlem Nocturne* in Fasoli's tenor, although the contrast of moods never jolts. It is likely Jelly Roll Morton would not recognize his *Chicago Breakdown,* as the horns reconstruct the theme from fragments while Tommaso layers in tactile *arco* effects. *Piano Sequenza* juxtaposes an Ayleresque dirge with march-like material, and *Ornette or Not* captures the inherent optimism of its namesake. In sum, a stylish and fresh perspective from an underrated musician.                                               **AL**

# Gateway

New review
**Homecoming**  John Abercrombie (elg); **Dave Holland** (b); **Jack DeJohnette** (d). ECM Ⓕ 1562 (73 minutes). Recorded 1994.

⑧ ❿

**Homecoming** is a reunion of old bandmates, but it has elements of a new enterprise too. The trio has an ancient pedigree, producing in its first incarnation (1975-7) two albums for ECM – **Gateway** and **Gateway 2**. Reflecting no doubt the cultural tenor of the times, the first edition of **Gateway** concentrated on the interior world, producing hippie chamber jazz. That introspective element is still evident on the new record, typically on Abercrombie's *Short Cut,* but elsewhere two things – the reconciliation of art jazz with r&b (a marriage typified by M-Base) and the return of the jazz standard – seem to have moderated the music. These effects are manifested in muscular riff tunes like Holland's *How's Never* (shades of Led Zeppelin), the inclusion of tunes that function like conventional jazz standards (*Short Cut* and even a blues, *7th D*) and, generally speaking, more chromatic harmony, a warmer emotional climate and a more robust, focused approach. The passing years haven't done the players' techniques any harm either. Abercrombie, historically a rather reticent player, has developed new musical sinew in recent times, putting it to good use in a blazing solo on *How's Never* and in some magnificent comping during the drum *ad lib* on the 10/4 Latin piece *Modern Times.* DeJohnette, always a fine drummer, plays his cymbals like tuned percussion, the sound captured to crisp perfection by ECM's exacting recording engineer. A subsequent album, **In The Moment** (ECM), places more emphasis on free improvisation.                                                            **MG**

# Charles Gayle                                                                                      1939

**Consecration**  Gayle (ts, bcl); **William Parker** (vc, vn); **Vattel Cherry** (b); **Michael Wimberley** (d). Black Saint Ⓕ 120138-2 (68 minutes). Recorded 1993.

⑧ ❽

In a jazz world cosily reassured by the neo-classicist movement, Gayle is one of the ultimate 'outcats'. Born in Buffalo, NY, he had early piano lessons but is self-taught on saxophone. He jammed with the likes of Archie Shepp and Pharoah Sanders in the sixties but then, as now, was basically a loner. He moved to New York City in the seventies and has played on streets and in subways ever since. His more recent association with the Knitting Factory has brought him to more serious notice and he now has the beginning of a recording portfolio.

This CD does not feature his idiosyncratic piano but it suggests that, whether he used tenor, bass clarinet or blow torch, his music would have the same incendiary qualities. His style does owe something to Albert Ayler's world of the sixties but he sets his own guidelines and is indisputably virtuosic. Thoughts of the field holler are evoked on *O Father*; *Rise Up* is an unashamed *cri de coeur,* while *Justified* has an ineluctable rhythmic thrust that is almost frightening. His bass clarinet on *Thy Peace* navigates more gentle waters but it is his wild freedoms, intimidating power and melody demolitions that have made him one of jazz's most potent non-conformists.                                                               **BMcR**

# Gianni Gebbia

**Outland** Gebbia, (ss, as, prepared sax); **Lelio Giannetto** (b); **Vittorio Villa** (d); **Massimo Simonini** (turntables, kbds, objects, v). Splasc(h) Ⓕ 315-2 (55 minutes). Recorded 1990.

⑦ ❽

Gebbia is one of a new generation of unheralded, adventurous Italian (in his case Sicilian) jazz musicians influenced by the flood of various post-war styles. One common decision has been to blend folk musics and local colour into their improvising, and Gebbia is comfortable in such modal surroundings, often at rhapsodic tempos. He can also spray notes at will and is unafraid of noise for its own sake. His primary sax is the soprano, and there is little doubt that the music of Steve Lacy, Anthony Braxton and Wayne Shorter helped point him in that direction. But his search for additional colours has led him on previous recordings to include didjeridu (an Australian aboriginal wind instrument) and Sicilian voices, as well as electronics of his own devising. Here, Simonini is the wild card, manipulating turntables and found-sound samples to play havoc with the trio. His electronics seldom mirror the acoustic instruments; he is at his most effective and most shocking injecting a sampled melismatic vocal on the North African-tinged *Shamal*, sound splurges in *Zero in Geometry*, or cartoonish hi-jinx in *Outland*. The sometimes over-extended performances may evoke atmosphere in lieu of invention, but Gebbia's music should be of interest to those looking for an alternative to conventional (i.e. American) jazz. **AL**

# Herb Geller
1928

New review
**Plays the Al Cohn Songbook** Geller (as, ss); **Tom Ranier** (p, cl, bcl, ts); **John Leitham** (b); **Paul Kreibach** (d); **Ruth Price** (v). Hep Ⓕ CD2066 (75 minutes). Recorded 1994.

⑥ ❽

Californian Geller was firmly identified with the West Coast progressives during the fifties but during the course of the next decade relocated to Germany, which he has used as a base ever since. He and his late wife Lorraine Geller made records with EmArcy in the fifties, but such opportunities became less frequent in Europe, so this latest Hep effort is a welcome arrival. It is doubly welcome for being a carefully thought-out programme rather than the usual hotchpotch of standards with a thrown-together rhythm section. Geller of course knew Cohn, so it is natural that he would want to pay tribute to a highly talented but curiously neglected song-writer and arranger. Cohn's saxophone work is justly celebrated, but Geller effortlessly demonstrates here that Cohn's more formal musical thinking had much to offer the improviser curious enough to seek it out. Geller's roots in Parker and the old Californian scene certainly aid his empathy with the material, and while there is a rather anodyne quality to the Hollywood recording, not helped when pianist Ranier overdubs his own rather pallid reed solos, Geller always impresses with his spirit and his imagination. In addition to Cohn's originals, there are pieces by Johnny Mandel and Geller himself. Vocalist Price appears on three tracks. It might have been less. **KS**

# Stan Getz
1927-91

**Stan Getz at the Shrine** Getz (ts); **Bob Brookmeyer** (vtb); **John Williams** (p); **Bill Anthony** (b); **Art Mardigan**, **Frank Isola** (d). Verve Ⓜ 513 753-2 (70 minutes). Recorded 1954.

⑧ ❻

This Los Angeles concert was recorded when the group had matured into a singularly fine improvising band. Getz paid the lowest wages he could get away with and was lucky to enrol such giants of the time as Brookmeyer and Williams. Having taken Bob Brookmeyer into his band, Getz let the valve trombonist hold sway with a powerful influence over both the band's repertoire and over Getz's own playing. The spirit of Kansas City jazz reigned within a neo-bop group. There was always more to Getz's talents as a leader than has been acknowledged and the sensitive selection of material reaches its acme in Al Cohn's *Tasty Pudding*, a mournful theme which should have become a jazz standard. Brookmeyer the composer is represented by *Open Country*; Johnny Mandel, briefly in the quintet on trombone before Brookmeyer, by the stomping *Pernod*. The concert was recorded during a tour which included the Gerry Mulligan Quartet, wherein Brookmeyer, Anthony and Isola had all done time. In fact Isola was still a member of Mulligan's group, and there was some friction between leaders over the drummer's appearance on the two studio recorded tracks here, a fetching version of the superior ballad *We'll Be Together Again* and a romping version of Basie's *Feather Merchant*. Getz emerged butterfly-like from his 'cool' period at this time, and this is a fine example of his Brookmeyer-inspired commitment to mainstream jazz. Finally, CDs displaying the original piano style of John Williams are to be winkled out like truffles. The opportunity to pick this one up from above ground should not be missed. **SV**

New review
**East of the Sun: The West Coast Sessions** Getz (ts); **Conte Candoli** (t); **Lou Levy** (p); **Leroy Vinnegar** (b); **Stan Levey**, **Shelley Manne** (d). Verve Ⓕ 314 531 935-2 (three discs: 228 minutes). Recorded 1955-7.

⑦ ❿

If West Coast jazz means slightly awkward polyphony, this is the stuff. Candoli and Getz sometimes just don't work well together – even on *S-h-i-n-e*, featuring a pellucid, epic solo by Getz which is one for the books (his own playing on these sessions is fabulous). Much has been made (by Getz and by historians) of the fact that, despite the title of the first LP represented on the set, this was not anaemic 'West Coast Jazz' – it was in fact being played by red-blooded East Coasters out West for a career change. The tunes strengthen the point – East-Coast bop workouts like *Four* and *A Night in Tunisia* are included. Nevertheless, it has that upright, fugal quality that one associates with cool jazz. The later sessions are preferable because the air is cleaner; Getz seems more comfortable without the presence of another horn. The material continues to be well-chosen bop and show standards.

It gets the full Verve reissue treatment, with alternative takes and false starts; these draw closer attention to the artistry of the leader and also of Lou Levy, whose spiky Bud Powell-school solos, containing the rhythmic *frisson* Getz avoids, are generally worth a second listen. **BR**

### Stan Getz and J.J. Johnson at the Opera House  Getz (ts); **Johnson** (tb); **Oscar Peterson**
(p); **Herb Ellis** (g); **Ray Brown** (b); **Connie Kay** (d). Verve Ⓜ 831 272-2 (73 minutes). Recorded 1957.

✓     ⑩ ❻

None other than Johnson himself has recently alluded to the "circus atmosphere" that surrounded many Jazz-at-the-Philharmonic performances. In this case, the excitement was fully earned, the natural product of imaginatively matching some extrovert and more restrained players. The blends of Getz and Johnson as featured voices, the Peterson trio and Kay in support, and this front line with this rhythm section inspires each member of the sextet to memorable contributions. Great ballad features balance more hard-driving jams in an environment in which *My Funny Valentine* inspires burning creativity. They sounded so nice, Norman Granz recorded them twice – in stereo at Chicago's Opera House, then eight days later in mono at the Los Angeles Shrine Auditorium – and released both versions in similar packaging without indicating the difference. The CD has the entire superior Chicago set, plus four of the L.A. tracks. **BB**

### Focus  Getz (ts); **John Neves** (b); **Roy Haynes** (d); **The Beaux-Arts Quartet** and other unidentified
strings; **Hershey Kay** (dir). Verve Ⓜ 821 982-2 (38 minutes). Recorded 1961.

✓     ⑩ ❽

**Focus** is unlike any other saxophone-and-strings record ever made. Getz and the composer Eddie Sauter devised an entirely new musical form for this one record, and it was never subsequently taken up by anyone, not even Getz himself. Sauter wrote what amounted to a complete composition for small string orchestra, plus bass and drums, with a lot of space in it, and left Getz to complete the picture. The result is a glowing work of remarkable cohesion and depth, yet one which can be enjoyed by absolutely anyone.

The time-honoured way of writing for saxophone and strings is to treat the saxophone like a ballad singer, packed around with strings in the form of a soft cocoon or pillow. There is absolutely nothing wrong with this method, as Ben Webster, Zoot Sims and many others have proved over the years, but **Focus** showed that it was not the only way. Whereas most string arrangers drew their inspiration from the nineteenth-century Romantics, Sauter seems to have drawn his mainly from Bartók. The result is a spikey, energetic work, relieved by moments of deep, contemplative calm. One of the seven movements (*I'm Late, I'm Late*) is cast in the form of a mini-double concerto for Getz and his favourite drummer, Roy Haynes. Another (*I Remember When*) is a kind of pastoral idyll. It is almost impossible to believe that music of such clarity, emotional breadth and formal elegance can have been created by a method so untried and risky. For Getz himself, **Focus** represented a crucial moment, the moment when everything about his playing began to grow and deepen. It spread like some vast, luxuriant plant until, by the end of his life, it had outgrown the confines of jazz itself. **DG**

### The Girl From Ipanema – The Bossa Nova Years  Getz (ts); with the following collective
personnel: **Doc Severinsen, Bernie Glow, Joe Ferrante, Clark Terry, Nick Travis** (t); **Ray Alonge** (frh); **Tony Studd, Bob Brookmeyer, Willie Dennis** (tb); **Gerald Sanfino, Ray Beckenstein, Eddie Caine, Babe Clark, Walt Levinsky, Romeo Penque** (f, cl, bcl); **Hank Jones, Steve Kuhn** (p); **Jim Hall, Tommy Williams, Keter Betts, George Duvivier, Don Payne, Gene Cherico** (b); **Johnny Rae** (d); **Jose Paula** (tamb); **Carmen Costa** (cabassa); **Charlie Byrd, Luiz Bonfa, Kenny Burrell, Laurindo Almeida, João Gilberto** (g); **Gene Byrd** (g, b); **Antonio Carlos Jobim** (g, p); **Gary Burton** (vb); **Luiz Parga, Jose Paulo, Buddy Deppenschmidt, Bill Reichenbach, Paulo Ferreira, Jose Carlos, Dave Bailey, Milton Banana, Joe Hunt, Helcio Milito, Edison Machado, Jose Soorez** (d, perc); **Maria Toledo, Astrud Gilberto, João Gilberto** (v). Verve Ⓜ 823 611-2 (four discs: 221 minutes). Recorded 1962-4.

⑩ ❻

Getz was not the first jazz musician to involve himself in Brazilian music but he probably did more to popularize it internationally than any other. Although his first LP in the Brazilian idiom did not actually carry the words "bossa nova" anywhere on its sleeve, it nevertheless sparked off interest in this blending of the music of North and South America. This four-CD set (complete with booklet) brings together all of the bossa nova music which Getz recorded for the Verve label and is virtually the equivalent of five LPs (**Jazz Samba**, **Big Band Bossa Nova**, **Jazz Samba Encore**, **Getz/Gilberto** and **Getz/Almeida**) plus various other tracks including five previously unissued performances. The best tracks are in the majority, that is the small band titles where Stan blends so beautifully with the guitar work of João Gilberto, Charlie Byrd and Laurindo Almeida as well as providing ideal support to the voices of João and Astrud Gilberto and the fine singing of Maria Toledo. At a time when jazz seemed in danger of turning in on itself, Getz came up with albums of pure melody, allied to the intriguing, shifting rhythms of Brazil. This is the definitive collection of bossa nova material by the master, including the original versions of songs such as *Desafinado* and *The Girl from Ipanema*. Much of this music was recorded on 30ips tape initially and the discovery of the original master tapes in most instances means that the intimate group sounds have been retained in pristine condition. A classic collection. **AM**

---

**Sweet Rain** Getz (ts); **Chick Corea** (p); **Ron Carter** (b); **Grady Tate** (d). Verve Ⓜ 815 054-2
(37 minutes). Recorded 1967.

✔️ ⑩ ❾

*Sweet Rain* was a revelation on its first issue, some 27 years ago; it showed an abrupt change for Getz, away from any involvement in the by then evaporated bossa-nova craze, away from the sometimes lightweight elegance of the quartet with Burton, towards a new interest in more flamboyant expressivism. On Corea's piece *Litha*, for example, he continually distorts his tone, creating boiling, bubbling rages of notes as the composition alternates between its two halves, one at medium, one at fast tempo. That this piece is modal in the manner of Miles and Coltrane, and that the rhythm section here has the elasticity of both men's groups, cannot also have been coincidental. Getz was reacting, in his own way, to the prevailing spirit of the times.

The rhythm section is exemplary in its support, with Grady Tate producing drumming which is both memorable and enjoyable in its own right while not being distracting. Corea paces Getz with amazing exactitude, feeding him ideas, moods, alternatives, while also being prepared to react to his every nuance. Carter is impeccable. With *O Grande Amor* and *Con Alma*, Getz is re-interpreting old territory, but he seems intent on doing so from a radically different vantage point. The title track, a Mike Gibbs composition, brings forth a performance of unearthly beauty. **KS**

---

**The Dolphin** Getz (ts); **Lou Levy** (p); **Monty Budwig**, **Victor Lewis** (d). Concord Ⓕ CCD4158
(46 minutes). Recorded 1981.

❾ ❽

Recorded live at San Francisco's Keystone Korner in May 1981, as Getz was in the process of setting up residence in the Bay area, this remains one of the tenor saxophonist's most evocative testaments to the capacity of jazz as a medium of transcendent melodic expression.

The repertoire, with its lyric lines and provocative harmonic grids, is perfection; so too is Getz's rhythm section. Indeed, if jazz is music's quintessential form for intimate and yet dynamically interactive conversation, discussants Getz, Levy, Budwig and Lewis provide a textbook example of mainstream interlocution elevated to the level of art. Two of the loveliest examples of Getz's melodic invention are his exquisite readings of Johnny Mandel's haunting ballads, *A Time for Love*, and *Close Enough for Love*. Clifford Brown's bebop anthem *Joy Spring* unfolds with similar mellifluence, albeit at a loping medium gait. Throughout the rhythm tandem of Levy and Budwig, Lewis whispers powerfully. Levy also deserves credit for his exuberant yet disciplined solo work which provides an effective foil for Getz's inspired limning. Also of note are Getz's poignant rhapsodizing on *My Old Flame* and his lithe Latinizations of Luiz Eca's sleek title track and *The Night Has a Thousand Eyes*.

Regardless of tempo or rhythmic pattern, Getz again proves himself a sublime yet always swinging classicist. **CB**

---

**Anniversary** Getz (ts); **Kenny Barron** (p); **Rufus Reid** (b); **Victor Lewis** (d). EmArcy Ⓕ 838 769-2
(70 minutes). Recorded 1987.

✔️ ❽ ❽

This Copenhagen concert exemplifies what Stanley Dance dubbed 'mainstream' jazz – standards and blues played in a style which naturally and seamlessly combines the values of swing (the genre) and hard bop. Barron and Lewis are among the most creatively sympathetic accompanists in modern jazz, always suggesting new ideas to the soloist. Like Reid they frame everything in terms of emphatic but relaxed swing. The burping, amplified bass sound is about the only real problem, endemic to period concert recordings.

By 1987, Getz's gorgeous tone had deepened slightly – as with many tenor players, his sound became more lustrous as he approached 60 – and he sounds as elegant as ever, with delicacy and manly grace at odds with the popular image of Getz the prickly, difficult leader. *Stella by Starlight* is buoyant, a war-horse played without the cynicism repetition can breed. Billy Strayhorn's meditation on his own mortality, *Blood Count*, gets an especially plaintive reading, yet the pathos Getz mines is more ennobling than self-pitying. Some jazz musicians sound like they love their instruments, some like they love themselves. Whatever his failings, Getz played like he loved music, loved art. There is a good sequel from the same concert, *Serenity*, but *Anniversary* is the cream. **KW**

# Tiziana Ghiglioni

**SONB** Ghigliono (v); **Enrico Rava** (t); **Giancarlo Schiaffini** (tb); **Steve Lacy** (ss); **Gianluigi Trovesi** (pic cl, bcl); **Umberto Petrin** (p); **Attilio Zanchi** (b); **Tiziano Tononi** (d, perc). Splasc(h) Records ℗ CDM3702 (61 minutes). Recorded 1992.

⑧ ❽

Italy's best-known jazz singer, Tiziana Ghiglioni has worked with Paul Bley, Chico Freeman, Mal Waldron and with many of her countrymen. **SONB** is a reunion of sorts, since she previously recorded with Lacy in 1986, Rava in 1987 and Schiaffini in 1989. Together with Trovesi, they take turns here to play with Ghiglioni and her regular trio. Lacy gets most space, playing on seven tracks, while the others are given two apiece. As well as these four guests, the disc features four composers too: Lacy, again the main contributor with five pieces, Horace Silver, Ornette Coleman and Mal Waldron, whose lovely Ellington tribute *Duquility* closes the set. A versatile singer who sounds at ease with both standards and free-form, Ghiglioni treads the middle-ground here. Variety comes in the individual way she treats each song: breathily intimate on *Peace*, jaunty and extrovert on *Gospel*. Perhaps she's most impressive in her wordless duets with Trovesi's clarinets on *Art* and *Utah*, the former all sensuous swing, the latter breaking into comic quasi-operatic exchanges. Lacy is his usual imperturbable self, sweet-toned and austere by turns; his two solo tracks are exquisite miniatures. The curious title is an acronymic amalgam of the subtitle, **Something Old**, **Something New**, **Something Borrowed**, **Something Blue**. **GL**

# Michael Gibbs

**Big Music** Lew Soloff, Allan Rubin, Earl Gardner, Ian Carr (t); John Clark (frh); Dave Bargeron, David Taylor (tb); Gibbs (tb, p); Dave Tofani, Julian Argüelles, Bob Mintzer, Chris Hunter, Lou Marini, Jim Odgren (reeds); Django Bates, Brad Hatfield, Dave Bristow (kbds); John Scofield, Bill Frisell, Kevin Eubanks, Dave Fiuczynski, Duke Levine (g); Kai Eckhardt (b); Bob Moses, Bill Martin, Ben Wittman (perc). ACT ℗ 9231-2 (45 minutes). Recorded 1988-90.

⑨ ❽

Big bands have come a long way since Fletcher Henderson's of the twenties and while the lineage is by now shattered, Gibbs continues to show that large groups are today as valid as what used quaintly to be known as combos. This is a welcome reissue from 1989 with an added track, an exquisite duet between Julian Argüelles and Django Bates, recorded in 1990. Gibbs has always been a composer of great vision and the disparate elements he draws into his music include rock, reggae and the eponymous Third-World music. He was always closest of the younger composers to putting a hand on the muse of Gil Evans, but the vivid colours and the fathomless energy of his recordings leads him on from his guru to the point where his music suffers from only one serious fault – its lack of exposure to a wide audience. As always his themes here are strong and original and an invaluable gift to his soloists. The percussion section with Bob Moses is also a powerful attribute. Scofield, long a Gibbs associate, is pungent on *Watershed* and *Adult*. *Mopsus*, with solos from the trombones, is a tribute to Gil Evans. **SV**

# Terry Gibbs

**Dream Band Volume 1** Gibbs (vb); Al Porcino, Ray Triscari, Conte Candoli, Stu Williamson (t); Bob Enevoldsen, Vern Friley, Joe Cadena (tb); Joe Maini, Charlie Kennedy (as); Bill Holman, Med Flory (ts); Jack Schwartz (bs); Pete Jolly (p); Max Bennett (b); Mel Lewis (d). Contemporary Ⓜ CCD7647-2 (53 minutes). Recorded 1959.

⑦ ❹

Terry Gibbs's natural effervescence was one of the vital elements of the late-forties Woody Herman Herd, and whenever he has had the opportunity he has put together a big band for a record or club date. Most of the tracks here come from once-a-week engagements at the Seville Club in Hollywood where the owner could only afford a quartet. The fact that all the high-powered players were prepared to play at the club for minimum payment is an indication of the collective enthusiasm of the men involved. This is a very exciting band playing very exciting music; the only drawback being that much of the programme is cast in the same mould as regards tempo and general atmosphere. There is a relentlessness to the music (spread across no less than five albums now, for those who are interested in the complete output), which is a little wearying in bulk. The best way to approach such discs is to pick out three or four titles at one sitting rather than sit through close to an hour of sustained excitement. Gibbs solos on nearly every track but there are plenty of others' voices to be heard (*Avalon* sports both Richie Kamuca and Bill Perkins on tenor). Spread over the five albums are arrangements by Bill Holman, Med Flory and Bob Brookmeyer, plus others by Marty Paich, Manny Albam and Al Cohn. Wally Heider's engineering has caught the in-person spirit to perfection. **AM**

# Peter Giger

New review
**Jazzz** **Giger** (d, perc); **Gerd Dudek** (reeds); **Vitold Rek** (b). B&W Music Ⓔ BW029 (63 minutes). Recorded 1992.

⑦ ❽

Giger is a free spirit who considers that the full drum set is an orchestra in its own right. His career began in the late sixties in Switzerland, where he played nightly percussion sessions with Jerry Chardonnens and Daniel Mauer. This 'Drum Club' attracted German trombonist Albert Mangelsdorff and resulted in Giger's move to Frankfurt where he has since lived. His Family of Percussion has showcased players such as Doug Hammond and Trilok Gurtu and Giger now claims to have relinquished all interest in playing scored or commercial music. That contention is not entirely supported by this CD. It features superbly, floating and arhythmic works like *Rue de la Tour* and *Zbigi* as well as ferociously free items such as *Henrik's Choice*. In contrast, it also offers an isolated title such as *Sweet and Short* that takes him on a 'matched grip' trip, close to the verticality and rigidity of rock. On balance, he is a genuinely flexible musician and this 1992 date has the further bonus of Dudek's versatile reed work. The saxophonist's creative flair is in evidence throughout and the group sympathy achieved by the three men involved is remarkable by any standard. **BMcR**

# Astrud Gilberto
1940

**Look to the Rainbow** **Gilberto** (v); with orchestras arranged and conducted by: **Gil Evans, Al Cohn**; **The Walter Wanderley Trio**. Verve Ⓜ 821 556-2 (45 minutes). Recorded 1966.

⑧ ❽

Astrud Gilberto is one of the few popular singers of modern times to use absolutely no vibrato whatsoever. It was this which created that first impression of pubescent artlessness, an effect confusingly and delightfully at odds with the sophistication of the songs she sang. She chose the right moment to appear. In 1963, the year of her hit recording of *The Girl from Ipanema*, bookstalls happened to be doing a brisk trade in paperback copies of *Lolita*.

This CD consists largely of her third and best solo album, with arrangements by Gil Evans. As one might expect, the settings are bold and original: one piece features that strange and plangent Brazilian folk instrument, the berimbau, or musical bow, while another reproduces the sound of a carnival band which moves across the stereo picture from right to left (it was a year before the same effect appeared on the Beatles's **Sergeant Pepper**, to be hailed as a unique stroke of genius). The early to mid-sixties was Evans's great period, when his instinct for instrumental timbre and texture was drawing unimagined riches from studio orchestras judiciously laced with jazz soloists. One of these was Johnny Coles, who plays a delectable trumpet solo, in the Michel Legrand song *I Will Wait for You*. Evans was an agonizingly slow writer, which explains why two of the numbers are arranged in his style by Al Cohn, with a flair that goes beyond pastiche. The six tracks added for this CD edition come from Astrud Gilberto's fourth album, **A Certain Smile, A Certain Sadness**, accompanied by Brazilian organist Walter Wanderley. **DG**

# Dizzy Gillespie
1917-93

**The Complete RCA Victor Recordings** **Gillespie** (t, v); with a collective personnel of: **Dave Burns, Elmon Wright, Lammar Wright, Benny Bailey, Matthew McKay, Ray Orff, Willie Cook, Benny Harris** (t); **Taswell Baird, William Shepherd, Ted Kelly, Andy Duryea, Sam Hurt, Jesse Tarrant, J.J. Johnson, Charles Greenlea** (tb); **John Brown, Howard Johnson, Ernie Henry** (as); **James Moody, Joe Gayles, Don Byas, Big Nick Nicholas, Budd Johnson, Yusef Lateef** (ts); **Cecil Payne, Al Gibson** (bs); **Milt Jackson** (vb); **John Lewis, Al Haig** (p); **John Collins, Bill DeArango** (g); **Ray Brown, Al McKibbon** (b); **Joe Harris, J.C. Heard, Kenny Clarke** (d); **Chano Pozo** (cga, perc, v); **Sabu Martinez** (perc); **Kenny Hagood, Johnny Hartman, Joe Carroll** (v); **The Teddy Hill Orchestra**; **The Lionel Hampton Orchestra**; **The Metronome All-Stars**. RCA Bluebird Ⓜ 66528-2 (two discs: 129 minutes). Recorded 1937-49.

✅ ⑧ ❽

There are three 1937 tracks by the Teddy Hill band featuring Gillespie, and one from Hampton's studio aggregation where Gillespie is prominent. There are also two takes each of two numbers from the Metronome All-Stars of 1949. The rest of the collection comes from the big bands and small groups led by Gillespie which recorded for Victor between February 1946 and July 1949. The recordings reflect typical major-label reactions to a recently underground phenomenon, combining the ground-breaking pieces such as *Night in Tunisia*, *Manteca* and *Good Bait* with the more lightweight (and hopefully more commercially successful) clowning in which Gillespie loved to indulge. That said, the bulk of the music is quintessential early bop, with Gillespie's post-California septet replacing the L.A.-mired Parker with Don Byas, who is impressive on both takes of Monk's *52nd Street Theme*, while the innovative charts of the big band also feature key tracks with congas by Chano Pozo.

Gillespie's Victor sides as a leader are pre-dated by his small-group Musicraft recordings of 1945 (see below), but it is on Victor that the big band first appeared and continued to flourish. Many of the charts from this collection have become hallmarks of the bop style and deserve their classic status. This is an important reissue, charting The Way Ahead for all those who cared to listen at the time. Sound quality, never that good on the originals, is enhanced by some deft transfer techniques. **BP**

---

**Shaw 'Nuff** Gillespie (t, v, ldr) with personnel including: **Dave Burns**, **Kenny Dorham** (t); **Charles Greenlea** (tb); **Charlie Parker**, **Sonny Stitt**, **Howard Johnson**, **Scoops Carey** (as); **Dexter Gordon** (ts); **Leo Parker**, **Pee Wee Moore** (bs); **Milt Jackson** (vb); **Clyde Hart**, **Al Haig**, **John Lewis** (p); **Remo Palmieri** (g); **Curly Russell**, **Slam Stewart**, **Ray Brown** (b); **Big Sid Catlett**, **Cozy Cole**, **Kenny Clarke**, **Joe Harris** (d); **Gil Fuller** (v). Musicraft Ⓜ MVSCD53 (58 minutes). Recorded 1945/6

✓ ⑧ ⑥

After leaving the Billy Eckstine Orchestra in 1944, Gillespie settled into playing in the clubs along New York's 52nd Street. It was the street that hosted jazz of every persuasion, but more significantly allowed old to either blend or contrast with new. It was left to the recording studios to document the proposed merger and this CD provides an insight into the way in which the emerging boppers tended to distance themselves from most of the swing-era giants. Outstanding swing players like Slam Stewart suddenly sounded very pedestrian; of the outsiders, only the likes of Catlett and Hart seemed to fully grasp the new requirements. For his part, Gillespie was playing magnificently; he has stunning solos on *Blue 'N' Boogie*, *Hot House* and *Oop Bop Sh'Bam*. Parker's contributions to *Dizzy Atmosphere* and *Groovin' High* are no less impressive as both men advance jazz into a new era of complex harmonic investigations and more oblique rhythmic patterns. These developments notwithstanding, Gillespie's recent experience with Eckstine had fired his interest in presenting bop on a wider canvas. On five titles he insinuates his bop lines into an existing tradition with only the minimum of adjustment to the big-band frameworks required to accommodate him. Some of the music here is duplicated on the Savoy label Gillespie reissue, *Groovin' High*. The sound quality is better here, and you also get an extra 20 minutes of music. **BMcR**

---

**Dizzy Songs** Gillespie (t); **Don Byas** (ts); **Hubert Fol** (as); **Bill Tamper**, **Nat Peck** (tb); **Arnold Ross**, **Raymond Fol**, **Wade Legge** (p); **Joe Benjamin**, **Pierre Michelot**, **Lou Hackney** (b); **Bill Clark**, **Pierre Lemarchand**, **Al Jones** (d); **Joe Carroll** (v). Vogue Ⓜ 115464-2 (74 minutes). Recorded 1952/3.

⑩ ⑧

These 24 delightful tracks (four of them alternative takes) date from Dizzy's visits to Paris in 1952 and 1953. Coming as they did hard on the heels of his combative and radical big-band bebop of the late forties, they revealed for the first time his flair for melody and relaxed swing. The heart of the collection is a series of improvisations on standard tunes, such as *Somebody Loves Me* and *Sweet Lorraine*, in which Dizzy is virtually the only soloist. The tone is broad and juicy and the melodic line remarkably un-boppish, apart from a sparing use of double-tempo phrases and the odd flattened fifth or augmented ninth. From the moment of its foundation in 1948, Vogue records and their jazz director Charles Delaunay made a point of recording visiting American musicians in informal settings and with the minimum of 'production'. The results added up to a valuable and distinctive body of work, of which these sessions are among the very best. **DG**

---

**Diz and Getz** Gillespie (t); **Stan Getz**, **Hank Mobley** (ts); **Oscar Peterson**, **Wade Legge** (p); **Herb Ellis** (g); **Ray Brown**, **Lou Hackney** (b); **Max Roach**, **Charlie Persip** (d). Verve Ⓜ 835 559-2 (48 minutes). Recorded 1953/4.

⑧ ⑥

Eight of these tracks were made in Los Angeles while Getz and Gillespie were on tour with a Stan Kenton package show and Max Roach was working at the Lighthouse with Howard Rumsey's All Stars. With the efficient and reliable Peterson Trio providing a foundation it was easier to find common ground with songs such as *Exactly Like You* rather than try to produce new, original material, and the two best tracks are the opening ones, both of which are Ellington compositions. On *It Don't Mean a Thing* the ultra-fast tempo puts the soloists on their mettle and it is surprising to find how well Getz (at his coolest in the early fifties) rises to the challenge. Gillespie was apparently never off form in or out of a recording studio, and his solo work throughout is noteworthy, especially his control with a mute. He plays conga drum on part of *Siboney* and does not sing (despite the notes). *One Alone* was recorded in New York the following year by Dizzy's regular band, a fairly lightweight number with a short solo from the tenor player listed as "Earl Mabley"! A useful example of how Gillespie invariably succeeded in pulling together seemingly disparate elements on recording sessions, this compact disc is typical of the 'all-star' dates organized by Norman Granz. **AM**

---

**Dizzy Gillespie at Newport** Gillespie (t, v); **Lee Morgan**, **Ermit Perry**, **Carl Warwick**, **Talib Daawud** (t); **Melba Liston**, **Al Grey**, **Chuck Connors** (tb); **Ernie Henry**, **Jimmy Powell** (as); **Billy Mitchell**, **Benny Golson** (ts); **Pee Wee Moore** (bs); **Wynton Kelly**, **Mary Lou Williams** (p); **Paul West** (b); **Charlie Persip** (d). Verve Ⓜ 513 754-2 (73 minutes). Recorded 1957.

⑧ ⑧

Although Gillespie has been the subject of many CD collections it is unlikely that there has been a more lively and humour-filled one than this. He leads a spirited, loose big band and his own playing is at its most mature and uncompromising. It was soon after this period that he understandably drew in his horns as far as trumpet playing was concerned, so that we are privileged to enjoy one of his last flat-out performances. The atmosphere of the open air concert adds to the excitement of this most vivid of concerts. This group, about to be disbanded, was the remains of the one Gillespie put together for State Department tours and had lost only one major soloist – altoist Phil Woods. The solos of Al Grey and Billy Mitchell were driven by the supercharged drumming of Persip. Confirmation that Wynton Kelly was a good big-band pianist as well as a soloist comes in his playing behind Gillespie on the magnificent interpretation of *I Remember Clifford*. Mary Lou Williams replaces Kelly to play three extracts from her *Zodiac Suite*. Both her writing and playing are fresh and contemporary, and the band roars back in response to her piano solos. The ten-minute re-creation of *Cool Breeze*, more like a hot tornado, roars along at a tremendous tempo, with Al Grey indulging in the double-tempo soloing which he uses to try to convince his audiences that he is playing bebop rather than straight mainstream. There is no such doubt about the flaring Gillespie solo which follows and builds ecstatically as the band (and Kelly) build the tension behind him. Gillespie drops out to let the newly emergent Lee Morgan solo with considerable fire on *Night in Tunisia*.     **SV**

**Duets with Sonny Rollins and Sonny Stitt**  Gillespie (t); **Sonny Rollins** (ts); **Sonny Stitt** (as, ts); **Ray Bryant** (p); **Tommy Bryant** (b); **Charlie Persip** (d). Verve Ⓜ 835 253-2 (60 minutes). Recorded 1957.

⑧ ❼

Gillespie's career has so far been inadequately covered by CD issues and reissues. Whole sections of his best period lie undisturbed in various record companies' vaults while inferior performances have been repeatedly reissued. In the absence of vast swathes of masterpieces recorded for Verve, Philips and Solid State (who between them own such gems as **An Electrifying Evening**, **Perceptions**, **The New Continent** and **At the Village Vanguard**, to name a mere handful), we can buy this as a good representation of Gillespie, relaxed and jamming with friends. This is a better buy than its companion-piece, **Sonny Side Up**, recorded a week later, if only because extra material on the CD adds no less than 20 extra minutes to the original LP, while **Sonny Side** is still only a mediocre 38 minutes in duration. (**Sonny Side**, however, does have the famous and heart-stopping unaccompanied Rollins solo on *The Eternal Triangle*.) The music itself is fine: Diz is full of good notions and his execution is magnificent. In a period when he could often be ruminative during solos, he lights up here. Stitt is a more comfortable partner than Rollins, in the sense that he fits in better with Gillespie's conception of the overall performance, but Rollins is in the typically aggressive, searching form of this period. The rhythm section is exemplary, with Bryant contributing some neat solos. Recording sound is much improved.     **KS**

**New review**

**Gillespiana/Carnegie Hall Concert**  On Gillespiana: **Gillespie, John Frosk, Ernie Royal, Clark Terry, Joe Wilder** (t); **Urbie Green, Frank Rehak, Britt Woodman** (tb); **Paul Faulise** (btb); **James Buffington, Al Richman, Gunther Schuller, Julius Watkins** (frh); **Don Butterfield** (tba); **Leo Wright** (f, as); **Lalo Schifrin** (p, arr); **Art Davis** (b); **Jack Del Rio** (bgo); **Candido Camero** (cga); **Willie Rodriguez** (timbales); **Chuck Lampkin** (d); on two tracks substitute **William Lister** and **Morris Scott** for **Richman** and **Buffington** (frh). On **Carnegie Hall Concert**: **Gillespie** (t, v); **Frosk, Terry, Nick Travis, Carl Warwick** (t); **Faulise, George Matthews, Arnet Sparrow, Woodman** (tb); **John Barrows, Richard Berg, Buffington, Schuller** (frh); **Butterfield** (tba); **Wright** (f, as); **Schifrin** (p, arr); **Davis** (b); **Ray Barretto, Julio Collazo, Jose Mangual** (perc); **Lampkin** (d); **Joe Carroll** (v). Verve Ⓜ 519 809-2 (75 minutes). Recorded 1960-1.

⑥ ❿

Schifrin was 28 and a soundtrack composer for Argentinian films when Gillespie hired him for **Gillespiana**, in an attempt to give his sound a make-over. The result was an unwieldy fusion of cool and hot – as if the sensibilities of Gil Evans and Stan Kenton were battling it out. Schifrin's composing and arranging ideas are based on predictable see-saws between sinuous, harmonized vamps and fanfares that tend toward the garish; this is the man who wrote *Mission Impossible*. (It only makes one marvel all the more at the best of the Evans/Davis collaboration; Stanley Crouch famously called Evans's arrangements "high-level television music," but the phrase seems more applicable to this material.) The horn ensemble passages are lumpy, and the synthesis of Latin music with jazz a strange Disney-world dilution of both; this was recorded at the height of America's obsession with making its own pop culture seem internationalist and somewhat highfalutin'. Yet Gillespie's quintet at the centre of the circus still sounds great; solos by the leader as well as Art Davis (in *Blues*) and Leo Wright (in *Prelude*) have great personality and articulation.

  **Carnegie Hall Concert**, recorded the following year with most of the same personnel and Schifrin arrangements on pieces by Gillespie, is another matter. The tunes are looser, with fewer and better intrusive ensemble columns holding up the small-band architecture. It has neither the compositional ambition of the earlier record nor its pitfalls. *Kush*, however, remains trimmed through its original LP edit to just 4 minutes, and the rest of the unissued material from the concert is not here.     **BR**

**Dizzy Gillespie's Big 4**  Gillespie (t); **Joe Pass** (g); **Ray Brown** (b); **Mickey Roker** (d). Pablo Ⓜ OJC443-2 (44 minutes). Recorded 1974.

Gillespie's personality cost him the respect of many critics and listeners, who considered him not serious enough once jazz grew more introverted and abstract. Yet Gillespie was as intellectual an improviser as any of his successors, and he remained a deeply moving ballad player. The present set, one of producer Norman Granz's most inspired showcases for Gillespie in the trumpeter's Pablo period, gets an after-hours feeling by using Pass's guitar rather than piano. Even a flag-waver like *Russian Lullaby* sounds intimate, though it and the rest of the date are hardly lacking in energy. The rhythm section (Granz's usual suspects) play as well here as they did anywhere, and the trumpeter unleashes cliché-free improvisations that were as fresh and challenging as any trumpeter's of the period. There is a brief and lovely *September Song*, a delicate *Jitterbug Waltz*, and a *Hurry Home* that was one of the first things to hit my sound system when I learned of Gillespie's passing. **Big 4**, which tended to go unnoticed like much of Gillespie's later playing, argues that his later years were also filled with music of great beauty. **BB**

## John Gilmore 1931

**Blowing in from Chicago** Gilmore, **Clifford Jordan** (ts); **Horace Silver** (p); **Curly Russell** (b); **Art Blakey** (d). Blue Note Ⓜ CDP8 28977-2 (47 minutes). Recorded 1957.

⑧ ⑧

Although he actually co-leads this session with Clifford Jordan, it is listed here under John Gilmore's name as one of those rare occasions where he is out from under the shadow of Sun Ra. This was in fact the recording début of both saxophonists, fresh out of the Windy City; Jordan was born there, Gilmore brought there as an infant, and they were classmates under the legendary music instructor Captain Walter Dyett at DuSable High School. Chicago has a rich tradition of muscular, extroverted tenor saxists, including Gene Ammons, Johnny Griffin, Eddie Harris and Von Freeman (all of whom studied under Dyett), and Gilmore and Jordan fill the bill at this stage of their careers. With the dead-on New York rhythm section of Silver, Russell and Blakey, this is a prototypical hard-bop date, capturing a level of excitement you seldom hear today (due at least in part to engineer Rudy Van Gelder's classic Blue Note sound). Both saxists are well-versed in bebop lore, as the quotes and licks sprinkled throughout *Billie's Bounce* show, yet the variety of tunes authored by Gigi Gryce, Jordan and Silver prevent them from playing by rote. Jordan's tone is a touch grainier than it would later become, and his lines tend to tumble forward from exuberance; Gilmore's sinewy phrasing barely anticipates his subsequent freer approach. The only complaint I can muster is against the constant, annoying sizzle of Blakey's ride cymbal; otherwise, this is a classic fifties blowing date well worth hearing. **AL**

## Egberto Gismonti 1947

**Danca das Cabecas** Gismonti (g, p, wood f, v); **Nana Vasconcelos** (perc, berimbau, corpo, v). ECM Ⓕ 827 750-2 (50 minutes). Recorded 1976.

✔ ⑧ ⑧

Gismonti was on the leading edge of world-music synthesis that has recently opened jazz to diverse ethnic influences. A trained pianist and self-taught guitarist who studied with Nadia Boulanger and played pop music in his native Brazil, he was drawing on diverse compositional and improvisational resources long before such eclecticism became fashionable. While he has made several later recordings for ECM in solo, duo and quartet formats, as well as with the trio Magico, his first album for the label remains his most intense and expressive. In ten keenly-shaped yet spontaneous-sounding pieces, played primarily on eight-string guitar, Gismonti moves in focused bursts of melody, sometimes ruminative, sometimes explosive, with Vasconcelos's percussion slipping in and out for just the right emphasis. While the atmospherics associated with such music are present, there is also more impulse and grit than usual, making **Danca das Cabecas** more appealing to jazz fans, and a definitive example of how the jazz spirit can inform the creative music of other cultures. **BB**

## Jimmy Giuffre 1921

**The Jimmy Giuffre 3** Giuffre (cl, ts, bs); **Jim Hall** (g); **Ralph Peña**, **Jimmy Atlas** (b). Atlantic Ⓜ 790981-2 (47 minutes). Recorded 1956-7.

⑧ ⑥

Giuffre, the contributor of the famous *Four Brothers* to Woody Herman's Second Herd, a composition which defined a whole period of that band's history, has led a varied career. After a stint with Herman he settled on the West Coast and became a Lighthouse All-Stars regular, also moonlighting as a honkin' rhythm & blues tenor player in Shorty Rogers's apocalyptic (and unattributed) studio band, Boots Brown and His Blockbusters. By 1956, when this album was made, Giuffre had carved out a fascinating contemporary niche for himself, operating at low voltage – and low volume – in this drummerless, pianoless trio. The achieved intimacy had a great deal to do with the quick public acceptance of his work, and with the initial release of this LP he had a minor hit on his hands. The song *The Train and the River*, here given its first recording, became a talking-point of both the 1957 CBS TV special, *The Sound of Jazz*, and Chuck Wein's film of the 1958 Newport Jazz Festival, *Jazz on a Summer's Day*.

This CD reissue has greatly improved the recording sound, and in the process has helped delineate the interplay and natural balance between the three equal participants in this music. Giuffre's breathy, low-register clarinet playing, although derided at the time, has a wonderful, casual warmth, Hall wraps Giuffre's lines in a continual thread of golden chords, and Peña perfectly anticipates every shift of musical direction. In retrospect, the only change between this group and the radical trio of 1961 is in the style, not the process. The CD contains two tracks from a previously unissued session, recorded a year after the initial LP. Now that Neshui Ertegun, the CD's producer, is gone, one wonders whether the whole session, or any other Giuffre Atlantic, will ever see the light of day. **KS**

---

**1961** Giuffre (cl); **Paul Bley** (p); **Steve Swallow** (b). ECM Ⓕ 849 644-2 (two discs: 92 minutes). Recorded 1961.

⑩ ❽

This set is a reissue of the Verve albums **Fusion** and **Thesis**, recorded in March and August of 1961 by the Jimmy Giuffre Three. Giuffre had already led a drummerless trio with Jim Hall and Ralph Peña some five years earlier, but the three studio albums he made with Bley and Swallow (the Columbia album **Free Fall** followed in 1962) represented a more radical break with jazz tradition. Free, abstract, with no regular tempo, these records went farther out than anyone (except perhaps Cecil Taylor) had then ventured. And whereas other free players of the period tended towards the fiercely declamatory, The Giuffre Trio created quiet, alert, sensitive music that set out the blueprint for a free-form chamber jazz.

Although **Free Fall** (recently reissued) was the record on which, to quote Giuffre "I let everything go", the impulse towards abstraction is already well advanced on the two 1961 records. Even so, the mostly improvised music here always starts from a head and often explores a specific mood or idea. The trio's interplay shows unusual empathy and their attention to textural detail, together with the spacious feel of their music, anticipate the early experiments of the AACM. A further bonus is the presence of four Carla Bley tunes, notably the bright, Monkish *Ictus* and a dreamy *Jesus Maria*. ECM have done a splendid job of enhancing the sound quality and have also added three previously unreleased tracks. However, *Used to Be*, a track from the **Fusion** LP, has mysteriously vanished and the original version of *Trudgin'* (also from **Fusion**) has been replaced by an alternative take, again without explanation. These anomalies aside, **1961** makes newly available two LPs which were among the first masterpieces of a truly post-bebop jazz. **GL**

# Ben Goldberg

New review

**Junk Genius** Goldberg (cl, bcl); **John Schott** (g); **Trevor Dunn** (b); **Kenny Wollesen** (d). Knitting Factory Works Ⓕ KFW160 (54 minutes). Recorded 1994.

⑦ ❼

The clarinet's resurgence in modern jazz has been widely publicized via the exploits of the late John Carter, Don Byron, Louis Sclavis and the rediscovery of Jimmy Giuffre. Ben Goldberg is a young New Yorker committed to the slender black stick, making his mark in a number of against-the-grain groups which aggressively redesign traditional styles. He is a founding member of the New Klezmer Trio, which explores the overlapping spheres of influence between that exhilarating folk music and jazz. He has recorded with drummer Wollesen in a duo that offers skeletal versions of Monk tunes. Then there is this quartet, which plots a somewhat hallucinogenic course through the bebop song book of Parker, Powell, and Gillespie. There's a trace of Naked City's icon-smashing plugged-in thrash mentality to their method, though they never approach nihilism – rather, the exuberance of bop's revolutionary origins is translated to more recent degrees of dissonance, discontinuous rhythms, and asynchronous phrasing. They maintain the roller-coaster excitement – and danger – of edge-of-the-precipice lines like *Shaw 'Nuff* and *Un Poco Loco*, but are equally liable to turn a tune inside-out or distort it with carnival mirrors, as they do with *Confirmation* and *Hot House*. At the rhythmic core there's less of an insistent swing than a varied pulse, throbbing and sometimes cantankerous, which seems to capture more of the extreme urgency and abandon of Bird and Bud than any of the younger neo-cons have yet mustered. **AL**

# Larry Goldings

New review

**Whatever it Takes** Goldings (org, clav, p); **Maceo Parker**, **David Sanborn** (as); **Joshua Redman** (ts); **Fred Wesley** (tb); **Peter Bernstein** (g); **Richard Patterson** (elb); **Bill Stewart** (d). Warner Bros Ⓕ 9362-45996-2 (65 minutes). Recorded 1995.

⑧ ❾

Larry Goldings is best known for his work in the r&b-inflected organ trio heard on John Scofield's 1993 **Hand Jive**. Here he follows a broadly similar muse, though with hardly any of the abstraction that colours most Scofield albums and with rather more populism – expressed in such soul staples as *Big Brother*, *If You Want Me to Stay* and *Boogie On Reggae Woman*. Goldings's adoption of the classic organ trio sound is yet another manifestation of today's ubiquitous retrospection, but, as in Scofield's band, a new spin is put on the old idiom, mostly notably in the harmony of such Goldings originals as *Slo-Boat* and *Up for Air*. The album is very listenable throughout, but perhaps the most fun is to be had from the seventies funk readings. In this respect the crisply grooving *Boogie On* is a standout, with excellent rhythm work by Goldings and soul authenticity from two-thirds of the JB Horns – Parker and Wesley. It's interesting to note, however, that the more live, raw and vocalized tone belongs not to Parker, who is arguably the greater r&b icon, but to David Sanborn. There are also appearances by Joshua Redman, as convincing here as when he plays bebop, and some relatively restrained playing from Peter Bernstein, except on *Yipes!*, where he throws caution to the wind in fours with the leader.　　**MG**

## Vinny Golia

**Commemoration**　Golia (pic, f, cl, ss, bs, bss); **Mark Underwood, John Fumo, Marissa Benedict, Rob Blakeslee** (t, flh); **Mike Vlatkovich, Bruce Fowler, George McMullen, Phil Teele** (tb); **William Roper** (tba); **Emily Hey** (pic, f); **Kim Richmond, Steve Fowler, Bill Plake, David Ocker** (reeds); **Wayne Peet** (p, syn, cond); **Harry Scorzo, Jef Gauthier** (vn); **Greg Adamson, Matt Cooker, Jonathan Golove, Dion Sorrell** (vc); **Ken Filiano, Joel Hamilton** (b); **Alex Cline** (d, perc); **David Johnson, Brad Dutz** (vb, mba, perc); **Stephanie Henry** (cond). 9 Winds Ⓟ NWCD0150/60 (two discs: 120 minutes). Recorded 1991/2.

⑧ ❼

One of the best-kept secrets in jazz, California visual artist, composer and multi-instrumentalist Vinny Golia's Large Ensemble has been active since 1982, having recorded two multi-LP sets and three CD releases, to little or no acclaim. One of the problems may be that Golia's provocative writing owes little to the prevailing canons of big-band orthodoxy; the addition of strings, mallet instruments and unusual wind and brass combinations (*Mahlow*, for example, features tuba, bass trombone and bass saxophone) makes the Large Ensemble more of a chamber music group than a swinging big band, although they can swing when called upon to do so. Most of the 11 compositions on this two-disc set take their time to brew, which allows Golia gradually to integrate soloists into the music rather than have them interrupt its progress. Golia's sombre moods and sharply etched up-tempo lines inhabit a territory somewhere between the orchestral conceptions of Charles Mingus and Anthony Braxton, but the way he orchestrates for alternately subtle and dramatic colour and texture is entirely his own. A case in point is *Tumulus or Griffin*, which begins as if an illustration of Gothic architecture and builds to a fantastic multi-layered climax. As a painter, Golia has a trained eye for line, contrast and chiaroscuro; his ear is no less acute.　　**AL**

## Benny Golson　　1929

**This is for You, John**　Golson (ts); **Pharoah Sanders** (ts); **Cedar Walton** (p); **Ron Carter** (b); **Jack DeJohnette** (d). Timeless Ⓟ CDSPJ235 (43 minutes). Recorded 1983.

⑦ ❼

Benny Golson's playing career falls into two distinct phases, themselves separated by a dozen or so years in which he virtually gave up performing to work as a composer and arranger. The best of his earlier recordings, often made in the company of Art Farmer, have yet to reappear on CD. **This is for You, John** is a particularly enjoyable album from his later period, which commenced in the late seventies. It is also among the more personal of the many recorded tributes to John Coltrane, for Golson had been Coltrane's regular jamming partner when the pair were growing up in forties Philadelphia. Most of the tracks touch on the tenorists' friendship in some guise, from *Page 12*'s recreation of the complex bebop lines they played together as young men to *Times Past*'s evocation of the lilting, surging tunes on which Coltrane liked to fashion his more rhapsodic solos. The Trane link is underlined by the presence of Pharoah Sanders, whose abrasive tone is an excellent foil for the leader's more liquid sound.

　　Golson's ballad feature, *A Change of Heart*, reveals his talents as both player and composer. A floating dream of a tune, so subtly shaped it sounds almost abstract, he performs it with such deftness – of phrasing and timing – that it recalls one of his chief tenor influences, the great Lucky Thompson. Lehár's *Vilia*, also recorded by Coltrane, makes an unlikely but charming finale.　　**GL**

## Eddie Gomez　　1944

**Gomez**　Gomez (b); **Yasuaki Shimsu** (ts); **Chick Corea** (kbds); **Katumi Watanabe** (g); **Steve Gadd** (d). Denon Ⓟ DC8562 (46 minutes). Recorded 1984.

⑥ ❽

Because of the difficulties of smooth articulation on the instrument, the bass remained the least viable of the solo jazz instruments until the arrival of Jimmy Blanton in 1940. From then on virtuosos like Ray Brown, Charles Mingus and Red Mitchell gradually expanded the instrument's voice to a point where the grand masters of today, Gomez very much amongst them, have an almost saxophone-like fluidity in their lines. However, the bass does not have the emotional palette of the saxophone, and showcase albums like this one are to be taken as rare wine.

Gomez has an equal eloquence throughout the full range of his instrument and demonstrates that it is not just possible, but desirable to use amplified acoustic bass in preference to the purpose-built electric bass. Like his successor and peer Marc Johnson, Gomez developed as an individual voice in the Bill Evans trio. Evans had already matured the ill-fated Scott LaFaro there, and there is no doubt that his closely knit trios, developed over years rather than months, had a profound effect on the bassists. Gomez's tone is plump and full and his *arco* work on the out-of-tempo *Zimmerman* is a dark contrast to the powerfully plucked basses on the multi-dubbed *Mez-Ga*, a duet with Gadd. Corea plays delicate acoustic piano solos on a couple of the tracks and it is only on his own *Ginkakuji* that he employs his multitude of electronics. **SV**

# Nat Gonella 1908

**Nat Gonella and His Georgians** Gonella (t, v); **Bruts Gonella, Johnny Morrison** (t); **Albert Torrance, Ernest Ritte** (cl, as); **Pat Smuts, Don Barrigo** (ts); **Harold Hood, Monia Liter** (p); **Jimmy Mesene** (g); **Charlie Winter, Tiny Winters** (b); **Bob Dryden** (d). Flapper Ⓜ PASTCD9750 (66 minutes). Recorded 1935-40.

⑥ ❺

After some years in the trumpet section of British dance-bands led by Billy Cotton, Roy Fox and Lew Stone, Gonella formed his own slightly smaller ensemble, the Georgians. Their repertoire suggests a showband like Cab Calloway's, mixing standards like *Nagasaki* and *On the Sunny Side of the Street* with novelty hot numbers such as *Someone Stole Gabriel's Horn* or the hillbilly song *The Man Who Comes Around*. Torrance, Smuts and Hood contribute sprightly swing solos a little in the manner of sidemen in Fats Waller's or Skeets Tolbert's groups, but the dominant character of the music lies in Gonella's trumpet playing, deeply influenced by Louis Armstrong's, and his unobtrusive London-accented singing. Occasionally, as in *Tiger Rag*, he matches the excitable audacity of the young Armstrong, but more often he and his companions show the decent restraint that has thwarted so much promising English jazz. This is not an outstanding selection of Gonella's work and the remastering is muddy, but it gives an adequate picture of his band's repertoire and style. Three 1940 tracks are by the New Georgians, with similar instrumentation but an entire change of personnel. **TR**

# Paul Gonsalves 1920-74

**Gettin' Together** Gonsalves (ts); **Nat Adderley** (c); **Wynton Kelly** (p); **Sam Jones** (b); **Jimmy Cobb** (d). Jazzland Ⓜ OJCCD203-2 (40 minutes). Recorded 1960.

⑧ ❽

It is hard to think of a jazz musician who was as generally underestimated as Gonsalves was. He emerged from the saxophone section of the Duke Ellington Orchestra to become famous for one of his least trenchant solos, the 27 choruses which he blew on Duke's *Diminuendo and Crescendo in Blue* at the 1956 Newport Jazz Festival, and was forever more linked to up-tempo tenor marathons. In truth, Gonsalves was one of the more creative musicians within the Ellington ranks and although he was firmly rooted in the Ben Webster tradition, he brought consistently fresh thought to Ellington's works.

He made half a dozen outstanding albums away from the Ellington influence (one with Sonny Stitt, **Salt & Pepper** on Impulse!, has recently reappeared), and this one is probably his best. His supporting musicians came from the Miles Davis (Kelly and Cobb) and Cannonball Adderley (Jones and Nat Adderley) quintets, and Kelly in particular is responsible for the virtuous tenor playing which results. There are exquisite, tenor ballad performances of *I Surrender, Dear* and *I Cover the Waterfront*, and a most refreshing treatment of *Yesterdays*. That the other musicians also enjoyed the invigorating surroundings is evinced by the way they and Gonsalves pile into the up-tempo pieces here. Perhaps this was Gonsalves's true masterpiece. **SV**

# Denis Gonzalez 1954

**New review**

**Stefan** Gonzalez (t, pkt t, flh, perc, v); **John Purcell** (f, bf, as, bcl, ehn, syn, v); **Malachi Favors** (b); **Henry Franklin** (b, v); **W.A. Richardson** (d, v). Silkheart Ⓕ SHCD101 (43 minutes). Recorded 1986/87.

⑧ ❽

A second-generation Mexican-American, Gonzalez settled in Dallas in 1976 and two years later founded DAAGNIM, the Dallas Association for Avant Garde and New Impressionistic Music. He used the same acronym for the label he set up in 1979 and for which he made his first recordings. **Stefan**, **Namesake** and **Debenge-Debenge**, three discs released by the Swedish Silkheart label in the mid eighties, finally established him as a major force in new music. The latter two discs are well worth hearing, not least because Gonzalez assembled such intriguing line-ups: **Namesake** has

Charles Brackeen and Douglas Ewart, **Debenge-Debenge** Brackeen again, plus the New Orleans father-and-son pairing of Kidd and Marlon Jordan. However, **Stefan** remains his finest artistic achievement. The music flows beautifully, Gonzalez and Purcell keeping a perfect balance between finesse and fire. Purcell is an ideal front-line partner for Gonzalez, his bass clarinet and flutes a supple counterpoint to the trumpeter's breathy attack and darting abstractions. The disc has such good tunes too: Purcell's attractive *Deacon John Ray*, Gonzalez's capricious *Hymn for Don Cherry* and his atmospheric title track, which mysteriously segues from ethereal calm to New Orleans street dance. *Doxology*, from Gonzalez's series of reworked hymn-tunes, closes the set with a rousing emotional flourish.　　　　　　　　　　　　　　　　　　　　　　　　　　　　　　　　　　　　　　**GL**

# Jerry Gonzalez　　　　　　　　　　　　　　　　　　　　　　　　　　　　1949

**Rumba Para Monk**　Gonzalez (t, flh, perc); **Carter Jefferson** (ts); **Larry Willis** (p); **Andy Gonzalez** (b); **Steve Berrios** (d, perc). Sunnyside Ⓕ SSC1036D (72 minutes). Recorded 1988.

**⑧ 8**

A conscious attempt to demonstrate Thelonious Monk's often neglected indebtedness to Cuban rhythms, **Rumba Para Monk**, courtesy of its uncontrived arrangements and the enthusiastic commitment of all its participants, triumphantly vindicates the truth of the late composer/pianist's assertion that "Jazz is New York man. It's in the air." A passionate and eloquent champion of all Latin Musics, Jerry Gonzalez, a New York-based Puerto Rican, has managed a rare feat; he has produced a tribute album which genuinely grants the listener a new perspective on the work of its dedicatee. A representative example of Monk's compositions – *Monk's Mood*, *Nutty*, *Ugly Beauty* among them – are filtered through Latin arrangements and instrumentation, and the result is a joyous celebration not only of the durability and versatility of the tunes themselves, but also of the subtle power and infectious exuberance of Latin rhythms, ranging from (as the album's excellent booklet-notes point out) the mozambique employed on *Bye-Ya* to the guiro on *Little Rootie Tootie*. This last is a particular delight, featuring Gonzalez's muted trumpet over percussive train effects and Larry Willis's pianistic 'bell', but throughout Gonzalez's respect for and sensitivity to the nuances of Monk's tunes are demonstrated in a series of startlingly idiosyncratic but entirely appropriate arrangements. The quality of the soloing occasionally does not quite fulfil the promise inherent in the arrangements, but this is a minor quibble, given the originality and sheer panache of the project as a whole.　　　　　　　　　　　　　　　　　　　　　　　　　　　　　　　　　　　**CP**

# Brad Goode　　　　　　　　　　　　　　　　　　　　　　　　　　　　　1964

**Shock of the New**　Goode (t); **Lin Halliday**, **Ed Petersen** (ts); **Jodie Christian** (p); **Fareed Haque** (g); **Dennis Carroll**, **Angus Thomas**, **Rob Amster** (b); **Jeff Stitely**, **Paul Wertico**, **Bob Rummage** (d). Delmark Ⓕ DD440 (44 minutes). Recorded 1988.

**⑥ ❼**

A first-call trumpeter for session work and club dates around Chicago, Goode has made a reputation for himself at a young age because of his crisp technique, versatility and ability to keep up with fast company. He acknowledges Clifford Brown as a major influence and constructs clean, curving lines often reminiscent of Red Rodney. His début album, however, like many début albums, is a mixed bag. In an effort to display his various interests, Goode has included a fusion novelty number and a pair of trumpet-plus-strings tunes that border on muzak. The straight-ahead blowing tunes reveal Goode's real potential. *The New Blues*, for example, allows him to flaunt his bright, brash tone and fluent chops. There is a version of *Old Folks* that erases any lingering sentiment, with Goode biting and smearing notes in his solo. A reliable Chicago piano veteran, Jodie Christian gets little space to showcase his sophisticated wares, but of most interest may be Lin Halliday. One of those locals who fell between the cracks, he is an attractively insular player with a dry, whispery tone and a habit of phrasing like a man looking over his shoulder. Halliday's playing may entice fans of obscure bop tenors like J.R. Monterose and Allen Eager to listen up here.　　　　　　　　　　　　**AL**

# Benny Goodman　　　　　　　　　　　　　　　　　　　　　　　　　1909-86

**The Birth of Swing**　Goodman (cl); **Bunny Berigan**, **Pee Wee Irwin**, **Mannie Klein**, **Sterling Bose** (t); **Red Ballard**, **Jack Lacey**, **Murray McEachern** (tb); **Toots Mondello**, **Hymie Schertzer** (as); **Art Rollini**, **Vido Musso** (ts); **Frank Foeba**, **Jess Stacey** (p); **George Van Eps**, **Allan Reuss** (g); **Harry Goodman** (b); **Gene Krupa** (d). RCA Bluebird Ⓜ ND90601/3 (three discs: 205 minutes). Recorded 1935/6.

✓　　　　　　　　　　　　　　　　　　　　　　　　　　　　　　　　　**⑧ 8**

There is a case for claiming that swing, as a musical and social phenomenon, was born on July 1st, 1935. On that day Benny Goodman's new and still struggling band recorded Fletcher Henderson's arrangement of Jelly Roll Morton's *King Porter Stomp*. By any standards this three-minute work is a little masterpiece, from Bunny Berigan's opening trumpet solo, through constant changes of texture and dynamics, to the exultant riff ending. When success broke over Goodman and the band later that year it was numbers like this that the crowds wanted, and which set the pattern for the following decade.

These three discs contain the band's entire output in its first two years of existence and there is a freshness about the best pieces that was rarely recaptured later. The combination of Henderson's elegant imagination and Goodman's fanatical attention to detail produced a stream of wonderfully sharp-edged and uplifting performances: *Down South Camp Meeting*, *When Buddha Smiles*, *Somebody Loves Me*, etc. The other main arranger was Jimmy Mundy, whose *Swingtime in the Rockies* could stand as the archetype of riff-based dance numbers. Notable soloists during this period, apart from Berigan and Goodman himself, include Jess Stacey, Jack Teagarden and the heavyweight Vido Musso. The vocalists here were both teenagers at the time: Helen Ward was the band's regular singer and Ella Fitzgerald guested on the last session of 1936.

Admittedly this is a hefty package, representing only a brief period in Goodman's career, and it just misses a number of important events, such as the arrival of Harry James and the arranger Eddie Sauter. What we need is a really good one-volume anthology for the general listener which covers the entire Victor years, but there is not one (the two single-volume Harry James sets which cover subsequent Goodman events miss the best of this one); so this remains an essential item. **DG**

---

## Live at Carnegie Hall   Goodman (cl); Harry James, Ziggy Elman, Bobby Hackett, Gordon 'Chris' Griffin, Cootie Williams, Buck Clayton (t); Red Ballard, Vernon Brown (tb); Johnny Hodges (ss, as); Hymie Schertzer, George Koenig (as); Babe Russin, Arthur Rollini, Lester Young (ts); Harry Carney (bs); Lionel Hampton (vb); Jess Stacy, Teddy Wilson, Count Basie (p); Allan Reuss, Freddie Green (g); Harry Goodman, Walter Page (b); Gene Krupa (d); Martha Tilton (v). Columbia Ⓜ 450983-2 (two discs: 103 minutes). Recorded 1938.

⑨ ❹

Goodman's commercial success in the late thirties aroused the latent snob that lurks in the bosom of so many jazz musicians. As well as being an outstanding jazz clarinettist, Goodman was also an accomplished classical performer and, perhaps because of this, felt the need to legitimize the jazz side of his music by fronting a jazz concert in Carnegie Hall. This CD provides authentic documentation of "The Night of January 6, 1938", a vital date in American musical history. Goodman was himself inspired, fully involved in *One O'Clock Jump*, in spikey reverence to Larry Shields on *Sensation Rag*, in parody of Ted Lewis on *When My Baby Smiles at Me* and totally at ease with Count Basie and Duke Ellington's men on the jammed *Honeysuckle Rose*.

His elegant trio and quartet performances with Hampton, Wilson and Krupa make a major contribution and his big band takes care of all the heavy duty parts. Hackett pays homage to Bix Beiderbecke on *I'm Coming Virginia*, James tips his hat to Louis Armstrong on *Shine* while Krupa tears into the amazing *Sing Sing Sing*. The Ellington message is delivered by the Duke's men on *Blue Reverie*; there are excellent solo interludes by Young, Basie, Hodges and Brown, showboating efforts from Elman and Griffin and pleasant vocal interludes by Tilton. Despite the daunting prospects that the concert must have presented, the outcome was tremendously successful. Carnegie is now a regular venue for such concerts, but this ground-breaking effort should be in every collection, despite the low-fi sound. It is not widely known that Goodman's 1939 return to Carnegie Hall was also preserved on discs, some of which appeared recently on a budget CD compilation. **BMcR**

---

## Benny Goodman Sextet Featuring Charlie Christian (1939-41)   Goodman (cl); Christian (g); Cootie Williams (t); Georgie Auld (ts); Lionel Hampton (vb); Fletcher Henderson, Johnny Guarnieri, Dudley Brooks, Kenny Kersey, Count Basie (p); Artie Bernstein (b); Nick Fatool, Harry Jaeger, Jo Jones, Dave Tough (d). Columbia Ⓜ CK45144 (55 minutes). Recorded 1939-41.

⑧ ❽

Oklahoman Charlie Christian was among the first guitarists effectively to employ amplification as a means of equalizing volume levels with horn players, pianists and drummers. With the decibel playing-field thus levelled, Christian, who like all swing era guitarists had been limited to four-to-the-bar comping, suddenly had the technical means for viable soloing. That Christian should have become the leader of this loud mini-revolution is a consequence of the entrepreneurial acumen of John Hammond who in 1939 brought Christian to Goodman's attention. And while Christian had the right musical stuff, it took the national platform provided by Goodman's band to make the transition possible.

These landmark tracks also figured significantly for Benny Goodman, who expanded on the success of his mid-thirties trio and quartet recordings with the sextet and septet sides of 1939-41 with Christian. What may surprise some first-time listeners is Christian's rather limited role, but considering that the enlarged Goodman small groups featured not only the leader, but also Lionel Hampton, Count Basie and Cootie Williams, what becomes clear is Goodman's generosity in sharing the spotlight on tracks whose average length is only three minutes. Yet even in the half-chorus breaks of *Poor Butterfly* we hear "the father of modern jazz guitar" clearly anticipating things to come. We also hear a supple accompanist whose relaxed rhythmic pulse bears comparison to Freddie Green, for 50 years the heartbeat of the Basie Band. **CB**

---

## B.G. in Hi-Fi   Goodman (cl); with Chris Griffin, Ruby Braff, Bernie Privin, Carl Poole, Charlie Shavers, Bobby Donaldson (t); Will Bradley, Cutty Cutshall, Vernon Brown (tb); Hymie Schertzer, Paul Ricci (as); Boomie Richman, Al Klink (ts); Sol Schlinger (bs); Mel Powell (p);

Steve Jordan (g); **George Duvivier** (b); **Jo Jones, Bobby Donaldson** (d). Capitol Ⓜ CDP7 92864-2 (64 minutes). Recorded 1954.

⑧ ❽

At the time of these November 1954 sessions Goodman was leading a small group containing Shavers and Powell, so the big band was just a studio-assembled unit. Many of the dozen arrangements were taken from the old book and had been scored originally by Fletcher Henderson, but this excellent band of professionals attacks them with enthusiasm, so what might well have been a tired re-creation emerges as a thrillingly fresh experience. Braff was added as a soloist only, the remaining solos being taken by Brown on trombone, Richman (fine, rich-toned tenor), Powell and Goodman himself. Benny clearly felt happy with the band, for his solos are scintillating, sailing high over the ensemble and contributing to the building excitement on tunes such as *Jumpin' at the Woodside*. The eight small-group titles are gems, with marvellous piano from Powell, and Braff in great form on *Rock Rimmon*. *Rose Room* and *What Can I Say After I Say I'm Sorry* are minor classics; here the instrumentation is reduced to clarinet, piano and drums only. The CD contains four previously unissued tracks (including a superb quintet version of *Slipped Disc*), and the music is programmed in chronological order of recording. Capitol's high standard of recording and CD transfer make this a most attractive issue. **AM**

**New review**
### The King of Swing: Rare Recordings from the Yale University Music Library Goodman
(cl); **Joe Newman, Doc Cheatham, Bernie Privin, Mannie Klein, Conrad Gozzo, Irv Goodman, Don Fagerquist, Charlie Shavers** (t); **Bill Harris, Lou McGarity, Joe Howard, Murray McEachern, Milt Bernhardt** (tb); **Toots Mondello, Herb Geller, Bud Shank** (as); **Zoot Sims, Flip Phillips, Buddy Collette, Dave Pell** (ts); **Chuck Gentry** (bs); **Bernie Leighton, Herbie Hancock, Marty Harris, André Previn, Hank Rowland, Russ Freeman, Mel Powell, Teddy Wilson** (p); **Eddie Costa, Lionel Hampton** (vb); **Attila Zoller, Les Spann, Leo Robinson, Barney Kessel, Tony Mottola, Al Hendrickson, Steve Jordan** (g); **George Duvivier, Al Hall, Al Simi, Leroy Vinnegar, Israel Crosby** (b); **Joe Marshall, Morey Feld, Bob Binnix, Frank Capp, Roy Burnes, Gene Krupa** (d); **Annette Saunders, Martha Tilton** (v). MusicMasters Ⓟ 01612-65130-2 (five discs: 297 minutes). Recorded 1954-67.

⑧ ❼

Equipped with a new *embouchure* and a thinner tone than in the days when he first came to fame, Goodman has often been written off by critics for the years that followed his full-time big band of the thirties. This collection of material from his private collection of tapes (now housed at Yale) spans the 'dead years' and shows that he was far from idle and still playing at a consistently high level for much of the fifties and sixties. There are some surprises, for example a 1954 version of his trio with Mel Powell and Morey Feld has more pep about it than the genuine trio (and quartet) reunion from 1963, with Powell prodding some inspired clarinet from Goodman, although the 1963 sides include some intriguing rehearsal eavesdropping. The 1954 trio was expanded to a sextet including Charlie Shavers, and this group produced some of the best of Goodman's latter-day recordings by matching an on-form Goodman with a particularly impressive group of sidemen. He also fronted some quite unusual groups – a 1966 sextet from New York's Rainbow Room has the unlikely pairing of Herbie Hancock and Doc Cheatham in the same line-up. While that group stuck to relatively orthodox repertoire, a sextet with Bill Harris and Flip Phillips from 1959 includes Nat Adderley and Neal Hefti compositions alongside Goodman's staple fare of old favourites (not least because Benny simply 'borrowed' Harris's and Phillips's Florida sextet complete with charts for the recording date). The big band makes just one appearance across this set of five CDs, with former Goodman regulars mingling with Californian session players who had cut their teeth with Kenton and Herman; otherwise this is all Goodman small groups of varying sizes. There isn't the kind of innovation here that so often elevated Goodman's thirties recordings from the capable to the magical, but there is plenty of evidence that if you caught Goodman on a good night any time from the early fifties to the late sixties, there were few, if any, clarinettists in the world who could touch him. **AS**

# Mick Goodrick
1945

**Biorhythms** Goodrick (elg); **Harvie Swartz** (b, elb); **Gary Chaffee** (d). CMP Ⓕ CD46 (54 minutes). Recorded 1990.

⑥ ❽

Mick Goodrick is hardly a jazz household name, having been anchored in Boston by a teaching gig for some two decades, but any of the post-1970 crop of guitar heroes associated with Berklee School – Abercrombie, Scofield, Frisell, Stern, Metheny and the like – will vouch for his skill and influence. Goodrick's music straddles several worlds, from the monochrome asceticism heard on **In Pas(s)ing** (a recently reissued 1978 set for ECM) to the more visceral, funkier style heard in his later recordings with Jack DeJohnette's Special Edition and Gary Thomas's Seventh Quadrant.

All shades of his wide-ranging style are represented here, from the chorale-like chord solo which opens the set through the sometimes awkward funk of *Thramps* (Swartz does not sound too happy with the electric bass) to the nineties bop of *H.D.&L.* and the atonal, pointillist textures of the aptly titled *Something Like That Kind of Thing*. Occasionally Goodrick's guitar sounds shrill, his phrasing a mite effortful, but the set's rough edges lend it a certain charm and it remains the most comprehensive statement yet from a father figure of what may be recognized as the seventies school of Boston guitar players. **MG**

## The Goofus Five

**1926-7** Chelsea Quealey (t); **Abe Lincoln**, **Al Philburn** (tb); **Bobby Davis** (cl, ss, as); **Sam Ruby** (ts); **Adrian Rollini** (bss, gfs); **Irving Brodsky**, **Jack Russin** (p); **Tommy Feline** (bj); **Herb Weil** (d); **Ernest Hare**, **Les Reis**, **Ted Wallace**, **Beth Challis** (v). Timeless Historical Ⓜ CBC1-017 (73 minutes). Recorded 1926/7.

⑥ ❼

Needless to say, The Goofus Five rarely played as a quintet, and invariably recorded with between seven and eight pieces. As a small group within the larger dance-band, the California Ramblers, they were a disciplined, driving good-time unit with an unusually propulsive rhythm section given a good deal of its life by the extraordinary Adrian Rollini, who was soon to carve an indelible niche on a series of classic recordings with Bix Beiderbecke. Rollini aside, the jazz content is relatively light. In Quealey the group had a good trumpet lead with a full tone and the ability – probably learned from Beiderbecke – to carry a melody gracefully. That said, his improvisation is pretty basic, although it is still a few steps ahead of either Lincoln or Davis, who sound hesitant every time they move away from the simplest paraphrase of the melody.

The Goofus Five, for all their limitations, are a very enjoyable unit, and while all the vocalists without exception have little to offer the listener, the instrumental side of things will bring a smile to your face and get you tapping your foot. **KS**

## Dexter Gordon                                             1923-90

**On Dial: The Complete Sessions** Gordon, Wardell Gray, Teddy Edwards (ts); with a collective personnel of: **Melba Liston** (tb, arr); **Charlie Fox**, **Jimmy Bunn**, **Jimmy Rowles** (p); **Red Callender** (b); **Chuck Thompson**, (d). Spotlite Ⓜ SPJCD130 (63 minutes). Recorded 1947.

⑧ ❻

When these titles were recorded Gordon was *the* tenorman-in-residence at Los Angeles's Central Avenue jazz establishments. He was already dubbed 'Vice-Pres' and was having a considerable influence on all local saxists, including the young Art Pepper. Producer Ross Russell placed on record the two-tenor 'battle', *The Chase*, which was a nightly show-stopper at the Bird-In-the-Basket restaurant when Gordon and the brilliant Wardell Gray locked horns. A week prior to the *Chase* record date Russell formed a quintet around Dexter using a trombonist from Gerald Wilson's big band in the dual role of arranger and soloist; even at this early stage in her career Melba Liston gives a very clear indication of her talent. Later quartet sessions for Dial produced some gorgeous ballads, including a fine *Talk of the Town*. On the last Gordon date before the recording ban came into force at the end of December 1947, Ross Russell tried to recreate the initial excitement of *The Chase* but this time with Dexter and Teddy Edwards but some of the magic had evaporated and *The Duel* lacks the impact of the earlier battle; the session comes to a close with *Blues in Teddy's Flat* played by just Edwards and the rhythm section. Gordon was hardly an under-recorded soloist but these Dial tracks have a special place in his discography, freezing in time a most important and exciting period of post-war jazz development. This CD contains all surviving alternative takes and benefits from excellent programme notes contained in a separate booklet. **AM**

New review
**The Complete Blue Note Sessions** Gordon (ts); with a collective personnel of: **Freddie Hubbard**, **Donald Byrd** (t); **Kenny Drew**, **Sonny Clark**, **Barry Harris**, **Bud Powell** (p); **Paul Chambers**, **Niels-Henning Ørsted Pedersen** (b); **Philly Joe Jones**, **Art Taylor**, **Billy Higgins** (d). Blue Note Ⓜ CDP8 34200-2 (six discs: 445 minutes). Recorded 1961-5.

⑨ ❿

Dexter Gordon was a true giant. Although he never attained the status of either Sonny Rollins or John Coltrane, who both credited Gordon as a major influence, Gordon's place in jazz history as "the first bebop tenor saxophonist" is secure. More importantly, Gordon's music continues to sound as fresh and vital as it did when first recorded. Part of that is due to his majesterial sound and agile technique. That his work continues to 'live' is also a consequence of an attitude that was both serious and fun, provoking a deceptively complex range of reactions, causing one to think as well as smile, and to tap a foot. In considering his rich recording legacy, one can point to just about any point in Gordon's career and justifiably say, "amen!" Still, Gordon's distinguished tenure with Blue Note (1961-5) marked a particularly fruitful period. As caught in such Blue Note classics as **Clubhouse** and **Go!**, Gordon's towering command with its still palpable *joie de vivre* was also pivotal in jump-starting a career that in the fifties had been derailed by drugs. Gordon, as indicated by the title of his 1961 Blue Note début, was back and **Doin' Alright**.

In this meticulousley remastered six-disc reprise, Gordon orates with Olympian authority. On ballads, whether his signature *You've Changed* or the poignant *Serenade in Blue*, Gordon's *bel canto* tenor moves effortlessly between his voluptuous lower and plaintive higher registers. For boppish romps like the rowdy *Second Balcony Jump*, the Big Man struts with aplomb. Along the way, jazzdom's most prolific quote-master again proves the equal of Bartlett. An unusually fascinating booklet includes revealing correspondence between Gordon and Blue Note producers Francis Wolff and Alfred Lion. Also, at the end of several discs, we hear Gordon speaking on such subjects as bebop and Charlie Parker. In sum, a life-affirming *magnum opus* by a charter member of the post-war jazz pantheon. **CB**

**Go!** Gordon (ts); **Sonny Clark** (p); **Butch Warren** (b); **Billy Higgins** (d). Blue Note Ⓜ CDP7 46094-2 (38 minutes). Recorded 1962.

⑧ ❽

Dexter Gordon sounds exactly like what he was; a big, confident, forceful man. There was little subtlety in his playing, but prodigious swing, ingenuity and an engagingly obvious sense of humour. This is one of the glories of jazz, the fact that it is a medium which so directly expresses the personality. In Dexter's case this took the form of a curiously deliberate articulation, each phrase delivered with a delighted thump, only just in time. The humour found expression in a succession of unlikely quotations, fitted with devilish cunning into whatever tune happened to be receiving attention at that moment. In this set, for instance, you will find bursts of *Mona Lisa*, *My Heart Stood Still*, *The Mexican Hat Dance*, *Five O'Clock Whistle* and *Three Blind Mice*.

**Go!** comes from Dexter's very best period, the early sixties. It is entirely typical and a delight from beginning to end. The rhythm section is particularly good, Sonny Clark being one of the sharpest-eared pianists in the business. On more than one occasion he picks up the melodic thread at the end of Dexter's solo and keeps it spinning intact – a rare feat. The sound is exceptionally good, as is usual with Blue Note at this time. **DG**

**New review**
**The Panther** Gordon (ts); **Tommy Flanagan** (p); **Larry Ridley** (b); **Alan Dawson** (d). Prestige Ⓜ OJCCD770-2 (44 minutes). Recorded 1970.

⑨ ❼

Gordon hit his creative peak in the sixties and continued to play with great power and authority well into the following decade, during which time the public at large caught up with the significance of what he had been doing all those years and made him a hero on his return to the USA in 1976. During his years of residence in Europe he had been playing as well as ever, but few had paid a great deal of notice. Records such as this one were made regularly on Gordon's infrequent trips back to the States for club and festival appearances and have mostly been overlooked ever since. This is a shame, for **The Panther** is vintage Gordon, finding him with his usual barn-door tone, muscular rhythmic gait and deliberate note production all functioning perfectly, his tendency to lag too far behind the beat when too well prepared with Dutch courage not apparent at any point in the proceedings. The selection of material is an unremarkable mix of Gordon originals and evergreens (Gordon's *Valse Robin*, a real jazz waltz, is one of his better efforts) but he and his backing group handle everything with the same care and concern which raises these performances well beyond the perfunctory. Indeed, the rather compressed recorded sound aside (pretty much standard for Prestige recordings at this time), this could easily pass muster as a late Blue Note Gordon effort. One of the few caveats I can level is at Alan Dawson's insistence on repeatedly playing triplet patterns on his snare for much of *Body and Soul*, no matter what anyone else is doing; strange from a drummer renowned for his responsiveness and sensitivity. That aside, this record will give many hours of listening pleasure to those carrying a torch for big-hearted post-bop tenor titans. **KS**

# Honi Gordon
1936

**Honi Gordon Sings** Gordon (v); **Ken McIntyre** (f, as); **Jaki Byard** (p); **Wally Richardson** (g); **George Duvivier** (b); **Ed Shaughnessy** (d). Prestige Ⓜ OJCCD1783-2 (34 minutes). Recorded 1962.

⑤ ❺

Honi Gordon's recording career has not been extensive. She recorded with the family vocal group (the Gordons) for Mingus's Debut label in 1953 and continued to record from time to time for Mingus over the next decade and a half. Her father, George Gordon, directed his family singers and was a poet of sorts. His aim was to merge poetry and melodic line into compositions that stimulated spontaneous improvisation. His most convoluted piece on this album is *My Kokomo*; a relative of the poetry-meets-jazz vocalese of Lambert, Hendricks and Ross.

The nine tracks on offer here are Honi's only album under her own name, but it is a tribute to her vocal skills that she has a stellar backing group, with Byard and Richardson outstanding. Her voice is accurate but veers towards blandness, not helped by a narrow, lowish range. Even so, in a low-key way she navigates the twists and turns of her father's tortuous compositions, and her singing lingers in the mind like melancholy mist. At this distance in time she sounds most accomplished on the standards *Ill Wind* and *Why Try to Change Me Now?* (the latter with brilliant Byard moments). George Gordon's work sounds too contrived for comfort. **AS**

# Joe Gordon

**West Coast Days**  Gordon (t); **Richie Kamuca** (ts); **Russ Freeman** (p); **Monty Budwig** (b); **Shelly Manne** (d). Fresh Sounds Ⓕ FSCD1030 (57 minutes). Recorded 1960.

⑥ ❹

Gordon was a player who made a nonsense of the East and West divide in American jazz by being prominent in both arenas. He worked in his native city of Boston with Sabby Lewis and Georgie Auld and gigged alongside visitors such as Charlie Parker, Lionel Hampton, Art Blakey and Don Redman. He was in Dizzy Gillespie's big band for the 1956 tour of the Middle East and in 1958 he moved to California. There he teamed up with Harold Land, Dexter Gordon and Barney Kessel before becoming a permanent member of Shelly Manne's quintet. This CD suggests that his tidy articulation and lightly ringing tone was better suited to the reserved temper of the West Coast's brand of hard bop. His approach to *Summertime* is typical, with an improvisation that keeps well in the centre of the thematic safety net. An essential lyricism ensures his almost saxophone-like fluency and one senses that he is guarded against the dramatically angular phrase. The undulating contours of the *Poinciana* line surprisingly inspire a greater show of motive power but the Gordon on this live Lighthouse Club date is trading mainly in understatement. He certainly made better recordings but these are, as yet, unavailable on CD. The bonus here is two 1960 titles by a Richie Kamuca Quartet with Scott LaFaro.   **BMcR**

# Simon Goubert

New review

**L'Encierro**  Goubert (d, elp); **David Sauzay** (ss, ts); **Jean-Michel Couchet** (ss, as); **Arrigo Lorenzi** (ss); **Michel Graillier** (p); **Stephane Persiani** (b). Seventh Records Ⓕ A18 (52 minutes). Recorded 1995.

⑦ ❼

While young America stampedes in the direction of jazz's new traditionalism, there are still outposts of the Empire where older forms of expression hold true. Goubert's Frenchmen remain stubbornly true to the modalities of mid-sixties John Coltrane and seventies McCoy Tyner at a time when if you know what you're about, you don't venture past 1960 as far as Coltrane compositions go. Considering the vast overdose of such music we all suffered in the seventies and eighties, this CD comes as a refreshing surprise, and the players on it, pretty much unknown outside France, acquit themselves very well indeed within their self-imposed boundaries, their three-horn arrangements adding considerable sparkle to the occasion. Leader Goubert continually calls the troops to battle, stoking a fire under even the most laid-back soloist, although even he turns gentle on the pretty ballad (a feature for the trio) *Jacqueline*. The weirdo *Ultime Appel* and the gentle *Wayne's Way*, where Sauzay sticks to soprano backgrounds for pianist Graillier, bring a nice variety to the proceedings.   **KS**

# Dusko Goykovich

**Soul Connection**  Goykovich (t, flh); **Jimmy Heath** (ts); **Tommy Flanagan** (p); **Eddie Gomez** (b); **Mickey Roker** (d). Enja Ⓕ ENJ80442 (71 minutes). Recorded 1993.

⑧ ❽

Goykovich was born in what was then Yugoslavia and found his way across the Atlantic with Marshall Brown's International Youth Band after working for some years in Germany. He studied at Berklee College and subsequently worked with the orchestras of Maynard Ferguson, Woody Herman and Kenny Clarke-Francy Boland. He is, with Rolf Erison and the late Jimmy Deuchar, one of the three leading post-war European jazz trumpet soloists, and **Soul Connection** is certainly his best small-group recording. Made in New York, it has a virtually unbeatable rhythm section and, on five of the nine tracks, a very on-form Jimmy Heath. Dusko received help and encouragement as a young player from Miles Davis and this album is dedicated to "Miles and his spirit". It is the spirit, rather than the letter, of Davis's teachings which is manifest here. All but *I'll Close My Eyes* are Goykovich originals and his *Ballad for Miles* is one of the most sensitive and moving of all the tributes to the trumpeter. The originals have a haunting Balkan feeling, beautifully interpreted by the full group (it's no accident that Goykovich's latest CD is called **Balkan Connection**). This is an excellent example of post-hard-bop jazz by five quite outstanding musicians. The recording quality captures the music with clarity and sympathy, making this a highly recommended release.   **AM**

# Teddy Grace

**Teddy Grace**  Grace (v); **Bobby Hackett, Charlie Shavers, Max Kaminsky** (t); **Jack Teagarden, Sonny Lee, Brad Gowans** (tb); **Buster Bailey, Pee Wee Russell** (cl); **John Sandola, Bud Freeman** (ts); **Dave Barbour, Eddie Condon** (g); **Frankie Froeba, Billy Kyle, Dave Bowman** (p); **Haig Stephens, Delmar Kaplan, Pete Peterson** (b); **Al Sidell, O'Neil Spencer, Morey Feld** (d). Timeless Ⓜ CBC1-016 (62 minutes). Recorded 1937-40.

Teddy Grace was a well-connected Southern belle who, for a dare, stood up to sing with the band at a country club dance. Within a year she was a professional vocalist and a few years later made her recording début. That was 1937. For three years she recorded with the best (see above) and then stopped. The rest of her extraordinary story is told in the notes to this CD, so fascinating that they are one of the reasons for buying it. She had a sweet voice and an in-born sense of swing almost at the Peggy Lee level. But her real talent was for the blues. I can think of no white woman who sings the blues as easily or as authentically as Teddy Grace; in this regard she is the female equivalent to Jack Teagarden. They were both Southerners, and this leads to the reflection that geography, rather than race, could be the determining factor. Whatever the case, this collection rehabilitates an important lost voice. **DG**

## Robert Graettinger 1923-57

**New review**

**Stan Kenton Plays Bob Graettinger: City of Glass** The Stan Kenton Orchestra; collective personnel includes: **Kenton** (p); **Buddy Childers**, **Ray Wetzel**, **Al Porcino**, **Maynard Ferguson**, **Conte Candoli**, **Pete Candoli**, **Shorty Rogers** (t); **Milt Bernhart**, **Eddie Bert**, **Billy Byers**, **Bill Russo**, **Bob Burgess**, **Frank Rosolino** (tb); **John Graas** (frh); **Gene Englund** (tba); **Art Pepper**, **Bob Cooper**, **Bud Shank**, **Lennie Niehaus**, **Bill Holman**, **Lee Konitz**, **Richie Kamuca**, **Herb Geller** (reeds); **Laurindo Almeida**, **Sal Salvador** (g); **Eddie Safranski**, **Joe Mondragon**, **Don Bagley** (b); **Shelly Manne**, **Don Lamond**, **Frank Capp**, **Stan Levey**, **Carlos Vidal** (d, perc); **June Christy** (v); plus string section. Capitol Ⓜ CDP8 32084-2 (63 minutes). Recorded 1947-53.

One of the phantoms of modern jazz, Bob Graettinger's brief career consisted primarily of the dozen or so compositions and arrangements he scored for Stan Kenton's Progressive Jazz and Innovations In Modern Music orchestras. Full of sharp dissonance and abrupt, colliding rhythms, Graettinger's writing mystified the musicians, confused the critics and alienated most listeners. Kenton himself was a staunch supporter, however, and today, more than 40 years and several musical revolutions later, Graettinger's unique sound world seems to be among the most imaginative and prophetic of his time. But there's a question of whether his music was jazz at all. Certainly, *House of Strings*, composed solely for Kenton's string section, reveals barely any discernible trace of popular song writing – this is classical music by design. In *A Cello, an Orchestra and a Thought*, the music develops along lines that are classical in character and organization, while incorporating propulsive jazz rhythms and improvised solos. The undeniable excitement in pieces like *Incident in Jazz* and *Thermopylae* arise from the tension between episodes of swing and non-swing, bracing polyphony, jagged melodic contours and the almost antagonistic rhythms and harmonies. *City of Glass* was his masterpiece. Influenced by Stravinsky's polytonality and layered orchestration, Bartók's string voicings and Varèse's blocks of sound and clashing textures, the four-movement composition reflects Graettinger's view of an architecture of the future, seen from a cubist's multiple perspectives and through various stages of illumination. It also evokes the psychological problems man may have in existing there. Perhaps the true measure of his originality emerges most immediately in his arrangements of standard tunes like *Everything Happens to Me* and *You Go to My Head*, where the familiar melodies are given bizarre counterpoint by caustic harmonies, drastically unrelated episodes and nightmarish ambience. Graettinger's music, in all its urgent, anxious momentum, explosive climaxes, and surrealist interludes may seem cataclysmic, claustrophobic, or merely incongruous; it's also exhilarating and strangely beautiful. Graettinger wrote his music for Kenton, but *City of Glass* has been given a recent dusting-down on CD by Gunther Schuller and the Ebony Band (Channel Crossings). **AL**

## Jerry Granelli 1940

**Another Place** Granelli (d); **Julian Priester** (tb); **Jane Ira Bloom** (ss); **David Friedman** (vb, mba); **Anthony Cox** (b). VeraBra Ⓔ vBr 2130-2 (51 minutes). Recorded 1992.

San Franciscan drummer Granelli has been making fine music with others – including Vince Guaraldi, Ralph Towner and John Handy – for over 30 years. As it is, this is by no means Granelli's first album – there are two worthy attempts on the ITM label – and it demonstrates most forcefully that Granelli is of the Paul Motian school to the extent that he is offering much more than sheer physical and percussive presence to the music. Here, he supplies the concept and shapes this unusually resourceful band in a manner which continually offsets the soloists in the most provocative light. This enables each composition to be fully fleshed out and paced so that each performance is properly formed and balanced.

Additionally, it is a treat to have Julian Priester back on record. This man has been in the shadows for far too long, and here he is given a setting which perfectly suits his velvet tone and angular melodic conception. Both Bloom and Friedman also solo imaginatively, with Friedman adding a distinctive colour through his extensive use of the marimba. This is first-rate modern music, played with immense style and no little commitment, with improvisatory egos nicely in check. Granelli's latest album, **Broken Circle** (Intuition), depicts the world of the U.S. Indians, but remains less impressive musically than this one. **KS**

# Darrell Grant

**The New Bop**  Grant (p); **Scott Wendholt** (t); **Seamus Blake** (ts, ss); **Calvin Jones** (b); **Brian Blade**
   (d). Criss Cross Ⓔ 1106CD (70 minutes). Recorded 1994.

⑦ ❾

Grant comes with a recommendation from his idol, Horace Silver, who in the sleeve-notes praises
Grant's burgeoning compositional talents. Everything about his album complements the Silver
tradition, including the eloquent two-horn front line. Grant manages original composition like *The
Blues We Ain't No More*, very much based on Silver mores, while *Don't Stray*, a mournful ballad,
draws forth a Milesian solo from Wendholt. Although eight of the 12 compositions are his, one still
could wish for more. But then we would have missed this imaginative reading of Ellington's *Come
Sunday*. Blake has a fat, almost mainstream tone which is heard at its best on that track. *Rebop* is a
tantalizing one-minute fragment which has a potent chase between the horns before it fades. More
substantial is the ten-minute *Water Dreams,* a mini-suite including an unusual improvisation on *How
Deep Is the Ocean* and a powerful Cuban-inspired composition by the leader. The latter, subtitled
*Agua Profunda*, is driven by powerfully rhythmic piano in the Eddie Costa area of the keyboard and
is notable for one of Wendholt's most inflammatory solos as well as more hard-edged tenor from
Blake. Grant's robust solo is tremendously impressive. Silver's right: this ranks with Silver.     **SV**

# Stephane Grappelli

1908

**Grappelli Story**  Grappelli (vn, p); with the following collective personnel: **Bill Shakespeare,
   Stan Andrews** (t); **Dennis Moonan, Frank Weir** (reeds); **Charlie Pude, Frank Baron, George
   Shearing, York de Sousa, Maurice Vandair, Raymond Fol, Marc Hemmeler, Michel Legrand** (p);
   **Django Reinhardt, Roger Chaput, Eugene Vees, Jack Llewellyn, Chappie D'Amato, Syd
   Jacobson, Joe Deniz, Dave Wilkins, Alan Hodgkins, Rene Duchaussoir, Pierre Cavalli, Leo Petit,
   Diz Disley, Ike Isaacs, Philip Catherine, Larry Coryell** (g); **Harry Chapman** (h); **Arthur Young**
   (novachord); **Reg Conroy, Roy Marsh, Michel Hauser** (vb); **Louis Vola, George Senior, Hank
   Hobson, George Gibbs, Joe Nussbaum, Coleridge Goode, Benoit Quersin, Pierre Michelot, Guy
   Pedersen, Lennie Bush, Eberhard Weber, Lisla Eckinger, Andrew Simpkins, Nils-Henning Ørsted
   Pedersen** (b); **Eugene Pini, Stanley Andres** (vn); **Tony Spurgin, Al Philcock, Jock Jacobson, Dave
   Fullerton, Jean-Louis Viale, Jean-Baptiste 'Mac Kac' Reilles, Alan Levitt, Daniel Humair, John
   Spooner, Kenny Clare, Rusty Jones** (d); **Beryl Davis** (v). Verve Ⓜ 515 807 2 (two discs: 174
   minutes). Recorded 1938-92.

⑧ ❻

A comprehensive survey of Grappelli's work, culled from sources available to PolyGram and
commencing with some Quintet of The Hot Club sides made for Decca during a visit to London
in 1938. The conjunction of Grappelli and Reinhardt was unique; it is brought into sharp focus
with two duets, *It Had to Be You* (on which Stephane doubles on piano and violin) and the
intimate *Nocturne*. Guitars have always figured prominently on Grappelli's recording dates, but
subsequent to the break between the two principals, the chugging sound of the string-laden
QHCF has usually been replaced by the lighter effect of a more orthodox rhythm section. A brief
revival of the Grappelli-Reinhardt partnership in 1946 (again in London for Decca) produced
the lovely *Nuages,* but Stephane was already looking for new inspiration. His strong sense of
melody and a hard, aggressive approach on the faster tempos is well demonstrated here. An
indication of the violinist's awareness of jazz in the wider sense is evident in his choice of material
which takes in Sonny Rollins's *Pent Up House* and John Lewis's *Django* from a fine 1962 session
represented here. *Darling je vous aime beaucoup* is quite hilarious and has a deliberately funny
vocal by Grappelli. In the seventies Steph did an LP with George Shearing (the two worked
together frequently in the early forties), the source of two tracks immediately preceding the 1979
*Sweet Chorus*, which sets the violinist in between youngsters Philip Catherine and Larry Coryell.
Overall Grappelli's work is in a class of its own, albeit a little florid at times, but few other
musicians have enjoyed such a long and distinguished career in jazz. A recommended issue with
generous playing time.     **AM**

# Milford Graves

1941

**Percussion Ensemble**  Graves (d, perc); **Sunny Morgan** (d, perc). ESP-Disk Ⓜ 1015-2
   (35 minutes). Recorded 1965.

⑧ ❼

An important second-generation free drummer, Graves worked with the New York Art Quartet,
Albert Ayler, Don Pullen and the Jazz Composer's Orchestra in the sixties. More recently he has been
involved in teaching, but this CD reissue shows him in the naked spotlight of the percussion duo.
Fortunately, the sound separation is good and Graves comes at the listener from the right speaker. All
of his trade marks are here; his mobility around his entire kit and his expert use of the auxiliary

percussion paraphernalia to flesh out the textures. There is obviously no orthodox thematic continuity, a fact emphasized by the absence of tune titles (well, they are all called *Nothing*), but both men pursue a policy of story-telling on the drums. Neither uses points of strict punctuation and it is instructive to hear how both create the feeling of abstract calibration that was to offer a state of free flow to horn players soloing above it. Although a lesser-known figure, the late Sunny Morgan comes over as a player of near-equal stature.                                   **BMcR**

## Georg Gräwe                                                                      1956

**Chamber Works 1990-2** Gräwe (p); Horst Grabosch (t); Melvyn Poore (tba); Michael Moore (cl, bcl); Phil Wachsmann (vn); Ernst Reijseger (vc); Anne Le Baron (hp); Hans Schneider (b); Gerry Hemingway (d); Phil Minton (v). Random Acoustics Ⓟ 003 (50 minutes). Recorded 1991/2.

⑧ ❽

Georg Gräwe's music is difficult to categorize; in fact, the name of his self-produced record company, Random Acoustics, might be the best clue to how he views the problem himself. One of a younger generation of Europeans who are equally adept at improvisation and composition, Gräwe is working in an area where those two disciplines overlap, or blur. As an improvising pianist, he can be best heard in the Gräwe/Reijseger/Hemingway trio (they have recorded for hatART, Music & Arts and other labels). But as a composer, he has written memorable pieces for the ten-piece GrubenKlang Orchestra, and contingents of smaller groups, as on **Chamber Works 1990-2**. Although many of Gräwe's compositional techniques are based in contemporary classical procedures, by using musicians well versed in free improvisation he obtains striking results from small details and intimate gestures. Both *15 Duets* and *Flavours A* here are good examples. On the former, the six musicians improvise in the various possible duo combinations, but their statements are kept as brief as to create a music of constantly changing colour, character and perspective. Likewise, *Flavours A* consists of violin, tuba and piano whispering aphorisms and minuscule variations of pitch and timbre. *Variations Q* is a reworking of a piece for the larger ensemble, performed by a livelier, more interactive quartet. Gräwe acknowledges the musicians' contributions of what he calls "extended interpretation" in bringing his music to life.                                                                **AL**

## Wardell Gray                                                                    1921-55

**Memorial, Volumes 1 and 2** Gray (ts); Clark Terry, Art Farmer (t); Sonny Criss, Frank Morgan (as); Dexter Gordon (ts); Teddy Charles (vb); Al Haig, Phil Hill, Jimmy Bunn, Hampton Hawes, Sonny Clark (p); Tommy Potter, John Richardson, Billy Hadnott, Harper Crosby, Dick Nivison (b); Roy Haynes, Art Mardigan, Chuck Thompson, Larry Marable (d); Robert Collier (cga). Prestige Ⓜ OJCCD050/1-2 (two discs, oas: 59 and 64 minutes). Recorded 1949-53.

⑧ ❻

In 1949 Gray recorded his most popular track (the blues *Twisted* which was later lyricized by Annie Ross) and must have seemed well on the way to becoming the most successful bop-tinged tenorman of the next decade. By comparison with Gene Ammons and Dexter Gordon, who had reinforced a basic Lester Young approach with the harder sound of Charlie Parker, Gray (like Sonny Stitt) softened the Parker style with reminiscences of Young. Sadly, Gray followed Stitt along the drug trail and spent the first half of the fifties under-employed on the West Coast until his untimely death.

For the CD edition, each volume (available separately) includes several additional takes originally available only on unofficial issues, the inferior sound being carried over where presumably the masters have been lost. But this is by far the best representation of Gray's slender discography. Vying with the *Twisted* session, a 1952 date with the young Art Farmer and Hampton Hawes has everyone on form, while a 19-minute jam with fellow Basie sideman Terry and friendly rival Dexter is energizing. The Milt Jackson-influenced Charles's sextet date has the first jazz recordings of latterly rehabilitated Frank Morgan, then just 19, but the best news throughout is Gray.                                                          **BP**

## Bennie Green                                                                    1923-77

**Blows His Horn** Green (tb); Charlie Rouse (ts); Cliffe Smalls (p); Paul Chambers (b); Osie Johnson (d); Candido (cga). Prestige Ⓜ OJCCD1728-2 (40 minutes). Recorded 1955.

④ ❻

The advent of the LP may have given musicians a chance to stretch out, but it also led to a lot of not-bad not-good two-front-line-plus-rhythm blowing sessions. Fashionably there was also a conga player, who came in for the faster numbers and laid out on the ballads, unless they doubled the tempo on the ballad whereupon he would stub out his cigarette and leap into action. The advent of J.J. Johnson is also supposed to have liberated the trombone, but in hindsight Johnson's dry, gentlemanly tone led to a lot of slightly desiccated stylists like Bennie Green, and the trombonists who now shine out of the fifties are those who like Jimmy Knepper went their own way, not J.J.'s. This record never really gets anywhere, nor really tries; it is a museum piece, to be placed in a glass case marked "Mid-fifties modern jazz sophisticated horns 'n' rhythm session" and got out and dusted occasionally, so that we can marvel at what people found exciting in those days. **MK**

## Benny Green
1963

**New review**

**Kaleidoscope**  Green (p); **Antonio Hart** (as); **Stanley Turrentine** (ts); **Russell Malone** (g); **Ron Carter** (b); **Lewis Nash** (d). Blue Note Ⓔ CDP8 52037-2 (57 minutes). Recorded 1996.

Blue Note shepherded a line of great pianists which included Bud Powell, Thelonious Monk, Horace Silver, Sonny Clark and, on occasion, Bobby Timmons. There is no one in the younger generation who deserves to continue that line better than Green, despite the fact that there appear to be more good young pianists about than players of the other instruments, even accounting for the last shower of trumpeters. Perhaps it is because Green refers back more firmly to earlier days. It is no criticism to note that his work often reflects elements of Powell, Timmons, Gerald Wiggins and even Garner and Tatum, as well as more contemporary sources such as Tyner and Hancock.

This new record is perhaps his most impressive yet, and one of the few where he conclusively escapes the power-trio approach of most of his former dates. Altoist Hart is featured on four tunes and plays out of his skin, reflecting a staggering maturity on both ballads and up-tempo screamers such as the title track. Turrentine crops up on three tracks, and guitarist Malone appears on two, one of which (*The Sexy Mexy*) is a classy Blue Note patent groover. Green shows a considerable growth in his ability to bring the depths of ballads to the surface, giving himself more time than previously to do so, and making himself in the process a more rounded player. This is a mightily impressive disc. **SV**

## Bunky Green

**Healing the Pain**  Green (ss, as); **Billy Childs** (p); **Art Davis** (b); **Ralph Penland** (d). Delos Ⓔ DE4020 (66 minutes). Recorded 1989.

Delos is an American company more usually asociated with classical music recordings than jazz, but we can all be grateful that they crossed the great divide and made this one. Green is not exactly a household name, although he has been making records since the sixties at least, most notably for the old Chess/Argo/Cadet group based in Chicago. He went through a stage of playing quite funky music which won him few friends among jazz pundits, but he has always been an intelligent and articulate man who could express with absolute clarity exactly what he was trying to achieve on any given piece of music. This album carries a dedication to his parents, both of whom died shortly before the sessions for it were held, and the choice of tracks is certainly dominated by that dedication, whether it is *The Thrill is Gone*, *I Concentrate on You* or *Goodbye*. Tempos are for the most part slow, and a mood of longing and despairing love hangs over Green's playing. The album is very moving, and Green plays with terrific intensity of a type more normally associated with latter-day Art Pepper. Although he plays both soprano and alto, he favours the latter. He long ago carved a highly individual style on both instruments, and is capable of both the simplest and most complex of improvisational approaches. A fine album. **KS**

## Grant Green
1931-79

**Idle Moments**  Green (g); **Joe Henderson** (ts); **Bobby Hutcherson** (vb); **Duke Pearson** (p); **Bob Cranshaw** (b); **Al Harewood** (d). Blue Note Ⓜ CDP7 84154-2 (64 minutes). Recorded 1963.

Grant Green made many fine – and poor – albums for Blue Note (many of both type are currently on CD), but this is the best. It has a certain indefinable, but quite tangible, atmosphere to it, something which existed just for the hours these musicians assembled for this project. The title track, which opens the album, properly sets the mood: it is a very slow blues-based line written by pianist Duke Pearson, and one with intriguingly altered changes which suggest other things to the soloist and, ultimately, the listener. If anyone wanted to define music for the small hours, then this is it. Each soloist plays in the most relaxed, soulful manner, completely free from artifice or grandstanding, each digging a little further into the mood. It is 15 minutes long, but not for a second does it drag, so perfectly is it judged.

The rest of the date keeps up the standard, with an energetic, forward-reaching feel to *Jean de Fleur*, an enigmatic and tautly elegiac atmosphere to one of the most successful readings of John Lewis's *Django* outside the original, and a distinctly hard-boppish edge to the medium-tempo *Nomad*. In all, a remarkably unified session, with fresh, unhackneyed improvising and a special group 'feel' to the whole proceedings. There really must have been something in the air that night. The record has been marked a half-star short due to the inclusion of 20 minutes' worth of alternative takes which disrupt the flow of the original album, and really should have been added at the end of the CD programme. **KS**

# Burton Greene

1937

**New review**

**Burton Greene Quartet** Greene (p); **Marion Brown** (as); **Henry Grimes** (b); **Dave Grant, Tom Price** (d); on one track add **Frank Smith** (ts). ESP-Disk Ⓜ 1024-2 (44 minutes). Recorded 1965.
⑥ ❼

Greene made a considerable if short-lived impact in New York's avant-garde circles during the mid sixties, then relocated in Europe, first in Paris and finally in Holland, where he still lectures at Utrecht's Conservatoire. Greene's talent is indisputable and his technique secure, having been classically trained in both theory and piano at Chicago's Arts Academy before plumping for jazz. Meeting bassist Alan Silva, he moved to New York and quickly became part of the burgeoning free-music scene there, joining the Jazz Composers Guild in 1964 and becoming part of that year's 'October Revolution in Jazz'. His association with ESP-Disk began with this album, a second record being made by his working trio during a short stint as Patty Waters's backing group in spring 1966. They also appeared on both Patty Waters's ESP-Disk albums. The **Quartet** record is Greene's most memorable as a leader, partly because of Brown's stimulating and precise presence, partly because the excitement of discovery is quite clearly in the air and Greene is intelligent enough a musician to spread that excitement to ballads (*Ballade II*) as well as the more rumbunctious material – a rare event in the New York avant-garde of the time. The group works well together, listening and responding at appropriate points in the music. Tenorist Frank Smith (who also made an album for ESP-Disk at around this time) appears for a few high-energy, cliché-ridden minutes on *Taking it out of the Ground*, thus confirming posterity's subsequent silence on his part. **KS**

# Dodo Greene

**New review**

**My Hour of Need** Greene (v); **Ike Quebec, Eddie Chamblee** (ts); **Grant Green** (g); **Edwin Swanton, Sir Charles Thompson** (org); **Johnny Acea** (p); **Herbie Lewis, Milt Hinton, Wendell Marshall** (b); **Jual Curtis, Billy Higgins, Al Harewood** (d). Blue Note Ⓜ CDP8 52442-2 (59 minutes). Recorded 1962.
④ ❼

Greene was brought to Blue Note's attention by tenorist and sometime A&R man for the label, Ike Quebec. Her roots in gospel are undisguised and her previous records had reflected that. This, her only album for Blue Note, show her to be a pre-Nancy Wilson Nancy Wilson, belting the lyrics and enunciating like crazy. She sings accurately, has a big voice and is not afraid to emote. Past that, I'm afraid, there is little more to write. There are four different but equally discreet line-ups from four different sessions, spread over eight months. Ike Quebec is the common denominator for all of them, and his obbligatos and solos are the only possible reasons for this album ever being reissued. **KS**

# Guillermo Gregorio

1941

**New review**

**Approximately** Gregorio (cl, as); **Eric Pakula** (as, ts); **Mat Maneri** (vn); **Pandelis Karayorgis** (p); **John Lockwood** (b). hatART Ⓕ CD6184 (55 minutes). Recorded 1995.
⑧ ❾

Gregorio recorded **Approximately**, his first disc as leader, at the age of 54. Born in Buenos Aires, he worked as an architect, wrote about design and modern music and performed in both contemporary classical and jazz groups. In 1986 he left Argentina, living first in Germany then settling in the United States. Though he had long led his own groups, his only commercial recordings prior to **Approximately** were as a member of Franz Koglmann's Pipetet. Gregorio shares Koglmann's fondness for the 'white line' of Cool Jazz and Third Stream improvisers. There are similarities in his music to the gentle abstractions of Jimmy Giuffre's 1961 trio and Gregorio is also much influenced by Tristano school saxophonists Lee Konitz and Warne Marsh, the latter of whom he studied with in the mid eighties. On **Approximately**, Gregorio is joined by four Boston-based musicians who fit perfectly into his austerely beautiful sound-world. This is a music of intimate exchange: wraiths of melody hang in the space, instruments step softly in unison or intricate counterpoint, eerie rumbles and scurries come and go. Barely audible at times, introspective, subtly nuanced, **Approximately** is a disc that requires – and repays – the closest attention. On headphones, a masterpiece. **GL**

# Sonny Greenwich

1936

**Live at Sweet Basil** Greenwich (g); **Fred Henke** (p); **Ron Seguin** (b); **Andre White** (d). Justin
Time Ⓕ JUST26-2 (60 minutes). Recorded 1987.

⑧ ❽

Jazz guitarists are a dime a dozen these days, and Coltrane-influenced saxophonists come even
cheaper. But Greenwich, a reclusive Canadian who performed briefly with John Handy and Wayne
Shorter in the sixties, and who seems to pop up every ten years or so, just when you have abandoned
hope of ever hearing him again, is worth his weight in gold as a Coltrane-influenced guitarist. He is
also one of very few jazz musicians to have realized the harmonic potential of Stephen Sondheim's
music – witness his spiralling interpretations on his previous album. On theme statements, his
phrasing is so Coltrane-like you can imagine the rise and fall of his breath. *You Go to My Head*, this
live set's ballad, is not nearly as mesmerizing, but the faster numbers are satisfying emotional
workouts, and you would be able to tell that *Libra Ascending* – perhaps the most effervescent of them
– was dedicated to Coltrane even without reading Greenwich's brief sleeve-note. Occupying a niche just
to the left of Grant Green and just to the right of Sonny Sharrock, Greenwich is an elusive figure who
always leaves you wanting to hear more. **FD**

# Al Grey

1923

**Al Meets Bjarne** Grey (tb); **Bjarne Nerem** (ts); **Norman Simmons** (p); **Paul West** (b); **Gerryck
King** (d). Gemini Ⓕ GMCD62 (60 minutes). Recorded 1988.

⑧ ❽

Grey's considerable playing experience takes in employment with the big bands of Lucky Millinder,
Benny Carter, Lionel Hampton, Dizzy Gillespie and Count Basie as well as numerous tours with
JATP. As a group leader he favours the trombone-tenor front-line and has worked with partners such
as Jimmy Forrest and Buddy Tate, but few have bettered this one-off session with Norway's
outstanding mainstreamer, the late Bjarne Nerem. Backed by the rhythm section then working with
singer Joe Williams (which also supported Harold Ashby on his Gemini date) the two men create fine
music in a variety of moods and tempos. Nerem gets close to the spirit of Lester Young in places and
produces a superlative version of *Blue and Sentimental*. Grey makes adroit use of mutes, especially the
rubber plunger, but his brazen open sound gets close to the tone we associate with Bill Harris. The
title tune is a beautifully relaxed blues and the sound of the quintet has been well captured in this
session held in Oslo's Rainbow studio. **AM**

# Carola Grey

1969

**New review**

**Girls Can't Hit** Grey (d); **Rich Keller** (ss, ts); **Werner Neumann** (g, elg); **Martin Kalberer** (kbds);
**Paul Tietze** (elb). Guests: **Paul Koji Shigihara** (elg, gsyn); **Ina Stock** (ehn). Lipstick Ⓕ LIP8945-2
(48 minutes). Recorded 1996.

⑨ ❾

In her last album, **The Age of Illusions**, Carola Grey proved that she could not only drive but reinvigorate
hard-bop material. Now, home again in Germany, she springs more surprises, having moved towards a
wider-ranging repertoire with a strong rock and fusion element. Her compositions – eight of the nine
are hers – display a variety of influences, with Indian rhythm patterns inspiring the brief drum solo
*3/3/3/5/5/5/4/4*, and yet other world music providing the impetus for the ethereal introduction and
Spanish main section of *It's All Good*. However, most of the record concerns itself with funkier, more
urban textures. *Don't Play It Again Sam*, for instance, sounds like an update on Eddie Harris's *Freedom
Jazz Dance*, and *Room 201* is a hell-for-leather roadhouse blues. The latter has excellent work from
guitarist Werner Neumann, an old colleague from Grey's Cologne days, and he is also remarkable on
the opening *Bits & Pieces*, his hot, over-driven tone a refreshing antidote to the soft, chorused tones so
often associated with fusion guitar. The other soloists do acceptable work but won't worry the New York
sidemen on Carola's last date. On balance a solid and rewarding move forward for a talented woman
who shows on the heavy metal title track that girls can hit just as hard as they need. **MG**

# Della Griffin

**Travellin' Light** Griffin (v); **Houston Person** (ts); **Randy Johnson** (g); **Stan Hope** (p); **Cameron Brown**
(b); **Michael Carvin** (d). Muse Ⓕ MCD5496 (49 minutes). Recorded 1992.

⑥ ❻

For many years Della Griffin played drums and sang in her own band at various Harlem clubs,
keeping a career going during the twilight years for jazz in the seventies and eighties. She was
something of a local legend but not known beyond her home patch. A traffic accident ended her
percussion playing and she relaunched her career as a singer, aiming at a wider audience than her

quarter of Manhattan. Her début album is produced, with great taste, by Person, whose 20 years with Etta Jones have taught him how to back a singer, and it is his contributions in particular that make this more than an ordinary album. He builds up a rapport with Griffin that is a model of how to accompany a singer without stealing the limelight, yet to play so ravishingly in what Buck Clayton called the 'windows' as to command attention. Griffin's voice has echoes of Billie Holiday's style and phrasing, although it is fanciful to suggest she sounds as Billie might have, had she lived another few decades, despite a 'lived-in' tone, and the sense of worldly experience with which she delivers her lyrics. Hope is outstanding in a strong rhythm section, and this is a commendable first album. **AS**

## Johnny Griffin 1928

**The Congregation** Griffin (ts); **Sonny Clark** (p); **Paul Chambers** (b); **Kenny Dennis** (d). Blue Note
Ⓜ CDP7 89383-2 (37 minutes). Recorded 1957.

⑧ ❼

Griffin is still active, both live and in the recording studio, and continues to produce good and varied albums, but the ones which made his reputation are those he recorded as a sideman with both the Blakey and Monk groups and a string of burning dates for Blue Note in the late fifties, the most famous of which, **A Blowing Session** (featuring both Coltrane and Mobley), is currently unavailable on CD. So **The Congregation**, from the same year as the triple-tenor album, will have to serve as substitute. And no mean substitute it is, with Sonny Clark (at that time more or less permanently nailed to Van Gelder's piano stool when it came to Blue Note sessions) at the keyboard and Paul Chambers providing pulsation. Griffin, one of the great speed merchants (he and 'Lockjaw' Davis ran a terrifying twin-tenors band for a few years – there was a recent Prestige reissue of **Tough Tenor Favorites** (1962) which more than adequately represents that pairing), surprisingly opts for medium swingers on five of the six tunes here, but his busy, bustling style and unburnished tone retains sufficient bite and content to keep the listener happy and involved. Besides, the medium tempos give Griffin the perfect excuse to double-up at will.

To say this is typical late-fifties Blue Note fare is not to denigrate it, but to give it a proper perspective. If you like hard bop, then this is a safe bet. This CD reissue is the album's first appearance in true stereo, and there is a seven-minute bonus track, *I Remember You*. Which makes the original LP playing time desperate. **KS**

**New review**
**The Little Giant** Griffin (ts); **Blue Mitchell** (t); **Julian Priester** (tb); **Wynton Kelly** (p); **Sam Jones** (b); **Albert Heath** (d). Riverside Ⓜ OJCCD136-2 (34 minutes). Recorded 1959.

⑧ ⑧

In 1959, having gigged already with the Jazz Messengers and Thelonious Monk, Johnny Griffin was still relatively new to the New York scene, where he had built a reputation as a saxophonist tailor-made for the informal jam session around which many recordings were built. Throughout the time he recorded for Riverside things gradually changed until he led a studio big band and recreated Billie Holiday songs in front of a string section. This is half-way there. Arrangements by a fellow-Chicagoan, the pianist Norman Simmons, make full use of the front line, especially on his own quite intricate compositions. Of these, *The Message* gets the best performance. A kind of way-out gospel theme, it lets Griffin charge over some stop-time passages before cruising at medium tempo and finding plenty of room for those querulous squawks in the high register that so enlivened his solos. He is just as excitingly inventive on his own *63rd Street Theme*, a blues closely related to the tune that became *Blues for Dracula*. The only mild complaint is Heath's rather heavy drumming on a couple of tracks. **RA**

## Henry Grimes 1935

**The Call** Grimes (b); **Perry Robinson** (cl); **Tom Price** (d). ESP-Disk Ⓜ 1026-2 (34 minutes).
Recorded 1965.

✔ ⑧ ❼

A Juilliard student, Grimes's early musical grounding was in r&b bands. He later worked with Anita O'Day, Gerry Mulligan and Sonny Rollins before getting involved with sixties avant-garde. This CD comes from that period and portrays Grimes as an outstanding talent. *For Django* is evidence of his writing talent but, whether racing out behind the clarinet line or soloing with strength and genuine harmonic originality, it is his highly original bass playing that stands out. Both *arco* and *pizzicato* work excel and in the former role he deploys notes, bent in the manner of a horn, avoiding the string player's normal slurs and achieving the changing density associated with the saxophone. Robinson is at times rhythmically predictable but he was an important figure in changing the vernacular of his instrument, producing a new sound in the process. On *For Django* and *The Call*, in particular, he shows his talent for taking fragments of the theme and working them in theoretical circles, from germ ideas and free development, back to the original. While he is doing this, Grimes and Price provide a rhythmic contradiction, yet they do achieve a form of integration in the process. Grimes was amongst the first of the free bassists to demand this front-line status. **BMcR**

# Tiny Grimes
1916-89

**Callin' the Blues** Grimes (g); **J.C. Higginbotham** (tb); **Eddie 'Lockjaw' Davis** (ts); **Ray Bryant** (p); **Wendell Marshall** (b); **Osie Johnson** (d). Prestige Ⓜ OJCCD191-2 (40 minutes). Recorded 1956.
⑦ ❽

A native Virginian, Grimes's career began as a pianist and dancer in the cabaret clubs of Washington DC. In 1939, he switched to guitar and almost immediately became one of the pioneers of amplification on the instrument. His progress was such that, by 1943, he had reached a level of technical proficiency sufficient to persuade pianist Art Tatum to include him in his first trio. He recorded with Charlie Parker in 1944 and, in the early fifties, contributed to the world of rock 'n' roll with his Rockin' Highlanders. His métier, however, was small, blues-based bands with their roots in the swing era. This CD shows that his rock experience had some influence on his later jazz perspectives, particularly when he chooses to use the odd riff cliché in his ensemble frames. His own solos are the real thing, however, ploughing timeless blues furrows and never with more sincerity than in the ribs 'n' greens grind of *Blue Tiny*. His jazzier and perhaps more extrovert side is better illustrated by the romping *Air Mail Special*, where he builds his lines with care born of wide, musical experience but still swings prodigiously. The flamboyant Bryant matches Grimes blow for blow but all six men do enough to convince even the superficial listener that what sounds 'ordinary' is actually musicians doing what they know best and doing it very well. **BMcR**

# Don Grolnick
1947-96

**Nighttown** Grolnick (p); **Randy Brecker** (t); **Joe Lovano** (ts); **Marty Ehrlich** (bcl); **Steve Turré** (tb); **Dave Holland** (b); **Bill Stewart** (d). Blue Note Ⓕ CDP7 98689-2 (57 minutes). Recorded 1991.
⑧ ❽

Pianist-composer Don Grolnick, though perhaps best known for his provocative fusionistic writing and playing with the Brecker Brothers Band of the mid seventies, was also a no-nonsense modernist whose acoustic piano attack borrowed from the spartan solo style of Bill Evans as well as the thumping chordal accompaniments of McCoy Tyner. Here, in an astringent post-bop date, Grolnick penned a gallery of compelling soundscapes. There is *Heart of Darkness*, where Lovano's steely tenor walks the pianist's mean streets with a noirish swagger worthy of the hard-boiled Humphrey Bogart, and *Genie*, a magic carpet ride through swirling, mysterious atmospheres 'shot' in the aural equivalent of stutter-frame, cyber-space, quasi-slow-motion. There is also a standard, Cole Porter's *What is This Thing Called Love?*, veering between a Latinized matinée stroll across Roseland's dance floor and a desperate marathon chase down Broadway in the wee small hours of the morning. Throughout there are powerful ensemble and solo contributions by Randy Brecker, Steve Turré and Joe Lovano's haunting tenor. Grolnick's decision to add the reedy raspiness of Marty Ehrlich's bass clarinet was another master-stroke. **CB**

# Steve Grossman
1951

**Standards** Grossman (ts); **Fred Hanks** (p); **Walter Booker** (b); **Masahiro Yoshido** (d). DIW Ⓕ DIW908 (57 minutes). Recorded 1985.
⑦ ❽

Grossman's period in Miles Davis's band in 1970 is his most-quoted biographical fact. He also worked with Lonnie Liston Smith and Elvin Jones, but was certainly one of the first formerly orthodox saxophonists to be classified as a jazz/rock fusionist. The eighties saw him record many scratch sessions, with him playing powerfully but with too little preparation before reaching the studio. The fault applies rather less with **Standards** and little is also heard here of Grossman the fusionist. This is the Rollins-inspired hard-bop tenor saxophonist, demonstrating a considerable mastery of his horn and a sense of timing that pays scant attention to normal bar division. He does however show several faces. *When I Fall in Love* has him luxuriating back to the Ben Websterish world of the sixties; the theme is reshaped, paraphrased and adjusted rather than developed. *Autumn Leaves* and *Mr Sandman*, in contrast, are explored in an oblique manner with Grossman building away from the theme and using each motif as a stepping-stone to the next, rather than as an immediate route back to the harmonic base. The rhythm section is faithfully guided by Booker's bass and the light-fingered logic of Henke, but as a team it is functional rather than inspired, and seems to ignore Grossman's more extravagent excursions into the rhythmic void. **BMcR**

# George Gruntz
1932

**Blues 'n' Dues Et Cetera: The New York Sessions** George Gruntz (p, ldr); **Marvin Stamm, Bob Millikan, Randy Brecker, Michael Mossman, Jon Faddis, John D'earth, Wallace Roney, Ray Anderson, Art Baron, Dave Taylor, Dave Bargeron** (t); **John Clark, Jerry Peel** (flh);

Dave Bargeron, Jim Pugh (euph); Howard Johnson (tba); Chris Hunter, Bob Mintzer, Bob
Malach, Jerry Bergonzi, David Mann, Alex Foster, Roger Rosenberg (reeds); John Scofield (g);
Mike Richmond (b); Adam Nussbaum (d). Enja Ⓕ 6072-2 (67 minutes). Recorded 1991.

⑧ ⑩

Formed in 1972 with Gruntz as music director and chief writer/arranger, the George Gruntz Concert
Jazz Band is an exuberant players' ensemble in which an annually shifting international cast of
hand-picked improvisers are given plenty of elbow-room for gritty, no-nonsense treks on the wild
side. It is also a highly disciplined unit combining the best attributes of both Basie and Ellington
along with the modernistic palette of Gil Evans. Indeed, Gruntz's ability to incorporate even rap –
as he does in *Rap for Nap* with trombonist/jazz-rapper Ray Anderson – is reminiscent of Evans's
capacity to creatively amalgamate the big-band heritage and the latest of pop music trends with
equal amounts of irony and appreciation. Like Evans, Gruntz uses post-bop electric guitar to
advantage on tracks like the mysterioso *Forest Cathedral*, featuring the wailing John Scofield.
Gruntz's organization is also open to newcomers like trumpeter Wallace Roney, who is given prime
time on *Datune*.

Throughout, the GGCB's experimentalism is balanced with its appreciation of tradition and its
sense of *joie de vivre*. Indeed, the GGCB's capacity to surprise and tickle as well as to swing like mad
is frequently astonishing. MPS have recently reissued a compilation of some of the band's best
recorded efforts between 1975 and 1981: this is well worth seeking out in its own right and also for
the perspective it casts on Gruntz's current work.                                                    **CB**

# Dave Grusin                                                                                    1934

**The Gershwin Connection**  Dave Grusin (kbds, ldr); Sal Marquez (t); Eddie Daniels (cl); Eric
Marienthal (as); Gary Burton (vb); George Gershwin, Chick Corea, Don Grusin (kbds); Lee
Ritenour (g); John Patitucci (b); Dave Weckl, Sonny Emory (d); David Nadien (concertmaster);
Ettore Strata (cond). GRP Ⓕ GRD2005 (60 minutes). Recorded 1991.

⑦ ⑧

Pianist/composer Grusin is one of the key figures of the eighties West Coast fusion movement. He is
a top TV and film composer with an Academy Award for Robert Redford's *The Milagro Beanfield
War* (1988). He is also a successful producer whose GRP label, co-founded with partner Larry Rosen,
was one of the record industry's great eighties success stories, although both men have subsequently
departed the label.

Here, Grusin's affection for what Alec Wilder calls "The American Popular Song" is refracted
through often poignant settings for Gershwin classics like *'S Wonderful* and *Our Love Is Here to
Stay*. The stylistic range runs from a hauntingly modal *My Man's Gone Now*, with a quintet
featuring Grusin's Tyneresque flurries, Marquez's crackling trumpet and Marienthal's plaintive
alto, to a more fusionistic launch for *There's a Boat Dat's Leavin' Soon for New York*. Also
appealing are buoyant readings of *Soon* with Daniels's eloquent clarinet, and *Fascinating Rhythm*
with Burton's quicksilver vibes.

The tracks, like the bulk of GRP's commercially successful, studio-massaged jazz, are highly
choreographed. Yet Grusin's arrangements are attractive, and there is much spontaneity. For contrast,
there are two solo piano tracks, one by Gershwin, a poignantly articulated *That Certain Feeling* via
piano roll; and, *Nice Work If You Can Get It* in which Grusin's acoustic ruminations bespeak a man
who like Gershwin has had the good fortune to achieve his own fair piece of 'nice work'.            **CB**

# Gigi Gryce                                                                                   1927-83

New review
**The Hap'nin's**  Gryce (as); Richard Williams (t); Richard Wyands (p); Julian Euell (b); Mickey
Roker (d). Prestige New Jazz Ⓜ OJCCD1868-2 (40 minutes). Recorded 1960.

⑧ ⑧

Jazz effectively borrowed Gigi Gryce from classical music for a period of ten years. He had studied
with some of the greatest teachers in the world and composed three symphonies and a variety of
chamber music. He became associated with Clifford Brown and some of the younger jazz musicians
in 1953 and went on to write most effective jazz arrangements for some of the greats, notably Dizzy
Gillespie, who recorded Gryce's beautiful *Reminiscing* on one of his finest albums. Gryce gave up
jazz and returned to classical music as composer and teacher in the year that this album was
recorded. It is a fine farewell, showing him as a torrid Parker-inspired soloist, well partnered here
by the remarkable Richard Williams, a man with a trumpet tone like the side of a house. Gryce was,
not unnaturally, compared unfavourably with Parker as an altoist, but he was a technically gifted,
attacking player with his own kind of persuasiveness. His soloing was less abstruse than his writing:
over a springy rhythm section his playing is to the mainstream side of modernity. The
underestimated Wyands plays several good solos.

It's fitting that Gryce should bid good-bye with such a robust session: his loss to jazz was to be
lamented, but his early death was a blow to music in general.                                    **SV** | 243

# Vince Guaraldi

1928-76

**Jazz Impressions of Black Orpheus** Guaraldi (p); Monty Budwig (b); Colin Bailey (d).
Fantasy ⓜ OJCCD437-2 (39 minutes). Recorded 1961.

⑦ ❺

Guaraldi was never really given an even break by the critics of the time. While he himself would never have claimed to be a moving spirit of the music, or someone with a truly original, creative voice, he brought great taste and discernment to whatever he did, and the arrangements on this album of the music from the 1959 film, *Black Orpheus*, combine the lithe elegance of Brazilian music with the drive and dynamism of piano trio jazz. His style was rooted deep in the West Coast of the fifties (he didn't spend three years with Cal Tjader for nothing), but his instinct for melody set him apart and eventually led to him having a major hit single, which is included on this album. An example of his genuine empathy with Brazilian music, and his equally real sensitivity as a pianist, is his reading here of Jobim and Bonfa's beautiful *Manha de Carnaval*, recorded before the deluge of cover versions let loose by the Getz/Byrd labum of the following year. The second side of the original LP (the last four tracks here), by the way, has nothing to do with the film or Brazil. **KS**

# Lars Gullin

1928-76

**Volume 1: With Chet Baker** Gullin (bs); Baker (t); Arne Domnerus (as, cl); Rolf Billberg, Bjarne Nerem (ts); Dick Twardzik, Gunnar Svensson, Rune Ofverman (p); George Reidel, Jimmy Bond (b); Egil Johansen, Peter Littman, Nils-Bertil Dahlander (d); Caterina Valente (v) and others.
Dragon ⓕ DRCD224 (74 minutes). Recorded 1955-6.

⑧ ❽

One of the most original of the European giants, Gullin was one of the most eloquent of all the baritone players. Unusually his playing was not obviously influenced by Harry Carney or Gerry Mulligan, and unlike them he didn't emphasize the barrel-chested quality of the instrument, preferring to play it with smooth flexibility as though it were a tenor. All of his work was of a high standard which has not dated and his playing seemed unimpaired by the narcotics which bedevilled so much of the rest of his life. This album serves as a fine collection of his inventive sounds, both as soloist and composer, and is also to be relished for the way in which it illustrates him at home in his natural habitat, playing with other world-class Swedes like Rolf Billberg and Arne Domnerus. Chet Baker and Dick Twardzik, on the European visit which was to take Tzwardik's life six days after his work here, slipped easily into Gullin's company, and both are at their most confidently creative on the underrated Bob Zieffs *Brash*. They shine again on *I'll Remember April*, which contains the only flaw in the album, a listless scat vocal by the usually excellent Caterina Valente. The reviewer has for some years pursued every available recording of Gullin's and has yet to be disappointed. Dragon are providing a welcome service in keeping so much of his work in their catalogue. **SV**

# Russell Gunn

1971

**New review**
**Young Gunn** Gunn (t); Sam Newsome (ts); John Hicks (p); Peter Washington (b); Cecil Brooks III (d). Muse ⓕ MCD5539 (58 minutes). Recorded 1995.

⑧ ❾

The nineties seem to be the decade of hot new trumpet players in the same way that the eighties were the decade of bright young saxophonists. Russell Gunn is the newest name to appear – and would have been an obvious recruit for the Jazz Messengers, had Art Blakey still been with us. Aged 24, he was born in St Louis and attended Miles Davis's old school, although his childhood ambition was to become a rap artist. However, the school band was trained by Ron Carter, who got hold of him at an impressionable age and spotted his talent. He plays with astonishing maturity, not just the fast-flying stuff but feathery ballads and mellow blues, too. This splendid début also alerts us to another talent to watch, in the shape of saxophonist Sam Newsome. **DG**

# Trilok Gurtu

1951

**Living Magic** Gurtu (d, perc, v); Jan Garbarek (ss, ts); Daniel Goyone (kbds); Nicolas Fiszman (b, g); Tunda Jegede (kora, v); Shanthi Rao (veena); Nana Vasconcelos (perc). CMP ⓕ CD50 (43 minutes). Recorded 1990-1.

⑧ ❿

Gurtu came to prominence in the late seventies and early eighties in a succession of striking partnerships with jazz musicians, including Charlie Mariano, Barre Phillips, Nana Vasconcelos and Jan Garbarek. The latter two appear to good effect on this record.

Gurtu, born in Bombay and with a formidable course of instruction in classical Indian music behind him, has come to jazz through hearing records, and his own albums tend to veer one way or the other, with a solidly jazz-based content or music predominantly displaying Indian music characteristics. This is an album closer to jazz than to Eastern music, and a heady mix it turns out to be. Gurtu's complete mastery of even the most remote time signature gives this music considerable rhythmic depth and complexity, suggests a logical musical role or area for each instrument to play within, and gives the soloist a remarkably rich tapestry of sound to glide over or dig into, as the whim (or the arrangement) takes them. Of the improvisors, only Garbarek need detain us for long, but when he takes centre stage, the album locks into top gear and really earns its grading. Gurtu's albums which followed this one, including his current release, **The Glimpse** (CMP), have moved progressively away from jazz and towards the embrace of world music. **KS**

# Charlie Haden 1937

New review

**Liberation Music Orchestra** Haden (b); **Mike Mantler** (t); **Don Cherry** (c, f); **Roswell Rudd** (tb); **Bob Northern** (frh, bells); **Howard Johnson** (tba); **Gato Barbieri** (ts, cl); **Dewey Redman** (ts, as); **Perry Robinson** (cl); **Sam Brown** (g, thumb p); **Carla Bley** (p); **Paul Motian**, **Andrew Cyrille** (d, perc). Impulse! Ⓜ IMP11882 (52 minutes). Recorded 1969.

Ⓥ ⑩ ❽

This beautiful album of contrasting moods, fine solo comment and distinguished writing belongs in all collections. Haden's sterling work with Ornette Coleman had established him as the doyen of free bassists but this 1969 recording was his first as a leader. It was inspired by the music of the Spanish Civil War and it reflects Haden's serious political commitment. The unifying aspect is the Spanish tinge, overtly apparent on *El Quinto* but unmistakably omnipresent. *Ché* and *Circus* were arranged by Haden, the remainder by Bley, but all are attended by an Ellington/Strayhorn-type cohesion. At times, such as the *Drinking Music* interlude and during the flamenco guitar passage on *El Quinto*, the mind is drawn to Mingus's **Black Saint** but this remains a work of artistic caprice and all of its motivations are Haden's. Even his bass solos evoke images of the camp fire and his masterful outing on *Ché* matches the horn solos for melodic ingenuity and power. As a comparison, Rudd makes a virtue of simplicity with a jazz-drenched theme statement on *We Shall Overcome*. *Circus* has Shepp-type densities and, although Cherry's bamboo flute meanders ineffectually on *Ché*, he more than compensates with superb cornet on *El Quinto*. **BMcR**

**"Closeness" Duets** Haden (b); **Ornette Coleman** (as); **Keith Jarrett** (p); **Alice Coltrane** (hp); **Paul Motian** (d). A&M Ⓜ CDA0808 (39 minutes). Recorded 1976.

⑧ ❼

This early date as a leader is both absorbing and instructive, because it becomes in one sense a guided musical tour of Haden's past, and in another sense a virtuosic display of the type Haden has no desire to include in one of his large-group recordings, where other concerns are paramount.

Thus you get a lot more of Haden the instinctual player here, trading felicities with his four partners, conjuring extraordinarily full musical landscapes behind their statements of his themes (this is especially true of the duet with Alice Coltrane, *For Turiya*), and indulging in energetic dialogue within the improvised sections. The most immediate quality to be appreciated on a Haden album is the depth and beauty of his rich, dark tone. It is instantly identifiable and inimitable. The second unique quality he possesses is an enormous authority in his playing. He rarely opts for complicated, helter-skelter lines in his own work, preferring the simplicity of the perfect choice of note. His authority resides in the fact that invariably he does make the perfect choice.

Each duet is utterly different in tone and content, and this is what Haden wished: each reflects the past work carried out with these artists, and in the case of the duet with Ornette, Haden's theme consciously imitates those wild, exciting Coleman tunes of the L.A. years. A disc for those with wonder in their souls. **KS**

**The Ballad of the Fallen** Haden (b, ldr); **Don Cherry** (pkt t); **Michael Mantler** (t); **Gary Valente** (tb); **Sharon Freeman** (frh); **Jack Jeffers** (tba); **Steve Slagle** (f, cl, ss, as); **Jim Pepper** (f, ss, ts); **Dewey Redman** (ts); **Carla Bley** (p, glockenspiel, arr); **Mick Goodrick** (g); **Paul Motian** (d, perc). ECM ⑫ 811 546-2 (52 minutes). Recorded 1982.

⑧ ❾

If Spanish Civil War songs inspired Charlie Haden to record his first Liberation Music Orchestra album, it was the more immediate fact of US involvement in El Salvador that spurred him to re-form the orchestra a dozen years later and make a second album. **The Ballad of the Fallen** takes its title from a poem found on the body of a Salvadorean student murdered by the US-backed National Guard. When set to music it became a popular folk song; it is played here as an instrumental. The disc also includes resistance songs from Chile and Portugal, several more Spanish Republican tunes and three new pieces – Haden's *Silence* and *La Pasionaria* and Carla Bley's ominously titled *Too Late*.

Bley plays as central a role here as she did on the first album. Her arrangements fashion a cohesive style for music that ranges from the desolation of *Too Late* (her duet with Haden) to the brass-led defiance of *The People United Will Never Be Defeated*. It is a better-recorded set than Liberation Music Orchestra; the arrangements are smoother, the solos more focused. But its moods are sombre, lacking the raucous sixties optimism that gave the first album its extraordinary lift. Haden's bass remains a small flame of hope – tender, reflective, always melodic. **GL** 245

New review
**Quartet West: Now Is the Hour** Haden (b); **Ernie Watts** (ts); **Alan Broadbent** (p, arr); **Laurance Marable** (d). Verve Ⓕ 529 827-2 (60 minutes). Recorded 1995.

⑦ ❾

From his tumultuous forays with Ornette Coleman and Don Cherry to the thunderous Liberation Orchestra, Charlie Haden has always exerted a presence. Who, though, would have predicted that some of Haden's finest work would come from his residency in Los Angeles and its principal centre of pop culture, Hollywood? Over a span of ten years and five albums, Haden has successfully plumbed the expressive musical link between Hollywood and jazz in a unique style aptly dubbed 'jazz noir'. His vehicle is the extraordinary Quartet West featuring tenor saxophonist Ernie Watts, pianist Alan Broadbent and drummer Larance Marable. Here, Haden says that "I just wanted to do a really beautiful record." That beauty is most manifest in exquisite tracks with a French string ensemble playing charts arranged and conducted by Alan Broadbent, currently setting the standard for the genre. There are haunting originals such as Haden's *Here's Looking at You*, a tip-of-the-hat to Humphrey Bogart, and Broadbent's *When Tomorrow Comes*, a poignantly plush noirish soundscape. A brief reprise of Lennie Tristano's *Requiem* leads to a spirited quartet romp through Charlie Parker's *Back Home Blues*. Turning sentimental dross into gold, Haden's *pizzicato* limning of *Now Is the Hour* is a heart-breaker embellished by Broadbent's evocative strings and Watt's plaintive tenor. In all, another landmark from one of contemporary music's most innovative groups. **CB**

## Tim Hagans

New review
**Audible Architecture** Hagans (t); **Bob Belden** (ts); **Larry Grenadier** (b); **Billy Kilson** (d). Blue Note Ⓕ CDP8 31808-2 (67 minutes). Recorded 1994.

⑦ ❼

Whatever may be said about other cities, New York remains the magnet to attract most jazz aspirants, although Hagans's progress towards that goal was more tortuous than most. He had been on the road with Stan Kenton and Woody Herman, worked in Europe with Thad Jones and Ernie Wilkins and made his recording début as a leader in 1983. Yet on his return from Europe, he chose to continue the 'dues-paying' process in Cincinnati and then to teach at Berklee before making the big move in 1986. Since then, work with Joe Lovano, Bob Belden and Gary Peacock has introduced him to a wider audience and, as this CD shows, produced a fine trumpeter and composer. *Garage Bands* and *Family Flowers* are the best of his seven originals but his solo response to all of the material is that of a relaxed, lyrical and self confident horn man. On *You Don't Know What Love Is* these talents are matched by his creative flair; *I Hear a Rhapsody* and *Shorts*, in particular, demonstrate an articulation in which every note is cleanly hit, even in the fastest passages. All of his solos have a spring in their step and, with Grenadier and Kilson the propulsive support duo here, a piano is never missed. Hagans still works out of New York but his more recent involvement on the festival tour bodes well for the future. **BMcR**

## Bob Haggart
1914

**Lawson/Haggart Jazz Band – Singin' the Blues** Haggart (b); **Yank Lawson** (t); **George Masso** (tb); **Joe Muranyi** (cl, ss); **John Bunch** (p); **Bucky Puzzarelli** (g); **Jake Hanna** (d). Jazzology Ⓕ JCD193 (69 minutes). Recorded 1990.

⑥ ❽

Bass player, composer, arranger and frequent poll-winner, Haggart was a Bob Crosby Band original before moving to the world of radio and television. In 1968 he was, with Lawson, instrumental in the formation of the World's Greatest Jazz Band; a unit devoted to keeping the Crosby spirit alive. Despite the unfortunate name foisted upon it, the WGJB employed the likes of Billy Butterfield, Vic Dickenson, Bud Freeman, Bob Wilber and Ralph Sutton during its 13-year life. The band here is its logical successor and features several musicians with WGJB experience. The choice of material does appear a trifle hackneyed but, with Lawson adroitly ignoring the Bix Beiderbecke connection on the title track, all the soloists de-Wallering *Blue Turning Grey* and the smooth trombone of Masso irradicating the earthy, Kid Ory memory on *Muskrat Ramble* the Lawson/Haggarts put their own brand on everything. Haggart, with his supple rhythmic instructions, is at the heart of an ideal rhythm section and there are two guest appearances from the pleasing Barbara Lea. The "Legendary Lawson/Haggart Jazz Band" is certainly a better and more descriptive label than the World's Greatest Jazz Band. **BMcR**

## Jerry Hahn
1940

**Time Changes** Hahn (g); **David Liebman** (ss); **Phil Markowitz, Art Lande** (p); **Steve LaSpina** (b); **Jeff Hirschfield** (d). Enja Ⓕ ENJ9007-2 (51 minutes). Recorded 1993.

⑥ ❽

Hahn made a terrific impact in the mid sixties as a member of the John Handy group with Michael White on violin which became one of the decade's major jazz successes. He continued into the seventies with the Jerry Hahn Brotherhood but by mid-decade was back in his hometown of Wichita, Kansas, teaching at the University and writing about music. This is his first headlining album in over 20 years, and it finds his sound and conception largely intact, the continuity with his youth still discernible. He describes himself as "a jazz player who loves the blues", and a direct affinity with latter-day John Scofield is immediately apparent here, even though they may have arrived at similar conclusions from vastly different starting-points. There is plenty of space to compare, with the two pianists between them managing just five appearances over ten tracks (saxophonist Liebman is on just two). Frankly, Hahn is at his best just accompanied by bass and drums, where he has the most flexibility of support and can go whichever way he wants. His serpentine improvising lines and his elusive sound do not always sit with the immediate sonics and harmonic patterns of the piano, and on the bright-tempo *The Method*, pianist Markowitz quite simply cannot make the tempo. That problem aside, this is a useful return to the studio by Hahn, with the ballads perhaps impressing most. **KS**

# Al Haig

1924-82

**Ornithology** Haig (p): **Jamil Nasser** (b); **Frank Gant** (d). Progressive Ⓕ PCD 7024 (42 minutes). Recorded 1977.

⑥ ❻

Haig was one of the first (and best) of the young pianists who took to bebop in the mid forties. He worked and recorded with, among others, Charlie Parker, Stan Getz and Wardell Gray, turning in beautifully crafted solos in which compression was the name of the game. After a period of time away from the limelight he came back in the seventies as a fully mature concert performer, and it is a source of regret that many of his finest albums for the Interplay and Spotlite labels have either not been transferred to the CD format or, in the case of the Interplays, are available only in Japan. This is a CD version of an LP titled **Reminiscing**, boosted by the addition of *Body and Soul* which is actually a feature for Nasser. Despite this, there is enough of Haig's wonderfully apt interpretations of classic bebop tunes such as *Shaw 'Nuff*, *Marmaduke* and *Blue Bird* to make this a memorable album. The delicacy of his work on Ellington's *Daydream* reminds us of another dimension and the only question mark hangs over the prominence given to Nasser in the instrumental balance. Haig came up with bass players such as Tommy Potter and Curley Russell, whose throbbing lines kept a respectful distance from the piano in terms of audio perspective. Nasser is a fine technician (Haig rated him very highly), but on a programme made up principally of bebop tunes the strong bass presence is sometimes anachronistic. **AM**

# Nathan Haines

New review

**Shift Left** Haines (ts, as, kbds); **Kevin Field** (elp, seq); **Peter Woods** (vb); **Joel Haines** (g); **Richard Hammond** (b, elb); **Mickey Ututaonga** (d); **Miguel Figuentes**, **Tony Hopkins** (perc); **Manuel Bundy** (tt); **Sonny Sagala**, **Paul Fuemana** (v). Verve/Polydor Ⓕ 527150-2 (53 minutes). Recorded 1994.

⑤ ❽

Haines is a talented but not particularly distinctive saxophonist, the real interest in this record lying in his imaginative combining of the improvisatory jazz tradition (there are many overtones of early seventies fusion music on this disc) with current performance and recording techniques, including rhythm tracks, turntable twitches, spoken vocals in the rap style and various nods in the direction of world music at large. It often combines to sound like a backing track waiting for something to happen, but at least it has reached a stage where the background is capable of being in sympathy with a structured melody or solo when it comes along. A recent American release on the Verve label by The Grassy Knoll failed to break out of its rock and popular music forms and connect with the small amount of genuine improvisation which took place. This music is probably best not listened to too carefully, perhaps when dancing, though it may in parts be too subtle for the latter option. **KS**

# Halfway House Orchestra

New review

**The Complete Recordings 1925-8** Albert Brunies (t); **Leon Roppolo** (cl, as); **Sidney Arodin** (cl); **Charlie Cordella** (cl, ts); **Joe Loyacano** (tb, as); **Mickie Marcour**, **Red Long** (p); **Bill Eastwood**, **Angelo Palmisano** (bj); **Chink Martin** (b, bb); **Leo Adde**, **Emmett Rogers** (d). Jazz Oracle Ⓕ BDW8001 (67 minutes).

⑥ ❽

The Halfway House was a supper club situated approximately equidistant from New Orleans and Lake Ponchartrain. It was a single-storey building with a spacious dance floor surrounded by tables or diners. This tells us much about the music made by the band that played there; a band containing several jazz worthies but, of necessity, obliged to compromise their music for the sake of the patrons' dancing requirements. This CD contains all known recordings by the Halfway House Orchestra including some sides originally rejected and one title which first emerged as a single in Australia. The leader is Albert 'Abbie' Brunies, a fine lead trumpeter whose early work on this release has much of the earthy simplicity and attack of NORK legend Paul Mares. Later recordings suggest a move toward more Bixian lyricism but he always remained a man in charge of the ensemble. Pick of the reed men is Roppolo, whose neat breaks and gentle clarinet solo on *Barataria* give no hint of his impending committal to the Louisiana State Asylum. His 1925 replacement Cordella was a rhythmically predictable but tidy improviser who was more at home on obvious jazz material such as *Maple Leaf Rag*. Arodin, the clarinettist after 1927, was a more modern player but his presence alongside a more sophisticated rhythm section on the final eight titles must be balanced against the corny material used. The quality of the remastering of this obscure material is first class.　　**BMcR**

# Adelaide Hall　　1904-93

**Hall of Memories: Recordings 1927-39**　Hall (v); with a collective personnel of: **Bubber Miley, Louis Metcalf, Jabbo Smith, Pike Davis, Demas Dean, Charlie Teagarden, Manny Klein, Wardell Jones, Shelton Hemphill, Ed Anderson, Bill Coleman, Bobby Martin** (t); **Joe Nanton, Herb Flemming, George Washington, Henry Hicks, Billy Burns** (tb); **Henry Edwards** (tba); **Jimmy Dorsey** (cl); **Carmello Jejo, Albert Socarras, Gene Mikell** (cl, as); **Harry Carney** (cl, as, bs); **Rudy Jackson, Frank 'Big Boy' Goudie** (cl, ts); **Joe Garland** (cl, ts, bs); **Otto Hardwicke** (ss, as, bs); **Willie Lewis, George Johnson** (as); **Joe Hayman** (as, ts, bs); **Crawford Wethington** (as, bs); **Raymond Usera** (ts, vn); **Duke Ellington, George Rickson, Joe Turner, Francis Carter, Art Tatum, Edgar Hayes, Herman Chittison** (p); **Fats Waller, Fela Sowande** (org); **Larry Gomar** (vb); **Fred Guy, Benny James** (bj); **Dick McDonough, John Mitchell** (g); **Wellman Braud, Hayes Alvis, Louis Vola** (b); **Sonny Greer, Jesse Baltimore, O'Neill Spencer, Ted Fields** (d). Conifer Ⓜ CDHD169 (54 minutes). Recorded 1927-39.

⑥　❹

Adelaide Hall's career is a paradox. Many jazz musicians, singers and entertainers lost ground by coming to Europe in the twenties and thirties, whereas Adelaide (in common with very few others, Josephine Baker being one) used her European move to prolong and sustain a career that had already teamed her with some of the world's finest jazz musicians before she left the US. This disc is an excellent cross-section of her pre-war work, from her wordless vocals with Ellington's orchestra to her duos with Fats Waller at HMV's mighty Compton organ. Her delivery lacks the edge of Alberta Hunter, but she had the same vaudevillean ability to interpret a song. Her best work here is with the piano duet backing of Francis Carter and either Joe Turner or Art Tatum, where the uncluttered setting allows her lyrics to shine, but gives plenty of space for some first-rate piano stride. The transfers (by John R.T. Davies) make the most of the source material available, but not all the selection was as well recorded in the first place as the Victors of Ellington or Millinder, so the overall quality is a little uneven.　　**AS**

# Bob Hall　　1942

**Alone With the Blues**　Hall (p, v); **Tom McGuinness** (g, b); **Rob Townsend** (d); **Hilary Blythe, Linda Adams** (v). Lake Ⓕ CD44 (54 minutes). Recorded 1995.

⑥　❽

Hall has established himself as one of Britain's leading boogie woogie pianists, and his encyclopaedic knowledge of the genre, coupled with his technical facility, means that he combines authentic performances of less well-known works by the likes of Montana Taylor, Peter Johnson and Cripple Clarence Lofton with original compositions of his own. The core of this album is a set of unaccompanied piano solos, with Johnson's *Blues on the Downbeat* and Lofton's *Sixes and Sevens* standing out. Hall's blues singing is a shade lightweight, though pleasant enough, and the tracks of his own vocals and those with backing singers are peripheral to the main strengths of this disc. Solo, or backed up by McGuinness (whose steel guitar playing has a suitably plaintive ring) and Townsend, Hall has the right timing and feel in his playing to keep the spirit of boogie alive. His original compositions explore all the ingredients that make boogie a varied rather than a narrowly similar genre, from single-note bass patterns to walking basses and train-like chords, and suggest that Hall is a worthy companion to the boogie composers of yore.　　**AS**

# Edmond Hall　　1901-67

**New review**

**Edmond Hall 1937-44**　Hall (cl); **Billy Hicks** (t, v); **Sidney De Paris, Emmett Berry** (t); **Fernando Arbello, Vic Dickenson** (tb); **Cyril Haynes, James P. Johnson, Eddie Heywood, Teddy Wilson** (p); **Meade Lux Lewis** (cel); **Leroy Jones, Charlie Christian, Jimmy Shirley, Al Casey, Carl Kress** (g); **Al Hall, Israel Crosby, Billy Taylor, Johnny Williams** (b); **Arnold Boling, Big Sid Catlett** (d); **Red Novo** (vb); **Henry Nemo** (v). Classics Ⓜ 830 (75 minutes). Recorded 1937-44.

❽　❼

Ed Hall played Albert system clarinet but that was where his allegiance to the clarinettists of his hometown, New Orleans, ended. He played with Chris Kelley and Jack Carey while in his teens and later had spells with the legendary Buddy Petit and Eagle-Eye Shields. It was not until his move to New York in 1928 that his real personality began to emerge, however, and by then a good case could be made for seeing his stylistic inspiration as coming from Benny Goodman. This CD, mainly from the World War II years, would certainly support such a contention. It demonstrates similar approaches to Hall's solo construction, his use of Goodmanesque phrase shapes and his comparable instrumental facility. Like the Chicagoan, his blues playing occasionally sounded superficial; strong in line but gaining in emotional impact more from his acrid tone than from any deeper personal involvement. The rest of his band was stacked impressively, however, and here he conducts his *High Society* responsibilities with aplomb. *Royal Garden Blues* shows the quality of his attack while the effortless swing of *Jammin' in Four* is the work of a natural jazzman. The value-added extras on this album include excellent acoustic guitar from Christian, fine trumpet by De Paris and Berry, sparkling piano by Wilson and cultured vibes from Norvo. Hall is more than their equal throughout and, although his work in later years with the Louis Armstrong All Stars was distinguished, this CD examines his most impressive period. **BMcR**

## Jim Hall 1930

**New review**
**Concierto** Hall (g); **Paul Desmond** (as); **Chet Baker** (t); **Roland Hanna** (p); **Ron Carter** (b); **Steve Gadd** (d). CBS Associated Ⓜ ZK40807 (50 minutes). Recorded 1975.

⑧ ❽

Jim Hall is one of the gurus of modern jazz guitar. A talented veteran whose deep *résumé* includes landmark collaborations with the likes of tenor saxophonist Sonny Rollins, pianist Bill Evans and flügelhornist Art Farmer, Hall possesses a warm intimate sound, a uniquely understated and sophisticated harmonic palette and a gift for flowing lyric invention. Although the guitarist has evolved a denser style in more recent projects such as **All Across the City** (Concord CCD4384-2), here, we meet Hall, melodic minimalist *par excellence*.

In this now-classic 1975 date originally recorded for Creed Taylor's CTI label, we confront music whose tonal warmth and lyric grace embody what aestheticians once called "the beautiful". With like-minded souls such as Paul Desmond, Chet Baker and Roland Hanna, Hall flows with a kind of classicism that is downright Mozartian. For modern swing, there is the horn-less quartet reading of the Ellington-Strayhorn gem, *Rock Skippin'*, a previously unreleased track. *You'd Be So Nice to Come Home To* flows in similarly effortless fashion with Desmond and Baker in top form. The second movement of Joaquín Rodrigo's *Concierto de Aranjuez*, while borrowing from the Miles Davis-Gil Evans version, remains an atmospheric masterpiece and an exemplar of lyric restraint. Also included is an alternative take of Jane Hall's *The Answer is Yes*, a jaunty minor theme. **CB**

**New review**
**Live at Town Hall, Volume 1** Hall (g); **Bob Brookmeyer** (vtb); **Gerry Mulligan** (bs); **Gary Burton** (vb); **Don Thompson** (p, arr); **Steve La Spina**, **Ron Carter** (b); **Terry Clarke** (d). MusicMasters Ⓟ 5050-2 (67 minutes). Recorded 1989.

⑦ ❽

Hall is a player at the heart of jazz. Most of the things he does are skilled, in irreproachable taste and totally loyal to the historic roots of the music. While he is undoubtedly moved as a Charlie Parker disciple, you can also hear Teddy Bunn and Eddie Lang in his style. The first six tracks are felicitous duets between Hall and – two each – Carter, Brookmeyer and Mulligan. Carter opens the soloing on *Alone Together* and the intimate spotlight reveals just what a giant he is on his instrument. Hall follows him modestly but with his usual eloquence, then provides a setting for the languid musings of Bob Brookmeyer – renewing a musical partnership which goes back over 30 years. Hall had never played duets with Mulligan before, and he lays back to let Mulligan exert his authority on *All the Things You Are*. The baritone playing is vigorous, a fine counterpoint soon emerging between the two men.

The final three tracks occupy almost half the album and add a string quartet. They are badly compromised in jazz terms. Had the momentum of the first six tracks been maintained instead, then the album would have rated 9, but the descent into cold experiment is a new one for Hall, and the music lacks emotional content. There is a volume two, also on MusicMasters, for those who wish to hear the entire concert. **SV**

## Bengt Hallberg 1932

**Yellow Blues** Hallberg (p). Phontastic Ⓟ PHONCD7583 (60 minutes). Recorded 1987.

⑧ ❽

Sweden's Bengt Hallberg is one of the most gifted, technically accomplished and least prejudiced pianists jazz has produced. From his early recordings with American visitors such as Clifford Brown and Stan Getz, his work with fellow Swedes Lars Gullin and Arne Domnerus and his own solo and trio albums he has established a reputation as a musician of world class. **Yellow Blues** was recorded at the Royal Academy of Music in Stockholm (Hallberg is a member of the Academy) and 17 of the 18 tracks are adaptations of the music of the Värmeland province of Sweden (the other track is the title blues, written by Bengt). Värmeland is obviously rich in composers and native folk music; Hallberg's treatments of the pieces are so ingenious, so inventive and so beautifully played that this is a CD which deserves the largest of audiences. Bengt's use of *accelerando* and *rallentando*, his most expressive sense of touch and continuity of ideas sets him apart from many jazz pianists. He includes a version of *Ack Värmeland Du Skona* (better known in jazz circles as *Dear Old Stockholm*, the song he recorded with Stan Getz in 1951). Gert Palmcrantz's engineering has perfectly captured the full range of the piano. **AM**

## Lin Halliday                                                                1939

**East of the Sun** Halliday (ts); Ira Sullivan (t, flh, ts, f); Jodie Christian (p); Dennis Carroll (b); George Fludas (d). Delmark Ⓕ DE45864 (64 minutes). Recorded 1992.

⑤ ❼

Halliday, originally from Arkansas, has been playing professionally for more than three decades, and his career has seen him settled in places as far apart in America as Hollywood, Wisconsin, Nashville and New York (where in the early sixties he was a member of the Maynard Ferguson band). His style relies heavily on Rollins and Mobley for the way in which he approaches thematic development or negotiates chord changes, his sound also nestling closely between these two players. So much so that, for all Halliday's skill and commitment, the flood of echoes from other people's solos gets in the way of a proper perception of his talents. Nevertheless, he is a fluent and knowledgeable saxophonist who is expertly supported by a rhythm section in which pianist Jodie Christian is a standout. Multi-instrumentalist Ira Sullivan spreads himself rather thinly on this date, and has been heard to better advantage elsewhere. **KS**

## Chico Hamilton                                                             1921

**Gongs East!** Hamilton (d); Eric Dolphy (as, f, cl, bcl); Dennis Budimir (g); Nathan Gershman (vc); Wyatt Ruther (b). Discovery Ⓜ DSCD831 (38 minutes). Recorded 1958.

⑧ ❽

The Chico Hamilton Quintet was one of the most popular modern jazz units of the fifties; in addition to appearing in the noted jazz documentary *Jazz on a Summer's Day* (1958), it was also featured, dramatically as well as musically, in Alexander Mackendrick's stunning *film-noir* study of Big Apple corruption, *The Sweet Smell of Success* (1957). Hamilton, reflecting experiences with such lyrical artists as Lester Young, Lena Horne and Gerry Mulligan, built his highly appealing fifties quintets around a chamber-music-like approach, with its inclusion of such then-unusual instruments as cello, flute and bass clarinet. Hamilton also introduced such emerging talents as Paul Horn, Eric Dolphy, Ron Carter and, at a later stage, Charles Lloyd, Gabor Szabo and Larry Coryell.

Here, in an ebullient yet carefully modulated session from 1958, Hamilton's group weaves its way through highly choreographed charts that include plenty of elbow-room for Dolphy, the date's principal soloist. Although Dolphy was soon to become an important figure of the nascent avant-garde, here we meet a disciplined player who, while taking chances, meshes perfectly with the Third Stream tendencies of compositions such as Nat Pierce's *Far East* in which Dolphy's flute melds with Nathan Gershman's cello before romping over the changes. Fred Katz's *Nature by Emerson* is a reflective ballad in which Dolphy's surprisingly glossy alto evokes the legacy of Johnny Hodges. Hamilton, while finessing the subtle rhythmic textures, adds nuance and colour through his expert brush and stick work. **CB**

**Man from Two Worlds** Hamilton (d); Charles Lloyd (f, ts); George Bohanon (tb, four tracks); Gabor Szabo (g); Albert Stinson (b). Impulse! Ⓜ GRP11272 (68 minutes). Recorded 1962/3.

⑥ ❼

There lurk behind this title not one but two separate albums, recorded more than a year apart. The earlier (and better) disc was called **Passin' Thru**, and represented one of Lloyd's earliest exposures on record. Since being part of the original Gerry Mulligan Quartet, Hamilton had specialized in bringing to the fore a formidable number of gifted young players – Buddy Collette, Paul Horn, Eric Dolphy, Ron Carter, Charles Lloyd and Gabor Szabo up to this point, with Larry Coryell to follow in short order. In that sense, Lloyd in this band was part of an ongoing process. As the group's musical director, he had a great opportunity to formulate his ideas, and this on-the-job experience was soon to pay enormous dividends when he formed his own quartet featuring young Keith Jarrett and Jack DeJohnette. *Forest Flower*, the composition which did it for Lloyd at Monterey in 1965 (q.v. Lloyd), is here in a stiff and rather unconvincing version, hampered by the inflexible sonics of Szabo's wooden-sounding guitar. In fact Szabo, soon to go on to considerable commercial success, is the weak link in general on the 1963 cuts, his intonation often suspect and his role ill-defined.

The earlier **Passin' Thru** avoids these problems through Hamilton's more assertive playing and the presence of trombonist George Bohanon, who can carry the ensemble lines with Lloyd and give Szabo a more chordal and rhythmic role. Szabo also solos more conventionally, avoiding the self-conscious gipsy imitations which were soon to overcome him. Lloyd plays with terrific drive, his every solo full of earthiness and the excitement of discovery. This is Hamilton's chamber jazz concept working at its best, and it is still worth hearing today.                                                                                   **KS**

## Ed Hamilton

New review
**Planet Jazz** Hamilton (g, b, org, kbds, p); **George Howard** (ss); **Dave Falciani** (p); **Stanley Clarke**, **Charles Famborough**, **Vince Fay** (b); **Pat Petrillo**, **Lenny White** (d); **José Rossy**, **Todd Schietroma** (perc); **Loretta Boyer** (v). Telarc Jazz Zone Ⓕ 83387 (60 minutes). Recorded 1995.

⑦ ❾

Multi-instrumentalist Hamilton is first and foremost a guitarist and his thinking is in line with classical players like John Williams, who have attempted to cross-fertilize the pure tone of an acoustic instrument with some of the possibilities offered by a fusion background. In his own solos Hamilton (who grew up in Philadelphia and went on to the Manhattan School of Music) is clearly an exceptional jazz guitarist and here and there he takes off on a passage of unashamed swing. But he is concerned in his writing and arranging to explore a different context; for the most part he succeeds, avoiding the musical wallpaper of a lot of synthesizer-dominated sessions and achieving a coherent and individual identity across the dozen tracks of the album. None of this is great music, but it is a well-executed exploration of the territory that preoccupies Hamilton, whose own multi-instrumental talents are well up to the job.                                                                                   **AS**

## Scott Hamilton                                                                                   1954

New review
**East of the Sun** Hamilton (ts); **Brian Lemon** (p); **Dave Green** (b); **Allan Ganley** (d). Concord Ⓕ CCD4583 (63 minutes). Recorded 1993.

❾ ❾

Scott Hamilton is a swing tenor player who happens to have been born long after the swing era was officially declared dead and buried. His very existence challenges all kinds of hallowed assumptions about jazz and progress. His steady growth as an artist refutes charges of pastiche, and his evident success and popularity act as a constant irritant to fashionable advanced opinion. He has made around 30 albums under his own name, not to mention many with other artists, such as Rosemary Clooney and Ruby Braff. This CD finds him in the company of his 'British band', the trio which accompanies him on his twice-yearly UK tours. He says that he has sometimes played with equally good rhythm sections, but never a better one. The programme for this disc was mostly chosen by a poll among the readers of Japan's *Swing Journal* and represents a typical Hamilton set – ten standards and an original blues. Warm, fluent, smilingly magisterial, he surpasses himself here – and the rhythm team live up to everything he says about them.                                                                                   **DG**

## Gunter Hampel                                                                                   1937

**The 8th of July 1969** Hampel (p, vb, bcl); **Anthony Braxton** (as, cbcl, snino s); **Willem Breuker** (as, ts, bcl, ss); **Arjen Gorter** (b); **Steve McCall** (d); **Jeanne Lee** (v). Birth Ⓕ 001 (68 minutes). Recorded 1969.

⑧ ❽

American and European free-jazz scenes have gone separate ways in recent decades (although one should not oversimplify; cross-pollination quietly continues), but there was a short period, beginning in 1969 with a wave of Chicago avant-gardists taking up residence on the continent, when the intermingling of style and players was common. This historic meeting of Chicagoans Braxton and McCall, New Yorker Lee, Holland's Breuker and Gorter (still working together in Breuker's Kollektief) and German multi-instrumentalist Hampel, shows how total that blending could be.

Some of this music is rumbunctious and dissonant in the prevailing free-jazz manner, but not all of it. Atmospheric improvising was already common among the Chicagoans, who often set the tone. But it is Lee's cool, almost uninflected singing, with or without words, which really gives this date its distinctive flavour. The free scene produced few singers and fewer good ones; Lee is the best of the lot. There were not many free vibraphonists either – the instrument is not particularly assertive – but Hampel was always one of the best and most outgoing (his dippy, syncopated piano figure underpinning on *We Move* is less satisfying). This CD reissue adds alternative takes to four out of five tunes.   **KW**

## Lionel Hampton                                                                                   1909

**1937-8, 1938-9, 1939-40** Hampton (vb, p, d, v); **Ziggy Elman, Cootie Williams, Jonah Jones, Harry James, Walter Fuller, Irving Randolf, Dizzy Gillespie, Henry 'Red' Allen** (t); **Benny Carter**

(t, as, cl); **Rex Stewart** (c); **Lawrence Brown, J.C. Higginbotham** (tb); **Mezz Mezzrow, Eddie Barefield, Edmon Hall** (cl); **Omer Simeon** (cl, as); **Johnny Hodges, Russell Procope, Earl Bostic, Toots Mondello** (as); **Vido Musso, Herschel Evans, Budd Johnsonn, Chu Berry, Coleman Hawkins, Ben Webster** (ts); **Edgar Sampson, Harry Carney** (bs); **Jess Stacy, Clyde Hart, Billy Kyle, Spencer Odum, Joe Sullivan** (p); **Allan Reuss, Danny Barker, Charlie Christian, Wesley Prince, Al Casey, Freddie Green, Oscar Moore** (g); **Harry Goodman, John Kirby, Billy Taylor, Milt Hinton, Artie Bernstein** (b); **Gene Krupa, Cozy Cole, Sonny Greer, Jo Jones, Alvin Burroughs, Big Sid Catlett, Zutty Singleton, Nick Fatool** (d). Classics Ⓜ 524, 534, 562 (three discs, oas: 72, 70 and 70 minutes). Recorded 1937-40.

✅       ⑩ ❼

What makes the Hampton Victors such a special studio series is the large number of musicians involved. It anticipates the Jazz-at-the-Philharmonic mix-and-match policy while showcasing one of the most remarkable of all jazz musicians. Hampton is heard on these three CDs as the master vibraphone player, superbly relaxed on *Singin' the Blues,* fiercely attacking on *Hot Mallets,* lyrically poetic on *I Surrender Dear* and endlessly inventive in almost every solo he takes. His honestly forthright drumming is heard to good advantage on *Drum Stomp* and *Big Wig in the Wigwam,* while his excellent but underrated singing is never better displayed than on *Object of My Affections* and *After You've Gone.* His somewhat boring piano playing blights *Rock Hill Special* and *Central Avenue Breakdown,* but compensation for these is found in his special contrapuntal moments. His vibes work with Berry on *Sweethearts on Parade,* his response to Catlett's rhythmic thrust on *Haven't Named It Yet* or his rhythmic freedom over the Carter-arranged reeds on *I'm in the Mood for Swing* speak for themselves. In addition, the trumpets boast the sometimes brash Elman, the powerful Jones, the smouldering Williams, the bubbling Gillespie and the irascible Stewart. Carter stars on trumpet, clarinet and alto and there are also outstanding reed contributions from Hodges, Berry, Hawkins, Bailey and the unsung Mondello. **BMcR**

---

**Flying Home**  Hampton (vb, p, v); **Ernie Royal, Karl George, Joe Newman, Cat Anderson, Roy McCoy, Joe Morris, Lamar Wright Jr, Snooky Young, Wendell Culley, Dave Page, Al Killian, Jimmy Nottingham** (t); **Fred Beckett, Sonny Craven, Harry Sloan, Al Hayes, Booty Wood, Vernon Porter, Andrew Penn, Allen Durham, Abdul Hamid, John Morris, Jimmy Wormick** (tb); **Marshall Royal** (cl, as); **Ray Perry** (as, vn); **Earl Bostic, Gus Evans, George Dorsey, Herbie Fields, Bobby Plater, Ben Kynard** (as); **Illinois Jacquet, Dexter Gordon, Al Sears, Arnett Cobb, Fred Simon, Jay Peters, Johnny Griffin** (ts); **Jack McVea, Charlie Fowlkes** (bs); **Milt Buckner, John Mehegan, Dardanelle Breckenridge** (p); **Irving Ashby, Eric Miller, Billy Mackel** (g); **Vernon Alley, Vernon King, Charles Harris, Ted Sinclair** (b); **George Jenkins, Fred Radcliffe, George Jones** (d); **Dinah Washington** (v). MCA/Decca Jazz Ⓜ MCAD42349 (50 minutes). Recorded 1942-5.

✅       ⑧ ❽

Hampton left Benny Goodman to form his own band in 1940, but remained under contract to RCA through the following year. This anthology captures the beginning of his successful period with Decca, and producer Orrin Keepnews does an admirable job of salvaging Hampton's more substantial performances from the period without totally neglecting the boisterous side of his music that made him such a commercial success (and such an important figure in the jazz-to-r&b transition of black popular music). A glance at the personnel reveals that the Hampton band was a breeding ground for both young modernists and the mainstream yeomen who would keep bands like Ellington's and Basie's going for the next few decades. Among the essential titles included here are *Flying Home* with the classic Illinois Jacquet solo and *Flying Home No. 2* with Arnett Cobb, flag-wavers – Hamp's *Boogie Woogie* (featuring the leader's two-finger piano) and *Hey! Ba Ba Re Bop* – plus Dinah Washington's salty *Blow Top Blues* with a septet taken from the band. Pianist Milt Buckner, who contributed several arrangements, is the unsung hero of this affirmative and very swinging collection. For a more comprehensive (though inevitably less thorough) look at the Hampton Decca years you could do a lot worse than purchase **Hamp** (GRP), a two-CD box which covers the years 1942-63, but which cannot be described as an essential purchase. **BB**

---

**The Paris Session 1953**  Hampton (vb); **Walter Williams** (t); **Al Hayse, Jimmy Cleveland** (tb); **Mezz Mezzrow** (cl); **Clifford Scott, Alix Combelle** (ts); **Claude Bolling** (p); **Billy Mackell** (g); **William Montgomery** (b); **Curley Hamner** (d). Vogue Ⓜ VG655609 (55 minutes). Recorded 1953.

     ⑧ ❻

The band that Hampton brought to Europe in 1953 was full of young men who were destined for greatness; players such as Clifford Brown, Art Farmer, Quincy Jones, Gigi Gryce and Alan Dawson. Hampton decreed that there should be no unauthorized recording dates during the tour; fortunately this stipulation was ignored and even while this 'authorized' jam session was taking place in one Paris studio, a big band using much of the rest of the Hampton orchestra was at work in another. But this was no mere jam session, it was a high-powered social occasion and, surprisingly, the music matched the event. Hampton was given complete freedom in terms of material and lengths of tunes (*Free Press Oui* which uses the chords of *I Found a New Baby,* runs for nearly 13 minutes). He also insisted on bringing in Mezzrow while the two French musicians, Combelle and Bolling, emerged as stars in their own right. The five full-group performances have solos of a generally acceptable standard from everyone, even if things get a little out of hand at times. But the three tracks by just Hampton, Billy Mackell and William Montgomery achieve classic status. **AM**

**Reunion at Newport, 1967** Hampton (vb, p, d, v); with a collective personnel of: **Snooky Young, Jimmy Nottingham, Joe Newman, Wallace Davenport** (t); **Al Grey, Garnett Brown, Britt Woodman, Dave Gonzalez, Walter Morris** (tb); **Benny Powell** (btb); **Ed Pazant, George Dorsey, Frank Foster, Dave Young, Jerome Richardson** (saxes); **John Spruill, Tete Montoliu, Oscar Dennard, Milt Buckner** (p); **Billy Mackel** (g); **George Duvivier, Peter Badie** (b); **Steve Little** (d); **Eddie Chamblee** (d); **Illinois Jacquet, Eddie Chamblee** (ts); **Eddie Chamblee** (d); **Scoville Brown** (cl); **Bobby Plater** (as); **Curtis Lowe** (bs); **Maria Angelica** (castanets). RCA Bluebird Ⓜ 66157-2 (71 minutes). Recorded 1956/67.

⑥ ❹

The Newport set was originally released under the title **Newport Uproar!**, which still seems entirely appropriate when re-appraising this CD. For 50 years Hampton has been leading a take-no-prisoners big band with feet firmly in both the chutzpah and jazz camps. Some bands have been better than others, depending mostly on who the soloists and section leaders were at any given time. This band was a special one, pulled together as a one-off for the Newport Festival and containing many old Hampton hands. The excitement is palpable and the recording balance certainly lets you know there was an excited crowd present. The set is nicely varied, with *Thai Silk* being a romantic setting for Hampton and *Meet Benny Bailey* bringing out the best in Joe Newman. By the time the inevitable *Flying Home* is reached, everybody is suitably tired and emotional, and Illinois Jacquet boots them all home in vintage style. The encore, a reprise of *Greasy Greens*, adds little to the first version. The sound, always poor on vinyl, is still very thin.

The last five tracks bring onto CD a most peculiar disc, probably the weirdest thing Hamp has ever made. The album was cut in Madrid while the band was on the Spanish leg of a seven-month tour of Europe and the Near East (they had played to 19,000 in a Barcelonan bull ring the week before). Hamp had spent a reputed 48 hours in a Flamenco nightspot and had come across Maria Angelica there. As Hamp said, "I dug her the most. I said to myself, 'Man, you got to get this together with the band.' So we did." Well, not quite: the recording quality is primitive in the extreme, Maria's castanets dominate the whole date, and Flamenco Swing was still a fledgling art when this date happened. The presence of Tete Montoliu on two tracks aids things considerably, but, as David Drew Zingg wrote in the original booklet-notes, "This is a crazy, mixed-up album." Amen. Hamp must have *really* dug that castanet player.                                                                                 **KS**

New review
**Mostly Ballads** Hampton (vb); **Lew Soloff** (t); **John Collani, Harold Danko** (p); **Bill Moring, Milt Hinton, Peter Washington** (b); **James D. Ford, James Madison** (d); **Richard Haynes, Philip Markowitz** (syn). MusicMasters Ⓔ 5044-2 (69 minutes). Recorded 1989.

⑦ ❾

Hampton is the soloist most of the way in these 12 numbers, recorded over three sessions with differing personnel. At 76 he had abandoned the wilder excesses of showmanship, such as jumping on drum kits, but the musical faculties were still on fine form. The original album was conceived as a companion piece to an earlier one entitled **Mostly Blues**. The atmosphere is quite subdued, with Hamp playing the tune virtually straight in the opening chorus before proceeding to some typically bravura improvisation. As is the case with him, the best bit is often the coda, in which one idea leads to another and his only problem seems to be how to stop. At the end of one of these, he can be heard chuckling delightedly. The other musicians have little solo space, and the synthesizer was a mistake. Apparently, it was the idea of producer Teo Macero, who contributes a few originals. No one could claim this as vintage Hampton, but it affords some nice moments                    **DG**

# Slide Hampton                                                                                1932

**Dedicated to Diz** Hampton (tb, ldr, arr); **Jon Faddis, Roy Hargrove** (t, flh); **Steve Turré** (tb); **Douglas Purviance** (btb, tba); **Antonio Hart** (ss, as); **David Sanchez** (ss, ts, f); **Jimmy Heath** (ts); **Danilo Perez** (p); **George Mraz** (b); **Lewis Nash** (d). Telarc Jazz Ⓔ CD83323 (72 minutes). Recorded 1993.

⑦ ❻

Slide Hampton and the Jazz Masters, to give this group its full title, was born in early 1993 of an idea shared by Slide Hampton and Dizzy Gillespie's manager Charles Fishman. It was conceived as a small big band (12 pieces) which could perform the compositions associated with the masters such as Gillespie, Parker, Ellington and Monk, all in imaginative new arrangements specially tailored for the band by Slide Hampton. It was a great idea on paper, and the resulting CD (recorded live at the Village Vanguard) shows that Hampton has created an unusually persuasive book.

This should hardly surprise the long-term follower of Hampton's career. A good if unspectacular soloist, Hampton's forte has always been creating charts honed to perfection for forces such as the one assembled on this date. He first came to prominence with Lionel Hampton, Lloyd Price and Maynard Ferguson, and in 1959 he formed his Octet, a group which brought him considerable attention and which crystallized his clean, powerful approach to arranging, one which, like Gerry Mulligan, left considerable room for good soloists to stretch out. His later group, World of Trombones, understandably had less room for solos (there were nine trombonists to cater for), but in recent years he has been performing mostly with quintets. Thus it is good to welcome him back to his natural milieu on this date. The recording quality may not be wonderful (it is about par for the Vanguard), and the band may be a little rough in places, but it is all there, and the soloists – all of whom can claim a meaningful association with Gillespie – create a worthwhile tribute to a great man and his music.          **KS**

# Herbie Hancock                                                                    1940

**Maiden Voyage**   Hancock (p); Freddie Hubbard (t); George Coleman (ts); Ron Carter (b); Tony Williams (d). Blue Note Ⓜ CDPB21Y46339-2 (42 minutes). Recorded 1964.

✓                                                                              ⑩ ❽

Hancock made many fine albums in the sixties, and this one is so often paraded in front of the public as a genuine jazz classic (and just as regularly debunked by those anxious to appear better informed) that one could be forgiven for wondering why it would need yet another recommendation. The answer to that runs along the lines of the type of music played by the band on **Maiden Voyage**. It is generally quiet, relaxed, contemporary mid-sixties jazz, aware of the turmoil of change around it but happy to stay within clear parameters. Of course four-fifths of the line-up were in the Miles Davis quintet at the time, but this is the least Milesean album of all the ones this rhythm section made with this trumpeter. The members of the group are clearly comfortable with each other, and there are no unseemly dramas: mutual support is the rule. Hancock's compositional and arranging skills see to that.

George Coleman in particular solos strongly, his warm, clear tone and truly original melodic sense combining to create a series of timeless improvisations. Being relatively unadventurous musically, Coleman in general is underrated, and his period with Miles (he was the one between Mobley and Shorter), which saw him at his peak, won him few friends. This is a shame: he was capable, on occasion, of playing to Getzian standards. This is one of the occasions. No one else falls below such relative values on their own instruments. Need I reiterate it? I will, anyway: a classic.          **KS**

**New review**
## Mwandishi: The Complete Warner Bros. Recordings   Hancock (p); Johnny Coles, Joe Newman, Ernie Royal, Eddie Henderson (t); Garnett Brown, Benny Powell, Julian Priester (tb); Ray Alonge (frh); Joe Henderson, Joe Farrell (ts, f); Benny Maupin (ss, bcl, alto f); Arthur Clark (bs); Eric Gale, Billy Butler, Ron Montrose (g); Patrick Gleason (syn); Buster Williams, Jerry Jermott (b); Albert 'Tootie' Heath, Bernard Purdie, Billy Hart (d); George Devens, Leon Chancler, Jose Ares, Victor Pontoja (perc); Candy Love, Sandra Stevens, Della Horne, Victoria Domagalski, Scott Beach (v). Warner Archives Ⓜ 945732-2 (two discs: 125 minutes). Recorded 1969-72.

                                                                              ⑨ ❽

Bedazzled! This collection competes with the best of Weather Report and with Davis albums like **In a Silent Way** as a documentation of the best of electronic jazz. The three LP albums it includes chronicle three of the most important years in Hancock's career. The pianist had already made his mark in jazz during his period in Miles Davis's band of the mid sixties and he became Davis's most effective disciple. He exercised a considerable intellectual influence on contemporary jazz with seminal acoustic Blue Note albums like **Takin' Off** and **Maiden Voyage**. The first of the three albums in this Warner set, **Fat Albert Rotunda**, has him leading a 14-piece band that includes conventional players like Joe Newman, superb on *Wiggle-Waggle*, hard boppers such as Joe Henderson and Johnny Coles, and rock-influenced players like Gale and Butler. Coles's ballad playing of *Jessica* (wherein Hancock plays orthodox piano) has all the charm of his similar features with Gil Evans. By the time of the second album (originally **Mwandishi**) Hancock is a committed and expansive electrician and the horns of Eddie Henderson and Benny Maupin add invention and colour to the explosive sounds from Hancock's arsenal. The dry-sounding trombone of Julian Priester makes a good contrast and his solos, in their comparative logic, similarly contrast with the trumpet fireworks from Henderson.

By now Hancock's music demands performances which become ever longer – the longest, *Wandering Spirit Song*, runs for 21 minutes. The beauty of the music is such that it needs to be allowed to develop to the full, and much of it is impressionist. Maupin contributes some good writing, but it is the leader who is remarkably expressive. The final album, **Crossings**, continues to develop the format. Some opinion has it that Hancock's next-but-one album, **Headhunters** (1973), which resulted from his switch to Columbia, was his best in the electric arena, but the joyous and pristine inventiveness of the Warner Bros. material gives it a unique edge, uncompromised at the time of issue by the 'jazz-rock' tag that was to give Hancock such huge commercial success in the immediate years that followed.          **SV**

**Headhunters**   Hancock (elp, clav, syn, pipes); Bennie Maupin (ss, ts, saxello, bcl, af); Paul Jackson (elb, marimbula); Harvey Mason (d); Bill Summers (perc). Columbia Legacy Ⓜ 471239-2 (42 minutes). Recorded 1973.

✓                                                                              ❽ ❽

When he left Miles Davis, Herbie Hancock (driven perhaps by pressure of reputation) felt he ought to produce a jazz masterpiece. The critically well-received 'space music' of his early seventies sextet resulted, but when these records reduced parties to silence, Hancock chose a more populist path and, ironically, turned out a seminal recording. In essence, **Headhunters** was an attempt to produce an instrumental paraphrase of the music of Sly Stone, James Brown and other soul artists, and Hancock's grasp of the infectious polyrhythmic counterpoint typical of that style is confirmed by the funk staple *Chameleon*. Soul has its dull moments too, and they are here in the corny update of *Watermelon Man* and the drowsy tone-poem *Vein Melter*. However, although the aim had been to produce dance music, jazz kept surfacing, and *Sly*, the best track here, provides a fresh and invigorating modal setting for Hancock's polytonal jazz style. Jackson's motoring, dotted-crotchet bass lines and Mason's restless bass drums and urgent, 16th-note hi-hat and cymbal figures are a wonder in themselves, but Hancock ices the cake with improvisation as volatile as any he produced in a straight-ahead context. In the midst of this careering, hothouse jazz, the insistent, funky clavinet becomes an irritating superfluity.　　　　　**MG**

**A Jazz Collection** Hancock (p); **Wynton Marsalis, Freddie Hubbard** (t); **Wayne Shorter** (ss, ts); **Chick Corea** (p); **Ron Carter** (b); **Tony Williams** (d). Columbia Ⓜ 467901-2 (76 minutes). Recorded 1977-82.

Ⓐ⑧ 🅑⑧

This album covers a cross-section of Hancock's jazz activities between his hit singles *Chameleon* (1973) and *Rockit* (1983). Three groups are represented, most notably VSOP – Hubbard and Shorter being teamed with the ex-Miles rhythm section of Hancock, Carter and Williams in a powerful *Nefertiti*. The same rhythm section backs Wynton Marsalis in an early-eighties touring band (caught here in Japan) while the disc is rounded out with some sublime piano duos between Hancock and Corea.

Some critics felt Hancock lost touch with jazz when he struck commercial success in disco and funk, but on this showing he is as assured and original as in his dominant performance in Tavernier's film *'Round Midnight*. The tune of that name is the most impressive of the Marsalis quartets, with some deft manipulation of the tempo resulting in a power surge of acceleration out of Monk's ballad. Wynton overuses one device of punching out a series of descending high notes, but his playing on this and Monk's *Well, You Needn't* is otherwise impressive. For sheer uninhibited joy, musicality and quick-fire exchange of ideas, nothing compares with the Corea/Hancock duet on *Liza*, where the two pianists seem to operate as one, recreating the magic of their concert appearances.　　　　　**AS**

**Mr Hands** Hancock (p, kbds, syns, d); **Bennie Maupin** (ts); **Wah Wah Watson** (g); **Paul Jackson, Byron Miller, Jaco Pastorius, Ron Carter, Freddie Washington** (b); **Harvey Mason, Leon 'Ndugu' Chancler, Alphonse Mouzon** (d); **Bill Summers, Sheila Escovedo** (perc). Columbia Ⓜ 471240-2 (41 minutes). Recorded 1982.

Ⓐ⑥ 🅑⑧

By the early eighties, Hancock's funk flirtation had been fully exploited. After the popular success initiated by the hit album **Headhunters** and solidified by a string of chart-topping albums and singles, he accepted that his jazz roots had spread into areas that embraced the VSOP message, the acoustic duets with Corea and even a solo acoustic piano recording for Sony Japan, as well as the overriding fusion ethic of the early seventies. On this album all of the tunes are by Hancock, and this gives him a firm controlling hand in a very varied programme. The emphasis remains on dance qualities inspired by Sly Stone, but titles like *Calypso* are pure jazz aimed at the heads of the jazz cognescenti rather than at the dancing feet of club-dwellers. Certainly *Just Around the Corner* and *Shiftless Shuffle* present a synthesis of both elements, with creative solos over a strong rhythmic base: clearly, Hancock was not trading in comfort music. He relished the challenge the electronic world offered, but he was a jazzman of such stature that it became a foregone conclusion that he would successfully surmount any difficulties of integration between the two. Meanwhile, anyone who can sit through this album oblivious of the music's dance potential would have to be in need of orthopaedic assistance.　　　　　**BMcR**

**New review**

**The New Standard** Hancock (p); **Michael Brecker** (ts, ss); **John Scofield** (g); **Dave Holland** (b); **Jack DeJohnette** (d, perc); **Don Alias** (perc); **Sam Riney, Gary Herbig, Gene Cipriano, William E. Green** (reeds); **Lester Lovitt, Oscar Brashear** (t, flh); **Suzette Moriarty** (frh); **Maurice Spears** (btb); **Lili R. Haydn, Margaret R. Wooten, Richard S. Greene** (vn); **Cameron L. Stone** (vc). Verve Ⓕ 529 584-2 (71 minutes). Recorded 1995.

Ⓐ⑦ 🅑⑨

Intersections between jazz and pop, though the bane of purists, have served an important function by making improvisation accessible to larger, non-jazz oriented audiences. Sometimes they have even opened genuinely new musical vistas. Here, Hancock offers a quasi-covert polemic for considering a 'new standard' through jazz-textured renderings of such recent pop-rock successes as Peter Gabriel's *Mercy Street* and Prince's *Thieves in the Temple*. With the addition of subtly scored strings in such Hancock/Bob Belden charts as *When Can I See You* by Kenny 'Babyface' Edmonds, seductive currents swirl ominously *à la* Charlie Haden's Quartet West. In sprints like the romping take on Stevie Wonder's *You've Got It Bad Girl*, Hancock and company breathe fire. Featuring an all-star cast – Brecker, Scofield, Holland, DeJohnette and Alias – Hancock suggests that there is jazz potential even in lines as seemingly recalcitrant as *All Apologies* by Nirvana's Kurt Cobain. In Sade's *Love is Stronger Than Pride* we hear echoes of such previous Hancock jazz-pop summits as *Fat Albert Rotunda*. Though uneven, Hancock's brief for the 'new standard' is nonetheless worth considering. **CB**

## Craig Handy 1962

**Introducing Three for All + One**  Handy (ts, ss); **David Kikoski** (p); **Charles Farnbrough** (b); **Ralph Peterson** (d). Arabesque Ⓕ AJ0109 (53 minutes). Recorded 1993.

⑧ ❽

Tenor saxophonist Craig Handy is a rollicking modernist, a big-toned player whose arabesques reflect the melodic wit and rhythmic panache of Sonny Rollins as well as the loping neo-bop swingingness of Dexter Gordon. Like Rollins, Handy has a zesty imagination capable of reconfiguring pop standards such as *Spinning Wheel*, Blood, Sweat & Tears' mega-hit, rendered here as a harmonically spartan Rollins-esque trio track for tenor, bass and drums. It is pithy and perky, and bubbling with Handy's distinctive barrel-chested brio.

The University of North Texas alumnus uses Gordon-like broad-strokes in the balladic stroll through Gordon Jenkins's *P.S. I Love You*. For Marvin Hamlisch's *One!*, his tenor slashes with sheets-of-sound abandon while the lean Jarrett-like jabs of pianist Kikoski keep things bright and swinging. His foray on Farnbrough's lithe *Amy's Waltz* spotlights this Coltrane-inflected soprano. Also impressive are the trio version of Joe Henderson's harmonically challenging *Isotope* and the quartet take on Kikoski's haunting lamentation, *Chant*. Handy, as evidenced in the roller-coaster ride called *To Woo It May Concern* and in the solo flight, *West Bank: Beyond the Berlin Wall*, is a composer to reckon with as well. **CB**

## John Handy 1933

**New review**

**Live at the Monterey Jazz Festival**  Handy (as); **Michael White** (vn); **Jerry Hahn** (g); **Don Thompson** (b); **Terry Clarke** (d). Koch Jazz Ⓜ 7820 (46 minutes). Recorded 1965.

⑧ ❼

John Handy made a considerable impact when he joined the Mingus aggregation which embarked upon the epochal 1959 series of recordings for Columbia and then went on to record and play a series of famous dates in New York at the dawn of the sixties. By the time Handy left to pursue a solo career he was already marked out as an individual alto stylist with a wonderfully singing tone and an advanced musical approach. None of this bore fruit in the public's eye until the then-new Handy group's début in front of 7,000 people at the 1965 Monterey Festival, an event thankfully recorded for posterity. The unusual line-up (electric guitar and violin: no piano) was the hit of the festival (as Mingus's big band had been in 1964, and Charles Lloyd's Quartet would be in 1966), playing two long and spirited numbers and incorporating many lessons learned from Mingus himself, especially the use of swirling counter-rhythms and moorish melodies and arabesques. Handy's ability to passionately sing a melody proved to be the golden thread which held a combustible ensemble sound together and the band became enormously influential during the formative period of the embryonic jazz-rock scene (which was two years away from any formal acnowledgement of its existence). This reissue by Koch is well overdue, and shames the owners of the masters, Columbia (who have a further three Handy LPs from this period, every one of them fine in their own way, languishing in their archives), who have never thought to do this in the 15 years CD has been with us. This is an enjoyable and important album; considering the track-record on its availability, buy it while you can. **KS**

## Roland Hanna 1932

**Impressions**  Hanna (p); **Major Holley** (b); **Alan Dawson** (d). Black & Blue Ⓕ 59 753-2 (54 minutes). Recorded 1979.

⑥ ❻

'Sir' Roland Hanna is another of the gifted products of America's Rust Belt, being born and raised in Detroit. Initially self-taught, he progressed eventually to Juilliard, from whence he graduated to professional life. His most famous stint as a sideman is the early-sixties one with Charles Mingus, but for years now he has divided his time between work as a leader and sessions with the New York Jazz Quartet.

This trio date is of the typical Black & Blue tradition, recorded in their 'open air studio' in Nice. All three musicians stretch out and play what they please, and with such a disciplined team as this, the results are just fine. Hanna's style, whether solo (as on *Body and Soul* here) or in a trio, remains essentially a 'modern conservative' one, with roots as much in Milt Buckner and Art Tatum as in

Powell or Monk. This makes his foray into Coltrane's *Impressions* that much more interesting; the return to the piano from the saxophone of this sliver from Debussy's *L'Isle Joyeuse* has a peculiarly apposite excitement, set to a sprightly jazz rhythm by the superb Alan Dawson. **KS**

# Annette Hanshaw

1910-85

**New review**

**The Twenties Sweetheart** Hanshaw (v); **Red Nichols** (c, t); **Miff Mole** (tb); **Jimmy Lytell** (cl); **Adrian Rollini** (bs, gfs, hfp, cel); **George Bohn** (cl, as); **Joe Venuti** (vn); **Irving Brodsky** (p, bj, bb); **Willie White**, **Frank Signorelli**, **Rube Bloom** (p); **Eddie Lang** (g); **Harry Reser** (bj); **Ray Bauduc** (d); **Vic Berton** (d, chimes). Jasmine Ⓜ JASMCD2542 (64 minutes). Recorded 1926-8.

⑥ ❼

Born into a comparatively wealthy family, Hanshaw was never forced to compromise her style or approach. From her earliest days she was fascinated by any singer 'bending' a melody and her own style grew from this interest. She had a light voice, but she employed rhythmic nuances that could transform a pop song into something at least strongly related to jazz. On this CD, titles such as *Somebody to Love* and *Get Out and Get Under the Moon* display a subtle but personal form of jazz phraseology and it is not unreasonable to trace a line of influence from the Hanshaw of the middle twenties to the style of Mildred Bailey. What was important, in the early years of her career, was the quality of her backing groups. The Redheads were Nichols's group and there was quality work from Mole and Lytell. The Original Memphis Five continued that tradition, the Four Instrumental Stars/Sizzlin' Syncopators had the fulsome talents of Rollini, Venuti and Lang, while Brodsky's brand of sanitized stride and Lytell's clean-cut clarinet made them an ideal support duo. Her financial independence meant that she never had to endure unworthy musical backings. She retired at the age of 28 because it suited her and she is reputed to have lived in fine style until her death. **BMcR**

# Mick Hanson

1948

**New review**

**Do You Have a Name?** Hanson (elg); **Kevin Flanagan** (ts); **Brian Dee**, **Gordon Beck** (p); **Mike Carr**, **Jay Denson** (org); **Len Skeat** (b); **Chris Dagley**, **Bobby Worth** (d). Spotlite Ⓕ SPJCD555 (77 minutes). Recorded 1995-6.

⑧ ❾

It is a little surprising to find that this British admirer of Wes, Pat Martino and Johnny Smith hasn't made his recording début as leader before now. Although his influences and approach are familiar, the 48-year-old Hanson scores through sheer musicality and good taste. Except for a few slack periods when ballads or duets are juxtaposed, the selection and sequencing are perfect. I particularly liked the exotic colour added by Milton Nascimento's *Vera Cruz* to a set which otherwise ploughs a familiar bop, blues and ballads furrow. Variety is also created by the use of contrasting instrumentation – guitar and piano trio, guitar, tenor and rhythm, guitar/organ combo and guitar and piano duet – all without producing any sense of unevenness. Twists in the arrangements, like the dark, 'foggy' introduction to *Foggy Day*, also help to reduce the idiomatic predictability of the material, but even an unremarkable arrangement of *I Thought about You* has a freshness and presence so often missed in such dates. There are good contributions from the sidemen, Flanagan a specialist in gritty Hawkins-style excursions and Brian Dee particularly exciting on *Here's That Rainy Day*. A creative post-bop guitar session with a warm, smoky, club ambience. **MG**

# Fareed Haque

**New review**

**Opaque** Haque (g, elg, gsyn); **Jonathan Paul** (b); **Mark Walker** (d); **Hamid Drake** (perc). Blue Note Ⓕ CDP8 29270-2 (44 minutes). Recorded 1995.

⑥ ❽

This, Haque's third album and second for Blue Note, confirms his talent and stature as a brilliant guitar technician with toes in a number of stylistic camps and a degree of comfort in whatever genre he selects. For the most part on this record he sticks to one of a number of acoustic guitar options, often with discreet electric guitar overdubs to beef up the backing or decorate a melody he is etching with his front-line acoustic. Sometimes the whole thing veers towards the techno-driven fusion overkill of Di Meola and friends at their worst, while at other times one feels a little blanded-out, but when the composition matches Haque's instrumentalist skills, then the interest does not flag. Such a piece is *Duet 2*. In this delicate waltz Haque touches a number of resonances, including Spanish and Latin music, but the character of the song is strong enough for him to guide his own course. Likewise his improvisation can use similar elements yet not sound like Charlie Byrd on a bad day. Yet the following track, *Never Ending*, which sounds as if it evolved from a fretboard pattern exercise, is too close to some McLaughlin/Mahavishnu epics of the past to get off the ground. Haque is making superior and pleasant music. If on top of this he evolves a stronger musical identity then he's going to be on to something. **KS**

# Bill Hardman
1933-90

**What's Up** Hardman (t); **Junior Cook** (ts); **Robin Eubanks** (tb); **Mickey Tucker** (p); **Paul Brown** (b); **Leroy Williams** (d). SteepleChase Ⓕ SCCD31254 (68 minutes). Recorded 1989.

⑦ ❾

Converted from swing-era influences by hearing Charlie Parker as a teenager, Hardman became a 'first call' trumpeter who graced the bands of Jackie McLean, Art Blakey, Charles Mingus and Horace Silver throughout the fifties and sixties. In the next decade he led Brass Company and began a fruitful musical association with Junior Cook. In his earlier days his bubbling lines made him sound like a bop version of Freddie Jenkins, but as he matured, more of the hard-bop lean burn became apparent. This CD is by his working band, augmented by Eubanks, and it documents the music of Hardman's last few years with some accuracy. The programme, with only one Hardman original, is well chosen, and the trumpeter continually demonstrates his adaptability. His easy lyricism is heard on *I Should Care*, his puckish humour on *Whisper Not* and his well-chosen aggression on *Yo What's Up*. His five blues choruses on *Room's Blues* are well engineered and full of genuine feeling: as all of this session develops, it becomes obvious that this is a commodity always available in Hardman's musical storehouse. It all makes for a performance that gives no hint of the trumpeter's imminent and untimely demise.
**BMcR**

# Roy Hargrove
1970

**New review**

**Family** Hargrove (t); **Ron Blake** (ts, ss); **Stephen Scott** (p); **Rodney Whitaker** (b); **Gregory Hutchinson** (d); with guests **Wynton Marsalis** (t); **Jesse Davis** (as); **David 'Fathead' Newman** (ts, f); **John Hicks**, **Ronnie Mathews**, **Larry Willis** (p); **Walter Booker**, **Christian McBride** (b); **Jimmy Cobb**, **Lewis Nash**, **Karriem Riggins** (d). Verve Ⓕ 527 630-2 (79 minutes). Recorded 1995.

⑧ ❽

A former member of Generations and Jazz Futures, Hargrove is now very much the finished article and he finds himself at the head of the post-Marsalis neo-classic ratings. For him this is a double-edged sword. The quality of his jazz playing is obviously ratified but the honour implies a return to roots, rather than a movement toward the cutting edge of music. His current work confirms how meaningless such assessments really are. Hargrove is a player of consummate instrumental ability, inherent rhythmic dash and full emotional commitment. Reality attends every bar he plays and, if the inspiration for his music is the hard bop of Clifford Brown, Horace Silver and the Jazz Messengers, it acts only as a starting-point. Entitled **Family**, this CD illustrates that fact while honouring the people closest to him. It was culled from a total of 42 titles recorded over four days in the company of his peers. The core quintet's familiarity breeds success; they move as one and, although it is obviously Hargrove's date, all contribute wholeheartedly. In terms of the guests, there is the bonus of variety. Marsalis crosses the most friendly of swords on *Nostalgia*, Davis wrings every ounce of feeling from *Polka Dots and Moonbeams*, while Booker is a superbly lyrical partner in the *Ethiopia* duo. Hicks displays the structural logic of his style on *Pas de Trios*, while the muted trumpet and flute meeting of Hargrove and Newman recalls the Joe Newman/Frank Wess team of the fifties. Over it all, Hargrove's superb tone on trumpet and flügelhorn complements the ideas he conjures from the material and completes this picture of a highly distinctive player.
**BMcR**

# Billy Harper
1943

**Black Saint** Harper (ts); **Virgil Jones** (t); **Joe Bonner** (p); **David Friesen** (b); **Malcolm Pinson** (d). Black Saint Ⓕ 0001 (41 minutes). Recorded 1975.

⑧ ❽

I first encountered Billy Harper's playing on a Lee Morgan LP released in 1972; his tenor solos were thoughtful, articulate, unusually contoured and immediately impressive. They include one solo teeter-tottering on a repeated honk that brought to mind Arnett Cobb and their shared 'Texas tenor' roots. It was only later that I noticed the album's two most attractive compositions were from Harper's pen. One of them, *Croquet Ballet*, a waltz with challenging melodic twists and turns, appears on this disc. But this has proven indicative of Harper's career since then. Although this and a pair of Japanese LPs from the late seventies enhanced his reputation, he remains better known as a valuable sideman in groups led by Max Roach, Art Blakey, Thad Jones/Mel Lewis, Gil Evans and Randy Weston than as a leader himself. One wonders why. This is enormously exciting music. Extending the concept of Coltrane's arpeggiated 'sheets of sound', Harper flexes his muscles on the opening *Dance, Eternal Spirit, Dance!* Here, and on the anthemic *Call of the Wild and Peaceful Heart* (where the unusual 9/8 meter creates a surging momentum), it is trumpeter Jones's task to relieve the tension Harper's chromatic exuberance builds, with pianist Bonner a romantic foil, comping in the rich, ringing style McCoy Tyner popularized during this period.

Worthy of rediscovery.
**AL**

# Herbie Harper

**Two Brothers**  Harper (tb); **Bill Perkins** (ts, bs, f); **Larry Koonse** (g); **John Leitham** (b); **Laurance Marable** (d). VSOP Ⓕ #80CD (51 minutes). Recorded 1989.

⑧ ❽

The combination of saxophone and trombone as a front line is a mightily rewarding one, and the expected clash between the similar ranges of trombone and tenor seldom happens. Brookmeyer and Getz made the most memorable pairing, but the leaders of the Harper-Perkins Quintet are joyously compatible. This group has a completely fresh sound, spiced by the use of a guitar instead of a piano.

The album is also important because it gives Harper, trombonists' trombonist *par excellence*, a rare chance to be heard at length. His beautiful tone, developed from long years in big bands and the studios, is better than ever, and his smooth legato work is set off by Perkins's astringent tenor (Perkins, who had previously followed his Rollins muse, was at this time re-orienting because he had discovered that his fans wanted his older Lester Young-based style). Unique treatments of Russ Freeman's *The Wind*, Brookmeyer's *Dirty Man* and Hefti's *Fred* are only the beginning, while *The Touch of Your Lips* in a most imaginative treatment is just one of a selection of unhackneyed standards.

The rhythm section is ideal and a just celebration of this quintet demands more space than is available, so this pressing recommendation will suffice.                                    **SV**

# Tom Harrell

**New review**
**Labyrinth**  Harrell (t, flh, p); **Don Braden** (tb); **Kenny Werner** (p); **Larry Grenadier** (b); **Billy Hart** (d); **Joe Lovano** (ts); **Gary Smulyan** (bs, bcl); **Steve Turré** (tb); **Rob Botti** (ob); **Leon Parker** (perc). RCA Victor Ⓕ 68512-2 (67 minutes). Recorded 1996.

⑧ ❽

Harrell's instrumental ability is totally compatible with his improvisational process. His range is unspectacular but he has a beautiful tone, relaxed delivery and a sense of phrase organization that means that he is rarely hurried into error. Early experience on the West Coast led to tours with Stan Kenton and Woody Herman in his early twenties. He worked with Horace Silver, Cecil Payne and Lee Konitz then in 1983 began a tour of duty with Phil Woods that lasted six years. Since then, Harrell has worked consistently on the festival circuit. This album features a multi-track piano and trumpet duet by Harrell alone, four titles by his working quintet of the time and a further five with invited guests. *Darn That Dream* demonstrates that he is not an impressive pianist but that, as a trumpeter, is not unhinged by pedestrian backing. The quintet titles feature Harrell as an excellent horn man, happiest at thrusting medium tempo but playing with fulsome grace and with an attack that is amiable but never flaccid. Comparable solos by Werner and Braden offer fine support and Lovano and Turré are the pick of the guests. Harrell wrote nine of the ten titles and they show him to be a pleasing tunesmith. His arrangements add a further dimension and, particularly with the larger unit, he makes good use of the means available. There is evidence enough here to show why Harrell is rated as a musicians' musician.                        **BMcR**

# Barry Harris

**Live at Maybeck Recital Hall**  Harris (p). Concord Ⓕ CCD4476 (53 minutes). Recorded 1990.

⑧ ❽

Although solidly grounded in bebop, Harris has always shown that he does not suffer from tunnel vision as far as music is concerned. This fine album from Concord's 'Maybeck Hall' series of unaccompanied pianists at work and in front of a small audience is strongly recommended. Solo piano is challenging for the pianist (richly satisfying for the listener), but Harris is obviously at home in this setting. One of his early LPs for Riverside was a solo album, with one title, an original named *Mutattra*, giving a clue to Barry's idol if you reverse the spelling. There are graceful, ruminative readings of songs such as *It Could Happen to You* and *Gone Again*, a tribute to Monk in the opening chorus of *All God's Children* (before the tempo shifts up to about 80 bars a minute) and a moving version of the Bud Powell ballad *I'll Keep Loving You*. Just as dramatic is Harris's total recall of *Parker's Mood*. A short ballad medley opens with a splendid version of Richard Rodgers's *It Never Entered My Mind* which slides surprisingly but logically into the *Flintstones* theme! The closing track is a tune Art Tatum liked to play, *Would You Like to Take a Walk?*, a fitting end to a fascinating solo recital.                        **AM**

# Beaver Harris

**Beautiful Africa**  Harris (d); **Grachan Moncur III** (tb); **Ken McIntyre** (as, bn, f); **Rahn Burton** (p); **Cameron Brown** (b). Soul Note Ⓕ 121002-2 (40 minutes). Recorded 1979.

⑥ ❽

After moving to New York from Pittsburgh in 1962, Beaver Harris played for a remarkable number of leaders, including Sonny Rollins, Albert Ayler, Roswell Rudd and Thelonious Monk. His spell as the driving force behind Archie Shepp's explosive quintet was the most noteworthy, but Harris was always an extremely adaptable drummer. In 1968 he formed the 360° Music Experience with Moncur and pianist Dave Burrell, and this highly musical CD gives a fine example of Harris's own propulsive style as well as the group's well-balanced musical stance. All of the players here were at one time associated with the free-form leaders of the sixties, but all play better in this more orthodox musical environment. The tunes were written by group members and, apart from the odd pan-tonal flourish from McIntyre and Burton, the treatment they receive is straight-ahead jazz. Burton shows the odd flash of Horace Silver on *African Drums* and *Love and Hate*. Moncur is selectively laconic on *Love and Hate* and at his loose-limbed best on *Baby Suite*, while McIntyre's flute lights up *Aladdin's Carpet*. Brown makes good solo statements on *Love and Hate* and *Baby Suite* and Harris is relaxed and swinging throughout. *Drums for Milan* is just what it claims to be, but there is no percussion overkill.              **BMcR**

## Bill Harris                                                                    1916-73

**Woody Herman Live 1957 Featuring Bill Harris, Volume 1**  Herman (cl, as, v); **Bill Berry,
  John Coppola, Bill Castagnino, Andy Peele, Danny Styles** (t); **Harris, Bobby Lamb, Willie Dennis**
  (tb); **Jay Migliori, Jimmy Cook, Bob Newman** (ts); **Roger Pemberton** (bs); **John Bunch** (p); **Jimmy
  Gannon** (b); **Don Michaels** (d). Status Ⓕ STCD107 (56 minutes). Recorded 1957.

⑧ ❻

Two of the trombonists who held sway in the thirties, J.C. Higginbotham and Dickie Wells, were responsible for the schools of the following decade, variously led by Bill Harris and J.J. Johnson.
Harris eschewed Johnson's machine gun-like precision for an emotional shaggy-dog style of trombone playing which, at its best, was one of the most exciting sounds in jazz. Harris was a man full of contradictions. On the one hand he was shy and retiring, while on the other he was an incurable practical joker and a blustering giant of a trombone soloist who could transform a performance with a few violent smears on his horn. He was also a formidable section leader. His introspective ballad performances, represented here by *Let's Talk*, managed to be exquisite as well as powerful.
The CD under review is particularly apposite since it provides an opportunity to hear Harris playing lead in the section as well as soloing. Take into account that Bobby Lamb and Willie Dennis were uncommonly devoted disciples and that the Herman band, little known in this version, was on particularly good form, then this Status volume, one of two, becomes essential listening. The recording quality is good for a live session and it is further remarkable in that it was recorded on a single mike suspended over the band.              **SV**

## Bill Harris                                                                    1925-88

**The Fabulous Bill Harris**  Harris (g, v, recitation); with, on one track: **Howard University
  Ensemble**. VSOP Ⓕ 66CD (62 minutes). Recorded 1957-86.

⑧ ❽

Not to be confused with the trombonist of the same name, Bill Harris made a considerable impression on many listeners with his solo acoustic guitar albums for the EmArcy label in the late fifties. This CD has nothing to do with any earlier releases and comes from a variety of dates and locations including the Kennedy Centre, New York's Village Gate and San Francisco's Blues Alley. The choice of material is wide-ranging, taking in Django Reinhardt (an impressive *Nuages* running for nearly 11 minutes), Bach (Segovia's arrangement of the Prelude in D Minor), John Coltrane (*Syeeda's Song Flute*) and Big Bill Broonzy (*Key to the Highway*). A couple of (fortunately) short tracks which should have been left on the editing room floor are devoted to Harris's recitations on the subject of Ma Rainey and jazz bands. Harris also has some difficulties with playing the complex line of *Syeeda's Song Flute*, but overall there is enough good, orthodox acoustic guitar playing here to justify the rating.              **AM**

## Craig Harris                                                                   1953

**Shelter**  Harris (tb, didjeridu); **Edward E.J. Allen** (t); **Don Byron** (cl, bcl); **Anthony Cox** (b);
  **Pheeroan AkLaff** (d); **Rod Williams** (p); **Tunde Samuel** (v). JMT Ⓕ 870008-2 (43 minutes).
  Recorded 1986.

⑦ ❽

"Why weren't there any trombonists on Coltrane's *Ascension*?" Craig Harris once asked, and in so doing identified himself with those trombonists like Roswell Rudd and Grachan Moncur III who redefined the horn in the light of its earliest jazz progenitors. Harris himself blows burry, hot trombone, nurtured in dynamic bands led by Abdullah Ibrahim, Sun Ra and David Murray. But these experiences also taught him the value of arranging and scene-setting, and at times the music on Shelter is reminiscent of the modernist side of the Blue Note catalogue circa 1964-5. That is, the piquant voicings and slippery, shifting metres of tunes like *Cootie* and *Sound Sketches* are impressive, although they seem to keep the band from erupting into a Mingus-like frenzy. Harris is partial to programmatic themes for his albums, here connecting the plight of underdeveloped Third World countries with that of the American homeless. Tunde Samuel's vocals on *Africans Unite* and *Shelter* may remind you of Leon Thomas, as the band finds an infectious groove and builds a rewarding head of steam. Harris makes good (if slightly restrained) use of his quality personnel; Byron's background in klezmer bands lets him slide through and around the modalities effortlessly and Allen's best workout is in a late-Miles mode on *Sound Sketches*. Attractive music just short of outstanding.   **AL**

## Eddie Harris                                                    1936-96

**Artist's Choice: The Eddie Harris Anthology**  Harris (ts, ets, p, reed t, v); with a collective personnel including: **Benny Bailey**, **Joe Newman**, **Snooky Young**, **Ray Codrington**, **Don Ellis** (t); **Bennie Powell** (btb); **King Curtis**, **'Fathead' Newman** (ts); **Haywood Henry** (bs); **Jodie Christian**, **Cedar Walton**, **Milcho Leviev** (p); **Richard Abrams** (elp); **Joe Diorio** (g); **Melvin Jackson**, **Leroy Vinnegar**, **Ron Carter**, **Rufus Reid** (b); **Richard Smith**, **Billy Higgins**, **Billy Hart**, **Grady Tate**, **Paul Humphrey** (d); **Ray Barretto** (perc). Rhino/Atlantic Ⓜ 271514-2 (two discs: 150 minutes). Recorded 1961-77.

**⑥ ❼**

Chicagoan Harris started on piano and clarinet but soon shifted to saxophone. Stationed in Germany during his stint in the army, he came into contact with Don Ellis, Leo Wright, Quincy Jones, Cedar Walton and Don Menza, among others, and this helped set him on the road to the type of music he would become famous for. His first hit, the *Theme from Exodus*, was recorded for Vee Jay records; this eventuall led to a contract with Atlantic, which was to be his company for the next decade or more. There he recorded *Freedom Jazz Dance* (a complex line over a simple vamp, and a title which Miles Davis also recorded) and *Listen Here*, the latter being another substantial hit. He was to have another million-seller in tandem with Les McCann with *Compared to What?* (not in this selection), pulled from the **Live at Montreux** album and released as a single. After that, business stayed much the same.

Harris had a light, alto-like tone and a phenomenally complete technique. He had a thorough grasp of modern jazz history and was able to play in virtually any style, but he tended to stick for the most part to mixing jazz-funk rhythm and phraseology together with the occasional harmonic sequence or line which would not have been out of place in early-sixties progressive jazz. As such he was something of an enigma, as is this collection, which mixes the hits (including the original Vee-Jay recording of the *Exodus* theme) with his rigorous workouts on Coltrane's *Giant Steps* and *Steps Up*, which Harris describes as "another intervallic tune" and features Don Ellis on his last recording session. Whichever your preference (and you may just like the lot), there is never the chance of mistaking Harris for anyone else; nor is there the chance of finding him playing music he has no interest in or commitment to. Both qualities are rare and should be accorded due respect. It is only to be expected that the sound quality is variable over such a long stretch of recording time, especially when it comes to the horrible bass sounds that studios insisted on producing in the late seventies.   **KS**

**There Was a Time (Echo of Harlem)**  Harris (ts); **Kenny Barron** (p); **Cecil McBee** (b); **Ben Riley** (d). Enja Ⓕ 6068-2 (59 minutes). Recorded 1990.

**⑨ ❽**

"Underachiever" is a dubious term which has entered the language via the social sciences; applied to oneself, it amounts to self-flattery masquerading as self-flagellation. But there is no other word for Harris, a tenor saxophonist with a paradoxical combination of gifts: a tone as airy as Paul Desmond's, an attack as bruising as Gene Ammons's and an understanding of harmonic relationships almost as keen as Sonny Rollins's. Since scoring a hit single with a jazz version of the theme from the movie *Exodus* in 1961, Harris mostly gave his audience the sort of tepid funk he presumed them to want. Over the decades he indulged in electronics, stand-up comedy, scat and mouthpiece gimmickry of a sort that enabled him to do an eerie Billie Holiday impersonation on one of his live albums. Every once in a while, however, he refrained from this, and when he did, there are few improvisers whose work is as viscerally or intellectually satisfying. Most of his better recordings are out of print on vinyl and have never been available on CD. The CD listed here might be the best Harris album of all, if only for the push he receives from a superb rhythm section and the gem of a solo he turns in on Victor Young's *Love Letters* – a solo which creates the illusion of being delivered in a rush, though Harris is phrasing well behind the beat.   **FD**

## Gene Harris                                                      1933

**New review**

**Brotherhood**  Harris (p); **Ron Escheté** (elg); **Luther Hughes** (b); **Paul Humphrey** (d). Concord Ⓕ CCD4640 (58 minutes). Recorded 1992.

**⑦ ❾**

Having established a successful formula, Gene Harris and Concord have wasted no time in capitalizing on it. This, Harris's sixth quartet album in about as many years (many of them recorded in the early part of that period), differs hardly at all from its predecessors. At the core of Harris's style, and the secret of his popularity with both jazz and general audiences, is his propensity for making virtually anything sound like a blues. This is effected by having the drummer play simple, crisp shuffle figures with plenty of emphasis on the offbeats and by introducing blues licks at frequent intervals, although on the gospel sequence, *The Brotherhood of Man*, and the outright rock'n'roll of *This Little Light of Mine* such modifications are unnecessary. Despite changes in Harris's rhythm team, guitarist Ron Escheté has been a constant, and shrewdly so, since his unambitious but tastefully developed solos are one of the quartet's major assets. In its quieter moments (on such ballad reflections as *September Song* and *When You Wish Upon a Star*) the record suggests the sort of cocktail jazz Harris might have produced in the late seventies as Musical Director at the Idanha Hotel in Idaho, but the sort of party which would have the guests swinging from the chandeliers never seems far away.  **MG**

## Lafayette Harris, Jr

**New review**
**Happy Together** Lafayette Harris, Jr Trio featuring **Melba Moore Harris** (p); **Dwayne Dolphin** (b); **Cecil Brooks III** (d); **Melba Moore** (v). Muse Ⓕ MCD5541 (62 minutes). Recorded 1995.
Ⓢ Ⓞ

On this, his second Muse CD as a leader, Philadelphia-born Lafayette Harris, Jr applies his airy, tripping piano sound to a programme equally divided between straightforward originals and material from a variety of sources. The opening track, *Happy Together*, written by Gary Bonner and Alan Gordon, from the little-known group the Magicians but made famous by the Turtles in 1966, provides some engaging moments, combining Harris's light, springy approach – a sort of cocktail-lounge version of Ahmad Jamal – with the brisk, supple drumming of producer Brooks and the discreet bass of Dolphin, but overall this is a pleasant yet unremarkable album. Harris's compositions, even the inevitable blues-album closer, never look like stretching anyone concerned; the trio's visits to standard fare such as Bill Carey's *You've Changed* are professional but distinctly unadventurous; the solo Scott Joplin feature, *Solace*, provides a welcome change of pace and style, but never really catches fire. Melba Moore, moreover, betrays her inexperience in jazz singing on all her four tracks, the Billie Holiday classic, *Lady Sings the Blues*, receiving a particularly unappealing treatment that steadfastly ignores all the song's pathos and subtlety.  **CP**

## Vandy Harris, Jr.     1941

**New review**
**Pure Fire** Harris (ts); **Robert Griffin** (t, flh); **Isaiah Jackson** (tb); **Boaz McGee** (bs); **Maia** (f, pic, v); **Ken Chaney**, **Jodie Christian** (p); **Malachi Favors**, **Thaddeus Expose** (b); **Aye Aton** (d, perc); **Art T. Burton** (perc); **Shawn Wallace**, **Kevin McIlvaine** (v). Katumbi Ⓕ 9001 (74 minutes). Recorded 1996.
Ⓖ Ⓞ

Chicago runs its own musical underground, nurturing a body of players who show no inclination to become part of the New York or general world scene. One such man is Harris; born in Louisiana but brought up in Chicago. As a young saxophonist he sat in with the likes of Muddy Waters, and his professional career took off in the Joseph Jarman sextet. A taste of commercialism with organist Jack McDuff persuaded him that his artistic interests were best served by the musical integrity of the AACM. This CD examines Harris the individual but also provides a useful blueprint for all generations of AACM players. It acknowledges the juxtaposition of their free and more organized jazz and the way in which the blues soul of the City has survived into their nineties product. The less pleasing moments occur when the soul vocal elements misfit the jazzier ensembles or when Griffin's technique fails to keep abreast of his improvisational thinking. The best is found in the variety of Harris's scores and in the fine ensemble reading they receive. There are pleasing flute and piano interludes as well as gambolling counterpoints involving all of the horns. It is the power and range of the leader's own solos, with his big tone and fine Traneish stance, that provides the highlights.  **BMcR**

## Donald Harrison     1960

**Full Circle** Harrison (as, v); **Cyrus Chestnut** (p); **Mark Whitfield** (g); **Dwayne Burno** (b); **Carl Allen** (d). Bellaphon/Sweet Basil Ⓕ 660 55 003 (53 minutes). Recorded 1990.
Ⓖ Ⓞ

Born in New Orleans, Donald 'Duck' Harrison studied at Southern University and the Berklee College of Music. More significantly, he joined the Art Blakey Academy when he became a Jazz Messenger in 1982. His current work suggests that it is his place of birth and his sojourn with the drummer that make him the player most heard on this CD. His melodic delivery on *Bye Bye Blackbird* displays a character that is uniquely of the Crescent City. The related jump blues style of *Hold It Right There* has the same roots, and contrasts to his ease with *Let's Go Off*, an orthodox hard-bop 12-bar that could have come from the Blakey repertoire.
Harrison is already a versatile player, his intonation is accurate, he plays with relaxation and has an unforced improvisational manner. He is at home with the Latin elements here and on *Nature Boy* shows that he is as aware of a tune's structure as he is of its changes. The balladeer is heard on *Good*

*Morning Heartache* and on his own *Infinite Heart*. On both he moves well away from the parent theme and demonstrates how to produce a replacement as pleasing as the original. Chestnut and Allen are at the heart of a highly sympathetic support team for one of the truly original young saxophone voices. **BMcR**

## Nancy Harrow

**Lost Lady** Harrow, **Vernel Bagneris** (v); **Phil Woods** (cl, as); **Dick Katz** (p); **Ray Drummond** (b); **Ben Riley** (d). Soul Note Ⓕ 121263-2 (48 minutes). Recorded 1993.

⑥ ❼

Harrow has made a number of albums over the years, starting with her Candid and Atlantic efforts at the dawn of the sixties, and continuing with albums such as this and its immediate predecessor, **Secrets** (Soul Note). Yet she has been passed over without comment in the major jazz encyclopaedias and dictionaries. Which is doubly odd in that her latter-day career has seen her blossom into a song-writing talent to be reckoned with. There is nothing original in the style of the pieces she has created here – they are in the broad tradition of Porter, Gershwin, Rodgers and Hart and their ilk – but the unusual element is that this album was conceived as a whole, in order to tell the story to be found in a Willa Cather novella, *A Lost Lady*. To do this she has created two narrating voices and used Vernel Bagneris to take the male narrating role.

Harrow has a small voice and a relatively rudimentary technique, although her ear is good and she sings in tune. Bagneris, a good, live performer, seems less at ease in front of a studio mike and rather too aware of the words he has to deliver, but his good feeling communicates itself. The supporting musicians play with taste and sensitivity. A good record, interesting from its own point of view, but not one which will change your life. **KS**

## Antonio Hart

1969

**New review**

**Here I Stand** Hart (as, ss, arr); **James Hart** (p, org); **John Benitez** (elb, b); **Nasheet Waits** (d); with appearances from the following: **Patrick Rickman** (t); **Robin Eubanks** (tb); **Mark Gross** (f, as); **Amadou Diallo** (ts); **Shirley Scott** (p, org); **John Ormond** (b); **Pernell Saturino** (perc); **Jessica Care Moore** (v). Impulse! Ⓕ IMP 12082 (56 minutes). Recorded 1996.

⑧ ❿

This, Hart's first for the Impulse! label after a trio of fine records for Novus, finds him developing in a number of directions. What's so impressive is that he shows an equal degree of assuredness about each direction, no doubt due to the intense preparations he imposed upon himself and his working band before they got to make these recordings. The basic quartet is augmented or substituted from time to time by guest musicians, with Shirley Scott ("one of the icons of the music", according to Hart) appearing twice, on organ for a brisk work-out on *Flamingo*, on piano Hart's original, *Like My Own*, a bluesy tribute to his recently appointed Godson. Elsewhere, reggae, salsa and other cultural influences are registered and used, but this is one of those rare instances where it's not like watching someone try on different suits of clothes, just in case they fit. Hart has assimilated the genres he is delving into and made them natural outlets for his own clearly defined musical personality. In the only really stillborn track, Jessica Care Moore delivers a rap-style poem over an M-Base-type rhythm on *The Words Don't Fit in My Mouth*, and although the words themselves are interesting, there is little rhythmic or cadential connection to the music sliding by beside them: it's like having the radio on two channels at the same time. That aside, Hart's rich, keening tone is caught beautifully throughout by the crisp, full recording, and his band respond superbly to his wishes. He also consistently plays the soprano in tune – something which has been sadly lacking on many records by other young players I've heard recently. Hart seems to have pushed Coltrane to the fore in his learning curve at present, so that his own style is less attached to that of Cannonball Adderley's than before. This has not decreased the pleasure to be found, only made it more intriguing. Hart is a seriously good musician: this latest album proves it beyond doubt. **KS**

## Billy Hart

**Amethyst** Hart (d); **John Stubblefield** (ss, ts); **David Kikoski** (p); **Marc Copland** (kbds); **Mark Feldman** (vn); **David Fiuszynski** (g); **Santi Debriano** (b). Arabesque Jazz Ⓕ AJ01505 (67 minutes). Recorded 1993.

⑤ ❼

Hart made a considerable impact as the drummer in Mwandishi, Herbie Hancock's pre-**Headhunters** sextet, along with Bennie Maupin and Eddie Henderson. He already has a couple of albums as leader to his credit, but this latest is the only one on CD. It is a good record, played by expert musicians, but there is little on it which cuts through in a way that makes you glad you bought it. For the most part, themes are played across a variety of vamps or suspended tempos, then everybody lines up for their solos, then the theme is re-stated, then the track stops. Only Debriano's *El Junque* and Feldman's *Asylum* have what could be termed a definable atmosphere which calls to be explored by the players, but then little is done to develop that atmosphere while everyone tries to keep out of each soloist's way. The shortest of the seven tracks on the album is just a handful of seconds less than seven minutes, while four of them are comfortably over ten. With that sort of length, more thought needed to be put into the shaping of the music if the album was not to pall long before it finished.             **KS**

# John Hart

**New review**
**High Drama**  Hart (g); **Chris Potter** (ss, ts); **Marc Copland** (p); **Jay Anderson** (b); **Jeff Hirshfield** (d). Concord Ⓔ CCD4688 (64 minutes). Recorded 1995.

⑦ ⑧

A guitarist in his thirties, who has recorded with Jack McDuff and Terumasa Hino and appears on a couple of Chris Potter's albums, John Hart is commendably hard to classify. His tunes and arrangements are contemporary in mostly avoiding old-fashioned 4/4 and he extracts a slight twang from an otherwise uniformly metallic sound. At the same time, his lines are more cool than jazz-rock and he never tries to show off. Potter guests on four tracks, notably on Hart's *Ozone*, one of those Ornette Coleman-type tunes as filtered through John Scofield, and on Billy Strayhorn's *Isfahan*, both among the better tracks. Hart has clearly taken trouble with the programming, giving another original *Who Killed Mr Lucky* a rolling, boogaloo beat and reworking the rhythmic background on the standard *I'll Never Be the Same*. Plenty of neat interplay within the rhythm section, with Copland given many chances to shine.             **RA**

# Johnny Hartman

1923-83

**I Just Dropped by to Say Hello**  Hartman (v); **Illinois Jacquet** (ts); **Hank Jones** (p); **Kenny Burrell**, **Jim Hall** (g); **Milt Hinton** (b); **Elvin Jones** (d). Impulse! Ⓜ IMP11762 (33 minutes). Recorded 1965.

⑧ ⑧

Hartman made less than half a dozen albums, and must have counted himself lucky to survive the outrageous booklet-note to this one, flatulently written by some long-forgotten disc jockey ("I cannot say that I have liked and played every recording that Johnny Hartman has made ..."). Judged by this album and the relaxed and lyrical one he recorded with John Coltrane (recently reissued in a cleaned-up and lavishly packaged version), he was a good jazz singer whose warm bass-baritone showed the influence of Billy Eckstine and Joe Williams in its pitch, also spreading out to include Sinatra's phrasing. The songs are well chosen and most of them rarely sung – *Stairway to the Stars*, *If I'm Lucky* and *A Sleepin' Bee* are well delivered and Hartman even manages to create an original version of *In the Wee Small Hours of the Morning*. The voice is richly melodic and the timing that of a jazz musician born and bred. The accompaniment is spiced by the two guitarists. Jones solos with his usual light touch on the title track, and Jacquet is suitably voluptuous whenever he enters.

The album has been re-mastered and put in the new Impulse! sleeve, but remains essentially untouched. Another worthy Hartman album, from the early seventies, **I Remember Trane** (Capitol), has recently reappeared.             **SV**

# Mark Harvey

**New review**
**Paintings for Jazz Orchestra**  Harvey (t, p, cond); **Jeanne Snodgrass**, **K.C. Dunbar** (t); **Bob Pilkington**, **Jay Keyse** (tb); **Jeff Marsanskis** (btb); **Marshall Sealy**, **John Patton** (frh); **Ari Cheatham**, **Peter Bloom**, **Phil Scarff**, **Brad Jones**, **Eric Hipp**, **Joel Springer**, **Tom Hall** (reeds); **Richard Nelson** (g); **Ken Filiano** (b); **John Funkhuser** (b, p); **Jerry Edwards** (elb); **Harry Wellott** (d); **Craig Ellis** (perc); **Donna Hewitt-Didham** (v). Leo Lab Ⓔ CD014 (67 minutes). Recorded 1993-4.

⑦ ⑧

Harvey has been a trumpeter, composer and band leader since the mid sixties. Based in Boston, he has worked with George Russell, Gil Evans, Sheila Jordan and Marilyn Crispell. In 1973, he became the founder and Musical Director of Aardvark. This jazz orchestra has an innovative policy, takes its inspiration from its leader and, through him, from a tradition that stems from John Cage and the black American avant-garde. All the music on this CD is by Harvey and it presents *Paintings*, six pieces dedicated to American abstract painter Stuart Davis and *Convergences*, a series of duets built into a total band piece in the London Jazz Composers' manner. The *Painting* arrangements leave only modest space for soloists but they are structured in such a way as to contain the freedoms they develop. The counterpoints are well organized and the odd static moments are balanced by passages that display a flowing ease. The best of the duos on *Convergence* team Cheatham's tenor with Filiano's bass and Nelson's guitar with Edwards's electric bass. Its prime impact, however, is as a complete unit and this is a genuinely contemporary, big jazz band reflecting like its leader a musical world populated by the ideas of men as diverse as Duke Ellington, John Cage and Charles Ives. **BMcR**

# Michael Hashim

1956

New review

**Keep a Song in Your Soul** Hashim (ss, as, arr); **Claudio Roditi** (t); **Richard Wyands** (p); **Dennis Irwin** (b); **Kenny Washington** (d). Hep Ⓕ CD2068 (65 minutes). Recorded 1996.

⑧ ❿

Although known chiefly as a repertoire specialist – previous projects have included tributes to Billy Strayhorn (**Lotus Blossom**, 1990), an exploration of Hammond organ jazz (**A Blue Streak**, 1991) and a collaboration with UK musicians (**Transatlantic Airs**, 1995) – Michael Hashim elevates all he plays far above the realms of dot-reading glibness courtesy of an infectious enthusiasm for, and detailed knowledge of, the entire jazz tradition, from early collective improvisation through swing to bop and beyond. Here, in the company of the fiery but disciplined Brazilian trumpeter Claudio Roditi, veteran Prestige stalwart, pianist Richard Wyands, and long-time associates, Dennis Irwin and Kenny Washington, and under the eye of the master, Rudy Van Gelder, Hashim applies his Johnny Hodges-inspired alto and his agile soprano to compositions by, and songs associated with, Fats Waller. From the jaunty opening title track through the lush ballad, *Two Sleepy People*, to an imaginatively latinized *Honeysuckle Rose*, Hashim brings his customary brio to all he plays – infusing some of his alto work in particular with a boppish urgency reminiscent of, say, Sonny Criss – as well as his considerable arranging skills, ensuring that even the most familiar of Waller's tunes are given fresh lustre. **CP**

# George Haslam

1939

New review

**Argentine Adventures** Haslam (bs, tarogato, pinkuyo); **Enrique Norris** (t); **Fernando Barragan** (sicu, ocarinas, quena, perc); **Daniel Harari** (f, ss, ts); **Sergio Paulucci** (as, v); **Ruben Ferrero** (p, pianica); **Quique Sinesi** (g); **Pablo Blasich**, **'Mono' Hurtado** (b); **Horacio Lopez**, **Sergio Urtubei** (d); **Horacio Straijer** (mba, silbato, perc); **Tim Short** (cga); **Mirta Insaurralde** (v). Slam Ⓕ SLAMCD304 (68 minutes). Recorded 1991-93.

⑧ ❼

After leading the Siger Band in the eighties, Haslam decided to move "more into improvised music" and set up his own label to document the results. Slam has since developed into one of the UK's premier small labels, featuring a wide spectrum of mostly British improvisers. Haslam's own releases have included duos with Paul Rutherford (**1989 and All That**) and Mal Waldron (**Waldron-Haslam, Two New**) plus the début recording of the British Saxophone Quartet (**Early October**, with Elton Dean, Paul Dunmall and Simon Picard). **Argentine Adventures** presents another facet of Haslam's catholic tastes. Recorded during his regular visits to Argentina in the nineties, it details his meetings with a variety of Buenos Aires-based musicians and their mutual attempts to graft jazz-based improvisation on to indigenous forms such as the tango and the vidala. Despite odd moments when the players sound fazed by unfamiliar idioms, the CD is a fascinating collection of what the locals called "Etno jazz". This piquant hybrid runs the gamut from Mirta Insaurralde's stirring folk-jazz vocals to Fernando Barragan's evocative Bolivian pipes. There's even an incendiary version of Coltrane's *Affirmation* on which tenorist Sergio Paulucci suddenly breaks into scat vocals! The sequel disc, **Argentine Adventures Part 2**, is also recommended. **GL**

# Stan Hasselgard

1922-48

**The Permanent Hasselgard** Hasselgard, **Benny Goodman** (cl); **Rolf Ericson** (t); **Tyree Glenn** (tb); **Wardell Gray** (ts); **Red Norvo** (vb); **Arnold Ross, Teddy Wilson, Barbara Carroll, Kjeld Bonfils** (p); **Barney Kessel, Billy Bauer, Chuck Wayne, Al Hendrickson** (g) and others. Phontastic Ⓕ PHONTNCD8802 (70 minutes). Recorded 1945-8.

⑧ ❻

Although it includes less of Hasselgard's recordings with Benny Goodman than other albums, the Phontastic gives a comprehensive portrait of the clarinettist's short career since the first dozen tracks were done in Sweden before he left for the USA. These show him to be an accomplished Goodman disciple as yet untouched by bebop, and they also display the very high jazz standards which Hasselgard and the other Swedish musicians had achieved.

It was in 1947 that Hasselgard emigrated to the US. and eventually, in a most extraordinary move by Goodman, became co-opted into the Benny Goodman Septet as second clarinet. By then he had become a confident bop player, more comfortable in this role than many other exponents who tried so hard to popularize the clarinet as a bop instrument. (Goodman made a half-hearted attempt. It is interesting to compare Hasselgard and Goodman on the second version of *All the Things You Are* where they each solo and then duet. It seems likely that Goodman hired the young man so that he could study

Hasselgard's bebop playing at close hand.) The last track, *Cottontop*, introduced by Hasselgard himself, was recorded less than a week before his death and shows him completely fluent in the bop idiom.   **SV**

# Hampton Hawes

1928-77

**New review**

**For Real** Hawes (p); **Harold Land** (ts); **Scott LaFaro** (b); **Frank Butler** (d). Contemporary
Ⓜ OJCCD713-2 (46 minutes). Recorded 1958.

⑨ ❽

A minor classic, this impeccable session finds both Hawes and Harold Land in top form. This was before Land fell under the influence of Coltrane, and his characteristically round phrases, delivered with a slight, charming stutter, blossom in the light of Hawes's accompaniment. He can be quite a busy accompanist, perhaps not always the soul of discretion, but invariably interesting. There is something of Horace Silver in his stabbing, percussive chords. All six numbers are excellent, from the ballad-tempo *Wrap Your Troubles in Dreams* to the speedy *Crazeology*. In the latter, the drumming of Frank Butler can be enjoyed at its crispest, along with LaFaro's lightweight bass. There might have been more from this beautifully matched quartet, but soon after this session Hawes was arrested on a drugs charge and sent to prison for five years.   **DG**

**As Long as There's Music** Hawes (p); **Charlie Haden** (b). Verve Ⓔ 513 534-2 (70 minutes).
Recorded 1976.

⑧ ❻

This album grew out of the series of duets Charlie Haden recorded for release on the two albums, **"Closeness" Duets** (A&M; q.v. Haden) and **The Golden Number** (Artists' House). When Hawes died in May 1977 of a cerebral haemorrhage, Haden went back to the session tapes and found sufficient material to release this critically acclaimed album. This is its first appearance on CD. It comes with three extra tracks, all alternative readings of songs present on the LP version. Haden and Verve have commendably added the extra tracks to the end of the CD, thereby not interrupting the playing order of the original album.

The extra intimacy of the duet format allows an especially direct link between the two musicians, and both are sufficiently inventive and sensitive to thrive from such a link. Haden's clear thematic logic impresses in each of his solos here, while the insouciance of Hawes's lines keeps his clear, vibrant musical personality in perfect focus throughout. Their easy gambol through Ornette's *Turnaround* is a particular joy, but the two Hawes originals, the ballad *Irene* and the latin-tinged *Rain Forest*, both have a disarming simplicity emanating from their subtle sophistication.   **KS**

# Coleman Hawkins

1904-69

**The Complete Recordings, 1929-41** Hawkins (ts); accompanied by: **his Orchestra**, **All Star Jam Band**, **Trio and the Chocolate Dandies**; **Mound City Blue Blowers**; **Henry 'Red' Allen**; **Horace Henderson**; **Benny Goodman**; **The Ramblers**; **Michel Warlop**; **The Berries**; **Benny Carter**; **Jack Hylton**; **Metronome All Star Band** and **Count Basie**. Affinity Ⓜ CDAFS1026-6 (six discs: 430 minutes).

⑧ ❻

The comprehensive treatment accorded here to Hawkins's early work is amply justified, for the tenor giant was as fundamental to jazz saxophone as Armstrong to jazz trumpet. The title of this otherwise exemplary boxed set is slightly misleading, since recordings by the Fletcher Henderson band, with Hawk still a member until 1934, are excluded. What is here is everything else, including that band's six tracks led by Horace Henderson and small groups from the band (led by Hawkins himself and 'Red' Allen).

Already by 1933 Hawk had perfected a couple of personal styles, the rhythmic but flowing 'hot' approach that others had merely attempted on saxophone, and the luxuriant balladry, for example on *I've Got to Sing a Torch Song* (disc two), which – with only Armstrong as inspiration – he created from the ground up. After Hawkins's five-year stay in Europe, the ballad style flowered with the artistic and sales success of *Body and Soul* (disc five). This was greeted as a triumph within the enclosed jazz world, but was largely ignored by record producers and, without the fascinating multiple takes of the 1940 Commodore session, the last period covered would be thin indeed.

Three CDs' worth, forming the core of the set, document the European sojourn. Because he was justly treated as a star in Europe, he was recorded more often and frequently accorded more space on individual tracks, seeming to expend more energy to make up for sometimes inadequate accompaniments. Although a natural outgrowth of his commanding musical personality, this bore fruit triumphantly in the sessions with fellow-expatriate pianist Freddie Johnson and in examples of Hawkins's little-known composing ability, such as *A Strange Fact* and *Netcha's Dream* (both with The Ramblers). Even the several recordings with Benny Carter, also in Europe for two years, find Hawk carrying all before him, for instance on the famous *Crazy Rhythm*. Hawkins's historical position as the fount of all worthwhile saxophone playing is underlined by the contrast of the opening track, *Hello Lola* (which clearly influenced Bud Freeman, the earliest convincing 'non-Hawkins' stylist) with

*One O'Clock Jump* and *Feedin' the Bean* from the closing sessions. These latter make a convincing case for Hawk's parentage of the Southwestern blues/riff style which begat Lester Young. But it is unnecessary to listen for such academic reasons – each of the 142 tracks has something worth hearing, mostly from Hawk himself. Much of the Victor material gathered herein and much else not in this collection is obtainable either on **Body and Soul** (RCA) or **Retrospective** (RCA). **BP**

New review

**Coleman Hawkins 1943-4**  Hawkins (ts); Budd Johnson (bs); Cootie Williams, Bill Coleman, Roy Eldridge, Dizzy Gillespie, Vic Coulsen, Ed Vanderveer (t); Art Tatum, Ellis Larkins, Eddie Heywood, Teddy Wilson, Clyde Hart (p); Al Casey, Jimmy Shirley (g); Oscar Pettiford, Billy Taylor (b); Shelly Manne, Max Roach, Cozy Cole, Big Sid Catlett (d). Classics Ⓜ 807 (71 minutes).

A look at the sidemen may be all you need to ascertain that this disc must be heard. But it's important for other reasons as well: this incredibly urbane stuff was laid down hurriedly on independent labels – Commodore, Signature, Brunswick, Keynote, Apollo – after the end of the AFM recording ban, and you can hear bop experimentation wafting into the rhythm. The sound quality of the earlier of two Signature session is a little damaged, but does it matter? *How Deep Is the Ocean* contains a continuous, magisterial Hawkins solo, and even *Stumpy*, marred by a few note fluffs, is Hawkins in pure kaleidoscopic overdrive. The Signature sides from late December 1943 – *Crazy Rhythm*, *Get Happy*, *The Man I Love*, *Sweet Lorraine* – shimmer on every hearing. Oscar Pettiford's hustling bass solos, contributing much to the group's swing, and Eddie Heywood's crisp phrasing, create a serious air; one gets the impression that they're giving it all they've got. Hawkins, on *The Man I Love*, solos through two extended, rock-solid choruses, contributing to a track I'd put before the 1939 *Body and Soul* – partly because the ground is made so fertile by Heywood and Pettiford before he steps up for his turn. When the disc proceeds next to the lovely but more lighthearted Keynote sessions with Roy Eldridge and Teddy Wilson, you find yourself catching your breath. (The 78 disc for *The Man I Love* had to be issued at 12 inches instead of ten; producer Bob Thiele didn't want to cut off what he must have known was a masterpiece.) After that, there's the big-band session which has been called the first legit bebop recording: *Woodyn' You*, with chord changes that sound comparatively exotic, as well as a charging Dizzy Gillespie, and *Bu-Dee-Daht*. Today these won't catch anyone by surprise, but the music is an important historical link from swing to the revolution. Sound, overall, is muffled on the CD; these are typically so-so Classics transfers. But since the material isn't easily available otherwise, grit your teeth and get it. **BR**

**Hollywood Stampede**  Hawkins (ts); with a collective personnel: Howard McGhee, Miles Davis (t); Vic Dickenson, Kai Winding (tb); Sir Charles Thompson, Hank Jones (p); Allan Reuss (g); Oscar Pettiford, John Simmons, Curley Russell (b); Denzil Best, Max Roach (d). Capitol Ⓜ CDP7 92596-2 (49 minutes). Recorded 1945/7.

The dozen titles which Coleman Hawkins recorded for Capitol in Hollywood at the beginning of 1945 are among the very finest he made throughout his long and fruitful career. He had recently been working in New York with Thelonious Monk and was clearly very interested in the new ideas of the incipient boppers, Howard McGhee amongst them. McGhee, Thompson, Best and Pettiford comprised Hawk's regular band at the time and the library contained a number of pieces which, in retrospect, effectively bridged the gap between swing and bebop. Tunes such as *Rifftide and Stuffy* became closely identified with Hawkins but the programme also contained sumptuous ballad readings such as the superlative *What is There to Say?*, a close contender for second place after *Body and Soul* as one of Hawk's most impressive performances. These 12 tracks demonstrate again what a high standard Capitol had achieved in recording terms by 1945. The clarity and immediacy of this music, although in mono, is actually superior to a lot of later stereo recordings. The CD is fleshed out with four tracks done two years later for Aladdin Records by an ephemeral band that Hawkins took on a number of bookings. Musically these are good, although the recording quality is a little lower. Miles Davis solos on *Bean-a-Rebop*, but the most memorable moments are the leader's. **AM**

**Encounters Ben Webster**  Hawkins, Ben Webster (ts); Oscar Peterson (p); Herb Ellis (g); Ray Brown (b); Alvin Stoller (d). Verve Ⓜ 823 120-2 (36 minutes). Recorded 1957.

This album, a classic latter-day Hawkins set, comes from a mammoth recording session in October 1957 which also produced the album **The Genius of Coleman Hawkins** (Verve 825 673-2). The difference between the two is that Webster is absent from **The Genius**. On the set under consideration Hawkins and Webster manage to keep competitiveness to a minimum, and the resultant music has a relaxed, quiet warmth which is wholly beneficial. The opening track, *Blues for Yolanda*, contains a blistering Hawkins solo which reaches a climax wherein the tenorist is literally shrieking high-note phrases on his horn. Webster, unperturbed, follows with a disarmingly relaxed, beautifully poised effort which nevertheless keeps the listener spellbound. For the rest of the record, both saxophonists produce gloriously sensuous ballad readings (Hawkins, aware of Ben's mastery in this area, is much less dismissive of melodic expression than he usually was by this stage of his career) and lightly swinging medium-tempo interpretations of standards such as *You'd Be So Nice to Come Home to* and *Shine on Harvest Moon*. The rhythm section extends a level of support all the more extraordinary for its discretion and complete absence of showiness.

The only carp I have here is that, with a playing time which barely stretches to CD capacity, and with a late-seventies vinyl reissue of this material setting a laudable precedent of including all the material from this pairing, there are two tracks left off here, one of them being the bewitchingly pretty *Maria*. Both tracks were originally assigned back in the fifties to **Coleman Hawkins and His Confrères**, but surely they could have been added to this set? They were the only tracks on that album with Webster present.   **KS**

**With Roy Eldridge at the Opera House**  Hawkins (ts); **Eldridge** (t); **John Lewis** (p); **Percy Heath** (b); **Connie Kay** (d). Verve Ⓜ 521 641-2 (74 minutes). Recorded 1957.

⑧ ❽

For many years these recordings posed a great puzzle. They were on two LPs, with some numbers in mono and others in stereo, and several were identical on both discs. In fact, two concerts were recorded, one in Los Angeles and one in Chicago, and they are both on this CD. Hawkins plays superbly, using that rather irascible mode of address that he adopted in the fifties. His long, heavily accented lines pursue the harmonies relentlessly through every conceivable permutation, and it is quite impossible to resist the power of his biting tone and unremitting swing. Eldridge, too, seems in a somewhat peppery mood. He resorts even more than usual to sudden stratospheric shrieks, the kind that had had such an effect on his young acolyte, Dizzy Gillespie, and hurls himself into solos with a recklessness which would bring instant disaster to a lesser artist. The blistering effect of these two is heightened by the suave self-possession of the rhythm section, which is actually three-quarters of the Modern Jazz Quartet. And that is where the great attraction lies; jazz played by artists of this age and calibre is a drama of character and personality as much as anything else. They reveal themselves through the music. A long additional track features others on the same concert bill – J.J. Johnson, Stan Getz, Lester Young, Oscar Peterson – but it is the interplay between Hawkins and Eldridge that really matters.   **DG**

**Hawk Eyes**  Hawkins (ts); **Charlie Shavers** (t); **Ray Bryant** (p); **Tiny Grimes** (g); **George Duvivier** (b); **Osie Johnson** (d). Prestige Ⓜ OJCD294-2 (46 minutes). Recorded 1959.

⑧ ❻

As Hawkins entered his last decade his tenor sound was angry, harsh and stripped of adornment. This coincidentally allowed him, in sound at least, to keep up with the contemporary hard-boppers. The exception here is in a softly wistful statement of *La Rosita*. However, the 14-minute blues *C'mon In* is a towering and menacing example of his craft at its best. Opening with teak-like tenor over double bass, the piece builds gradually until Shavers enters with a blood-vessel bursting solo which, for him, is pretty well stripped down to essentials. His second solo on the piece is an unexpectedly delicate and tasteful essay. Bryant was a couple of generations younger than Hawkins, but he was already a veteran of Jo Jones's trios; here he shows complete maturity in everything he does. *I Never Knew* is a previously unissued track which must have been excluded from the original for space reasons and not for any dip in quality, for it has a marvellously buoyant and driving solo from Hawk, plus robust but tasteful piano, while Shavers wrestles himself to the floor with a brazen solo which has a fleeting but effective touch of half-valving at its conclusion. You could never fall asleep to this album, but if somehow you managed such a feat, the remarkable honk with which Hawk starts his second tirade on *I Never Knew* would abruptly awaken you and your neighbours.   **SV**

**Supreme**  Hawkins (ts); **Barry Harris** (p); **Gene Taylor** (b); **Roy Brooks** (d). Enja Ⓕ ENJ-9009-2 (65 minutes). Recorded 1966.

⑧ ❻

Recorded live in Baltimore in 1966, at a time when his playing was reported to be erratic at best, **Supreme** catches Coleman Hawkins on a night that gloriously reaffirms his greatness. It's true that the gruffly muscular tone has taken on a querulous edge, that the bustling rhythmic assurance has been infiltrated by a degree of hesitancy, but in their place has come an economy of means that bespeaks a man still at the peak of creativity. Every pared-down, beautifully-weighted phrase has the rightness of a Zen painter's brush-stroke, the wisdom of 45 years' playing distilled into the *essence* of tenor mastery. What's more, Hawkins sounds like he's enjoying himself, his grizzled lyricism imparted with the playfulness of an old dog who knows there are no more tricks to learn. The set comprises mostly standards – *Lover Come Back to Me*, Monk's *In Walked Bud* – plus a lovely reading of Quincy Jones's ballad *Quintessence*; the pick-up rhythm trio, with Gene Taylor, Roy Brooks and Hawkins's then-regular pianist Barry Harris, provide sensitive support. Inevitably, there's a version of *Body and Soul*, through which Hawk ambles with a gruff inventiveness, the site of the warrior's most historic victory transformed once more. Despite the poor sound quality, **Supreme** is an apposite title.   **GL**

# Erskine Hawkins    1914-93

**And His Orchestra 1936-8**  Hawkins, **Wilbur 'Dud' Bascomb**, **Marcellus Green**, **Sammy Lowe** (t); **Edward Sims**, **Robert Range** (tb); **William Johnson** (as); **Jimmy Mitchelle** (as, v); **Paul Bascomb**, **Julian Dash** (ts); **Haywood Henry** (cl, bs); **Avery Parrish** (p); **William McLemore** (g); **Leemie Stanfield** (b); **James Morrison** (d); **Billy Daniels**, **Merle Turner** (v). Classics Ⓜ 653 (67 minutes).

⑥ ❼

At the age of 20, Hawkins went with the Alabama State College band to New York. Two years later he assumed the band's leadership and began recording almost immediately. He continued to lead a big band until the early fifties and, significantly, his last orchestra contained several of the sidemen who had started with the 'Bama State Collegians and who are featured extensively on this CD. As a band, it was not significant: Lowe was a useful arranger in the Sy Oliver manner and most of the remaining charts were by Parrish. They enjoyed considerable popularity with black audiences, but items such as *I'll Get Along Somehow* are almost mawkishly sentimental. The band were at their most comfortable with medium-tempo items like *Uproar Shout* or *Big John Special*. The outstanding soloists were the forthright Dud Bascomb, the fleet Dash and the gifted Parrish but, not surprisingly, most of the solo space fell to the leader. In his more restrained moments Hawkins played powerful, Louis Armstrong-inspired trumpet, but there were times, as on *Dear Old Southland*, where he became incontinently exhibitionistic. The final four titles, with a fuller ensemble, are the strongest and arguably represent the Hawkins orchestra at its peak. **BMcR**

## Vaughan Hawthorne-Nelson                    1968

**New review**

**Emergence** Hawthorne-Nelson (as); Nick Ramm, Salvatore Bonafede (p); Jeremy Brown, Bruno Destrez (b); Matt Skelton, Aldo Romano (d). TML Records Ⓕ TML001 (72 minutes). Recorded 1995-6.

⑥ ❽

Hawthorne-Nelson first came in front of the wider public in the mid eighties as Vaughan Hawthorne, when two albums made at that time presented him as part of the young English generation of modern players spearheaded by Courtney Pine. After finishing that decade by graduating from the Berklee College of Music he dropped from view for a while and studied Counselling Psychology instead. This led to a long-term professional commitment to teaching disturbed adolescents, and the music career was not resumed in any organized way until 1995. This and a companion album, **The Gift** (featuring Jean Toussaint), announce his return. His tone has more edge, his attack is more telling (a legacy perhaps of his time studying with Bobby Watson), and he finds more variety in his rhythmic and harmonic approach, though at times the Coltrane legacy is overwhelming (*A Tale of Tomorrow*). There are still intonation problems to be dealt with (many of the unison passages with piano leave him wanting in this area), but this album's energy and enthusiasm shows Hawthorne-Nelson to be on the right path for an altogether more significant musical career than last time around. **KS**

## Louis Hayes                    1937

**New review**

**The Super Quartet** Hayes (d); Javon Jackson (ts); Kirk Lightsey (p); Essiet Essiet (b). Timeless Ⓕ CDSJP424 (58 minutes). Recorded 1994.

❽ ❽

One of the finest small-band drummers in jazz, Louis Hayes provided the drive behind two leading hard-bop groups of the early sixties – the Horace Silver and Cannonball Adderley Quintets – and later played with the bands of Oscar Peterson and McCoy Tyner, as well as co-leading a group with Freddie Hubbard and Joe Henderson. Such a curriculum vitae speaks for itself. No one can get quite so many gradations of tone out of a top-cymbal as Louis Hayes, nor generate more propulsion by simply playing four even beats to a bar. He moves the Super Quartet along in fine style. Each of the eight numbers is packed with excellent playing, especially from Kirk Lightsey, whose long sojourns in Europe may have kept him from receiving due credit at home. Jackson is a forward and imaginative soloist, although with a tendency to play flat towards the top of his range, while Essiet follows the sensible Sam Jones practice of tucking in close beneath the drums and laying down a neat, unpretentious line. **DG**

## Tubby Hayes                    1935-73

**For Members Only** Hayes (ts, fl); Mick Pyne (p); Ron Matthewson (b); Tony Levin (d). Master Mix Ⓕ CDCHE 110 (71 minutes). Recorded 1967.

❽ ❽

Tubby Hayes possessed an awesome talent. The combination of a remarkably fast brain and a flawless technique manifested itself in a garrulous, pugnacious, completely unstoppable flow. These 12 numbers by his last quartet all come from BBC Radio Two live sessions and benefit from the presence of enthusiastic studio audiences. There is an added sparkle to everyone's playing, Tubby's in particular.

Of all the posthumous Tubby Hayes releases, this is probably the best. It reveals what a complete artist he was, both as a composer and a player. The slow ballad *Dedicated to Joy* is especially good, as is the characteristically bravura *Off the Wall*. This was the time when new and looser forms were being explored by jazz musicians, and towards the end of his life Tubby Hayes was cautiously expanding his horizons in this direction. Probably his most complete achievement in this area was the extended composition *Mexican Green*, which he originally recorded for Fontana. The version here is every bit as good as the one released on LP, if not better. **DG**

# Graham Haynes 1960

**The Griots' Footsteps** Haynes (c, kbds); **Steve Williamson** (ts, ss); **Cheick Tidiane-Seck, Don-Dieu Divin, Luis Manresa** (kbds); **Laroussi-Ali Djamel** (g); **Brigitte Menon** (sitar); **Lyra Menon** (tbra); **Vincent Othieno, Noel Ekwabi** (b); **Brice Wassy** (d, v); **Jorge Amorim, Daniel Moreno, Chief Udoh Essiet** (perc). Verve Ⓕ 523 262-2 (60 minutes). Recorded 1994.

⑥ ❻

Haynes is one of the more conceptually savvy jazz funksters, with an ear for fluid forms and plausible syntheses of different traditions. On this session, recorded in Paris with an aggressively international cast, his limber cornet soars over a near-cinematic montage of string-synth washes, de-natured blues, organ riffs, South Indian string drones, talking drum and ethnofunk beats. The players develop their complex rhythmic interaction by ear, which is why Haynes's music breathes more freely than the electric jazz of contemporaries like his one-time associate Steve Coleman. But Haynes is also a sound democrat: some background textures are thick and juicy, some banal synth clichés. It is a little closer to Jon Hassell than seventies Miles. Graham's fan Don Cherry pioneered this jazz-meets-the-Third-World stance, and Haynes echoes Cherry's declarative pentatonics and vulnerable, human tone. He also has a younger man's chops. This disc is far from perfect: it is way too long, and dead patches abound. That said, the cornettist crafts shapely phrases even when harmonic motion is nil – sometimes following the arabesques of sung Islamic prayers – and executes complex bent-note figures without self-congratulation. He is worth hearing even in an uneven setting. **KW**

# Roy Haynes 1926

New review

**Out of the Afternoon** Haynes (d); **Roland Kirk** (ts, manzello, strich, f); **Tommy Flanagan** (p); **Henry Grimes** (b). Impulse! Ⓜ IMP11802 (38 minutes). Recorded 1962.

⑥ ❻

Haynes had been a drummer at the top of his profession for a decade by the time this session was scheduled by the then-fledgling Impulse! label, so the idea of his having his own date (not many drummers got the chance in those days) was not so odd. What is odd is that it still sounds a very good record, largely because of the care Haynes showed in choosing his colleagues, especially the mercurial and explosive Kirk. Haynes displays the skills and panache which made him a favourite with Stan Getz, Steve Lacy, Eric Dolphy, John Coltrane and Charlie Parker during that era, combining the elegance and precision of Max Roach with some of the single-minded drive of Blakey. But that alone would not be enough to justify this album's reappearance; Kirk does that all by himself. No surprise there, I guess. This is hardly the multi-reedman's most inspired session, but he plays with feeling and expressive colour, toying with themes before good-naturedly pulling them to pieces (especially *Fly Me to the Moon*). The rest of the band keep their respectful distance and let him get on with it, Grimes and Flanagan playing with accustomed elegance. The recording quality is down on Van Gelder's usual standards, there being rather too much reverb and a few rather mad rushes of blood to the head where instruments suddenly zoom up and down in the mix. **KS**

# Kevin Hays 1968

New review

**Go Round** Hays (p, elp); **Steve Hall** (ts); **Seamus Blake** (ts, ss); **Doug Weiss** (b); **Billy Hart** (d, cga, perc). Blue Note Ⓕ CDP8 32491-2 (69 minutes). Recorded 1995.

⑦ ❽

When Blue Note launched its series of recordings by young musicians, Hays was an early choice. Even during his Connecticut-based school days he had taken energy from New York and, via jam sessions, had secreted himself into the City's jazz scene. Three albums with SteepleChase arrived in the early nineties to announce a prodigal talent and he subsequently worked with Benny Golson, Donald Harrison and Sonny Rollins. This CD presents him as pianist, leader and composer and, with the limited personnel numbers involved, as a useful arranger. As a pianist, he is circumspect without being withdrawn, his harmonic variety hints at Herbie Hancock and his clarity of line accommodates a loose-limbed rhythmic feel. The quality of his improvisation on the reflective *Early Evening* demonstrates an inquiring mind, an uncharacteristic freedom meets the pantonal challenge of *Sutra*, while his electric piano builds up a strong groove on the title track. Hart is never predictable in a flexible and imaginative rhythm section and both saxophonists make telling contributions. Hays recently took "listening to jazz recordings" out of his programme. Here the resulting introspection would seem to have made him a highly focused performer. **BMcR**

# Jimmy Heath

**New review**

**On the Trail** Heath (ts); **Wynton Kelly** (p); **Kenny Burrell** (g); **Paul Chambers** (b); **Albert 'Tootie' Heath** (d). Riverside Ⓜ OJCCD1854-2 (38 minutes). Recorded 1964.

⑧ ❽

Somehow, Jimmy Heath has missed out on the wider acclaim his talent as a saxophonist deserves. A Philadelphian contemporary of John Coltrane, he was part of the forties bebop scene with Howard McGhee and, later, Dizzy Gillespie. Since then he has become better known as Percy Heath's younger brother ('Tootie' being the youngest) and as the writer of tunes Miles Davis recorded over several years. One of these is *Gingerbread Boy* (spelled "box" on the insert), a blues theme vaguely similar to *Freedom Jazz Dance* (which it partnered on **Miles Smiles**) that soon hits a lively blues groove.

The rest mixes Heath's minor blues *Cloak and Dagger* and the medium-tempoed *Projects*, which he charges through somewhat in the manner of Dexter Gordon, with such standards as the title piece and a driving *All the Things You Are*. Heath's straight-ahead style, closer to Sonny Stitt than to Coltrane, with a rounded tone exuding a hint of fur-lined warmth, ticks over engagingly at the head of an excellent rhythm section, Burrell's effortless solos being the icing on the cake. **RA**

# Ted Heath

**New review**

**At Carnegie Hall and First American Tour** Heath leading **Bobby Pratt, Bert Ezzard, Duncan Campbell, Eddie Blair** (t); **Wally Smith, Don Lusher, Jimmy Coombes, Ric Kennedy** (tb); **Les Gilbert, Ronnie Chamberlain** (as); **Henry McKenzie** (cl, ts); **Red Price** (ts); **Ken Kiddier** (bs); **Frank Horrox** (p); **Johnny Hawksworth** (b); **Ronnie Verrell** (d). Limelight Ⓜ 820 950-2 (67 minutes). Recorded 1956.

⑧ ❼

Although the Americans thought that they didn't want it, the Heath band went to the United States in the first of the crazy and convoluted exchanges contrived by the AFM and the British MU. This was to forestall the hysterically held idea that American musicians visiting England would steal work from the British. In order to enable Stan Kenton to tour Britain it was necessary for a similar number of British musicians to tour the States. No better first group could have been chosen than this one, for because of it American audiences came to realize that European jazz could be as skilled as their own and, more importantly, that our musicians were not necessarily clones of their own.

It is fortunate that Decca went to the trouble of recording the Carnegie Hall concert, for it remains the best testimony to the musical virility of Heath's band and of some of its fine composers, notably Kenny Graham, a brilliant and inventive writer whose *King's Cross Climax* included here is taken from his "Australian Suite". Individual soloists play with worthy inventiveness and the sections are magnificent. Heath ran a tight ship and it paid off handsomely, although he did belong to the "once-the-solo's-on-a-popular-hit-record-don't-change-it" brigade.

Most of the band's commercial music is eschewed in favour of the jazz side, and ballad performances like *Memories of You* by trumpeters Pratt and Ezzard remain undated by the passing years. **SV**

# Mark Helias

**New review**

**Loopin' the Cool** Helias (b); **Ellery Eskelin** (ts); **Regina Carter** (vn); **Epizo Bangoura** (djembe, perc); **Tom Rainey** (d). Enja Ⓔ ENJ9049 2 (63 minutes). Recorded 1994.

⑧ ❽

The latest in a string of excellent Enja releases from one of the most cogent and powerful bassists in contemporary jazz, **Loopin' the Cool**, like its predecessors **Desert Blue** and **Attack the Future**, employs a band comprising some of the most original and innovative soloists around to intepret a rich variety of Helias compositions, some sparked by his previous associations with his colleagues in BassDrumBone, trombonist Ray Anderson and drummer Gerry Hemingway, and by former employers such as drummer Ed Blackwell. The front-line pairing of Carter and Eskelin, in particular, brings a pleasing textural originality to the sound mix, and the consistently musical contributions of Rainey (a drummer of the Paul Motian school, as alert to the tuning as to the rhythmic disposition of his drums), plus his excellent rapport with percussionist Bangoura, render the whole album taut and whip-smart, yet are relaxed enough where necessary to accommodate the almost playful extemporizations of the querulous Eskelin.

Both the tenor player, whose gruffly expressive tone is reminiscent of that of the vastly underrated Sydney-based saxophonist, Bernie McGann, and the graceful but gutsy Carter are clearly rising stars in the jazz firmament, but overall it is the intelligent, always vigorous compositions of Helias that mark this album out as definitive jazz for the nineties: polyglot, multi-referential, but hard-driving and even joyous. **CP**

# Gerry Hemingway

**New review**
**Perfect World** Hemingway (d, electronics); **Michael Moore** (as, cl, bcl); **Wolter Werbos** (tb); **Ernst Reijseger** (vc); **Mark Dresser** (b). Random Acoustics Ⓕ RA019 (61 minutes). Recorded 1995.

⑧ ❽

One of the most thoughtful, intelligent and inventive musicians working in the New Music field, Hemingway is not 'just' a percussionist. He's recorded solo drum recitals, sometimes including an electronic component of his own devising, worked in a long-standing, rumbunctious trio with trombonist Ray Anderson, and, most notably, was for many years an integral part of the Anthony Braxton Quartet. The long and fruitful association with Braxton no doubt furthered his interest in alternative modes of expression and construction and Hemingway's own quintet reflects these concerns in fresh, vital ways. In poker terms, the band is a handful of wild cards – Werbos is a particularly uninhibited trombonist; Reijseger a classically-trained cellist with a Dadaesque demeanour; Moore the reed-playing traditionalist; Dresser the solid anchor; and Hemingway the conjurer always with a new trick up his sleeve. Of the albums they've recorded to date for hatART and Random Acoustics, **Perfect World** is a good example of their stylistic range. *Sinsulu* was inspired by South African kwela rhythms, *N.T.* shows a rough-and-tumble aggressiveness, and *Village of the Virgins* is a really obscure piece of Ellingtonia. *Perfect World* and *Little Suite*, each 20-plus minutes, show the band at its most ambitious – multi-sectional works displaying various layers of instrumentation, multiple tempos, counterpoint, free jazz interaction, bop ensemble intricacy, and unaccompanied solo excursions. There are times when the thematic material and connecting tissue seem somewhat slight stretched to such lengths, until attention is diverted by a powerful solo episode. The band has its own unique identity – not often the case in these days of mix-and-match *ad hoc* groups – which is much more than the sum of its not inconsiderable parts. **AL**

# Julius Hemphill

**Big Band** Hemphill (ss, as); **David Hines, Rasul Saddik** (t); **Frank Lacy, David Taylor** (tb); **Vincent Chancey, John Clark** (frh); **Marty Ehrlich** (ss, as, f); **John Purcell, John Stubblefield** (ss, ts, f); **J.D. Parran** (bs, f); **Jack Wilkins, Bill Frisell** (g); **Jerome Harris** (elb); **Ronnie Burrage** (d); **Gordon Gottlieb** (perc); **K. Curtis Lyle** (narr). Elektra/Musician 960831-2 (61 minutes). Recorded 1988.

⑧ ❻

Through much of the early part of his recording career, Julius Hemphill favoured lean, uncluttered settings for his eloquent alto – frequently duos with like-minded cohorts such as Oliver Lake or Abdul Wadud, or piano-less trios or quartets with cello replacing bass. His moody, lavish compositions for the World Saxophone Quartet were an outgrowth of his early overdubbed solo works, programmatic 'audiodramas' like *Blue Boye* and *Roi Boye and the Gotham Minstrels*. Such extravagant gestures are carried over into his writing for big band, with unusual instrumentation put to unconventional use. Most accessible are the ballads; *For Billie* finds his piquant lead alto awash in muted brass and five flutes, while the winding melody of *Leora* must conjure with a minimal, static background reminiscent of Steve Reich. Cagey free-bop lines contrast with noirish episodes in *At Harmony* and *C/Saw* – the latter indebted in some structural way to Coltrane's *Bessie's Blues* (is there a hidden clue in the title?). But on the debit side are *Bordertown*, a visit to Hemphill's Texas roots via a strained soprano line, refracted harmonies, and a backbeat that threatens to go on forever, and *Drunk On God*, a lengthy pastiche of styles meant to illuminate a shamanistic poem. Altogether, an ambitious but flawed programme. **AL**

# Eddie Henderson

**New review**
**Inspiration** Henderson (t, flh); **Grover Washington, Jr** (ss); **Joe Locke** (vb); **Kevin Hays** (p); **Ed Howard** (b); **Lewis Nash** (d). Milestone Ⓕ MCD9240-2 (72 minutes). Recorded 1994.

⑧ ❼

After more than a decade of limited exposure, Eddie Henderson has gained renewed visibility in the nineties. His sideman work on CDs with leaders such as Kenny Barron, Billy Harper, Mulgrew Miller, Bill Stewart and McCoy Tyner has generated belated interest in his playing, which is out from under the Miles Davis shadow that blanketed much of Henderson's own personality during his years with Herbie Hancock's Mwandishi band. This album, the first of two by Henderson under his new Milestone contract, is intended as a tribute to his favourite musicians, and its willingness to go beyond trumpet players and incorporate music by Barron, Harper, Tyner, Bobby Hutcherson and Joe Henderson is one key to its appeal. Another is the cohesive rhythm section, with impressive young pianist Hays especially lucid and Locke's vibes adding unexpected colours. Henderson plays with channelled energy and loads of ideas, and appears to be making up for lost time; and Washington takes good guest turns on two of the ten tracks. While the follow-up album **Dark Shadows** (Milestone

MCD9254-2) also has its strengths, I prefer this one for the inclusion of such worthy compositions as *Jinriksha, Oliloqui Valley* and *Peresina*.                    **BB**

# Fletcher Henderson                    1897-1952

**A Study in Frustration**  Selective personnel including: **Fletcher Henderson, Horace Henderson** or **Fats Waller** (p); **Louis Armstrong, Rex Stewart, Henry 'Red' Allen, Roy Eldridge** (t); **Charlie Green, J.C. Higginbotham, Jimmy Harrison, Benny Morton** (tb); **Buster Bailey** (cl); **Don Redman, Benny Carter, Russell Procope, Hilton Jefferson** (as); **Coleman Hawkins, Ben Webster, Chu Berry** (ts); **John Kirby, Israel Crosby** (b); **Walter Johnson, Big Sid Catlett** (d). Columbia Ⓜ 57596 (three discs: 194 minutes). Recorded 1923-38.

⊘                                                                              ⑧ ❻

Henderson was an unlikely man to be the one who evolved and formalized the conventional line-up of the big band in jazz – trumpets, trombones, reeds and rhythm section. In his personal life and as a band leader Henderson was largely ineffectual, his brother was a much better pianist, and colleagues like Don Redman and Benny Carter were much better band leaders. In another place it could be argued that most of the credit which accrued to Henderson should have gone to Don Redman, who wrote magnificent arrangements for the band and undoubtedly provoked Henderson's compositional innovations.

Never mind that; it was all done under Henderson's name, and it was he who gave house room to Louis Armstrong, Coleman Hawkins, Roy Eldridge and Chu Berry at the burgeoning point of their careers. Henderson chose musicians well and wrote good arrangements for them to play. Even the earliest of these 64 tracks, done before there were any major soloists, holds much of interest. Armstrong electrified the band when he joined in 1924 and, on the nine tracks on which he is featured, shows by his tone, ideas and abilities to swing that he was light years ahead of the rest of the band, which sounds leaden by contrast. Later Coleman Hawkins matured within the band and created the first chapter in the history of the tenor saxophone. His 1933 *Queer Notions*, featuring himself and trumpeter 'Red' Allen, (the only two musicians in the band who could really understand the composition) was a decade ahead of its time and the first example of avant-garde jazz. In the later bands the emergent Roy Eldridge and Chu Berry treat the music like a great playground for their solos. It is amazing to find such a body of well-written music with such a consistently high level of soloists.

Henderson eventually abandoned his own orchestra and took his arrangements to Benny Goodman, who added another dimension to them and made all the money.            **SV**

**Tidal Wave**  Henderson, **Horace Henderson** (p, arr); **Russell Smith, Bobby Stark, Rex Stewart, Irving Randolph, Henry 'Red' Allen** (t); **Claude Jones, Benny Morton, Keg Johnson** (tb); **Buster Bailey** (cl); **Russell Procope, Harvey Boone, Edgar Sampson, Hilton Jefferson, Benny Carter** (cl, as); **Coleman Hawkins, Ben Webster** (cl, ts); **Clarence Holiday, Lawrence Lucie** (g); **John Kirby, Elmer James** (b, tba); **Walter Johnson** (d). MCA/Decca Ⓜ GRD-643 (61 minutes). Recorded 1931-4.

                                                                               ⑧ ❽

With a decent press agent, Fletcher Henderson might have been annointed 'King of Swing'. Indeed, by the mid twenties, Henderson was leading the archetype for all swing groups at New York's fabled Roseland Ballroom. Though starting out and functioning primarily as a dance band, Henderson's ensemble got an important jazz boost with the addition of Louis Armstrong in 1924-5. Also pivotal was arranger Don Redman, whose charts bubbled with riffs and call-and-response exchanges that would become hallmarks of the thirties big-band sound. When Redman left in 1927, Henderson took over the principal arranging chores, developing a lean yet supple approach that swung with power and panache.

In this sparkling compilation of 21 tracks from the band's 1931-4 tenure with Decca, we catch a well-drilled ensemble, a stable of outstanding soloists and a batch of Henderson charts like *Sugar Foot Stomp* that still make your feet want to dance. Among the soloists, Coleman Hawkins, then establishing the tenor sax as a front-line solo 'voice', was central to the band's success. Trumpeters Red Allen and Rex Stewart and a young Benny Carter on alto sax also shine. Ironically, the title track was written and arranged by Russ Morgan. Though a clever novelty number demonstrating the reeds' digital dexterity, it throws into relief (as do the charts of brother Horace and Carter) Henderson's sleek, power-packed take on tunes such as *Wrapping' It Up* and *Shanghai Shuffle*. Indeed, Henderson classics like *Down South Camp Meetin'* (heard here in its original 1934 incarnation) would soon help America's popular music swing and Benny Goodman its 'King'.            **CB**

# Horace Henderson                    1904

**Horace Henderson and His Orchestra, 1940**  Henderson (p); **Emmett Berry, Harry 'Pee Wee' Jackson, Gail Brockman, Nat Bates** (t); **Harold Johnson** (t, v); **Ray Nance** (t, vn); **Edward Fant, Nat Atkins, Joe McLewis, Leo Williams, Archie Brown** (tb); **Dalbert Bright** (as, cl); **Willie Randall,**

Howard Johnson, C.Q. Price (as); Elmer Williams (ts); Dave Young (ts); Mosey Gant (ts); Bob Dorsey, Lee Pope (ts); Leonard Talley (bs); Hurley Ramey, Leroy Harris (g); Jessie Simpkins, Israel Crosby (b); Oliver Coleman, Debo Mills (d); Viola Jefferson (v). Classics Ⓜ 648 (69 minutes). Recorded 1940/41.

Ⓖ **❻**

Horace Henderson, brother of Fletcher, led big bands for more than 40 years. He was a useful pianist, an accomplished arranger and over the years he provided charts for Benny Goodman, Don Redman, The Casa Loma Orchestra, Rommy Forsey and Earl Hines as well as for his better-known brother. This CD offers the only sides made by Horace Henderson's working band, a band that he had recently 'inherited' from Nat Towles. His arrangements were in some ways more subtle than Fletcher's; *Do-Re-Mi* and *I Still Have My Dreams* give an idea of the contrasts in his style; the former a texturally aware fun number and the latter a reserved version of the inter-section call and response system. His soloists were impressive, with Nance's violin particularly strong on *Kitty on Toast*, Young's tenor flying the Coleman Hawkins colours on *Shufflin' Joe* and Berry conspicuous throughout, especially on the declamatory *Turkey Special*. Henderson's own piano also displays understated finesse, perhaps rather obviously striding on *Flying a Whing-Ding* but elsewhere taking the more judicious Teddy Wilson route. Crosby's Blantonian bass and some of the trombone parts remind one of the great forties Ellington Band; for a short time this Henderson Orchestra, with its close attention to collective dynamics, could be discussed in the same breath. Four Fletcher Henderson titles from 1941 complete the programme. **BMcR**

# Joe Henderson

1937

**The Blue Note Years** with a collective personnel of: **Henderson** (ts); **Hubert Laws** (f); **Leo Wright, Eric Dolphy, James Spaulding, Jerry Dodgion, Jerome Richardson, Steve Wilson** (as); **Jerome Richardson, Eddie Daniels** (ts); **Pepper Adams** (bs); **Kenny Dorham, Blue Mitchell, Lee Morgan, Carmell Jones, Donald Byrd, Freddie Hubbard, Woody Shaw, Snooky Young, Al Porcino, Denny Moore, Marvin Stamm** (t); **Johnny Coles** (flh); **Curtis Fuller, Garnett Brown, Tony Studd, Benny Powell, Jimmy Knepper, Bob Burgess, Julian Priester** (tb); **Grant Green, Eddie Wright** (g); **Bobby Hutcherson** (vb); **Herbie Hancock, McCoy Tyner, Andrew Hill, Duke Pearson, Barry Harris, Tommy Flanagan, Horace Silver, Steve Kuhn, Cedar Walton, Roland Hanna, Renee Rosnes** (p); **Freddie Roach, Larry Young** (org); **Butch Warren, Gene Taylor, Eddie Khan, Bob Cranshaw, Richard Davis, Teddy Smith, Steve Swallow, Ron Carter, Herbie Lewis, Buster Williams, Ira Coleman** (b); **Tony Williams, Pete LaRoca, Roy Brooks, Al Harewood, Roy Haynes, Billy Higgins, Clarence Johnston, Albert 'Tootie' Heath, Elvin Jones, Roger Humphries, Mickey Roker, Joe Chambers, Mel Lewis, Al Foster, Billy Drummond** (d). Blue Note Ⓜ CDP7 89287-2 (four discs: 278 minutes). Recorded 1963-90.

Ⓝ **❽**

Since hitting the scene in 1962 with Brother Jack McDuff, Henderson has built a body of work placing him at the post-war tenor sax summit with such titans as Sonny Rollins, John Coltrane and Stan Getz. Henderson's singular style, while drawing on Rollins's rhythmic serendipity, Coltrane's sheets-of-sound and Getz's ethereal lyricism, also calls on rhythm 'n' soul and the 'harmolodic' free-falls of Ornette Coleman. However, it's the saxophonist's pliant sound – at once bluesy and hip, as well as lush and cool – that makes Henderson immediately identifiable. In this four-hour, four-disc boxed anthology culled from Henderson's initial dates for Blue Note in 1963 to a 1990 session with pianist Renee Rosnes, Henderson emerges as a consistently engaged and innovative player able to respond with apt élan whatever the setting or style. Henderson's Blue Note oeuvre encompasses seven albums as a leader and 30 albums as a sideman. Here, 26 of the 36 tracks consist of dates led by Kenny Dorham, Blue Mitchell, Grant Green, Andrew Hill, Lee Morgan, Freddie Roach, Horace Silver, Duke Pearson, Pete LaRoca, Larry Young, Bobby Hutcherson, McCoy Tyner, Herbie Hancock and the Thad Jones-Mel Lewis Orchestra, all from the sixties. The package is thus as much a retrospective of Blue Note's glory years as of Henderson. Among the gems are Henderson-penned standards *Blue Bossa* and *Recorda Me* from **Page One** (1963), the saxophonist's Blue Note début as a leader, and a rousing *Isotope* from **The State of the Tenor, Volume 1** (1985). Definitive. **CB**

**The Milestone Years** Henderson (ts); with various groups comprising: **Mike Lawrence, Woody Shaw, Oscar Brashear** (t); **Nat Adderley** (c); **Grachan Moncur III, Julian Priester, Curtis Fuller** (tb); **Jeremy Steig, Ernie Watts** (f); **Hadley Caliman** (f, ts); **Lee Konitz** (as); **Kenny Barron, Don Friedman, Joe Zawinul, Mark Levine, Joachim Kühn** (p); **Herbie Hancock, George Cables, Hideo Ichikawa, George Duke** (p, elp); **Alice Coltrane** (p, hp); **Patrick Gleeson** (syn); **Michael White** (vn); **George Wadenius, James Blood Ulmer, Lee Ritenour** (g); **Ron Carter, Victor Gaskin, Stanley Clarke, Kunimitsu Inaba, Dave Holland, Charlie Haden, J.F. Jenny-Clark, David Friesen** (b); **Ron Carter, Alfonso Johnson** (elb); **Louis Hayes, Jack DeJohnette, Roy McCurdy, Lenny White, Motohiko Hino, Leon Chancler, Daniel Humair, Harvey Mason** (d); **Airto Moreira, Carmelo Garcia, Bill Summers** (perc); **Flora Purim** (v). Milestone Ⓔ 8MCD-4413-2 (eight CDs: 587 minutes). Recorded 1967-76.

Ⓖ **❽**

Henderson's improvisatory style has changed little since his introduction to the recording studio by Kenny Dorham in 1963 (see above). On this collection, made for the Milestone label over the best part of a decade, he reveals a wide interest in a multiplicity of settings for his music and his playing, but his identity remains static. This in part explains why his years at Milestone were for the most part financially unrewarding – popular music, with jazz following in its wake, went through cataclysmic changes, and many musicians changed with it to stay afloat – and why, ultimately, his stylistic intransigence has lately paid off in a big way. By then, he had certainly paid his dues, as the simple fact of him being a sideman for most of the years contained within this box points out.

Henderson excels in both the hard-bop milieu he responded so positively to while in the Horace Silver band, and in the relative freedom which modality can bring to a player. His playing on compositions recorded previously for both Blue Note and Silver, such as *Mamacita*, *The Kicker* and *Mo' Joe*, has a warmth and relaxation which can sometimes on more straightforward sessions be replaced by diffidence and a reliance on personal cadences. This is most clearly evident in his work on the Lighthouse Cafe gig with his working band from 1970, where the general fire and excitement to be found around him does not seem to translate to the leader; perhaps leadership and solo duties did not sit easily with him. Either way, his next live date for the label, with a pick-up rhythm section in Japan in the summer of 1971, produced arguably his best playing for Milestone, and his best since the remarkable **Inner Urge** on Blue Note from 1964.

Later Milestone studio efforts switch sometimes uneasily between electric and acoustic stools, seemingly attempting to follow the paths opened up by Miles Davis, Herbie Hancock and Tony Williams. Henderson plays with undiminished vigour, and his choice of musicians is ever perspicacious, but it is at times hard to escape a period-piece feeling to the musical forms and patterns being investigated. The ballad *Black is the Colour* elicits warm, tender sax playing from Henderson, but the arrangement sounds second-hand, all swirls and sound-cushions *à la* Miles, 1969-1970. The October 1973 effort, **Canyon Lady**, finds a variation to this sequence, placing as it does Henderson in front of a set of fine Latin-based big and mid-sized band arrangements, and the saxophonist responds with great sensitivity. A similarly oblique departure took place in the same month, when Henderson joined up with Alice Coltrane and Michael White for **The Elements**, a record anticipating world music by more than a decade. Another live date – recorded in Paris and released as one side of **Black Narcissus**, with weird electronic additions by Patrick Gleeson and a studio session marrying fusion beats with acoustic band arrangements completes Henderson's Milestone years, and the sense of momentum which began the package has largely evaporated.

This fascinating collection gives a general clue to what happened to the majority of jazz musicians between 1967 and 1976, especially when you consider the anodyne version of *My Cherie Amour* to be found on **Black Miracle**, the tenorist's last album for the label. Henderson always plays well, always stays true to his own music, but the latter half of his career here is the musical equivalent of trying on endless new suits in an attempt to get an image the wearer is happy with. Perhaps the first one was the best after all. **KS**

---

**So Near, So Far (Musings for Miles)** Henderson (ts); **John Scofield** (g); **Dave Holland** (b); **Al Foster** (d). Verve Ⓕ 571 674-2 (73 minutes). Recorded 1992.

⑥ ❽

In this Miles tribute, Henderson and his producers have concentrated on less well-worn if not completely overlooked Miles tunes. Thus, in place of *So What*, *All Blues*, *Blue and Green*, *Nardis* and the like, such infrequent visitors to the repertoire as *Miles Ahead*, *Flamenco Sketches*, *Teo*, *Side Car*, *Circle* and *So Near, So Far* get rare and (given the pre-funk Milesian inspiration) generally rarefied inspections. In an album which seems mellow even at quick tempos, the treatment of the orchestral piece *Miles Ahead* is intriguing, the suave sonorities of the big group transferring quite convincingly to the smaller ensemble. As far as performance is concerned, Scofield is consistent if routine, and Holland is a particularly melodic and appealing soloist. Henderson, a widely influential and recently much-fêted stylistic cousin to Coltrane, is at his best on the outstanding *Swing Spring*, still plying the signature licks that he perfected on Blue Note in the sixties, although playing perhaps with less timbral variety and bite than in those days. This album garnered generally ecstatic reviews on release, but despite the unusual material, the dust is likely to settle on a thoroughgoing if unexceptional sixties-style session. **MG**

---

New review

**Joe Henderson Big Band** with a collective personnel including: **Henderson** (ts); **Lew Soloff, Marcus Belgrave, Virgil Jones, Freddie Hubbard, Idrees Sulieman, Jimmy Owens, Jon Faddis, Nicholas Payton, Byron Stripling** (t); **Robin Eubanks, Kfane Zawadi, Jimmy Knepper, Douglas Purviance, Conrad Herwig, Keith O'Quinn, Larry Farrell, Dave Taylor** (tb); **Bob Porcelli, Pete Yellin, Craig Handy, Joe Temperley, Dick Oatts, Steve Wilson, Tim Ries, Garry Smulyan** (reeds); **Ronnie Matthews, Chick Corea** (p); **Christian McBride** (b); **Louis Nash** (d); **Bob Belden** (cond). Verve Ⓕ 533 451-2 (60 minutes). Recorded 1992-6.

⑧ ❽

This album, taken with **Sonny Rollins and the Big Brass** and John Coltrane's **Africa Brass**, completes a most appropriate triptych. While Henderson hasn't yet achieved the major status as a jazz influence that the other two are, he is linked with each of them and responds with similar relish to the foil provided by the big band. He has a looser approach and tends to ride with the band rather than declaim against it as the others did. The result, as in *Without a Song*, is both powerful and pleasing. Despite the two-year gap between the recording of three tracks and then of the other six, the tenor soloing is remarkably consistent and charismatic. Henderson has a self-editing eloquence which is in contrast to the more-than-a-minute introduction written by Slide Hampton to his piece *Inner Urge*. This seems unconnected to the piece itself and has all the pretence of some of the worst pseudo-classical Kenton. However, most of the arranging is done by Henderson and Bob Belden and is outstanding. Corea, McBride and Louis Nash light up the sessions they're on. Hubbard plays a Gillespie-like solo of unusual restraint on *A Shade of Jade* from 1992 with a couple of clinkers perhaps auguring the decline that was to come. Nicholas Payton, so-called modern, plays poised mainstream trumpet which would not have disgraced Joe Newman.  **SV**

## Rosa Henderson

1896-1968

New review

**Complete Recorded Works, Volume 2** Henderson (v); **Rex Stewart** (t); **Harry Smith, Elmer Chambers, Howard Scott** (c); **Teddy Chambers** (tb); **Don Redman** (cl, as); **Coleman Hawkins** (ts); **Bob Fuller** (cl); **Fletcher Henderson, Porter Grainger, Edgar Dowell, Cliff Jackson** (p); **Charlie Dixon** (bj); **Lincoln M. Conaway** (g); **Ralph Escudero** (bb); **Kaiser Marshall** (d). Document Ⓜ DOCD5402 (70 minutes). Recorded 1924.

⑥ ❼

Born Rosa Deschamps, Henderson began touring the vaudeville circuit before the age of 20. She formed a duo and later married partner Slim Henderson. Under her own name and various other pseudonyms she enjoyed a recording career that spanned from 1923 to 1931. During that time, she worked in many prestigious New York reviews and played in the 1928 *Show Boat* in London.

As this CD shows, she was a strong singer, stylistically located in that indefinable hinterland between jazz and blues. Titles such as *Papa Will Be Gone* and *Clearing House Blues* illustrate the strength of her singing, while her jazz-shaped phraseology is more evident on *How Come You Do Me, My Right Man* and *Do That Thing*. Her diction was far more precise than many of her earthier contemporaries but she delivered her lyrics with power and conviction. Her reputation ensured quality support and there are many outstanding accompanists here. Fletcher Henderson (no relation) provides his full nine-piece Club Alabam Orchestra with Redman's alto and Hawkins's tenor on *Do That Thing*. His Jazz Five features Chambers's assured and driving lead as well as Nixon's adapted tailgate trombone, while his star cornettist Smith presents his understated credentials on two titles. Her five tracks with just the pianist are models of integration, perhaps more than all the others confirming the degree of jazz input to be found in Rosa's music as she made her contribution to vaudeville blues lore.  **BMcR**

## Scott Henderson

**Spears** Henderson (g); **Pat Coil** (kbds); **Brad Dutz** (mallets, perc); **Gary Willis** (elb); **Steve Houghton** (d). Relativity Ⓟ 88561-1030-2 (44 minutes). Recorded 1988.

⑥ ❽

Led Zeppelin was one of Henderson's earliest and strongest musical influences, and the rock-blues sonorities of that group have informed both his playing and writing, especially on Tribal Tech's last three albums, **Nomad, Tribal Tech** and **Illicit**. This record comes from an earlier period, when Henderson's jazz influences were more prominent. Although he relishes the power and immediacy of rock, it is clear from his playing in this group, or with Chick Corea's Elektric Band or The Zawinul Syndicate, that he has a firm grasp of bebop and the Coltrane idiom. Thanks – or no thanks – to record company advice, his music acquired a dense, homogeneous texture on the later albums. **Spears**, by contrast, is lightly woven, with plenty of dynamic shading, a broad instrumental palette, airy compositions and sharply focused solos. Weather Report, Jaco Pastorius's Word Of Mouth band and Chick Corea's jazz-rock are discernible in the writing, and Gary Willis has almost certainly studied Pastorius's bass guitar style. Henderson's tone and melodic concept often suggest a loose, bluesy reading of Allan Holdsworth. The opening track, *Caribbean*, is a particularly effective example of both his writing and soloing.  **MG**

## Jon Hendricks

1921

**Freddie Freeloader** Hendricks, Judith Hendricks, Aria Hendricks, Kevin Fitzgerald Burke, Al Jarreau, George Benson, Bobby McFerrin, The Manhattan Transfer (v); **Randy Sandke, Wynton Marsalis, Lew Soloff** (t); **Britt Woodman, Al Grey** (tb); **Jerome Richardson** (as); **Frank Foster, Stanley Turrentine** (ts); **Joe Temperley** (as, ts, bs); **Andy Stein, Al Rogers** (vn); **Barry Finclair** (va); **Larry Goldings, Tommy Flanagan** (p); **Romero Lumbambo** (g); **Andy McCloud, George Mraz, Tyler Mitchell, Rufus Reid** (b); **Clifford Barbaro, Jimmy Cobb, Duffy Jackson** (d); **Ron McBee** (perc); **Margaret Ross** (hp); **Count Basie Orchestra**. Denon Ⓟ 81757 6302-2 (59 minutes). Recorded 1989-90.

⑧ ❽

Too many of Hendricks's projects, with and without Lambert and Ross, have been undermined by questionable intonation and the sameness of albums dominated by vocalese. This project had the budget to bring in talented guest singers and strong instrumental soloists, ensuring stronger vocals and welcome variety from track to track. Hendricks also chose his material well – *Jumpin' at the Woodside* and two originals with the Basie band; the title track with McFerrin, Jarreau and a very agile Benson taking one solo apiece; Stanley Turrentine's *Sugar* with the composer and Wynton Marsalis blowing; a pair of Monk tunes with support from Tommy Flanagan's trio; and a pair of Armstrong classics for his own family-based vocal group. Everyone had a lot of fun, as well as the necessary studio time to keep vocal clams to a minimum. Brian Lee, who did much of the original engineering, also did an unobtrusive job of mixing the various parts, which were often recorded separately.

Hendricks still has the knack for setting lyrics to instrumental solos; additionally in this case, one can listen without wincing through stretches of faulty execution. Hendricks's latest, **Boppin' at the Blue Note** (Telarc 1996), is a live album with many of the faults endemic to live albums. **BB**

## Michele Hendricks

**Me and My Shadow**  Hendricks (v); **James Williams, David Leonhardt** (p); **Ray Drummond** (b); **Marvin 'Smitty' Smith** (d). Muse Ⓕ MCD5404 (59 minutes). Recorded 1990.

④ ❽

Hendricks's third album, like its predecessors, finds her contrasting scat singing with ballads. She has inherited her father's (Jon Hendricks) agility and accuracy of voice and this enables her to use scat without the embarrassment which often accompanies the forays into the genre by so many others (perhaps Armstrong was the only one secure in the style). Ballads are Miss Hendricks's forte. *But Beautiful*, treated conventionally, is a beautiful reading and *Misty*, treated at twice its normal tempo, comes off with great success. The rolling ostinato with which James Williams opens *Summertime* confirms that this is to be a collection of most individual interpretations. The singer is fortunate in having the backing of such a skilled regular group and she can relax into it as a member of it, rather than as a cabaret singer with accompaniment. **SV**

## Ernie Henry                                                               1926-57

**Seven Standards and a Blues**  Henry (as); **Wynton Kelly** (p); **Wilbur Ware** (b); **Philly Joe Jones** (d). Riverside Ⓜ OJC1722-2 (40 minutes). Recorded 1957.

⑦ ❽

Ernie Henry is a footnote in the jazz history books. From 1947 to the mid fifties he was a sideman with the likes of Tadd Dameron, Max Roach, Illinois Jacquet and Dizzy Gillespie, until his career peaked with his recorded solos on Monk's *Ba-Lue Bolivar Ba-lues-are* and *Brilliant Corners*. A year (and less than a handful of recordings) later, he was dead at 31. As he was still developing as a musician, we can only speculate on what would have been his mature voice, but what can be heard, if only momentarily, on recordings like this is inviting. Like John Jenkins and Jackie McLean, Henry was discovering personal alternatives of tone and phrasing to the overwhelming influence of Bird. He flashes the requisite bop chops on *I Get a Kick out of You* and *Lover Man* (the occasional intonation problems add charm), but seems more comfortable with the sentiments of *Soon* and *Like Someone in Love*, staying close to the melody and singing through his horn. The respectful way he plays *Sweet Lorraine* without trying to modernize his phrasing is reminiscent of Benny Carter, and his most winsome passages occur as he stretches out on the blues, *Specific Gravity*. The reliable rhythm section keeps everything on an even keel and, thanks to the succinctness of Henry's solos, there are plenty of opportunities to enjoy Ware's warm and pithy playing. **AL**

## Woody Herman                                                             1913-87

**Blues on Parade**  Herman (cl, as, v); with the following collective personnel: **Clarence Willard, Kermit Simmons, Steady Nelson, Mac MacQuordale, Bob Price, Cappy Lewis, John Owens, Ray Linn, George Seaburg, Billie Rogers, Charlie Peterson** (t); **Joe Bishop** (flh); **Neal Reid, Toby Tyler, Bud Smith, Vic Hamman, Jerry Rosa, Tommy Farr, Walter Nimms** (tb); **Murray Williams, Don Watt, Joe Estrin, Ray Hopfner, Joe Denton, Herb Tompkins, Eddie Scalzi, Jimmy Horvath, Sam Rubinowich** (as); **Saxie Mansfield, Bruce Wilkins, Pete Johns, Ronnie Perry, Nick Caiazza, Sammy Armato, Mickey Folus, Herbie Haymer, Pete Mondello** (ts); **Skippy De Sair** (bs); **Nick Hupfer** (vn); **Horace Diaz, Tommy Linehan** (p); **Chick Reeves, Hy White** (g); **Walter Yoder** (b); **Frank Carlson** (d). MCA/Decca Ⓜ GRD-606 (60 minutes). Recorded 1937-42.

⑧ ❻

Herman's first band was a co-operative unit formed out of the Isham Jones orchestra. This 20-track CD documents the growth of "The Band That Plays The Blues" in near-chronology and contains two previously unissued tracks (although some doubt exists over whether or not this particular take of *Farewell Blues* was included on an old Coral LP). From those earlier beginnings, when Woody was playing (and sometimes singing) such pieces as Morton's *Doctor Jazz*, to the final track, a 1942 Dizzy Gillespie composition and arrangement titled *Down Under,* is a fascinating evolutionary study. The band got stronger and more exciting (try *Woodsheddin' with Woody*, for example) and much of the library came from within the Herman ranks, particularly from the busy pen of flügelhorn player Joe Bishop.

The CD contains a number of Woody's winners, commencing with the original 1939 version of *Woodchoppers' Ball* and, of course, the famous *Blue Flame*. There are two titles by the Woodchoppers (including *River Bed Blues*) and two more by the Four Chips which allow us to hear the leader's attractive, Jimmy Noone-like clarinet to advantage. A number of CDs exist comprising Herman selections from the American Decca archive, but this one is probably the best and certainly the most comprehensive.                                                                          **AM**

---

**Best of the Big Bands** Herman (cl, as, v); with **The First Herd** (Sonny Berman, Chuck
  Frankhauser, Ray Wetzel, Pete Candoli, Conte Candoli, Shorty Rogers, Carl Warwick,
  Conrad Gozzo, t; Bill Harris, Ralph Pfeffner, Ed Kiefer, tb; Sam Marowitz, John LaPorta, cl,
  as; Pete Mondello, Flip Phillips, ts; Skippy DeSair, bs; Ralph Burns, p, arr; Jimmy Rowles, p;
  Marjorie Hyams, vb; Billy Bauer, g; Chubby Jackson, b; Dave Tough, Don Lamond, d); **The
  Second Herd** (Shorty Rogers, Ernie Royal, Bernie Glow, Stan Fishelson, Marky Markowitz, t;
  Earl Swope, Ollie Wilson, Bob Swift, tb; Sam Marowitz, as; Herbie Steward, as, ts; Stan Getz,
  Zoot Sims, ts; Serge Chaloff, bs; Fred Otis, p; Gene Sargent, g; Walter Yoder, b; Don
  Lamond, d; Ralph Burns, arr). Columbia Ⓜ 466 621-2 (52 minutes).
  Recorded 1944-7.

⑤ ❻

Of all the great big-band recordings, Woody Herman's First and Second Herd classics for Columbia have consistently been some of the most ill-treated and sloppily presented on CD. This disc is the only current release covering the crucial mid-to-late-forties period of studio recordings (a better one, though still far from perfect, has recently been deleted by the British Charly label), and although the playing time is acceptable, the choice of material is scandalously idiosyncratic. A simple illustration will suffice: on this disc we are presented with a jokey re-arrangement of Khachaturian's *Sabre Dance* from his "Gayaneh" Ballet. It's close to embarrassing. This is chosen (along with other oddities) in preference to *The Good Earth, Bijou, Your Father's Moustache, Wild Root, Steps, Igor, Fan It, Sidewalks of Cuba, Lady McGowan's Dream* (either part), *Panacea, Woodchopper's Ball, Back Talk, Four Brothers* or any section of *Summer Sequence*. None of the above sides are currently on CD.

What *is* here includes *Apple Honey, Caldonia, Blowin' Up a Storm, Goosey Gander, Happiness Is A Thing Called Joe, Everywhere* and *Northwest Passage*. Considering the unusually good sound on the original 78rpm recordings, the remastering is, at best, adequate, while the complete lack of recording dates or personnel is shoddy in the extreme. Until the excellent old vinyl boxed set, **The Thundering Herds** (or a decent approximation of such) makes its début on CD, this miserable eking-out of some of big-band jazz's most prized treasures will have to suffice.                                        **KS**

---

**Keeper of the Flame** Herman (cl, as, v); **Ernie Royal, Bernie Glow, Stan Fishelson, Red Rodney,**
  **Shorty Rogers** (t); **Earl Swope, Bill Harris, Ollie Wilson, Bob Swift** (tb); **Sam Marowitz** (as); **Al
  Cohn, Zoot Sims, Stan Getz, Gene Ammons, Buddy Savitt, Jimmy Giuffre** (ts); **Serge Chaloff** (bs);
  **Terry Gibbs** (vb); **Lou Levy** (p); **Chubby Jackson, Oscar Pettiford, Joe Mondragon** (b); **Don
  Lamond, Shelley Manne** (d); **Mary Ann McCall** (v). Capitol Ⓜ CDP7 98453-2 (58 minutes).
  Recorded 1948-9.

✔                                                                              ⑩ ❽

Woody Herman formed his Second Herd, featuring the celebrated three-tenors saxophone section, in 1947. It recorded its first sides for Columbia in great haste in December of that year, in order to beat a recording strike due to begin on January 1st, 1948. The strike dragged on for most of the year, and it was not until December 1948 that the band could record again, this time for Capitol. This disc contains its complete Capitol recordings.

So much for history. The one undeniable classic here is *Early Autumn*, composed by Ralph Burns as a kind of afterthought to his suite *Summer Sequence* and featuring the tenor saxophone of the 21-year-old Stan Getz. The effect of this one piece is difficult to overestimate, not only on Getz, or even on the tenor saxophone style, but on the direction taken by modern jazz during the fifties. Together with the Miles Davis band of the same period (also recorded by Capitol), it defined the ideals of restraint and purity of tone which were summed up in the term 'cool'. Alongside this, and complementary to it, was the influence of bebop. There was a brief popular craze for bebop at the time, which found its expression mainly through the medium of fashion accessories like berets and dark glasses and a few musical trade marks, such as Gillespie-type scat vocals. Probably the best of all these pop-bop records was Herman's recording of George Wallington's *Lemon Drop*, an exhilarating, headlong affair featuring brief but crackling solos by Chaloff, Swope, Rodney, Gibbs and Herman. This disc is important both for its musical excellence and its historical significance.                                                                      **DG**

**New review**

**Jazz Masters No. 54** Herman (cl, as, v); **Bill Chase, Paul Fontaine, Dave Gale, Ziggy Harrell, Gerry Lamy, Billy Hunt, Danny Nolan, Larry Ford, Dusko Goykovich** (t); **Jack Gale, Eddie Morgan, Phil Wilson, Bob Rudolph, Henry Southall, Kenny Wenzel, Bob Stroup** (tb); **Gordon Brisker, Larry Cavelli, Sal Nistico, Bobby Jones, Bill Perkins, Carmen Leggio, Jack Stevens, Gary Klein, Andy McGhee, Raoul Ramero** (ts); **Gene Allen, Frank Hittner, Nick Brignola, Tom Anastas** (bs); **Nat Pierce** (p); **Chuck Andrus** (b); **Jake Hanna** (d). Verve Ⓜ 529 903-2 (69 minutes). Recorded 1962-4.

⑨ ❾

Generally considered to have been the best edition of the Herd led by Herman after the Four Brothers band, the Swinging Herd of 1962-4 grew out of one of Woody's periodic engagements at New York's Metropole and refused to go away. It was built on the formidable rhythm section of Pierce, Andrus and Hanna, the latter two producing for the sixties as dynamic a pairing as Chubby Jackson and Don Lamond had achieved in the forties. Andrus's ability to produce a glowing big sound at breakneck tempos gave the rhythm great depth, especially on a piece like *Caldonia*, hi-jacked at twice its earlier speed to become a vehicle for the flawless tenor of Nistico, who leaves even Woody's vocal floundering in his wake. With Bill Chase pushing the boundaries of the brass section upward and outward, and some impressive soloing from him and trombonist Wilson, the band was strong in every section. As ever it played Woody's characteristic mix of old and new, with Ellington swing standards jostling with archaic tunes like *Jazz Me Blues* or up-to-the-minute standards like Mingus's *Better Get It In Your Soul*, but all of them infused with such powerful energy and enthusiasm that the whole repertoire took on a consistency of feel. Despite the Verve tag, this is actually a cross-section of Woody's Philips recordings from the period, among which the bright recording quality is exceptionally good on the band's live dates at Basin Street West, giving the listener a clear sense of eavesdropping on the most exciting big band of the early sixties in action. **AS**

**Woody's Winners** Herman (cl, as); **Gerald Lamy, Dusko Goykovich, Bobby Shew, Don Rader, Bill Chase** (t); **Henry Southall, Frank Tesinsky, Donald Doane** (tb); **Gary Klein, Sal Nistico, Andy McGhee** (ts); **Tom Anastas** (bs); **Nat Pierce** (p); **Anthony Leonardi** (b); **Ronnie Zito** (d). Columbia Ⓜ 468454 2 (44 minutes). Recorded 1965.

⑧ ❽

Each edition of the Herman Herd usually managed to produce a blockbuster and **Woody's Winners** is certainly that. The infectious elation captured here is all the more imposing when one remembers that the Herman Herd delivered this kind of punch to its live audiences every night.

Nat Pierce was the spark plug, both in rehearsing and arranging for the band, and his rolling piano, mixing elements of stride, Basie and Ellington styles, is better displayed on this album than on any other. Herman's facetious identification of Pierce as Mary Lou Williams has caused reviewers and listeners difficulties ever since. The ten-minute *Opus de Funk*, Pierce's arrangement of Horace Silver's tune, swings as fiercely as any big-band performance one can recall, and apart from good solos by Pierce, Klein and Goykovich, it contains a powerful one from Henry Southall which has gone unacknowledged (and remains so on this CD reissue) since the album was first released on LP. The trio of ballads is quite overwhelmed by the quintet of flag-wavers. **SV**

# Vincent Herring

1966

**Don't Let It Go** Herring (ss, as); **Scott Wendholt** (t); **Cyrus Chestnut** (p); **Jesse Yusef Murphy** (b); **Carl Allen** (d). MusicMasters Jazz Ⓕ 65121-2 (54 minutes). Recorded 1994.

⑧ ❿

Herring is a young musician who is maturing at a frightening rate. Lucky enough to be discovered while still a teenager and installed in Nat Adderley's band for close to five years, his natural affinity with brother Cannonball's sound and style was perhaps heightened more than would otherwise have been the case. Nevertheless, he was leading his own dates at the dawning of the nineties and a steady progression of albums (and record labels) now reach the point where clear signs of maturity are evident on every level. Interestingly, Herring does it here with musicians who have often cropped up on his records before, including the fine pianist Chestnut and the accomplished drummer and leader Carl Allen.

What has happened to Herring now that he has reached this stage is, as Benny Golson points out in his long and detailed booklet-notes, that he has developed his own sound and his own personal mix of the past. He has also been writing some uncommonly good songs for his band to play. Often in the minor key, they stay within a relatively restricted harmonic ambit, but are beautifully arranged between the members of the group, and the melodies are fresh. Herring no longer goes hell-for-leather from the first note of a solo, and his pacing of all aspects of the music on this disc is exemplary. The album hangs together as a single identity very well indeed. Of his band, pianist Chestnut perhaps stands out due to his unerring choice of chord voicings and his wonderfully weighted hands, but no-one is below par, and the group works beautifully as a complete unit. An understated yet rewarding record, and an important step forward for Herring. **KS**

# Fred Hersch

**Passion Flower: the Music of Billy Strayhorn**  Hersch, **Nurit Tilles** (p); **Drew Gress** (b); **Tom Rainey** (d); **Andy Bey** (v); string orch **/ Eric Stern** (cond). Nonesuch Ⓕ 79395-2 (63 minutes). Recorded 1995.

⑦ ❽

Hersch has had a formidable reputation as a pianist for several years, but lately has entered a phase of intense creativity both as a pianist and composer and arranger. His regular trio and guests are well represented in regular jazz mode on a release like **Point in Time** (Enja 9035-2), but this is an altogether more ambitious project, partially inspired through conversations with Strayhorn's biographer. In it, Hersch seeks to explore many aspects of Strayhorn's music in settings ranging from solo piano to string orchestra, and from trio to piano-and-vocal or piano duet. Andy Bey's haunting evocation of *Something to Live For* reveals Hersch as a challenging accompanist, and Hersch's solo versions of *Lotus Blossom* and *Pretty Girl* are more lyrical than on many of his earlier albums, where edginess, sheer technique and dazzling pace have tended to obscure the more meditative side of his character. Despite the strings, Hersch proves here that he's still at his most impressive in the context of the trio, with accomplished versions of *Rain Check* and *UMMG*. Overall, his re-examination of Strayhorn is well worthwhile, illuminating the composer's character independently from Ellington, and producing one genuinely unusual idea, well worth further exploration, in the stimulating piano duet with Tilles on *Tonk*.   **AS**

# Conrad Herwig

1959

**New York Hardball**  Herwig (tb); **Richie Beirach** (p); **Ron McClure** (b); **Adam Nussbaum** (d). Ken Music/Bellaphon Ⓕ 660 56 002 (43 minutes). Recorded 1989.

⑧ ❽

American college bands have been attacked with boring regularity for producing technically accomplished but characterless musicians; Conrad Herwig, who studied at North Texas State, is one player who proves conclusively the foolishness of that position. Clark Terry warned us, when Herwig was in his big band, to "be on the lookout for a new giant" and now, thanks to Ken Music, which has recorded three dates led by Herwig, the work of one of the most individual and gifted of contemporary musicians is being more widely heard. Like Woody Shaw on the trumpet, he has transferred Coltrane's technically demanding polytonal vocabulary to the trombone with impressive rigour; in addition he has absorbed some of the language of Bartók, Berg and others. Allied to that is an extraordinary control and facility, a range of timbral resources as expressive as that of the human voice and a thematic sense so powerful that it enables him to render chromatic material as musically as if it were a mere pentatonic. This recording is also marked by unusually cohesive ensembles and fine playing by Herwig's mentor, the vastly underrated Richie Beirach. There is barely a dull moment here, but the throwaway brilliance of Herwig's arrangement of *I'm Getting Sentimental over You* is a particularly good place to start.   **MG**

# John Hicks

1941

**Gentle Rain**  Hicks (p); **Walter Booker** (b); **Louis Hayes** (d). Sound Hills. Ⓕ SSCD8062 (59 minutes). Recorded 1994.

⑦ ❽

Hicks became part of the New York scene in 1963. He graduated from the Betty Carter academy of musical life and was distinguished in action with the Jazz Messengers as well as with Woody Herman. In the eighties he joined freedoms with the likes of Arthur Blythe, David Murray and Hamiet Bluiett to round out his pliancy of outlook. He was never an empty chameleon but it was this adaptability that opened doors for him. This CD has him 'insider' dealing rather than at the cutting edge, but it also shows how he applies his technique to the needs of the material, to the stylistic bias of the environment in which he finds himself and to the musical predilections of his colleagues. His chordal strength is emphasized on *We'll Be Together Again*, *Hi-Fly* shows just how supple his sense of swing becomes, while *Goodbye Pork Pie Hat* establishes the theme statement as the basis of the performance. *Ruby My Dear* captures the wonderful air of resignation implied by the melody line while on the title track Hicks plays romantically without becoming maudlin. Tracing Hicks's musical lineage would take you from Teddy Wilson via Bud Powell to Tommy Flanagan and beyond, but Hicks knows few limitations. He is now a readily identifiable pianist whose only operating criterion is quality.   **BMcR**

# Eddie Higgins

**Those Quiet Days**  Higgins (p); **Kevin Eubanks** (g); **Rufus Reid** (b). Sunnyside Ⓕ SSC 1052D (57 minutes). Recorded 1990.

⑦ ❺

Higgins is a pianist whose touch and conception immediately communicates itself as someone who came up in the fifties, rather than a later era. His models are not Hancock, Tyner, Evans and Corea; from him you hear the tidiness of structure, the articulation of Tatum, Powell, Shearing and Garner. This is not his first album: that was made in 1957. But it is the first in some time. On it, he breaks with the convention (or tyranny) of the piano-bass-drums format and opts for a guitar and bass instead. This was an inspired idea, for it opens up the music to more unusual influences on its direction in each piece, and it also makes the musicians work together in freshly minted ways, rather than rely on Pavlovian sequences and reactions. All three musicians thrive in this situation, with Eubanks in particular sounding free and swinging, his lines seeking out unusual harmonic nuances in a similar way to Jim Hall's methodology. Higgins himself plays through this set of originals and old favourites with enormous confidence.

For Bill Evans fans looking for a change of scenery.                                                  **KS**

# Andrew Hill                                                                           1937

**Judgment!** Hill (p); **Bobby Hutcherson** (vb); **Richard Davis** (b); **Elvin Jones** (d). Blue Note Ⓜ
   CDP8 28981 2 (48 minutes). Recorded 1964.

⑩ ❽

Of all the great artists to have had significant parts of their careers documented by Blue Note recordings, Andrew Hill has been by far the worst served in the reissue stakes. Even his two fine albums made at the dawn of this present decade for the reborn label have been deleted, while not only the entire extent of his unissued material lies inactive and unheard in the Blue Note vaults, but the vast bulk of his brilliant series of sixties releases are either deleted or await their 15 CD-minutes in the sun. Thankfully, **Point of Departure** (see below) remains available (probably due to the presence of one Eric Dolphy and one Joe Henderson), but of the rest, just this one remains. Grab it while you can, because the music is little less than sensational. And if you need any convincing, play either the opener, *Siete Ocho* (logically, a piece in 7/8), which goes directly from a theme-over-ostinato bass and Hutcherson solo to a boiling explosion of drums from Elvin Jones. If you still feel obstinate about it, try the ballad *Alfred*, dedicated to Blue Note's founder, Alfred Lion. It is one of the most beautiful tunes to have come out of jazz in the past 50 years, an ingenious construction worthy of Monk, and must melt even the most obdurate potential buyer's heart.

After those two, anything else would necessarily have a sense of anti-climax, but each extra piece has reasons for further fascination, if you give it a chance. The title track, for example, has a wonderfully sinuous and insinuating melody. Hill has a unique pianistic voice, has an identifiable compositional style, and is worth the effort of discovering. As we go to press, news has arrived from EMI announcing the reissue of Hill's **Smokestack** album. Now, if only Blue Note could get around to **Compulsion!** (they probably will, now that Mosaic have done it in their boxed set).              **KS**

**Point of Departure** Hill (p); **Kenny Dorham** (t); **Eric Dolphy** (f, as, bcl); **Joe Henderson** (f, ts);
   **Richard Davis** (b); **Tony Williams** (d). Blue Note Ⓜ CDP8 4167-2 (51 minutes). Recorded 1964.
✅

⑩ ❽

Andrew Hill's still underrated yet superb body of work for Blue Note from 1963-70 epitomized the movement which sought to combine elements of freedom (primarily an evasion of the tyranny of bar lines and rhythmic regularity) with an expansive concept of composition (including unusual, often juxtaposed metres, modal areas rather than strict chord changes, and less rigid rhythmic relationships). An excellent pianist with an individual, mosaic-like manner, he nevertheless recorded with eight different instrumental combinations during this period, expanding and diversifying his expressive ambitions. **Point of Departure** is especially noteworthy for the quality of the compositions and the contributions of the ensemble. Dolphy, in his characteristic way, extends Hill's often ambiguous harmonic framework even further; Henderson's probing, focused style is more attuned to the music's intricacies – a dramatic contrast to Dolphy's jolting expressionism. Dorham responds to the freedom offered with a moving introspection; Davis and Williams are responsible for the relaxed feel and flow. But Hill's organization of voicings, colours, and polyrhythms (more an extension of Herbie Nichols than Monk in this regard) is masterful – this music is not just written, it is scored for sextet; a music of nuance, complexity and consequence.                                **AL**

**Shades** Hill (p); **Clifford Jordan** (ts); **Rufus Reid** (b); **Ben Riley** (d). Soul Note Ⓕ SN 1113 CD
   (44 minutes). Recorded 1986.

⑩ ❾

After leaving Blue Note in 1970, Andrew Hill continued to record for a number of labels, but it was not until 1986's **Shades** for Soul Note that he made an album to stand alongside the best of his sixties work.

Hill has cited Tatum, Powell and Monk as primary influences. Memories of Monk are certainly to the fore on **Shades**, both in the tribute, *Monk's Glimpse*, its dancing lines punctuated by percussive stabs, and in the skipping phrases of *Chilly Mac*. Yet Hill remains very much his own man, his shifting tempos and fragmented lines the surface-play of a deeply thoughtful music that can be lit by flashes of lyricism or darkened by turbulent anxiety. On **Shades** the moods are mostly happy, thanks in part to Clifford Jordan's warm-toned tenor, which sails through the music with a beautiful delicacy. Reid and Riley are also superb, the latter's cymbals consistently whisking up the beat. They are heard to best advantage on the two trio tracks, *Tripping* and *Ball Square*, where Hill is at his most probingly idiosyncratic. The real gem, though, is *La Verne*, a dedication to his wife that Hill has recorded several times. Here Jordan's deft, swinging phrases coax a new tenderness from the tune, casting a spell of rhapsodic magic that envelops even Hill's more private solo. **GL**

## Buck Hill                                                                                  1928

**I'm Beginning to See the Light**  Hill (ts); **Jon Ozment** (p); **Carroll Dashiell** (b); **Warren Shadd** (d). Muse Ⓕ MCD 5449 (52 minutes). Recorded 1991.

⑦ ⑧

Born and bred in Washington DC, Hill was playing professionally at the age of 15. He worked at several clubs in his hometown during the fifties and recorded with Charlie Byrd in 1959. He played sporadically during the sixties but emerged in the next decade to establish himself as a leading saxophone light in Washington. There is little doubt that, by shunning the limelight of New York, he has retarded a promising career but, as this CD shows, he is a talented player. His solo on *Lullaby of Loosdrecht* gives notice of his structural awareness, *Warm Valley* is a model of tonal consistency while the urgent *Mitzi* shows that he knows how to bear down on the beat. The title track is taken with good-humoured swing and, like most of his playing, exhibits an inner strength. He can be a busy player but there are few superfluous arpeggios and he is concerned mainly with providing the bare bones of each musical story. To add interest, he uses the odd very personal phrase shape and ensures that his stories take some unpredictable turns. Despite his absence from the main arena, he does have albums such as this to campaign for him. **BMcR**

## Teddy Hill                                                                              1909-78

**Uptown Rhapsody**  Hill (ts, ldr, v); **Bill Dillard, Bill Coleman, Roy Eldridge, Frankie Newton, Shad Collins, Dizzy Gillespie** (t); **Dicky Wells** (tb); **Russell Procope** (cl, as); **Howard Johnson** (as); **Chu Berry, Robert Carroll** (ts); **Cecil Scott** (ts, bs); **Sam Allen** (p); **John Smith** (g); **Richard Fulbright** (b); **Bill Beason** (d); **Beatrice Douglas, Bill Dillard** (v). Hep Ⓜ HEPCD 1033 (72 minutes). Recorded 1936-7.

⑧ ⑥

Roy Eldridge and Dizzy Gillespie played their first solos on record with Teddy Hill (and in Dizzy's case, these were his first-ever recordings); it was also Hill who, in 1940, became manager of Minton's club in Harlem where the young beboppers tried out their first musical experiments. This CD comprises all 26 issued sides by the Hill band, splendidly remastered by John R.T. Davies and programmed in chronological order. It helps to place the band in perspective, for although it may not have possessed the 'name' value of other Harlem bands of the period, it had more than its fair share of soloists, particularly in the brass department. Eldridge rips off a fine solo on the opening *Lookie, Lookie, Lookie Here Comes Cookie* and Gillespie's exciting chorus on *King Porter Stomp* just over a year later shows where his allegiance lay at the time. The final six tracks are by the band which Hill brought to Europe, with Dillard, Collins and Wells joining in on the classic Paris sessions with Django Reinhardt. But the work of pianist Sam Allen should not be overlooked, nor the fine solos from Chu Berry on the first session. **AM**

## Earl Hines                                                                             1903-83

**The Chronological Earl Hines and his Orchestra 1928-32**  Hines (p, v); **Shirley Clay, George Mitchell, Charlie Allen, George Dixon, Walter Fuller** (t); **William Franklin** (tb, v); **Louis Taylor** (tb); **Lester Boone, Toby Turner, Cecil Irwin, Darnell Howard, Omer Simeon** (reeds); **Claude Roberts** (bj, g); **Lawrence Dixon** (g); **Hayes Alvis** (bb, v); **Quinn Wilson** (b); **Benny Washington, Wallace Bishop** (d); **Alex Hill, Irwin, Alvis, Reginald Foresythe** (arr). Classics Ⓜ 545 (71 minutes). Recorded 1928-32.

⑥ ⑥

Hines was the first pianist to deliver his instrument from the inheritance of ragtime. For all their captivating right-hand melodies, James P. Johnson and Hines's contemporary Fats Waller were bound by the regular beat of their left-hand rhythm section. But the influence of Armstrong's trumpet lines on Hines's right (he claimed his distinctive style was formed before working with Louis, but he can hardly have been unaware of his records) also liberated his left, forcing it to become less regular and to dialogue with the right hand.

In 1928 he was not quite as adventurous as subsequently (*A Monday Date*, especially in the QRS version, recalls Waller), but this playing was absolutely revolutionary in the context of the times. What distinguishes this reissue is the gathering together – seemingly for the first time ever – of the eight QRS sides and the four Okehs, all performed unaccompanied and all within a couple of weeks of his 25th birthday. His early big-band tracks which follow are crude indeed by comparison, and not a patch on later editions. But, even despite the surface noise of the opening tracks and the frequent distortion of the piano sounds, their historical importance is matched by their joyous dynamism. **BP**

**Earl Hines and His Orchestra 1932-4 and 1937**  Hines (p); with the following collective personnel: **Charlie Allen, George Dixon, Walter Fuller, Milton Fletcher** (t); **Louis Taylor, William Franklin, Trummy Young, Kenneth Stuart** (tb); **Darnell Howard, Omer Simeon** (cl, as); **Cecil Irwin, Jimmy Mundy, Budd Johnson** (ts); **Lawrence Dixon** (g); **Quinn Wilson** (b); **Wallace Bishop** (d); **Walter Fuller, Herb Jeffries, Valaida Snow, Madeline Green** (v). Archives Of Jazz Ⓑ 3801022 (44 minutes). Recorded 1932-7.

⑥ ❻

These 16 titles were recorded when Hines and his orchestra were the star attractions at Chicago's Grand Terrace. Some of the earlier material is trite (*Why Must We Part?* is a lachrymose ballad which was presumably on the then-current 'plug' list), but invariably Hines's own piano interludes lift the entire level of the performances.

This was a good band with a fine trumpet soloist in Walter Fuller (he also sings effectively) and a pleasing tenor soloist, Cecil Irwin. On *Cavernism*, Jimmy Mundy's first arrangement for Hines, there is a splendid violin chorus from Darnell Howard, and on one of the 1934 sessions there are a couple of vocals by Herb Jeffries. But it is Hines himself who invariably catches the ear with his immensely assured solo work. Perhaps the best tracks of all are *Love Me Tonight* and *Down among the Sheltering Palms*: these are piano solos of great value. The whole CD interlocks well with the Hines chronology on the Classics label, for these are alternative takes, some of them very rare, thereby avoiding duplications. Inevitably there are a few clicks and pops on the tracks dubbed from test pressings, but the overall sound is good.     **AM**

New review
**Another Monday Date**  Hines (p); **Eddie Duran** (g); **Dean Riley** (b); **Earl Watkins** (d). Prestige Ⓜ PRCD24043-2 (76 minutes). Recorded 1955-6.

⑧ ❼

Hines's four years with the Louis Armstrong All Stars took him from 1947 to 1951 but provided him with only limited artistic satisfaction. The early fifties found him on the West Coast and, if anything, in even less appropriate Dixieland circumstances. The first stirrings of the mainstream revival were beginning to be felt, however, and this CD draws from two important LPs made in 1956. Hines probably knew little of such a movement at the time, but literally by playing as he always had, he became part of it. His sense of form, the mixture of power and restraint and the rhythmic diversity of his playing gave him a timeless style with all the instrumental accoutrements in place. It becomes most obvious when his note placements are set against the predictable brush work of drummer Watkins, especially on accommodating Fats Waller material like *Squeeze Me* and *Ain't Misbehavin'*. On the final 12 titles Hines plays solo. Given such freedom, his mental time-machine takes over and he continues to take audacious metronomic liberties while maintaining his improvisation momentum. Hines was clearly ready for the further triumphs ahead.     **BMcR**

New review
**Grand Reunion**  Hines (p); **Roy Eldridge** (t); **Coleman Hawkins** (ts); **George Tucker** (b); **Oliver Jackson** (d). Verve Ⓜ 528 137-2 (two discs, nas: 90 minutes). Recorded 1965.

✔  ⑩ ❽

Originally released on two separate vinyl albums for the Mercury jazz subsidiary Limelight, this date has for a long time been seen as a high point in the latter-day Hines discography, after his triumphant 1964 rehabilitation into the professional jazz fraternity at a series of New York concerts. Recorded at the Village Vanguard where Hines was enjoying a week-long residency with Hawkins opposite the Charles Mingus Quintet, it was given added spice by the presence for the Sunday shows of guest Roy Eldridge. Neither horn man had recorded with Hines in decades. All three men were born leaders and intensely competitive, so their friendly rivalry had a keen edge during the week in question and each man was careful to be at or near their personal best when the tape recorders were rolling. The repertoire selected was well known to all three, with the Hines trio reeling off two superbly relaxed, endlessly creative medleys, one comprised of Fats Waller tunes, the other relating to the Grand Terrace club of the thirties where Hines had held forth. Both Hawkins and Eldridge, often paired at Norman Granz concerts in the past, display their undiminished gifts on five tracks apiece, sharing just two of them, old mid-tempo war-horses *C-Jam Blues* and *Take the 'A' Train*. Eldridge brings a stark eloquence to *The Man I Love*, while Hawkins makes his ballad choice, the previously unissued *Just One More Chance*, a relaxed and friendly affair. What every note of this brightly burning album reinforces is that back in the sixties pre-bop jazz still had adventure and humanity to offer those who could bother to listen attentively. That lesson still holds good today.     **KS**

**Plays Duke Ellington**  Hines (p). New World Ⓟ 361/62-2 (two discs: 121 minutes). Recorded 1971-5.

✔  ⑩ ❽

Hines's last great phase began in 1964, when critic Stanley Dance persuaded him to begin performing solo; the unaccompanied recordings he made in this period are the distillation of everything he had ever learned and played: masterworks. Hines had always been a radical. More than any other pianist he liberated the left hand from stride and ragtime's march-rooted oompah patterns – a bass-register revolution more profound than his oft-cited, 'trumpet-style' right hand. On *Squeeze Me*, Earl's antic left alternately clonks asymmetrical runs like Bud Powell and bounces classic stride patterns; Hines compresses decades of jazz history into one cut, one style. His independence of hands, most striking on *Caravan*, harks back to early days when he patterned each hand's moves after a different Pittsburgh piano hero.

This is not typical late Hines in that he was unfamiliar with many of the 20 Ellington tunes he essayed, some of them rather obscure (you can hear him turning a page of music early on in *Take Love Easy*). But he stretches out enough to get comfortable – a couple of tracks run ten minutes – and his excursions highlight the similarities between his stride-rooted, bass-jabbing style and Duke's. It is a painless history lesson, and a thoughtful appreciation of a composer and pianist Hines greatly admired.     **KW**

## Terumasa Hino                                                                       1942

**New review**

**Unforgettable**  Hino (c); **Cedar Walton** (p); **David Williams** (b); **Michael Carvin** (d). Blue Note
ⓒ CDP7 81191-2 (58 minutes). Recorded 1993.

⑦ ❾

A veteran of the thriving sixties Tokyo jazz scene, trumpeter Terumasa Hino has staked out a significant career at the vortex of New York City's swirling jazz scene. A devotee of Miles Davis, Hino's horn crackles with an energy reminiscent of the master's late-fifties/early-sixties acoustic playing. The Davis influence can also be discerned in Hino's skittering, high-register flurries, his mid-range, half-valve smears and low register growls. But with his bold, brassy sound and the experience picked up through collaborations with Jackie McLean, Gil Evans, Dave Liebman and Elvin Jones, Hino has emerged as one of the most original of the post-Miles trumpeters.

Here, with brilliantly subtle support from pianist Cedar Walton, bassist David Williams and drummer Michael Carvin, Hino imprints his impassioned signature on a set of standards. Although ballad tempos predominate, Hino's brassy yet mellow cornet rings with a heart-on-sleeve verve incorporating what he describes as "the spirit of kamikaze". Still, when he limns such indelible lines as *I've Never Been in Love Before*, Hino's fire burns with Vesuvian intensity. So, too, his tributes to Miles, *Bye Bye Blackbird* and *My Funny Valentine*. In an album of memorable tracks, the cornettist's heartfelt take on Charlie Chaplin's bittersweet *Smile* is "unforgettable".     **CB**

## Milt Hinton                                                                        1910

**Laughing at Life**  Hinton (b, v); with the following collective personnel: **Jon Faddis** (t, flh); **Harold
Ashby** (ts); **Richard Wyands**, **Derek Smith** (p); **Lynn Seaton**, **Brian Torff**, **Santi Debriano**, **Rufus
Reid** (b); **Alan Dawson**, **Dave Ratajczak**, **Terry Clarke** (d). Columbia ⓒ 478178 2 (54 minutes).
Recorded 1995.

⑥ ❽

Hinton made his first records in 1933 and is arguably the most recorded bass player in the history of jazz. That in itself is remarkable but even more noteworthy is the fact that, at the age of 84, he has such a 'modern' sound and forward-looking approach. There are, for example, four trio tracks here (two with Smith and Dawson, two with Wyands and Ratajczak) which are propelled along with enormous power by Milt who obviously enjoys playing in this context. He takes three pleasant, if lightweight, vocals and on the closing *The Judge and the Jury* leads a four-man bass 'choir' of musicians, all considerably younger than himself. Yet he remains one of the most respected of all New York-based musicians, for he has been a part of so many developments in jazz. The men chosen for this CD are people he admires greatly and the opening *Child Is Born* featuring Milt and Jon Fadds is beautiful. Harold Ashby plays his part on four tracks, including a gorgeous *Prelude to a Kiss*; in the absence of Ben Webster one gets the impression that Ashby was Milt's second choice. Good, varied mainstream music; add another mark if you are not averse to the occasional bass solo.     **AM**

## Jutta Hipp                                                                         1925

**New review**

**With Zoot Sims**  Hipp (p); **Jerry Lloyd** (t); **Zoot Sims** (ts); **Ahmed Abdul-Malik** (b); **Ed Thigpen**
(d). Blue Note Ⓜ CDP8 52439-2 (54 minutes). Recorded 1956.

⑥ ❻

Hipp was born in Leipzig, later moving to Munich before trying her luck in New York in the mid fifties. That her luck held is amply demonstrated by this and other record dates at the time for Blue Note (there were two vinyl albums of her trio at the old Hickory House club). By 1958, however, she had decided to return to both Germany and her earlier love, fine art, and abandoned professional music-making. This album reveals her to be an adequate post-Powell pianist who has also listened closely to Teddy Wilson, but not a player of any great individuality. If it weren't for the presence of an in-form Sims there would be little reason for its reissue, with trumpeter Lloyd offering not much more than Chet Baker in second gear (Lloyd went back to cab driving soon after the date). Also, although the bass and drums of Malik and Thigpen are first rate, tape-stretch on the masters has resulted in considerable wow on the cymbal sound. But Sims makes it all worthwhile, playing with driving, Lester-like force on *Just Blues* (based on Young's *New D. B. Blues*) and wondering tenderness on *These Foolish Things* (one of two CD bonus tracks). **KS**

# Steve Hobbs

**On the Lower East Side** Hobbs (vb, mba); **Kenny Barron** (p); **Peter Washington** (b); **Victor Lewis** (d). Candid ⓕ CACD79704-2 (65 minutes). Recorded 1993.

⑧ ⑧

Hobbs is a 30-something vibes and marimba player from Raleigh, NC, where he still works regularly. This is, apparently, his third release. He is not one of the Gary Burton vibes-as-piano persuasion, relying instead on crisp and crystalline single-note lines, in the Milt Jackson tradition. His use of the marimba is far more urgent and assertive than usual for this instrument and his break-neck marimba version of *The Song Is You* constitutes one of the high spots of a fine programme. The rhythm section (do those guys ever stop working?) is as good as usual – which means perfect. Recordings like this serve to remind us that the majority of jazz musicians, even very good ones like Steve Hobbs, go largely unappreciated, simply because they work away from New York or Los Angeles, or have not been associated with big names at some time or other. **DG**

# Art Hodes
1904-93

**Pagin' Mr Jelly** Hodes (p). Candid ⓕ 79037-2 (58 minutes). Recorded 1988.

⑧ ⑦

How ironic that a white, Russian-born, Chicago-bred pianist in his eighties became one of the last masters of a disappearing style of blues playing. Always a competent, devoted disciple of South Side pianists ranging from the sophisticated, especially Earl Hines, to the earthy, in this case the equally incomparable Jimmy Yancey, Hodes's art grew more personal, more pleasingly idiosyncratic with age. This intimate programme, dedicated to another of Hodes's idols Jelly Roll Morton, finds him approaching the ragtime-influenced pieces like *Grandpa's Spells* with a calm, crisp articulation and only a touch of whimsy, although still likely to highlight an unusual progression in the bass line or add his own tag. He takes a few more liberties with the non-Morton material, joking with quotes in *Ballin' the Jack* and coaxing bluesy passages out of the march-step *High Society*. He really shines on the blues, however, whether his own tribute *Gone Jelly Blues* or *Mamie's Blues* (here mistakenly credited to Morton; he attributed it to Mamie Desdume) – both gorgeously slow, sparse and saturated with atmosphere. Like Yancey, he is unafraid to take his time, alter the dynamics of his phrases, or find a particularly tart harmony and let it ring, much as Monk would do. Hodes never dazzled with his technique, but his vast experience allowed him to interpret this material with a wealth of associations, allusions, and simple eloquence. It may not be trendy, but it is timeless, and as Art used to say, "The records got released, and no one got hurt." **AL**

# Johnny Hodges
1907-70

**Passion Flower 1940-6** Hodges (as, ss) with **Duke Ellington** and his Famous Orchestra and small groups drawn from it, including: **Cootie Williams**, **Ray Nance** (t); **Rex Stewart** (c); **Lawrence Brown**, **Joe 'Tricky Sam' Nanton**, **Juan Tizol** (tb); **Otto Hardwick** (as); **Barney Bigard** (cl, ts); **Ben Webster** (ts); **Harry Carney** (bs); **Duke Ellington**, **Billy Strayhorn** (p); **Fred Guy** (g); **Jimmy Blanton** (b); **Sonny Greer** (d). RCA Bluebird ⓜ 66616-2 (70 minutes).

✓ ⑩ ⑧

A first-rate selection of Hodges's work as a member of Ellington's orchestra and as a small-group leader. Both his musical personae are well represented, the swoony romantic and the cryptic swinger, and the majority of the 22 tracks are classics of Ellingtonia in any case, so you can't go wrong. Among the delights are *That's the Blues Old Man*, an early ancestor of *Happy Go Lucky Local* and the last number Hodges ever recorded on soprano, beautifully poised small-group swingers such as *Good Queen Bess*, *Squatty Roo* and *Goin' out the Back Way*, and the almost criminally sensuous *Warm Valley*. Inevitably, there are many overlaps with other editions, but these change so often that keeping track of them is impossible. It is worth pointing out, however, that this CD follows neatly on from Black & Blue's **Johnny Hodges & his Orchestra: 1937-9** making them a very handy pairing. **DG**

**Used to be Duke** Hodges (as); **Harold 'Shorty' Baker** (t); **Lawrence Brown** (tb); **Jimmy Hamilton** (cl, ts); **John Coltrane** (ts); **Harry Carney** (bs); **Call Cobbs**, **Richie Powell** (p); **John Williams** (b); **Louis Bellson** (d). Verve 849 394-2 (48 minutes). Recorded 1954.

⑧ ⑦

Johnny Hodges's 42-year stint with the Ellington orchestra was interrupted just once: from 1951 to 1955 he led his own small ensembles, recording several fine albums for the Norgran label. These LPs were reissued by Verve, then in 1989 resurfaced, still on vinyl, as a Mosaic box-set. Presumably Verve will eventually release all of it on CD, but to date **Used to be Duke** is the only disc to have appeared.

A strong Ducal influence pervaded Hodges's Norgran dates. **Used to be Duke** is atypical in having only one Ellington tune (*Warm Valley*), but a line-up that includes four of Hodges's ex-orchestra colleagues (Baker, Brown, Carney, Hamilton) is par for the course. The blues exerts a strong influence too. The masterly *Sweet as Bear Meat* is taken at what Stanley Dance has called "a relaxed, sauntering tempo" of a kind almost peculiar to Hodges; the punchier riffing of *Burgundy Walk* and the title track reflects the fifties taste for r&b. Hodges brings an urbane elegance to the blues, while *Warm Valley* is all melting balladry, and the zestful *Sunny Side of the Street* finds him slipping in and out of double-time with consummate ease. There is nothing superfluous in his playing, just a stream of supple phrases, beautifully poised and unfailingly melodic. **GL**

---

**Back to Back/Side by Side**  Hodges (as); **Harry Edison**, **Roy Eldridge** (t); **Lawrence Brown** (tb); **Ben Webster** (ts); **Duke Ellington**, **Billy Strayhorn** (p); **Les Spann** (g, f); **Sam Jones**, **Al Hall**, **Wendell Marshall** (b); **Jo Jones** (d). Verve Ⓜ 823 637-2/821 578-2 (two discs, oas: 46 and 52 minutes). Recorded 1958/9.

⑩ ❽

One of the most significant late-period small groups, **Back to Back** and 16 minutes of **Side by Side** came from the same sessions, with Duke on the piano and billed accurately as co-leader. Until such time as they are combined on a single CD, both original albums need to be recommended.

All seven tracks on the first and one item on the second (Waller's *Just Squeeze Me*) are old war-horses, composed by neither Hodges nor Ellington but freshened remarkably by the combination of the altoist with ex-Basie-ite Edison (and indeed Duke with Jo Jones). Hodges knew how to play simple with supreme effectiveness, and the skeletal arrangements on such as *Wabash Blues* or *Loveless Love* take much of their flavour from Ellington's piano. Of the two Ducal themes on **Side by Side**, he lifts the entire performance of *Stompy Jones* by his dialogue with Jones, while the other, *Goin' Up*, is a 1943 Ellington item never previously recorded in the studio and marking Duke's first use of the flute.

Six septet items on **Side by Side** recall the group Hodges led during the first half of the fifties, but the addition of Verve contract artists Eldridge and Webster is an undoubted plus. Two laid-back standards (*Let's Fall in Love* and the unusually structured *Just a Memory*) are a diversion from the main course of four blues at different tempos. A reminder that Hodges virtually founded instrumental rhythm & blues in the late thirties is Strayhorn's repetition of a single figure throughout the joyous *You Need to Rock*. **BP**

---

**And Wild Bill Davis**  Hodges (as); with, on disc one: **Wild Bill Davis** (org); **Dickie Thompson**, **Mundell Lowe** (g); **Milt Hinton**, **George Duvivier** (b); **Osie Johnson** (d); on disc two: **Lawrence Brown** (tb); **Bob Brown** (ts, f); **Wild Bill Davis** (org); **Dickie Thompson** (g); **Bobby Durham** (d). RCA Jazz Tribune Ⓜ ND89765 (two discs: 79 minutes). Recorded 1965/6.

⑧ ❼

Hodges made a large number of albums with Wild Bill during the sixties, spreading them between two companies – RCA and Verve. Few of them are available in any form at the present time, so we must welcome such reissues. The first CD is a 1965 studio session and finds Hodges at his most relaxed and sumptuous, his tone beautifully captured by the RCA technicians and faithfully balanced against the might of Davis's instrument. Wild Bill occasionally threatens to overwhelm anyone within earshot, and once or twice is a little too adept at imitating Fats Waller's organ timbres, but apart from that he is enthusiastic and supportive, often showing surprisingly attentive and discreet backing to Hodges. The lack of a second horn is in fact a bonus, allowing Hodges all the room he needs.

The second CD stems from an engagement at Grace's Little Belmont, Atlantic City, where Davis had a residency and from whence came a contemporaneous live album featuring the organist's trio with tenorist Bob Brown on a couple of tracks. Until recently this was available on American Bluebird as a single CD, which had a previously unissued version of *Just Squeeze Me* to bolster a not overwhelming amount of playing time. The music here is not so finely balanced, or finely recorded (too much stereo separation, a fair amount of bottom-end distortion and far too much audience chatter) as the 1965 session, but it has its moments, especially a sprightly *Good Queen Bess*. But why have BMG France put this out with the extra track missing, especially when, as the playing time now stands, this entire package could have been fitted onto one CD? **KS**

---

# Bendik Hofseth                                                                 1962

New review
**Metamorphoses**  Hofseth (saxes); **Michael Mainieri** (vb); **Eivind Aarset** (elg); **Anders Jormin** (b); **Talvin Singh** (ta); **Jon Christensen** (d); **Paolo Vinaccia** (perc). Verve/Sonet Ⓔ 527789-2 (49 minutes). Recorded 1994.

If a mischievous ECM engineer were to sample any of Hofseth's bleating, vibrato-laden lines and splice them into a Jan Garbarek record, only the most avid Garbarek disciple would spot the difference. However, where Garbarek's chief concern of recent years has been folk music of the Nordic and other varieties, his fellow Norwegian Hofseth has ventured across the great northern ocean and imported some distinctly American blood into his music, in the form of more electronic noise, faster and firmer beats, Breckerish tenor licks and a less bleak emotional landscape. The ethnic elements are nevertheless strongly represented on this live recording by the tabla playing of Talvin Singh and in the folky melodies, but the presence of the urbane vibist and former Hofseth employer Mike (now apparently Michael) Mainieri and the tough fusion guitar of Eivind Aarset speaks clearly of New York. Indeed, Hofseth's association with Mainieri in Steps Ahead might explain the similarity between some of Hofseth's writing and the country-inflected numbers which entered Steps Ahead's book in the mid eighties. Garbarek fans may want to test the record anyway, but in general terms it probably could do with a wider range of expression. After a while, the alternation between drifting, ruminative introspection and vigorous folk-inspired reels wears a bit thin.                **MG**

# Jay Hoggard                                                                         1954

**New review**

**A Night in Greenwich Village**  Hoggard (vb); **Geri Allen** (p); **Anthony Cox** (b); **Marvin 'Smitty' Smith** (d). Muse Ⓕ MCD5556  (69 minutes). Recorded 1987.

⑦ ❼

Hoggard is an accomplished vibraphonist who has been recording under his own name since his early twenties without ever making a very consistent impression. However, a case can be made for his Muse albums of the last decade having done him more justice than his early efforts, and for this 1987 live date (though only recently issued) as being one of the very best.

It manages to combine his ability in chord-based improvisation, his interest in the more ethnomusicological aspects of the marimba family, and his apparent admiration for the work of Bobby Hutcherson. It does so in the context of just five long pieces (*A Night in Tunisia* is the shortest, but still lasts over 12 minutes) and Hoggard's three originals are skeletal but absorbing. *Comfort in the Storm* begins with a couple of minutes of vibes completely unaccompanied, but the techniques and musicality involved make the moment utterly gripping. It goes without saying that an extended session such as this could not succeed without a sympathetic but challenging rhythm section, and that is certainly the case here. The playing is excitingly loose, and Geri Allen in particular summons all her knowledge and energy to provide an excellent foil to Hoggard.                **BP**

# John Högman                                                                       1953

**New review**

**Good Night Sister**  Högman (ts, bs, syn); **Ulf Johansson** (tb); **Knud Jörgensen** (p); **Nils-Erik Sparf** (vn, va); **Thomas Arnesen** (g); **Bengt Hansson** (b); **Johan Dielemans** (d). Sittel Ⓕ SITCD9202 (64 minutes). Recorded 1992.

⑥ ❽

Stockholm-born Högman moved with his family to Uppsala at the age of eight, which has served as his base ever since. On this, a rare excursion as a leader, Högman reveals himself as a tenorist with a deep-throated Rollins-esque tone and a conception closer to old-fashioned mainstream than to bop and after. Even the presence of the occasional pop or funk beat cannot hide this basic orientation. This, however, is hardly a drawback in a modestly conceived but enjoyable and spirited journey through warm and good-natured repertoire mostly from the leader's pen. Trombonist Johansson appears but twice, yet is able to make a mark and help in creating a strong impression of diversity on the album. Sparf appears just once, providing backing on the ballad *November Söndag*, while Arnesen brings his guitar to three songs, giving an added texture and a blues-driven line to *Anders Påse* and a bossa sway to *A Sentimental Gentleman*, but the focus is clearly on Högman, who seems a thoroughly confident and individual voice and who is bound to give pleasure to those listeners who enjoy a characterful but comfortable ride through the musical landscape.                **KS**

# Allan Holdsworth                                                                   1946

**New review**

**None Too Soon**  Holdsworth (elg, gsyn); **Gordon Beck** (p); **Gary Willis** (elb); **Kirk Covington** (d). Cream Ⓕ 400-2 (51 minutes). Recorded 1996.

⑩ ❾

Holdsworth has been noted in recent years for hi-tech, highly complex fusion writing which tends to conjure the image of a clattering, highly automated factory production line, but those who recall with relish his showings in various nearly mainstream settings around London in the late seventies, prior to his emigration to California, will welcome this superb record as if it were the

Holy Grail. The title seems apposite, since this session, setting Holdsworth as the lead voice in a programme rich in conventionally arranged standards with acres of blowing space, is the record many of his followers must have dreamed of since the early days. The appetite was perhaps whetted by **Truth in Shredding**, the 1990 collaboration with Frank Gambale which got close to bop blowing in covers of early Shorter and Corea tunes, but **None Too Soon** is the genuine article, presenting Holdsworth's staggering solo voice in satiating profusion over an uncluttered, purring rhythm section. *Countdown*, *Isotope*, *Inner Urge* and *How Deep Is the Ocean* are typical of the stylistic remit, and if Holdsworth's soloing on the last named is an outstanding episode, it is the peak of a session which rarely dips below the stratospheric. There are fine solos too from Beck and Willis, but predictably Holdsworth steals the show. The synthaxe, by the way, is used only moderately, mainly for backgrounds. **MG**

## Billie Holiday

1915-59

**The Voice of Jazz** Holiday (v); Roy Eldridge, Buck Clayton, Bunny Berigan, Jonah Jones, Frankie Newton (t); Bobby Hackett (c); Benny Morton, Dickie Wells, Jack Teagarden, Trummy Young (tb); Benny Goodman, Cecil Scott, Irving Fazola, Artie Shaw, Edmund Hall, Buster Bailey (cl); Hilton Jefferson, Johnny Hodges, Tab Smith, Benny Carter (as); Lester Young, Ben Webster, Joe Thomas, Babe Russin (ts); Teddy Wilson, Joe Bushkin, Sonny White (p); Lawrence Lucie, Dave Barbour, Al Casey, Freddie Green, John Collins, Allan Reuss, Bernard Addison (g); John Kirby, Milt Hinton, Artie Bernstein, Walter Page (b); Cozy Cole, Jo Jones, Gene Krupa, J.C. Heard, Yank Porter (d). Affinity Ⓜ CD AFS BOX 1019-8 (eight discs: 559 minutes). Recorded 1933-40.

⑩ ❽

Billie Holiday's achievement was to take popular songs, purge them of sentimentality and raise them to expressive heights unimagined by their composers. She had the techniques and instincts of a jazz musician, and is both the greatest jazz singer and the greatest interpreter of American song.

This boxed set contains Billie's earliest and best records, most of them made in an informal, small-band setting, surrounded by the best jazz musicians of her generation. The finest pearls in the collection are those pieces where Lester Young plays as Billie sings. Their lines are so close together you expect them to trip each other up, but they never do; they simply move as one, gracefully and in perfect accord. Apart from Armstrong in his prime, there is no more optimistic, spirit-lifting sound in jazz. These discs follow Billie's career into its second stage, when she was being taken up by the intelligentsia and characterized as a tragic figure, a wronged woman and a kind of universal human doormat. Her repertoire changes suddenly and quite markedly to slow, doom-laden ballads, torch songs of the most despairing kind, and of course, the famous *Strange Fruit*, a poem set to music on the subject of lynching in the Deep South.

In all, there are 189 tracks here; some are alternate takes, but not many. Because there are so many great classics here, it really is worth getting the full set rather than seeking a one-volume anthology, none of which are particularly good. The remastering and presentation here is also greatly in advance of the single-CD series issued by the owners of the masters, Columbia, so it is a worthwhile investment from every point of view. **DG**

**New review**

**Love Songs** Holiday (v) with: Shad Collins, Charlie Shavers, Emmett Berry, Buck Clayton, Jonah Jones, Harry Edison, Roy Eldridge (t); Benny Morton, George Hunt, Dan Minor (tb); Buster Bailey, Edmond Hall, Jimmy Hamilton (cl); Lester Young, Vido Musso (cl, ts); Tab Smith (as, ss); Ben Webster, Babe Russin (ts); Eddie Heywood, Claude Thornhill, Teddy Wilson, Kenny Kersey, Joe Sullivan (p); John Collins, Al Casey, Allan Reuss, Freddie Green (g); Walter Page, John Kirby, Milt Hinton (b); Kenny Clarke, Cozy Cole, J.C. Heard, Jo Jones, Gene Krupa (d) and others. Columbia Ⓜ 483878-2 (47 minutes). Recorded 1937-42.

✓ ⑩ ❽

"I wonder what the poor people are doing tonight?" Fats Waller famously reflected. Listening to this Holiday single-CD concentration instead of one of the boxed sets, no doubt. It's a good collection, even if the 16 tracks leave space for half as many again on the disc, but then the poor are used to that. Columbia have resisted the temptation to go for all the all-out classics here, although there are some like *Them There Eyes* and *The Very Thought of You*. Instead they've included some of the less famous but still good numbers, renovated to greatness by the singer and her cohorts, which here frequently include Buck Clayton, Teddy Wilson and Lester Young. The dead hand of Eddie Heywood put paid to the orchestrations when his band accompanied Billie. He's only let loose on one here, *All of Me*, but it's largely rescued by Billie and a good tenor solo by Lester Young (omitted from the personnel on the sleeve, by the way). It's often thought that the uniquely high standard of the instrumentalists on Billie's recordings was due to the selection (usually by Teddy Wilson) of top solo players. But the way people like Babe Russin and Vido Musso raise their game in her company, it's difficult to believe that everyone was not inspired by the enchantment of the singing. **SV**

**The Quintessential Billie Holiday, Volume 9** Holiday (v); Bill Coleman, Shad Collins, Roy Eldridge, Emmett Berry (t); Benny Morton (tb); Jimmy Hamilton (cl); Leslie Johnakins, Eddie Barefield, Ernie Powell, Lester Boone, Jimmy Powell, Hymie Schertzer (as); Benny Carter (as, cl); Georgie Auld, Lester Young, Babe Russin (ts); Sonny White, Eddie Heywood, Teddy Wilson (p); Ulysses Livingston, John Collins, Paul Chapman, Al Casey, Gene Fields (g); Wilson Myers, Ted Sturgis, Grachan Moncur III, John Williams (b); Yank Porter, Kenny Clarke, Herbert Cowans, J.C. Heard (d). Columbia Ⓜ CK47031 (55 minutes). Recorded 1940-2.

✅ ⑩ ❻

For those torn between the early, smooth-voiced Holiday or the later, tortured one, on this last volume from her first Columbia period she is poised between the two. The music can be decidedly melancholic: *Solitude* and *Am I Blue?* are effectively slightly too slow, and the suicide-themed *Gloomy Sunday* is ages away from the blithe young Billie of a few years earlier. She was now 26.

Still, the swinging small groups follow her established model. Eight of 18 tracks are with Teddy Wilson, including a fine *I Cover the Waterfront* where the introductory verse swings as hard as the rest. There are classics here: the original *God Bless the Child*, Holiday's own fine lyric; a buoyant *It's a Sin to Tell a Lie*; the fussing-over-baby charmer *Mandy Is Two*, words by Johnny Mercer, no piece for a juvenile; one of Lady's rare blues, albeit a fancy one – W.C. Handy's *St. Louis Blues*. Her melismatic phrasing is so personal, it's odd to hear her bend conventional blue notes there.

Critics may complain about Holiday's lacklustre material, but this fairly representative slice is clinker-free (not even *Jim* sounds corny). We sometimes talk of early and late Holiday as different people; this Billie is both, and integrated: the soaring voice of youth seasoned with a deeper personal understanding. **KW**

**The Complete Original American Decca Recordings** Holiday (v); with a collective personnel of: Joe Guy, Rostelle Reese (t); Lem Davis (as); Bob Dorsey (ts); Joe Springer, Billy Kyle, Bobby Tucker (p); Tiny Grimes, Jimmy Shirley, Mundell Lowe (g); Thomas Barney, Billy Taylor, John Levy, John Simmons (b); Kelly Martin, Kenny Clarke, Denzil Best (d); Louis Armstrong (v). MCA/Decca Ⓜ GRP26012 (two discs: 151 minutes). Recorded 1944-50.

✅ ⑩ ❽

For once an album title is correct; these are the complete recordings Billie made for Decca, including nine previously unissued tracks and others which only saw the light of day briefly on Japanese or German LP compilations. All of the music has been lovingly restored to near-perfect conditions (allowing, in some instances, for worn source material) and the 80-page booklet which is part of the package is packed with relevant information on personnels, actual times of the sessions, background stories by supervisor/producer Milt Gabler and many rare photographs. Billie's Decca recordings have often received short shrift from critics but this set of 50 tracks, made over a five-and-a-half year period, makes it clear that Miss Holiday was singing as well as she ever did during her career, often better in fact, and the strings and studio bands were not Decca's idea but Billie's. She saw herself as a star and demanded star treatment, and was no longer content with a casual gig with a handful of jazzmen grouped around Teddy Wilson's piano. There are gems to be found here, apart from the expected *Lover Man* and *Porgy* (plus a previously unissued take of *My Man*); the 1947 version of *Easy Living*, for example, is the equal of the 'classic' 1937 record of the song even though there are no instrumental solos. And the two tracks on which Billie duets with Louis Armstrong are beyond category. This set renders all other compilations from the Decca period obselete and is essential in the overall assessment of Billie's unique artistry. It is worth noting that, as this new edition goes to press, the Commodore Holidays have been returned to CD availability through the auspices of GRP/MCA in the form of a two-CD boxed set, thus plugging a long-lamented gap. **AM**

**The Complete Billie Holiday on Verve** Holiday (v); with a selected collective personnel of: Howard McGhee, Buck Clayton, Joe Guy, Charlie Shavers, Joe Newman, Harry 'Sweets' Edison, Roy Eldridge, Joe Wilder (t); Trummy Young, Jimmy Cleveland (tb); Buddy DeFranco (cl); Tony Scott (cl, p); Willie Smith, Benny Carter (as); Illinois Jacquet, Wardell Gray, Charlie Ventura, Coleman Hawkins, Lester Young, George Auld, Flip Phillips, Paul Quinichette, Budd Johnson, Ben Webster, Al Cohn (ts); Danny Bank (bs); Red Norvo (xyl); Milt Raskin, Ken Kersey, Bobby Tucker, Oscar Peterson, Carl Drinkard, Beryl Booker, Sonny Clark, Billy Taylor, Jimmy Rowles, Wynton Kelly, Mal Waldron, Hank Jones (p); Dave Barbour, Tiny Grimes, Barney Kessel, Freddie Green, Jimmy Raney, Billy Bauer, Kenny Burrell, Barry Galbraith, Billy Byers (g); Charles Mingus, Curly Russell, Al McKibbon, Ray Brown, Red Mitchell, Leonard Gaskin, Artie Shapiro, John Simmons, Aaron Bell, Joe Mondragon, Joe Benjamin, Milt Hinton (b); Davie Coleman, J.C. Heard, Jackie Mills, Alvin Stoller, Elaine Leighton, Cozy Cole, Chico Hamilton, Larry Bunker, Jo Jones, Don Lamond, Osie Johnson (d); Ray Ellis and his Orchestra. Verve Ⓜ 517 658-2 (ten discs: 722 minutes). Recorded 1945-59.

⑧ ❼

Critics have had a field day with the post-war career of Billie Holiday. There are two basic positions adopted: the first is that her career was spoiled by the overly commercial backdrops given her by American Decca in the forties, and by the time she got back to small-group jazz recordings with Norman Granz, her voice was shot to pieces. The second position is that her later recordings are a triumph of spirit and artistry over acute physical and personal handicaps, and in fact offer deeper insights into the human condition than any of her earlier recordings. Both positions reveal more about the critics who form these opinions than about the artistry of Holiday. For she, along with just a handful of jazz singers, deserves to have her entire recorded output accorded the same degree of study and hard-won insight usually reserved for the very greatest figures in their respective fields, be that Mozart, Picasso or Rilke, Armstrong, Parker or Ellington.

This collection covers a greater time-span than any other single-label set can (the Columbia is from 1933 to 1942; the Decca from 1944 to 1950, while the Commodore sides cover just a handful of years), and therefore shows a more complete picture of the artist than any other. The earliest concert sides on the first disc (all taken from Jazz At The Philharmonic appearances from the forties) find her in perfect voice and in mostly outgoing and ebullient mood, whatever the character of the songs perfomed. Her various accompaniment is also variously successful, although Charles Mingus is conspicuous on bass on the very first track, *Body and Soul*, from 1945. Verve's attempt to be exhaustive in its coverage of Holiday's Verve years has led to the inclusion of an entire disc (fourth disc) and all but three tracks from the sixth disc which for the first time bring home-made Holiday rehearsal tapes before the public. The sound quality is not very good, although the insights are fascinating for the dedicated Holiday fan. It is definitely not for casual listening, however.

Also available here is the 1956 Carnegie Hall concert, which generally finds her in good voice and well focused on her material, and the 1957 Newport Jazz Festival set where her voice is scratchy and her delivery uncertain. The set ends with the sessions she made with a Ray Ellis orchestra which contains both sympathetic obbligato jazz soloists and a string section, thereby combining, to her way of thinking at this stage of her career, the best of both worlds.

As a document of jazz history, this is a vital set to acquire. As a ten-disc set of entertainment for those more inclined to a casual approach to music, it is something to avoid. The standard of presentation, packaging and documentation (there is a 220-page booklet included in the set) is exemplary, and an object-lesson to all those who would care to embark on similar enterprises. **KS**

**New review**

**Lady in Satin** Holiday (v); collective personnel, including: **Mel Davis**, **Billy Butterfield**, **Bernie Glow** (t); **Urbie Green**, **Tom Mitchell**, **J.J. Johnson** (tb); **Gene Quill** (as); **Ed Powell**, **Tom Pashley**, **Romeo Penque**, **Phil Bodner** (reeds); **Hank Jones**, **Mal Waldron** (p); **Barry Galbraith** (g); **Milt Hinton** (b); **Janet Putman** (hp); **Bradley Spinney** (xyl); **Osie Johnson**, **Don Lamond** (d); unknown str, choir; **Ray Ellis** (arr, cond). Columbia Ⓜ CK65144 (45 minutes). Recorded 1958.

✔ ⑧ ❼

**Lady in Satin** is Holiday's most controversial recording; it can still polarize opinions like few other jazz discs. Whereas her preceding sessions for Norman Granz had been with small jazz groups, Holiday moved to Columbia specifically to make a 'strings' album with Ray Ellis, whose work she admired. By this time, however, her voice was all but shot and the contrast between the plush strings, pure soprano choir and Holiday's croaking recitatives can be extremely discomfiting. Many critics have found the disc too pathetic: the case against was put most starkly by John Chilton, who wrote that "the vocal sounds seem as private and distressing as photographs of a hopeless medical case". Others, including numerous musicians (and Holiday herself), have claimed **Lady in Satin** as one of her most moving records, its soul-bearing performances matched by her incomparable gift for interpreting lyrics. Certainly she transforms several of the mawkish songs here into gripping emotional soliloquies of farewell and loss. Listeners may still find the results intensely depressing, but there is a kind of triumph too in the way she transmutes the vicissitudes of her life into her last remaining source of power – an art that reaches beyond artistry and defies analysis. When she sings "I'll hold out my hand, and my heart will be in it", you believe it's the truth. **GL**

# Dave Holland
1946

**Extensions** Holland (b); **Steve Coleman** (as); **Kevin Eubanks** (g); **Marvin 'Smitty' Smith** (d). ECM Ⓕ 841 778-2 (59 minutes). Recorded 1989.

⑧ ❾

Holland was born in Wolverhampton but left the UK for America in 1968 at the behest of Miles Davis. He swiftly established himself as a leading talent on bass and cello and hit an early peak with his 1972 LP **Conference of the Birds**, made with Anthony Braxton and Sam Rivers. In the eighties Holland led his own group (originally a quintet that featured Kenny Wheeler and Julian Priester) and recorded a series of well-received albums for ECM. Later releases such as **Triplicate** and **Extensions** showed him moving away from the previous, Mingus-inspired ensembles towards a more fluid, expansive form of music, a trend continued on 1996's **Dream of the Elders**.

Holland has cited Ornette Coleman's strong melodic lines as a major influence on his composing and it is not difficult to hear the Coleman Quartet's Atlantic LPs as a model for **Extensions**. Eubanks adds watercolour daubs of chords at times, but often saxophone, bass and guitar simply play lines, lending the music an attractive sense of space and flow as snippets of melody float and circle over a skittering pulse. Steve Coleman's alto has never sounded more eloquent and his funk-driven *Black*

*Hole* jumps and jolts with elastic charm. But it is Holland who lays the foundation of the record's success. His bass, and his compositions (notably the lovely *Procession*), sparkle with grace and intelligence in ECM's pellucid acoustic. **GL**

**Dream of the Elders** Holland (b); **Steve Nelson** (vb); **Eric Person** (as, ss); **Gene Jackson** (d); **Cassandra Wilson** (v). ECM Ⓕ 821 572-2 (77 minutes). Recorded 1995.

⑧ ⑩

Dave Holland is a complete musician. A bassist of rare invention and subtle virtuosity, he first became known through his exemplary work with such British players as John Surman, Humphrey Lyttelton, Tubby Hayes, Ronnie Scott and Kenny Wheeler. When Miles Davis persuaded the young Englishman to join him in 1968, Holland became an international presence. In the seventies, the bassist established a reputation in the avant-garde through his involvements with Circle (Chick Corea's free-jazz quartet with Barry Altschul and Anthony Braxton) and Gateway (John Abercrombie's trio with Jack DeJohnette). In the mid seventies, Holland anchored Stan Getz's far-reaching quartet.

Here, Holland enlarges on his recent **Triplicate** and **Extensions** with a highly-evolved quartet featuring saxophonist Eric Person, vibraphonist Steve Nelson and drummer Gene Jackson. Working from open-ended compositions by the leader, everyone soars. On the sharply angular title track, for instance, the burnished blend of alto and vibes gives way to tumbling solos buoyed by Holland's popping bass and Jackson's jabbing drums. Holland's lyrical expansiveness is perhaps best displayed in the aptly entitled *Lazy Snake*, in which the leader's *arco* undulations lead to leisurely, languorous uncoilings. Holland's evocative setting of Maya Angelou's *Equality*, as intoned by Cassandra Wilson, is a poetic plea to "take the padding from [our] ears." So, too, is Holland's latest opus, a truly inspired and artful work. **CB**

# Rick Hollander

**The Music of Hoagy Carmichael** Hollander (d); **Tim Armacost** (ts); **Walter Lang** (p); **Will Woodard** (b); Concord Jazz Ⓕ CDD4666 (60 minutes). Recorded 1994.

⑦ ⑧

"We were searching for a concept, a theme," says Armacost. "We ended up doing Hoagy because his music offered so much variety to us as an instrumental group." Not because Carmichael's compositions were particularly good on their own, then? But let us not be curmudgeonly, as Carmichael was (on one of his albums he tried to get an Art Pepper alto solo replaced by his own whistling). Carmichael's library is a wonderful one for an instrumentalist to work with, even though the most recent composition, *Ivy*, is 50 years old. Although Hollander seems to think it important that he is recognized as a pianist and although he contributed some good charts, it seems irrelevant since he sticks to drums. His idea of an up-tempo *Stardust* works well and Armacost has a good tenor romp, taking advantage too of the similarly imaginative variations on *Hong Kong Blues*. Lang and Armacost are both effective soloists and it's interesting to compare this less radical but more soundly-based performance with Armacost's own album (q.v.). Lang arranged *Baltimore Oriole* and appropriately graces it with a beautiful solo. **SV**

# Red Holloway                                            1927

**Brother Red** Holloway (ts); **Alvin 'Red' Tyler** (bs); **Brother Jack McDuff** (org, p); **George Benson** (g); **Wilfred Middlebrooks** (b); **Tommy Shelvin** (elb); **Joe Dukes** (d). Prestige Ⓜ PRCD24141-2 (69 minutes). Recorded 1964.

⑦ ⑦

Holloway has always been a player who made meaningless any line of demarcation between jazz and blues. A Chicago native, he was inherently comfortable in all blues fields and in his early years was at ease backing blues singers. The fact that some of the material heard on this CD originally appeared under McDuff's name provides the first suggestion that this combo's stance extended beyond the blues. The parallel with Jimmy Smith studio groups using horn(s) and guitar is immediately apparent, although it is instrumental blues such as *Something Funny*, *Rail Head* and the stomping *Brother Red* that ensure that Holloway's *modus operandi* is made clear. With his earthy sound and brusque delivery, he is certainly happier with such material. It is only on titles such as *No Tears* when his tone adopts a more luxurious quality, bringing him to the brink of bathos, that his stylistic identity becomes blurred. His biggest commitment to pure jazz forms came during the five years he spent in partnership with Sonny Stitt during the late seventies. Since then, it is albums such as the 1989 **Locksmith Blues** (Concord CCD4390) that have shown him be increasingly comfortable with jazz majors such as Clark Terry. Perhaps his creativity within his self-made kingdom between r&b and jazz is Holloways's special ploy. There are certainly few contenders for the crown he wears with ease. **BMcR**

# Ron Holloway

**Struttin'** Holloway (ts); plus personnel, including: **Mac Gollehon** (t); **Chris Battistone** (flh); **Kenny Barron, Larry Willis** (p), **Dr Lonnie Smith** (org); **John Scofield, Marlon Graves, Paul Bollenback** (g); **David Williams** (b); **L'Nar Brantley** (elb); **Victor Lewis** (d), **Steve Barrios** (perc), **Seema Sugandh** (v); **Larry Willis** (arr). Milestone ⑤ MCD9238-2 (62 minutes). Recorded 1995.

⑥ ⑨

This, Holloway's second record for Milestone, represents progress for the saxophonist in that his penchant for diversity is more successfully integrated into his personal style and approach. Holloway has the big, bustling tenor sound usually associated with tenor 'n' organ groups, and this approach can be found alive and well on a version of *I Found a New Baby* which includes Scofield and Smith. But Holloway is also capable of phrasing a melody to make it his own, even in a Latin-based quasi-elevator music song (perfect for daytime radio, I would guess) like the one which kicks off the album, *Amazon River*, although I for one could have done without the Burt Bacharachian flügelhorn treatment of the theme after Holloway's initial statement. Other things attempted include a beautiful duet with Kenny Barron on the standard *Where Are You?*, a recherché stab at Milesian funk on *Jungle Strut*, and a soulful session with a quartet led by Larry Willis on the timeless *How Long Has This Been Going On?*, a long-time tenor ballad favourite. Holloway's version of Tadd Dameron's *Soultrane* is another high spot, helped along by Dr Lonnie, while the final track, *Cobra*, is a Holloway original dedicated to Miles. It involves use of classical Indian instruments and techniques married to some funky bits reminiscent of Miles *circa Tutu*. For all the exotica, Holloway's roaring sax remains the track's best asset. **KS**

# Bill Holman
1927

**Bill Holman Band** Holman (ts, arr); **Carl Sanders, Frank Szabo, Don Rader, Bob Summers** (t, flh); **Jack Redmond, Bob Enevoldsen, Rick Culver, Pete Beltran** (tb); **Lanny Morgan, Bob Militello** (ss, as, f); **Bob Cooper, Dick Mitchell** (ss, ts, f); **Bob Efford** (bs, bcl); **Rich Eames** (p); **Barry Zweig** (g); **Bruce Lett** (b); **Jeff Hamilton** (d). JVC ⑤ 3308-2 (59 minutes). Recorded 1987.

⑦ ⑧

One of the best-respected and in-demand big band arrangers of the last 40 years, Holman has written for, among others, Maynard Ferguson, Buddy Rich, Woody Herman, Sarah Vaughan, films and television, although the bulk of his best and most adventurous work was done in the fifties for Stan Kenton (which can be heard on the highly recommended Mosaic multi-disc set, **Stan Kenton – The Complete Capitol Recordings of the Holman and Russo Charts**). Due to the unavailability on CD of **The Fabulous Bill Holman** (originally on Coral), this JVC session offers the best example of latter-day Holman. He was accused of swinging too hard for Kenton's taste, and he maintains that standard here in the punchy style of post-war mainstream arranging he helped develop. Characterized by ingenious sectional scoring, his charts balance brilliance with tact, agility with craft. Although a fine composer in his own right, as shown on the flagwaving *Front Runner* and the quirky *The Real You*, he likes to take a familiar piece of material and open its seams, inserting counter-themes and bravura episodes. This works well with *St Thomas*, highlighting Holman's gift for thematic variation, and *I Mean You*, with its piquant three-soprano front line. The approach is less successful on a pop song like *Isn't She Lovely?* and the intimate elegy *Goodbye Pork Pie Hat*. The orchestra plays the charts with crisp precision; the soloists may not exhibit the personality of his collaborators of the Kenton days, but they remain faithful to the character of the music. **AL**

# Richard 'Groove' Holmes
1931-91

**Blues All Day Long** Holmes (org); **Cecil Bridgewater** (t); **Houston Person** (ts); **Jimmy Ponder** (g); **Cecil Brooks III** (d); **Ralph Dorsey** (perc). Muse ⑤ MCD5358 (40 minutes). Recorded 1988.

⑦ ⑧

In the absence of the certified classic **Groove**, recorded in 1961 for Richard Bock's Pacific Jazz and featuring Ben Webster on sax, which has been both released and deleted on CD, this is as good a taste of the B3 solid sender as you are likely to hear. It finds him in utterly typical musical territory, mixing smoothly-rolling blues numbers with tasteful performances of old standards. It also finds him with a distinctly superior bunch of supporting stars, with saxophonist Person also doubling as producer. The treatment of *These Foolish Things* shows a deal of forethought and draws a sustained and touching ballad display from Person, with his caressing of the melody being particularly affecting.

Holmes always saw himself as a distinct cut above the average Hammond groove merchant, and his skilful deployment of a large sonic range on his instrument shows that he worked hard for that distinction. Even the boogaloo-type treatment of *Killer Joe* finds him experimenting with sound in a refreshing rather than a clichéd way, driving along the beat with deft touches and slick footwork. Bridgewater responds by playing a deeply bop-rooted solo in the manner of his better work with Max

Roach. By and large, this is typical of the overall approach taken by Holmes and his sidemen, and it makes for an intelligent and above-average organ-plus-horns workout. Holmes made albums after this, but it remains a high point in his output.                                                                                     **KS**

# Adam Holzman

**Manifesto**  Holzman (syn, p, elp, d-prog, v); **Aaron Heick** (ss, as); **Mitch Stein** (elg, v); **Mike 'Dino' Campbell**, **Jane Getter** (elg); **Freddy Cash Jr** (elb); **Juju House** (d, pc, v); **Marin Sander-Holzman** (v); **The L.D.A. Crew.** Lipstick Ⓕ LIP89033-2 (56 minutes). Recorded 1995.

⑨ ❾

Adam Holzman will be known as a keyboard linchpin in the Miles Davis band in the eighties, and here he follows a similar electronic style but with rather more sophistication and complexity than was evident in the Davis band. Where Davis was frequently happy with grooves with minimal variation, Holzman has written some quite brilliant compositions which show a great mastery of electronic instrumentation and orchestration, of studio production, and of idiomatic colours from jazz to funk, hip-hop, house and so forth. These elements are all manipulated and blended with exceptional skill and imagination to create a constantly entertaining masterpiece of contemporary fusion. Holzman's rich arrangements (there are one or two co-compositions) are a joy in themselves, but despite the fact that everything seems to be preordained down to the last detail, the music still has a great sense of spontaneity, with brief solos from Holzman, Heick, Stein and Campbell dovetailed into the constantly evolving ensemble fabric. The packaging, in a voguish tin box, is not so good – distinctive, and appropriate to Holzman's brassy, urban, industrial sound, but leaving a lot to be desired in practical terms. However, that's a small complaint about an otherwise very good issue. Outstanding tracks to sample are the beautiful soul ballad *Janeway* and *Bully 4 U*, an exemplar of concentrated thematic development.                                                                                     **MG**

# Yuri Honing

**Star Tracks**  Honing (ts); **Tony Overwater** (b); **Joost Lybaart** (d). Jazz In Motion Ⓕ 992010-2 (45 minutes). Recorded 1996.

⑧ ❾

Honing and his pals are yet another manifestation of the extraordinary level of jazz talent coming out of northern Europe these days. This programme, chosen by the Honing trio to bring a truly contemporary flavour to their interpretations of what Herbie Hancock terms "new standards", includes workouts on music by Björk, Sting and Abba. The album opens with a hypnotic statement of *Isobel*, a track from Björk's current album, and closes with a reprise of *True Colors*, the Tom Kelly-Billy Steinberg hit. The tenor-bass-sax trio, a staple in jazz for over 50 years, brings this music to a new and pulsing life, and much of the playing has a wonderfully haunting quality through the expert use of space by the three players. Honing's tone is full but capable of a full range of sonic variations, from whisper to blare, and he has a definite talent for the carrying of a melody. This unpretentious, unselfconscious but imaginative and open-minded album will be much in my CD player over the next little while, that's for sure. I can only urge you to do the same thing.                                                                                     **KS**

# Bertha Hope

**Elmo's Fire**  Hope (p); **Eddie Henderson** (t); **Junior Cook**, **Dave Riekenberg** (ts); **Walter Brooker** (b); **Leroy Williams** (d). SteepleChase Ⓕ SCCD31289 (56 minutes). Recorded 1991.

⑧ ❽

In many respects a re-creation of the small-group session of an earlier era – quirky boppish themes delivered in a slightly sour ensemble sound followed by a brisk round of solos before a theme restatement – **Elmo's Fire** nevertheless has three great strengths. The first is the playing of Bertha Hope herself; a considered, unspectacular but intriguing soloist, she proceeds through her subtle extemporizations with almost cat-like care and delicacy. This approach works extremely well on her own compositions, an extended blues and a relaxed bossa nova, and brings new life to her late husband's faintly Monkish minor classics *Bellarosa* and *Elmo's Fire*. The second is the presence of tenor saxophonist Cook, one of the finest and most neglected of the bop-influenced mainstream players. His most obvious influence is Dexter Gordon, whom he closely resembles not only in tone and overall approach, but also in his predilection for unexpected but felicitous musical quotations. On **Elmo's Fire**, he demonstrates his grandiloquent, foggy sound to perfection. The third is the inclusion of Elmo Hope's tricky, idiosyncratic compositions, like those of Herbie Nichols never quite accorded the acclaim they deserved during his life, but sounding fresh as ever over 25 years after his premature death. Henderson has an unusual, smeary trumpet sound, but it is appropriate in this context, and all those present contribute to a quietly competent but surprisingly subtle album.                                                **CP**

# Elmo Hope

1923-67

**Elmo Hope Trio**  Hope (p); **Jimmy Bond** (b); **Frank Butler** (d). Contemporary Ⓜ OJCCD0477-2 (44 minutes). Recorded 1959.

⑧ ❼

"Elmo truly had a touch of genius. I was in awe of him." If Harold Land's tribute to the still little-known Hope sounds a shade extravagant, listen to the pianist's trenchant contributions (as player and composer) to Land's classic album **The Fox** and to his own records, such as the two-volume **Last Sessions** or this trio set, made during a four-year stay in Los Angeles at the close of the fifties.

Hope's major influences were Bud Powell (a childhood friend) and Thelonious Monk, although as with those men (and the similarly neglected Herbie Nichols) his style was a distinctly personal distillation of bebop. His abrupt right-hand runs, in which strings of notes seem almost to jostle against each other, give a bright rhythmic bounce, heard to good advantage on **Trio** on the blues-based *B's A-Plenty* and the Latin-ish *Something for Kenny*, which also boasts a striking hands-on-kit solo by the redoubtable Frank Butler. The album's highlight is a reading of the Van Heusen-Burke standard *Like Someone in Love*, its dreamy tread cueing a series of skittish feints at the melody line by Hope. He is not a spectacular player, but the cumulative effect is richly inventive.    **GL**

# Claude Hopkins

1903-84

**Monkey Business**  Hopkins (p, ldr); with a collective personnel of: **Albert Snaer, Sylvester Lewis, Shirley Clay, Jabbo Smith, Lincoln Mills** (t); **Ovie Alston** (t, v); **Fernando Arbello, Fred Norman, Floyd Brady, Vic Dickenson** (tb); **Edmond Hall** (cl, as, bs); **Gene Johnson, Chauncey Haughton, Ben Smith** (as); **Bobby Sands** (ts); **Walter Jones** (g); **Henry Turner, Abe Bolar** (b); **Pete Jacobs, George Foster** (d); **Orlando Roberson, Baby White** (v). Hep Ⓜ HEPCD1031 (64 minutes). Recorded 1934.

⑥ ❻

Hopkins had an eventful and interesting early life which included a tour of Europe with Sidney Bechet and Josephine Baker in 1925. During the thirties he led one of Harlem's most popular dance bands, with long residencies at the Cotton Club and Roseland Ballroom. The 23 titles assembled here date from this period, and while Hopkins himself was very modest about the band's solo strength in later years (he singled out Edmond Hall as the only outstanding soloist) it was a very efficient unit with a light ensemble sound and a crisp attack, particularly in the popular 'call and response' ensemble passages. Ovie Alston was a good Armstrong-inspired trumpeter and singer, while Hall performed well on both clarinet and baritone. But Hopkins's own piano playing (well featured here on *Three Little Words*, for example) was everything that a band leader's keyboard work should be. In Sands he had a most impressive Hawkins-like tenor saxophonist, and the 1937 titles benefit from the solo playing of Clay, especially on the fine *Church Street Sobbin' Blues*. Inevitably there are several vocal tracks (Orlando Roberson's falsetto singing will appeal immediately to connoisseurs of the unusual) but the fine remastering has enabled us to get a truly representative taste of pre-war Harlem.    **AM**

# Glenn Horiuchi

1955

New review

**Calling Is It and Now**  Horiuchi (p); **Francis Wong** (ts); **Anders Swanson** (b); **Jeanette Wrate** (d). Soul Note Ⓕ 121268-2 (65 minutes). Recorded 1993.

⑦ ❻

Horiuchi is part of a movement, based primarily in California and also including saxophonist Fred Ho and pianist Jon Jang, that uses jazz to make a statement about Asian-American culture. As with the others, Horiuchi often includes pointed references in his titles; but his music had grown into freer areas in the four years separating this album from its Soul Note predecessor, **Oxnard Beet** (121228-2), and the Japanese scales and other Asian touches are now simply options among many that the mutable compositions pursue. Art Lange's booklet-notes expand on this point, and signal the album title's echo of Cecil Taylor, although the music has a rather different weight that suggests Horiuchi is also paying attention to West Coast models like Horace Tapscott and Andrew Hill. Wong, the lone hold-over from the earlier Horiuchi quartet, has made his sound more flexible, and the leader has the assurance to play around and through the rhythm section. Wrate's lucid ideas and mobility do much to sustain a flow in a music that displays maturity, growth and more thorough integration of (as well as less dependence upon) what may strike jazz listeners as the exotic strains in Horiuchi's concept.    **BB**

# John Horler

1947

New review

**Gentle Piece**  Horler (p); **Phil Lee** (g); **Dave Green** (b); **Spike Wells** (d) Spotlite Ⓕ SPJCD542 (67 minutes). Recorded 1992.

⑧ ❾

John Horler is one of Britain's finest jazz pianists, a superb accompanist and an endlessly inventive soloist. Musicians consistently name him among their favourites, yet you will seek in vain for his name in any jazz encyclopaedia, even British ones. His style is unashamedly based on Bill Evans, which means that he deals in harmonic subtlety and delicate shading, not sound and fury. This collection of 11 numbers, standards and originals, is divided among solos, trios and piano-guitar duets of remarkable rapport. They will serve as an excellent introduction to his great gifts and may even persuade you to seek out his live performances, which are always enjoyable.          **DG**

## Shirley Horn

**New review**
**Loving You** Horn (p, v); **George Mesterhazy** (kbds, p, g); **Steve Novosel** (b); **Steve Williams** (d); **Alex Acuña** (perc). Verve Ⓕ 537 022-2 (53 minutes). Recorded 1996.

⑦ ❾

Horn's latter-day records have been universally lauded and commercially successful, and during the nineties she has maintained a remarkable consistency of effort. Each project is tackled on its own merits and with its own themes, and Horn's inimitable vocals, never much more than a whisper and with little attempt to create a sustained melodic line, have revealed to a new audience a depth of interpretative emotion and intelligence rarely found in any era. Horn has recently been alternating between small-group, guest-star and orchestra albums, and this time it's the turn of the small-group, slow-burn approach (in an intelligent twist on an old recipe, the previous album, **The Main Ingredient** – Verve, 1995 – had included some heavyweight guests and had attempted to re-create the open-house atmosphere of Horn's own kitchen when her friends turn up to relax, jam and eat). Horn continues to pick superior songs with grown-up lyrics, although the emphasis here is on the first flush of love, the 'up'-ness love can deliver, rather than the down sides (although this is touched upon in songs like *Someone to Light Up My Life*). That she can do this effortlessly at ultra-slow tempos shows her musical strength. The synthesized noodlings of Mesterhazy are the only real drawback here, their occasional entrance giving the music a sentimental edge. Horn simply doesn't need such props. The occasional mid-tempo track could help things along a little, however.          **KS**

## Wayne Horvitz

**Miracle Mile** Horvitz (kbds, p); with **The President**: **J.A. Deane** (tb); **Doug Weiselman** (cl, ts); **Denny Goodhew** (saxes); **Stew Cutler**, **Bill Frisell**, **Elliot Sharp** (g); **Ben Steele** (g, sampler); **Kermit Driscoll** (elb); **Bobby Previte** (d). Elektra Nonesuch Ⓕ 79278-2 (48 minutes). Recorded 1991.

✔ ❿ ❽

Wayne Horvitz is one of the talents to have emerged unscathed from the Knitting Factory in New York, moving on now from small local labels to a deal with a major label like Elektra. Where this has no doubt helped most is in the recording budget, for this ambitious album is very fully realized indeed. Each of the eight tracks here is an individual entity, with no great continuity between them beyond the musical forces employed. Horvitz often uses riffs, ostinato lines and repetitious slivers to keep the music moving on (in fact, *Variations on a Theme by W.C. Handy*, the theme being *St Louis Blues*, is entirely taken up by progressive modifications of riffs and lines which run the length of the piece). *Yuba City*, in contrast, uses repetition merely as a backcloth to hang the often fierce improvising and sound-painting he elicits from his group. *An Open Letter to George Bush* sounds more like a lament for a vanished America, *à la* Charlie Haden's Liberation Music Orchestra recordings, reiterating simple but moving harmonies, while the title track has an enigmatic progression on keyboards, a fifth interval in the treble clef having its harmonic base constantly modified by where the pedal points land. A sax takes an impassioned solo in the B section of the song.

This is jazz from a very different angle, but it is essential listening for those interested in what those today who are stretching the form are actually achieving.          **KS**

## Kid Howard                                                                    1908-66

**George Lewis Ragtime Band of New Orleans** Howard (t); **Jim Robinson** (tb); **George Lewis** (cl); **Alton Purnell** (p, v); **Lawrence Marrero** (bj); **Alcide Pavageau** (b); **Joe Watkins** (d, v). American Music Ⓕ AMCD 24 (52 minutes). Recorded 1953.

⑥ ❻

Initially a drummer, Howard played in the twenties with Chris Kelly and Isaiah Morgan. The former gave him cornet lessons, and by the end of the decade he was leading his own band on the instrument. In the thirties he worked with Jim Robinson and Capt John Handy. When the New Orleans revival began, Howard joined George Lewis on his first recording session with a full band in 1943. This CD was made at a time when he was working only intermittently and was no longer the powerful Armstrong-inspired player he had been in the thirties. He was now a more diffident performer, with a querulous vibrato and a lacklustre delivery. Fortunately the Lewis band at the time would not have welcomed a powerhouse player, and for all his technical frailty, Howard integrated perfectly. His uncomplicated lead was rhythmically assured and the somewhat thin tonal quality of his trumpet suited this particular front line well. He is exposed on slower items like *Tin Roof Blues* and *Just a Closer Walk*, but when the tempo moves up on the likes of *Sensation Rag* and *Precious Lord*, he contributes considerably to the overall balance of the ensemble. Ironically, following a serious illness in 1960, he landed a Preservation Hall spot and, up to the time of his death, played as well as at any time in the previous 20 years. **BMcR**

# Noah Howard                                                                    1943

**At Judson Hall**  Howard (as, bells); **Ric Colbeck** (t); **Dave Burrell** (p); '**Sirone' (Norris Jones)** (b); **Catherine Norris** (vc); **Robert Kapp** (d). ESP-Disk Ⓜ 1064-2 (38 minutes). Recorded 1966.

⑧ ➏

Born in New Orleans, Howard's early influences were Johnny Hodges and Charlie Parker. After hearing Ornette Coleman, he moved to California and teamed up with other second-generation free-form players such as Byron Allen and Sonny Simmons. This CD was made after his move to New York in 1965 and rates with any recording he ever made. His enthusiasm for free playing was on the up and his early eclecticism had provided him with a very personal style. His playing displays a sense of the dramatic and, in both *This Place Called Earth* and *Homage to Coltrane*, passages of motif declension building are juxtaposed with fiery and longer-lined forays. The *Homage* owns little to Coltrane but it does have the same spiritual intensity, and in this he is particularly helped by Kapp's Graves-like drum torrent. There is a real input from Colbeck, a highly talented young British trumpeter who later committed suicide, as well as from Burrell, whose modification of the Cecil Taylor message is of intrinsic value to the group. Not surprisingly Howard dominates and, although his later work with Archie Shepp, Sun Ra, Sonny Sharrock and Frank Wright has distinct merit, October 1966 in Judson Hall was a very special occasion. **BMcR**

# Freddie Hubbard                                                                1938

**The Artistry of Freddie Hubbard**  Hubbard (t); **Curtis Fuller** (tb); **John Gilmore** (ts); **Tommy Flanagan** (p); **Art Davis** (b); **Louis Hayes** (d). Impulse! Ⓜ IMP11792 (43 minutes). Recorded 1962.

⑧ ➓

"If someone were to ask how rising young jazzmen in New York were playing on a good get-together in 1962, this album would provide a succinct answer", is Dan Morgenstern's assessment of **The Artistry of Freddie Hubbard**, and 30 years on it is possible to add that the music has also triumphantly stood the test of time. A front line consisting of two Jazz Messengers, Hubbard and Curtis Fuller, augmented by John Gilmore, long-time Sun Ra associate, backed by a first-class rhythm section and engineered by Rudy Van Gelder, promises a great deal and delivers in spades. Three Hubbard originals – *Bob's Place*, a quintessential hard-bop vehicle; *Happy Times*, a bubbling, joyous theme; and *The Seventh Day*, a more complex affair incorporating punning references to sevenths and rests – are complemented by two classics, *Caravan* and *Summertime*, and provide excellent springboards for exuberant, youthfully ebullient improvisation from all participants. Hubbard, equally assured at either extreme of the trumpet's range, and possessed of an exhilarating, crackling, fiery tone, demonstrates just why so many tipped him at the time as the new trumpet prospect. Fuller is slyer in approach, but just as virtuosic and exciting. Gilmore shows why he is frequently seen as Coltrane's major influence, exhibiting an obsessive fascination with small cycles of notes and playing with passionate intensity throughout. Overall, this is a definitive early-sixties East Coast jazz session, faultlessly recorded and newly repackaged. **CP**

**New review**

**The Body and the Soul**  Hubbard (t); **Wayne Shorter** (ts, arr, cond); with septet – add **Curtis Fuller** (tb); **Eric Dolphy** (f, as); **Cedar Walton** (p); **Reggie Workman** (b); **Louis Hayes** (d); with big band – add **Al DeRisi, Ernie Royal, Clark Terry** (t); **Melba Liston** (tb); **Bob Northern** (frh); **Robert Powell** (tba); **Seldon Powell, Jerome Richardson** (ts); **Charles Davis** (bs); **Philly Joe Jones** (d); with strings – add ten-piece string section, substitute **Ed Armour, Richard Williams** (t) for DeRisi, Royal and Terry. Impulse! Ⓜ IMP11832 (37 minutes). Recorded 1963.

⑦ ➑

Hubbard made a long series of records for Blue Note from the dawn of the sixties up to 1966, when he moved to Atlantic and the prospect of a more commercially rewarding career. Many of these were outstanding small-group recordings, especially those coming towards the end of the Blue Note years such as **Breaking Point** and **Blue Spirits**. Much of this legacy was made available on CD in the late eighties but little of it is in the current Blue Note catalogue, which instead carries titles such as the ho-hum double live **The Night of the Cookers**, recorded in 1965 at the Club La Marchal with Lee Morgan as co-leader, where the shortest track clocks in at a few seconds less than 20 minutes (members, don't get weary), or **Ready for Freddie**, a 1961 small-group studio date which has nice touches but hardly catches fire, despite the presence of Elvin Jones. Neither of these albums would displace **The Artistry of Freddie Hubbard** (reviewed above) or this album, an ambitious project conceived to give a soulful and well-rounded picture of a star trumpeter in mostly reflective mood. **The Body and the Soul** remained Hubbard's only album with large forces until well into the seventies and his CTI period, when **First Light** showed he had not lost his way with a ballad, but this largely-ignored earlier effort has an integrity of its own. It is built around balladry, with six of the nine performances opting for slow tempos (even Ellington's *Chocolate Shake*, recorded by the composer as a jaunty dance theme, here becomes a brooding soliloquy), and Hubbard is spotlighted in septet, big band and big band-with-strings settings. Apart from the trumpeter, only pianist Walton gets more than a token solo, although Dolphy, on the blues, *Clarence's Place*, takes a short alto solo which is so extreme as to be almost Dadaistic, and is priceless for just that reason. Hubbard himself is on utterly commanding form, his technique flawless, his range excitingly complete, his imagination poised and on fire. His way with a ballad is not flashy, but committed and persuasive. Shorter's arrangements are for the most part competent and occasionally inspired (the septet reading of *Body and Soul* being just that), with his inexperience in the area also noticeable, especially on a turbulent theme like *Thermo* (part of the Jazz Messengers book of the day) where unison saxophones, distantly recorded, lack the crackle and fire of the Messengers' own versions. Still, this is a minor problem in an overall package of music which, 30-plus years on, grabs your attention and your imagination. **KS**

**New review**

## The Freddie Hubbard and Woody Shaw Sessions
Hubbard (t, flh); **Shaw** (t); **Kenny Garrett** (as); **Mulgrew Miller** (p); **Cecil McBee**, **Ray Drummond** (b); **Carl Allen** (d). Blue Note Ⓜ CDP8 32747-2 (two discs: 102 minutes). Recorded 1985-7.

⑧ ❽

The early eighties found Hubbard trying to live down his fusion reputation of the previous decade. He had kept his hard-bop hand in with V.S.O.P in the late seventies but the legacy of electric funk and over-arranged disco music was not easy to shed. The shadow of Creed Taylor hovered for longer than he would have wished and several overused clichés had become unwelcome trademarks. This double CD sets its sights on just the right target and has the advantage of a production team which includes arranger Don Sickler and engineer Rudy Van Gelder. The two sessions were 18 months apart and, except for the bassist, have identical line-ups. Both rhythm sections are powerful and supportive, Garrett steals more than one scene but it is the challenge of Shaw that pushes Hubbard firmly along the right road. However friendly they may be, there is always a gladatorial element in the meeting of trumpeters and Shaw was never a player to roll over and die. Hubbard parades all of his assets; the brassy tone, strength in all registers, subtle vibrato and a loping, rhythmic gait attend every solo. He nurtures the pretty melody of *Sao Paulo*, is masterful on *Calling Miss Khadija*, wrings a maximum emotional affect from *Lament for Booker* and literally flows with ideas on *Hub Tones*. The session certainly put the wheels back on the career-wagon and showed that, when conditions were advantageous, Hubbard was still a substantial trumpeter. **BMcR**

## Topsy
Hubbard (t); **Kenny Garrett** (as); **Benny Green** (p); **Rufus Reid** (b); **Carl Allen** (d). Enja Ⓔ ENJ7025-2 (63 minutes). Recorded 1989.

⑥ ❽

This is the most successful Hubbard session for quite some time, and at least part of the reason lies in the repertoire. Since the late sixties, such pop songs as were included on his albums (and those of many other artists) had been recent 'chart' material, which has seldom proved either suitable or stimulating – an honourable semi-exception in this respect being the Sting song, *Fragile* on **Times Are Changing** (Blue Note). Here the first four tunes are from the thirties (including the Basie-popularized title track and *As Time Goes By*) while the most recent are fifties items, such as *All Of You* and J.J. Johnson's *Lament*.

Hubbard adopts a relaxed approach, whatever the tempo, and the rhythm section combines youth and experience to inspiring effect; as a result, the trumpeter is not overly flamboyant but warms to his task most satisfyingly. It may well not have been his own choice but the marketing considerations of the Japanese producer that dictated the Miles Davis-associated harmon-mute on every track; nevertheless, the emotional spectrum is quite wide. Add the excellent work of guest altoist Kenny Garrett on his three numbers, and what seems at first glance an unambitious assignment is carried out with all Hubbard's considerable authority. **BP**

# Spike Hughes
1908-87

**High Yellow** Hughes (b); with the following collective personnel: **Norman Payne**, **Chick Smith**, **Jimmy Macaffer**, **Bruts Gonella**, **Billy Higgs**, **Billy Smith**, **Red Allen**, **Shad Collins**, **Leonard Davis**, **Bill Dillard**, **Howard Scott**, **Leslie Thompson** (t); **Leslie Thompson**, **Lew Davis**, **Bill Mulraney**, **Dickie Wells**, **Wilbur De Paris**, **George Washington** (tb); **Harry Hines**, **Billy Amstell**, **Dave Shand**, **Philip Buchel**, **Harry Hayes**, **Buddy Featherstonehaugh**, **Benny Carter**, **Howard Johnson**, **Wayman Carver**, **Coleman Hawkins**, **Chu Berry** (reeds); **Billy Mason**, **Billy Munn**, **Eddie Carroll**, **Luis Russell**, **Red**

**Rodriguez** (p); **Alan Ferguson, Lawrence Lucie** (g); **Ernest Hill** (b); **Ronnie Gubertini, Bill Harty, Sid Catlett, Kaiser Marshall** (d); **Claude Ivy** (chimes). Largo Ⓕ 5129 (60 minutes). Recorded 1930-3.

⑧ ❻

It simply was not possible to confine Spike Hughes's talents and enquiring mind to just one musical form and his three-year involvement with jazz in the early thirties probably gave him all he wanted, although he continued to write provocative and valuable criticism for years after laying down his bass. By the closing months of 1930 his jazz interests had moved away from the 'white' small groups of Red Nichols and Venuti-Lang; he had become enamoured of the orchestral works of Duke Ellington. Hughes was able to deploy his arranging talents to greater effect and his best-selling record of the day was the two-part *Harlem Symphony* included here, a release devoted to Spike's own compositions and including nine of the 14 tracks he recorded in New York in 1933 with what was, in fact, Benny Carter's orchestra. This had a stellar personnel which included Coleman Hawkins, Chu Berry, Red Allen, Dickie Wells and Sid Catlett. Largo have grouped together the seven pieces (including *Harlem Symphony*, *Six Bells Stampede* and *Elegy*) used in the ballet *High Yellow*, first staged in June 1932. This was certainly the very first conjunction of ballet and jazz but the titles made in New York will have the strongest appeal, especially *Donegal Cradle Song* and *Arabesque,* with their magnificent contributions from Hawkins. All tracks have been carefully remastered by John R.T. Davies.    **AM**

## Daniel Humair                                                                1938

**Edges**   Humair (d); **Jerry Bergonzi** (ss, ts); **Aydin Esen** (p); **Miroslav Vitous** (b). Label Bleu
   Ⓕ LBLC 6545 (50 minutes). Recorded 1991.

⑧ ❽

Geneva native Humair, one of the great jazz drummers on any continent, usually displays his skills as an accompanist, or in such collective groups as the Kuhn/Jenny-Clark/Humair Trio or Quatre. This disc gives him a rare opportunity to function as a leader; rather than monopolizing the situation, he has done an inspired job of blending performers and material. The talented international quartet plays music from a variety of jazz composers (including Joachim Kühn, Franco d'Andrea, Michel Portal and George Gruntz) and interprets each piece, rather than merely using them as excuses for casual blowing. What results is an uncommonly balanced programme where we appreciate Humair's empathy for each soloist. The empathy is real: he and Bergonzi have grown to know each other, and pianist Esen is also moved to more interesting playing than on his own Columbia album. Vitous, who works with Humair in Quatre, lets his bold ideas pivot through the structures naturally over the drummer's flowing time. Humair, one of the most beautiful drummers to watch when he plays, conveys the dance-like grace of his conception, even in the heat of a performance like *Monitor*.    **BB**

## Helen Humes                                                                1913-81

**Songs I Like to Sing!**   Humes (v); **Al Porcino, Ray Triscari, Stu Williamson, Jack Sheldon** (t); **Harry Betts, Bob Fitzpatrick** (tb); **Art Pepper** (cl, as); **Ben Webster, Teddy Edwards** (ts); **Bill Hood** (bs); **André Previn** (p); **Barney Kessel** (g); **Leroy Vinnegar** (b); **Shelly Manne** (d). Contemporary
   Ⓜ OJCCD-171-2 (42 minutes). Recorded 1960.

⑦ ❾

Humes emerged from near-retirement in 1959 to make appearances and recordings that were greeted with fervent enthusiasm even by sober critics. The sweetness, accuracy and musicality of her voice had not declined since her time with Count Basie's orchestra in the thirties, nor been coarsened by the raucous blues that maintained her career after World War II – a period excellently documented on **Be-Baba-Leba** (Whiskey, Women and ... RBD701). For this album, arranger Marty Paich booked a 14-piece band of leading West Coast players; Sheldon, Pepper and Webster take most of the solos. Humes dresses a classy selection of standards, such as *Don't Worry 'Bout Me, You're Driving Me Crazy* and *Love Me or Leave Me*, without fuss or frippery, allowing the lyrics to tell their tales and adding a judicious minimum of decoration. *My Old Flame* and three others are arranged for jazz quintet (with Webster as tenor soloist) and string quartet. Humes's first recordings were racy blues, and her best-known number *Million Dollar Secret* (reprised here) another, yet she resisted being typecast in that idiom, maintaining that her favourite songs were ballads. She promoted that side of her repertoire on several subsequent recordings, all of them good, but none as spontaneously happy as **Songs I Like to Sing!**    **TR**

## Alberta Hunter                                                                1895-84

**Young Alberta Hunter: The 1920s and 1930s**   Hunter (v); **Charlie Shavers** (t); **Louis Armstrong, Elmer Chambers** (c); **George Brashear** (tb); **Buster Bailey, Don Redman, Ernest Elliott** (cl); **Sidney Bechet** (cl, ss); **Lil Armstrong, Fletcher Henderson, Eddie Heywood, Eubie Blake** (p); **Fats Waller** (org); **Buddy Christian, Charlie Dixon, Wellman Braud** (b). Jass Ⓕ J-CD6
   (67 minutes). Recorded 1921-40.

⑥ ❹

Clarity of diction, forceful delivery, a voice that is sweet and hard by turns, and the ability to bring a narrative song to life made Alberta Hunter one of the very best of the classic blues singers. She wrote *Downhearted Blues*, which she performs here, though less forcefully than most of the other pieces on the disc. Alberta was in Europe during the late twenties and early thirties, and this collection draws together the best of her American work from either side of that visit. The later sides, from 1939 and 1940, are a pointer to her mature style. Chief among them are four solos with pianist Eddie Heywood, which range from the mournful *The Love I Have for You* to the gutsy *My Castle's Rockin'*. At her best, she acts out a vocal character, and her reading of *Fine and Mellow* is the opposite to Billie Holiday's tragic lament,yet avoids sacrificing the song's intensity. Only the transfers let this collection down, as they are muddier than the few of these tracks that have surfaced in other anthologies. **AS**

# Charlie Hunter

**New review**
**Ready ... Set ... Shango!** Hunter (eight-string g); **Calder Spanier** (as); **Dave Ellis** (ts); **Scott Amendola** (d). Blue Note Ⓕ CDP8 37101-2 (53 minutes). Recorded 1996.

⑥ ⑧

Guitarist Hunter came to jazz through rock, rap and funk, discovering it on his own through the records of Charlie Christian and Charlie Parker. His own career path took him into the industrial rap band, the Beatnigs, and then on to the Disposable Heroes of Hiphoprisy, who reached their zenith when they landed the support slot on a U2 tour of America. A move into jazz gave Hunter more musical rewards, the Charlie Hunter Trio quickly landing a contract with Blue Note. Their first album, **Bing, Bing, Bing!** (not a tribute to Bing Crosby, as far as one can establish) met with sufficient popular response to merit a new record, made by what had now, with the addition of altoist Calder Spanier, become a working quartet. This is it. It suggests a settling of style (one of the distractions of the first had been its nervy inability to resist the temptations of eclecticism), and the two horns have some nice routines worked for themselves, taking some of the front-line burden from Hunter, but some problems remain. Tenorist Ellis is still in the thrall of Michael Brecker, with the new man, Spanier, setting all the pace with his alto solos. Meanwhile, Hunter is happy to play an eight-string guitar, which obviates the necessity for a bass player, but it means that, for the most part, the bass lines remain simple vamps or pedal tones, more useful to the repetitions of rock and soul than to the improvised music Hunter is now dealing with, and while his chorded accompanying and solos are deft and full of a jazz sensibility, the overall effect is one of constraint rather than restraint. It's a little like Scofield with sunglasses on: hip but a little too cool. Hunter's band has released a subsequent album, **Natty Dread** (Blue Note), focusing on Bob Marley's music, to which the same comments apply. **KS**

# Per Husby
1949

**New review**
**If You Could See Me Now** Husby (arr, cond); **Earl Gardner**, **Michael Leonhart** (t); **Jim Pugh** (tb); **Peter Gordon** (frh); **Howard Johnson** (tba); **Jerome Richardson**, **Chris Potter**, **Frank Wess**, **Scott Robinson** (reeds); **Ted Rosenthal** (p); **Bucky Pizzarelli** (g); **Jay Leonhart** (b); **Grady Tate** (d); **Karin Krog**, **Georgie Fame** (v). Gemini Ⓕ GMCD89 (68 minutes). Recorded 1995.

⑨ ⑩

Jazz is full of labours of love, some good, some bad. This is one of the good ones, though it makes a painful start in that the charming *On a Misty Night* begins with George Fame having severe difficulty centring his notes. Once that rocky start is out of the way, the listener with an ear for mellifluous big band sounds is in for a considerable treat, for what this album does is dust down and update a whole treasure trove of Tadd Dameron compositions and arrangements, with a couple of Per Husby originals thrown in for good measure. Husby is a long-term Dameron devotee, as can be seen from the fact that one of the first men he contacted in New York (where the record was made) to help him bring the project to fruition was one of the leading lights behind Dameronia, Frank Wess. The studio big band is ridiculously laden with talent and performs with precision and *élan*, with soloists such as Richardson, Potter, Pugh and Leonhart. The charts are beautifully balanced by exciting solos. The writing is, of course, beautifully transparent, every line clearly etched, while the clean recording helps the listener follow such subtle beauties. This is a labour of love, and it works. **KS**

# Bobby Hutcherson
1941

**Components** Hutcherson (vb); **Freddie Hubbard** (t); **James Spaulding** (as, f); **Herbie Hancock** (p); **Ron Carter** (b); **Joe Chambers** (d). Blue Note Ⓜ CDP8 29027-2 (41 minutes). Recorded 1965.

⑧ ⑧

Vibraphonist Bobby Hutcherson is a player deserving far greater recognition. Originally inspired by Milt Jackson, Hutcherson, while borrowing from Jackson's inimitable blues-cum-bop bag, has developed a remarkably broad and pliant style. The Los Angeles native received his initial baptisms with Curtis Amy, Charles Lloyd, Al Grey and Billy Mitchell. It was his 1961 move to New York and a batch of outstanding Blue Note dates with protean players such as Jackie McLean, Grachan Moncur III, Grant Green, Andrew Hill and Eric Dolphy that put him on the map. Here, in his second date for Blue Note as a leader, Hutcherson's compelling breadth is revealed in tandem with some of Blue Note's then youngest and hottest new stars.

The first four tracks, Hutcherson originals, speak with an edgy, no-nonsense neo-bop voice reminiscent of Blakey's Jazz Messengers. On the title tune, ensembles snap like a whip, unleashing inspired solo flights. A contrast is *Tranquillity*, a shimmering soundscape whose introduction features a surprisingly ethereal Hutcherson. *Little B's Poem* is a charmingly lithe waltz with Spaulding's breezy fluting, while *West 22nd Street Theme* is a slow stroll featuring Hutcherson's and Hubbard's bluesy bop-isms. Most surprising are the remaining four tunes by Joe Chambers, galvanizing amalgams of bop and free jazz that alternately groove, float, flutter and fly to the heavens. In all, it is a diverse and alluring set spotlighting the multi-dimensional Hutcherson and a group of peers whose alert simpatico and derring-do still raise goose-bumps.                                                    **CB**

---

**Solo/Quartet**  Hutcherson (vb, mbas); **McCoy Tyner** (p); **Herbie Lewis** (b); **Billy Higgins** (d).
  Contemporary Ⓜ OJCCD425-2 (45 minutes). Recorded 1981-2.

⑧ ⑧

Hutcherson made his reputation with a long sequence of brilliant albums for the Blue Note label, starting in the early sixties and coming to an end with the demise of the original Blue Note jazz programme in the mid seventies. Of those 15 or so vinyl releases, just two – **Components** and **San Francisco** – are currently available (the other Blue Note now available is **Oblique**, a mid-sixties session which went unissued at the time, and is certainly not essential Hutcherson). The L.A.-based vibes player has since continued his recording career with Contemporary, Landmark and Timeless.

This early-eighties session contains most of the best things about Hutcherson's playing. On what was originally the first side of an LP, but now is just the first three tracks of a CD, Hutcherson plays solo, with a deal of double-tracking utilized as well. His musical thinking has always been much broader than that of someone who just waits for his turn to solo, and he uses this natural arranger's sensibility to brilliant effect on the pieces where the vibes, glockenspiels and marimbas are built up track by track into cohesive and swinging wholes. The remarkable thing about these tracks is that they remain utterly transparent in texture and completely devoid of clutter. The quartet sides are more conventional in concept, and Hutcherson's roots in the Milt Jackson vocabulary more clearly evident, but his originality of approach is just as certain, as is the intensity of vision he brings to everything he does. Hutcherson's is a major voice in the music and this album is a significant achievement in his career.                                                    **KS**

---

**Cruisin' the Bird**  Hutcherson (vb); **Ralph Moore** (ts, ss); **Buddy Montgomery** (p); **Rufus Reid** (b);
  **Victor Lewis** (d). Landmark Ⓕ LCD 1517-2 (53 minutes). Recorded 1988.

✔️                                                    ⑧ ⑧

This is just the record to play to anyone who is fond of announcing the imminent death of jazz. Everything about it is distinguished; the bass and the drums function together with the ease and familiarity of a long-standing relationship, the piano lays down clear but unobvious harmonies, and both front line soloists play with relaxed brilliance. You might expect a band of veterans like Hutcherson to perform at this level, in this timeless style which is beyond fashion, but Ralph Moore was born in 1956, the year Rollins made **Saxophone Colossus**. Hence the reason to be cheerful about the future. In form, this is a simple quintet blowing session, recorded over two days, made up of originals and standards and very lightly arranged. The result is sparkling music. Hutcherson's whole career is dotted with such works and they have rarely received the praise they deserve. **Cruisin' the Bird** is one of the great jazz records of the eighties.                                                    **DG**

# Dick Hyman                                                                          1927

---

**Music from My Fair Lady**  Hyman (p); **Ruby Braff** (c). Concord Jazz Ⓕ CCD4393 (53 minutes).
  Recorded 1989.

⑧ ⑧

Hyman is a repository of early jazz and jazz-related piano styles, which made him the perfect composer to work on Woody Allen's period comedy, *The Purple Rose of Cairo*, one of several films he has scored. Stylistic diversity is Hyman's strength; in the fifties he worked with swing veteran Red Norvo, modernist Tony Scott, and Dixieland revivalists. In the sixties, he was one of the first to record on synthesizer. His partnership with cornettist Braff, dating from 1974, brings out Hyman's best. In person, he is quiet and composed, Braff an outspoken cut-up. Before the microphones, they switch personalities: Braff plays with warm elegance (a weakness for witty quotes notwithstanding); Hyman prods him using any workable strategy.

This is the most satisfying of their duo albums, not least because Lerner's and Loewe's 1956 show may have been the last Broadway musical with more than two songs worth whistling. Hyman can break into Waller-style stride (fast *With a Little Bit of Luck*), careen like Earl Hines (*I'm an Ordinary*

*Man*), walk 4/4 bass lines (*Wouldn't It Be Loverly*), or echo Darius Milhaud's chromatic Brazilian pieces of the twenties (*Rain in Spain*). But there is nothing musty about their playing fifties music, twenties style, in the eighties: it breathes fresh air. **KW**

# Abdullah Ibrahim 1934

**Echoes from Africa** Ibrahim (p, v); **Johnny Dyani** (b, v). Enja Ⓕ ENJ3047-2 (32 minutes). Recorded 1979.

⑧ ❽

Although best known as a solo pianist and group leader, Ibrahim also has a number of duo albums to his credit. These include sets with Gato Barbieri, Johnny Dyani, Max Roach, Archie Shepp and Carlos Ward. **Echoes from Africa** is the second of his two records with Dyani, a fellow South African totally conversant with Ibrahim's musical roots and whose bass has an elemental power to match the leader's driving piano. *Namhanje*, a traditional folk-song, shows how well they work together, the piano's rich rolling drama underpinned by a strong bass pulse as their voices sing out in exhortation. *Lakutshonilanga*, by Mackay Davashe, shares the plaintive beauty of Ibrahim tunes such as *The Wedding*, although here the pianist embroiders the melody line with tiny percussive dissonances that point to his love for Thelonious Monk's music. Ibrahim's own *Zikr* is devotional music, a genre he has been exploring since his conversion to Islam: over growling *arco* bass, the men's hushed voices rise up in undulating lines of prayer.

The CD's drawback is a playing time of only 32 minutes. Enja should consider coupling **Echoes from Africa** with Ibrahim's and Dyani's 1973 **Good News from Africa**, as both LPs could be accommodated on a single disc. **GL**

**Ekaya** Ibrahim (p, ldr); **Dick Griffin** (tb); **Carlos Ward** (f, as); **Ricky Ford** (ts); **Charles Davis** (bs); **Cecil McBee** (b); **Ben Riley** (d). Blackhawk Ⓕ BKH50205CD (38 minutes). Recorded 1983.

⑧ ❼

Capetown-born Adolph Johannes Brand converted to Islam in 1968 and became Abdullah Ibrahim, but by that time he had already become known internationally as Dollar Brand. No matter, it is the music which is important and this CD, released originally on the Ekapa label, features the group which calls itself Ekaya which means "home" in several South African languages. There is a very strong thread of African music in the six titles and the work of the American jazzmen is exactly in context. In fact Carlos Ward sounds for all the world like a native-born South African (he was, in fact, born in the Panama Canal Zone); it is Ward who is one of the strongest featured voices here, playing with the verve and dancing quality found in the work of the late Kippie Moeketsi, a remarkable South African alto saxist. Ibrahim has surrounded himself with men who are very sympathetic to his work (five of the six tunes and all of the arrangements are by the pianist); and the rhythm work of Ben Riley is so imaginative that one realizes he was never given sufficient scope when working with groups such as the Thelonious Monk Quartet or the Lockjaw Davis-Johnny Griffin band. Inevitably Ibrahim is not featured at length with the group, but his personality manifests itself throughout this fascinating programme of genuine Afro-American music. **AM**

**African River** Ibrahim (p); **Robin Eubanks** (tb); **John Stubblefield** (f, ts); **Horace Alexander Young** (ss, as, picc); **Howard Johnson** (bb, tba, bs); **Buster Williams** (b); **Brian Adams** (d). Enja Ⓕ ENJ6018-2 (46 minutes). Recorded 1989.

✔ ⑧ ❽

In retrospect, Ibrahim's somewhat prodigious output must be rated as inconsistent; outstanding solo albums such as **African Piano** (Japo CD600002) and **Ode to Ellington** (West Wind 2020CD) must be weighed against poor items where the pianist's insistent chordal emphasis has led into somewhat static areas. His work with the American free-players in the late sixties occasionally lacked direction and his more recent partnership with Carlos Ward often foundered through no fault of his own. Fortunately, more is now being heard of his arranging skill in medium-sized groups and this CD is a superb example. Despite the American emphasis in the personnel, the arrangements consistently capture the South African 'high life' spirit. The piano plays a prominent part and there is a textural depth that speaks of the leader's wide musical experience, as well as his awareness of the need to surprise in jazz writing. There is something of the Ellington tone-poem about *Joan – Capetown Flower* and evidence of Ducal voicings on other titles. Ibrahim's own hypnotic fervour remains an important ingredient in titles such as *Toi-Toi* and *Chisa* but, with quality solos in particular from Williams on *African River*, Eubanks on *Joan* and *Duke 88*, Young on *Duke 88* and Stubblefield and Johnson literally throughout, this is a perfectly balanced mix of the prepared and the extemporized. **BMcR**

**No Fear, No Die (s'en fout la mort)** Ibrahim (p); **Frank Lacy** (tb); **Horace Alexander Young III** (f, ss, as); **Ricky Ford** (ts); **Jimmy Cozier** (bs, cl); **Buster Williams** (b); **Ben Riley** (d). Enja/Tip Toe Ⓕ 88815-2 (45 minutes). Recorded 1990.

⑧ ❿

On this, the soundtrack album to Claire Denis's eponymous film, Ibrahim combines his twin fascinations for Ellington and African music into a compelling, lazy, sensuous tapestry of sound.

The opening track, *Calypso Minor*, sets a brooding, spare mood similar to that often caught in later years by Ellington when he was casting a spell of mystery and vague unease. Ford does a manful impersonation of Gonsalves, Lacy of Britt Woodman. This theme, with its dominant ostinato bass pattern, gets a reprise at the end, this time in brighter colours and retitled *Calypso Major*. The music is pellucid, every note has its proper place, and Ibrahim gives us the core of its meaning. The Ellington connection is even stronger on the second track, *Angelica*, one of Duke's tunes which first saw the light of day on his 1963 small-group date with Coltrane. This is a jolly treatment of a colourful theme, stressing the Latin and West Indian rhythmic angle inherent in the melody. On this disc Ibrahim manages to convey the best of his two dominant musical worlds, avoiding the siren calls of both – imitation of a master or the repetition of static patterns past the point of interest and into tedium. His writing for his group is consistently resourceful, bringing especially bright colours to the unison themes, while his own piano playing is concise, taut and laden with meaning. The horns all deliver their section work convincingly. Of the soloists, only Ford really pulls his weight, but this is a small drawwback to a generally very positive and enjoyable programme of music. **KS**

## ICP Orchestra

**Performs Nichols and Monk** **Misha Mengelberg** (p, arr); **Ab Baars** (ss, as); **Michael Moore** (as, cl); **Wolter Wierbos** (tb); **Maurice Horsthuis** (va); **Ernst Reijseger** (vc); **Han Bennink** (d); **George Lewis** (tb) on Monk programme only; **Toon de Gouw** (t); **Garrett List** (tb); **Larry Fishkind** (tba); **Sean Bergin** (as); **Paul Thermos** (as); **Steve Lacy** (ss) on Nichols programme only. ICP ⓕ 026 (72 minutes). Recorded 1984/6.

⑩ ❽

The ICP Orchestra was originally formed in the seventies as a Dutch version of Globe Unity, although under the guidance of the remarkable Misha Mengelberg it grew into a more versatile and still volatile ensemble. These two stimulating sessions expand upon the small group arrangements of tunes by Thelonious Monk and Herbie Nichols recorded under Roswell Rudd's leadership in 1982. As a pianist Mengelberg is fully capable of mirroring Monk's inimitable timing and acidic harmonies, but as an arranger his own brilliant vision intrudes – for example, in the unrelated atonal episode which interrupts the swinging performance of *Four In One* or the non-tempered, atmospheric introduction to *Misterioso* – preventing these versions from remaining merely rote recreations. Mengelberg himself perfectly characterizes the musicians' contributions as "uninhibited," and their tart, often thematically tangential solos slip in and out of context in these always unpredictable arrangements. Mengelberg may extend vamps, eliminate chord changes, adopt even more outrageous harmonies than in the original, and add extreme splashes of colour by use of instruments like cello, tuba and soprano sax, but he is ever-faithful to the *spirit* of Monk's unique style and wit.

His radical redesign of Nichols's pieces do no harm to their inherent lyricism, and the presence of Steve Lacy acts as an additional grounding force. But there is nevertheless a constant tension, a pulling apart and reformation, that energizes the arrangements and identifies Mengelberg's brilliance and individuality. Like John Zorn at his best, Mengelberg is able to recontextualize the originality of the music in a time when our ears have grown accustomed to dissonance and rhythmic quirks – an essential antidote to musty neo-conservative revivalist attitudes. **AL**

## Klaus Ignatzek

1954

New review

**Silent Horns** **Ignatzek** (p); **Claudio Roditi, Gustavo Bergalli** (t); **Jean-Louis Rassinfosse** (b); **Jorge Rosse** (d). Candid ⓕ CCD79729 (71 minutes). Recorded 1994.

⑦ ⑨

Hailed in his native Germany as one of the most talented musicians on that country's jazz scene, critics elsewhere have never been quite so sure about Ignatzek. Despite impeccable credentials that have him paying his dues with visiting US stars whilst at the University of Oldenburg, then completing his studies in the jazz program at Arizona State, his work has often seemed like a brilliant collage of post-bop styles rather than something truly original. In his last-but-one album, **The Answer** (Candid CCD79534), he set about confounding his critics with this reedless line-up, featuring a two-trumpet front line with prodigious solo skills and limiting the necessity for ensemble playing.

His pairing with Roditi goes back earlier and has inspired some of Roditi's best recorded playing. Here, on a set of originals paying tribute to some of bop's finest trumpeters (all now dead – hence the album title), Ignatzek continues the good work, the identity of this quintet now firmly established, and the particular chemistry between his trumpeters producing some challenging and absorbing solos. Roditi's is the more mature voice, aptly supported by the rhythm team. Ignatzek's all-round talent as bandleader and composer is obvious, and his solo playing (especially on a nimble *Calling Mr Gillespie*) now has the marks of maturity. Max Bolleman's first-rate recording quality deserves mention. **AS**

# Irakere

**Live at Ronnie Scott's** Jesus 'Chuchu' Valdes (p, ldr); **Juan Monguia, Adalberto Moreno** (t); **Orlando Valle, Caesar Lopez, Carlos Averhoff** (reeds); **Carlos E. Morales** (g); **Carlos del Puerto** (b); **Oscar Valdes** (v, perc); **Enrique Pla, Miguel 'Anga' Diaz** (perc). World Pacific Ⓕ CDP7 80598-2 (61 minutes). Recorded 1991.

⑦ ❼

Here, the exuberant 11-strong Irakere is caught live in a tumultuous 1991 date recorded at Ronnie Scott's Club, London's fabled jazz mecca. Led by Jesus 'Chuchu' Valdes, the juggernaut's peppery pianist and chief composer, Irakere is an open-ended yet disciplined ensemble with lots of wide open spaces for soloists to range and roam freely. Since its establishment in Havana in 1973, Irakere has been an incubator for fine soloists such as Paquito D'Rivera and trumpeter Arturo Sandoval, who both defected in the early eighties for solo careers in the US. That tradition continues, especially in the inspired work of saxophonists Carlos Averhoff and Caesar Lopez, and flautist Orlando Valle. In a programme of Valdes originals, the band smokes with Caribbean fire. Even on the ballad *When My Heart Sings* there is a larger-than-life, heart-on-sleeve lyricism that sets everything in motion. On *Looking Up*, the band struts with an infectious street-wise swagger keyed to Lopez's surging alto *à la* Gil Evans-vintage David Sanborn. Valdes, who attacks the keyboard with a brio similar to that of Monty Alexander and Michel Camillio, is a constant source of soloistic heat, especially in the tempestuous *Neurosis* in which he includes a number of Maynard-isms in an oblique but no less sincere tip-of-the-hat to fellow bandleader Maynard Ferguson. **CB**

# Mark Isham

1951

**New review**
**Blue Sun** Isham (t, c, flh, el); **David Goldblatt** (p, elp); **Steve Tavaglione** (ts); **Doug Lunn** (elb); **Kurt Wortman** (d). Columbia Ⓕ 481304 2 (61 minutes). Recorded 1995.

⑦ ❾

As a frequent underscorer in the Hollywood film studios, Isham must be used to working to bespoke briefs and he applies the same method to his Columbia début. Here, his self-assigned model is Miles Davis's **Kind of Blue** and accordingly the mood is introspective, tempos rarely stray above a creep, and Isham's pale and interesting horn, either open or muted, dominates the soundscape. The only things that betray the record's modernity are the electric bass (even then played with great subtlety), the electric piano on *Tour De Chance* (derived from later Miles: say, **Filles de Kilimanjaro**) and harmonic sequences and rhythms (mostly Latin and rock – no swing) which are post-1959.

Conceptually then, only a few surprises, but the interpretation and execution is impeccable. Lovers of Miles's lyricism will relate quickly to Isham's sullen tone and thoughtful delivery, and it's good to hear Steve Tavaglione, who has so far been a well-kept secret on the West Coast fusion scene, both excelling in an uncharacteristically poetic setting and getting major label exposure. Witness his contrasting tonal approaches throughout and his exquisite range and control on *Barcelona*. One could suspect Isham of preciosity: the music is 'performed' rather than 'played', the insert-note seems to depict the leader as a lifestyle model and often enough his Windham Hill new-age roots show. But the modish veneer is just that; there's substance below the surface. **MG**

# Iskra 1903

**New review**
**Iskra 1903** Paul Rutherford (tb); **Philipp Wachsmann** (vn); **Barry Guy** (b). Maya Ⓕ MCD9502 (58 minutes). Recorded 1992.

⑨ ❽

Named after the house organ of Lenin's Bolshevik Party during the early days of the Russian revolution ('iskra' translates as 'spark'), the original configuration of Iskra 1903 consisted of first-generation British, free improvisers Rutherford, Guy and guitarist Derek Bailey. They released a stunning two-LP set of 1970 and 1972 performances on Incus (deserving of immediate reissue) as well as an even rarer 1973 recording for Deutsche Grammophon. In the hiatus between then and now Bailey has been replaced by violinist Wachsmann and though the fragile interpersonal dynamics from which this music so vibrantly feeds have shifted somewhat, the realignment has in fact revitalized their outlook and efforts.

They specialize in expansive, detailed, large-form improvisations of inherently dramatic – rather than technical – impetus; individual contributions approach the state of musical narrative, lending a variety of episodes to each of the four pieces here. Over the years Rutherford has grown even more loquacious, able to appear brash and laconic in the same breath. Wachsmann adds a wry sense of lyricism and percussive pluck. Animated by bassist Guy's energetic resourcefulness, the trio's contagious interplay highlights quick-witted repartee and remarks on the fly, which occasionally assemble into something resembling a theme – normally anathema in such spontaneous circles. **AL**

# Itchy Fingers

**Full English Breakfast**  Matt Wates (as); **Pete Long** (as, cl); **Andy Panayi** (ss, as, ts); **Dave O'Higgins** (ts); **Mike Mower** (ts, bs, cl, f). Enja Ⓕ ENJ7085-2 (51 minutes). Recorded 1992.

⑧ ❽

In contrast to their previous (third) album, **Live in Europe**, **Full English Breakfast** presents the UK's leading saxophone quartet with the opportunity to exploit a range of studio techniques, most importantly overdubbing, to produce their most intricate and polished work to date. Time signatures can be anything from 7/8 through 15/16 to 4/4 (and that is just one piece, *The Dome*), and the intricacy of leader/composer Mike Mower's arrangements occasionally militates against his band achieving the exuberant informality characterizing the work of say, Bobby Watson's 29th Street Saxophone Quartet, but this album generally hits a workable balance between composition and improvisation. Thus, alongside the elaborate formality of *Svea Rike*, a Mower composition commissioned by a Swedish classical saxophone quartet and containing a bare minimum of improvisation, Itchy Fingers are versatile enough to present *This Time's Hard*, a 5/8 piece held together by a drum machine and climaxing in an absorbing tenor duel between Andy Panayi and the uniformly excellent Dave O'Higgins. They then follow that with *The Crillon Controller*, featuring a bluesy, airy alto solo from Matt Wates. Overall, the album is at its most enjoyable on tracks like these last two – and, in particular, a highly intelligent version of *Night in Tunisia*, when the band lets their hair down a bit; the prevalence of tricksy arrangements elsewhere tends to over-egg the pudding somewhat, but then full English breakfasts are traditionally hard to digest, if ultimately extremely nourishing.     **CP**

# Jackie & Roy

1928/1921

**New review**

**Jackie and Roy Forever**  Jackie Cain (v); **Roy Kral** (v, p); **Peter Ecklund** (t); **Matt Haviland** (tb); **Bob Franceschini** (ts, f, cl); **Erik Lawrence** (bs, f); **Lynn Seaton**, **Dean Johnson** (b); **Rich Derosa** (d) plus string quartet. Music Masters Ⓕ 01612 65128-2 (47 minutes). Recorded 1995.

⑧ ❿

When this splendid CD was recorded Cain and Kral had been working together for 47 years and married for 46. As with Cleo Laine and John Dankworth, it is impossible to imagine them apart. They have become a kind of composite individual, consisting of a piano and two voices, with a rapport that is quite uncanny. Frank Sinatra once remarked that "you could tune a piano to Jackie Cain's voice", so exact is her intonation. Add to this the inventive harmonies and immaculate synchronization and you have a truly remarkable phenomenon. There is a version here of that fine Wolf-Landesman song *Spring Can Really Hang You Up the Most*, first recorded by them in 1955, and there is little to choose between the two renditions. Of all their time-defying feats this is the most amazing.     **DG**

# D.D. Jackson

1967

**New review**

**Rhythm Dance**  Jackson (p); **John Geggie** (b); **Jean Martin** (d). Justin Time Ⓕ JUST89-2 (64 minutes). Recorded 1996.

⑦ ❽

Jackson made his début as a leader in 1994 with **Peace-Song**, which found him with this trio plus employer David Murray on sax. Clearly he and his record company feel that the disc had sufficient impact to warrant a trio album with Jackson unequivocally as the selling point. As noted previously, Jackson has played around New York with some exacting leaders, including Dewey Redman, and also took a course of music tuition from the late Don Pullen. This latter mentor still exerts a great influence over Jackson's approach, both technically and emotionally. Jackson has that same ability to move suddenly and dramatically between the most *avant* of keyboard pummellings to an elegant and rhythmically uncluttered melody, all usually over a contant pulse. In this he is not moving into uncharted territory; more just keeping pace with the contemporary tendency to use many eras of jazz from which to extract a coherent statement. Like many young pianists (Terrason, Keezer and Green, for example) Jackson has terrific facility and occasionally torrential feelings to express, and this flair makes it easy to feel well disposed towards this set. Jackson is not yet particularly comfortable with the nether regions of a ballad, preferring to rough the listener up a little with some hairy speeds and oblique juxtapositions, but while excitement alone cannot sustain an entire career, there's enough of that quality here to make one look forward to the next instalment.     **KS**

# Ed Jackson

1959

**Wake Up Call**  Jackson (as, arr); **James Zoller** (t, f); **Tom Varner** (frh); **Clark Gayton** (tb); **Rich Rothenberg** (ts); **John Stetch** (p); **Dave Jackson** (b); **Steve Johns** (d); **Jamie Baum** (f). New World CounterCurrents Ⓕ 80451-2 (70 minutes). Recorded 1994.

New York saxophonist/composer Jackson has been making appearances on recordings since the beginning of the eighties, enjoying stints with Jaki Byard's Apollo Street Stompers and Roy Haynes's quintet before making international waves with the 29th Street Saxophone Quartet. This is his début as a leader, and it has a great deal more going for it than the vast majority of débuts. His musical language is fully formed as both a composer and an improviser. He understands the sonorities of the instruments he combines here in superb arrangements, mostly with his own originals but also, with notable imagination, to Monk's *Played Twice* (John Stetch contributes the arrangement for the Richard Rodgers standard, *Have You Met Miss Jones?*).

In some respects Jackson conjures memories of Charles Mingus's Jazz Workshop alchemy in the way he combines his own material with re-thought standards he has particular affection for. He is interested in extended form as well as an individual balance between scored and improvised sections. There is also a healthy amount of interchange and dialogue between all the musicians involved: this is not an exercise in the horns queueing up for their solo spots either side of a theme statement. Much more happens than that, and the unwinding of each tale told is a consistent stimulation to the listener. This is not 'difficult' music at all, but it rewards close attention and repeated hearings.　　**KS**

# Javon Jackson

**New review**
**A Look Within** Jackson (ts); **Fareed Haque** (g); **Peter Washington** (b); **Billy Drummond** (d); on two tracks add **Dr Lonnie Smith** (org); on one track add **Cassandra Wilson** (v). Blue Note Ⓕ CDP8 36490-2 (57 minutes). Recorded 1996.

This, Jackson's second as a leader for Blue Note, shows a considerable growth and broadening of his creative aspirations. Retaining Haque, Washington and Drummond from his first line-up but this time dispensing with piano (Dr Lonnie does his organ thing on two tracks, but elsewhere there are no keyboards), Jackson revels in the sparseness and in the exoticisms Haque can so naturally bring to a session. There are many touching moments on this disc, not least the moving ballad *Memoria e fado*, but Jackson also demonstrates on *Zoot Allures* that he has not lost interest in chasin' the train, leading a compelling up-tempo gallop with customary zest. What he seems to have had most success with in the year or so since his last album is developing a wholly convincing balladeer's approach, and while it still may lean rather heavily on the dark brusqueness of Joe Henderson, it carries enough distinguishing traits to be recognizable as Jackson and no one else. Latinate, groovy, exotic or other, each number here receives just treatment and a wholly committed performance from a thoroughly integrated group, led from the front by a tenorist with much of interest to relate. One to keep for the very next rainy day.　　**KS**

# Milt Jackson　　1923

**Plenty, Plenty Soul** Jackson (vb); **Joe Newman** (t); **Jimmy Cleveland** (tb); **Cannonball Adderley** (as); **Frank Foster**, **Lucky Thompson** (ts); **Sahib Shihab** (bs); **Horace Silver** (p); **Percy Heath**, **Oscar Pettiford** (b); **Art Blakey**, **Connie Kay** (d); **Quincy Jones** (arr). Atlantic Jazz Ⓜ 781269-2 (42 minutes). Recorded 1957.

The star of the Modern Jazz Quartet, and before that a sideman with Dizzy Gillespie and Woody Herman, Jackson is still the vibraphonist most able to sound like a wind instrument, rather than a novelty effect whose main appeal is visual. The two sessions here feature all-star sextet and nonet line-ups within which Jackson's status as a 'horn-player' is triumphantly confirmed, especially in the larger group where Blakey's 'big band' drumming is a challenge and a complement to all concerned. The brief but pithy comments of Adderley and Basie sidemen Newman and Foster are excellent. In particular, Thompson's solos on the sextet sides exemplify his peak period, which includes other sessions with Jackson for Atlantic and Savoy. Jones's arrangements are crucial to the mellow sound of both sets, including the only up-tempo number, *Boogity Boogity*, which has the same melody as his more famous ballad *The Midnight Sun Never Sets*. Nat Hentoff's updated notes are definitive, on both Jackson and the then-new term, 'soul', though the booklet fails to include Silver in the sextet line-up. Happily, the overdubbing which enables Milt to duet with himself briefly on *Blues at Twilight*, lost in at least one earlier reissue, is duly restored.　　**BP**

**Bags & Trane** Jackson (vb); **John Coltrane** (ts); **Hank Jones** (p); **Paul Chambers** (b); **Connie Kay** (d). Atlantic Jazz Ⓜ 781368-2 (57 minutes). Recorded 1959.

The vibraphone does not need a better interpreter than Milt Jackson. His robust and direct manner with the instrument is much more astute than the fey approach evinced by Gary Burton and more incisive than that of the voluble Lionel Hampton. Atlantic provided a myriad of settings for Jackson when he was under contract to them in the early sixties – this one in late 1959 came a couple of months after a similar pairing of Jackson with Coleman Hawkins. The resultant music is often stark and economical, more like hessian than silk. But benign warmth flows through the jumping *Three Little Words* and Coltrane is at his softest on *The Night We Called It a Day*. He moves happily in Jackson's blues-drenched homeground and plays more open and less self-conscious tenor than was often the case, producing a virtuous set of mainstream tear-ups which is probably the nearest Coltrane ever came to a frolic. It would have been difficult to improve on the rhythm trio. Three tracks, Jackson's *Blues Legacy*, the standard *Stairway to the Stars* and a stalwart version of Harry Edison's *Centrepiece*, which previously appeared elsewhere on vinyl, have been added to the original album. **SV**

---

**New review**

**Memories of Thelonious Sphere Monk** Jackson (vb); **Monty Alexander** (p); **Ray Brown** (b); **Mickey Roker** (d). Pablo Ⓜ OJCCD851-2 (42 minutes). Recorded 1982.

⑦ ❽

Recorded at Ronnie Scott's club in London shortly after the death of Thelonious Monk, the album includes a tribute in the form of a Monk tune featuring each musician in turn. Medleys don't usually come off on record but this succeeds better than most. The other factor that might have affected Jackson's playing was the recent revival of the Modern Jazz Quartet after an absence of seven years. This makes the inclusion here of *Django*, a tune he must play on most gigs with the MJQ, somewhat surprising. However, he seems inspired by the powerful lift imparted by the rhythm section, different to what he would expect from the MJQ, to produce one of his most propulsive solos on the tune without losing any of the usual suppleness of phrase. He maintains his form on the other numbers, a blues and a gospel-type piece, in what stands as a good account of his more extrovert side. **RA**

---

**The Prophet Speaks** Jackson (vb); **Joshua Redman** (ts); **Cedar Walton** (p); **John Clayton** (b); **Billy Higgins** (d). On three tracks **Joe Williams** (v). QWest/Reprise Ⓕ 245591-2 (74 minutes). Recorded 1994.

❽ ❿

Jackson is now comfortably into his seventies, but there is no lessening of his creative fire: the flow of improvisatory ideas is as strong as ever. This may not be the greatest record he has been involved in, but it is a very good one and equal to any he has made under his own name for many years. This is in part due to the superb empathy to be found within the rhythm section, Walton and Higgins moving as one with Jackson at every turn in the music. As for the vibist himself, he always plays to his strengths, with the blues and balladry being two which get ample coverage here. Jackson has an uncanny ability to make his instrument sing a melody, his gradations of touch and his minute rhythmic shifts giving great expressivity to the simplest line. Examples of such moments abound throughout the programme. Jackson often has guest saxophonists on his dates, and this time it is Joshua Redman, who makes his presence felt in an entirely appropriate way on six of the 12 tracks, two of which also have the veteran singer Joe Williams vocalizing with unusual restraint and directness. Redman makes full use of his versatility, concentrating on the blues-based part of his style and using a full, sensuous tone to good expressive effect. In this he fulfils the function once taken up by, say, Jimmy Heath on some of Jackson's sixties albums (one of which has been included as a filler on last year's Impulse! reissue, **Statements**). It's also nice to see Jackson continuing his long-standing affair with Monk's music, both *Off-Minor* and *Blue Monk* getting the treatment here. **KS**

# Oliver Jackson

1933-94

**Billie's Bounce** Jackson (d); **Irvin Stokes** (t); **Norris Turney** (as); **Claude Blake** (p); **Ali Jackson** (b). Black & Blue Ⓕ 59183-2 (70 minutes). Recorded 1984.

⑤ ❽

A stalwart of the Detroit modern scene of the forties, Jackson formed a duo with Eddie Locke in 1948 and for five years worked as a variety act called Bop and Locke. He moved to New York in 1956 and, after playing at the Metropole for a time, found himself being called repeatedly for mainstream gigs. He played with leaders such as Buck Clayton, Benny Goodman and Earl Hines, and in 1969 formed the JPJ Quartet. In more recent years he had been a member of George Wein's Festival All Stars. This CD gives a good impression of his driving and always swinging style. There remains an edge to his playing that reminds the listener of his bop beginnings, but he is an ideal partner for the uncomplicated trumpet of Stokes and the gently flowing alto of Turney. Appropriately, the odd drum bombs are dropped on *Billie's Bounce* and *Yardbird Suite*, while the softly contoured aspects of *I Don't Know About You* are exploited in a more relaxed manner. Jackson's timing is very good, his ride cymbal always suitably pushy. This musicianly, if unspectacular, session shows him to have been an all-round professional. **BMcR**

# Willis Jackson

1928-87

**Bar Wars** Jackson (ts); **Charles Earland** (org); **Pat Martino** (g); **Idris Muhammad** (d); **Buddy Caldwell** (perc). Muse Ⓕ MCD6011 (46 minutes). Recorded 1977.

✓

Willis 'Gator' Jackson (he got his nickname from a hit 45 he had with the Cootie Williams band in 1948, *Gator Tail* ) started his career as an out-and-out bar-walking honker. His early sides certainly lack nothing in excitement, but are rather short on invention (a goodly sample of his work at this time is available on **Call of the Gators**, Delmark CD DD460). Possibly realizing that this approach would limit his long-term career, he developed his playing much in the same way as did the 'daddy of all honkers', Illinois Jacquet. By the time this 1977 Muse album was recorded, Jackson had long achieved mastery of the idiom he worked in: the tenor-and-organ combo.

**Bar Wars** gets top rating simply because tenor-and-organ records do not come better than this. Jackson's full, warm tone is ideally captured by – who else? – Rudy van Gelder. He plays the ballads in a way which suggests direct descent from the Herschel Evans-Gene Ammons school of sax playing (there is a beautiful version of *Blue and Sentimental* here), and on the medium-tempo swingers he is exciting without being repetitive and boorish. In all this he is superbly backed by Earland, who shadows his every phrase, and Pat Martino, who contributes some very tasty solos indeed. It was also an inspired day for Idris Muhammad at the drum kit. The CD contains two extra tracks, both alternative takes of numbers on the original vinyl release. **KS**

# Illinois Jacquet                                                                 1922

**Flying Home – Best of the Verve Years** Jacquet (ts); with the following collective personnel: **Russell Jacquet, Joe Newman, Elmon Wright, Lammar Wright, Harry Edison, Roy Eldridge** (t); **Henry Coker, Matthew Gee** (tb); **Ernie Henry, Earle Warren, Count Hastings, Cecil Payne, Ben Webster** (reeds); **Carl Perkins, Hank Jones, Johnny Acea, Sir Charles Thompson, Jimmy Jones** (p); **Count Basie, Hank Jones, Gerry Wiggins, Wild Bill Davis** (org); **Freddie Green, Oscar Moore, John Collins, Joe Sinacore, Irving Ashby, Herb Ellis, Kenny Burrell** (g); **Blakey, Shadow Wilson, Jimmy Crawford, Osie Johnson, Al Bartee, Jo Jones, Johnny Williams** (d); **Chano Pozo** (perc). Verve Ⓜ 521 644-2 (80 minutes). Recorded 1951-8.

⑧ ❻

On the basis of some deliberately orchestrated crowd-rousing solos, principally with early editions of Norman Granz's JATP units, Jacquet has been unjustly dismissed in some critical circles as a musician of little consequence. In fact his playing contains all the elements of a significant soloist in the great tenor tradition, taking in the strength of Hawkins, the breathiness of Webster on ballads and the inventive melodic continuity of Lester Young. This excellent compilation from his Verve years, put together by Brian Priestley, plays for just a few seconds under one hour and 20 minutes and contains some of his best titles, including two by a studio-assembled big band (*Boot 'Em Up* and *Bluesitis*) and the lengthy *Kid and the Brute,* where he shares the tenor spotlight with Ben Webster. It also contains *Lean Baby* and *Port of Rico*, made in 1952 with Count Basie (as a sideman) playing organ. These titles triggered off a host of sessions featuring tenor and organ. Three tracks come from a neglected album (never issued in Britain) pairing Jacquet with Roy Eldridge and the quality of the supporting musicians throughout is exemplary. A fine issue. **AM**

**The Blues: That's Me!** Jacquet (ts, bn); **Wynton Kelly** (p); **Tiny Grimes** (g); **Buster Williams** (b); **Oliver Jackson** (d). Prestige Ⓜ OJCCD614-2 (41 minutes). Recorded 1969.

⑦ ❼

Jacquet, the inventor of tenor saxophone hysteria back in the early forties and a big star by the end of that decade, had become a reformed character by the time of his long series of records for Norman Granz in the fifties. On those, his Texas tenor tone and swagger was placed in the context of other jazz legacies, in particular those of his predecessors in the Basie band, Lester Young and Hershel Evans. Unfortunately, little of his vast Verve fifties output is on CD (see above).

This date is not entirely typical: his preferred company for much of the sixties and seventies was organist Milt Buckner, and he rarely uses musicians born of the sixties, but here we find ex-Miles pianist Kelly and young tyro Williams on bass. Yet it all gels the way it should, bound together by the common language of the blues. Kelly has the disadvantage of playing a poorly-tuned instrument, but still solos spiritedly. Jacquet seems impervious to any form of setback and plays with great conviction, both at the ultra-slow tempo of the long title track and the racy clip of *Still King*. His bassoon playing on *'Round Midnight* is tuneful, dignified and astonishingly natural. Tiny Grimes lays out on this track, but pulls his weight elsewhere. **KS**

# Ahmad Jamal                                                                     1930

**At the Pershing** Jamal (p); **Israel Crosby** (b); **Vernell Fournier** (d). Chess Ⓜ MCAD9108 (58 minutes). Recorded 1958.

⑦ ❼

A number of pianists, prominent among them Erroll Garner and Oscar Peterson, came to fame without any CV of years spent toiling behind famous hornmen before striking out on their own. Like them, Jamal soon received endorsement from hornmen – in his case, from Miles Davis, no less – and went on to become extremely influential, possibly more than even Garner or Peterson. This was because of his updating of Garner's block-chords to make them compatible with post-bop of all kinds and his dramatic use of space and his ability to ride on top of the rhythm section, instead of driving it like his more swing-derived forebears.

That he appeared to be 'taking it easy' (an accusation also sometimes levelled at Miles) is easily understood when listening to his classic trio with fellow Chicagoan Crosby, who made his début with Fletcher Henderson in 1936. The simplified Latin rhythm of *Poinciana*, a revision of Jamal's 1955 version with guitarist Ray Crawford, is so hypnotic that the pianist's imaginative ideas can be displayed rather than developed. On some tracks the same approach combines with upper-register tinkling and over-obvious changes of dynamics to be positively annoying, but elsewhere the subtle chord voicings sustain interest, and they quite clearly were of sufficient interest to a new generation of pianists for them to adopt a similar approach. **BP**

---

**The Awakening** Jamal (p); **Jamil Nasser** (b); **Frank Gant** (d). Impulse! Ⓜ IMP12271
(41 minutes). Recorded 1970.

⑧ ❼

Jamal's most famous album is his live date at The Pershing, **But Not For Me**, and that record certainly caught him at his first peak. There is plenty of recorded evidence to suggest that the pianist reached a second peak at the close of the sixties, when his style was freer and more adventurous but his framework was basically unaltered. Virtually all of this work is not currently on CD (**Extensions**, on Argo/Chess, and **At the Top**, on Impulse! are two cases in point), but **The Awakening** fits comfortably into this grouping.

Jamal, a superb technician, is also master of the vamp (a single figure which is sustained or repeated for large sections of a piece), and uses many vamp variants to pace and organize familiar material in new and imaginative ways. On this disc Jamal uses vamps, pedal tones and pianistic pauses in his inimitable fashion, but he also plays a great deal more piano than in the past. A vehicle such as *I Love Music* is almost entirely a piano solo, couched in Tatum-like swirls of notes: just the middle section picks up the trio at a sedate tempo, which Jamal pulls about almost to breaking. Herbie Hancock's *Dolphin Dance* is made to sound as if it were written for Jamal, so natural is its treatment, while Oliver Nelson's *Stolen Moments* is given great respect and played with power and dignity. **KS**

New review
**Chicago Revisited – Live at Joe Segal's Jazz Showcase** Jamal (p); **John Heard** (b); **Yoron Israel** (d). Telarc Jazz Ⓕ CD83327 (60 minutes). Recorded 1992.

⑧ ❼

Thirty-four years after the residency at Chicago's Pershing lounge where Jamal's best-selling album, including a seven-minute *Ponciana*, was recorded, this is an attempt to re-create the chemistry by eavesdropping on another live Chicago session by Jamal's trio. In the intervening years Jamal has produced a steady stream of recordings, most of them above average, despite some less artistically successful forays into fusion. This album restates his importance as a jazz pianist. Jamal acknowledges Erroll Garner as an early influence, and refines Garner's sense of drama into a unique blend of pianistic flair and minimalism. On a straight-ahead bop track like Clifford Brown's *Daahoud*, Jamal invests his relentlessly swinging performance with continual dramatic touches, but underlying them is a sense of dynamics that builds on a potent use of quiet. When bass and drums still almost to silence, Jamal wills his listeners to concentrate, and he produces constantly inventive motifs to decorate the clear development of his dramatic ideas. His improvisation is not a headlong rush, the imposition of such compositional devices as form, dynamics and thorough melodic restatement evident in an apparently spontaneous process. A subsequent album, **I Remember Duke, Hoagy and Strayhorn** (Telarc Jazz) takes the process further in a more measured studio setting, but its bias towards ballads makes it a less-rounded effort than this live session. **The Essence** (Birdology), released in two volumes, is perhaps the equal of this Telarc document, but one has to make a choice somewhere. Not so much Chicago revisited, then, but a statement of the far-from-wasted years of experience since the Pershing in 1958. **AS**

# Bob James
1939

---

**Explosions** James (p, tapes, samples); **Barre Phillips** (b); **Robert Pozar** (d, perc). ESP-Disk
Ⓜ 1009 (35 minutes). Recorded 1965.

⑩ ❼

Unless you knew otherwise, there is no way you would connect the man who made this album with the one who has in the past two decades added a new dimension to the concept of wallpaper music in jazz. James came to jazz in the early sixties as a thoroughly schooled musician, and his first album (**Bold Conceptions**, Mercury 1962) demonstrated the sort of imaginative rethinking of bop formulas which a number of pianists (Jaki Byard, Roger Kellaway) were playing around with at that time. This, his next effort, is about as far removed from that as the Globe Unity Orchestra is from Fletcher Henderson. For four out of the five tracks there is not a single metric jazz beat kept by the trio (the one exception has the trio playing cocktail jazz as an ironic comment on the taped radio commercials being used at the same time). All but one track uses taped electronic effects and what was then called 'musique concrète', but is now probably best known as 'found art' or 'samples' – that is, sounds and noises taken from the natural world. If this all sounds very esoteric, it is; but James and his trio keep such an iron grip on the form and drama of each piece that the album is completely gripping from beginning to end. A point of clarification: the CD release perpetuates a titling confusion from the original vinyl issue. Track one, *Explosions*, is mistitled *Peasant Boy*; track three, *An On* (the only completely acoustic performance, and misspelt here as *And On*), is mistitled *Explosions*; track four, *Peasant Boy*, is mistitled *An On*. The other two tracks are actually what they say they are.    **KS**

# Harry James                                                          1916-83

**New review**

**Verve Jazz Masters 55**  James, John Audino, Ollie Mitchell, Nick Buono, Bob Rolfe, Rob Turk, Larry Maguire, Vern Guertin, Jack Bohannon, Dick Cathcart, Sam Conte, Mike Conn, Bill Mattison, Fred Koyen (t); Ray Sims, Bob Edmondson, Ernie Tack, Vince Diaz, Joe Hambrick, Dick Leith, Joe Cadena, Dick McQuary (tb); Matty Matlock (cl); Willie Smith, Herb Lorden, Pat Chartrand, Joe Riggs, Larry Stoffel (as); Corky Corcoran, Sam Firmature, Bob Poland, Jay Corre, Modesto Briseno, Dave Madden (ts); Ernie Small, Bob Achilles (bs); Jack Perciful (p); Dave Koonce, Terry Rosen, Guy Scalise, Dempsey Wright (g); Joe Comfort, Russ Phillips, Red Kelly (b); Charlie Persip, Jackie Mills, Buddy Rich, Tony DeNicola, Jake Hanna (d). Verve Ⓜ 529 902-2 (55 minutes). Recorded 1960-4.

**⑨ ❽**

Abandoning his more florid trumpet work, as he did from time to time, James became inordinately proud of this band – rightly so. Under his authority it became very much a creature of the arrangers, notably Ernie Wilkins and Neal Hefti, and took on a Basie-like feel. Despite the number of names listed above, the personnel remained pretty constant (another matter of pride for James) and the sections, particularly the saxophone sections, were quite outstanding. The corner men were, apart from the leader, Willie Smith, Corky Corcoran, Ray Sims and Jack Perciful and a glance at the names of the eminent drummers will confirm the superiority of the rhythm section. Of most interest are two breathtaking, previously unissued arrangements by Ralph Burns, *Homage to Swee' Pea* and *Rose Bud*, which, set in the lovely arrangements, have solos from James, Sims and Smith. Smith's brilliance as a section leader is demonstrated everywhere, but notably in the sax chorus on *Blues Like*. "How on earth did they manage", asked Jake Hanna "with the two biggest egos in the world, Harry and Buddy Rich, in the band at the same time?". James's own solos reflect the virtuosity generations of trumpeters have marvelled at, coupled to a solid and tasteful instinct for improvising. Verve have left themselves enough material by this band to make up two more equally good CDs. The sooner the better.    **SV**

# Jon Jang

**Self Defense!**  Jang (p); John Worley Jr (t, flh, perc); Jeff Cressman (tb, perc); Melecio Magdaluyo (as, ss, f, perc); Francis Wong (ts, f, dizi); Jim Norton (bcl, ss, f, dizi); Mark Izu (b, sheng); Anthony Brown (d, perc); Susan Hayase (taiko). James 'Frank' Holder (perc). Soul Note Ⓟ 121 203-2 (75 minutes). Recorded 1991.

**⑧ ❽**

Along with saxophonist Fred Houn and pianist Glenn Horiuchi, pianist/composer Jang is at the forefront of the flourishing Asian-American jazz movement. Each writes extended works which express their community's dissatisfaction with the subtle and not so subtle forms of racism that have pervaded post-Second World War US society. Here, titles like *Never Give Up!* (dedicated to Jesse Jackson and the Rainbow Coalition), *Redress* and *Reparations Now!* from his 30-minute *Concerto for Jazz Ensemble and Taiko*, relate Jang's socio-political agenda. But the music itself warrants attention as an original blend of multicultural elements. Jang's orchestrations include Asian instruments like the sheng (a Chinese bamboo mouth organ), dizi (flute), and taiko (Japanese drum) to fascinating effect. His multiple flute and piano voicings in *Never Give Up!* may be reminiscent of Toshiko Akiyoshi, but the rhythmic impetus is via Mingus, and on Dizzy's *A Night in Tunisia* Japanese drum riffs join with the Latin percussion. The Asian influence is heard even more directly through the pentatonic scales of Jang's *Concerto* and the traditional Chinese and Japanese tunes, *Butterfly Lover's Song* and *Ichikotsu-cho*, respectively. Such ambitious arranging, along with strong soloists like Wong, Magdaluyo, Brown and Jang himself, should help bring the music's message to a larger audience. **AL**

# Denise Jannah

**New review**

**I Was Born to Love You**  Jannah (v, per); John Eckert, Byron Stripling, Roger Ingram, Allan Rubin (t); Britt Woodman, Earl McIntyre, Art Baron (tb); Javon (ts); Gary Smulyan, Dick Oatts, Paquite D'Rivera, Charlie Pillow, Craig Handy, James Riggs, Lou Marini (cl, f, etc.);

**Howard Johnson** (tba, bcl); **John Campbell, Cyrus Chestnut** (p); **Lynn Seaton, Steve Kirby** (b); **Dennis Mackrel, Yoron Israel** (d); **Daniel Sandownick** (perc); **Bob Belden, Jon Schapiro** (arr, cond); **Bert Van Den Brink** (arr). Blue Note ℗ CDP8 33390-2 (69 minutes). Recorded 1995.

⑧ ❿

Denise Jannah is a Dutch-Surinamese singer, enormously accomplished and with a beautiful, mid-range voice. For this, her début album for a US company (she made a number of records for Timeless in Holland), Blue Note pushed the boat out in a quite heroic manner, providing a big New York studio band, name soloists, arrangers and all the trimmings. I only wish I liked it better. I wish that the featured tenor soloist had not been the angular Javon Jackson. I wish Denise Jannah had not elected to sing *Bye Bye Blackbird* in 12/8, or *A Night in Tunisia* in 5/4. I wish everybody had not tried quite so hard to impress us. On the other hand, the arrangements are a delight, especially Schapiro's woodwind voicing and Belden's warm orchestral sound. And Ms Jannah's devotion to the classic American song is evident from her choice of material and imaginative use of long-disused verses. She will make better, more relaxed albums than this. **DG**

# Guus Janssen

**Dancing Series** **Janssen** (p); **Herb Robertson** (t); **Wolter Wierbos** (tb); **Vincent Chancey** (frh); **Ab Baars** (ss, ts, cl); **Paul Termos** (as); **Jacques Palinckx** (g); **Maurice Horsthuis** (va); **Ernst Reyseger** (vc); **Raoul van der Weide** (b); **Wim Janssen** (perc). Geestgronden ℗ 1 (64 minutes). Recorded 1988.

⑧ ❽

As a composer, Holland's Guus Janssen does not have the reputation of fellow countrymen Maarten Altena, Willem Breuker or Misha Mengelberg, but he certainly shares their predilection for provocation and humour. His ensemble includes a couple of American ringers in Robertson and Chancey, but the rest are among Holland's best – and they have to be to negotiate the high-wire balancing and razor-sharp axe-juggling of Janssen's deliciously unpredictable scores. The tongue-in-cheek titles survey dance forms from the seventeenth-century French passepied to street-beat Hip Hop, but audience participation may not be advisable. Moods, colours, tempos and rhythms all change at the drop of a beat, with quick-cutting *à la* cinematic montage; incongruous episodes are bashed together or flow in bizarre compromise, repetitious riffs collide with hasty polyphony or sizzling solo outbursts. Highlights are a *noir*-ish ballad (*Slow Fox*), a phantasmagorical *Mambo* and a satirical *Jojo Jive*, heavy on the growl and wah-wah brass and slappy doo-wah rhythms. On the debit side are an inchoate *Incourante* and an over-parodied pair of *Pogo*s which succumb to mumbling, terrorist landmines and cavalry fanfares. Still, highly recommended to those listeners unafraid of the whimsical deconstruction and reconstruction of conventional jazz. **AL**

# Joseph Jarman 1937

**Song for** **Jarman** (as, recitation); **Bill Brimfield** (t); **Fred Anderson** (ts); **Christopher Gaddy** (p, mba); **Charles Clark** (b); **Thurman Barker, Steve McCall** (d). Delmark ℗ DD410 (51 minutes). Recorded 1966.

⑧ ❼

This, Jarman's recording début as a leader, predates the formation of the Art Ensemble of Chicago by nearly two years. The disc's personnel, while never a working band as such, reflects the period's emphasis on experimenting with varying instrumental combinations. Anderson and Brimfield are long-time partners; adding them to Jarman's active quartet completely changed its emotional balance. Jarman has always been partial to theatrical presentations, and even on disc the drama of this music is palpable. The opening version of Anderson's *Little Fox Run* is forceful and determined, with the two drummers providing a rhythmic torrent and the cumulative power of the horns a squalling force of nature. Limited to the quartet, *Non-Cognitive Aspects of the City* integrates Jarman's existential poetry with a sensitive, highly-organized and changing environment of related activity – Gaddy's florid piano gestures, Clark's power and *arco* prowess, Jarman's wailing post-Dolphy alto eventually soothing harsh nerves. On both *Adam's Rib* and *Song for* the tension is thick, with emotions barely held in check despite the growing flux of details. The return of *Little Fox Run*, as encore, now sounds like a shout of affirmation and exuberance. The tragically early deaths of Gaddy and Clark was to destroy this group and send Jarman to Europe with the Art Ensemble. In sub-sequent albums under his own name Jarman's vision would expand and blossom; still, this vibrant music documents a portion of the vital musical experimentation within the early days of Chicago's AACM. **AL**

# Al Jarreau 1940

**Al Jarreau: 1965** **Jarreau** (v); **Cal Bezemer** (p); **Gary Allen** (b); **Joe Abodeely** (d). Bainbridge Ⓜ BCD2037 (43 minutes). Recorded 1965.

⑦ ❼

This engagingly rough recording catches Al Jarreau when he was still a graduate student in psychology at the University of Iowa and moonlighting as a jazz singer at the Tender Trap in nearby Cedar Rapids. It also places Jarreau with the Tender Trap's house rhythm section, with whom he worked regularly. It is not surprising, then, that there is a gritty yet relaxed kind of serious fun at work.

Jarreau's wonderfully supple voice shines throughout, and what a pleasure it is to hear a jazz vocalist who sings in tune and who really swings. Jarreau, at the age of 25, had also developed into an effective story-teller whose renderings of tunes like *This Masquerade is Over* and *Come Rain or Come Shine* connect with a dramatic impact that is neither over-the-top nor too close-to-the-vest. And in a genre in which scatting is assumed to be the essential criterion necessary to be called a jazz singer, it is refreshing to hear Jarreau take flight, as with *Stockholm Sweetnin'*, in a musically convincing manner derived from the bop-crobatics of Jon Hendericks and Dave Lambert. Although Jarreau went on to develop an intriguing repertory of mouth and body sounds, here the focus is straight-ahead. Pianist Bezemer, bassist Allen and drummer Abodeely also deserve credit for their restrained and sensitive support. **CB**

# Keith Jarrett 1945

**Fort Yawuh**  Jarrett (p); **Dewey Redman** (ts, mus); **Charlie Haden** (b); **Paul Motian** (d, perc); **Danny Johnson** (perc). Impulse! Ⓜ MCAD33122 (42 minutes). Recorded 1973.

⑧ ❻

When Jarrett was younger, before his varied interests and lofty pronouncements obscured matters, his inspirations were easy to hear: the Ornette Coleman quartet's harmonic rambling, and pianist Paul Bley's adaptation of it; Coltrane's and Bill Evans's free-tempo ballads; gospel piano and the rolling-chord grooves of Ramsey Lewis and Vince Guaraldi.

On this live Village Vanguard set, different tracks highlight different sources: *De Drums* is the pop-piano finger-snapper, where Motian's defiantly loose pulse forestalls monotony. (*If the*) *Misfits* (*Wear It*'s) theme is explicitly Ornette-ish, no surprise as Redman and Haden are long-time Coleman sidemen. Redman is well displayed with an impassioned multiphonic played/sung tenor on *Misfits*, and a short, deft solo on his usually intractable double-reed musette, on *Fort Yawuh*.

The music is eclectic, but because each member of the quartet has a strong personality, they sound like a band (Johnson was not a regular, and plays an ancillary role). The pianist's trademark rubato phrasing is everywhere evident, but his ruminations are less ponderous and prone to self-parody than elsewhere. The stylistic gulf between Jarrett's 'American' and 'European' seventies quartets is not as great as commonly assumed. But on a good night like this, the Yanks had more juice. **KW**

**Belonging**  Jarrett (p); **Jan Garbarek** (ss, ts); **Palle Danielsson** (b); **Jon Christensen** (d). ECM Ⓕ 829 115-2 (47 minutes). Recorded 1974.

✓ ⑩ ⑩

Keith Jarrett's biographer, Ian Carr, refers to **Belonging** as "one of the greatest quartet recordings in jazz because everything about it is superlative: the compositions, the free-flowing interplay, the level of inspiration and the brilliantly focused improvising of all four musicians". This is a verdict with which contemporary jazz *aficionados* wholeheartedly agreed, **Belonging** and Jarrett immediately garnering a clutch of awards across Europe, Japan and America. Recorded in two days after minimal rehearsal, all the tracks – first takes – are perfect vehicles for demonstrating both the strengths of the soloists (Garbarek's sonorous, anthemic keening, Jarrett's intense lyricism) and the truly astonishing empathy characterizing the Scandinavian rhythm section. Jarrett's slower compositions, *Blossom* and the beautiful two-minute title track, verge on sound-poetry; his up-tempo pieces are jaunty and often irresistibly joyous. The album as a whole is a faultless vindication of Jarrett's reputation for producing complex and subtle but wholly accessible music, delightful to jazz specialists and casual listeners alike.

The quintessential European-quartet Jarrett recording, it not only gave its name to this particular band but set new standards for quartet jazz. Simply indispensable. **CP**

**The Köln Concert**  Jarrett (p). ECM Ⓕ 810 067-2 (66 minutes). Recorded 1975.

✓ ⑧ ❻

Well, this is it. This is the live solo recording by Keith which showed that one man could sustain a whole record, that one man improvising without a touch of electronics could capture a generation, that one man dancing between the borders of jazz and classical music could make friends with both sides, but above all it is the record which sold millions for ECM and thus funded the rise of one label and the style of music which became associated with it. When you think of the players before Jarrett who had shown allegiance to both jazz and classical music, and how they have been forgotten or abandoned (Jacques Loussier, Gunther Schuller, Phil Sunkel, and so on), you get a measure of just how resourceful Keith Jarrett was. This is still hypnotic, shifting, beautiful music. Will it ever sound dated? I suspect not. **MK**

**Mysteries: The Impulse Years 1975-6** Jarrett (p, wood-f, osi drum); **Dewey Redman** (ts, mus, perc); **Charlie Haden** (b); **Paul Motian** (d, perc). On first and second discs, add **Guilherme Franco** (perc). Impulse! Ⓜ IMPD4-189 (four discs: 232 minutes). Recorded 1975-6.

⑧ ❽

As young present-day jazz musicians scramble to reinvent free jazz by adding structure and shake up the straight-ahead scene by using looser procedures to build pieces, the late music of Jarrett's great American quartet – they would break up a year after this set's **Bop-Be** session – seems ever more prescient. It is the antithesis of the popular Bill Evans school of modern jazz: it has grooves, a fluid manner of orienting a theme statement around a rhythm scheme, long sections in no particular key. That's not to say these four records – **Shades**, **Mysteries**, **Byablue** and **Bop-Be**, presented here with extra takes to fatten the discs – aren't also marked by anachronisms. All that redeems *Flame*, with its wood flute and Chinese musette, is Motian's compelling rhythmic ideas; the rest is joylessly well-intentioned one-worldism. And sometimes Jarrett's solos embody such a late-romantic swoon that they lose the throb, to the point at which the music seems more relevant as performance art than jazz. But the music is stuffed by vigorous playing on vigorous ideas, enough for a generation of musicians to chew on. The music synthesizes Ornette's melodic obsession with Paul Bley's weightless drift and the two later discs (including Redman's *Mushi Mushi*, recently covered on Billy Drummond's excellent Dubai CD) are the most valuable for their compositional contributions by all members. **BR**

**At The Deer Head Inn** Jarrett (p); **Gary Peacock** (b); **Paul Motian** (d). ECM Ⓕ 1531 (66 minutes). Recorded 1992.

⑧ ❾

The nineties have seen Jarrett take a new angle on himself. By that I do not mean he has de-constructed his music or reinvented himself or anything quite so drastic. But it would seem that he has done a lot of thinking about his own output, because it tends to be more clearly delineated into 'types' or 'streams' than previously. Hence we get a Jarrett album of old masters, classical music interpretations, or a Jarrett album of standards interpretations, or we get a Jarrett solo recital. Recently there was Jarrett the self-historian giving us a complete warts-and-all night at New York's Blue Note, complete on six ECM CDs. Less often, we may get an album of his compositions, most of which fall loosely into an 'art music' approach. Clearly the man's pursuits are as varied as ever, but what seems less in evidence is the idea of just setting to and seeing what happens (like on the classic **Changes** album from 1983). There is nothing wrong with any of this: it is merely an observation on where Jarrett may be heading as a musician. Certainly at the present time his albums of standards interpretations outweigh the rest, and this one remains the current pick of the bunch. Which is just slightly odd, because it is not the usual Standards trio with DeJohnette, but a throwback to the seventies band which featured Paul Motian so consistently. This does the music no harm at all, Motian's rhythmic colour and propulsion unerringly centring the musical spotlight on the soloist. There is a great sense of peace and well-being in this live set, recorded at one of Jarrett's teenage haunts: no one forces the pace or distorts the contours of the music. Everything breathes naturally, so to speak. Examples abound, but *You Don't Know What Love Is* is spellbinding. So, grunts and squeaks aside, this is exemplary music-making. **KS**

# Bobby Jaspar

1926-63

**With George Wallington, Idrees Sulieman** Jaspar (ts, f); **Sulieman** (t); **Wallington** (p); **Wilbur Little** (b); **Elvin Jones** (d). Riverside Ⓜ OJCCD1788-2 (46 minutes). Recorded 1957.

The Belgian tenorist was a brilliant player whose career mirrored that of Tubby Hayes right down to the two men both dying after heart surgery at similar ages following a long period of narcotics abuse. Both men had a built-in swing to their playing which was almost unique in European players of the time. Jaspar, who was married to the singer Blossom Dearie, became, as did Hayes, very popular with American musicians to the extent that he worked for both J.J. Johnson and Miles Davis (Little and Jones were in Johnson's group with Jaspar at the time of this recording). He is revealed in this straight blowing session as a fine soloist and a gifted flautist on *My Old Flame*. Sulieman, present on three of the seven tracks, already had experience working with Monk and Coleman Hawkins amongst others. He plays with great fire here and Wallington, a familiar to this kind of quintet, provides adequate support. Wallington was to leave music shortly after this date. **SV**

# André Jaume

1940

**Musique Pour Huit: L'oc** Jaume (as, ts, f); **Jean-François Canape** (t, flh); **Yves Robert** (tb); **Jacques Veille** (btb); **Michael Overhage**, **Heiner Thym** (vc); **François Mechali** (b); **Gerard Siracusa** (d). hatART Ⓕ 6058 (55 minutes). Recorded 1981.

⑧ ❽

This French multi-reed player has shown his prowess on a wealth of discs from his own CELP label, where he favours duos (partners have included Jimmy Giuffre, Charlie Mariano, Daniel Humair and Raymond Boni) and trios (notably one with Joe McPhee and another, exploring Ornette material, with Charlie Haden) that inspire his increasingly intimate style. But this earlier date gives a broader, more imaginative view of his original music. The striking compositions present a tug-of-war between arranged and freely improvised elements, performed by musicians sensitive to the spontaneity of the moment but who may miss that last measure of urgency. The strings bring a post-Bartók chamber music feel to pieces like the slightly melancholy *Blue Note* and *L'oc*, a tone poem of stark themes and shifting textures. Jaume's playing at this stage is reminiscent of Archie Shepp's reconsideration of the tradition, with split notes and stretched tones striking sparks. Most impressive, however, is the music's concentration on ensemble interplay and uncommon ideas, as the unusual instrumentation offers fresh colours. It is a pure, European concept, the kind of sound and perception that probably would not occur to an American jazzman. **AL**

# Jazz at the Philharmonic

**Jazz at the Philharmonic: The First Concert (1944)** Collective personnel: **Shorty Sherock** (t); **J.J. Johnson** (tb); **Illinois Jacquet, Jack McVea** (ts); **Nat King Cole** (p); **Les Paul** (g); **Red Callender, Johnny Miller** (b); **Lee Young** (d). Verve Ⓜ 521 646-2 (63 minutes). Recorded 1944.

**⑨ ❻**

This, the inaugural JATP concert (and one which set in train a highly successful series of Granz promotions which would continue for over 25 years), happened to inspire some of the most typical jam session playing of any JATP set. The line-up may not be the most spectacular of impresario Norman Granz's career (his 1946 concert series, currently reissued under Charlie Parker's name, had Coleman Hawkins and Lester Young on the same bill, plus Parker and Willie Smith, with Buck Clayton, Al Killian and Dizzy Gillespie variously keeping trumpet fans happy), but the music is absolutely irresistible. The rhythm generated by Nat Cole and Les Paul in tandem with Red Callender on bass and Lester's brother Lee Young on drums is impossible not to tap your feet to. Cole and Paul, by the way, indulge in a continuing series of one-upmanship games from track to track which have both men laughing out loud at various points, and it is arguable that in their own solos not only do they occasionally outshine the two tenors and J.J., but they play some of the best jazz of their lives.

But of course it is Illinois Jacquet who became a tenor-sax hero (or zero, depending on your point of view) by his high-note screeches and frenziedly expressionistic solos here. What he was doing was nothing new for him – after all, his *Flying Home* with Hamp was already two years in the past – but the sheer intensity and ebullience he brings to his work here is breathtaking. He also invents some pretty meaty normal-register work and his solos are consistently well formed. The other tenor, Jack McVea, is a fine Lester Young-style swing player who refuses to be intimidated by Jacquet and who on *Tea for Two* takes a driving and eloquent solo. Johnson, overtaken by all the excitement, plays with little of his later poise but is enjoyable nonetheless. Shorty Sherock appears on a couple of tracks and does nothing to lower the temperature. For anyone interested in locating the soul of jazz *circa* 1944, then this is no bad place to start. In fact, I'd even go so far to say it is required listening. **KS**

**J.A.T.P. In Tokyo** Collective Personnel – i) **JATP All-Stars: Roy Eldridge, Charlie Shavers** (t), **Bill Harris** (tb), **Willie Smith, Benny Carter** (as), **Ben Webster, Flip Phillips** (ts), **Oscar Peterson** (p), **Herb Ellis** (g), **Ray Brown** (b), **J.C. Heard** (d); ii) **Oscar Peterson Trio: Peterson** (p), **Ellis** (g), **Brown** (b); iii) **Gene Krupa Trio: Benny Carter** (as), **Oscar Peterson** (p), **Gene Krupa** (d); iv) **Ella Fitzgerald** with **Raymond Tunia** (p), **Ellis** (g), **Brown** (b), **Heard** (d) and **The JATP All-Stars**. Pablo Live Ⓜ 2620-104-2 (two discs: 144 minutes). Recorded 1953.

**⑧ ❻**

JATP was a jazz institution all over the world for close on 20 years (they even made it to Australia in 1960). Norman Granz, a bright and resourceful man with the drive and taste to want only the best and want them on stage all at the same time found a formula which the world's audiences responded to enthusiastically until the whole idea of the jam session withered and died in the white heat of change in the sixties. Granz recorded JATP extensively and released many hours' worth of concerts on his Norgran, Clef and Verve labels, much of which has never been transferred to CD (although at the present time, Verve are rumoured to be preparing a *de luxe* boxed set of the entire forties JATP tapes in their possession). Granz, however, kept much of the material back, and when he started his Pablo label in the seventies, he began issuing selected concerts. This was one of them, and possibly the best of the Pablo bunch.

It follows time-honoured JATP procedure, starting with a jam session, moving on to a ballad medley, then giving over to small group sessions (here it's the Peterson and Krupa groups). After the interval Ella would come on for a set, to be joined at the end by the jam session all-stars for a last-number rave-up. A simple formula, but one which worked for years and gave us all many memorable moments. Hearing people such as Willie Smith and Benny Carter, at length, on the same stage together, or Roy Eldridge and Charlie Shavers doing battle, is something to treasure. No one does such unselfconscious things today, and jazz is the poorer for it.                                    **SV**

## The Jazz Crusaders

**Freedom Sound**  Wayne Henderson (tb); Wilton Felder (ts); Roy Gaines (g); Joe Sample (p); Jimmy Bond (b); Stix Hooper (d). Pacific Jazz Ⓜ CDP7 96864-2 (47 minutes). Recorded 1961.

⑧ ❽

The irony of a band with the name Jazz Crusaders being in the vanguard of those deserting jazz for commercial funk in the seventies is given a further twist by the contents of this, their début album, for it concentrates on the sort of jazz – gospel-tinged hard bop with an emphatic backbeat – which became relatively commercial in the eighties, filling dance floors and sparking something of a jazz revival among the young. **Freedom Sound** was recorded by this group of mainly Houston-born musicians on their arrival on the West Coast, and it combines an infectious freshness and enthusiasm with the relaxed, comfortable groove that results from long association. It is full of ringing, declamatory themes impeccably played, including the anthemic title tracks and the rousing opener *The Geek* – even the theme from the film *Exodus* – but the chief attraction is the group's overall sound, which is clean and neat with tasteful, tuneful soloing and well-judged, imaginative arrangements set against the crispest rhythm section imaginable. In that sense, little changed in these men's careers, because those elements were at the heart of their later successes. The disc contains two bonus tracks, extended alternative takes of *MJS Funk* – a reference to the band's previous name, the Modern Jazz Sextet – and *Coon*. Blue Note have recently reissued the mid-sixties Pacific Jazz set **Live at the Lighthouse** (Blue Note/Pacific Jazz), which is also very fine.                              **CP**

## Jazzensemble des Hessischen Rundfunks

New review

**Atmospheric Conditions Permitting**  Jazzensemble des Hessischen Rundfunks featuring: Thomas Heberer (t); Albert Mangelsdorff (tb); Tony Scott, Karel Krantgartner (cl); Michel Pilz (bcl); Joki Freund (ts, as, ss); Heinz Sauer (ts, as, syn, ss, bs); Christof Lauer (ts, ss); Emil Mangelsdorff (f, as, ss); Günter Kronberg (bs); Lee Konitz (as); Theodossij Spassov (kaval); Jamie Torres (charango); Peter Ponzol (ss); Bob Degan (p); Rainer Brüninghaus, Aki Takase (kbds); Werner Pirchner (vb); Bill Frisell, Volker Kriegel (g); Gunter Lenz, Eberhard Weber, Buschi Niebergall (b); Ralf-R Hübner (d); Paul Loven (perc). ECM Ⓕ 1549/50 (71 minutes). Recorded 1967-93.

⑦ ❾

When Horst Lippman founded the Jazzensemble des Hessischen Rundfunks in 1958, he envisaged a musical workshop in which members could experiment freely without the spectre of commercial obligation. The outlook was 'modern' and since its inception more than 2,000 recordings have been made. Some founder members remain to the present day, but as this CD shows, more than a quarter of a century has seen a quite extraordinary guest list. It has also seen line-ups of various sizes and of diverse, musical intent. A Scott/Krantgartner clarinet exchange takes place in a nonet setting on *Bagpipe Song*, Weber's bass and Frisell's guitar take their compatibility to beautiful ends in an octet reading of *Niemandsland* and Freund's tenor and composing skills guide a nonet through a tasteful requiem for the late Günter Kronberg on *Incantation for an Alto Player*. Loven shows that solo percussion can be quietly conversational on *Krötenbalz*, solos by Mangelsdorff's trombone and Sauer's tenor dominate a quintet's *Blues, Eternal Turn On*, while Konitz fronts a nonet again on *Noldes Himmel*. Torres's charango and Sauer's tenor make a powerful team for a trio's *Concierto de Charangojazz*, the nonet reappears to support fine vibraphone from Pirchner on *Traurigkeit* and again on *Manipulation*, where Spassov's quaint kaval shows that anything goes. This is perhaps the organization's watchword. Creative licence abounds and, in the cross-section available here, the suggestion is that the Jazzensemble des Hessischen Rundfunks found the musicians to take advantage of that fact.                              **BMcR**

## The Jazztet

**Blues On Down**  Art Farmer (t); Tom McIntosh (tb); Benny Golson (ts); Cedar Walton (p); Tommy Williams (b); Albert Heath (d). Chess Ⓜ GRP18022 (67 minutes). Recorded 1960/1.

⑦ ❽

The Jazztet was a band which should have made it big. Its leaders Art Farmer and Benny Golson had been sidemen in all the right bands, including Gerry Mulligan for Farmer and Art Blakey for Golson, both men were first-rate soloists, and Golson was a seriously gifted composer. The band inhabited a stylistic area defined by Blakey, the Adderleys and the type of well-drilled group

J.J. Johnson was running, and all those groups were conspicuously successful. So what happened? It seems to have been a case of the times moving on just when these guys caught up. With the advent of Ornette, with Coltrane's emergence as a leader, with Sonny Rollins's reinvention and Miles's blossoming under modality, what Golson and Farmer had to offer – beautifully-crafted small-group arrangements of quality material, and a mainstream approach to improvisation which was conspicuous in its lack of flash and shallowness – was not what was in demand. So the band broke up after a few years and a number of fine albums, some for Chess/Argo and the remaining ones for Mercury.

Does the reissued music live up to the memories, then? By and large, yes. These men are playing uncompromising jazz, they express themselves with conspicuous taste and an admirable clarity, and the rhythm section settle to a groove at every tempo. What's more, the front line are invariably in tune. This is warm, sophisticated music with much to offer the careful listener, and it wears its age very well. Any track will demonstrate this, but Golson's *Five Spot After Dark* is an especially good place to start. **KS**

**New review**

**Back to the City** Art Farmer (flh); Benny Golson (ts); Curtis Fuller (tb); Mickey Tucker (p); Ray Drummond (b); Marvin 'Smitty' Smith (d). Contemporary Ⓜ OJCCD 842-2 (57 minutes). Recorded 1986.

⑧ ❽

This and the subsequent **Real Time** (also Contemporary) were recorded on the same two nights at Sweet Basil in New York. The original Jazztet was formed by Farmer and Golson in 1959. Its great strengths were Golson's compositions and Farmer's meltingly beautiful flügelhorn. The times were not propitious for such restrained and craftsmanlike music and the band lasted only three years. Golson went into session writing and Farmer moved to Europe. In 1982, the world having come partly to its senses, the pair re-formed the Jazztet and the revived group enjoyed a life more than twice as long as the original's. The passage of years had made Farmer's playing even more delicately beautiful, and in each of these numbers it is his appearance one waits for. Golson's own style, formerly a subdued variant of Lucky Thompson, had coarsened somewhat and Curtis Fuller's trombone had grown much more assertive. The result is a wilder, hairier but still recognizable variant of the old Jazztet. Golson's tunes, such as *Whisper Not* and *Are You Real?* retain their charm, and Art Farmer is a constant delight. **DG**

# Eddie Jefferson
1918-79

**Letter From Home** Jefferson (v); Clark Terry, Ernie Royal, Joe Newman (t); Jimmy Cleveland (tb); James Moody (f, as); Johnny Griffin (ts); Arthur Clark (bs); Barry Galbraith (g); Joe Zawinul, Wynton Kelly, Junior Mance (p); Sam Jones (b); Osie Johnson, Louis Hayes (d). Riverside Ⓜ OJCCD 307-2 (38 minutes). Recorded 1962.

⑥ ❻

There have been a number of claimants for the position of 'first' in the field of what became known as 'vocalese'; that is, the adding of words to a recorded jazz solo, but it seems likely that Jefferson was the originator. King Pleasure (born Clarence Beeks) seems to have beaten Eddie to the punch only in terms of getting on record first.

Cannonball Adderley, who often worked in an informal A&R capacity for the old Riverside label, was behind the making of this album, which includes Adderley's *Ja-Da*-like tune, *Things Are Getting Better*, and while there are some of Jefferson's vocalese excursions, there are also a number of straightforward examples of Eddie's attractive and musicianly singing. He was associated with James Moody for some time (he was Moody's vocalist and road manager in the late fifties) and *Back In Town* (based on *I Cover the Waterfront*) and *I Feel So Good* (or *Body and Soul*) use Moody's recorded solos as the basis for Jefferson's singing. One of the best vocalese tracks here is *Bless My Soul*, a very accurate transcription of Charlie Parker's stunning solo on his Savoy recording of *Parker's Mood*. Ernie Wilkins wrote all of the arrangements and most of the instrumental solos are by Johnny Griffin, although Jimmy Cleveland gets a chorus to himself on the title track. Incidentally, Manhattan Transfer (q.v.) included their version of Jefferson's *Body And Soul* on a latter-day tribute. **AM**

# Billy Jenkins
1954

**Scratches of Spain** Jenkins (g, vn); Chris Batchelor, John Eacoti, Skid Solo (t); Iain Ballamy, Steve Buckley, Dai Pritchard (saxes); Dave Jago (tb); Ashley Slater (v, btb, tba); Dave Cooke (elg); Django Bates (kbds); Jimmy Haycraft (vb); Jo Westcott (vc); Tim Matthewman (elb); Simon Edwards (b); Dawson, Steve Argüelles, Roy Dodds (perc). Babel Ⓔ BDV9404 (39 minutes). Recorded 1986.

⑤ ❼

Jenkins has been a part of the London jazz scene for a good 15 years, having previously graduated from the 'art-rock' scene of the late seventies and early eighties. This part of his career is perhaps best summed up by the albums he made with the band Burlesque. Most of his jazz and improvisational work has been performed, issued or published under the auspices of his own Voice of God Collective; much of it carries a double edge where the listener is not quite sure whether the joke is on the musicians or the audience.

The Babel label itself is jokey in the same way as *The Beano*. Jenkins's album plagiarizes the distinctive Gil Evans/Miles Davis **Sketches of Spain** cover and the insert-note has schoolboy jokes like "bigtime saxophones" and "juvenile trombone". It may well once have amused Molesworth, but few others nowadays will have a great deal of patience with it. The mostly joyful music is much better than one might have expected: Jenkins plays wailing guitar and clapped-out violin, the latter some way advanced from the Stuff Smith demolition school of virtuoso playing. The personnel reads like a spin-off of Loose Tubes and includes Django Bates on keyboards. The arrangements are mannered but lifted by some robust solo contributions. Ashley Slater's trombone enlivens *Benidorm Motorway Services* and there are powerful saxophone solos on *Bilbao*. Dai Pritchard contributes three minutes of beautifully played clarinet to *Barcelona* which is indistinguishable from the work of the late Jimmy Hamilton. After that the track, pinned by a martial drum rhythm, quickly becomes tiresome. The best track is *Cooking Oil*, a moving piece dominated by *arco* cello from Jo Westcott. **SV**

# John Jenkins 1931

New review

**John Jenkins with Kenny Burrell**  Jenkins (as); **Burrell** (g); **Sonny Clark** (p); **Paul Chambers** (b); **Danny Richmond** (d). Blue Note Ⓜ CDP8 52437-2 (51 minutes). Recorded 1957.

⑤ ❼

This album is also known simply as **John Jenkins** (the title used above only appears on the back of the original cover). Jenkins was a hard-blowing Parkerite who played as consistently out of tune as Jackie McLean and consequently was often compared to him at the time. It is fair to say that McLean won the musical argument hands down, Jenkins never really progressing past his Parker mannerisms and eventually by the mid sixties leaving the music scene. The real interest here lies in the rhythm section, with Clark, Chambers and Richmond forming a formidable unit at any tempo Jenkins decides to nominate. Clark is uninspired as a soloist (he has played much better elsewhere) but is brilliant behind both Jenkins and Burrell, while bass and drums have a real buoyancy to their beat. Burrell is fluid in his own solos but his unison melodies with Jenkins mostly fail to gel, his rhythm sounding strangely stilted. Not one of Blue Note's more enduring legends. **KS**

# Leroy Jenkins 1932

New review

**Themes and Improvisations on the Blues**  Jenkins (vn); **Frank Gordon** (t); **Jeff Hoyer** (tb); **Vincent Chancey** (frh); **Henry Threadgill** (f); **Don Byron** (cl); **Marty Ehrlich** (bcl); **Janet Grice** (bn); **Myra Melford** (p); **Laura Seaton, David Soldier** (vn); **Ron Lawrence** (va); **Mary Wooton** (vc); **Lindsey Horner** (b); **Thurman Barker** (d); **Tania Leon** (cond). CRI eXchange Ⓟ CD663 (61 minutes). Recorded 1992.

⑧ ❽

Jenkins joined Chicago's AACM in 1965 and quickly began to devise new personal languages for the violin. In the late sixties he played with Anthony Braxton and Leo Smith in the Creative Construction Company, then in 1971 co-founded the Revolutionary Ensemble with Sirone and Jerome Cooper. That group broke up in 1977 but Jenkins has remained active on many fronts: he's played solo concerts, composed for the JCOA, toured with Cecil Taylor, experimented with electronics, written opera and recorded several small-ensemble sets for Black Saint, notably **Mixed Quintet** and **The Legend of A.I. Glatson**. **Themes and Improvisations on the Blues** focuses on Jenkins the composer, a role also explored by many of his AACM colleagues; like them, he is especially adept at blending improvised and notated episodes. For much of the title track, performed by the Soldier String Quartet, one player is left free to improvise; for *Monkey and the Dragon*, Jenkins's solo violin is the free element, the 'monkey' that 'takes stabs' at the chamber orchestra 'dragon'. In contrast, *Panorama 1*, played by the closely-attuned quintet of Jenkins, Byron, Chancey, Ehrlich and Threadgill, is mostly free. Jenkins may take jazz and blues a long way from home on this CD, but the journey is highly original and always enthralling. **GL**

# Ingrid Jensen 1967

**Vernal Fields**  Jensen (t); **Steve Wilson** (ss, as); **George Garzone** (ts); **Bruce Barth** (p); **Larry Grenadier** (b); **Lenny White** (d). Enja Ⓟ ENJ9013-2 (65 minutes). Recorded 1994.

⑥ ❽

Jensen is a young trumpeter with a full brass tone and a fiery attack. She has picked a very talented team to back her on her début album, with Steve Wilson already forging a successful solo career and

Lenny White being a well-established master of the drums. Jensen's version of *Ev'ry Time We Say Goodbye* shows what she has learned from Art Farmer (someone she has seen play many times in Vienna) about how to caress a ballad. She is equally adept at taking a standard and giving it a fresh face, as she does with *I Love You*, where a vamp over a suspended chord gives it the type of suspense so beautifully exploited by Miles on mid-tempo ballads in the early sixties. Jensen operates in a modern mainstream style, not moving very far from the type of music being created by Davis, Hubbard, Morgan, Farmer and their ilk in the sixties. She does it well, has an impressive maturity of thought and execution, and we will undoubtedly hear more from her. **KS**

# Jan Johansson
1931-68

**Longing**  Collective personnel: **Lennart Aberg** (ldr, cond); **Lars Lindgren, Bertil Lovgren, Bosse Broberg, Jan Allan** (t); **Sven Larsson, Runo Ericksson** (btb); **Lennart Aberg, Joakim Milder, David Wilczewski, Erik Nilsson, Rune Falk, Arne Domnerus, Claes Rosendahl, Jan Kling** (reeds, f); **Bobo Stenson** (p); **Rune Gustafsson** (g); **Dan Berglund, George Riedel** (b); **Egil Johansen** (d). Phono Suecia Ⓕ PSCD74 (62 minutes). Recorded 1966/93.

⑧ ❽

The 13 tracks comprising this CD are actually played by the Swedish Radio Jazz group but, fittingly, it is Jan Johansson's name which is displayed most prominently. Swedish pianist-composer Johansson was killed in a road accident in 1968 at the age of just 37. He played both on and off record with Stan Getz and Oscar Pettiford but it was as a writer that the Jazz Group remembered him. This outstanding band interprets Jan's music with expertise and care well above the line of duty, achieving a unique ensemble blend to produce some of the freshest and most intriguing voicings. Johansson had a love and understanding of Scandanavian folk music and this element of his work is present here. There are no spurious attempts to manufacture a North American dialect, for this is original music written and played by men with an all-round knowledge of jazz. The tone colours are gorgeous, the solo playing of men such as Aberg, trumpeters Jan Allan and Bosse Broberg and the piano work of Bobo Stenson are all exactly in context. Scandinavia continues to produce quality jazz of such originality that only those with tunnel vision fail to recognize the fact. The final track, *Langtan* (Longing), dates from 1966 and was written for the Mai Zetterling film **Night Games**. It makes a fitting postscript to an important release. **AM**

# Budd Johnson
1910-84

**New review**

**Let's Swing!**  Johnson (ts); **Keg Johnson** (tb); **Tommy Flanagan** (p); **George Duvivier** (b); **Charlie Persip** (d). Prestige Swingville Ⓜ OJCCD1720-2 (43 minutes). Recorded 1960.

⑦ ❾

Johnson's unaccompanied opening to the first track, *Serenade in Blue*, is worth the price of the album alone, it being a marvellously conceived introduction and summation of the song's content and Johnson's own lyrical yet bravura approach to playing, including trills and unusual harmonic choices. What's more, he doesn't put a foot wrong once the band enter, delivering a masterful ballad treatment. Not that Johnson is a slouch at any tempo, as *I Only Have Eyes for You*, rendered at a jaunty pace, proves. Johnson was one of the few saxophonists of his era (he played with George E. Lee's orchestra in 1929) to convincingly grow with the times, modifying his first mature style, which was essentially swing-based, into a unique amalgam of swing and post-swing influences, all delivered with a tone which owes as much to Lester Young and his followers as it does to Hawkins and his. Johnson is a player never stuck for ideas, and he has the rare gift of being able to run one idea seamlessly into another, thereby accomplishing a smooth and logical flow to his improvisation which is the envy of many lesser players. His brother, Keg, certainly hasn't got it, although he possesses a blustery tone and can swing along nicely, and while pianist Flanagan also possesses the secret, his is a more discreet art. On this date he keeps his solo talents mostly under wraps, instead helping Duvivier and Persip stoke the flames under Johnson on swingers such as *Downtown Manhattan* and offering little gems to the grateful saxophonist on a ballad such as *Someone to Watch over Me*. There should be many more Johnson albums like this but there aren't, so get it while you can, as Tampa Red once said. **KS**

# Bunk Johnson
1889-1949

**1944**  Johnson (t); **Jim Robinson** (tb); **George Lewis** (cl); **Lawrence Marrero** (bj); **Alcide 'Slow Drag' Pavageau** (b); **Sidney Brown** (bb); **Baby Dodds** (d); **Myrtle Jones** (v). American Music Ⓕ AMDC3 (61 minutes). Recorded 1944.

✓ ⑦ ❹

Jonnson's penchant for embellishing the truth led to misconceptions regarding his music. It is most unlikely that he played with Buddy Bolden. He was, however, a prominent figure in the jazz of New Orleans. He left that city in 1915, toured with minstrel shows, circus and theatre bands before dental problems forced him to retire in the middle of the thirties. His discovery, rehabilitation and revived recording career was an important landmark in jazz history. This disc helps explain why Johnson was never entirely happy with the circumstances in which he found himself. He was a professional musician who resented being seen as a folk figure and he preferred to play pop tunes of the day such as *You Wore a Tulip* and *There's Yes! Yes! In Your Eyes* rather than *Tiger Rag*, *The Saints* or other items from the traditional repertoire. He was further disenchanted by the choice of musicians in the band and he certainly considered himself superior to his front line partners. The amazing thing is that the outcome of the American Music sessions is basically good. The ensemble integration on *Darktown Strutter's Ball* and *Panama* is beautifully balanced and Johnson's simplistic but heartfelt solos on *Careless Love* and *Alabama Bound* are the work of an emotionally fired and skilful musician. What he sounded like in valve trombonist Frank Duson's Band in 1910, we will never know.                                                                                                    **BMcR**

# Charlie Johnson                                                       1891-1959

**The Complete Charlie Johnson Sessions**  Johnson (p, arr); **Gus Aiken, Leroy Rutledge, Jabbo Smith, Thomas Morris, Sidney De Paris, Leonard Davis** (t); **Regis Hartman, Charlie Irvis, Jimmy Harrison, George Stevenson** (tb); **Ben Whittet** (cl, as); **Edgar Sampson** (as, cl, vn, arr); **Alec Alexander** (ts, cl); **Benny Waters** (as, ts, arr); **Benny Carter** (cl, as, arr); **Bobby Johnson** (bj); **Cyrus St Clair, Billy Taylor** (bb); **George Stafford** (d); **Monette Moore** (v). Hot 'N' Sweet Ⓜ FDC5110 (78 minutes). Recorded 1925-9.

⑦ ❻

His first band having been formed in 1918, Johnson was already established when he took a band into the newly opened Small's Paradise Club in New York City in 1925. This CD covers Johnson's entire recorded output, although his tenure at the club was very much longer. The 1925 band was somewhat primitive, with Hartman a rustic but well-featured soloist and Sampson's reed scoring predictable and clumsy. Matters had improved greatly by 1927, however, with Waters bringing greater co-ordination to the arrangements and the considerable talents of Smith breathing fire into titles like *Charleston is the Best Dance of All* and *Birmingham Black Bottom*. The organizational skills of Carter were employed in 1928, but later that year those duties had returned to Waters and to a now more accomplished Sampson in what was the best Johnson band to record. De Paris excelled whether open or tightly muted and he is outstanding on *The Boy in the Boat* and *Hot Bones and Rice*, where he preaches through a plunger with a passion perhaps rivalled only by King Oliver or Bubber Miley. Despite this, he is matched here blow-for-blow by Harrison. The trombonist's innovatory importance has been cursorily dealt with in most jazz histories but, although it must be weighed against that of George Brunies, Miff Mole, Charlie Green and Jack Teagarden, the 1928 Harrison had progressed jazz playing on his instrument beyond the stage achieved by his rivals.

This CD highlights his declamatory style, his naturally coherent sense of solo construction and his effortless swing. More importantly, it demonstrates the immediacy of his playing and the way in which his improvisations evolved on each recording date. Sadly, with Harrison replaced by Washington, Johnson's last recording was in 1929. He remained at Small's until 1938 but, disillusioned with music, retired in 1940.                                                                               **BMcR**

# Howard Johnson                                                          1941

**New review**
**Gravity!!!**  Johnson (tba, pw, arr); **Joe Daley** (euph); **Dave Bargeron** (euph, tba), **Tom Malone, Nedra Johnson, Earl McIntyre, Carl Kleinsteuber, Marcus Rojas, Bob Stewart** (tba); **Raymond Chew** (p); **Paul Shaffer** (kbds); **George Wadenius** (g); **Bob Cranshaw** (b); **Melissa Slocum** (elb); **Kenwood Dennard, Kenny Washington** (d); **Victor See Yuen** (perc). Motor/Verve Ⓔ 531 021-2 (65 minutes). Recorded 1995.

⑦ ❾

Gravity is a tuba group which has existed in various forms and with varying line-ups since Johnson marshalled New York's finest in 1968 to begin a series of weekly gigs at Slug's and even appear at the Fillmore East in 1969. The band has waxed and waned over the years and personnel inevitably has shifted. For a long time the ensemble was dormant while people pursued other musical interests, but Johnson claims "the audience ... were always solidly there. We tried the big labels, the independent labels, the European and the Japanese labels. Frankly nobody had the vision until now ... I never let anyone refer to Gravity as my former band or as a failed band. It's always been there ... ."

The impact of multiple tubas (and the occasional euphonium) is both soothing and surprising. Soothing because, in terms of human warmth and mellowness, the tuba played like these musicians play it even out-does the trombone; surprising because of the incredible range (and technical security within that range) the instruments encompass in executing these charts and taking their solos. The material selected is very 'safe', as if the record company, shocked at its own audacity in allowing Johnson to realize his dream, then took no chances with the repertoire. So *Stolen Moments* is here, along with Don Pullen's take on *Freedom Jazz Dance*, called *Big Alice*, plus a few other well-grooved swingers and ballads such as *Kelly Blue*, *'Round Midnight* and *Yesterdays*. More enlightening is *Appointment in Ghana*, Jackie McLean's little-heard classic, and two Johnson originals. This good-natured and enjoyable disc is ideal for anyone with modern mainstream tastes. **KS**

# James P. Johnson
1894-1955

**Snowy Morning Blues** Johnson (p); **Eddie Dougherty** (d). MCA/Decca Ⓜ GRP16042 (58 minutes). Recorded 1930-44.

⑧ ⑧

Although a decade younger than the long-lived Eubie Blake, Johnson is acknowledged as the great master of the 'Harlem stride' piano style. Like Blake, he composed several of the early standard songs to come from the jazz milieu (such as *Old-Fashioned Love* and *If I Could Be With You*) and solo piano showstoppers. Among the latter, the classic *Carolina Shout* inspired not only Ellington and Basie in their formative years as pianists, but also his student, Fats Waller, who did the most to popularize his style and material.

The set begins with four 1930 solo tracks, including a subtle transformation of the then new *What is This Thing Called Love?* while the remaining duo sessions from 1944 consist of tunes by Johnson himself and Waller (the first jazz figure to be celebrated on record immediately after his premature death). While the Waller tunes are slightly less imaginative than the versions Johnson made without the doughty Dougherty, they underline the imagination both pianists brought to bear on their own and others' material. Rhythmic and textural nuances may go unnoticed behind the melodic variation and surging swing, but they do much to illustrate the difference between the more stilted ragtime and this early jazz style. **BP**

# J.J. Johnson
1924

**The Eminent Jay Jay Johnson, Volumes 1 and 2** Johnson (tb); **Clifford Brown** (t); **Hank Mobley** (ts); **Jimmy Heath** (ts, bs); **John Lewis, Wynton Kelly, Horace Silver** (p); **Charles Mingus, Paul Chambers, Percy Heath** (b); **Kenny Clarke** (d); **Sabu** (perc). Blue Note Ⓜ CDP7 81505/6-2 (two discs, oas: 38 and 61 minutes). Recorded 1953-5.

✔ ⑨ ❺

If Johnson's output in the late forties had been about convincing fellow musicians and critics that bebop was feasible on the slide trombone, his work in the early fifties did very much more than prove it. Volume 1 here is a truly full marks performance, although both CDs can be rated as good as anything he has ever done. Traditional trombone techniques have long since been abandoned and there are even moments when Johnson embraces an almost saxophone-like cadence. On Volume 1 his fluency and trumpet-like articulation light up *Turnpike* and *Get Happy*, *Loverman* confirms his infallibly accurate intonation while *It Could Happen to You* could be taken as a model for a concert feature number. The presence of the young and confident Brown is an added bonus. Volume 2 embraces two sessions. The first, with Johnson the only horn, provides *Time After Time* and *Too Marvellous for Words* as evidence of his harmonic insight and both justify the description of instant composition. The strong hands of Silver are introduced to good effect on the second recording date but Johnson's *Pennies from Heaven* (the originally issued version) and the superbly restrained *You're Mine You* solos are standouts and are as fine an example of trombone improvisation as one could find. At this juncture the Johnson career looked to be set fair. **BMcR**

**The Great Kai and J.J.** Johnson, **Kai Winding** (tb); **Bill Evans** (p); **Paul Chambers**, **Tommy Williams** (b); **Roy Haynes, Art Taylor** (d). Impulse! Ⓜ IMP12252 (42 minutes). Recorded 1960.

⑧ ⑧

Although the partnership started almost accidentally (Bennie Green was the original choice to duet with Johnson on the first LP – on Savoy – by the trombonists) J.J. and Kai got a lot of mileage out of the group. They had gone their separate ways when Impulse! reassembled the duo at the end of 1960 for this album, but to hear them sliding smoothly into the routines makes it sound as if the group was still gigging. The vibratos are beautifully matched, the dynamics are superbly rehearsed and executed and the choice of material ideal for the instrumentation. Winding is on the right channel throughout with J.J on the left, a fact which has to be remembered occasionally when the two start carving the solos up into four bar lengths. *I Concentrate On You* is a masterpiece of mute swapping and there is humour too in *Going, Going Gong!*, an updated sequel to the previous *Gong Rock* from the duo's Bethlehem LP. The rhythm sections are perfect in this context and the solos by Bill Evans, although fairly brief, are gems of lucidity and compression. This was a little band which succeeded in combining marvellous musicianship with good humour and a lot of jazz playing. Impulse! have remastered and repackaged this CD since the last Guide, reprinting the original booklet-notes in readable type size: a definite bonus over the previous CD incarnation, for they are both literate and informative. They were written by pianist Dick Katz, who once worked with Jay and Kai. **AM**

**Proof Positive** Johnson (tb); **Harold Mabern, McCoy Tyner** (p); **Toots Thielemans** (g); **Arthur Harper, Richard Davis** (b); **Frank Gant, Elvin Jones** (d). Impulse! Ⓜ GRP11452 (41 minutes). Recorded 1964.

⑦ ❼

Johnson is the author of several major big band jazz scores: Miles Davis and Gil Evans recorded *Lament*, while Dizzy Gillespie commissioned and recorded an entire album of his music, **Perceptions**. Until recently, this side of his art was represented on CD by the excellent **Say When** album of mid-sixties recordings for RCA, but this is now deleted. **Proof Positive** is from a similar period, but finds Johnson stretching out unexpectedly in the opposite direction. Here he is prepared to take long solos and push himself to the limit in improvising. Being the only horn, he has deliberately put himself under scrutiny, and in general he comes out ahead. The long opening track, Davis's *Neo* (aka *Teo*), finds Johnson soloing all the way, and while the group which plays on all but one track here – Mabern, Harper and Gant – are somewhat conservative and possibly ill at ease, Johnson is quite happy to dominate proceedings. Which is all to the good, because he is remarkably versatile and consistent, moving from ballads (*Gloria, My Funny Valentine*) to funky jazz waltzes (*Blues Waltz*) to medium tempo swingers (*Stella by Starlight, Lullaby of Birdland*) without once stepping out of character or showing signs of strain or distortion of his basic musical personality. He also proves to be a lot more dynamic than the common perception: it was the imitators who lacked his range, his fire and precision, and gave the J.J. Johnson school of trombone playing a bad name. The originator was always something else: the proof positive is here. **KS**

---

**New review**

**Tangence** Johnson (tb); **Wynton Marsalis** (t); **Laurie Holloway** (p); **Louis Stewart** (elg); **Chris Lawrence** (b); **Terry Jenkins** (d); orchestra dir/arr by **Robert Farnon**. Verve Ⓔ 526 588-2 (57 minutes). Recorded 1994.

⑧ ❿

It is not widely realized that Johnson, along with being a leading jazz trombonist, has pursued a modestly successful career as a composer, arranger and musical director. In this sphere he has taken as his exemplar the great light music composer, Robert Farnon. It is hardly surprising, therefore, that he should have described this production, in which his solo trombone is accompanied by a 50-piece orchestra, arranged and conducted by Farnon himself, as a "dream come true". Johnson, then aged 70, certainly took full advantage of the occasion. His playing has ripened with the years, its hard-edged clarity rounded and softened into a warm purr. Suffused with the golden glow of Farnon's strings it becomes the aural equivalent of a misty sunset. One element of his style remains unchanged: even in the slowest and most lyrical passages there is scarcely a trace of vibrato. Among the 12 pieces are a wonderfully tender version of Benny Carter's *People Time*, a bravura *Malaguena* and an original blues, *Opus de Focus*, which is a trombone-bass duet with Chris Lawrence. The orchestral playing is prodigiously accomplished and the recording perfect. Marsalis plays well on his three guest numbers, but it was quite unnecessary to include him. **DG**

# Pete Johnson

1904-67

**Pete's Blues** Johnson (p); **Hot Lips Page** (t); **J.C. Higginbotham, Clyde Bernhardt** (tb); **Albert Nicholas** (cl); **Don Stovall** (as); **Ben Webster, Budd Johnson** (ts); **Jimmy Shirley** (g); **Al Hall, Abe Bolar** (b); **J.C. Heard, Jack Parker** (d); **Etta Jones** (v). Denon/Savoy Ⓜ SV0196-2 (38 minutes). Recorded 1946.

⑥ ❼

For 1946 this was rather an ingenious concept record. Johnson opens the session with a piano solo and is joined by musician after musician, track by track, until an octet has been assembled. The order of the day is blues, and all the participants contribute characteristic solos. The last five tracks feature a mostly different and more Basie-like eight-piece band, but the emphasis on blues and boogie material never weakens.

This is a pleasant record that gives a fair impression of Johnson in one of his common contexts, but the listener concerned to hear him in the round will need to look further. The authoritative boogie-woogie duets with Albert Ammons are on **Barrelhouse Boogie** (RCA Bluebird ND88334), but Johnson's most influential pieces, the ones that boogie-woogie practitioners still test themselves by, are the early forties solos and trios like *Dive Bomber, Death Ray Boogie* and *Kaycee Feeling*, which combine thematic invention and rhythmic intensity. These are presently most easily found on **Genius of Boogie Woogie** (Giants of Jazz CD53053), an inexpensive compilation which also has work by Albert Ammons, Meade Lux Lewis, Jimmy Yancey and others. **TR**

# Pete Jolly

1932

**New review**

**Yeah!** Jolly (p); **Chuck Berghofer** (b); **Nick Martinis** (d). VSOP Ⓔ 98CD (65 minutes). Recorded 1995.

❿ ❿

This trio gives the lic to the belief that familiarity breeds staleness. These three men have been playing together for more than 30 years and the music they produce has the freshness and vitality of a newly created trio. Pete Jolly has been a mainstay of jazz in California since he made his first appearances there with Shorty Rogers in the fifties. This is the best album he has made thanks to the conjunction of some important elements; a good studio with a knowledgeable engineer (Jim Mooney at Sage & Sound), a talented and helpful producer (Dick Bank) and a dozen choice tunes. There are six jazz works by men such as Horace Silver (including the title track), George Wallington, Benny Harris and the like and another half-dozen quality songs such as *The Man I Love*, *Wonder Why* and *Ill Wind*. Jolly has recorded some of these tunes on earlier albums but they all warranted second visits, notably George Wallington's two-tempo *Variations*. The pianist has always possessed an enviably crisp touch and highly accurate digital dexterity. When the tempo is up there is no stopping this trio, with Martinis's marvellous drumming and Berghofer's unfailingly apt choice of notes. This is a piano trio record to cherish; they don't come any better. **AM**

# Elvin Jones                                                                     1927

**It Don't Mean a Thing** Jones (d); **Nicholas Payton** (t); **Delfeayo Marsalis** (tb); **Sonny Fortune** (ts, f); **Willie Pickens** (p); **Cecil McBee** (b); **Kevin Mahogany** (v). Enja Ⓕ ENJ8066-2 (59 minutes). Recorded 1993.

⑦ ❽

Jones came to prominence on the Detroit scene with brothers Hank and Thad. His style, a composite of Max Roach's bebop tradition, Art Blakey's aggression and his own massive inspiration, recommended him to John Coltrane. From 1960, he was the ideal drummer for the tenor giant, delivering the cross rhythms and irregular accents that released him from the role of 'pulse provider' and put him in competition with his leader. After leaving Coltrane in 1965 he began leading his own groups, the name Jazz Machine was adopted and this CD, not so named, offers an example of the musical style he fostered. Each player responds to Jones's special brand of turmoil in his own way. The mixture of off-centre rhythmical shifts and oblique snare accentations adds drama to Fortune's plaintive flute on *Zenzo's Spirit*. It also adds body to McBee's inventive bass on *It Don't Mean a Thing*, leaving no doubt that neither would have sounded as substantial with a routine percussionist. Never routine, Jones is a master of propulsive playing. This pushes Payton to his best work on *Fatima's Waltz* and, although Marsalis responds rather less positively, one cannot discount the inhibition factor. Jones is one of the great drum innovators, a jazz icon who must seem daunting to a young musician. **BMcR**

# Etta Jones                                                                     1928

New review

**My Gentleman Friend** Jones (v); **Benny Green** (p). Muse Ⓕ MCD5534 (45 minutes). Recorded 1994.

⑥ ❽

For several of her recent Muse albums, Etta Jones has fronted a band led by her long-time associate, tenorist Houston Person, in which Benny Green was frequently the pianist. Now, Person forsakes the tenor for the producer's chair, and Green himself is the sole accompanist. The material is almost all ballad-based, and despite some characteristically brilliant playing from Green, the album badly needs more variety. Jones's voice has settled in the middle register, and she tends to shorten her phrases, which gives a disjointed feel to the lyrics – quite acceptable on an up-tempo romp, but wearisome in a whole set of medium-paced songs. She deconstructs melodic lines – *Because of You* is unrecognizable – and occasionally breaks words between or across syllables, so that on *For Once in My Life*, the word "make" somehow gets split into two parts. This having been said, Jones is very effective at conveying the meaning of the lyrics, and she communicates an experienced and slightly care-worn character, well-versed in the ups and downs of life. She is marginally better represented by the greater variety on *Reverse the Charges* (Muse MCD5474) from 1991-2, with Person's little band, but that album doesn't include quite such splendid examples of Green as his solo on *Happiness is a Thing Called Joe* from the present album, which grows magnificently at the stateliest of tempos. **AS**

# Hank Jones                                                                     1918

New review

**Great Jazz Trio: The Standard Collection, Volume 1** Jones (p); **Mads Linding** (b); **Billy Hart** (d). Limetree Ⓕ MCD0031 (54 minutes). Recorded 1988.

⑧ ❽

There is a Volume 2 (MCD0032) which differs only in that it runs for two minutes longer, but never mind the width, feel the quality. It is invidious to choose between the two albums in the same way that it is invidious to choose between any two Hank Jones albums. He is one of the most sensitive, intuitive and tasteful musicians in jazz and is as near to perfection as both a soloist and an accompanist as makes no matter. Which doesn't leave much to say. Now nearing his eighth decade, he has been the bench-mark for jazz pianists since the early fifties, although he had begun to make his mark even before that. Any album which features Jones as a sideman is usually of a high quality. Some great pianists, such as Kenny Barron, for instance, have been hired to appear on albums by inferior artists. Although he is usually outstanding in any performance, this doesn't seem to have happened to Jones, and his presence is an assertion of quality. The Great Jazz Trio has gone through numerous permutations, including the original one of Jones with Ron Carter and Tony Williams. The latest line-up does not disappoint. The material here includes such unlikely tunes for a bop-derived pianist as *After You've Gone* and *St Louis Blues*, but as ever the material doesn't matter since everything is transformed by the Jones touch.                                                                                                **SV**

## Jo Jones                                                                                          1911-85

**Jo Jones Special**  Jones (d); **Emmett Berry** (t); **Benny Green, Lawrence Brown** (tb); **Lucky Thompson** (ts); **Rudy Powell** (as, cl); **Nat Pierce, Count Basie, Pete Johnson** (p); **Freddie Greene** (g); **Walter Page** (b). Vanguard Ⓔ 662 132 (42 minutes). Recorded 1955.

⑧ ❽

Given instruction by Fess Whatley drummer, Wilson Driver, Jones worked with Walter Page's Blue Devils in Oklahoma city and with Jeter-Pillar's Orchestra in St Louis. He was in the film *Jammin' the Blues* in 1944, made many tours with Jazz at the Philharmonic and, in later years, was in constant demand when swing-based rhythm sections were assembled for club, concert or record dates. His status as one of jazz music's greatest drummers, however, stems from the pre-eminent part he played in the 'All-American Rhythm Section' of the Count Basie Orchestra. This CD features that rhythm quartet as well as players steeped in that tradition. It shows how Jones discounted the bass drum as a pulse provider and used his gapped hi-hat to produce a lighter, more flexible rhythmic impetus. It features his superb work with brushes, his dragged rim-shot timing and his bass drum endorsements as well as other devices that inspired the bebop drummers. Basie (or Pierce), Green, Page and Jones almost breathed as one man in the Count Basie Orchestra and they slot into that groove here. Recorded at the time when the forgotten men of the 'mainstream' were being given an opportunity to record, this session has outstanding solo work by Thompson, Green and Berry.                       **BMcR**

## Jonah Jones                                                                                         1909

**At the Embers**  Jones (t); **George Rhodes** (p); **John Browne** (b); **Harold Austin** (d). RCA Victor Ⓜ 18523-2 (46 minutes). Recorded 1956.

⑥ ❽

Looking back, it seems almost outlandish that a good mainstream trumpeter, playing straight-forward, swinging versions of the best tunes, should have been not only vastly popular but a fashionable figure of New York nightlife – yet that was Jonah Jones in the later fifties. His quartet was virtually a fixture at the Embers Club, and his albums sold literally in millions. This one epitomizes his approach – terse, muted theme statement, slightly florid piano solo, possibly a half-chorus of drums, trumpet solo and the theme again to round it off. Rarely does any number exceed four minutes. Jones was born in 1909 and inevitably, given his age, an Armstrong adherent. He is particularly fond of the long, Louis-style *glissando*, which he uses rather liberally, and he has acquired some of the Master's clipped authority. This is music designed to be played in a social context, not listened to in hushed reverence, but this does not make it an inferior product. The relevant distinction is of that between decorative art and fine art. This is good decorative art.                                      **DG**

## Leroy Jones                                                                                         1958

New review

**Props for Pops**  Jones (t, v); **Craig Klein** (tb); **Glenn Patscha, Richard Phipps, Thaddeus Richard, Harry Connick Jr** (p); **Kerry Lewis, Reginald Veal** (b); **Gerald French, Shannon Powell** (d). Columbia Ⓔ 465141-2 (62 minutes). Recorded 1995-6.

⑧ ❿

The latter-day New Orleans trumpeter dedicates his second CD to Louis Armstrong. Most of the numbers are what Louis used to call "good ol' good ones" – *Struttin' with Some Barbecue, Someday You'll Be Sorry, Jeepers Creepers* – along with a few strangers, like Horace Silver's *The Preacher*. There is nothing of the revivalist about Leroy Jones and his approach is full of apparent contradictons, with New Orleans ensembles leading into solos inspired by Clifford Brown and vaudeville songs from the twenties suddenly sprouting decidedly boppish background riffs. Everyone involved, including Jones's old boss, Harry Connick, is a native of New Orleans, where such musical diversity is regarded as perfectly natural. One thing which should not be overlooked is the band's technical accomplishment. Nothing could be further from the earnest incompetence of some 'purist' trad bands than this snappy, disciplined ensemble. Leroy Jones, like his great predecessor, regards himself as a jazz entertainer. His live show is fun and guaranteed to raise the spirits; the recorded version is almost as good. **DG**

# Oliver Jones                                                    1934

**A Class Act** Jones (p); **Steve Wallace** (b); **Ed Thigpen** (d). Justin Time Ⓕ Just41-2 (50 minutes). Recorded 1991.

⑤ ❽

For many years involved as an accompanist to pop singer Ken Hamilton, Jones did not return to full-time jazz involvement until 1980. Since then he has made a considerable name for himself on the festival circuit. This CD is typical of his output and shows him to be a player with a dazzling technique. His solos are well designed and when the mood takes him he can swing remorselessly. He is most at home, however, with the less tempting challenge of very positive themes like *Everybody's Song But My Own* or *Very Early*. In the former he relaxes to let the melody breathe through his improvisation, while in the latter he rocks gently in waltz time. He is never totally convincing with the Baptist rock of *Tippin' Home from Sunday School* or *Hymn to Freedom* and he is just a shade heavy-handed with *Stan Pat Calypso*. Where he is least impressive is in his showboating approach to titles like *Mark My Time* or *Scrambled*, where his style recalls Oscar Peterson and the lack of content found in that giant's early work is replicated. He is well supported by Wallace and Thigpen, a logical choice in the circumstances, and together they have produced a proficient and musical release. **BMcR**

# Philly Joe Jones                                                1923-85

**Drums Around the World: Big Band Sounds** Jones (d); **Lee Morgan, Blue Mitchell** (t); **Curtis Fuller** (tb); **Herbie Mann** (f, pic); **Cannonball Adderley** (as); **Benny Golson** (ts); **Sahib Shihab** (bs); **Wynton Kelly** (p); **Sam Jones, Jimmy Garrison** (b). Riverside Ⓜ OJCCD1792-2 (49 minutes). Recorded 1959.

⑧ ❼

Philadelphia-born Joe Jones (who added 'Philly' to his name in order to avoid being confused with veteran drummer Jo Jones) is one of the important links bridging the drums' stylistic shift from the swing era's essentially time-keeping mission to the bebop period's stress on a more rythmically independent approach and an expanded soloistic role. Despite the shift, time-keeping has remained the drummer's basic job, and no one did it better than Jones, who studied with Cozy Cole, one of the masters of steady four-to-the-bar swing. In the forties Jones also came under the sway of Max Roach, the bebop drum pioneer who, along with Kenny Clarke, helped set the stage for modern jazz drumming. Having absorbed both traditions, Jones became a sought-after sideman playing for such diverse stylists as Charlie Parker, Billie Holiday, Lee Konitz and Miles Davis.

Here, in a fascinating 1959 date that helped establish Jones as a leader following his tenure with Davis, Jones pursues a thematic programme based on a tour of international rythms. *Land of the Blue Veils*, for example, evokes the Orient while Jones's unaccompanied *Tribal Message* conjures up the African tradition. There is also a boppish batch of home cooking in Tadd Dameron's *Philly J.J.* and Benny Golson's *Stablemates*. Along with well-crafted horn charts, there are great solos from Cannonball Adderley, Lee Morgan, Blue Mitchell and, of course, the singular Philly Joe Jones. **CB**

# Quincy Jones                                                    1933

**This is How I Feel About Jazz** Jones (arr, cond); **Art Farmer, Bernie Glow, Ernie Royal, Joe Wilder** (t); **Urbie Green, Jimmy Cleveland, Frank Rehak** (tb); **Herbie Mann** (f); **Phil Woods, Gene Quill, Benny Carter, Art Pepper, Herb Geller, Charlie Mariano** (as); **Lucky Thompson, Zoot Sims, Buddy Colette, Bill Perkins, Walter Benton** (ts); **Jack Nimitz** (bs); **Milt Jackson** (vb); **Hank Jones, Billy Taylor, Lou Levy, Carl Perkins** (p); **Paul Chambers, Charles Mingus, Red Mitchell, Leroy Vinnegar** (b); **Charlie Persip, Shelly Manne** (d). Impulse! Ⓜ GRP11152 (67 minutes). Recorded 1956-7.

⑧ ❽

Jones, with his use of woodwind and original voicings, was one of the first to break away from the restrictions of the Fletcher Henderson big band line-up. Although his innovations were not as significant as, say, those of Gil Evans, he played a major role in establishing the big band sound from the fifties onwards. His arrangements are most original and here provide wonderful settings for some of the finest soloists of the day, notably Phil Woods (who had a long and close association with Jones), Lucky Thompson and Milt Jackson. An outstanding track amongst the six which make up the 1956 New York session is *Evening in Paris*, scored especially for Zoot Sims and drawing out some of Sims's finest ballad work. An 11-minute *Walkin'* displays the young Art Farmer at his best, to be followed by commanding solos from Lucky Thompson, the three trombones, Phil Woods (on devastating form throughout) and Hank Jones. Every track from the session is a classic.

The six tracks included here from a Jones album originally entitled **Go West Young Man** are variously arranged by Jimmy Giuffre, Lennie Niehaus and Charlie Mariano, and Jones's involvement here is minimal. Nevertheless there is stalwart work from the four alto soloists on one set and from the three tenors on the other, so there is much to enjoy. If it's more of the same that you want after listening to this album, Impulse! have recently reissued **Quintessence** (IMP12222). **SV**

## Richard M. Jones                                                     1889-1945

New review
**1923-7** Jones (p); **Shirley Clay, Dave Nelson, Willie Hightower** (c); **Preston Jackson, Henry Clark, John Lindsay** (tb); **Albert Nicholas** (cl); **Artie Starks, Fred Parham** (cl, as); **Warner Seals** (ts); **Johnny St Cyr, Ikey Robinson, Bud Scott** (bj); **Rudy Richardson** (d); **Lillie Delk Christian** (v). Classics Ⓜ 826 (68 minutes). Recorded 1923-7.

⑥ ❺

Richard M. Jones was one of jazz's most important mercenaries. His musical education was in the Storyville section of New Orleans, where he played tuba with Claiborne Williams, then cornet and alto horn with the Eureka Brass Band before settling down as a pianist and band leader in his own right. His move to Chicago saw a broadening of his horizons and he gained a reputation as composer, music publisher, talent scout and, most significantly, the brains behind recording projects for the Okeh label. In this capacity he was involved in the legendary Louis Armstrong Hot Five dates, and many of the titles on this CD were made for that company. Two 1923 items are a good introduction to his solo work: one takes him on an amiable blues curve while the other offers janglingly commercial ragtime. *Spanish Shawl* from 1925 is perhaps more representative of a style that deals in note displacement rather than melodic redevelopment and involves little in the way of real improvisation. His arrangements for the larger editions of his Jazz Wizards are suitably functional but they do accommodate the limitations of his sidemen in the best possible manner. The identity of the piano soloist on *Phillips Street Stomp* leaves room for some debate, but the driving barrelhouse piano on *All Night Shags*, the spirited jazz injection behind the slender vocal talents of Christian and the quality solos on *Mushmouth Blues* and *29th and Dearborn* are undoubtedly by Jones and are the work of an accomplished artisan. **BMcR**

## Sam Jones                                                                1924

**Visitation** Jones (b); **Terumasa Hino** (c); **Bob Berg** (ts); **Ronnie Mathews** (p); **Al Foster** (d). SteepleChase Ⓕ SCCD31097 (56 minutes). Recorded 1978.

⑥

Sam Jones was not a bassist with ambitions to lead from the front, and here, except for a gently-paced theme and solo on Paul Chambers's *Visitation*, he remains where he is most comfortable, generating propulsive bass lines in tandem with a sometimes rather noisy Al Foster. The somewhat thin sound, imported from the original analogue session, perhaps relieves Jones's lines of some resonance, but it does not obscure some very fine bebop playing, in particular by Bob Berg. At this time Berg was at the top of his game in the straight-ahead mode he pursued before joining Miles Davis in the early eighties, and his flawlessly structured solo on the title track is a model example of the post-Coltrane style, demonstrating his acute melodic sense to perfection. The often overlooked trumpeter Terumasa Hino is similarly incandescent, if a little less coherent, and Ronnie Mathews is not unlike Cedar Walton, another pianist who played often with Sam Jones. SteepleChase strove to make this 1988 CD reissue a special event by adding three alternative takes. One of these was the first take of *Visitation*, and it shows that as far as Bob Berg's solos are concerned, this first issued take was the right one. **MG**

## Thad Jones                                                              1923-86

**Début** Jones (t); **Frank Wess** (f, ts); **Hank Jones, John Dennis** (p); **Charles Mingus** (b); **Kenny Clarke, Max Roach** (d). Début Ⓜ OJCCD625-2 (64 minutes). Recorded 1954/5.

⑧ ❻

Many will bracket Jones's name with that of Mel Lewis and remember him as co-leader of a very musicianly big band. They will also recall his compositions and arrangements and, perhaps, his *Pop Goes The Weasel* quotation in his *April In Paris* solo with Basie. But the fact is that Thad was an exceptional player by any standards and Charles Mingus called him "the greatest trumpet player that I've heard in this life". The tracks on this CD were made by Mingus for his own Debut label at a time when Jones was with Basie. The trumpet playing is little short of breathtaking in both conception and delivery. Thad had the exciting qualities of Navarro and Gillespie but a technique which enabled him to hit every note so cleanly that even the semiquavers stood out like the strokes of a bell. *I Can't Get Started* is dramatic as Thad plays his trumpet line against the stark sound of Mingus's bass in the first chorus. In the final analysis, these tracks must figure as some of the finest solo playing Jones ever recorded. The CD benefits from extra takes of *Get Out Of Town* and the exciting blues, *One More,* from the quartet date with the virtually unknown John Dennis on piano. The remastering is well handled and the quartet tracks are pristine but some of the quintet titles, notably *Sombre Intrusion*, suffer from an inherent muddiness due to the original and rather crude overdubbing of additional trumpet, tenor and flute lines. **AM**

---

**Basle, 1969** Jones (t, arr); Snooky Young, Al Porcino, Richard Williams, Danny Moore (t); Eddie Bert, Jimmy Knepper, Cliff Heather, Ashley Fennell (tb); Jerome Richardson, Jerry Dodgion, Joe Henderson, Eddie Daniels, Pepper Adams (saxes); Roland Hanna (p); Richard Davis (b); Mel Lewis (d). TCB Ⓕ TCB02042 (68 minutes). Recorded 1969.

⑧ ❻

Jones's arranging talent remained underexposed during his Basie period but burst into full flower after he moved into studio work in the mid sixties. While still using trumpets, trombones and saxes as separate sections (unlike Gil Evans), Jones was able to incorporate the full range of post-bop humour and virtuosity. Fellow New York studio musicians who populated the truly all-star line-up of his and Lewis's band were delighted with his writing and the loose-hinged performance it required, originally meeting just for once-a-week live rehearsals. This previously unissued Swiss Radio recording of the band's very first European tour has nearly all the original heavyweights on board (co-lead trumpeter Jimmy Nottingham dropped out, only to be replaced by the exceptional Porcino). The exciting rhythm section with Hanna and the adventurous bass work of Davis makes its presence felt immediately on one of two tracks featuring long solos by Henderson. Other prominent soloists include Williams, Knepper (on *A-That's Freedom*) and Thad himself (on *Come Sunday* as scored for singer Joe Williams), while Hanna has an Ellingtonish unaccompanied solo before the closing *Groove Merchant*. Though the band's five-CD Mosaic set is the best bet for collectors, and although this album has a slightly too ambient sound, it nevertheless packs a hefty punch. **BP**

# Vince Jones

**Here's to the Miracles** Jones (v, t); James Greening (tb); Tim Hopkins (ts); Barney McAll (p, elp, syn); Jonathan Zwartz (b); Peter Jones, Andrew Gander (d); Fabian Hevia (perc). Intuition Ⓕ INT3198-2 (52 minutes). Recorded 1996.

⑦ ❼

Australian Jones has been a headliner in his own country for over a decade and has been assiduously touring both Europe and America over the past few years. He has made close to a dozen albums, of which five have been released internationally, writes most of his own material and runs a tight ship when it comes to his own bands. His vocals are out of the Mark Murphy/George Fame tradition, though he has a vocal range and timbre of his own, and his trumpet playing is clean and no-nonsense, the songs precisely structured along traditional jazz/funk lines. The music is natural and unaffected, and it is possible that Jones's albums are more enjoyable once the listener has experienced his band live, so that the reflected memory increases the pleasure. The single-minded dedication to high standards in a difficult popular music area marks Jones out from so many of his contemporaries, and he deserves our encouragement and attention. Moreover, his records are old-fashioned fun. **KS**

# Cennet Jönsson

**Ten Pieces** Jönsson (ss, bcl); Staffan Svensson (t); Sven Berggren (tb); Joakim Milder (ts); Dan 'Gisen' Malmqvist (bcl, cbcl); Mats Rondin (c); Jacob Karlzon (p); Christian Spering (b); Peter Danemo (d); Lisbeth Diers (perc). Phono Suecia Ⓕ PSCD94 (64 minutes). Recorded 1995.

⑧ ❽

A nine-piece suite (the "ten" in the title refers to the suite as a whole, which constitutes the tenth piece), commissioned by the Plektrum Jazz Society to mark the tenth anniversary of the Lund Jazz Festival in southern Sweden, this lively, rich work vindicates those who lament the comparative neglect of Swedish jazz outside Scandinavia. Admirers of Jönsson's work in his most familiar context, Helge Albin's superb Tolvan Big Band, will be unsurprised to learn that this suite concerns itself as much with subtleties of timbre and texture as with covering stylistic ground from post-bop through fusion to free improvisation. Jönsson is a highly skilled exploiter of his resources, whether he is pitching scurrying high-register cello against boppish horns (*Bebopmania*), setting his own dignified soprano and Staffan Svensson's jaunty trumpet to a woozy tattoo opening out into free-ish improvisation (*Odd Slippers*), or allowing the band its head on a bright, percussive fusion-tinged theme (*Dance Children, Dance!*). Such a multi-textured work, exploring such a wide variety of moods, might easily have failed to cohere; **Ten Pieces**, courtesy chiefly of Jönsson's compositional and arranging skills, but also thanks to the enthusiasm and commitment of his zesty tentet, triumphantly avoids such a pitfall. **CP**

# Scott Joplin 1868-1917

**Treemonisha** **Carmen Balthrop** (sop); **Betty Allen** (mez); **Curtis Rayam** (ten); **Willard White** (bass); **Houston Grand Opera Chorus and Orchestra / Gunther Schuller**. Deutsche Grammophon Ⓜ 435 709-2 (two discs: 90 minutes). Recorded 1975.

⑧ ❽

*Treemonisha* was Joplin's second opera (the earlier *A Guest of Honor* has been lost) and he spent the last decade of his life desperately trying to get it produced. A run-through in a Harlem rehearsal hall – minus orchestra and staging – proved a flop. This was as close as Joplin came to hearing his opera, for his mental state, already affected by syphillis, was deteriorating rapidly. Late in 1916 he was committed to an asylum, where he died the following spring.

More than 50 years later, thanks to the revival of interest in Joplin's music, *Treemonisha* was rediscovered. In 1972 came a semi-professional performance in Atlanta, with an orchestration by the African-American composer, Thomas Jefferson Anderson. Then in 1975 the Houston Grand Opera mounted the first fully professional production, with arrangements and orchestration by Gunther Schuller (a piano-vocal score, published in 1911 by Joplin himself, is all that remains of the original opera). This mid-price two-CD set is a reissue of the 1975 recording by the Houston cast. Brief notes and the libretto (also by Joplin) are included, but DG have not replicated the excellent documentation of the original LP issue.

Schuller conducts a lively performance, with Balthrop and White outstanding among the singers. His orchestration proves credibly idiomatic, opting for light textures and nimble pacing. Both plot and libretto have been criticized as undramatic, but Joplin's homespun moral fable was surely intended less as a realistic story than as a ritual celebration of community, a vision of salvation through education. It has its moments of spectacle – the corn huskers' dance, the climactic real slow drag – and the music is beguiling. *Treemonisha* is not a ragtime opera. It draws on ragtime as it does on gospel, barbershop quartets, folk dances and the European opera tradition. But in particular it draws on Joplin's extraordinary capacity to blend these influences into a coherent and affecting personal language. **GL**

**King of Ragtime Writers** Player piano rolls by unidentified period musicians. Biograph Ⓕ BCD110 (55 minutes). Created 1900/60.

⑥ ❻

This and its companion albums, **The Entertainer** (BCD101) and **Elite Syncopations** (BCD 102), consist of careful transfers of original piano rolls to new copies, played at corrected speeds and checked for authenticity against the published manuscripts. The whole area of piano roll recordings is a minefield, and not worth entering in great depth here; suffice it to say that these transfers are of good quality, although on this volume none of the very few rolls which Joplin himself made are present (they are on the earlier ones).

The biggest single problem with rolls is a lack of touch and gradations of tone: only the most sophisticated pianola companies tackled this problem (Ampico, and the like), and their results were invariably reserved for the classical celebrities of the day. So things here can get a little wearisome after a time, and I would recommend small doses of this CD, rather than long draughts. The big advantage, however, is that the rhythmic emphasis is authentic. These rolls were made long before jazz, with its concomitant radical modifications to the very nature of syncopation, was properly formulated, so the concept of syncopation present on this CD is pre-jazz, and adheres much more closely to, for example, what non-jazz composers created in their own cakewalk imitations, and to the earliest recorded ragtime and jazz piano players.

If you prefer a modern filter on the music, then 70 minutes of Joshua Rifkin's sensitive and ground-breaking 1970 recordings are available on **Piano Rags** (Nonesuch 79159-2). **KS**

# Clifford Jordan 1931-93

New review

**Down through the Years** **Jordan** (ts); **Dizzy Reece, Stephen Furtado, Dean Pratt, Don Sickler** (t); **Kiane Zawadi** (euph); **Brad Shigeta** (tb); **Jerome Richardson, Sue Terry** (as); **Lou Orensteen, Willie Williams** (ts); **Charles Davis** (bs); **Ronnie Mathews** (p); **David Williams** (b); **Vernel Fournier** (d). Milestone Ⓕ MCD9197-2 (59 minutes). Recorded 1991.

⑧ ❽

Chicago tenorman Clifford Jordan first made his mark in the late fifties/early sixties when he worked with Horace Silver, Max Roach and Charles Mingus. **These are My Roots**, a Leadbelly tribute on Atlantic, was later followed by **In the World** and **Glass Bead Games**, both released on the Strata East label that he co-ran. In the seventies and eighties he worked with pianist Cedar Walton, contributed to Andrew Hill's excellent **Shades** and recorded the late-night **Royal Ballads** for Criss Cross. From 1990 Jordan led a weekly big band at Condon's in New York. **Down through the Years**, one such date, has an irresistible good-time feel, band tightly swinging, soloists fiercely declamatory. Jordan is chief writer and soloist, though trumpeter Dizzy Reece is featured too and there's a delightful swagger through Ellington's *Don't Get Around Much Anymore*. Jordan's tenor rampages through *Highest*

*Mountain*, talks tenderly on *I Waited for You*, affirms the faith at Charlie Parker's *Last Supper*. There are echoes at times of Von Freeman's dark, gnarled grain, of Wardell Gray's legato flow, but mostly Jordan is an individualist with a big, friendly tone and distinctively daubed phrases. "I like to kinda float", he once explained. "Abstractly. Put some brush strokes over the music." **GL**

## Duke Jordan

1922

**Trio and Quintet** Jordan (p); **Percy Heath** (b); **Art Blakey** (d); plus on five tracks: **Eddie Bert** (tb); **Cecil Payne** (bs). Denon/Savoy Ⓜ SV0149 (45 minutes). Recorded 1955.

⑧ ❻

Duke Jordan will always be remembered for his elegant introductions and solos on Charlie Parker's series of recordings for Dial. In later years he emerged as a composer in his own right, with tunes such as *Jor-Du* (originally called *Minor Escamp*), *Scotch Blues, Flight to Jordan* and *Forecast*. Although he has made many albums in Denmark for the SteepleChase label, this CD, recorded originally for Signal, remains one of his best. Opening with four trio numbers (including *Forecast*), Jordan soon establishes himself as a truly melodic improviser. The focus remains firmly on the piano, for Art Blakey respectfully scales down the volume of his playing for the occasion (although he has a most inventive chorus on *Night in Tunisia*). The fifth track is a solo version of *Summertime* which shows how successfully Jordan can operate on his own. The following five tracks add the warm-toned, flexible trombone playing of the underrated Eddie Bert and the fine bebop baritone playing of Payne (who also demonstrates his emotional ballad approach on *Two Loves*). The transfers to CD are clear but one of Blakey's cymbals obtrudes at times. **AM**

## Louis Jordan

1908-75

**Let the Good Times Roll – The Complete Decca Recordings 1938-54** Jordan (v, cl, as, bs); **Elks Rendezvous Band** (Courtney Williams, t; Lem Johnson, cl, ts; Clarence Johnson, p; Charlie Drayton, b; Walter Martin, d); **Tympany Five** (Freddie Webster, Eddie Roane, Aaron Izenhall, Harold Mitchell, Emmett Berry, t; Oliver Nelson, as; Stafford Simon, cl, as; Josh Jackson, Eddie Johnson, ts; Arnold Thomas, Wild Bill Davis, Bill Doggett, p; Carl Hogan, Bill Jennings, g; Al Morgan, Jesse Simpkins, Dallas Bartley, Bob Bushnell, b; Shadow Wilson, Slick Jones, Joe Morris, d); **Bing Crosby, Louis Armstrong, Ella Fitzgerald, Martha Davis** (v). Bear Family Ⓕ BCD15 557 (nine discs: 562 minutes). Recorded 1938-54.

⑧ ❼

For the majority of Louis Jordan's more casual fans, I am sure the highlights disc (below) will suffice. However, this *de luxe* boxed set is a monumental achievement by Richard Weize's small Bear Family label. Jordan is always paid lip-service for steering a popular new route between the increasingly beleaguered jazz fraternity of the war years and the successively detached popular market, which was becoming ever more reliant on vocalists or novelty records. Without Jordan, Basie, Lionel Hampton and Lucky Millinder it is difficult to imagine the r&b/jump scene evolving out of this morass in quite such a positive way. Of course Jordan had his models (I am sure he learned a lot about entertainment from Fats Waller) and his formulas, but he was always a complete professional, and a highly exciting alto saxophonist to boot.

The Jordan formulas tend to wear thin if you attempt too much of this set at once: the inane lyrics and shuffle rhythms become tiresomely monotonous. But a judicious usage of the box will reveal a cornucopia of music which repays the effort of sifting through the candyfloss. American Decca, of course, recorded all of Jordan's biggest hits, and they are all here. Also included are fascinating vocal duets with Bing Crosby, Louis Armstrong and Ella Fitzgerald (the latter take up the ninth disc, the only disc which runs under 70 minutes: it was not until the initial compilation was manufactured that Bear Family obtained clearance to include the Fitzgerald duets in the package. There is some 20 minutes worth of them.)

The accompanying 48-page booklet is lavish by any standards, and includes a complete Jordan/Decca discography plus a long essay with copious photographs, in both colour and mono, many of them very rare indeed. This is a labour of love and deserves our admiration. If you buy this you will never need another Jordan record. **KS**

**Five Guys Named Moe** Jordan (as, ts, v); **Eddie Roane, Aaron Izenhall, Bob Mitchell, Harold Mitchell** (t); **Josh Jackson, James Wright, Eddie Johnson** (ts); **Arnold Thomas, Wild Bill Davis, Bill Doggett** (p); **Carl Hogan, James Jackson** (g); **Dallas Bartley, Jesse Simpkins, Billy Hadnott** (b); **Walter Martin, Shadow Wilson, Eddie Byrd, Joe Morris** (d). MCA Ⓜ DMCL1718 (49 minutes). Recorded 1942-9.

✔ ⑧ ❽

Issued in response to the success of the musical *Five Guys Named Moe*, this compilation focuses on well-known numbers such as *Ain't Nobody Here But Us Chickens, Let the Good Times Roll* and *Saturday Night Fish Fry* – songs that find Jordan at his happiest and most characteristic, playing master of ceremonies at euphoric celebrations of black nightlife. His music is sometimes called jump blues, but its connections with the blues idioms of his day are only occasional. Both the musical forms and the language of his songs display a variety and sophistication few blues artists could command. We may discern closer analogies in the music of small Harlem swing groups of the thirties like Lil Armstrong's, but the more we look for a line that leads to Jordan, the more inexorably we are drawn to conclude that he was *sui generis*. The line from Jordan, on the other hand, is clear to see: without him the early, white rock and roll of a Bill Haley is barely imaginable.

Another good, if overlapping, selection from Jordan's Decca years is the budget-price **Jump Jive!** (Music Club MCCD085), as is the mid-priced compilation on the Cool Note label, while many of the songs on **Five Guys Named Moe** are reprised in their fifties Mercury versions on the mid-price **No Moe! The Greatest Hits** (Verve 512 523-2). Both RCA and EMI/Aladdin have late-forties collections which, although they date from Jordan's less hit-strewn years, contain fine music. **TR**

## Marlon Jordan                                                     1970

**The Undaunted**   Jordan (t); **Tim Warfield** (ts); **Eric Reed** (p); **Tarus Mateen** (b); **Troy Davis** (d).
Columbia Ⓕ CK 52409 (60 minutes). Recorded 1992.

⑥ ❼

Born in New Orleans, Jordan had the difficult task of following the success stories of Wynton Marsalis and Terence Blanchard. These two excellent trumpet sons of his city had tempted scribes to make overly romantic comparisons with the King Oliver, Freddie Keppard and Louis Armstrong lineage. Jordan has not been fazed by such talk; he made his record début at the age of 18 and was a prominent member of the fine 1991 edition of Jazz Futures. Previous recording dates had shown Jordan as comparatively immature, his solos restricted by his obsessive concern for musical accuracy and devoid of what Lester Bowie called "good wrong notes". This CD is well titled because it does begin to break down that last barrier. His almost earthy look at Coltrane's powerful *Village Blues* and his angry, muted attack on *In and Out* put content before the empty virtuosity that blighted some of his earlier work. The showboater does surface on the ugly *Confrontation*, and his growling solo on *Laurie's Mood* comes over as slightly inappropriate, but this is a young man 'on the up' and he is already exhibiting great flexibility, as well as a widening emotional range. Judging by this, his best CD to date, he seems set fair to make his mark. **BMcR**

## Sheila Jordan                                                     1928

**Portrait of Sheila**   Jordan (v); **Barry Galbraith** (g); **Steve Swallow** (b); **Denzil Best** (d). Blue Note
Ⓜ CDP7 89002-2 (39 minutes). Recorded 1962.

⑨ ❾

A product of the Detroit school and influenced by Charlie Parker, Jordan studied under Lennie Tristano and was married to pianist Duke Jordan, with whom she often worked in the fifties. This CD was Blue Note's first by a woman singer and it presents her at her best. She is a jazz singer who manages to combine respect for the meaning of the lyrics with an improvisational sense that makes every solo an investigative process. She has a horn player's awareness of phrase formation and delivery, and she uses her skill with note displacement as the key to her ability as a swinger. She makes sparing use of melismatic effects and this is best appreciated by listening to a title such as *Am I Blue?* On this, *When The World Was Young, Willow Weep for Me* and the other slow items, Jordan's smooth projection shows how she spurns the overly decorative. She turns her odd pitch aberration to advantage on *Dat Dere* but swings throughout with genuine accuracy. Her diction is impeccable, her feeling for dynamics excellent and she responds best to this type of small group. Jordan at her best, as she is here, is one of the finest of all female jazz singers. **BMcR**

## Stanley Jordan                                                    1959

**Magic Touch**   Jordan (g); **Onaje Allan Gumbs** (kbds); **Wayne Brathwaite** (elb); **Charnett Moffett**
(b); **Peter Erskine**, **Omar Hakim** (d); **Sammy Figueroa**, **Buggsy More** (perc); **Al DiMeola** (cym).
Blue Note Ⓕ CDP7 46092-2 (54 minutes). Recorded 1985.

④ ❻

This was the album that launched Stanley Jordan on an amazed world. The world was amazed because it thought that nothing new could be done with the guitar, and here was young Stanley retuning the thing in fourths and playing melody lines with both hands by 'hammering on', which gave rise to such contrapuntal effects that the record sleeve begged you not to think that anything had been overdubbed. Eventually it transpired that however fast and cleverly Jordan could play, what he was playing was actually a bit old-fashioned and cosy. He was a bit like a footballer who could dribble like a star but not actually get the ball in the goal, and after a few sensational years Stanley dropped out of the public eye. But this record shows you what it was all about, back in those innocent days when a jazz guitarist was thought smart if he kicked off a record with a Beatles song like

*Eleanor Rigby*. **MK**

# Julian Joseph

**In Concert at the Wigmore Hall** Joseph (p); **Johnny Griffin** (ts); **Eddie Daniels** (cl); **Alec Dankworth** (b); **Jason Rebello** (p – one track only). East West Ⓕ 0630-11370-2 (78 minutes). Recorded 1994.

⑦ ❼

Joseph's third album is a change of pace from its predecessors, and commemorates what were claimed as the first-ever jazz concerts at the Wigmore Hall (although Evan Parker and Derek Bailey recorded an album there as long ago as 1975). The rhythm section of Joseph and Dankworth – is the Wigmore not licensed for percussionists? – plays on three tracks with Johnny Griffin and three with Eddie Daniels, a piquant contrast. My distinct preference is for Griffin's mellow playfulness (including numerous quotations such as the Big Ben chimes and *Country Gardens*) over the collected calm of Daniels, although the instrumental control of both is equally impressive. The longest track is a rather diffuse duet on *Maiden Voyage* by Joseph and Jason Rebello, while the *Solo Medley* covers more ground and generates more energy, especially on the closing *Just One of Those Things*. If his work with Branford Marsalis and at Ronnie Scott's with men such as George Coleman hadn't already made the point, this certainly proves Joseph's excellence in modern mainstream settings. Joseph's subsequent album, **Universal Traveller** (East West), is a trio date of high standards and superb sound quality, but which does little to redefine either his own image or the piano trio concept in modern jazz.
**BP**

# Martin Joseph

**More Light** Joseph (p). Cantus Ⓕ CA005-2 (49 minutes). Recorded 1995.

⑥ ❺

Joseph was active on the British jazz-rock scene of the sixties before relocating to Rome in the early seventies. There he moved gradually towards a more wholly jazz-based musical output and began a music teaching career which continues today. He also developed a long partnership with multi-instrumentalist Eugenio Colombo. By the late eighties Joseph felt the need to move on once more, this time to South America, where he found Peru to be most congenial to his artistic needs. Both teaching and performing in concert with many different musicians continue to dominate his itinerary. This album is a sustained creative effort, *More Light* being a suite in 13 pieces, using the 12 tones of the scale to give a shape to the work (the thirteenth piece is "without tonality"). Three short unrelated pieces round the album off. Joseph shows a multifarious collection of musical roots, including people such as Lennie Tristano, Mal Waldron and Thelonious Monk as well as modern, western classical composers. He has a clear conception of what he is about and is not afraid to rely on pause and space. The music is complex but not difficult, Joseph clearly investing great store in the value of melody. The recording quality is not great, the piano being somewhat distanced, while the instrument itself sounds as if it has seen better days. Nowwithstanding such small problems, however, this is a stimulating set.
**KS**

# Vic Juris

**Night Tripper** Juris (g); **Phil Markowitz** (p); **Steve La Spina** (b); **Jeff Hirschfield** (d). SteepleChase Ⓕ SCCD31353 (67 minutes). Recorded 1994.

⑥ ❽

Juris's regular contributions to albums by other leaders tend to favour a conventional guitar tone in contrast to the rather spacey sound he opts for on much of his album. Here he keeps his clean semi-acoustic tone to a minimum, and it's not until a crystal-clear version of his own *For Harry* towards the end of the album that it's obvious how much he avoids it elsewhere. For the most part, his tone and sound mirrors his collaborations with John Etheridge, rather than the metallic edge of his other frequent associate, Birelli Lagrene. The playing, as one would expect from this most sought after of session guitarists, is exemplary, especially on Juris's own four compositions, including the title track (which has nothing at all to do with Dr John). Juris has a particularly fleet style, and his lines are picked up well by Markowitz who is a regular musical partner. La Spina's bass solos are rather packed with notes and his tone suffers slightly in the recording, but he is a sound foil for Juris in the ensembles, as is Hirschfield. Nothing here is exceptional and Juris himself is the main point of interest in what is for the most part a workmanlike session.
**AS**

# Kamikaze Ground Crew

**Madame Marie's Temple of Knowledge** Doug Weiselman (ldr, ss, ts, bs, cl, perc); **Gina Leishman** (ldr, as, bcl, pic, acc, p, toy-p, v); **Steven Bernstein** (t, slide-t, c, flh); **Jeff Crossman** (tb);

**Ralph Carney** (as, ts, cl, toy-p); **Bob Lipton** (tba); **Danny Frankel** (d, perc, whistle). New World
Ⓕ 80138-2 (62 minutes). Recorded 1991/2.

⑥ ❽

This mainly San Francisco-based septet share a musical catholicity that relates to their experience in multi-media spheres such as theatre and circus work. Individual members have played with Robin Holcomb, Wayne Horvitz, Carla Bley and Peter Apfelbaum, who was on the Crew's previous New World album, **The Scenic Route**. Co-leaders Weiselman and Leishman are reed specialists, although Leishman also plays piano and sings on one track, and the five horns are supported most of the time by a relatively conventional drums and tuba rhythm section. They use jazz sounds and techniques while simultaneously inhabiting Mexican border towns, Weimar Berlin and the Middle East; the result is like a mixture of Charles Mingus and Kate Westbrook. The closing arrangement of *You Are My Sunshine* – one to put alongside George Russell's 1962 version (q.v. Russell) – is the only piece not written by the co-leaders. The lack of a strong solo voice robs the result of a jazz cachet, although trombonist Jeff Crossman (featured only on the long *Blue Lake Dances*) comes close, but the writing and its performance is convincing and entertaining.                                          **BP**

# Richie Kamuca                                                                    1930-77

**Tenors Head On**  Kamuca (ts); **Bill Perkins** (ts, bcl, f); **Pete Jolly**, **Hampton Hawes** (p); **Red Mitchell** (b); **Stan Levy**, **Mel Lewis** (d). Pacific Jazz Ⓜ CDP7 97195-2 (63 minutes). Recorded 1956.

⑥ ❻

Kamuca envied Perkins's ability to play ballads with consummate beauty, whilst Perkins felt that he could not match Kamuca's natural and irrepressible swing. The chance to make close comparisons shows that any stylistic weaknesses are at most a matter of fine tuning. Both men were in thrall to the playing of Lester Young even more than their eminent predecessors Stan Getz, Zoot Sims and Al Cohn (Perkins was later to become a Rollins disciple, but public demand forced him to return to his original image). Both had also shone brightly in the ranks of the Woody Herman and Stan Kenton orchestras. If there is a fault in these typically smooth West Coast sessions it lies in the reticence of the main exponents to go for the jugular. The result is a tight-knit series of improvisations made the more effective by the outstanding rhythm sections. How much would Young himself have benefited from such stimulating accompaniment? Amongst a preponderance of up-tempo performances, *I Want a Little Girl* and *Sweet and Lovely* stand out for their beauty. The latter has an effective setting of Perkins's bass clarinet against a high register statement of the theme by Kamuca's tenor.          **SV**

# Shake Keane                                                                     1927

**Real Keen**  Keane (flh); **Henry Holder** (kbds); **John Kpiaye** (g); **Dennis Bovell** (b, d machine, kbds); **Angus Gaye**, **Jah Bunny** (d); **Geoffrey Scantlebury** (perc). LKJ Ⓕ CD001 (37 minutes). Recorded 1991.

⑦ ❻

As befits a man whose nickname is derived from a love of poetry and Shakespeare, Keane is an essentially lyrical trumpeter. He came to prominence in England in the mid fifties, worked with Joe Harriott and Michael Garrick in the sixties and, in the next decade, moved on to Europe, the Kurt Edelhagen Orchestra and the Clarke-Boland Big Band. He has always led a somewhat Bohemian life and was persuaded to remember his Caribbean roots by a postman he met in Somerset. This CD is the outcome and it shows that its sub-heading *Reggae Into Jazz* is not misplaced. Keane uses the instant throb of reggae as a background and overlays it with a sparkling display of swinging flügel-horn playing. He brings a variety of moods to what is ostensibly a limiting form. On *Gorby Gets Them Going* long drawn out notes lend an arhythmic aspect to a form that is basically rigid; *Tiananmen Square* mixes a little rebellion with a lick of resilience, while *Prague 89* is treated with sad lyricism. *Rift* is the angriest title, but on this form, Keane would be at home in any musical situation.          **BMcR**

# Geoff Keezer                                                                    1970

New review
**Trio**  Keezer (p); **Steve Nelson** (vb); **Neil Swainson** (b). Sackville Ⓕ SKCD2-2039 (70 minutes). Recorded 1993.

⑧ ❾

Pianist Geoff Keezer is one of the young lions from the eighties whose initial promise continues to evolve. A winner of an International Association of Jazz Educators Young Talent Award in 1987, Keezer first gained notoriety as the last pianist to work with Art Blakey's Jazz Messengers, an experience which Keezer credits as having taught him how to lead a band, not with words, but by example. Stylistically, he is a contemporary modernist. Blessed with a fluid, unforced technique, Keezer reveals influences ranging from the bop of Bud Powell and harmonic lyricism of Bill Evans to the tempestuous fire of McCoy Tyner. Here, in a set of dialogues with vibraphonist Steve Nelson and bassist Neil Swainson, we are treated to exuberantly interactive performances recorded at the

Montreal Bistro, Toronto. For a sample of Keezer's bop-generated heat, the trio's ironically brisk take on Charlie Parker's *Relaxin' at Camarillo* is exemplary. As a balladeer, Keezer's solo medley of *Darn That Dream* and *Sophisticated Lady* reveal a tartly lush concept that impresses as much by what is not played as by what is actually heard. Keezer's thunderous mid-tempo reading of Monk's *Epistrophy* is another bright moment. So, too, the flying-wedge run-down of Sonny Stitt's *Eternal Triangle*.     **CB**

## Roger Kellaway                                                              1939

**Fifty-Fifty**  Kellaway (p); **Red Mitchell** (b); **Brad Terry** (whistling). Natasha Imports ℗ NI4014 (50 minutes). Recorded 1987.

⑧ ❻

Jazz duos, rare in the fifties, have become quite fashionable these days, and one of the reasons for this, oddly, is the licensing laws. In Britain you can present a duo without going through the bureaucracy necessary for a trio, which explains all those duos at the Pizza Express over the years, and it seems that New York's weird cabaret laws say something of the same sort – at any rate, this duo was formed for an engagement at Bradley's there, and the result is as good as anything you are likely to hear when bass and piano get together. Kellaway is a sparkling, quirky pianist who is not afraid to do something silly like *Take The A Train* at funereal pace (and it works) or invite someone called Brad Terry to come and whistle on *Doxy* in bop style (and it works). Mitchell does not have quite the mobility that this sort of close-quarter encounter demands – it would be great to hear Kellaway with Nils Pedersen or Miroslav Vitous – but he is wonderfully solid and does some nice double-stopping. *'A' Train* is the best track, but the opening *Gone With the Wind* is very good and the final *St Thomas* never loses momentum, even when Mitchell is tapping rather than plucking his solo.     **MK**

## Wynton Kelly                                                               1931-71

**Kelly Blue**  Kelly (p); **Nat Adderley** (c); **Bobby Jaspar** (f); **Benny Golson** (ts); **Paul Chambers** (b); **Jimmy Cobb** (d). Riverside Ⓜ OJCCD033-2 (57 minutes). Recorded 1959.

⑧ ❽

The vitality of Kelly's piano work is under-recognized these days, even though he had a considerable long-term influence through his recordings on, among others, Miles Davis, Hank Mobley and Wes Montgomery. Maybe he is best appreciated by contrast with front-line instrumentalists, hence his high reputation as an accompanist, but the recent reissue of his early **Piano Interpretations** (Blue Note, from 1951) underlines how individual was his particular slant on bebop piano. This album was made just after he joined Davis, and takes five selections as trio performances. Here Kelly is responsible for setting up his own contrasts between different themes and between theme and improvisation, while his rhythm section colleagues of the next seven years abet his surging, inventive approach to standards such as *Do Nothin' Til You Hear from Me* (an addition for the CD edition) and *On Green Dolphin Street*. The remaining three tracks (one a new alternate take) add the three horns and feature an intriguing blend of personalities who seldom worked together. The title-number, later covered by Cannonball Adderley, is slight but brilliantly arranged for the forces available, bringing out everyone's best solos. Throughout the 27 minutes by the sextet, Kelly's driving but responsive accompaniments complement his own featured spots.     **BP**

## Rodney Kendrick

**New review**
**Dance World Dance**  Kendrick (p); **Graham Haynes** (c, flh); **Arthur Blythe** (as); **Bheki Mseleku** (ts); **Patience Higgins** (bs, bcl); **Tarus Mateen**, **Michael Bowie** (b); **Yoron Israel** (d); **Chi Sharpe** (perc). Gitanes Verve ℗ 521 937-2 (61 minutes). Recorded 1993.

⑦ ❽

The tributaries that flowed into New York's early nineties mainstream were many and various. The rock powered M-Base, the Knitting Factory experimentation and the neo-classic revival each contributed heavily to the main swell. On this CD Kendrick is the catalyst in the coming together of these disparate sources and he has put a New York stamp on musicians coming from the extremes of California and South Africa. To facilitate this, he undertakes the majority of the composing chores and also provides the arrangements. These offer impressive templates for the soloists and again Kendrick scores personally with some fine, percussive and Horace Silver-like piano playing. The sidemen respond well, with Haynes at times incisive, at others lyrical. Blythe solos with absolute authority throughout, Mseleku introduces his pleasingly oblique tenor statements on *We Need Mercy* and *Little Sweeter*, while Higgins makes his point on *Totem*. The core rhythm section of Kendrick, Mateen and Israel kick-start everything in an uncompromising manner and the addition of auxiliary percussion does nothing to lessen their impact. The whole, with its broad stylistic spread, suggests an update of the JATP attitude, and it serves as a reminder that the present New York scene is as socially cosmopolitan and musically catholic as it has ever been.     **BMcR**

# Stan Kenton

1911-79

**Retrospective** Kenton (p, ldr); with a collective personnel including: **Ray Wetzel, Chico Alvarez, Buddy Childers, Shorty Rogers, Maynard Ferguson, Conte Candoli, Stu Williamson, Sam Noto, Vinnie Tano, Jack Sheldon, Marvin Stamm, Gary Barone, Jay Daversa** (t); **Fred Zito, Kai Winding, Skip Layton, Eddie Bert, Harry Betts, Milt Bernhart, Frank Rosolino, Bob Fitzpatrick, Milt Gold, Kent Larsen, Carl Fontana, Don Sebesky, Dee Barton** (tb); **Gene Roland, Ray Starling** (mph); **Gene Roland** (ss); **Boots Mussulli, George Weidler, Art Pepper, Bud Shank, Lee Konitz, Dave Schildkraut, Charlie Mariano, Lennie Niehaus, Gabe Baltazar** (as); **Red Dorris, Vido Musso, Bob Cooper, Richie Kamuca, Zoot Sims, Bill Perkins, Dave Van Kriedt, Sam Donahue, Don Menza** (ts); **Bob Gioga, Don Davidson, Marvin Holladay** (bs); **Laurindo Almeida, Sal Salvador, Ralph Blaze** (g); **Eddie Safranski, Don Bagley, Pete Chivily** (b); **Bob Varney, Shelly Manne, Jerry McKenzie** (d); **Anita O'Day, June Christy, Nat King Cole, Chris Connor, Ann Richards, Jean Turner** (v). Capitol Ⓜ CDP7 97350-2 (four discs: 263 minutes). Recorded 1943-68.

**⑩ ⑧**

This is the most successful and comprehensive selection from the body of work which Stan Kenton recorded over the 25-year period which commenced in 1943. It illustrates clearly how Kenton was always anxious to provide a platform for young writers and there are some splendid scores here from Shorty Rogers (*Viva Prado*, *Jolly Rogers*, *Art Pepper*), Bill Holman, Bill Russo, Gene Roland, Bill Mathieu, Dee Barton, Johnny Richards and, of course, Pete Rugolo who was the 'Strayhorn' to Stan's 'Ellington'. From those opening bars of *Artistry in Rhythm* on the first of the four discs this is music which evokes an era and the tireless dedication of a man. Compiler Ted Daryll has not spared us the occasional failure (there is one movement from Bob Graettinger's over-ambitious *City of Glass* suite) but most of the music has its part in a history of orchestral jazz and the wealth of soloists listed above is an indication of the quality of the improvisers Stan employed to add spice to the arrangements. The four-CD set comes in a box with an 88-page booklet which contains full discographical information, details of soloists and arrangers and a selection of historic photos. Strongly recommended to those looking for an accurate picture of Kenton's music. Well mastered and digitally transferred.     **AM**

**New Concepts of Artistry in Rhythm** Kenton (p, ldr, narr); **Conte Candoli, Buddy Childers, Maynard Ferguson, Don Dennis, Ruben McFall, Bob Fitzpatrick, Keith Moon, Frank Rosolino, Bill Russo, George Roberts** (t); **Lee Konitz, Vinnie Dean, Richie Kamuca, Bill Holman, Bob Gioga,** (reeds); **Sal Salvador** (g); **Don Bagley** (b); **Stan Levey** (d); **Derek Walton** (perc); **Kay Brown** (v). Capitol Ⓜ CDP7 92865-2 (44 minutes). Recorded 1952.

**⑦ ❼**

Kenton, the Richard Wagner of big band jazz, was an indefatigable champion of musical extremes. Seemingly intent on organizing the largest, loudest and highest jazz group on the planet, Kenton hit the mark with the 43-piece Innovations In Modern Music Orchestra of 1950. Dismissed for its decidedly unjazzy pomposity, Kenton returned to the 1949 'Progressive Jazz' format with a 21-strong group of all-stars for **New Concepts of Artistry in Rhythm**. It is a mixed, although always provocative, affair. At one extreme is *Prologue (This is an Orchestra!)*, in which Kenton, portraying a paternalistic despot (that is, himself), orates a self-important brief on his musical aims; there are also condescending intros for the players which have a god-like omniscience comparable to that of Charlton Heston playing Moses. At the other end, exuberant numbers like Bill Holman's *Invention for Guitar and Trumpet* and Gerry Mulligan's *Swing House* prove that, in spite of the critics, Kenton's bands could swing with the best. Indeed, the downsizing of the Innovation Orchestra's doggedly determined modernistic approach actually helped make Kenton's 21-piece group texturally leaner and rhythmically more supple. It also created greater elbow room for the band's great soloists, namely Konitz, Kamuca, Ferguson, Rosolino and Salvador. Even some of the overtly 'progressive' tracks, like Gene Roland's *Lonesome Train*, simmer nicely – in this case due to Kay Brown's smouldering vocals.     **CB**

**Stan Kenton in Hi-Fi** Kenton (p) with: **Maynard Ferguson, Pete Candoli, Sam Noto, Ed Leddy, Vinnie Tanno, Don Paladino** (t); **Milt Bernhart, Carl Fontana, Bob Fitzpatrick, Kent Larsen, Don Kelly** (tb); **Skeets Herfurt, Lennie Niehaus** (as); **Spencer Sinatra, Bill Perkins, Vido Musso** (ts); **Jack Nimitz** (bs); **Ralph Blaze** (g); **Don Bagley** or **Red Mitchell** (b); **Mel Lewis** or **Shelly Manne** (d); **Chico Guerrero** (perc). Capitol Jazz Ⓜ CDP7 98451-2 (60 minutes). Recorded 1956-58.

**✔**

**⑧ ❽**

The group of Kenton musicians who started what was known as 'progressive' jazz in the mid forties spread out to occupy a considerable area of the West Coast jazz scene, and Kenton continued to create a musical commotion until his death. This disc is a pulling together and a re-creation of the music from the first decade of his career. It is enormously successful, and the massed ranks of Kenton's brasses and saxophones have seldom been better served on a single album. The compositions, many of them by Pete Rugolo, are among the best and most memorable of the leader's variable career. All the bombast and pretentiousness is here, but so too is the sheer power and discipline of a great band. Once one accepts that there was a dimension missing from Kenton's music it becomes easier to relax and enjoy it, particularly when as here there is the bonus of some excellent solos from Carl Fontana (the trombone was Kenton's favourite instrument) and section work of a quality rarely found elsewhere. **Kenton in Hi-Fi** is a warts and all job, with the leader's cloying piano on the pretentiously-titled *Concerto to End All Concertos* retained in all its full horror. But even this is made acceptable when Maynard Ferguson and the band enter to kick the hell out of the piece. These recordings feature men who solo with an authority which was missing from the inferior bands of Kenton's last decade.  **SV**

## Robin Kenyatta
1942

**Blues for Mama Doll** Kenyatta (ts); François Coutourier (p); Reggie Johnson, François Laizeau (b); Jean-Pierre Arnaud, Jean-Paul Celea (d). Jazz Dance Ⓕ 01 (54 minutes). Recorded 1987/9.
⑥ ❼

This curious CD – which does not even possess a catalogue number – collates Kenyatta's performances from two separate sessions in Switzerland. It is produced by Kenyatta, with the 1987 tunes coming from a radio studio session and the 1989 efforts from the Cully Jazz Festival. Kenyatta sticks to tenor throughout (which is a little surprising, considering his long history on the alto), and sounds a good deal like Archie Shepp. In fact, his speech-like inflections on *In Your Own Sweet Way* made me double-take, convinced that in fact this really was Shepp after all.

Kenyatta came to the fore rapidly in the late sixties, and took a memorable alto solo on Bill Dixon's only album as a leader in that decade, **Intents and Purposes**, on RCA of all labels. It indicated a unique talent. Subsequent projects under his own name never quite reached those levels again, and the seventies and eighties saw him spending much of his professional life funkin' it up in much the same manner as another alto original, John Handy, did. Both outings on this disc are in the tradition, and Kenyatta plays with commitment and verve. The backing trios are on both occasions sympathetic and professional, with Coutourier being impressive as a soloist in his own right. But the saxophonist unnerves me: if the emcee did not announce Kenyatta to the audience at the beginning of this disc I would put money on it being Shepp on a good day.  **KS**

## Freddie Keppard
1890-1933

**New review**

**The Legend** Keppard, James Tate, Elwood Graham (c); Fayette Williams, Fred Garland, Eddie Vincent, Eddie Ellis (tb); Angello Fernandez, Jimmie Noone (cl); Johnny Dodds, Buster Bailey, Clifford King, Joe Poston (cl, as); Norval Morton, Jerome Pasquall (cl, ts); Adrian Robinson, Antonia Spaulding, Kenneth Anderson, Jimmy Blythe, Arthur Campbell, Tiny Parham (p); Jimmy Bell (vn); Erskine Tate, Stan Wilson, Johnny St Cyr (bj); Bill Newton, Sudie Reynaud (b); Jimmy Bertrand, Bert Greene, Andrew Hilaire, Jasper Taylor (d, perc). Topaz Ⓕ TPZ1052 (70 minutes). Recorded 1923-7.
⑥ ❹

Falling chronologically between Buddy Bolden and Joe Oliver, Keppard played a formative part in New Orleans's transition from ragtime to jazz. He co-led the legendary Original Creole Orchestra and, in 1916, was reputed to have declined a recording opportunity, the year before the Original Dixieland Jazz Band made the 'first' jazz records. He briefly occupied the second cornet chair in the Oliver band before the arrival of Louis Armstrong but unfortunately all of his recordings were made when he was past his prime. This CD offers some of his best, but his presence on every track is far from certain and his playing is inconsistent. He is buried in the Tate Vendome Orchestra's poorly-balanced ensemble but fortunately his work with Cook is considerably better. With the Dreamland Orchestra he plays fine preaching cornet and in Cook's smaller Gingersnaps group his shapely lead is often interchangeable with his solo line. The two Jazz Cardinals tracks are the pick of the eight Paramount label items and *Stock Yard Strut* shows the power and creativity of which he was capable. The ragtime legacy of his earlier days is still evident in his faintly vertical phrase shapes but an element of acquired rubato has updated the style. This is especially true of his bluesy playing on the two *Salty Dog* takes, although in the process it confirms that the remaining Paramounts are almost certainly not Keppard's work. This is a slightly confusing issue but Topaz's booklet-notes do acknowledge the doubts and it does not alter the fact that Keppard was a seminal jazz figure whose music should be in all representative collections.  **BMcR**

## Barney Kessel
1923

**Red Hot and Blues** Kessel (g); Bobby Hutcherson (vb); Kenny Barron (p); Rufus Reid (b); Ben Riley (d). Contemporary Ⓜ CCD14044-2 (61 minutes). Recorded 1988.
⑦ ❽

Kessel appeared in the legendary *Jammin' the Blues* film, made by Gjon Mili in 1944. He went on to record with the likes of Charlie Parker and Lester Young, played in several big bands and was a stalwart with Jazz at the Philharmonic. In the seventies he was a vital part of the Great Guitars Group and continued to lead small groups devoted to jazz with a bebop flavour and a cosmopolitan aspect. As this CD shows, Kessel is a sympathetic combo member and a natural improviser who builds his solos with careful attention to their overall symmetry. He has occasionally allowed himself to be trapped in empty virtuoso situations as a weaver of pretty patterns, but here, with a forthright and driving rhythm section and with the creative challenge of Hutcherson to stimulate him, he does not coast for a moment. His uncharacteristically convoluted solo on *Barniana*, his intriguing re-balancing of *You've Changed* and his joyful blues playing on the rollicking *Blues for Bird* are three standout performances from a three-day session which maintained consistently high standards. Kessel is a player who responds to positive musical stimulation and he certainly gets it here.                **BMcR**

## Steve Khan                                                                                    1947

**Crossings** Khan (g); **Michael Brecker** (ts); **Anthony Jackson** (elb); **Dennis Chambers** (d). Verve
   Forecast Ⓕ 523 269-2 (69 minutes). Recorded 1993.
                                                                                    ⑥ ❽

One of the unanswered questions of recent jazz history concerns Steve Khan's abrupt metamorphosis in 1981 from the hard-rocking fusion player who produced memorably penetrating work on The Brecker Brothers's **Back to Back** and Steely Dan's **Gaucho** into the relatively low-key small group player heard on this and a host of other records over the past 12 years. Nevertheless, although he has scaled down the intensity of his playing, Khan continues to work the fusion seam, using deep chorusing on his guitar and giving all the numbers here – eight standards and two originals – a Latin treatment. The sense of exoticism is enhanced by the stealthy, tastefully understated playing of fellow former Steely Dan sideman and unsung pioneer of the low bass guitar, Anthony Jackson, and by percussionist Manolo Badrena.
   One of the hazards of Khan's current style is a tendency for the soft, unfocused sound of his guitar to become cloying after a while, but the presence of Michael Brecker's unfailingly incisive tenor on three tracks adds a contrast missing from hornless albums by the band.                **MG**

## Carol Kidd

**Crazy for Gershwin** Kidd (v); **Mark Bailey** (c); **David Newton** (p); **Nigel Clark**, **Dominic
   Ashworth** (g); **Fraser Spiers** (hca); **Miles Baster**, **Peter Markham** (vn); **Michael Beeston** (va);
   **Ronnie Rae** (b); **Tony McClennan** (d). Linn Ⓕ AKD026 (56 minutes). Recorded 1993.
                                                                                    ⑥ ❻

It is hard to come up with a new or refreshing angle on music which is as frequently performed as the seven Gershwin tracks that form the core of this 14-track album. Carol Kidd succeeds in doing so, at least in part due to the sensitivity of her accompanists, Ray and Newton (who both solo briefly from time to time, Newton also acting as musical director). The album also benefits from the thought and care that have gone into the settings. Using a pair of acoustic guitars and a harmonica, in addition to the basic jazz trio, creates a light, springy backdrop for the material, treading a careful path between out-and-out jazz interpretation and a style more suited to the musical stage. On a number of tracks the Edinburgh String Quartet blend effortlessly with singer and regular accompanists, giving the same *gravitas* in this simple setting as would a full string section. The recording is clear and clean, devoid of echo and effect, and Ms Kidd sensibly relies on art not artifice to interpret not only Gershwin but equally distinguished songs by McHugh and Fields, Harold Arlen and Henry Mancini.                **AS**

## Franklin Kiermyer                                                                             1956

**Solomon's Daughter** Kiermyer (d); **Pharoah Sanders** (ts); **John Esposito** (p); **Drew Gress** (b).
   Evidence Ⓕ ECD22083 (60 minutes). Recorded *c*1994.
                                                                                    ⑦ ❽

Born in Canada, Kiermyer got his first set of drums at the age of 12. Adulthood found him as part of the Montreal jazz scene but, after a period of commuting, he settled in New York. Unsure of the future, he was delighted to be recommended to Esposito. Their partnership rapidly fostered their mutual interests; Kiermyer's quick admiration for John Coltrane (and by inference Elvin Jones and Rashied Ali), became a major factor in his career. This CD endorses that devotion and points to the importance that Kiermyer places in the jazz of the sixties. His well-established rapport with Esposito and Gress offers flexibility, and his choice of Sanders, an extension of the Trane tradition, is both logical and challenging. Kiermyer wrote all of the material and, although he imbues it with his own personality, he captures the spiritual values established by the Coltrane/Sanders partnership. In some ways he favours the Ali path, but he remains the extrovert musical thespian, acting for the benefit of all. Sanders is free to play with unbridled passion and the music is, in places, powerfully hostile. Kiermyer is looking back to the sixties without nostalgia, selling its intensity from a contemporary

sales list.                **BMcR**

# David Kikoski

**Dave Kikoski** Kikoski (p); **Essiet Essiet** (b); **Al Foster** (d). Sony Epicure ⓕ EPC478174-2 (60 minutes). Recorded 1994.

⑥ ❿

Kikoski has been garnering strong press notice for the past half-decade, after his becoming part of the Roy Haynes band (Haynes appeared on his first release on the Freelance label, **Presage**). This new effort, for the jazz wing of the Epic label, offers brilliant recorded sound, greatly sympathetic companions in Essiet and Foster, and some burning piano playing from the leader (notably on Coltrane's *Giant Steps*). It also features a cover design so appallingly conceived that the record company have had to add a sticker to the jewel-case with the pianist's name on it, so as to help potential buyers to spot it in the racks.

Kikoski deserves more than this because, although he is another of the unending stream of pianists whose roots lead back to the triumvirate of Hancock, Corea and Evans, he has great natural flair, considerable harmonic dexterity and imagination, and a sense of excitement at the music which he is creating. All of which makes for pleasant and occasionally moving listening. Maybe the next one will see the breakthrough. **KS**

# Bob Kindred

New review

**Hidden Treasures** Kindred (ts, bs); **Clark Terry** (t, flh); **Richard Stoltzman** (cl); **Dave Samuels** (vb); **Fred Sherry** (vc); **Bill Charlap**, **Bill Mayes** (p); **Todd Coolman**, **Sean Smith**, **Dave Finck** (b); **Tim Horner**, **Grady Tate** (d); **John Kaye** (perc). Milan ⓕ 35731-2 (65 minutes). Recorded 1995.

⑥ ❽

Kindred was born in Philadelphia, a town that has produced a list of tenor saxophonists including Stan Getz, Benny Golson, Jimmy Heath and Richie Kamuca. Kindred was less well known but, like many of his contemporaries, he did time with the popular organ trios. He also toured with several big bands, the most notable being that of Woody Herman. On this CD we hear the man who, many years later, is a ubiquitous figure on the New York club scene. Perhaps reflecting that fact, the programme is concentrated on the ballad end of the spectrum. Fortunately Kindred does this rather well. His is a style built on the fundamental techniques as they apply to the main stream of jazz, as opposed to the self-imposed limitations of 'mainstream jazz'. He paints with light musical brush strokes and titles such as *Autumn Nocturne*, *Blood Count* and *Crazy He Calls Me* have an unashamed romanticism. *Merry Go Waltz*, his one track on baritone, introduces an avuncular stateliness, *Veles Igades* gets a gentle Getzian exploration and *Mr Magoo* suggests the jocular but at no time is the creative flow retarded. This is not so much a retro trip as it is a saxophonist playing in a way that is, for him, a musical way of life. **BMcR**

# Morgana King

1930

**For You, For Me, Forever More** King (v); with orchestral accompaniment featuring: **Chauncey Welsch** (tb); **Hank Jones** (p); **Al Caiola**, **Mundell Lowe** (g); **Rick Hayman** (arr). EmArcy Ⓜ 514 077-2 (36 minutes). Recorded 1956.

⑥ ❻

In later years Morgana King's voice has dropped in range, and she has developed a very individual delivery. Yet little in her more recent repertoire transcends this early session, cut before her twenty-fifth birthday, where her voice is remarkable for its clarity and perfection. She takes few liberties with line or lyric, and when she does, such as on the gravelly phrase "sweet chickadee" on *It's De-Lovely*, she foreshadows her more recent style. This is clear, uncomplicated cabaret singing, with just enough depth in her girlish talcum-powder voice to avoid the bland. The ambitous restructuring she brought to later songs like her 1963 *Taste of Honey* can only be glimpsed in her style here, but this is one of the better EmArcy vocal albums from the mid fifties, despite its very short playing time. **AS**

# Peter King

1940

New review

**Tamburello** King (as, ss, perc); **Steve Melling** (p, kbds); **James Hallawell** (kbds); **Alec Dankworth** (b, perc); **Stephen Keogh** (d). Miles Music ⓕ MMCD083 (63 minutes). Recorded 1995.

⑨ ❾

With this extraordinary production King's reputation as a jazz saxophone virtuoso and an improviser of near-genius must now be extended to include composition. By this I do not mean simple theme-writing, at which he has always been adept, but the creation of extended works. The heart of this CD is a sequence of linked pieces dedicated to the memory of Ayrton Senna, the racing driver who, King claims in his insert-note, "elevated driving to the level of an art form". By the bold use of electronic colour, 'live' effects and vibrant rhythmic energy he evokes scenes and moods with a delicacy reminiscent of Gil Evans. Just as impressive are the two adaptations from the classical repertoire – "Dido's Lament" from Purcell's *Dido and Aeneas*, and the principal theme from Bartók's Second Violin Concerto. This is a milestone work, rather like Getz's **Focus**, in which King, while remaining a jazz musician, reaches out beyond jazz to new and wider territory. His own playing on both alto and soprano saxophones is as impressive as ever and brilliantly complemented by the others.    **DG**

## John Kirby                                                                   1908-52

**The John Kirby Sextet**  Kirby (b); **Charlie Shavers** (t); **Buster Bailey** (cl); **Russell Procope** (as); **Billy Kyle** (p); **O'Neil Spencer** (d); **Maxine Sullivan** (v). Columbia Ⓜ 472184-2 (two discs: 129 minutes). Recorded 1939-41.

⑦ ❽

This best-known line-up of the Kirby Sextet was celebrated for its translations into a 'chamber jazz' style of classical themes from Grieg (*Anitra's Dance*), Chopin (*Minute Waltz*), Dvořák (*Humoresque*) and Schubert (*Serenade, Who is Sylvia?*), as well as of folk melodies like *Little Brown Jug* and *Molly Malone*. The legacy of these polished performances has been a certain critical impatience: like the Modern Jazz Quartet later, the band has been perceived as too genteel for its own good. Its more polite side is most aptly employed in the accompaniments to *St Louis Blues, If I Had a Ribbon Bow* and four other songs by Maxine Sullivan, a limpid and graceful singer. Considerable skill, much of it Shavers's, went into the group's arrangements, and there is much variety of tone colour. Yet some of the band's instrumental pieces seem to exhibit good manners at the expense of good jazz. Shavers, though a greatly gifted player, tended to tiptoe rather than stride or swagger, muted in both senses, while Procope readily lapsed into parsonical bleating. But when the group had done with its bland drawing-room exchanges and settled to the lively jazz discussions of *Effervescent Blues* and *Jumpin' in the Pump Room*, or the exceptionally vivacious *Front and Center* and *Opus 5* (all written or co-written by Shavers), it became a more daring organization altogether. This French Columbia set is complete for its period: an admirable survey.    **TR**

## Andy Kirk                                                                   1898-1993

**Mary's Idea**  Collective personnel on 18 tracks: **Harry Lawson**, **Paul King**, **Earl Thompson**, **Clarence Trice**, **Harold Baker** (t); **Ted Donnelly**, **Henry Wells**, **Fred Robinson** (tb); **John Harrington**, **John Williams**, **Dick Wilson**, **Earl Williams**, **Don Byas**, **Rudy Powell**, **Edward Inge** (reeds); **Mary Lou Williams** (p, arr); **Claude Williams** (vn); **Ted Brinson**, **Floyd Smith** (g); **Booker Collins** (b); **Ben Thigpen** (d, v); **Pha Terrell**, **Harry Mills** (v); on two tracks: **Harold Baker** (t); **Ted Donnelly** (tb); **Edward Inge** (cl); **Dick Wilson** (ts); **Mary Lou Williams** (p, arr); **Booker Collins** (b); **Ed Thigpen** (d). MCA/Decca Ⓜ GRD622 (59 minutes). Recorded 1936-40.

⑧ ❽

In the first half of the thirties Andy Kirk led a popular band in the Midwest, operating out of Kansas City, but his band became a much better-known proposition thanks to the records he was asked to make from 1936 onwards. This release concentrates on that period; by this time Kirk had the talented Mary Lou Williams in the band, playing fine two-handed piano as well as writing much of the library. She and tenor saxist Dick Wilson were the band's strongest soloists, a fact borne out here, for this CD contains most of Kirk's best recordings. The ensemble sound is light and attractive, swinging gently in an unforced manner. Pha Terrell, Ben Thigpen and Harry Mills (from the Mills Brothers) have a few vocals but it is the keyboard work of Mary Lou and her most attractive arrangements which lift the band to the heights. She was always a forward-looking writer and her *Walkin' and Swingin'*, which opens this collection, contains an ensemble phrase which later became known as *Rhythm-a-Ning* (credited to Thelonious Monk) and *Opus Caprice* (Al Haig). *Baby Dear* and *Harmony Blues* are by a septet comprising the band's soloists and rhythm section made originally under Mary Lou's name, for inclusion in Decca's **Kansas City** album. These are fine examples of small band jazz, with outstanding trumpet from Harold Baker. The remastering has been achieved using the NoNoise system, giving a clean, sharp sound, although some tracks seem to cut off in peremptory fashion at the end.    **AM**

## Rahsaan Roland Kirk                                                           1935-75

**Kirk's Work**  Kirk (ts, mzo, str, f, siren); **Jack McDuff** (org); **Joe Benjamin** (b); **Arthur Taylor** (d). Prestige Ⓜ PR7210 (34 minutes). Recorded 1961.

⑨ ❽

Blind from the age of two, Kirk began his musical career as a tenor saxophonist in r&b bands. His main claim to fame – playing three instruments at once – came about while he was still a teenager with his own Vibration Society, a band he led for more than 15 years. As this CD shows, his tenor could range from the forthright on *Makin' Whoopee* to the outright romantic on *Too Late Now*. The manzello, a relation of the soprano, was often his story-telling horn in a piece where the tenor had stated the melody, while the alto-like stritch, heard here on *Skater's Waltz*, was used more sparingly. By structural amendments to the tenor, adroit false fingering and sustained drones, he transformed all three into a one-man saxophone section. On *Funk Underneath*, his flute and growling voice-over effect added another dimension to his playing, and it was one that none of his copyists have ever quite matched, possibly because it is a hopeless task to bring the same degree of spirit and verve to the job that Kirk could manage. As a soloist on a single horn, Kirk would not perhaps have attracted so much publicity, but the three-into-one flights were wholly musical, Kirk was not one given to parading gimmicks, and he was, incidentally, one of the most visually exciting of all jazzmen. He would have won his audience regardless of his choice of instrument. **BMcR**

---

**We Free Kings** Kirk (f, ts, mzo, str, siren); **Richard Wyands**, **Hank Jones** (p); **Art Davis**, **Wendell Marshall** (b); **Charlie Persip** (d). Mercury Ⓜ 826 455-2 (43 minutes). Recorded 1961.

✔ ⑧ ❻

Whenever you sat and watched Roland Kirk, before or after he became Rahsaan Roland Kirk, you could not help wondering if people who had never seen him would ever have any idea of the impact in the flesh or, after his death, whether people could hear on record the sounds he made you hear in person. Even now it is hard to know. When you listen to this early Kirk record it all seems to be there – the growling flute, the three-reed interludes, the moaning and groaning – but do you hear it on the record, or does the record merely act as a nudge to the memory? I think it is actually all there. The opening blues, *Three for the Festival*, is quite electrifying after 30 years, not so much for Kirk's one-man reed section, though that still gets you smiling and feet-tapping, as for the flute work. His unison blowing and humming still manages to get the hairs on the back of the neck doing a dance, and the stop time solo (which, unaccountably, starts in the fifth bar of a 12-bar blues) is just wonderful. The very slow blues on this record, *You Did It, You Did It*, is only two-and-a-half minutes long, but anyone who can play the blues like that does not need more than two-and-a-half minutes. He was to make bigger and splashier records, but I would hate to be without this one. **MK**

---

**"Rahsaan" – The Complete Mercury Recordings** Kirk (f, ts, str, mzo, siren); **Kirk Quartet** (Richard Wyands, Wynton Kelly, Andrew Hill, Harold Mabern, Tete Montoliu, Horace Parlan, Jaki Byard, p; Art Davis, Richard Davis, Niels-Henning Ørsted Pederson, b; Charlie Persip, Roy Haynes, Walter Perkins, J.C. Moses, Elvin Jones, d; Sonny Boy Williamson, hca); **Orchestra** (Virgil Jones, Richard Williams, Joe Newman, Clark Terry, Ernie Royal, t; Charles Greenlea, Jimmy Cleveland, Kai Winding, Melba Liston, tb; Don Butterfield, tba; Julius Watkins, Bob Northern, Willie Ruff, frh; Phil Woods, Zoot Sims, James Moody, Budd Johnson, Jerome Richardson, reeds; Harold Mabern, Lalo Schifrin, p; Kenny Burrell, Jim Hall, g; Richard Davis, Milt Hinton, Art Davis, George Duvivier, b; Albert Heath, Osie Johnson, Ed Shaughnessy d); **Benny Golson**, **Quincy Jones** (arr); **All-Stars** (Virgil Jones, t; Tom McIntosh, tb; Tubby Hayes, James Moody, ts; Walter Bishop Jr, Harold Mabern, p; Sam Jones, Richard Davis, b; Louis Hayes, Walter Perkins, d). Mercury Ⓜ 846 630-2 (11 discs: 565 minutes). Recorded 1961-5.

⑩ ❽

This is a boxed-set fully worthy of its subject. Roland Kirk (the 'Rahsaan' was not added until after he left Mercury/Limelight and went to Atlantic Records) spent five very fruitful years with the label, and it is arguable that he made his very best albums there, although such gems as **Volunteered Slavery** and **The Inflated Tear**, both Atlantic dates, would also have to be taken into consideration in such a list. When he arrived at Mercury in late summer 1961 he was known locally around New York as the guy who tore it up with Mingus for a few months. By the time he left the label he was an internationally established star. This collection includes such classic albums as **We Free Kings**, **Domino**, **Reeds and Deeds**, **Meets the Benny Golson Orchestra**, **Kirk in Copenhagen** and **Gifts and Messages** on the Mercury label, and **I Talk with the Spirits**, **Rip**, **Rig & Panic** and **Slightly Latin** from the Mercury jazz subsidiary, Limelight. The extra material here (and we are truly blessed that it isn't just a case of bucketfuls of alternative takes) comes from a Tubby Hayes album on Smash records (a Mercury subsidiary), an Eddie Baccus Smash date, three Mercurys and one Limelight album by Quincy Jones, plus a couple more Mercury compilations. The record which is most tellingly fleshed out here is the Copenhagen album. Originally just six tracks were released: here there are no less than 16, covering two whole CDs in the set. Kirk, working with a European band which includes Tete Montoliu and NHØP, and on a couple of numbers jamming furiously with no less a guest than Sonny Boy Williamson, gives the listener some inkling of just what a devastating live performer he was.

Also included here is arguably Kirk's greatest single album, **Rip, Rig & Panic** (see below), plus the exquisite and sadly unappreciated all-flute album, **I Talk with the Spirits**, featuring Kirk's old Mingus ally Horace Parlan, and which includes the nearest thing to a hit Kirk ever had: *Serenade to a Cuckoo*. The booklet which comes with this package is well laid out, and carries a full Kirk Mercury discography. The only thing which annoys me about this set (and it is a mistake repeated on the single-issue version reviewed below) is the misspelling throughout of the first track on **Rip, Rig & Panic**, *No Tonic Pres*. Lester Young's nickname has somehow acquired an extra "s" to become "Press". Considering the long explanation of the rationale behind the title from Kirk himself in the original LP booklet-notes, this oversight is, to put it mildly, baffling. **KS**

**Rip, Rig & Panic/Now Please Don't Cry, Beautiful Edith**  Kirk (ts, f, mzo, str, perc, siren);
**Jaki Byard**, **Lonnie Liston Smith** (p); **Richard Davis**, **Ronnie Boykins** (b); **Elvin Jones**, **Grady Tate**
(d). Emercy Ⓜ 832 164-2 (68 minutes). Recorded 1965-7.

✓                                                                                                    ⑩ ⑩

Combining two of the multi-instrumentalist's finest recordings, this compilation is a superb showcase
for the unique artistry of Roland Kirk, packed with virtuosic idiosyncrasy but based, as always, on
his encyclopaedic knowledge of and enthusiasm for the entire jazz tradition from Fats Waller through
Lester Young to Charles Mingus and free music. 1965's **Rip, Rig & Panic** features Kirk with probably
the most sympathetic rhythm section he ever encountered; Jaki Byard, a fellow Mingus adherent, is a
perfect foil for the leader, equally adept in all modes from stride to avant-garde piano; Richard Davis
has a tigerish fluency particularly well adapted to Kirk's approach; Elvin Jones is, by turns, superbly
aggressive and delicately controlled. On material ranging from the famous Lester Young tribute, *No
Tonic Pres,* through the multi-referential but strangely homogeneous *From Bechet, Byas and Fats* to
the archetypal Kirk stormer *Slippery, Hippery, Flippery*, Kirk produces his customarily unpredictable
but peerlessly flamboyant virtuosity on instruments ranging from tenor, through stritch (an archaic
straight alto) and manzello (a soprano-type saxophone), to flute, sirens and various percussion
instruments, including a breaking pane of glass.

The result is simply one of the finest recorded group performances in the music, one of the few
sessions where everything gels perfectly. The 1967 session, originally released on Verve, is a less stellar
affair, but like **Rip, Rig & Panic** ranges through an astonishing variety of jazz forms; a blowsy, slow
blues, charming ballads, gospel-influenced material and plaintive laments, all filtered through Kirk's
irreplaceably original vision. Both sets are available in The Complete Mercury box reviewed above,
but if you want just a single CD of the man, this is it. **CP**

---

**The Inflated Tear**  Kirk (ts, cl, f, ehn, mzo, str, whistle, perc); **Ron Burton** (p); **Steve Novosel**
(b); **Jimmy Hopps** (d); **Dick Griffin** (tb). Rhino/Atlantic Ⓜ 790045-2 (38 minutes). Recorded
1967.

                                                                                                     ⑧ ⑥

Before the Art Ensemble of Chicago declared its intention to encompass music "from the ancient to
the future," decades before Wynton Marsalis and his disciples developed a pan-stylistic historicism
spanning old New Orleans and modern modal jazz, visionary Rahsaan had his own inclusive music
policy. His 5/8 theme, *A Handful of Fives,* sounds remarkably Brubeckian; *Black and Crazy Blues*,
employing english horn and tenor sax, is a funeral dirge that turns into a bar-room blues and back
again. On the frothy *A Laugh for Rory*, Kirk plays/sings the distinctive flute multiphonics which have
been widely imitated by other jazz and rock flautists (such as Jethro Tull's Ian Anderson). He also
anticipates the Art Ensemble by making atmospheric use of little percussion instruments on the title
track. As on Ellington's *Creole Love Call*, rendered down and dirty, Kirk roughly harmonizes on two
saxes at once – a speciality.

The stylistic range and exuberant execution confirm Rahsaan's expansive sensibility; his
able backing trio can follow him anywhere. In a way, Rahsaan's sophistication, playfulness and
receptiveness to many styles would come to be his undoing. His later Atlantic recordings became
increasingly r&b oriented; this slick and pretty, raw and powerful date is among his last great
sessions. **KW**

---

**Does Your House Have Lions?**  Kirk (ts, bs, bass sax, str, mzo, flexaphone, cl, f, nose f, pic, t,
reed t, ehn, black mystery pipes, hca, whistle, hmn, perc, music box, bird sounds, v); **Charles
Mingus**, **Jaki Byard**, **Hilton Ruiz**, **Trudy Pitts**, **Richard Tee**, **Ron Burton**, **Sonelius Smith**, **Hank
Jones**, **Lonnie Smith** (p); **Doug Watkins**, **Henry Pearson**, **Bill Salter**, **Vernon Martin**, **Steve Novosel**,
**Ron Carter**, **Major Holley**, **Metathias Pearson** (b); **Robert Shy**, **Bernard Purdie**, **Khalil Mhridi**,
**Charles Crosby**, **James Madison**, **Jimmy Hopps**, **Sonny Brown**, **Oliver Jackson**, **Harold White** (d).
Various horns, strings and percussion on individual tracks. Rhino/Atlantic Jazz
Ⓜ R2-71406 (two discs: 138 minutes). Recorded 1961-76.

                                                                                                     ⑦ ⑧

Rahsaan Roland Kirk was a beloved figure to many musicians and listeners alike, because of his
great spirit and humour as well as his enormous energy and improvisational skills. Over the course
of his unfortunately abbreviated career he recorded for a number of labels, with varying results.
Inevitably, however, his strongest dates were the simplest ones: those on which he was able to draw
upon a love and deep knowledge of the jazz tradition while extending it with soulful variations and
madcap imagination. His connection with Atlantic Records was the final stage of his career and,
Stanley Crouch's persuasive booklet-note argument notwithstanding, not the most musically
rewarding. Much is written here about the 'complete freedom' Kirk was given in these sessions, and
it is unfortunate that the selection of material on these two discs was apparently meant to impress
the listener with the breadth of his conceptions rather than the depth of his playing. For Kirk, jazz
was a popular music, and he was able to inject tunes ranging from the commercial (*I Say a Little
Prayer*) to the spiritual (*Old Rugged Cross*) with unapologetic power and exhilaration. He had no
qualms about appropriating melodies from The Beatles or medieval folk tunes, Stevie Wonder or
Dvořák, and finding the humour, pain and dignity in each. Few could match the sheer

expressiveness of his tenor saxophone playing. But there were certainly times when his instrumental prowess could not inspire merely competent sidemen, or invigorate bland material and humdrum arrangements, as is too often the case here, where the choice of performances overemphasizes Kirk's multi-instrumentalism, vaudevillian slapstick, and experimental eccentricities rather than his considerable musical abilities. The result is a view of a wildy expressionistic artist at his most colourful instead of his most profound. **AL**

## Kenny Kirkland 1955

**Kenny Kirkland** Kirkland (p, kbds); **Roderick Ward** (as); **Branford Marsalis** (ss, ts); **Charnett Moffett, Chris McBride, Andy Gonzalez, Robert Hurst** (b); **Jeff 'Tain' Watts** (d); **Steve Berrios** (d, perc); **Don Alias, Jerry Gonzalez** (perc). GRP Ⓕ 96572 (63 minutes). Recorded 1990.

Ⓖ Ⓗ

The presence of synthesizers on several tracks might suggest typical GRP sweetening of the jazz pill, but by and large this is uncompromised modern jazz from one of the most consistent American inheritors of the Hancock-Tyner-Jarrett legacy. In any case, notwithstanding his long purist gig with Wynton Marsalis in the early eighties, Kirkland has never made any secret of his timbral promiscuity. Thus here the electronically orchestrated samba, *Celia,* is sandwiched between *Steepian Faith*, which swings with the stealth of Wayne Shorter's *Deluge*, and *Chance*, a bright, swinging waltz of similar stylistic vintage. Elsewhere, Shorter's *Ana Maria* and Kirkland's own *Revelations* reveal Kirkland's delicate, introspective side and the brisk *Mr J.C.*, while carrying Shorter's compositional imprint, features strong Coltrane-style tenor from Kirkland's long-time associate Branford Marsalis. Perhaps the freshest playing here is in *When Will the Blues Leave?*, which is fired by Roderick Ward's loose-limbed amalgam of Ornette and Coltrane, and in Monk's *Criss Cross*, arranged as a Latin piece complete with tuned percussion. **MG**

## Yoshiko Kishino 1960

New review
**Fairy Tale** Kishino (p); **Marc Johnson, Eddie Gomez** (b); **Peter Erskine, Lewis Nash** (d); on three tracks **Michael Brecker** (ts). GRP Ⓕ 98362 (58 minutes). Recorded 1995.

Ⓖ Ⓗ

Kishino has experienced a rapid rise to prominence in Japan, her Bill Evans-inspired style bringing her quick appreciation and a number of awards. Kishino's chordal approach reflects the late American, but her rhythmic sense is less circumscribed than Evans's, it being more in keeping with later keyboard stars such as Chick Corea or Keith Jarrett; certainly, her forceful emphases in melodic statement, her *ritardando* and her *cantabile* owe more to the later players than to the jazz impressionist supreme. Kishino has unerringly clean execution and an unsentimental approach, even when playing pretty songs such as *Someday My Prince Will Come*, and this bodes well for her development. She doesn't attempt to dazzle through transcendent technique or wacky conceptions of familiar things; she just sticks to working the groove travelled profitably by many before her, and the substantial musical content she manages to provide, with the help of two separate bass and drum teams, shows that musical integrity can still win through. Michael Brecker decorates three songs, most especially *Stella By Starlight*, but Kishino really doesn't need the GRP cheer squad call-out: she is capable of sustaining our interest in her own right. **KS**

## John Klemmer 1946

**Waterfalls** Klemmer (ts, ss); **Mike Nock** (p); **Wilton Felder** (b); **Eddie Marshall** (d); **Victor Feldman** (perc); **Diana Lee** (v). Impulsc! Ⓜ MCAD33123 (41 minutes). Recorded 1972.

Ⓗ Ⓗ

Critics have often damned Chicago-bred saxophonist John Klemmer with faint praise. Thus, while his technical prowess has been noted, his overall work has often been qualified as "uneven" or "derivative." In this seminal 1972 date, recorded live at the Ash Grove in Los Angeles, Klemmer is revealed as a moving player of extraordinary talent and vision.

The first thing one notes is his exceptional use of the echoplex. As employed in the two solo *Preludes*, Klemmer's electrified tenor spews sounds that spill and splash, leaving sonic rainbows suspended in the mist. Equally impressive is his poignant balladry on *Waterfall*. Here, he soars with an ethereality reminiscent of Stan Getz. In the aptly titled *Centrifugal Force*, his tenor explodes outward with Trane-like intensity. On soprano, Klemmer's laser lyricism signals *There's Some Light Ahead*.

Supple fusionistic force fields are energized by electric pianist Mike Nock, electric bassist Wilton Felder, drummer Eddie Marshall, percussionist Victor Feldman, and singer Diana Lee whose haunting vocalese on *Utopia* takes us to a lush, exoticized Eden. At the centre of each vortex is the volcanic lyricism of the estimable John Klemmer. **CB** 339

# Eric Kloss

1949

New review
**Eric Kloss and the Rhythm Section** Kloss (as, ts); **Pat Martino** (elg); **Chick Corea** (p, elp); **Dave Holland** (b); **Jack DeJohnette** (d). Prestige Ⓜ PRCD24125-2 (79 minutes). Recorded 1969/70.

④ ❽

Like the buildings of the period, which fell into tatty decay almost as soon as they were put up, much jazz of the hippie era is sorry stuff – tuneless, shapeless and endless. It was the misfortune of Eric Kloss to reach the age of 20 in 1969 and, after a solid series of records with people such as Jaki Byard, Booker Ervin and the like, to be given his big break with a couple of albums accompanied by Miles Davis's then-current rhythm section. Both those albums, **To Hear is to See** and **Consciousness**, are contained on this CD. The blind former child prodigy is a fine player on both alto and tenor, with a lot of technique and a fertile imagination, but the material is useless and, without Miles's firm hand, Corea and company prance about interminably, playing rhythm-games with dinky little riffs. Everyone had been so unnerved by the rock explosion that the only course seemed to be to adopt some of its characteristics. That or give up all pretence of coherence and play 'free'. The hapless Kloss has a go at each of these strategies, with the expected results. It is a great shame, and begs the question as to why, of all Kloss records, these were the first chosen for CD transfer. If he had been born 20 years later he might have had a good career. **DG**

# Earl Klugh

1954

**The Earl Klugh Trio, Volume 1** Klugh (g); **Ralphe Armstrong** (b); **Gene Dunlap** (d). Warner Bros Ⓕ 926750-2 (51 minutes). Recorded 1991.

⑦ ❽

Klugh has been at the top of his profession for many years, but little of the music he has played in the past 15 years has had much jazz content: if anything, jazz was used as a flavouring, much as Lee Ritenour was using it. Both guitarists, though, have recently come back to jazz, albeit in very different ways. This album finds Klugh sticking exclusively to acoustic guitar and well-worn standards such as *Bewitched*, *I'll Remember April*, *Insensatez* and *Too Marvellous for Words*. His playing reminds one of a number of players from an older generation, and in that sense it is a backward-looking album which certainly makes no attempt at all to break new ground. That said, the playing is of a very high standard indeed: Klugh's fabled technique enables him to articulate any idea which comes his way, but more than that, he plays very tastefully at all stages: there is no flash and superficiality, and no obvious catering for people who just want to hear the melody and nothing else. Klugh also communicates a great deal of warmth, and clearly cares deeply for these songs. He is expertly supported in every mood and at every tempo by his colleagues. There is also a Volume 2 in this series now available which maintains these standards. A later album which unfortunately doesn't is the misleadingly titled **A Sudden Burst of Energy**, which is perfect music for insomniacs. **KS**

# Martin Klute

New review
**Swing** Klute (b); **Mark Edwards** (p); **Paul Cavacuiti** (d). Top Cat Ⓕ TCF1731 (60 minutes). Recorded 1994.

⑤ ❼

This is conventional piano-bass-drums trio jazz by a young British group. Klute and Edwards cut their teeth with Tommy Chase while Cavacuiti has absorbed US influences at first hand when working in America. The recording is a live, uncut analogue affair, made in the Church of St John the Baptist, Pinner. The discovery is Edwards, a pianist of verve and skill who takes risks, has no fear of jumbling influences into an eclectic *mélange* of his own and remains consistently interesting (and entertaining). Cavacuiti uses dynamics more effectively than many a British mainstreamer, keeping to a quiet supporting role when required, but opening up with an attack and volume often missing from piano trios. With the exception of one original from Klute the fare is mainly standards, but the treatments are sufficiently original to remain unhackneyed. **AS**

# Jimmy Knepper

1927

**Special Relationship** Knepper (tb) with, on seven tracks: **Joe Temperley** (ts, bs); **Derek Smith** (p); **Michael Moore** (b); **Billy Hart** (d); on five tracks: **Bobby Wellins** (ts); **Peter Jacobsen** (p); **Dave Green** (b); **Ron Parry** (d). HEP Ⓕ CD2012 (78 minutes). Recorded 1978/80.

⑧ ❽

Although his name is almost inextricably linked with that of Charles Mingus, it would be a gross inaccuracy to assume that Jimmy Knepper has no other claim to fame. He is, quite simply, one of the most individual of all trombone soloists and certainly one of the most experienced with all manner of bands ("the worse the music, the better they play" he remarks). This long-playing CD contains nearly all the tracks from two Hep LPs, the first jointly made under the leadership of Knepper and Joe Temperley in New York, the second commemorating a short British tour with Bobby Wellins in 1980. The session with Temperley shares the solo honours fairly evenly and Joe responds to the challenges of pure bebop (*Yardbird Suite*) and the writing of Duke Ellington on *Aristocracy of Jean Lafitte* (from the *New Orleans Suite* and taken in waltz time) and *Sophisticated Lady*. The rhythm section has the crisp 'New York' sound but the British trio is equally excellent, with well-selected and long bass notes from Dave Green and splendid piano from the underrated Pete Jacobsen. Wellins's unique keening sound makes an ideal foil for the warm-toned, agile trombone of Knepper who came up with three distinctive originals for the date including a Parker-like blues *Gnome on the Range*. The stark *'Round Midnight* is a duet featuring Wellins and Jacobsen. **AM**

## Franz Köglmann                                                                 1947

**New review**
**We Thought About Duke** Köglmann (t, flh); **Rudolf Ruschel** (tb); **Raoul Herget** (tba); **Tony Coe** (cl, ts); **Lee Konitz** (as); **Burkhard Stangl** (g); **Klaus Koch** (b). Hat Hut Ⓟ ARTCD6163 (56 minutes). Recorded 1994.

⑧ ❽

The Vienna-based Köglmann is best-known as a composer and arranger, his reputation for originality established by a series of recordings for Hat Hut in the eighties that included **About Yesterday's Ezzthetics** (currently out of the catalogue) and **The Use of Memory**. His music tends to the esoteric, making reference to the visual arts, poetry, modernist composers and what he has called "a white line" of jazz improvisers, such as Bix Beiderbecke, Lennie Tristano and Paul Desmond. Köglmann cites their "considered design, lucid coolness, detached lyricism" as qualities he aspires to, whether playing with his jazz chamber orchestra, the Pipetet, in small groups or with guest artists who on record have included Ran Blake, Bill Dixon and Steve Lacy. **L'Heure Bleu**, his finest recording to date, is now unavailable, but its successor, **We Thought about Duke**, has much to commend it, not least Tony Coe's superb clarinet work. Köglmann's reworkings of Ellington are fairly radical, a ploy that adds little to masterpieces like *Ko-Ko* and *The Mooche* but certainly uncovers the striking beauty to be found in lesser-known gems such as *Lament for Javanette*, *Zweet Zurzday* and Billy Strayhorn's inconsolable *Dirge*. **GL**

## Hans Koller                                                                    1921

**Out on the Rim** Koller (snino s, ss, ts); **Wolfgang Puschnig** (as); **Martin Fuss**, **Warne Marsh** (ts); **Klaus Dickbauer** (ts, bs); **Bernd Konrad** (as, bss). In & Out Ⓟ 7014-2 (69 minutes). Recorded 1984-91.

⑥ ❽

Viennese-born Koller has been a prime mover on the German jazz scene since the early fifties, playing with a string of top German and visiting American instrumentalists. Since the sixties he has been very involved in saxophone workshops, so the line-up on this, his latest record and his first in a decade, should come as no great surprise. Neither should it be suprising that the level of technical ability is very high amongst all the players here, with precision virtually taken for granted on even the most complex passages. The music tends to the ascetic, with lone, bleak tunes emerging from complex passages and helter-skelter solo lines. Two dedications mark the album like book-ends, the music starting with *In Memoriam Stan Getz* and finishing with *Warne Marsh (In Memoriam)*, a 1984 duo with the master saxophonist and his only appearance on the disc. This music is not easy, but nor is it so wild and woolly as to be an assault on the ears. It is complex, and reveals its subtleties slowly. Have patience and you will be rewarded. **KS**

## Krzysztof Komeda                                                              1931-69

**New review**
**Astigmatic** Komeda (p); **Tomasz Stanko** (t); **Zbigniew Namyslowski** (as); **Gunter Lenz** (b); **Rune Carlson** (d). Power Bros Ⓟ 00125 (47 minutes). Recorded 1965.

⑨ ❼

Dead at 38, pianist Komeda was a musical icon in his native Poland. This CD is the reissue of an LP that enjoyed a cult following and, to put it into its European perspective, was made within three months of the Spontaneous Music Ensemble's first record. In Stanko, Namyslowski and Lenz, it had three men who became major figures in the European free music scene but it was the remarkable Komeda who made it such an important landmark. His professional début was in 1956 and he made an unremarkable album of standards in 1961. He had been metaphorically touched by Bill Evans, Eric Dolphy and John Coltrane, however, and by 1965 had moved into freer areas, both as composer and player. *Kattorna* was written for a film but shows the way in which Komeda used Polish folk sources, classical elements and Monk-like eccentricities in his own piano concept. *Svantetic*, with its sombrely majestic opening, is inspirational to Stanko and Namyslowski but it is the title track that fires the whole project. It is orchestrated by Komeda's modest yet meaningful piano and dwells in emotional vales and peaks as the occasion demands. Each melodic strain elicits its own response, there is not a trite phrase in sight and the contrapuntal interactions achieve an almost Mingusian intensity. Only two albums followed and, four years later, Komeda collapsed in America. Although he returned to Poland in a state of coma, he never recovered.  **BMcR**

# Klaus König

**Time Fragments**  Mark Feldman (vn); Reiner Winterschladen (t); Kenny Wheeler (flh); Jörg Huke (tb); Michel Godard (tba); Robert Dick (f, pic); Frank Gratkowski (f, ss, as); Matthias Schubert (ob, ts); Wollie Kaiser (ss, bcl); Stefan Bauer (mba); Mark Dresser (b); Gerry Hemingway (d); König (cond, arr). Enja ⓕ ENJ8076-2 (54 minutes). Recorded 1994.

⑦ ❽

König belongs to a forward-looking tradition in jazz which hasn't had a great deal of encouragement outside of Europe since Stan Kenton hung up his spurs and Don Ellis rediscovered common time. Not that König's music, or his orchestra, sounds much like either of those musicians, but there is possibly a similarity of intent, if nothing else. In a sense it is an Apollonian, intellectual approach gone very skewed indeed, with Dionysian elements constantly being ushered in at the joins. The booklet which accompanies this music folds out to something like six times its closed size and is crowded with essays and even diagrams of how the music is structured and how and where its themes interlink and disperse. Conventional musical notation is mostly avoided, and the substitutes become something of an art form in themselves. The subtitle to the project is "Seven Studies in Time and Motion". Each but the last piece carries a dual dedication, emphasizing the perceived links between classical and jazz music – Berg/Mingus; Monk/Bartók; Threadgill/Mahler and so on. The music when actually listened to becomes something of a collage – not so surprising when you consider what has come before – but the accomplished musicians involved give the music a consistent voice which would be impossible to achieve otherwise. This is music to be closely considered first and reacted to later; which is no bad thing. In the long-postponed wedding between European art music and jazz, this is a positive communication between the two families of the bride and groom. Unfortunately, König has subsequently gone on to cross wires with the self-conscious and misconceived **Reviews**, which makes the fatal mistake of being quite long and relying heavily on humour.  **KS**

# Lee Konitz

1927

**Subconscious-Lee**  Konitz (as); Warne Marsh (ts); Lennie Tristano, Sal Mosca (p); Billy Bauer (g); Arnold Fishkin (b); Shelly Manne, Denzil Best, Jeff Morton (d). Prestige Ⓜ OJC186-2 (40 minutes). Recorded 1949/50.

✔                                                                        ❿ ⑦

Although he had previously recorded as part of the Claude Thornhill Orchestra, this album, consisting of four separate sessions, was Konitz's first under his own name. The timing was serendipitous; the initial date, with Tristano, Bauer, Fishkin and Manne, took place just a few months before Tristano's legendary Capitol recording, and only days before Konitz waxed with the first of Miles Davis's **Birth of the Cool** sessions. More than 40 years later the results remain spectacular, a slice of jazz history. The effortless manner in which Konitz negotiates the labyrinthine contours of *Tautology* and *Progression* is a tonic; the music combines bebop intricacy with different rhythmic accents and fresh harmonies (*Subconscious-Lee*, based on altered chords to *What is This Thing Called Love?* has proven especially durable over the years). The next four tunes, with *alter ego* Warne Marsh, include telepathic counterpoint and a breathtaking unison on Marsh's treacherous roller-coaster *Marshmallow*. In contrast to such dazzling invention, *Rebecca*, a duet with Bauer's lithe guitar, is an unbroken thread of pure, fragile melody. Blending elements from Benny Carter, Johnny Hodges and Lester Young in the face of Bird, Konitz's fluid, uninhibited spontaneity and vulnerable, nearly transparent tone set him in good stead for a career of consistently inspired, risk-taking improvisation.  **AL**

New review
**Lee Konitz Meets Jimmy Giuffre**  Konitz (as); with a collective personnel including: Giuffre (cl, bs, arr); Tony Miranda (frh); Danny Bank (f); Hal McKusick (as); Ted Brown, Warne Marsh (ts); Bill Evans (p); Buddy Clark (b); Ronnie Free (d); orchestras under the direction of Bill Russo, Ralph Burns and Giuffre; Südwesfunk Orchestra, Baden-Baden, Woflram Röhig (dir). Verve Ⓜ 527 780-2 (two discs: 151 minutes). Recorded 1951-9.

⑦ ❻

Konitz's name at the head of this set is something of a flag of convenience, for Verve have taken the
opportunity to collate no fewer than four old albums under one slim-line double-CD title. The four

concerned are Ralph Burns's old 10" LP, **Free Forms**; **Lee Konitz With Strings**; **Lee Konitz Meets Jimmy Giuffre** and, lastly, **Jimmy Giuffre Piece for Clarinet and String Orchestra/Mobiles**, on which Konitz does not appear. Most of the music was recorded in the space of a year, 1958-9, with just the Ralph Burns material dating from 1951. When Burns made his album Cool was well established on the West Coast, but Third Stream was unheard-of; by the time the other LPs were made, Third Stream was a constnat talking-point among musicians and critics (most of them hated it). For an interesting insight into Third Stream's gestation, the booklet of a recent Columbia reissue, **The Birth of the Third Stream**, which features works from Giuffre, John Lewis, J.J. Johnson and Gunther Schuller and was originally recorded in 1956 on two separate LPs as **Modern Jazz Concert/Music for Brass**. Meanwhile, back to Konitz. The with-strings album highlights the altoist's limpd tone and gift for melodic phrasing; the Ralph Burns music is rather dated and hardly competes with what Burns did for Herman in the forties. The album with Giuffre is probably the pick of the bunch, although the sheer cream involved in that non-aggressive bunch of saxophone tones makes one occasionally wonder, and the up-tempo and the bluesy numbers such as *Palo Alto* and *Somp'm Outa' Nothin'* tend to fare best. The album featuring Giuffre out front with his own orchestral pieces is sometimes intriguing, sometimes plain hard work. There is not a great deal of common ground with the jazz tradition as it was then understood on this last set of sessions. The deliberate paleness of sound and emotional input, spread over two well-filled CDs, tends to give the listener – long before the music stops – the raging desire to go out and eat an enormous underdone steak. **KS**

---

**Live at the Half Note** Konitz (as); **Warne Marsh** (ts); **Bill Evans** (p); **Jimmy Garrison** (b); **Paul Motian** (d). Verve Ⓜ 521 659-2 (two discs: 97 minutes). Recorded 1959.

✔                                                                                        ⑧ ⑧

For most of his career Lee Konitz has been saddled with a reputation for chilly abstraction. This was undeserved but understandable in view of the contrast between his limpid, unemphatic style and the vehemence of hard bop, which was the height of jazz fashion at the time of this live recording. His style had changed hardly at all since the late forties, when he and Warne Marsh were members of the coterie of young players which clustered around that severe guru, Lennie Tristano. Konitz and Marsh had been perfecting their unique form of interplay over the same period, and their act never sounded tighter than it does here. The deftness with which the two of them weave and twine their lines, aided by the impeccable match of their tones, is truly phenomenal. A further recommendation is the rhythm section. Instead of the studied blandness or neutrality of the Tristano school, this team, an early version of the Bill Evans Trio, leans quite hard on the beat, creating a superb feeling of momentum. How this remarkable session came to languish unissued between 1959 and 1994 is a mystery. **DG**

---

**Zounds** Konitz (as, ss, v); **Kenny Werner** (p, syn); **Ron McClure** (b); **Bill Stewart** (d). Soul Note Ⓕ 121219-2 (55 minutes). Recorded 1990.

                                                                                         ⑧ ⑧

The one consistent factor in Konitz's chequered career has been his unswerving devotion to improvisation – he has always regarded it as a prime duty to be creative. This CD certainly upholds that principle and, in the sense that much of it champions the ideal of spontaneous composition, it is very much nearer to the Lennie Tristano *Intuition* session in the late forties than to any more obvious source. Known tunes such as *Prelude to a Kiss* and *Taking a Chance on Love* are of special interest, being orthodox extemporizations only in that they start with a known theme. The solos follow the changes in a quite devious way, although Konitz is happy to return to them when his own personal meanderings are exhausted. The bench-marks by which the album should be judged are the excellent *Zounds* and *Synthesthetics*, where all four players allow themselves the utmost freedom and in the process produce a collection of extended phrases that could, in their own right, be compositions of the future. Not even on his own *Blue Samba* does Konitz ignore the freedom ethic, and with a rhythm section that involves itself to the extent of being very much more than a rhythm section, he has documented his current career with some style. **BMcR**

# Diana Krall

---

New review
**All For You** Krall (v, p); **Russell Malone** (g); **Paul Keller** (b); add on one track each **Benny Green** (p); **Steve Kroon** (perc). Impulse! Ⓕ IMP11642 (59 minutes). Recorded 1995.

                                                                                         ⑧ ⑩

The subtitle of this, Krall's third disc as a leader, is "A Dedication to the Nat King Cole Trio". The music Krall's trio makes is worthy of such a dedication. Of all the young female vocalists presently on the scene, Krall is able to cut through the surface of a song and deliver its essence to the unsuspecting listener. That essence can be fun as well as hardship or heartache, but her smoky timbre and easy delivery gives her a wonderful, understated intimacy, achieved without undue flash, while her innate musicality allows her to add small variations to a song's original course. In this way she stamps her own authority on the music in the manner of a McRae or – well, a Cole. The trio she appears with here is her working band and it became familiar with the Cole-inspired selection during a summer season around US clubs. The understanding this engendered is greatly in evidence and the group plays as one, moving to each cadence and inflection with a perfectly realized integration. Cole's artistry is lovingly invoked in this collection, but Krall's interpretations can be enjoyed on their own terms. A fine pianist whether accompanying herself or soloing, on *If I Had You* she duets movingly with a perfectly understated Benny Green. Krall is no longer promising great things – she's delivering them. **KS**

## Wayne Krantz                                                           1956

**Long to Be Loose** Krantz (g); Lincoln Goines (elb); Zach Danziger (d). Enja Ⓕ ENJ7099-2 (62 minutes). Recorded 1993.

⑧ ❾

Wayne Krantz made several impressive if stylistically unexceptional showings as a sideman with fellow guitarist Leni Stern in the late eighties, but on his second album as leader he has stumbled on something quite fresh. You have heard everything here somewhere before – in the wry harmonic abstraction of Scofield's late seventies funk, in thousands of country licks, in the Strat rattle of Mark Knopfler, in the riffing of Led Zeppelin – but where it might have seemed no further permutations were possible, Krantz has hammered out a new configuration of the old verities. It is fusion, and one which draws on some quite disparate resources, but thanks to his assured sense of form, pacing and mood, even the most oblique juxtapositions seem to flow together. His goal was to find a new direction for the time-worn guitar-bass-drums format, and in Goines and Danziger he has two players able to interpret his often demanding, heavily through-written charts with skill and sympathy. The result is an exhilarating, always intriguing hour of trio music, and a comprehensive exposition of modern guitar playing. Krantz's second album, **Two Drink Minimum** (Enja), is also impressive. **MG**

## Ernie Krivda                                                           1945

New review
**Sarah's Theme** Krivda (ts); Jeff Halsey (b); Bob Frazer (g). Creative Improvised Music Projects Ⓕ CIMP102 (69 minutes). Recorded 1995.

⑥ ❽

As a young man, Krivda's greatest problem was reconciling his father's love of classical music with his own liking for jazz. At high school he switched from clarinet to saxophone and began to take an interest in the hard boppers. At his father's insistence, he declined a spot at the all-jazz Berklee and completed his studies at the more cosmopolitan Berea College in Ohio. He remained, however, a voracious jazz listener and his realm of interest extended in the late sixties to the records of John Coltrane and Eric Dolphy. In the late seventies his first recordings as a leader in New York certainly reflected the influence of Coltrane, in tone and delivery if not always in content. Since that time most of his musical activities have taken place back in his home town in Cleveland and, as this live 1995 New York recording shows, his style has returned to its more pure bop beginnings. His tone on titles such as *Interlude No. 2* and *Pacific Echoes* has assumed a lighter timbre, at times almost pointing toward the sound of Stan Getz or Al Cohn. The absence of a drummer serves this purpose well. The quality of his attack remains constant but it is now directed by an improvisational method, couched in the unwritten rules of bebop rather than the headlong harmonic extensions of Coltrane. **BMcR**

## Karin Krog                                                             1937

New review
**Jubilee – the best of 30 years** Krog (v) with a collective personnel including: Jan Garbarek, Dexter Gordon, Bjarne Nerem, Archie Shepp, Warne Marsh (ts); John Surman (bs, syn); Egil Kapstad, Kenny Drew, Jon Balke, Bengt Hallberg, Roger Kellaway (p); Kurt Lindgren, NHØP, Arild Andersen, Red Mitchell (b); Jon Christensen, Beaver Harris (d); The Don Ellis Orchestra, Palle Mikkelborg and Orchestra. Verve Ⓜ 523 716-2 (two discs: 148 minutes). Recorded 1964-91.

⑧ ❼

There are very few singers who can claim to cover the range of music the Norwegian Karin Krog has so convincingly managed in the past three decades. With that in mind, plus her absolute insistence on never over-singing, instead choosing to sing only the essential notes (and always in the right places), it is hardly surprising she has attracted so many first-rate musicians for her record dates. Her approach eschews the grand statement, giving her clear timbre and precise delivery a deceptively cool poise which never deserts her even in the midst of a blues with Archie Shepp breathing down her every phrase (*Sing Me Softly of the Blues*). With the Don Ellis Orchestra she again provides a perfect counterpoint, retaining her vocal identity while all hell breaks out around her. This collection traces her singing from the orthodox niceties of 1964's *Lover Man* and *By Myself* to her fascinating work with John Surman and Palle Mikkelborg. Krog is still far too active and vital a musician to be decribed as an institution, but the integrity of her artistic vision as revealed by these two well-filled discs qualifies her for any number of lifetime achievement awards, should she want them. **KS**

# Gene Krupa

**Drum Boogie** Krupa (d, ldr) **and His Orchestra**, including: **Norman Murphy**, **Torg Halten**, **Rudy Novak**, **Shorty Sherock** (t); **Pat Virgadamo**, **Jay Kelliher**, **Babe Wagner** (tb); **Clint Neagley**, **Musky Ruffo** (as); **Walter Bates** (ts); **Sam Musiker** (cl, ts); **Bob Kitsis** (p); **Ray Biondi** (g); **Buddy Bastien** (b); **Irene Day** (v); **Jimmy Mundy** (arr). Columbia Legacy Ⓜ 473659-2 (50 minutes). Recorded 1940-1.

⑥ **❻**

Krupa left Benny Goodman's employ in spring 1938 and quickly pulled a big band together under his own name. The early sides were short on subtlety and long on drums, but the fans got the message and Krupa's popularity was asssured. His records for Brunswick emphasized the killer-diller approach he had got such praise for when with Goodman. Two years down the line, however, with a change of record company, Krupa finally felt the need to jettison an image which had become something of a strait-jacket, where each number had to top the last. This collection reflects that increasing moderation, and although the leader's drums are ever-prominent, the musicianship around him is allowed to blossom and dynamics are carefully observed.

For a man whose visual impact was so enormous, it is always surprising to hear just how much of that flair came across intact on his records. Krupa may have been criticized for being somewhat unsubtle, and at times his work with Goodman could be unswinging, but on this selection there is no doubt about his ability alternately to kick his band along or to ride close behind it, keeping things lightly swinging. Strange that some of his hits are boogies, because the band itself isn't very good at playing boogie or shuffle beat (pianist Kitsis is quoted in the notes as saying "God, but I hated boogie-woogie", and it shows). Still, it helped keep his name in front of an adoring public, and Krupa was able to keep his unoriginal but accomplished band successful, just as Chick Webb had with nursery rhymes a couple of years previously. Soon after the last session on this CD was recorded, Roy Eldridge and Anita O'Day were to join the band and give it a completely new lease of life. **KS**

# Joachim Kuhn/Rolf Kuhn

New review

**Brothers** Joachim Kuhn (p); **Rolf Kuhn** (cl). VeraBra Ⓕ vBr2184 2 (62 minutes). Recorded 1994.

⑥ **❾**

The fact of being born almost 15 years apart has meant that the Kuhn brothers arrived at similar musical conclusions from different directions. As the older, clarinettist Rolf melded the swing era influences of his forties education with the bop of his maturing years. He worked in various big bands, embraced Cool jazz and approached freer climes with some stealth. Joachim, a virtuoso pianist, entered Paris's jazz auditorium in the late sixties. He flourished in the turmoil of fusion, hard bop and free jazz, although his eclecticism occasionally obscured his true *métier*. From the sixties onward, they often worked together without actually nailing their colours to one stylistic mast. This CD gives them considerable licence. It transports them from the classically-inclined *Opal*, with its controlled, contrapuntal parts and taped background support, to *Saturday Blues* with its perambulating mobility and its avoidance of regimented bar lines. There is something consciously iconoclastic in most of what they do. It is obvious in the Thelonious Monk-like angularities of *Loverman* and *Ev'ry Time We Say Goodbye* but none of their solos are blatant. The secret of the effortless way in which their melodic lines interact might be the fact that Rolf originally studied piano and Joachim is an accomplished alto saxophonist. One of Joachim's best piano records, the 1980 solo effort **Snow in the Desert**, has recently been reissued by WEA. **BMcR**

# Steve Kuhn

**Oceans in the Sky** Kuhn (p); **Miroslav Vitous** (b); **Aldo Romano** (d). Owl Ⓔ 056CD380056-2 (57 minutes). Recorded 1989.

⑥ **❽**

The impenetrable purple-on-black printing on the back of the CD case would be a poor inducement to investigate any recording, but those with a taste for elegant yet often impassioned piano trio music should not be discouraged; the packaging is no reflection on the clarity and colour of the music it contains. The session's treasures are revealed a few minutes into the opening number, Ivan Lins's *The Island*. Kuhn first came to attention in John Coltrane's quartet (he preceded McCoy Tyner) and he has also enjoyed a long, creative friendship with Sheila Jordan. On ths album Kuhn at first plays with a precision and lyricism which reflect his rigorous classical training and his taste for Erik Satie, Bill Evans and the like, but as his beautifully contoured solo gathers pace, he produces muscular, probing, intensely swinging right hand lines in the style of Bud Powell. There is more of the same, but faster, and worrying the piano's highest octave at length, on the next item, Kenny Dorham's *Lotus Blossom*. Several other tracks, hewing a gentler line, are less substantial, and Carlos-Jobim's *Angela* offers more than a glimpse of Kuhn the cocktail pianist. But when he is good, he is compelling, and his pursuit of the perfect swing is hardly hindered by the presence of two deft and sympathetic colleagues. **MG**

# Charles Kynard

**Reelin' With the Feelin'/Wa-Tu-Wa-Zui** Kynard (org, elp); **Wilton Felder** (ts); **Joe Pass**, **Melvin Sparks** (g); **Carol Kaye**, **Jimmy Lewis** (b); **Paul Humphrey**, **Idris Muhammed**, **Bernard Purdie** (d); **Virgil Jones** (t); **Rusty Bryant** (ts). Beat Goes On Ⓜ CDBGPD055 (74 minutes). Recorded 1969/70.

⑤ ❻

Kynard, along with many others, carved a career for himself playing funky organ at the end of the sixties, usually with some form of backbeat, and with a liberal helping of blues changes. At the time these two albums were recorded jazz was under siege, and most journeymen players like Kynard were attempting to appeal to the younger audience in the hope of achieving financial survival. So their usual riffs and routines were dressed up in quasi-soul or rock forms (much here is only one step away from King Curtis sessions, or James Brown without the vocals). It was only the improvisations which pushed this music into the jazz arena. Indeed, on the first date, Wilton Felder plays thoroughly contemporary tenor, unafraid to acquaint his listeners with subtle harmonic routes through dead-ordinary changes. Joe Pass, on the other hand, pretty well capitulates to the simplistic approach, and does it half-heartedly, too, only shining when given a bossa beat and the more sophisticated harmonic basis of *Be My Love* to solo over. The second date is painfully under-rehearsed, with Jones and Bryant often unable to phrase together on the simple song 'heads'. Kynard has, meanwhile, moved closer to out-and-out soul, and much of this date could have been played by Junior Walker and The All-Stars. The use of Melvin Sparks instead of Pass accelerates this process. Of all the players here, predictably only Jones plays with what could be called a jazz inflexion and awareness of passing tones. Kynard's electric piano playing robs him of his usual energy and shows his musical thought to be essentially unoriginal. I would imagine that, today, this would be music to dance to in clubs, so things have come full circle. It serves its purpose, and when Felder or Jones solos, occasionally surpasses it. **KS**

# L.A. 4

**New review**
**Executive Suite** Bud Shank (as); **Laurindo Almeida** (g); **Ray Brown** (b); **Jeff Hamilton** (d). Concord Jazz Ⓕ CCD4215 (42 minutes). Recorded 1982.

⑧ ❾

Four strong characters give the L.A. 4 a power and range of expression which is much wider than the line-up would suggest. The basic factor is the contrast in temperament between Shank, who wails passionately on the alto and is one of the best players in the world, and Almeida, who is a controlled virtuoso guitarist. The roles of Ray Brown and Jeff Hamilton are perfectly taken and the result is a group which plays with great passion and contrast of mood. The opening *Blues Wellington* is a fine example, with Shank's driving voice contrasted with a delicate out-of-tempo guitar solo, pressured by accompaniment from growling *arco* bass. *Arco* bass again on Almeida's impressionistic *Amazonia*, where Shank's flute emerges as a Dr Jekyll to the Mr Hyde of the alto. Although it is capable of very detailed and complex playing the quartet remains a very committed jazz group and it is irritating to see it sometimes dismissed as 'twee'. Perhaps the delicate essay on Bach's *Simple Invention* contributes to this idea, although Bach would have liked the pulse of Ray Brown's bass and would have had to own that it was jazz. Shank stands revealed as a master flautist. The twee label sometimes also befalls the Modern Jazz Quartet, the nearest parallel and a similarly committed jazz group. Both groups are in fact classic jazz groups made up of giants. **SV**

# Dean Laabs

**Invisible Maniac** Laabs (t); **Jeff Song** (elb, kayagum, g); **Matt Turner** (vc, kbds); **Dan Stein** (kbds); **John Mettam** (perc). Asia Improv. Records Ⓕ AIR0018 (73 minutes). Recorded 1993.

⑤ ❽

The playing of Laabs and Song could be seen as belonging to a less than clearly defined musical genre. Academically trained, experienced in jazz, contemporary improvised music, rock and its many relatives, they are producing music drawing from all of these sources. Laabs served as a composer/artist in residence in his hometown of Wisconsin before moving to the Boston area. He has been playing throughout New England since 1988 and his partnership with Song has proved to be very fruitful.

This challenging CD has its slightly pretentious lows in the rock-style prevarications of *Lucy, Lucy Talkin' Twice* and in the static percussion interlude on *Namu*, but these are balanced by some fine trumpet by the joint leader. He has a distinctive tone and is at his best when he allows his lyricism to carry through his harmonically liberated solos. On *Parting With Regret*, he conjures up a mood of plaintive resignation and, although he essays little in the way of overt passion, there is a soulfulness in all he does. The atmospherics of *The Canal* are unconvincing but this is primarily clean-lined free jazz with the emphasis on control. Drummer Mettam's occasional journeys into the frenetic are isolated and irrelevant, but this is New Age music with attitude. **BMcR**

# Steve Lacy

**The Straight Horn of Steve Lacy**  Lacy (ss); **Charles Davis** (bs); **John Ore** (b); **Roy Haynes** (d). Candid Ⓜ CD9007 (37 minutes). Recorded 1960.

⑦ ❽

At the time this record was made Steve Lacy was one of the very few soprano players around, and also one of the few players (white or otherwise) to enlist enthusiastically under the colours of Monk and Cecil Taylor, composers of all but one of the tunes on this CD. What was most extraordinary about this allegiance was that Lacy had come almost directly from the ranks of the Dixielanders in converting to this new music, and it shows in his playing. Not that he has any Dixieland licks in his solos; rather that he has no preconceptions about how to play modern. His somewhat inconsistent front line partner, the baritone player Charles Davis, has a whole range of bop mannerisms to offer which now sound almost quaintly dated, but nobody had taught Lacy the tricks of the trade, so you get on this record a rather rare sound in jazz: someone working it out for himself how he should sound. The effect is cerebral, but fascinating, as he carves his way into the unknown, almost deliberately choosing the notes *en route*, using his musical intelligence and not his reflexes. Worth hearing, even at this distance from the event. Roy Haynes's drumming, especially on *Air*, is crisp and attentive. **MK**

**School Days**  Lacy (ss); **Roswell Rudd** (tb); **Henry Grimes** (b); **Dennis Charles** (d, perc). HatART Ⓕ CD6140 (55 minutes). Recorded 1963.

Following his comparative success with synthetic Dixieland, Lacy spent two years studying and playing with avant-garde guru Cecil Taylor. He had, however, always been fascinated by the work of Thelonious Monk and had welcomed the chance to join him in the early sixties. Monk's lessons were delivered on site and for Lacy it became another graduate course. It was perhaps inevitable that the group he led from 1961 to 1964 should mine this rich field of music and the appropriately-titled **School Days**, with its full programme of Monk compositions, documents the changes that were accommodated within Lacy's style. Themes were approached in a straight manner, but both Lacy and Rudd take more liberties than is usual in readings of *Melodious Thunkery*. Rudd's bucolic ramblings on *Brilliant Corners* and *Monk's Mood*, the almost folk-like quality of Lacy on *Monk's Dream* and the jaunty gait of both on *Bolivar Ba-Lues-Are* suggests that Dixieland experience attended the range of expression they used. In support Grimes gives a fine exhibition of 'changes' bass playing and Charles keeps time surefootedly.  For Lacy it proved to be a natural launching pad for the next stage of his career: his take-off into even freer musical areas. **BMcR**

**Remains**  Lacy (ss). HatART Ⓕ CD6102 (64 minutes). Recorded 1991.

⑨ ❾

Lacy began playing solo in 1972 after hearing Anthony Braxton's **For Alto**, the first-ever album of solo saxophone music. Together with Braxton, Roscoe Mitchell and Evan Parker, he has become one of the outstanding solo saxophone recitalists in contemporary jazz, although unlike the other three he has not developed a specifically 'solo music', preferring to play solo versions of tunes he also performs in other contexts. **Remains** is a fine exhibition of his solo skills, its stark beauty traversing a typically varied set of material. *Tao* is Lacy's earliest surviving piece, a six-part suite begun in 1967 and still in the process of "elaboration and realization". Its evolution exemplifies his *modus operandi* of building improvisations around a structural germ, often a simple sing-song phrase (as on *Bone* here), then reworking the music – adjusting the pulse, reshaping the contours – until all its possibilities have been teased out.

A second long piece, *Remains*, is mostly notated and "explores the nature of decay", its austere poetry showing why Lacy has been called "the Samuel Beckett of the soprano saxophone". *Afterglow*, a bright Kansas City blues, and *Epistrophy*, reveal his friendlier aspects, the latter a happy example of his gift for refashioning Monk tunes to often brilliant effect (see too his Soul Note discs **Only Monk** and **More Monk**). **GL**

**New review**
**Vespers**  Lacy (ss); **Tom Varner** (frh); **Steve Potts** (ss, as); **Ricky Ford** (ts); **Bobby Few** (p); **Jean Jacques Avenal** (b); **John Betsch** (d); **Irene Aebi** (v). Soul Note Ⓕ 121260-2 (51 minutes). Recorded 1993.

⑨ ❽

Steve Lacy has an affinity for poetry, ancient and modern, and the wisdom and fantasy that can be found therein. As early as 1967 he began setting texts from the *Tao Te Ching* of Lao-Tzu to music, which eventually became his suite of songs, *The Way*. Subsequently he's arranged his chiselled melodies to enhance excerpts from the notebooks of George Braque (*Tips*) and the cut-up poems of Brion Gysin (*Songs*), devised song cycles using Russian poets like Akhmatova and Mandelstam (*Rushes*) and the American Robert Creeley (*Futurities*), as well as possibly hundreds of individual songs from a wide range of poetic sources, examples of which have been scattered throughout his recordings. With **Futurities** (hatART) currently unavailable, **Vespers** is probably the most ambitious and successful of his vocal settings now available on CD. Though there's nothing specifically religious about the music or text of **Vespers**, the title suggests the sanctity of evening worship, and in fact it has been performed in churches separate from any official service. The seven poems, by Bulgarian poet Blaga Dimitrova, are the sort of verse Lacy appreciates – deceptively direct, with nuance and irony suggesting subtler interpretations – and he strengthens their delivery by never masking or distorting them for musical effect. The words become another strand of the fabric, equal to but not overshadowing the instrumental solos, and with an added measure of meaning. By expanding his group to include Tom Varner's french horn and Ricky Ford's tenor sax, he broadens his own signature ensemble sound with appealingly darker colours and thicker textures. **AL**

## Guy Lafitte

1927

**Joue Charles Trenet**  Lafitte (ts); **Marc Hemmeler, Hank Jones** (p); **Milt Buckner** (org); **Jack Sewing, George Duvivier** (b); **Philippe Combelle, Sam Woodyard, J.C. Heard** (d). Black & Blue Ⓕ 59 190 2 (55 minutes). Recorded 1977-84.

⑥ ❽

Lafitte has never had to rely on music for a living, and he seems to have recorded only when attracted by the musical company or intrigued by the concept. For all that, his work on record does not offer the rewards his abilities promise. Probably his most satisfying album is this programme of songs associated with the much-loved French singer, Charles Trenet, not least because the unfamiliarity of the tunes as jazz vehicles allows the listener to concentrate, without the distraction of recognizable procedures, on his sensitive and at times ravishing explorations. His playing recalls Coleman Hawkins yet his approach is drier, more restrained in expression, less rhapsodic. The core 1984 session with Hemmeler, Sewing and Combelle is augmented by three 1977 tracks with Buckner and Woodyard and one from 1978 with Jones, Duvivier and Heard. The seventies readings of *Bonsoir Jolie Madame* and *Que Reste-t-Il de Nos Amours* (which, translated, became *I Wish You Love*) find Lafitte wrapping the notes with Ben Websterish breaths, and they have an air of wistfulness absent from the more trenchant versions of 1984. Apart from the bright *France Dimanche* the prevailing tempo is that of the ballad, and this seems to be where Lafitte is happiest. **TR**

## Bireli Lagrene

1966

**Standards**  Lagrene (g); **Niels-Henning Ørsted Pedersen, Dominique DiPiazza** (b); **André Ceccarelli** (d). Blue Note Ⓕ CDP7 80251-2 (69 minutes). Recorded 1992.

❽ ❽

French guitarist Bireli Lagrene is a young master of the neo-bop mainstream. Initially influenced by his guitarist father and grandfather as well as his family's gipsy background, the seven-year-old Bireli came under the sway of the idiosyncratic style of Django Reinhardt. As a teenager, he played with swing legends Benny Goodman, Stephane Grappelli and Benny Carter; at the other end of the stylistic spectrum he also helped stoke the jazz-rock fires of Jaco Pastorius.

Here, in a stunning 1992 session with virtuoso bassist NHØP and dynamic drummer Andre Ceccarelli, Lagrene adds sheen to a set of glistening standards which includes *Softly, As In a Morning Sunrise, Stella By Starlight* and *Ornithology*. In contrast to many recent 'standards' projects, Lagrene hews closely to each tune's original melodic and harmonic contours; yet, with his unflagging inventive flow and sensitivity to shadings of timbre, texture and dynamics, the guitarist gives each tune a fresh, 'first-time-through' feel. Lagrene is a virtuoso capable of non-stop torrents of precisely structured tones. At heart, though, he is a romantic whose medium is a music that breathes deeply. He also possesses one of jazzdom's most beautiful guitar sounds, and one which is comparable to the late Jim Hall's. **CB**

## Cleo Laine

1928

New review

**Solitude**  Laine (v) with the **Duke Ellington Orchestra** directed by **Mercer Ellington**; **Barrie Lee Hall, John Longo, Tony Barrero, Ron Tooley** (t); **Bradley Shigeta, Gregory Royal, Art Barron, Raymond Harris** (tb); **Charlie Young, Mark Gross, Patience Young, Zane Zacharoff, Shelley Paul, Jay Brandford** (reeds); **Thomas 'TJ' James** (p); **Stephen Fox** (g); **Hassan Ash-Shakur** (b); **Rocky White** (d); **John Dankworth** (as, cl, cond). RCA Victor Ⓕ 68124-2 (63 minutes). Recorded 1994.

❽ ❿

This disc was greeted with somewhat muted praise when it appeared, but on examination most of the criticism boiled down to the complaint that 'the Duke Ellington Orchestra' was not actually Duke Ellington and his Famous Orchestra or anything much like it. Give or take bits of preaching trombone, *à la* Tricky Sam, and other Ellingtonian effects, this is true, but hardly fair or reasonable comment. The orchestra is a very good New York session band, with some excellent soloists and a finely integrated ensemble sound. The arrangements are mostly by John Dankworth, with one by Stan

Tracey and one by Ed Harvey. The title song is built around Duke's 1941 solo piano recording, a hazardous undertaking that comes off beautifully. In fact, there is not a single clumsy or inappropriate move in the whole affair. Cleo Laine's voice continues to be a source of wonder, not because of her astounding range, but because it has such a lovely natural timbre. She also has the rare and still-precious gift of eloquent simplicity. **DG**

# Oliver Lake 1942

**Compilation** Lake (saxes); **Geri Allen, Frank Abel** (p); **Fred Hopkins, Santi De Briano, Billy Grant** (b); **Anthony Peterson, Alphonia Tims** (g); **Pheeroan akLaff, Andrew Cyrille, Gene Lake, Brandon Ross** (d); **Jawara** (perc). Gramavision Ⓕ GV79458-2 (63 minutes). Recorded 1982-8.

⑨ ❽

Another student from St Louis's Black Artist's Group, Lake is probably best known for his involvement in the seventies loft movement and his pre-eminent role in the World Saxophone Quartet. This CD presents a selection from four previously issued albums and spans a period of six years. *Sun People*, from the 1982 **Jump Up**, shows that a jaunty funk base is not the ideal environment for his carousing free lines. In contrast, *France Dance*, from the 1986 **Gallery**, reassures the listener that there is nothing wrong with jauntiness if that climate is created by Allen, Hopkins and akLaff, and Lake is in a strongly creative mood. The Dolphy-like *Olla's Blues,* from the same date, offers Lake's more laid-back character and, like *Gano Club* from the 1988 **Otherside** date, shows how he makes judicious use of bluesy distortion. *We're in the Moment* is the pick of the 1987 **Impala** release, and it takes him on a chromatic path, one which is populated by more devious harmonic turns. The selection of titles is excellent and, judged as a whole, this CD accurately introduces newcomers to a man who knows how to balance his playing between a search for melodic freedom and a loyalty to the structural limits of a theme. **BMcR**

---

**New review**
**Dedicated to Dolphy** Lake (as); **Russell Gunn** (t); **Charles Eubanks** (p); **Belden Bullock** (b); **Cecil Brooks III** (d). Black Saint Ⓕ 12044-2 (54 minutes). Recorded 1994.

❽ ❽

This is not the first nod in Dolphy's direction from Lake, but it is perhaps the one most nearly cast in his predecessor's own image. Lake has chosen a quintet which can echo the line-up and inclinations of the famous but short-lived Dolphy/Booker Little Quintet of summer 1961 as well as, in trumpeter Gunn and drummer Brooks, the outward urge of **Out to Lunch** (there are two Dolphy compositions from that date represented here). Lake himself is one of a very small number of saxophonists who show a real grasp of the inner workings of Dolphy's sound and style, and this programme is a very handsome tribute indeed, partly because Lake is able to use his own strongly individual approach to bring fresh meaning to these updates, and partly because Lake already has so much of Dolphy's sensibility in his music. Others who have attempted similar tributes have been unable to put enough distance between their neo-bop ideas and themselves to make a proper marriage between their own music and Dolphy's, for while Dolphy unmistakably arose from the Parker/Gillespie tradition, his was a genuine advancement of and from that style and those concerns, and his music can only be fully appreciated once this simple fact is fully appreciated. On track after track Lake balances incisiveness and romance with a jovial belligerence in precisely the manner Dolphy did, adding his own tradition, especially that of the blues, with its unique 'cry'. On the blues *245* Lake really does holler on his horn, moulding Dolphy's language into a burning yet entirely appropriate improvisation of his own. Lake's own compositions dovetail nicely into the overall shape of the session, using chordal movements and melodic displacements typical of a Dolphy composition, along with those clever rhythmic punctuations he so often employed. This is a tribute of the best kind, couched in the unique language that the original helped forge. **KS**

# Ralph Lalama 1951

**New review**
**You Know What I Mean** Lalama (ts); **George Cables** (p); **Dennis Irwin** (b); **Leroy Williams** (d). Criss Cross Jazz Ⓕ CD1097 (64 minutes). Recorded 1993.

⑥ ❽

Lalama is a bustling, no-nonsense tenor player who can eat up any tempo and come back for more. He possesses a big tone and an authoritative, purposeful way of investigating the structure of a song which speak volumes about the many dues he has paid in order to reach the point of making his début CD as a leader. A member since 1983 of the Thad Jones-Mel Lewis Orchestra which played Monday nights at the Village Vanguard, Lalama reveals himself here to be a fine if not particularly wide-ranging or expressive modern mainstream player, prone to a one-paced approach but still capable of considerable excitement and undoubtedly at his best at high tempo, ripping into songs such as Wayne Shorter's *Lester Left Town* and Ellington's *Take the Coltrane*. On this disc he is ably supported by Cables in particular and the whole rhythm team in general. No prisoners are taken. **KS**

# Andrew Lamb

**Portrait in the Mist** Lamb (ts); **Warren Smith** (vb, d, perc); **Wilber Morris** (b); **Andrei Strobert** (d). Delmark Ⓕ DE479 (63 minutes). Recorded 1994.

⑥ ⑧

Born in North Carolina but raised in New York City, Lamb studied at the State University. He honed his skills at the Chelsea Performing Arts Studio before its closure marked the end of the loft movement. In the instrumental sense, the claimed influence of Lester Young, Charlie Parker and Roland Kirk is not apparent, but he also lists John Coltrane, Sonny Rollins, Archie Shepp and Albert Ayler as spiritual mentors. This CD provides greater support for these latter claims, although it does present a tenor saxophonist whose solos cover a wide, stylistic area. Titles such as *Negretta Mia*, *Portrait in the Mist* and *Eccentricity* show how he states his theme then gradually deconstructs it before moving outward along his varied chosen routes. The straight-ahead solos from vibist Smith are self sufficient and the busily shifting but orthodox rhythm team of Morris and Strobert serve tunes, improvisational developments and the freer tirades as required. **BMcR**

# Bobby Lamb

**Trinity Fair: Bobby Lamb Meets Bob Florence (with Trinity Big Band)** Lamb (dir, tb); **Kenny Wheeler, Dave Peers, Jeremy Moore, Damian Simpson, Darren Wiles, Stephen Jones, Alistair Walker** (t, flh); **Mark Nightingale, Phil Hyde, Matthew Horner, Alex Hewins, Owen Rees, Peter North** (tb); **Jonathan Rees** (tba); **Dave Laurence, Huw Evans, Marcus Bates, Steve Reading** (frh); **Simon Hutchings, Ian Collinson, Peter King** (as); **Pelham Wood, Jason Mathias** (ts); **Kate Osborne, Julian Costello** (bs); **Matthew O'Regan** (p); **Jerome Davis** (b); **Mark Allis** (d); **Fabian Beard, Jason Hollings** (perc); **Bob Florence** (comp, arr, p); HEP Ⓕ CD2064 (52 minutes). Recorded 1993.

⑦ ⑨

Favourable reviews of big band dates are often described in terms of energy, enthusiasm and excitement. Clichés, yes. But with dates like this, such conventions communicate clearly. Here, the pot bubbles with charts by the wonderful Bob Florence, the swinging students of London's Trinity College of Music, and three inspired guests, Pete King, Kenny Wheeler and Mark Nightingale. Directing traffic is Bobby Lamb, Trinity's Director of Jazz and a veteran of tromboning tenures with Woody Herman, Buddy Rich and Stan Kenton. The first of the five Florence lines is *Party Harty*, a palpitating flagwaver. The title tune, a high octane adventure book-ended by the composer's probing piano, frames neon-lit flights by Nightingale, King and Wheeler. A ballad built on the three-note theme of B, B and C, salutes, yes, the *BBC*. Also included are spirited readings of Don Menza's *Samba De Rollins* and George Handy's *Forgetful*. Like the student bands of such noted jazz programs as the University of North Texas, the youthful musicians of Trinity play with the *élan* of seasoned pros. **CB**

# Lambert, Hendricks and Ross

**Sing a Song of Basie** Dave Lambert, Jon Hendricks, Annie Ross (v); **Nat Pierce** (p); **Freddie Green** (g); **Eddie Jones** (b); **Sonny Payne** (d). Impulse! Ⓜ GRP11122 (31 minutes). Recorded 1957.

⑧ ⑧

In 1957 Lambert, Hendricks and Ross undertook a project to sing the instrumental parts of certain Count Basie compositions in the company of ten other singers. In the event the exercise failed, but the three prime movers decided to do the job on their own. This CD shows how, with the aid of multi-tracking, they succeed in following the Eddie Jefferson and King Pleasure tradition of fitting words to horn sounds. The very positive nature of the arrangements used by the Basie orchestra of the period helped enormously and the sheer musicality of the LHR team ensured a successful outcome. The support players used were ideal, with Pierce on piano and the unit completed by Basie's then-current rhythm section. All of the 'lyrics' save for *Everyday* were written by Hendricks, and for their part the singers managed to reproduce the demanding twists of horn techniques with surprising ease. Highlights are Hendricks's reading of Wardell Gray's *Little Pony*, Ross's Buck Clayton trumpet part on *Fiesta in Blue* and Joe Newman's trumpet on *Down For The Count*, but the full ensemble are handled with equal skill. Were these singers the forerunners of today's rappers? **BMcR**

# Lammas

**The Broken Road** Tim Garland (ss, ts, f, syn, p); **Don Paterson** (g); **Steafan Hannigan** (bodhran, Uillean pipes, whistle, perc); **Mark Fletcher** (d); **Christine Tobin** (v). EFZ Ⓕ CD1015 (61 minutes). Recorded 1995.

⑦ ⑧

Lammas are always for convenience's sake dubbed a 'folk/jazz' band, for they exhibit both the keening earnestness of Celtic folk music – from Scotland, Brittany and Ireland – and the unpredictable inventiveness of improvised jazz. From their first eponymous album (a trio recording featuring special guest Kenny Wheeler, on FMR) onwards, the band have proved adept at producing an attractively accessible sound which fuses the two traditions, and with the addition, for their latest two EFZ CDs, **This Morning** and **The Broken Road**, of Dublin-born singer Christine Tobin and piper/percussionist Steafan Hannigan, the blend is now near-perfect, the music entirely natural-sounding yet highly original. Lammas's material ranges from plangent folk reels and vocal laments enlivened by vigourous, jazzy improvisation to almost straightforward jazz pieces made utterly distinctive by the textural range resulting from the band's unusual folk instrumentation. In Christine Tobin, too, they have a singer equally at home with the plaintive purity demanded by Gaelic ballads and the sophisticated improvisational virtuosity required for jazz singing. **The Broken Road**, for its poise and assurance, is their best album so far, though **This Morning** runs it a very close second. **CP**

# Byard Lancaster                                                          1942

**Worlds**  Lancaster (ss, as, ts, bcl); **Alfie Pollitt** (p); **Jim Dragoni** (g) **Kenny Davis** (b); **Webb Thomas** (d); **Keno Speller** (perc). Gazell ⓕ GJCD4005 (49 minutes). Recorded 1992.

⑥ ❻

Lancaster followed a familiar path for those who came to their first maturity in the sixties. After completing music studies in Boston and New York, he embraced the burgeoning New York avant-garde scene, appearing and recording with, among others, Bill Dixon, Sunny Murray and Sun Ra. The seventies saw a considerable retreat across a whole range of radical music activities, jazz being no exception, and Lancaster came to rest for six years in the McCoy Tyner group. This was clearly a formative experience, as the Tyner/Coltrane stylistic axis, leavened with borrowings from the James Brown brigade, Caribbean music and his own past playing, has remained the core around which his playing revolves. This is shown here by his opening the CD with a spirited eight-minute version of *My Favourite Things*. However, he goes on to encompass funky blues, funk and bop into the mixture, so by the end we have a clear view as to where Lancaster stands today. There is even a solo soprano piece, *Internal Security*. The musicians on **Worlds** are largely from Lancaster's home town of Philadelphia, and have long been his associates, so there is a high degree of unity in their playing. **KS**

# Harold Land                                                             1928

**Harold in the Land of Jazz**  Land (ts); **Rolf Ericson** (t); **Carl Perkins** (p); **Leroy Vinnegar** (b); **Frank Butler** (d). Contemporary Ⓜ OJCCD162-2 (48 minutes). Recorded 1958.

⑧ ❻

At this period Harold Land's tone, articulation and turn of phrase were all instantly recognizable – similar in some ways to Hank Mobley but with more edge to the sound. Later, like so many others, he fell under the influence of John Coltrane and his playing lost some of its sly charm. As Dr Johnson said of Milton, it is better to admire Coltrane than to imitate him. This disc (a CD transfer from the original LP, with one additional track) catches Land at his best and most characteristic. Among other attributes he had the knack of making interesting shapes out of mid-tempo tunes in minor keys, something which eluded many of his contemporaries. There is a splendid example here in *Grooveyard*. This set also contains one of Land's best slow ballad performances, *You Don't Know What Love Is*, in the course of which he grows positively expansive. The Perkins-Vinnegar-Butler rhythm section, working as a semi-regular team, was one of the best on the West Coast at the time, while Rolf Ericson's bright and nimble trumpet provides a perfect foil for Land. **DG**

# Art Lande                                                               1947

New review
**Skylight**  Lande (p, perc); **Paul McCandless** (ss, ehn, ob, bcl, wf); **David Samuels** (vb, mba, perc). ECM ⓕ 531 025-2 (40 minutes). Recorded 1981.

⑤ ❿

With Lande there is a temptation to pronounce on his music on the basis that it is quintessential ECM atmospherics first, jazz second. The presence of reed player McCandless, a veteran of many New Age sessions under his own name, hardly reduces this possibility. Yet to leave Lande in such a position would be to do him an injustice. During the seventies he played with a number of leaders in the possession of impeccable jazz credentials, among them Steve Swallow and Ted Curson, while a period with Jan Garbarek helped confirm his ever-widening musical interests. For the past decade or more Lande has alternated performing with professional music teaching on both sides of the Atlantic. **Skylight** is not his greatest moment. The album's main deficiency is a lack of percussion; without this the interplay does tend to become sterile after the first few minutes, with none of the three men capable of sufficient momentum to beguile the listener into not noticing the lack. The sounds are often pretty, sometimes intriguing, but don't stay in the mind very long. This is a sophisticated, elegant album which punches well below its emotional weight in a musical area inhabited by the likes of Garbarek and Surman.                                                                         **KS**

# Eddie Lang                                                                                          1904-33

**A Handful of Riffs** Lang (g); with a collective personnel of: **King Oliver** (c); **Leo McConville** (t); **Tommy Dorsey** (t, tb); **Bill Rank** (tb); **Jimmy Dorsey** (cl, as); **Izzy Friedman** (cl, ts); **Hoagy Carmichael** (p, cel, perc); **Arthur Schutt, Frank Signorelli, J.C. Johnson** (p); **Lonnie Johnson** (g); **Joe Tarto** (b); **Stan King** (d). ASV Living Era Ⓜ CDAJA5061 (64 minutes). Recorded 1927-9.

⑧ ❽

Lang is, beyond argument, the first great guitarist in jazz. There is a case for going further and calling him the first great guitarist in American popular music, and most of the exhibits required for putting that case are on this record. The first half is concerned less with the values of improvisation or hot jazz than with material that reveals Lang's technical powers as a guitarist: the masterly shaping of notes, his practically faultless fingering and immense chordal vocabulary. The Rachmaninov *Prelude* and the standard songs, *Jeannine* and *There'll Be Some Changes Made*, are performances without fireworks yet full of light, space and grace. Lang's most startling recordings – and they are still that, 65 years later – are the duets with blues guitarist Lonnie Johnson. In *Bullfrog Moan* Lang's low chords evoke froggy plops and croaks, while in the faster title track and *Two-Tone Stomp* the players maintain interdependent lines of some complexity with enormous *élan*. Their comparative restraint on the quartet sides, *Jet Black Blues* and *Blue Blood Blues* tactfully supports the simple, affecting blues cornet of King Oliver. The selection concludes with five band numbers featuring some of New York's leading jazz professionals at their most trenchant, Tommy Dorsey contributing a remarkably low-down trumpet solo to *Hot Heels*. Lang's rhythm playing is, as always, exemplary. He died before he was 30, a less resonant and romanticized fate than his contemporary Bix Beiderbecke's, but perhaps not much less of a loss to jazz.                                                                         **TR**

# Don Lanphere                                                                                      1928

**Go Again** Lanphere (ss, ts); **Jon Pugh** (t); **Jeff Hay** (tb); **Marc Seales** (p, syn); **Chuck Deardorf** (b); **Dean Hodges** (d); **Jay Clayton** (v). Hep Ⓕ HEP2040 (63 minutes). Recorded 1987-8.

⑧ ❽

Lanphere has had two separate careers with the first coming to an abrupt halt in 1951 when he was arrested for heroin addiction. Prior to that he had been active in New York jazz circles and had done two recording sessions with Fats Navarro, the second of which produced the tunes *Stop* and *Go*. After running the family music business he emerged from his native Washington State in 1982 with a fine band of comparative youngsters (heard here) and has made a number of albums for release on the Hep label. *Go Again* harks back to the Navarro session and is a brisk workout on the chords of *The Way You Look Tonight*, with assured solos by all. Pugh in particular is on spectacular form through-out, constructing fleet trumpet lines which lift the excitement level on the faster tempos. Hay was a late arrival and caused Lanphere to enlarge his quintet and add trombone parts to his arrangements. Eight of the 11 tracks are by the sextet and *Darn That Dream* is by just tenor, bass and Clayton, who succeeds in staying perfectly in tune. Lanphere takes considerable care to produce an album which gets well away from the ordinary, and older jazz enthusiasts will be pleased to know that the occasional hints of Parker and Lester Young show that Don has not forgotten that first career phase.       **AM**

# Ellis Larkins                                                                                      1923

**A Smooth One** Larkins (p); **George Duvivier** (b); **J.C. Heard** (d). Black & Blue Ⓕ 59 123 2 (52 minutes). Recorded 1977.

⑥ ❻

Larkins has always succeeded in keeping a relatively low profile both at the keyboard and in terms of the availability of his records. He will be remembered by many for the successful LPs he made with Ella Fitzgerald and Ruby Braff on which his impeccable sense of taste and knowledge of correct chords added greatly to the professionalism of the music. This CD dates from one of his rare visits to Europe (he appeared at the Nice Festival with singer Joe Williams) and it is easy to understand why he has been rated so highly as an accompanist to vocalists and as an entertainer on the supper-club circuit. With the strong, warm sound of Duvivier's bass Larkins tends to use the upper half of the keyboard, leaving Heard to keep perfect time, usually with brushes. This is the kind of music which cannot be faulted, but by the same token it seldom raises the temperature above blood heat. One of the most successful tracks is a beautiful solo version of the Benny Carter song, *Blues in My Heart*, a comment which also applies to the solo, *Day Dream*, one of the two previously unissued titles added to the original LP to make up this compact disc.                                                                         **AM**

# Pete LaRoca

**Basra** LaRoca (d); **Joe Henderson** (ts); **Steve Kuhn** (p); **Steve Swallow** (b). Blue Note Ⓜ CDP8 32091-2 (41 minutes). Recorded 1965.

⑧ ❼

LaRoca, who like Steve Kuhn had a short stint in the first version of John Coltrane's classic quartet (the bassist was Steve Davis, and Elvin Jones and McCoy Tyner were soon drafted in), has only made one album as a leader, and this is it. It is hardly more than he deserves, for he was at the time of its recording a fiery and forward-looking drummer with an unusually broad musical vision. Born Pete Sims, he adopted his more musicianly professional name in the fifties, and it suits his explosive, Elvin Jones-derived style. He quit the music scene by the end of the sixties, but his small recorded legacy is a worthwhile one. **Basra** has never been reissued since its initial release, and has consequently acquired a semi-legendary status. Two tracks from it were included in the Blue Note Henderson retrospective, but the album here is complete. At the time of the recording, the rhythm section was then functioning as three-quarters of the Art Farmer Quartet, and the substitution of Henderson for the lyrical trumpeter/flügelhornist gives the music a wider dynamic range and a more exploratory feel. Kuhn is an unusually resourceful and imaginative pianist with a conception more original than most, and this early stage of his career finds him crammed full of ideas both as a soloist and as an accompanist. He can play with great fire, but his ballad work is outstanding here. All in all, then, **Basra** is an album that was taken for granted on first release, but now sounds like exactly the type of exploratory, urgent album made at the cutting edge of the modern mainstream which is virtually impossible to record any more, because all the discoveries were subsequently claimed and the new musical soil trampled into submission. **KS**

# Steve LaSpina
1954

**New review**
**When I'm Alone** LaSpina (b); **Billy Drewes** (ss, as, ts); **Vic Juris** (g); **Marc Copland** (p); **Jeff Hirschfield** (d). SteepleChase Ⓕ SCCD31376 (65 minutes). Recorded 1995.

⑦ ❽

Born in Texas, but raised in Chicago, bassist Steve LaSpina moved to New York in 1979 for gigs with Marian McPartland and the Mel Lewis Jazz Orchestra. With his deep resonant sound, precise intonation and supple swingingness, LaSpina has also lifted bandstands with Stan Getz, Toots Thielemans, Joe Williams, Dave Liebman, Steve Kuhn, Richie Beirach, Chet Baker, Bob Brookmeyer, Pat Martino, Zoot Sims and Al Cohn. In recent years, he has worked steadily with guitar legend Jim Hall. In this, his third date as a leader for SteepleChase, LaSpina ascends to the summit with a hearty band of New Yorkers. With guitarist Vic Juris adding postmodern electronics *à la* Scofield and Frisell, LaSpina and long-time friends Drewes, Copland and Hirschfield coalesce around a septet of striking originals. While completely at ease in reframing standard fare such as Benny Carter's *Only Trust Your Heart*, in originals like LaSpina's *Soaring* there's an interactive immediacy that bespeaks an inspired as well as shared vision. Indeed, as Drewes's tenor and Juris's chorused-up guitar unfurl and flutter above seas of roiling rhythms, one realizes that supersonic speeds are not necessary for music to 'soar'. In sum, a testament to LaSpina's status as a world-class player poised at the cutting edge of the contemporary mainstream. **CB**

# Yusef Lateef
1920

**The Centaur and the Phoenix** Lateef (f, ob, ts, argol); **Clark Terry** (t, flh); **Richard Williams** (t); **Curtis Fuller** (tb); **Tate Houston** (bs); **Josea Taylor** (bn); **Joe Zawinul** (p); **Ben Tucker** (b); **Lex Humphries** (d). Riverside Ⓜ OJCCD721 (38 minutes). Recorded 1960.

✔ ⑩ ❼

Lateef's long and varied career as a leader is well covered on records, but at the present moment that legacy is peculiarly ill-served on CD. Of his long-standing relationships with various labels (Savoy, Prestige, Impulse! and Atlantic for starters), only the Prestige material has been reissued in any depth on CD. So this Riverside reissue would be welcome even if it was a lesser achievement than it actually is. This was his first opportunity to write for a larger ensemble than just a five- or six-piece, and he manages to seize the opportunity with relish and abundant imagination. Medium-tempo swingers full of flair and unusual progressions lie in close proximity to moody, angular slower pieces, or pastoral sketches such as *Summer Song*. This is a fully realized album, from the opening power and urgency of *Revelation*, with its stabbing ensemble figures and preaching tenor from Lateef himself, through to the weird tenderness of *Iqbal*, written for Lateef's young daughter.

Lateef has been on the wrong end of a fair amount of criticism; occasionally his albums have justified it, betraying an attitude close to indifference to the end result. Yet there are plenty which point to his passionate and continuing commitment to experiment, expression and beauty, and a few which achieve and sustain a very high level of artistry. Of the handful currently on CD, this stands above the others as a testament to his real musical stature. **KS**

**Eastern Sounds** Lateef (ts, f, ob); **Barry Harris** (p); **Ernie Farrow** (b, rabat); **Lex Humphries** (d).
Prestige Ⓜ OJCCD612-2 (40 minutes). Recorded 1961.

⑥ ❽

The peripatetic wind-player was here recorded for the Prestige Moodsville series. Thus the album contains Alex North's *Love Theme from Spartacus* – Bill Evans the pianist also included it in his **Conversations With Myself** from two years later – but Lateef goes one better by adding Alfred Newman's *Love Theme from The Robe*, played on oboe and flute respectively. Nevertheless, most Moodsvilles consisted of very familiar standards and uniformly slow tempos, so Lateef was in fact countering expectations in a number of ways. Much of the material is original and the only other exception, the tenor ballad *Don't Blame Me*, is played without any obvious reference to the well-known theme. In fact Lateef's tenor work, which was featured with Cannonball Adderley at this period, is prominent here and reveals an individual tone and uncluttered musical thinking.

The vaguely exotic thematic approach, which earlier was acknowledged by Coltrane in his scalar explorations and set the tone for much sixties jazz, is evident in the modal basis of the originals. In the opening and closing tracks Ernie Farrow, the future Alice Coltrane's brother, uses the single-stringed rabat, in the first case alongside Lateef's Chinese clay flute.                                    **BP**

**Live at Pep's** Lateef (ts, f, ob, shenai, argol); **Richard Williams** (t); **Mike Nock** (p); **Ernie Farrow** (b); **James Black** (d). Impulse! Ⓜ GRP11342 (61 minutes). Recorded 1964.

❽ ❽

Lateef's career falls into two distinct phases. As Bill Evans he played his own brand of extrovert tenor in the bands of Dizzy Gillespie, Lucky Millinder and Hot Lips Page. In 1950, he returned to Detroit, embraced the Moslem faith, adopted the name of Yusef Lateef and re-evaluated his musical outlook. Initially the eastern element in his music seemed little more than a veneer, lending an exotic flavour to the improvisational method of a good journeyman bebopper. This was perhaps true of albums such as **Other Sounds** (New Jazz OJCCD399-2) from 1957, but by 1964, the effects of Third Stream projects and free-form experimentation were more widely felt and more modest aspects had entered the fabric of Lateef's playing. The use of the 12-note row recurs on this album, but it is the way that his soulful shenai is Americanized on *Sister Mamie*, his highly vocalized flute deals with *Slippin' and Slidin'* and the way he captures genuine blues feeling with the plaintive sound of the oboe on *See See Rider* that distinguishes this CD. It was not a synthesis of cultures that had any universal effect but Lateef made a statement in the sixties that was unquestionably valid. There are three more tracks here than on the original vinyl release, although all of the music here has been available before.          **BMcR**

# Andy LaVerne                                                                            1947

**First Tango in New York** LaVerne (p); **Joe Lovano** (ss, ts); **Steve LaSpina** (b); **Bill Stewart** (d). Musidisc Ⓕ 500472 (48 minutes). Recorded 1993.

❽ ❽

It is something of a surprise to find two Andy LaVerne originals apparently tacked on to the end of what is basically a standards album, since the New York pianist is a distinguished composer, having once produced a symphony for his one-time leader Stan Getz. Nevertheless, the mature, finely honed, occasionally quite exquisite sound of the band on these standards, which range from a burly, vigorous *You and the Night and the Music* through a slow-burning, moody *Goodbye* to a fluent but neat *Melancholy Baby*, more than justifies this policy. LaVerne is a supremely cultured pianist, equally adept at sparkling solo improvisational flights, discreetly mellifluous comping and leading a tight, virile rhythm section, but it is saxophonist Joe Lovano who makes perhaps the most memorable contributions. His playing on the album's six standards is uniformly cogent and controlled, his smoky, warm tenor incorporating swing, bop and even occasional avant-garde influences to produce an entirely personal and instantly identifiable sound. His artistry, and his rapport with fellow ex-Herd member LaVerne, put **First Tango in New York** far ahead of similar standards-oriented ventures. **CP**

# John Law                                                                               1961

New review
**Giant Leaves (Autumn Steps)** Law (p); **Tim Walls** (b); **Paul Clarvis** (d, perc). FMR Ⓕ CD32 VO896 (55 minutes). Recorded 1995.

⑥ ❼

The title interchange between John Coltrane's *Giant Steps* and Johnny Mercer's *Autumn Leaves* introduces the type of challenge that Laws enjoys. As a youngster, London-born Law was not slow to exploit his prodigal talents. He studied classical piano and composition in Vienna and in his home town and he turned to jazz in his early twenties. A successful 1992 Council Tour of Belorussia and Lithuania kick-started his career and he is now an established figure on the European tour scene. This album has him displaying both his instrumental talents and his writing skills. Despite the strategic borrowing on the two title tracks, all of the tunes are his and they provide good improvisational incentives. Law the soloist parades his accurate articulation, showing impressively clean note production at the bass end of the instrument. Wells and Clarvis take full advantage of the solo licence available. They also provide balanced, contrapuntal support when required and, as the deliberately static mood of *Two-Elf Town* demands, produce ensemble colour as well as rhythmic impetus. Law is as comfortable with free as he is with 'inside' jazz; he rejects banal performance formulas and, as his growing discography shows, values creativity above surface musical gloss.                          **BMcR**

# Hubert Laws                                                                                        1930

**The Laws of Jazz/Flute By Laws** Laws (f, pic); **Chick Corea, Rodgers Grant** (p); **Sam Brown**
   (g); **Jimmy Owens, Marty Banks** (t); **Garnett Brown, Benny Powell, Tommy McIntosh** (tb); **Richard**
   **Davis, Chris White, Israel 'Cachao' Lopez** (b); **Bobby Thomas, Jimmy Cobb, Ray Lucas** (d);
   **Carmelo Garcia, Victor Pantoja, Raymond Orchart, Bill Fitch** (perc). Rhino/Atlantic Jazz Gallery
   Ⓜ R2 71636 (68 minutes). Recorded 1964.

⑦ ⑧

With Herbie Mann already under contract, Atlantic cornered the sixties market in jazz flute with the 1964 signing of Hubert Laws. A virtuoso player with classical training at Juilliard and the chops to cut regular gigs with the New York Philharmonic and the Metropolitan Opera, Laws got his first jazz experience in his home town of Houston with high school friends who eventually grew up to become the Jazz Crusaders. Here, we catch Laws at the onset of his recording career in his first outings as a leader on Atlantic. **The Laws of Jazz**, recorded in 1964 but not issued until 1965, was an impressive début. With spare yet supple backing by pianist Chick Corea, bassist Richard Davis and drummer Bobby Thomas, Laws proved in *Miss Thing* that he could stroll with a funky strut, *à la* Mann. Even more telling was his lovely ballad treatment of *All Soul* and the perky piccolo spicings of *Black Eyed Peas and Rice*. His follow-up album, **Flute By Laws** (yet another punny title) released in 1966, sets the flautist's quicksilver flights against pungently Latinized horn charts also by Laws. Again, Laws's appealingly low-key virtuosity is ably abetted by Corea's effective and economical comping.      **CB**

# Yank Lawson                                                                                       1911

**Something Old, Something New, Something Borrowed, Something Blue** Lawson (t);
   **George Masso** (tb); **Johnny Mince** (cl); **Lou Stein** (p); **Bucky Pizzarelli** (g); **Bob Haggart** (b); **Nick**
   **Fatool** (d). Audiophile Ⓕ APCD240 (41 minutes). Recorded 1988.

⑥ ⑧

A trumpeter with his heart in Dixieland jazz, Lawson's early career included spells with Wingy Manone and Ben Pollack. In 1935 he became a founder member of the Bob Crosby Orchestra, a reluctant big band that always found time for items like *Come Back, Sweet Papa*, *Royal Garden Blues* or others from the Dixieland 'song book'. Often in the company of Haggart, Lawson has continued to play with men associated with this style and he played a major part in the formation, in 1968, of the World's Great Jazz Band (*sic*). This CD features players associated with the WGJB and effectively showcases the work of the trumpeter. His brassy tone and team leading qualities are evident throughout and his strong blowing style, devoid of histrionics, is an obvious motivating factor in the playing of his sidemen. Not always the hard-hitting front runner, he resorts to old world, preaching horn on *What Else is New*, while on *Come Back, Sweet Papa* he produces a stop-time chorus of real class, slightly dragging at the coat tails of the beat and keeping just a little in reserve. A 77-year-old is perhaps justified in protecting his 'chops', but Lawson gives value, even if it is in shorter bursts.                              **BMcR**

# Nguyên Lê

**Miracles** Lê (g, danh tranh, programming); **Art Lande** (p); **Marc Johnson** (b); **Peter Erskine** (d).
   Musidisc Ⓕ 500102 (57 minutes). Recorded 1989-90.

⑧ ⑩

Although much of Nguyên Lê's plangent, spangly-toned solo guitar playing is somewhat reminiscent of John Scofield's in overall sound and approach, his personal strengths – an ability to coax an attractive range of surprising sounds and textures from pleasant but unremarkable themes, and a confident fluency and infectious exuberance as both soloist and leader mark this album out as worthy of sustained attention. Of course, the importance of a rhythm section comprising three of the most experienced practitioners in this area of music, operating in the fertile area bounded by fusion on one side and jazz on the other, is difficult to overestimate: pianist/educator Art Lande draws on experience with everyone from Steve Swallow through Jan Garbarek to Ted Curson; Marc Johnson collaborated most famously with Bill Evans and Stan Getz before producing his seminal **Bass Desires** album with Scofield and Bill Frisell. But it is Peter Erskine who holds the album together, justifying his reputation as one of the world's leading jazz and fusion drummers with a sustained performance of great power and subtlety, notable not only for its felicitous use of a stunning variety of percussive sounds and effects, but also for the delicacy and control of his more straightforward time playing. Drawing as it does on a strikingly original selection of sounds, from electronic, synthesized washes and splashes to the traditional Japanese danh tranh, **Miracles** is a highly enjoyable and accomplished album.　**CP**

# Barbara Lea
c1930

**Lea in Love**　Lea (v); **Johnny Windhurst** (t); **Dick Cary** (ah, p, arr); **Ernie Caceres** (cl, bs); **Garvin Bushell** (ob, bn); **Jimmy Lyon** (p, cel); **Adele Girard** (h); **Al Casamenti**, **Jimmy Raney** (g); **Al Hall**, **Beverley Peer** (b); **Osie Johnson** (d). Prestige Ⓜ OJCCD1742-2 (37 minutes). Recorded 1957.
⑥ ❻

"I believe in jazz and singing but not necessarily in jazz singing" wrote Lea in the notes to this album, one of a handful she made in her brief contract with Prestige. Along with her eponymous sister album (Prestige OJCCD1713-2) this is a collaboration with trumpeter Johnny Windhurst and multi-instrumentalist Dick Cary. Lea disproves her apparent disenchantment with "jazz singing" by revealing a voice rich in nuance and subtlety, as adept at timing a well-turned lyric as other singers are at wordless scatting. She had chart success with her gallic *Autumn Leaves* and Cole Porter's *True Love* (somewhat dominated by Adèle Girard's harp) and both are here, but as jazz performances they are outclassed by *We Could Make Such Beautiful Music* and *The Very Thought of You*, the former dominated by Windhurst's clean Bixian trumpet, the latter by Jimmy Raney's guitar, and both set by Cary to use the unusual instrumental tone colours of double reeds and alto horn to add depth and texture.　**AS**

# Lee Ann Ledgerwood

**You Wish**　Ledgerwood (p, syn); **Jeremy Steig** (f); **Bill Evans** (ts, ss); **Eddie Gomez** (b); **Steve LaSpina** (b); **Danny Gottlieb** (d). Triloka Ⓕ 187-2 (53 minutes). Recorded 1991.
⑦ ❽

The list of pianists who have played at Bradley's Piano Bar in New York is impressive. The superb instrument is perhaps the magnet, but the late Bradley Cunningham saw to it that only musicians worthy of the task enjoyed the privilege. Ledgerwood was one such player and her exposure at Bradley's was important to a career that had begun in kindergarten and embraced classical training. She came through the Berklee Academy of jazz know-how, arrived in New York in 1982, became a familiar face at Bradley's and has since played throughout the city.

This CD is not a recording début but is her first as a leader. It shows her good touch, fine attack and an improvising style unconcerned with musical euphemisms. Melodic ideas are developed on their own merits and, as the title track illustrates, piano solos are designed to accommodate progress reports from bass and drums. *Nardis* establishes her imaginative use of the synthesizer and the reflective *I Want to Talk About You* shows that, even at slow tempo, she has no need to rely on rhythmic support. *Taisho Pond* and *You Wish* mark her out as a fine composer and suggest hers is a writing style that grows from her improvisational method.　**BMcR**

# Mike LeDonne

**New review**
**Common Ground**　LeDonne (p); **Dennis Irwin** (b); **Kenny Washington** (d). Criss Cross Jazz Ⓕ CD1058 (59 minutes). Recorded 1990.
⑥ ❽

LeDonne is a neat and decisive pianist with a solid technique and an admirable musical temperament. At the time this record was made his trio was a working unit and the togetherness shows in its smooth and joyful music-making. The style of the jazz played is such that, had this record been released 30 years ago, LeDonne would have been accused of copying Bobby Timmons and Les McCann, among others. As it is, today he sounds up to date. The music here is not earth-shaking, but none of it is sub-standard. Those in need of good piano trio jazz can add this to the list.　**KS**

# Jeanne Lee
1939

**You Stepped Out of a Cloud**　Lee (v); **Ran Blake** (p). Owl Ⓕ 055CD (58 minutes). Recorded 1989.
⑧ ❽

Lee met Blake while studying dance at Bard College, and in 1961 they made a recording for RCA, **The Newest Sounds Around**, which was hailed by some observers as the most innovative vocal record since the Sarah Vaughans of the forties. Lee has worked with the likes of Gunter Hampel, Archie Shepp, Anthony Braxton and Cecil Taylor but has always kept a spiritual link with Blake. This CD renews that feeling in musical terms and scales similar artistic heights. It emphasizes the rare empathy that exists between these two creative spirits and displays them as painters in sound. They embark on a journey of half tones and shading as they add their own subtle tints to each shared melodic sound pattern. Lyrics are not robbed of their meaning, but they are felt rather than expressed vehemently.

Lee's timing on *Mysterioso Rose* and *I Like Your Style* is distinctly Monkish. *You Go to My Head* takes a more Lee Konitz-like route, most especially in its tone and off-centre note placement. Her rubato is further exploited on her unaccompanied *Newswatch* which leaves no doubt that she is a creatively uncompromising jazz singer of the highest order. **BMcR**

## Julia Lee

1902-58

**Ugly Papa** Lee (p, v) with various bands including: **The Tommy Douglas Orchestra**; **The Bob Dougherty Orchestra**, and groups with **Geechie Smith, Ernie Royal** (t); **Vic Dickenson** (tb); **Henry Bridges, Dave Cavanagh, Gene Carter** (ts); **Nappy Lamare, Jack Marshall, Jim Daddy Walker, James Scott** (g); **Billy Hadnott, Harry Babasin, Leonard Johnson** (b); **Sam 'Baby' Lovett, Bill Nolan, Corky Jackson** (d). Jukebox Lil Ⓕ RBD603 (45 minutes). Recorded 1945-57.

⑥ ❻

Julia Lee spent the formative years of her life in Kansas City, and this fortuitous circumstance governed the style of her music for the vast majority of her career. Although a professional singer and entertainer from the early twenties onwards, she was a latecomer to success, not moving much out of KC and consequently remaining a local rather than national act. She was renowned for the salacious side of her nightclub act, and much of this sauciness filtered onto her recordings when she finally made her studio début. This came in 1944 (two sides cut in 1923 were never released) when she was already 42 and a throwback to a style of singing fast either updating to r&b or disappearing altogether. Yet she, along with Nellie Lutcher, a singer from Georgia with a not dissimilar style but a singularly different voice, made a special combination of boogie, swing and the then-popular 'jump' style to register serious commercial success in the next five years.

The tracks on this compilation for the most part avoid the crassest end of her sexually audacious lyrics (there's no *My Man Stands Out* or *Don't Come Too Soon* here, although we are treated to *King Size Papa*), most of which were made at the end of the forties when her career began to fade. The vast majority of tracks fall into the 1945-50 period, just three coming after that, with the single 1957 track, *Bop & Rock Lullaby*, featuring a heavy back-beat absent elsewhere, though the sax solo is undiluted mid-forties Arnett Cobb. Good fun and fine, if basic, musicianship all round. **KS**

## Keiko Lee

New review

**Kickin' It** Lee (v); **Renee Rosnes** (p); **Ron Carter** (b); **Grady Tate** (d); on various tracks add **Claudio Roditi** (t); **Lee Konitz** (as); **Ole Matheison** (ts); **Valtinho Anastacio** (perc) and a woodwind section of **Bob Magnuson, Lawrence Feldman, Roger Rosenberg**. Columbia Ⓕ 485135-2 (51 minutes). Recorded 1996.

⑤ ❾

With a line-up like this it's clear Sony mean business with Ms Lee, a Korean singer who has been touring the world to promote her jazz credentials. I'm not sure if there's a legitimate tradition in jazz of husky-toned singers with suspect intonation, but if there is, Ms Lee fits right in there. As one would expect, the rhythm section flows along smoothly and flawlessly at any tempo and gives Lee's Nancy Wilson-cum-June Christy vocals exemplary support. The guest soloists crop up here and there and do nice things, and the whole thing sounds like a groovy little vocal session from the early sixties. But just as there is much good musicianship and hip arrangements of stock standards, there are times when style overwhelms substance. *Come Rain or Come Shine* as an easy-swingin' finger-snapper? Has she grasped the meaning of the lyrics? At least *How Long Has This Been Going On?* gets the slow-drag treatment (and a nice solo from Matheison), although her intonation is at its most fragile here. A worthy and professional effort, then, in these days of world-jazz shared language. But sometimes you wonder why anyone still wants to do it when this less than overwhelming session is the result. **KS**

## Peggy Lee

1920

**Beauty and the Beat!** Lee (v); **George Shearing** (p); **Toots Thielemans** (g); **Warren Chaisson** (vb); **James Bond** (b); **Roy Haynes** (d); **Armando Peraza** (cga). Capitol Jazz Ⓜ CDP7 98454-2 (39 minutes). Recorded 1959.

⑧ ❻

It can only be snobbery towards their 'popular' status that nourishes the theory that the likes of Lee and Sinatra are not jazz singers. A singing (and swinging) performance such as this concert recording is more rewarding than many a 'dedicated' jazz album. Miss Lee has the knack of sounding spontaneous but in fact every vocal and visual nuance is premeditated and polished to perfection. With that in mind, the latest version of this album reveals that the 'in concert' announcements were dubbed on the day after the event and that even the photograph on the sleeve was concocted in the studio. No matter; the music of both Lee and Shearing is beyond reproach, reaching its zenith in a previously unissued studio duet version (done the day after the concert) of *Nobody's Heart*, a surprisingly neglected Richard Rodgers ballad. Amongst the good songs are two instrumentals from Shearing, who was just beginning to feel his oats as one of the giants of jazz piano. **SV**

# Ranee Lee

**You Must Believe in Spring** Lee (v); **Guido Basso** (t, flh, hca); **Pat LaBarbera** (ts); **Tilden Webb** (p); **Richard Ring** (g); **Ray Brown** (b); **Ed Thigpen** (d). Justin Time Ⓕ JUST88-2 (62 minutes). Recorded 1996.

⑥ ❽

With a bass and drum team like the one above, you wouldn't expect too many problems with regard to swinging, and indeed the rhythm glides beautifully throughout. The pianist is competent, the guitarist ok-ish, so they don't get in the way. The problem with this, Lee's third album for Justin Time, is that everybody's been too nice to the sidemen, resulting in, for example, an opening track (a sprightly *Secret Love*) which contains not just sax and trumpet solos, but opens with a poor guitar solo and also includes a chorus apiece for the pianist and drummer. Lee sings for just two minutes of a song lasting close to six. Things get better as the disc wears on, no better than when Ray Brown walks Lee alone through the opening statement of *Nice and Easy* or keeps company with Brown and Thigpen at the beginning of *Angel Eyes*, but she really could have done without all these solos from such undistinguished improvisers. More background arrangements, please, and less padding next time around. Lee's fine sound, impressive control and emphatic but not hyperbolic stylizations deserve no less. The *Stolen Moments* arrangement would point the way, where at least the solos make some sort of sense, though it should have been two, not three, after Lee's nicely moody scatting. **KS**

# Michel Legrand 1932

**Legrand Jazz** Legrand (arr, cond); **Miles Davis, Ernie Royal, Art Farmer, Donald Byrd, Joe Wilder** (t); **Frank Rehak, Billy Byers, Jimmy Cleveland, Eddie Bert** (tb); **James Buffington** (frh); **Herbie Mann** (f); **Gene Quill, Phil Woods** (as); **Ben Webster, John Coltrane, Seldon Powell** (ts); **Jerome Richardson** (bs, cl); **Teo Macero** (bs); **Eddie Costa, Don Elliot** (vb); **Betty Glamann** (hp); **Bill Evans, Nat Pierce, Hank Jones** (p); **Paul Chambers, George Duvivier, Milt Hinton** (b); **Major Holley** (b, tba); **Don Lamond, Kenny Dennis, Osie Johnson** (d). Philips Ⓜ 830 074-2 (38 minutes). Recorded 1958.

⑧ ❽

This is a good example of an orchestrator moving a collection of soloists out of their usual milieux and stimulating them anew with his writing. When it is borne in mind that this music was created at the time when Quincy Jones was at his peak, it becomes almost (but not quite) understandable that this collection was largely overlooked, despite all the star names. It works on many levels. The writing is inventive and well voiced. The idea of wedding Miles Davis and John Coltrane to unlikely tunes like Armstrong's *Wild Man Blues* and Waller's *Jitterbug Waltz* was a good one, for this is material which can be handled in any idiom. Davis's response is completely unruffled, and his wistful solos will appeal to anyone who values his work from the period. He has *Django* to himself. Coltrane is intimidating on *Jitterbug* in contrast to Woods, who is his usual outgoing self. Woods and the ill-starred Gene Quill are to be found in full flight on *Night In Tunisia* which also has characteristic fireworks from Jimmy Cleveland and a much-to-be-prized solo from Joe Wilder, along with the other practised trumpeters on the session. Evans appears on the four tracks with Davis and Coltrane and shows his ability in a large group, away from the intimacy of the smaller groups which were to dominate in the rest of his professional life. Webster gives a towering performance, opening *Blue and Sentimental* in an unaccompanied duet with Rehak. He is at his most voluptuous here, in stark contrast to the driving, tearing solo on *Rosetta*. *Don't Get Around Much Anymore* is given to Mann's flute, but the four trombone chases in the long *Rosetta* have much more of the red meat of jazz. **SV**

# Urs Leimgruber

**Live at Montreux 1987** Leimgruber (ts, ss); **Don Friedman** (p); **Palle Danielsson** (b); **Joel Allouche** (d). B&W Music Ⓕ BW016 (71 minutes). Recorded 1987.

⑦ ❼

Leimgruber was born in Switzerland and initially played in r&b groups. He became interested in jazz, studied at the Swiss Jazz School in Berne and acknowledges Miles Davis and John Coltrane as early influences. He formed a quartet called OM in 1972, taking its name from Coltrane's contention that "OM was the sound from which everything originated". Their publicity of the time described them as 'electricjazz' although, despite the implications, most of their recordings during the seventies showed them to be a workmanlike, straight quartet with only limited references to jazz-rock in which the leader performed consistently as a powerful saxophonist and fine bass clarinettist. Reflexionen was formed in the early eighties with American pianist Don Friedman and, while staying shy of free music's outer fringes, continually took the music to the cusp. This CD benefits from Friedman's panoramic punctuations in a loose limbed quartet format. It proffers the type of inexact frame that suits Leimgruber, although the saxophonist's more free-ranging work can be found on **Ungleich** (HatART CD6049) where he appears solo or in the company of bassist Adelhard Roidinger.   **BMcR**

# Peter Lemer                                                                    1942

**Local Colour**  Lemer (p); **Nisar Ahmed Khan** (ts); **John Surman** (bs, ss); **Tony Reeves** (b); **John Hiseman** (d). ESP-Disk Ⓜ 1057-2 (43 minutes). Recorded 1966.

⑥ ❻

British-born Lemer studied jazz piano with Paul Bley and Jaki Byard, as well as classical piano at the Royal Academy of Music. He has worked with big bands and bebop combos as well as with fusion musicians. He is also well known for his work with the men who launched the country's free music movement in the sixties. This CD comes from that era and also features the emerging talent of Surman and the eccentric but colourful ramblings of Khan. Even then, Lemer's own piano style was the product of fairly wide experience and he exerts a strong influence on all involved on this recording date. His articulation is clean, he has a distinctive touch as well as an innate ability to swing. Despite superficial similarities, his playing is somewhat divorced from the Cecil Taylor school. His solos are less abstract and their direction, if not actually signposted, is reaffirmed by harmonic hints as the solo progresses. His comping behind the soloists is percussive and (as he shows on *In And Out*) at times startlingly inspirational. The under-recorded Reeves provides a firm musical chassis and, although Hiseman had not yet grasped the full implications of this music, the album shows British free-form jazz at an important early stage of development.   **BMcR**

# Brian Lemon                                                                   1937

New review
**A Beautiful Friendship**  Lemon (p); **Warren Vaché** (t, v); **Roy Williams** (tb); **Dave Cliff** (g); **Dave Green** (b); **Martin Drew, Allan Ganley** (d). Zephyr Ⓕ ZECD4 (63 minutes). Recorded 1995.

⑧ ❾

Few artists have a label exclusively dedicated to their works, as Zephyr is to Lemon, but the pianist comes nearer than most to deserving one. Appropriate too, that he should be found in the company of the cream of British musicians. They come no better than the players on this album, and with their American guest Vaché at the top of his prodigious form this becomes an album to excite superlatives in the reviewer's breast. The tunes are also from Rolls Royce and the solos they generate are both exciting and immaculately communicated. Lemon's rolling talent, both in solo and accompaniment, is by now legendary. Roy Williams is internationally accepted as a giant and it is ironic to compare the acclaim showered upon him with the indifference jazz buffs seem to have to Dave Cliff, one of the most talented and tasteful players in the world. Green is also lionized world-wide, notably by other bass players (usually a good sign) and if ever it was required to show someone the true strength of jazz in the UK, then this album would be a good place to start.   **SV**

# Stan Levey                                                                    1925

**Quintet**  Levey (d); **Conte Candoli** (t); **Richie Kamuca** (ts); **Lou Levy** (p); **Monty Budwig** (b). VSOP Ⓕ # 41CD (30 minutes). Recorded 1957.

⑤ ❻

This is the archetypal West Coast session. It proceeds so smoothly it could be on tramlines, and has as much roughage in it as childrens' breakfast cereal. Nobody plays badly, everybody swings, but nobody gets worked up into a sweat either, and few moments of music here stay in the memory past the end of the track. Which is another way of saying that this pleasant but unremarkable record is an audio definition of the word mediocre, although that is perhaps being a little harsh on Kamuca, a good tenor player who has certainly risen to much greater things than he manages here, however pretty his tone may be.

If you like your jazz to go down smoothly without touching the sides, this will be your idea of heaven, though you'd better listen closely, as heaven doesn't last very long.   **KS**

# Milcho Leviev                                                                 1937

**Blues for the Fisherman**  Leviev (p); **Art Pepper** (as); **Tony Dumas** (b); **Carl Burnett** (d). Mole Jazz Ⓜ CDMOLE1 PLUS (70 minutes). Recorded 1980.

⑧ ❽

Although this is an Art Pepper recording in all but name, Bulgarian pianist Milchio Leviev's unhurried, deeply thoughtful playing, capable both of sustaining a subtly chiming accompanying role under Pepper's extended improvisations and of slowly building unspectacular but deeply-felt soloing, makes an indispensable contribution to the group's overall sound. Recorded at Ronnie Scott's at the height of the alto player's hard-won rehabilitation, **Blues for the Fisherman** documents an archetypal Pepper live set: a mixture of plaintive, slowish blues numbers and affectingly simple heart-on-sleeve ballads, spiced up with brisk boppish material. Pepper's is one of the most intimate saxophone styles in the music, earnest, confiding, almost painfully personal, conveyed through a unique and instantly identifiable combination of breathless flurries interspersed with sustained single notes terminating in a melancholy vibrato effect. The combination of a familiar and highly accomplished rhythm section – Carl Burnett is an old Pepper hand and Tony Dumas has stints with Joe Henderson and Nat Adderley to his credit – and a strongly supportive audience makes for a highly enjoyable, relaxed and informal session of airily accessible music.                                            **CP**

# Lou Levy                                                                                        1928-

New review

**By Myself**  Levy (p). Verve/Gitanes Jazz Ⓕ 522 510-2 (51 minutes). Recorded 1994.

⑦ ❾

Lou Levy is a musicians' musician. Graced with an ego that has allowed him to put each project ahead of compulsions to 'star', Levy has forged a gilt-edged career comping for notables like Sarah Vaughan, Peggy Lee and Ella Fitzgerald. He has also held down the piano chair for Stan Getz, Benny Goodman and Supersax. When helming his own small groups, it is a lyricized version of the bop-inflected lexicon of Bud Powell that has prevailed.

In this leisurely outing, Levy's self-effacing solo style works small miracles. Thus, in an era possessed by the narcotizing thrills of speed and sensory overload, Levy stands out by virtue of his understated approach. How refreshing to hear a pianist who allows lines to breathe, whose piquancy is as much a matter of knowing what to omit as what to play. This use of space as a means of articulation is effectively exemplified in Levy's balladic tracing of *How High the Moon*, a tune usually co-opted for high-velocity athletic drills. In his graceful programme of standards, Levy's pastel renderings of *Easter Parade*, *Embraceable You* and *Everything Happens to Me* resonate as exemplars of tasteful restraint and quiet melodic charm.                                                                         **CB**

# George Lewis                                                                                  1900-68

**Trios and Bands**  Lewis (cl); **Louis 'Kid Shots' Madison**, **Avery 'Kid' Howard** (t); **Jim Robinson** (tb); **Alcide Pavageau**, **Ricard Alexis**, **Chester Zardis** (b); **Lawrence Marrero** (bj); **Baby Dodds**, **Edgar Moseley** (d). American Music Ⓕ AMCD4 (60 minutes). Recorded 1943-5.

⑦ ❷

When the deterioration of New Orleans's post-war economy encouraged a mass migration of the city's outstanding jazzmen, Lewis remained. During the twenties he worked with the Eureka Brass Band, the Olympia Orchestra and with the likes of Buddy Petit, Red Allen and Kid Rena. He first worked with Bunk Johnson in the thirties but he was the producer's choice to support the trumpeter as the New Orleans style was revived in the forties. It was not the happiest of stylistic weddings and this CD supports the theory that Lewis's best work was done elsewhere. By the standards of contemporaries Dodds, Noone and Simeon, Lewis had a thin sound, but it was a soulful, sweet tone that could wring emotion from almost any material. His introduction to *Over the Waves* does come dangerously near to maudlin sentimentality but moving hymns like *Lead Me Saviour* are more representative. His trio playing throughout is commendable and he successfully overcomes the at-times stiff rhythmic backgrounds. Two of the full band titles are blighted by Madison's fumbling technique and suspect intonation, but Lewis's partnership with Howard on the final three items is far more fruitful. The series of recording dates shows that Lewis's outright dismissal by the technique-conscious moderns is no more justified than is the incontinent praise heaped upon him by the passionate traditionalists.                                                                                  **BMcR**

New review

**Jazz at Vespers**  Lewis (cl); **Avery 'Kid' Howard** (t, v); **Jim Robinson** (tb); **Alton Purnell** (p); **Lawrence Marrero** (bj); **Alcide 'Slow Drag' Pavageau** (b); **Joe Watkins** (d, v). Riverside Ⓜ OJCCD1721-2 (42 minutes). Recorded 1954.

⑦ ❽

In the 12 years following Lewis's first appearance on record with Bunk Johnson he became identified as the leading clarinettist of the New Orleans revival. This line-up is the band that was his touring group for much of the fifties and it has the cohesion and swing of a regular working group, qualities absent from many of Lewis's earlier efforts for American Music. The best work by this band was recorded at Bakersfield, California, and in Rudy Van Gelder's studio for Blue Note, but with that material currently unavailable except in a Mosaic three-volume set, this session comes closest in spirit, style and content. Recorded during one of Lewis's many visits to Oxford, Ohio (several albums of live material are issued on American Music), this was a church concert, and all the material is based on spirituals or hymns. To start with, Watkins's brushes and the hushed tones of the brass suggest the band will be cowed by the atmosphere, but soon on *Bye and Bye* Watkins is playing his familiar press-rolls, he and Howard swaggering through vocals as if they were playing a back-of-town juke joint. Howard and Robinson use the occasion to employ mutes more than usual, but without inhibiting Howard's explosive flurries into the upper register, or Robinson's tailgate foils to Lewis's delicate clarinet lines. Purnell is slightly under-recorded but the sound is otherwise excellent, giving a clear and faithful impression of the band most imitated by revivalists for the past 40 years. **AS**

## George Lewis 1952

**New review**
**Changing with the Times** Lewis (tb); **Douglas Ewart** (shakuhachi, cl, bcl, reeds, didgeridoo, perc); **Daniel Koppelman, Ruth Neville** (p); **Jeannie Cheatham** (p, org, v); **Mary Oliver** (va, v); **Peter Gonzales III** (perc); **Bernard Mixon, Jerome Rothenberg, Quincy Troupe** (v). New World Records Ⓕ 80434-2 (65 minutes). Recorded 1973.

⑨ ❾

Since completing his studies with the AACM in the mid seventies, Lewis has worked chiefly with avant-gardists such as Anthony Braxton, Steve Lacy and Evan Parker. His long association with reeds virtuoso Douglas Ewart has been documented on a series of fine Black Saint recordings, most notably the excellent **Homage to Charles Parker**. His pioneering work in computer music – he has programmed a computer to improvise – can be sampled on his **Voyager** disc with Roscoe Mitchell. **Changing with the Times** is unique among Lewis's recordings in that it features his musical settings for a variety of spoken texts. These include poems by Rothenberg and Troupe plus prose narratives by both Lewis himself and his father, George T. Lewis. The latter's *Changing with the Times* is the disc's centrepiece, a 25-minute soliloquy delivered with consummate skill by Mixon. Lewis's music – part-composed, part-improvised – subtly enhances the different texts, the players weaving their comments through the narratives with acuity and wit. In its sensitive marriage of music and text, **Changing with the Times** is arguably the most cogent synthesis to date of jazz and story-telling traditions. **GL**

## John Lewis 1920

**Grand Encounter: 2° East, 3° West** Lewis (p); **Bill Perkins** (ts); **Jim Hall** (g); **Percy Heath** (b); **Chico Hamilton** (d). Pacific Jazz Ⓜ CDP7 46859-2 (35 minutes). Recorded 1956.

⑧ ❺

This album, Lewis's first under his own name, brought his composition *2° East, 3° West* to the world, and for that alone we ought to be thankful. The disc displays all the usual qualities associated with the pianist/composer: restraint, a high degree of organization, delicacy, perceptive accompaniment of soloists, a relaxed feel. This last quality is amply displayed on his feature, *I Can't Get Started*, where he unhurriedly unveils his treatment of the beautiful theme, subtly alters its harmonic accompaniment then builds a leisurely, spare but well-structured solo on top. Perkins is in a decidedly romantic frame of mind on this record, displaying in equal measure his admiration for Lester Young and Stan Getz, while Hall is quite withdrawn, even for him. Hall's solo on *2° East, 3° West* is an intriguing exercise in minimalism in a blues context, but he leaves Lewis and Perkins to take the lion's share of solo space.

An album of almost casual beauty, it has a very low emotional temperature, but rewards close study. The recording (mono only) is not great – the instrumental balance being decidedly unhappy – but it is no worse than contemporary albums on Atlantic. **KS**

**The Wonderful World of Jazz** Lewis (p, ldr); **Jim Hall** (g); **George Duvivier** (b); **Connie Kay** (d); **Herb Pomeroy** (t), **Paul Gonsalves** (ts); **Herb Pomeroy** (t); **Gunther Schuller** (frh); **Eric Dolphy** (as); **Benny Golson** (ts); **Jimmy Giuffre** (bs). Rhino/Atlantic Ⓜ 790979-2 (56 minutes). Recorded 1960.

⑩ ❽

John Lewis's presence on record or the concert platform has always brought a sense of dignity. For years he guided the MJQ as the power behind the throne, often allowing Milt Jackson to take the spotlight. This CD version of a long-unavailable LP is especially valuable and contains two previously unissued titles, one by the basic quartet (Tadd Dameron's *If You Could See Me Now*) and Arif Mardin's *The Stranger* by the nonet, which means we hear a new, explosively exciting alto solo from Eric Dolphy. But most of the satisfaction to be obtained from the CD is the careful, often understated piano playing by Lewis, one of the least demonstrative but most effective keyboard players in jazz. Like Basie, he concentrates on the notes that matter, allowing them to stand alone with plenty of space around them. The most memorable track is the longest: *Body and Soul* is over 15 minutes of timeless perfection. Paul Gonsalves spins out a tenor solo of such warmth and invention that it rivals even the classic Coleman Hawkins version, thanks largely to the prodding, sensitive piano backing from Lewis. This is a five-star performance by any standard. The sound is good with just a hint of tape hiss in places; a small price to pay for the retention of the original recording characteristic. Recommended without reservation. **AM**

# Meade Lux Lewis

1905-64

**1927-39/1939-41** Lewis (p, cel); with a collective personnel including: **J.C. Higginbotham** (tb); **Albert Arnmons, Pete Johnson** (p); **Teddy Bunn** (g); **Walter Page, Johnny Williams** (b); **Jo Jones, Sid Catlett** (d). Classics Ⓜ 722/743 (two discs, oas: 72 and 70 minutes). Recorded 1927-41.

✔️ ⑧ ❺

Lewis was not the first boogie boogie pianist, but he had one of the earliest successes with the style when his first version of *Honky Tonk Train Blues* was released at the end of the twenties. A Chicagoan, Lewis had spent his youth in Kentucky before returning to his home town and linking up with his friend Albert Ammons. Out of luck and money, by 1927 he was reduced to driving cabs, but the release of *Honk Tonk Train Blues* that year enabled him to attempt music as a career. This met with only partial success and it was not until his appearance at John Hammond's famous Carnegie Hall concert of 1938 that he was able to sustain his career's momentum.

He recorded briefly for a number of companies at the dawn of the thirties, but the intense bout of recording for Blue Note which began in 1939 perhaps stand as his best work, although a 'live' set from a mid-forties Jazz at the Philharmonic concert (doubtless to be dealt with on a subsequent Classics release) is thrillingly immediate and worth seeking out. On these discs we have the complete Blue Note output, mixed with other sides made for Vocalion, Victor and Solo Art. The sound quality is not brilliant (the originals are generally poor), but Lewis's unusually large stylistic range is immediately apparent. While he could keep his left hand rolling around in boogie patterns all night long, he tried many different approaches, echoing other players as disparate as Earl Hines and James P. Johnson, moving between stride and blues patterns at will. His work with the Higginbotham group on *Basin Street Blues* shows him to have a strong grasp on jazz piano practice, and he fits smoothly into the rhythm section.

Athough his powerful boogie duets with Ammons and Johnson are rightly enthused over, his most affecting work is done alone. *Far Ago Blues* is a wistful, regretful blues performance which incidentally has an almost complete statement of the melody to *Blue Monk* some decade or so before that famous piece was first brought before the public. It should be noted that on some tracks here Lewis plays the celeste, an instrument for which he retained an affection throughout his career. Lewis is a musician who has more complexity of thought and execution than he is often given credit for, and these two CDs are an essential purchase for those who wish to comprehend the development of piano in the years between the Jelly Roll Morton Victors and Charlie Parker's first records with the Jay McShann band. **KS**

# Mel Lewis

1929-90

**The Definitive Thad Jones** Lewis (d); **Earl Gardner, Joe Mosello, Glenn Drewes, Jim Powell** (t); **John Mosca, Ed Neumeister, Douglas Purviance, Earl McIntyre** (tb); **Stephanie Fauber** (frh); **Dick Oatts, Ted Nash** (as); **Joe Lovano, Ralph Lalama** (ts); **Gary Smulyan** (bs); **Kenny Werner** (p); **Dennis Irwin** (b). MusicMasters Ⓕ 5024-2 (52 minutes). Recorded 1988.

⑧ ❻

Thad Jones loved to spread himself when he wrote, but never wasted a note. The band he led with Lewis was one of the greatest in the whole pantheon of jazz; after Jones's death Lewis carried on the tradition using younger musicians. Naturally he kept most of Thad's writing in the book and the five titles here are well-chosen examples. Lewis rightly trusted his audience's attention span. *Three in One* runs for 13 minutes and *Little Pixie,* another variation on *I Got Rhythm,* for more than 15.

The Jones/Lewis band had the pick of the crop of contemporary New York musicians of all styles. Lewis's band had younger men of similar stature, particularly in soloists Dick Oatts and Joe Lovano, but the sections also play with outstanding finesse and this is a worthy tribute to Jones. His writings were far too good to waste, and are ideal for new generations of musicians to cut their teeth on.

All of which makes this sound like a worthy album rather than an enjoyable one. That is unfair: it is filled with fire from the drums up. **SV**

# Ramsey Lewis

1935

**Live** Lewis (p); **Eldee Young** (b, vc); **Isaac 'Red' Holt** (d). Stereo Ⓑ JHR73524 (70 minutes). Recorded 1965.

④ ❻

The first half of this CD was originally released as an album called **The "In" Crowd**, and it sold more than a million copies. The mid sixties were a good period for Lewis; the soul-jazz movement was firmly in place and the Chicagoan's churchy, rolling style was just right for that climate. He had become fully established, had a consistent personnel and was full of confidence. His large following had begun to demand the same tunes rather too frequently, but he was equipped with a formula that worked. Technically he was a good player, but his improvisational processes were predictable and this repetitive approach became wearing even to the dedicated listener. As his popularity waned in the seventies he tried keyboards and the world of funk. His return to the acoustic instrument in the eighties did not see him return to critical favour, but although he is still a popular performer he remains a figure somewhat on the jazz fringe. Despite the claim on the CD, the final seven titles were recorded at the Lighthouse on Hermosa Beach. **BMcR**

**Ivory Pyramid** Lewis (p); **Mike Logan** (kbds); **Henry Johnson** (g); **Charles Webb** (b); **Steve Cobb** (d, perc). GRP ⓕ 96882 (48 minutes). Recorded 1992.

⑤ ❽

One man's meat ... . Depending on your point of view, this is either a highly successful marriage of contemporary rhythms with the type of melody and chord sequence one would normally find in popular music written 40 years ago, or it is a cliché-ridden sell-out. Lewis has been riding this dichotomy of opinion for the whole of his career and it shows no sign of abating. One thing not at issue is the man's talent: he has a great deal of that, and the technique to match it. He plays acoustic piano exclusively on this disc, allowing his mostly electronically-powered working group to supply backdrops which really only have their parallel in the type of accompaniment once supplied to George Shearing and Nat King Cole. 'Lush' is the word.

Lewis gives tantalizing glimpses of what he is truly capable of as a soloist on track after track, but does not sustain it, preferring to pull back into understatement and well-turned phrases. His ear is very good and he has a developed orchestral sense, but he has chosen to use it for the most part to create sophisticated popular music with a touch of jazz. That is not his fault, but he could do otherwise. I get the feeling this brings us back to the opening dilemma. **KS**

# Vic Lewis
1919

**Vic Lewis West Coast All Stars Play the Music of Bill Holman, Volume 1** Lewis directing **Conte Candoli, Jack Sheldon** (t); **Rob McConnell** (vtb); **Andy Martin** (tb); **Ron Loofbourrow** (frh); **Bud Shank, Lanny Morgan, Lennie Niehaus** (as); **Bob Cooper** (f, cl, ts); **Bill Perkins** (f, ss, bs, bcl); **Mike Lang, Alan Broadbent, Dudley Moore** (p); **John Clayton** (b); **Jeff Hamilton** (d); **Ruth Price** (v). Candid ⓕ CCD79540 (61 minutes) Recorded 1989.

⑧ ❽

Each winter Vic Lewis goes to California and persuades the West Coast 'giants' to record for him for scale (standard union fees). No matter how it is done, we can only be grateful for the results. Holman, for example, is shamefully underexposed on record, running an artistically successful rehearsal big band for the best part of 20 years during which time it has done little but rehearse.

Holman specializes in an oblique look at familiar melodies. *Yesterdays* and *Easter Parade* are re-composed in this way, both stretched out at length to allow potent series of solos. Candoli is brutally powerful on the Kern tune, which is also distinguished by a maverick and forceful bass-clarinet solo from Perkins and wistful valve trombone from the excellent McConnell. Both tenors grace *Easter Parade*, taking advantage of another aspect of Holman's writing, the opportunity to swing. Holman's originals are splendid, with a particularly attractive slow theme for the multi-tempo *As We Speak*. Previously issued on Mole CD14, this new version of the album has been re-edited and completely rebalanced by Bill Perkins, with a second version of *Oleo* being added. **SV**

# Willie Lewis
1905-71

**New review**

**And His Entertainers 1936-8** Lewis (as, v, dir); **Bill Coleman** (t, v); **Arthur Briggs, Jack Butler, Theodore Brock** (t); **Billy Burns, Eugene d'Hellemmes** (tb); **Joe Hayman** (as, ts, bs); **George Johnson** (as); **Frank 'Big Boy' Goudie** (cl, ts); **Fletcher Allen, Roscoe Burnett** (ts); **Herman Chittison** (p); **John Mitchell** (g); **Louis Vola, Wilson Myers** (b); **Ted Fields, Tommy Benford** (d); **Jean Tranchant, Greta Keller** (v). Classics Ⓜ 847 (73 minutes). Recorded 1936-8.

⑦ ❼

Lewis was one of the American band leaders who made a bigger impact abroad than at home. He was born in Texas, studied at the New England conservatory in Boston and crossed the Atlantic with the Sam Wooding Orchestra. When the band was broken up in 1931, he returned to the USA but had soon re-formed on his own behalf and, for most of the thirties, led a band in Europe. Lewis called his group the Entertainers and there are plenty of novelty vocals on this CD to remind us that in 1936, jazz and popular music were comfortable bed-fellows. Tranchant's and Keller's contributions are disposable but this does not devalue Lewis's band of roving troubadours. In Coleman and Chittison it had major league players and in Goudie a reed man of substance. On paper, the rhythm section hinted at better things. There are moments when the light bounce of *Organ Grinder's Swing* and *Swing Time* becomes a chug, but Chittison is excellent and, on balance, it was a fine band. After World War II Lewis virtually deserted his music, holding down a 'day job' until shortly before his death. **BMcR**

# David Liebman 1946

New review

**Return of the Tenor: Standards** Liebman (ts); **Phil Markowitz** (p); **Vic Juris** (g); **Tony Marino** (b); **Jamey Haddad** (d). Double-Time Records Ⓕ DTRCD109 (71 minutes). Recorded 1996.

⑦ ❽

"Coming to terms with the big horn has been looming in my head as a kind of mid-life challenge", writes a reflective Dave Liebman. Dropping the tenor in the early eighties in order to deflect comparisons with the transcendent John Coltrane, Liebman focused his energies on the soprano saxophone, an instrument that he – along with Steve Lacy and Jane Ira Bloom – has made his own. But as this galvanizing outing makes clear, Liebman has beat back his tenor demons to re-embrace the big horn with vigor and *élan*. In his thoughtful annotations, Liebman adds that with tenor, "I go more directly head to head inside the music." Liebman, in fact, sounds perfectly at home. And, yes, while there are echoes of Coltrane in the side-slipping *Secret Love*, Liebman emerges his own man. Throughout the powerful blowing date devoted to standards, the saxophonist uses an ear-grabbing mix of duo, trio, quartet and quintet settings spotlighting pianist Phil Markowitz, guitarist Vic Juris, bassist Tony Marino and drummer Haddad, Liebman's highly *simpatico* working group since 1991. In the process, the masterful Liebman reclaims his place as one of jazzdom's most compelling and individual tenorists. **CB**

# Kirk Lightsey 1937

**Temptation** Lightsey (p); **Freddie Hubbard** (t); **Santi Debriano** (b); **Eddie Gladden** (d); **Jerry Gonzalez** (perc). Timeless Ⓕ CDSJP257 (51 minutes). Recorded 1987.

⑦ ❽

His earliest reputation was established as a sensitive accompanist to singers, but Lightsey emerged as a soloist in the mid sixties with combos led by Sonny Stitt and Chet Baker. In the eighties his career development continued and was furthered by periods spent under the leadership of Dexter Gordon, Jimmy Raney, Clifford Jordan and with the Leaders Co-operative Group. He also began to record as a leader himself, and this CD finds him in the company of Hubbard as well as three men with whom he works regularly. The programme is made up of three Hubbard originals, one Thelonious Monk classic and two standards. All receive thorough jazz treatment, with themes stated clearly and improvisationed examinations conducted in style by the two principals. The pianist's work is consistently good and shows his dynamic awareness in solos that grow in creative and rhythmic tension as they progress. His handling of *Evidence*, a Monk theme developed without reference to the basic Thelonious piano vocabulary, is typical, but every little phrase speaks of an individuality with which he has not always been credited. Hubbard is on daunting form on this date, but Lightsey is not inhibited by it, in fact producing some of his most imaginative patterns in support of the trumpeter's work. **BMcR**

# Abbey Lincoln 1930

**Talking to the Sun** Lincoln (v); **Steve Coleman** (as); **James Weidman** (p); **Billy Johnson** (b); **Mark Johnson** (d); **Jerry Gonzalez** (perc); **Arlene Knox**, **Bemshee Shirer**, **Naima Williams** (v). Enja Ⓕ 79635-2 (39 minutes). Recorded 1983.

⑩ ❽

Lincoln's trademark as a singer is her lack of artifice – her way of experiencing a song and expressing to the listener what the words and melody mean to her, in the most direct and honest means possible. After a start as a lounge singer in the fifties, she became a singing spokeswoman for the civil rights movement, participating on her then-husband Max Roach's **We Insist** and **Percussion Bitter Sweet**. In the nineties, relatively late in her career, she has acquired something approaching a mass following on the strength of a trio of albums for Verve which have surrounded her with all-star accompanists. Her most satisfying album, though, may be this one for Enja, which features her working band of the period. **Talking to the Sun** includes material by Villa-Lobos, Johnny Mandel and Stevie Wonder, as well as *You're My Thrill*, an erotic chant of a song that Lincoln owns, iconic interpretations by Billie Holiday and Chet Baker notwithstanding. What gives this disc its edge, however, are Lincoln's own songs. *People on the Streets* might be the most empathic song ever written about the homeless, but it takes second place to the title song, in which the orb around which the earth revolves is given human qualities and compared to a lover – the implication being that no man under the sun could be as steadfast as the singer desires. As is also true of Betty Carter, Lincoln has been so celebrated as a singer that her gifts as a lyricist have gone overlooked. In their unpretentious way, the lyrics here approach poetry. So does Lincoln's delivery of them. **FD**

**A Turtle's Dream** Lincoln (v); Roy Hargrove (t); Julien Lourau (ts); Pat Metheny (g, elg); Kenny Barron (p); Christian McBride (b); Victor Lewis (d); string section. Verve Ⓕ 527 382-2 (69 minutes). Recorded 1994.

⑧ ❿

Lincoln's voice, fibrous and warm, seems to improve with age, and so does her command of time, which was always formidable. She gives the impression of being an entirely self-sufficient and self-sustaining artist. She wrote most of the songs, and most of the arrangements, too. They are thoughtful without being pretentious and she delivers them with a confidence delicately tinged with irony. This and other recent albums show that Abbey Lincoln has succeeded in escaping both from her own type-casting as a radical-political performer and from the general type-casting of modern women jazz singers as imitation Billie Holiday-plus-soul. The band here is a delight, particularly Hargrove and the young French saxophonist Julien Lourau. **DG**

## Nils Lindberg
1933

**Sax Appeal and Trisection** Lindberg (p, arr) leading: Idrees Sulieman, Jan Allan (t); Eje Thelin (tb); Rolf Billberg (as); Harry Backlund (ts); Lars Gullin, Erik Nilsson (b); Sture Nordin (d) and others. Dragon Ⓕ DRCD220 (67 minutes). Recorded 1960-3.

⑧ ❽

Seven of the titles on this album were made at Lindberg's début session as composer/arranger. The first day in the studio was a disaster and Lindberg had to beg for a further four hours the next day. It was then that the seven included here, all first takes, were recorded. The three giants of the saxophones, Backlund, Billberg and Gullin, sail through the finely written charts with an easy serenity, and *Just A Take*, an improvised track recorded at the end of the session, turns out to be a variation on *Yesterdays* with some well-oiled baritone from Gullin, later joined in some nice interplay by Billberg on alto. The more ordered tracks by an 11-piece make up the **Trisection** suite and again display Lindberg's bias towards the saxophones in his original writing and in the solo space allocated to them. However *Ars Gratia Artis* features a free solo from one of the two great Scandinavian trombonists, Eje Thelin (Ake Persson was the other). Thelin has a more conventional solo on *Joker* which also has a tough tenor solo from Backlund. There is melodic trumpet from Sulieman and a piano solo from Lindberg which seems to draw its inspiration from Eddie Costa and, as with much of Lindberg's work, Hank Jones.

Those looking for a more up to date sample of Lindberg's artistry will be in for a treat should they purchase his solo piano album, **Alone With My Memories** (Dragon). A superbly sustained and consistently beautiful record, it has Lindberg giving intensely-felt, committed performances of his own compositions. **SV**

## Erica Lindsay
1955

**Dreamer** Lindsay (ts); Howard Johnson (tba, bs, flh); Francesca Tanxley (p); Anthony Cox (b); Newman Baker (d); Robin Eubanks (tb). Candid Ⓕ CCD79040 (45 minutes). Recorded 1989.

⑥ ❽

Lindsay is a large talent both as a composer and as a player, but this album is not really delivering all that it promises. The leader plays to a high level and comes across as a saxophonist with sufficient of her own voice to be called distinctive, although the ghost of Coltrane hovers nearby. What she brings to the music, however, is a tangible desire to communicate emotionally, however sophisticated her own concepts may be. This communication certainly takes place when she is soloing or stating themes (drummer Baker is also at his best when backing her), and Howard Johnson can never be anything less than one hundred per cent. But the rest of the supporting cast sound a little perfunctory occasionally, while at other times somewhat lacking in imagination (surely there isn't just the McCoy Tyner patented method for comping and soloing in 6/8?). The three stars are mostly for Lindsay; let's hope for more consistent things to come. **KS**

## Jeanette Lindström

**Another Country** Lindström (v); Örjan Hultén (ts); Torbjörn Gulz (p); Dan Berglund (b); Magnus Öström (d, perc). Caprice Ⓕ CAP21480 (68 minutes). Recorded 1995.

⑦ ❽

This is an impressive record, partly because Lindström is a good singer, but mostly because the Jeanette Lindström Quintet which plays on it is a well-rehearsed, coherent and interactive group of musicians which manages to create a real identity for itself. Lindström has a light, agile voice and a surprising ability to dig into the rhythm and swing a song's lyric along (many singers are content to glide on top of whatever pulse their support group is already providing). She is not the world's greatest interpreter of lyrics, but she is not merely facile: there is a nice feeling of commitment in her singing, allied to the sense of joy in what she is doing which often gets covered by more grandiloquent singers with layers of showbiz knowingness and posing. The quartet of musicians behind her are first-rate, saxophonist Hultén worthy of an album to himself, while pianist Gulz applies countless felicities to the music behind the singer. The material is made up of originals and covers of American-period Weill. If this was a record by a new US singer's band it would win every award going. **KS**

## Rudy Linka
1960

**Czech it Out!** Linka (g); George Mraz (b); Marvin 'Smitty' Smith (d). Enja Ⓕ ENJ9001-2 (53 minutes). Recorded 1994.
⑦ ❿

Linka came west from Czechoslovakia in 1981, studied under a string of Americans including Red Mitchell and John Abercrombie, settled in America and began recording as a leader as the nineties dawned. This, his fourth date as a leader, shows increasing maturity and the ability to sustain interest in an exposed format, that of the trio. Of course it helps that his fellow musicians are such powerful identities, able to fill the spaces with intelligent and meaningful note-choices, but the spotlight rightly falls mostly on Linka.

He helps his own cause by showing himself equally adept at playing jazz on both electric and acoustic six-string guitars (a feat suprisingly few guitarists manage convincingly), and while he sticks by and large to an undistorted tone and a linear approach, he constantly exhibits the sort of wide harmonic knowledge and resourcefulness usually associated with the likes of Jim Hall. His ease with the blues also suggests a familiarity with Scofield. Seven of the nine tunes here are Linka originals, and each is designed to showcase a different aspect of his improvisatory skill, while *How Deep is the Ocean?* and *Love Letters* find him conversant in traditional modern jazz guitar language. Linka has a lot to offer the serious listener. **KS**

## Booker Little
1938-61

**Out Front** Little (t); Eric Dolphy (f, as, bcl); Julian Priester (tb); Don Friedman (p); Art Davis, Ron Carter (b); Max Roach (d). Candid Ⓜ CD9027 (44 minutes). Recorded 1961.
❿ ❼

Booker Little came to prominence with the Max Roach Quintet (he worked alongside tenor player George Coleman), playing with that group at the 1958 Newport Jazz Festival when he was just 20 years old. By the time of this, his last album as a leader, he had developed at a phenomenal rate, becoming a resourceful composer as well as a uniquely gifted trumpeter. While his style and sound came directly from the late Clifford Brown, he was one of very few to take Brown's legacy and make something new with it.

**Out Front** is conceived as a display album for Little: all the tracks are his own compositions and the front line of three horns allows the trumpeter to investigate harmonic combinations unusual in jazz, mostly involving dissonance. There is also considerable experimentation with different metres, sometimes within one piece. His beautiful tone and ear for melody, as well as Roach's inspired drumming, keep this from becoming a dry or ugly exercise, and Little solos convincingly throughout. Dolphy is the other principal soloist, with his alto work on *Moods in Free Time* still coming across as some of his fiercest and most free. But Little is the main attraction, and his playing here often has a beauty which is breathtaking. **KS**

## Charles Lloyd
1938

**Forest Flower/Soundtrack** Lloyd (ts, f); Keith Jarrett (p); Cecil McBee, Ron McClure (b); Jack DeJohnette (d). Rhino/Atlantic Ⓜ R2 71746 (77 minutes). Recorded 1966-8.
⑧ ⑧

One of the seminal figures of the sixties, Memphis-born Charles Lloyd forged a unique style conjoining the blues of his hometown, the modal forays of John Coltrane and at times an almost folk music-like lyricism. In Los Angeles, Lloyd studied composition at the University of Southern California and came into contact with Eric Dolphy and Ornette Coleman. His star rose through important gigs with Gerald Wilson, Chico Hamilton and Cannonball Adderley, during which Lloyd made a pivotal shift from alto to tenor. Along with Coltrane's influence, the impact of Lloyd's years as an altoist can be heard in his penchant for the tenor's upper register and his gauzy, mystical tone.

In 1966, Lloyd and his newly-formed quartet with Jarrett, McBee (later replaced by McClure) and DeJohnette became a *cause célèbre*. Appealing to rock as well as jazz audiences, Lloyd's kaleidoscopic soundscapes encompassed bucolic meditations as well as cascading freefalls. It was fresh, even audacious, and bubbling with sounds-of-surprise. Lloyd's top-drawer status was solidified with the landmark **Forest Flower**, recorded at the Monterey Jazz Festival in 1966, but released in 1967. The mesmerizing title track became Lloyd's anthem. In *Sorcery* and *Sombrero Sam*, Lloyd proved himself a compelling flautist in the soaring, open-ended manner of Jeremy Steig. Equally impressive is the quartet's hand-in-glove interplay and Jarrett's sparkling pianistics *sans* grunts and groans. **CB**

---

**The Call** Lloyd (ts); **Bobo Stenson** (p); **Anders Jormin** (b); **Billy Hart** (d). ECM Ⓕ 517 719-2 (77 minutes). Recorded 1993.

⑨ ❿

Lloyd begins this, the album before his latest, **All My Relations** (ECM), with a song called *Nocturne*, and immediately the listener is overwhelmed by its affinity with Coltrane's *After The Rain*. Lloyd always did have a passing resemblance to the older man, but here it is spelled out quite deliberately. His tone has never been richer (perhaps it has never been this well recorded before?), and he sings the melody line on his horn.

Not that the saxophonist has not played melodically before; his phenomenal popular success in the mid sixties, after a useful training in the Chico Hamilton band which also nurtured Gabor Szabo, was based as much on his memorable extended sketches – *Forest Flower*, for example, always sounded as if it were going somewhere, evolving, rather than being used as a stock item for a bunch of guys to jam on – as on the phenomenal talents which made up the original Charles Lloyd Quartet: Lloyd himself, Keith Jarrett, Ron McClure and Jack DeJohnette.

Most of the great Lloyd albums from the sixties, all on Atlantic, are currently unavailable on CD. This new album is deliberately looking back to that time. In a short note to the purchaser, Lloyd refers to an occasion in France in 1966 when "a group of mystics with saxophones initiated me into their society". That group was the Ellington sax section, and certainly this whole album has the ineffable mood of relaxation and peace which Ellington small groups often achieve. Although individual solos or tracks on his classic sixties albums may reach headier heights than anything here, I doubt whether Lloyd has surpassed this album as a sustained effort. The group (his current working band) is, to these ears at least, a more integrated unit than the one which brought Petrucciani to international attention, and Lloyd's own playing is at a new peak. **KS**

# Joe Locke

1959

**New review**

**Moment to Moment** Locke (vb); **Billy Childs** (p); **Eddie Gomez** (b); **Gene Jackson** (d). Milestone Ⓕ MCD9243-2 (57 minutes). Recorded 1994.

⑥ ⑨

Listening to a less familiar player working with well known material allows the listener easier access to the player's improvisation talent. Locke is hardly a mystery man but, considering the range of his talent, he remains a comparatively obscure figure. He grew up in New York State, initially studied piano and drums and switched to the vibraphone at the age of 13. He moved to the city in 1981 and since then has been something of a first call man for the likes of Eddie Henderson, Marvin 'Smitty' Smith and the Mingus Big Band. This CD has him reworking material by Henry Mancini and progressing a reputation earned by a series of fine recordings released on SteepleChase in the nineties. Not written with jazzmen in mind, Mancini's music does present a certain challenge. It is, however, one that Locke is happy to meet. On the ballads he puts the brooding resonance of his tone to good effect. Whatever the tempo, he drives across bar divisions, using his long lines to blunt any of the over-genteel contours that might confront him. He is at his most creative on a beefed-up *Charade*, *Days of Wine and Roses* and the title track but nothing that he plays could be taken as ill-considered. **BMcR**

# Mornington Lockett

---

**Mornington Lockett** Lockett (ts, p, b); **Jonathan Gee** (p); **Laurence Cottle** (b); **Ian Thomas** (d, b); **Jim Mullen** (g – two tracks); **Sarah Jane Morris** (v – one track) EFZ Ⓕ EFZ1006 (58 minutes). Recorded 1993.

⑥ ⑧

The young Scottish musician celebrated here was for a couple of years the second saxophonist in Ronnie Scott's group. He shows his paces in what is predominantly a quartet context and, like many début albums, it has something of the sampler about it, with different tracks coming from different directions. The two pieces with Mullen are an altered blues (seemingly with jazz-bar crowd noises dubbed in) and a promising version of *Lush Life*, which loses direction slightly after going into a steady tempo. Apart from an excellent Rollinesque *I Got Rhythm*-type number (*Laphroaig*) with just Cottle and Thomas, the rest has Jonathan Gee and includes two versions of an acoustic duo with Gee called *Demusiado* – wittily subtitled *Satie Mix* and *Debussy Mix*.

The more funky items are also well carried off and have Lockett wailing expansively in a manner that even the record compares to Mike Brecker. The whole is expertly recorded, if in that rather dry way typical of British studios which robs the music of its impact, but only Sarah Jane Morris's vocal on the Etta Jones speciality, *Don't Go to Strangers*, seems a waste of space. **BP**

# Didier Lockwood

1956

**New York Rendez-Vous** Lockwood (vn); **Dave Liebman** (ss – four tracks); **Gil Goldstein** (acc – two tracks); **Mike Stern** (g – one track); **Dave Kikoski** (p); **Dave Holland** (b); **Peter Erskine** (d). JMS ⑤ 075-2 (56 minutes). Recorded 1995.

⑦ ❽

The genealogy of French excellence in the field of jazz violin has extended from Grappelli to the present day and has apparently been confirmed by the donation of actual instruments from the veteran to the younger Jean-Luc Ponty, then onward from Ponty to Lockwood, his junior by a further 14 years. But even if the listener is not averse to Ponty's love-affair with fusion, his output over the years and the company he keeps have often been anti-climactic. Lockwood, on the other hand, has gone from strength to strength, and this latest all-star album in a series for the JMS label is probably his best to date. The occasionally intriguing tone-colours are of less interest than the 'blowing' of all concerned and the original compositions by Lockwood and four others (some of which are glimpsed in manuscript on the cover photo). The leader is easily the most compelling post-bop violinist currently active and, despite a comparative lack of renown, seems content to quietly demonstrate his superb ability on occasions such as this splendid album. **BP**

# Martin Löfgren

**Flow** Löfgren (d, perc); **Jonas Knutsson** (ss, as, bs); **Lars Jansson** (p, syn); **Yasuhito Mori** (b). Amigo ⑤ AMCD875 (55 minutes). Recorded 1995.

⑥ ❿

Löfgren is a Swedish drummer with long experience in recording studios (he produces here): hence, no doubt, the choice of Oslo's Rainbow Studio, beloved of ECM's Manfred Eicher, for the making of this superbly-recorded disc. The music itself could easily fit into the ECM release policy, being content to follow in the paths of musicians like Jan Garbarek, Bobo Stenson and so many others of the ECM brigade. That is not to say the music is poor: it is excellently played, sophisticated and very attractive, giving many moments of pleasure. In the final analysis, however, it is deeply unoriginal, and one may as well have the originals these men are imitating. **KS**

# Giuseppi Logan

1935

**More Giuseppi Logan** Logan (f, as, bcl, p); **Don Pullen** (p); **Reggie Johnson**, **Eddie Gomez** (b); **Milford Graves** (d). ESP-Disk ⓜ 1013-2 (39 minutes). Recorded 1964/5.

④ ❹

Logan was a significant theorist and fellow-traveller during the New York avant-garde jazz explosion of the early and mid sixties. Trained at New England Conservatory, he later went against most of the accepted tenets of instrumental expertise in an attempt to win a new approach to music. His first album for ESP-Disk (simply titled **Giuseppi Logan**) is so laboured in its perverseness that, through no fault of his accompanying musicians, it becomes quite painful to listen to at times. A left-over from that date on this disc (*Wretched Saturday*) gives ample demonstration of the point. However, there was more to Logan than that record suggested, and the first two tracks on this album, recorded live at a concert in New York's Town Hall (the same gig where Ayler's *Bells* was recorded), are quite presentable. Logan restricts himself to some atmospheric flute and bass clarinet arabesques, leaving the others to get down to business. They do this very well indeed, and it is a shame that the recording quality on these two tracks is very poor. That Logan was quite capable of producing memorable music is evident from his role on Roswell Rudd's 1966 album **Everywhere**, where his own composition *Dance of Satan*, so poorly played on the above self-titled album, gets a rousing performance. **KS**

# London Jazz Composers Orchestra

1970

**Portraits** Barry Guy (b, dir); **Henry Lowther**, **Jon Corbett** (t); **Marc Charig** (c); **Paul Rutherford**, **Radu Malfatti**, **Alan Tomlinson** (tb); **Steve Wick** (bb); **Howard Riley** (p); **Trevor Watts**, **Evan Parker**, **Simon Picard**, **Peter McPhail**, **Paul Dunmall** (reeds); **Phil Wachsmann** (vn); **Barre Phillips** (b); **Paul Lytton** (d). Intakt ⑤ CD035/1994 (two discs: 115 minutes). Recorded 1993.

⑧ ❽

The London Jazz Composers Orchestra is a band that matches improvisation with structured writing in a way that dispenses with the word 'paradox'. Formed in 1970, it has continually sought to provide cohesive direction to solo or small group freedoms under an orchestral banner. Following the band's initial success, an overtly academic route was pursued; pointing the music toward atonality and introducing certain restrictive practices. The period was brief and a degree of constructive mutiny led the band back to more righteous values.

This CD ideally illustrates leader Guy's current performance principles. He is helped by the quality of solos, while group sequences that he uses smooths their path with orchestral textures to suit each situation. Typical is the way that Wick is cossetted on *Study III* and the manner in which almost Ellingtonian calm eases the path for Corbett on *Crackle*. Sheer drama showcases Parker on *Triple*, light counterpoint is the tool in use on *Sunnyman*, while the entire orchestra bellows on *Five Pieces*. The important point is that the solo interludes and combo cameos are organic entities, vital to the musical progress of every work. They ensure that the formal and the free are balanced and explain how the LJCO confronts the concept of 'jazz orchestra'.                                                                    **BMcR**

# Eddy Louiss                                                                                                        1941

New review
**Conference De Presse, Volume 2** Louiss (org); **Michel Petrucciani** (p). Dreyfus Jazz
Ⓔ FDM36573-2 (62 minutes). Recorded 1994.

⑦ ❼

The second volume of two culled from the same three nights, these tracks were recorded in a Paris nightclub shortly after the initial encounter of the 53-year-old organist and the pianist who was 21 years his junior. It is a piquant combination, for the younger partner has a vivid attack at the keyboard and an all-consuming technical facility. The lesser-known Louiss is a veteran of work with Stan Getz, Les Double-Six and Jean-Luc Ponty (for the last-named association, see two live trio sets led by drummer Daniel Humair reissued by Dreyfus). By contrast with Petrucciani he has fairly modest dexterity, a rather veiled organ sound and, I believe, still plays his bass-lines with the left-hand rather than the pedals, further restraining an instrument which could easily submerge the piano. In fact the duo get on excellently, dividing their programme between warhorses such as *Caravan* and *Summertime* and originals, including a version of Petrucciani's *Rachid* which is now in waltz-time. The pianist is not without a certain exhibitionism but, as this adds to the joyous nature of the performance in addition to highlighting Louiss's more stolid virtues, it's hard to resist. A subsequent Dreyfus Louiss release, **Flomela**, covering his earlier career in the studio, is something of a curate's egg.                                                                                                      **BP**

# Joe Lovano                                                                                                        1952

New review
**Quartets Live at the Village Vanguard** Lovano (ts, ss, c-ms); **Tom Harrell** (t, f); **Mulgrew Miller** (p); **Anthony Cox**, **Christian McBride** (b); **Billy Hart**, **Lewis Nash** (d). Blue Note Ⓔ CDP8 29125-2 (two discs: 128 minutes). Recorded 1994-5.

⑨ ❽

As Jazz Musician and Tenor Saxophonist of the Year, Lovano dominated the 1995 Down Beat polls. It was a well-earned endorsement of an excellent journeyman who has become a major soloist almost by the back door. He was with Herman's Herd in the seventies, Mel Lewis in the eighties, as well as touring with Carla Bley in 1983. The last several years have seen him emerge as a leader, first-call player and a musical maverick welcome in all circumstances. John Scofield, Paul Motian, Charlie Haden and the Smithsonian Repertory have all acknowledged his value but it is as master of his own destiny that he has flourished. This CD provides evidence of his wide emotional and stylistic range. The 1995 material (the second disc) has Lovano fronting an orthodox rhythm trio, with Miller ensuring an organized atmosphere and McBride and Nash lending muscle to the saxophonist's solos. An adventurous spirit prevails throughout but titles such as *Reflections* and *Sound of Joy*, in particular, are models of post-bop quartet integration. The 1994 date (the first disc) essays greater freedoms. The absence of piano gives Lovano more licence and even the familiarity of *I Can't Get Started* is no barrier to the improvisatory determination he shows. The later date produced fine jazz but the 1994 session looks destined to be an important landmark in the Clevelander's career. He could be considered the finest player not to appear in the *Grove Dictionary*.                                              **BMcR**

# Allen Lowe

New review
**Woyzeck's Death** Lowe (ts); **Randy Sandke** (t); **Roswell Rudd** (tb); **Ben Goldberg** (cl); **Andy Shapiro** (p, syn); **Jeff Fuller** (b); **Ray Kaczynski** (d). Enja Ⓔ ENJ9005-2 (68 minutes). Recorded 1994.

⑦ ❽

Before becoming involved in playing as a professional, Lowe had worked as a jazz journalist, concert producer and booking agent. He has been Director of Jazz New Haven since 1990 and worked with players as diverse as David Murray, Doc Cheatham, Julius Hemphill and Jimmy Knepper. This CD is by his working band and includes both his nine-movement tribute to German playwright Georg Büchner and two colourful pieces by group member Rudd. Lowe's approach on tenor is unusual but effective; his timing is a mixture of Rollinsesque angularity and swing era plushness and he puts his ideas together with some diligence. Careful to avoid stylistic stereotypes, he moves from free-fall on *Sun On Her Bones* and *Voices in the Fiddles* to a more lyrical approach on *Hard Gray Sky*. In support, Sandke is a man for all seasons; he is Dixie-like of tone, mainstream of phrase-shape but more open in terms of solo organization. Rudd, of similar stylistic extremes, includes smouldering intensity, natural creativity and declamatory power in his group input. Lowe has made several albums in the nineties but more than any other **Woyzeck's Death** provides the blueprint for his playing, writing and group-leading qualities. **BMcR**

# Frank Lowe 1941

New review

**Bodies & Soul** Lowe (ts); **Tim Flood** (b); **Charles Moffett** (d). Creative Improvised Music Projects
ⒻCIMP104 (64 minutes). Recorded 1995.

**⑨ ⑧**

The Memphis-born Lowe worked in the Stax record shop as a teenager, digging blues, soul and saxophonists Gene Ammons and Chu Berry. Inspired by Coltrane, he moved to New York in the mid sixties to play free jazz and worked with Sun Ra. Later he studied the jazz tradition and all kinds of contemporary musics and has recorded with a wide range of artists, among them Billy Bang, Lawrence 'Butch' Morris and Leo Smith. Lowe's estimable 1984 **Decision in Paradise** featured Don Cherry and the trumpeter's spirit hovers over this new trio session. His elegant tune *Art Deco* is included, as is Lowe's tribute *Don One*. In his notes Lowe thanks Cherry for showing him "the pure joy one gets from just playing the music" and that joy suffuses this set. Moffett's drums swing and dance gleefully throughout and bassist Flood makes a (very) quietly effective CD début. The diffident Lowe is a superb player. Despite his tenor's visceral tone, he's basically a lyrical improviser who favours terse, jingling phrases that stay close to the melody. Though he can cavort with gusto, he's at his most compelling here on Phillip Wilson's lovely ballad *For Louie*, the tenor caressing the tune with a gruff tenderness that is spellbinding. **GL**

# Mundell Lowe 1922

**The Mundell Lowe Quartet** Lowe (g); **Dick Hyman** (p, org); **Trigger Alpert** (b); **Ed Shaughnessy**
(d). Riverside Ⓜ OJCCD1773-2 (37 minutes). Recorded 1955.

**④ ⑥**

In the mid fifties Lowe and Hyman were anchoring the rhythm sections of numerous New York studio bands for radio and TV, and this quartet got together (rather as Bud Shank's groups did on the West Coast) to escape the studio grind and play some jazz. This is an only partially successful escape, and recapture seems imminent throughout, as both men's nonchalant studio technique and chameleon tendencies keep hi-jacking the best jazz moments with displays of stunning superficiality. When things start cooking, however, the jazz is very good indeed. Low and Hyman pace each other through a series of chase choruses on *All of You*, while *Yes, Sir, That's My Baby* features the whole group, Shaughnessy's drum accents underpinning the theme and Alpert's accomplished bass work before launching him into a clattery solo on his rims. Lowe's guitar work is on par with Raney or Kessell, and his quote-laden solo on *Cheek to Cheek* is masterly. Hyman sounds better on piano, his organ work owing more to Reginald Dixon than Jimmy Smith. He never gets the volume changes right, sounding too abrupt, and his mock church playing on *Bach Revisited* is too pious for comfort. **AS**

# Jimmie Lunceford 1902-47

**Rhythm is Our Business** Lunceford (ldr, as, v); **Eddie Tomkins, Tommy Stevenson, William
Tomlin, Paul Webster, Gerald Wilson, Snooky Young** (t); **Sy Oliver** (t, v); **Henry Wells, Russell
Bowles, Elmer Crumbly** (tb); **Eddie Durham** (tb, g); **Trummy Young** (tb, v); **Willie Smith** (as, cl, v);
**Dan Grissom,Ted Buckner** (as, cl); **Farl Carruthers** (bs, as, cl); **Laforet Dent, Ed Brown** (as); **Joe
Thomas** (ts, cl, v); **Edwin Wilcox** (p); **Al Norris** (g); **Moses Allen** (b); **James Crawford** (d). ASV
Living Era Ⓜ CDAJA5091 (71 minutes). Recorded 1933-40.

**⑧ ⑥**

Observers of the day claim that Lunceford's band was the greatest show band working in Harlem during the thirties and that its section work was never less than immaculate. The latter comment is certainly borne out on the two dozen tracks selected for this truly representative collection by compiler Vic Bellerby. With Willie Smith leading the reed section and men such as Sy Oliver and Edwin Wilcox both writing for and playing in the band it was certainly a most musicianly orchestra. Lunceford was obviously concerned with putting on a show at the dancehalls, but there was still room for a sizeable jazz content too. Bellerby's selection creams off the best of the latter (the Lunceford discography is certainly not without dross, but none of it is here). This CD contains two of the Duke Ellington numbers which the band used in its earlier days, Willie Smith's arrangement of *Sophisticated*

*Lady* (with Smith playing the theme immaculately on clarinet) and Oliver's score of *Black and Tan Fantasy*, with fine growl trumpet from Sy. The collection also includes two popular Oliver arrangements in *Margie* and *'Tain't What You Do*, but the peak of jazz involvement is the classic *Uptown Blues* with solos from Smith on alto and trumpeter Snooky Young. The transfer from 78s is good.     **AM**

## Jan Lundgren

1966

**New review**

**Stockholm Get-Together**  Lundgren (p); **Herb Geller** (as); **Lars Lundstrom** (b); **Anders Langerlof** (d). Fresh Sound Ⓕ FSR5007CD (66 minutes). Recorded 1994.

⑧ ❾

This is a session that almost got away. It took place near the end of a short tour of Sweden by Hamburg-based Herb Geller and Jan Lundgren's Trio. Done in a small studio with an upright piano it was intended originally as a memento of Herb's visit but in Los Angeles producer Dick Bank heard a copy of the tape and immediately set the wheels in motion to have the music prepared for issue. Those who remember Geller's work from the fifties (**Darn That Dream** on Jazz Studio Two for starters) will be overjoyed to learn that his playing here is the equal – and often superior to – anything he has done in the past. That flawless and big, warm tone is heard on a dozen performances including the neglected George Shearing tune *Conception* and Lundgren, despite his comparative youth, knows them all. He leads a faultless trio which gives Geller just the helpful support a soloist of his stature has a right to expect. He has a knowledge of jazz tradition which belies his years and will certainly gain further acclaim when his work becomes better known, through records such as this and his own trio recording, **Conclusion** (Passport TCD521). In short this is a marvellous example of Swedish-American jazz co-operation.     **AM**

## Carmen Lundy

**Self Portrait**  Lundy (v) with a collective personnel including: **Gary Herbig** (f, ss); **Ernie Watts** (ts); **Cedar Walton** (p); **John Clayton** (b); **Ralph Penland** (d); orchestras arranged and conducted by **Jeremy Lubbock**. JVC Ⓕ JVC2047-2 (59 minutes). Recorded 1994.

⑥ ⑧

Lundy has a superb, richly-dark alto voice, great timing and perfect diction. She has chosen a goodly bunch of tunes to work out on here, and her selection of supporting musicians could hardly be bettered. Her approach reminds me occasionally of the young Abbey Lincoln, and from time to time the more arch and unappealing side of that singer's work can also be found in Lundy's delivery. It may not be coincidental that her best singing tends to come on her own material, where the collective weight of past interpretations doesn't have to be grappled with. That said, she makes a very fair pass at *My Favorite Things*, rarely associated in jazz with someone interpreting the lyrics; more with swirling saxophone flights. But then, the very fact that Coltrane has so dominated this song's jazz image means that Lundy has a pretty clear run at it. Watts takes a biting Brecker-inspired tenor solo on this track.

There is plenty to recommend: for one thing, the orchestra only crops up from time to time (I'm not entirely convinced she knows what to do with an orchestral accompaniment: she seems a touch unsure of her angle on a song when it oozes around her), and the trio is light and sure. Lundy only needs to deepen her interpretations to move up alongside the best of the current jazz vocal crop.     **KS**

## John Lurie

**New review**

**Men With Sticks**  Lurie (ss, as); **Billy Martin** (perc); **Calvin Weston** (d). Made to Measure Ⓕ MTM34CD (50 minutes). Recorded 1992.

⑨ ⑧

If evidence were needed of John Lurie's extraordinary talent, playing freely for 35 minutes with just percussion for company would be a daunting task for any of the world's leading improvisers. On *If I Sleep the Plane Will Crash* Lurie makes short work of it. Martin and Weston beat an intricate but steady rhythm, varying only in texture and intensity, and let the soprano saxophone do the rest. Shifting between strained sounding but perfectly executed split-tones, fast passages of false fingering that seem to lie somewhere between Evan Parker's solo work and **Stellar Regions**-period John Coltrane, and sections of delicate, fractured melody, shifting to the alto for the final, introspective six minutes, Lurie doesn't allow a single dull moment. The track is an unexpected masterpiece. The rest of the album is split between the much shorter *Men With Sticks (Noble Version)* and *Schnards Live Here*. After the extraordinary performance that comes before them one feels there might be little left to say. But the title track, once again working over a steady percussive beat, contains some fleet and attractive alto saxophone work. **Men With Sticks** is a free project with all the clarity and single mindedness to convert the sceptical and does Lurie's reputation no harm at all.     **LC**

# Nellie Lutcher

1912

**The Best of** Lutcher (p, v); plus trios made up from the following: **Ulysses Livingstone**, **Nappy Lamare**, **Irving Ashby**, **Hurley Ramey**, **Stanley Morgan** (g), **Billy Hadnott**, **Truck Parham**, **Benny Booker** (b); **Lee Young**, **Big Sid Catlett**, **Alvin Burroughs**, **Earl Hyde** (d). Capitol Ⓜ CDP8 35039-2 (53 minutes). Recorded 1947-9.

⑧ ❽

Nellie Lutcher, sister of r&b saxophonist Joe Lutcher, was born in the hamlet of Lake Charles, Louisiana, probably in 1912 (although Nellie herself claims 1915), and by the late twenties was already a proficient enough pianist to help out Ma Rainey when her regular accompanist dipped out of the show one night in Lake Charles. Her career stuttered along even after a move to Los Angeles in 1935, and she alternated between nightclub headliners and bread-and-butter sidelining until 1947. Considering that she was a contemporary of Ella Fitzgerald, Mildred Bailey, Billie Holiday and Lee Wiley, she had to wait a long time for her turn. When it came, however, her success was immediate. Her unique, coy, fun-filled voice, her occasionally *risqué* lyrics and her forthright piano style combined to win her an eager audience in both the US and Europe. For a period of two years after her 1947 signing to Capitol she could do no wrong and the vast majority of her best work stems from that time. In a sense she took over from Fats Waller in offering the listener an opportunity to come in on the joke she is having, leaving no barrier at all between herself and her audience, although her musical style and delivery is much closer to Nat Cole's than to Waller's.

That she was capable of more than teasing is made clear at regular intervals in her recordings, with *Cool Water* and *My Mother's Eyes* being resonant examples. Of these two fine songs, only the latter appears here (one of the two omissions which makes this a less than complete "Best of", the other key absence being *There's Another Mule in Your Stall*), but this compilation otherwise avoids blotting its copybook. The remaining hits and favourites are here, including *Hurry On Down*, *He's a Real Gone Guy*, *Lake Charles Boogie* and *Fine Brown Frame*, so this is by a very long distance the best Lutcher compilation currently available. It is also greatly helped by the fact that Capitol had in the forties one of the best studios anywhere in civilization at the time, and the transfers here reflect that fact. All in all, then, this is one not to be missed. **KS**

# Bobby Lyle

**Rhythm Stories** Lyle (kbds); **Larry Cohn** (syn); **Gerald Albright**, **Everette Harp**, **Kenny Garrett**, **Kirk Whalum** (s); **Michael 'Patches' Stewart** (flh); **Paul Jackson Jr**, **Dwight Sills**, **Ray Fuller**, **Danny Jacob**, **Carl Burnette**, **Peter White** (g); **Larry Kimpel**, **Reggie Hamilton**, **Marcus Miller**, **Stanley Clarke** (b); **Sonny Emory** (d); **Lenny Castro** (perc). Atlantic Jazz Ⓕ 782590-2 (59 minutes). Recorded 1994.

⑦ ❾

At first it seems that Bobby Lyle – noted for his arranging, instrumental and production work in the dance field – has here delivered another package of slick soul – rich in brassy, high-end tonalities and slamming, if clichéd, funk riffs. However, it becomes apparent before very long that substantial musical muscle is being flexed behind the glossy exterior. As the album progresses, he reveals quite a powerful conceptual imagination too, melding on *Funk Street*, for example, hip hop beats and bebop harmony. His good taste is confirmed by his choice of soloists, with sly harmonic tricks from Kenny Garrett on *Funk Street*, and, unexpectedly, from Everette Harp on *Don't You Know*. There's more unadulterated jazz, highlighting Lyle's occasionally Tynerish piano, on the Latin and swing *Anthem*. *B's Mood*, featuring the maudlin Kirk Whalum, might be little more than a farrago of mainstream soul gestures and *Tonight We Love* a similarly forgettable episode, but the banal material throws the good stuff into sharper relief, and it's the latter that remains in the mind. **MG**

# Brian Lynch

1956

**At the Main Event** Lynch (t); **Ralph Moore** (ts); **Peter Bernstein** (g); **Melvin Rhyne** (org); **Kenny Washington** (d); **Jose Alexis Diaz** (perc). Criss Cross Ⓕ 1070CD (58 minutes). Recorded 1991.

⑦ ❽

Brian Lynch's trumpet has graced the small groups of Horace Silver and Charles McPherson; he broadened this experience in the big bands of George Russell, Mel Lewis and Toshiko Akiyoshi and, most significantly, was the last trumpeter in the Jazz Messengers. In the early nineties he gained in reputation by filling the difficult space created by Tom Harrell's departure from the Phil Woods Quintet. The impression given on this CD is of a 'working' band; in his notes, Lynch talks of the jazz of his youth and the clubs that sired it. To endorse it, the orthodox hard bop of the 1986 album, **Peer Pressure** (Criss 1029 CD) is replaced by more functional 'club' music.

Rhyne plays an important part, his ensemble backgrounds being assured and his solos well articulated and buoyant. Moore plays with similar authority and Bernstein signals that he is an emerging talent. This is Lynch's album, however, and he is a confident and versatile player. His tonal quality is highlighted on *Cry Me a River*, his uncompromising attack is a feature of *Blues for Woody* and *Nite 'Vidual*. The extent of his improvisational ability is showcased in imaginative solos on *Ecaroh* and the title track, but throughout, his flair for logical thought and unpredictable delivery complements that for swinging. This is jazz from the nineties that provides a continuous link with the early sixties. **BMcR**

## Gloria Lynne

New review

**Miss Gloria Lynne ...** Lynne (v); **Harry Edison** (t); **Sam 'The Man' Taylor** (ts); **Eddie Costa** (p, vb); **Wild Bill Davis** (org); **Kenny Burrell** (g); **Milt Hinton**, **George Duvivier**, **Tom Bryant** (b); **Jo Jones** (d). Evidence Ⓕ ECD22009 (36 minutes). Recorded 1958.

⑥ ❽

Lynne enjoyed a career stretching over three decades after being discovered by and recording this album for the Everest label when that company was enjoying a relatively brief flirtation with jazz. Lynne's gospel roots are never too far away, being spelled out for all to hear on her version of *Without a Song,* made a hit a little later on by that other gospel-influenced singer, Ray Charles. But with a band boasting Jo Jones she has little difficulty swinging the rest of the repertoire, which includes chestnuts like *Perdido*, *Bye Bye Blackbird*, *April in Paris* (using a scaled-down version of the Basie arrangement) and *Stormy Monday*. That Lynne deserves the august company she keeps here there can be little doubt, her variant turns of phrase and her general rhythmic suppleness being a constant pleasure. She also understands how to use her voice effectively, eschewing the blowtorch approach of some singers of that time and opting for intelligent use of dynamics. Of the backing musicians Edison shines for his typically apposite obbligatos and swinging solos, while Eddie Costa is superb in everything he does. Sam Taylor, a driving saxophonist equally at home in the jazz or r&b genres and pitifully under-represented on CD, adds his persuasive voice at the appropriate moments. The rest of the cast contribute skilfully, though the session seems to have been unusually tough on bass players. In reissuing this old LP Evidence have reproduced the kitschy original sleeve, a classic of bad taste and artifice, fully worthy of preservation and just possibly an influence on David Lynch. **KS**

## Jimmy Lyons

1932-86

**Give It Up** Lyons (as); **Enrico Rava** (t); **Karen Borca** (bn); **Jay Oliver** (b); **Paul Murphy** (d). Black Saint Ⓕ BSR0087CD (45 minutes). Recorded 1985.

⑧ ❼

Jimmy Lyons spent 25 years as loyal collaborator-cum-interpreter to Cecil Taylor, whom he met in 1960 and in whose groups he then played until his death in 1986. During that period Lyons also led his own groups from time to time, though he made only a handful of records under his own name. **Give It Up** is the last and arguably the best of these, although its predecessor, **Wee Sneezawee**, runs it close.

The main appeal of **Give It Up** is that it is such a good group record. Rather than go for extended solos, Lyons sets up a series of animated conversations in which Rava's mercurial trumpet and the grainy cry of Borca's bassoon bob and weave around his propulsive alto in playful call-and-response chases. For all its busy surfaces, however, there is a broad seam of lyricism running through the music that is finally openly acknowledged on the closing *Ballada*, a passionate, singing elegy with distant echoes of *Parker's Mood*. Charlie Parker was Lyons's chief influence and it was through Lyons's alto – coursing, sinuous, bluesy – that Parker's rhythmic assurance was first translated into a freer context. **Give It Up** allows the listener to savour the tough-minded elegance which is Lyons's trademark. **GL**

## Johnny Lytle

1932-96

**The Loop/New and Groovy** Lytle (vb, ldr); **unknown** (p, b); probably **'Peppy' Hinnant** (d). BGP Ⓜ CDBGPD961 (70 minutes). Recorded 1966.

⑥ ❹

Lytle cut his musical teeth in his father's band in Springfield Ohio and as drummer with Ray Charles and Gene Ammons. When he switched to vibes in 1953 he moved inexorably towards dancehall-based soul jazz, backed by organ, bass and drums but occasionally working alongside Johnny Griffin or Frank Wess, and often with star sidemen like bassists Milt Hinton, Bob Cranshaw or Major Holley. He cut the two albums that comprise this CD for Tuba, a minor Detroit-based label, during the unparalleled explosion of small, independent soul record companies in the fifties and sixties. The fuzzy sound, the artificial echo, and the dreamy quality of the playing, especially on the medium-paced *Selim*, made the records a cult among jazz-dance enthusiasts, and before this reissue the originals had become expensive collectors' items. The legend, cultivated by rarity, is overstated on this evidence, but Lytle has a deft vibraphone style and a sound that is quite unlike Hampton, Jackson or Burton, though at times close to Bobby Hutcherson. This is unpretentious, straight-ahead rhythmic playing, with solos designed to entice the listener onto the dance floor. Standards like *The More I See You* and *Time After Time* are more rewarding than Lytle originals like *The Snapper* and *Possum Grease*. **AS**

## Harold Mabern

1936

**New review**
**The Leading Man** Mabern (p); **Christian McBride**, **Ron Carter** (b); **Jack DeJohnette** (d); on one track each add: **Bill Mobley** (t); **Bill Easley** (as); **Kevin Eubanks** (g). Columbia Ⓔ 477288-2 (62 minutes). Recorded 1992-3.

⑦ ❽

Mabern has been a professional for four decades and in that time has consistently commanded the respect of his peers, being an accompanist of choice for talents as diverse as Miles Davis, Roland Kirk, Wes Montgomery and The Jazztet. He himself places great store by being able to play the blues, get inside the blues form and play the soul of the music, like Charlie Parker and other greats of Mabern's own youth did. The leaders who hired him all understood the importance of that legacy, as did his mentor as a pianist, Phineas Newborn Jr. This album, like 1989's **Straight Street** made for DIW and later given release in the US and Europe by Columbia, shows him to be thoroughly versed in the full range of jazz tradition and capable of supplying appropriate music for whatever musical setting he has devised for the largely jazz standard-led repertoire used here. There are nods to Montgomery (*Full House*, a duet with Kevin Eubanks), Parker (*Au Privave*) and, as on **Straight Street**, John Coltrane (the much covered *Moment's Notice*, again a duet, this time with Christian McBride), while Wayne Shorter weighs in with *Yes and No*. Mabern has three of his own songs, where he shows his affinities with McCoy Tyner, but he is such a complete player that it is easy to admire him for the masterly touch he brings the music of his own accord. **KS**

## Cecil McBee

1935

**Mutima** McBee (b); **Tex Allen** (t, flh); **George Adams** (ts); **Allen Braufman** (as); **Art Webb** (f); **Onaje Allen Gumbs** (p, kbds); **Cecil McBee Jr** (elb); **Jimmy Hopps**, **Allen Nelson** (d); **Lawrence Killian** (pc); **Michael Carvin** (p); **Jaboli Billy Hart** (perc); **Dee Dee Bridgewater** (v). Strata East/Bellaphon Ⓔ 660-51-006 (45 minutes). Recorded 1974.

⑦ ❽

Having already made a name for himself in Detroit, McBee moved to new York in 1964. Since that date, a list of the leaders for whom he has worked would read like a who's who of contemporary jazz. Comfortable with bop, modal or free jazz, he has consciously served all with his special brand of bass skill, whether with finger or bow. This CD finds him at the helm of his own ship, playing his own compositions and with the personnel of his choice. Stylistically, the music comes from the New York loft scene of the seventies, committed to strong melodic lines but with soloists essentially free to exploit them as seems appropriate.

Cut in one day, the session was built around *Mutima (forces unseen)*. This title track is a well-structured work by McBee, evoking the spirit and culture of black Africa while allowing the solo roster free reign. Gumbs and the horn men make particularly ferocious progress on *Life Waves*, perhaps the archetypal loft jam number, and transform *Tulsa Black* from a funky languor to the mood of a free rambler with faked all-in passages to match. If proof of McBee's instrumental skills is required, it is to be found in the superb backgrounds of *Life Waves* and in his inspired 'duet' with himself *From Within*. **BMcR**

## Christian McBride

1972

**New review**
**Number Two Express** McBride (b); **Gary Bartz**, **Kenny Garrett** (as); **Kenny Barron**, **Chick Corea** (p); **Steve Nelson** (vb); **Jack DeJohnette** (d); **Mino Cinelu** (perc). Verve Ⓔ 529 585-2 (64 minutes). Recorded 1995.

⑧ ❽

The display of virtuosity came on McBride's first album for Verve done a year earlier. By the time of this recording he had been so much in demand that he had matured into a veteran and this is a better-balanced album which doesn't place the prime emphasis on bass solos. But it does help to have one of the best bassists in the world in the rhythm section and this album, which almost inevitably becomes yet another showcase for the modest but brilliantly accomplished Kenny Barron, makes a well-tailored platform for the soloists, with Bartz and Garrett coming out equal in the race for the saxophone laurels, although Garrett is only on two of the ten tracks. He is the more original player, with Bartz still holding strongly to the Coltrane line. McBride has, in addition to Barron, the luxury of three beautiful performances from Chick Corea, most notable on his own *Tones for Joan's Bones* and an ideal drummer in Jack DeJohnette. McBride continues to grow as a composer (five of the compositions are his) and writes an intelligent account of the music in the booklet, which otherwise has the apparently mandatory list of people whom the artist wishes to thank. He should do this in private, since it is no business of the listener's.                                                                                      **SV**

# Les McCann                                                                                          1935

**Swiss Movement**  McCann (p, v); **Benny Bailey** (t); **Eddie Harris** (ts); **Leroy Vinnegar** (b); **Donald Dean** (d). Rhino/Atlantic Ⓜ 272452-2 (48 minutes). Recorded 1969.

⑥ ❼

Born in Kentucky, McCann settled in California after leaving the navy and, armed with a Pacific Jazz contract, found that his rolling, bluesy piano style fitted neatly with the soul/jazz movement that was underway in the sixties. **The Truth** and **On Time** were typical albums as his version of the 'baptist rock' became a trademark. By the close of the sixties his popularity had overrun jazz's boundaries, and his new contract with Atlantic reflected that fact. This CD is a reissue of what was a best-selling album and includes an extra track, *Kaftan*, hitherto unavailable on CD. The line-up is impressive and their collective potential, at one of the biggest jazz festivals and in front of an enthusiastic audience, was unlimited. In the event, the outcome is mixed; Bailey injects personal spice into *Compared to What* and *You Got it in Your Soulness* and Harris gambols along in his usual manner on *Cold Duck Time* but the leader's work, not favoured by the recording, lacks its usual presence. His Fats Domino-type vocal puts across the social message of *Compared to What* but, although his solos on *Cold Duck Time* and *Generation Gap* take him on his churchified route, one finds oneself looking for more content. The set at Montreux was paced reasonably well, with the groovy ballad, *Kathleen's Theme* eliciting Harris's best playing of the evening, but a hastily designed set by a thrown together band often sounds just that. For a more complete picture of McCann's abilities we will have to wait for some of the better Pacific Jazz or Limelight albums of the early and mid sixties to be reissued.                           **BMcR**

**New review**
**On the Soul Side**  McCann (p); **Jeff Elliott** (t, flh); **Keith Anderson** (as); **Abraham Laboriel** (b); **Tony St James** (d); on one track each, add: **Eddie Harris** (ts); **Lou Rawls** (v). MusicMasters Ⓕ 65112-2 (63 minutes). Recorded 1994.

⑦ ❾

As with many successful artists, Les McCann has found it hard to move on from his fans' perceptions of him as the hip soul man of the close of the sixties and beginning of the seventies. His work today still incorporates similar elements, especially his marriage of gospel and soul harmonic progressions and his reliance on a solid groove in which to create his inimitable partterns, but he casts his stylistic net wider today, as this album shows. Tunes like *Back Rub* and *Ignominy* (featuring Eddie Harris) make it feel like old times again, with McCann digging deep into his sanctified bag, but *Early Riser* is a beautiful and sophisticated ballad, while *Vu Jadé* is unlike anything I've heard from McCann before, being more like some of Bud Powell's sombre pieces of the early fifties, or Miles with Wayne Shorter. His band on this album is well rehearsed and play with great spirit, adapting to the varied demands of the leader. This is a superior album as McCann discs go, which makes it very good indeed.            **KS**

# Ron McClure                                                                                       1941

**New review**
**Never Always**  McClure (b); **Don Friedman** (p); **Billy Hart** (d). SteepleChase Ⓕ 31355 (71 minutes). Recorded 1994.

⑧ ❾

The late Philip Larkin's collected jazz criticism takes frequent swipes at bass solos – they are boring, self-indulgent, and frequently inaudible, and often played by musicians markedly inferior as improvisers or technicians than those around them. No better proof of the wrong-headedness of this view could be found than in this trio, built around the bass playing of McClure, whose long list of credits begins with the famous Charles Lloyd quartet of the sixties and tends to veer in the direction of jazz-rock, rather than the relatively straightforward mainstream on display here. His own trio mixes standards and originals with a succession of pieces by other bassists including Gary Peacock, Miroslav Vitous, Red Mitchell and Paul Chambers, but most notably, Scott LaFaro, who has exerted a clear influence on McClure. The range and interest of the compositions suggest that a listener prey to the Larkin stereotype might also fail to realize just how a bassist's knowledge of structure provides the right ingredients to write impressive and absorbing music. LaFaro's *Gloria's Step* has Friedman and McClure interlocking phrases, nodding toward Bill Evans, but mainly showing McClure's ability to play lines that are genuinely pieces of collective improvisation without ever losing sight of the bass-line function. The tonal variety of Friedman's playing on McClure's album makes this a better than average piano trio: small group jazz with the bass in a prominent but responsible role.            **AS**

# Rob McConnell

1935

**Our 25th Year** McConnell (tb); **Arnie Chycoski, Steve McDade, John MacLeod, Guido Basso, Dave Woods** (t, flh); **Alistair Kay, Bob Livingston, Jerry Johnson** (tb); **Ernie Pattison** (btb); **Gary Pattison, James McDonald** (frh); **Moe Koffman, John Johnson** (f, cl, ss, as); **Eugene Amaro** (f, cl, ts); **Rick Wilkins** (cl, ts); **Bob Leonard** (f, cl, bcl, bs); **Don Thompson** (p); **Ed Bickert** (g); **Steve Wallace** (b); **Terry Clarke** (d); **Brian Leonard** (vb, perc). Concord Jazz Ⓕ CCD4559 (60 minutes). Recorded 1993.

⑥ ❽

When Canadian-born McConnell formed Boss Brass in 1968 it was a group without a reed section. They were added in 1971 and the band has gained in reputation since that date. They made their American début at the 1981 Monterey Jazz Festival and won a Grammy in 1984 with **All In Good Time**. This CD celebrates their twenty-fifth year and is typical of their work. The players are highly professional, the arrangements are mainly good, with *Imagination* the best here, and the solos are always up to an acceptable standard. The best individual efforts on this session come from the leader, imaginatively positive on *4BC* and *TO2*, Bickert, who has original ideas regarding *Broadway*, and Don Thompson puts his own decorative brand on Evans's *My Bells*. Basso, who basks in the comfort of the *Imagination* chart, is the pick of the trumpets, while Amaro is the best sax on view. Over-busy arrangements, such as those on *Nightfall* and *TO2*, are not the rule, but there are moments when the band's ability to swing is restricted. This is even missing on *Flying Home*, but with live dates being very different from recorded efforts, it could be that they do not fully respond to the studio. A similar judgement can also be passed on the recent **Even Canadians Get the Blues** (Concord). **BMcR**

# Susannah McCorkle

**From Bessie to Brazil** McCorkle (v); **Randy Sandke** (t, flh); **Robert Trowers** (tb); **Dick Oatts** (as, f); **Ken Peplowski** (ts, c); **Alan Farnham** (p); **Howard Alden** (g); **Kiyoshi Kitagawa** (b); **Chuck Redd** (d). Concord Jazz Ⓕ CCD4547 (60 minutes). Recorded 1993.

⑧ ❽

McCorkle is a singer whose shining virtues include the insight she brings to lyrics, the wholesome sexuality she projects, and her refusal to take gratuitous liberties with a song in the name of jazz. She first attracted attention for the excellent series of lyricist songbooks for Inner City and Pausa in the early eighties. None of these has yet appeared on CD. Her albums since then have been more eclectic in their range of material, and this has sometimes worked against them. Along with **No More Blues** from 1989, this is the most successful of her efforts for Concord Jazz. The Brazilian numbers are fairly lightweight, but McCorkle turns in winning interpretations of several standards, including Harold Arlen and Johnny Mercer's *Hit the Road to Dreamland*. What is more remarkable, she manages to make Rupert Holmes's *The People That You Never Get to Love* and Paul Simon's *Still Crazy After All These Years* sound like trenchant, modern, urban blues songs. Best of all, though, is her version of the Bessie Smith-associated *My Sweetie Went Away*, on which she evokes Bessie without resorting to caricature. *Thief in the Night*, which attempts to do the same for Ethel Waters, is less convincing because it is a little too reverential. The accompaniment provided by Music Director Farnham and the others is overcrowded enough in places to make you wish that Concord would acknowledge McCorkle's relationship to cabaret and record her with just a pianist. **FD**

# Jack McDuff

1926

New review
**The Honeydripper** McDuff (org); **Jimmy Forrest** (ts); **Grant Green** (g); **Ben Dixon** (d). Prestige Ⓜ OJCCD222-2 (38 minutes). Recorded 1961.

⑧ ❾

This is the second of two fine studio dates McDuff made for Prestige with Jimmy Forrest in the tenor role. McDuff may be better known for his wild sessions from around this time with Willis Jackson, Red Holloway and Harold Vick (such as **Live!** or **Hot Barbecue**, both of which have recently been reissued), but the two Forrest sessions, especially this one, are hard to beat for drive, flair and inventiveness within a relentlessly grooving *métier*. McDuff, once a pianist but persuaded by Jimmy Smith's success to swap to the Hammond B3, is famous for his burning, medium tempo grooves, and such pieces as *Whap!* and the title track, Joe Liggins's old shuffle-beat, *The Honeydripper*, threaten to wear your shoe leather out before they're over. Yet no one sticks to grinding out endless lines of licks and clichés, least of all Forrest, who is inspired throughout, generating great excitement but constantly avoiding the obvious or the banal. Green is more aggressive than usual, his tone fraying and distorting juicily on the harder groovers, while McDuff has a field day, whether supporting or soloing. While it is correct to stress the groove-juice qualities of this album, however, it would be a real oversight to neglect the more mainstream approach adopted for songs such as the moody *I Want a Little Girl* or the Henry Mancini number, *Mr Lucky*, where the sophistication of the musicians shines through. McDuff continues to record fine records in a very similar vein for a variety of labels today, but I doubt if he has ever bettered this one. **KS**

# Malcolm Macfarlane

**The Mulford-MacFarlane Group: Jamming Frequency** Macfarlane (g); Pete Murray (kbds); Phil Mulford (elb); Mike Bradley (d). Bridge Ⓕ BRGCD13 (59 minutes). Recorded 1994.

⑧ ❽

If anyone still wonders why good money is spent on jazz education they will find an answer in this musicianly and imaginative British fusion group, which is composed entirely of well-schooled alumni of the National Youth Jazz Orchestra.

The co-principles are both strong soloists, Macfarlane in particular working an attractive seam which ranges from clean, crisp Stratocaster lines to warm distorted tones, but like most fusion groups, the MMG places most emphasis on composition and arrangement. As well as essaying a variety of styles, from the mellifluous Metheny-esque samba of *Bar Italia* to the heavy-duty Scofieldian funk of *Mr T.P.*, the composers are careful to extract a broad range of texture, timbre and dynamic variation from relatively small forces, writing continuously evolving compositions rather than sketchy preambles to strings of solos. Thus instead of them appearing in dull sequential form over largely unvarying rhythms and textures, solos emerge as organic elements in ingeniously constructed compositions. This may seem an uncool constraint on the hallowed soloist, but for the listener it is a good deal more fun than a thousand unstructured blowing choruses. **MG**

# Bobby McFerrin

1950

New review

**The Best of** McFerrin (v) with various personnels including: Scott Weindholt (t); Bob Mintzer (bcl); Chick Corea, Herbie Hancock (p); Russell Ferrante (p, kbds); Judd Miller (syn progs); Paul Jackson Jr (g); Jimmy Haslip (b); William Kennedy (d); Paulinho De Costa (perc); Manhattan Transfer, Jon Hendricks (v). Blue Note Ⓜ CDP8 53329-2 (55 minutes). Recorded 1986-90.

⑦ ❽

McFerrin hit the popular music world's headlines when his *Don't Worry, Be Happy* was a hit on both sides of the Atlantic, along with the album **Simple Pleasures**, from which it had come. *Don't Worry* is included here, of course, along with McFerrin's other well-known single, *Thinkin' About Your Body*, originally located on the album, **Spontaneous Inventions**. McFerrin never really followed up commercially on the wave of popularity propelled by these efforts, perhaps worried by the implications for his artistic career: tellingly, his next release of consequence, **Play**, was a live duet album with Chick Corea which showed both men rising to the challenge of creating spontaneous variations out of each other's inventions. McFerrin has since moved to Sony, where he has been experimenting – to mixed results – with wordless vocals added to mainstream classical repertoire. Meanwhile, back at jazz station zero, Blue Note have decided it's time for a "Best of".

McFerrin has a clean and easy control of a voice with a wide range but not spectacular depth; he can move it around at will and give it sudden crescendos and decrescendos without wavering from pitch (he has a phenomenal ear) or losing his natural voice quality. His awareness of what is going on around him when he is in the presence of other musicians is made very clear during the tour around his Blue Note years here, and while the material from **Bang Zoom** is largely constructed as a passive support for his vocals, the extracts from **Spontaneous Inventions** and **Play** find him fitting seamlessly with his peers and colleagues, from Manhattan Transfer to Herbie Hancock. As far as career summaries go, this one covers McFerrin's jazz years pretty capably, although the two earlier Elektra Musician albums are also worth seeking out. The playing time is not exactly over-generous. **KS**

# Bernie McGann

**Ugly Beauty** McGann (as); Lloyd Swanton (b); John Pochee (d). Spiral Scratch Ⓕ 0010 (54 minutes). Recorded 1991.

⑧ ❼

McGann finally stopped being Australian jazz's best-kept secret when he played briefly in the US during the eighties, alerting the keen-eared there to a talent which, had it been settled closer to New York, would long ago have been accorded world-wide acclaim. As it is, McGann has been a first-rate altoist playing around the razor's edge of bebop and freer styles since the mid sixties, and he long ago evolved a personal mode of expression which makes both his sound and his angle of approach instantly recognizable.

This trio date, one of a lamentably few number of records McGann has made under his own name in a long career, gives him plenty of room to expound on the improviser's art and very few places to hide. Playing Monk without a piano, for example, is usually left to the likes of Steve Lacy, but McGann is completely at ease with *Ugly Beauty*. *Without a Song* was memorably covered by Rollins but here McGann fashions a set of personal paraphrases which recast the tune in his own image, while *Daydream*, long synonymous with Johnny Hodges, is approached from such a different angle, both emotionally and architecturally, that McGann pretty much reinvents the environment within which the melody exists. In all this he is helped enormously by Swanton and Pochée, both of whom have long been masters on their instruments. This may not be the easiest CD in the world to find (it will in all likelihood be a special import) but it is worth the bother.　　　　　　　　　　　　　　**KS**

# Howard McGhee　　　　　　　　　　　　　　　　　　　　　1918-87

**New review**

**The Complete Dial Sessions** McGhee (t); James D. King, Teddy Edwards, James Moody (ts); Vernon Biddle, Jimmy Bunn, Dodo Marmarosa, Hank Jones (p); Milt Jackson (vb); Arvin Garrsion (g); Bob Kesterson, Ray Brown (b); Roy Porter, J.C. Heard (d). Spotlite ⓔ SPJCD131 (69 minutes). Recorded 1945-7.

⑧ ❹

The last edition of this Guide carried a review of the deeply flawed Denon reissue of McGhee's Savoy sides of 1947-8, and suggested that his better playing of the period lay elsewhere. Since then Spotlite have effected their transfer of the old McGhee Dial masters to CD. These document McGhee's sensational form during his formative bebop days on the West Coast. Four 1945 tracks cut for Philo and later released by Dial feature two tenors (Edwards and King) trading punches, but the sound quality is poor and McGhee is jostling for room, leaving pianist Vernon Biddle to make the deepest musical impression. Two 1946 tracks recorded at the session made famous by Charlie Parker's collapse and subsequent nervous breakdown, and cut after Bird had left the studio, feature McGhee soaring thrillingly at manic tempos, demonstrating his full, bold tone and characteristic harmonic choices on standard changes. The trumpeter's last West Coast session for Dial was in October 1946 and featured a well-integrated quintet (with Edwards again on tenor and Dodo Marmarosa on piano) playing typically boppish themes. McGhee's playing is more identifiably using Gillespie as a model than is usual for him, but on the intriguing *Up in Dodo's Room* the unusual chord progression challenges him to a more typical improvised statement. The last ten tracks come from a 1947 New York date with James Moody, Milt Jackson and Hank Jones, and McGhee generates considerable excitement while being fired up himself by outstanding work from Ray Brown and J.C. Heard, both of whom are more adept at bop rhythmic nuances than their Californian counterparts. Anyone wanting to see why McGhee was for a while an alternative trumpet model to Gillespie, Davis and Navarro will get an unequivocal portrait of a vital talent from these sides.　　　　　　**KS**

**Maggie's Back in Town!** McGhee (t); Phineas Newborn Jr (p); Leroy Vinnegar (b); Shelly Manne (d). Contemporary ⓜ OJCCD693-2 (43 minutes). Recorded 1961.

⑧ ❽

Trumpeter Howard McGhee is one of the players who figured prominently in the transition from swing to bebop. Though he had studied clarinet, he fell in love with trumpet and started playing in mid-west territory bands in the late thirties. Following stints with Lionel Hampton and Andy Kirk, McGhee was ushered into bebop's inner circle by Dizzy Gillespie. A quick learner, he soon found himself playing with Charlie Parker as well as with Charlie Barnet and Coleman Hawkins. In 1949, Down Beat designated him 'Best Trumpeter'. Drug-related problems kept him mostly off the scene during the fifties, but when he returned in 1960, there was if anything a new maturity. His tone was more burnished, and while he could still dazzle with lightning licks, he was also willing to let the music breathe. Here, on one of his finest dates, McGhee is given hand-in-glove support by the amazingly inventive Phineas Newborn Jr and the supple, steady team of Leroy Vinnegar and Shelly Manne. With his full yet edgy tone and torrid technique ablaze, McGhee relentlessly pursues the blues in *Demon Chase*. He smoulders on the poignant *Willow Weep for Me* and *Summertime*, and flies passionately through fallen trumpeter Clifford Brown's *Brownie Speaks*.　　　　　　　　　　　**CB**

# Chris McGregor　　　　　　　　　　　　　　　　　　　　　1936-90

**New review**

**Live at Willisau** McGregor (p); Harry Beckett, Marc Charig, Mongezi Feza (t); Nick Evans, Kadu Malfatti (tb); Dudu Pukwana (as); Evan Parker, Gary Windo (ts); Harry Miller (b); Louis Moholo (d). Ogun ⓔ OGCD001 (66 minutes). Recorded 1973.

⑧ ❽

Chris McGregor and his fellow Blue Notes (Johnny Dyani, Mongezi Feza, Louis Moholo, Dudu Pukwana) settled in London in 1965, preferring exile to South African apartheid. Long a big band fan – "I love the colours and the energy flow of big groups" – McGregor's early idol was Duke Ellington. Later, after seeing Albert Ayler perform live in 1966, he was inspired to extend the big band tradition into freer areas. Brotherhood of Breath, formed in 1970, was the result: Blue Notes at the core, supplemented by a crop of the capital's more adventurous players. Recordings for RCA and Ogun in the seventies were followed by discs for In & Out and Virgin, these eighties sets showing a move towards what McGregor called a more 'African' sound that comprised lighter textures and tighter structures. This evolution was still underway when McGregor died in 1990, at the age of 53. **Live at Willisau** catches the Brotherhood in early, freer phase, a wildly exciting amalgam of fiery solos, rumbustious ensembles, gleefully stomping rhythms. McGregor's mission-school roots are audible in the hymnlike *Ismite is Might*; elsewhere melodic kwcla (*Tunji's Song*), neo-Ducal swing (*Kongi's Theme*) and carousing freeform (*Funky Boots*) jostle together in joyful profusion. The CD adds five tracks not on the original LP issue. **GL**

## Jimmy McGriff 1936

**Blues Groove** McGriff (org); **Hank Crawford** (as); **Wayne Boyd** (g); **Vance James** (d). Telarc Jazz Ⓕ CD83381 (67 minutes). Recorded 1995.

⑥ ❾

Organist Jimmy McGriff, who describes himself as a 'blues' rather than a 'jazz' player, is – whatever the nomenclature – an exemplar of the power of positive swing. With a gritty, toe-tapping approach falling somewhere between the virtuosic flights of Jimmy Smith and the r&b soulfulness of Booker T of the MGs, McGriff remains atop the 'chicken and chitlins' circuit with appearances that lift bandstands as well as spirits. Here, McGriff is joined at the bluesy hip by alto saxophonist Hank Crawford, a frequent and long-standing collaborator. With guitarist Wayne Boyd and drummer Vance James, McGriff and Crawford roast a savoury batch of soul jazz standards. Starting with the organist's *Movin' Upside the Blues* and ending with a churchy treatment of Joe Zawnul's *Mercy, Mercy, Mercy*, McGriff swings with an economy reminiscent of Basie. Indeed, he lets the music 'breathe'. In place of the customary B-3 preferred by virtually all the greats of jazz organ, McGriff plays Hammond's new XB-3, which replicates the sound of the no longer manufactured B-3 while adding an array of MIDI sounds which McGriff tastefully exploits. **CB**

## Kalaparusha Maurice McIntyre 1936

**Forces and Feelings** McIntyre (f, cl, ts, little instruments); **Sarnie Garrett** (g); **Fred Hopkins** (b); **Wesley Tyus** (d); **Rita Omolokun** (v). Delmark Ⓕ DE425 (55 minutes). Recorded 1970.

⑥ ❼

McIntyre was a founder member of Chicago's AACM in 1965 and appeared in concerts and on records with the likes of Roscoe Mitchell, Muhal Richard Abrams and Lester Bowie. By the end of that decade he was leading his own bands. This, his second album as leader (the first, 1969's **Humility in the Light of the Creator**, is also on CD) features his group, The Light; later in the seventies he worked extensively with drummer Jerome Cooper. McIntyre has never enjoyed the larger reputation his undoubted instrumental abilities deserve, but then the context within which he has normally worked has not been conducive to such acceptance as the aforementioned AACM colleagues gradually won for themselves. His work with this group tends to move in the world of 'happenstance', and everybody either plays flat-out or quietly together, with few instances of a contrast between fiercencss on one instrument and restraint on another. But then this was the time of freedom in jazz, as McIntyre's original booklet-notes vividly recall: "Wesley Tyus ... is highly underrated because of his approach to the music which is completely free, not undisciplined but universally free in the sense that he can do anything he wants to because he thinks with a system which is completely unorthodox technically but perfectly natural which makes him miles ahead of any percussionist I know." The point is worth debating, I guess, but it gives the reader a reasonable fix on what these musicians are up to. The singer's contributions, by the way, are as embarrassingly inept as one would expect from free music singers of this period. There are two previously unissued tracks here, *Behold! God's Sunshine!* containing lyrics which will transport you back to those long summers of love and smoke hazes. **KS**

## Ken McIntyre 1931

**Introducing the Vibrations** McIntyre (f, as, bcl, ob, bn); **Terumasa Hino** (t); **Richie Harper** (p); **Alonzo Gardner** (b); **Andrei Strobert** (d); **Andy Vega** (cga, perc). SteepleChase Ⓕ SCCD31065 (40 minutes). Recorded 1976.

⑧ ❽

In 1961 Ken McIntyre concluded that a teaching career made better sense than trying to survive as a full-time musician. As a result, his appearances on disc have been limited. He did record with Bill Dixon, Eric Dolphy and Cecil Taylor in the sixties and also played with Charlie Haden's Liberation Music Orchestra in the eighties and nineties. The best examples of his work currently on disc, however, are the five recordings he made for the SteepleChase label between 1974 and 1978.

McIntyre is not only a virtuoso multi-reeds player, one of the few convincingly to use oboe and bassoon in jazz contexts, he is also a distinctive composer whose tunes are full of surprising melodic and rhythmic twists. **Introducing the Vibrations** provides a fine showcase for his talents: *Shortie*'s quirky funk and the haunting *Clear Eyes* demonstrate his versatility writing, while his playing encompasses mellifluous oboe, acerbic alto sax (with traces of a Charlie Parker influence) and a keening bass clarinet solo that sharpens the poignancy of *Theme*. Guest Hino proves a sympathetic trumpet foil and the remaining 'Vibrations' are engagingly effective. Most of McIntyre's compositions here date from the fifties: someone should record his more recent material. **GL**

## Dave McKenna

1930

**New review**
**Easy Street** McKenna (p). Concord Jazz Ⓕ CCD4657 (57 minutes). Recorded 1994.

⑦ ❽

Some pianists excel as band pianists, others as unaccompanied soloists. McKenna excels in both roles, and has developed an individualistic solo style that serves as well in the hotel lounges and nightclubs which are a regular part of the lone pianist's lot, as on festival stages. His walking bass lines and deft right-hand figures are unexceptional until McKenna inserts a layer of chords between them, and just as stride pianists amaze the listener by popping a counter melody between the 'oompah' tenths of the left hand and the formulaic patterns of the right, McKenna seems to be able to keep his left hand in two places at once. He eases his way through ballads like *Street of Dreams* or the title track with a sensuous feel for where the lyrics should be, meanwhile storming his way through the up-tempo pieces with the swinging momentum that has made his band playing so sought after. He's been making records like this for nearly three decades and while there are occasional falters, the innate musicianship and taste in his playing carry the day. Unusually for McKenna, there are no medleys here (like Ralph Sutton, his live sets frequently include a medley that builds pace and excitement over several tunes); instead there's a McKenna trademark – a whole sequence of songs built around the 'street' theme of the title track – just as he might string together a club set. **AS**

## Red McKenzie

1899-1946

**1935-7** McKenzie (v); Eddie Farley, Bunny Berigan, Dave Wade, Jonah Jones (t); Bobby Hackett (c); Mike Riley, Al Philburn, Vernon Brown (tb); Slats Long, Sid Stoneburn (cl, ts); Forest Crawford, Paul Ricci, Sid Trucker (cl); Babe Russin, Dave Harris (ts); Adrian Rollini (bss); Conrad Lanoue, Frankie Froeba, Frank Signorelli, Raymond Scott, Fulton McGrath (p); Eddie Condon, Arie Ens, Carmen Mastren, Dave Barbour, Dick McDonough (g); George Yorke, Sid Weiss, Lou Shoubee, George Hnida, Artie Shapiro, Pete Peterson (b); Johnny Powell, Vic Engle, Stan King, Johnny Williams (d); Al Sidell (d, vb). Timeless Ⓜ CBC1-019 (69 minutes). Recorded 1935-7.

⑤ ❻

The early thirties saw the demise of the Mound City Blue Blowers and **1935-7** presents McKenzie's Rhythm Kings and Orchestra of the middle thirties. On the strength of his singing, it is unlikely that such music would have survived into the CD era. A natural baritone, he delivered the lyrics with punctilious accuracy, his intonation was good and his timing very much of the era. He sang the lyrics as if he meant them and he avoided both euphoria and unreal sadness. He was not, however, a jazz singer; he sang the songs as written and took no liberties with the composer's required cadence.

What makes this a worthwhile issue is the quality of the McKenzie sidemen. His comb/paper playing is not heard here but, in its original form, it was intended to imitate the trumpet part of the ensemble. Because of this, he enjoyed the company of good trumpeters and there is outstanding playing by Berigan on eight titles. Despite restricted space, there is also fine playing by Jones on two, Hackett on four and, the surprise, some lyrical Red Nichols-inspired work by Farley on eight more. The clarinet of Slats Long and piano contributions by Froeba and Signorelli are an added bonus and the spirit of **1935-7** is perfectly captured. **BMcR**

## Ray McKinley

1910-95

**New review**
**The Class Of '49** McKinley (d, v); Nick Travis, Larry Forand, Bill Hodges (t); Vern Friley, Dave Pittman, Irv Dinkin (tb); Bobby Jones (as); Harvey Nevins (as, cl); Bunny Bardach, Ernie Perry (ts); Deane Kincaide (bs, arr); Joe Cribari (p); Jim Thorpe (b); Paul Kashian (d); Eddie Sauter (arr). HEP Ⓕ CD4 (74 minutes). Recorded 1949.

⑦ ❽

Jazz discographies and reference books tend to ignore McKinley's bands after 1947 and, admittedly, his output for RCA in the late forties was hardly inspiring. This CD gives a rounded picture of the 1949 orchestra taken from two recording sessions done for radio transcription purposes, that is – under normal studio conditions. Although there are comedy or show numbers here (*Down the Road Apiece*, *Arizay*) there is also a lot of excellent big band jazz featuring soloists such as Nick Travis, the Bill Harris-like trombone of Vern Friley and tenor saxist Bunny Bardach. Best of all, perhaps, are the arrangements of Eddie Sauter (he wrote half of the numbers heard here) plus a couple by veteran

Dean Kincaide, who also takes a few baritone solos. Sauter's Borderline is cast in the Bijou mould and there are some flaring up-tempo swingers such as Pete's Cafe. There are some unexpected 'concert' arrangements by Sauter including an extended *Stardust* and a quite beautiful *Laura*, all of which help to put the McKinley band in its correct place in the pecking-order of post-war dance bands. **AM**

## McKinney's Cotton Pickers

**The Band Don Redman Built** John Nesbitt, Langston Curl, Joe Smith, Leonard Davis, Sidney De Paris, George 'Buddy' Lee (t); Rex Stewart (c); Claude Jones, Ed Cuffee (tb); Don Redman, Milton Senior, Jim Dudley, Benny Carter (cl, as); George Thomas (cl, ts, v); Prince Robinson, Ted McCord (cl, ts); Coleman Hawkins (ts); Todd Rhodes, Leroy Tibbs (p); Fats Waller (p, cel); Dave Wilborn (bj, g); Ralph Escudero, Billy Taylor (bb); Cuba Austin, Kaiser Marshall (d). RCA/Bluebird Ⓜ ND90517 (65 minutes). Recorded 1928-30.

✅      ⑧ ❽

With William McKinney as business manager, McKinney's Cotton Pickers came into being in 1926. In trumpeter Nesbitt the band had a fine arranger and he must take credit for the band's original musical personality. In 1927, however, the band took on Don Redman as musical director, and by the time they began recording one year later they had begun to develop a new identity. As this CD demonstrates, the band responded to Redman's charts with enthusiasm. Stomping performances such as *Crying and Sighing* and *Stop Kidding* were models of their kind, showing that the arranger had freed himself from the restrictions of section harmonies. The soloists were not the band's strongest point but Claude Jones, John Nesbitt and Redman do make some worthwhile contributions. While at the Greystone Ballroom in Detroit, their activities overlapped with the Jean Goldkette Orchestra and band members were occasionally interchanged. Redman was attracted to this practice and himself introduced Benny Carter, Coleman Hawkins and Fats Waller for guest spots on sessions that produced outstanding performances like *Miss Hannah* and *Wherever There's a Will*. The band's last recording was in 1931, and by 1933 it had ceased to exist. During its heyday it had been a band to stand comparison with Duke Ellington, and was seen by many as superior to Fletcher Henderson. Bill McKinney did try to keep a band of sorts together, but in 1941 quit the music business altogether. **BMcR**

## Hal McKusick      1924

New review
**Now's the Time** McKusick (as, bcl); with a collective personnel of: Art Farmer (tp); Frank Socolow (as); Dick Hafer (ts); Jay Cameron (bs); Eddie Costa, Bill Evans (p); Barry Galbraith (g); Milt Hinton, Paul Chambers (b); Gus Johnson, Connie Kay, Charlie Persip (d). Decca Ⓜ GRD651 (62 minutes). Recorded 1957-8.

⑧ ❼.

Though not considered a heavyweight instrumentalist the Massachusetts-born McKusick did combine the virtues of modesty, restraint, and intelligence. Most important, however, was the company he kept. Scattered recordings for Bethlehem, Prestige, RCA and Decca invariably included first-class sidemen like Farmer, Costa, Hinton, Galbraith and Evans. While his taste for the unorthodox may have resulted from the adventurous scores he played whilst a member of the Boyd Raeburn and Claude Thornhill orchestras, he probably also sensed an inability to hold his own among conventional blowing sessions. Thus McKusick sought colourful, out of the ordinary settings leaning towards chamber jazz for his cool musings and this led him to collaborations with arrangers like Manny Albam, Gil Evans and especially George Russell. In fact, most of this same line-up had recorded in 1956 (under Russell's name) such masterpieces as *Concerto for Billy the Kid*, *Night Sound* and *Ezz-thetic*.

The material on this reissue is taken from four sessions resulting in two LPs, **Cross Section – Saxes** and **Hal McKusick Quintet Featuring Art Farmer**. Russell contributes the stark blues *Stratusphunk* and two edgy, reharmonized standards, while other superb arrangements include Ernie Wilkins's suave blending of saxes on *Whisper Not* and Jimmy Giuffre's pessimistic *It Never Entered My Mind*, a frightening four-minute psychological portrait exquisitely scored for bass clarinet, muted trumpet, and Evans's rivetingly minimal piano commentary. Less interesting today are George Handy's pieces, with sometimes silly twists amid an innocuous swing and blithe sectional blending. The remaining seven tunes are simpler vehicles for Farmer's pungent playing across a rhythm section weaned on Count Basie. There's little tension to the blues numbers (Evans was not a blues player) and a few tunes approach the fluffiness that gave much of West Coast jazz a bad name. But there's still enough of interest here to keep McKusick's reputation alive and remind listeners of other successful dates, such as his **Jazz Workshop** (RCA), which included Russell's *The Day John Brown Was Hanged*, Gil Evans's *Blues for Pablo* and *Jambangle*, and other pieces of historical significance and lasting value. **AL**

# John McLaughlin

**Extrapolation**  McLaughlin (g); **John Surman** (ss, bs); **Brian Odges** (b); **Tony Oxley** (d). Polydor
Ⓜ 841598-2 (41 minutes). Recorded 1969.

✅         ⑩   ⑧

This, the Yorkshire-born guitarist's first album as leader, not only set the agenda for UK jazz-rock, but also showcased a composing and instrumental talent which would be of crucial importance on the US musical scene in the seventies, illuminating albums by Tony Williams, Miles Davis and Carla Bley and storming the citadels of both critical and commercial success as leader of the Mahavishnu Orchestra. Like the seventies work of UK-based composer-bandleaders Mike Westbrook and Mike Gibbs, *Extrapolation* is a beguiling and satisfying mix of jazz-rock with elements of freer jazz, but it is the truly original blend of McLaughlin's guitar with John Surman's superb baritone saxophone which gives the album its unique sound. The compositions range from relatively straightforward slow-burners, through the haunting 11/8 *Arjen's Bag* to feverish free-for-alls. Throughout, McLaughlin's angular clanging chords and blistering runs and Surman's tenacious virtuosity – twin flames constantly stoked by the perfect rhythm section of Tony Oxley and Brian Odges – mark this as one of the most accomplished and influential début recordings in jazz history.      **CP**

---

**Inner Mounting Flame**  McLaughlin (g); **Jerry Goodman** (vn); **Jan Hammer** (kbds); **Rick Laird**
(b); **Billy Cobham** (d). Columbia Ⓕ CK31067 (46 minutes). Recorded 1970.

✅         ⑩   ⑧

This album, officially released as being by the Mahavishnu Orchestra, could only have been McLaughlin's date. It is his vision, his intensity, his urgency and tortured lyricism which gives the music its character, and while drummer Billy Cobham plays so dazzlingly and with such an overwhelming density of sound that he made his reputation overnight from this one disc, he is always following the guitarist's lead. As such, this band has the same rhythmic fulcrum as most of the greatest jazz combos – that between the leader and the drummer.

There is very little music which carries the burning, steely intensity of this first album: utterly humourless and completely relentless, it demands total submission from the listener and is as wildly exciting as an uncontrollable adrenalin rush. On reflection, the joins in the music show a little, and the seeds of the group's eventual demise are present here, including their collective inability to write music which aspires beyond the episodic. But on this first album, these qualities are still part of the good things the group brought to the world, and are used to generate drama and rework the musical vocabulary: even the relative weakness of Jerry Goodman as a soloist in this context becomes a release from the power of the other players, and his sweet tone helps the ballads to involve the listener.

An album, then, which is very much more than the sum of its parts.      **KS**

---

New review
**After the Rain**  McLaughlin (g); **Joey DeFrancesco** (org); **Elvin Jones** (d). Verve Ⓕ 527 467-2
(57 minutes). Recorded 1994.

⑩   ⑨

In this inspired date of October 1994, McLaughlin pays tribute to the legacy of John Coltrane. Eschewing the ethereal *Angst* of his Mahavishnu days, and urged on by organist Joey DeFrancesco and drummer Elvin Jones, McLaughlin swings with modal abandon. Given the brooding intensity of McLaughlin's past work and the original versions of such Coltrane-associated classics as *Naima* and *My Favorite Things*, what is most surprising is the session's *joie de vivre*. Whether a ballad like *Sing Me Softly of the Blues* or a sleek burner such as *Take the Coltrane*, there's a palpable camaraderie which carries echoes of the Tony Williams LifeTime workout on *Big Nick* at the dawn of the seventies and which probably explains the glow of the guitarist's smiling countenance on the album's cover.

Another surprise is the session's lyricism. Even on Mongo Santamaria's *Afro Blue* and Ellington's *Take the Coltrane*, the impassioned playing unfolds along lithe, supple lines. This is music that breathes – yet another surprise given the capacity of guitar and organ to sustain one into infinity. Also appealing is the blend between McLaughlin's chorused-up guitar and Francesco's Hammond B-3 organ, a spatialized sound with pulsating depth. Aside from repertoire, the link to Coltrane is further tethered through the presence of Elvin Jones. Along with Coltrane themes such as *Crescent* and *After the Rain*, there are two impressive McLaughlin themes, *Encuentros* and *Tones for Elvin Jones*.      **CB**

---

New review
**The Promise**  McLaughlin (g, elg, kbds); **Jeff Beck** (elg); **Paco de Lucia, Al Di Meola, Philippe Loli** (g); **Joey DeFrancesco** (t, org); **Michael Brecker** (ts); **David Sanborn** (as); **Tony Hymas, Jim Beard** (kbds); **Pino Palladino, James Genus, Sting** (elb); **Yan Maresz** (b); **Mark Mondesir, Dennis Chambers, Vinnie Colauita** (d); **Zakir Hussain** (ta); **Nishat Khan** (sr, v); **Trilok Gurtu, Don Alias** (perc); **Stephanie Bimbi, Mariko Takahashi, Susana Beatrix** (v). Verve Ⓕ 529 828-2 (73 minutes). Recorded 1995.

⑨   ⑨

Apart from offering over an hour of virtually flawless music, this excellent CD functions simultaneously as a retrospective on the last quarter century of jazz (much of which corresponds to McLaughlin's own career) and as the culmination of a remarkable renascence for one of Britain's greatest jazz exports. That rebirth began with the Free Spirits trio of **Tokyo Live** and the same group is featured to great effect on the blues, *Thelonius Melodius,* in which McLaughlin demonstrates once again the rich fruit of intensive jazz woodshedding at the turn of the eighties. However, McLaughlin's bewilderingly fast guitar playing is only one component in a continuously revolving kaleidoscope of musical colours and it is this wide stylistic range, realized with the help of a cast of stars, which puts this record ahead of its predecessors. The itinerary includes r&b with Jeff Beck, bebop with the trio, a mini guitar concerto, eighties-style Miles funk and Spanish, Asian and chamber guitar recitals, but the centrepiece is *Jazz Jungle,* a demonic, hernia-inducing out-funk rave-up in which McLaughlin shows he is still more than a match for the hottest of New York crews, in this case one featuring Michael Brecker, Dennis Chambers, and James Genus. **MG**

# Jackie McLean                                         1932

---

**Lights Out** McLean (as); **Donald Byrd** (t); **Elmo Hope** (p); **Doug Watkins** (b); **Art Taylor** (d). Prestige Ⓜ OJCCD426-2 (46 minutes). Recorded 1956.

⑧ ❽

When this session took place both McLean and Byrd were already playing with the kind of assurance normally associated with older, more experienced players. In fact both were just 23 at the time (and bass player Watkins was only 21), clear evidence that they were destined for greatness. The album title takes its name from the fact that the long, eponymous blues was played with the studio lights dimmed in order to provide an increased atmosphere of relaxation. It certainly worked and *Lights Out* is a splendid performance, drenched with the blues feeling that hallmarked so much of Charlie Parker's work. This is living, vital music by determined young men and it still possesses the original urgency more than three decades later. There is little in the way of written, or even pre-planned, arrangements throughout the date, but the strength and quality of the solo playing is the major factor. The themeless *Lorraine* is actually an examination of the chords of *Embraceable You* with a few references to Bird's Dial versions. Watkins, who was to be killed in a tragic motor accident almost exactly six years after this session, shows just how fine a bass player he was and Rudy Van Gelder's engineering captures all the nuances of the music to perfection. The transfer to CD is excellent. **AM**

---

**Destination Out!** McLean (as); **Grachan Moncur III** (tb); **Bobby Hutcherson** (vb); **Larry Ridley** (b); **Roy Haynes** (d). Blue Note Ⓜ CDP8 32087-2 (35 minutes). Recorded 1963.

✔                                                        ⑩ ❿

McLean has enjoyed a long and illustrious career, but there is little doubt that his best and most original recordings were made during the time he was contracted to Blue Note. Apart from the outstanding appearances he made from time to time as a sideman on the dates of others, there is hardly a duff session from **Jackie's Bag** through to **Demon's Dance**, a period of close to ten years. Within that time-span is a sequence of ground-breaking titles, starting perhaps with **A Fickle Sonance** (1961) and including **Let Freedom Ring**, **One Step Beyond**, this title, **Right Now!** and **New & Old Gospel** (which had Ornette on trumpet and which recently reappeared on CD), where McLean was creating music in a new form and free from cliché, either that of the immediate past (bop) or the then-present (the so-called avant-garde). In a sense he was one of the key inheritors of the progressive banner from people like Mingus and John Lewis, using new structures, finding new subject-matter and creating new musical backdrops and textures upon which to improvise.

On this album, as on **One Step Beyond** (released on CD but now deleted), trombonist/composer Grachan Moncur III is the key collaborator, contributing three of the four compositions, while Bobby Hutcherson, also a hold-over from the previous session, gives the music his uniquely spare, flowing accompaniment. The crucial difference between the two records is the substitution of Haynes for Tony Williams (who had by then joined Miles's band). Williams brought a wildly exhilarating (and occasionally downright astonishing) concept of time-keeping to **One Step Beyond**, and Haynes, for all his accomplishment, simply cannot compete with that level of originality and inspiration. Still, everything else is as before, and although **One Step Beyond** would be the Basic Jazz Library recommendation if it were still available on CD, this is an entirely acceptable substitute. **KS**

---

New review

**Hat Trick** McLean (as); **Junko Onishi** (p); **Nat Reeves** (b); **Lewis Nash** (d). Blue Note Ⓕ CDP8 38363-2 (54 minutes). Recorded 1996.

⑨ ❾

Improvisation is by nature a slippery thing and greatness can be especially elusive – even to those who have proven their mettle countless times. Why is this the best Jackie McLean album since his classic Blue Note recordings of the sixties? Who can say for sure? It may have something to do with artistic indecision: how far to take the post-Ornette Coleman freedoms which spiced his most adventurous playing of that decade? Did time off to concentrate on teaching interrupt his creative evolution? Did inspiration flag as a result of less-than-challenging sidemen, or dull material, or even health problems? Not that it matters; the point is that over a near-30-year period McLean recorded a number of discs, some exciting and some dull, but none with quite the fire, intensity, and brilliance of this one. His biting, tart tone is still intact and he sets out like a man with something to prove. There are no other horns to get in the way, and in Onishi he's paired with a pianist occasionally reminiscent of his part-time partner, the late Walter Davis Jr – one who is capable of providing a solid harmonic framework as well as spinning off some fresh, oblique variations. The rhythm section is supportive, never showy. Among the tunes are some McLean classics (*Little Melonae* and *Bluesnik*), a couple connected to former employer Miles Davis (*Solar* and *Will You Still Be Mine?*), a witty Onishi original, blending *Sweet Georgia Brown* with echoes of Bud and Monk (*Jackie's Hat*), and a poised, moving tribute to Billie Holiday (*Left Alone*). Only a pair of misjudged, harsh ballads bring down the rating a notch. But throughout the programme McLean offers edgy, passionate solos with an individual attitude that separates him from Konitz, Desmond, Pepper or any other of his post-Parker alto peers. **AL**

# Rene McLean 1947

**In African Eyes** McLean (ss, as, ts, f); **Hugh Masekela, Prince Lengoasa** (flh); **Moses Molelekwa, Themba Mkhize, Rashid Lanie** (p); **Jonny Khumalo, Jonny Chancho, Prof. Themba Mokoena, Bheki Khasa** (g); **Bakhiti Khumalo, Fana Zulu, Vcitor Masondo** (b); **Sello Montwedi, Ian Herman, Lulu Gontsana** (d); **Jon Hassan, Papa Kouyate, Bill Summers, Zamo Mbuto** (perc). Triloka Ⓕ 203 195-2 (47 minutes). Recorded 1992.

⑦ ❽

Rene McLean would long ago have established himself as an individualist saxophonist if it were not for the fact that his father, Jackie, is still going strong and making fine music. As it is, Rene perhaps doesn't get the critical attention he deserves. This new album certainly shows that he is a careful musical thinker and listener, drawing as it does deeply from the well of contemporary African instrumental music. McLean recorded the album in Johannesburg, and many of the pieces on the date are from the backing musicians themselves. It is to McLean's credit that he went alone to this assignation and worked entirely with local musicians (Hugh Masekela is the exception, but then he came from there to start with), thereby not approximating the highly inflected jazz feel which African musicians create, but immersing himself within it.

The emphasis is very much on the ensemble rather than the individuals; although there are solos from McLean, his flügelhornists and pianists, they are made very much to fit into the fabric of sound built up around them. There are many felicitous moments to be heard in this long programme, but the most important overall conclusion is that this joining of two different strands of musical culture is a happy success. **KS**

# Jim McNeely 1949

**East Coast Blow Out** McNeely (p, arr); **John Scofield** (g); **Marc Johnson** (b); **Adam Nussbaum** (d) and the **West Deutschen Rundfunks Big Band**. Lipstick Records Ⓕ LIP89007-2 (53 minutes). Recorded 1989.

⑧ ❽

Best known as a one-time pianist in the Stan Getz Quartet, McNeely is also a music teacher of prodigious experience. His music is broadly in the post-Gil Evans-Thad Jones field and, like Mike Gibbs he weaves contemporary ideas into classic big-band pieces. His main weapon in doing this is the playing of guitarist John Scofield, a virtuoso with fundamental jazz values, who has also played a similar role to this with Gibbs. Both Scofield and Marc Johnson are somewhat larger than life in that they transcend comparison with other instrumentalists. McNeely's charts are long (three over 11 minutes and the other two over seven) and give Scofield plenty of scope to combine with the band. On this showing McNeely is as gifted at composing and arranging as he is at playing the piano. There is some refined writing for the band in *Skittish*, which features the three major soloists, and the WDR band interprets the scores with great precision and fire. An unaccompanied passage by Scofield, who plays with considerable vigour, culminates in a delicate entry by the band which typifies McNeely's discriminating creation of stimulating settings. **SV**

# John McNeil 1947

New review
**Look to the Sky** McNeil, **Tom Harrell** (t, flh); **Kenny Barron** (p); **Buster Williams** (b); **Billy Hart** (d). SteepleChase Ⓕ SCCD31128 (57 minutes). Recorded 1979.

⑧ ❾

Both of these splendid trumpeters served periods with Horace Silver's band and both subsequently worked around the New York scene in much the same company. So it is hardly surprising that there are many similarities in their styles and approaches, and this makes them excellent duettists. The opening number, *Chasing the Bird*, literally develops into a chase which ends in the two trumpets tumbling inextricably around for a chorus, and it is simply impossible to tell which is which. At other times, such as during the gentle *Look at the Sky*, their separate personalities come over strongly, with Harrell playing the smoother lines with a mellower tone. McNeil excels in the crackling, fiery, up-tempo, but there is little to choose between them when it comes to sheer quality. The gold-standard rhythm section performs with all the expected panache. In fact, the only let-down is the photograph on the back cover, taken at the session and revealing that flared trousers were still in vogue among New York musicians as late as 1979. This CD reissue of the original Steeplechase album has two alternative takes added. SteepleChase have also reissued another very good McNeil album from the same year, **Faun** (SCCD31117), in which he is partnered by saxophonist Dave Liebman.     **DG**

# Jimmy McPartland                                                       1907-91

**That Happy Dixieland Jazz**  McPartland (c, v); **Charlie Shavers** (t); **Cutty Cutshall** (tb); **Bob Wilber** (cl, ts); **Ernie Caceres** (cl, bs); **Dick Cary** (p, arr); **George Barnes** (g); **Harvey Phillips** (tba); **Joe Burriesce** (b); **George Wettling** (d). RCA Living Stereo Ⓜ 118518-2 (35 minutes). Recorded 1959.
⑧ ❼

McPartland was a cornettist whose style didn't ossify around early (and doomed) attempts to sound and play like Bix Beiderbecke. In this he was different from many contemporary white players, let alone the players who came to the fore on both sides of the Atlantic in the Revivalist phase of the forties and fifties. Indeed, when it comes to Dixieland, as opposed to trad (original or revivalist), it is Chicago, with its marriage of front-line polyphony and tightly arranged performances with a rhythmic thrust which is closer to swing than to classic jazz, from whence the major stylistic influence or thrust came.

McPartland shares the lead role here with Charlie Shavers, a self-confessed Armstrong worshipper whose bright tone, easy technique and imaginative variations help keep afloat this ramble through the usual repertoire. Pianist Katz contributed the arrangements, and they hover between recreating the Bix & Tram sound when Adrian Rollini was present and going for a more straightforward mainstream approach. McPartland himself plays cleanly and with a deal of fire, while the spacious stereo recording helps concentrate the listener's attention by giving clarity to the often quite dense lines woven by the group. McPartland's vocals come from somewhere between Jack Teagarden (phrasing) and Jimmy Rushing (range and timbre).     **KS**

# Marian McPartland                                                      1920

**Piano Jazz with Guest Bill Evans**  McPartland, **Bill Evans** (p). Jazz Alliance Ⓕ TJA12004 (60 minutes). Recorded 1978.
⑨ ❽

Marian McPartland, one of Britain's great gifts to American jazz, is a musicians' musician. Recognized as one of the New York scene's most accomplished and versatile pianists, her tenures at the Embers and Hickory House during the fifties and sixties are now the stuff of legend. During the past 15 years, McPartland has been busy establishing yet another facet of her outstanding career as host of the radio programme, "Piano Jazz". Whether sitting (and playing) opposite Dave Brubeck, Dizzy Gillespie or Eubie Blake, McPartland has proved an ideal intermediary, coaxing rare insights and performances from a who's who of jazz stars which continue to illuminate our understanding of jazz from a perceptive insider's position.

Thanks to The Jazz Alliance, a subsidiary of Concord Records, we now have access to a growing catalogue of "Piano Jazz" programmes originally aired in North America on National Public Radio. "What's really nice about the series," McPartland notes, "is that people who've wanted copies of the programme can now get them." Indeed, until released on CD, the Bill Evans broadcast of November 6th, 1978, was the most coveted of the "Piano Jazz" bootlegs. The programme typifies McPartland's congenial and informative talk and play format. In the Evans programme, as we learn something of the pianist's ideas on reharmonization, we hear telling examples in spontaneous performances of *In Your Own Sweet Way* (a stirring Evans-McPartland duet) and *Waltz for Debby* (a fascinatingly prolix Evans solo). McPartland's "Piano Jazz" is destined to be one of music's most valued documents, a living history told by those who played and lived it.     **CB**

**Piano Jazz with Guest Dizzy Gillespie**  McPartland (p); **Gillespie** (t, p). The Jazz Alliance Ⓕ TJA-12005 (57 minutes). Recorded 1985.
⑩ ❻

The eighteenth volume of McPartland's radio series arrived the day I wrote this; and Volume 5, with Gillespie talking and playing both trumpet and piano easily remains my favourite to date. Some listeners may prefer more music and less talk, although the real value of these shows is when historical and musical information is exchanged – and no one was more willing to share such knowledge (even with critics) than Dizzy. The deep intelligence and musicality that pervaded his personality and his life shine through here, offering an experience similar to any conversation Gillespie participated in where a piano was at hand. My guess is that the justifiably celebrated fourth volume, with Bill Evans, will receive the most choices; but anyone who has the **Complete Fantasy** Bill Evans boxed set already has that one. **BB**

**New review**

**Live at Yoshi's Nitespot** McPartland (p); **Bill Douglass** (b); **Glenn Davis** (d). Concord Ⓕ CCD4712 (71 minutes). Recorded 1995.

⑧ ❾

Few active musicians in jazz have a more catholic taste than Marian McPartland. On this typical club programme she includes tunes by Ellington, Monk, Parker, Ornette Coleman, Stephen Sondheim, Clare Fischer and a forgotten tune from 1935, *Chasing Shadows* by Benny Davis and Oliver Silver. Her regular "Piano Jazz" programme on National Public Radio has kept her in touch with the finest and most individual keyboard players (and allowed her to play duets with them) so her instrumental expertise is kept at a very high pitch. In fact it is this very consistency which sometimes results in her being under-appreciated. She is never off form, knows the right chords of thousands of tunes, works extremely well as soloist or leader of a trio and must be rated as one of jazz's best performers active today. The Concord catalogue contains many CDs by Marian, all of a very high level, and it is a matter of personal choice as to their selection. This one benefits from a good live recording quality, sensitive accompanists and a beautiful set of tunes (her interpretation of Ellington's *Warm Valley* is the best since Stan Getz's). **AM**

## Joe McPhee
1939

**Topology** McPhee (c, ts); **Radu Malfatti** (tb, el); **André Jaume** (ts, bcl); **Daniel Bourquin** (as, bs); **Irène Schweizer** (p); **Raymond Boni** (g); **Michael Overhage** (vc); **François Mechali** (b); **Pierre Favre** (perc); **Tamia** (v). hatART Ⓕ CD6027 (64 minutes). Recorded 1981.

⑦ ❽

McPhee did not take up the tenor saxophone until after his first recording on trumpet in 1967. From 1969 to 1971 he lectured at the Vassar College for Black Studies on "The Revolution in Sound" before transferring for some time to Europe. A series of records for the then Hat Hut label documented that part of his career and they highlight his progress on saxophone, with circular breathing, leg-muting and other instrumental devices to show what contact with the likes of Steve Lacy and Evan Parker had inspired. This CD from 1981 is the finished article, with McPhee presenting the full emotional range of his style on brass and reeds. *Age* is his excursion into a form of tenor terror, *Blues for New Chicago* takes his cornet into Roscoe Mitchell's sixties sound experiments, while the whole band's performance of *Pithecanthropus Erectus* perpetuates the Charles Mingus-held belief that every time a piece is played it should develop. McPhee's investigation of this Mingus classic is imbued with a friction-induced luminescence as the individual horns make their own brand of abrasive contact with each other. *Violets for Pia* is story-telling from the old school, while *Topology* is an acknowledgement of his regular trio's work. None is governed by a set series of rules, and they confirm McPhee as one of the most expressive and stylistically versatile of avant-garde musicians. **BMcR**

## Charles McPherson
1939

**New review**

**Come Play with Me** McPherson (as); **Mulgrew Miller** (p); **Santi DeBriano** (b); **Lewis Nash** (d). Arabesque Jazz Ⓕ AJ0117 (61 minutes). Recorded 1995.

⑧ ❾

A fine, reliable, post-Bird altoist with flashes of brilliance – that's McPherson, who came out of Detroit (a hothouse jazz community) as a hardcore ornithologist and developed a wider range of harmonic and rhythmic strategies due in large part to an extended tenure in the University of Mingus. His playing today – fluid, full of finesse, and eminently tasteful – is the result of three decades of experience on the ever-changing jazz scene. Thus on standard material like *Get Happy* or *Darn That Dream* he's resourceful and still finely calibrated, injecting passages of Mingus-like exhilaration, venturesome chromaticism, or even a smidgen of fifties r&b, with an authority and authenticity you don't hear in the younger neo-con players. His own tunes, including the mellow *Lonely Little Chimes*, a playful *Marionette* (not to be confused with the Billy Bauer tune) and the Caribbean lilt of *Pretty Girl Blues*, fall outside of hard-bop orthodoxy. So why isn't he better known? Maybe because of an uneven, sketchy recording career. This is a fine showcase for his talents and with pianist Miller supplying his usual excellent contribution it will hopefully make up for some of that neglect. **AL**

## Carmen McRae
1922-94

**Here to Stay** McRae (v); with various personnel including: **Billy Strayhorn**, **Dick Katz** (p); **Herbie Mann** (f); **Mundell Lowe** (g); **Wendell Marshall** (b); **Kenny Clarke** (d); **Ernie Wilkins Orchestra**

with **Jimmy Maxwell**, **Richard Williams**, **Ernie Royal** (t); **Jimmy Cleveland**, **Billy Byers** (tb); **Phil Woods** (as); **Zoot Sims**, **Budd Johnson** (ts). MCA/Decca Ⓜ 16102 (53 minutes). Recorded 1955-9.

⑧ ❾

Beginning her career with Benny Carter in 1944, McRae later sang with Count Basie and Mercer Ellington. She had a spell as intermission singer at Minton's Playhouse and made her début as a leader in 1954. This CD includes some of her finest work and finds her dovetailing well with Wilkins's fine big-band arrangements, sitting comfortably with her own quartet, and overcoming bizarre instrumentation (flute and accordion included) to make *Yardbird Suite* one of her more memorable performances. As befits a devoted Billie Holiday fan, she is a naturally inventive singer. Her muscular delivery can sometimes have the 'caged animal' intensity found in *It's Love*, but this is contrasted by *Supper Time*, a heartfelt rendition in which her jazz artistry is perfectly balanced with the meaning of the lyrics. Her control at slow tempos is exemplary and her easy vibrato adds warmth to all performances. It is interesting to hear how even the opening theme statements are slightly modified and given different points of emphasis. Her improvisations never become too tortuous, however, and they are certainly free from the rhetorical excesses that confuse the work of some singers. More was to be heard of her clever scat singing later in her career, but by 1959 she was already the finished article, as this CD attests. **BMcR**

---

**The Great American Song Book** McRae (v, p); **Jimmy Rowles** (p); **Joe Pass** (g); **Chuck Domanico** (b); **Chuck Flores** (d). Atlantic Jazz Ⓜ 7-81323-2 (72 minutes). Recorded 1970.

✓

⑧ ❽

Considering how well she succeeds with her material it is perhaps surprising to note that Miss McRae has neither a big range nor a beautiful voice. Most singers have one or the other or, in the case of the Ellas and Sarahs, both. So Miss McRae on paper is no match for Peggy Lee or Anita O'Day.

Happily she doesn't sing on paper, and her talents for sound and imaginative improvisation are what sell her recordings. Her voice is unbeautiful in a way that Charlie Parker's alto tone was (when compared with Hodges or Jefferson). She made a direct bridge between the singing of Billic Holiday and the harmonic innovations of bebop and this makes her a singer who gets deeply into her material rather than just adding a veneer to it. More than any other vocalist she extemporizes like an instrumental and, unlike most 'instrumental' singers, her work is not flawed by artifice or histrionics. This generous collection puts her in a crucible with the sparest but most accomplished setting any singer could ask for. Rowles was as good an accompanist as any and a distinguished improviser. Those qualities were also present in the work of Joe Pass, whose cushion for the singer on *What Are You Doing for the Rest of Your Life?* is perfectly conceived. It is unlikely that McRae ever recorded a better collection than this one, done live in Los Angeles. She certainly never received better backing. **SV**

---

**Carmen Sings Monk** McRae (v); **Clifford Jordan**, **Charlie Rouse** (ts); **Eric Gunnison**, **Larry Willis** (p); **George Mraz** (b); **Al Foster** (d). RCA Novus Ⓔ 3086-2 (66 minutes). Recorded 1988.

⑧ ❽

Thelonious Monk's music places a special burden on improvisers; generally interpreters lean toward Monk's angularity and blocky harmonies in order to integrate the written and improvised parts of a performance. McRae goes against the grain, emphasizing the beauty of Monk's melodies. About half the selections are ballads, including *'Round Midnight*, *Ruby, My Dear* and *Ask Me Now*. She makes it work; at age 66, her voice was surprisingly limber, heavier but no less pleasing than in the fifties.

The two pianists do not imitate the composer, taking their stylistic cues from the leader's smooth approach. McRae's effective foils are tenor saxists Charlie Rouse, a Monk sideman for over a decade (he is on two live cuts), and Clifford Jordan, who was playing exceptionally well in the eighties, and whose dramatic use of space and silence suggests how much he learned from Monk. Between Jordan's elliptical improvising and McRae's sensitivity to the composer's melodies, they do Monk justice.

The lyrics, by Jon Hendricks, Abbey Lincoln and others, are not in Monk's league; you don't mind that McRae slurs a few words. But the lyrics are good for one thing. Even Monk fans have trouble remembering which melody goes with which title; this disc enables you to learn the names of 14 of them. **KW**

# Jay McShann

1909

---

**Blues from Kansas City** On three tracks **McShann and His Orchestra**: **McShann** (p) **Harold Bruce**, **Bernard Anderson** (t); **Joe Baird** (tb); **Charlie Parker**, **John Jackson** (as); **Bob Mabane**, **Harry Ferguson** (ts); **Gene Ramey** (b); **Gus Johnson** (d); **Walter Brown** (v); on three tracks **Jay McShann Trio**: **McShann** (p); **Gene Ramey** (b); **Gus Johnson** (d); **Walter Brown** (v); on eight tracks add **Leonard Enois** (g); on seven tracks **Jay McShann Orchestra**: **McShann** (p); plus: **Bob Merrill**, **Jesse Jones**, **Willie Cook** (t); **Alonzo Pettiford**, **Alfonso Fook**, **Lawrence Anderson** (tb); **Rudy Jackson**, **Rudolph Dennis** (as); **Paul Quinichette**, **Fred Culliver**, **Bill Goodman** (ts); **Rae Brodely** (bs); **Leonard Enois** (g); **Gene Ramey** (b); **Dan Graves** (d). MCA/Decca Ⓜ GRP16142 (61 minutes). Recorded 1941/2.

⑦ ❻

The three tracks which the McShann band made while Charlie Parker was with them guaranteed its immortality. They also somewhat distorted the legacy which McShann's aggregation had to offer, for this was indeed a band straight out of the Basie and Kansas City tradition, and Parker at this stage was very much under the spell of Lester Young. What Parker went on to become has made these brilliant examples of Kansas City-style blues and swing into some form of harbinger of bop. They may be, but hindsight is a wonderful thing, and they sound more like backward glances at a tradition which was already fading. Just how conservative McShann was is indicated by the long string of small-group sides which follow *Swingmatism*, *Hootie Blues* and *Dexter Blues*. This is a cross between the Basie quartet sides for Decca and an Albert Ammons or Pete Johnson boogie date, with vocals from Walter Brown to match.

McShann was and is a capable pianist with a fine swing beat in both hands. His band plays straightforward arrangements of simple tunes, almost invariably blues-based and often with a shuffle beat from the drums. The small-group sides could do with another horn to liven things up a little, especially as the ubiquitous Walter Brown was hardly the most inspired of blues vocalists. What the later band represented here desperately needed was what Basie had in abundance: fine soloists. Parker had moved on and McShann would not progress without him. **KS**

# Jack McVea                                                                    1914

**Two Timin' Baby**  McVea (as, ts); **Cappy Oliver, Jesse Perdue, Sammy Yates, Russell Jacquet, Joe 'Red' Kelly** (t); **Melba Liston** (tb); **Marshall Royal** (cl); **Wild Bill Moore** (ts); **Bob Mosley, John Shackleford, Call Cobbs, Tommy Kahn** (p); **Irving Ashby, Gene Phillips** (g); **Frank Clarke** (b); **Rabon Tarrant** (d, v). Jukebox Lil Ⓕ RBD612 (48 minutes). Recorded 1944-7.

⑥ ❻

McVea was a competent saxophonist, arranger and bandleader who appeared at the first Jazz-at-the-Philharmonic concerts in 1944 and whose early recording career, in the second half of the forties, was shaped by the demands of the Californian record industry. Independent labels with low budgets found him a reliable and craftsmanlike producer of small-group blues, boogies and novelty numbers patterned on more successful contemporaries like Louis Jordan. McVea was sometimes able to commission names like Marshall Royal or Maxwell Davis, who arranged *House Party Boogie,* but most of his work was done with a core of little-known journeyman players like pianist Kahn and drummer Tarrant, the featured blues-singer on about half the tracks here. The general effect is similar to that of local contemporaries like Roy Milton and Joe Liggins. *Bulgin' Eyes,* a brisk if formulaic jump number, scores a few more jazz points than usual. The earlier and slightly better collection, **Open the Door Richard** (Jukebox Lil JB-607), has not yet been transferred to CD. At last report, McVea was playing clarinet in a strolling band at Disneyland. **TR**

# Teo Macero                                                                   1925

New review
**Teo  Macero** (ts); **Teddy Charles** (vb); **Mal Waldron** (p); **Addison Farmer** (b); **Jerry Segal** (d). Prestige Ⓜ OJCCD1715-2 (37 minutes). Recorded 1957.

⑤ ❻

Macero's name has become so closely associated with Miles Davis, through his quarter-century as Davis's trusted record producer, that his own considerable body of work is largely unknown. He was a close associate of Charles Mingus in the Jazz Composers' Workshop and a moving spirit, along with Gunther Schuller, in the Third Stream movement, which set out to fuse elements of jazz and European classical music. This subdued set with the Prestige Jazz Quartet (same line-up as the then all-conquering Modern Jazz Quartet) represents only a tiny segment of a busy and varied creative life. The notes list him as playing only tenor saxophone, but there are moments when it sounds uncannily like an alto, not merely in pitch but also in timbre. His approach is clearly based on early Stan Getz, but with more angular phrasing and a tone that is, if anything, even paler and more piping. The six original tunes, by members of the group, are all slightly abstract variations on the American ballad, quite attractive in a chilly kind of way. This was the jazz avant-garde of 1957 and is of mainly historical interest today. **DG**

# Kevin Mahogany

New review
**You Got What It Takes**  Mahogany, **Jeanie Bryson** (v); **Benny Golson** (ts); **James Williams** (p); **Michael Formanek** (b); **Victor Lewis** (d). Enja Ⓕ ENJ9039-2 (55 minutes). Recorded 1995.

⑦ ❾

It sounds too good to be true, but Mahogany is his real name and it suits his voice to perfection. Its timbre is deep, rich and solid, reminiscent of the young Joe Williams. Now aged 37, Mahogany has matured impressively and with this, his third CD, establishes himself among the finest contemporary jazz singers. His taste in material is adventurous and he approaches each song with a lightness of

touch which some of his contemporaries would do well to emulate. I would also recommend
Mahogany's 1993 Enja CD **Double Rainbow**.                                              **DG**

# Mike Mainieri                                                                    1938

**New review**

**An American Diary** Mainieri (vb, MIDI-v, mba, xyl, p, chimes, whistle); **Joe Lovano** (ss, ts, acl);
   **Eddie Gomez** (b); **Peter Erskine** (d, perc). NYC Ⓕ 6015-2 (67 minutes). Recorded 1994.

⑧ ❾

Although he was professional by the mid fifties (**Playtime**, a recent reissue on Charly Le Jazz 47,
has him playing accomplished bop vibes with the 1960 Buddy Rich Septet), Mike Mainieri is now
most often associated with the sometimes very commercial fusion of Steps Ahead. This intriguing
session is something of a departure then, since it explores the esoteric realms usually occupied by
Mainieri's fellow vibists Gary Burton (notice the Burton-style bent notes on the jazzed-up reading
of Roger Sessions's *Piano Sonata No. 1*) and Bobby Hutcherson. Mainieri says that the project
stems from the musical dualism he developed as a youth in a household split between 'longhairs'
and 'jazzers' (a divide far less imaginable now that jazz has almost emptied the classical library in
its search for new expression). The resulting 'diary' integrates those opposing forces by turning
pieces by American composers such as Copland, Sessions, Bernstein and Barber into jazz vehicles,
but it also recognizes Frank Zappa (*King Kong*) and includes some suitably idiomatic pieces by
group members. Those who have long held that Mainieri is one of the most talented and versatile
vibists of his generation will not be surprised to learn that like art-jazz master Lovano he handles
this generally abstract material with great flair.                                      **MG**

# Bob Malach

**Mood Swing** Tom Harrell (t); **Bob Malach** (ts); **Bob Mintzer** (bcl); **Russ Ferrante** (kbds); **Dr John**
   (p, v); **Robben Ford** (elg); **Eddie Gomez** (b); **Will Lee** (clb); **Vinny Colaiuta**, **Charley Drayton**, **Steve
   Gadd** (d). Go Jazz R Ⓕ vBr 2045 2 (59 minutes). Recorded 1990.

⑧ ❽

Bob Malach is one of the least exposed of the New York school of white post-Coltrane tenor
saxophonists typified by such players as Michael Brecker, Bob Mintzer and Bob Berg. Here his
pared-down version of the Brecker style receives a long-deserved airing in a programme which
reflects his interest in a wide variety of music, from New Orleans r&b to the semi-swing of Bob
Mintzer's *Mr Fone Bone* and Russ Ferrante's *Whistle While You Walk*. His versatility is illustrated
by his equal ease with the Latin modalism of *In Your Eyes*, which prompts some skilfully handled
polytonal Traneisms, and the unashamed bar-room sentimentality of his duo with Dr John on *I'm
True*, where he proves the perfect accompanist, embellishing the vocal with taste and sensitivity.
The supporting cast are faultless, though it would have been nice to have heard more from Tom
Harrell, who is inexplicably limited to a brief but finely wrought obbligato on *In Your Eyes*. On
one level this may appear as easy listening jazz, but the wide range of mood and strong playing
give it a seductive appeal.                                                              **MG**

# Radu Malfatti

**Ohrkiste** Malfatti (tb); **Reiner Winterschladen** (t); **Martin Mayes** (flh); **Melvyn Poore** (tba); **John
   Butcher** (ss, ts); **Wolfgang Fuchs** (bcl); **Peter Van Bergen** (cl, bcl); **Phil Wachsmann** (vn); **Karri
   Koivukoski** (va); **Alfred Zimmerlin** (vc); **Wolfgang Güttler** (b); **John Russell** (g); **Fred Van Hove** (p).
   ITM Ⓕ 950013 (74 minutes). Recorded 1992.

❾ ❽

Note that there is no drummer among the 13-piece ensemble listed above – it is one indication that
Radu Malfatti's music is less concerned with controllable tempos or regularity of pulse than with
sounds that breathe at irregular intervals. A well-travelled veteran in European and British free music
circles (ranging from a trombone/bass duo with the late Harry Miller to participation in Brotherhood
of Breath), Malfatti has assembled an impressive body of like-minded improvisers who follow his
scores through varied compositional instructions if not strict notation, and their selflessness on behalf
of such indeterminate events is convincing and gratifying. The result is music of gradual growth, terse
details and silences filled with often unrecognizable colours and forms – everything is a surprise. The
two long multi-sectional works (*Notes* and *Graukanal*) create a marvellously intense, dynamically
modulated tension between unpredictable improvisational gestures and compositional direction and
unity. More chamber music ensemble than traditional big band, the instrumentation, although
sectionalized (reed trio, brass quartet, string quartet, guitar and piano), belies such rigid
compartmentalization; the fluid, amorphous sound mass may be closer in character and spirit to
music from composers like Ligeti, Xenakis and Varèse than Ellington or even Gil Evans.
Comparisons aside, this is difficult but fascinating, frequently magical music.          **AL**

# Russell Malone

1963

**Black Butterfly** Malone (g); **Gary Motley** (p); **Paul Keller** (b); **Peter Siers** (d); on two tracks add **Steve Nelson** (vb). Columbia Ⓕ 474805-2 (63 minutes). Recorded 1993.

⑦ ❾

This, Malone's second album for Columbia, is a fair-sized advance on the first, where he spread himself too far and too thinly, playing many different types of guitars and musical styles and completely filling every crevice in the music with himself. **Black Butterfly** sees no dropping back from previous playing standards but a considerable increase in musicality and maturity. Malone, late of Harry Connick Jr's band among others, has incredible chops, as he demonstrates on Wes Montgomery's *Jingles*, taken at a ferocious tempo which he stays completely on top of. But as with George Benson, speed is not the only requirement for a complete technique, and the easy medium-tempo stroll of *Kenny* (after Kenny Burrell) finds the guitarist capable of relaxed invention. Pianist Motley is given a chance to shine on Enrico Pieranunizi's *Dee's Song*, and Malone delivers an intense, hushed portrait of his young daughter on *After Her Bath*. Malone is a stylist without being the creator of a new style, but within those parameters he is exceptional. **KS**

# Junior Mance

1928

**Junior Mance Trio at the Village Vanguard** Mance (p); **Larry Gales** (b); **Ben Riley** (d). Riverside Ⓜ OJCCD2042 (43 minutes). Recorded 1961.

⑦ ❽

Discounting purely generic players, Junior Mance is about as much of a blues pianist as anyone in jazz (though there was a time when Ray Bryant could have given him a good tussle for the title). Later albums have illustrated more fully the span of his abilities, but they have seldom, if ever, captured the effervescence and young man's bullishness of this début appearance at the famous New York club. Though only one tune-title (*Smokey Blues*) admits it, blues form and blues feeling are spread over this record like a mulch, from the rocketing opener, *Looptown*, through Johnny Griffin's *63rd Street Theme* to the Basie band's *9.20 Special*. Even *Girl of My Dreams*, a dance-band tune from the twenties that Mance picked up from his one-time employer Dizzy Gillespie, rocks to a beat that Louis Jordan might have counted off. Mance's trenchant phrasing, crisp attack and fondness for soulful figures lend this record a precise location in time and style, close to the contemporary work of Horace Silver and cheek-by-jowl with that of Cannonball Adderley, whose first band Mance worked with for almost two years. The 1980 trio session **Smokey Blues** (JSP CD219) can also be recommended for a quieter display of many of the same characteristics. **TR**

# Joe Maneri

1927

**Three Men Walking** Maneri (reeds); **Mat Maneri** (elvn); **Joe Morris** (elg). ECM Ⓕ 531 023-2 (67 minutes). Recorded 1995.

⑦ ❾

The music of New Yorker Joe Maneri represents a meeting place for the theories of Schoenberg and Berg, free jazz and the routine 'day-job' business of wake, bar mitzvah and social intercourse. Maneri wrote a piano concerto for the Boston Symphony in 1960 and in 1965 worked with Gunther Schuller in an Ornette Coleman dedication at Carnegie Hall. He became theory and composition professor at the New England Conservatory in 1970, has written a book on microtonal studies but, since the mid-eighties, has been increasingly involved in his own specialized brand of jazz. In eliminating the bass and drums, used on the excellent **Get Ready to Receive Yourself** (Leo Lab CD010), this album has further highlighted the linear aspect of his music. The listener's instruction course is, on this occasion, provided by the standard *What's New* and the way in which the Haggart/Burke classic is ushered into microtonal territory is illuminating. The remainder of the titles are by members of the trio and these men all sing from the same hymn sheet. Joe's approach to all of his horns is similar, although his tenor takes him nearer to orthodoxy and his alto tends to swing more lightly. It is his clarinet, however, superb on *Calling*, *Let Me Tell You* and the title track, that shows the full value of the man. **BMcR**

# Mat Maneri

**In Time** Maneri (elvn); **Panis Karayorgis** (p). Leo Lab Ⓕ 002 (62 minutes). Recorded 1993.

⑧ ❽

Thanks to the New England Conservatory of Music, the Berklee School of Jazz and other academies of higher learning, the Boston area has long been a training ground for young musicians. Maneri and Karayorgis exemplify the city's free-thinking experimental contingent, exhibiting musical maturity and ability far beyond their years. Attracted initially to the Tristano legacy of harmonically deceptive linear improvisation, Karayorgis adds the elliptical phrasing and rhythmic irregularity of Monk for a style refreshingly free of swing or bop clichés. Maneri is the son of the unjustly neglected saxophonist and microtonal tactician, Joe Maneri; his plugged-in violin can sound dark and rich as a cello or offer a feathery evanescence that enhances his oblique sense of tonality. Their duo is based upon responsive support and an almost telepathic interaction, with a wealth of fascinating melodic details emerging from sparse, halting, wildly chromatic manoeuvres. Conventional swing attitudes don't apply here; they substitute an introspective ebb and flow of delicately etched, exquisitely proportioned ideas that are often left unresolved, hanging in the air like unanswered questions. The danger is that their dialogue might be heard as mumbling, their subtlety as solipsistic. But even if Maneri's moody *Blue Seven* will never be confused with Rollins's classic of the same name, the two hauntingly deconstructed versions of Monk's *Ugly Beauty* illustrate their ingenuity and sincerity. **AL**

# Albert Mangelsdorff                                                    1928

New review

**Three Originals** Mangelsdorff (tb); **Heinz Sauer** (ts, as); **Wolfgang Dauner** (p); **Gunter Lenz, Eddie Gomez, Leon Francioli** (b); **Ralf Hübner, Elvin Jones** (d). MPS Ⓜ 529090-2 (two discs: 134 minutes). Recorded 1970-82.

⑧ ❽

Mangelsdorff came to prominence in Germany in the early fifties as an outstanding J.J. Johnson stylist. After touring Asia in 1964 he became increasingly involved with the free movement in jazz. This set documents his progress through a productive 12 years of his life and presents material that originally appeared on three LPs. The first from 1970 suggests an acquaintance with the New York Art Quartet and shows Mangelsdorff moving from the sveltely mobile to the gutterally assertive as the case demanded. Themes still had a directional role to play but he had already moved some distance along the freedom road. By the time of the second session (1978), he had brilliantly incorporated Paul Rutherford's voice-over technique and his total mastery of multiphonics was in place. In creative terms, his ability to improvise was neither boosted nor retarded by this device but it did mean that he had a broader range of options. As if to prove it, solos on *Wart G'Schwind* and *Three Card Milly*, with Dauner's piano prominent, turn the clock back to more boppish times. The 1982 session reinstates the freedom ethic. Mangelsdorff's themes still point the way but solo routes take rapid leave of the designated path, embracing slurring, melodic contradictions and presenting the kinds of deliberate confutations that make following their progress a challenge to the listener. All three sessions display his awesome technical command of the trombone, an aspect of his playing that he has carried through to the present. **BMcR**

# Chuck Mangione                                                        1940

New review

**Spring Fever** Mangione (t); **Sal Nistico** (ts); **Gap Mangione** (p); **Frank Pullara** (b); **Vinnie Ruggieri** (d). Riverside Ⓜ OJCCD767-2 (41 minutes). Recorded 1961.

⑥ ❽

This CD presents a fine young trumpeter potentially on the brink of a major career in jazz. Mangione had paid his dues in the bands of Woody Herman, Maynard Ferguson and Art Blakey but, instead of taking the pure jazz route, he saw a 'niche in the market' and, throughout the seventies, switched to flügelhorn and played gentle original tunes and standards to a formula. These softly contoured pieces, often with a Latin flavour, essayed little in the way of improvisation but took him into sales figures normally associated with pop music. No instrumental concessions were made; Mangione remained a good musician and it must be conceded that his uncomplicated, sanitized jazz did introduce a whole generation to the real thing. It was just that, in the early sixties, the Jazz Brothers, with brother Gap, were unobtrusively producing albums as good as this. It shows the leader's sober restraint on ballads like *What's New*, his lightly bristling attack on *Spring Fever* but there is no doubt that there was a controlled element in all he did. Later albums such as **Recuerdo** (OJCCD495-2) had more potent rhythm sections and, on this date, some of the thunder is stolen by the articulate Nistico. There is, however, enough from the leader's horn to suggest that the real Mangione stood up too early. **BMcR**

# Manhattan Transfer

**The Best of Manhattan Transfer** Tim Hauser, Cheryl Bentyne, Alan Paul, Janis Siegel, Laurel Masse (v); **Randy Brecker, John Faddis, Marvin Stamm** (t); **Quentin Jackson, Wayne Andre** (tb); **Jerry Dodgion, Dave Sanborn** (as); **Mike Brecker, Seldon Powell** (ts); **Don Grolnick** (p, elp); **Ira Newborn** (g, mus. dir.); **Andy Muson** (b); **Roy Markowitz** (d). Atlantic Ⓜ 781582-2 (44 minutes). Recorded 1975-81.

⑧ ❽

The dilemma of close harmony groups such as Manhattan Transfer and Singers Unlimited is that they usually fall between two stools. Far too musicianly and hip for the wider audience to appreciate, they are also treated with suspicion by older jazz enthusiasts. But there is so much to enjoy which can only be rated as jazz that those committed enthusiasts who ignore these records are the losers. This "Best of" collection is the CD equivalent of an LP and, in turn, draws its dozen tracks from five previous albums. It contains the astonishing *Four Brothers*, on which Hauser, Masse, Paul and Siegel (Cheryl Bentyne was a later replacement for Laurel Masse) contrive to sing Jon Hendricks's lyrics to the original instrumental solos by Zoot Sims, Serge Chaloff, Herbie Steward and Stan Getz. *Body and Soul* is a quite marvellous recreation of Coleman Hawkins's classic performance, complete with a careful transcription of Gene Rodgers's piano introduction. But the unforgivably sloppy presentation gives none of this information and restricts itself to a listing of titles and singers' names. Mike Brecker takes the tenor solo on *Operator*, Ira Newborn is the sensitive guitarist on *Java Jive* and the closing *Nightingale Sang in Berkeley Square* is a perfect example of *a cappella* singing. Recommended. **AM**

# Herbie Mann                                                                                        1930

**The Evolution of Mann: The Herbie Mann Anthology** Mann (f); with a collective personnel of: Leo Ball, Doc Cheatham, Jerry Kail, Ziggy Schatz, Pedro Paulo, Clark Terry, Marky Markowitz, Joe Newman, Jimmy Owens, Wayne Jackson (t); Mark Weinstein, Quentin Jackson, Sam Burtis, Barry Rogers (tb); Paulo Moura (as); King Curtis, Ed Logan, Andrew Love, David 'Fathead' Newman (ts); Pepper Adams, James Mitchell (bs); Charlie Palmieri, Antonio Carlos Jobim, Sergio Mendes, Bill Evans, Chick Corea, Jimmy Wisner, Bobby Wood, Barry Beckett, Richard Tee, Pat Rebillot (p); Bobby Emmons (org); Baden Powell, Durval Ferreira, Mundell Lowe, Al Gorgoni, Charlie Macey, Larry Coryell, Sonny Sharrock, Reggie Young, Eddie Hinton, Duane Allman, Cornell Dupree, Jerry Friedman, Bob Mann, Hugh McCracken, Jeff Mironov, Hux Brown, Rod Bryan, Nick Woodland, Ricardo Silveira (g); Nabil Totah, Juan Garcia, Ahmad Abdul-Malik, Ben Tucker, Otavio Bailly, Jr, Chuck Israels, Earl May, Joe Macko, Mike Leech, David Hood, Richard Davis, Reggie Ferguson, Chuck Rainey, Andy Muson, Willie Weeks, Al Gorry, Tony Levin, Jackie Jackson, Gary Unwin, Paul Socolow (b); Rudy Collins, Dom Um Ramau, Paul Motian, Bruno Carr, Mel Lewis, Don McDonald, Reggie Ferguson, Bernard Purdie, Gene Christman, Roger Hawkins, Aynsley Dunbar, Steve Gadd, Rick Marotta, Michael Richard, Martin Harrison, Ricky Sebastian, Buddy Williams (d); Johnny Rae, Ray Mantilla, Ray Barretto, Michael Olatunji, Willie Rodriguez, Chief Bey, Carlos 'Patato' Valdes, Warren Smith, Phil Krauss, Ralph MacDonald, Armen Halburian, Rubins Bassini, Elmer Lewis, Tessie Coen, Joe Spector, Cyro Baptista (perc); Jose Andreu, Daniel Gonzalez, Joe Silva, Stephane Grappelli (vn); Johnny Rae, Hagood Hardy, Dave Pike, Roy Ayers (vb); Maya Angelou, Dolores Parker, Rannelle Broxton, Cissy Houston, Eunice Peterson, Sylvia Shemwell, Jerry Rix (v). Rhino/Atlantic Gallery Ⓜ R2 71634 (two discs: 138 minutes). Recorded 1960-92.

**⑥ ❼**

Herbie Mann deserves credit for making the flute a full-fledged jazz voice. Indeed, his funky chart-busters *Comin' Home Baby* (1961) and *Memphis Underground* (1969), helped create a boom in flute sales and lessons. From Mann on, reedmen had to prove themselves on flute as well as sax as fans and musicians alike embraced the instrument. In addition to popularizing various amalgams of rock and jazz, Mann was in the vanguard of American exponents of the bossa nova. Mann, a global traveller responsive to indigenous musics, was one of the first American jazzmen to incorporate African rhythms and Japanese melodies, making him a trail-blazer leading to what in the late eighties would be called world music.

In this two-disc anthology spanning 1960-92, we catch Mann's varied personas from the Muscle Shoals nitty gritty of the genuinely infectious *Memphis Underground* to the enraptured Brazilian insouciance of *One Note Samba* with composer Jobim wafting the vocal. Mann's most engaging and enduring works float simple melodies atop rhythmically charged undercurrents. On more ambitious fare, such as *I Love You* with the Bill Evans Trio, results are tentative. And though much of the commercialized jazz-rock of Mann's Atlantic career is decidedly dated, it nonetheless provides a revealing snapshot of the musical changes then blowing in the wind. By the end of the sixties, Mann had been eclipsed by a phalanx of new flute stars such as Hubert Laws and Charles Lloyd. Still, his place in jazz history is secure as the chief popularizer of jazz and jazz-pop flute. **CB**

---

New review

**Peace Pieces** Mann (f); Randy Brecker (flh); Bruce Dunlap (g); Eddie Gomez, Paul Socolow (b); Louis Nash, Ricky Sebastian (d); Sammy Figueras (perc). Kokopelli Ⓕ KOKO1306 (51 minutes). Recorded 1995.

**⑧ ❿**

At the beginning of the nineties Mann started up his own label, Kokopelli (he had previously demonstrated his A&R acumen with Vortex, the late-sixties Atlantic Records spin-off which brought the world début albums from Keith Jarrett, Steve Marcus, Robin Kenyatta and Tower of Power, amongst others). After a number of modest successes he has come up with a concept which gives him a unifying theme and an excuse to range far and wide over his different musical interests. The theme here is Bill Evans (with whom Mann made one of his most committed jazz records for Atlantic, **Nirvana**), and the range is the natural ambit of the tunes authored by Evans. This allows Mann, a dedicated eclectic and true connoisseur, to bring fresh and imaginative settings to familiar Evans themes such as *Funkarello* (nicely latinized), *Turn Out the Stars* and *We Will Meet Again* (with acoustic guitar), while *Blue in Green* becomes a beautifully balanced dialogue between a harp, an enchantingly voiced bank of overdubbed flutes and an eloquent flute soloist. A similar experience is in store for the listener on the enticingly scored *Peace Piece*. In his self-penned appendage to Orrin Keepnews's booklet-notes, Mann stresses the personal importance of this project, stating "It demanded a deeper level of understanding and a more disciplined command of my instrument than I have previously been willing to risk. The result has been deeply gratifying and has provided me with a new standard." I believe him, and I think the proof is there for anyone willing to give this record an unbiased listen. Mann's own commitment and enthusiasm is evident at every turn in the music, and while he is not the world's most imaginative improviser, his solos here are full of little delights. Brecker, by the way, appears on just a handful of tracks in a mainly supporting role, while the alternative bass-and-drums team of Socolow and Sebastian, a hold-over from his regular group, appear on the two latin-tinged tracks only. **KS**

# Shelly Manne                                                        1920-84

**Shelly Manne and His Men Live at the Blackhawk, Volumes 1-5** Manne (d); Joe Gordon
(t); **Richie Kamuca** (ts); **Victor Feldman** (p); **Monty Budwig** (b). Contemporary Ⓜ
OJC656/7/8/9/60-2 (five discs, oas: 280 minutes). Recorded 1959.

⑩  ❼

Shelly Manne was by a long way one of the most tasteful and open-minded musicians in jazz history. He led a very high percentage of outstanding albums, of which **2**, **3**, **4** on Impulse! (see below) and **Checkmate** on Contemporary (not on CD at present) spring to mind. Yet none of them is more valuable than this then unprecedented documentation of a band at work in a nightclub. Contemporary released four volumes on LP, and they have been classics since their first appearance. The CD release carries extra material on each volume (usually, alternative versions of already released tracks), plus a whole new volume (Volume 5, of course) of previously unissued material.

The band on this recording just happens to have that perfect balance few groups ever achieve, and even fewer achieve with a microphone nearby. Nobody is out to cut anyone else, everyone is proficient on their instruments and at ease with the material (a mixture of group originals and standards), and the level of inspiration is high. Kamuca is a particularly warm and involving tenor player, with great tonal beauty but none of the enervation often to be found on the West Coast, while Gordon combines audacious ideas with superb execution. Feldman is, of course, little short of a genius.

Everybody should have at least one of these albums on their shelves, not because the music is important, but because it is so damn enjoyable. **KS**

**2, 3, 4** Manne (d); **Coleman Hawkins** (ts, p); **Eddie Costa** (p, vb); **Hank Jones** (p); **George Duvivier**
(b). Impulse! Ⓜ GRP11492 (42 minutes). Recorded 1962.

⑧  ❽

A combination of inventiveness and eccentricity makes this a unique and classic album. The playing is largely of the stream-of-consciousness variety, but that should not deter the faint-hearted, for these men, giants all, communicate with great clarity and skill.

In such a setting Coleman Hawkins would be expected to dominate, but a lot of the time the initiative is taken by Manne. It is important to accept that Manne was the most un-drummer-like drummer in that he used his instruments in a most musical way and was never remotely overbearing. He worked in partnership with those he accompanied and, although a superlative big-band player, his forte was the intimate small group. Most of these he found on the West Coast, but these performances were done in New York with the locals.

Hawkins was at his most inspired and plays both tenor and piano in the amazing duet *Me and Some Drums*. Costa, whose piano work is both beyond value and unjustly rare, plays on only two of the seven tracks with his typical muscular locked-hands rumble appearing two minutes into *Lean on Me*. **SV**

# Wingy Manone                                                        1900-82

**1927-34** Manone (c, t, v); with, on four tracks **Hal Jordy** (cl, as); **Bob Sacks** (ts); **Johnny Miller**
(p); **Steve Brou** (g); **Arnold Loycano** (b); **John Ryan** (d); **Earl Warner** (v); on two tracks **Wade**
**Foster** (cl); **Bud Freeman** (ts); **Jack Gardner** (p); **Gene Krupa** (d); on two tracks **Frank**
**Teschemacher** (cl); **George Snurpus** (ts); **Art Hodes** (p); **Ray Biondi** (g); **Augie Schellange** (d); on
two tracks **George Walters** (cl); **Joe Dunn** (ts); **Maynard Spencer** (p); **Dash Burkis** (d); on four
tracks add to previous personnel: **Miff Frink** (tb, bj); **Orville Haynes** (b); **Bob Price**, **Ed Camden**
(t). Four tracks with **Matty Matlock** (cl); **Eddie Miller** (ts); **Gil Bowers** (p); **Nappy Lamare** (g, v);
**Harry Goodman** (b); **Ray Bauduc** (d); on four tracks **Dicky Wells** (tb); **Artie Shaw** (cl); **Bud**
**Freeman** (ts); **Jelly Roll Morton**, **Teddy Wilson** (p); **Frank Victor** (g); **John Kirby** (b); **Kaiser**
**Marshall** (d). Classics Ⓜ 774 (67 minutes). Recorded 1927-34.

⑧  ❻

Born in New Orleans, Manone was an exact contemporary of Louis Armstrong and there were many occasions throughout his life when his trumpet and cornet playing echoed that of Louis. In 1935 he had a massive record hit with *Isle of Capri* and subsequent recordings often contained elements of burlesque, but this excellent CD groups together seven 'pre-*Capri*' sessions of lasting interest. The first of two Chicago dates finds Wingy in the company of Bud Freeman, Gene Krupa and 'Jumbo' Jack Gardner, although the absence of a bass player tends to overemphasize Gene's drumming. The next date had Art Hodes and Frank Teschemecher (as if to reinforce Wingy's jazz credentials) while a 1930 session produced *Tar Paper Stomp* by Manone, a tune which became better known years later as *In the Mood*. There is an outstanding New York date on which the trumpeter teamed with other white New Orleans musicians in the persons of Eddie Miller, Nappy Lamare and Ray Bauduc and which is hallmarked by the clean ensemble playing. The final session on the CD has one of the most unexpected line-ups in jazz and includes Dicky Wells, Artie Shaw, Jelly Roll Morton and Bud Freeman, but the music has cohesion and clarity. In fact Manone's solo on *Never Had No Lovin'* from this session is one of his best in the Armstrong vein. Wingy conquered the tragedy of losing an arm in a road accident as a boy and was able to laugh when, years later, Joe Venuti gave him, as a birthday present, one cufflink in a box!      **AM**

## Michael Mantler
1943

**New review**

**Cerco un Paese Innocente** Mantler (t); **Jan Kohlin, Benny Rosenfeld, Palle Bolvig, Henrik Bolberg Pedersen, Lars Togeby** (t, flh); **Vincent Nilsson, Steen Hansen, Kjeld Ipsen** (tb); **Giodano Bellincampi** (btb); **Axel Windfeld** (btb, bb); **Jan Zum Vohrde** (f, ss); **Michael Hove** (f, cl, ss); **Uffe Markussen** (cl, bcl, f); **Bob Rockwell** (cl, ss); **Flemming Madsen** (cl, bcl, f); **Kim Kristensen** (p); **Nikolaj Bentzon** (syn); **Bjarne Roupé** (g); **Marianne Sorensen** (vn); **Mette Winther, Gunnar Lychou** (va); **Helle Sorensen** (vc); **Thomas Ovesen** (b); **Jonas Johansen** (d); **Ethan Weisgard** (perc); **Mona Larsen** (v). ECM Ⓔ 527 092-2 (62 minutes). Recorded 1994.

⑥ ❽

Despite his involvement with the Jazz Composers Orchestra, his work with Steve Lacy, Jazz Realities and his membership of Charlie Haden's Liberations Orchestra, Mantler remains a figure on the jazz fringe. This suite of *Songs and Interludes* has followed the lead given by his 1987 **Many Have No Speech** and has backgrounds that showcase the poetry of acclaimed Italian Giuseppi Ungaretti. Mantler has enlisted the services of Larsen's voice, several chamber string players and the 'untypical' Danish Radio Big Band. The compositions are imaginative and are underwritten by Mantler's knowledge of and sympathy for serialism. The arrangements are superbly realized by Ole Kock Hansen's orchestra and the mixture of sadness and drama is effectively balanced. Very little jazz is elicited, however, and, although there are useful interludes by solo strings, Roupé's guitar, Mantler's trumpet and Kristensen's piano, there is a clinical quality about the performance which is not helped by a high-pitched reed section and a politely mechanical rhythm team that seems guarded when it should perhaps be dictatorial. Ungaretti's work was always concerned with the human condition with an emphasis on loneliness, love, loss and death. Mantler has accommodated this emotional climate but his success is at the expense of the more obvious jazz qualities available to a big band.      **BMcR**

## Steve Marcus
1941

**Smile** Marcus (ss, ts); **John Hicks** (p); **Christian McBride** (b); **Marvin 'Smitty' Smith** (d). Red Baron Ⓜ JK53751-2 (53 minutes). Recorded 1993.

❽ ❾

Marcus made his first impact on the jazz scene back in the late sixties, becoming known internationally through his stints with Larry Coryell and Herbie Mann. The latter sojourn brought him his first date as a leader, on Mann's Vortex label, and for a while Marcus was a member of the short-lived jazz-rock boom which quickly foundered between the twin stools of Fusion and Soul. Escaping into the big-band ranks, Marcus worked successfully with Woody Herman before settling down for a 12-year stint with Buddy Rich's outfit, where he also took over much of the arranging work.

This present album, the second and decidedly superior of his latter-day records, has him essaying into the deepest saxophone waters, and generally acquitting himself creditably. The programme here is given over largely to compositions by, or closely associated with, greats such as Parker, Gillespie, Rollins, Coltrane and Dolphy. Marcus is far from overawed by precedent, and is quoted in the booklet-notes as saying each song chosen has long been a personal favourite, so there is nothing arbitrary here. Marcus has no evident technical weaknesses, his tone and conception is a personal amalgam of Coltrane and Rollins, and he has more than just heat and sound to communicate. The cohesion of his own approach and of the group he has chosen to play with is a definite plus, and although the set could have done with a few less bass solos, the album as a whole gives us much to admire and enjoy.      **KS**

## Rick Margitza

**Work It** Margitza (ss, ts); **James Williams** (p); **George Mraz** (b); **Billy Hart** (d). SteepleChase Ⓔ SCCD31358 (59 minutes). Recorded 1994.

Margitza came to international attention with a brace of albums on Blue Note, both of which fell into the 'promising' category without managing to suggest how the tenorist would escape from under the Coltrane shadow. This latest effort, on SteepleChase, suggest he's seen the way ahead. He's still using Coltrane's language, but the examples of people such as Joshua Redman and Don Braden in their combination of many different influences and their preference for a softer, rounder tone than most post-Coltrane tenors of the older generation preferred, seem to have helped Margitza to a more personal stance. That said, Margitza's one essay on soprano, Coltrane's *Your Lady*, is still wholly cast in the master's mould.

Having such mature players in the band behind him may have helped focus his mind. Mraz's powerful pulse and judicious note-choices leave Hart free to react dynamically to Margitza, while Williams is a discreet but unending font of ideas. His work on *My Foolish Heart* avoids the obvious, and sidesteps the Bill Evans legacy, but still manages to be both affectingly pretty and quietly supportive. All of which is captured by a pleasingly natural recorded sound typical of SteepleChase's high standards.     **KS**

# Charlie Mariano     1923

**Jyothi** Mariano (ss, f); **Karnataka College of Percussion**: **R.A. Ramamani** (v, tbra); **T.A.S. Mani** (mridangam); **R.A. Rajazopal** (ghatam, marsing, konakkal); **T.N. Shashikumar** (kanjira, konakkal). ECM Ⓟ 811 548-2 (46 minutes). Recorded 1983.

⑧ ❽

Although musical collaborations between West and East frequently result in the strengths of both traditions being diluted to form a bland pap bearing little resemblance to either, *Jyothi* is strong enough in its ambition and overall direction to avoid such a dilution. This success is possibly due to the fact that the necessary accommodation appears to have operated mostly in one direction; Charlie Mariano, with extended musical studies in Japan (while married to Toshiko Akiyoshi), Malaysia and India behind him, is undoubtedly one of the most versatile and open-minded jazz musicians on the planet, and on both flute and soprano here he manages to complement perfectly R.A. Ramamani's pure, silken vocals and the College's almost miraculously empathetic percussion work. As other, less successful experiments in similar fields have shown, mere virtuosity is not enough: the understanding and sympathy that comes only from proximity and study (*à la* John McLaughlin) is a prime requisite. Deprived of a jazz musician's familiar chord sequence structure upon which to improvise, Mariano demonstrates no unease, simply submerging himself (like the other members of this excellent ensemble) in an organic whole whose overall effect is infinitely greater than the sum of its parts. There are therefore no gratuitous displays of virtuosity, no grandstanding, no star turns here, and the result is that this meditative but intense music is served by the musicians rather than vice versa.     **CP**

# Dodo Marmarosa     1925

New review
**On Dial – The Complete Sessions (1946-7)** Marmarosa (p); **Howard McGhee**, **Miles Davis** (t); **Charlie Parker** (as); **Teddy Edwards**, **Lucky Thompson** (ts); **Arvin Garrison** (g); **Harry Babasin** (vc); **Bob Kesterson** (b); **Roy Porter**, **Jackie Mills** (d). Spotlite Ⓟ SPJ-(CD)128 (64 minutes). Recorded 1946-7.

⑧ ❼

Even in the midst of the talented tide of musicians who emerged during the mid forties, Marmarosa stood out as exceptional. Although the music here is serious bebop the pianist's devotion to Art Tatum is revealed at every turn, and he plays with a phenomenal speed and clarity of thought. He regarded himself handicapped by his small finger span, but no such flaw is apparent to the listener. This is a typically well-produced Spotlite album (re-issue collections include full details in a separate 16-page booklet provided with each album) which adds four tracks outside of the claimed scope of the programme. These are two aircheck piano solos and, most interestingly, two serial improvisations by Marmarosa, well ahead of contemporary jazz thought, which were never intended for issue. Eleven of the tracks, by Marmarosa's trio, use *pizzicato* cello instead of bass to good effect and it is here that the pianist spills out the cornucopia of his luminous talent. There are six tracks by Howard McGhee's sextet, all of which include potent piano solos, but none more impressive than the lightning-speed *Dilated Pupils*. There is a unique take of *Ornithology* (under the title *Bird Lore*) by Parker's septet wherein Parker stepped back to let Marmarosa take the solo which should have been for the alto. The track is duplicated on Spotlite's album of Parker **Dials** (q.v.), and McGhee appears again on the collection under the trumpeter's name. This is a sensible move for completeness on Spotlite's part and, given the ample playing time of the label's issues, shouldn't deflect anyone from acquiring the three historic collections.     **SV**

# Joe Marsala     1907-78

**1936-42** Marsala (cl); on two tracks **Pee Wee Erwin** (t); **Frank Signorelli** (p); **Carmen Mastren** (g); **Artie Shapiro** (b); **Stan King** (d); on three tracks **Marty Marsala** (t); **Ray Biondi** (vn);

Joe Bushkin (p); Adèle Girard (hp); Eddie Condon (g); Artie Shapiro (b); Danny Alvin (d); on four tracks **Condon** and **Alvin** out, replaced by **Jack LeMair** (g, v) and **Buddy Rich** (d); on four tracks **Bill Coleman** (t, v); **Pete Brown** (as); **Carmen Mastren** (g); **Gene Traxler** (b); **Dell St. John** (v); on four tracks **Marty Marsala** (t); **Ben Glassman** (as); **John Smith** (ts); **Dave Bowman** (p); **Adèle Girard** (h); **Carmen Mastren** (g); **Jack Kelleher** (b); **Shelly Manne** (d); on four tracks **Max Kaminsky** (t); **George Brunies** (tb); **Dick Cary** (p); **Carmen Mastren** (g); **Haig Stephens** (b); **Zutty Singleton** (d). Classics Ⓜ 763 (65 minutes). Recorded 1936-42.

**⑧ ❻**

The clarinet playing of Jimmy Noone was an early and continuing influence on Joe who, with his brother Marty, was born in Chicago but found jazz fame in New York. This CD collects together six complete sessions under Joe's name made during the period when he was working clubs, principally the Hickory House, and using the pick of the New York-based jazzmen. His wife Adèle adds an unusual but attractive tone colour with her harp playing on three dates. Marsala's own clarinet playing is lucid, clear-toned and melodic; the varying instrumentations mean that the music is never repetitious and in many ways this music is the very essence of the Golden Age of small band swing. On one date, supervised by Leonard Feather (predictably all four tunes are Feather's own), Marsala shares the front line with two other highly individual players in the persons of Bill Coleman and Pete Brown. Another date boasts a nine-piece group with proper arrangements for the ensemble and some effortless low register work from Marsala on a delightful *I Know That You Know*. The final session, dating from 1942, leans heavily on the Condon form of 'Nicksieland' jazz and finds Marsala flanked by Max Kaminsky and George Brunies. Two sessions mark the recording début of two important drummers, Buddy Rich and Shelly Manne. **AM**

# Branford Marsalis

1960

**Scenes in the City** Branford Marsalis (ss, ts); **John Longo** (t); **Robin Eubanks** (tb); **Mulgrew Miller**, **Kenny Kirkland** (p); **Ron Carter**, **Ray Drummond**, **Charnett Moffett**, **Phil Bowler** (b); **Marvin Smith**, **Jeffrey Watts** (d); **Wendell Pierce** (narr); **Ed Williams** (radio announcer). Columbia Ⓕ CK38951 (41 minutes). Recorded 1983.

**⑨ ❿**

Although he had recorded prominently with his brother trumpeter Wynton Marsalis, and with Art Blakey and the Jazz Messengers, saxophonist Branford Marsalis's 1983 début as a leader still stands as a remarkable maiden voyage. Though only 22 at the time of the first of the two sessions comprising the album, Marsalis shows incredible maturity and an uncanny absorption of the lexicons of John Coltrane and Sonny Rollins. Indeed, in the tumultuous *No Backstage Pass*, Branford evokes the Rollins legacy in a furiously dense, motivically constructed solo nudged by Carter's pendulous bass and Smith's swift brushes. Coltrane's sheets-of-sound intensity is refracted in *Solstice*, Branford's 7/4 reworking of Trane's *Equinox*.

The title track, Mingus's *Scenes in the City*, is an aural collage that today might be classified as 'performance art'. A confessional glimpse into the psyche of a black jazz fan of the fifties, it embraces snippets of period radio newscasts, a collection of 'wild' sounds recorded in Greenwich Village, and Branford's stirring sextet. We also get the 'voice' of Mingus's alter ego through the device of a narrator who concludes: "You see, I love jazz music." So, too, does Branford, who in spite of tasting the heady lotus fruit of show-biz fame and fortune – first with Sting, then as leader of the Tonight Show Band – is still one of the era's most absorbing jazz voices. **CB**

**Buckshot LeFonque** Marsalis (ss, as, ts, d prog); with a collective personnel including: **Roy Hargrove**, **Chuck Findley** (t); **Matt Finders** (tb); **Delfeayo Marsalis** (tb, p); **Kenny Kirkland** (p); **Greg Phillinganes** (kbds); **David Barry**, **Kevin Eubanks**, **Ray Fuller**, **Nils Lofgren**, **Albert Collins** (g); **Robert Hurst**, **Darryl Jones**, **Larry Kimpel** (b); **Jeff 'Tain' Watts**, **Chuck Morris** (d); **Mino Cinelu**, **Vicki Randle** (perc); **DJ Premier** (d prog), **Maya Angelou**, **Blackheart**, **Uptown** (v); **Clare Fischer** (string arr). Columbia Ⓕ 476532 2 (two discs: 113 minutes). Recorded 1994.

**⑧ ❿**

This just might turn out to be the **Bitches Brew** of the current jazz generation. Like Miles's epoch-marking album, it is a sprawling double-disc, full of half-developed and fascinating ideas. Again like Miles's initial electric forays, very little of the elements Marsalis pulls together into this huge musical stew could be described as newly minted: they've all been around for a number of years now. But it's the mix which is new and absolutely electrifying. Many musicians have been on the cusp of this sort of thing for a while, and in related fields a number have already been there (Bill Laswell, Eno, Prince *et al*) but Marsalis is one of the few jazz musicians with sufficient scope, knowledge and interest in the world outside to even want to attempt such a synthesis. What he can effortlessly pull off is a track with a sampled funky drum pattern, over which runs a rap vocal which then seamlessly segues into a fully fledged and scored sax-section figure which would not disgrace Woody Herman (and which in turn launches more lyrics, then a sax conversation where one of the horns quotes Monk). This all happens on *Breakfast at Denny's (Uptown Version)*. On *Breakfast at Denny's (Live Version)*, rhythm scratches and Hancock-inspired electric piano support some finely etched, laconic tenor work from the leader. The second disc has various different versions and mixes of the 'original' pieces to be found on disc one. So we have no less than four remixes of *No Pain, No Gain*, one with a wicked heavy metal riff guitar supporting a lightning-quick rap from *Uptown*.

Meanwhile, if you really want to scare yourself to death and you know your Coltrane, try *The Blackwidow Blues*: in the first 40 or so seconds there is an object lesson in Marsalis's methods on this album, and Elvin Jones has never before sounded like this.

This is an important album. Even if you hate it, it is an important album. It doesn't matter that Buckshot LeFonque is an old Cannonball Adderley pseudonym: all that proves is that, apart from having a sense of history, Branford's also got a sense of humour. **KS**

---

**New review**

**The Dark Keys** Marsalis (ss, ts); **Reginald Veal** (b); **Jeff 'Tain' Watts** (d); with guests **Joe Lovano** (ts) and **Kenny Garrett** (as). Columbia Ⓕ 486668-2 (62 minutes). Recorded 1996.

⑧ ❽

Unlike his unsullied sibling Wynton, Branford has slept frequently with the enemy – he played with Sting, he was a regular in The Tonight Show band and he has recently led his own funk group, Buckshot LeFonque. However, like a penance, he has kept up his jazz dues in parallel with his pop work and he takes that route on this issue. Branford was once very keen on Wayne Shorter, but in recent years Coltrane and Ornette Coleman seem to have been his chief inspirations, and so it is here. The opening track is based on an inversion of Coltrane's *A Love Supreme* motif, and Branford's tenor playing mostly recalls Coltrane, but while he sounds like him on soprano on *Judas Iscariot*, his approach on the higher horn is more varied, suggesting Steve Lacy on *Hesitation* and Ornette on *Lykeif*. The absence of a chordal instrument and the harmonic vagueness of much of the material leads to blandness on occasions, but the contrapuntal passages with Joe Lovano on *Sentinel*, Kenny Garrett's compelling, logical solo on *Judas Iscariot* and the provocative, orchestral Jeff 'Tain' Watts anywhere lend welcome colour. An honest if derivative modern jazz record, passionately and proficiently played, though not perhaps one for those who know Branford only through Buckshot LeFonque. **MG**

# Ellis Marsalis                                                                                               1934

---

**New review**

**A Night at Snug Harbor, New Orleans** Marsalis (p); **Tony Dagradi** (ts, ss); **Rick Margitza** (ts); **Bill Huntington** (b); **David Lee Jr**, **Art Blakey** (d); **Nicholas Payton** (t); **Donald Harrison** (ts). Evidence Ⓕ ECD22129 (72 minutes). Recorded 1989.

⑦ ❼

Born in New Orleans, Ellis is the father of the Marsalis clan, as well as being one of his hometown's leading educators. This CD provides an ideal starting place to examine the man and his art. It was recorded at the time of the 1989 Jazz and Heritage Festival, presents the leader as pianist and composer and features several of his protégés in action, at one of the town's outstanding clubs. The spirit of the jam session prevails, *Jitterbug* presents 15-year-old Payton on an early learning curve as guest-drummer Blakey injects his own devils. Altoist Harrison augments the parent quintet impressively on tenor but there is plenty of opportunity to assess Marsalis. Not an easy pianist to categorize, he uses bebop as he does other styles. It can be a means of expression or equally a colouring agent to be employed in a style born of his background. He is a pianist who comes to terms with his material rather than trying to change its substance and he is inevitably in the full comfort zone with his own *Nothin' But the Blues*. He displays latent urgency in the modal atmosphere of *The Call*, puts meaning into *Some Monk Funk* and shows the basics, with his orthodox reading of a standard such as *The Very Thought of You*. The flow of jazz from New Orleans seems to be as ineluctable as the river that runs through it and, with Marsalis still at the wellspring, the future seems assured. If, once this album has been assimilated, you are moved to explore later albums, then the studio-originated **Whistle Stop** (Columbia, 1994), featuring Marsalis fronting a quartet including son Branford and Jeff 'Tain' Watts, is full of bristling modern-mainstream creativity. **BMcR**

# Wynton Marsalis                                                                                           1961

---

**Wynton Marsalis** Marsalis (t); **Branford Marsalis** (ss, ts); **Kenny Kirkland**, **Herbie Hancock** (p); **Clarence Seay**, **Ron Carter**, **Charles Farnborough** (b); **Jeff 'Tain' Watts**, **Tony Williams** (d). Columbia Ⓜ 468708-2 (42 minutes). Recorded 1981.

⑥ ❽

Prompted by this début album, jazz critics have spent much of Marsalis's career trying to define his original contribution. He has not created a new style (although he has aroused a movement of historical and stylistic awareness, as well as politicizing many of the current critical debates) and his technically perfect, but to many ears rather cold, trumpet has a chameleon quality that would not make him immediately identifiable on first hearing except in the context of his own more recent Sextet compositions. Here he flits from the Milesian (especially when accompanied by the ex-Davis rhythm section of Hancock, Carter and Williams) to the Morganesque. His ballad playing (notably on *Who Can I Turn To?*) is exceptionally mature for his then 20 years. As the album that marked his emergence from Blakey's talent school to the world stage in his own right, this is important, but since Marsalis's playing was still developing (even if its eventual destination is still unclear), the sum of its parts is substantially greater than the whole. **AS**

**Hot House Flowers** Marsalis (t); **Branford Marsalis** (ss, ts); **Kent Jordan** (f) **Kenny Kirkland** (p); **Ron Carter** (b); **Jeff Watts** (d); **Robert Freedman Orchestra**. Columbia Ⓕ CK39530 (42 minutes). Recorded 1984.

⑧ ⑧

Haydn's *Trumpet Concerto* at 14, Jazz Messenger at 19, record date leader at 20 and first musician to win a Grammy for both jazz and classical work, Marsalis could not fail. In fact, he didn't. It is just that his success has been misunderstood to some extent. By 1984 he was suffering from the expectation syndrome. This CD gets ⑧ ⑧ because it succeeds in all it sets out to do. Freedman's luxurious textures are not an empty background wash; they are worthy support figures for a trumpeter with something to say about a series of fine tunes and equipped with the technique, tone and imagination to do it well. Unfortunately, critics and lay press alike had discovered Marsalis and were looking for classical perfection of execution. This they get and it would be difficult to imagine a more faultless reading of *Lazy Afternoon*, *Melancholia* and *I'm Confessin'*. What it lacks is the kind of fire in the belly of which Marsalis is eminently capable. *When You Wish Upon a Star* threatens to prove the point as he cuts loose, but these arrangements are not about to allow him space to continue, so brother Branford comes in and the strings re-establish the calm. When this session took place, the composition of superb Ellingtonian-type suites and the best of his breathtaking solo performances had still to come. It does, however, monitor a corner turned. **BMcR**

**Citi Movement** Marsalis (t); **Todd Williams** (ss, ts); **Wes Anderson** (as); **Wycliffe Gordon** (tb); **Eric Reed** (p); **Reginald Veal** (b); **Herlin Riley** (d); plus **Herb Harris** (ts); **Marthaniel Roberts** (p). Columbia Ⓕ CK53324 (two discs: 123 minutes). Recorded 1992.

✅ ⑩ ⑩

**Citi Movement** is the music written by Wynton Marsalis for Garth Fagan's ballet *Griot New York*. The composer's challenge was, in his own words, "to write a piece that could come close to dignifying their [the dancers'] grace". It is in three parts, all broadly illustrative of the black American experience: *Cityscape*, a musical impression of city life; *Transatlantic Echoes*, an examination of black history; and *Some Present Moments of the Future*, which explores jazz's response to this century, from Buddy Bolden to John Coltrane and beyond. But the bare bones of the piece, thus dispassionately (and somewhat distortingly) laid out, give no impression of the wealth of creative imagination Marsalis has expended on the composition; a short cut to conveying a sense of this would be to compare it, as Stanley Crouch does in his booklet-notes, with the work of Duke Ellington (for its scale, dignity and grace) and of Charles Mingus (for its superb use of the septet format, the ease and familiarity with which it draws on the whole of jazz and blues for its means of expression, and – crucially – for its exuberance and vitality, expressed through effortlessly negotiated time-signature changes and its plethora of musical references, from spirituals, blues and New Orleans polyphony through swing, to modal, bop and beyond). In **Citi Movement** Marsalis has produced a work of great importance, both in the context of his own career and in the broader context of the music generally, since it unequivocally demonstrates the power, subtlety and complexity of the music when sensitively allied with other art forms. **CP**

**In This House, On This Morning** Marsalis (t); **Wycliffe Gordon** (tb); **Wessell Anderson** (as); **Todd Williams** (ts, ss); **Eric Reed** (p); **Reginald Veal** (b); **Herlin Riley** (d); on one track **Marion Williams** (v). Columbia Ⓕ 474552-2 (two discs: 115 minutes). Recorded 1992-3.

⑧ ⑧

The sheer volume and diversity of Wynton Marsalis's recorded output can make the listener a little blasé; equally the confrontation with a two-CD set of his septet playing nearly two hours of a work purporting to present an evocation of a service at an Afro-American church may not cause the pulse rate to quicken. But in fact this is a quite breathtaking display of Wynton's mastery as both instrumentalist and composer. Stanley Crouch's excellent notes should be read in conjunction with the music, but even without them the listener will surely be impressed by Marsalis's uncanny knack of producing the kind of ensemble sounds seldom heard since Duke Ellington's earlier works. The parallel with Ellington is heightened by the playing of trombonist Wycliffe Gordon, who would have been at home sitting alongside 'Tricky Sam' Nanton. The sheer breadth of the ensemble work, the tone colours and the unity of the solo playing will bring to mind such episodic Ducal works as *Black, Brown & Beige*. The actual shapes of some of the written melodies sound fresh simply because Marsalis is using the kind of intervals and hard-to-play octave jumps often avoided by trumpeters. Yet the music is never pretentious; Marsalis is not trying to prove his superiority, but his mastery of both form and technique gives his writing a freshness which is invigorating. **In This House** is worthy of consideration by anyone interested in both the tradition and contemporary direction of jazz. **AM**

# Tina Marsh

**The Heaven Line** Marsh (v, ldr); **Martin Banks**, **Dennis Gonzalez**, **Larry Spencer** (t); **Randy Zimmerman**, **James Lakey** (tb); **Jay Rozen** (tba); **Alex Coke** (f, ts); **Greg Wilson** (as, ts);

John Mills (bs); Bob Rodriguez (p); Ken Filiano (b); Billy Mintz (d). CreOpMuse Ⓟ 002 (74 minutes). Recorded 1992/3.

⑦ ❼

Tina Marsh has led the Texan large ensemble CO2 for the past 15 years and this recording of it comes from a live concert in Austin, Texas. It picks up on a jazz tradition which stuttered and virtually died with the ending of the sixties, only to be re-formulated by brave outfits like Toshiko Akiyoshi's various bands and the Thad Jones-Mel Lewis group. Marsh's band are unafraid to mix a variety of styles and techniques to create long-form acoustic music tailor-made for an imaginative big-band setting. In that sense, they perhaps find echoes in the work of units such as George Grunz's Big Band and the defunct British aggregation, Loose Tubes. These two made very exciting music live, but their recorded legacy generally doesn't quite capture that fire.

Marsh's group uses the killer-diller punch much more sparingly and takes different kinds of musical chances: the use of near-silence in Marsh's own *Cloud on Cloud, Movement ll: Sally's Storm* is a risky thing indeed, but its place in the overall structure of the piece makes it work brilliantly. The scoring, mostly undertaken by Rodriguez, Filiano and Zimmerman, is fresh, at times beautifully transparent, and at no time awkward or bombastic, even when the group is really wailing. The brass writing is especially crisp. For a singer, Marsh is exceedingly backward in coming forward, mostly preferring to use her voice as a wordless lead or part instrument. Her improvisation on Lakey's *Circle* is neither too long nor too exhibitionist, though she certainly gives her voice a workout. This is a record which improves with each listening, and while there are no standout soloists, Marsh's Texans deserve our attention. **KS**

# Warne Marsh
1927-87

**New review**
**Noteworthy** Marsh, Ted Brown (ts); Sal Mosca, Ronnie Ball (p); Sam Jones, Jim Hughart, Ben Tucker (b); Roy Haynes, Nick Ceroli, Jeff Morton (d). Discovery Records Ⓟ DSCD945 (69 minutes). Recorded 1956/77/79.

⑨ ❼

A student and disciple of Lennie Tristano, Warne Marsh thought that players should try to reach beyond ego to "purely musical expression" and he shared the pianist's belief in a total dedication to music, vowing "to play only what I want to play". This idealism kept him out of the recording studios and jazz clubs for long periods, especially in the sixties, though he did record more frequently towards the end of his life. His chief stylistic features – subtle time, oblique phrasing, a sinuous gracefulness – were derived from his saxophone heroes Charlie Parker and Lester Young, but already by the fifties had been refined to the point where he had become a brilliant and highly original improviser. **Noteworthy** comprises the 1979 LP **How Deep/How High** (with Mosca, Jones and Haynes), most of the 1977 LP **Warne Out** (with Hughart and Ceroli) plus three 1956 tracks with Brown, Tucker and Morton. The real gems here come from **How Deep/How High**, where Marsh is partnered by the hugely underrated Sal Mosca, a fellow Tristanoite whose understanding of harmony and rhythm is no less profound than the saxophonist's. Their four duos are an intimate masterclass in improvisation, while two live tracks with Jones and Haynes elicit more exuberant responses, Marsh twisting outrageously through *Background Music* before he and Mosca redesign *She's Funny That Way* with a feinting, lyrical invention that is as daring as it is beautiful. **GL**

# Claire Martin
1967

**New review**
**Off Beat** Martin (v); Mark Nightingale (tb); Anthony Kerr (vb); Martin Taylor (g); Gareth Williams (p); Arnie Somogyi (b); Clark Tracey (d). Linn Ⓟ AKD046 (69 minutes). Recorded 1995.

⑥ ❼

The fourth in a series of albums that confirm Martin's reputation as one of Britain's brightest and best jazz singers, this one stems from live recordings made at Ronnie Scott's Club in London. Whereas the previous albums have benefited from Linn's exemplary studio sound, this has some shortcomings, particularly in the way the vocals themselves are captured, with an excess of echo diminishing the unusually clear sound of her voice. This is, however, a minor cavil, since the performances themselves demonstrate just how well Martin sings in a live session. Kerr and Nightingale each guest on a couple of tracks and Taylor offers the sole accompaniment to the beautiful and measured closing track, *Some Other Time*. Everything else is by Martin's trio, Williams being jointly responsible with the singer for the arrangements. Mark Nightingale shines on *Comes Love* (in which Martin cannot avoid mirroring the classic Ella Fitzgerald/Louis Armstrong version, but acquits herself admirably nonetheless). Overall, Martin proves her outstanding musicianship is growing apace, mixing exquisite pitching and timing with an ability almost unrivalled in Britain at present to interpret lyrics. Once more her material is drawn from a combination of familiar and unexpected sources, Stevie Wonder jostling with Irving Berlin, and it is the internal balance of the set almost as much as the polished performances of all concerned that make this an unusually satisfying album. **AS**

# Sara Martin

New review

**In Chronological Order, Volume 1 (1922-3)** Martin (v); **W.C. Handy** (dir.); **Tick Gray**, **Tom Morris** (c); **Sylvester Bevard** (tb); **Clarence Williams**, **Shelton Brooks** (p, v); **Clarence Johnson**, **Charlie Hillman** (p); **Eva Taylor** (v). Document ⓔ DOCD5395 (74 minutes). Recorded 1922-3.

⑥ ❹

Martin is remembered as much for her extrovert stage persona as for her singing. In her live performances she set her own standards; the theatre darkened, illuminated only by candles, then Martin entered, moving dramatically across the stage as she moaned the blues. Her singing by the late twenties had become powerful and compelling, although its histrionics did bring her repeatedly to the brink of bathos. At the time of this CD her voice was somewhat lighter. She did not begin singing professionally until widowed for the second time at the age of 32, when initially her higher pitched voice and careful pronunciation made her a less convincing blues singer. It is her supporting musicians that make her early work of special significance. There is little of note in the pedestrian Williams accompaniments but, in view of the controversy that once raged between Jelly Roll Morton and W.C. Handy, it is instructive to evaluate the Handy Orchestra from this period. It is heard here on three titles, recorded while Martin was touring with the band. On this evidence, Morton was correct in seeing Handy as a *poseur*. Cornettist Gray was later to play with King Oliver but here he leads the ensemble in a stiff, somewhat Johnny Dunn-like manner and the band sounds typical of most early-twenties New Yorkers still awaiting their jazz injection from New Orleans's avant-garde. Fellow New Yorker Morris does offer more in the way of rubato to help the singer out but Martin's best days were still ahead of her. **BMcR**

# Stu Martin

New review

**Live at Woodstock** Martin (d, syn); **John Surman** (bs, ss, bcl, syn). Beat Goes On Ⓜ BGOCD290 (37 minutes). Recorded 1974.

⑦ ❼

Martin was a world traveller as well as a musician of great versatility. He supplied the powerhouse drum needs of Count Basie and Duke Ellington, throttled back to a whisper for singers Tony Bennett and Blossom Dearie, and battled in the hard-bop turmoil of groups led by Sonny Rollins and Donald Byrd. He spent many years in Europe as both teacher and player and it was during that period that he became part of the brilliant group, The Trio, with Surman and bassist Barre Phillips. It was also the time when this recording was made and when both men's conversancy with each other and with the requirements of such music was put to good effect. The klaxon metronome at the start of this CD comes as something of a surprise but it opens the way to an excellent, loose-limbed recital in which each musician plays an equal part. All of the writing is their own and it encourages a degree of rivalry and, at times, allows paired synthesizers to meet head to head. The best moments are to be found when Martin's cleverly fractured percussion is snapping at Surman's heels and both men are on their favoured instrument. Neither can enjoy a moment's complacency, but this is the joy of the freedoms to be found in such challenging music. **BMcR**

# Pat Martino

**Consciousness** Martino (g); **Eddie Green** (elp, perc); **Tyrone Brown** (elb); **Sherman Ferguson** (d, perc). Muse ⓔ MCD5039-2 (39 minutes). Recorded 1974.

⑥ ❽

Unlike such peers as John McLaughlin and Larry Coryell, Pat Martino remained largely immune to the explosion of the guitar's resources occasioned by rock. He touched on fusion in the mid seventies with his group Joyous Lake, but his chief inspiration remained the unadorned bop combo sound of Wes Montgomery. However, although he adopted Montgomery's general approach, including a dark tone, the mature Martino played faster and denser than did Wes, and rarely used his idol's trade mark octave and chord soloing style. Where Wes refined and extended on bebop, Martino was one of the first jazz guitarists to successfully apply Coltrane's modal style to the guitar. Thus his playing is more scalar than chordal, and marked by extensive chromatic embellishment and connection of scale tones. It has its formulas, and his sometimes unrelieved 16th-note phrasing can want rhythmic variety, but, on *Impressions* and the breathless 12-bar *On the Stairs* his chromatic lines generate staggering harmonic and kinetic energy. Martino's career was wrecked in 1980 when undiscriminating fate dealt him a cerebral aneurism, and he has made tenacious efforts to rekindle the old fire, but on the evidence of recent recordings the formidable form heard here has yet to be recovered. **MG**

# Hugh Masekela

New review

**The Lasting Impressions of Ooga Booga** Masekela (t, v); **Larry Willis** (p); **Harold Dotson**

(b); **Henry Jenkins** (d). Verve Ⓔ 531 630-2 (79 minutes). Recorded 1965.

⑦ **❽**

Among Masekela's earliest work that followed his move from South Africa via Britain to the USA, this is a conjunction of two MGM LPs, which together documented an inspired evening at the Village Gate in New York. It is perhaps his most straightforwardly jazz-orientated album currently in catalogue. Devotees of Masekela's latter-day fusion albums will find the origins of that style here, in the more overtly African material played by what is otherwise a driving and effective hard-bop quartet. Masekela's own playing was still at the chrysalis stage – some clear outlines of his subsequent style are apparent through the carapace, but the outline resembles some aspects of Freddie Hubbard or Lee Morgan. Amid the original compositions by Masekela and his then wife, Miriam Makeba, are pieces by Herbie Hancock and the quartet's pianist Larry Willis, and these show the extent to which Masekela was exploring the integration of genres, with African and Latin themes mingling with more obviously American material. His own *Mixolydia* is a case in point, nodding at Miles and Coltrane, but with a trumpet solo that moves in an ever more African direction. In his more recent recordings, Masekela still occasionally lets loose his passionate, intense solo style, but this album is one of his most consistent, with its heart clearly on its sleeve. Oh, and the title? **Ooga Booga** is Masekela's impression of the standard dialogue given to African characters in the B-movies of the day. **AS**

# Steve Masakowski

New review

**Direct AXEcess** Masakowski (g); **David Torkanowsky** (p); **Hank Mackie** (g); **James Singleton**, **Billy Huntingdon** (b); **Brian Blade** (d). Blue Note Ⓔ CDP8 31108-2 (57 minutes). Recorded 1994.

⑧ **❾**

Masakowski combines an awareness of the guitar tradition with his New Orleans heritage in this accomplished disc which pays tribute to the late Joe Pass. Playing the acoustic guitar bequeathed to him by the late Danny Barker, Masakowski produces a faultless reading of Hoagy Carmichael's *New Orleans*, while on the electric seven-string instrument he reflects the latter-day Crescent City of Dr John and The Meters with *Burgundy*. His own compositions, by and large, pass muster and the mixture of New Orleans-inspired material, originals and standards works to achieve a well-balanced album. His tone on both electric and acoustic instrument is glowing and warm, reflecting his interest in Pass, but also catching nuances of men like Jim Hall and Kenny Burrell, which is a contrast to the rather spacey Scofield-inspired sound in vogue with many of Masakowski's contemporaries. In a quartet setting Masakowski effortlessly holds the lead, but his best moments here are in two unaccompanied solos that realize his full potential. **AS**

# Cal Massey                                                        1927-72

**Blues to Coltrane** Massey (t); **Julius Watkins** (frh); **Hugh Brodie** (ts); **Patti Brown** (p); **Jimmy Garrison** (b); **G.T. Hogan** (d). Candid Ⓜ CD9029 (41 minutes). Recorded 1961.

⑧ **❻**

Massey was a heartbreakingly unlucky musician. His luck was so bad that this, his only album as a leader in a career spanning 30 years, was never released in his lifetime: a victim of the early demise of the original Candid label in 1961, it had to wait until the mid eighties for its first full release (one track, in edited form, appeared on the Candid sampler LP, **The Jazz Life**). Considering all the blowing sessions thrown onto the market in the late fifties, the failure of this carefully prepared album to see the light of day is all the sadder. A painfully out-of-tune piano aside, everything slots perfectly into place and each soloist has something meaningful to say. Each track is a Massey composition: that he was a superior composer and arranger is attested by the many songs and settings of his recorded by the best players of his generation and beyond, from Charlie Parker to John Coltrane to Lee Morgan and Archie Shepp.

His trumpet style is related to the lyricism of Johnny Coles, although he seems not to have had the overall technical security Coles enjoys; yet his vulnerability somehow makes his playing that much more affecting. His companions here are all good, interesting players, with Brodie soloing strongly in the manner of early Coltrane (a pleasant change from the post-**Giant Steps** acolytes) and Julius Watkins, as always, arresting in his ideas. **KS**

# Zane Massey                                                       1957

**Brass Knuckles** Massey (ss, ts); **Hideiji Taninaka** (b); **Sadiq M. Abu Shamid**, **William Parker** (d). Delmark Ⓔ DD464 (47 minutes). Recorded 1992.

⑧ **❽**

Were it not for critic/producer Nat Hentoff the jazz world at large may not have been aware of the talents of Cal Massey as a trumpeter and composer (although Archie Shepp did much at the end of the sixties to commit Massey's compositions and arrangements to disc). It was Hentoff who was responsible for Massey's only album, **Blues to Coltrane** (see above). Zane is Cal's son, a young man who grew up in a household where it was not unusual to find men such as Coltrane and Cedar Walton rehearsing with Massey Sr. Tuition from people like Frank Foster and Jimmy Heath, plus the encouragement of his father, has resulted in Zane's emergence as a powerful, confident soloist whose music is thankfully devoid of the filibustering self-indulgence of many post-Coltrane players. Although he has worked and recorded with Sun Ra, Ronald Shannon Jackson and Roy Campbell, this disc is Zane's début as a leader and there have been few more impressive beginnings. The eight-tune programme contains two of his father's works, *Message from Trane* and *Assunta* (the latter is the only track on which he plays soprano). The Japanese bass player Taninaka produces a full, rich sound reminiscent of the great Leroy Vinnegar and Wilbur Ware, and the compactness of the trio makes this a unit which has the flexibility to cover a range of expression. **AM**

# Ronnie Mathews 1933

New review

**Shades of Monk** Mathews (p); **Buster Williams** (b); **Kenny Washington** (d). Sound Hills
Ⓕ SSCD8064 (55 minutes). Recorded 1994.

⑥ ❾

Something of a curate's egg, this one. For a start, in a disc titled **Shades of Monk** there are just three out of ten compositions by Thelonious, with a light-hearted amble through *Sweet & Lovely*, an old standard also recorded by Monk, as a makeweight. The rest of the session is taken up by two Buster Williams songs (the ballad *Christina* and the jazz standard *Toku-Do*), a Mathews original, a rarely-covered Wayne Shorter piece (*Marie Antoinette*) and an old Duke Pearson theme (*Is That So*). There is no doubting Mathews's complete understanding of the Monk songs he plays and the other two do nothing wrong, but once Monk is left largely behind, the coherence of the project – and therefore of the album – begins to crumble. In the end we are left with a pleasant piano trio record where everything is well played and nothing much apart from the Monk readings remains in the memory after the disc stops turning. Which is the case with 90 per cent of piano trio records, so Mathews, a veteran of such bands as those of Lee Morgan, Freddie Hubbard, Max Roach and Art Blakey, is in good company. **KS**

# Keiji Matsushima

New review

**Brand New** Matsushima (t); **Don Braden** (ts); **Bob Bargad** (p); **Peter Washington** (b); **Billy Drummond** (d). Alfa Jazz Ⓕ ALCB3903 (62 minutes). Recorded 1995.

⑥ ❿

Matsushima is a Japanese trumpeter in his early twenties who excels in tone and execution and operates in the area of jazz once populated by Art Blakey and Blue Note records during the sixties. Virtually the whole repertoire of ten songs was in Blakey's sixties band book (Matsushima's two originals *could* have been), and what wasn't was recorded by Blakey's ex-band members for Blue Note. That aside, this exercise in reclamation is immaculately performed and Matsushima has real fire in his belly, sounding for all the world like the young Freddie Hubbard on a good night. Braden plays up to his usual high standard, and the rhythm team don't let anyone down. OK, then; you know what to expect, and you know whether it will suit you, so that's enough from me. **KS**

# Turk Mauro 1944

New review

**Hittin' the Jug** Mauro (ts, bs); **Dr Lonnie Smith** (p, org); **Jeff Grubbs** (b); **Duffy Jackson** (d).
Milestone Ⓕ MCD9246-2 (63 minutes). Recorded 1995.

⑥ ❾

New Yorker Mauro Turso (inadvertently dubbed 'Turk' by a forgetful bandleader one night) was a confirmed jazz fan by his mid-teens, standing outside clubs at night to see his heroes. After a string of gigs in and around New York, in the mid seventies he joined Billy Mitchell's outfit, where he often played baritone and also came to know Dizzy Gillespie, who eventually took him into his own group. Later Mauro did time with the Buddy Rich band before spending a number of years in Paris, finally returning to New York in 1994. His tenor style owes a considerable – and freely acknowledged – debt to Gene Ammons and swinging players such as Zoot Sims and Sonny Stitt. His sound is broad and deep, much more so than most modern stylists, and his phrasing alternates between mainstream and hard bop. He is of the 'tough but tender' school, a characteristic which is emphasized by his work on baritone, and his unsentimental approach means that the ballads are usually very prettily done in great broad strokes of phrasing. The up-tempo numbers tend to be less memorable, but they still do enough to excite, so this is a record which is hard to dismiss as lightweight. It is unpretentious, honestly played music and everyone involved gives of their best.

Smith alternates between piano and organ, with Grubbs dropping out when the Hammond is being used. Everything stays funky, though, whichever way it goes.  **KS**

## Maximilian

New review
**What I'm Doing Now ... Must Be Done**  Johan Maximilian Sievert (elb); **Jerry Bergonzi** (ss, ts); **Ido Yanai** (elg); **Gunther Kuermayr** (p, kbds); **Marc Gratama** (d). X-Records Ⓕ CD96031 (62 minutes). Recorded 1994.

⑦ ❾

Veteran Coltrane disciple Jerry Bergonzi provides a point of reference in this set by otherwise little known players, but it would be a mistake to make predictions about the record's contents from his presence. He flexes his Coltrane muscle at accomplished length on the Corea-like *North End*, the title blues and the closing *I Hear a Rhapsody*, but these tracks are exceptions in an album which generally favours a cooler approach. All compositions except *Rhapsody* are by the bassist-leader and the majority follow the lugubrious ECM model, with particularly doleful examples in *The Baltic Sea*, *Ballad for the Poor* and *Homelonging*. There are, therefore, many meditative episodes with stark, chilling harmony and little sense of movement or development; even the samba, *The Searcher*, is muted in the Metheny manner. Those with a taste for such low intensity music should give the record a hearing, but those who get more thrills from post-Coltrane bop may find that although Bergonzi and the Scofieldian Yanai do excellent work in that style on two or three occasions, that isn't enough to justify purchase. Others may of course find it the perfect mix, and bass specialists might benefit from checking out the leader's poetic if technically restrained solo on *Homelonging*.  **MG**

## Tina May

New review
**Time Will Tell ...**  May (v); **David Newman** (p); **Mick Hutton** (b); **Clark Tracey** (d, arr); with, on two tracks each **Alan Barnes** (as, bcl); **Don Weller** (ts); **John Mead** (kbds); on three tracks **The Lochrian String Quartet**. 33 Records Ⓕ 33Jazz029 (64 minutes). Recorded 1995.

⑦ ❾

With this, her fourth album as a leader, May takes a significant step in her career. Previous to this she has produced likeable records with much good singing and attractive repertoire. Here, although she has used much the same cast as on her previous outings, the message has deepened, and there is an assurance to all that is performed which proclaims her new maturity as an interpretative artist. The arrangements, whether for the string quartet or for the jazz quartet (there is also a largely convincing duo arrangement of *Do Nothing 'Til You Hear from Me*, voice and bass clarinet), are fashioned with her emotional and timbral imprint in mind, she sounds comfortable in all she does, and there is no over-extension of her facilities in an ill-judged attempt to impress. An astute and sometimes electrifying live performer, May has now fully grasped the different art of creating a lasting impression through the agency of the recording studio. Her ease with *'Round Midnight*, recently given a modern twist by Cassandra Wilson, shows that she is able to approach songs on their own terms and not be overwhelmed by their history, lending her light, clean timbre to a song of mystery and producing a satisfying portrait of the early hours. In this and elsewhere her supporting quartet is flawless, with Newton particularly sensitive in his accompaniments. The diversity of the excellent Tracey arrangements tends to disguise a certain sameness of approach from the singer which will probably resolve itself in time (hence the title?), but, for now, this is an admirable statement of where May is presently and where she intends to go.  **KS**

## John Mayer

New review
**John Mayer's Indo-Jazz Fusions**  Mayer (comp, cond, vn); **Dave Smith** (t); **Anna Brooks** (as); **Steve Tromans** (p); **Jonathan Mayer** (sitar); **Peter Moore** (tbra); **Chris Featonby** (b); **Andrew Bratt** (d); **Ranjit Singh** (tabla). Nimbus Ⓕ NI5499 (58 minutes). Recorded 1996.

⑥ ⑦

Long before world music and ethnic eclecticism there were John Mayer's early sixties experiments with joining Classical Indian theory to jazz extemporization. The key figure in the early attempts was altoist Joe Harriott, whose fiery, striking improvisations had already set British jazz on its ear and awakened the interest of Atlantic Records in the US. Predictably enough, when the Indo-Jazz Fusions project became widely popular it was Harriott who garnered most of the praise. Mayer, who admits today that writing for jazz musicians did not come easily at that time, was seen as merely the provider of the canvas and eventually found a position as Professor of Composition at Birmingham Conservatoire. Well, now the canvas is back, without the late and lamented Harriott, to be judged on its own merits. The concept has shifted little since its heyday, with a noticeably higher level of integration between the two musical spheres, but without a soloist strong enough to grab the listener's attention and make the whole thing come alive. Curiously, after three decades in existence, this blend of two cultures still sounds tentative, still sounds like the early days of an idea. Perhaps these guys need to loosen up a little, mix the elements – let the tabla rip, for example, behind the sax. Otherwise it still comes across as if it were the M.J.Q. in funny suits and on their very best behaviour.   **KS**

## Bill Mays
1944

**New review**
**An Ellington Affair**  Mays (p); **John Goldsby** (b); **Lewis Nash** (d). Concord Ⓕ CCD4651 (57 minutes). Recorded 1994.

⑥ ❾

The opening *I'm Just a Lucky So and So* begins with a burst of startlingly anachronistic boogie woogie. Mays is too accomplished a pianist and too inventive a composer and arranger not to bring some fresh ideas and individual idiosyncrasy to the Ellington songbook, and he draws his inspiration from the full gamut of jazz piano history. This makes him a thoroughly entertaining and interesting pianist, and when teamed with a trio as well balanced as this, the results are rewarding. The ballads (notably *Day Dream*) stand out as Mays's best work on the disc. Yet, in some respects, his very versatility works against him, and the sublime confidence and professionalism with which he approaches every track suggests the lack of an individual voice. It would be hard to listen to this in a blindfold test and identify anything that marks him out in terms of touch, tone or timing. Instead, the interest in his playing comes from his very considerable ability to present jazz ideas in a cogent and intelligent framework, and to use a particularly wide keyboard vocabulary in doing so. This in itself is a substantial achievement, well worth recognition in its own right. Mays has four other Concord albums to his name, including a set in the esteemed Maybeck series (CCD4567).   **AS**

## Lyle Mays
1953

**Fictionary**  Mays (p); **Mark Johnson** (b); **Jack DeJohnette** (d). Geffen Ⓕ GEFD24521 (65 minutes). Recorded 1992.

⑨ ❾

Pianist Lyle Mays, though best known for his electronic keyboard work with various editions of guitarist Pat Metheny's popular fusion group, is also an exceptional acoustic pianist. Here, in the good company of Johnson and DeJohnette, Mays may often evoke the Bill Evans lineage, but remains his own man. As is also the case in the pianistics of Richie Beirach, one hears the luminescent colours and subtly washed lines of turn-of-the-century composers such as Scriabin, Ravel and Debussy, especially in the picaresque title tune.

There is also a harder, neo-bop edge in tracks like *Sienna*, where the furious pace seems as driven as that of that fabled city's annual Palio horse race around the Piazza del Campo. Contrastingly, there are lyric meditations such as the poignant *Something Left Unsaid* and the aptly titled *Bill Evans*. Interactions between Mays, Johnson and DeJohnette are deep, touching on the profound. Considering the status of all three players, that should perhaps be no surprise. However, it is Mays whose seal finally provides the authorial stamp on this sublime exhibition of the art of the modern piano trio.   **CB**

## Robert Mazurek

**New review**
**Badlands**  Mazurek (t); **Eric Alexander** (ts); **John Webber** (b); **George Fludas** (d). Hep Ⓕ 206 (75 minutes). Recorded 1994/5.

⑥ ❽

Mazurek is a very capable trumpeter in the orthodox jazz-pedagogy vein of the last 15 years; his charging hard-bop compositions, like *Badlands*, sound like they could be dropped whole into a Freddie Hubbard record from 1962. His clear lines bear a trembling, long-note Miles Davis affinity on ballads; he's an accomplished player, but the tunes chosen for this record, including over-recorded standards like *Angel Eyes* and *Ev'ry Time We Say Goodbye* offer a glimpse of him still in the tribute stage. Alexander is a similar kind of player, his broken phrases evoking Joe Henderson, but with undeniable warmth and commitment. It's classicism from top to bottom, but well performed.   **BR**

## Medeski, Martin and Wood

**Shack-Man**  John Medeski (org, p, elp); **Billy Martin** (d, perc); **Chris Wood** (b, hca, wood f). Gramavision Ⓕ GCD79514 (55 minutes). Recorded 1996.

④ ❽

Although Medeski, Martin and Wood have been acclaimed for their "daring genre-smashing" among Manhattan's self-consciously progressive East Village community, this, their third album for

Gramavision, echoes **Friday Afternoon in the Universe**'s triumph of style over content. The trio's attitude, presumably one they share with their audience, is routinely post-modernist, a concern simultaneously to demonstrate an awareness of tradition (in this case early seventies Miles, the organ trio, and – shorthand for real jazz roots – the acoustic bass) and a serious embrace of the avant-garde. Nice concept, but in MMW's case the musical substance is slight to say the least, amounting to an agglomeration of somewhat skewed r&b riffs and free-ish interludes in which spontaneity and self-expression are favoured over the stuffy and prohibitive old values of form and development. The resultant music smacks a little too clearly of self-consciousness and artful poses to merit musical analysis. For an example, check out *Bubble House*. **MG**

# Myra Melford

**New review**
**The Same River, Twice**  Melford (p); **Dave Douglas** (t); **Chris Speed** (ts, cl); **Erik Friedlander** (vc); **Michael Sarin** (d). Gramavision Ⓕ GCD79513 (62 minutes). Recorded 1996.
**⑥ ❼**

Melford came to public attention during long hours spent at the Knitting Factory and has since made a number of CDs under her own name. The previous two with hatART illustrated her talents applied to a piano trio and a group context. Since then she has moved to Gramavision, who have put her in a studio with her group to record a selection of her latest works. Her compositional style continues to evolve and clarify itself, and the pieces here involve considerable intricacies, both in terms of ensemble playing and overall construction. The unusual line-up makes for pleasing sonorities, especially in a piece such as *Crush*, when Douglas is often muted, giving a strangely middle-heavy balance to the ensemble. Melford's music continues to be resolutely abstract, only occasionally settling for long periods into metred time. As before, her own improvising remains the least convincing part of her creativity, although she can generate considerable excitement using methods not dissimilar in places to Cecil Taylor's. Douglas, however, takes the solo honours (try *Changes*, for example). Recorded sound is good, but the piano is in need of a tune. **KS**

# Gil Melle                                         1931

**Primitive Modern/Quadrama**  Melle (bs); **Joe Cinderella** (g); **Billy Phillips**, **George Duvivier** (b); **Ed Thigpen**, **Shadow Wilson** (d). Prestige Ⓜ OJC1712-2 (68 minutes). Recorded 1956-7.
**⑥ ⑧**

During the fifties Melle was identified with the modernist side of jazz. He acknowledged being influenced by contemporary composers like Bartók and Varèse, but outside of the uncommon care he took to structure his pieces there is little overt evidence, and he never lost the desire or ability to swing. Recordings for Blue Note early in the decade found him playing tenor sax with a cool Getzian demeanour, but soon the baritone became his main instrument. This disc generously combines two LPs. Without trombonist Eddie Bert, his front-line partner on the Blue Notes, the quartet arrangements take on a more intimate character, with a greater emphasis on interplay between the baritone and guitar. On the first album, **Primitive Modern**, Melle plays with a light, velvety tone and attractive ideas, and guitarist Cinderella offers a flexible harmonic balance, in unison, counterpoint, or as accompanist. By the time of the second date, a year later, Melle's tone had grown a touch more gruff and Mulliganesque with Cinderella adopting a Barney Kesselish twang. In retrospect, except for some unusual rhythmic accents and a soupçon of dissonance, the music is not all that experimental, and remains easily likeable, whether it is a mellow *In a Sentimental Mood*, the open-textured *Dominica*, or a full-bodied *It Don't Mean a Thing*. **AL**

# George Melly                                         1926

**Frankie and Johnny**  Melly (v); **John Chilton** (t); **Ron Rubin** (p); **Eddie Taylor** (d). D Sharp Records Ⓕ DSHCD7001 (49 minutes). Recorded 1992.
**⑥ ⑧**

In the first part of his career Melly confined himself to reworking classic blues (usually the ones sung largely by women) in a macabre manner, becoming in effect a singing version of the cartoonist Charles Addams. When he and his current trumpeter/musical director John Chilton formed their liaison more than two decades ago, the two men set about broadening the range of Melly's material to incorporate Broadway songs and other popular pieces. Melly, with his superbly jigged histrionics, has always provided the most spectacular visual display on the British scene. Over the years he has cultured his voice to move away from the earthy shouting of his early years. This album, his best yet, represents the fruition of his and Chilton's efforts. The material is treated with sophistication and Melly's gallows humour still manifests itself when the opportunity offers.

The backing by John Chilton's Feetwarmers is essential to Melly's success. Chilton is a fine trumpeter and he plays several good solos, displaying also an instinctive feel for obbligato. He and pianist Rubin shepherd the singer through each track. Rubin is a particularly delicate blues player and this is probably the best example of his work on disc. Chilton's arrangements exploit the limited line-up to the full and his composition *Living on My Own* has real poignance, bringing out the best in the singer. Melly's cheerful bawdiness is another element in his repertoire and it is unleashed on a handful of these tracks.                                                                                                                          **SV**

# Vince Mendoza                                                                                                          1960

**Sketches** Mendoza (cond, arr); **Andy Haderer, Rob Bruynen, Klaus Osterloh, Rick Kiefer, John Marshall** (t); **Dave Horler, Henning Berg, Bernt Laukamp, Roy Deuvall** (tb); **G. Kedves, L. Rasch, M. Putnam** (frh); **H. Waldner** (tba); **Dave Liebmann** (ss); **Charlie Mariano, Heiner Wiberney, Harald Rosenstein** (as); **Olivier Peters, Rolf Romer** (ts); **Jens Neufang** (bs); **Frank Chastenier** (p); **Nguyên Lê** (g); **Dieter Ilg** (b); **Peter Erskine** (d). ACT Ⓟ 892 152 (63 minutes). Recorded 1993.

⑥ ❽

Despite a rather uneasy integration of flamenco with big-band jazz, Mendoza's previous album **Jazzpaña** was nominated for a Grammy and marked him out as an arranger of originality and power. Raw flamenco has too much strength of its own to be happily contained in a formal band setting, and much of Mendoza's writing sounds contrived, yet it brought him sufficient recognition that this new collaboration with the WDR Big Band is liberally labelled 'The Man from **Jazzpaña**." This is a far more effective disc in its own right, solving a different compositional problem; how to set almost free improvisation in a formal structure. The Cologne musicians produce a near-perfect example of section discipline and, driven by Erskine's *tour-de-force* drums plus some excellent guest soloists, the results are exhilarating. Some unusual voicings and pairings ebb and flow in the eight-movement suite written for the album, but the whole thing is prefaced by Ravel's *Pavane*: a showcase for Mariano's sumptuous alto and Dave Liebmann's upwardly mobile soprano.                                                **AS**

# Misha Mengelberg                                                                                                    1935

**Who's Bridge** Mengelberg (p); **Brad Jones** (b); **Joey Baron** (d). Avant Ⓟ 038 (60 minutes). Recorded 1994.

⑧ ❽

Never one to travel in a straight line when there are curves to consider, the Russian-born, Dutch-bred Misha Mengelberg is a brilliant composer, arranger and pianist, fluent in a wide variety of twentieth-century musical styles. He has written for classical ensembles, but his work in jazz allows him to bring together his eclectic interests. Like the Dadaists, Mengelberg constantly seeks to erase the boundary between the 'serious' and the 'humorous'. His arrangements for the ICP Orchestra, the Berlin Contemporary Jazz Orchestra and other large ensembles often use elements of collage, slapstick and repetition to confuse and delight listeners. Working in the traditional piano trio, here, allows him affectionately to parody its conventions – those established by Art Tatum, Bill Evans and Oscar Peterson – distorting but never destroying them completely. Mengelberg flits from style to style within a single tune – sometimes from phrase to phrase, as in *Rumbone*, where he plays funky chords in one hand and atonal clusters in the other, or *Gare Guillemans*, which at first glance could be a fifties Broadway show tune, until his solo gradually deconstructs the theme down into a few stumbling pitches and then smoothly shifts back into the groove. Monk is a major influence, as can be heard in the leaping intervals and theme interruptions of *Romantic Jump of Hares*, and the lovely, unexpected, angular chords and lyrical line of *Peer's Counting Song*. This programme is the closest Mengelberg has yet come to the jazz mainstream and the blend of playfulness and precision is always engaging. A pity about the gaffe in the title.                                                                              **AL**

# Helen Merrill                                                                                                           1930

**Collaboration** Merrill (v); **Lew Soloff** (t); **Shunzo Ono** (t, flh); **Jimmy Knepper** (tb); **Dave Taylor** (btb); **Danny Bank** (f, bcl, bs); **Phil Bodner** (f, af, ss); **Chris Hunter** (f, cl, ob, ss, as, pic); **Wally Kane** (bcl, bn); **Roger Rosenberg** (bcl); **Gil Goldstein** (p, kbds), **Harry Lookofsky** (vn); **Lamar Alsop** (vn, va); **Harold Colletta, Theodore Israel** (va); **Jesse Levy** (vc); **Joe Beck, Jay Berliner** (g); **Buster Williams** (b); **Mel Lewis** (d, perc); **Gil Evans** (arr, cond); **Steve Lacy** (ss-2). EmArcy Ⓟ 834 205-2 (45 minutes). Recorded 1987.

✔                                                                                                                       ⑩ ⑩

A singer whose cool timbre resembles that of Chris Connor or June Christy, but who brings her emotions much closer to the surface, Merrill has surrounded herself with superior musicians throughout her career – her album with Clifford Brown from the fifties compares favourably with Sarah Vaughan's date with him from the same period. We have Merrill to thank for what amounted

to Evans's last hurrah as an arranger. **Collaboration** is a remake of **Dream of You**, Merrill's 1956 album with Evans which is said to have inspired **Miles Ahead** and Evans's subsequent albums for Miles Davis. Because failing health prevented Evans from writing new charts for this reunion with Merrill, he recorded two new versions of 11 of the 12 songs from **Dream of You**. If anything, these remakes swim deeper emotional currents than the originals, and they certainly sound more like Evans's work than most of what he recorded with his own wayward big band in the last decade of his life. The heartstopper is *Anyplace I Hang My Hat is Home*, a prime example of how an Evans arrangement could make a great song even better: with its unlikely combination of boogie-woogie rumble and existential *douleur*, it sounds like something written by Meade Lux Lewis and Jean Paul Sartre, instead of by Harold Arlen and Johnny Mercer. Steve Lacy's solos on two tracks are an inestimable bonus, but the star soloist is Merrill, a class act who has rarely sounded better than she does here.
**FD**

# The Messengers

**New review**

**Barungwa**  Prince Lengoasa (t); **Bheki Mbatha**, **Andy Rogers**, **Neil Yates** (tb); **Chris Bowden** (as, ts), **Mckoy Mrudata** (ts, f); **Ian Price** (ts); **Mick Foster** (bs); **Moses Molelekwu** (p); **Mxolise 'Dave' Mayekana** (g, v); **Peter Martin**, **Jeremy Shaw** (g); **Ike Leo** (b); **Andrew Missingham** (d); **Simpiwe Matole** (mba); **Pops Mohamed** (Mbira, didjeridu); **Gabriel Mabe Thobejane** (perc); **Themba 'Max' Mntambo**, **Wendy Mseleku**, **Nozipho Nguse**, **Faca Khulu**, **Ngxabhisho Khubheka** (v). B&W
Ⓔ BW070 (52 minutes). Recorded 1995.

⑥ ❽

This international collaboration, co-ordinated by Missingham, is far more than the meeting of three British-based musicians (Bowden, Leo and Missingham) with three South African counterparts (Mntambo, Molelekwa and Mayekana) for an intense fortnight of recording. One by one, many more of South Africa's individual jazz voices came to the studios and in overdubs or foundation backing tracks added their parts to the album, until it became a complex kaleidoscope of sound. The joyful singing and catchy backing (built on Leo's bass lines) of *Siyahamba* best exemplifies the happy spirit of collaboration on the album. Other tracks have a range of sound effects included (from the opening and irritating telephone to voice commentaries that sound like out-takes from *Yellow Submarine*) which detract from the music but these apart, this is an entertaining album with strong world music connections and an overall South African feel. Notable among the participants is keyboard player Molelekwa.
**AS**

# Pat Metheny                                                                                       1954

**Travels**  Metheny (g); **Lyle Mays** (p, syn); **Steve Rodby** (b); **Dan Gottlieb** (d); **Nana Vasconcelos** (perc, v). ECM Ⓕ 810 622-2 (two discs: 96 minutes). Recorded 1982.

⑧ ❽

Metheny as guitar synthesizer whizz, composer, arranger, restless improviser, ambient soundscape constructor and above all virtuosic lyrical jazz guitar hero: 1982's **Travels** has it all, and all live at that. By this stage, Metheny's partnership with keyboardist and composer Mays was several albums old, and the magic they weave – a magic as successful commercially as artistically – was at its peak. Arguably, as the Pat Metheny Group has developed (and it has notched up a good five or so albums since **Travels**) the lushness of the arrangements and precision of the playing has taken the music further into the instrumental rock category and further away from any sort of jazz base, but no such criticisms could be levelled at the music they were making together on their 1982 world tour. Old favourites dating right back to the group's 1978 eponymous début, and then-recent but now-classic pieces like the achingly lovely ballad *Are You Going with Me?*, as well as material still not recorded elsewhere (most notably the dazzling guitar/synth freak out of *Song for Bilbao*) all get an airing. Of special note are the contributions of the extraordinary Brazilian percussionist and berimbau specialist Vasconcelos, who débuted on the group's Grammy-winning **Offramp**, and who brings a rhythmic vitality and textural earthiness to the group's sound that helps make this album unique in the guitarist's entire canon.
**SH**

**The Road to You – Live in Europe**  Metheny (g, gsyn); **Lyle Mays** (kbds); **Steve Rodby** (b); **Paul Wertigo** (d); **Armando Marcal** (perc); **Pedro Aznar** (v). Geffen Ⓕ 24601 (74 minutes). Recorded 1992.

⑦ ❽

The Pat Metheny Group has been responsible for some pretty boring albums in recent years, however nice the subtleties may have been. This album, taken from their 1992 European tour, re-establishes some muscle in their playing, touches base with some of their best-known compositions of the past, and conjures echoes of one of their best past efforts, the ECM album, **Travels**, from ten years ago. Tunes such as *First Circle, Last Train Home* and *Third Wind* get new workouts here, and Metheny himself plays them with a great deal more variety in tone and approach than he did the more standard jazz repertoire on the disappointing 1990 trio album with Dave Holland and Roy Haynes, **Question and Answer**. One still gets the impression that occasionally Metheny finds certain complex fingerboard patterns utterly irresistible, so that phrases come out in the most unlikely places and for no particular musical reason. Yet, on balance, there are a lot more good things going down than poor, and even though the material needs close attention to detail before it will reveal its true character, there is enough spirit in the highly professional playing of all Group members to make the effort rewarding. **KS**

**New review**

**We Live Here** Metheny (g, elg, gsyn); **Lyle Mays** (p, kbds); **Steve Rodby** (b, elb); **Paul Wertico** (d); **David Blamires** (v); **Mark Ledford** (v, flh, t); **Luis Conte** (perc). Geffen Ⓕ GED24729 (67 minutes). Recorded 1994.

⑦ ❾

Pat Metheny has never been a man for half-measures. At one end of the scale the mellifluous easy-listening productions of the Pat Metheny Group have been innocuous enough to attract mainstream radio play, but at the other, Metheny's unlikely admiration for Ornette Coleman has led to moments – and albums, like **Song X** – which demand more than casual engagement. This record, following as it does the grim thrash-metal extravaganza **Zero Tolerance for Silence**, is the perfect demonstration of that artistic schizophrenia. Although nothing unusual in general terms, the record is a departure for Metheny in being his first substantial adventure into funk rhythms, inspired in this case by trendy hip-hop drum loops. The basic material – often just a strolling funk bass riff – is flimsy, but the production is effective and there are some excellent guitar breaks in the Grant Green-Wes Montgomery tradition – especially on *Here to Stay* and *The Girls Next Door*. However, after the refreshingly bluesy early tracks, the record does tend to subside into the histrionic Brazilian-style fare that has made the Metheny Group a stadium attraction around the world. A good record, with some superb passages, but some sort of compromise between **Zero Tolerance** and this would at once integrate and maximize Metheny's range of expression. **MG**

# Hendrik Meurkens

**Slidin'** Meurkens (hca); **Dado Moroni**, **Mark Soskin** (p); **Peter Bernstein** (g); **David Finck**, **Harvie Swartz** (b); **Tim Horner** (d). Concord Ⓕ CCD4628 (63 minutes). Recorded 1994.

⑥ ❽

Meurkens was born in Hamburg of Dutch parents, attended Berklee College in Boston and taught himself to play the vibraphone. He plays harmonica here, as he has done on his three previous CDs on the Concord label. Many jazz enthusiasts, including the present writer, have quite serious reservations about the harmonica, preferring to relegate it to film soundtracks or blues bands. However Toots Thielemans, Max Geldray and now Hendrik Meurkens will cause a re-examination of long-held opinions if one adopts the view that these men play music first and foremost. Meurkens seems to have overcome most of the technical problems, although he admits in his notes to the difficulties in playing *legato*. His solos have all the interest of a good improvising saxophonist and he had taken care in his choice of companions, selecting men whose work complements the sound of the harmonica. Peter Bernstein is an excellent guitarist, both pianists (they play on six tracks apiece) are sensitive and inventive players while Horner is simply one of the most tasteful and intelligent of drummers. The music is based on good standards such as *All of You*, tasteful originals and two timeless jazz standards, Oliver Nelson's *Stolen Moments* and Kenny Barron's *Voyage*. If the listener is prepared to set aside preconceptions and prejudice he will be repaid with some fine music. Similar sentiments can be voiced for the follow-up album, **October Colours** (Concord). **AM**

# Mezz Mezzrow
1899-1972

**The King Jazz Story, Volume 2** Mezzrow (cl); **Sidney Bechet** (ss, cl); **Hot Lips Page** (t, v); **Sammy Price**, **Fitz Weston** (p); **Pops Foster**, **Wellman Braud** (b); **Sid Catlett**, **Baby Dodds**, **Kaiser Marshall** (d); **Pleasant Joe**, **Coot Grant**, **Douglas Daniels** (v). Storyville Ⓜ STCD8213 (77 minutes). Recorded 1945-7.

⑧ ❻

Mezz Mezzrow was a much maligned man who more literally than most lived for jazz. His prime skill was in propagandizing the music and organizing record dates, and his efforts in this direction with regard to Tommy Ladnier and Sidney Bechet should not be underestimated. Although his clarinet technique was limited, he excelled within its boundaries, and his instinctive support and obbligatos behind Bechet could not be bettered, with the result that he held the book of jazz open while Bechet wrote some of the greatest words in it.

The King Jazz label was Mezzrow's own, and while the recordings were predominantly of himself with Bechet (the versions of *Where Am I?*, *I'm Speaking My Mind* and *I Want Some* have declamatory Bechet at his most powerful), he gave Sam Price the opportunity to record some of his best solo tracks, and these are scattered throughout this and the other four volumes of King Jazz issues (Storyville STCD8212, 8214 and 8215) are every bit as good as this one, whilst STCD4104 is at variance only in being the sole CD with a playing time under 70 minutes.

Singers like Pleasant Joe and Coot Grant inhabited the backwaters in jazz, but thanks to Mezzrow they have their day here. Mezzrow's recorded comments on the music pop up between some of the tracks, and while they are an hilarious anachronism, they are heartfelt if misguided.          **SV**

## Joakim Milder

New review
**Sister Majs Blouse**  Milder (ts); **Sorje Fredriksson** (comp); **Bobo Stenson** (p); **Palle Danielsson** (b); **Fredrik Noren** (d). Mirrors Ⓕ MICD 002 (63 minutes). Recorded 1993.

⑨ ❾

Although Sorje Fredriksson made few records during his short life he was one of Sweden's most influential tenor saxists and composers. He was an early inspiration for the outstanding Milder, surely one of the most striking saxophonists playing today. The rhythm section here is one with which worked and which he used when recording. After Sorje's death his scores were entrusted to Palle Danielsson. Five of the 11 works here have never previously been recorded and the complete programme of music is a valuable insight into Swedish jazz. The conception is remarkable, the more so since this is music originally composed around 30 years ago. There is a haunting Scandinavian feeling which is heightened by the keening sound of Milder's tenor, sometimes uncannily like that of Britain's Bobby Wellins. Unlike so many contemporary tenor players, Milder does not believe in producing strings of notes for their own sake and there is an economy to his playing which is very welcome. It also focuses attention on his ideas and consistent tonal production. The title track is a fine blues written in the closing weeks of Fredriksson's life. All four men contribute equally to a memorable example of Swedish jazz, past and present.          **AM**

## Ron Miles

New review
**My Cruel Heart**  Miles (t); **Fred Hess** (ts); **Karl Miles** (f); **Al Moore** (org); **Todd Ayres**, **Rudy Lowe** (g); **Artie Moore** (b); **Rudy Royston** (d). Gramavision Ⓕ GCD79510 (56 minutes). Recorded 1995.

⑥ ❾

Miles seems in some oblique way to be out of Ornette Coleman via Bill Frisell and John Zorn. This album was produced by Wayne Horvitz, which gives another clue to its lineage. Miles has a secure if not overwhelming technique, a full sound and a penchant for melody, as well as a hankering after combining disparate (and often grating) sounds to create the backdrop for the improvisation. Sometimes it's two riff-driven guitars; other times it's a skewed bass ostinato; at other points again it may be an infernally tilted drum pattern. Whatever, there is usually a lot of space in the music (certainly there is harmonically) through which to grasp the slivers of melodic continuity issuing from Miles, tenorist Hess, or whoever else may be in the spotlight (Eric Miles's twinned flute on the title track, for example). This is a sombre album, and at times the word 'bleak' also comes to mind. The silence around a melodic statement that Ornette can manage also happens here, and it is significant that Bill Frisell is apparently featured on the forthcoming **Woman's Day** (Gramavision), while Miles has joined the Frisell band for its next European tour. Not the cheeriest music you'll ever encounter, but at least he doesn't sound like yet another Miles clone.          **KS**

## Glenn Miller                                                                    1904-44

**The Essential Glenn Miller**  Miller (tb, ldr); with a collective personnel including: **Dale McMickle, Bob Price, Legh Knowles, Clyde Hurley** (t); **Glenn Miller, Al Mastren, Paul Tanner** (tb); **Hal McIntyre, Wilbur Schwartz** (cl, as); **Gabe Gelinas** (as, bs); **Al Klink, Stanley Aronson** (ts); **Tex Beneke** (ts, v); **Chummy McGregor** (p); **Richard Fisher** (g); **Rowland Bundock** (b) **Maurice Purtill** (d); **Ray Eberle, Marion Hutton, Jerry Gray, Glenn Miller** (v). RCA Bluebird Ⓜ 66520 2 (two discs: 150 minutes). Recorded 1939-42.

⑧ ⑧

Listening to *In the Mood* for the millionth time in preparation to write about this compilation, I happened on an entirely banal but useful thought: this really is just *Woodchopper's Ball* with an asymmetrical riff thrown over the verse. Which makes you wonder about the relationship between Woody's original and Wingy Manone's *Tar Paper Stomp*; which also led me to think about the isolation ward Miller's music is often pushed into by jazz writers. Many critics would dispute the need to have *any* Glenn Miller records in a Guide of this nature – and indeed he is not in some recent ones I've seen – but this would seem more to be pique at his continued popularity than any really objective judgement. Miller, an adroit leader and arranger but a so-so instrumentalist and poor improviser, often recorded songs and ditties with only a tangential link to jazz, but then so did Harry James and Nat King Cole, and nobody denies them their jazz standing.

There are literally hundreds of Miller compilations on the market at present, but I've chosen this one because it has a good playing time, is mid-price, has much of the essential jazz-based Miller (*Little Brown Jug, Tuxedo Junction, Pennsylvania 6500, In the Mood, A String of Pearls* and *American Patrol*, for example), as well as all the hits and is released by RCA Bluebird, who own the original masters. This is an important point, because the producer of this quite lavish edition, Paul Williams, writes in the CD booklet "we examined every metal part still remaining in our vaults (masters, moulds and stampers) together with some test pressings ... After extensive restoration work, we were able to work with the original takes on all but three of the selections." The difference in quality over previous releases is marked, as a quick check against a predecessor such as **The Ultimate Glenn Miller** reveals. The full recording and personnel details are also available in the booklet, along with lots of pictures and a good essay from Colin Escott.

Some of the material included here is well beyond the realms of jazz, and if anyone should want just the instrumentals with clear jazz content, a sister reissue, **Swinging Instrumentals** (Bluebird 66529 2) should suffice. If anyone happens to want the *complete* RCA Glenn Miller, 1938-42, then that is also currently available, on no fewer than 13 CDs and in a deluxe black box (RCA Bluebird ND90600) containing a 140-page booklet which exhaustively documents the civilian band from 1938-42. You have been warned ...                                                                                      **KS**

## Marcus Miller                                                                           1959

**Tales** Miller (v, f, g, p, kbds, bcl, elb, programming); **Michael 'Patches' Stewart** (t); **Kenny Garrett** (as); **Joshua Redman** (ts); **Hiram Bullock**, **Dean Brown** (elg); **Bernard Wright** (syn, org, kbds, marimba); **Poogie Bell**, **Lenny White** (d); **Lalah Hathaway**, **Joe Sample** (v); **Me'Shell NdegeOcello** (v, syn); **Bashiri Johnson** (perc samples); **David Ward** (programming). Dreyfus Ⓕ FDM36571-2. Recorded 1995.

④ ❽

Miller's mid-eighties début as leader, in which he posed Jacko-like atop a stack of hackneyed disco clichés, sat uncomfortably with his burgeoning reputation as one of the hippest young bassists in New York. Unfortunately, on the evidence of his last two solo records, not a lot has changed, certainly not enough to meet the high expectations attendant on the man who was indispensable to the success of David Sanborn's last all-electric records and who conceived and almost singlehandedly realized Miles Davis's final studio triumphs.

It is probably a warning sign that Miller has an extra-musical agenda for **Tales**. Its nature is hardly significant but it may explain the record's mystifying musical moribundity. The drum programming, all either slow or mid-tempo, is dense and static, there is little attempt at dynamic variation, the bass, dominant in themes and solos, is slapped and popped in an archaic mid-eighties style, several tunes seem to work the same pedestrian chord sequence and others are largely unmodified readings of seventies soul standards. There is some mild jazz interest from Garrett and Stewart, but one of the most successful pieces is Me'Shell NdegeOcello's *Rush Over* – good soul, but not much to do with jazz.    **MG**

## Mulgrew Miller                                                                         1955

**Wingspan** Miller (p); **Kenny Garrett** (as, f); **Steve Nelson** (vb); **Charnette Moffett** (b); **Tony Reedus** (d); **Rudy Bird** (perc). Landmark Ⓕ 1515-2 (54 minutes). Recorded 1987.

⑧ ❽

The names McCoy and Herbie dog younger pianists; these days, Tyner or Hancock are almost inescapable influences. Miller absorbed a lot of both, Tyner especially, but the Mississippi-born, Memphis-schooled pianist's style has also been shaped by bluesy southern roots and by significant stints with leaders Mercer Ellington, Betty Carter, Woody Shaw, Art Blakey and Tony Williams. Mulgrew's lines are graceful and flowing, sometimes long and intricate, yet tolling middle-register chords keep his flights tethered. **Wingspan**, his first non-trio album, demonstrates that Miller the leader does not follow the example of any former employer too closely. He writes fetching tunes, conspicuously the up-tempo romp, *Wingspan*, and *One's Own Room*, with lovely unisons for flute and vibes floating over a static bass line.

With Garrett's pungent alto up-front (the ballad *You're That Dream* makes effective use of his sour, keening long tones) Miller gets to show off his propulsive comping. Nelson's Hutcherson-like drifting lines contrast sharply with Miller's grounded chords; the two do not snarl each other up. The vibist makes a particularly strong statement on *I Remember You*, the only non-original. But then bringing out the best in sidefolk is a hallmark of any good leader.                                            **KW**

## Punch Miller                                                                       1894–1971

**Punch Miller's New Orleans Band 1957** Miller (t, v, ldr); **Eddie Morris** (tb); **Simon Frazier** (p); **Ricard Alexis** (b); **Bill Bagley** (d). 504 Ⓕ CD34 (57 minutes). Recorded 1957.

⑤ ❷

Miller was a widely acclaimed trumpeter, not best served by some of the recordings he left. He featured in New Orleans with Kid Ory, Jack Carey and Jelly Roll Morton in the twenties and worked New York and Chicago in the thirties and forties. His recording début was in 1925 but it was not until 1941 that he fronted his own studio session. He settled in New Orleans in 1956 and was best known for his playing with George Lewis and for the 1971 film, '*Til the Butcher Cut Him Down*.

His earliest influence had been Louis Armstrong and Miller was (then) blessed with a comparable attack. His moments of daring rivalled Jabbo Smith, his solos avoided the easy route and he had the power to carry even the most pedestrian ensemble. Little is available on CD and his latter-day playing is uneven. Restricted by a modest rhythm section and hampered by a fumbling trombone colleague on this CD, he faces an uphill battle. His powerful lead on *You Rascal You*, the swing he generates on *Sheik of Araby* and *Royal Garden Blues* recalls the master of the past, however, and he says enough on *All of Me* to endorse his reputation as an improviser. **BMcR**

## Lucky Millinder

1900-66

**Lucky Millinder 1941-2** Millinder (v, dir); **William Scott, Archie Johnson, Nelson Byrant, Freddy Webster, Dizzy Gillespie** (t); **George Stevenson, Donald Cole, Eli Robinson, Floyd Brady, Edward Morant, Sandy Williams, Joe Britton** (tb); **Billy Bowen, George James, Ted Barnett, Tab Smith** (as); **Buster Bailey** (cl, as); **Stafford Simon, Dave Young** (ts); **Ernest Purce** (bs); **Bill Doggett, Clyde Hart** (p); **Sister Rosetta Tharpe** (v, g); **Trevor Bacon, Sterling Marlow** (g); **Abe Bolar, George Duvivier, Nick Fenton** (b); **Panama Francis** (d). Classics Ⓜ 712 (61 minutes). Recorded 1941-2.

⑦ ❻

Millinder was not a musician, but notable sidemen such as Gillespie have spoken of his exceptional talent as a conductor. He first became a band leader in 1931, toured Europe in 1933, and in the following year assumed the leadership of the Mills Blue Rhythm Band. In 1940 he assembled his own band for a spot at the Savoy Ballroom and the tracks on this CD come from that period. It was music for dancers, but there were also jewels for the listener; all editions of the band had good rhythm sections and solos by Simon on *Apollo Jump*, Stevenson on *Slide, Mr Trombone*, Doggett on *Let Me Off Uptown*, Smith on *Little John Special* and Gillespie on *Mason Flyer* and *Little John Special* are highlights. Most of all, there is Tharpe's swinging guitar and stunningly secularized gospel vocals on *That's All, Trouble in Mind, Rock Me* and *Shout, Sister Shout* where she intones that "there ain't no reason why a band can't swing" and, as an endorsement, gives the band a Jimmy Rushing-like lift whenever she is featured. Millender led bands into the fifties and later stayed in touch with the music industry as a disc jockey. However, it was his romping band of the early forties for which he will be best remembered. **BMcR**

## Mills Blue Rhythm Band

**Rhythm Spasm** Wardell Jones, Shelton Hemphill, Ed Anderson, Eddie Mallory (t); **Harry White, Henry Hicks, George Washington** (tb); **Charlie Holmes** (cl, as); **Gene Mikell** (as); **Joe Garland** (cl, ts, bs); **Crawford Wethington** (as, bs); **Edgar Hayes** (p); **Benny James** (bj, g); **Hayes Alvis** (b, bb); **O'Neill Spencer** (d). Hep Ⓜ CD1015 (73 minutes). Recorded 1932-3.

⑦ ❼

The Mills Blue Rhythm Band has with some justification been identified as a Cab Calloway Orchestra clone. One suspects that Manager Irving Mills's 'control' of the Calloway and Ellington orchestras led to his manipulating the MBRB virtually as an available second choice to bookers. Such a situation was unfortunate, because this was a very good band. They were pushed along by a lively rhythm section and the roster of soloists was impressive. Anderson, an up-dated King Oliver rather than a Louis Armstrong devotee, shone with both open horn or as a passionate growler. Washington, as fiery as Jimmy Harrison on *Kokey Joe* or as suave as Dorsey as the occasion demanded, was an all-purpose trombonist; Garland excelled on both clarinet and tenor, while Hayes continually proved himself to be amongst the best pianists of his generation. The one drawback was that the MBRB may have been said to lack real personality as a band. It was not instantly recognizable and used a team of arrangers who too often produced charts which sounded like 'stocks', the off-the-shelf arrangements shunned by any band with ambition. White's *White Lightning*, Hayes's *The Growl* or Benny Carter's *Jazz Cocktail* are exceptions, but the band's overall anonymity was due not to what it played but rather to how its sidemen were asked to play it. **BMcR**

## Charles Mingus

1922-79

**Pithecanthropus Erectus** Mingus (b, ldr); **Jackie McLean** (as); **J.R. Monterose** (ts); **Mal Waldron** (p); **Willie Jones** (d). Atlantic Jazz Ⓜ 781456-2 (36 minutes). Recorded 1956.

❼ ⑩ ❼

There are classics and there are the extra-special ones. In terms of fifties and sixties jazz, **Kind of Blue** and **A Love Supreme** are the most oft-quoted examples of the latter group. There is a strong case to be made for adding **Pithecanthropus** to the list, although many would put **Blues and Roots** or **The Clown** before this one if a choice were to be made of Mingus's late-fifties Atlantic material. Sadly, **The**

**Clown**, which includes *Haitian Fight Song* and *Reincarnation of a Love-Bird* (not to mention the extra material from the session released finally on **Tonight at Noon**), is not currently on CD, while **Blues and Roots** is covered below. These facts notwithstanding, it is on this date that Mingus recorded some ground-breaking music and gave a clear indication of where his concerns in small-group music-making would lie for the next decade.

The title track is usually singled out as the most provocative composition here, with its programmatic qualities and its imitations of bestial screams. It certainly re-enacts drama, and its cyclic form allows the story to be told in a cohesive way which avoids the usual jazz pitfall of opening theme-solos-end theme. The onslaught of the sixties has drained away the shock of this music, but the content is still intact. This revolves around the dynamism inherent in the interaction between soloist and arrangement, and here *Pithecanthropus* is largely better off than **The Clown**, with stronger soloists all round (with the sole exception of **The Clown's** Jimmy Knepper). Yet to dwell on *Pithecanthropus* is to unfairly downgrade the sly charms of *A Foggy Day (In San Francisco)*, the beautiful and moving ballad *A Profile of Jackie*, with its utterly typical Mingus melody and counterline, and the remarkable *Love Chant*. At 15 minutes, *Chant* is the longest track on the album, but it never once falters, being a simple but ingeniously constructed exercise in extended form which finds the whole group engaged in inspired melodic and rhythmic interplay. **KS**

---

**East Coasting** Mingus (b, ldr); **Clarence Shaw** (t); **Jimmy Knepper** (tb); **Shafi Hadi** (as, ts); **Bill Evans** (p); **Dannie Richmond** (d). Bethlehem Ⓜ BET6014-2 (39 minutes). Recorded 1957.

⑧ ⑥

Nothing was ever placid in Mingus's life, and the three LPs he made in 1957 with more or less the same group (two for Bethlehem, one for RCA) are remarkable not only from the standpoint of the music itself, but also for the fact that the recordings took place at all. This CD is a literal transferral of the original Bethlehem **East Coasting** LP to the digital format: the other Bethlehem vinyl release, **A Modern Symposium of Music and Poetry**, is available on a separate CD (BET6015-2). Considering the playing time of this disc, it is conceiveable that both LPs would have fitted onto one CD. Be that as it may, the music is at least available. In retrospect, having Shaw, Knepper, Hadi, Evans and Richmond in his band simultaneously gave Mingus the broadest and most exciting palette to work from; each was an individual both in sound and ideas. Like Ellington, Mingus drew on their individuality to enhance his writing. Without these men this music would sound very different, and the tempestuous atmosphere of the rehearsals and performances must have contributed to the overall success of the music, hard though it may have been for those on the receiving end of Mingus's often brutal criticisms. There is a fragile beauty to *Celia* and a hectic, headlong excitement to the *Blues Conversation* in its final choruses, where a round of four-bar exchanges by the front line gets pared down to one bar apiece. This CD is vital in any serious consideration of Mingus's music, for it reveals much about both the leader and his men. As we go to press RCA Victor have reissued the CD of **New Tijuana Moods**, recorded in this same year and another essential record in any assessment of Mingus's overall achievement. **AM**

---

**Mingus Ah Um** Mingus (b); **John Handy III**, **Shafi Hadi** (as); **Booker Ervin** (ts); **Horace Parlan** (p); **Willie Dennis**, **Jimmy Knepper** (tb); **Dannie Richmond** (d). Columbia Ⓜ 450436-2 (46 minutes). Recorded 1959.

✓ ⑩ ⑥

This comes from a magic period when jazz was oozing with self-confidence. Bop had matured into modern jazz. Men like Mulligan, John Lewis and Mingus were using the language of jazz to make bigger statements. College kids felt bereft if they didn't have a few Brubeck, Miles or Mingus LPs in their collection. Rock still meant Elvis, or Buddy Holly. Everything looked good for jazz. Nobody knew that round the corner lay the Beatles, the rock explosion, free jazz and a lot of lean years for jazz musicians.

There is no better record from this era to show how a masterful composer/leader like Charles Mingus could create a series of miniatures which would satisfy anyone looking for either excitement or structure. Mingus could create near-abstract patterns. He could also get close to the heart of gospel and the blues, as in the joyous *Better Get It in Your Soul*. He could play the bass like a demon. And he was, quite unusually for the time, aware of jazz history; at least four of the tracks are tributes to such different musicians as Lester Young, Charlie Parker, Duke and Jelly Roll Morton. This record swings lightly and croons softly; it is very humorous and intensely serious. It is also one of the great jazz records of all time. **MK**

---

**Blues and Roots** Mingus (b); **Jimmy Knepper**, **Willie Dennis** (tb); **Jackie McLean**, **John Handy** (as); **Booker Ervin** (ts); **Pepper Adams** (bs); **Horace Parlan**, **Mal Waldron** (p); **Dannie Richmond** (d). Atlantic Jazz Ⓜ 781336-2 (38 minutes). Recorded 1960.

✓ ⑧ ⑧

Mingus was a gifted leader of men and a composer of substantial power. His pieces are notable for their originality and his interpretations of them for the expression of his deep passion. His self-defined role as a freedom fighter was no doubt aided by his inborn bloody-mindedness.

This album is one of his most passionate and exciting and is the one which first infected the general jazz audience with his message. The band is as good as any he ever led, with Ervin, Knepper and

Richmond being the Mingus equivalent of Ben Webster, 'Tricky Sam' Nanton and Sonny Greer. Ellington was Mingus's muse, with Parker also generating strong inspiration. Mingus was of course his own Jimmy Blanton and is one of the exceptions to the rule that bassists should accompany and not solo. His driving, hard plucked solos put the bass on equal terms with the horns. Opening with *Wednesday Night Prayer Meeting*, this collection has much of the gospel music influence from Mingus's youth. The use of the colours in his small orchestra is extraordinary, benefiting here from the presence of Pepper Adams. Mingus relishes the lower register of the baritone and Adams makes a fine complement to the bassist's prime soloist, Booker Ervin, he of the declamatory ideas, dry tone and gymnastic solos. Knepper was peculiarly good on all the Mingus albums on which he appeared taking all the trombone solos except the one on *Prayer Meeting*, where Dennis, a similarly radical player with an absorbing style, shows that he too was steeped in the Mingus idiom. The antithesis of Miles Davis's **Kind of Blue** album and recorded a year later, this ranks with the latter album as an example of the best music of the period.     **SV**

**Mingus at Antibes** Mingus (b, p); **Ted Curson** (t); **Eric Dolphy** (as, bcl); **Booker Ervin** (ts); **Dannie Richmond** (d); **Bud Powell** (p). Rhino Atlantic Ⓜ 790532-2 (72 minutes). Recorded 1960.
⑩ ❻

Much as Mingus idolized Ellington, he knew you didn't need a big band to sound like one. The Antibes quintet is the musical equivalent of three movie cowboys who defend a fort by making all the noise of a battalion. On these loose live pieces, one or two horns will function as a section, riffing behind a soloist to egg him on. These classic blues-and-gospel-drenched performances support the contention that Mingus got more impassioned performances from sidemen than they got on their own (Dolphy's own LPs from the period are noticeably more conservative). He and Mingus converse on 'talking' bass clarinet and bass. Curson's hard-driving attack and Ervin's blues-soaked timbre and sensibility were also perfect for the band. It frequently achieves a telepathic elegance, as on *Folk Forms No. 1*, a magnificent blues collectively improvised around a rhythmic figure played by Mingus and his alter ego Richmond.

Here and elsewhere, this fluid approach to quintet dynamics looks forward a decade to the Art Ensemble of Chicago. *I'll Remember April* – featuring the great pianist Powell, sounding spry despite his continuing personal problems – demonstrates Mingus's time, plump sound and solid lines, and his ability to push soloists hard without tripping them. This is small group music of uncommon power.     **KW**

**Charles Mingus Presents Charles Mingus** Mingus (b); **Ted Curson** (t); **Eric Dolphy** (bcl, as); **Dannie Richmond** (d). Candid Ⓜ CD9005 (46 minutes). Recorded 1960.
✔
⑩ ❼

Recorded with the studio lights turned off to simulate the ambience of a nightclub, **Charles Mingus Presents Charles Mingus** captures the spontaneous and intimate fire of live performance. The group, which had been playing with Mingus during his long residency at the Showplace (in Greenwich Village), were familiar with both the material and each other. Their rapport is instantly apparent on *Folk Forms No. 1*, a freewheeling piece built on a brief rhythm pattern. The ensuing mêlée is wildly exciting – dashing ensembles, *a cappella* flourishes, frenetic altercations – at its centre a magnificent Mingus solo. Similar dialogues of form and freedom run – in and out of tempo – through the other pieces. Mingus and Richmond hold everything together with uncanny empathy, Curson blows with new boldness, Dolphy's volatile alto soars into the outer reaches of tonality.

Two of Mingus's best-known tracks are here: *Original Faubus Fables* (the definitive, uncensored version) is his put-down of the Arkansas governor who opposed integration; *What Love*, famous for its bass/bass-clarinet 'conversation', is a duet based on speech patterns that erupts into a slanging-match. A very humorous piece, it shows Mingus extending the range of instrumental expression just as his experiments with time and form were extending the parameters of group improvisation. Fiercely played, intensely felt, daringly conceived, **Charles Mingus Presents Charles Mingus** is one of his essential albums.     **GL**

**Oh Yeah** Mingus (p, v); **Jimmy Knepper** (tb); **Roland Kirk** (ts, mzo, str, f, siren); **Booker Ervin** (ts); **Doug Watkins** (b); **Dannie Richmond** (d). Atlantic Jazz 90667-2 (68 minutes: 46 music; 24 interview). Recorded 1961.
⑧ ❽

If the practice of reissuing old material in CD format is to earn any respectability, opportunities to correct anomalies connected with previous vinyl issues must be seized with both hands. The extraordinary material from this December 1961 session – particularly valuable because Mingus plays piano rather than bass throughout, and sings the odd blues – was issued on vinyl, split between **Oh Yeah** and one half of **Tonight at Noon**. A CD reissue could have created something approaching a masterpiece, albeit an eccentric and unusually rumbustious one, even by Mingusian standards, simply by collecting together again all the material – conveniently CD-length – from that original session and issuing it as recorded. Instead, Atlantic have unearthed a 24-minute conversation between Nesuhi Ertegun and Mingus and included that where '*Old' Blues for Walt's Torin*, *Invisible Lady* and *Peggy's Blue Skylight* should have been. This beef – and it's a big one – aside, what remains is well worth having: wailing, blowsy, wonderfully overblown blues; church music given the unique Mingus treatment; a humorous Fats Waller tribute, all performed by Mingus regulars at the peak of their powers. Roland Kirk is a delight throughout: raw, emotional and totally unpredictable; Booker Ervin is his perfect foil, all contained passion; Jimmy Knepper produces several solos of great warmth and quirky humanity; Mingus himself plays utterly distinctive piano, oddly phrased and percussive, and he sings the occasional blues in an affecting, high smoky whisper. The session as issued here, however, tilts too far towards the humorous; the missing tracks would have restored the balance and created a near-perfect album – as it is, what remains is a highly entertaining novelty.					**CP**

**The Black Saint and the Sinner Lady** Mingus (b, p, arr); **Rolf Ericson, Richard Williams** (t); **Quentin Jackson** (tb); **Don Butterfield** (tba); **Charlie Mariano** (as); **Dick Hafer** (ts, f); **Jerome Richardson** (ss, bs, f); **Jaki Byard** (p); **Jay Berliner** (g); **Dannie Richmond** (d). Impulse! Ⓜ IMP11742 (39 minutes). Recorded 1963.

✓								⑩ ⑩

A classic album standing at the intersection of Mingus's staggeringly individual small-group work and his generally less original writing for big band. Not only for reasons of size, the ensemble manages to combine the loose discipline of the very greatest large units with the controlled freedom associated with Mingus at his best. Although possibly conceived for a larger band (some of the material was originally prepared for use in the abandoned **Epitaph**, where it is titled *Ballad (In Other Words, I Am Three)*, the music was probably tried out and worked over by the unit which recorded it during the weeks preceding the session.

Described by its composer as ballet music, this is a single work in four tracks or six 'movements', linked in a complex manner determined partly by tape-editing and creative use of an overdub by Mariano. Although he is the chief soloist (in what has been described as the performance of a lifetime), there is also excellent work from the two trumpets, Spanish guitarist Berliner and trombonist Jackson, whose Ellington echoes are the other unforgettable sound of the piece. While also echoing other Mingus works, the summation of his concerns here makes this a peak experience. **BP**

New review

**Mingus, Mingus, Mingus, Mingus, Mingus** Mingus (b, p, arr); **Eddie Preston, Richard Williams, Rolf Ericson** (t); **Britt Woodman, Quentin Jackson** (tb); **Don Butterfield** (bb); **Jerome Richardson** (ss, bs, f); **Eric Dolphy** (as, f); **Charles Mariano** (as); **Dick Hafer** (ts, f, ob); **Booker Ervin** (ts); **Jaki Byard** (p); **Jay Berliner** (g); **Walter Perkins, Dannie Richmond** (d). Impulse! Ⓜ IMP11702 (46 minutes). Recorded 1963.

									⑨ ⑧

This CD, from a highly productive period of Mingus's career, came about more as a marketing idea than a pre-conceived project. It combined material recorded during the **Black Saint** session with titles cut at a later date and using a similar sized but, if anything, superior line-up. In reality the mood of the **Black Saint** enterprise is retained on the two remainder titles, but although deprived of its single theme motivation, the later recording date shows with equal clarity that Mingus could adapt widely diverse material to a larger band. He returned to older compositions such as *Haitian Fight Song*, *Goodbye Pork Pie Hat* and *Better Git in Your Soul* (all retitled, possibly for copyright reasons) and gave them treatments suitable to this 11-piece unit. He drew on his love of Ellington to showcase his own powerful bass on *Mood Indigo* and he used orchestral textures that were ideal for a personnel which balanced four reeds with four brass, bottoming out with a tuba. The outcome is an album reflecting its contemporary setting and confirming that there were various musical blades at the cutting edge of jazz in the early sixties.					**BMcR**

**Right Now: Live at the Jazz Workshop** Mingus (b); **John Handy** (as); **Clifford Jordan** (ts); **Jane Getz** (p); **Dannie Richmond** (d). Fantasy Ⓜ OJCCD237-2 (47 minutes). Recorded 1964.

									⑩ ⑧

There is much of Charles Mingus the composer, arranger, virtuoso soloist and ensemble leader on his many classic albums. The galvanic effects of the Mingus/Dannie Richmond rhythmic section is less scrupulously preserved; recording studios simply did not encourage the all-out time bending that the pair generated in person (but hear *Folk Forms No. 1* on **Mingus Presents Mingus**). **Right Now** captures this in a surprisingly bold nightclub set. This was actually a quartet, with former sideman Handy added on *New Fables* (an opened-up *Fables of Faubus*) only. Not the most imposing of personnels, with the little-known Jane Getz and the already-journeyman Clifford Jordan. Those who paid belated attention to Jordan at the end of his career will love this album, where he plays as extravagantly and well as anywhere on record. While the free-to-funky *Fables* is great, the other lengthy piece, *Meditations (for a Pair of Wire Cutters)* puts the larger orchestral versions to shame and reaches a fiery plateau during Jordan's solo that makes it an indispensable part of the Mingus legacy.	**BB**

**Let My Children Hear Music** Mingus (b); **Lonnie Hillyer, Joe Wilder, Snooky Young** (t); **Julius Watkins** (frh); **Jerry Dodgion, Charles McPherson** (as); **Bobby Jones** (ts); **Sir Roland Hanna** (p); **Charles McCracken** (vc); **Ron Carter, Richard Davis, Milt Hinton** (b); **Danny Richmond** (d); **Sy Johnson** (arr); **James Moody** (ts). Columbia/Legacy Ⓜ CK48910 (60 minutes). Recorded 1971.

✓								⑩ ⑧

The incomplete personnel listing is from various other sources in addition to the CD booklet – you'd think that after 20 years CBS would have got it right. The label also should have reprinted in its entirety Mingus's original liner-essay, instead of boldfacing selected passages within an admittedly more informative essay by George Kanzler. Packaging aside, however, there's nothing to complain about here. Along with two live albums from France and the publication of his autobiography, *Beneath the Underdog*, **Let My Children Hear Music** announced Mingus's return to activity following a drawn-out bout with clinical depression. This is Mingus with the weight of the world upon his shoulders, but nobody ever brooded with such heroic physical force, or swung harder while so doing. Combining the structural abstraction of Mingus's work from the early fifties with the fulmination and combustibility of his **Pithecanthropus Erectus**, Eric Dolphy, and **Black Saint and the Sinner Lady** periods, this music can be interpreted as Mingus's attempt to sum himself up as he neared the age of 50. Significantly, a few of the pieces are reworkings of earlier ones, with *The Chill of Death* dating all the way back to the composer's adolescence. Although solos generally take second place to compositional layering, there are animated simultaneous improvisations between Hillyer, Jones and McPherson in various combinations – and between Mingus and Moody on a shouting stop-time shuffle called *Hobo Ho* which (according to Kanzler's notes) was pieced together from various takes by producer Teo Macero, but gives the illusion of being a carefree, one-take performance. Given its focus on composition, it is no surprise that this is the favourite Mingus album of many of the most ambitious composers to emerge from jazz in the last two decades. What tends to draw in the average listener, though, is the dark emotional undercurrent of this music, signified by the low brass on *The Shoes of the Fisherman's Wife* and six *arco* basses on *Adagio ma non Troppo*. **FD**

---

**New review**

**Changes One/Changes Two** Mingus (b), **George Adams** (ts, v), **Jack Walrath** (t), **Don Pullen** (p), **Danny Richmond** (d); add, on **Changes Two**: **Jackie Paris** (v), **Marcus Belgrave** (t), **Sy Johnson** (arr). Rhino/Atlantic Ⓜ R271403/4 (two discs, oas: 45 and 43 minutes). Recorded 1974.

⑧ ❽

Half the pieces on these two separate CDs have become important staples of the posthumous Mingus Big Band repertory, and for good reason: both albums, taken from the same sessions, spotlight a mature composer who seems to have gotten some of his inimitable shock tactics out of his system. It is a reflective Mingus and a mournful one (Ellington had died seven months earlier). These were the last recordings before his health seriously failed him, and the music has the reach of a statement: there are several different tunes within the huge constantly double-and-half-timing suites like *Orange Was the Color of Her Dress, Then Silk Blue* and *Sue's Changes*. Mingus at his best is full of bloody-minded drama, and a sense of foreboding permeates even a minor jam vehicle like Walrath's *Black Bats and Poles*.

Despite the probable tension inherent in the last gasp of a classic rhythm section against younger players who came along after the paradigm shift of Coleman and Taylor, the young members keep reflecting Mingus's own image: classicists, but ready to let passion take them away from comfortable melodies. This is especially true of Pullen, who balances Ellingtonian flourishes at the ends of the instrument with adrenaline flares in *Sue's Changes*. The piano has a few out-of-tune keys throughout, and *Devil Blues* (on **Changes One**), with George Adams's blues shouting, seems like a classic Mingus throwaway, at odds with the grandeur of all the rest. Still, it's an enthusiasm indulged by a working band whose single-take recording method (if Nat Hentoff's claim in the booklet-notes are to be believed) transmitted the excitement of a club gig. This should be collected in one double-CD set. **BR**

# Mingus Big Band

---

**Mingus Big Band 93** Collective personnel: **Randy Brecker, Ryan Kisor, Jack Walrath, Lew Soloff, Chris Kase** (t); **Art Baron, Sam Burtis, Dave Taylor, Ku-umba Frank Lacy** (tb); **Alex Foster, Steve Slagle** (as); **Chris Potter, John Stubblefield, Craig Handy** (ts); **Ronnie Cuber, Roger Rosenberg** (bs); **Joe Locke** (vb); **Kenny Drew Jr** (p); **Mike Formanek, Andy McKee** (b); **Marvin 'Smitty' Smith, Victor Jones** (d); **Ray Mantilla** (cga); **Ronnie Cuber, Jack Walrath, Sy Johnson, Charles Mingus** (arr). Dreyfus Jazz Ⓕ FDM36559-2 (78 minutes). Recorded 1993.

⑩ ❽

This is such a successful evocation of Charles Mingus's music that it deserves a place in any collection of Mingus records. All too often 'tribute' albums are pale copies of the original, sometimes produced to cash in on the name of a major departed figure, but the Mingus Big Band grew out of a 'workshop' unit which started to perform in September 1991 in New York's Time Cafe. It has the advantage of containing several men who actually played with Mingus, soloists such as Ronnie Cuber, Jack Walrath and arranger Sy Johnson. All ten numbers were composed by Mingus over a fairly long period (the CD contains a version of the 1947-vintage *Mingus Fingers*, for example), and in a number of cases the original Mingus arrangements have been used. But there is a vitality to the music, a raw, flaring passion which demands to be heard. Everyone involved is deeply committed to the Mingus concept, and the newer musicians include a fine wah-wah trombonist in Art Baron, some excellent saxophone soloists and Kenny Drew Jr, continuing the distinguished tradition of his late father at the keyboard. The final stamp of approval is the presence of Mingus's widow, Sue, who produced the album and presumably chose the musicians to be heard here from the pool of approximately 100 who have played at the Time Cafe workshop. That pool, by the way, is now more widely represented on the newest release from the Mingus Big Band, **Live in Time** (Dreyfus, 1997), recorded on a couple of wildly exciting nights at Fez under Time Cafe and including a Mingus composition, *Number 29*, never recorded by the man himself. **AM**

## Bob Mintzer

1953

**Departure** Mintzer, Lawrence Feldman, Bob Malach, Roger Rosenberg, Peter Yellin (saxes, f); Marvin Stamm, Laurie Frink, Tim Hagens, Bob Millikan, Mike Mossman (t, flh); Dave Bargeron, Mike Davis, Keith O'Quinn, Dave Taylor (tb); Phil Markowitz, Jim McNeeley (p); Michael Formanek (b); Lincoln Goines (elb); Peter Erskine, Jon Riley (d); Sammy Figueroa (perc). DMP Ⓔ CD493 (64 minutes). Recorded 1992.

⑧ ❿

Bob Mintzer's avowed aim in making **Departure** was to focus on "counterpoint and elaborate syncopation ... to expand on the concept of taking an orchestral approach to improvisation and groove music." Extremely experienced not only in the big-band field – his credits include stints with Buddy Rich, Hubert Laws, Louie Bellson and, most crucially, the Thad Jones-Mel Lewis band – but also in classical music, playing with the New York Philharmonic, the Brooklyn Philharmonic and the American Ballet Theatre, Mintzer brings to his composing and arranging for his own big band an open-minded, eclectic approach which has borne fruit here in a rich, vigorous and fresh-sounding album, packed with ideas and bursting with vitality. The material ranges from the driving opener, *Dialogue*, a musical conversation between Mintzer's tenor and Jon Riley's drums, through a semi-humorous 'production number', *The Big Show*, with its simple, growling riff; the evergreen Victor Feldman classic *Joshua*, to *Horns Alone*, where the rhythm section drops out and allows the horns to exploit Mintzer's extensive experience in and enthusiasm for chamber music, in his own words "particularly Bartók, Stravinsky and early music". In addition to Mintzer's own breadth of experience, the album also draws on New York's street rhythms, Latin, rock – even children's songs – and the result is a thoroughly contemporary-sounding big-band romping enjoyably through an original and varied repertoire. **CP**

## The Missourians

**Cab Calloway and The Missourians, 1929-30** Calloway (v); Roger Quincey Dickerson, Lammar Wright, Reuben Reeves (t); De Priest Wheeler, Harry White (tb); George Scott, William Thornton Blue (cl, as); Andrew Brown (cl, ts); Walter Thomas (cl, ts, bs); Earres Prince (p); Morris White (bj); Jimmy Smith (bb); Leroy Maxey (d). JSP Ⓔ JSPCD328 (74 minutes). Recorded 1929/30.

⑦ ❻

The Missourians were one of the most animated territory bands. Beginning life in St Louis as Wilson Robinson's Syncopators, adopted as the Cotton Club Orchestra in New York, they became the Missourians at the end of 1927. They were never the most imaginative of bands and, as this CD shows, their attempts at plagiarism are somewhat transparent. They borrow Bennie Moten's *South* to shore up *You'll Cry for Me*, they use distinctly Ellingtonian voicings on *Prohibition Blues* and lift *Stoppin' the Traffic* from McKinney's Cotton Pickers's *Milenberg Joys*. There is more than a hint of the Fletcher Henderson reed section on several titles, yet the band could be electrifyingly exciting. Maxey and Smith are at the heart of a highly propulsive rhythm section and they assist superbly growling trumpet solos by Dickerson, shapely clarinet work by Blue and punchy trombone fundamentals from Wheeler. The take-over by Calloway in 1930 did dilute this dynamic musical cocktail to some extent and eccentric scats on *Viper's Drag* or good jazz vocals like *Happy Feet* hardly compensate. Nevertheless, for a short time, the Missourians were a unit that, if only for their vitality, seriously rivalled the contemporary Ellington, Henderson and Luis Russell bands. **BMcR**

## Blue Mitchell

1930-79

**Big Six** Mitchell (t); Curtis Fuller (tb); Johnny Griffin (ts); Wynton Kelly (p); Wilbur Ware (b); Philly Joe Jones (d). Riverside Ⓜ OJCCD615-2 (43 minutes). Recorded 1958.

⑧ ❻

Mitchell had a warm, burnished sound and roots in the work of Fats Navarro and, perhaps, Clifford Brown. This was his first album as a leader, a heavyweight date which finds him in full control of his playing and not subjugated by the machine-gun style of Philly Joe Jones's drumming nor the powerful tenor work of Johnny Griffin, a man usually capable of cutting any new soloists down to size. The most impressive track is also the longest, Benny Golson's 2/4 time *Blues March* (this was the anthem-to-be's initial recording). But there are no weak tracks in this seven-tune programme, and Blue features himself with just the rhythm section on a slow tempo version of *There Will Never Be Another You*, showing off his tone and a fine vibrato control. The rhythm section is as good as one has a right to expect, but Wilbur Ware's bass lines are unusually subdued, which may be a fault in the original balance. Otherwise there is the bright immediacy associated with hard-bop recordings of the period.

Shortly after this session Mitchell joined the Horace Silver Quintet, at which point his career took off, but this initial recording remains one of his best. **AM**

# Red Mitchell
1927-92

**Red Mitchell-Harold Land Quintet: Hear Ye!!!! Hear Ye!!!!** Mitchell (b); **Land** (ts); **Carmell Jones** (t); **Frank Strazzeri** (p); **Leon Petties** (d). Atlantic Jazz Ⓜ 781376-2 (39 minutes). Recorded 1961.

⑧ ❻

Red Mitchell became closely associated with the West Coast movement in the fifties, but was originally from New York. His approach to the bass was always more hard-driving and imaginative than most of the Californian set. Like many of his generation he came up through the big bands, playing with both Chubby Jackson and Woody Herman before coming to prominence with the Gerry Mulligan Quartet. A measure of his enquiring musical mind is that he was one of the few to record with Ornette Coleman before the latter's successful move to New York. Mitchell's partner on this record (and in this group), Harold Land, was another player whose approach hardly fitted the West Coast stereotype, being the tenor player in the Clifford Brown-Max Roach Quintet for close to two years, then going on into the sixties and seventies in a creative musical partnership with Bobby Hutcherson which is excellently documented on records.

The quintet these two shared was together only briefly as a working unit, making this one album. It is a classic hard-bop session, combining exceptionally strong compositions from both Land and Mitchell with a fully formed group sound and exciting soloing from the two principals and the gifted trumpeter Carmell Jones. The opening track, Land's *Triplin' Awhile*, deserves to be much better known and is the type of tune the inner ear simply cannot dislodge for hours afterwards. Other pieces have a similar effect. Land plays with precision and purpose, while Jones has a flair and a sense of excitement rare in the bop trumpet circles of the time, which with rare exceptions (Morgan, Hubbard, Dorham, Mitchell) had already ossified into stylization and cliché. That excitement is shared by the whole group. Buy a copy and share it with them. **KS**

# Roscoe Mitchell
1940

New review
**Sound** Mitchell (as, cl, rec, little instruments); **Lester Bowie** (t, flh, hca); **Lester Lashley** (tb, vc); **Maurice McIntyre** (ts); **Malachi Favors** (b); **Alvin Fielder** (d). Delmark Ⓕ DE408 (68 minutes). Recorded 1966.

✔ ⑨ ❼

*Sound* was not only Roscoe Mitchell's first recorded effort, but the first official release by a member of Chicago's AACM (Association for the Advancement of Creative Musicians). As such it is a seminal album, carrying within its three compositions many of the seeds for what was to come from that key avant-garde organization, including the Art Ensemble of Chicago and the avant-pop loonings of Lester Bowie. To a public grappling with the full-frontal shriekings of the Albert Ayler-led New York school, the Chicago approach was a radical departure, calling for all sounds and musical fragments to be equally considered as material to be moulded into new and strikingly different forms. The methodology of that moulding was also different, using as a basis the idea of a group functioning as one body of sounds and silences, collectively and equally bringing about the creation of an organic totality called a performance. Often these totalities, contained within a composition such as the title piece here, or the cheeky and affectionate *Ornette*, would utilize a broad cross-section of jazz's history within its duration, and each instrument would swap roles endlessly in an attempt to create a rounded and fully-realized message. Thus the music could be registered at the absolute extremities of sound creation, from the barest whisper of an instrument's tonality to a ranting, tumbling, screaming explosion of cacophany. Of the three works here, *The Little Suite* comes closest to later AACM practice in its seamless combination of theme, extemporization and collective effort. *Sound*, though more immediate in its ability to shock and excite the listener, eventually has to be seen (as does *Ornette*) as a piece using the conventional jazz formula of initial theme-solos with accompaniment-closing theme. That having been said, there can be no doubt that Mitchell's solo on the original take of *Sound* is one of jazz's great treasures. For the CD generation Delmark have kindly included a previously unissued version of *Ornette*, plus two complete takes of *Sound* (the original LP version was a composite edit between the two). **KS**

New review
**Hey Donald** Mitchell (f, snino s, ss, as, ts); **Jodie Christian** (p); **Malachi Favors** (b); **Albert 'Tootie' Heath** (d, perc). Delmark Ⓕ DE475 (57 minutes). Recorded 1994.

⑨ ❽

The nineties have seen Mitchell continue as a creative force on a number of fronts. In 1992 his jazz-oriented Note Factory recorded the fine **This Dance is for Steve McCall** on Black Saint; in 1993 his New Chamber Ensemble, with vocalist Thomas Buckner, recorded **Pilgrimage**, a set of more notated material, for Lovely Music. Then in 1994 Mitchell returned to Chicago to record only his second disc for Delmark

– nearly 30 years after he had made his groundbreaking début **Sound** (see above) for the same label. On **Hey Donald** he's joined by AACM colleagues Christian and Favors plus veteran drummer Heath. The tracks fall neatly into three categories. The four free-form ensembles are seething tumults locked around Mitchell's wailing soprano. A quartet of mainstream compositions includes **Walking in the Moonlight**, a romantic tenor stroll written by Mitchell's father, and the title track, a jaunty swinger dedicated to late saxophonist Donald Myrick, an AACM founder-member. Mitchell's four duets with Favors are special: long-time associates in the Art Ensemble of Chicago, their telepathic intimacy conjures a gripping dialogue. If **Sound**'s spiky radicalism has given way to a more relaxed mastery, **Hey Donald** shows that Mitchell's music can still be as intensely challenging as it is enjoyable. **GL**

## Bill Mobley

New review

**Triple Bill** Mobley (t, flh); **Billy Pierce** (ts, ss); **Bill Easley** (as, cl, f); **Kenny Barron** (p); **Christian McBride** (b); **Alan Dawson** (d); **Ron McBee** (perc). Evidence Ⓕ ECD22163-2 (59 minutes). Recorded 1993.

⑦ **7**

This New York-based trumpeter and flügelhorn player is joined by a couple of other Bills on the front-line of what seems a fairly orthodox sextet. A lot of these American theme-solos-theme bop and post-bop dates result in skilful but dull sessions so **Triple Bill** is something of a find. A good part of the fun certainly comes from the choice of sidemen – Kenny Barron has perfected his immaculate yet spirited approach in some fine company over a number of decades, Christian McBride is the man of the moment on bass, and deserves to be, and Alan Dawson (who died, sadly, in 1996) proves an attentive drummer. But Mobley (no relation to Hank) has spent much of his musical career in arrangement and it shows, as he takes full advantage of the textural possibilities offered by the unusual combinations of instruments. Flügelhorn, soprano saxophone and flute make an attractive ensemble sound on *Prelude*, and the flügelhorn, clarinet and tenor saxophone combination on *Mulgrew's Motif* manages to sound close to a big band. *49th Street* – a superb composition – is a busy bop tune led by muted trumpet and blasted through with incredible poise and virtuosity before a muscular tenor solo. While the best tracks are original tunes, there is also a nice trip through Cole Porter's *I Concentrate on You*, with alto saxophonist Easley and tenor saxophonist Pierce swapping eights in another example of what makes this project different. **LC**

## Hank Mobley

1930-86

**Soul Station** Mobley (ts); **Wynton Kelly** (p); **Paul Chambers** (b); **Art Blakey** (d). Blue Note Ⓜ (37 minutes). Recorded 1960.

✅ ⑩ **8**

This is Mobley's masterpiece and one of the great jazz records, on a par with Rollins's **Saxophone Colossus**. Hank Mobley has been consistently undervalued because his prime virtues – elegance, rhythmic poise, warmth of tone, subtlety of nuance – fell out of fashion just as he was reaching his maturity. A former member of the Miles Davis Quintet and the Jazz Messengers, he was as well qualified as it was possible to be, a master of both the chromatic and modal approaches to improvisation. One number here, *This I Dig of You*, demonstrates how he could move between the two with absolute stylistic consistency. The tune alternates eight bars of a single scale with eight bars of chromatic changes, the first winding up the tension and the second releasing it. The sheer agility with which he exploits this musical drama would alone be enough to place him in the highest company.

Listen also to his brisk, spare statement of the theme to *Remember,* the clear, measured lines in the stop-time choruses of the blues *Dig Dis*, the calm, knowing exploration of *If I Should Lose You.* This CD conveys better than any other the purity of Mobley's imagination and the vigorous candour of his expression. **DG**

## The Modern Jazz Quartet

**Odds Against Tomorrow** Milt Jackson (vb); **John Lewis** (p); **Percy Heath** (b); **Connie Kay** (d). EMI/UA/Blue Note Ⓜ CDP7 93415-2 (33 minutes). Recorded 1959.

✅ ⑩ **7**

If you will excuse the pun, it is odd that two of the MJQ's greatest records are derived from John Lewis film soundtracks; most jazz groups usually provide rather sub-standard fare when it comes to music for films. But this is to reckon without John Lewis, the group's artistic director, and the remarkable creativity of this group. Both this album and the other (**One Never Knows** – Atlantic, not yet transferred to CD) gave the group some of their most challenging material to play. This present album contains the original version of what was to become one of the MJQ's most-requested concert items, *Skating in Central Park*, as well as memorable themes in *A Cold Wind is Blowing* and *Odds Against Tomorrow* itself.

The MJQ were often accused during their first 15 years together of an overly precious and

unswinging approach to their material. This album has a very small dynamic range, and is mostly *piano* or *pianissimo*, but the music is very intense, the improvising inspired (in the case of Jackson, it is certainly some of his best and most authoritative work on records), and the band really *do* swing when the occasion requires it. Lewis's arrangements, dealing as they do with just four instruments, are marvellously imaginative, evoking an unusually full range of images and feelings for the listener. In this case, economy certainly does pack a punch.                                                    **KS**

**New review**

**Lonely Woman** John Lewis (p); Milt Jackson (vb); Percy Heath (b); Connie Kay (d). Atlantic
Ⓜ 90665-2 (42 minutes). Recorded 1962.

⑨ ❽

Small pleasures abound with the MJQ, and this is surely one of their most finely detailed records. Milt Jackson is the extrovert, easily enjoyed, but John Lewis shouldn't be dismissed by anyone enamoured of famously hip idols like Sonny Clark or Dick Twardzik; without those pianists' abrupt pull-up-short rests, he nonetheless achieves a floating discourse, highly rhythmic with only the tiniest of left-hand interjections, full of space and the accomplished improviser's trick of not seeming bound by the tune. (Hear the second chorus on the *Lamb, Leopard* solo for Lewis's eccentricity.) The Ornette Coleman title track – the quietest piece on the record – is fine MJQ in itself, despite a somewhat genteel smoothing-out of the original's ragged grief. The best pieces here are the three quartet-size reductions of pieces originally written by Lewis for orchestra, *Animal Dance*, *Fugato*, and *Lamb, Leopard*, whose moods are darker and more nuanced. Finally, arrangement is the group's key attribute. Every piece comes fitted with drop-outs, changed-up rhythms, and an exquisite attention to timbral combination that anyone can spot.          **BR**

**Echoes** John Lewis (p); Milt Jackson (vb); Percy Heath (b); Connie Kay (d). Pablo Ⓜ CD2312.142
(45 minutes). Recorded 1984.

✓                                                                                 ❽ ❽

In 1974, after 22 years of playing and recording, the MJQ disbanded, but by 1981 requests for its reformation, particularly from Japanese bookers, had become too insistent to ignore. This CD is a studio-recorded reunion comprising six tracks, with three compositions by John Lewis, two by Milt Jackson and Percy Heath's *The Watergate Blues*, which is a feature for the composer's rich, warm-toned bass. The return of the four men has resulted in music which carries on, seamlessly, from the pre 1974 albums. Lewis is still the controlling factor and the temperature of the music is fairly mild, but the quartet was never designed to allow a free spirit to take off on an unscheduled series of improvised choruses. At the same time Milt Jackson's solos, within the constraints of the MJQ formula, are masterpieces of concision played over a near-perfect backing. On the opening vibes choruses in *Connie's Blues*, for example, Lewis's chords are an object lesson in piano accompaniment, each of them weighted perfectly to achieve the right amount of springiness. Tempo changes, even drum accents, appear to be rehearsed, the quartet always achieving the correct internal balance. If jazz can be said to have its equivalent of chamber music, this might be it. Nat Hentoff has written some good notes but Pablo have seen fit to print them white-on-black and reduce the original LP sleeve to a quarter of its size, so a magnifying glass may be needed.          **AM**

# Cody Moffett

**Evidence** Moffett (d); Wallace Roney (t); Kenny Garrett (as); Antoine Roney, Ravi Coltrane (ts);
Kenny Drew Jr (p); Charnett Moffett (b). Telarc Jazz Ⓕ CD83343 (57 minutes). Recorded 1993.

⑥ ❽

The young drummer is the son of Charles Moffett who used to play with Ornette Coleman in the sixties, and this début album features him with varying small groups, all including his more famous brother Charnett on bass. The permutating personnel consists of another pair of siblings (impressive trumpeter Wallace Roney and Shorteresque tenor Antoine Roney), a couple of sons of the famous (Kenny Drew Jr and Ravi Coltrane, who appears to be the tenor player who doubles on soprano and who has also recorded a couple of double-header albums with Antoine Roney), and a rank outsider, the altoist Kenny Garrett.

The programming is a cornucopia of fairly short performances of jazz standards by such as Gillespie, Davis, Rollins, Monk and Coltrane, the latter's *Equinox* being sadly in the wrong key with the wrong bass figure. Even the more recent repertoire consists of minor classics (Freddie Hubbard's *Red Clay* and Cedar Walton's *Bolivia*), with only one old pop-song (*Beautiful Love*) and, more surprisingly, only one original piece by each Moffett. The leader's drumming is reliable rather than recognizable but it will, like the names of his colleagues, be a guarantee of quality on future releases.          **BP**

# Louis Moholo                                                                  1940

**Exile** Moholo (d, v); Claude Deppa (t, flh, v); Sean Bergin (ts, f, concertina); Steve Williamson (ts,
as); Frank Douglas (elg); Paul Rogers (b); Thebe Lipere (perc, v). Ogun Ⓕ OGCD003
(63 minutes). Recorded 1990/1.

⑥ ❽

As a member of Chris McGregor's Blue Notes, Moholo arrived in London in 1965. Initially a bebop band, the Blue Notes had already begun to explore freer musical climes. Moholo's role in this development was important and his powerful style proved itself equally effective at the heart of McGregor's Brotherhood Of Breath big band. Work with diverse figures such as Steve Lacy, Peter Brötzmann, Elton Dean and Keith Tippett chronicles his development during the seventies and eighties but he always retained his South African connection. Its sheer rhythmic strength is evident throughout this CD and with Moholo, Lipere and Rogers at full bore, it is a powerful potion. Moholo's drumming style has been likened to Elvin Jones but, as his 'toppy' driving work on *Dudu Pukwana* and *Plastic Bag* demonstrates, it is a style tempered by high life elements at all times. His compositions are similarly African in their tone and his excellent Viva-La-Black band play them with a rare élan. The ensembles are a trifle untidy in places, the singing on *Kwa Langa Kumandi* amateurish and Douglas's solo style a little incongruous but this is real music with the emphasis on communication and the spirit, one of joy. **BMcR**

## Mokave

New review

**Afriqué** Larry Karush (p); Glen Moore (b); Glen Velez (perc); with John Bergamo, Junior Homrich, Bob Fernandez (perc); Pedro Eustache (bf). AudioQuest Music Ⓟ AQCD1024 (57 minutes). Recorded 1993.

⑦ ⑧

Like Glen Moore's most celebrated band, Oregon, Mokave inhabit a capacious musical terrain incorporating territory bordering on jazz, world and folk musics. Larry Karush and Glen Velez have previously collaborated on Steve Reich projects; Velez and Glen Moore worked together in Oregon's spawning ground, the Winter Consort. Unsurprisingly, given the band's collective pedigree, Mokave's overall sound is a heady, eclectic mix of translucent piano playing, purring bass and skilfully selected percussion. Their original material ranges from joyous, dancing Moore themes sensitively interpreted by Karush and lovingly embellished by Velez (who, as sleevenote writer W. Patrick Hinely remarks, is – if Trilok Gurtu is Elvin Jones – the Paul Motian of percussionists for his intense musicality), to Karush's slightly more broad-based, ambitious compositions, which are as liable to draw on African music as on freely improvised jazz. The two non-band member compositions included here are John Abercrombie's deceptively simple *Parable* and Scott LaFaro's lightly tripping melody, *Gloria's Step*; the latter showcases Moore's sonorous sound to perfection, but it is the band's extraordinary musical rapport which enables them – like Oregon – to create a coherent musical statement from such a rich diversity of traditions. **CP**

## Moses Molelekwa

New review

**Finding One's Self** Molelekwa (p, kbds); Timothy Prince Lengoasa (t, flh); McCoy Mrubata (ss, as, ts, f); Vivian Thulani Majola (ss, ts); Sidney 'Ace' Mnisi (ts); Soyaphi Louis Mhlanga (g); Fana Zulu, Janji Mayo, Sibusiso Victor Masonda (b); Lulu Gontsana, Vusi Mhumalo (d); Bassie Mahlasela Mattanyane (perc); Sipho Maboya, Max Ngcobo (v). B&W Ⓟ BW053 (56 minutes). Recorded 1994.

⑥ ⑧

In South Africa Molelekwa is already recognized as a major force in jazz piano and he has toured outside his home country with Hugh Masekela and Julian Bahula. He has made surprisingly few recordings, although his presence is notable on the **Barungwa** album reviewed elsewhere in this Guide. This is his first disc under his own name. For such a dynamic performer, rather too many of the tracks focus on his melancholy and reflective compositions, not helped by a piano in Johannesburg's Downtown studios that was clearly going further out of tune as the sessions progressed. The best examples of Molelekwa's playing are in the raffishly up-tempo *Ntate Moholo* (Grandfather), and the unaccompanied stately, gospel-tinged *Marabi A Aremogolo* and its sequel *Bo Molelekwa*. Because of the relative sameness of the material the remainder of the album is just a little less vibrant than it should be, but it is nevertheless as good a first album as many performers have made, and no doubt the precursor of many more to come from Molelekwa. **AS**

## Grachan Moncur III                                                             1937

**Some Other Stuff** Moncur (tb); Wayne Shorter (ts); Herbie Hancock (p); Cecil McBee (b); Tony Williams (d). Blue Note Ⓜ CDP8 32092-2 (41 minutes). Recorded 1964.

✅                                                                                           ⑩ ⑧

Moncur, son of the swing bassist, first made his mark with the Ray Charles band at the beginning of the sixties. After that, a stint with The Jazztet gave him some much-needed exposure and led to his work with altoist Jackie McLean. This in turn led him to Blue Note, who recorded him both with McLean and – just twice – as a leader. The first album, **Evolution**, has already been and gone as a CD reissue, and the music it had to offer was not far from what McLean's own band of the time (1963) was playing. A glance at the personnel on this album would perhaps lead you to believe that a Miles Davis-minus-Miles date would ensue: after all, Blue Note were by this time specialists at such things. This album, however, truly is some *other* stuff.

There are just four tracks (two per side of the old vinyl release) and the opener, *Gnostic*, immediately plunges us into the type of music which, along with Eric Dolphy's **Out to Lunch**, some Andrew Hill albums and the early Bobby Hutcherson dates, suggested that Blue Note really did have an alternative thoery of avant-garde jazz to propose to the world at large. Using a slow, simple melody, it is woven together by the extraordinary patterns Hancock uses and anticipates by close to a decade the type of 'space music' musicians would explore via synthesizers in the seventies and eighties. *Thandiwa* is a more conventional triple-time piece, but again, with *The Twins*, we have a miracle of sustained invention, this time collective, where the reactions between each soloist and the rhythm team, their bending of time and metre, have to be heard to be believed. Listening to the Shorter solo here, with its dense interlocking with Hancock, McBee and Williams, one wonders what worlds the Miles group could have developed into had the leader been amenable. *Nomadic* finishes the album, and it's a setting created for a Williams drum solo. Moncur comments in the notes "I thought it would just be nice to have a relaxed drum solo ... that would be soothing." Quite an extraordinary idea, and perhaps the only way to end this completely out-of-the-ordinary album. **KS**

# Thelonious Monk
1917-82

**Complete Blue Note Recordings** Monk (p); with various personnel including: **Idrees Sulieman, George Tait, Kenny Dorham** (t); **Danny Quebec West, Sahib Shihab, Lou Donaldson** (as); **Lucky Thompson, Sonny Rollins, John Coltrane** (ts); **Milt Jackson** (vb); **Gene Ramey, Bob Paige, Al McKibbon, Nelson Boyd, John Simmons, Paul Chambers, Ahmed Abdul Malik** (b); **Art Blakey, Max Roach, Shadow Wilson, Roy Haynes** (d); **Kenny Hagood** (v). Blue Note Ⓜ CDP8 30363-2 (four discs: 208 minutes). Recorded 1947–58.

✅ ⑩ ⑧

This major boxed set contains Monk's first recordings as a leader, made between 1947 and 1952, plus a session with Sonny Rollins from 1957 and a recently rediscovered 1958 live recording with John Coltrane from New York's Five Spot Café. As well as proving that Monk was one of the handful of truly great jazz composers, on a par with Morton and even, at times, with Ellington, these early pieces bear out an uncomfortable truth – namely that the best jazz records have often been produced under the worst conditions. They were held in a cheap New York studio, with little time and a piano badly in need of tuning, yet the results are superb: spare, cogent and uniquely haunting. The original version of *'Round Midnight*, Monk's most famous composition, illustrates perfectly how original a composer he was. The piece is now established as a minor standard, and because of its slow tempo most people play it as a romantic ballad. But listen to this performance and you will hear it as the composer heard it – sombre and menacing, a thing of flitting shadows and midnight fears. The nervous atmosphere is sustained by having the melody passing unpredictably from one instrument to another, by ghostly piano runs on the whole-tone scale, even by the slightly sour intonation. It reminds us that, after Ellington, Monk is the great impressionist composer of jazz. He never surpassed early works like *'Round Midnight*, *Misterioso* and *Evidence*, although he did equal them later. Their very bareness reveals the great originality of his mind and the completeness of his vision. The alternate takes included here offer added insight into his creative process. The inclusion of the poor-fidelity Five Spot recordings (taken from a private tape made by Coltrane's wife, Naima) is a decidedly questionable decision by the present-day Blue Note powers-that-be, whatever the music's undoubted historical significance. **DG**

**The Unique Thelonious Monk** Monk (p); **Oscar Pettiford** (b); **Art Blakey** (d). Riverside Ⓜ OJCCD064-2 (38 minutes). Recorded 1956.

✅ ⑩ ⑧

With a programme comprising seven standard tunes, this is an ideal introduction to the quirky, unexpected approach that Monk used. The material is familiar, the treatments are certainly not. There is a glancing, oblique quality to the theme statements of songs such as *Tea for Two* and *Honeysuckle Rose,* for example. On the former Pettiford introduces the verse *arco* then Monk moves into the chorus, subtly reharmonizing the song to suit his individual recasting of the melody. It is a little like taking a watch apart to see what makes it work; Monk was always concerned with the insides of tunes and he would often state the melody with such care that it would sound as if he was playing it for the first time. *Memories of You* (played as an unaccompanied solo) and *You Are too Beautiful* benefit from the charm of his apparent 'discovery' of these songs as he goes along. The fact of the matter is that his musical vocabulary was immense and his method of improvisation was well rooted in the swing era, where musicians played the tune 'as written' before carefully moving away from it. Art Blakey was always the perfect drummer for Monk, and Pettiford's surging bass lines provide him with the foundation he needed on what is, without doubt, one of his most important trio records. **AM**

**Brilliant Corners** Monk (p, cel); **Ernie Henry** (as); **Sonny Rollins** (ts); **Clark Terry** (t); **Oscar Pettiford** (b); **Max Roach** (d); **Paul Chambers** (b). Riverside Ⓜ OJCCD026-2 (43 minutes). Recorded 1956.

✅ ⑩ ⑧

This is one of Monk's most impressive band records, and it followed the trios which, as at Blue Note and Prestige, had opened his account with Riverside the previous year. It includes three then-new and challenging compositions that, contrasting with the deceptive concision of the early Blue Notes, show

Monk letting the soloists have their head within his carefully constructed enclosures. These players include the neglected Henry and the masterly Rollins, who had gained considerably in authority in the two years since he had last recorded with Monk, largely as a result of constant work in the group of Max Roach. Roach too is on excellent form here, collaborating with the pianist to vary the textures behind the improvisations, nowhere more than in the title track which is one of the relatively few examples of Monk giving his soloists a specifically rhythmic hurdle to negotiate.

It is a pity the bass is consistently under-recorded and that the piano intro to *Ba-lues Bolivar Blues-are*, missing from earlier reissues, was not restored; equally, the gradual settling of the pitch in the first half-minute of *Pannonica* could be rectified with modern technology. But such reservations are insignificant beside the strength of the music.                                        **BP**

---

**Monk's Music** Monk (p); **Ray Copeland** (t); **Gigi Gryce** (as); **Coleman Hawkins**, **John Coltrane** (ts); **Wilbur Ware** (b); **Art Blakey** (d).Riverside Ⓜ OJCCD084-2 (48 minutes). Recorded 1957.
✅                                                                                    ⑧ ❼

The music here is hard to beat, but in historical terms this is a tantalising and frustrating issue. It stands as a huge signpost in what was then regarded as modern jazz in that Coleman Hawkins, who had been Monk's mentor and employer during the 1940s, was present along with John Coltrane, then just beginning to take the music forward in a way which would make him Hawkins' replacement as the main influence on tenor saxophone playing. Incredibly, apart from what is here, Monk recorded only three further tracks with Coltrane, even though the tenorist was part of Monk's quartet for almost a year.

Monk's work is crisp and beautiful and his solos on these splendid themes (all but one are his) are amongst his finest work. A Monk session leaves the soloists uniquely exposed, and even Hawkins has occasional problems, although his interpretation of *Ruby, My Dear* ranks with his wonderful Capitol output of the mid-1940s. Gryce is rather swiped by the backwash, while Copeland operates at a fairly safe and thus unambitious level.

That apart, there is a constant moment to each track which probably indicates that things were going to Monk's liking. When that happened in the quartet wlth Rouse there was a burning and unmissable exhilaration in the music. Here that indicator is replaced by a deep underlying satisfaction which is just as palpable. The commendable recording quality helps to make this album indispensable to a serious collection of Monking.                                        **SV**

---

**The Thelonious Monk Orchestra at Town Hall** Monk (p); **Donald Byrd** (t); **Eddie Bert** (tb); **Robert Northern** (frh); **Jay McAllister** (tba); **Phil Woods** (as); **Charlie Rouse** (ts); **Pepper Adams** (bs); **Sam Jones** (b); **Art Taylor** (d). Riverside Ⓜ OJCCD206-2 (53 minutes). Recorded 1959.
✅                                                                                    ⑩ ❻

The orchestrations of six Monk tunes that Hall Overton produced in collaboration with the composer remain a marvel, full of the restless energy of Monk's piano and quartet and matched by a brash sound from the tentet that is both tinny and just right. Monk's basic group of the time featured the wide bottom of Sam Jones's and Art Taylor's time-playing, and the head-first logic of tenor saxophonist Charlie Rouse, who had only recently arrived. They power the massive locomotive of the Monk orchestra through haunting versions of *Monk's Mood* and *Crepuscule with Nellie*, hard bop jams of *Off Minor* and *Friday the 13th*, a signature *Thelonious* and pièce de résistance *Little Rootie Tootie* that features an arrangement of Monk's 1952 solo for the full band. One might have wished that Bert, Woods and Adams had a bit more solo space, and Byrd a bit less. Still, this was an exciting occasion that actually worked, and a key event in Monk's ascension to his position of pre-eminence among postwar American artists. The CD reissue supplements the original vinyl release with the complete version of *Thelonious* and second encore take of *Rootie*.                        **BB**

---

**Big Band and Quartet in Concert** Monk (p); **Charlie Rouse** (ts); **Butch Warren** (b); **Frank Dunlop** (d); with an ensemble comprising: **Thad Jones** (c); **Nick Travis** (t); **Steve Lacy** (ss); **Phil Woods** (as, cl); **Gene Allen** (bs, cl); **Eddie Bert** (tb); **Hall Overton** (arr). Columbia/Legacy Ⓜ C2K57636 (two discs: 108 minutes). Recorded 1963.
                                                                                    ⑨ ❽

Monk's landmark December 30, 1963 Philharmonic Hall concert at New York's Lincoln Center came at the height of Monkmania, when the pianist was being lionized by the popular press as well as by jazzophiles. Though calling the ten-piece ensemble a 'big band' was hyperbolic, especially given the horn section's primarily supportive role, the broader palette made possible by Monk's commercial as well as artistic success was greeted by the jazz press with wine and roses. Today, the spartan yet pungent enlargements of classic Monk lines like *Evidence*, *Epistrophy*, *Four in One* and *Misterioso* resonate with a timelessness that like all of Monk's music, simultaneously embracing the past as it points towards the future.

This was Monk's second venture with an expanded ensemble. Like the 1959 Town Hall concert, the task of fleshing out Monk's deliciously quirky lines and 'weird' harmonies fell to the under-appreciated Hall Overton. Indeed, it was Overton's ability to both preserve and magnify Monk's stylistic eccentricities, the angular lines and biting phrases, that is largely responsible for the project's enduring appeal. Monk was obviously inspired. So, too, were the members of his working quartet, especially tenor saxophonist Charlie Rouse. Also praiseworthy is the energized soloing of Phil Woods and the ensemble's overall empathy for this sublimely grand project. It should be noted that the 1964 release was severely edited to accommodate the LP format. For this CD reissue the entire concert, including previously deleted drum solos, has been restored. **CB**

---

**It's Monk's Time** Monk (p); **Charlie Rouse** (ts); **Butch Warren** (b); **Ben Riley** (d). Columbia Ⓜ 468405-2 (48 minutes). Recorded 1964.

✅ ⑩ ⑩

It's not only because I am very partial to *Lulu's Back in Town* that I'm going to sing the praises of this album. I happen to believe that it is one of Monk's best, and it is certainly among the best-recorded (I can only think of the follow-up studio album, **Monk**, as having recording quality to match this one). But *Lulu* does get things off to a flying start. Monk begins with an unaccompanied quasi-stride routine, played on a deliberately out-of-tune piano, doing wonderfully mischievous things to the song (such as slipping a semitone down on the last beat of the first measure of the melody proper, thereby rendering the jaunty mood of the song fit only for a bar-room scene) before coming to a pedal point, slowing almost to a stop, then swapping pianos and launching the quartet full tilt into a burning medium-tempo rendition. Under one of Rouse's best-ever solos, Monk is exceptionally busy and authoritative, prodding away at the harmonic base of the ditty. At the close, Thelonious returns to his bar-room relic and gets lugubrious. Beautiful.

The rest of the date keeps on or near this level, with two quite sane solo excursions on old standards (*Memories of You* and *Nice Work If You Can Get It*), plus vital updatings of some relatively untouched early Monk material (*Brake's Sake* and *Shuffle Boil*). Monk sounds very happy. Rouse is also in oustanding form, his sound warmer and more varied in expression than is often the case, his patterns refreshingly free of cliché. Warren and Riley, beautifully recorded, do everything right. **KS**

---

**The London Collection, Volumes 1-3** Monk (p); **Al McKibbon** (b); **Art Blakey** (d). Black Lion Ⓜ BLCD760101/116/142 (three discs, aas: 153 minutes). Recorded 1971.

⑧ ❽

This London session was Monk's last studio date. A decade of illness and neglect awaited him, but there was no hint of the troubles to come on this night of glorious music-making, which included Monk's first trio performances for 15 years, his first recordings with Art Blakey for 14 years and his best solo playing since 1959's **In San Francisco**.

The session, which began with a Monk solo and concluded with the trio, lasted for six hours. Volume One of this three-CD series (the discs are also available separately) collects nearly all of the solo masters, Volume 2 nearly all of the trio masters. The third disc comprises mostly alternate takes, though it also has the only takes of *The Man I Love*, *Something in Blue* (both solo) and *Introspection* (solo and trio), plus the nine-minute solo improvisation *Chordially*. The latter is actually Monk trying out the piano at the beginning of the evening and, as Brian Priestley remarks in his insert-notes, "what is fascinating is that Monk, being a composer, is unable to carry out this routine task without at the same time experimenting with chord densities and creating potential new melodies".

Even so, the third disc is perhaps best left for completists. Volumes 1 and 2, however, are near-essential items in the Monk discography and contain some of the liveliest, most engaging playing of his later years. Blakey has often been described as the ideal drummer for Monk: if he sounds a little busy here at times, perhaps that was the spur necessary to keep Monk fully extended. The music is certainly compelling and the rhythm section remains surefooted through both the bright flow of *I Mean You* and more complex feintings of *Evidence*, *Misterioso* and *Criss Cross*. The solo disc is better still, as Monk rings out the dissonances on *Trinkle Tinkle*, *Jackieing* and *Loverman*, turns reflective for *Darn That Dream*, negotiates the intricacies of *Little Rootie Tootie* and allows himself a little dry humour at the close of *Nice Work If You Can Get It*. This is and you should. **GL**

---

# Thelonious Monk Jr                                                                 1949

---

**New review**

**The Charm** Monk Jr (d); **Don Sickler** (t); **Willie Williams** (ts, ss, f); **Bobby Porcelli** (as, f); **Ronnie Mathews** (p); **Scott Colley** (b). Blue Note Ⓕ CDP7 89575-2 (57 minutes). Recorded 1995.

⑥ ❽

Thelonious Monk Jr grew up around Charlie Parker, Dizzy Gillespie and John Coltrane but later listened to Sly Stone, Jimi Hendrix and the Rolling Stones. He led a disco-orientated band called T. S. Monk but, into his forties, decided to take a jazz plunge. He was perhaps inhibited by his father's reputation but has since made steady progress. He is not a drummer distinguished by subtleties of rhythmic shading although, in rather an obvious way, he does swing. The ghost of his r&b background has still to be laid in its entirety but his activities on the festival circuit with a reasonably stable personnel have paid dividends. The Mathews, Colley, Monk team has achieved a good degree of integration, the band has advanced since the 1991 unit of **Take One** (CDP7 99614-2) and Sickler's arrangements on the likes of *Marvelous Marvin* and *Highest Mountain* serve the sextet well. His father's music still seems to be Monk's biggest barrier. At least the choice of tempo for *Bolivar Blues* is better but, despite Mathews's sensitive solo, the group fail to capture the loping intensity that made the original irresistable. Sickler is the most consistent soloist but Monk now has a hard bop band with its own identity. **BMcR**

# J.R. Monterose 1927-33

**A Little Pleasure** Monterose (ss, ts); **Tommy Flanagan** (p). Reservoir Ⓕ RSRCD109 (46 minutes). Recorded 1981.

⑧ ❽

Monterose, not to be confused with the Los Angeles-based tenor saxist Jack Montrose, was a needlessly neglected player who succeeded in keeping a remarkably low profile in terms of records for years. He is hardly well represented now, and this fascinating release is a CD reissue of an LP. When Monterose cropped up on record in the fifties with his single Blue Note album and on his appearances with Mingus and Kinny Dorham's Jazz Prophets his sound was often hard-edged, but during his eight years in Europe (1967-75) his tone, and his playing, mellowed somewhat. This is the most intimate of settings, with a close microphone set-up giving the listener the impression that he is sitting next to the two musicians. Monterose still had the "Phase One Coltrane" sound, sometimes overlaid with the scooped-out tone of Don Lanphere, but he was a fully rounded soloist with a warm approach to ballads (his *Never Let Me Go* here is a gem) and an easy sense of swing when the tempo increases. Flanagan is the ideal pianist in this context, always harmonically correct and with an enviable gradation of touch. The CD contains what are probably Monterose's only recorded examples of his soprano playing; on the title tune, Coltrane's *Central Park West* and *A Nightingale Sang in Berkeley Square*. He produced a unique and oboe-related sound. Recommended without reservation. **AM**

# Wes Montgomery 1923-68

**The Incredible Jazz Guitar** Montgomery (g); **Tommy Flanagan** (p); **Percy Heath** (b); **Albert Heath** (d). Riverside Ⓜ OJCCD036-2 (44 minutes). Recorded 1960.

✔ ⑩ ❻

After Charlie Christian there was Wes Montgomery. His impact on jazz critics with the World Pacific LP **Montgomery Brothers and Five Others** was universal. Apart from his undoubted musicianship and improvising abilities, he had perfected a trick of playing phrases in unison octaves (although it should be pointed out that Django Reinhardt had also done this during the thirties). **The Incredible Jazz Guitar** is one of the best albums he ever made and is thankfully free from added strings or an organ to cloud the beautiful tone of his instrument. He attacks the Sonny Rollins tune *Airegin* at a tempo which would leave many lesser players gasping, yet he works all his ideas out to logical conclusions. There are four originals included in this eight-tune programme, and two of them, *Four on Six* and *West Coast Blues,* have gone into the library of lasting jazz standards. Both use unexpected time signatures although the former, which commences in 4/4 against 6/8, reverts to common time for the improvised choruses. The rhythm section is faultless but spatially a little distant in the overall recording balance. This does not detract, however, from Wes's incredible guitar playing. **AM**

**Impressions: The Verve Jazz Sides** Montgomery (elg) with the orchestras of **Johnny Pate**, **Oliver Nelson** and **Don Sebesky** and small groups featuring **Jimmy Smith** (org); **Wynton Kelly** (p); **Paul Chambers**, **Ron Carter** (b); **Ray Barretto** (cga); **Grady Tate**, **Jimmy Cobb** (d). Verve Ⓜ 521 690-2 (two discs: 152 minutes). Recorded 1964-6.

✔ ⑩ ❽

Wes's orchestral work for Creed Taylor is quite reasonably regarded as one of the great jazz betrayals, and certainly things don't get off to a particularly good start in this double-CD collection, with Johnny Pate's arrangements of *West Coast Blues* and *Caravan* sounding like Sunday night at the Palladium. But the compilers have striven for damage-limitation, and things quickly look up with three Oliver Nelson big band arrangements which give Wes a chance to get up a head of steam, plus such Wes and Jimmy Smith classics as the cooking hothouse blues *James and Wes*. But Wes's Verve best – now, finally, available complete – is reserved to last.

As Pat Metheny says in the insert note, **Smokin' at the Half Note** "is the absolute greatest jazz-guitar album ever made", and it is here in total on disc two. Even the stoutest atheist could believe that divine inspiration was in the Half Note that night. On *No Blues*, Wes produces 24 ceaselessly inventive choruses, working perfectly finished bop phrases and imaginatively varied blues riffs into a flawless grand design. The Kelly trio is invested with the same muse and the result is 13 of the richest minutes in jazz, worth the price of this CD alone. **MG**

# Montgomery Brothers

New review

**Groove Yard** Wes Montgomery (g); **Buddy Montgomery** (p); **Monk Montgomery** (b); **Bobby Thomas** (d). Riverside Ⓜ OJCCD139-2 (39 minutes). Recorded 1961.

⑧ ❾

Wes was the *raison d'être* for the Brothers, who came from Indianapolis. They had all worked together there originally as The Mastersounds. Wes Montgomery was a natural virtuoso who had celebrity thrust upon him. His style, like that of most contemporary guitarists, was derived from that of Charlie Christian, but Montgomery also used devices from Reinhardt, notably the gipsy's use of unison octaves. His sound was more individual because, against the fashion of the day, he used his thumb rather than a plectrum. This recording is of particular interest because it presents him in an uncompromising jazz setting. He gravitated naturally to a trio with organ and unfortunately, as is their wont, the organists were not usually able to express themselves with comparable élan. Later he was picked up by jazz faddists in the recording industry and they provided him with a series of unsuitable settings which compromised his artistry. This session with the Montgomery Brothers, one of his earliest, remains one of his best. In the face of his pre-eminence it should not be overlooked that his brother Buddy is an admirable pianist. **SV**

# Tete Montoliu

**Songs for Love**  Montoliu (p). Enja Ⓔ ENZ2040 2 (43 minutes). Recorded 1974.

⑧ ❽

An unpretentious record – just one man sitting and playing mostly ballads – but one that grows on you. His version of *Here's That Rainy Day* is utterly convincing. His reworking of John Lewis's *Django* is equally satisfying, though it is hard to go too far wrong with *Django*, which is one of the few modern jazz compositions which really are compositions and have structures which stand up by themselves. The only tune that doesn't work is *Gentofte 4349*, probably because it is the only up-tempo one and therefore the only one on which you really miss the bass and drums. Otherwise this Catalan musician (I am sure he would object to being called Spanish) shows that he is a complete pianist; odd that he is not mentioned more when people draw up their lists of favourites. **MK**

# James Moody

1925

**Hi Fi Party**  Moody (as, ts); Dave Burns (t); William Shepherd (tb); Numa 'Pee Wee' Moore (bs); Jimmy Boyd (p); John Latham (b); Clarence Johnson (d); Eddie Jefferson (v). Prestige Ⓜ OJCCD1780-2 (47 minutes). Recorded 1955.

⑧ ❽

James Moody, in spite of the implications of his surname, is one of the most ebullient forces in all of jazz. Indeed, while a complete and totally dedicated jazz musician, Moody is also a natural entertainer who can, if the situation warrants, keep dancing feet happy and an audience smiling. Part of that ability was undoubtedly nurtured by Moody's long-standing association with Dizzy Gillespie, with whom he frequently and significantly teamed.

Moody's initial impact was felt in the late forties with his group, The Moderns: this band can be heard sharing a current Blue Note CD with a young Art Blakey. In 1955, when this swinging little-big-band date was waxed, Moody had patterned his alto style largely after Charlie Parker. For tenor, the weather vane was Lester Young, though Moody subsequently incorporated John Coltrane's modernist primer into his unique and energetic approach; flute was also added later. But here Moody impresses mainly with a musically sophisticated attack that also reflects such then-popular r&b performers as Earl Bostic, Bull Moose Jackson and Screamin' Jay Hawkins.

Moody, Burns and Shepherd – who had worked together in Gillespie's big band – handle the bulk of soloing chores with gusto and good cheer. It is a tightly knit ensemble with a loose, relaxed feel and a solid book that includes challenging originals like Benny Golson's *Big Ben* and John Acea's *Little Ricky*. There's a swinging romp through *There Will Never Be Another You* and a vocal, *Disappointed*, from Eddie Jefferson, who primarily served as Moody's road manager. All in all, an upbeat and consistently pleasing date. **CB**

New review

**Return From Overbrook**  Moody (as, ts, f) with a big band arranged by Johnny Pate and with a small group composed of Johnny Coles (t); William Shepherd (tb); Pee Wee Moore (bs); Jimmy Boyd (p); John Lathan (b); Clarence Johnson (d); Eddie Jefferson (v). Chess Ⓜ GRP18102 (64 minutes). Recorded 1956-8.

⑥ ❻

This CD is made up of two reissued LPs which don't really sit very comfortably together. The first ten tracks comprise an album made in 1958 with a big band arranged by Johnny Pate, where Moody is showcased playing standards against a remarkably stiff and strident background. The original album was called **Last Train from Overbrook**, and it was regarded as Moody's comeback record after a time recovering at Overbrook Sanitorium from his previous lifestyle. The arrangements are so unsuited to Moody's grainy and quite human timbre that he often gets lost to the listener as wave upon wave of stilted brass or sax figures swamp the audio. The small-group session from two years earlier which makes up the last ten tracks here was originally called **Flute'n The Blues**, and is a more relaxed affair, where the relatively rudimentary figures provided by Coles, Shepherd et al stay nicely tucked into the background and provide an undistracting cushion for the Moody sax and flute. Coles gets several chances to shine, showing his still-forming style to be more indebted to Clifford

Brown than later in his career, and trombonist Shepherd is also heard at length. Eddie Jefferson sings some of his own lyrics on three tracks, adding little to the overall quality of the music and making things too hip for words. Moody is generally in very good fettle, especially on tenor (making a nonsense of the title), displaying his fine melodicism and his consummate musicianship in his usual understated way. **KS**

# Whistlin' Alex Moore
1899-1989

**New review**
**From North Dallas to the East Side** Moore (p, v, whistling). Arhoolie Ⓕ CD408 (77 minutes). Recorded 1947-69.

⑧ ❼

The word that most immediately springs to mind about this CD and its sole contributor is 'authenticity'. When critics Paul Oliver and Chris Strachwitz found him in Dallas in 1960 he had been out of the recording limelight for a lengthy period. What was significant was that the man who began his recording career in 1929 and subsequently worked the honky tonks, speakeasies and bars of Dallas had not changed in his musical outlook. It might be presumptuous to suggest that he was playing better than ever, but on the three recording dates (1947, 1960 and 1969) on this album there is no variation in quality. Moore is a rough-hewn Texas singer but it is his varied piano skills that earn him a place in this jazz guide. His roaring boogie know-how is amply displayed on *July Boogie*, *Alex's Boogie* and *Boogie in the Barrel*. His ability to drag at the tempo on a down-home, earthy blues brings a tension and reality to *Back to Froggy Bottom* and *West Texas Woman*. There is an idiosyncratic stride quality to *Alex's Wild Blues*, while his driving attack in the barrelhouse manner brings drama to *New Miss No-Good Weed*, *Alex's Blues* and *You Say I am a Bad Feller*. His whistling is heard on only two tracks, but he is a fine and strident performer in this somewhat lost jazz art. In fact it typifies the man; a musician to whom playing jazz was akin to breathing. **BMcR**

# Michael Moore
1954

**New review**
**Chicoutimi** Moore (cl); **Fred Hersch** (p); **Mark Helias** (b). Ramboy Ⓕ 06 (58 minutes). Recorded 1993.

⑧ ❽

Moore was born in California, studied at Boston's New England Conservatory then relocated to Amsterdam in 1982. Now established on the Dutch improvising scene, he's recorded with Maarten Altena, fellow expatriate Curtis Clark and the ICP Orchestra. He is also a regular member of both the Clusone Trio and Gerry Hemingway's American/Dutch quintet. He's led his own groups too; line-ups have included Herb Robertson (**Horne Game**), Alex Maguire (**Negligé**) and Marilyn Crispell (**MGM Trio**), the releases appearing on his own Ramboy label. **Chicoutimi** pays homage to the Jimmy Giuffre 3, specifically to their 1961 recordings **Fusion** and **Thesis**. Moore's trio lovingly recaptures many of that music's characteristics: its floating melody-lines and spacious feel (*Anomalous Soul*, *Open, Still ...*, *Chicoutimi*), its cool urgency (*Abdomen*, *Trident*), its delicate playfulness (*Grace*, *Be Careful*). They are more skittish, less focused than the Giuffre 3, lacking their model's gift for bracing abstraction, and occasionally drift towards the bland. But there are some fine moments too, with the clarinet particularly adept at evoking a fragile sensuality. Moore also cites the 1980 Lee Konitz/Gil Evans duets as an inspiration, that source most evident perhaps on *Rebus*, with its simple, repeating phrases in tightly-wound counterpoint. **GL**

# Oscar Moore
1912-81

**Oscar Moore** Moore (g); **Carl Perkins** (p); **Joe Comfort** (b); **Lee Young** (d); **Mike Pacheco** (perc). VSOP/Tampa Ⓕ #34/22CD (51 minutes). Recorded 1954.

⑥ ❺

If Oscar Moore is known to a wider public, it is only as the guitarist in the Nat King Cole Trio between 1937 and 1947. He combined the intricacy and instrumental sound of Les Paul with the harmonic attack of Charlie Christian, and was a highly-regarded player during his years with Cole. He left Cole to pursue a solo career but was diverted into his brother Johnny's group, the Three Blazers. It was downhill all the way from there, and within a year of recording this, one of only four albums as a leader from his whole career, he was working as a bricklayer.

He doesn't sound like someone who should be laying bricks. In fact, his humour and complete professionalism make him a likeable musical personality without being the type you would never forget. Pianist Perkins more neatly fits into the latter category, being one who promised much and died young. His playing here is considerably mellowed, and he often seems to be consciously mimicking Cole's piano style. A modest, competent album (in fact, it combines two old vinyl dates, from Tampa and from Skylark) which will help while away the time. **KS**

# Ralph Moore

**Who It Is You Are**  Moore (ts); **Benny Green** (p); **Peter Washington** (b); **Billy Higgins** (d).
Denon/Savoy Ⓔ CY75778 (70 minutes). Recorded 1993.

⑦ ❽

London-born Moore moved to California at the age of 15. He studied at Berklee in Boston, MA, before moving to New York in 1980. He was a sideman with Horace Silver and the Mingus Dynasty band and also worked with Dizzy Gillespie, Freddie Hubbard and J.J. Johnson. His earliest recordings exhibited more individual personality than some critics were prepared to allow but he was determined to break through as a leader in his own right. This status he realized in the mid-eighties and this CD, like its recent predecessors, finds him in good company. His playing is now very assured and titles like *Skylark* demonstrate the extent to which his breathing patterns accommodate his solo conception and not vice versa. He employs a wide dynamic range and his control of vibrato is emphasized on *But Beautiful*. Despite his original background, *Testifyin'* suggests that he has more than a little gospel in his soul, while *Yeah You* confirms that a spicing of contemporary funk need have no detrimental effect. Moore is also a useful composer, with *Esmeralda* in particular showing the extent to which his solos follow his theme shapes. They proclaim a musician whose improvisations combine the logical with the spontaneously creative. **BMcR**

# Airto Moreira

**The Other Side of This**  Moreira (v, perc); **Mickey Hart**, **Zakir Hussain**, **Babatunde Olatunje**, **Kitaro**, **Vikku Vinayakaram** (perc); **Dr. Verna Yater**, **Flora Purim**, **Caryl Ohrbach**, **Rose Solomon**, **Cheryl McEnaney** (v);  **Frank Colon**, **Giovanni Hidalgo**, **Diana Moreira**, **Justine Tons**, **Margaret Barkley**, **Leah Martino**, **Amrita Blair**, **K.C. Ross**, **Jana Holmer** (v, perc). Rykodisc Ⓔ RCD10207 (59 minutes). Recorded 1992.

⑧ ❽

Mickey Hart, drummer with legendary San Franciscan psychedelic rockers The Grateful Dead and all-round drumming historian-philosopher-spokesperson, claims that Airto Moreira "literally created the role of percussionist in the West." This is, of course, a little extravagant, but Hart is always deadly serious on the subject of percussion, and there is no doubt that the Brazilian Moreira (commonly recognized as simply 'Airto'), one-time member of Miles Davis's trail-blazing seventies-period electric doom-jazz group and founder member of Chick Corea's Return to Forever (just about the other end of the entire fusion spectrum), has been one of the most consistently astonishing and yet satisfying drummers in recent jazz, and never a musician to let his awesome technique get in the way of the music. **The Other Side of This**, a document of 1992 sessions organized and ultimately produced by Hart, is at first sight far removed from the electric jazz of Airto's youth. A purely percussion and vocals recording, the album pulls together percussion music and its practitioners from cultures as diverse, musically and geographically, as India, the US and Brazil, and this clearly with pan-global, deeply spiritual intentions. If this sounds a tad New Agey, rest assured; the spontaneity, virtuosity and sheer bravado of the performances make for hugely enjoyable listening. **SH**

# Frank Morgan

**Listen to the Dawn**  Morgan (as); **Kenny Burrell** (g); **Ron Carter** (b); **Grady Tate** (d). Antilles Ⓔ 518 979-2 (52 minutes). Recorded 1993.

⑧ ❽

This arresting and well put together album is a magnificent cameo by Morgan, who returned to the limelight only relatively recently after years of obscurity. On three compositions he is backed by Burrell alone, giving a soft chordal cushion for Morgan's breathy, delicate but hard-edged alto. Morgan is a player who picks up the threads of Charlie Parker's work and weaves them into an entirely different pattern from the Bird-influenced players of the fifties and sixties, excels in this intimate dialogue, his flurries of notes decorating an essentially ballad style in a completely personal way. When Ron Carter and Grady Tate add their almost telepathic skills to the rhythm section, the result is a light (but far from lightweight) and apparently effortless piece of music making that repays re-listening. Frank Morgan's years away from the public eye were hard and difficult. His playing has a lyric intensity rare in soloists who have no autobiographical pain or beauty to express. The altoist has recently moved to the Telarc label, and his latest from there, **Bop!**, features him winding the musical clock back effectively with the help of the Rodney Kendrick Trio. **AS**

# Lee Morgan

**The Best of Lee Morgan**  Morgan (t); **Jackie McLean**, **Gigi Gryce** (as); **Hank Mobley**, **Joe Henderson**, **Wayne Shorter**, **Benny Golson** (ts); **Pepper Adams** (bs); **Herbie Hancock**, **Barry Harris**, **Bobby Timmons**, **Harold Mabern**, **Ronnie Mathews**, **Sonny Clark**, **Wynton Kelly** (p); **Paul**

**Chambers**, **Larry Ridley**, **Bob Cranshaw**, **Doug Watkins**, **Victor Sproles**, **Butch Warren** (b); **Billy Higgins**, **Philly Joe Jones**, **Art Taylor**, **Charlie Persip** (d). Blue Note Ⓜ CDP7 91138-2 (73 minutes). Recorded 1957-65.

✔ ⑧ 🎱

There is no doubt that hard bop is one of the least pretentious and most trenchant forms of jazz expression. Its ugly name embraces a wealth of fine jazz music and Lee Morgan became one of its greatest practitioners. As far as can be ascertained Morgan never recorded a bad solo. Fortunately his short career was crammed with recording sessions and, since most of them were recorded for Blue Note by Rudy Van Gelder, their quality is high on all counts.

Morgan matured in Art Blakey's Jazz Messengers and it is notable that, although Blakey is not present on any of these sessions, his high standards and the general aura of good feeling generated by the Messengers permeates these nine tracks. Morgan's earliest influence was Clifford Brown, his near-contemporary, but he was not as agile as Brown and his playing had mainstream qualities in it – his half-valve work could, for instance, have come from listening to Rex Stewart. Some of the pieces here reflect the Blue Note penchant for funky blues – the medium must have made a fortune for the company – but tracks like *The Sidewinder* and *The Rumproller* are nevertheless filled with uncompromising solos of the highest calibre.

Morgan's five-minute work-out on a solo feature, an r&b ballad by Buddy Johnson called *Since I Fell For You*, is a trumpet jazz classic by anyone's standards and would serve as a marvellous introduction to a minor jazz giant. **SV**

---

**The Sidewinder** Morgan (t); **Joe Henderson** (ts); **Barry Harris** (p); **Bob Cranshaw** (b); **Billy Higgins** (d). Blue Note Ⓜ 821Y 84157-2 (41 minutes). Recorded 1963.

⑧ 🎱

This album has been accorded such iconic status in certain circles that it's worth reminding ourselves that most of the music on it doesn't in fact fit the funky jazz scene at all. In that at least it is a typical Blue Note product of its period. The label had been starting Horace Silver and Art Blakey records with funky gospel-tinged hard bop tracks for years, then leaving the musicians free to pursue whatever they wanted for the remainder of the disc. The only difference here is that the LP's side two also kicks off with another funky little number, so you get two for the price of one.

Not that such music doesn't suit Morgan and his band perfectly: after all, the trumpeter himself came up with the tune, so he clearly felt good about it. All that aside, everyone plays well here, whether they are funking it up or hitting a more mainstream groove. Morgan and Henderson mesh very well – well enough for the front line to remain intact when the follow-up, **The Rumproller**, came to be made (the title track of which is on the compilation above), and for Henderson to then be hired by Horace Silver as a replacement for the departing Junior Cook. I was going to make this part of the Basic Jazz Library, but then the compilation album above has the tracks off it everybody talks about, plus a more rounded picture of Morgan's career, so that's maybe a better place to start. Meanwhile, seek out the now-deleted **Search for the New Land**, a very different type of Morgan album from the same period. Morgan's late-period masterpiece, **Live at the Lighthouse** (Blue Note) has also been reissued, and its multiple-CD set contains two hours of extra music. Made with his working band of the early seventies (Bennie Maupin on reeds), it is also highly recommended, though every track is *long*. **KS**

# Joe Morris

1955

---

**New review**

**No Vertigo** Morris (g, elg, mand, banjouke). Leo Lab Ⓕ CDLR226. (77 minutes). Recorded 1995.

⑥ ❼

Since jazz's convenience marriage with rock, the term "jazz guitarist" has come to mean many things to many listeners. Morris has consummated his own part in the musical ceremony and can unquestionably be classified by the term. He is an original player and his background embraces blues, fusion and work with the less extreme sixties horn men. In home town Boston he exercised his stylistic predilections but has more recently made impressive albums with altoist Rob Brown (**Illuminate**, Leo Lab) and clarinettist/altoist Joe Maneri (**Three Men Walking**, ECM). This solo CD shows how he paints attractively in monochrome, putting the emphasis on the picture and not on how he decorates it for presentation. His improvisational methods are best demonstrated on the acoustic guitar and *Equilibrium* and *Balance Point* can be taken as yardsticks. The electric guitar avails him of more *legato* movement but in the main he shuns this and the sound of the axe is all that distinguishes the 'straight' from the 'plugged-in' instrument. *Long Carry*, on the banjouke (a ukulele with a banjo head), takes us on a percussive journey that endorses Morris's stylistic ambition and growing stature. **BMcR**

# Lawrence 'Butch' Morris

1940

---

**Dust to Dust** Morrls (cond); **Vickey Bodner** (ehn); **J.A. Deane** (tb, elect.); **Marty Ehrlich** (cl); **John Purcell** (o); **Janet Grice** (bn); **Myra Melford** (p); **Wayne Horvitz** (kbds, elp); **Brian Carrott** (vb);

Jason Hwang (vn); **Zeena Parkins** (hp); **Jean-Paul Bourelly** (g); **Andrew Cyrille** (d). New World
Ⓕ 80408-2 (61 minutes). Recorded 1990.

⑦ ❽

As a cornettist Morris was prominent on the West Coast before moving to New York and becoming involved with the loft movement of the seventies. He lived and worked in Paris for some time, but once back in America, he became increasingly involved with 'conduction', his own very special musical form. As this CD shows, the conductor becomes an organic part of the ensemble. He initiates rhythmic, melodic and harmonic changes and actually develops new musical structures while the piece is being performed. It is essentially a collective form, although Bourelly on *Othello B*, Ehrlich on *Long Goodbye* and Purcell on *Othello A* show how solos can be an integral part of an ensemble whole. The degree of Morris's conductive involvement is not always immediately apparent, a quandary complicated by the fact that he wrote all of the originals and that each of them has his distinctive stamp. They range from pastoral restraint to multiphonic turbulence, but there is no descriptive intent. It is an essentially orchestral form, with no theme-and-development system. It certainly accommodates the juxtaposition of musical anger and gentle beauty, and provides jazz with another important performance option. **BMcR**

# Thomas Morris                                               1898-c1949

**When a 'Gator Hollers** Morris (c); **Rex Stewart, Jabbo Smith** (c); **Geechie Fields, Charles Irvis, Joe Nanton** (tb); **Ernest Elliott, Happy Cauldwell, Bob Fuller** (reeds); **Mike Jackson** (p, v); **Lee Blair, Buddy Christian** (bj, g); **Bill Benford** (bb); **Wellman Braud** (b); **unknown** (d). Frog Ⓕ DGF1 (79 minutes). Recorded 1926.

⑥ ❹

A cornettist who made a recording début in 1922, played with Sidney Bechet in Clarence Williams's Blue Five, passed on his know-how with mutes to Bubber Miley and made more than one hundred and fifty recordings, deserves greater recognition. His style was personal if unspectacular and he played a significant part in the early New York scene. His timing lacked the rubato of the Oliver-Ladnier-Armstrong lineage but, like Johnny Dunn and others of the New York school, he coloured his more rigid delivery with muted effects that gave the impression of greater elasticity.

The titles on this CD come some time after his first breakthrough, but with improved recording quality they do show a more polished performer. *King of the Zulus* suggests that he had listened constructively to the New Orleans avant-garde but his powerful lead through the tempo changes of *Blues for the Everglades*, his well-organized solo on *PDQ Blues* and his preaching blues accompaniment on the title track are not the work of a primitive. In the thirties he quit music, working at Grand Central Station before joining a religious order. His contribution to jazz may appear modest but he was a significant figure in a New York scene trying to cope with the New Orleans jazz of the First World War and beyond. **BMcR**

# James Morrison

**Two the Max** Morrison (t, tb, flh); **Benny Green** (p); **Ray Brown** (b); **Jeff Hamilton** (d). East/West
Ⓕ 77125-2 (58 minutes). Recorded 1991.

⑧ ❽

Of all the current crop of young Australian instrumentalists, Morrison seems to have most successfully flown the coop, as is evidenced by both the music and the musicians on this album as well as by the label he is recording for. Morrison is equally adept on all three of his instruments and certainly lacks nothing in confidence: the opening track here, Jeff Hamilton's *Max*, has a stop-time structure which Morrison exploits wickedly with out-of-tempo half-valve growling. He then seamlessly devolves back into the hard-swinging rhythm section at the appropriate moment. No hesitant seconds there, for trumpeter or rhythm section. Of course, Ray Brown has been doing things like that to perfection all his working life, but this band he and Morrison are guiding breathes like a working unit rather than the studio pick-up outfit it actually is.

*Honeysuckle Rose* has a delicious duet opening between Brown and a flügelhorning Morrison before the piano and drums saunter in. During Morrison's long and engaging stint in the spotlight on this track, hints of a decided liking for Clark Terry become evident. In this he may be unusual amongst trumpeters and flügelhornists, but Terry is an excellent musician to take as any sort of model, and the relatively unexplored territory thus made available gives Morrison a head start on many other players.

His trombone playing equally glances back towards similarly pivotal figures with stylistic feet in both swing and bop camps – players such as Frank Rosolino and Jimmy Knepper – but what is most evident is that Morrison is building on the vocalized tradition of horn playing, whichever instrument he chooses for any given track. Terry's stint with Ellington places him in a similar stream, and both Rosolino and Knepper have a wonderful facility with smears and glissandos used as an adjunct to their melodic developments, so the patterns of Morrison's heritage seem remarkably consistent. As does this nicely-paced and immaculately executed showcase album. **KS**

# Jelly Roll Morton

**The Pearls** Morton (p, comp); with various groups including: **George Mitchell**, **Ward Pinkett**, **Ed Anderson**, **Edwin Swayzee**, **Sidney de Paris** (t); **Kid Ory**, **Gerald Reeves**, **Geechy Fields**, **Charlie Irvis**, **Claude Jones** (tb); **Omer Simeon**, **Barney Bigard**, **Darnell Howard**, **Johnny Dodds**, **Russell Procope**, **George Baquet**, **Albert Nicholas** (cl); **Stump Evans**, **Paul Barnes**, **Joe Garland**, **Walter 'Foots' Thomas**, **Sidney Bechet**, **Happy Cauldwell** (saxes); **Johnny St Cyr**, **Bud Scott**, **Lee Blair**, **Lawrence Lucie** (bj); **John Lindsay**, **Wellman Braud** (b); **Andrew Hilaire**, **Baby Dodds**, **Tommy Benford**, **Manzie Johnson**, **Zutty Singleton** (d). Bluebird Ⓜ ND86588 (73 minutes). Recorded 1926-39.

✓  ⑩ ⑧

Where do we begin our praises for Jelly Roll Morton's work? We might mention the endless variety which he contrives to draw from the seven instruments of the standard New Orleans dance band, the individual brilliance of the players, even the high quality of the recording, quite remarkable for such an early date. But more important than these is the almost physical sense of vitality and relish for life that fills the air when Morton's music is playing.

Finest of all is the sequence of pieces by Morton's Red Hot Peppers recorded between September and December 1926, beginning with the sublime *Black Bottom Stomp,* the first fully-realized composition in the jazz idiom and still among the finest, meticulously prepared yet sounding free as air. If the composition of European classical music resembles architecture, the composition of jazz is more akin to gardening; the materials have a life of their own and the composer's work is to trim, shape and combine them – which is exactly how these masterpieces were produced.

It would be difficult to compile a better anthology of 23 Morton pieces than this. Along with the complete 1926 sequence it includes, among others, *Shreveport Stomp,* its hideously demanding solo clarinet part faultlessly played by Omer Simeon, the haunting *Deep Creek* and two songs of yearning nostalgia from Morton's last years. The digital restoration does justice to the already excellent mono recording. **DG**

**His Complete Victor Recordings** Morton (p, v, arr); with the following collective personnel: **George Mitchell** (c); **Ward Pinkett**, **Ed Anderson**, **Edwin Swayze**, **David Richards**, **Boyd 'Red' Rosser**, **Red Allen**, **Bubber Miley**, **Sidney De Paris** (t); **Kid Ory**, **Gerald Reeves**, **Geechie Fields**, **William Cato**, **Charlie Irvis**, **J.C. Higginbotham**, **Wilber De Paris**, **Claude Jones**, **Fred Robinson** (tb); **Sidney Bechet** (cl, ss); **Omer Simeon**, **Ernie Bullock** (cl, bcl); **Barney Bigard**, **Darnell Howard**, **Johnny Dodds**, **George Baquet**, **Albert Nicholas** (cl); **Russell Procope** (cl, as); **Paul Barnes** (ss); **Walter Thomas** (as, bs); **Stump Evans** (as); **Joe Thomas** (cl, ts); **Joe Garland**, **Happy Cauldwell** (ts); **Rod Rodriguez** (p); **J. Wright Smith**, **Clarence Black** (vn); **Johnny St Cyr**, **Lee Blair**, **Barney Alexander** (bj); **Will Johnson**, **Bernard Addison**, **Howard Hill**, **Lawrence Lucie** (g); **John Linsday**, **Pops Foster**, **Billy Taylor**, **Wellman Braud** (b); **Quinn Wilson**, **Bill Benford**, **William Moore**, **Harry Prather**, **Pete Briggs** (tba); **Andrew Hilaire**, **Baby Dodds**, **Tommy Benford**, **Manzie Johnson**, **William Laws**, **Paul Barbarin**, **Zutty Singleton**, **Cozy Cole**, **Bill Beason** (d); **Lew LeMar** (v); **Marty Bloom** (sound effects). RCA Bluebird Ⓜ ND82361-2 (five discs: 342 minutes). Recorded 1926-39.

✓  ⑩ ⑧

Morton's place in jazz history is assured, for he was its first real composer/arranger. He himself claimed that he had invented jazz itself, and while this is clearly an overstatement, the fact remains that his own organizational methods are still in use today. This is beautifully exemplified on this set of over 100 tracks covering his most important and productive sessions for RCA Victor. There are a number of alternative takes here (all known to Morton experts, incidentally) but most of them simply reinforce the fact that Jelly had the music worked out in advance of the first attempt; there was little room for spontaneous improvisation on a Morton date. The first tracks, cut at a morning session in a Chicago hotel, are classics, with Morton leading a hand-picked band of mainly New Orleans-born musicians through *Black Bottom Stomp, Smoke House Blues* and two takes of *The Chant,* the latter written by the young white pianist Mel Stitzel. This was the beginning of Jelly's purple patch, when virtually everything he recorded had something beyond what others could achieve, however hard they tried. In 1927 Morton headed for New York, where the recordings he made still show the class and care of his Chicago dates, for Jelly used nothing but the best available musicians, men who were formally trained as well as being fine jazz soloists.

But the thirties were not kind to Morton, and nine years elapsed in between these and his subsequent Victor dates; yet his 1939 comeback titles are excellent, four of them featuring both Albert Nicholas and Sidney Bechet. The CDs also contain three attractive trio sessions, with the clarinets of Johnny Dodds, Barney Bigard and Omer Simeon featured on various titles.

The importance of the Morton Victors cannot be overstated, and while this five-CD boxed set has a lot to commend, including a 60-page booklet giving complete recording information, the production is flawed. Both *Freakish* and *Original Jelly Roll Blues* are listed as existing on the discs in two takes, but in each case take two is repeated and the first takes are therefore absent. The album title is also misleading; "his complete Victor recordings" actually refers only to those under Morton's own leadership, and a replanning of the masters could surely have given us the eight tracks under Wilton Crawley's name, the two by Lizzie Miles and the four by Billie Young, all of which have Jelly Roll at the keyboard. For such a significant set it would have been worth sweeping aside any commercial considerations and opting for a six-CD compilation. The sound is generally acceptable, but RCA's much vaunted 'NoNOISE' reprocessing system is not a complete success. There are occasional and disturbing increases in volume during ensemble passages and the notes admit that some (unspecified) tracks have been taken from "early (fifties and sixties) tape transfers". These caveats notwithstanding, the set is recommended as a vital and vibrant slice of jazz history. **AM**

---

**The Library of Congress Recordings** Morton (p, v, speech). Affinity Ⓜ CDAFS1010-13
(three discs: 231 minutes). Recorded 1938.

⑧ (see below)

The first recorded jazz 'documentary' resulted from the Depression-era interest in 'folk music'. Alan Lomax had been making field recordings of a wide range of folk artists for several years for the Library of Congress when he discovered the once-successful pianist/bandleader, working in utter obscurity in the nation's capital.

The talking and playing reflects Lomax's unawareness of Morton's personal achievements, concentrating to a large extent on his reminiscences of New Orleans, of otherwise unknown pianists around the country, and the influence of ragtime, folk-song and European music. This is fascinating stuff, enhanced by the fact that it all comes out Mortonized. Fortunately, Jelly was not overmodest and includes around 20 of his own compositions (authorship being sometimes disputed), with interesting variations from the commercial versions and including a couple otherwise unknown. That these recordings were never intended for release is underlined by the perfunctory recording, full of distortion and with the balance between Morton's piano, voice and tapping feet varying wildly from session to session. The remastering on these discs minimizes the listener's problems and, while discs one and three have some speech with piano backing, omits virtually all the passages where Morton merely talks. For the above reasons this set is impossible to compare with the rest of this book, but it remains required listening for the historically minded. **BP**

---

**New review**

**Last Sessions: The Complete General Recordings** Morton (p, v); add on 12 tracks **Henry 'Red' Allen** (t); **Albert Nicholas** (cl); **Eddie Williams** (as); **Wellman Braud** (b); **Zutty Singleton** (d). On eight of these tracks add **Joe Britton** or **Claude Jones** (tb). Commodore Ⓜ CMD14032 (71 minutes). Recorded 1939-40.

⑧ ⑧

Somebody has finally done Commodore records proud. Its new owners are the GRP group, and the first set of releases include Billie Holiday, Pee Wee Russell, Lester Young and this, Jelly Roll's last testament. Beautifully packaged (there is a picture of the Commodore record shop on the disc and inside the jewel case and the old 1940s designs are reinvoked) and properly documented, this reissue series is something to treasure. In the case of Jelly, the sound transfers are the best I have heard from this set of recorded performances yet, better than the old Columbia/German Teldec remasterings and much superior to the Classics CD (which also split the piano solo sides over two discs). The solo piano sides may reveal little new about Morton, but they are some of my favourites in that they are utterly relaxed, completely idiomatic and show Morton to be entirely in command of his music and his facilities. Here was a man at peace with his talent, his past and his music. On the faster numbers he generates tremendous drive, while his slower pieces have wonderful subtleties of interpretation regularly floating to the surface. His light baritone vocals on a handful of tracks are charming and, in the case of *Don't You Leave Me Here*, quite moving. The small-group sides are more problematic, finding both Jelly and Red Allen in fine form but seemingly more at odds as the music wears on and the gap between Morton's conception and the rest of the band seems to grow. The ensemble is disciplined and the drive is there, but the band is veering towards swing and Morton won't hear it. These are the songs of experience, and 1926 is now a long way away. **KS**

# Bob Moses

**Time Stood Still** Moses, Bill Martin (d), Mike Peipman, Miles Evans (t); Rob Scheps, Bob Gay, Ole Mathisen, Rafael Moses, Stan Strickland, Evan Ziporyn (reeds); Brian Carrot (vb); Duke Levine, Tisziji Munoz (g); Jamshied Sharifi (kbds); Yossi Fine, Matthew Garrison, Wesley Wirth (b); Bill Martin, Ben Wittman, Simone Haggaig (perc); Luciana Souza, Alvin Roberts (v); Jimmy Slyde (tap dancer). Gramavision Ⓕ R2 79493 (60 minutes). Recorded 1993-4.

⑧ ⑧

Drummer Bob Moses is a musical mystic, a metaphysical time-traveller whose open-ended forays emcompass and yet transform essences derived from the giants of the realm, "the powerful, ubiquitous spirits of Monk, Trane, Duke, Mingus, Rahsann, etc." Moses comes with solid credentials. Indeed, his charged percussive alchemy has provoked Larry Coryell, Gary Burton, Rahsaan Kirk, Jack DeJohnette, Dave Liebman, Mike Gibbs and Pat Metheny to some of their most ambitious explorations. Here, Moses continues the kind of large-ensemble, multi-cultural probe first initiated in **Bittersweet in the Ozone** (1975).

It's an adventure that traverses time and space. In *Prelude*, using a technique Moses calls "simul-circular loopology", the air is simultaneously still and vibrant. For *Felonious Thunk*, a funky backbeat and aphoristic rap pay Dadaistic tribute to the aforementioned Thelonious Monk. Wesley Wirth's cosmic bass carries the day in a heartfelt tribute to *Jaco* (Pastorius). The lyric playfulness of *Gregarious Chants* with Brian Carrot's vibes solo conjures up echoes of Moses' days with Burton. Also arresting are the Gil Evans-like orchestral colours of *Elegant Blue Ghosts* with Rob Scheps's plaintive tenor and Miles Evans' jabbing trumpet. Throughout, the members of the Boston Philharmonic prove worthy companions to Moses's grand and compellingly idiosyncratic quests.                                                                                               **CB**

# Bennie Moten                                                                                    1894-1935

**Kansas City Orchestra 1923-17/1930-2** Moten (p, ldr); with a collective personnel of: **Lammar Wright, Harry Cooper, Ed Lewis, Paul Webster** (c); **Oran 'Hot Lips' Page, Joe Keys, Dee Stewart, Booker Washington** (t); **Thamon Hayes** (tb, v); **Dan Minor** (tb); **Eddie Durhan** (tb, g); **Woody Walder** (cl, ts); **Harlan Leonard** (cl, ss, as); **Eddie Barefield** (cl, as); **La Forest Dent** (as, bs, bj); **Jack Washington** (cl, as, bs); **Ben Webster** (ts); **Ira 'Buster' Moten** (p); **Count Basie** (p, v); **Sam Tall, Leroy Berry** (bj); **Vernon Page** (bb); **Walter Page** (b); **Willie Hall, Willie McWashington** (d); **William Little, Jimmy Rushing, Josephine Garrison, Sterling Russell Trio** (v). Classics Ⓜ 518/9 (two discs, oas: 70, 69 minutes). Recorded 1923-32.

✓                                                                                               ⑧ ⑧

Moten represents yet another stumbling block to the 'jazz up the river from New Orleans' theory. Born in the ragtime heartland of Missouri, he played baritone horn before switching to piano in his teens. In the early twenties he led a quintet, but by the time he made his recording début in 1923, this had become a sextet. The collective playing on *Elephant Wobble*, from the first CD above, shows how far removed the band's uncompromising ensemble sound was from the accepted Louisiana formula. Admittedly the 1925 band's arrangements used unison cornet breaks in the manner of the King Oliver Creole Jazzband on titles such as *South*, but the similarity ended there. Moten was certainly not helped by Walder's eccentric clarinet style, but the arrival of Leonard in his reed section in 1924 gave him other options. The 1926 nonet did bear a superficial resemblance to Oliver's Savannah Syncopators, but the pulse of the band was altogether different, with the Moten band maintaining its 'rural' identity by retaining a place for the banjo-picker and giving a hint of the chicken-reel. Changes were becoming more obvious, however, and the band was moving ever closer to the even four-beat, rhythmic pattern as more accomplished sidemen joined the band and the outlook became more sophisticated.

The second CD shows that, by 1930, the band had been enriched by the arrival of Lips Page's driving trumpet, Basie's powerful piano, Durham's cultured guitar and forthright trombone, as well as by Rushing's already outstanding jazz singing. The introduction of string bassist Walter Page also transformed his rhythm section from its still slightly rustic verticality into a more flexible unit, one perfectly equipped to deliver the four-beat bass in its natural form. Durham's loose-limbed arrangements were a further asset, and the Luncefordesque mobility of the *Milenberg Joys* chant provides lasting evidence of the band's influence on those that came after. With the new foundation, Lips Page gained in stature and his masterful playing on *Toby*, *Moten Swing* and *Prince of Wails* made him a serious rival to Louis Armstrong as the trumpet king. The Hawkins-inspired Webster strengthened the reed section as well as the band's solo strength, and the young Rushing produced little masterpieces of jazz singing like *New Orleans*. The December 1932 *Two Times* was the band's last recording; Moten died from complications following a tonsillectomy. Fortunately for us, Basie was on hand to carry on the tradition.                                                                     **BMcR**

# Paul Motian                                                                                    1931

**Reincarnation of a Love Bird** Chris Potter (as, ts); Chris Cheek (ts); **Kurt Rosenwinkel, Wolfgang Muthspiel** (g); **Steve Swallow** (elb); **Paul Motian** (d); **Don Alias** (perc). jmt Ⓕ 514016-2 (54 minutes). Recorded 1994.

                                                                                                ⑧ ⑧

Paul Motian was once noted for his abstraction, but like many of his peers he has responded at length to the new awareness of jazz's past. **Reincarnation** is yet another example of his sustained reconciliation with the modern mainstream, one which has already spawned imaginative tributes to Monk, Bill Evans and the Broadway repertoire.

Less resourceful or flexible individuals, discovering or re-discovering bebop, have been happy enough just to do it, but while **Reincarnation** includes such familiar fare as *Half-Nelson*, *Two Bass Hit*, *Ornithology* and *'Round Midnight*, Motian thoroughly reinvents the old standards in a way that Parker, Gillespie, Mingus et al would have been bound to salute. The combination of such non-idiomatic timbres as distorted and chorussed guitar (the resultant legato actually very bebop), post-bop harmonic vocabulary and a joyously sprawling delivery produces music as vibrant and fresh as its inspirations and distinctly non-neoclassical. Indeed, in a world where imitation is too often equated with authenticity, **Reincarnation** is a rare, genuinely creative reading of bebop, easily the most impressive of Motian's recent retrospectives.                                                            **MG**

# Mound City Blue Blowers

**Mound City Blue Blowers** **Red McKenzie** (v, comb); **Bunny Berigan, Yank Lawson** (t); **Al Philburn** (tb); **Eddie Miller , Forrest Crawford** (cl, ts); **Sid Trucker** (cl, as); **Frank Signorelli, Gil Bowers** (p); **Nappy Lamare** (g, v); **Dave Barbour** (g); **Bob Haggart, Sid Weiss, Pete Peterson, Mort Stuhlmaker, Harry Goodman** (b); **Ray Bauduc, Dave Tough, Stan King** (d). Timeless Ⓜ CBC1-018 (73 minutes). Recorded 1935-6.

⑥ ❻

The Blue Blowers centred on McKenzie, a vocalist who made his name by making the paper and comb an acceptable jazz instrument. He was so expert at this that he could lead a band in the trumpet role without any apparent diminution of power. Additionally he was a very good in-tune singer who, although he sounds a bit ripe now, had a big influence on Bing Crosby. His most famous recordings were in 1929 with the Blue Blowers featuring Coleman Hawkins and Pee Wee Russell in profound ground-breaking roles. This third-generation version of the band (the first was a quartet of paper and comb, kazoo, banjo and a suitcase played as drums) finds McKenzie surrounded by the embryonic Bob Crosby band, plus worthy citizens like Berigan and Tough.

The jazz is light and invariably delightful. Berigan and Lawson played great lead and solo and Miller was a typically melodic New Orleans player, albeit better equipped technically than a lot of them. The light rhythm sections provide springy support for the soloists while instrumentals like *High Society* and *Muskrat Ramble* present some very good ensemble playing between the front line of Lawson and Miller. This is a treasure-house of little-known music from the dawn of the swing era.     **SV**

# Alphonse Mouzon

**New review**
**Mind Transplant** **Mouzon** (d, kbds); **Tommy Bolin, Lee Ritenour, Jay Graydon** (g); **Jerry Peters, Rocky Grace** (kbds); **Henry Davis, Stanley Sheldon** (elb). RPM Ⓜ 116 (53 minutes). Recorded 1974.

⑥ ❼

Mouzon began his recording career in 1969 with Gil Evans on his Ampex album, but he first came to prominence in 1971 as the first in a long line of drummers for Weather Report. His reputation as a bulldozing, powerhouse player with Larry Coryell's electric Eleventh House, competing hard with the likes of Mahavishnu's Billy Cobham, and strident belief in unflagging self publicity, much of it of the ridiculous 'who's fastest variety', gained him a Blue Note solo deal in 1974. Street-funk flavoured albums like **The Essence of Mystery** and **Funky Snakefoot** (all out of print) became the label's biggest sellers of the period, but **Mind Transplant** was aimed unashamedly at the burgeoning Mahavishnu/Cobham jazz-rock audience, with a knowing steal in Bolin from Cobham's début album, **Spectrum**.

Mouzon compacted his mastery of rudiments, polyrhythms, speed and power into an engine of unstoppable force and he never lets you forget it. Track titles like *Nitroglycerin*, *Absorbic Acid* and *Mind Transplant* give plenty of clues as to the mood and velocity. But Mouzon's compositions keep the tension bubbling, giving the grooves a riveting tautness over which the guitarists pile on a series of terse ostinato riffs while the keyboards weave a dense, choppy undercurrent. One-dimensional it may be but as an early example of a genre that is undergoing something of a renewed interest, it's a period piece of rough charm. This reissue offers a 15 minute meandering studio jam of wavering quality as a bonus for CD buyers.     **JN**

# Bheki Mseleku

1955

**New review**
**Star Seeding** **Mseleku** (ts, p, g, v); **Charlie Haden** (b); **Billy Higgins** (d). Verve Ⓕ 529 142-2 (72 minutes). Recorded 1995.

⑧ ❽

Perhaps nervous that the then relatively unknown Mseleku needed bolstering by some star names, Verve jam-packed his last album, **Timelessness**, with other well-known musicians. As it was, Mseleku's remarkable talent carried the show, and this time Verve have provided him with what must be the ideal setting for not only his inspired piano playing, but his other instruments and vocals. Haden produces basslines that for all their apparent simplicity follow the subtle and supple twists and turns of Mseleku's keyboard work, while Higgins is rhythmically perfect whether adding a delicate solo on brushes to *Melancholy in Cologne* or underpinning the pent up energy of the multi-tracked *Thula Mtwana*, where Mseleku plays saxophone, piano and guitar as well as overdubbing the vocal. Mseleku is still an instantly recognizable individual voice on piano, but his ability to move into the jazz mainstream was apparent from **Timelessness** and here is even more marked, especially on *L.A. Soul Train Blues*, on which he accompanies his own tenor in a quartet where (were they not the same person) both pianist and tenorist would stand out as exceptional.     **AS**

# Jim Mullen

**Soundbites** Mullen (elg); **Dave O'Higgins** (ts); **Lawrence Cottle** (elb); **Ian Thomas** (d).
EFZ Ⓕ 1003 (52 minutes). Recorded 1992.

⑥ ❽

Ten years ago, Scots-born stringsman Jim Mullen suffered the usual neglect reserved for domestic prophets. There were a few albums with the late-lamented funk band Morrissey-Mullen, one or two sideman dates and, in 1983, **Thumbs Up**, a début solo album for Coda Records. But since 1990 things have got better. The sideman gigs have increased and Mullen has recorded two albums as leader in as many years. There was 1990's **Into the 90s**, a funk set on the sadly short-lived Six Strings And A Plank Of Wood label, and then in late 1992 came **Soundbites**, a set which registers a return to straight-ahead values while simultaneously retaining the funky, visceral quality which has made Mullen a favourite with local audiences for almost two decades. Although Mullen has consciously tried to curb the effect when preparing the eight strongly-written originals here, John Scofield clearly remains a prominent late influence, and it is a credit to his exceptional musicianship that on several tracks he is able to so faithfully replicate Scofield's melodic curves and chord movement and voicings. However, the guitar solos remain distinctively Mullenian, the singing lines and phlegmy tone inimitable. Fellow EFZ signatory Dave O'Higgins plays the Joe Lovano role superbly but uses Michael Brecker as his solo model, and there is impeccable support from two redoubtable London rhythmatists. **MG**

# Gerry Mulligan

**Best of Gerry Mulligan with Chet Baker** Mulligan (bs): **Chet Baker** (t); **Bobby Whitlock**, **Carson Smith**, **Henry Grimes** (b); **Chico Hamilton**, **Larry Bunker**, **Dave Bailey** (d). Pacific Jazz Ⓜ CDP7 95481-2 (49 minutes). Recorded 1952-7.

✔

❽ ❽

The first Gerry Mulligan Quartet had one of the most completely realized sounds in jazz. The roles of the four instruments, the blend of their tones, the balance of solo and ensemble, the choice of tempo and control of the general mood – all these are judged to perfection. Since there is no piano to add harmonic colour, each part stands out sharply, contributing an active and coherent strand to the pattern. Above all, it is an attractive sound – tuneful, good-humoured and welcoming – qualities that remain undimmed to this day.

This is a good selection from the quartet's three ten-inch albums of 1952-3 (plus one track from the 1957 reunion date), a typical half-and-half mixture of standards and originals, with some of the best tunes *(Walking Shoes, Nights at a Turntable*, etc.*)* being Mulligan's own. His baritone playing is at its most agile and debonair, his lines simple but never obvious. Baker, an infant phenomenon of 22, displays a harmonic-melodic flair that is a little short of genius at times. He follows his ear unhesitatingly, occasionally getting into tight corners, from which he extricates himself nimbly. In this he is uncannily like Bix Beiderbecke. He is also a master of the winsome ballad, of which there are several examples here, including the celebrated *My Funny Valentine*. The original bright mono recording is faithfully transferred to CD. **DG**

**What is There to Say?** Mulligan (bs); **Art Farmer** (t); **Bill Crow** (b); **Dave Bailey** (d). Columbia Ⓜ 475699-2 (41 minutes). Recorded 1958-9.

❽ ❽

Farmer spent less than a year with the Mulligan Quartet; it is unfortunate that his term of service was so short, for the recorded evidence shows that he was an ideal partner. His dry, precise sound and clean articulation, added to a well-schooled musical background, gave his playing a different approach to that of Chet Baker, whose intuitive playing and warm tone had made such a huge impact on jazz of the fifties. This is in every way an excellent album, benefiting from the accuracy of the ensemble playing and the steady, reliable time keeping of Crow and Bailey. There is a freshness to the music which has withstood the passage of the years and even when the quartet turns the clock back to look at a Mulligan 'hit' of six years earlier, the brooding *My Funny Valentine* with Crow's dramatic bass line descending in semi-tones behind the horns, the listener is soon aware of the individuality of Farmer rather than someone trying to sound like Chet Baker. These four men could produce a quite astonishing drive on the up-tempo material and there is just such a feeling on *Festive Minor, As Catch Can* and *Blueport*. The harmonic understanding of Mulligan, Farmer and Crow enables them to imply the sound of rich, full voicings, rendering absurd the blurb on the back of the package which states that "a piano-less small-group sound ... serves as a reminder that Mulligan was interested in chordless jazz well before the innovative Ornette Coleman". **AM**

**And the Concert Jazz Band Featuring Zoot Sims** Mulligan (bs, p); **Don Ferrara**, **Conte Candoli**, **Nick Travis** (t); **Bob Brookmeyer** (vtb, p); **Willie Dennis**, **Alan Ralph** (tb); **Gene Quill**, **Bob Donovan** (as); **Zoot Sims**, **Jim Reider** (ts); **Gene Allen** (bs, cl); **Buddy Clark** (b); **Mel Lewis** (d). Europe 1 Ⓕ 710382/3 (two discs: 91 minutes). Recorded 1960.

❽ ❹

The Concert Jazz Band was one of Mulligan's greatest achievements. It came to deserved fame at the end of what was surely the most magnificent decade in big band jazz, when orchestras led by Quincy Jones, Duke Ellington, Gil Evans and Count Basie amongst others had set new standards in the skilful interpretation of quality arrangements. Mulligan transferred the idea of the piano-less rhythm section to the big band with sometimes perilous results. Pivoting a 14-piece on bass and drums required caution as well as skill and sometimes the music sounds inhibited as a result. That is the only qualification which can be made about this exhilarating concert recorded in the Paris Olympia for French radio. The concert atmosphere is relaxed compared to a studio date, and the soloists are given their heads – *Piano Blues* runs for 21 minutes, *Moten Swing* for 13 and *Blueport* for 11. Zoot Sims and Bob Brookmeyer are at their wailing best, as is Mulligan when he plays baritone, and they make a small but formidable solo team. On piano Mulligan is long-winded and, given that he is an eccentric pianist who functions simply as a soloist and never as a constructive rhythm section member, has a tendency to self-indulgence. But let us not carp at his genius. This is an enjoyable album reflecting the freshness and excitement which the Concert Jazz Band brought into big band jazz. It served to awe and startle us until the Thad Jones-Mel Lewis Orchestra came along five years later.       **SV**

**New review**
**Dragonfly**  Mulligan (bs); **Ryan Kisor** (t); **Warren Vaché** (c); **Grover Washington** (ss, ts); **Dave Grusin**, **Ted Rosenthal** (p); **Dave Samuels** (vb); **John Scofield** (g); **Dean Johnson** (b); **Ron Vincent** (d); plus brass section of **Luis Bonila**, **Bobby Milliken**, **Jim Pugh**, **Byron Stripling**, **Dave Taylor**. Telarc Jazz Ⓕ CD83377 (63 minutes). Recorded 1995.

⑨ ❿

This is an unusually beautiful record; I say unusually because most Mulligan dates have their fair share of beauty in them, but this one has more than its fair share. It's the recipient of that rare sense of well-being when all the participants are at ease with their roles and happy with the music they are playing. It is apparent from the booklet notes by Mulligan himself that this is due in no small part to the large amount of careful pre-planning he and his pre-production team put in. Pushed for time in a busy schedule, Mulligan handed over much of the arranging work on his new material to Slide Hampton and Mike Mossman, both of whom did outstanding jobs. All three thought long and hard about which guest star would fit which new piece best, which song the brass ensemble would augment, which they would be best out of. The result is a perfect balance being struck for each tune. *Backstage* has the intimacy of the quartet with vibes and trumpet added, while *Little Glory*, at the same tempo, is cushioned by brass as well. *Listening to Astor* has a more plaintive air (and distant echoes of the music Mulligan wrote and recorded many years ago for the film *I Want to Live*) and this is highlighted by discreet but stark brass writing. Throughout, Mulligan plays with even more sensitivity and persuasiveness than usual, caressing his melodies and evolving his soloistic ideas with rare grace. His regular quartet moves with him in total unity, the music-making seamless. This is a quiet, discreet record for the most part, as full of joy as it is of pain, but its triumph is none the less substantial for that. What a beautiful *vale* he left for us all.   **KS**

# Mark Murphy
1932

**Bop for Kerouac**  Murphy (v); **Richie Cole** (as, ts); **Bruce Forman** (g); **Bill Mays** (p); **Bob Magnusson**, **Luther Hughes** (b); **Roy McCurdy**, **Jeff Hamilton** (d); **Michael Spiro** (perc). Muse Ⓕ MCD5253 (39 minutes). Recorded 1981.

⑥ ❽

Singer Mark Murphy is perhaps America's last self-consciously hip hipster. And while there is something oddly out-of-time and out-of-place in this 1981 pre-postmodern ode to Beat Generation chronicler Jack Kerouac (and also with Murphy himself), it is an anachronistic blip that is nice to have around, especially for anyone who passed through the roiling cultural currents of the fifties. The biggest stretch in this project is Murphy's reading of an excerpt from Kerouac's *On The Road* as a set-up for *Ballad of the Sad Young Men*, a strangely moving yet pathetic performance of Las Vegas proportions.

The theme is amplified on *Be-Bop Lives (Boplicity)*, a tribute to the giants of the genre that, while often musically lithe and heartfelt, teeters on the brink of parody. Murphy's problem here, and throughout his career, is the carefully cultivated, hipper-than-hip persona, where 'hip' is expressed by the white Murphy largely through an appropriation of black mannerisms that border, albeit unintentionally, on caricature. But regardless of how outrageous his posture may appear, Murphy prevails by dint of his sincerity. We believe that he believes. Murphy is also a singer with whom to reckon. He is a wonderful balladeer in the Tony Bennett-Jack Jones tradition, as demonstrated on *You Better Go Now*, and though his scatting is somewhat laboured, he swings like mad and has great intonation. Here, he benefits from the inspired ebullience of Richie Cole, Bruce Forman, Bill Mays and friends.   **CB**

# David Murray
1955

**Hope Scope**  Murray (ts, bcl); **Hugh Ragin**, **Rasul Siddik** (t); **Craig Harris** (tb); **James Spaulding** (as, f); **Dave Burrell** (p); **Wilber Morris** (b); **Ralph Peterson Jr.** (d). Black Saint Ⓕ 120 139-2 (44 minutes). Recorded 1987.

✔ ❿ ❽

Murray has spent the better part of nearly two decades securing a reputation as one of the most vibrant soloists in jazz, with many duo, trio, and quartet dates as evidence. But the octet, first recorded in 1980 and intermittently thereafter, is undoubtedly the best showcase for the full measure of his talents. Each of these recordings contains something of merit; this is the most recent and in some ways the best. Murray's writing for the band has been at a consistently high level, but at this point the ensemble seems tighter, and just as exciting, than any previous edition. The upbeat swagger of *Ben* (for Ben Webster, one of his touchstones on tenor), with wah-wah brass and jolting background figures, could be a contemporary view of the Ellington jump bands (Murray himself suggests that Ragin and Saddik fill the Cat and Cootie roles, respectively). *Lester*, for Lester Young, is a romantic ballad with warm, willowy chromatic tenor cushioned on a bed of brass and flute. The title tune winds through episodes of chattering horns, free polyphony, and a pogo'ed ending. For the first time Murray allows outside contributions, and Harris's *Same Places New Faces* roars congenially. Murray's his own best soloist, but Harris and Spaulding let off sparks when let loose. A powerful sample of one of the best bands of the eighties and nineties.. **AL**

---

**Ming's Samba** Murray (bcl, ts); **John Hicks** (p); **Ray Drummond** (b); **Ed Blackwell** (d). Portrait Ⓕ
  PRT465457-2 (40 minutes). Recorded 1988.

⑨ ❾

Sandwiched between his eighties recordings for Black Saint and his later series of works for DIW, **Ming's Samba** was the result of Murray's brief flirtation with a major US label (Portrait being part of Columbia). Whether by chance or design, it contains some of his most ebullient, accessible music.

Murray's ongoing re-examination of the tenor tradition – moving back through Ayler, Gonsalves, Hawkins – has been filtered through the avant-garde techniques he learned early in his career. On this CD he employs a full range of contemporary vocabulary – tonal distortion, overblowing, huge intervallic leaps – to breathe new life into familiar territory. His tenor swarms over the music with irrepressible bravura, *Ming's Samba*'s latino swing and *Rememberin' Fats*' barrelhouse opened up by rampaging solos and fiery group interaction. The sauntering *Walter's Waltz* has Murray on bass clarinet, recalling Eric Dolphy's arabesque abstractions. Murray is not a great innovator, but **Ming's Samba** should leave no one doubting his phenomenal prowess as a player. **GL**

## Sunny Murray

1937

**Sunny Murray** Murray (d); **Jacques Coursil** (t); **Jack Graham** (as); **Byard Lancaster** (as); **Alan Silva** (b). ESP-Disk Ⓜ 1032-2 (52 minutes). Recorded 1966.

⑦ ❹

A surprise guest on a Cecil Taylor session in 1961, Murray played with John Coltrane and later made a vital contribution to Albert Ayler's sessions for ESP in the middle sixties. He lived for some time in Paris, working with most of the American expatriates in the city, but after returning to New York in the seventies he performed in the company of the younger loft movement musicians in a style that had withdrawn from its arhythmic concentration and assumed the more obvious mantle of bop. This CD finds him in his more pioneering days and marks his début as a leader. As with the Ayler sessions, it shows him to be one of the first drummers to pass the pulse-carrying function of the conventional drummer over to the listener. His style's legato flow made few vertical contacts with the music and, in fact, Coursil's trumpet lines do more to calibrate the music than do either Murray of his similarly free partner Silva. As a consequence, the collective passages are sometimes incontinently frenetic, Coursil is on no fixed route and neither saxophonist seems able to embrace free melodic development in the motif-building sense. The colourful sound banks they do produce are sustained by a Murray-inspired rhythmic background, but they do not always seem to respond with the flexibility that the drummer offers them. Most of the themes are rudimentary, though *Giblets* raises a smile.

The star rating is based almost entirely on the strength of Murray's drumming. Recording quality is not good. **BMcR**

## Music Revelation Ensemble

New review

**In the Name of ...** Sam Rivers (f, ss, ts); **Arthur Blythe** (as); **Hamiet Bluiett** (bs); **James Blood Ulmer** (g); **Amin Ali** (elb); **Cornell W. Rochester** (d). DIW Ⓕ DIW885 (59 minutes). Recorded 1993.

⑧ ❽

Ulmer formed the Music Revelation Ensemble in 1971 but they didn't record until 1980. By the mid-eighties, with Jamaaladeen Tacuma and Ronald Shannon Jackson in the line-up, they'd become a rather unwieldy supergroup. **Elec. Jazz**, recorded in 1990 with a revised personnel of Ulmer, David Murray, Ali and Rochester, marked a turning point, the music at last showing shape and purpose and Ulmer clearly calling the shots again as group leader. **In the Name of ...** builds on that success, its three guest saxophonists bringing welcome variety to the core trio's relentless rhythmic attack. Ulmer studied with Ornette Coleman in the seventies and has utilized the latter's theory of harmolodics to re-think rhythm-section roles. Guitar, bass and drums rarely provide conventional accompaniment here and often solo simultaneously, giving the music a frantic, cluttered feel. Ulmer's acrid, blues-roots guitar, pushed at times to extremes of tonal distortion, adds to the listener's initial sense of disorientation. The saxophonists appear on separate tracks. Bluiett's baritone exudes menace on *The Dawn*, but Rivers is the most telling contributor; his soprano laces *In Time*'s heavy propulsion with a slippery sharpness, his flute wafts like a lost soul through the trio's power-metal scrum on *Mankind*.          **GL**

## Wolfgang Muthspiel                                                                  1965

**New review**
**Loaded, Like New** Muthspiel (g, elg, g syn); **Tony Scherr** (b, elb); **Kenny Wolleson** (d); **Don Alias** (perc). Amadeo ℗ 527 727-2 (60 minutes). Recorded 1995.

⑧ ❾

At this late stage in the history of the instrument it's difficult to imagine what fresh individual niches are left for the new guitarist to exploit. Unless, that is, you are the prodigious Austrian Wolfgang Muthspiel. Muthspiel is not immune to influence; there are strong elements of the modern American style in his playing – some of his guitar synth work has echoes of Bill Frisell or Allan Holdsworth, and when he plays straight-ahead on his semi-solid Ibanez Artist, his awareness of the playing of that other Ibanez-wielding fretworker John Scofield is transparent. However, Muthspiel comes from another tradition – he has a sound classical grounding – and while the Scofield influence is strong, especially on the nervy swinger *Rocket* and the ballad *Shorter,* it is clear that for Muthspiel the contemporary New York sound is just one part of a broader musical vocabulary which encompasses a superb classical technique (put to carelessly virtuosic use on an oblique solo reading of Lennon and McCartney's *All My Loving)* and an idiosyncratic line in guitar synth manipulation *(Shift To The Rite)*. Muthspiel is a guitar master and this record, one of a number by Muthspiel on PolyGram's Austrian subsidiary Amadeo, is a modern guitar masterpiece. His subsequent release, **Perspective**, which features him with a trio made up of Marc Johnson and Paul Motian, is similarly outstanding and emphasizes the American side of his music's nature.          **MG**

## Amina Claudine Myers                                                              1943

**Salutes Bessie Smith** Myers (p, org, v); **Cecil McBee** (b); **Jimmy Lovelace** (d). Leo ℗ CDLR103 (45 minutes). Recorded 1980.

⑦ ⑧

Myers performed with gospel groups while still at school and even today it shows in everything she does. In Chicago she played with many visiting stars before becoming involved with the Association for the Advancement of Creative Musicians. Her involvement in the free form movement of that city continued after her move to New York and, latterly, Europe, and she has recorded with Lester Bowie, Muhal Richard Abrams and Frank Lowe. This CD, made at a time when she was actually touring with a gospel group, reflects her wide interests. She sings Bessie Smith tunes in her own light and soulful, rather than bluesy, way. She treats *It Makes My Love Come Down* to her rolling style of piano playing and takes *The Blues Straight to You* very close to Tamla-Motown soul. The main piece, however, is *African Blues*, with straight-ahead piano but with Myers moaning an 'African' part. It is full of melismatic extravagance all of which takes the performance into a different creative field, equally powerful and possibly more demanding. Myers is a difficult artist to classify, but her gospel roots have made it possible for her to branch out to all jazz-and-blues-related areas.          **BMcR**

## Simon Nabatov

**Tough Customer** Nabatov (p); **Mark Helias** (b); **Tom Rainey** (d). Enja ℗ 7063-2 (74 minutes). Recorded 1992.

⑧ ⑧

First things first: don't let the truly dumb cover of this album put you off. This is challenging, exciting, well-worked-through jazz from a trio of players who know and like each other's approach. Nabatov was born in Moscow and left there for New York in 1978. Although he still has a base there, in the eighties he relocated to Europe, where he now centres his operations.

Nabatov's piano playing and compositions show the signs of a classical training, both in his impeccable technique and in his quest for musical structures which balance classical form with jazz freedom. In this he shares similar concerns with the Denny Zeitlin of the sixties, and also Dave Brubeck, both of whom are effective composers as well as comprehensively equipped pianists. Nabatov's touch is firm and precise and he is a sophisticated musical thinker, always able to work through any harmonic sequence he initiates and come up with worthwhile ideas. The record is composed of originals (five by Nabatov, two by Helias), so they are charting their own territory and nobody else's. Good thing, too: we don't need any more Evans or Hancock clones.          **KS**

# Naked City

**Grand Guignol**   John Zorn (as, v); Bill Frisell (elg); Wayne Horvitz (kbds); Fred Frith (b); Joey Baron (d); Yamatsuka Eye, Bob Dorough (v). Disc Union/Avant Ⓕ AVAN002 (62 minutes). Recorded 1992.

⑧ ❾

Like most Naked City records, **Grand Guignol**, an aural depiction of the degradations of the Parisian horror show of the same name, thrives on the dark, disquieting underbelly of human experience. The brutal noise of free jazz is a major means to the expression of this condition, but composer John Zorn is interested in its sound and intensity rather than its form (or lack of it). Thus the often hilarious roaring, shrieking and retching of Yamatsuka Eye, the wild, apoplectic skirling of Zorn's alto and the slabs of thrash metal from Frisell's guitar are used as packets of sound in what appear to be precisely defined arrangements. No doubt in evocation of the schizoid tension between public calm and private turmoil, a few seconds of apocalyptic racket will butt directly onto a snatch of complacent lounge-bar country and western. Such bathetic, comic juxtapositions are a typical Naked City technique, but this record is wider ranging than the five or so other recordings by the group. In addition to 30-odd hard little nuggets of expression of the sort outlined above (many lasting less than half a minute), there is extra and contrasting interest in Zorn's arrangements for small band of Debussy, Scriabin, Lassus, Ives and Messiaen.   **MG**

# Zbigniew Namyslowski

1939

**Quartet**   Namyslowski (as); Adam Matyszkowicz (Makowicz) (p); Janusz Kozlowski (b); Czeslaw Bartkowski (d); Power Bros Ⓕ 33861-2 (52 minutes). Recorded 1966.

⑧ ❼

Namyslowski is an eclectic whose career has literally traced jazz history. A child prodigy on piano, he switched to cello at 12 and studied musical theory in Warsaw. He played tailgate-style trombone with a traditional band while still a teenager and, at the same time, worked in modern groups on cello. In 1960, he switched to alto, came under the spell of John Coltrane, Sonny Rollins and Ornette Coleman and made a considerable impact as an altoist in London in 1964. This CD, made shortly after that trip, gives a good impression of his work at the time and marks a high spot in a varied career. He wrote all of the material and it shows how effectively the solo Namyslowski takes Colemanesque excursions away from and back to each theme. He is a player of power and authority and throughout declares his consistent emotional involvement. Szafa, in particular, shows potential ferocity but on every title he swings assertively. He made important records with Krzysztof Komeda (**Astigmatic**) in the sixties and, in the seventies, led a quintet with tenor man Tomasz Szukalski (**Kujaviak Goes Funky**) that made an impressive job of reproducing the American fusion style. He remains active but is not producing work quite as dramatic as **Quartet**. **BMcR**

# Lewis Nash

1958

**Rhythm is My Business**   Nash (d); Steve Nelson (vb); Mulgrew Miller (p); Peter Washington (b); Ron Carter (pic b); Steve Kroon (perc); Teresa Nash (v). Evidence Ⓕ ECD 22041-2 (64 minutes). Recorded 1989.

⑥ ❽

A well-recorded set of material designed by Nash to be "challenging but also soothing". The challenge is sporadic, though with musicians of this quality everything is well, if not spectacularly, played. Nash himself is reckoned to be one of the brightest and best drummers on today's scene and his own work here is exemplary, from the startling, almost Blakey-esque solo he interpolates into the relaxed blues *106 Nix* to his brushwork on Don Pullen's ballad *Sing Me a Song Everlasting* or Arlen-Mercer's *Shining Hour*. Pullen's piece has a long and thoughtful solo from Nelson and Miller is conspicuous for the high level of his contributions throughout (Ron Carter appears on just one track, giving his piccolo bass a solo outing). These are the main solo moments on the disc. It is a well-crafted début but not as exceptional as Lewis's contribution to albums by many others might lead one to expect. Since it was recorded, both time and Lewis's playing have marched on. Evidence only finally brought the session out in 1993 so a new solo album from Nash is long overdue.   **AS**

# Gilles Naturel

**Naturel**   Naturel (b); Stephane Belmondo, Francois Chassagnite (t); Guillaume Naturel, Lionel Belmondo (ts); Jacky Terrasson, Laurent de Wilde (p); Simon Goubert, Peter Gritz (d). JMS Ⓕ 18676-2 (49 minutes). Recorded 1994.

**⑤** **❽**

Since the initial ferocity of the trad-versus-bop wars of the sixties, the French scene has been relatively free from sectarian extremism. In its case, it hardly needed to have a neo-classical bop revolution because so many of its better players seem at home in most jazz environments. The group on this CD, led by bassist Gilles, is typical. It has American guests such as former Taylor's Wailer Terrasson but the tone of the music could be considered totally international. Flowing Zoot Simsish tenor from brother Guillaume graces all but one track. He is reflective in *Little World* but is equally happy in the craftier manoeuvres of *The Feeling of Jazz.* Trumpets add a little steel to four items and it is Belmondo's adventurous walk through *Ray's Blues* and Chassagnite's well planned outing on *I Had a Dream* that captures attention. Gilles is an excellent leader of the rhythm section, as well as being a good soloist in his own right and his solos on *Nice Reed* and *Trois Bornes* put the emphasis on melodic development. There is perhaps too much emphasis on slow to medium pace pieces but, with nobody prepared to make loquacity a virtue, it is pitched at a level ideal for the chosen idiom. **BMcR**

# Fats Navarro
1923-50

**New review**

**Complete Blue Note and Capitol Recordings of Fats Navarro and Tadd Dameron** Navarro, Miles Davis, Howard McGhee (t); J.J. Johnson, Kai Winding (tb); Ernie Henry, Sahib Shihab (as); Wardell Gray, Allen Eager, Dexter Gordon, Sonny Rollins, Charlie Rouse, Ben Lundy (ts); Cecil Payne (bs); Benny Goodman (cl); Milt Jackson (vb, p); John Collins, Mundell Lowe (g); Tadd Dameron, Bud Powell, Gene DiNovi (p); Nelson Boyd, Curly Russell, Tommy Potter, Clyde Lombardi (b); Shadow Wilson, Kenny Clarke, Roy Haynes, Mel Zelnick (d); Diego Ibarra, Vidal Bolando (perc); Rae Pearl, Kay Penton (v). Blue Note Ⓜ CDP8 33373-2 (two discs: 114 minutes). Recorded 1947-9.

 **⑨** **❼**

The work of Fats Navarro was a formative influence on Clifford Brown and through him on generations of jazz trumpeters. His bell-like tone, crackling articulation and above all his astonishing fluency placed him alongside Gillespie and Miles Davis as a major force in bebop and post-war modern jazz generally. His early death, at 26, makes his discography a short one, and the contents of this double-CD set represents a sizeable portion of it. Many of the tracks find him in the company of Tadd Dameron, a composer and bandleader with whom he had a close rapport. In such typical pieces as *The Squirrel* and *Ladybird* Navarro's broad, commanding sound gives definition to the ensemble while his solos are unfailingly bold and striking. A session with fellow trumpeter Howard McGhee, an almost equally strong and authoritative player, is particularly exciting. But even this is surpassed by the set recorded under the leadership of Bud Powell on August 8th, 1949, which also features the young Sonny Rollins, a few weeks short of his twentieth birthday. The inclusion of alternate takes and an excellent illustrated booklet make this an important ingredient of the basic jazz library. **DG**

**New review**

**With the Tadd Dameron Band** Navarro (t); Kai Winding (tb); Rudy Williams (as); Allan Eager (ts); Milt Jackson (vb); Tadd Dameron (p); Curly Russell (b); Kenny Clarke (d). Milestone Ⓜ MCD47041-2 (62 minutes). Recorded 1948.

**⑨** **❹**

Despite its issue under Navarro's name, this recording is by the Dameron Band. Navarro appears on only the first ten titles (of 13) but the quality of his contribution explains the situation perfectly. More significantly, this CD provides a superb example of the trumpeter in the work place; in this case, playing at New York's Royal Roost, something of a home fixture for Dameron at the time. It also provides positive evidence that, without the aid of the 'in-house' safety net, he plays with the same assurance and produces a finished product every bit as immaculate as in the studio environment. It was perhaps inevitable. Navarro never dealt in clichés; his solos have cohesion that suggests careful preparation but, in terms of execution, they sound totally spontaneous. This was especially evident at the Roost and comparison with the two versions of *Good Bait* illustrates the way in which he confronted the same material by taking it into different areas of investigation. In the primitive atmosphere of these recordings, his mastery seems even more apparent. His speed never impaired his creative flow but this live performance seems to put his emotional commitment into sharper relief. **BMcR**

# Oliver Naylor
1903

**New review**

**1924-5** Naylor (p, dir); with his Seven Aces: Edward 'Pinky' Gerbrecht (c); Charles Hartman (tb); Bill Creger (cl, as); Newton Richardson (ts); Jules Bauduc (bj); Louis Darrough (d); with his orchestra – Gerbrecht (c); Pete Bellman (tb); Jerry Richel (cl, as); Jack Howard (as); Lester 'Gilly'

**Bouchon** (cl, ts); **Bob Zurke** (p); **Bauduc** (bj); **Carl Hansen** (b); **Darrough** (d). Retrieval Ⓕ RTR79008 (58 minutes). Recorded 1924/5.

⑥ ❽

Nayor and his Seven Aces have rarely been writ large in the history of early jazz, but the Alabaman ran a young and enthusiastic band at the start of the twenties which reached New York's Roseland Ballroom in early 1924 and then went on to make records for Gennett in New York. The band hovers between conventional white notions of 'hot' music for the time and real jazz (the arrangements are often pedestrian, even though the tempos are rarely below 'spirited'). There is no denying, however, the rhythmic zest and drive supplied by Bauduc (father of the drummer Ray Bauduc) and Darrough, and this probably accounts for the majority of their jazz feeling. There is little real improvisation going on here, with most of the leads played straight, although Gerbrecht deploys the mute *à la* Oliver with endearing regularity, and clarinettist Creger has been listening to Dodds with some assiduity. The more these sides are listened to, the more the music sounds for the most part rehearsed, the solos memorized, the performances leaving little to chance. That account for the unusually clean execution on track after track, as well as the overall spirit of the sides (and the unusually good recording quality, considering the date, lovingly brought to CD by John R.T. Davies), but it means that we are moving dangerously close to good-time music here, rather than jazz, whatever Brian Rust may claim in his cogent and persuasive booklet-notes. The collective ensembles are clean and sunny, everyone keeps out of each other's way admirably, and one would be a fool not to be able to enjoy this music. I find it difficult to credit it much more signifiance than that, though.  **KS**

# Buell Neidlinger

1936

**New review**

**Blue Chopsticks**  Neidlinger (vc); **Hugh Shick** (brass); **Marty Krystal** (reeds); **Richard Green** (vn); **Jimbo Xoss** (va). K2B2 Records Ⓕ K2B2 3169 (63 minutes). Recorded 1994.

⑨ ❾

Neidlinger's career exemplifies his dictum that "to be a complete musician, one must play all styles". A valuable contributor to Cecil Taylor's groundbreaking records of the late 1950s, Neidlinger has since played in symphony orchestras, led a bluegrass band and continues to perform jazz on bass and cello. **Blue Chopsticks** is Neidlinger's very personal tribute to his friend Herbie Nichols. When the pianist was dying of leukemia in 1963, Neidlinger promised one day to record a disc of his compositions arranged for horns and strings (something Nichols had always wanted to hear). I doubt Nichols had in mind this rather bizarre line-up, or Neidlinger's bluegrass-inflected arrangements, but I suspect too he would have liked the results. The strings are sharp to Nichols's deft rhythmic motifs, the horns decorate his flowing lines with daubs of solo colour. The compositions are wonderful, with such distinctive masterpieces as *2300 Skidoo*, *Love*, *Gloom*, *Cash*, *Love* and *Query*. As Roswell Rudd has said of Nichols's music, "What incredible lyricism! What soulfulness! What grace!"  **GL**

# Oliver Nelson

1932-75

**Blues and the Abstract Truth**  Nelson (arr, ts, as); **Eric Dolphy** (as, f); **Freddie Hubbard** (t); **George Borrow** (bars); **Bill Evans** (p); **Paul Chambers** (b); **Roy Haynes** (d). Impulse! Ⓜ IMP 11542 (47 minutes). Recorded 1961.

✓ ⑧ ❽

This was Oliver Nelson's finest hour, when his gifts as a composer and arranger intersected most happily with the jazz spirit of the age. At times there is a slight air of **Kind of Blue** about the music, at others a whiff of Mingus, but the bright, confident simplicity of the writing is archetypal Nelson. Having only four front-line instruments, he uses great ingenuity to extract more tonal variety from them than many arrangers could get out of twice that number. Particularly delightful is his voicing of the melody in *Stolen Moments,* with its plangent semitones at the centre of the chord, and the call-and-response effect utilized in *Hoe-Down*. Both these devices were subsequently done to death by all and sundry, but the original still sounds as fresh as ever.

Nelson's choice of musicians was impeccable: Dolphy had just broken the surface and was obviously a major talent, with Hubbard just behind him. Evans was already universally admired by musicians, but then only beginning to become well known to the listening public as a result of his time with Miles Davis. The real surprise, however, turned out to be Nelson's own rumbustious tenor playing, which often upstages the lot of them.  **DG**

**Sound Pieces**  Nelson (ss, arr); with a big-band personnel on three tracks of **John Audino**, **Ollie Mitchell**, **Conte Candoli**, **Bobby Bryant**, **Al Porcino** (t); **Richard Leith**, **Mike Barone**, **Ernie Tack**, **Dick Noel**, **Bill Byers** (tb); **Gabe Baltazar**, **Bill Green**, **Bill Perkins**, **Plas Johnson**, **Jack Nimitz** (reeds); **Bill Hinshaw**, **Richard Perissi** (frh); **Red Callender** (tba); **Mike Melvoin** (p); **Ray Brown** (b); **Shelly Manne** (d); a quartet personnel on remaining tracks of **Steve Kuhn** (p); **Ron Carter** (b); **Grady Tate** (d). Impulse! Ⓜ GRD103 (55 minutes). Recorded 1966.

⑧ ❽

In contrast to his most celebrated recorded work, **Blues and the Abstract Truth**, which featured Oliver Nelson on tenor fronting a small ensemble, **Sound Pieces** features the late composer on soprano – then returning to prominence in jazz courtesy of Steve Lacy and John Coltrane – in front of what must rank as some of his finest orchestral writing and, from a different session, with a quartet. There are three orchestral pieces, all rich, vigorous and subtle, and featuring the cream of West Coast studio musicians, including Conte Candoli on trumpet, the late Red Callender on tuba, Ray Brown on bass and Shelly Manne on drums. The title track is a wonderfully rumbustious affair, written for the Stuttgart Radio dance band and later performed by Stan Kenton's Neophonic Orchestra, and its drama, propulsion and intensity are echoed by the TV theme *The Lady from Girl Talk*, which successfully attempts to mimic the sound of chattering conversation. The third orchestral selection, *Flute Salad*, is more ethereal, accurately described by Nelson himself as "essentially melodic", a try-out for his just-beginning career as a writer of film and TV scores.

The rest of the album is a quartet session featuring the unusual rhythmic clatter of Steve Kuhn on piano and a superb rhythm section, Ron Carter and Grady Tate. Nelson's soprano snakes sinuously above their solid foundation and the two bonus tracks (originally issued on the double-vinyl **Three Dimensions** Nelson compilation), Thelonious Monk's *Straight No Chaser* and Nelson's own *Example 78*, bristle with imaginative energy. By demonstrating just what an accomplished instrumentalist and composer Nelson was, **Sound Pieces** underlines the tragedy of his early death from a heart attack at the age of 43. Nelson's earlier orchestral and small-group records for Prestige, including the outstanding suite **Afro-American Sketches**, are now on CD and deserve to be in your collection. **CP**

## Phineas Newborn Jr.                                                              1931-90

**Harlem Blues** Newborn (p); **Ray Brown** (b); **Elvin Jones** (d). Contemporary Ⓜ OJCCD662-2
(38 minutes). Recorded 1969.

⑧ ❽

Something of a multi-instrumental prodigy, Newborn finally settled for the piano and established a reputation as a brilliant soloist. He had experience with Lionel Hampton before moving to New York in 1956, where he worked for a time with Charles Mingus. He moved to Los Angeles in 1960, but unfortunately his career took a bad turn on the West Coast as ill health and a hand injury made him less active. He was less able to display his breathtaking technique, but his playing on this CD seems to benefit from the physical restrictions forced upon it. There is no diminution of strength or reduction of fluency evident in the Baptist rock atmosphere of *Harlem Blues* or in the headlong drive of *Cookin' at the Continental*. He handles the strange middle eight of *Sweet and Lovely* with imagination and plays *Tenderly* and *Stella By Starlight* with an emotional depth not always evident in his more flamboyant days. In this he is helped considerably by the challenging yet sympathetic input from Brown and Jones. It is as if the need to be less exhibitionistic forced him to re-examine his goals, to put content before rhetorical embellishment and, as a result, to be a better balanced musician. He did not always maintain this standard; although various comebacks were signalled, subsequent records proved less satisfying.                                                                **BMcR**

## New Departures Quartet

**New Departures Quartet** Bobby Wellins (ts); **Stan Tracey** (p); **Jeff Clyne** (b); **Laurie Morgan**
(d). Hot House Ⓕ HHCD1010 (44 minutes). Recorded 1964.

⑧ ❻

Stan Tracey's exquisite jazz suite **Under Milk Wood** (reviewed under Tracey's entry, and one of the most outstanding British jazz records) didn't just fall out of an empty sky. For almost two years beforehand the quartet that made it (with the exception of drummer Jackie Dougan) had been appearing regularly with poets Michael Horowitz and Pete Brown in their jazz and poetry venture New Departures. In the summer of 1964 critic Victor Schonfield produced this session, with a texture so similar to the more famous suite that it is rather like a second helping of something particularly delicious. On the original sixties Transatlantic album there were two other tracks, but Hot House producers Pete Fincham and the late Ed Dipple chose instead to replace them with a previously unissued version of *Let Them Crevulate* (a Wellins/Tracey collaboration that they subsequently recorded for a different label). This is vintage Tracey, his asymmetric chords and jagged rhythms offset against Clyne's rock-steady bass lines and acting as a voluptuous cushion for Wellins. These are the definitive versions of Wellins's *McTaggart* and *Culloden Moor*, the composer's tenor investing both themes and variations with a spacious melancholy.                                                    **AS**

## David 'Fathead' Newman                                                           1933

**Back to Basics** Newman (f, as, ss, ts); **Pat Rebillot, George Cables, Hilton Ruiz** (kbds); **Jay
Graydon, George Davis, Lee Ritenour** (g); **Abraham Laboriel, Wilbur Boscomb** (elb); **Idris
Muhammad** (d); **Bill Summers** (perc). Milestone Ⓜ MCD9188-2 (50 minutes). Recorded 1977.

⑤ ❽

Born in Dallas, a near-contemporary of Ornette Coleman and a man who worked with Buster Smith as well as Coleman, Newman never became involved in the free-form revolution that had its birth in that city. Experience with Lowell Fulson and T-Bone Walker pointed him in the direction of the r&b field, but he had the technique in reserve to enable him to work comfortably with top bop men when the opportunity arose. This CD has him in the company of highly professional sidemen such as Cables, Ruiz, Ritenour and Muhammad and bridging his two worlds with perhaps an eye to the commercial potential of such a release. This aspect is most evident in his alto work on *Knocks Me Off My Feet* or *Clouds*; less obvious when his driving tenor takes on *Blues for Ball*. The more subtle side of his personality is heard on *Save Your Love for Me* on soprano, or on *Keep the Dream Alive*, where his flute just avoids crossing the border into the musically saccharine. His earlier records for Atlantic with the likes of Ray Charles generally show him at his best. **BMcR**

# Joe Newman
1922-92

**Jive at Five**  Newman (t); **Frank Wess** (ts); **Tommy Flanagan** (p); **Eddie Jones** (b); **Oliver Jackson** (d). Prestige Swingville Ⓜ OJCCD419-2 (37 minutes). Recorded 1960.

**⑧ ❽**

Warm, fat tones seem to abound amongst jazz musicians from New Orleans, and trumpeter Newman's was one of the fattest. Fired by Louis Armstrong, he became one of the major soloists in the second generation Basie band of the fifties and, with Buck Clayton and Ruby Braff, one of the outstanding mainstream voices of the period.

He recorded prolifically and his sessions were divided between the polished and well scored and the informal 'blowing session' as captured here (Newman had not played with Flanagan or Jackson until the day of this recording). Newman's regular partnership with Basie colleague Wess was highly productive and more refined sessions with Newman muted and Wess on flute produced some unique jazz voicings. Here Wess confines himself to robust tenor. Newman plays fine, cascading solos and takes the only ballad, *More Than You Know*, as a feature.

At the time, Eddie Jones was having difficulties in the Basie band with the incumbent drummer, Sonny Payne. Jackson is a much lighter player and, in tandem with Flanagan, produces a light sound in the rhythm section which enables the two horns to improvise with easeful eloquence. **SV**

# New Orleans Owls
1922–9

**The Owls Hoot**  Bill Padron (c); **Red Bolman** (c, v); **Frank Netto** (tb); **Benjamin 'Benjy' White** (cl, as, dir); **Irvine 'Pinky' Vidacovitch** (cl, as); **Lester Smith** (ts); **Edward 'Mose' Ferrer, Sigfre Christansen** (p); **Rene Gilpi** (bj, g); **Nappy Lamare** (g); **Dan LeBlanc** (bb); **Earl Crumb** (ldr); add four tracks by: **New Orleans Rhythm Kings** (Paul Maures, c, Santo Pecora, tb, Charles Cordella, cl); four tracks by: **John Hyman's Bayou Stompers** (John Hyman, Johnny Wiggs, c, Charles Hartman, tb, Elery Maser, cl, Monk Hazel, d). Frog Ⓕ DGF2 (78 minutes). Recorded 1925-7.

**⑤ ❹**

The New Orleans Owls are a good example of the white Crescent City bands of the period. They came into being in 1922 and drew the majority of their personnel from the Invincibles String Band. Players certainly made the transition to horn playing with some ease, although it was outsiders Padron and LeBlanc that put the backbone into the musical carcass. Padron in particular was impressive and this CD is littered with muted cornet solos, owing far more to Joe Oliver and Paul Mares than to Nick La Rocca. *Piccadilly* and *Tampeekoe* presents the unit's dance-band persona but on obvious jazz standards such as *Eccentric* or *That's A Plenty* Padron and White produce solos of genuine merit and serious improvisational intent. None of the saxophone work is of similar quality, however, and Vidacovitch's naïve alto solo on *Meat on the Table* typifies their lack of jazz know-how. The Owls' final recording session in 1927 finds them saddled with inappropriate arrangements and perhaps unsure of their position in a changing jazz world. They bring some life to *Goose Pimples* but within two years they were to disband. Excluding the unissued *Zero*, all of their known titles are here and the album is completed by a latter-day New Orleans Rhythm Kings band and Hyman's Bayou Stompers. **BMcR**

# New Orleans Rhythm Kings

**N.O.R.K and Jelly Roll Morton**  Paul Mares (c); **George Brunies** (tb); **Leon Ropollo** (cl); **Jack Pettis** (c-ms, ts); **Glenn Scoville** (as, ts); **Don Murray** (cl, ts); **Elmer Schoebel, Jelly Roll Morton, Mel Stitzel, Kyle Pierce** (p); **Steve Brown** (b); **Chink Martin** (bb); **Lou Black, Bob Gillette** (bj); **Frank Snyder, Ben Polack** (d). Milestone Ⓜ MCD47020-2 (74 minutes). Recorded 1922/3.

✅ **⑧ ❻**

The New Orleans Rhythm Kings were a very influential group, even if the source of their own inspiration is less clear. Their choice of material and the town of their origin could explain why the Original Dixieland Jazz Band is their oft-quoted role model. The fact remains, however, that they sound nothing like Nick La Rocca's band. Even allowing for the five year time difference, NORK had advanced ODJB's jazz playing techniques by some distance. Mares had always claimed King Oliver as his mentor and, as this CD demonstrates, NORK had more of that band's *legato* mobility than it did the upright rigidity of the ODJB. With Pettis dominant, numbers like *Discontented Blues* and *Oriental* are little more than dance items but the majority of the band's output is jazz of a high standard. Mares's fine lead is typified by his work on titles like *Eccentric* and *Sweet Lovin' Man*, while Ropollo is consistently inventive in a style that eschews the empty arpeggio running of many of his contemporaries and, on *Tiger Rag* and *Tin Roof Blues*, displays timing that is surprisingly Doddsian. Brunies, like Miff Mole and Charlie Green, a forgotten man when the birth of jazz trombone is discussed, is a remarkable player, subtle in solo on *Tin Roof Blues* and an emsemble master throughout. Morton's involvement remains something of a mystery and his organizing hand is more prominent than his solo piano. His presence is felt rather than asserted but the NORK were a band that needed little outside support. **BMcR**

## Sam Newsome
1965

**Sam I Am** Newsome (ts); **Steve Nelson** (vb); **Mulgrew Miller** (p); **James Genus** (b); **Billy Drummond** (d). Criss Cross ℗ 1056 (61 minutes). Recorded 1990.

⑦ ❽

Newsome began playing tenor when he was admitted to his school's jazz band at the age of 13. A friend's record collection introduced him to Sonny Rollins, John Coltrane and Ornette Coleman, as well as to earlier figures such as Ben Webster and Lester Young. He then won a Kool Jazz Festival Scholarship that led him to Berklee College and to playing offers in the Boston area. He was with Donald Byrd in 1987 and, at the time of this session, was about to join Terence Blanchard's hard hitting quintet. His suitability for that particular post is made more than evident on this CD, where he matches himself against the most powerful of rhythm sections. His slow-burn treatment of *Vein of Trane* does full justice to the dedicatee, the rollicking gait of *Indiana* evokes thoughts of Sonny Rollins, while *I Thought about You* takes a laconic mainstream route, treating the ballad to the most relaxed of examinations. Newsome is certainly an accomplished technician but his playing refutes the contention held by some observers that all of today's 'new wave' young men lack emotional involvement and historical perspective. This CD suggests that he has Lester Young's pork-pie hat in his wardrobe, even if it is decked out with a nineties hat-band. **BMcR**

## David Newton
1958

**Eye Witness** Newton (p); **Dave Green** (b); **Allan Ganley** (d). Linn Records ℗ AKD015 (48 minutes). Recorded 1990.

A clear-toned pianist with an approach whose neatness and delicacy verge on fastidiousness, David Newton's limpid style is particularly well suited to accompanying singers, and he is frequently still to be found in that role, backing label-mates Carol Kidd and Claire Martin, and 33 Records's Tina May. In recent years he has launched himself into a solo career, recording three albums in quick succession for Linn Records, two with stellar UK rhythm sections, the third, **Return Journey** (1992), a solo effort featuring his own gently romantic compositions. Eye Witness, by the shortest of heads, is the pick of the bunch, courtesy of the control Newton exerts upon it of his besetting sin – a slight tendency to gush – and thanks to the balance it contains of slow-burning ballads (a Newton speciality) and more vigorous fare written by Herbie Hancock (*Eye of the Hurricane*) and Newton himself (*Ol' Blue Eyes*, a relaxed walking blues opener, and the attractively jaunty title track). Thus, although Newton's playing is still chiefly remarkable for the burnished, luminous clarity he brings to such material as **Angel Eyes** and **Stars in My Eyes**, both he and his elegant, utterly dependable rhythm section generate considerable swing on the more up-tempo pieces, and **Eye Witness** is something of a high-water mark in recent UK mainstream jazz. The Eyes have it. **CP**

## Frankie Newton
1906-54

**Frankie's Jump** Newton (t); **Edmond Hall, Mezz Mezzrow** (cl); **Pete Brown, Russell Procope, Gene Johnson, Tab Smith, Stanley Payne** (as); **Cecil Scott, Kenneth Hollon** (ts); **Don Frye, James P. Johnson, Kenny Kersey** (p); **Richard Fullbright, John Kirby, Johnny Williams** (b); **Cozy Cole, O'Neil Spencer, Eddie Dougherty** (d); **Clarence Palmer, Slim Gaillard, Leon LaFell** (v); **John Smith, Frank Rise, Al Casey, Ulysses Livingstone** (g); **Dickie Wells** (tb). Affinity Ⓜ CDAFS1014 (64 minutes). Recorded 1937/9.

⑧ ❻

Newton's bands epitomized the very best of the little 'jump' units to be found in pre-war Harlem clubs. Newton played on Bessie Smith's last record session and also worked for some time with Billie Holiday, so his jazz credentials were never in doubt. He was a lyrical player with great taste and a natural sense of what was right in both solos and arrangements. This is an essential compilation, bringing together the products of six beautiful sessions featuring men such as Pete Brown, Ed Hall and Cecil Scott. Also included are Slim Gaillard's very first vocals on record (*There's No Two Ways Bout It* and *'Cause My Baby Says It's So*), which are balanced by the 'crooning' of Leon LaFell on Ralph Rainger's lovely song *Easy Living*. (For collectors of the bizarre, LaFell also inserted himself into a Johnny Hodges session about this time!) The album abounds with highlights, but mention must be made of the 1939 date with Mezzrow, James P. Johnson and Al Casey, from which comes the fine *Rompin'*. The transfers are from 78s using the CEDAR process and while the sound is never less than acceptable (and often very good), the compilers were obviously at the mercy of the source discs. **AM**

## James Newton                                                                                              1953

**New review**

**Suite for Frida Kahlo** Newton (f); **Pedro Eustache** (f, bf, bcl, ts); **Julie Feves** (bn); **George Lewis**, **George McMullen** (tb); **Kei Akagi** (p); **Darek Oleszkiewickz** (b); **Sonship Theus** (d, perc). AudioQuest Music Ⓕ AQ1023 (57 minutes). Recorded 1994.

⑧ ⑧

Inspired by Eric Dolphy, Newton has developed into a virtuoso flautist; inspired by Ellington and Mingus, he has also won acclaim as a composer and arranger. His 1981 solo CD **Axum** (ECM) is a brilliant display of technique and invention on the flute family. His recordings for Gramavision and Blue Note later in the eighties revealed his growing talents as a composer, especially **The African Flower**, an Ellington tribute, and **Romance and Revolution**, dedicated to Mingus. **Suite for Frida Kahlo** allows Newton to shine in both roles. The opening tracks feature the bravura flautist, his rich tone slipping gracefully through the gorgeous ballad, *The Price of Everything*, then engaging Lewis's rumbustious trombone on the fiery duet, *Elliptical*. The four-movement, eponymous suite, though initially inspired by Kahlo's paintings, also shows Newton the composer incorporating a range of influences that bridge the jazz/classical divide: John Carter, Villa-Lobos and Takemitsu are among the names he invokes. For the suite, Eustache and Feves bring their darker sonorities to the line-up and Newton makes astute use of this extended tonal palette, using a versatile personal language that runs the gamut from *The Broken Column*'s stabbing anguish to *Frida*'s soulful dignity. **GL**

## New York Art Quartet

**New York Art Quartet** Roswell Rudd (tb); **John Tchicai** (as); **Lewis Worrell** (b); **Milford Graves** (d); **LeRoi Jones (Amiri Baraka)** (recitation on one track). ESP-Disk Ⓜ 1004-2 (43 minutes). Recorded 1964.

⑧ ⑥

This underrated cooperative band formed in 1964 from the city's burgeoning New Thing scene; Tchicai, Rudd, and later NYAQ bassist Reggie Workman had recorded together on Archie Shepp's **Four for Trane**, and the altoist and trombonist joined Albert Ayler on the **New York Eye and Ear Control** date. But as an ensemble the NYAQ adopted neither Shepp's theatrical nor Ayler's extreme brands of expressionism, developing instead an almost classical sense of compositional design that balanced their focus on freedom. Their unanimity is striking; once beyond the initial theme each composition is based upon spontaneity and instrumental equality. Textures change constantly, from four-part polyphony to unaccompanied solos and all combinations in between. Due to the group's rhythmic flexibility, the time expands and contracts, demanding – and receiving – acute responsiveness from each musician. A clue to their cohesive interaction is Rudd's *Rosmosis*, suggesting the music's fluid density and exchange of position within its flow. Tchicai's willowy, lyrical phrasing contrasts with Rudd's exciting expressionism, and together they luxuriate in linear improvising, buoyed by Graves's waves of sound and Worrell's thoughtful foundation. Free music of drama and finely wrought proportion. **AL**

## New York Voices

**What's Inside** Peter Eldridge, Caprice Fox, Laurence Kinham, Darmon Meader, Kim Nazarian (v); **Claudio Roditi** (t); **Jay Ashby** (tb, perc); **Andy Erin** (p); **Randy Landau** (b); **Tommy Igoe** (d). GRP Ⓕ 97002 (53 minutes). Recorded 1993.

⑦ ⑧

Vocal groups have not had an easy time of it in jazz, those enjoying the most successful careers having to usually criss-cross-over between the popular style of the day and straight-ahead jazz styles. This young group is no exception but happily everything it attempts it does with panache and good musical taste. Thus the opening track, *All Blues*, has an excellent and accurate arrangement by Darmon Meader (it even uses an arpeggio'd quotation from the piano accompaniment by Bill Evans of Miles's solo from the original recording) and while the lyrics are not deep or meaningful, they're not a liability either.

Of course other vocal outfits have beaten this path before (just as others have also treated soul classics like *Ain't No Sunshine* to this type of approach), and the most obvious models are LHB and Manhattan Transfer, so what New York Voices do isn't markedly original. The original compositions are the tracks most removed from the above models. But, be it on originals or covers, they blend beautifully, phrase accurately, and generally avoid tasteless elaboration and grandstanding. This alone makes **What's Inside** a highly enjoyable experience, as does the general lack of saccharine sentimentality. The musical accompaniments are highly competent, and everything is attacked with great spirit. The chancy idea of actually using Ella Fitzgerald's 1947 scat vocal for the central section of *Lady Be Good* (logically enough delivered as a tribute to Ella) in fact works very well (the rhythm tracks are – mercifully – perfectly matched, and it means no one has to imitate Ella.

This is an impressively disciplined and varied album from a group with a jazz future.     **KS**

## Herbie Nichols                                         1919-63

**The Art of Herbie Nichols**  Nichols (p); Al McKibbon, Teddy Kotick (b); Art Blakey, Max Roach (d). Blue Note Ⓜ CDP7 99176-2 (65 minutes). Recorded 1955/6.

⑩ ❽

A splendid representation of the archetypal 'musician's musician'. It has 14 original pieces excerpted from the five sessions (available complete on a five-LP Mosaic set) which, his Bethlehem sessions aside, constitute almost his entire legacy; two of the items not issued at the time are included.

Spending his working life as an obscure backing pianist, Nichols created works which, until the eighties, were thought to be irredeemably bound up with his own playing style. This was often compared to his friend and contemporary Thelonious Monk – he was the first person to praise Monk in print – but is gentler and more flowing. He is also similar in being best-known for a ballad, called by the singer who added lyrics (and used the title for her book) *Lady Sings the Blues*. There is also a distant Ellington-Strayhorn influence; despite their diverging development, *Third World* could be a rewrite of *'A' Train*, while *Spinning Song* starts out on *Chelsea Bridge*.

Younger musicians such as Misha Mengelberg, Geri Allen and the annotator of this album, Roswell Rudd, have perpetuated Nichols's memory, but these recordings, with their highly creative percussion parts, are the equal of Monk's fifties trios with the same drummers.     **BP**

## Red Nichols                                           1905-65

**Rhythm of the Day**  Nichols (c); with a collective personnel including: Charlie Teagarden, Manny Klein (t); Miff Mole, Glenn Miller (tb); Jimmy Dorsey, Adrian Rollini, Benny Goodman, Fud Livingston (reeds); Arthur Schutt, Lennie Hayton (p); Eddie Lang, Dick McDonough, Carl Kress (g); Vic Berton (d); Joe Venuti (vn) and others. ASV Living Era Ⓜ CDAJA5025 (59 minutes). Recorded 1924-32.

⑥ ❻

It isn't often that jazz historians openly apologize for anything to their readers, but in the second volume of his long-running history of jazz, Gunther Schuller admits that he had many protests over his brusque treatment (in the first volume) of the music of Red Nichols. Schuller says that in the light of this lobbying he has listened again to Nichols's records and now feels he did the man an injustice.

Poor old Red Nichols. He has always suffered. Suffered from not being Bix Beiderbecke, not being black, not being an influence on other jazz players, not drinking himself to death. But what he did do was good enough; he surrounded himself with the best white New York musicians in the late twenties and evolved a brittle theatrical style of jazz which never got within hailing distance of any deep feeling, but did create attractive little miniatures. The number of records he made then and the number of angry letters Schuller got 50 years later shows that Nichols had and has a big fan club. This collection shows the pluses of the Nichols approach – a bright, shallowly swinging feel, some quirky original arranging and some oddball tunes among the pop stuff. As 1930 approached the bands got bigger and more cumbersome (it's the Jelly Roll Morton story all over again), but even then, in 1929, there was the unexpected bonus of Jack Teagarden and Glenn Miller running in tandem. All but forgotten ten years later, Red Nichols must have rubbed his eyes at the world-wide popularity of Glenn Miller, his erstwhile employee.     **MK**

## Lennie Niehaus                                         1929

**The Octet No. 2**  Niehaus (as); Stu Williamson (t); Bob Enevoldsen (vtb); Bill Holman (ts); Jimmy Giuffre (bs); Pete Jolly (p); Monty Budwig (b); Shelly Manne (d). Contemporary Ⓜ OJCCD1767-2 (40 minutes). Recorded 1955.

⑧ ❽

Niehaus came to attention through his work with Stan Kenton, both as alto soloist and arranger. His move away from the playing side of jazz is a source of regret, although his behind-the-scenes work on the soundtrack music for the Clint Eastwood film **Bird** was valuable. This is actually the third album he did for Lester Koenig's Contemporary label, and it has the classic West Coast sound, with its beautifully played ensemble passages, tight voicings, and a rhythm section sparked by Manne's highly imaginative drumming. Niehaus's tone is an amalgam of Parker and Benny Carter, warmer than that of Lee Konitz but lacking the emotion of Art Pepper. Lennie's arrangements certainly pack a great deal into a comparatively small space (the longest of the dozen tracks is just four minutes), such as the clever key changes in the last chorus of *Love is Here to Stay*. There are four originals by Niehaus, and his *Circling the Blues* succeeds in revolving the chords of the blues through 12 keys with Lennie himself modulating from B to E then to A and into D before leading the ensemble into G. Everyone is given a chance to solo, the music retaining the freshness it possessed when it first appeared on LP.                                                                                    **AM**

## Judy Niemack

**Heart's Desire**  Niemack (v); **Kenny Barron** (p); **Eric Friedlander** (vc). Stash Ⓕ STCD548
(57 minutes: ) (57 minutes). Recorded 1991.

⑨ ⑧

A tangential Tristano-ite by virtue of having studied with Warne Marsh, this young singer has developed a following among French hard-bop devotees on the strength of two discs she recorded for Freelance in the late eighties. This American release gives a better sense of her wide range. Coming across as a Barbra Streisand without the hysterics (although the influence of Sheila Jordan is also discernible), Niemack gives *Over the Rainbow* what might be its definitive interpretation. Combining the best of both worlds – a cabaret singer's respect for melody as written and a jazz singer's eagerness to have a go at it – she unearths a lyric to Monk's *Well, You Needn't*, takes the twitter out of Joni Mitchell's *All I Want*, and scats the bridge of Richard Rodgers's *The Sweetest Sounds* with genuine élan. Friedlander provides an effective one-man string section on a few tunes, including a lovely reading of Dave Frishberg's title tune. Barron displays the same sensitivity behind Niemack as he displayed behind Stan Getz. This is one of the finest vocal albums of recent years.                                                                                    **FD**

## Mike Nock

1940

**Dark and Curious**  Nock (p); **Tim Hopkins** (ts, recorder, v); **Cameron Undy** (b); **Andrew Dickeson** (d). veraBra Ⓕ vBr2074-2 (49 minutes). Recorded 1990.

④ ⑥

Nock, in many ways, is a down-under version of Joe Zawinul. He also came to jazz from far afield (in Nock's case, New Zealand), initially arrived in the US to attend Berklee College, and relocated to the West Coast before founding an even earlier electric jazz-rock group. The Fourth Way was less successful than Weather Report, though, and Nock soon returned to the piano in acoustic settings. Since 1985, he has been based in Australia, where this set was recorded by his quartet. While more satisfying jazz can be heard on his 1981 trio album **Ondas** (ECM 829 161-2), where he works with Eddie Gomez and Jon Christensen, or on a Tomato quintet date yet to appear on CD, this session represents a broader range of his compositional interests, placing some of the trans-national notions of **The Fourth Way** in an acoustic context (*Dance of the Global Village*, for instance). The playing is workmanlike – one wishes Tim Hopkins would let loose more in his tenor solos. Hopkins also reads an original poem on the title track, while Nock applies clusters in the background. The studied nature of much of this music is indicative, though Nock does have the capacity to transcend the poses.                                                                                    **BB**

## Jimmie Noone

1895-1944

**New Orleans Jazz Giants 1936-40**  Jimmy Noone, Johnny Dodds, Edmond Hall (cl); **Red Allen, Natty Dominique, Guy Kelly, Charlie Shavers** (t); **Preston Jackson, Benny Morton** (tb); **Pete Brown** (as); **Francis Whitby** (ts); **Lil Armstrong, Richard M. Jones** (p); **Teddy Bunn, Lonnie Johnson** (g); **Israel Crosby, Pops Foster, Johnny Lindsay** (bs); **Baby Dodds, Tubby Hall, Zutty Singleton, O'Neil Spencer** (d). JSP Ⓕ JSPCD336 (79 minutes). Recorded 1936-40.

✔                                                                                    ⑧ ⑧

It was rare for the clarinettist Jimmy Noone to achieve his potential. Too often his voluptuous and immaculate tone was directed at cloying performances of trivial tunes. Uniquely, ten of the 14 tracks by him on this album have him at his best and the apparently perverse setting of him against emergent young mainstream giants Charlie Shavers and Pete Brown works wonderfully, reaching its ultimate in *Four or Five Times*, a classic which is graced, as are 14 of these titles, by the eloquent acoustic guitar playing of Teddy Bunn. By this period the veteran Noone was an anachronism, as was Johnny Dodds, but the eight sides under the leadership of the latter contain his only recorded work since the twenties, and although often ragged, they bulge with hot and potent improvisation.

Four tracks featuring the comparative youngster Edmond Hall in a band which doubles under the leadership of Henry Allen and Zutty Singleton are amongst the first to display his waspish tone at its best, and his smooth agility and facile mastery of the registers show how Noone and Dodds had been left behind. Splendid trumpet from Allen and trombone from the neglected Benny Morton earn these tracks a place with the rest of the classics on an album of remarkable value. Like other JSP issues the body of the sound on the original 78s has been preserved in transfer by the gifted engineer John R.T. Davies. Some of the bigger companies could benefit from his example. **SV**

# Fredrik Norén

New review

**One Day in May** Norén (d); **Magnus Broo** (t); **Fredrik Ljungkvist** (ts); **Torbjorn Gulz** (p); **Filip Augustson** (b). Mirrors Ⓕ MICD004 (66 minutes). Recorded 1995.

⑧ ❾

Like the late Art Blakey, Swedish drummer Fredrik Norén likes to lead a band made up of young musicians. This is good example of the 'youth-experience' mix with Norén very much in charge but never obtruding in a boorish way. A trumpet-tenor-and-rhythm line-up led by the drummer has become closely identified with hard bop but there is a great deal more to this quintet. Most of the writing comes from within the band and although there is a considerable amount of free playing during the improvised sections everything is still linked to the basic chorus construction. Ljungkvist is one of the breed of newer Swedish tenors and is at home with a limited harmonic base; he builds his solos on short phrases, developing the ideas over the constantly shifting rhythmic tensions and releases. Norén controls the band from the drummer's stool very much as Tony Williams did with Miles Davis. Of the younger men Augustson is perhaps the most impressive, using a huge bass sound to lay down very authoritative lines. Lina Nyberg sings on *Someone to Watch over Me* and includes the verse with the support of just Magnus Broo's trumpet. The final track finds the band very much at home with Monk's *Trinkle Tinkle*, trumpet and tenor playing the theme with great accuracy and feeling for the music. **AM**

# Red Norvo                                                                  1908

**Jivin' the Jeep** Norvo (xyl); **Bill Hyland, Stewart Pletcher, Louis Mucci, George Wendt** (t); **Leo Moran, Eddie Sauter** (tb); **Frank Simeone** (as); **Slats Long, Hank D'Amico** (cl, as); **Len Goldstein** (as); **Charles Lamphere** (as, ts); **Herbie Haymer** (ts); **Joe Liss, Bill Miller** (p); **Dave Barbour, Red McGarvey** (g); **Pete Robinson** (b); **Mo Purtill** (d); **Mildred Bailey, Lew Hurst** (v). Hep Ⓜ CD1019 (64 minutes). Recorded 1936/7.

⑧ ❻

Norvo, after a series of unflattering jobs at the end of the twenties, joined the Paul Whiteman Orchestra in 1929 on the recommendation of his sweetheart and subsequent wife, Mildred Bailey. For much of the early thirties he played around New York, and made at least one immortal session in 1933 (not included here) where he coupled his arrangement of Bix's *In a Mist* with his own Ravel-influenced *Dance of the Octopus*. At the beginning of the period covered by this CD, Norvo was married to Bailey and leading his own small orchestra. He had singlehandedly wrested the xylophone from the clutches of vaudeville (much as Hawkins had done with the tenor sax a decade previously) and had taken on board as an arranger Eddie Sauter, a singularly gifted musician with a significantly different approach from the predominating swing style of the time.

The music which resulted from all this has a passing resemblance to the Teddy Wilson aggregations, often featuring Billie Holiday, which were being made for Brunswick at this time, but Norvo's was always the more formal band. Bailey, no match for Billie as an extemporizing singer, required a firmer arranging hand and got it from Sauter, delivering some of her happiest and most memorable performances in the process, while Norvo showed just why connoisseurs regard him as one of the great unrecognized improvisers of jazz. His incredible freedom over the regulation swing beat, his limitless technique, and his familiarity with several improvisatory procedures (paraphrase, theme-and-variations, etc.) are all to be savoured. This is not the most obvious music from the swing era, but it is some of the most rewarding for those prepared to break the surface. **KS**

**The Red Norvo-Charles Mingus-Tal Farlow Trio, Volume 2** Norvo (vb); **Farlow** (g); **Mingus** (b). Vintage Jazz Classics Ⓜ VJC1008-2 (78 minutes). Recorded 1943-50.

⑧ ❹

This trio's mixture of lilting melody and bebop improvisation is unique. The music is devoid of crowd-pleasing elements and maintains an unusually high standard of improvisation. From his earliest ventures on vibraphone in the thirties Norvo always showed a subtlety on the instrument which kept him from depending on the raw rhythmic impact of Lionel Hampton. He usually kept to a tighter sound than Hampton's, probably something of a throwback to his earliest days on the xylophone.

The speed and facility of the trio at first frightened both Farlow and Mingus; "Tal used to quit every night," Norvo recalled. The setting gives Tal Farlow every opportunity to play and his radiant solos are amongst the best recorded by a guitarist during the bebop period.

There are 30 tracks here by the trio of 1949-50 and three added tracks by a Norvo Septet backing Helen Ward on recordings for V-disc. These last tracks are, however, very poorly recorded and are mostly of interest for some early Flip Phillips tenor. **SV**

# NRG Ensemble

**This is My House** Mars Williams, Ken Vandermark (reeds); Kent Kessler (b); Brian Sandstrom (b, g, t); Steve Hunt (d, perc). Delmark Ⓕ DE485 (67 minutes). Recorded 1995.

⑧ ❽

Under the leadership of the late Hal Russell (q.v.) the NRG Ensemble was formed and flourished. Since his unfortunate passing in 1992 the band has added irrepressible multi-reedman Vandermark and continues to present a whimsical and cathartic brand of cutting-edge jazz. Realizing the impossibility of reproducing Russell's surrealistic humour, they now have focused even more on group strengths – volcanic ensemble intensity capable of heaven-storming cacophony or sustained rock-steady grooves, surprisingly varied compositional structures and a broad range of instrumental textures (supplemented here on two tracks by violinist Dan Scanlan and short-wave radio manipulator Don Meckley). Indeed, Hal's larger-than-life presence may have inadvertently obscured some band talents now allowed to blossom. In addition to his passionate soloing, Mars Williams emerges as a composer of merit and mystery – his *Whirlwind* progresses through various mesmerizing levels of form and feeling. Another characteristic piece is Vandermark's *Cut Flowers*, a theme of Braxtonian contours and unconnected interludes where twin bassists Kessler and Sandstrom hold the pulse together, allowing Steve Hunt's effervescent drums to *push* rather than support the soloists. As if on a constant adrenaline rush the band finds deep significance in the turbulent area between tumult and tranquillity, order on the brink of chaos. **AL**

# Lina Nyberg

**So Many Stars** Nyberg (v, arr); Magnus Broo, Marten Lundgren (t); Dicken Hedrenius (tb); Catharina Fridén (f); Amanda Sedgwick (cl, as); Fredrik Ljungkvist (ss, ts); Charlie Malmberg (bs); Anders Persson (p); Christian Spering (b); Magnus Öström, Anders Kjeilberg (d); Temmel Quartet. Prophone Ⓕ PCD030 (68 minutes). Recorded 1995-6.

⑦ ❼

Nyberg is a young Swedish vocalist and composer/arranger who has her own definite slant on music. Eight of the 13 selections here are self-penned, the others coming from as disparate a collection as Jimmy Rushing, Lerner/Loewe and Sergio Mendes. Nyberg constantly varies her instrumental line-up, sometimes using just piano trio, sometimes a string quartet and drums, sometimes a small big band. Other tracks feature a septet backing with typical trumpet or sax solos interspersing her vocals. The arrangements are always imaginative, the improvising spirited, with the tenor solo by Lindqvist on Nyberg's *My Castle* worthy of Maurice McIntyre at his most fiery. *On the Street Where You Live* becomes a quasi-James Brown funk strut. Nyberg's own vocals range from quirky to chillingly effective, her voice small and range limited but her expressiveness unfettered. She has a naturally musical phraseology and can re-align well-known melodies in a graceful and exciting way. This is no mere vocalist-plus-accompaniment ho-hum release: a lot of thought and talent has been expended to fill the music with imagination, honesty and flair. Nyberg's quixotic lyrics are good, too. **KS**

# Anita O'Day

1919

**Pick Yourself Up** O'Day (v); Harry Edison (t); Larry Bunker (vb); Paul Smith (p); Barney Kessel (g); Joe Mondragon (b); Alvin Stoller (d); Buddy Bregman Orchestra. Verve Ⓜ 517 329-2 (66 minutes). Recorded 1956.

⑧ ❽

Anita O'Day is incapable of singing anything which is not jazz, *vide* her attempt here at making a hit record with the almost unjazzable *Rock 'n' Roll Waltz*. Let us hasten to add that the tune's presence is an aberration and that most of the 21 songs are ideal material for O'Day.

Her long career reached its peak in the fifties and sixties when she recorded for Verve. Her very best session (with the Gary McFarland Orchestra) remains unissued on CD, but her Verve performances which are already on CD are of uniformly high quality.

O'Day takes to herself the freedom of an instrumentalist more than any other of her peers. Impeccable timing and imagination make her improvisations exceptionally fine, and her dexterity with fast numbers is matched by the beautiful poise of her ballad singing. Her voice is mannered with some of the soft rasp of Billie Holiday, but she justifies any of her quirks with the high quality of her beautifully crafted jazz performances. Incidentally, the date's arranger Buddy Bregman has been consistently undervalued, usually by being cast in the shade of Nelson Riddle. His orchestras are always good and his arrangements sometimes rival Riddle's. He uses good soloists sparingly: Bob Cooper makes a lovely entry after the cool brass ensemble on *I Never Had a Chance*. Harry Edison heads the typical Verve small group on five tracks. This band could have been much improved by the substitution of regular pianist Jimmy Rowles for Smith. **SV**

# Chico O'Farrill

**Pure Emotion**  O'Farrill (arr, cond); **Victor Paz, Michael Mossman, Jim Seeley, Dan Collette, Tim
  Ouimette** (t); **Gerald Chamberlain, Papo Vasquez, Robin Eubanks, Earl McIntyre** (tb); **Mario
  Rivera, Bob Franceschini** (ts, ss, f, cl, bcl); **Lenny Hambro, Rolando Briceno** (as, f, cl, bcl); **Pablo
  Calogero** (bs); **Jeffrey Scott, Sharon Moe** (frh); **Arturo O'Farrill Jr** (p); **Andy Gonzales** (b); **Jerry
  Gonzalez** (cga); **Steve Berrios** (d, perc); **Manny Oquendo, Elisabeth Monder** (perc). Milestone Ⓕ
  MCD9239-2 (50 minutes). Recorded 1995.

⑦ ❽

Cuban-born trumpeter O'Farrill earned a reputation as a composer and arranger in the post-Second
World War jazz worlds of Dizzy Gillespie, Stan Kenton, Charlie Parker and Machito (these activities
have recently been extensively documented on a two-CD Verve reissue, **Cuban Blues: The Chico
O'Farrill Sessions**, a collation which covers no less than six separate Clef and Norgran albums
O'Farrill did for Norman Granz). He was for some time a musical director for CBS, wrote for pop
figures such as David Bowie and produced a large number of evocative commercial jingles. He was
also successful as a leader, but this album is his first jazz release for some 30 years. It perhaps
disappoints in that it fails to up-date his stylistic stance but it satisfies fully as a retrospective,
maintaining the rhythmic verve, musical conviction and Cuban identity of his finest efforts. For the
job he has assembled a large orchestra, with 11 in the brass team for *La Cucaracha*. There are notable
solos from Calogero's baritone (*Igor's Dream* and *Perdido*), Hambro's alto (*Pure Emotion*),
Franceschini's tenor (*Get Me to the Church*), Rivera's tenor (*Obscuridad*) and Mossman's trumpet (*El
Loco Blues*). It is the ensemble and its members' readings of the parts, however, that impresses most;
the reeds have a full-bodied mobility and the brass punches its weight in a timeless manner as the
various Latin forms are presented. Bolero, mambo, gujira, guaracha and guaguanco are the grist to
O'Farrill's mill, but it is his Cuban upbringing and swing input that ratifies the finished product as
outstanding big-band jazz with a Cuban accent.  **BMcR**

# Claus Ogerman

**Featuring Michael Brecker**  **Randy Brecker** (t, flh); **Michael Brecker** (ts); **Robben Ford, Dean
  Parks** (g); **Alan Pasqua** (kbds); **Marcus Miller, Abraham Laboriel, Eddie Gomez** (b); **Vinnie
  Colaiuta, Steve Gadd** (d); **Paulinho DaCosta** (perc). GRP Ⓕ GRD9632 (44 minutes). Recorded
  1991.

⑧ ❽

Since recording **Gate of Dreams** together in the late seventies, Claus Ogerman and Michael Brecker
have had a special rapport particularly since producer Tommy Lipuma brought them together again
in 1982 for a full orchestral Ogerman composition, **Cityscape** (Warner Bros). On the latter, a
somewhat subdued, melancholy, but strangely affecting saxophone concerto, Brecker plays with his
customary virtuosic eloquence throughout, imbuing Ogerman's deceptively accessible music with an
unusual mix of blustering power and sonorous dignity. On this later recording, Brecker again
performs fautlessly, his grainy, sophisticated sound perfectly complemented by his collaborators, the
cream of contemporary fusion musicians. As might be expected from an album masterminded by a
man equally at home in the classical and jazz worlds, with a string of compositions for the likes of
Carlos Jobim, Bill Evans and Oscar Peterson behind him, this is by no means conventional fusion
fare. Ogerman has used his pool of musicians (Gadd, Miller and DaCosta all also appear on
**Cityscape**) chiefly as providers of a sound palette for five startlingly original compositions, and the
strength of the album derives from the variety of textures, ranging from light washes of synthesized
sound to muscular, vigorous backdrops enlivened by energetic percussive effects, against which
Michael Brecker is able to demonstrate just why he is regarded as one of the undisputed masters of
contemporary saxophone technique.  **CP**

# Dave O'Higgins

**The Secret Ingredient**  O'Higgins (ss, as, ts, bs); **Robin Aspland** (p, elp); **Alec Dankworth** (b);
  **Gene Calderazzo** (d) with **The Electra Strings**. EFZ Ⓕ 1020 (62 minutes). Recorded 1996.

⑧ ❽

Dave O'Higgins has made three previous albums for EFZ, two involving UK-based rhythm sections,
and one – **Beats Working for a Living** – with a stellar New York band featuring vibes player Joe Locke.
O'Higgins's down-to-earth professionalism fits in well with his label's overall philosophy (EFZ stands
for Ego-Free Zone), and his reward is this ambitious project involving the Electra Strings, skilfully
arranged by his former Itchy Fingers collaborator, Mike Mower. The album's overall conception was,
O'Higgins notes, inspired by Coltrane's **Ballads** and the various albums produced by Miles Davis with
Gil Evans, but in mood, the string-assisted tracks bring to mind Art Pepper's **Winter Moon** rather

than **Miles Ahead** and its like. The bustling ebullience O'Higgins exuded on previous albums, and in his stints with Roadside Picnic and Gang of Three, has been largely replaced here by a more mature, restrained sound on both tenor and soprano, and, likewise, the normally volcanic Gene Calderazzo (who has energized the London jazz scene with his vigorous but supple drumming since settling there) restricts himself to whispering brushes for much of this tasteful set. There are only two O'Higgins originals, but the remaining pieces – Billy Strayhorn's *Chelsea Bridge*, Rodgers and Hart's *You Are Too Beautiful* and Neal Hefti's *Girl Talk*, lovingly embellished by Mower's lush string arrangements, plus a selection of quartet tracks including a plangent version of *Dedicated to You* – have been judiciously chosen to showcase the musical empathy of one of the UK's most listenable working bands.     **CP**

## Toru 'Tiger' Okoshi                                                                1950

**Two Sides to Every Story**  Okoshi (t); **Mike Stern** (g); **Gil Goldstein** (p); **Dave Holland** (b); **Jack DeJohnette** (d). JVC Ⓕ 2039-2 (66 minutes). Recorded 1994.

⑥ ❽

Okoshi made his first recording in his homeland Japan in 1971 before moving to America the following year. There he rapidly came to public notice with Gary Burton and made his US recording début, with guitarist Baird Hersey in 1977. He also led a band of his own, playing strident, hard-hitting trumpet with Miles Davis's group as role model and stylistic guide for his 'Baku' brand of jazz-rock. In fact, his own playing was some distance from Davis. Okoshi delivered clean-cut power, where Davis dealt in implication; Okoshi was outspoken and his approach was patently more vertical.

Although it was a style with its own appeal, this album, with its outstanding rhythm section and basically hard-bop policy, suggests that this might be a more productive route for him. His fusion mode translates easily into straight-ahead blowing and his full-frontal trumpet on titles like *Finders Keepers* and *What It Was* illustrate this perfectly. On the debit side, his blues playing on *Monday Blues* remains too verbose, but his more restrained, muted work on the waltz, *Yuki No Furu Machi O,* and the relaxation he displays on the album's title track point to a direction that could serve him better in future.     **BMcR**

## Old and New Dreams

**A Tribute to Blackwell**  **Don Cherry** (t); **Dewey Redman** (ts); **Charlie Haden** (b); **Ed Blackwell** (d). Black Saint Ⓕ 120 113-2 (48 minutes). Recorded 1987.

⑧ ❽

Old and New Dreams, formed in 1976 by four former Ornette Coleman alumni, continued up to the recent death of drummer Blackwell to champion the beautiful free jazz that its initiator has now largely abandoned. In the process, the band has continually produced jazz that maintains the high compositional and improvisation standards set by the instigator. Three of the tunes on this CD are Coleman originals and *Dewey's Tune* sounds as if it could have been another. The formula for performance also follows the classic quartet's pattern, allowing reasonably lengthy horn solos on every track. On this occasion it is Redman who is the pick of them; in each solo he draws questions from the parent theme and answers them convincingly. His journeys away from each original motif can become tortuous as he moves from an easily identifiable point of departure to a solo conclusion that is less obvious.

This was not a good period for Cherry, but here he plays well. His plaintively whispy tone is exploited to good effect on *Law Years* and, most especially on *Street Woman*, we have the 'old' Cherry dancing through his solos in a waywardly perverse, yet naturally appealing way. Haden and Blackwell formed the best of all Coleman's excellent rhythm teams and there is no lowering of standards as Old and New Dreams perpetuate the original Coleman ethos.     **BMcR**

## Maggie Olin

New review
**Land of Me**  Olin (p, kbds); **Hans Ulrik** (ss, ts); **Hans Andersson** (b); **P.A. Tobin** (d); on three tracks add **Torben Waldorff** (g). Prophone Ⓕ PCD031 (58 minutes). Recorded 1995.

⑦ ❾

Born in the 1960s, Olin graduated from Berklee in 1988 and returned to Europe to take up a freelance musician's life, playing with Maria Schneider and John Abercrombie, among others. Since then she has made considerable progress as a composer, pianist and leader of her own group, the Maggie Olin Quartet, the latest edition of which is on this record. The band plays in what could roughly be termed the modern European style, halfway between Jan Garbarek's bands and, say, Lee Ann Ledgerwood. The music is intelligently mapped out, thoughtfully arranged and always has a story to tell. Ulrik's tenor playing owes much to Garbarek and Brecker, but the urgency of his own feelings makes him worth listening to. Olin herself plays spare but angular, precise piano, often within complex and intricate small-group arrangements, unusual metres and asymmetric compositional layouts. The music is easy to approach and engrossing when concentrated upon, so don't be scared.     **KS**

# King Oliver

**King Oliver's Jazz Band 1923** Oliver, **Louis Armstrong** (c); **Honore Dutrey** (tb); **Johnny Dodds** (cl); **Lil Hardin** (p); **Bud Scott** (bj); **Baby Dodds** (d); on eight tracks add: **Johnny St Cyr** or **Bud Scott** (bj); **Charlie Jackson** (b). Jazz Archives Ⓑ 15746-2 (44 minutes). Recorded 1923.

✔                                                                        ⑩ ❹

Nowhere on the sleeve or in the booklet-notes of this album are you told as much, but these are all 15 of the famous Oliver band Okeh sides. Why this should be something worth noting has everything to do with the greatly superior sound quality of the Okeh recording process over the contemporaneous Gennett. Oliver recorded his band for both labels in 1923 and although the resultant music is glorious in both instances, the listening pleasure is greatly enhanced on the Okehs for the simple reason that you can hear it so much better. Indeed, this CD seems to be an improvement on the excellent job achieved by World Record Club on their vinyl transfers of the early eighties, so there is an added reason to acquire this disc.

So much for the sound quality (or lack of it – these, after all, are still imperfect acoustic-process recordings); what about the music? Stepping aside from its historical importance for a moment (the Oliver band was the greatest living example of the New Orleans outdoor tradition when it made these Chicago recordings), this music is so full of invention, spirit and wit that it is still a lesson in creativity to anyone who cares to listen. The dual lines worked out for the two cornets by Oliver and Armstrong are fascinating enough, but add the brilliant accompanying figures of Johnny Dodds and the overall cohesion-through-interplay, on a remarkably supple rhythmic base, and you have a heady musical brew. Something else of which Oliver is also a master is drama and contrast (on a personal level he displays this in his various tonal distortions through the use of mutes and growls), and there are countless times (the most famous is probably *Snake Rag*) where this happens. It is worth remembering that Oliver – as opposed to Armstrong – was a song-writer of some significance, and his overall sense of form is reflected in the way his band functions here.                                          **KS**

**Sugar Foot Strut** Oliver (c); **Bob Shoffner, Tick Gray** (t); **Kid Ory, Jimmy Archey** (tb); **Albert Nicholas, Barney Bigard, Darnell Howard, Stump Evans, Johnny Dodds, Omer Simeon, Arville Harris** (reeds); **Luis Russell, Clarence Williams, Richard M. Jones** (p); **Bud Scott, Leroy Harris** (bj); **Bert Cobb, Cyrus St Clair** (tba); **Paul Barbarin** (d). MCA/Decca Ⓜ GRP16162 (64 minutes). Recorded 1926-8.

⑧ ❻

This is the band which Oliver formed following the break-up of his Creole Jazz Band. The Creole Jazz Band had played pure New Orleans dancehall music and its records, in effect, launched jazz on the world. The Dixie Syncopators was an entirely different kind of band, an early form of the standard American dance orchestra, arranged in sections and playing mainly from written parts, with improvised solos interspersed. Even so, it was still a band of New Orleans players capable of producing that loose, rolling beat and those hot, blues-inflected solos which the rest of the world was only just beginning to get the hang of (compare this with the stiffness of the contemporary Fletcher Henderson band).

At their best, in numbers like *Wa Wa Wa* and *Too Bad*, the Syncopators are magnificent and Oliver's bright, clear-toned cornet comes through clearly for the first time, thanks to the new electrical recording process. The only trouble is with the arrangements. The craft of jazz-arranging was still at a very crude stage, and there is a great deal of footling around with tricky breaks and novelty effects, not to mention some truly appalling saxophone playing by men who were nearly all superb New Orleans Creole clarinettists. Nevertheless, these are classic recordings in a well-chosen and very effectively transferred selection.                                          **DG**

# Orchestra Improvista

**Nino Rota Fellini** **Michel Marre** (t); **Yves Robert** (tb); **Doudou Gouirand** (as, ss); **Gérard Pansanel** (g, mand); **Michel Godard** (bb); **Antonello Salis** (p, acc); **Jean Jacques Avenel** (b); **Joël Allouche** (d). deux Z Ⓕ ZZ84121 (56 minutes). Recorded 1995.

⑥ ❽

Since the inception of LPs, theme albums have occupied a favoured place in the catalogues of many record companies. This one is dedicated to composer Nino Rota and takes into account that worthy's association with filmmaker Federico Fellini. The compositions from band members reflect this mood and, likewise, pay tribute to the partnership. Unfortunately, it is at times at the expense of jazz qualities. Most of the men involved have excellent credentials and, knowing their past performances, one might have expected greater commitment to the freedom ethic. Such routes are denied them, however, and the need to sustain the mood of the overall project erodes emotional input and deflects the musicians from the ideal implicit in the band's name. The marching band elements and the French cabaret atmosphere of certain titles is especially stultifying and, despite fine work by Avenel, affects the rhythm section adversely. Robert has an outstanding solo on *Nuits Romaines*, Salis takes a freer line in his *Intermezzo D'Antonello* and Marre's expressive trumpet convinces on *Theme 8½*. The all too brief *Tubatteria* is a fine duet for tuba and drum but Gouirand's own solos are unconvincing. Finally, it is the self-imposed obligation to a theme that dominates and, as a result, the music produced is pleasant, rather than inspired. **BMcR**

# Oregon

**Oregon** **Paul McCandless** (ss, ob, f, ehn, bcl, musette); **Ralph Towner** (kbds, g); **Glen Moore** (b, va, p); **Collin Walcott** (perc, sitar, v). ECM Ⓕ 811 711-2 (45 minutes). Recorded 1983.

⑧ ❿

Few, if any, ensembles so successfully incorporate such a welter of musical influences as the jazz chamber group Oregon. Formed in 1970 from four former members of the Paul Winter Consort, Oregon assemble their adventurous but utterly distinctive music from astonishingly diverse sources, classical, so-called 'world' music and jazz chief among them. From a bewildering array of available instrumentation – the group members play around 70 instruments between them – and exploiting both the improvisational latitude of jazz and the attention to nuance and dynamic subtlety commonly associated with classical music, Oregon construct closely worked sound-sculptures of great textural variety and harmonic originality. Their material ranges from composed tunes with flowing, sinuous themes set against a wash of synthesized and percussive sound to improvised pieces involving, say, a viola, oboe and hand drums or sitar and Indian-style vocals. The result might be a mite ethereal for some tastes, and titles like *Beside the Brook* and *There Was No Moon That Night* misleadingly locate the group as New Age pioneers, but the skill, commitment and patent sincerity of the musicians shines through everything they do, and on this, their definitive album, made for ECM with its customary flawless Eicher production, their considerable strengths are showcased to perfection. **CP**

# Original Dixieland Jazz Band

**The 75th Anniversary** **Nick LaRocca** (c); **Eddie Edwards** (tb); **Larry Shields** (cl); **Henry Ragas** (p); **Tony Sbarbaro** (d); **Benny Krueger** (as); **J. Russel Robinson** (p); **Frank Signorelli** (p); **Clifford Cairns**, **Eddie King**, **Al Bernard** (v). RCA Bluebird Ⓜ ND90650 (70 minutes). Recorded 1917-21.

⑦ ❼

It is an over-simplification to see the ODJB, unquestionably the first jazz band to record, as a mere copy of the Negro original. The black origins of jazz are indisputable, but the cross-fertilization of ideas between all ethnic groups, not least the Creoles, complicated the New Orleans situation. This CD shows the ODJB's early work for Victor as a mixture of inspired composition, strategic borrowing and ragged performance. The trumpet-trombone-clarinet line-up and its faintly hick version of the New Orleans ensemble satisfied the purist historians, but the actual performances were frequently untidy. LaRocca's cliché-laden lead was effective, however, and his willingness to leave the decoration to Shields and the punctuation to Edwards worked for the band. Titles such as *Livery Stable Blues*, *At the Jazz Band Ball*, *Tiger Rag* and *Fidgety Feet* became models for nearly all later recordings of these pieces, although the introduction of Krueger in 1920 produced sophistry rather than refinement. It was not until their return from Europe in 1921 that the band, now with the excellent Signorelli on piano, recaptured something of its early spirit. RCA Victor did a series of remakes in the thirties (available on an RCA Jazz Tribune two-CD set), but these are the genuine article. **BMcR**

# Jim O'Rourke

New review
**Acoustics** **O'Rourke**, **Henry Kaiser** (g); **John Oswald** (as); **Mari Kimura** (vn). Victo Ⓕ CD025 (62 minutes). Recorded 1993.

⑧ ❽

This album could have been listed under any of the names above, and in fact all four are given equal (and alphabetical) credit in the packaging. Which is as it should be; this is free improvisation of considerable nuance and concord, with a compatible vocabulary and consensual syntax. Limited to acoustic instruments, the music's intimacy and focus on detail is very much influenced by the British school – characteristically wispy violin, prickly guitar, breathy alto sax – though with telling differences. Both guitarists are liable to unexpectedly slide into John Fahey-style folk chording or fingerpicking (in *Aqua* Kaiser resorts to an actual chord progression!) which adds thematic elements seldom found in such rigorous improvisational environs. They are not confined to a single theory of development and take full advantage of multiple options including pointillistic polyphony, aggressive gestures and contrasting instrumental sonorities (for example, the harmonics versus bowed guitar effects on *To Chartreuse*). Most impressive are those moments (as on *Flesh*) where the music can be recognized as the audible sounds of the *mechanics* of improvising, via the instrument itself (ideas translated into sound). John Oswald (yes, the plunderphonic electrician) and Henry Kaiser, occasional collaborators since the seventies, are probably the most experienced and best known of these players, and Mari Kimura is a talented newcomer with the ability to offer long chromatic lines or short bursts of percussive plucking. O'Rourke has the highest visibility in New Music/Improvising circles right now, through his work with Company, Eddie Prevost, Günter Müller, and others, as well as his production work with alternative rock bands. As an improviser, he has an ear for microtonal sounds, bowed, plucked and rubbed from his acoustic guitar, and a very different approach – more ambient and compositional – on electric. He is certainly one to watch.　　　　　**AL**

# Niels-Henning Ørsted Pederson　　　　　　　　　　　　　　　　　1946

New review

**Those Who Were** Ørsted Pederson (b); **Ulf Wakenius** (g); **Victor Lewis** (d); **Johnny Griffin** (ts) on two tracks; **Lisa Nilsson** (v) on one track; **Alex Riel** (d) on two tracks. Verve Ⓟ 533 232-2 (55 minutes). Recorded 1996.

⑧　❽

Danish bassist Niels-Henning Ørsted Pederson began a prodigious career in his teens, was invited to join Count Basie when just 17, accompanied almost every leading American jazz musician to visit Copenhagen during the sixties and spent much of the seventies and eighties in Oscar Peterson's virtuoso trio. He has grown into one of the world's leading double bassists – a gifted technician and brilliant soloist who can play the massive instrument with the dexterity of a guitarist.

A worthy celebration of his gifts, **Those Who Were** presents the bassist in a variety of formats and features the sparkling, characteristically European guitar work of Ulf Wakenius, an underrated musician with a similar post-Reinhardt clarity to the better-known Philip Catherine. It opens with an immaculate, lightly swinging version of Gershwin's *Our Love Is Here to Stay*, the tune played on the bass with strummed guitar accompaniment. Pederson contributes a rowdy samba (*Wishing and Hoping*) and a lovely jazz waltz called *Friends Forever*. The only blues on the album, *The Puzzle*, happens to also be a vehicle for fast-fingered hard-bop tenor saxophonist Johnny Griffin, who proves himself a demonstrative presence. The rhythm section rises to the challenge, swinging hard, and Wakenius muffles his tone to play some Kenny Burrell-style blues. Pederson, a walking bass master and inspired soloist, has clearly done this somewhere before.　　　　　**LC**

# Anthony Ortega　　　　　　　　　　　　　　　　　　　　　　　1928

**New Dance!** Ortega (as); **Chuck Domanico**, **Bobby West** (b); **Bill Goodwin** (d). hatART Ⓟ 6065 (70 minutes). Recorded 1966/7.

⑧　❽

This disc combines **New Dance!** and **Permutations**, two remarkable LPs by this Mexican-American from Los Angeles, a one-time Lionel Hampton sideman then working with Gerald Wilson's big band. These duo (with Domanico) and trio (West and Goodwin) performances parallel contemporary developments – Ornette Coleman's elastic approach to song form, the eerie openness of Albert Ayler's trio – but Ortega sounds like neither saxophonist. His plaintive but muscular sax sound and ensemble dynamic set him apart.

These intimate settings convey a great sense of mood, often stark and melancholy, on both original tunes and lightweight fare like *The Shadow of Your Smile*, a ten-minute free dialogue with Domanico, who is an unusually nimble and full-sounding *arco* player and a close listener. There is a constant air of discovery about these pieces, meditative as chamber music but full of risk. Every detail sounds revealed to both players and listeners simultaneously. Exquisite as these recordings are, there is nothing similar among Ortega's rare later albums. Like other West Coast jazzers, thereafter he devoted most of his energies to anonymous studio work. However his (credited) solos waft memorably across the soundtrack to John Cassavetes's 1980 film *Gloria*.　　　　　**KW**

# Kid Ory　　　　　　　　　　　　　　　　　　　　　　　　1886-1973

**Ory's Creole Trombone** Kid Ory (tb, v); with a collective personnel including: **Mutt Carey** (c, t); **King Oliver**, **Bob Shoffner**, **George Mitchell** (c); **Louis Armstrong** (c, v); **Dink Johnson**, **Johnny Dodds**, **Omer Simeon**, **Jimmie Noone** (cl); **Albert Nicholas**, **Billy Paige**, **Darnell Howard**, **Stump Evans** (cl, ss, as); **Barney Bigard** (cl, ss, ts); **Joe Clarke** (as); **Fred Washington**, **Luis Russell**, **Lil Armstrong**, **Jelly Roll Morton**, **Buster Wilson** (p); **Bud Scott** (bj); **Johnny St. Cyr** (bj, g); **Bud Scott** (g); **Bert Cobb** (bb); **Ed Garland**, **John Lindsay** (b); **Ben Borders**, **Paul Barbarin**, **Zutty Singleton**, **Andrew Hilaire** (d). ASV Ⓜ CDAJA5148 (76 minutes). Recorded 1922-44.

⑧　❻

This CD gathers together some of the finest and most representative examples of Kid Ory's unique tailgate trombone playing from his musically most productive years. The collection opens with *Ory's Creole Trombone* and *Society Blues,* dating from 1922 and generally considered to be the very first recordings by a black New Orleans band. Although probably more of historic than musical interest, the elements of Ory's style are clearly on display. His massive, powerful sound was always producing just the right notes in the ensemble and although many tried to copy him, none succeeded. He plays a vital role with the 'big' band of King Oliver, but some of his finest work will be found on the six tracks by what was in fact the Armstrong Hot Five minus Louis and with Joe Clarke added on alto. George Mitchell's cornet playing is excellent but obviously not on a par with that of Armstrong, yet Louis's absence seems to give the band a more balanced feeling. The fine recording balance allows us to savour the clarity of the New Orleans Bootblacks. Four tracks under Jelly Roll Morton's name a few months later reunited Ory and Mitchell for more classic music (listen to Kid on *Smokehouse Blues*) but a lack of interest in this kind of music caused Ory to leave the business for a decade. The final five tracks come from the Orson Welles-sponsored Mercury Theatre broadcasts and mark Ory's comeback with a fine band containing Jimmie Noone, who died a matter of days after the last of their titles were recorded. The music is exuberant good fun but Ory was already past his peak in creative terms, although he continued to lead excellent bands right into the sixties. **AM**

**New review**
**The Legendary Kid** Ory (tb); **Alvin Alcorn** (t); **Phil Gomez** (cl); **Lionel Reason** (p); **Julian Davidson** (g); **Wellman Braud** (b); **Minor Hall** (d). Good Time Jazz Ⓜ GTCD12016-2 (43 minutes). Recorded 1955.

⑦ ❼

The seeds of Ory's later musical harvest were sowed many years earlier. He led a well regarded band in New Orleans from 1912 to 1919 and, after moving to California in 1919, continued in that vein. The important landmarks in the second phase of his career are well documented above but it was the Mercury Theatre broadcasts that anticipated the music heard in the third part of the story. Ory had retired from music in 1933 but, when he did return, he was on hand to play a prominent part in the New Orleans revival. The new career stretched from 1942 to 1966 and this CD comes from the middle of that era. The early death of clarinettist Jimmie Noone in 1944 was a sad loss but his place was alternatively filled by the likes of Omer Simeon, Joe Darensbourg, Darnell Howard and Phil Gomez (heard here). The 1955 band was rather better than those featuring spectacular trumpeters such as Teddy Buckner or Red Allen and this session shows how well Ory balanced his own groups. The tailgate master was a limited soloist but he was an adept user of mutes, and titles like *Sugar Blues*, *There'll Be Some Changes Made* and *By and By* demonstrate his wise tempo selections, well judged exploitation of dynamic levels and his ability to bring the best out of his soloists. In a revivalist movement beset by a large number of amateurs, Ory was always a professional. **BMcR**

## Mike Osborne
1941

**Outback** Osborne (as); **Harry Beckett** (t); **Chris McGregor** (p); **Harry Miller** (b); **Louis Moholo** (d). Future Music Ⓕ FMRCD07-031994 (44 minutes). Recorded 1970.

⑧ ❽

A Guildhall School of Music graduate, alto saxophonist Osborne distinguished himself in the big bands of Mike Westbrook and Brotherhood of Breath. He was part of SOS with John Surman and Alan Skidmore and made up a stunning duo with Stan Tracey. Many listeners were introduced to his music during a five-year residency at London's Peanuts Club, but little more than ten years later his passionate musical voice had been silenced by ill health.

Jackie McLean was an early influence but, wooed by the greater freedoms of Ornette Coleman, Osborne evolved a style that acknowledged both. Little of his work is currently available but this CD shows him to be a distinctive and dynamic player. It marks him out as a saxophonist of creative consistency, natural lyricism and as one blessed with a poignancy of tone that instantly engages the listener. For Osborne, swinging was not something to be achieved; it was something he did instinctively. Rather than disrupt his line, startling intervallic leaps inspired his soloing process and made his entire style unpredictable. His note placements are especially deft and on *So It Is*, in particular, he benefits from a rhythm section as capable of grass-rustling subtlety as they are of gale-force challenge. **BMcR**

## Greg Osby
1960

**New review**
**Black Book** Osby (as, p, kbds); on three tracks **Mulgrew Miller** (p); **D.J. Ghetto** (tt); **Riva Parker**, **Sha-Key**, **Mustafo**, **Markita Morris**, **Bernard Collins Jr**, **Taj McCoy** (narr); **Calvin Jones** (b); on one track **Bill McClellan** (d). Blue Note Ⓕ CDP8 29266-2 (57 minutes). Recorded 1995.

⑦ ❽

Altoist Osby has made a considerable name for himself in the last few years by his association with Steve Coleman and others and guest appearances for Andrew Hill and Dianne Reeves. As shown in his earliest albums, his playing is potentially as versatile as Coleman's, despite a similar urge to be at the cutting edge. This is his third collaboration with rappers (the others being already unavailable in some territories). It is perhaps the most successful in some respects, with greater variety and indeed a softer edge to many tracks which, the hip-hop beats apart, fit easily within the tradition of jazz-and-poetry. Doubtless this is why the entire lyrics are printed in the accompanying booklet (with only one use of Miles Davis's favourite word), but there are many moments of purely musical interest. Two of the three tracks containing Mulgrew Miller are, to all intents, purely instrumental, with *Intuition*'s sampled rhythm-section consisting of bass and drums played with brushes, while there is an uncredited tenor sax at the start of *Mr. Freeman* (Chico?). Osby's contributions are inventive but often relegated to the back of the mix, presumably in the pursuit of a larger part of the young black audience.   **BP**

**New review**

**Art Forum**  Osby (ss, as); **James Williams** (p); **Bryan Carrott** (vb); **Lonnie Plaxico** (b); **Jeff 'Tain' Watts** (d); with, on two tracks: **Robin Eubanks** (tb); **Cleave Guyton** (f, ts); **Alex Harden** (bcl); **Darrell Grant** (p); **Marvin Sewell** (g). Blue Note Ⓔ CDP8 37319-2 (58 minutes). Recorded 1996.
⑩ ⑩

Although Osby has in fact described this album as something of an accident, that takes nothing away from its significance. He may have made it as a temporary diversion from his other musical concerns (eloquently expressed on the album reviewed above), but **Art Forum** (whether the pun was intended or not) is immensely accomplished modern acoustic jazz. Osby's musical personality shines through every note he plays, his lines are lucid and perfectly weighted, and he sounds utterly in control of what he is executing, however oblique, however simple. For the most part here he plays alto and is accompanied by a piano trio, with vibist Carrott appearing from time to time. His alto sound is one of the richest and purest since John Handy's. This is very much his band, and he dominates its mood and sound, much as he did when he brought a superb young trio to Ronnie Scott's in late 1996 to deliver blistering hour-long sets where each piece segued into the next seamlessly and each note was a perfectly-achieved artefact. Osby's writing (only Ellington's *I Didn't Know about You* and Billie Holiday's *Don't Explain* deviate from self-penned material here) is angular and refreshing, finding an insistent groove and sufficient twists and turns to hint at a lineage from Andrew Hill (with whom he has recorded), among others. Yet the leader's overwhelming presence swamps any idle thoughts of this being a record made in anyone else's shadow. You sense that, like Sonny Rollins, Osby here has an at times awesome empathy with his instrument and chosen material, moulding it at will into the mode of expression he requires. With the two aforementioned ballads he creates timeless but intensely personal statements in the great instrumentalists' tradition. One tune, *2nd Born to Freedom*, is a soprano sax-acoustic guitar duet lasting less than two minutes. A couple of pieces show a more experimental bent, couched in highly disciplined improvisational counterpoint. On two other tracks there is an expanded personnel, giving added colour and richness to the music, but the spotlight stays with Osby. This is as it should be, for he has a lot to say, and it is all of interest.   **KS**

# Johnny Otis
1921

**The Original Johnny Otis Show**  Johnny Otis Big Band: Otis (d, ldr, arr); **Teddy Buckner, Billy Jones, Loyal Walker, Harry Parr** (t); **Henry Coker, Eli Robinson, John Pettigrew, Jap Jones** (tb); **Gene Bloch, Bob Harris** (as); **Paul Quinichette, James Von Streeter** (ts); **Leon Beck** (bs); **Bill Doggett** (p, arr); **Bernie Cobbs** (g); **Curtis Counce** (b); on four tracks **Jimmy Rushing** (v); **Johnny Otis & His Orchestra**: Don Johnson, Lee Graves, John Anderson (t); George Washington (tb); Floyd Turnham (as); Lorenzo Holden, James Von Streeter, Big Jay McNeely (ts); Walter Henry, Bobby McNeely (bs); Devonia Williams (p, v); Johnny Otis (vb, v); Pete Lewis (g); Mario Delgarde (b); Leard Bell (d); Little Esther, Junior Ryder, Red Lyte, Mel Walker, The Robins, Preacher Lee Graves (v); Marilyn Scott (remaining tracks). Savoy Ⓜ SV-0266 (76 minutes). Recorded 1945/51.
⑦ ⑥

Otis has spent the vast majority of his 50-year career in the realms of r&b and soul, but his beginnings were in jazz, and jazz inflected everything he did up to the mid fifties at least. These sides, made for the Exclusive and Savoy labels and all recorded in L.A., are his first sessions, with the first date comprising three straight-ahead Basie-type jazz outings and the big ballad, *Harlem Nocturne*, a major juke hit at the time. The rest of the music on this CD (which duplicates a mid-seventies double-LP compiled by Bob Porter, but omits the final six tracks due to space limitations) veers between straight instrumental r&b and a range of vocal styles which move from blues to prototype fifties harmony groups. As such it has little place in this Guide, but there is enough jazz juice for it to be a fascinating parallel odyssey to what else was going on, and a valuable glimpse into the black hinterland between straight blues, chart-type pop and mainstream jazz: a hinterland which was eventually to become the mainstream of popular youth music as the fifties gathered pace.   **KS**

# Roberto Ottaviano

**Items from the Old Earth**  Ottaviano (ss); **Mario Arcari** (ob, ehn, ss); **Sandro Cerino** (cl, bcl, f, bf); **Martin Mayes** (frh); **Roberto Rossi** (tb, shells); **Fiorenzo Gualandris** (tba). Splasc(h) Ⓔ 332-2 (51 minutes). Recorded 1990.
⑧ ⑧

As his imaginative solo soprano saxophone album, various quartet dates, and featured sideman role in Franz Köglmann's Pipetet show, Ottaviano is a singular player with a warm lyric flow and almost classical sound. But this fine disc finds him in another format, fronting an ensemble of unusual breadth for jazz. Known as the Six Mobiles, the band's first LP was devoted to Mingus material, a remarkable début that emphasized their links to the jazz tradition. In this CD they expand into original territory, and it is the intricate writing which distinguishes the music. Each member contributes at least one composition and arrangement, no two are alike. The group can sound like a classical wind quintet or a brass band in an Italian piazza, and they swing when it's needed. At times the music threatens to become too genteel, but at that point they are liable to slide into a foot-tapping riff or just as easily dissolve into a prismatic polyphony. Such a democratic approach means that Ottaviano and the phenomenal oboist Mario Arcari must sacrifice solo space; the ensemble's interplay is a marvel, however. **AL**

## Oran 'Hot Lips' Page

1908-54

**Hot Lips Page and His Band, 1938-40**  Page (t, v); with on four tracks: **Ben Smith** (cl, as); **Sam Simmons** (ts); **Jimmy Reynolds** (p); **Connie Wainwright** (g); **Wellman Braud** (b); **Alfred Taylor** (d); on 12 tracks: **Bobby Moore, Eddie Mullens, Dave Page** (t); **George Stevenson, Harry White** (tb); **Ulysses Scott, Ben Williams** (cl, as); **Benny Waters, Ernie Powell** (ts); **Jimmy Reynolds** (p); **Connie Wainwright** (g); **Abe Bolar** (b); **Alfred Taylor** (d); **Delores Payne, Ben Bowers** (v); on six tracks: **Buster Smith** (cl, as); **Jimmy Powell** (as); **Sam Davis** (ts); **Jimmy Reynolds** (p); **Abe Bolar** (b); **Ed McConney** (d); **Romayne Jackson, The Highlanders** (v); on four tracks: **Eddie Barefield** (cl, as): **Don Stovall** (as); **Don Byas** (ts); **Pete Johnson** (p); **John Collins** (g); **Abe Bolar** (b); **A.G. Godley** (d); **Beal Morton** (v). Classics Ⓜ 561 (72 minutes). Recorded 1938-40.

⑥ ❻

Lips Page was a big star with the Bennie Moten and early Basie bands to the point where agent Joe Glaser signed him to an exclusive contract in which he would be featured in front of the Basie band. Unfortunately for Page, Glaser forgot to ask the Count first, so the trumpeter became the leader of his own small bands, notably those featured here on this excellent chronology. Louis apart, no one could better Lips as a blues singer-cum-trumpeter, and the tracks of the greatest value here are those using the 12-bar formula. The 12 tracks made for Bluebird with a 13-piece band are pleasant and efficiently performed (Page had a knack of discovering lesser-known but fine players such as pianist Jimmy Reynolds and tenor saxist Sam Simmons), but the meat of the collection is the ten tracks made in 1940 for Decca. Six of these have 'Professor' Buster Smith on alto, one of Charlie Parker's early idols. *Lafayette* and *South* are by a specially assembled band and were made for Decca's **Kansas City Jazz** album; there is a lurching increase in tempo in the last chorus of *South*, a remastering fault. That aside, the transfers are excellent. **AM**

## Tony Overwater

New review

**Motion Music**  Overwater (b); **Eric Vloeimans** (t); **Yuri Honing** (ts, ss); **Joost Lybaart** (d); **Joshua Samson** (perc); **Sylvia De Hartog, Regina Mester** (v). Jazz In Motion Ⓕ JIMCD001 (56 minutes). Recorded 1994.

⑥ ❽

Overwater is a committed jazz bassist. He has worked with David Murray, Dave Liebman and Sunny Murray. He formed the Jazz In Motion foundation and has successfully led his own groups. Perhaps his most personal contribution to jazz has been his free approach to cinema and its music. He sees his jazz as a parallel form and this CD, with the help of its useful and essential booklet, allows the listener to identify the singers and instrumentalists on each title and to relate them to the visual sequences listed alongside. De Hartog is an impressive scat singer and there are other parts that are either spoken or delivered in a form of jazz *Sprechstimme*. Honing's solos on *Georg*, *Snarl and Rattle* and *Renee*, in particular, are distinctive, while Vloeimans plays dramatically on *Death Row Seat* and expressively throughout. Overwater is very much the leader. The only reservation the listener may feel is that, because the whole project seeks to be faithful to the mood of the 'subjects', it leads the players away from improvisational quality in the orthodox sense. **BMcR**

## Makoto Ozone

1961

New review

**Nature Boys**  Ozone (p); **John Patitucci** (b); **Peter Erskine** (d). Verve Ⓕ 531 270-2 (60 minutes). Recorded 1995.

⑧ ❾

The word "virtuoso" tends to get bandied about lightly in the face of impressive technique, but there is no better description for Ozone, whose playing combines emotional depth, harmonic exploration and the re-examination of standards with a dazzling technical command of the piano. Away from their normal territory, both Erskine and Patitucci fall naturally into the piano trio format, and rise to all the challenges presented by Ozone. One of the nine tracks is an Ozone original (and it receives a contrastingly contemplative treatment), but the others are the staple standard fare of a piano-bass-drums trio, only propelled on to a higher plane than usual by the group's remarkable musicianship. *Lover Come Back to Me* is the most outstanding example of Ozone's playing, taken at a fast clip and culminating in an unaccompanied cadenza. One of the most impressive aspects of Ozone is his ability to set and maintain a musical direction, whilst adding passing allusions to other genres and styles that enrich the mixture, but never hijack his chosen route. A good example is on Mitchell Forman's *Gorgeous*, where gospel and soul overtones deepen an essentially ballad treatment, Patitucci shadowing every harmonic nuance and Erskine overlaying a soft shuffle above the basic pulse. **AS**

# Marty Paich

1925-96

**Moanin'** Paich (p, arr, leader); with a collective personnel of: **Conte Candoli, Jack Sheldon, Al Porcino, Frank Beach, Stu Williamson** (t); **Bob Envoldsen, George Roberts** (tb); **Vince DeRosa** (frh); **Art Pepper** (as); **Bill Perkins** (ts); **Bill Hood, Jimmy Giuffre** (bs); **Russ Freeman** (p); **Victor Feldman** (vb); **Joe Mondragon, Scott LaFaro** (b); **Mel Lewis** (d). Discovery Ⓜ DSCD962 (71 minutes). Recorded 1959.

⑥ ❼

Paich established his reputation during the fifties through his flexible and imaginative work for a string of top-flight singers, including Peggy Lee, Ella Fitzgerald, Anita O'Day and Mel Tormé. At the end of that decade he made a series of fine albums under his own leadership for Warner Brothers, and this CD compiles some of the better moments from those albums. Paich is a thoroughly schooled musician, having obtained a Masters in music from the L.A. Conservatory, and this schooling stands him in good stead when it comes to arranging the most advantageous mix of line and colour between brass and reeds on such pieces as *Violets for Your Furs* or Ellington's *Warm Valley*. During Pepper's solo on the former his backing is so beautifully sonorous that it becomes a pleasure in its own right. On the latter, Paich's swapping of the melody onto baritone sax is a nicely judged move.

The second half of the CD comes from Paich's tribute to Broadway, and although the trumpet section is not as brilliant, soloists such as Pepper, Giuffre and Feldman make up for it while LaFaro makes his presence felt. The charts are relaxed, transparent and pleasurable without being in the least challenging. CD sound is commendable. **KS**

# Eddie Palmieri

1936

**Palmas** Palmieri (p); **Brian Lynch** (t); **Conrad Herwig** (tb); **Donald Harrison** (as); **Johnny Torres, Johnny Benitez** (b); **Robbie Ameen** (d); **Richie Flores, Anthony Carrillo, Jose Claussell** (perc). Elektra Nonesuch Ⓔ 61649-2 (52 minutes). Recorded 1993.

⑦ ❿

Palmieri came up in New York surrounded by Cuban music and musicians, and saw Tito Puente as his mentor. He admits that he "hated jazz" when he was young. "All I wanted to hear was Latin." It wasn't until the close of the fifties that he started hearing and understanding jazz pianists like Bud Powell and Thelonious Monk, and began to appreciate what they were doing. By the mid sixties he was ready to begin incorporating what he liked into his own bands.

This album is an extension of those beginnings, combining what Palmieri calls "the Afro-Caribbean dance form and the instrumental jazz form without losing the individuality of the soloists' voices." This he certainly achieves, with an at times overwhelmingly powerful and complex rhythmic thrust, which is centred on his pianistic patterns, keeping buoyant anything the horns care to try out. There is an engaging vitality about the music and, though it occasionally becomes a little relentless, all one has to do is get up and dance around the room to it to appreciate its felicities all over again. **KS**

# Jorge Pardo

New review

**10 de Paco** Pardo (ss, f); **Chano Dominguez** (p); **Javier Colina** (b); **Tino de Geraldo** (d); **Luis Dulzaides** (perc); **Conchi Heredia, El Conde** (v, handclaps). Milestone Ⓔ MCD9229-2 (61 minutes). Recorded 1994.

⑦ ❾

Pardo has been a long-serving member of Paco de Lucia's band and, as the title suggests, this programme consists of ten pieces associated with the great guitarist. The music stands in a similar relationship to flamenco as the work of Astor Piazzolla does to tango. That is to say, its melodic, harmonic and tonal contours are derived from the original form, but they are combined with elements of jazz and contemporary concert music to produce something more universal and exploratory. The two sounds which dominate this CD are the flute of Pardo himself and the raw, open-air flamenco voice of Conchi Heredia. It is stimulating and exciting music, although from a strictly jazz point of view it is of limited relevance. **DG**

# Hartzell 'Tiny' Parham

1900-43

**New review**

**1928-30** Parham (p, cel, ldr); with a collective personnel featuring: **Punch Miller**, **Roy Hobson** (c);
**Charles Lawson**, **Ike Covington** (tb); **Charles Johnson** (cl, as); **Elliot Washington** (vn); **Charlie
Jackson** (bj); **Quinn Wilson**, **Milt Hinton** (tba); **Ernie Marrero** (d, wshbd), **Tommy Brookins** (v).
Timeless Historical Ⓕ CBC1-022 (two discs: 154 minutes). Recorded 1928-30.

⑥ ❽

Parham was born in Kansas City and spent his early years touring the Southwest as well as getting as
far afield as Hawaii and Cuba before finally settling in Chicago around the middle of the twenties. By
1926 he had begun his recording career, two years later débuting as a leader with the sides which start
this two-CD collection. Parham battled on through the Depression with his own band, although the
recordings had stopped in 1930, but by 1936 his style of music was regarded as *passé* and he took work
as a theatre organist to keep body and soul together. He was engaged in this profession on the night
of his demise in 1943, probably due to a heart attack (he was decidedly overweight for many years),
in the Kilbourn Hotel, Milwaukee, as he stood to walk away from the hotel organ.

The music here combines competent musicianship and high discipline with a penchant for the New
Orleans ensemble as proselytized by Jelly Roll Morton and a true understanding of the blues and its
importance to jazz. The arrangements are consistently varied and occasionally inspired, mixing the
materials to hand with a flair for the dramatic gesture which never descends to cornball high-jinks. Of
the soloists, the cornettists tend to come out on top, Punch Miller in particular giving the music
tremendous authority, but the tuba-based rhythm section must be given due praise for the smooth
forward motion it consistently generates. These guys could swing.                          **KS**

# Charlie Parker

1920-55

**The Complete Birth of Bebop** Parker (as, ts); with i) **Efferge Ware** (g); **Phil Philips** (d); ii)
various peronnels including: **Dizzy Gillespie**, **Billy Eckstine** (t); **Goon Gardner** (ts); **Hurley Ramey**
(g); **Oscar Pettiford** (b); plus Parker playing over 78rpm discs of **Hazel Scott**, **Benny Goodman
Trio** and **Quartet**; iii) **Dizzy Gillespie's Rebop Six** (Gillespie, t; Parker, as; Milt Jackson, vb; Al
Haig, p; Ray Brown, b; Stan Levey, d). Stash Ⓕ STCD535 (73 minutes). Recorded 1940-5.

⑥ ❷

When genius appears fully-fledged in all its astounding splendour, part of the afterglow of its effect is
to awaken interest in how such perfection came about. In the case of Charlie Parker, as opposed to
that of Lester Young, the trail has gradually become illuminated by the indefatigable researches of a
legion of Parker historians and fans. While Young's playing prior to his 1936 début on discs remains
a matter only of spoken testimony, we now have the unmistakable sounds of Parker's evolution
stretching back to 1940, still four years away from his first mature commercial recordings.

Group i) of the above comes from Kansas City. The first track is from 1940, presenting Bird
unaccompanied and in dreadful sound quality. The following four find him with guitarist Efferge
Ware. Between the two dates Parker made his first records with the Jay McShann Orchestra, lived
in New York as a freelance, then returned to his hometown. His feet are still firmly in swing soil
here, with little of the double-timing or rhythmic displacement of his later playing, but his
harmonic sense is already sophisticated. Group ii) finds Bird for the most part on tenor sax, and
his oft-remarked derivation from Lester Young is at its most obvious here; he even quotes whole
Young phrases in his solos. Yet there is also Herschel Evans and Coleman Hawkins in his
increasing exploration of extended chords. Sound quality is bearable most of the time. Group iii)
jumps to fully mature Parker and a fabulous session for Jubilee Radio in LA in good mono. Both
principals are in exciting form, with Parker fully emerged from the chrysalis he inhabits on the
earlier sides.

As a potted history of the birth of Charlie Parker, genius and revolutionary, this will do just nicely.
As an essay in recorded sound, worry later.                                              **KS**

**The Immortal Charlie Parker** Parker (as, ts); **Miles Davis** (t); **John Lewis**, **Bud Powell**, **Dizzy
Gillespie**, **Clyde Hart** (p); **Tiny Grimes** (g); **Curley Russell**, **Tommy Potter**, **Nelson Boyd**, **Jimmie
Butts** (b); **Max Roach**, **Harold West** (d). Denon/Savoy Ⓜ SV-0102 (54 minutes).
Recorded 1944-8.

✓                                                                                   ⑩ ⑥

A somewhat haphazard but nevertheless valuable selection of Parker material culled from his
Savoy sessions. For once a sleeve timing is overly modest; the duration is actually some eight
minutes longer than stated and the reason is that takes one and two of *Tiny's Tempo* and take one
of *Red Cross*, all from the 1944 Tiny Grimes session (Parker's first commercial small-group
recordings) are complete and not faded as have been previous reissues. Although the interest is
clearly Parker, these Grimes titles are excellent small-band pieces with fine piano from Clyde Hart
and steady time-keeping from West. *Now's The Time* is from the famous *Ko Ko* session (a blues
with a theme similar to *The Hucklebuck*) with a faltering 19-year-old Miles Davis partnering
Parker for the first time. Davis is present on all the other tracks but his playing on the 1947 and

1948 sessions is far more assured, the tone dry and distinctive. *Chasin' the Bird* has a contrapuntal theme (as does *Ah-Leu-Cha*, not included here), possibly an indication of Parker's desire to get away from convention. Four titles find him switching to tenor, slowing down his fast articulation slightly but still sounding light years ahead of the competition. The transfers are variable in quality but never less than acceptable. Some second-choice takes and breakdowns are included, but with Parker everything is worthy of study.  **AM**

---

**The Charlie Parker Story**  Parker (as); **Miles Davis** (t); **Dizzy Gillespie** (t, p); **Sadik Hakim** aka **Argonne Thornton** (p); **Curly Russell** (b); **Max Roach** (d). Denon/Savoy Ⓜ SV-0105 (35 minutes). Recorded 1945.

✅    ⑩ ❹

Bebop begins here! This disc contains Charlie Parker's first commercial date as leader, on November 26th, 1945. Parker's Savoy recordings, all made in the mid forties, are one of the main pillars of his oeuvre and have been reissued in many configurations over the years. The label is currently owned by Denon/Nippon Columbia, whose Parker CD reissue programme leaves a lot to be desired – such as, for example, a definitive collection of the original master takes (last available as a two-CD set on Savoy ZDS 8801, but withdrawn on the label's acquisition by Denon).

The Charlie Parker Story is a reissue of an LP that Savoy released in the mid fifties and comprises that first session in its entirety, complete with false starts, warm-up tracks and alternative takes. Denon have also included the original fifties LP artwork, which is ghastly, and the original sleeve-notes by John Mehegan, who wrongly identifies the musicians on several tracks. By reprinting these errors without a word of correction, Denon have done the jazz public a sloppy disservice. Mehegan assumed that Bud Powell plays piano on the date; in fact, although Powell had been booked to play, he didn't turn up and Dizzy Gillespie is the pianist on all tracks except for the three takes of *Thriving on a Riff* (which Morgan mis-calls *Thriving from a Riff*) and the first take of *Ko Ko*, where Sadik Hakim (then known as Argonne Thornton) takes over. Mehegan also speculates that Gillespie plays trumpet on a number of tracks, but this happens only on the two takes of *Ko Ko* that closed the session.

The whole event seems to have been somewhat chaotic. Parker has recurring trouble with his saxophone which 'squeaks' throughout; Miles Davis fell asleep on the floor; Hakim, who didn't have a union card, had to exit hurriedly when a union rep arrived. Yet from this shambles emerged undeniably brilliant music; specifically, the master takes of *Billie's Bounce*, *Now's the Time*, *Thriving on a Riff* and *Ko Ko*. The other tracks, some just seconds long, make up a fascinating document of a Parker recording session. However, with one or two exceptions, such as the lovely alto solo on *Meandering*, they will probably be of interest only to collectors.

The four masters are a fair example of Parker's repertoire at the time. *Billie's Bounce* and *Now's the Time* are blues, *Thriving on a Riff* is based on the chords of *I Got Rhythm*, *Ko Ko* on the chords of *Cherokee*, one of Parker's favourite tunes and one on which he had already been improvising for many years. The session's masterpiece, *Ko Ko*, is one of the high points of Parker's entire recording career; his headlong, convoluted lines are an astonishing display of saxophone virtuosity. The bebop revolution is usually seen as an expansion of jazz's harmonic language, but what *Ko Ko* makes clear is Parker's dynamic rhythmic invention – his dramatic entrances, quicksilver lines, daring resolutions. All are played at breakneck speed yet remain fluent, melodic and intrinsically musical.  **GL**

---

**Charlie Parker On Dial: The Complete Sessions**  Parker (as); **Dizzy Gillespie, Miles Davis, Howard McGhee** (t); **J.J. Johnson** (tb); **Lucky Thompson, Wardell Gray** (ts); **George Handy, Dodo Marmarosa, Jimmy Bunn, Russ Freeman, Erroll Garner, Duke Jordan** (p); **Arv Garrison, Barney Kessel** (g); **Ray Brown, Vic McMillan, Bob Kesterson, Arnold Fishkind, Red Callender, Tommy Potter** (b); **Stan Levey, Roy Porter, Jimmy Pratt, Doc West, Don Lamond, Max Roach** (d); **Earl Coleman** (v). Spotlite/Dial Ⓒ SPJCD4-101 (four discs: 257 minutes). Recorded 1946-7.

✅    ⑩ ❻

The iconic status of Parker's Dials is often bracketed with the Savoys overlapping the same period. On most of these studio sides, from *Diggin' Diz* to *How Deep Is the Ocean*, the altoist is at the peak of his powers – which contrasts starkly with the drowning-not-waving *Lover Man* solo. Material is impressively varied, including such unique Parker originals as *Yardbird Suite* and *Bongo Beep*, and (unlike the Savoys) several more standard ballads.

A further distinction between the Dial and the Savoy material is that all the studio alternative takes (presented here in exact chronological order) are complete performances, apart from two Parker excerpted solos on *Crazeology* and the *Famous Alto Break*, which Bird then re-created on the subsequent versions of *A Night in Tunisia*. Another brief contrast is the so-called 'Chuck Kopely' jam-session (13 minutes on disc one), which is the earliest instance of live work featuring only Parker's solos with the recording apparatus switched off during others' efforts. The studio sidemen, on the other hand, do far more than earn their keep, especially on the 40 tracks by the classic 1947 working group of Roach, Jordan, Potter and Davis (who probably wrote the unusual introduction to *Don't Blame Me*). The sound is somewhat variable, depending on the state of the source material, but is considerably improved over the 20-year-old Spotlite LPs. Parker's invention is so varied that there is no incentive to programme out multiple versions, although Spotlite have done that job for the listener recently by issuing a two-CD set of just the master takes. This handsome package, its combined notes by original and reissue producers substantially rewritten, does justice to the eternal flame of the music itself. **BP**

**Jazz at the Philharmonic, 1946** Parker (as); Dizzy Gillespie, Al Killian, Howard McGhee, Buck Clayton (t); Willie Smith (as); Charlie Ventura, Lester Young, Coleman Hawkins (ts); Mel Powell, Arnold Ross, Ken Kersey (p); Irving Ashby (g); Billy Hadnott (b); Lee Young, Buddy Rich (d). Verve Ⓜ 513 756-2 (73 minutes). Recorded 1946.

✅ ⑨ ❻

This CD, containing material never conceived as being under the leadership of the altoist, is anachronistic in that it offers a chance to hear extended solos by men such as Parker at a time when this was not normally possible. It also places Parker amongst the modernists of an earlier era and, in so doing, highlights the vast innovatory strides he had made away from them. The harmonic complexity of his playing is at odds with their swing-era orthodoxy, and this is brought into even sharper relief by his use of rhythmic accentuation that they find almost completely incompatible. The music comes from two concerts, but with the common factor that neither had a rhythm section ideally suited to Parker, Gillespie or McGhee. It is Parker, however, who most effectively shrugs off their retrograde pull. He is at his exacting best on *Lady Be Good*, and is calmly controlled on *After You've Gone* where, after a momentary false start, he takes a melody chorus that is a joy and then tops it with a stunning solo. The second concert finds him reaffirming his blues credentials on *JATP Blues* and swinging alongside the swingers on *I Got Rhythm*, which incidentally has a head-on cutting contest between the then-reigning tenor sax kings, Coleman Hawkins and Lester Young, plus some wonderful Buck Clayton trumpet. It must be said that Young plays gloriously at all tempos in this set, as do Hawkins and Clayton. In company such as this, Parker's roots show clearly. However, along with Gillespie and Monk, he was the way forward. **BMcR**

New review

**Confirmation: The Best of the Verve Years** Parker (as); Kenny Dorham, Roy Eldridge, Dizzy Gillespie, Red Rodney, Doug Mettome, Ray Wetzel, Charlie Shavers, Al Killian, Howard McGhee, Jimmy Maxwell, Al Porcino, Bernie Privin (t); Bill Harris, Lou McGarity, Bart Varsalona, Tommy Turk (tb); Hal McKusick, John LaPorta (cl); Benny Carter, Johnny Hodges, Willie Smith (as); Ben Webster, Flip Phillips, Lester Young, Coleman Hawkins (ts); Manny Albam, Danny Bank (bs); Oscar Peterson, Al Haig, Tony Aless, Thelonious Monk,Walter Bishop, Bernie Leighton, Arnold Ross, John Lewis, Stan Freeman, Hank Jones (p); Barney Kessel, Freddie Greene (g); Teddy Kotick, Charles Mingus, Ray Brown, Percy Heath, Curly Russell, Billy Hadnott, Tommy Potter (bs); Don Lamond, Lee Young, Kenny Clarke, Roy Haynes, Max Roach, Shelly Manne, Buddy Rich, J.C. Heard (d); Carlos Vidal, Luis Miranda (cga); José Manguel (bgo); Dave Lambert Singers, Ella Fitzgerald, Jerry Parker, Annie Ross (v ); Machito's Afro Cuban Orchestra. Verve Ⓜ 527 815-2 (two discs: 135 minutes). Recorded 1946-53.

⑨ ❽

It seems impertinent to reduce Parker's rating from ten to nine. This is only done to acknowledge the Savoy and Dial masterpieces. Fifty years on, Parker's music is now the meeting place where listeners from all extremes can agree. His diamond-like solos instantly trigger the switch and one still feels a sense of privilege and urgency as he imparts his message. This is a continuation of Verve's recycling of their ten-CD Parker set, with this fraction of it probably being the best. Where dilution of the master's work occurs it is done by illustrious co-soloists like Lester Young, Flip Phillips, Al Haig and Roy Eldridge. Additionally, although they are a mere diversion, there are interesting solos from Kenny Dorham and the long-lost trombonist Tommy Turk during a couple of jam session performances. The three tracks by the quintet with Gillespie and Monk display a good idea gone slightly awry: giants do not perhaps inspire each other automatically by their presence. There are awkward moments in the JATP performances which make them sound dated, but these are more than compensated for whenever Parker blows. Listening to each disc end-to-end is a most satisfying pleasure, allowing the listener to experience a vital part of the altoist's creative life. **SV**

**Bird: The Complete Charlie Parker on Verve** Parker (as, ldr); with a collective personnel of: Mario Bauzá, Buck Clayton, Paquito Davilla, Kenny Dorham, Harry Edison, Roy Eldridge, Dizzy Gillespie, Chris Griffin, Benny Harris, Al Killian, Howard McGhee, Jimmy Maxwell, Doug Mettome, Carl Poole, Al Porcino, Bernie Privin, Red Rodney, Charlie Shavers, Al Stewart, Ray Wetzel, Bobby Woodlen (t); Hal McKusick, John LaPorta (cl); Benny Carter, Johnny Hodges, Gene Johnson, Toots Mondello, Sonny Salad, Freddie Skerritt, Willie Smith, Harry Terrill, Murray Williams (as); Coleman Hawkins, Jose Madera, Pete Mondello, Flip Phillips, Hank Ross, Sol Rabinowitz, Ben Webster, Lester Young (ts); Manny Albam, Danny Bank, Leslie Johnakins, Stan Webb (bs); Artie Drelinger (reeds); Walter Bishop Jr, Al Haig, Rene Hernandez, Hank Jones, Ken Kersey, John Lewis, Thelonious Monk, Oscar Peterson, Mel Powell, Arnold Ross (p); Irving Ashby, Billy Bauer, Jerome Darr, Freddie Green, Barney Kessel (g); Ray Brown, Billy Hadnott, Percy Heath, Teddy Kotick, Charles Mingus, Tommy Potter, Roberto Rodriguez, Curly Russell (b); Max Roach,

Arthur Taylor, Lee Young (d); Machito, José Manguel, Luis Miranda, Umberto Nieto, Chano Pozo, Carlos Vidal (perc); Ella Fitzgerald, Dave Lambert Singers (v). Verve Ⓜ 837 141-2 (ten discs: 624 minutes). Recorded 1946-54.

**⑨ ⑧**

This extraordinary, ten-disc compilation of Charlie Parker's output for Verve provides a revealing longitudinal glimpse of the alto saxophonist. By including every available out-take and false-start, we get a sense of Bird's exceptional powers and also his very human fallibilities. For example, in a 1952 small-group setting for the Latin tune, *La Cucaracha*, we hear several fluffs and, interestingly, Parker's less fluid mesh with a surprisingly staid rhythmic section anchored by Max Roach. We also hear the controversial 1949 and 1950 string sessions which, while being the fulfilment of a Parker dream, sound rather clunky in spite of the saxophonist's spirited flights. More satisfying are big band tracks like *Night and Day*, where Bird soars above a solid rhythm section (Oscar Peterson, Freddie Green, Ray Brown and Don Lamond) and a no-nonsense arrangement by Joe Lipman.

Parker was one of the quintessential figures who redirected jazz from the arranger-determined large ensembles of the swing era to the virtuosic soloist-determined small bebop groups of the forties. It should not be surprising, then, that the set's musical core consists of the combo waxings with fellow bebop giants like Dizzy Gillespie, Red Rodney, Thelonious Monk, Walter Bishop Jr., Charles Mingus, Kenny Clarke and Max Roach. Also of value is the unearthing of Chico O'Farrill's *Afro-Cuban Jazz Suite* and some of the uninhibited jam sessions organized by Verve impresario Norman Granz. A meticulously prepared booklet by producer Phil Schaap, with complete discographic information, a collection of poignant photos and a warm appreciation by Dizzy Gillespie helps contextualize Bird's singular contribution. In sum, a must for Parker completists and those committed to understanding the evolution of modern jazz. **CB**

---

**The Quintet: Jazz at Massey Hall** Parker (as); Dizzy Gillespie (t); Bud Powell (p); Charles Mingus (b); Max Roach (d). Debut Ⓜ OJCCD044-2 (47 minutes). Recorded 1953.

✓ **⑧ ❺**

The story behind this album, recorded live at the famous concert in Toronto's Massey Hall, has become a mixture of myth and legend – how the five men dragged themselves through ice and snow to get to Toronto, how Mingus just happened to record the concert on his tape recorder, how the sparse audience realized they were present at a historic occasion, namely the conjunction of the five greatest individuals in bop ... No hint of all this on the CD notes, as there are no notes, just ads for other records. Even in the personnel, Charlie Parker is listed as 'Charlie Chan' on alto. Surely it is safe for Parker to come out from behind his pseudonym, now that he has been dead 40 years or so? Actually, the audience doesn't sound sparse but quite big and warm, and the recording is not at all bad for an *ad hoc* live recording, though the prominence of the bass does encourage you to believe those stories about Mingus overdubbing all his bass lines the following day.

The music is pretty damn good, without being quite breathtaking or superb. This is what a top-class bop group sounded like in the mid fifties; energetic, edgy, swirling, allusive, slightly neurotic and technically beyond anything that had gone before. There are six tunes, of which four are bop standards and two are standards-by-proxy (Kern's *All the Things You Are* and the Ellingtonian *Perdido*), and the concert conditions prompt the participants to try harder than they might in the studio. If it never quite takes off into the empyrean, maybe it's because all five were thinking unconsciously of the heavyweight boxing match they'd just watched on the television in the bar across the street. **MK**

# Eddie Parker

---

**New review**

**Everything You Do to Me** Parker (f, bf, kbds, p); Pete Saberton (p, kbds); Julian Nicholas (ts, ss, bcl); John Parricelli (g, elg); Steve Watts (b); Mike Pickering (d, perc). FMR Ⓕ CD29 (64 minutes). Recorded 1996.

**⑦ ⑨**

It's not surprising to find Eddie Parker, formerly of the adventurous British big band Loose Tubes, exploring whimsical material that straddles the folk, jazz and classical worlds. This mostly acoustic ensemble (Parricelli's guitar is the only amplified instrument) is driven by acoustic bass and drums and, when it has a regular pulse (about 70 per cent of the time), emphasizes odd-metered Latin and funk. However, the predominantly tense, oblique harmony and the flute lead give the music a classical resonance which is enhanced by things like the long piano and flute interlude in *Broken Spectre*, the sinister, darting atonality of *Auster*, the stark chromatic counterpoints of the accurately titled *Delirium* and the Debussyish introduction to *Variable Geometry*. The mood brightens and eases periodically, as in the mildly ironic *Wonky Chorinho/Twerp*, but this is not generally an easy ride. There's undoubtedly some skilled writing here, and, amidst Parker's composerly labours, space for effective solos from Saberton, Parricelli, Nicholas and the leader himself, but it's not clear that there's enough to hold the attention of the jazz listener for a whole hour. **MG**

# Errol Parker 1930

**A Night in Tunisia** Parker (d); **Philip Harper** (t); **Michael Thomas** (t); **Tyrone Jefferson** (tb); **Doug Harris** (ss); **Donald Harrison** (as); **Bill Saxton** (ts); **Patience Higgins** (bs); **Cary De Nigris** (g); **Reggie Washington** (elb). Sahara Ⓕ 1015 (56 minutes). Recorded 1991.

⑦ ❹

Born Ralph Schecroun in North Africa, Parker recorded with Kenny Clarke under his real name in 1948. For that session he played piano, although he later recorded on organ in the Jimmy Smith manner. In the early sixties he adopted his new name and in 1971 formed Sahara, his own record company. As the decade progressed, he became involved with his own unique brand of jazz and with many of New York's young 'tigers'. To help out with the Parker Experience's studio booking expenses, he at times multi-tracked on both piano and drums, but by the time he formed his Tentet in 1982, he had begun to concentrate mainly on the latter. This CD, with its strange recording balance, putting the drums up front, documents the jazz of the group very well. It shows the full scale of the ensemble arrangements and especially how Parker projects individuals as well as two voice conversations in solo form. These exciting dialogues enrich most titles and dovetail well with Parker's foreground drum parts and Washington's fender, the two instruments which bear the brunt of rhythmic responsibility in the keyboardless unit. The group's stylistic aspirations are best summarized in the contrast of formality and deliberate mayhem in *Ol' Man River*. **BMcR**

# Evan Parker 1944

New review

**Imaginary Values** Parker (ss, ts); **Barry Guy** (b); **Paul Lytton** (d, perc). Maya Ⓕ MCD9401 (63 minutes). Recorded 1993.

⑩ ❾

Undoubtedly one of the most exciting groups in all of contemporary music, this trio translates individual virtuosity into dazzlingly complex labyrinths of sound. Based upon an exquisite sense of ensemble empathy, their improvisations typically begin from three distinct points in space and dovetail in towards each other until they coalesce in a contrapuntal weaving of independent lines at feverish speeds. Making use of atonality and microtonality, irregular rhythms or polyrhythms, along with acute group dynamics, they offer a music of intense concentration and startling imagination. On tenor Parker seems closer to a 'jazz' sensibility – terse, diamond-hard phrases cut with a jeweller's precision, while his soprano playing is usually combined with circular breathing to create a self-contained counterpoint of interwoven lines and motifs (and hear what sensitive things Guy can add to such a seemingly impenetrable texture in *Distinction*). Guy provides parallel lines of activity, and the way his and Parker's *staccato* phrases stab and jab each other, gradually elongating pointillist flurries into melodic waves, is simply breathtaking. Paul Lytton is an especially sensitive percussionist, whose varied points of emphasis do not punctuate or calibrate time but redirect our perception of its flow. His unusual kit allows him to sound like slivered glass or distant thunder. **AL**

New review

**50th Birthday Concert** Parker (ss, ts); **Alex Von Schlippenbach** (p); **Paul Lovens** (d, perc); **Barry Guy** (b); **Paul Lytton** (d, perc). Leo Ⓕ CDLR212/3 (two discs: 80 minutes). Recorded 1994.

⑧ ❽

Although one of the finest of all solo saxophonists, Parker's masterful soliloquys deny him the opportunity for group interaction; an area of music in which he excels. His circular breathing solo technique gives him a sound constant, his mastery of multiphonics a wonderful gradation of tone and his 'false' fingering an open door to total control. It is his ear, however, that promotes his success with other musicians. Parker is a listener, sympathetic to fellow band members and receptive to their musical stimulations at all times. This two-CD set offers the opportunity to examine two aspects of this process, one with a well established trio of kindred spirits, the other with a unit displaying less consanguine aspirations. The second disc presents his established trio with Guy and Lytton. The players' familiarity causes no complacency and, in fact, *In Exultation* is a model of freely improvised contrapuntal music. There is no confrontational element on the first disc but it does demonstrate a change in emphasis as well as in instrumentation. Von Schlippenbach seems to be the trio member most in contact with the spirit of American jazz and with Cecil Taylor, in particular. Parker is neither boosted nor restricted by the fact; rather, he allows the music to explore a more epigrammatical route. Parker has on many occasions worked with medium-sized and larger orchestras, but these albeit dissimilar line-ups suggest that the trio is the ideal environment for him. **BMcR**

# John W. 'Knocky' Parker 1918-88

New review

**The Complete Piano Works of Jelly Roll Morton** Parker (p, h, cel); **George Pryor**, **Dick Brightwell** (b); **Marvin Montgomery** (bj); **Ruth Brightwell**, **Harvey Kindervater** (d). Solo Art Ⓜ SACD61/2 (two discs: 147 minutes). Recorded 1960-70.

⑦ ❺

Beware the plagiarist who essays the piano styles of Jelly Roll Morton, Count Basie and Thelonious Monk. All are comparatively easy to copy (badly) but the subtleties of their timing elude all but a very few. Dr Parker from the University of South Florida was, with Don Ewell and Keith Nichols, among the few to successfully confront the Morton code. This CD attests to the fact, although it is wrong in claiming to present the complete piano works of the New Orleans master. Nevertheless, using harpsichord, celeste and piano, Parker gets inside the music and escorts the listener on Morton's journey from ragtime composer to improvising modifier of the idiom. Parker offers readings of *The Pearls*, *Kansas City Stomps* and *King Porter Stomp* to show how Morton, the musical architect, produced piano pieces with orchestral realization in mind. He is not phased by Morton's Spanish tinge on *Mama 'Nita* and *The Crave*; neither is he daunted by test pieces such as *Shreveport Stomp*, *Freakish* and *Finger Breaker*. There are moments when tape splices take him rather uncomfortably from one instrument to another, and the rhythmic support could be considered unnecessary in places. What really matters is that Parker has avoided slavish copying, has captured the mood of the era and has gone some way to solving that indefinable mystery – Morton's timing. **BMcR**

# Leon Parker 1965

**Above and Below** Parker (d, perc, v); **Lisa Parker** (f); **David Sanchez, Mark Turner, Joshua Redman** (ts); **Jacky Terrasson** (p); **Ugonna Okegwo** (b); **Adam Cruz, Natalie Cushman** (perc); **Jay McGovern** (v). Epicure Ⓔ 478198-2 (47 minutes). Recorded 1994.

⑧ ❽

Despite earnest talk among the post-Marsalis generation about extending tradition, only the merest handful have travelled beyond reiteration of fifties and sixties hard bop. The enormously talented Leon Parker is one of that rare breed, and his intriguing perspective on acoustic jazz is amply evidenced in this striking début (a début, moreover, which has proved to be better than its follow-up release, **Belief**, where Parker prefers finely wrought, exotic percussion ensembles to jazz standards).

Parker's vibrant, virtuosic drumming is a joy in itself, but more importantly he is a drummer who genuinely leads from the drums at every level of the music. He does this not merely by being loud, but by realizing that rhythm is the most essential and only sufficient element of music: this allows him to compose and rearrange from the ground up. The five standards here are thus radically transformed, *Bemsha Swing* couched as a fusion of powerful hip-hop and breakneck swing, *You Don't Know What Love Is* reinvented by the application of a simple double-time Latin bass and drum ostinato and *Epistrophy* enlivened by constantly deceptive rhythmic sleights-of-hand as Parker shifts from rock to latin to swing. There are further delights in the originals, among them the title track, a solo recital for percussion, cymbal and voice which perfectly captures the intensity, conviction and invention of Parker's music. **MG**

# Maceo Parker

**Life on Planet Groove** Parker (as, v); **Fred Wesley** (tb); **Pee Wee Ellis** (ts); **Larry Goldings** (org); **Rodney Jones** (g); **Kenwood Dennard** (d); **Kym Mazelle** (v); **Candy Dulfer** (as); **Vinvent Henry** (as, b). Minor Music Ⓔ 801023 (76 minutes). Recorded 1992.

⑥ ❽

Parker and some of his sidemen were important members of James Brown's backing group, the JBs, and many of the routines found on this live album can be directly traced back to the James Brown stage show. Consequently, there may be a few eyebrows raised about this being included here. While it is true that the rhythms are associated with funk and soul, the album is predominantly instrumental, and the solos, while basic and relying on well-used blues paths through life, are fiery, exciting and rely on improvisation just as much as any trad jazz revivalist solo does.

Hair-splitting aside, this album packs a tremendous punch and portrays a very tight and super-efficient band delivering a killer-diller set to its fans. The section-work, while hardly intricate, is well-judged and completely compatible with the music. Each horn player has a distinct voice and the rhythm section hits an intoxicating groove. If Lionel Hampton had his time over again, starting now, this is what he would be doing. **KS**

# William Parker 1952

New review
**In Order to Survive** Parker (b); **Lewis Barnes** (t); **Grachan Moncur III** (tb); **Rob Brown** (as); **Cooper-Moore** (p); **Denis Charles** (d); **Jackson Krall** (perc). Black Saint Ⓔ 120159-2 (72 minutes). Recorded 1993.

⑧ ❼

Parker's interest in jazz was sparked by hearing his father's Ellington records. Later he discovered the energy-based musics of Albert Ayler, John Coltrane and Cecil Taylor, and this has remained a major influence. He played in a Taylor big band in 1973 and in 1980 joined the pianist on a regular basis, a relationship that continues to date. **In Order to Survive** was recorded live at New York's Knitting Factory. The long, clamorous *Testimony of No Future* suggests Taylor's influence, though the variegated textures and demarcated solos also diverge from the sustained intensity of the pianist's ensembles. *Testimony of the Stir Pot* is both claustrophobic and exciting, surly horns jabbed against palpitating piano riffs, while *Anast in Crisis Mouth Full of Fresh Cut Flowers* is a fraught ballad carried by Brown's imploring alto. *The Square Sun*, sound-painting in muted tones, features a superb bowed solo from Parker, whose dark pulse is both a foundation and a fount of energy throughout this gripping set.                                                                 **GL**

# Horace Parlan

**Little Esther** Parlan (p); **Per Goldschmidt** (bs); **Klavs Hovman** (b); **Massimo De Majo** (d). Soul
  Note Ⓟ 21145-2 (54 minutes). Recorded 1987.

⑥ ❽

A Pittsburgh native, Parlan has worked in the Charles Mingus Workshop, with 'Lockjaw' Davis/Johnny Griffin, Roland Kirk and Michal Urbaniak in a career of considerable variety. He is a second-generation bebop pianist and, as befits a man who includes Ahmad Jamal and Bud Powell amongst his prime influences, is a strongly chordal player. His is not a spare style, however, and, as *Snow Girl* shows, he does not waste time on empty rhetoric. His direction-pointing harmonies are supported by a good story-telling right hand and, as *Something for Silver* demonstrates, he has no reticence in the swing department.

Living away from the US in Denmark could have blunted his cutting edge, but here he is capably assisted by Hovman and De Majo, a Dane and an Italian conversant with the international jazz language. The sole horn is Goldschmidt, another Dane and a man whose relaxed solos show the influence of Gerry Mulligan and Serge Chaloff in about equal parts. Like his own solo playing, Parlan's accompaniment of a saxophonist is equally expert.                                **BMcR**

# Joe Pass                                                                            1929

**Portraits of Duke Ellington** Pass (elg); **Ray Brown** (b); **Bobby Durham** (d).
  Pablo Ⓜ PACD2310-716-2 (49 minutes). Recorded 1974.

⑦ ❽

Although he came to attention in the sixties and, thanks to Norman Granz, became virtually a household name in the seventies, Joe Pass was essentially a player of an earlier era, oblivious to the harmonic expansions going on around him. As this record shows, with the exception of a brief moment at 2' 14" into *Don't Get Around Much Anymore* when he seems to forget the background and follows a thematic muse which takes him briefly out of key, he makes a fetish of playing carefully on the chords and their upper extensions; even the occasional blues lick is castrated before delivery. When allied, as it often was in the seventies, to a weakness for whole records of chord-soloing, this inclination tended to create the impression of a person more interested in mechanics than musical expression. Given those reservations, this record offers a reasonable compromise (and a comprehensive view of Pass's seventies style) by mixing three *a cappella* pieces with six trio numbers. There are still times when digital verbosity clouds musicality, but on *In a Mellow Tone* Joe puts the gas up high and produces a compelling exposition of post-bop guitar, fours with Brown adding extra interest. However, none of it approaches the vibrancy of Pass's currently unavailable early sixties recordings for Pacific.                                          **MG**

**One for My Baby** Pass (g); **Plas Johnson** (ts); **Gerald Wiggins** (p, org); **Andy Simpkins** (b); **Tootie Heath** (d). Pablo Ⓜ 2310-936-2 (50 minutes). Recorded 1988.

⑧ ❾

Joe Pass was one of jazzdom's transcendent guitarists. Possessed with quick-silver virtuosity, Pass was a master of chording and finger-picking, techniques allowing him to evolve highly developed accompanying and solo skills. With his command of the classic American popular song and his ease with both bebop and swing, Pass, after a youthful bout with drugs, established his reputation in the sixties and early seventies with Les McCann, Gerald Wilson and Benny Goodman. Catching the ear of producer Norman Granz, Pass joined Granz's all-star Pablo roster and worked extensively with such label-mates as Oscar Peterson, Ella Fitzgerald and Dizzy Gillespie. His solo albums, starting with his celebrated **Pablodébut** (Virtuoso, 1973), cemented his reputation. Here, we catch the guitarist with tenor-man Plas 'Pink Panther' Johnson, pianist Gerald Wiggins, bassist Andy Simpkins and drummer Tootie Heath, a congenial and empathetic crew. Pass, who like Art Tatum was sometimes accused of technical excess, flows here like honey. Yes, there are moments of bravado. Still, the dominant mood is one of leisurely post-dinner conversation. Among the treats are a poignant *Ghost of a Chance* and palmy *Poinciana*. Even the romp through *The Song Is You* unfolds like a stroll in the park.      **CB**

# Jaco Pastorius

**Jaco Pastorius** Pastorius (elb); **Randy Brecker, Ron Tooley** (t); **Peter Graves** (btb); **Peter Gordon** (frh); **Hubert Laws** (pic); **Wayne Shorter** (ss); **David Sanborn** (as); **Michael Brecker** (ts); **Howard Johnson** (bs); **Herbie Hancock, Alex Darqui** (kbds); **Richard Davis, Homer Mensch** (b); **Narada Michael Walden, Lenny White, Bobby Economou** (d); **Don Alias** (perc); **Othello Molineux** (alto steel d); **Leroy Williams** (tenor steel d); **Sam and Dave** (v); **David Nadien, Harry Lokofsky, Paul Gershman, Joe Malin, Harry Cykman, Harold Kohon, Matthew Raimondi, Max Pollikoff, Arnold Black** (vn); **Selwart Clarke, Manny Vardi, Julian Barber, Al Brown** (va); **Charles McCracken, Kermit Moore, Beverly Lauridsen, Alan Shulman** (vc). Epic Ⓜ CDEPC81453 (43 minutes). Recorded 1975.

✔                                                                          ⑧ ⑧

Pastorius's introduction of himself to Joe Zawinul as the world's greatest bass player was not perhaps the most modest of opening gambits. However, Pastorius was no stranger either to bravado or egotism, and this extraordinary début showed that on a musical level none of it was insupportable. It declared a revolution in bass playing – apparent here in the exquisite use of harmonics on *Portrait Of Tracy*, the singing, lyrical flights, expressive slurring and gorgeous double and triple stops of *Continuum*, the urgent, funky drive of *Kuru*, and the casual bebop virtuosity of *Donna Lee* – but it also showed that these previously unimagined technical innovations were born of a broad orchestral conception and an innocent eclecticism which could fearlessly juxtapose Charlie Parker with soul singers Sam and Dave. Jaco's orchestral awareness is evident in an obvious way in his string and horn arrangements for *Come On, Come Over* and *Speak Like a Child*, but it is there too on a more extemporary level, in the way the placement of a single harmonic during the steel pan solo on *Opus Pocus* completely shifts the mood of the piece. It seems strange to mention Herbie Hancock's fine work on *Kuru* as an incidental delight, but this was Pastorius's day, and his brilliance here would eclipse greater men.                                                              **MG**

# John Patitucci

**Another World** Patitucci (b, elb); **Jeff Beal** (t); **Steve Tavaglione** (ss, ts, EWI); **Michael Brecker** (ts); **John Beasley** (p, syn); **Andy Narell** (steel pans); **Armand Sabal-Lecco** (elb, v); **Will Kennedy, Dave Weckl** (d); **Alex Acuna, Luis Conte, Will Kennedy** (perc); various backing vocals. GRP Ⓔ 97252 (52 minutes). Recorded 1993.

⑧ ⑧

As titles like *Ivory Coast* and *The Griot* and the presence of African bassist Armand Sabal-Lecco announce, this is Patitucci's African record. Several pieces, most effectively perhaps the darkly grooving title track, have a pronounced African flavour, but Patitucci's long-standing admiration for Weather Report is also frequently in evidence, as is shown by *Ivory Coast Part II* and *I Saw You*, where Tavaglione phrases Shorter-like along with the bass, and by the steel pan quotient of *Soho Steel*. GRP is not a label noted for its substance, but among its fusion signatories John Patitucci is one of the most satisfying. His writing is derivative but effective, and he always leaves plenty of space for good jazz soloists, including himself. Like his writing, his post-Coltrane solo vocabulary is commonplace, but no other electric bassist has a better command of it, and this fluency is allied to an immediately recognizable sound and a strong melodic sensibility. Any collector professing an interest in current bass players ought to have at least one Patitucci album, and this is as good as any.   **MG**

# Big John Patton

**Let 'Em Roll** Patton (org); **Grant Green** (g); **Bobby Hutcherson** (vb); **Otis Finch** (d). Blue Note Ⓜ CDP7 89795-2 (40 minutes). Recorded 1965.

⑧ ⑧

Patton made a substantial impact on the chitlins circuit in the US during the sixties, when so many organists clung to the coat-tails of Jimmy Smith, as he crossed over with a vengeance. Big John made his impact – and remains a pleasant memory for many listeners – because of his unfailing taste as a player and as a leader. He eschewed the more blatant bump and grind routines of many at that time, and continued to both write and improvise on attractive themes (an example here is *Latona*, which he was later to record more than once). Though his pedal patterns were not of the most varied type, his fresh approach to chording and his finely-attuned ear for the most attractive part of the Hammond B3 range of sounds kept the listener fully involved. By the end of the sixties he was also experimenting with stylistic syntheses undreamed of by any other organist except Larry Young, as the recently reissued **Understanding** (Blue Note) shows.

He is greatly helped here by a typically first-rate set of Blue Note sidemen, and for once the absence of a horn player may well be seen by many as a positive gain: certainly the sterling improvising and accompaniment of Green and Hutcherson keep this set continually on the boil, whether it is on the nicely paced blues inflections of *Shadow of Your Smile* or the more funked-up groove of Hank Mobley's *The Turnaround*. Green occasionally gets stuck on his own personal clichés during his solos, but his attack and bite are beyond reproach. Hutcherson, a player of great imaginative resources in every musical situation, is oustanding here.  **KS**

# Les Paul
1915

**Les Paul Trio**  Paul (g); Milt Raskin (p); Cal Goodin (g); Clint Norquist, Bobby Morrow (b); unidentified (v) on one track. Laserlight ⓑ 15 741 (43 minutes). Recorded c1947.

⑧ ❺

The personnel is courtesy of Paul; the disc does not list any, and the recording date might be off by a few years. Once described by *The New Yorker* as "the Thomas Edison of reverb", Paul owes his reputation as a progenitor of rock 'n' roll to his invention of the solid-body electric guitar and to his and Mary Ford's hit records of the early fifties, which more or less introduced the concept of overdubbing (these are available, along with plenty of period curiosities, on **The Legend and the Legacy**, a prohibitively priced Capitol four-disc boxed set). Short of making a pilgrimage to the Greenwich Village club where Paul's trio has held forth every Monday night since 1984, the way to discover his uncelebrated prowess as a jazz guitarist is to hear his subtle chase sequence with Nat King Cole on the inaugural **Jazz at the Philharmonic** blowout from 1944, or to pick up this budget-priced disc of dubious legality before it is driven off the market. In one sense, Paul is not really an improviser – his solos give evidence of being set pieces, although they're no less beguiling as a result of this. Although the group's sense of itself as an extroverted chamber group seems modelled on the Nat King Cole Trio, Paul's playful tremolo and steam-roller propulsion also reveal the influence of Django Reinhardt.  **FD**

# Cecil Payne
1922

**Patterns of Jazz**  Payne (bs); Duke Jordan (p); Tommy Potter (b); Art Taylor (d); Kenny Dorham (t). Denon/Savoy Ⓜ SV-0135 (44 minutes). Recorded 1956.

⑧ ❻

Payne started out on alto (he had lessons from Pete Brown) and this may account for his fluency on baritone, which he started to play in 1947. He was one of the very first bebop soloists on the larger horn and was featured with the Dizzy Gillespie band to good effect. The opening four titles here form an excellent introduction to his qualities as a major jazz soloist, opening with a jaunty *This Time the Dream's on Me* and including a warm-toned version of *How Deep Is the Ocean*; on ballads he shows off his vibrato control and manifests the breathy tone of Ben Webster on the upper reaches of the baritone. Adding Kenny Dorham on half of the titles does not increase the impact of the music greatly, for Payne is clearly in more confident mood than the trumpeter. The rhythm section is exactly in keeping with Cecil's playing (Jordan and Payne worked together on many occasions, going right back to their days with Roy Eldridge's big band) and the release is recommended as a good example of a fine baritone player who has often been in danger of being overlooked.  **AM**

# Nicholas Payton

New review
**Gumbo Nouveau**  Payton (t); Jesse Davis (as); Tim Warfield (ts); Anthony Wonsey (p); Reuben Rogers (b); Adonis Rose (d). Verve Ⓕ 531 199-2 (57 minutes). Recorded 1995.

⑦ ❿

Payton, who made his début while still a teenager with the 1994-recorded Verve album **From This Moment** (warmly welcomed by DG in the previous Guide), has continued to deepen his musicality and has come up with an album combining New Orleans and New York in an easy-feel and brilliant set of modern-mainstream performances of old-timey standards. This is Payton's updated **Satch Plays W.C. Handy**. His band here are mostly of his own generation, and there are no slackers: each man works hard for the overall group. Apart from the leader, whose gorgeous Clifford Brown-inspired tone and winning melodicism give the listener a warm feeling inside, the standout musician on the date is Anthony Wonsey. The pianist accompanies crisply (listen to his thoughtful work on *When the Saints Go Marching In*) and also has hundreds of his own ideas to express when it comes time for his solo. Payton sometimes comes close to the type of playing one has come to expect of Ruby Braff in his later years, so rooted in tradition is it. The saxophonists play well and don't send out too many ripples, while the rhythm team of Rogers and Rose do all the good things. If you're not expecting someone to point to the future and make it work, you're going to enjoy this album.  **KS**

# Paz

New review
**The Best of Paz**  Dick Crouch (perc, ldr); Brian Smith (ss, f); Ray Warleigh (as, f, af, pic); Geoff Castle (kbds); Phil Lee, Ed Speight (g); Ron Mathewson (b); Dave Sheen, Frank Gibson (d);

Simon Morton, Chris Fletcher, Martin Drew (perc). Spotlite ⓕ SPJCD554 (66 minutes). Recorded 1976-80.

⑧ ❽

British jazz-rock of the seventies was in a class of its own and, along with Nucleus and Soft Machine, Paz led the way. All three bands shared personnel, Smith and Castle working with Nucleus and Warleigh with Soft Machine, but while Nucleus largely remained true to leader Ian Carr's Milesian conception of jazz-rock and Soft Machine grew out of Robert Wyatt's conception of art-rock, Paz had more affiliations with the music of Latin America. Sometimes the percussion threatens to engulf events, but overall the feel across the three versions of Paz presented here is of a compulsively rhythmic music never better than when Sheen, Morton and Crouch are all hammering away together, as on *Yours Is the Light* from their first Spotlite album. Not having heard this music for almost two decades, I'd forgotten how flute-dominated many of the pieces were, again giving Paz a flavour distinct from its contemporaries. Warleigh's passionate alto is also a vital ingredient of the later line-up on pieces like *Laying Eggs*, which also has Speight's effects-pedal working overtime in creating a funk background. There's more-or-less straightforward jazz on offer too, with Rollins's *Everywhere Calypso*, and Crouch's waltz *I Can't Remember*. This is music well worth Tony Williams's efforts to anthologize and reissue, recalling the heyday of British jazz-rock. **AS**

## Annette Peacock

**I Have No Feelings** Peacock (v, p, syn); **Roger Turner** (perc). Ironic Records ⓕ IRONIC4CD (34 minutes). Recorded 1986.

⑧ ❾

Singer, composer and pioneer of synthesizer music, Annette Peacock has marked out a personal musical territory that draws on elements of jazz and pop while owing few obvious allegiances to either. She first attracted attention in the mid sixties, writing initially for bassist Gary Peacock, then for pianist Paul Bley. Both men, but especially Bley, have continued to re-interpret on record the compositions she gave them at that time. She toured with Bley, becoming one of the first to play synthesizer in concert and to develop a method to process her vocals electronically, as exemplified on her early albums as leader, **Revenge** and **I'm the One**. Settling in England in the mid seventies, she explored an idiosyncratic jazz-rock fusion on **X-Dreams**, then turned to a more abstract, improvised music for later releases on her own label, Ironic.

    **I Have No Feelings** is a particularly elegant set, its collation of fragmentary melodies carried by Peacock's finely honed vocals, minimal keyboards and the discreet, free percussion of Roger Turner. Her epigrammatic lyrics traverse romantic whimsy, political protest and, on *Not Enough* and *Nothing Ever Was, Anyway*, the wry philosophical detachment that has become her signature. Her singing can be both intimate and ethereal, while her music here comprises mostly fragile, dreamy tunes that seem to float by on a breeze, a perfect expression of her focus on the transitory. **GL**

## Gary Peacock

1935

**Tales of Another** Peacock (b); **Keith Jarrett** (p); **Jack DeJohnette** (d). ECM ⓕ 827 418-2 (49 minutes). Recorded 1977.

⑧ ❿

Peacock's endless list of credits includes vital work done with Paul Bley, Albert Ayler, Miles Davis and the Bill Evans Trio. The group heard on this CD represents another high point in his illustrious career, being together on and off for nearly ten years. All of the tunes are by Peacock and they are well suited to the musicians involved. Jarrett's notorious scene-stealing never surfaces: as well as he plays, it is never at the expense of his colleagues. Peacock's bass really sings on *Vignette*, his solo a model of adventurous, personal projection and group awareness. He is especially powerful on *Trilogy II* and the superb sonority of his full tone is never better displayed than on the aptly titled *Tone Field*. He lays down throughout the blueprint of the Peacock method; every solo stays logically on its directional rails, there is never an angular phrase and everything he plays has a buoyancy that could sustain a group of any size. With a trio such as this, there is obviously adequate solo exposure and Peacock puts it to full use. **BMcR**

## Duke Pearson

1932-80

**Sweet Honey Bee** Pearson (p, arr); **Freddie Hubbard** (t); **James Spaulding** (f, as); **Joe Henderson** (ts); **Ron Carter** (b); **Mickey Roker** (d). Blue Note Ⓜ CDP7 89792-2. (40 minutes). Recorded 1966.

⑥ ❻

Pearson was an unusually sensitive small-group arranger and pianist, and his talents also occasionally embraced big-band sessions for Blue Note. It is no surprise that this organized and disciplined man had, by the time of this date, begun helping producer Alfred Lion to prepare Blue Note recording sessions, and would eventually become for a time Blue Note's main producer.

Although Nat Hentoff's booklet-notes claim this as Pearson's best date for Blue Note, this is unfortunately not the case: his earlier record, **Wahoo**, is a much more cohesive and resourceful session, with consistently inspired solo work from the sidemen (who, incidentally, included both Spaulding and Henderson). **Wahoo** was reissued a number of years ago on CD, but is now once again unavailable. Yet there are some outstanding pieces here, and probably the one to treasure most is the exquisite 6/8 time ballad *After the Rain* (a Pearson original, and not the Coltrane ballad of the same name). Apart from that, and the intriguing voicing and harmonic movement of what sound on first acquaintance like very straightforward compositions (*Gaslight*, for example), probably the most noteworthy music comes from Hubbard, who at this time was playing with great warmth and imagination.

The recorded sound is not Van Gelder's best (there is rather a lot of reverb on the piano sound, in particular), but it is crisp and clean, so it is in the Blue Note tradition. Pearson was too good a musician to be completely overlooked as he is today. This album has sufficient of what made him special to be worth buying. **KS**

# Ken Peplowski 1958

New review
**It's a Lonesome Old Town** Peplowski (cl, ts); **Tom Harrell** (t); **Charlie Byrd** (g); **Howard Alden** (elg); **Allen Farnham**, **Marian McPartland** (p); **Greg Cohen** (b); **Alan Dawson** (d). Concord Ⓕ CCD4673 (59 minutes). Recorded 1995.

⑧ ❾

This is the eleventh CD released by Concord under Peplowski's name and each of them has had something new to offer. In this case it is a collaboration on three of the pieces with Tom Harrell, one of the most delicate and subtle of all contemporary trumpeters. His tone combines beautifully with the glossy sound of Peplowski's clarinet and strikes a piquant contrast with his full-blown tenor saxophone. As if this were not enough, Marian McPartland plays on three other numbers, including one of the most exquisite versions of *It Never Entered My Mind* that I have ever heard. Peplowski's two favourite guitarists, Howard Alden and Charlie Byrd, finally get to play together – Byrd contributing to a melting *These Foolish Things* – and the basic rhythm section of Farnham, Cohen and Dawson does them all proud. This is Peplowski's best CD so far. **DG**

# Art Pepper 1925-82

**Art Pepper Meets the Rhythm Section** Pepper (as); **Red Garland** (p); **Paul Chambers** (b); **Philly Joe Jones** (d). Contemporary Ⓜ OJCCD5338 (50 minutes). Recorded 1957.

✔ ⑩ ❽

Alto saxophonist Art Pepper, as revealed in his autobiography *Straight Life* (written with wife Laurie Pepper, 1979), more than paid his dues. Indeed, on the morning of this landmark 1957 session, Pepper was not even aware that the date had been scheduled. But like an archetypal fifties jazzer sent to the gig by Hollywood's Central Casting, Pepper – in spite of not having played for several weeks and going through tough times because of narcotics – played like an angel.

So, too, did the stellar rhythm section of pianist Red Garland, bassist Paul Chambers and drummer Philly Joe Jones. And though recorded in Los Angeles, none of the mannerisms of the so-called West Coast school is present. Indeed, there's a focused intensity that is never forced, especially at the medium and slower tempos of *You'd Be So Nice to Come Home to*, *Imagination*, *Star Eyes* and the Pepper-Chambers line called *Waltz Me Blues*. However, when flags start waving, as they do on *Straight Life* (based on the changes of *After You've Gone*), Pepper and friends soar; again, despite the brisk pace, all things flow, albeit with virtuosic élan.

The match of Pepper with the then-current Miles Davis rhythm section of Garland-Chambers-Jones was a stroke of genius. Everything clicks, from the breezy take on Gillespie's *Tin Tin Deo* to the hauntingly poignant *The Man I Love*. There is even a boppishly hip reframing of Tom Delaney's Dixieland classic, *Jazz Me Blues*. Throughout, it is Pepper, one of jazzdom's pre-eminent lyricists, who sails with melodic, indeed, poetic abandon. **CB**

**Art Pepper + Eleven: Modern Jazz Classics** Pepper (as, ts, cl); **Pete Candoli**, **Al Porcino**, **Jack Sheldon** (t); **Dick Nash** (tb); **Bob Enevoldsen** (vtb, ts); **Vince de Rosa** (frh); **Herb Geller**, **Charlie Kennedy**, **Bud Shank** (as); **Richie Kamuca**, **Bill Perkins** (ts); **Med Flory** (bs); **Russ Freeman** (p); **Joe Mondragon** (b); **Mel Lewis** (d); **Marty Paich** (arr). Contemporary Ⓜ OJCCD341-2 (55 minutes). Recorded 1959.

✔ ⑩ ❽

This album pointedly begins with a cover of Miles Davis's great **Birth of the Cool** vehicle, *Move*, by Denzil Best. The Miles nonet's sound and aesthetic heavily influenced Los Angeles jazz in the fifties; arranger Paich was a leading exponent of Cool's harmonic and timbral schemes, and had already provided splendid settings for singers Ella Fitzgerald and Mel Tormé.

Pepper, an altoist with a singing, stinging attack, responds beautifully to Paich's sleek expansions of jazz tunes by Monk, Gillespie, Parker, Rollins and others; charts designed to frame Art's solos (Paich's harmonized reed choruses on Dizzy's *Groovin' High* look back to Benny Carter and ahead to sideman Flory's Supersax group of the seventies). California's Pepper was no typical West Coaster; even then his flame burned hot, like Charlie Parker's. He shows an aggressive approach to rhythm, soaring over and slicing through the arrangements, many of which betray an admiration for Basie's band (Paich had written for Basie, too).

Pepper also leads the sax section on either alto or tenor, to which he brings the same burning conception, and displays his skills as an overlooked if cooler clarinettist on Bird's *Anthropology*. On this classic Coastal date Pepper did nothing wrong, and many things right. **KW**

**New review**

### The Complete Village Vanguard Sessions Pepper (as); George Cables (p); George Mraz (b); Elvin Jones (d). Contemporary Ⓕ 9CCD4417-2 (nine discs: 546 minutes). Recorded 1977.

⑦ ❼

One of the most frequently cited sets of LPs when people talked of the Art Pepper renaissance after his return to playing in the seventies were the three albums, **Thursday**, **Friday** and **Saturday Night at the Village Vanguard**. Later on a fourth, **More For Les**, was added. The remarkably high level of inspiration evident throughout these performances suggested that Pepper had been pulling out all the stops at this particular engagement, and now that this boxed set makes available all the surviving music for the first time, this impression is confirmed. This was Pepper's début as a leader in the Big Apple and his first-ever live recording, and he was determined to make it memorable. The booklet-notes, written by his wife Laurie, tell a story of madness, panic and turmoil behind the scenes as Pepper psyched himself into a condition where he could perform at his best and found people who could match him at that level, but the music itself refracts such turmoil, making it coherent, intensely human and entirely approachable. During the course of his engagement at the Vanguard in summer 1977 Pepper moved ever more into the realms of wild expressivity, using slurs, shakes and screeches through his alto to dig deep into the feelings he was wrestling with, and this process was encouraged by the intensely sympathetic support he is given here by Cables, Mraz and Jones. Elvin in particular, though he plays nothing one cannot find on other records by him, gives such careful and propulsive rhythmic life to every turn of phrase, whether on flyers (*Cherokee* – all three takes of it), medium-tempo bluesers (nine takes of *Blues for Heard*, for example) or ballads (*Over the Rainbow* and *Goodbye*, the latter played twice here), that it seems like these two have always played together, rather than finally made a record in the same band after all those years. There is a tremendous amount of music here, and it is advisable to take it a little at a time, not least because the playing is so intense, but there is no doubt that this is a box of music worth treasuring. If nine CDs of live Pepper sound daunting, however, then the three initial LP releases are also available as single CDs. **KS**

### Among Friends Pepper (as); Russ Freeman (p); Bob Magnusson (b); Frank Butler (d). Storyville Ⓕ STCD4167 (50 minutes). Recorded 1978.

⑨ ❽

1975's **Living Legend** was Pepper's first record as leader for 15 years. It heralded one of the great comeback stories in jazz and in *Lost Life* had a masterpiece to set beside his most affecting ballad performances. But better was to come.

Pepper rated **Among Friends** as possibly the most pleasant date he ever played. The music is relaxed, full of vim and suffused with a feeling of joyful group rapport. The session was a reunion of sorts, since both Freeman and Butler had played with Pepper in his first heyday, from 1955-1960. It was also a second 'comeback' for the altoist who, after making **Living Legend**, **The Trip** and **No Limit** in quick succession, had not recorded for a year due to health and drug problems.

The set showcases the main areas of Pepper's talent. The bright mercurial lines of *I'll Remember April* are handled with a fleet assurance that reveals his debt to Charlie Parker; a cool, wistful *'Round Midnight* exhibits the rhythmic poise and economy of phrase he brings to ballads; *Besame Mucho* shows how he can lace the most lilting tune with a tart poignancy.

Many of Pepper's late performances attain a genuinely tragic stature. **Among Friends** is refreshingly unassuming; he shows that personal happiness, no less than personal tragedy, can be an effective spur to making great music. This Storyville issue, by the way, includes an alternate take of *Blue Bossa* not on the original Discovery CD. **GL**

### The Complete Galaxy Recordings Pepper (as, cl); with a collective personnel of: Stanley Cowell, Hank Jones, Tommy Flanagan, George Cables (p); Cecil McBee, Ron Carter, Charlie Haden, Tony Dumas, Red Mitchell, David Williams (b); Howard Roberts (g); Roy Haynes, Al Foster, Billy Higgins, Carl Burnett (d); Kenneth Nash (perc). Galaxy Ⓕ 1016-2 (16 discs: 1,052 minutes). Recorded 1978-82.

⑩ ❽

For all of his early triumphs, there's much to be said for Art Pepper's final recordings, here collected. The last three-and-a-half years of his life were staggeringly prolific, and the level of artistry amazingly high. Of these 137 performances, 63 were unreleased on LP (nine of them were once available in

Japan), spread over ten recording sessions (two of them thoroughly documented live dates in Tokyo and Los Angeles clubs). As the only horn, Pepper is almost always in the spotlight, and he never falters. Over the years he remained fiercely competitive, if only with himself, and the inner conflict he felt put him on a quest that drove his music into such emotionally uplifting (and occasionally tortured) states as can be heard here. As such, the songs were merely vehicles; he returns to *Landscape* and *Mombo Koyama* five times each over the course of several sessions, for example, and many tunes receive two or three distinct interpretations. But his obsession would not allow him to repeat himself. His ballads are breathtaking, vulnerable and quizzical, wounded and wary. Up-tempo, he is exhilarating. If forced to choose a single favourite session I might take the 1979 date with Haden, Cables and Higgins since it includes three torch songs on unaccompanied alto and two of his plucky clarinet numbers. But I would hate to be without the final, gem-like duos with Cables or *Nature Boy*, a singular masterpiece with Tommy Flanagan's risky piano, or the increasingly vivid, vigorous live performances. Taken together, they emphasize the fact that few improvisers in jazz have been so ruthlessly open, immediate and rewarding as Art Pepper. **AL**

# Danilo Perez 1967

**New review**
**Panamonk** Perez (p); **Avishai Cohen** (b); **Terri Lyne Carrington**, **Jeff Watts** (d); on one track **Olga Roman** (v). Impulse! Ⓕ IMP11902 (52 minutes). Recorded 1996.

⑦ ❾

Perez has both phenomenal technical control and a musical imagination which allows him to do interesting things with that technique. This, his second album as leader and first for the renascent Impulse! label, is some distance in front of his début record for Novus, which at times allowed the programme to run away with the content. On **Panamonk** the Panamanian pianist combines the rhythms of the Hispano-Latin tradition with the compositions of Thelonious Monk. This is not the first time such an idea has been tried – Jerry Gonzalez's **Rumba Para Monk** (Sunnyside) demonstrated the links between Monk and Cuban rhythms with considerable success. The difference here is that, for all but one track, Perez sticks to the piano trio format, while occasionally leavening the Monk orientation with a couple of his own compositions such as *Hot Bean Strut* and *Mercedes' Mood*. His group reacts superbly to his requirements, and Perez himself asks no quarter. The project seems best suited to either very slow or very fast tempos, partly because there is less difficulty in escaping the original when space is either at a premium or no problem at all, and partly because one of Perez's few faults as a player is a tendency to play at one level, rather than look for lilt and dynamics. Hence a swaying medium-tempo calypso treatment of *Reflections* doesn't work because Perez himself can't get the music to ebb and flow. No doubt that sort of thing will come in time. **KS**

# Bill Perkins 1924

**New review**
**Quietly There** Perkins (ts, bs, bcl, f); **Victor Feldman** (p, org, vb); **John Pisano** (g); **Red Mitchell** (b); **Larry Bunker** (d). Riverside Ⓜ OJCCD1776-2 (48 minutes). Recorded 1966.

⑨ ❾

When the writer asked Bill Perkins why he never led bands of his own he was told "Because I'm a born follower." Maybe so, but in making an album devoted to the compositions of Johnny Mandel, Perkins has shown a shrewdness which has escaped many a leader. A programme of Mandel music means that half the points are in your bag before you start. Ballads like *Emily*, *A Time for Love*, *The Shining Sea* and *The Shadow of Your Smile* are amongst the most effectively sophisticated writings in popular music and Mandel's youth as a provider of jazz stomps and blues fills out Perkins's palette with *Groover Wailin'*, *Keester Parade* and *Something Different*. *Keester Parade* was a great favourite of the Herman sidemen of the fifties and Perkins digs into its funky blues with his baritone, while that smooth and elegant tenor makes the perfect voice for *Shining Sea* and the title track. Keen to follow the innovations of Sonny Rollins, Perkins lost his wondrous tenor sound soon after he made this recording and was never able to recapture it, so this album is important on those grounds, too. The bass clarinet goes truffle-hunting on *Emily*. *A Time for Love*, immortalized on tenor by Getz, is here handled with great delicacy by beautifully controlled flute, with Feldman's superb vibes enhancing the mood. Given the standards of the other musicians it can be seen that this is one of those albums which has everything going for it, including Perkins's own skilled settings of Mandel's music. **SV**

# Rich Perry 1952

**New review**
**To Start Again** Perry (ts); **Harold Danko** (p); **Scott Colley** (b); **Jeff Hirschfield** (d) SteepleChase Ⓕ SCCD31331 (66 minutes). Recorded 1993.

⑦ ❾

Tenor saxophonist Rich Perry is an impassioned yet thoughtful player whose style and tone suggest the twin influences of Sonny Rollins and Stan Getz. Though débuting here as a leader, the Cleveland, Ohio native has spent the last 20 years in the eye of New York's tornadic jazz scene. His big-band credits include Thad Jones/Mel Lewis, Bill Warfield, John Fedchock, Maria Schneider, Grover Mitchell and Bob Mintzer. As for small groups, Perry has lifted bandstands with Chet Baker, Richie Beirach, Steve Swallow, Jack McDuff and Bob Moses.

Here, in the company of his regular working group, Perry's programme of deserve-to-be-heard-more-often jazz tunes pleases as it provokes. In lines like Steve Lampert's *Aria*, Perry's explorations are accessible as well as adventurous. And though his style might be described as cutting-edge mainstream, it is a description that does little justice to the tenorist's uniquely agile twists and transcendent melodism. Other lines illuminated are Maria Schneider's *My Lament*, Thad Jones's *Three and One* and Harold Danko's *To Start Again*. The *tour de force*, Perry's tumultuous *Algae*, is a roller-coaster ride in which the tenorist's Rollins-esque rhythmatics and Getzian plaints burn with laser intensity.                                                                        **CB**

# Eric Person                                                          1963

**Prophecy** Person (as, ss, kbds, perc); **Cary De Nigris** (d); **Kenny Davis** (b). Soul Note Ⓟ 121287-2 (57 minutes). Recorded 1992/3.

Ⓖ Ⓗ

No stranger to big-band work, St Louis-born Person has the tone and arhythmic confidence identifiable with such activity. He has also worked with Kelvynator, Living Colour, Chico Hamilton's Euphoria and the Decoding Society and he happily acknowledges his r&b and soul listening experiences. More recently, he has worked with the World Saxophone Quartet and angled himself again toward jazz. This CD presents many aspects of his music. The likes of *Plummett*, *Next Love* and *Ancient Sun* use electronic aids to give body to the group sound and a fillip to its commercial appeal.

In contrast, *Up Against the Wall*, *Improvisation in Linear B*, *Interstellar Space Suite* and the title track are jazz directed solo performances. They make sparing use of multiphonics and circular breathing and they show Person to have admirable creative standards, an expressive tone and an awareness of dynamics. His whole approach would find sympathy with the M-Base collective; all means directed to the creative process are acceptable and an effort is continually made to relate to other contemporary musical forms. Here he uses tunes by John Coltrane and Wayne Shorter but he also provides eight of his own, even if three are not developed beyond the theme statement.   **BMcR**

# Houston Person                                                       1934

New review

**The Lion and His Pride** Person (ts); **Philip Harper** (t); **Benny Green** (p); **Christian McBride** (b); **Winard Harper** (d); **Sammy Figueroa** (perc). Muse Ⓟ MCD5480 (61 minutes). Recorded 1994.

Ⓖ Ⓘ

Houston Person is a heart-on-sleeve romantic whose blues-drenched saxophoning has spiced the grits-and-gravy organ trios of Johnny 'Hammond' Smith, Richard 'Groove' Holmes and Charles Earland. He's also enjoyed a long, productive association with singer Etta Jones. Though usually cast as a smoking backroom wailer, Person is a complete jazz player whose loping boppishness and playful probes bear comparison to the great Dexter Gordon. Whatever the style, Person can be counted on to connect with body and soul. Here, the venerable Person teams with a band of brash youngsters (Figueroa excepted) about a third his age. Instead of devolving into an inter-generational cutting session, there's a shared vision focused around an engaging set of standards. *Dig*, Miles Davis's boppish reframing of *Sweet Georgia Brown*, is an amiable, mid-tempo romp with appealing solo work by Person and trumpeter Philip Harper. *I Remember Clifford* showcases pianist Benny Green's expressive balladry. Also notable are the tasteful backdrops by Green, bassist Christian McBride, drummer Winard Harper and percussionist Figueroa. At centre though is the muscular Houston Person, a true tenor titan whose heart always sings, be it ballad, bossa or burner.   **CB**

# Bent Persson                                                         1947

New review

**Louis Armstrong's 50 Hot Choruses, Volumes 1 and 2** Persson (c,t) with the following collective personnel: **Bob McAllister, Jens Lingren, Kaj Sifwert** (tb); **Bo Juhlin** (tba, b); **Goran Eriksson, Mats Soderqvist, Ole Host, Tomas Ornberg** (reeds); **Christian Hopkins, Hans Hultman, Ulf Johansson, Ake Edenstrand** (p); **Goran Stachewsky, Holger Gross, Olle Nyman, Rune Lindberg** (bj, g); **Goran Lind** (b); **Christer Ekhe** (d); **Nils Rehman** (v). Kenneth Ⓟ 3411 (62 minutes). Recorded 1976/96.

Ⓘ Ⓗ

In 1927 Louis Armstrong recorded a series of breaks and solos on 50 wax cylinders. These were transcribed for publication by Melrose Music and the cylinders were subsequently lost. In 1974

Sweden's Bent Persson set himself the task of recording all of the solos, from the transcriptions, but fleshing them out as full band pieces. The original four LPs by Persson were received with universal acclaim, not just for the care and accuracy which had gone into the project but for the sheer exuberance of the music. In fact you can appreciate the music as it stands without delving too deeply into the academics. Persson does an amazing job of bringing those Armstrong solos and breaks to life, ably assisted by men such as Tomas Ornberg on clarinet and alto. The LPs are now appearing on CD but with the difference that some of the pieces have been re-recorded (in 1996), making the conversion a little complicated. Although called Volumes 1 and 2, this consists of a single CD, the volume numbers referring to the original LP issues. Collectors who have LP Volume 1, for example, will find that *Hot Notes*, *Sugar Babe*, *Steamboat Stomp* and *Sobbin' Blues* have not been converted to CD and that a newly recorded *Chimes Blues* has taken the place of the 1976 version. But all of the music is extremely enjoyable and full marks to Persson and Ulf Johansson for turning in such a fine trumpet-piano duet version of *High Society*. Indeed, full marks to all concerned for one of the most worthwhile examples of jazz archeology. **AM**

# Hannibal Marvin Peterson                                    1948

**Now's the Time**  Peterson (t, v); **John Hicks** (p); **Richard Davis** (b); **Tatsuya Nakamura** (d). King
  Ⓕ KICJ108 (56 minutes). Recorded 1992.

⑦ ❽

Another talented product of the North Texas State University assembly line, Peterson is one of the most multi-stylistic of trumpeters. For many years with Gil Evans, he is as much at home with free-formers such as Roswell Rudd, Enrico Rava and Pat Patrick as he is with stalwarts like John Hicks, Kenny Barron and Roy Haynes. As this CD shows, he has the confidence and technical facility to take on anything and any style. Here he also has the advantage of being with musicians endowed with similar instrumental gifts. It is just that, with Hicks's forceful, rippling piano, Davis's assured and full toned bass and Nakamura's fine timekeeping, there is less temptation to go outside. The situation does not, however, restrict Peterson's musical range. The pure-toned lyricist is heard on *In a Sentimental Mood*, the blisteringly hot bebopper marauds through *Now's the Time*, while the harmonic investigator makes a detailed interrogation of *Smoke Gets in Your Eyes*. In contrast, the doleful blues man protests through *Turquoise* before donning his clown's hat to jive *The Saints*. Although he brings a gospel fervour to his singing on *Glory, Glory Hallelujah*, he is not the most deeply emotional of trumpeters. It is almost as if he finds it too easy to play. **BMcR**

# Oscar Peterson                                    1925

New review
**The Song Is You**  Peterson (p); **Herb Ellis, Barney Kessell** (g); **Ray Brown** (b); **Ed Thigpen** (d).
  Verve Ⓜ 531 558-2 (two discs: 119 minutes). Recorded 1952-9.

✅        ⑨ ❾

It was part of Norman Granz's strategy for developing Oscar Peterson's career that he should record in as many genres as possible. One of these was the 'song book' format, which was proving such success for Ella Fitzgerald, and this double-CD pack contains a sizeable selection from Peterson's albums devoted to individual song-writers and performed in a slightly more subdued style than his usual work with his trio. Rather like Stan Getz in the same situation, Peterson makes up in elegance and expressiveness what he is obliged to sacrifice in invention and the results are almost universally charming. The critical reaction at the time was rather hostile. It is a common error among jazz critics to confuse lightness with triviality and solemnity with seriousness. It is perfectly possible to have serious light work, and that's what this is. The eight years covered by the series saw changes in Peterson's trio, first the replacement of Ellis with Kessell and then the arrival of Thigpen's drums in place of the guitar. These are all reflected in the music, although not as dramatically as in the full-blown jazz recordings. Everything is cooler and straighter, but the famous 'will to swing' is as evident as ever. Some of these tracks have not seen the light of day for 40 years, which is an additional recommendation. **DG**

**The Trio Live from Chicago**  Peterson (p); **Ray Brown** (b); **Ed Thigpen** (d). Verve Ⓜ 823 008-2
  (47 minutes). Recorded 1961.

⑧ ❻

Although the admirable Norman Granz had not always presented Peterson in the best possible light, his sale of the Verve label to MGM in 1961 did not look likely to improve the situation. New executive director Creed Taylor's normal method of showcasing soloists was some distance from Peterson's concept, but in the event, his methods were not imposed. It was Jim Taylor who produced this session and, to some extent, it was he who directed Peterson on a fresh career path. This Chicago date typifies his approach. Peterson is in ebullient mood and it is one of those sessions where his awesome technical command is subjected to the greater creative needs of improvisational forays such as *Never Been in Love Before*, *Sometimes I'm Happy*, and *Whisper Not*. He makes it all seem easy, with the underlying rhythmic thrust as evident at the meandering pace of *Wee Small Hours of the Morning* as it is on a medium-tempo driver like *Chicago*. Brown gives a magnificent display of both supportive as well as scrupulously accurate bass playing, while Thigpen, who arrived in the trio in 1959, adds the stiffening element not always evident in the previous partnership with guitarist Herb Ellis. This is, in fact, the ideal trio for Peterson and, with the added stimulation of a noisy live audience, all three are inspired to produce their best work. Verve have recently gathered all the London House material together into a five-CD ring-backed set with graphics so appalling they're barely decipherable. The music, of course, is compelling, and there is a great deal of unissued material to boot, but I would suggest that, for the casual Peterson fan, this original single CD selection is still the best way to do it.　　**BMcR**

**Night Train** Peterson (p); **Ray Brown** (b); **Ed Thigpen** (d). Verve Ⓜ 821 724-2 (45 minutes). Recorded 1962.

✓　　　　　　　　　　　　　　　　　　　　　　　　　　　　　　　⑩ ❽

When Herb Ellis decided to leave Peterson in 1958, Oscar did not think any other guitarist could adequately take Herb's place, so he changed the trio's instrumentation and hired drummer Ed Thigpen. The Peterson-Brown-Thigpen trio remained in being for five years and **Night Train** is arguably the best representative album the group made; it certainly proved to be the most popular in terms of sales figures. The transfer to CD was a logical step and the reproduction is excellent. Setting himself a programme of music closely associated with others was a self-imposed challenge for Oscar, but he knew exactly what he was doing. Four of the 11 tunes are by Duke Ellington (five, if you count *Night Train* which, although credited to Jimmy Forrest, is actually based on a couple of Ducal themes) and two are from the Basie book. Joe Higgins had a hit in the forties with *The Honeydripper* but it never swung as much as Oscar's version here. Peterson has come in for a lot of ill-judged criticism over the years, perhaps because he is so consistently good as a player. He has only infrequently featured as a composer, but this CD has his *Hymn to Freedom*, surely one of his finest pieces of musical architecture, building steadily to a climax before returning gracefully to the opening mood.　　**AM**

**Trio + One: Clark Terry** Peterson (p); **Clark Terry** (t, flh, v); **Ray Brown** (b); **Ed Thigpen** (d). EmArcy Ⓜ 818 840-2 (41 minutes). Recorded 1964.

　　　　　　　　　　　　　　　　　　　　　　　　　　　　　⑨ ❼

Peterson has of course been amongst the most gregarious as well as most prolific of recording artists and, as this album attests, there are some solid successes to count among the collaborative efforts. This date was one of his most popular at the time of its initial release, spawning as it did the hit track *Mumbles* and its follow-up, *Incoherent Blues*. Both of those tracks remain enjoyable today, Terry's inspired vocal babblings still able to raise a laugh from even the most curmudgeonly of listeners, but it is the more solid musical virtues of the union between the trio and guest which invite our continued respect and attention and earn this album its classic status. The opening title, Frank Loesser's *Brotherhood of Man*, finds the trio digging in deep behind a wailing Terry, blues-drenched near-vocalizations pouring from his instrument. The same is true of Peterson's *Blues for Smedley*, but then there is also the unadorned way Terry and the band treat the pretty melody of *Roundalay*. By this time, this edition of the Peterson trio had been in place for over half a decade, and it swung like no other. Terry is arresting all through, striking an imaginative musical angle on every track and playing with overwhelming conviction. This is one to keep the home fires burning.　　**KS**

**Exclusively for My Friends** Peterson (p); **Ray Brown, Sam Jones** (b); **Ed Thigpen, Bobby Durham**, **Louis Hayes** (d). Verve/MPS Ⓜ 513 830-2 (four discs: 238 minutes). Recorded 1963-8.

　　　　　　　　　　　　　　　　　　　　　　　　　　　　　⑦ ❽

Peterson tends to get either deified or trashed. I find his proficiency both amazing and limiting, and this mega-survey, originally released on six LPs, makes the point as well as any single collection. Among its strengths are uniformly superb sound on the 36 tracks, recorded over a six-year span in producer Georg Brunner-Schwer's Villingen villa; the informal flow of repertoire and mix of solo and trio performances; and the chance to sample various combinations of the sixties Peterson trios. The piano playing has a technical uniformity about it, though I disagree with the argument advanced by some that Peterson does not swing. He shows what happens to the virtuosity of Art Tatum when tempered by the leaner sensitivities of Nat Cole and surrounded by a strong if ultimately servile rhythm section. The best Peterson unit, with Brown and Thigpen, gets only six of the 26 trio tracks (check Thigpen's long-ride cymbal decay as a gauge of the recording quality) and, oddly, the Jones/Hayes combination a measly one. Peterson's trio concept was the norm that Evans, LaFaro and Motian exploded; after this extended exposure, one understands why it needed exploding. But Peterson sure can play, as the performances here, including 10 solo tracks from the end of the project, more than adequately demonstrate.　　**BB**

New review
**The More I See You** Peterson (p); **Clark Terry** (t, flh); **Benny Carter** (as); **Lorne Lofsky** (g); **Ray Brown** (b); **Lewis Nash** (d). Telarc Jazz Ⓔ CD83370 (64 minutes). Recorded 1995.

　　　　　　　　　　　　　　　　　　　　　　　　　　　　　⑦ ❿

Three years after Peterson's arrival on the Telarc label with an extended (indeed rather too extended) four-CD set of 1990 reunion tracks with his original trio at New York's Blue Note Club, in which little new was on offer, he suffered a serious stroke. His return to playing was for a time in doubt, but he worked doggedly to regain his skill at the keyboard, and although he was never likely to regain the dash of his Verve/Pablo period, this album is the best of what currently amounts to three post-illness sessions revealing a pianist operating at a level still technically far above most other current practitioners. Peterson's playing is a little more spartan, a little more right-hand dominated, and perhaps more contemplative than of yore, but he remains a challenging sparring partner as he trades fours with Brown, a perfect accompanist for Carter and a sparklingly on-form Terry, and a soloist who still commands the attention. Terry's playing ranges from his characteristic blues style on *Ron's Blues* to the down-home funky on the Bourbon Street anthem, *When My Dream Boat Comes Home*. Carter is as urbane as ever, despite the passing years, but the album belongs to Terry and Peterson, who between them rekindle the inventiveness present in their earlier collaborations.　　　**AS**

## Ralph Peterson                                                          1962

New review
**The Reclamation Project**  Peterson (d); **Steve Wilson** (ss); **Bryan Carrott** (vb, mba); **Belden Bullock** (b). Evidence Ⓕ ECD22113-2 (59 minutes). Recorded 1994.

❻ ❼

At Peterson's request Wilson only used his soprano on the record, which will strike some as a shame; his voice on the alto saxophone is so lithe and singular, and he sounds flatter and harder to distinguish from a ton of other post-Shorter players on the straight horn. But Wilson is not the primary focus. The rhythm section carries the music; Bullock's bass dictates themes and Carrott's not particularly well-recorded vibes create harmonies and atmosphere. A heavier-gauge drummer than Peterson is hard to find – he's got a little of Elvin Jones and a little of Al Foster in him, though he'd drown out either – and that creates sound problems here, though the band seems to respond well enough to him. Overall, this Fo'Tet record doesn't have the urgency of the earlier Blue Notes; the tunes aren't as strong, nor is the ensemble playing.　　　**BR**

## Michel Petrucciani                                                      1962

New review
**Flamingo**  Petrucciani (p); **Stephane Grappelli** (vn); **George Mraz** (b); **Roy Haynes** (d). Dreyfus FDM36 580-2 (55 minutes). Recorded 1995.

❽ ❾

I wonder how many times Stephane Grappelli has played *These Foolish Things*, that archetypal Mayfair ballad of the war years, when he was a star of blacked-out, subterranean London nightlife. It must be thousands, yet he still manages to infuse it with genuine sentiment – which is not the same thing as sentimentality. Most of the tunes here are old songs of similar vintage or older – *Sweet Georgia Brown*, *There Will Never Be Another You* and so on – and his playing is as blithe and fresh as it was more than half a century ago. In fact it is better, because Grappelli seemed to take on a new lease of life in the early seventies and his whole conception deepened and expanded. He and Petrucciani establish a great rapport, with the latter playing much more simply and lyrically than usual, and the result is both absorbing and enjoyable.　　　**DG**

## Oscar Pettiford                                                    1922-60

**Deep Passion**  Pettiford (b, vc); **Ernie Royal, Art Farmer, Ray Copeland, Kenny Dorham** (t); **Jimmy Cleveland, Al Grey** (tb); **Julius Watkins, David Amram** (frh); **Gigi Gryce** (as, arr); **Lucky Thompson, Benny Golson** (ts, arr); **Jerome Richardson** (ts, f); **Danny Bank, David Kurtzer, Sahib Shihab** (bs); **Tommy Flanagan, Dick Katz** (p); **Whitey Mitchell** (b); **Osie Johnson** (d); **Betty Glamman** (hp). Impulse! Ⓜ GRP11432 (68 minutes). Recorded 1956/7.

❻ ❽

The almost big band that Pettiford put together in 1956 was not employed frequently enough to keep a regular personnel, but it did make two LPs (the first in particular is excellent of its kind). It also preserved some of the few large arrangements by Lucky Thompson and some of the first by his replacement, Benny Golson. The forces at their disposal included four saxes, two trumpets, one trombone and two French horns. Watkins and Amram (two of the few constants through the band's six studio sessions, all gathered here) were mainly used in a much more punchy way than Claude Thornhill's ever were, and are given an up-tempo solo feature ensemble on *Two French Fries*. The harpist, spread thinly through nine of the 17 tracks, is only there for colouration but intriguing nonetheless.

Pettiford gets a reasonable amount of space for bass and cello solos, though by no means on every track, and the most affecting soloists are Farmer and Thompson, both on the first album's ten tracks. The second album seems on the whole less ambitious in its choice of material and arranging style, but it does contain a fine *I Remember Clifford* (featuring Kenny Dorham, unidentified in the notes) and Randy Weston's *Little Niles*, both classics of the period.　　　**BP**

# Jack Pettis

**His Pets, Band and Orchestra** Pettis (cl, c-ms, ts) with the following selected personnel: **Bill Moore, Phil Hart, Don Bryan** (t); **Frank Sarlo, Miff Mole, Tommy Dorsey, Jack Teagarden, Glenn Miller** (tb); **Phil Sharp, Don Murray, Dick Stabile, Benny Goodman** (cl); **Spencer Clark** (bss); **Al Goering, Frank Signorelli** (p); **Joe Venuti, Nick Gerlach** (vn); **Eddie Lang** (g); **Dick McDonagh** (bj, g); **Max Rosen** (tba); **Merrill Klein** (tba, b); **Harry Goodman** (b); **Sam Fink, Dillon Ober** (d). Kings Cross Records Ⓜ KCM005/6 (two discs: 146 minutes). Recorded 1926-9.

⑦ ❽

Just a few bars of the first title here will tell you that this is Windy City music: that indelible stamp of smart arrangements with deft, rhythmically punctuated cadences, rich saxophone harmonies, hot trumpet breaks and a driving, even rhythm with the strong suggestion of common-time, all can be found on the sides made by any number of permutations of the musicians above, spreading out, of course, to include Bix and Tesch and their minions. Pettis was born, it seems, in 1902, and had a brief time when his name meant something in jazz circles, though by the onset of the Depression he was headed on the road to obscurity (no one knows when or where he died, although Bud Freeman's recollection that he married an heiress may explain his complete withdrawal from his old pals' haunts).

The music here is joyful, driving and continually has a twinkle in the eye, even when the key is minor, and the soloists are perfectly aware of jazz phrasing and feel. Pettis does not come across as an overwhelming musical personality, but his peers rated him as the formulator of much of what was to be later recognized as the Chicago School of saxophone style and technique. If this is true, then his influence becomes central to jazz, considering Lester Young's early love of Teschemacher, who had emerged along with Freeman to dominate this school's approach by the end of the twenties. Jazz history is fine, and credit should go to those to whom it is due, but it doesn't alter the fact that this is hugely spirited and enjoyable music (the occasional cornball vocals aside) which can stand on its own merits as Chicago jazz of a high order, prehistoric, historic, obscure·or whatever. The John R.T. Davis transfers are, as ever, exemplary. **KS**

# Barre Phillips
1934

**Mountainscapes** Phillips (b); **John Surman** (ss, ts, bs, bcl, synth); **Dieter Feichter** (synth); **Stu Martin** (d, synth); **John Abercrombie** (g). ECM Ⓒ 843 167-2 (38 minutes). Recorded 1976.

⑦ ❽

This was an important album for both Phillips and ECM when it first came out. For one thing, it was the best-recorded and most articulate documentation of the newly resurgent trio with Surman and Martin; for another, it utilized the at-that-time new sound panoramas generated by the synthesizer. It also kicked off the still-intact recording relationship between Surman and ECM. Lastly, the edge and energy to be found here was paralleled in few other contemporaneous ECM projects (although Benny Maupin's **The Jewel in the Lotus** – not yet on CD – approached it from a rather different path) and gave the label enhanced credibility in the progressive music arena.

Phillips had for most of his career been establishing standards (his **Unaccompanied Barre** from 1968 was the first solo bass recital album in jazz-related music) and on ECM had previously made the delectable **Music for Two Basses**, a series of astonishing duets with Dave Holland. This album, however, was perhaps the most ambitious to date, because even though it had an episodic nature, there was a definite intention to link the movements of *Mountainscape* into a unified entity. Some of the parts are exquisite; others border on the ferocious. The sum of the parts? Still impressive, partly because the sectionalization has allowed the music more drama and more linear development than much of the more sprawling music which was being created at this time, and partly because it still sounds uncompromisingly thought-through. **KS**

# Joe 'Flip' Phillips
1915

**Flip Wails: The Best of the Verve Years** Phillips (ts); with a collective personnel of: **Howard McGhee, Harry Edison** (t); **Bill Harris** (tb); **Hank Jones, Oscar Peterson, Mickey Crane** (p); **Herb Ellis, Billy Bauer** (g); **Ray Brown** (b); **J.C. Heard, Buddy Rich, Jo Jones, Max Roach, Alvin Stoller, Louie Bellson** (d). Verve Ⓜ 521 645-2 (74 minutes). Recorded 1947-58.

⑧ ❻

Remarkably, Flip Phillips sounded as good at his 80th birthday celebrations as he does on these classic recordings made in his middle life. He moved rapidly from being a clarinet player with Frankie Newton and Pete Brown in Harlem to becoming one of the most adventurous tenor soloists of the forties and was a prime mover in the innovative Woody Herman First Herd. While still with Woody he recorded with Parker and Gillespie and his later experience with Jazz at the Philharmonic as stablemate to Lester Young (a particular friend and influence), Coleman Hawkins, Ben Webster and Illinois Jacquet rounded out his experience.

This collection of his work for Norman Granz excludes the JATP sessions. Those concerts were regarded as frantic, but retrospective listening reveals glorious music, often in ballad form, from Phillips and the others. The tracks here have a more compact and rehearsed feel to them. It is little known that Phillips is a good composer and arranger. That is confirmed by his few originals here and by the disciplined and lean music produced by his groups. Above all he is an expansive and eloquent soloist in the grand tenor tradition. He swings as hard as any of the mainstream players and would have been equally at home with Ellington or Basie as he was with Herman. His long-time friendship and musical partnership with Bill Harris is regrettably represented on only four of these 20 tracks, where they play with typical strength of character. This excellent collection deserves to bring Phillips's music to a much wider and younger audience, which would surely accept such timeless art. **SV**

## Enrico Pieranunzi                                                1949

**New review**
**The Night Gone By** Pieranunzi (p); **Marc Johnson** (b); **Paul Motian** (d). Alfa Jazz Ⓔ ALCB3906
(62 minutes). Recorded 1996.

⑧ ❾

Just a glance at the personnel will tell where this album's coming from. A dip into the CD insert brings the reader quickly to a quote from a Japanese music journal which spells it out: "The European answer to Bill Evans". Both the listener and Pieranunzi could have done without that. This superb Italian pianist has been making outstanding albums for a decade now, and this latest is no exception, although it is noticeable that recent efforts have conveyed a clear softening of the attack and a more understated way with an oblique or anti-contextual thought. Pieranunzi has technique to spare and a lively imagination, and clearly owes a considerable debt to players such as Evans, Herbie Hancock and Chick Corea, but his own amalgam of all these players is highly individualistic and worth close investigation. Emphatically no one's answer to anyone else, he has played regularly with Johnson, but this is his first in a trio setting with Motian, who maintains his usual impeccable standards. The repertoire here, apart from Pieranunzi's four compositions, could have turned up on any modern mainstream piano jazz record of the past 40 years, but the pianist manages to recast such old war-horses as *Body and Soul* and *Over the Rainbow* to reveal something unusually pertinent in them. His own pieces are thoughtful and expertly put together, with overtones of his classical training a constant presence. The trio play excellently together at all times, and throughout the disc one is aware of a superior musical intelligence guiding proceedings. That, along with the other qualities already noted, makes it pretty good, at least in my book. **KS**

## Billy Pierce                                                     1948

**Rolling Monk** Pierce (ts); **Donald Brown** (p); **Christian McBride** (b); **Billy Drummond** (d). Paddle
Wheel Ⓔ KICJ154 (58 minutes). Recorded 1992.

⑦ ❽

A Berklee graduate, Pierce began his musical career as something of a house saxophonist in Boston soul clubs. In 1980 he took one of the saxophone chairs as Art Blakey assembled a new and exciting edition of the Jazz Messengers and toured extensively with the drummer for two years. He returned to Boston in the eighties, worked with pianist James Williams and taught both privately and at Berklee. As the title of this CD indicates, he has taken on, in Sonny Rollins and Thelonious Monk, two of the music's strongest personalities. It speaks volumes for his melodic selectivity and rhythmic awareness that he emerges unscathed. The basic cadence of his style gives him a natural affinity with Rollins and by ignoring the fine details of the New Yorker's game plan he successfully puts his own trademark on titles like *Old Cowhand* and *Strode Rode*. There is no marauding away from the theme and it is this fact that makes his Monk readings similarly effective. On *Ugly Beauty* and *Epistrophy* in particular he uses the original framework as a guideline to his own improvisational path and it proves to be a considerable creative stimulant. Pierce is fortunate in not being touted as another neo-classical wonderman. He is a mainstream/modern professional with a voice of his own. **BMcR**

## Nat Pierce                                                      1925-92

**Easy Swing** Nat Pierce Band (Pierce, p; Doug Mettome, t; Urbie Green, tb; Med Flory, as;
Richie Kamuca, ts; Jack Nimitz, bs; Freddie Green, g; Walter Page, b; Jo Jones d); **Mel Powell
Band** (Powell, p; John Glasel, t; Jim Buffington, frh; Chuck Russo, cl, as, bs; Boomie Richman,
ts; Mundell Lowe, g; Joe Kay, b; Eddie Phyfe, d). Vanguard Ⓔ 662 133 (41 minutes). Recorded
1954/5.

⑥ ❻

Pierce was unique in starting his career as a progressively modern pianist in the late forties and later retrenching to the swing idioms of Basie and Ellington. He was notable also for his ten years as straw boss and musical director of the Woody Herman band. Here he uses Basie's original rhythm section and adds his own friends. Pierce's sense of time was so good that it is impossible to detect the seams when he 'does a Basie' (he actually appeared anonymously as Basie on some of the Count's records – now there is a problem for discographers!)

The music is feather-light swinging with a powder-puff punch (the classic Basie band rarely hit hard). The image is complemented by Kamuca's Lester Young-inspired tenor and there is a rare chance to hear the solo work of Doug Mettome, one of the finest players of the time. The more ubiquitous Urbie Green is on good solo form, too.

The five tracks by Mel Powell's unit are immaculately arranged and played by the unusual front line and employ a similar light touch. Apart from the piano, the feature for the eccentric french horn on *When Did You Leave Heaven?* is particularly appealing. **SV**

## Dominique Pifarely

**Oblique** Pifarely (vn); **Yves Robert** (tb); **Louis Sclavis** (cl); **Francois Coutourier** (p, syn); **Riccardo Del Fra** (b); **Joel Allouche** (d). Ida Ⓕ 034CD (61 minutes) Recorded 1992.

⑤ ❿

Oblique it certainly is. Pifarely has been associated with Sclavis for a number of years, and Sclavis appears here fleetingly. Pifarely has a nervous energy, married to a rhapsodic approach which it is hard to altogether escape on the violin. This gives him a thoroughly modern sound, especially when in the company of musicians who are prepared to stretch metred time to the point of extinction. Yet his ideas don't significantly move his playing away from the Central European tradition of the earlier part of this century. When left to his own devices, he sounds distinctly Bartókian as did Leroy Jenkins for a number of years early in his career. Perhaps it's a problem endemic to the instrument. Or perhaps not. Stuff Smith and Ray Nance never sounded like warmed-over Bartók.

The most arresting playing often comes from the pianist Francois Coutourier, who has the energy and technical command to match his ideas. He's also on just over half the CD, so he has time to make his mark, as opposed to the superb Sclavis and trombonist Robert, given two tracks each. He saves *Crepuscule With Nellie* from becoming a rewrite of Debussy's Violin Sonata, and for that alone he deserves our gratitude. **KS**

## Dave Pike                                                                                                1938

**Times Out of Mind** Pike (v); **Tom Rainier** (as, ts, p, synths); **Ron Eschete, Kenny Burrell** (g); **Luther Hughes, Harvey Newmark** (b); **Ted Hawke** (d). Muse Ⓕ MCD5446 (41 minutes). Recorded 1975.

⑥ ❻

Pike has led a varied creative life, playing with Paul Bley in the fifties and then having a six-year stint with flautist Herbie Mann in the early sixties, when Mann established himself as one of the most popular players in jazz. After a period of residence in Europe in the late sixties leading The Dave Pike Set (recently returned to the catalogue via the MPS CD, **Masterpieces**, selected from the Set's four 1969-70 albums for the German label), he returned to California in 1973, and has stayed based there since then. Probably because of his long tenure with Mann, Pike has never garnered a strong critical press, and so his real achievements as a vibraphonist and leader have gone mostly unnoticed. While his style is rooted in Milt Jackson and Cal Tjader, he has a smooth and varied technique, clear improvisational ideas, and a musical taste which leads him away from the crasser aspects of commercial musical life. This present album finds him with a talented small group which allows him plenty of blowing room and which has a strong rhythm section. Tom Rainer is definitely preferable on piano to saxophone, and when he sticks to his keyboards the band gels effortlessly. Burrell doesn't have a great deal to say in his solo spots but, that aside, the musicians all play with spirit. A likeable album of fusion-tinged modern jazz. **KS**

## Courtney Pine                                                                              1964

**To the Eyes of Creation** Pine (ts, bcl, ss, WX7); **Dennis Rollins** (tb); **Keith Waite** (f, perc); **Julian Joseph** (p, org); **Bheki Mseleku** (p); **Tony Remi, Cameron Pierre** (g); **Wayne Batchelor, Gary Crosby** (b); **Mark Mondesir, Peter Lewinson, Brian Abrams** (d); **Frank Tontoh** (d, perc); **Thomas Dyani, Mamadi Kamara** (perc); **Cleveland Watkiss, Juliet Roberts** (v). Island CID514044 2 (58 minutes). Recorded 1992.

⑥ ❽

None of Pine's recorded releases has done justice to the man. In person he gives uncompromising jazz performances and competes at the highest level. Unfortunately, a look at his overall output suggests that the promise of **Journey to the Urge Within** (Island CID9846) or the ethnic honesty of **Closer to Home** (Mango 846528) are neither better nor worse than **Realms of Our Dreams** (Antilles ANCD8756) which teams him with a top-flight American rhythm section. This CD at least tries to cover the full Pine canvas. It has powerful tenor outings on *Country Dance* and *Cleopatra's Needle*, his soprano takes a sensitive look at *Psalm* and *Redemption Song*, while *X-Caliber* is an excellent, if short, soliloquy. In contrast, his simple lines set against a Latin base reduce *The Healing Song* to little more than supermarket music and *Eastern Standard Time* is a pop dance song. The CD closes with *The Holy Grail*, a beautiful piece of music that, perhaps more than any other title, reminds us that Pine is an enigma, a writer with a classic book in him, but still writing paperbacks and, even then, unsure whether they should be romantic fiction or high drama.                    **BMcR**

## Armand J. Piron                                                                        1888-1943

**Piron's New Orleans Orchestra** Piron (vn, v, dir.); **Peter Bocage** (t); **John Lindsay** (tb); **Lorenzo Tio Jr** (cl, ts); **Louis Warnecke** (as); **Steve Lewis** (p); **Charles Bocage** (bj, v); **Bob Ysaguirre** (bb); **Louis Cottrell** (d); **Lela Bolden**, **Ida G. Brown**, **Willie Jackson** (v). Azure Ⓕ AZCD13 (78 minutes). Recorded 1923-6.

⑥ ❻

Although he was active at the turn of the century, the story of violinist Piron really begins when he replaced Freddie Keppard as leader of the star-studded Olympia Orchestra in 1912. King Oliver, Sidney Bechet and Zue Robertson were sidemen but extra-curricular publishing activities diverted Piron during the First World War. Fortunately, he continued to lead bands in New Orleans and his 1919 unit provided the nucleus for the twenties orchestra. The sessions that make up this CD came about when Piron accepted a residency in New York and represent a complete contrast to the power of the contemporary King Oliver band.

The basis of Piron's music was ragtime; the delivery was elegant and all of the best traditions of Creole musical etiquette were observed. The ensembles encouraged contrapuntal interplay but arrangements on the likes of *Bouncing Around* and *Mama's Gone, Goodbye* avoid tail-gate trombone patterns and rely on the tastefully relaxed lead of Bocage and the flowing clarinet and dancing breaks of Tio. A different balance is achieved on the trombone-less *Red Man Blues*, excellent violin and clarinet counterpoint illuminates *Lou'siana Swing* and the swing generated throughout is genteel. The odd over-arranged item like *Ghost of the Blues* takes the band to the fringe of jazz, but Piron's entire recorded output is on this CD and it documents an important stage of the ragtime and jazz overlap.                                                                          **BMcR**

## Bucky Pizzarelli                                                                        1926

**The Complete Guitar Duos** Bucky Pizzarelli, John Pizzarelli (g). Stash Ⓕ STCD536 (74 minutes). Recorded 1980/84.

⑥ ❻

The depth of tone and pitch of the seven-string guitar means that even when playing alone, as both father and son do from time to time on this compelling album of chamber jazz, the sound is far richer than on the average guitar solo album. Together, they pace each other perfectly, and bring a gently swinging grace to standards like *In a Mellotone* or *Love for Sale*, as well as less familiar fare such as their arrangement of Beiderbecke's *In a Mist*.

Perhaps it's a genetic peculiarity, but the only other duo who switch so effortlessly from accompaniment to solo, telepathically swapping roles, and challenging each other's ingenuity, are the brothers Boulu and Elios Ferré. Pizzarelli *père et fils* have this knack, although they apply it best to material different from their European counterparts: Django's *Nuages* is less fulfilling a performance than material drawn from Chick Corea or veteran guitarist Carl Kress. In general, after some kind of vamp introduction, Bucky leads off on the melody or digs straight into a solo. John's solos are less classically elegant, but when they trade fours or eights it fast becomes hard to tell who's who. They excel at medium tempo, never better than on the opener *Love for Sale*.                    **AS**

## John Pizzarelli                                                                         1960

**Naturally** Pizzarelli (v, g); **John Frosk, Anthony Kadleck, Michael Ponella, Jim Hynes** (t); **Clark Terry** (t, flh); **Bob Alexander, Mark Patterson, Wayne Andre, Paul Faulise** (tb); **Walt Levinsky, Frank Griffith** (as); **Scott Robinson, Frank Wess, Harry Allen** (ts); **Jack Stuckey** (bs); **Dominic Cortese** (acc); **Ken Levinsky** (p); **Bucky Pizzarelli** (g); **Martin Pizzarelli** (b); **Joe Cocuzzo, Tony Corbiscello** (d). RCA Novus Ⓕ 63151-2 (51 minutes). Recorded 1993.

⑧ ❽

Imagine a distinguished guitarist who is the son of a distinguished guitarist, a young, personable singer with a penchant for early Nat Cole and the courage to tackle Django's *Nuages* with the original French lyrics, and you have John Pizzarelli. Why he is not infinitely more famous than Harry Connick Jnr I cannot understand, unless it is simply a matter of being too hip.

This is Pizzarelli's third album, and his first with a big band. Among its high points are a guitar feature dedicated to Charlie Christian (*Seven On Charlie*), an impeccable unison guitar and scat blues (*Splendid Splinter*) and a Sinatra-style swinging ballad (*You Stepped Out of a Dream*). The versatility and accomplishment is quite staggering. His follow-up album, **Dear Mr Cole**, has more singing and less guitar, so this slightly earlier one has the preferred balance.                                    **DG**

# Bill Plake

New review
**South**  Plake (ts); **Craig Fundyga** (vb, mba); **Anders Swanson** (b); **Jeanette Wrate** (d, perc). Nine
    Winds Ⓕ NWCD0175 (55 minutes). Recorded 1994.

⑤ ❽

In some ways, the current West Coast scene is similar to that of the Cool movement of the early fifties. The local New Age jazz has the same studied serenity and, among the record companies involved, Nine Winds has been prominent in the dissemination of the message. Figures such as reed man Vinny Golia, drummer Alex Cline and trumpeter Rob Blakeslee have been noteworthy in the 1990's movement and Plake has worked in Golia's Large Ensemble. This CD looks at the combo approach to the subject. The placid air of the arrangements take them into an almost ECM-like calm and, even in quartet, there is a strong textural awareness. What makes this date somewhat different is that Plake seems determined to roughen up the fabric of the music. The gentility evaporates when he comes thrusting forward although, for all that overt aggression, he is not among the more inventive of improvisers. The listener is badgered into submission by the weight of the comment, rather than by the profundity of it. In the somewhat clinical world of New Age, this can be a welcome relief.                                    **BMcR**

# King Pleasure (Clarence Beeks)                                    1922-81

**King Pleasure Sings/Annie Ross Sings**  Pleasure, Betty Carter, The Dave Lambert Singers,
    Jon Hendricks, The Three Riffs, Blossom Dearie, Annie Ross (v); Ed Lewis, Merril Stepter (t);
    J.J. Johnson, Kai Winding (tb); Lem Davis (as); Charlie Ferguson, Lucky Thompson, Ray Abrams
    (ts); Danny Bank, Cecil Payne (bs); Ed Swanston, John Lewis, Jimmy Jones, Teacho Wiltshire,
    George Wallington (p); Ram Ramirez (org); Peck Morrison, Percy Heath, Paul Chambers, Leonard
    Gaskin (b); Herbie Lovelle, Kenny Clarke, Joe Harris, Teddie Lee, Art Blakey (d). Prestige
    Ⓜ OJCCD217-2 (47 minutes). Recorded 1952-4.

✔                                    ❽ ❻

Yes, King Pleasure has other compact discs all to himself; but 12 of the 16 performances here are his, and one of the two CD bonus tracks is the original recording of *Moody's Mood* (still called *I'm In the Mood for Love* here) with Blossom Dearie singing the second bridge. Initial versions of such other Pleasure vocal trademarks as *Parker's Mood*, *Red Top* (with Betty Carter) and *Jumpin' With Symphony Sid* are also included, not to mention the classics *Twisted* and *Farmer's Market* among the Ross titles. Both singers favoured tenor soloists (Ross likes Wardell Gray, Pleasure prefers Getz, Pres and Moody) and, as the collective personnel suggests, both had an ear for a supporting cast and a functional arrangement, as well as due reverence for the source material. In sum, one for the five-foot vocal shelf. The elusive Pleasure was never as consistent in his later recordings, where his voice shows wear – although **Golden Days** (OJC1722-2) should be consulted for the booklet-notes, where he declares himself "the saviour of humanity" in the second paragraph and proceeds cosmologically to out-Ra Sun Ra.                                    **BB**

# Steve Plews                                    1961

New review
**Live 95 – Made in Manchester**  Plews (p); **Duncan Mackay** (t); **Steve Waterman** (t, flh); **Liam**
    **Kirkman** (tb); **Ed Jones, Mike Hall** (ts, as); **Chris Garrick** (vn); **Steve Berry** (b); **Peter Fairclough**
    (d). ASC Ⓕ CD6 (60 minutes). Recorded 1995.

⑦ ❽

Plews is a composer who plays piano rather than the reverse. In 1994 he was awarded an Arts Council grant to allow him to tour with his group Ascension. Despite having no formal training, he has gained recognition as a classical composer and lectures on various musically-related subjects. This CD features him with Ascension and firmly wearing his jazz hat. It shows that, while he is not extending stylistic boundaries, he is producing individualistic music. All of the compositions are his and they show him as an imaginative writer, at ease with varied time signatures and with a natural, melodic feel. The group dispatch his work effortlessly and, in Mackay, Kirkman and the more experienced Jones and Waterman, it has an impressive solo roster. Plews's own piano is tested on *Sleepwalker* but he shows he has the technique for the job. As leader of Ascension he shows that his input is into the British neo-classical (bop) movement. He can integrate a violin line into a hard-bop atmosphere as easily as he does a bustling trumpet or a svelte trombone and he deports himself musically with the nonchalance of a musical traveller who already has many successful stamps on his passport.                                    **BMcR**

# Paul Plimley

**Kaleidoscopes** Plimley (p); **Lisle Ellis** (b). hatART Ⓔ CD6117 (58 minutes) Recorded 1992.

⑥ ⑧

I wonder if Ornette is feeling his age? Within the space of a few years there have been a number of recorded tributes and reinterpretations of his music. Soon they'll be calling *Ramblin'* a jazz classic. That aside, few pianists have ever attempted to come to grips with Ornette's songs, although Paul Bley has always been partial to them. That's a good reason to welcome this pianist's long and heartfelt look into the interior workings of such witty and entertaining pieces as *Poise*, *Moon Inhabitants* and *Chronology*, as well as the more heart-on-sleeve songs such as *Beauty is a Rare Thing* and *Peace*. In fact, *Beauty* becomes a direct descendent of Monk in the version here, which is a fascinating tranformation to behold.

Plimley and bassist Ellis have a fine understanding of each other's playing and of Ornette's music. Happily there is no attempt to bend the piano to an approximation of Ornette's intensely human saxophone cry, and this completely alien instrument becomes a continual object of fascination within these songs. Plimley, a great believer in space and the value of proper phrasing, comes across as a fine interpreter of this music and an original thinker. A commendable effort.          **KS**

# Jimmy Ponder                                                  1946

**Come On Down** Ponder (g); **Houston Person** (ts); **Lonnie Smith** (org); **Winard Harper** (d); **Sammy Figuera** (perc). Muse Ⓔ MCD5375 (45 minutes). Recorded 1990.

⑥ ⑧

Ponder is not exactly a household name, but just a glance at the other major players here will make you covet this album. This is the musical territory carved out by Jimmy Smith and Kenny Burrell in the mid sixties, and with the addition of tenor player Person, we have a worthy updating of that tradition. Organist Smith (not to be confused with Lonnie Liston Smith) in fact made one of the cult Blue Note organ records in the late sixties and had a long stint with George Benson. His playing here is driving but ever tasteful (witness his sensitive backing of Ponder on the ballad *Ebb Tide*), and he knows just what effects will work for which instrument he is accompanying. Ponder himself freely admits admiration for Wes Montgomery, though his own playing on this disc has a more liberal helping of r&b than Wes mostly showed. He has an easy and complete technique, a tone which is not too mellow, and he is also a driving accompanist. Tenorist Person, who produced this session, adds some worthily meaty solos in just the right spirit: sophisticated but with fire to spare.

This is a fine mainstream jazz album masquerading as just another good'n, and is a deal better than the subsequent **Something to Ponder** (Muse), where the spark is missing.          **KS**

# Jean-Luc Ponty                                                1942

New review
**Trio HLP, Volumes 1 and 2** Ponty (v); **Eddy Louiss** (org); **Daniel Humair** (d). Dreyfus Ⓔ 191018/36510-2 (two discs, oas: 46 and 50 minutes). Recorded 1968.

⑦ ⑥

Given the level of exposure that follows from an involvement in rock, Jean-Luc Ponty is inevitably best known for his work with such stadium-filling seventies ensembles as John McLaughlin's Mahavishnu Orchestra and Frank Zappa's Mothers of Invention. However, what he brought to those bands was a powerful jazz sensibility and those who tuned into that will find much more to enjoy in this largely forgotten set of standards, recorded live at the Caméléon club in Paris in the late sixties. Reflecting the preoccupations of the period, violinists such as Leroy Jenkins had begun to investigate the avant-garde potential of their instrument, and as the fragmentation in the latter part of *So What* illustrates, Ponty was not immune to the influence (a couple of years later he would explore free playing more fully in the Jean-Luc Ponty Experience), but his unique achievement – the expansion of the jazz violin's harmonic resources – is the main business of these two volumes. His adaptation of Coltrane's tonal style to the violin is delivered here with a spirited, raw tone, and in Louiss and Humair he has two colleagues fully attuned to his vision of modern jazz. The sound suffers from the primitive location setting, but it is quite acceptable and its rough and ready quality enhances the sense of spontaneity and discovery.          **MG**

New review
**King Kong** Ponty (elvn) with a collective personnel including: **Vincent DeRosa**, **Arthur Maebe** (frh); **Jonathan Meyer** (f); **Ian Underwood** (as, ts, cond); **Ernie Watts** (as, ts); **Gene Cipriano** (ob, ehn); **Donald Christlieb** (bn); **George Duke** (p, elp); **Gene Estes** (vb, perc); **Frank Zappa** (g); **Milton Thomas** (va); **Harold Bemko** (vc); **Buell Neidlinger** (b); **Wilton Felder** (elb); **Arthur Tripp III**, **John Guerin** (d). Blue Note Ⓜ CDP7 89539-2 (44 minutes). Recorded 1971.

⑥ ⑧

This album was originally made for World Pacific records, now owned by Capitol; hence the reappearance on Blue Note, of all labels. Ponty was a prodigy who managed to sustain a meaningful musical career after youth had gone. A supreme exponent of the violin and able to play the instrument in any musical ensemble, Ponty of choice moved into the embryonic world of jazz-rock and fusion as the early parallel experiments of Frank Zappa, Jimi Hendrix, Miles Davis, Larry Coryell and Tony Williams became objects of desire for other adventurous spirits. Perhaps more comfortable in the more structured world of Zappa than the free-for-all maelstroms Miles and his ex-sidemen were soon delving into, Ponty formed a close working relationship with Zappa which produced some classic cuts on Zappa's **Hot Rats** album as well as this definitive statement of both Zappa's formalist aspirations and Ponty's improvisatory gusto and all-round musicianship. The major work here is *Music for Electric Violin and Low Budget Orchestra*, which at 19 minutes wears out its welcome long before the end through its chronic inability to decide whether it is an orchestral work featuring violin soloist or whether it is a piece for violin and rhythm with a few orchestral bits tagged on for good measure. Much better is the title track and the quasi-elegaic *Twenty Small Cigars*, featuring, along with Ponty, a smoky-sounding Ernie Watts. Zappa's sense of humour can also wear rather thin, so *America Drinks and Goes Home* is today something of a victim of its own condescension. But Ponty plays spiritedly, whatever the musical environment. The story of his career? **KS**

## Odean Pope 1938

**Out for a Walk** Pope (ts, v); **Gerald Veasley** (elb); **Cornell Rochester** (d). Moers Music Ⓟ 02072 (67 minutes). Recorded 1990

⑨ ❿

In addition to working with Max Roach since 1979, this disciple of the enigmatic Philadelphia pianist Ibn Hassan Ali now leads two bands of his own. Pope's Saxophone Choir (heard to best advantage on **The Ponderer**, Soul Note 121229-2) recalls the legend that Coltrane embraced soprano as the 'top' range he heard but could not reach on tenor. Pope, another Philadelphia tenorist of mystical bent, likewise must have been tracking down secret overtones in convening a band including nine saxes. Perhaps the best way to describe Pope's trio with Rochester polyrhythm-a-ning on drums and Veasley going one step beyond Jamaaladeen Tacuma on six-string electric bass is to ask the unexposed listener to imagine a 'harmolodic' synthesis of jazz and funk as created by Coltrane rather than Ornette Coleman. Not that Pope is especially beholden to either: if anything, he is a Sonny Rollins man, as witnessed here by the the calypso gait of the title track and the deep, athletic subtone that Pope reveals on *Zip, Part 1*. At this point, Pope owes little to any of what one assumes were his formative influences. When he does evoke Coltrane, it is deliberately, as *Philly in 3*, where the resemblance to Coltrane is not superficial; it is a matter of Pope's penetrating cry, rhythmic intensity, and harmonic reach. **FD**

## Michel Portal 1935

New review
**Cinemas** Portal (bcl, ss, ts) with a collective personnel of: **Paolo Fresu** (t); **Laurent Dehors**, **Guillaume Orti** (saxes); **Rita Marcotulli** (p, syn); **Andy Emler** (syn); **Nguyen Le** (syn, g); **Richard Galliano** (acc); **Ralph Towner** (g); **François Moutin**, **Michel Benita** (b), **Linley Marthe** (elb); **Tony Rabeson**, **Aldo Romano** (d); **Doudou N'Diaye Rose**, **Mino Cinelu** (perc); **Juan Jose Mosalini** and his **Grand Tango Orchestra**. Label Bleu Ⓟ LBLC6574 (40 minutes). Recorded 1994-5.

⑧ ❿

Behind one of the most unprepossessing CD covers of recent years lurks a very fine album and one of my personal favourites of the past 12 months. Portal is an old hand at the woodwind game, having been playing professionally in France since the fifties. By the mid sixties he was firmly identified with the nascent jazz avant-garde on both sides of the Atlantic, although he remained based in France. His classical training allowed him a more diverse musical career than many, bringing him work in classical ensembles and as a film music composer. This last occupation brings us to the album in question. The themes all come from Portal's commissioned film music work. As he puts it, "I wanted to re-orchestrate, just a bit, this passing music. I wanted to play it with jazz friends, using the language of jazz ... It's not a jazz record, but an interplay of atmospheres. It's an interaction for jazz musicians." What Portal has done here is bring some miniature structures under the microscope of spontaneous invention, each piece receiving a different line-up of musicians. Only one ensemble plays unchanged on two tracks (featuring Freu, Orti, Portal, Marcotulli, Benita and Romano), while only one theme, the remarkable *Max Mon Amour*, gets two arrestingly different treatments, the first a multi-tracked bass clarinet foray by Portal, the second a more conventional small group workout by the band listed above, where Freu and Marcotulli take the solos. There is an extraordinary degree of variety to be found here (the track *Yeleen*, featuring N'Daiye Rose and Towner, has a wildly world-music quality, while *Docteur Petiot* sticks close to classic tango), but it is clearly identifiable as being the product of one creative mind. An arresting and highly creative one at that. **KS**

# Chris Potter

**Moving In** Potter (ss, ts, bcl); **Brad Mehldau** (p); **Larry Grenadier** (b); **Billy Hart** (d). Concord Jazz
Ⓔ CCD4723 (70 minutes). Recorded 1996.

⑦ ❾

Potter came to international attention while with Red Rodney's group at the tail-end of the eighties,
quickly making a sufficient impact to begin picking up sideman work with an impressive roster of
leaders, including the Mingus Big Band and Paul Motian's Electric BeBop Band, as well as tours to
Japan with Ray Brown. Potter has yet to progress to the point where he runs a permanent unit of his
own, but he plays on this, his fourth as a leader, as if he's been in that position for some time. On six
of the nine tracks he features his tenor playing, with two soprano features (a gorgeous slow reading
of *Give Me a Kiss to Build a Dream On* being the pick of them) and one (*Chorale*) for bass clarinet.
His Coltrane roots show most clearly on soprano, although he aims at a smoother tone than his
predecessor, and occasionally achieves a conversationalism not unlike Steve Lacy at his most lyrical.
His tenor playing is more completely asssimilated, his own approach and personality shining through
the lessons learned from elders such as Rollins, Coltrane, Henderson and perhaps Dexter Gordon. His
lines are sinuous, full of subtle shifts of emphasis and beautifully judged cadences; his pacing is
unusually acute, his rhythmic interest a long way above average. Add to this a sincere interest in
swinging and fashioning out some grittily attractive melodic improvisation and you get an impressive
presence which will sustain even 70 minutes of mostly original material (the songs are good, by the
way). His backing group is excellent and close-knit (even though pianist and drummer had not met
before), but the superb recording standard reached on Potter's last Concord date, *Pure*, is not quite
matched here, the drums being somewhat compressed and at times simply too low in the mix. That
said, Potter's sound on all three instruments is superbly caught and a joy to hear. **KS**

# Bud Powell

**The Complete Blue Note and Roost Recordings** Powell (p); **Curly Russell, Tommy Potter,
George Duvivier, Paul Chambers, Sam Jones, Pierre Michelot** (b); **Max Roach, Roy Haynes, Art
Taylor, Philly Joe Jones, Kenny Clarke** (d); **Fats Navarro** (t); **Sonny Rollins** (ts); **Curtis Fuller** (tb).
Blue Note Ⓜ CDP8 30083-2 (four discs: 277 minutes). Recorded 1947-63.

✓ ⑩ ❽

Powell's Blue Note years encompass the artistic brilliance, high drama and low comedy that were all
part of his art. The early trio classics – among them *Un Poco Loco* and *Parisian Thoroughfare* – show
his mastery of the harmonic and rhythmic displacements (and speed) of Charlie Parker, and close
voicings indebted to Monk. This is bebop piano at its freshest and purest (the earliest session here is
one of two that eventually turned up on Roost). That spare trio format, broken up by one session
for quintet, and one for an odd quartet with trombone, always spotlights piano, not to dismiss
the excellent support he gets from a succession of fine rhythm sections. Given Powell's psychological problems in the fifties, there is a tendency to dismiss his later sides as sad and fumbling,
although only one encore, recorded in Paris, postdates 1958 in this collection. It is time for
re-evaluation. There is a stark and pitiless economy to the dark minor pieces he then favoured, cut
with the unexpected lightness of change-ups like his cowboy lope *Buster Rides Again* and chipper
children's song *Borderick*. Good notes by Bob Blumenthal and Alfred Lion, marred only by aggressive
typesetting design. Sound is quite good; some sides have been speed-corrected from previous
issues. **KW**

**The Complete Bud Powell on Verve** Powell (p) with the following collective personnel: **Ray
Brown, Curly Russell, George Duvivier, Percy Heath, Lloyd Trotman** (b); **Max Roach, Buddy Rich,
Art Taylor, Art Blakey, Kenny Clarke, Osie Johnson** (d). Verve Ⓜ 521 669-2 (five discs:
314 minutes). Recorded 1949-56.

✓ ❽ ❻

Powell's personal downward curve is a well-documented and immensely sad fact, and it would be vain
to pretend that all the music in this set is consistently good or at times even passable. Yet there is little
of it which doesn't inform the listener, and the best of it not only excites and overwhelms, but it is at
the very centre of modern jazz piano. It is impossible to conceive of jazz history without the impact
of such impossibly heroic miniatures such as the 1950 trio version of *Tea for Two* (there are three takes
here), taken at a murderously fast tempo at which Powell manages to articulate amazing right-hand
leaps of the imagination. These were the textbooks for a generation. Likewise the rich invention and
deep feeling of the 1951 piano solos, such as *The Last Time I Saw Paris*, *Dusky 'n' Sandy*,
*Hallucinations* and, particularly, *Parisian Thoroughfare*.

As noted above, not everything here is even near this level, and there are times when Powell is clearly
not on the same planet as his accompanists: he meanders through well-known songs and forgets the
changes, or decides to play at a slightly different tempo, or simply cannot make his fingers do what
he wants them to (try *Crazy Rhythm* from 1955, where all of these things happen). Yet the intensity
of his vision always hovers (not always the case on the more or less contemporaneous Blue Note

sessions), and even when technique deserts him, there are the feelings. A 1954 version of *It Never Entered My Mind* is heartbreakingly sad, Powell's left-hand stabbing out ugly, darkened chord alterations which don't hint at personal pain, they scream it. But not all is doom and misery: much of the more ordinary performances, from 1956 for example, find Powell quite bouncy and almost fleet, audibly enjoying himself. He also gets in a couple of Monk pastiches (*Mediocre*, *Epistrophy*) which combine great eccentricity with occasional wry touches of humour.

This essential jazz set is compiled and documented in exemplary fashion (though Powell's name could have been more prominent on the cover), its essays and interviews giving worthwhile insights into the man and the music. The inside pictures are a treat as well. If you fancy a single disc of the Verve years then **The Genius of Bud Powell** is still available. But when it comes to the overall picture don't hesitate: buy this. **KS**

---

**Jazz at Massey Hall**  Powell (p); **Charles Mingus** (b); **Max Roach** (d). Debut Ⓜ OJCCD111-2 (35 minutes). Recorded 1953.

⑧ ⑥

Recorded primarily in May 1953 by Charles Mingus, the New Jazz Society of Toronto's justly-celebrated Massey Hall concert brought together four of the giants of bebop – Parker, Gillespie, Powell and Roach – along with Mingus. One of the concert's pinnacles was the trio segment featuring Powell, Roach and Mingus. Powell, the most significant of the early bebop pianists, suffered a series of debilitating psychiatric problems from 1945 until his death. Still, his influence was felt through a handful of indelible recordings, including this stunning Massey Hall date. Obviously stirred by being reunited with his erstwhile colleagues, Powell more than rose to the occasion. His trademark fleet-fingered right-hand runs combined with pungent left-hand accompaniment liberally bedeck George Shearing's *Lullaby of Birdland*, while the influence of Art Tatum is apparent in Powell's evocative treatment of *Embraceable You*. Throughout, Powell is buoyed by the supple rhythmic undercurrents supplied by Mingus and Roach. Some tracks on this album are reputed to be from night-club performances later the same year. **CB**

# Mel Powell                                                                                          1923

---

**Mel Powell Trios: Borderline/Thigamagig**  Mel Powell (p); **Ruby Braff** (t) or **Paul Quinichette** (ts); **Bobby Donaldson** (d). Vanguard Ⓕ 662223 (62 minutes). Recorded 1954.

⑧ ⑥

The voluntary exit of Mel Powell from playing jazz was an extended torture for his fans which endured from 1954, when he last made a substantial number of recordings, until the mid sixties when he irrevocably moved his talents to what we must call serious music and taught at music colleges. He revisited our music briefly in 1986 but was then laid low by a muscular disease which has trapped his playing abilities but not his spirit nor his fertile musical mind.

Whenever he recorded, even in the awesome presence of a giant like Goodman, Powell's solos stood out as the precious metal of jazz. His clean, clipped but eloquent playing, derived but yet far removed from Earl Hines and Teddy Wilson, had total authority and it was rare for him not to dominate any session on which he played. Here are two of his best on one CD reissue, with sparse groups which allow his full talent to emerge. Powell, a swing pianist by repute, ventures firmly into his own grounds in these interpretations and spins elegant inventions on pieces like *What's New?* and his own *Bouquet*. Sprinting, stride-like piano also abounds, as on *California Here I Come*.

The young Braff, so appropriate here with his melodic style, and the more experienced Paul Quinichette can but be carried along by the great talent, although neither is intimidated. Braff went on to even greater things, but Quinichette's seven performances must be regarded as his most substantial legacy. This is probably one of the finest piano albums of them all. **SV**

# Roy Powell                                                                                          1965

---

**A Big Sky**  Powell (p, kbds); **Richard Iles** (t, flh); **Rick Taylor** (tb); **Mike Walker** (g); **Iain Dixon** (ts); **Jake Newman** (b); **Steve Gilbert** (d). Totem Ⓕ CD101 (52 minutes). Recorded 1994.

⑧ ⑧

This extraordinarily accomplished recording shows that while London was congratulating itself on being the focus of Britain's eighties jazz renaissance, rather greater things were fermenting in the north-west. Improbably, Powell thanks his studies with Harrison Birtwistle at the Royal Northern College of Music and former employers Anthony Braxton and Mike Gibbs for lending inspiration to this record. It turns out that Braxton's input was philosophical rather than stylistic, and that is no surprise given that the basis of Powell's success is a virtuosic command of harmony and orchestration and their application to jazz-rock.

Using every imaginable resource to vary texture and motive, Powell produces an endlessly compelling parade of dynamic and dramatic variation within the idiom, drawing a seemingly impossible degree of detail from the instruments at his disposal. The soloists, among them the monstrously talented Mike Walker and a beautifully poised Iain Dixon, are icing on an already unimaginably rich confection. It would be surprising if a more comprehensively conceived electric jazz record were to be issued this side of the millennium. **MG**

## Preservation Hall Jazz Band

New review
**In the Sweet Bye and Bye** Wendell Brunious (t); **Dr Michael White** (cl); **Frank Demond** (tb); **Rickie Monie, Ellis Marsalis** (p); **Narvin Kimball** (bj); **Benjamin Jaffe** (b, helicon); **Joseph Lastie** (d). Columbia Ⓕ SK62363 (63 minutes). Recorded 1994-5.

⑥ ❼

Too often, the New Orleans jazz heard in the Crescent City today is an amalgam of ageing incompetence, stylistic incongruity and bad taste. Those who can play often lack a true affinity to the music and the band that performs at Preservation Hall sometimes has combined masters such as the late Willie and Percy Humphrey with inept square pegs in extremely round holes. This 1994 recording date avoids the worst aspects of these disasters. In Brunious it has an assured lead, a trumpeter schooled outside the idiom but now very much at home with it. His solos have genuine shape and make consistent, creative progress. White plays with moving commitment at slow tempo and, despite a somewhat stiff rhythmic concept, is an adroit ensemble voice. Demond has not advanced instrumentally over the years but he plays a useful tail-gate trombone and is important to the band's collective aspirations. The New Orleans bounce is achieved by a rhythm section in which the excellent Marsalis appears only twice. Kimball's faster solos bear a regrettable similarity to George Formby but on *He Touched Me* he redeems himself. The vocals are uniformly dreadful but the overall impression is of revivalist music, distanced from its true source by some 75 years but played with conviction and likely to be better than most. **BMcR**

## André Previn                                                          1929

**Shelly Manne and His Friends: My Fair Lady/André Previn and His Pals: West Side Story** Manne (d); Previn (p); Leroy Vinnegar, Red Mitchell (b); Manne (d). Contemporary/Ace Ⓜ CDCOPD942 (74 minutes). Recorded 1956/9.

④ ⑥

One of the favourite sports of jazz reviewers in the late fifties was (after Brubeck-bashing) the act of Previn-bashing. Brubeck-bashing was more fun, because Brubeck was the bigger star and had a higher profile, but Previn-bashing was also much enjoyed because Previn had committed the sin of being on the LP which sold more than any other in jazz history up to that time. It was **My Fair Lady**. To bash Previn you said he was facile, shallow, fleet, superficial and all those other things that suggest he was not drenched in the blues. You don't need to be drenched in the blues to do a version of *My Fair Lady*, of course, and it is hard to see now why everyone got so steamed up, or indeed why everyone bought this and the follow-up **West Side Story** record. Jazz musicians don't make records of 'the music from the show' any more (classical conductors do that now). Classical conductors don't make swinging (but facile) piano records any more; at least not often. Jazz records don't sell a million copies. How long ago it all was. But you may care to note that a better album of the *Fair Lady* tunes was made in the eighties by Ruby Braff and Dick Hyman. Now, that deserved to sell a million. **MK**

## Bobby Previte                                                        1957

New review
**Too Close to the Pole** Previte (d, v); **Cuong Vu** (t, v); **Curtis Hasselbring** (tb, v); **Andrew D'Angelo** (as, bcl, v); **Jamie Saft** (p, elp, org, clav, v); **Lindsey Horner** (elb, v). Enja Ⓕ ENJ9306-2 (72 minutes). Recorded 1996.

✓                                                                        ⑨ ⑨

From his initial mid-eighties recordings on the European label Sound Aspects onwards, composer/drummer/leader Bobby Previte has occupied a special place in contemporary music. His influences – like those of many of his so-called Downtown contemporaries – embrace everything from minimalism through avant-rock to film music, but at the centre of his music there is always a highly effective bustling, jazz-based energy. His various projects range from the overtly programmatic (**Music for the Moscow Circus**, recorded for Gramavision in 1990) through more straightforward jazz fare (generally interpreted by the various manifestations of his band Weather Clear, Track Fast) to ambitious, through-composed multi-textured music (played by another of Previte's ongoing bands, Empty Suits). **Too Close to the Pole** features the septet Weather Clear, Track Fast on five Previte originals, plus a stately arrangement of *The Countess's Bedroom* from Tchaikovsky's opera *Queen of Spades*, plus a hidden bonus track. Previte's compositions privilege textural variety and the slow journey towards rousing climaxes over jazz's conventional theme-solos-theme structure, but fans of all the above mentioned styles from which Previte draws inspiration, particularly admirers of the woozy rumbustiousness of Charles Mingus, will find something to their taste in this heady brew. **CP**

# Sammy Price

**And His Texas Blusicians 1929-41** Price (p, v, wbd, ldr); with a collective personnel including: **Douglas Finnell, Joe Brown, Eddie Mullens, Shad Collins, Bill Johnson, Chester Boone, Emmett Berry** (t); **Bert Johnson, Floyd Brady, Ray Hogan** (tb); **Lem Johnson** (cl, v); **Fess Williams** (cl, as); **Don Stovall** (as); **Ray Hill, Lester Young, Skippy Williams** (ts); **Percy Darensburg, Duke Jones, Bass Hill, Billy Taylor** (b); **Wilbert Kirk, Doc West, Herb Cowens, J.C. Heard** (d); **Effie Scott, Ruby Smith, Jack Meredith** (v). Classics Ⓜ 696 (71 minutes). Recorded 1929-41.

**⑧ ❻**

Price never exactly hit the headlines in his long career, but early on he was a gifted and tasteful swing-style pianist and small-group leader in the manner of Earl Hines and Count Basie. At various times after the Second World War he veered first towards out-and-out boogie woogie and later to jump-style r&b (with King Curtis on tenor). This disc contains all his sessions as a leader up to 1942, and it can be argued that this is the cream of his jazz-based work. Certainly the bands are tight, swinging and entertaining, with altoist Don Stovall contributing some fine solos on the 1940 sessions. Price also plays well on the 1941 dates featuring Lester Young, not then long out of the Basie band, and it is fair to say that the four sides featuring Young are consciously apeing the Basie small-group approach of the time. Price is certainly not an original stylist, but his well-tailored music and tidy arrangements make this a consistently entertaining disc. The sound quality is variable but bearable. **KS**

# Julian Priester

**New review**
**Keep Swingin'** Priester (tb); **Jimmy Heath** (ts); **Tommy Flanagan** (p); **Sam Jones** (b); **Elvin Jones** (d). Riverside Ⓜ OJCCD1863-2 (36 minutes). Recorded 1960.

**⑧ ❾**

Orrin Keepnews suggests in his insert-note that Priester had managed to escape the influence of J.J. Johnson at the time when he made this album. The first track then opens with a trombone solo which is one of the closest evocations of Johnson you could wish to hear! The early trombonists who escaped such a fate were Benny Green and Willie Dennis. The later ones were led by Bob Brookmeyer and Jimmy Knepper. This is not to censure Priester who was one of a generation of young players who, like Jimmy Cleveland, were blessed not only with Johnson's agility but also with beautiful tones. Priester's worth can be measured by the fact that, like Benny Green and Brookmeyer, he was invited to join the Duke Ellington Band; Priester played for Ellington for six months. He and Heath make an urgent and powerful front line and the five originals plus *Just Friends* and *Once in a While* provide a good platform for them. Three of the originals are features for trombone and piano with Sam and Elvin Jones masking up a rhythm section which, for the period, was as good as you could get. *Bob T's Blues* is a potent slow blues which could have come from any era and shows off the richness of Priester's tone, which is mellow rather than dry like Johnson's. The phrasing here is once again redolent of Johnson, though. Flanagan is such a consistently good improviser that it only needs to be said that he, like everyone else here, is exceptionally well recorded. **SV**

# Brian Priestley

**New review**
**Brian Priestley Salutes 15 Jazz Piano Greats** Priestley (p); on five tracks add **Don Rendell** (ss, ts). Spirits of Jazz Ⓕ CD09 0995 (66 minutes). Recorded 1995.

**⑦ ❼**

Not all that many jazz critics are also active jazz musicians, and of those who are, few are brave enough to record an entire album of predominantly solo piano. This collection by Brian Priestley (who is joined on five of the 15 tracks by saxophonist Don Rendell) is more than simply a brave attempt, it's an absorbing and interesting cross-section of the most innovative figures in the jazz piano canon. Most tracks are interpretations of pieces by other pianists, the balance are Priestley's own compositions celebrating Fats Waller and Erroll Garner. There are plenty of pianistic in-jokes, as one might expect from someone so immersed in the jazz tradition, so spontaneous and improvised quotes appear here and there throughout the whole disc. Overall, though, Priestley emerges as his own man. Two of the slower tracks on the disc steal the honours – a tender reading of Strayhorn's *Star-Crossed Lovers* with Rendell on tenor and a delicate version of McCoy Tyner's *You Taught My Heart to Sing*. **AS**

# Louis Prima

**Let's Swing It** Prima (t, v, ldr) with **His New Orleans Gang**: collective personnel includes: **George Brunies** (tb); **Sidney Arodin, Eddie Miller, Pee Wee Russell** (cl); **Claude Thornhill, Frank Pinero**

(p); **George Van Eps**, **Nappy Lamare**, **Gerry McAdams** (g); **Artie Shapiro**, **Jack Ryan** (b); **Stan King**, **Ray Bauduc** (d). Charly ⑧ CDCD1160 (65 minutes). Recorded 1934/5.

⑦ ❻

Prima is not these days primarily associated with jazz. His latter-day career in Hollywood and Vegas and on the Latin side of the music entertainment business constitute the more lasting memory. But his small groups of the thirties were an adroit mixture of a Dixieland not dissimilar to Bob Crosby's with the enjoyable hamming which was to gradually point the leader on a different career path. His trumpet playing was simple and entirely under the spell of Armstrong, but it was strong and effective when carrying a melody, while his vocals were always engaging, to say the least. Then there is the not inconsiderable achievement of having spawned *Sing, Sing, Sing* in 1936 – a song now indissolubly associated with Benny Goodman's dominance of the Swing Era. This chronological collection pulls up 12 months short of Prima's version, but there are plenty of jolly up-tempo rave-ups here to compensate. The clarinettists tend to impress most, but the real stars are the rhythm section, whose precise and buoyant teamwork make this a very disciplined and swinging outfit. Swing may be something of a misnomer if applied rigorously, because the two-beat rhythm points clearly to the Dixie mentioned above, but the music remains very danceable indeed. Although the playing time and price are attractive, why did Charly not give personnel details? The above listing is from Rust. **KS**

## Marcus Printup

**Unveiled** Printup (t); **Stephen Riley** (ts); **Marcus Roberts** (p); **Reuben Rogers** (b); **Jason Marsalis** (d). Blue Note Ⓕ CDP8 37302-2 (64 minutes). Recorded 1996.

⑦ ❾

This is a curiously conservative follow-up album to Printup's first for Blue Note. It shows the trumpeter to be supremely assured as a tehnician and comfortably ahead of his own fingers when it comes to thinking through his own improvisatory phrases, but many of the choices he is making as a player are ones reached by trumpeters fully 50 years ago: perhaps the retro neo-classicist movement has now moved beyond hard bop and Clifford Brown to the original boppers, especially Navarro? The other ghost often being invoked, especially on Printup's own compositions, is the soulful and brassy Lee Morgan, always an imaginative player and a fine role model if one were to be sought. Make no mistake – Printup is an attractive player, and nothing is wrong here. His band functions with grace and feeling (Riley sounds like a hybrid of Gonsalves and Mobley: yet another well-researched 'new' confluence of styles) and Roberts, of course, is masterful. As with so many of these classicist albums, however, there is a sense of emptiness by the end, as if the bottle and its label is beautiful but the wine has already been drunk. **KS**

## Clarence Profit                                              1912-44

**All the Solo and Trio Sides Plus Washboard Tracks** Profit (p solos) on six tracks; on a further six tracks add: **Billy Moore** (g); **Ben Brown** (b). On four tracks **Jimmy Shirley** (g) replaces **Moore**. On two tracks **Profit** (p) with **Harold Randolph** (kazoo); **Teddy Bunn** (g); **Bruce Johnson** (wbd, v); **Gladys Bentley** (v). On two tracks **Profit** (p) with **Taft Jordan**, **Dave Page** (t); **Ben Smith** (cl, as); **Carl Wade** (ts); **Steve Washington** (bj, g); **Ghost Howell** (b); **Jake Fenderson** (wbd, v); **Eddie Foster** (v). Memoir Ⓕ CDMOIR504 (62 minutes). Recorded 1930-40.

⑧ ❻

Jazz hagiography abounds with tales of unknown talent, many of the stories probably apocryphal, but in the case of Profit we have a genuinely underrated and influential figure who made only a handful of record dates. Memoir have done a considerable service by releasing virtually all of his known work on this CD (it is possible that he plays on other as yet untraced washboard sides) which reinforces the public opinions of men who heard him play. Oscar Peterson has credited Profit with being his main inspiration when he formed his own trio while Teddy Wilson placed Clarence's work immediately after that of Tatum, Waller and Hines. On the evidence of the solo and trio performances he was well ahead of his time both in conception and execution. Some of the runs and cadences are very Tatum-like on the solo titles while George Wallington's admiration for Profit is manifest in the first chorus of George's 1951 version of *I Didn't Know What Time It Was,* for this is virtually a note-for-note transcription of Clarence's solo. Profit is less visible on the four washboard titles but they are extremely good fun. The excellent and very informative notes are by another jazz pianist, Britain's Pat Hawes, making this a highly recommended release made up entirely of fascinating and stimulating keyboard playing. **AM**

## Dudu Pukwana                                              1938-90

**Cosmic Chapter 90** Zila: Pukwana (as, ss); **Lucky Ranku** (g); **Eric Richards** (b); **Roland Perrin** (kbds); **Steve Argüelles** (d); **Fats Ramoba Mogoboya** (cga); **Pinise Saul** (v). Ah Um Ⓕ 005 (59 minutes). Recorded 1989.

⑥ ❼

Many observers felt that Pukwana's records did not always reproduce the fervour of his live performances. Born in Port Elizabeth, he came to London as part of Chris McGregor's Blue Notes in 1965. He played an important part in the musical revolution of the late sixties and seventies; although he was never really part of the free jazz scene, he had a natural affinity with its players and, when the circumstances dictated, could identify with the more challenging principles. As straw boss of the Brotherhood of Breath big band he made a major contribution and both there and in the Blue Notes combo he enjoyed many memorable moments. This CD offers a typical performance by his group, Zila. This edition is a septet; Pukwana is its most creative instrumental voice and, despite the variety of its rhythmic flow he responds to its complexity with a wave-clipping line full of natural grace. World music devotees will warm to Saul's spirited vocal invocations but the more committed jazz listener might regard her input as space wasted.  **BMcR**

## Don Pullen

1941-95

**New Beginnings**  Pullen (p); **Gary Peacock** (b); **Tony Williams** (d). Blue Note Ⓔ CDP7 91785-2
   (49 minutes). Recorded 1988.

✔️

⑩ ❿

Although Pullen had previously recorded solo albums, as well as duets with the drummer Milford Graves and the tenor saxophonist George Adams, this was his first recording to utilize conventional trio instrumentation. But its instrumentation is the only thing conventional about **New Beginnings**, a disc deserving a place alongside classic trio recordings by Duke Ellington, Art Tatum, Herbie Nichols, Bud Powell, Thelonious Monk and Paul Bley. Pullen's genius lies in incorporating the percussive techniques associated with avant-garde piano into a mainstream setting; he is the after-the-fact transitional figure between Horace Silver and Cecil Taylor. His peripatetic keyboard style ensures variety, not only from track to track, but from phrase to phrase – as on *Once Upon a Time*, for example, where he spins an expansive waltz, then skewers it and gradually smashes it into little pieces. **New Beginnings** also reaffirms Pullen's status as a versatile composer who obviously learned a trick or two from Charles Mingus. The infectiously syncopated *Jana's Delight* could pass as a homage to Ahmad Jamal. *Reap the Whirlwind* recalls the agitated, open-ended performances that Pullen recorded with Giuseppi Logan in the sixties, but it is much better focused. In their alert responses to Pullen, Peacock and Williams show a resourcefulness that recalls the bassist's work with Bill Evans and Albert Ayler and the drummer's work with Miles Davis. Not another tedious exercise in eighties classicism – just a classic. (The timings add up to just over 37 minutes, although the actual total is as listed above. A rare instance of a label short-changing itself, rather than the consumer!)  **FD**

New review
**Sacred Common Ground**  Pullen (p); **Joseph Bowie** (tb); **Carlos Ward** (as, ts); **Santi DeBriano**
   (b); **J.T. Lewis** (d); **Mor Thiam** (perc); **Chief Cliff Singers** (v). Blue Note Ⓔ CDP8 32800-2
   (47 minutes). Recorded 1995.

⑦ ❾

This album was finished only a matter of weeks before Pullen's death from cancer, and in the light of some brilliantly introspective playing from Pullen on *Common Ground* it would be easy to see elements of it as a conscious attempt at his own epitaph. Pullen was always a player with a roving, restless musical imagination who maintained the iconoclasm of his early mentor, Charles Mingus. This unusual and compelling disc is his response to a commission from a Montana-based arts organization to create a score for a dance piece combining jazz with Native American music. A few tracks, including the opening *Eagle Staff*, suffer from the very range of Pullen's interests, the Indian chanting competing with the rhythms of Senegal and Brazil as well as straightforward jazz to provide more of a profusion or confusion than merely fusion. Elsewhere the varied sources combine into something that is the very essence of Pullen's beliefs about music: the most successful sections create their own landscape, the harshness of Kootenai and Salish chants blending with Latin percussion and hard-edged jazz to encapsulate the Native American experience in *River Song* and *Reservation Blues*. Here and there, apart from some measured and graceful solos, Pullen's piano emerges from the *mêlée* with some anguished swirls. He did not live to see the summer tour by the Garth Fagan Dance ensemble, but his last work proved to be something that they could be truly inspired by.  **AS**

## Bernard Purdie

1939

New review
**Soul to Jazz**  Purdie (d, ldr); **WDR Big Band** featuring: **Randy Brecker** (flh); **Nils Landgren** (tb);
   **Michael Brecker**, **Eddie Harris** (ts); **Dean Brown** (g); **Dave King** (elb); **Martin Moss** (v); **Gil
   Goldstein**, **Tom Malone** (arr). ACT Ⓕ 9242-2 (65 minutes). Recorded 1996.

⑥ ❿

To call this album schizoid is to put it mildly. Track one is a straightforward big band version of Bobby Timmons's *Moanin'*; track two is a funked-up vocal-plus-big band arrangement of Steve

Wonder's **Superstition**. Next up is a large-ensemble Cajun favourite, *Iko Iko*, replete with solo accordion. After Horace Silver's *Señor Blues* we get a full-blown slow soul treatment of *When a Man Loves a Woman* (maybe this track explains the presence of a fully naked female torso in the fold-out part of the CD booklet), Percy Sledge-type vocals and all. What's goin' on, Bernard? Well, of course Purdie has always been at home in both types of music, playing with Aretha Franklin, King Curtis, Albert Ayler and Dizzy Gillespie among others, so it's only natural that he would want to go both ways on a big-band opportunity such as this. Just how many listeners would be enthusiastic about such polarizations I'm not at all sure, especially as the arrangements of the soul pieces hardly disturb their original nature sufficiently for one to not have an immediate reaction of reaching the first and best down from the shelves for another airing. A shame, because the jazz tracks (including a hip workout on Eddie Harris's *Freedom Jazz Dance* with Harris himself soloing) are immensely enjoyable and infectious enough alone to have given Purdie all the airwave exposure he could need. **KS**

## Marc Puricelli

New review
**The Shade** Puricelli (p, kbds); **Erik Friedlander** (b); **Avery Sharpe** (d); **Tracy Silverman** (vn); **Turtle Island String Quartet**; **Vanessa Rubin** (v). MusicMasters Ⓕ 65146-2. Recorded 1995.

⑦ ❽

A glance at the personnel listing will tell you that something is up: rarely do we find violinists and string quartets as the sole (and solo) companions of a jazz piano trio. It is becoming increasingly common to mix compositional techniques and styles associated with Debussy and, say, Copland, with jazz performance and improvisational practice. The dominant mood is perhaps best described as pastoral, hardly a surprise given the instrumentation, with the bass (alternating between acoustic and electric) and drums giving the music urgency in pieces such as *Walk On* and *Downtown Earth*, the latter enjoying a healthy backbeat from time to time. Vanessa Rubin appears on just one track, *The Madcap Laughs*, and acquits herself well. Much of this music reminds one of a sixties collaboration between Gary McFarland and pianist Steve Kuhn, **The October Suite** (Impulse! – nla), only updated slightly in its idiom. Interesting may sound a put down, but this album is unusually so. **KS**

## Flora Purim 1942

New review
**Speed of Light** Purim (v); **Airto Moreira** (d, perc); **Jose Neto, Ricardo Silveira** (g); **Giovanni Hidalgo** (cga); **Changuito, Freddie Santiago** (perc); **Billy Cobham** (d); **Jovino Santos Neto, Krishna Booker, Domenico Camardella** (kbds); **Alphonso Johnson** (b); **Gary Brown, Randy Tico** (elb); **Diana Moreira** (perc, v); **Randall Parmley** (f). B&W Music Ⓕ 044 (52 minutes). Recorded 1994.

⑦ ❾

It makes sense that Purim and Moreira were rediscovered for the seventies-obsessed English rhythm mavens. It's not just that they're true relics of an old lifestyle; they really did devise a kind of geographically-indistinct trance-ambient that worked well for them in the George Duke period on records like **Open Your Eyes**. Purim's first recording in five years, **Speed of Light** continues their best and most shamelessly groovy aspects. It's still a fusion, but a floating, weightless kind, without a blizzard of notes. Her best passages are the wordless ones; Purim can still scat effectively, though the extreme edges of her voice have eroded and she has to ease in and out of high registers. Much of the album is updated versions of what you've heard from them before, but it also ranges over more purely rhythmic pieces like *This World*, thick with different drum timbres, and the relaxed dance groove, *Light as My Flo*. High production value throughout, and despite lapses into World-music kitsch, the truly spaced-out nature of the main collaborators keeps it fresh. **BR**

## Nick Purnell

**Onetwothree** Purnell (arr, ldr); **Kenny Wheeler, Paul Edmonds** (t, flh); **Mike Gibbs** (tb); **Ashley Slater** (btb, tba); **Ken Stubbs, Julian Argüelles** (ss, as, ts); **Django Bates** (kbds); **John Taylor** (p); **Mike Walker** (g); **Laurence Cottle** (elb); **Mick Hutton** (b); **Peter Erskine** (d); **Dave Adams** (perc). Ah Um Ⓕ 006 (57 minutes). Recorded 1990.

⑦ ❽

Purnell has gathered an impressive cast and given them material with which to show off their abilities as section men and soloists across a wide range of styles. His writing is not busy (the rhythm section is very active, but I doubt that it is too precisely scored in that fashion: most of the time I would presume directions and patterns rather than notes on paper), but it is full of colour and character, has a big personality and reaches across the gap between the speakers and the listener quite successfully.

Of the soloists, Wheeler surprises as usual, and Julian Argüelles continues to impress with his logic and consistency.

The strange thing about this album is that it is so identifiably from Britain: there is a definite humour or feel to the music which one only finds in Britain, and its elements include whimsy, surrealism, self-deprecation and a type of manic high spirits which none the less avoids the extremism of some continental European countries' conceptions. There is also an eclecticism which comes of the unusual cultural mix to be found in Britain. All this may sound by-the-by, but it helps explain the richness and boldness of the instrumental writing and soloing. The execution is not always spot on (there are the occasional sax section wobbles), but it is always done with commendable spirit. **KS**

## Tony Purrone                                                  1954

New review
**Electric Poetry** Purrone (elg); **Dave Anderson** (elb); **Ray Marchica** (d); **Bob Mintzer** (ts, bcl, EWI); **Ray Grappone** (perc). B&W Ⓔ BW028 (63 minutes). Recorded 1992.

⑤ ❽

As the title suggests, this album explores the tonalities offered by electric guitar and electric bass. Bob Mintzer plays tenor on one track, bass clarinet on another and synthesizer on a couple more, and the drums and percussion add additional timbres. Purrone, a veteran of the Heath Brothers band and a versatile guitarist who has worked with many other household names, has a good stylistic range and his solos range from the fleet to the introspective, for the most part above Anderson's grumbling six-string bass, making the most of its very lowest register. Anderson's playing is impressive and when he shifts up the fretboard for a middle-register solo he produces a warm guitar-ish tone that neatly complements Purrone's sound. Indeed the teamwork between these two players is what makes the album, although Mintzer's bass clarinet, holding down the bass riff with Anderson on *Cheeks* and then moving into a menacing solo before Purrone's own rock-tinged outing is another highlight. All the pieces are written by Purrone, and overall the electric landscape needs a little more variety to qualify for a higher rating, although most tracks taken on an individual level have something to commend them. **AS**

## Ike Quebec                                                  1918-63

**The Art of Ike Quebec** Quebec (ts); with a collective personnel of **Bennie Green** (tb); **Stanley Turrentine** (ts); **Sonny Clark** (p); **Freddie Roach, Earl Vandyke** (org); **Kenny Burrell, Grant Green, Willie Jones** (g); **Paul Chambers, Milt Hinton, Sam Jones, Wendell Marshall, Butch Warren** (b); **Art Blakey, Willie Bobo, Al Harewood, Billy Higgins, Wilbert Hogan, Philly Joe Jones** (d); **Garvin Masseaux** (chekere). Blue Note Ⓜ CDP7 99178-2 (64 minutes). Recorded 1961/2.

⑧ ❽

A heavy-toned tenor from the Hawkins/Webster lineage, Ike Quebec made nearly all of his best music in two brief recording stints for Blue Note. The first, from 1944-6, yielded the hit single *Blue Harlem*, but was followed by years of obscurity and drug problems. The second, from 1959 until his death from lung cancer in 1963, flowered into a swan-song of remarkable beauty and eloquence. In this period, Quebec recorded more singles, guested on LPs by artists such as Sonny Clark, Grant Green and Jimmy Smith, and made a series of outstanding albums as leader: **Heavy Soul, Blue and Sentimental, It Might as Well Be Spring, Easy Living** and **Soul Samba**, all but one of which were released in his lifetime.

This compilation is drawn almost entirely from those albums. The emphasis is on ballads, which were Quebec's *forte*, plus a couple of blues. Most are quartet tracks, nearly half of them with organ. A distinctive stylist, Quebec's deep-hewn sound was shaped by a delicacy of phrasing that forbade indulgence or sentimentality. The disc is a treasure-house of delights – the sensuous freight of his tone on *It Might as Well be Spring*, the sinuous elegance of *I've Got a Crush on You*, the tender fervour he imparts to *Flavela* – but it is still small recompense for not having the original albums on CD, although it is now possible to find CD reissues of **Heavy Soul** and **Soul Samba**, which are part of the Connoiseur series of Blue Note reissues (meaning they won't be around for long). **GL**

## Alvin Queen                                                  1950

**I'm Back** Queen (d); **Fablo Morgera** (t, flh); **Amadou Diallo** (ts); **James Weldman** (p); **Fred Hunter** (b). Nilva Ⓔ CDNQ3421 (62 minutes). Recorded 1992.

⑥ ❽

Drummer Alvin Queen ran a record label, Nilva, for most of the eighties, but got caught in between formats when it came to the exodus from vinyl to CD. Previously he had garnered a reputation with Stanley Turrentine before settling permanently in Switzerland and leading his own groups. His albums as a leader have all been on Nilva, but this one is the first to appear on CD. It is a brand-new session, recorded with his current group, and while bassist Fred Hunter is an old friend, newcomers

Diallo and Morgera both impress. Diallo is one of the few of his generation not to pay an excess of tribute to Coltrane in his solos: he has a tone and approach quite removed from that of the late giant's, and has ideas of his own. Queen is a model drummer in many ways, laying down appropriate and perfectly-grooved beats on every track. On *Sketch* he inserts a Blakey-type backbeat which instantly recalls the Messengers, while the drum solo, *Much Elvin and Max*, is exactly what its title would lead you to expect, apart from the fact that it's just a little over two-and-a-half minutes long. An excellently-paced and well-crafted record. **KS**

# Paul Quinichette
1916-83

**New review**

**The Kid from Denver** Quinichette (ts) with: **Joe Newman, Renaul Jones, Thad Jones** (t); **Henry Coker** (tb); **Bill Graham** (as, bs); **Nat Pierce** (p); **Freddie Green** (g); **Eddie Jones** (b); **Sonny Payne** (d); **The Gene Roland Septet** and **Sextet: Gene Roland, John Carisi** (t); **Rob Swope** (tb); **Dick Meldonian** (as); **Nat Pierce** (p); **Dudley Watson, Wendell Marshall, Oscar Pettiford** (b); **Walter Noland, Sonny Payne, Osie Johnson** (d). Biograph Ⓕ BCD136 (53 minutes). Recorded 1957-9.

⑦ ❼

If he could return to the time before he had heard Lester Young, then the listener could be forgiven for adjudging Paul Quinichette to be one of the greatest of all saxophonists. But he based his style so closely on Young's that he became his own worst enemy and was doomed to obscurity, despite the fact that he was an outstanding player who had a lot of originality as well as Lester in his improvising. His best platform was the Count Basie band of the fifties, where he was one of the star soloists. Moved from the Basie rostrum he tended to have anonymous and unworthy backings, but the first eight of the 12 tracks here show him five and six years after he had left Basie working with a stripped-down version of the Count's band. The majority of the numbers are features for his eloquence and the band, powered by the intuitive Sonny Payne, opens up to give solo space to Joe Newman, Thad Jones, the lumbering baritone of Charlie Fowlkes and an on-form Henry Coker. Nat Pierce was the usual Basie sound-alike and at this period Quinichette was actually working in Pierce's own band. Guitarist Green was also hired by trumpeter Gene Roland for the four similarly Basie tracks under his name and the rhythm section once again includes Pierce, this time complemented by the presence of Pettiford and Gus Johnson. The arrangements for the tracks under Quinichette's own name were originally written for the Basie band by men like Manny Albam and Ernie Wilkins. Roland, who wrote the inspired music for Kenton's **Adventures in Blues** album, did his own arranging and his scores are outstanding. **SV**

# Boyd Raeburn
1913-66

**New review**

**The Transcription Performances 1946** Raeburn (bs, ldr); **Ray Linn, Dale Pierce, Nelson Shellady, Zeke Zarchey, Carl Groen** (t); **Britt Woodman, Ollie Wilson, Freddy Zito, Hal Smith** (tb); **Wilbur Schwartz** (as, cl); **Harry Klee** (as, f); **Ralph Lee, Lucky Thompson, Gus McReynolds** (ts); **Dodo Marmarosa** (p); **Tony Rizzi** (g); **Joe Mondragon, Harry Babasin** (b); **Jackie Mills** (d); **David Allyn, Ginny Powell** (v). Hep Ⓕ CD42 (72 minutes). Recorded 1945-6.

⑦ ❽

Prior to 1945, the Boyd Raeburn Orchestra was a somewhat nondescript outfit, providing semi-sweet arrangements for dancers, featuring the Hodges-inspired altoist Johnny Bothwell and Ben Webster devotee Frank Socolow on tenor, occasionally spicing things up with a Count Basie-style flag-waver, usually from the pen of Ed Finckel. The story goes that a 1944 fire burned up many of the band's charts, and after Finckel left to join Gene Krupa, Raeburn relied more than ever on the bizarre talents of George Handy to redesign the band's identity. The material collected on this CD is not the studio recordings originally cut for Guild or Signature (later reissued on Musicraft) or Jewell (ditto, on Savoy), but performances waxed by the Standard Transcription Service specifically for radio play. So while there are a few of the earlier hard-driving swingers, like *Tush* and *Two Spoos in an Igloo*, many of the tunes are either novelty vocals, like the hipster *Are You Livin' Old Man?* and the Bing Crosby hit, *Personality,* sung by the suave and sexy Ginny Powell, or ballads such as *I Only Have Eyes for You* crooned by David Allyn. Though Bothwell and Socolow had both broken ranks by this time, the 1945 performances are energized by the marvellously oblique tenor sax of Lucky Thompson. None of the soloists at the 1946 session are his equal, but by this point Handy's arrangements are the real star. For example, he takes the title of *Out of This World* literally, disintegrating the melody with multiple keys, dissonances, strange disconnected background figures and odd interludes. Compositions like *Dalvatore Sally* and *Cartaphilius* are concert pieces as ambitious and unusual as anything Stan Kenton devised – with stop-and-start themes, fanfares and flourishes, merry-go-round rhythms, and frequent mood shifts. Today some sound impressive and others merely silly, but they do anticipate such jazz mavericks as Bob Graettinger and John Zorn. For a more complete picture of the historically undervalued Raeburn band, including the earlier unit with Bothwell, the later, lush writing of Johnny Richards, and more of Handy's outrageous concoctions (such as the psychedelic *Over the Rainbow*) one must look elsewhere; for now, this is the fullest single disc compilation available. **AL**

# Ma Rainey

1886-1939

**Ma Rainey** Rainey (v); **Joe Smith**, **Shirley Clay** (c); **Louis Armstrong** (t); **Charlie Green**, **Ike Rodgers** (tb); **Buster Bailey** (cl); **Coleman Hawkins** (bs); **Fletcher Henderson**, **Jimmy Blythe**, **'Georgia Tom' Dorsey** (p); **Tampa Red** (g, kz); **Charlie Dixon** (j); **Kaiser Marshall** (d). Milestone Ⓜ MCD47021-2 (72 minutes). Recorded 1924-8.

⑦ ❻

Evaluating Ma Rainey will never be easy. Early recording processes sapped the strength and weight of her voice, and even this tolerably remastered collection requires the listener to enhance the music with imagination.

Like Bessie Smith, Rainey worked almost entirely at slow or slowish tempos; unlike her, she seldom used anything but the conventional 12-bar blues verse, so her recordings are varied only by their subject-matter and accompaniments. Sombre or violent narratives predominate, as in *Chain Gang Blues*, *Black Eye Blues* and *Sweet Rough Man* ("every night for five years I've got a beatin' from my man ..."), though in *Prove It On Me* she asserts with spirit her right to choose her own sexual identity. Some of these songs so fixed themselves in the minds of their first listeners that whole verses would turn up, years later, in the compositions of other blues singers.

The earlier tracks employ line-ups with two or three horn-players, notably Armstrong (*See See Rider*) and Joe Smith, while the latest put Rainey with the piano and slide guitar of Georgia Tom and Tampa Red – who also accompany her in the Tub Jug Washboard Band, a novelty combination with banjo, jug and kazoo. **Ma Rainey's Black Bottom** (Yazoo 1071) is better remastered but contains only 14 tracks and is full price, giving the Milestone, weighing in at 24 tracks and a few pounds cheaper, the nod for value. **TR**

# Mark Ramsden

New review

**Above the Clouds** Ramsden (ss, as); **Steve Lodder** (org). Breathe Ⓟ 001 (67 minutes). Recorded 1995.

⑦ ❽

Inventive, unusual, intriguing, complex, unclassifiable, and original are all words that spring to mind, prompted by this collection of duets recorded in a suitably churchy atmosphere by Dill Katz at St Thomas's, Clapton Common, London. Ramsden's snaking soprano intertwines with the baroque tones of the church's eighteenth-century organ to create a personal and powerful statement by both musicians. The final track breaks the mood slightly with a string arrangement by Roland Perrin accompanying Ramsden in a lament for his late father, but even this is in keeping with the slightly sombre tenor of the album. Not all the music is by the duettists, since they also include some genuine baroque music for good measure, with the soprano taking a convincing solo role in music by Fiocco, Albinoni and John Stanley. Ramsden and Lodder flit from the past to the present in a series of smooth transitions, and produce their most effective music on their own compositions, notably Ramsden's *While the Pulse Still Beats* on which he plays alto. This partnership is as effective as Lodder's long-term musical relationship with Andy Sheppard, and the exploration of both men's common musical heritage provides territory all too often left untouched by improvising musicians. It is also worth noting the virtuoso qualities in Ramsden's two unaccompanied solos. **AS**

# Jimmy Raney

1927-95

New review

**A** Raney (g); **John Wilson** (t); **Hall Overton** (p); **Teddy Kotick** (b); **Art Mardigan** or Nick Stabulas (d). Prestige Ⓜ OJCCD1706-2 (47 minutes). Recorded 1954-5.

⑧ ❼

It took a while for Jimmy Raney, by all accounts not among nature's publicity hounds, to get the recognition he deserved. He was probably the first guitarist after Charlie Christian to develop a horn-like method of phrasing that was different, an approach that, consciously or not, pointed to the way Wes Montgomery phrased a few years later. It didn't help that Raney was not around much during the sixties: as his beautifully judged contributions to the 1956 Teddy Charles Tentet make clear, he would have easily justified the superior production values bestowed upon Montgomery and Kenny Burrell. Instead, he tended to get blowing dates such as the two here. The four quartet tracks include an extra guitar line weaving in and out of the themes, an effective contrast to the excellent solos in between. Though recorded later, the quintet tracks, with Wilson sympathetic on trumpet if not particularly memorable, conform to shellac-disc length. That's possibly a good thing, as Raney is by some distance the most interesting musician and merits the bulk of the space. His cool, gentle, long-lined solos sound even better today because nobody plays anything remotely like them.  **RA**

# Ernest Ranglin                                                    1932

**New review**

**Below the Bassline** Ranglin (g); **Monty Alexander** (p, melodica); **Gary Mayone** (kbds, perc); **Ira Coleman** (b); **Idris Muhammad** (d); with **Roland Alphonso** (ss, ts). Island Jamaica Jazz Ⓕ IJCD 524 299-2 (55 minutes). Recorded 1996.

Ⓖ ❽

Ernest Ranglin's career, ranging from stints in dance bands through spells providing quintet music for the cruise-liner trade, to his present status as revered elder statesman, is as representative as anyone's could be of developments in post-war Jamaican popular music. In his time, he has played swing, Cuban music and mento, and the closely related musics known as ska, rocksteady and bluebeat have all filtered through alongside them into the sound he produces on this album, a lively selection of classic Jamaican songs interpreted through reggae and jazz. Ranglin's lionization as a reggae legend has endeared him to today's *aficionados* of club sounds such as drum'n'bass, and the presence of the wonderfully eclectic pianist Monty Alexander will enliven this recording for jazz fans, but overall the relentlessness of the reggae rhythms lessens its musical appeal. The simplicity of the tunes, too, render them less than gripping as vehicles for improvisation, although both Ranglin, with his distinctive slithering, skittering guitar sound, and the playful but consistently cogent Alexander bring as much improvisational brio as possible to them. While those interested merely in the groove will find much to relish in the hypnotically repetitive rhythms produced by Coleman and Muhammad, much of the genuine jazz spirit discernible in flashes from the front-line soloists is stifled by them.  **CP**

# John Rapson

**New review**

**Dances & Orations** Rapson (tb); **Bobby Bradford** (c); **Bill Roper** (tba); **Anthony Braxton** (f, cl, cbcl, ss, as); **Wayne Peet** (p, syn, samples); **Alex Cline** (d, perc, v). Music & Arts Ⓕ CD923 (61 minutes). Recorded 1994.

❿ ❾

Raised on the West Coast, Rapson made several recordings for the Nine Winds label that showed his proficiency across the spectrum of modern jazz styles but gave little hint of the originality evident on **Dances & Orations**. The core of the disc is a series of brief improvised duets that Rapson recorded with Braxton in January 1994. Rapson then edited these tapes to create compositional frameworks for a further session in July 1994, at which a quintet (minus Braxton) played with, against or around the original duets, replayed either "as was" or in various transformed states – orchestrated, overdubbed, sampled (by Peet). Tapes of this second session were then edited and processed too, the result being a brilliant array of 'assembled' musics, improvised and notated fragments refigured via technological creativity into richly-textured collages of sound. Braxton's abstraction and Bradford's lyricism are the dominant solo voices but Rapson and Peet concoct some wonderful moments at the tape deck, extrapolating a New Orleans parade from a Braxton solo or building the ethereally lovely *Oblation: Albert Testifies, Hildegard Prays* layer by layer. Rapson cites Ellington's "communal composition" as a precedent: in spirit perhaps, but I know of no other music fashioned quite like this. **Dances & Orations** is beautiful and unique.  **GL**

# Enrico Rava                                                      1943

**Quatre** Rava (t); **Franco D'Andrea** (p); **Miroslav Vitous** (b); **Daniel Humair** (d). Gala Ⓕ 91030 (48 minutes). Recorded 1989.

❾ ❽

As befits a world-class trumpeter, Rava's impressive career has ranged from a sixties free jazz quartet alongside Steve Lacy to a tango-tinged eighties band with Argentinian bandoneonist Dino Saluzzi, from Lee Konitz to Carla Bley. But few settings have shown off his ravishing powers of invention any better than this spectacular group, which unites four all-stars from three different countries. Their sense of ensemble is pin-point accurate and remarkably flexible, making this the epitome of a listening band, the musicians able to respond immediately to each other's playing with imagination and authority. By subtly shifting rhythmic accents into a constantly varied progression of seamless episodes, the music remains continually fresh and engaging. This demands exquisite balance and awareness of spontaneous design, but the four seem to be in telepathic agreement. The way they interact, the harmonic framework and floating rhythm of the compositions, is reminiscent of the Miles Davis band of the mid sixties; in fact, Rava's burnished tone – alternately dark and lustrous – and his thrilling lyricism could be considered a personal homage to Miles. Combined with Humair's playful and propulsive drumming, D'Andrea's embroidery and Vitous's virtuosity, it accounts for the sublime sounds to be heard here. **AL**

# Lou Rawls

**New review**

**For You My Love** Rawls (v); Al Porcino, Anthony Terran, Bobby Bryant, Harry Edison, Freddie Hill (t, flh); Tom Shepard, Ed Kusby, Lew McCreary, Dick Leith, Kenny Shroyer (tb); Bill Green, Jim Horn (as, ts, f); Plas Johnson (ts, f); Don Abney, Gildo Mahones (p, org); Gary Coleman, Dale Anderson (vb); Barney Kessel, Howard Roberts, Walter Namuth (g); Jimmy Bond, Robert Haynes (b); Alvin Stoller, Melvin Lee (d); Joe Clayton (cga, perc). Capitol Jazz Ⓜ CDP8 28979-2 (44 minutes). Recorded 1964/8.

⑦ ❽

There is a large number of vocalists who are able to span the borderline between jazz and popular music, but it is fairly easy to sort out the ones whose music is both trenchant and jazz-loaded. Rawls is very much one of them. More urbane and sophisticated than Joe Williams, his blues don't have the latter's explosive impact, but on the other hand his ballads don't, as Williams's do, descend to bathos. He has a pleasing voice and an intelligent awareness of what treatment is best for the backing arrangements. Here those arrangements are of the highest class, since they are provided on the first session by Benny Carter and on the second by Benny Golson. The music is well chosen, typified by Golson's punchy reinterpretation of Ellington's *Squeeze Me* where the 'small' big band brings out the delicacy of the writing. The writing too absolves some of the lesser ballads, although none of these is intrinsically bad. There are token jazz war-horses like *Wee Baby Blues* and *Gee Baby*, but jazz solos are virtually absent, the best instrumental music being found in the section work and obbligatos by Plas Johnson and Don Abney. **SV**

# Jason Rebello

**Make It Real** Rebello (p); Wayne Batchelor (b); Jeremy Stacey, Darren Abraham (d); Thomas Dyani Akuru (perc); Maysa Leak, Maxi Jazz, Joy Rose, Donna Gardner, Cleveland Watkiss (v). BMG Ⓕ 122408-2 (64 minutes). Recorded 1994.

⑥ ❽

Although he has often shown himself to be one of the most able of the generation of British players spawned by the eighties jazz explosion, since the uncompromised fusion of his début album, Jason Rebello has become a musical fashion victim. His recent removal to a religious retreat, coupled with his departure from BMG, bespeaks a radical reassessment of what he has done so far.

This last BMG album moves in the right direction, featuring him almost exclusively on piano with only a hint of synthesized strings on one track, but the unadulterated jazz does not start to flow until the seventh out of 12 tracks, and even then Rebello seems to be pulling punches. Tracks one to six are dominated by soul or rap vocals, and one has to wonder at the reasoning which sees its inclusion. The jazz does take off on *Beautiful Day* and *Heartless Monster*, but it often fails to attain the intensity Rebello has produced in concert. Furthermore, although *Wait and See* has a light rock pulse, it seems a shame, given this taste for backbeats, that Rebello has not picked up on the radical reassessments of piano jazz being essayed by Ilg/Copland/Hirshfield and Leon Parker on issues reviewed elsewhere in this volume. **MG**

# Re-Birth Brass Band

**Feel Like Funkin' It Up** Kermit Ruffins (t, v, perc); Derrick Shezbie (t, perc); Derek Wiley (t, v, perc); Keith 'Wolf' Anderson (tb); Philip Frazier (bb, perc); John Gilbert (ts, v, perc); Keith Frazier (bass d, v, perc); Kenneth Austin (snare d, v, perc). Rounder Ⓕ CD2093 (46 minutes). Recorded 1989.

⑥ ❻

Formed by a group of high school friends in the Treme district of New Orleans in 1984, the Re-Births have followed the lead taken by the Dirty Dozen Brass Band. Like them, the Re-Births have added funkier, more extrovert elements to the tradition previously established for the marching bands of the city. They have introduced the jump blues, tempered with bebop material and more modern phraseology, but most essentially they have still retained the exuberant spirit of the music. There is still little to choose between their various issues, but this CD has an especially streetwise vitality and youthful verve. Both Frazier and Austin form the nucleus of an oft-augmented and highly effective rhythm section, while the horn duties are shared by Ruffins, Gilbert and Anderson. Gilbert, rumbustious on *Do Watcha Wanna* and *Big Fat Woman*, is the pick of the bunch, but their collective musical frailties do tend to be exposed on record. Ruffins's best solo is on *Leave That Pipe Alone* and Anderson scores on *Mexican Special*, but it is the collective good time cacophony of titles like *I'm*

*Walkin'* and *Shake Your Body Down to the Ground* that would be most likely to sell the band and its brand of jazz to an audience out to enjoy itself. **BMcR**

## Sonny Red (Sylvester Kyner) 1932-81

New review
**Out of the Blue** Red (as); **Wynton Kelly** (p); **Sam Jones, Paul Chambers** (b); **Roy Brooks, Jimmy Cobb** (d). Blue Note Ⓜ CDP8 52440-2 (72 minutes). Recorded 1959-60.

⑥ ❽

Red was one of the many post-war musicians who hailed from Detroit and environs – Yusef Lateef and the Jones brothers (Elvin, Hank and Thad) are among the others – and made his first impact in the early fifties as a member of fellow-Detroiter Barry Harris's band. By the late fifties Red had formed a close musical partnership with trombonist Curtis Fuller and the two of them had moved to New York to try their luck. Fuller soon found work, but Red scuffled, and only after further tours well away from the Apple did he land consistent jobs and a deal with Blue Note. Even after albums such as this present reissue Red never advanced to the front rank of players and well before his early death he was back in Detroit. None of this should deter people from sampling the pleasures of this record, which is couched in the bop language of younger players following Parker but also reveals listening from further afield, such as Lou Donaldson and Jackie McLean. He is a capable blues player with his own breathy, keening timbre, his light touch on medium-tempo treatments of standards revealing the cross-pollination of both Stitt and Parker in his approach, though faster tempos leave his technique exposed. His ballad playing, however, is a real treat, with his light sound exhibiting a spine-tingling sensitivity to his material and his phrasing on songs like *Stairway to the Stars* and *Stay as Sweet as You Are* drawing exquisite pictures of the songs' inner subjects. The CD reissue carries five extra tracks, all dating from the 1960 session with Paul Chambers and Jimmy Cobb accompanying, none of them remakes of the first session's tunes, so they're welcome additions. **KS**

## Freddie Redd 1928

**Music from *The Connection*** Jackie McLean (as); **Redd** (p); **Michael Mattos** (b); **Larry Ritchie** (d). Blue Note Ⓜ CDP8 89392-2 (39 minutes). Recorded 1960.
✔ ⑩ ❽
The peripatetic Freddie Redd is one of several musicians (including Dexter Gordon, Cecil Payne and Cecil Taylor) to have written and recorded a score for Jack Gelber's notorious off-Broadway chronicle of heroin addicts (including the members of the musical ensemble) waiting for the man. This is the best version of the best score (Redd, under the *nom de disque* I. Ching, re-recorded his seven compositions under Howard McGhee's name for Felsted within the year) and a definitive hard-bop programme. McLean's early phase reaches glorious fruition here, with acidic passion and stunning command of the chord changes, while Redd's seven tunes are structurally fresh, melodically indelible and ferociously swinging. They also hang together, similar yet singular, to create as complete an album's-worth of music as any composer/player offered at the time. Also of note is Redd's piano, a good-timey take on Powell and Monk that shares some of Horace Silver's rollicking quality while remaining quite distinctive. The obscurity of the rhythm section in no way reflects upon how hard it swings. **BB**

## Dewey Redman 1931

**Choices** Redman (as, ts, mus, v); **Joshua Redman** (ts); **Cameron Brown** (b); **Leon Parker** (d). Enja Ⓟ ENJ7073-2 (55 minutes). Recorded 1992.

⑧ ❽

Redman became known in the sixties working with Ornette Coleman and bearing a tenor style indebted to Ornette's playful alto (in the seventies, Dewey was in Keith Jarrett's American quartet). On this trio/quartet set, Redman features his own alto on two tracks heavily influenced by Coleman's playing and writing, although Dewey plays on tenor heft and a distinctly darker tone. On tenor for a ten-minute *Everything Happens to Me*, his sound is in the grand Hawkins tradition, and is remarkably straight-ahead. He plays the chord changes straight, something Coleman's band was not known for doing. *O'Besso*, a West African-flavoured vamp tune, is an extended showcase for – and one of his best recorded outings on – Chinese musette, a simple double-reed instrument of short range and precarious intonation.

Son Joshua joins in on the two tracks where his dad plays alto; Joshua and the rhythm duo get *Imagination* to themselves. He is a good balladeer, if not yet a match for his father. Dewey's best album as tenorist, ECM's **The Struggle Continues**, is not yet on CD, and his best work overall has depended on rhythm sections more ferocious than this amiable one. Even so, **Choices** is a strong statement from an uneven but underrated veteran. **KW**

# Don Redman
1900-64

**Don Redman And His Orchestra 1931-33** Redman (as, v); **Leonard Davis, Bill Coleman, Henry Allen, Shirley Clay, Langston Curl, Sidney De Paris** (t); **Claude Jones, Fred Robinson, Benny Morton** (tb); **Edward Inge, Rupert Cole** (cl, as); **Robert Carroll** (ts); **Horace Henderson, Don Kirkpatrick** (p); **Talcott Reeves** (bj, g); **Bob Yasguirre** (b, bb); **Manzie Johnson** (d); **Louis Deppe, Harlan Lattimore, Cab Calloway, The Mills Brothers** (v); **Bill Robinson** (tap). Classics Ⓜ 543 (70 minutes). Recorded 1931-3.

✔ ⑥ ❼

Redman was one of the most important jazz arrangers, a situation perhaps initially helped by the fact that he played nearly all of the instruments associated with jazz. He joined Fletcher Henderson in 1923 and for the next four years provided many of the band's best charts. He became musical director of McKinney's Cotton Pickers and in 1931 formed his own band. Although by no means the only major arranger by this stage, he put an indelible stamp on bands with which he was associated. The music on this CD comes from an influential period. It is imaginative, often descriptive and, although not as accomplished as the works in the latter part of the band's life, had the unmistakable Redman stamp. He produced impressionistic compositions such as his famous *Chant of the Weed*, plus novelty pieces such as *Shakin' the African* as well as rather too many vehicles for his own strangely emasculated vocals. The band's main problem at this time was that, despite a personnel which included such considerable figures as De Paris, Coleman, Allen and Jones, it had continuing intonation troubles. Ironically, by the time this had been eradicated, the band had lost much of its individuality. **BMcR**

# Joshua Redman
1969

**New review**
**Spirit of the Moment – Live at the Village Vanguard** Redman (ts); **Peter Martin** (p); **Christopher Thomas** (b); **Brian Blade** (d). Warner Bros Ⓕ 245923-2 (two discs: 148 minutes). Recorded 1995.

⑧ ❽

This is not Redman's latest album – 1996's disappointing **Freedom in the Groove** claims that spot – but it fully documents the extent of this brilliant player's abilities and progress. What's more, it does this in the most natural, unvarnished way by presenting him with his own band in front of an appreciative hometown audience. Of course there is a precedent to live down, stretching back through legions of tenor players including Joe Henderson, John Coltrane and Sonny Rollins, just to name the most obvious ones to make landmark recordings at the Village Vanguard (Hawkins chose the Village Gate for his), so this double album is a conscious statement of intent from today's leading young tenor. As such it reaffirms his incredible fecundity when it comes to improvised ideas, as well as his technical standard, which enables him to execute anything he wants at any time, much in the manner of Rollins at his most complete and imperious. He can eat up fast tempos, can caress a ballad, can burn up the rhythm section when they try to burn him, and he can dig into a medium tempo blues groove with the best of them. His spontaneous execution of every idea which comes his way is awesome, and only his reliance on other models at times lets the continuity of his playing be dissipated  for example, the Coltrane-like screaming and honking, connected by similarly Coltrane-ish snaking chromaticisms, which come at the climax of a long and very good solo on *Herbs and Roots*. This is a small point, not a debilitating one, and shows that Redman has still some space within which to grow, which is a good thing, considering his age. Something for us to look forward to then ... **KS**

# Dizzy Reece
1931

**New review**
**Asia Minor** Reece (t); **Joe Farrell** (ts, f); **Cecil Payne** (bs); **Hank Jones** (p); **Ron Carter** (b); **Charlie Persip** (d). Prestige New Jazz Ⓜ OJCCD1806-2 (36 minutes). Recorded 1962.

⑦ ❾

The previous Guide had Reece's 1958 album for Blue Note, **Blues in Trinity**, as an example of his work, but this recent reissue is a better record. Reece was born in Kingston, Jamaica, and among his schoolmates were Joe Harriott and Bogey Gaynair. He came to England in 1948 and dedicated himself to a career in jazz. By the late fifties his reputation had spread as far as the US, spurring Reece into a move to New York, where he made the Blue Note album noted above. Hard times came his way after that, and **Asia Minor** represents an oasis in a desert of work opportunities. By 1962 Reece had moved on considerably from his previous Jazz Messengers-based ideas, his bright trumpet work owing little to his namesake Gillespie, Miles Davis or Lee Morgan, his phrases and sound being recognizably his own within a modern jazz context. His compositions here are considerably past the elementary stage usually thought of in 1962 jazz circles as sufficient to hang a string of solos on, and his cohorts all pull together to make this a consistently superior date from every angle. **KS**

# Eric Reed

**New review**

**Musicale** Reed (p); **Nicholas Payton** (t); **Wycliffe Gordon** (tb); **Wessell Anderson** (as); **Ben Wolfe**,
  **Ron Carter** (b); **Gregory Hutchinson**, **Karriem Riggins** (d). Impulse! Ⓕ IMP11962 (65 minutes).
  Recorded 1996.

⑥ ❼

Two different groups here, recorded a little over a month apart in the spring of 1996. One group
contains Ron Carter, altoist Anderson and trumpeter Payton, while the other largely functions as a
trio, with trombonist Gordon turning up on just one track, *Baby Sis*. Reed's opening track is
dedicated to his erstwhile employer, Art Blakey, and is accordingly titled *Black, As In Buhaina*. The
theme itself is arresting, the playing easily imagined to be that coming from a latter-day Blakey line-
up. Reed has continued to progress as a pianist, broadening and deepening his range and expressivity,
and the idea to split the album between the two quite different bands certainly aids the listener in
seeing a more rounded pianistic and compositional talent. Sax and trumpet come across as oddly
tentative at times, especially on the Dolphy/Coleman tribute, *Pete and Repete*, a clever intertwining of
motifs and patterns which occasionally have a point of reference in the older mens' musics. But Reed
stands out as the dominant talent in these line-ups. Only right too, considering it's his sessions. Apart
from a tendency to get just a little too bland in the pursuit of legitimate tradition, this is engaging
music immaculately played. Could do with the occasional spot of inspired chaos, though.      **KS**

# Dianne Reeves

**Quiet After the Storm** Reeves (v); **Roy Hargrove**, **Gary Grant** (t); **Ron Blake** (ss, ts); **Everette
  Harp** (as); **Joshua Redman** (ts); **Hubert Laws** (f); **Dori Caymmi**, **Kevin Eubanks** (g); **George Duke**
  (kbds); **David Torkanowsky**, **Jacky Terrasson**, **John Beasley** (p); **Chris Severin** (b); **Billy Kilson**,
  **Terri Lyne Carrington** (d); **Luis Conte**, **Airto Moreira** (perc). Blue Note Ⓕ CDP8 29511-2
  (59 minutes). Recorded 1995.

⑧ ❽

Like many of her jazz-singing contemporaries (UK examples include Claire Martin, Tina May, Carol
Kidd and Ian Shaw), Dianne Reeves casts her net wider than conventional jazz standards and originals
in her search for material suitable for her attractively smoky voice. On this, her fifth EMI recording, she
switches between big band jazz, small group torch songs, sophisticated rock and ethnic music with great
aplomb, demonstrating a maturity and confidence not always apparent on earlier recordings. The
hallmark of this newfound assurance is the restraint with which she approaches all she sings. Her voice's
many individual strengths, from its unusual range through its textural variety to its sure dynamic
control, are kept firmly in check, held in reserve until the most telling moment for their deployment.
Thus, in the moody ballad, *Come Love*, she intelligently accentuates the contrasts inherent in the song's
lyrics by moving easily and unaffectedly between an attractively informal, insinuating warmth and
sudden eruptions of emotion; in *Country Preacher*, a tribute to Cannonball Adderley, she positively
smoulders; in Joni Mitchell's *Both Sides Now* she sustains interest through three wordy verses, despite a
murderously slow tempo, by the sheer emotional intensity which she invests in the performance.
Rounded out by an excursion into Brazilian music (an echo of her early experience with Sergio Mendes)
and a song recalling childhood experience, *Nine*, which just steers clear of sentimentality courtesy of
Reeves's patent sincerity, and featuring accomplished versions of standards such as *In a Sentimental
Mood* and *Detour Ahead*, this is Dianne Reeves's finest album by some distance.      **CP**

# Django Reinhardt

**Chronological, Volume 1** Stephane Grappelli (vn, p); **Reinhardt**, Joseph Reinhardt, Roger Chaput
  (g); **Arthur Briggs**, **Frank 'Big Boy' Goodie** (t, cl, ts); **Louis Vola** (b). JSP Ⓕ CD341 (75 minutes).
  Recorded 1934-5.

✔                                                                                        ⑧ ❽

The Quintet of the Hot Club of France has been badly served on record. The multitude of their LPs
were mostly taken from bad sources, such as poorly centred and badly pressed 78s. Often, later albums
were simply careless copies of the first, haphazardly-produced, LPs.

  The music on this CD has been restored from the best available 78 copies, which have been carefully
checked for pitch by the sound engineer Ted Kendall. His work is so good that it can literally be said
that Reinhardt has never been heard with such presence before. The guitarist's fingers can be heard
moving across the fingerboard, and there is a new resonance as he plucks each note. Kendall has
cleared away audio rubble, using the skills he learned from his mentor John R.T. Davies, and has
brought out sounds in the music which haven't been heard since the recordings were made in the
studio. This chronological collection has a handful of rather dated vocals, but every track on which
the singers appear is dominated by jazz solos from Reinhardt and Grappelli, and on the out-and-out
jazz tracks, the two men showed a combination of swing and virtuoso playing which must have
stunned their American contemporaries.

One might expect *Dinah* or *Lady Be Good* to sound hackneyed, but they emerge here as newly refreshed classics. This is Volume 1 of what is projected to be a major Reinhardt series. There have been five volumes to date, following on chronologically from this one.          **SV**

---

**Swing in Paris, 1936-40** Reinhardt (g); with a collective personnel including: **Rex Stewart** (c); **Bill Coleman**, **Philippe Brun** (t); **Benny Carter** (t, as); **Dicky Wells** (tb); **Barney Bigard** (cl); **Frank 'Big Boy' Goudie**, **Alix Combelle**, **Bertie King**, **Hubert Rostaing** (cl, ts); **Andre Ekyan** (as); **Coleman Hawkins** (ts); **Stephane Grappelli** (p, vn); **Joseph Reinhardt**, **Pierre Ferret**, **Marcel Bianchi**, **Roger Chaput**, **Eugene Vees** (g); **Eddie South**, **Michel Warlop** (vn); **Louis Vola**, **Eugene d'Hellemes**, **Wilson Myers** (b); **Pierre Fouad** (d); **Freddy Taylor** (v). Affinity Ⓜ CDAFS1003-5 (five discs: 327 minutes). Recorded 1936-40.

✓                                                                                    ⑩ ❼

Where to start with Django? With the chord playing that takes a bulldog grip on Coleman Hawkins's *Crazy Rhythm* and *Honeysuckle Rose*, or treads fearlessly alongside an Eddie South, a Bill Coleman or a Dicky Wells in the blues' remembered hills? With the single-string solos, audacious yet never fanciful, that spill out of dozens of performances? Or the combination of both in a masterly reshaping of a standard like *I'll See You in My Dreams*, where Broadway is translated to the Boul' Mich'? Or rather should we begin with that matchless sound, the bittersweet zither's ring that spirals from every note, like a waft of Chanel or a whiff of Gauloises?

For most of Reinhardt's admirers the story begins, as this collection does, with his recordings alongside the violinist Stephane Grappelli in the Quintet of the Hot Club of France. This was the first small-group jazz made outside the US that not only rivalled the music's originators in its execution but revealed something to them, and expanded the vocabulary of jazz by the originality of its conception. The only American musicians at all comparable with Grappelli and Reinhardt, namely Joe Venuti and Eddie Lang, never hit upon such twirling arabesques, never achieved that boulevardier's elegance, even at their most extravagantly imaginative.

Reinhardt was the first incontestably great jazz musician from Europe. As the list of musicians above shows, this is a conclusion several excellent American players had already arrived at in the thirties, and the sessions with Hawkins and Benny Carter or with Rex Stewart and Barney Bigard are collaborations of the highest quality. Stretched by the presence or the recollection of these visitors, the other European musicians, Combelle and Ekyan, Brun and Rostaing and their peers, play with fresh vigour without losing their essentially European character. This superb collection embraces Reinhardt's recordings in his own name, with the QHCF, and as an accompanist or sideman, for the HMV and Swing labels.          **TR**

---

**The Great Blue Star Sessions 1947-53** Reinhardt (g); with a collective personnel of **Joseph Reinhardt**, **Jean-Claude Forenbach**, **Eugene Vees** (g); **Michel de Villers** (as); **Eddie Bernard**, **Maurice Vandair** (p); **Willy Lockwood**, **Ladislas Czabanyck**, **Emmanuel Soudieux**, **Pierre Michelot** (b); **Al Craig**, **André Jourdan**, **Ted Curry**, **Jean-Louis Viale** (d); **Vincent Casino**, **Louis Menardi**, **Jo Boyer** (t); **André Lafosse**, **Guy Paquinet** (tb); **Michel de Villers** (cl, as); **Gerard Levecque** (arr); **Hubert Rostaing** (cl, as); **Rex Stewart** (c). Verve Ⓜ 835418-2 (two discs: 97 minutes). Recorded 1947-53.

⑥ ❻

Reinhardt went to America at the end of 1946 to undertake a not wholly successful tour with the Duke Ellington orchestra. He formed a quintet with Hubert Rostaing on his return and 25 of these 33 titles were made for the French Blue Star (later Barclay) record label in 1947. With clarinet in place of violin, the group sometimes takes on the quality of a sub-Benny Goodman unit, but there is no mistaking Django, even when he occasionally fights against the low-tech amplification that he elected to use at this time. But nothing can hide his unique genius and there is some magnificent blues playing to be heard on *Django's Blues* and its alternative take labelled *Love's Mood*. Bebop was beginning to impinge on Reinhardt's sensibility at the time and the fast *Moppin' the Bride* has all the hallmarks of a European jazzman's attempts to come to terms with a new development. The two titles with Rex Stewart added on cornet are pleasant but unmomentous, lacking the magic of the 1939 Feetwarmers session, but the final 1953 date is a complete success due to the superior rhythm section, recording quality and Django's mastery of the amplification problems. These eight titles have often received less than critical acclaim but *Blues for Ike, Manoir Des Mes Reves* and *September Song* are particular joys, while this 1953 version of *Nuages* is perhaps the best of all.          **AM**

---

# Emily Remler                                                                1957 91

---

**Transitions** Remler (g); **John D'Earth** (t); **Eddie Gomez** (b); **Bob Moses** (d). Concord Jazz Ⓕ CCD4236 (37 minutes). Recorded 1983.

✓                                                                                    ⑧ ❽

The breadth and range of Emily Remler's talent – **Transitions**'s title track alone moves easily between 4/4, 7/4 and 3/4 and incorporates Latin rhythms as naturally as its closing track uses African ones – is faultlessly displayed on this thoughtful, well-balanced album. The New York-born guitarist was a regular in Astrud Gilberto's band in the early eighties (**Transitions**'s opening track, *Nunca Mais*, is a tribute to her fellow band members) and her front-line collaborator, trumpeter John D'Earth, featured in a number of Latin bands in the same period. This experience explains the intelligent and uncontrived use of Latin and African sounds and rhythms on the album's Remler originals which marks the recording out from many contemporary efforts, where a characterless pastiche too often results from a similar process. Furthermore, Remler's unostentatious versatility and D'Earth's flaring but tasteful tone are perfectly complemented both by Eddie Gomez's sensitivity in accompanying roles and quiet assertiveness in solos and by Bob Moses's richly sympathetic drumming, so that although Remler clearly sets the agenda for the album, it is nevertheless very much a group effort. It is therefore as a leader eminently capable of thus drawing a variety of unusual sounds into the jazz mainstream – here represented by Sam Jones's *Del Sasser* – and for her ability to grant sympathetic collaborators the space everywhere evident on **Transitions**, that she will be most sorely missed.   **CP**

## Don Rendell                                                    1926

**If I Should Lose You** Rendell (cl, ss, ts, f); **Martin Shaw** (t, flh); **Richard Edwards** (tb); **Brian Dee**, **John Burch** (p); **Peter Morgan**, **Mario Castronari** (b); **Robin Jones**, **Bobby Worth** (d). Spotlite ⓕ SPJCD546 (60 minutes). Recorded 1990/1.

⑥ ❻

Rendell came up at the same time as Sims and Getz and similarly absorbed Lester Young's influence but, unlike the other two, Rendell also modified his style to acknowledge the innovations of Coltrane and Rollins. His tenor playing is good enough to make one wonder why he has not received the acclaim of, say, a Tubby Hayes, yet over the years his work with far better groups than the ones here has gone similarly unnoticed, so perhaps it is a case of counting your blessings. Rendell uses the soprano sax with purpose and an individual sound, which is refreshing after the routine struggling one sees with many tenorists. As well as tenor, *All Too Soon* features sparse, somewhat shrill 'saxophone player's clarinet' but Rendell's work on both saxes is well displayed on *Calas Vinas,* which also has a rare solo from Richard Edwards, a name to watch amongst British trombonists.   **SV**

## Return to Forever

**New review**

**Return to the Seventh Galaxy** Chick Corea (p, elp, org, syn, clav, mba, h, perc, v); **Joe Farrell** (ts, f); **Bill Connors**, **Al DiMeola** (g, elg); **Flora Purim** (v, pc); **Stanley Clarke** (b, elb, perc, org, syn, v); **Steve Gadd** (d); **Airto Moreira**, **Lenny White** (d, perc); **Mingo Lewis** (perc). Verve Ⓜ 533 108-2 (two discs: 148 minutes). Recorded 1972-5.

⑧ ❽

In large part, this is a compilation of familiar RTF back catalogue, but the two-disc, 19-track trip is made more worthwhile by the inclusion of four previously unissued airshot recordings – *Spain, After the Cosmic Rain* and *Bass Folk Song* from 1973 and *The Shadow of Lo* from 1975. *Spain* is particularly good, although the seeker after a representative RTF collection might be disappointed by the absence of the seminal original. But on balance, this is a sound, chronologically ordered perspective on RTF's progress from hippy Latin jazz combo (note how Corea's overdriven and wah-effected Fender Rhodes on the excellent 1972 *500 Miles High* and *Captain Marvel* points the way to the future in what is otherwise a conventionally equipped group) to high decibel stadium-rocking fusion band. This is a Polygram issue, so the group's début on ECM is unrepresented, but in focusing on the era around the watershed first electric album, **Hymn to the Seventh Galaxy**, it is true to its title and gives good weight to the time before bombast set in and the group lost its best guitarist, Bill Connors. Listen to the way he and Corea burn on the new *Spain*. The packaging is exemplary in the usual Verve way, with seventies-style graphics wryly responding to the retro mood of today.   **MG**

## Melvyn Rhyne                                                   1936

**Boss Organ** Rhyne (org); **Joshua Redman** (ts); **Peter Bernstein** (g); **Kenny Washington** (d). Criss Cross ⓕ 1080CD (62 minutes). Recorded 1993.

⑩ ❽

After getting over the shock of seeing who is making up the tenor part of the tenor 'n' organ set-up here, you may have bigger problems coping with the first track. It's a long, long blues, slow and blissful, midnight-cool, no one straining, no one grandstanding, everyone pulling their weight. Things haven't been like this for some time down funk city way. Blue Note gave up making records like this 30 years ago, and it comes as a sad commentary on the current Stateside scene that while this CD may have been recorded in New York, it was at the behest of a Dutch record label. Still, I don't care who makes albums this good, as long as someone does. There is such refinement here (it's not a mere blowing session on the first blues head arrangement anybody could think of) along with a real sense of continuity and understanding between the participants. People fit into the area they've been allotted, and with Rhyne keeping such good time with his feet, Washington sounds especially happy. Rhyne also eschews the more blatant stops on his instrument, keeping the groove mellow, the swing deep, letting the rhythm work for him rather than blasting everyone within reach. His comping for Redman is wonderfully supple, and he and guitarist Bernstein have a great understanding about the best ways to balance their support roles. Redman himself plays with controlled freedom and imagination, at all times sounding completely at home. This is a fine album in the tenor 'n' organ tradition. **KS**

## Buddy Rich

1917-87

New review

**Swingin' New Band/Keep the Customer Satisfied** Rich (d); Bobby Shew, John Sottile, Yoshito Murakami, Walter Battagello, John Giorgiani, John Madrid, Mike Price, George Zonce (t); Jim Trimble, John Boice, Dennis Good, Mike Waverley, Rick Stepton, Tony Lada, Larry Fisher (tb); Gene Quill, Pete Yellin, Richie Cole, Jimmy Mosher (as, cl, f); Jay Corre, Marty Flax, Pat LaBarbera, Don Englert (ts, f); Steve Perlow, Bob Suchoski (bs); John Bunch, Meredith McClain (p); Carson Smith, Rick Laird (b). BGO Records Ⓜ BGOCD169 (75 minutes). Recorded 1966-70.
⑧ ❻

By and large drummers fall into one of two categories – small group or big band players. Even Mel Lewis, almost at the pinnacle of the craft, was essentially a big band drummer and slightly less effective in quintet surroundings. Rich was the exception. He excelled at everything. This is not surprising, for if ever the supernatural came into play in jazz then it was at the hands of Buddy Rich. Even people who can't bear drummers must be amazed at his apparent infallibility, which went far beyond craftsmanship to the outer edges of instinct. His speed and dexterity were unapproachable and his jazz sense in respect of the horns who worked for him was similarly informed. He was a hard, some would say impossible, taskmaster who stopped at nothing to get what he wanted from a band. The evidence that his methods worked is here in the performances by these two big bands. Rich lubricates the music with dazzling panache and, despite the combination of an admirable group of emergent young musicians and a quite outstanding roster of arrangers (including Bill Holman, Phil Wilson, Oliver Nelson and Roger Neuman), easily monopolizes the limelight. Considering that the soloists include fine players like Gene Quill, Riche Cole, Jay Corre and Pat LaBarbara this is not an ideal situation, but it is inevitable. **SV**

## Red Richards

1912

New review

**Groove Move** Richards (p); Doc Cheatham (t); George Kelly (ts); Ole Lindgren (tb); Al Casey (elg); Jan Jankeje (b); Imre Kosegi (d). Jazzpoint Ⓕ JP10545 (59 minutes). Recorded 1994.
⑧ ❿

In the year this CD was recorded the ages of the four principal players – Richards, Kelly, Cheatham and Casey – added up to 329. They were among the few authentic players of the swing era still performing and it is heartening to hear them on such good form. Cheatham, in particular, is a human phenomenon; surely no 90-year-old trumpeter ever sounded as firm and purposeful as this. There is not a hint of a quaver in his sound and his lines are as trim and and elegant as ever. He even sings with the voice of a man in the prime of life. Kelly's tenor, strongly reminiscent of his contemporary, Buddy Tate, maintains just the right balance between asperity and ripeness. Richards, a virtuoso stride pianist, leads the rhythm section with practised ease. Casey's electric guitar is all mellow simplicity. The Hungarians Jankeje and Koszegi, mere youths of 50 or so, respond beautifully to Richards's lead, while the Danish trombonist, Ole Lindgren, sounds as though he was born in Harlem. A wonderful hour's music. **DG**

## Jerome Richardson

1920

New review

**Midnight Oil** Richardson (f, ts); Jimmy Cleveland (tb); Hank Jones (p); Kenny Burrell (g); Joe Benjamin (b); Charlie Persip (d). Prestige Ⓜ OJCCD1815-2 (35 minutes). Recorded 1958.
⑧ ❽

Always a bridesmaid, never a bride. Not quite the case, but almost. Jerome Richardson is the universal section man, rarely heard in solo but indispensable to bandleaders from Jimmy Lunceford and Lucky Millinder to Charles Mingus and Quincy Jones. He played lead alto in the Thad Jones-Mel Lewis band from its foundation in 1965 until 1970 when he became a Hollywood section man. Enormously gifted on all reeds and woodwind, he shows on this, then his first recording under his own name, that he is an attacking tenor soloist and eloquent flautist. *Minorally,* a big shout-up, is the only one to feature tenor, with the other four being played delicately on flute. The sextet is generally very tasteful. Hank Jones's fine piano is much aided by the fastidious and swinging guitar of Kenny Burrell and by another virtuoso, the underrated Cleveland. Blowing session perhaps, but a very polished one. **SV**

# Dannie Richmond

1935-88

**Three or Four Shades**  Richmond (d); **Jack Walrath** (t); **Kenny Garrett** (as); **Bob Neloms** (p);
  **Cameron Brown** (b). Tutu Ⓕ CD888120 (71 minutes). Recorded 1981.

⑥ ❺

Richmond began his musical career as an r&b saxophonist, but apart from a period in the early
seventies when he flirted with rock, his career was inextricably bound up with Charles Mingus, the
man and his music. In the early years the bassist was his leader, friend, inspiration and teacher, but
Richmond's style of loose-jointed drumming matured quickly. He had a total grasp of suspended
rhythms and his work in the fifties opened stylistic doors for drummers such as Andrew Cyrille and
Sunny Murray. After Mingus's death he played with Mingus Dynasty and, up to the time of his own
premature demise, with the superb George Adams/Don Pullen Quartet. This CD provides an excellent
overview of his style. It demonstrates clear melodic expressiveness and shows how he was able to
reconcile lyricism with an exciting cut and thrust which stimulated fellow band members. Walrath has
played with greater authority elsewhere, and the 1981 Garrett was comparatively inexperienced, but
the rhythmically assertive Neloms and the propulsive Brown were his natural bedfellows. Students of
Richmond's drumming will want to return to the Mingus classics and the Adams/Pullen band, but
this release gives an insight into the way in which he led from the drum stool.         **BMcR**

# Kim Richmond

**New review**

**Range**  Richmond (as); **Clay Jenkins** (t); **Joey Sellers** (tb); **Dave Scott** (p); **Trey Henry** (b); **Joe
  LaBarbera** (d). Nine Winds Records Ⓕ NWCD0172 (70 minutes). Recorded 1994.

⑧ ❽

The various members of the West Coast-based Richmond/Jenkins Ensemble have roots, like the
original mainstreamers, in big-band jazz ranging from Stan Kenton through Bill Holman to Buddy
Rich and Count Basie, and the music they make could be termed modern mainstream. Their
repertoire of smart post-bop originals leavened with the odd standard locates them in the musical
area occupied in the UK by the Guy Barker Sextet, but the textural and harmonic subtlety of the
band's arrangements brings to mind the work of the late Don Grolnick, and occasionally even
that of Maria Schneider. The original material ranges from straightforwardly snappy springboards
for solo workouts in rotation, in the conventional mainstream manner, to more ambitious multi-
hued pieces enlivened by subtle tempo changes and imaginative front-line instrumental combinations.
The overall group sound is firmly knitted together by the intensely musical, sensitive yet assertive
kit work of Bill Evans's last drummer Joe LaBarbera, but it is the tension between the formality
of the written material and the freedom with which it is interpreted by the agile but earnest
Richmond and the surefooted Jenkins that is the source of this consistently fine album's considerable
appeal.         **CP**

# Howard Riley

1943

**New review**

**Descending Circles**  Riley (p); **Elton Dean** (as, saxello); **Mario Castronari** (b); **Mark Sanders** (d).
  Blue Print Ⓕ BP221CD (57 minutes). Recorded 1995.

⑦ ❽

A product of David Baker's Indiana school of excellence, Riley established himself as a leading figure
on the European free music scene in the seventies and eighties. He worked with the London Jazz
Composers Orchestra as well as in duos with Elton Dean and fellow pianists Jaki Byard and Keith
Tippett.  Albums such as the fine 1990 **Procession** (Wondrous WM0101) demonstrated both the
quality of his writing and the versatility of his solo piano skills.  This CD has him in a well-integrated
quartet. *Veracity*, *Sunflower* and the title track offer further examples of his composing talents,
although he is equally at home in his development of Dean's tunes.  As a soloist he is not afraid to
acknowledge the past but the final product is both personal and cohesive. Monk-like irreverences,
Tayloresque flow and Ellingtonian grace attend his style and his imaginatively creative approach to
free improvisation on *Alignment* and *Glimpsing* offers a further endorsement of his inventive
flexibility. Taken together, the album's seven titles are a good example of a working quartet making
its own stylistic choices.         **BMcR**

# Lee Ritenour

1952

**Wes Bound**  Ritenour (g, perc); **Alan Broadbent** (p, arr); **Bob James** (p, kbds); **John Beasley** (kbds);
  **Dave Witham**, **Ronnie Foster** (B-3 organ); **Melvin Davis** (elb); **John Patitucci** (b); **Gary Novak**,
  **Harvey Mason**, **Steve Gadd** (d); **Cassio Duarte**, **Harvey Mason** (perc); **Maxi Priest**, **Phil Perry**,
  **Kate Markowitz**, **Carmen Twillie** (v); **Jerry Hey** (arr). GRP Ⓕ 97052 (54 minutes). Recorded 1992.

⑥ ❽

Encouraged perhaps by jazz's new cultural correctness, Lee Ritenour hastened along with a multitude of other errant jazzers in the late eighties to protest his long-standing fealty to the jazz mainstream. The first gesture in this direction was 1990's efficient **Stolen Moments**, featuring Rit's Gibson L-5 in a straight-ahead quartet. A couple of years on, feeling perhaps that he had seen jazz all right, Ritenour relaxed his jazzman's rigour and re-embraced funkier values on **Wes Bound**. Of course there could be no better model for compromised jazz than Wes Montgomery, and even when he was playing jazz rather than Creed Taylor's arrangements, Wes was funky. Five of the 11 tunes here are Montgomery's, and three of those are from his string-bound Verve period; of the other two, *4 On 6* is the most representative of hard-bopping Wes, and Ritenour rises to the occasion with penetrating jazz guitar, nudged along by Jerry Hey's superbly judged horn prompts. The six non-Wes tunes tend towards Earl Klugh's and George Benson's diluted readings of the Montgomery style, and bottom-out with Maxi Priest singing Bob Marley's maudlin love long, *Waiting in Vain*. Purists might prefer **Stolen Moments**, but for all its shortcomings, **Wes Bound** has a warmth missing from the earlier session; it also offers a fuller picture of Ritenour's blend of bop, blues and funk. **MG**

# Sam Rivers
1930

**Waves** Rivers (f, ss, ts, p); **Joe Daly** (tba, brh); **Dave Holland** (b, vc); **Thurman Barker** (d, perc). Tomato Ⓕ 269649-2 (44 minutes). Recorded 1978.

❽ ❽

Sam Rivers has not been well served by the advent of Compact Disc. Many of his best recordings have yet to appear on CD, including such outstanding items as 1965's **Fuchsia Swing Song** on Blue Note and the 1979 **Contrasts** on ECM. His early interests ranged across gospel, blues, bebop and classical music but the sixties saw him forging a personal jazz style via stints with Miles Davis, Andrew Hill and Cecil Taylor. In the seventies he recorded for Impulse!, became a leading light of New York's avant-garde loft scene and began a long association with Dave Holland that is heard to good advantage on **Waves**.

Rivers has likened this recording to the motion of waves, changing currents, changing flow; apt analogies for music that is in a constant state of flux, each track a series of fleeting exchanges, tempos and moods. Daley's tuba propels the beat, allowing Holland to wax melodic, while Barker is sensitive yet forceful. Rivers himself plays superbly; his tenor fiercely expressive on *Surge* and *Shockwave*, his flute slipping gently through *Torch*. Best of all is *Pulse* which begins with a lively tuba/bass duet, then settles into a rhythmic groove over which Rivers snakes hypnotic soprano. Abstract, funky, intense; *Waves* covers the spectrum in scintillating style. **GL**

# Max Roach
1924

**Deeds, Not Words** Roach (d); **Booker Little** (t); **Ray Draper** (tba); **George Coleman** (ts); **Art Davis** (b). Riverside Ⓜ OJCCD304-2 (44 minutes). Recorded 1958.

❽ ❼

This group played the 1958 Newport Jazz Festival and stayed intact for close on two years; it was not the first piano-less band Roach had tried, but it was the first one to receive widespread recognition. Roach had formed the group with the clear intention of establishing a very young band with a new direction, and he certainly hit the jackpot with Little and Coleman. By the time of this record's first release, Little was already being talked of as the most significant arrival on trumpet since the death of Roach's friend and erstwhile partner, Clifford Brown, while George Coleman, a fine technician with a beautiful melodic turn, would go on to perform brilliantly with Miles Davis, amongst others. Ray Draper has not made such a large mark on the music, but his arranging and compositional talents were considerable, and were vital in defining the character of this Roach group.

Back in 1958, piano-less modern jazz small groups were still unusual (Mulligan's 1952 band had remained very much the exception to the rule), so this was an important step forward. Listened to today, the lack of a harmony instrument certainly allows the overall contours of the music to emerge more clearly and the soloists to form their phrasing without undue harmonic interference. But it would perhaps have been interesting to hear the occasional harmonic interjection from the non-soloists, supplying different colours as the numbers progressed, rather than using them solely in the theme statements at the beginning and end of each piece. The CD carries an extra track, a duet between Oscar Pettiford and Max Roach made during Sonny Rollins's **Freedom Suite** sessions. One wonders then why it wasn't added to *that* album's reissue? **KS**

**We Insist! – Freedom Now Suite** Roach (d, arr); **Booker Little** (t); **Julian Priester** (tb); **Walter Benton, Coleman Hawkins** (ts); **James Schenck** (b); **Michael Olatunji, Ray Mantilla, Thomas Duvail** (perc); **Abbey Lincoln** (v). Candid Ⓜ CCD9002 (37 minutes). Recorded 1960.

✔ ❽ ❽

Many critics and fans were upset by the espousal of the civil rights movement by musicians – if musicians were espoused by the movement, fans and critics didn't mind so much – but the critics and fans, being white, could afford to condemn the politicization of art. This was in any case not new, as black jazzmen had been privately outspoken since at least the thirties (note the contribution of Coleman Hawkins to the present album), but the explicit connection dates from the late-fifties influence on jazz of gospel music in addition to blues. By 1960, it was possible for Roach to emulate his colleague Charles Mingus and attempt a musical depiction of the condition of blacks in the US and in Central and South Africa. Very different in tone from his quintet co-led by Clifford Brown, this group was descended from his 1958 album **Deeds Not Words** (and presaged the also-excellent **Percussion Bitter-Sweet**, recently reissued on CD), and has telling contributions from Little and Priester added to considerable rhythmic interest, with its opening and closing tracks in 5/4. But the most affecting voice is Lincoln's, heard on all five numbers; sometimes using the lyrics of Oscar Brown Jr, she also duets wordlessly with Roach on the powerful *Triptych*. **BP**

---

**To the Max**  Roach (d, perc); **Cecil Bridgewater** (t); **Odean Pope** (ts); **George Cables** (p); **Ronnell Bey** (v); **Uptown String Quartet** (Diane Monroe, Lesa Terry, vn; Maxine Roach, va; Eileen Folson, vc); **M'Boom** (Roy Brooks, Joe Chambers, Omar Clay, Eli Fountain, Fred King, Ray Mantilla, Francisco Mora, Warren Smith, perc); **John Motley Singers**. Enja ⓟ ENJ7021/2 (two discs: 100 minutes). Recorded 1990/1.

⑧ ❽

"If you're a creative artist, you have to have new ideas." In 1985 the man who had played bebop with Charlie Parker was following his credo by playing hip-hop with Fab Five Freddie. It was just the latest venture from the 40-plus years of tireless experimenting that have seen Max Roach develop into the most complete percussionist in jazz history. As well as continuing to lead his fine post-bop quartet, his projects in the seventies and eighties included working with gospel choirs and string quartets, co-founding the percussion ensemble, M'Boom, writing extended compositions and recording excellent improvised duos with avant-gardists Anthony Braxton and Cecil Taylor.

**To the Max** celebrates Roach's multi-faceted creativity and offers a splendid introduction to some of his current interests. The opening 30-minute suite *Ghost Dance* features his vocal writing; *A Little Booker* blends jazz and string quartets to dramatic effect; two exquisite solo pieces let his drums sing out with scintillating artistry. His regular group contributes four tracks of fierce, passionate bop, while M'Boom add enchanting percussion sonorities, *Street Dance* a carnival shuffle, *A Quiet Place* all chiming liquidity. Roach's trap drumming, meanwhile, remains superbly lean and crisp, his rapid-fire cymbal lines setting the pace throughout this hugely impressive and enjoyable set. **GL**

---

New review

**Max Roach with the New Orchestra of Boston and the So What Brass Quintet**  Roach (d), with the **New Orchestra of Boston** conducted by **David Epstein**; **Roach** (d), **Cecil Bridgewater** (t), **Frank Gordon** (t), **Marshall Sealy** (frh), **Steve Turrey** (tb), **Robert Stewart** (tba). Blue Note ⓟ CDP8 34813-2 (63 minutes). Recorded 1993/95

④ ❽

Fred Tillis's *Festival Journey*, the 51-minute classical piece that takes up most of the disc, is a draggy piece of mid-century modernism, with a good amount of stirring American symphonic bombast. But Roach drums throughout, and is the featured soloist (it was written with Roach in mind); it's refreshing to hear really persuasive rhythm – not necessarily jazz drumming, but are Roach's favourite polyrhythmic patterns necessarily jazz? – meshing with academic classical music. They don't make perfect partners, but Roach enlivens the piece. The only other item on the disc, *Ghost Dance*, is more to the point in terms of texture, though musical interaction is uninspired. It's mostly ostinato riffing in blues scales with mournful, drumless passages and various pairings-off inserted to keep it fresh. Composition and improvisation are in equal parts, but the arrangements are both weak and heavy-handed; a cold, unfinished feeling pervades the music. **BR**

# Yves Robert

1958

New review

**tout de suite ...**  Robert (tb); **Philippe Deschepper** (g); **Claude Tchamitchian** (b); **Alfred Spirli** (d); **Xavier Desandre** (perc). Deux Z ⓟ 84115 (56 minutes). Recorded 1994.

⑧ ❽

It may not sound much, but Robert is at the forefront of French jazz trombone playing. In fact, native French jazz has a lot going for it, not the least being an urgent desire to create its own series of unique hybrids in pairing jazz ideas and forms with more local folk and popular musics. Thus Robert has the fluidity and flexibility of technique and tone to seem a worthy heir to Mangelsdorff's trombone generation while at the same time able to compose a continuous suite covering a lot of stylistic ground and lasting close to an hour. He and Deschepper in the front line also make short work of interpolating such jazz standards as *Ornithology* and J.J. Johnson's *Lament* into the suite's tapestry, taking Parker's song at breakneck speed but underlaying it with a sampled swingbeat drum pattern before falling into contrapuntal improvisation against a real drummer's added backbeat. Sound strange? Just the French sense of humour, that's all, and considering the often po-faced approach to jazz and related musics both sides of the English-speaking Atlantic, no bad thing either. Johnson gets an altogether more dignified treatment, his moving theme reverently transcribed for muted trombone, guitar and bass. This only scratches the surface on a fascinating, entertaining disc.　　　**KS**

## Charles Luckyeth 'Luckey' Roberts　　　　　　　　1887-1968

**Luckey and The Lion: Harlem Piano** Roberts, Willie 'The Lion' Smith (p). Good Time Jazz
Ⓜ GTJCD10035-2 (44 minutes). Recorded 1958.

⑧ ❻

The usual definition of Harlem 'stride' piano focuses on the superimposition of formulaic right-hand patterns over a rhythmic 'oompah' bass played by the left in a more swinging version of ragtime. This is, however, simplistic. On this disc the boundaries of the genre are tested by two very different exponents. Roberts is a bravura stylist, his rapid-fire flourishes and flurries undimmed on this relatively late recording by the effects of a traffic accident and a stroke. His *Spanish Fandango* brings the Hispanic elements of East Harlem to bear on some of the formulas of stride, while his *Railroad Blues* is as effective a piece of onomatopoeic programme music as the more familiar efforts of the boogie-woogie players. *Complainin'* is the most unusual – but the most subtle – of Roberts's pieces, his mumbling interruptions of complaint breaking the flow of a forward-moving piece of conventional stride, much in the manner of James P. Johnson's *Riffs*. Smith's pretty ragtime-based pieces like *Morning Air* and *Relaxin'* break the mould in another way. The Lion favoured left-hand ostinatos, repeated chords and suspensions in preference to 'striding'. When he eventually unleashed the full power of his left hand, the effect was genuinely dramatic.　　　　　　**AS**

## Howard Roberts　　　　　　　　　　　　　　　1929-92

**The Real Howard Roberts** Roberts (g); Ross Tompkins (p); Ray Brown (b); Jimmie Smith (d).
Concord Jazz Ⓕ CCD4053 (47 minutes). Recorded 1977.

❻ ⑧

The title has at least two interpretations. It could refer to Roberts's delivery from the Californian studios after the best part of 20 years; or it could announce his return to the post-Christian mainstream after such early seventies forays into jazz-rock psychedelia as **Antelope Freeway** and **Equinox Elevator Express**. Either way, this typically well-behaved Concord date is how Roberts is most likely to be remembered. Despite occasional rock and blues inflections and 'modern' colourations with phase shift and swell pedal, he is captured here in his natural habitat, playing politely daring jazz guitar in the Kessel-Burrell mould.

Inevitably, a good deal of single string soloing ensues. This is serviceable enough but, unsurprisingly in a man used to providing guitar soundbites, the solos are somewhat short on grand design and dramatic contour. For Roberts at his most completely satisfying it is perhaps best to turn to the swaggering comping with which he propelled the Bobby Troup band in the mid fifties (audible on the recently-issued **Bobby Troup**: **The Feeling of Jazz**, on Starline SLCD9009).　　　　**MG**

## Marcus Roberts　　　　　　　　　　　　　　　1963

**Alone With Three Giants** Roberts (p). Novus Ⓕ PD83109 (64 minutes). Recorded 1990.

⑦ ⑧

If only by association, Roberts is seen as part of the neo-classical jazz school in America. He has, however, done a great deal more than investigate the roots of bebop and the work of the pioneers in that movement. In building a personal style he has taken his field of research far beyond that area. This CD has him Robertizing the work of three great pianist/composers from past jazz history. The choice is superficially obvious, but the way in which he confronts each challenge is edifying. He has to contain Jelly Roll Morton's suspended rhythms, he must successfully temper Duke Ellington's dangerously deceptive romanticism and harness Thelonious Monk's idosyncratic approach to harmony for his own ends. Each victory is different, as he masters Morton's Spanish tinge on *New Orleans Blues* and *The Crave*, contrasts Ellington's reverential *Prelude to a Kiss* and *Mood Indigo* with the stride master's *Shout 'Em Aunt Tillie*, and then captures Monk's arrogant stride on *Trinkle, Tinkle* and the slower *Pannonica*. Yes, it is an act of revivalism, but Roberts has shown great sympathy for each of his subjects. To present a coherent study of jazz using the multi-strained ragtime compositional form, the James P. Johnson and Fats Waller stride lineage, and music from the once-exclusive bebop club, is to register oneself as an important young player. Roberts has since left Novus and recorded a range of albums for Columbia, but none move past what he achieves here.　　**BMcR**

## Dick Robertson　　　　　　　　　　　　　　　1903

**And His Orchestra, 1937-9** Robertson (v); with a collective personnel of **Bobby Hackett** (c);
**Johnny McGhee, Ralph Muzzillo, Johnny Carlson** (t); **Al Philburn, Buddy Morrow, Jack
Teagarden** (tb); **Paul Ricci, Sid Trucker, Don Watt, Tony Zimmers** (cl); **Frank Froeba, Frank**

Signorelli (p, cel); **Frank Victor**, **Dave Barbour** (g); **Haig Stephens** (b); **Sammy Weiss**, **Stan King** (d). Timeless Ⓜ CBC1-008 (70 minutes). Recorded 1937-9.

⑥ ❻

Robertson wasn't much more than a mediocre singer with a modicum of jazz style, his light baritone most accurately described as 'pleasing', but he deserves to be remembered, if only for the fine Dixieland-style small groups he invariably assembled behind him for his recording sessions. His career in the studios lasted just seven years, but in that time he was prolific, cutting many more sides than could be contained on a single CD. This compilation was selected by Chris Ellis and remastered by John R.T. Davies, so you're getting pretty much the best from what is available.

It is the presence of Bobby Hackett which enlivens the first clutch of performances, his sound getting the listener's heart to race just a little when he enters. Other notable characteristics are a steady, stomping beat of the type favoured by Bob Crosby, slashing trombone work and dextrous clarinet fills. A January 1938 date finds Jack Teagarden's trombone combining elegantly with trumpeters McGhee and Muzzillo, while pianist Froeba, present on 15 of the 24 tracks, starts the vast majority of those with the same descending piano arabesque. If it was a private joke, it must have been wearing thin after a year or so. **KS**

# Herb Robertson

New review
**Sound Implosion** Robertson (t, flh, s posthorn, toys, v); **Dominic Duval** (b, prepared b); **Jay Rosen** (d, perc, v). Creative Improvised Music Projects Ⓕ CIMP110 (72 minutes). Recorded 1996.

⑥ ❽

Long-term associate Tim Berne once accused Robertson of trying not to be discovered. Although something of a refugee from the commercial world, that humorous defamation no longer applies. Robertson is an outstanding trumpeter, composer and jazzman and, within his field, he is well known. Born in New Jersey, he attended Berklee from 1969 to 1972 and on leaving formed a productive quartet with bassist Mark Helias. During the eighties he worked with saxophonist Berne and together they forged a uniquely positive style and recorded frequently. As befits a musical habitué of New York's Knitting Factory, Robertson is an unashamed iconoclast and he believes that all sounds are for the using. The standard *Deep Purple* directs the newcomer into the trumpeter's improvisational method and (like other titles) shows that his style represents an update of Rex Stewart's tonal manipulation, audacious overstatement and vocalized phrasing. Robertson never parades his technique but he uses it as a creative tool and he ensures that humour enriches rather than demeans his music. His use of soprano posthorn and various toys confronts the po-faced and their use serves the broader purpose, extending his tonal range and providing the 'noises' he deems necessary. **BMcR**

# Jim Robinson

1892-1976

**Classic New Orleans Jazz, Volume 2** Robinson (tb); **Kid Thomas**, **Ernest Cagnolatti**, **Tony Fougerat** (t); **Capt. John Handy** (as); **Sammy Rimington**, **Albert Burbank**, **Orange Kellin** (cl); **Bill Sinclair** (p); **Dick Griffith**, **George Guesnon**, **Father Al Lewis** (bj); **Dick McCarthy**, **'Slow Drag' Pavageau**, **James Prevost** (b); **Sammy Penn**, **'Cie' Frazier**, **Louis Barbarin** (d). Biograph Ⓕ BCD128 (57 minutes). Recorded 1964-74.

⑤ ❹

Returning from military service in 1919, trombonist Robinson spent more than ten years in Sam Morgan's excellent band in New Orleans. His playing with the band and later with Lee Collins and Kid Howard called for a modified version of the tail-gate tradition. It was the New Orleans revival of the late forties and the need to assume his place in the bands of Bunk Johnson, then George Lewis, that forced Robinson to return to the purer aspects of the style. As this CD with his own bands shows, he was highly successful. He provided the forthright punctuation and ensemble linkage that was required, putting greater emphasis on *glissando* effects and, on *Shake That Thing* and *Gasket Street Blues* in particular, showing the fine balance he could achieve. His solo work was less impressive and *Lady Be Good* and *Washington and Lee Swing* are typical of his rudimentary approach. The melody is lightly paraphrased, points of emphasis are adjusted but no real attempt is made to improvise. The simplified approach served his collective playing well, however, and although he may not have deciphered the somewhat cluttered ensemble patterns of the first six titles here, the remainder provide a yardstick by which New Orleans's revivalist trombone is judged. **BMcR**

# Orphy Robinson

1960

**When Tomorrow Comes** Robinson (vb, mba, perc); **Rowland Sutherland** (f, af, pic); **Tunde Jegede** (kora, vc); **Joe Bashorun** (p, kbds); **Dudley Phillips** (b); **Winston Clifford** (d, perc). Blue Note Ⓕ CDP7 98581-2 (59 minutes). Recorded 1991.

⑥ ❽

Although Orphy Robinson has been a regular feature on the UK scene for some time, both collaborating with Andy Sheppard and fronting his own bands, this was his début main-label recording as a leader. He shares the composing credits with keyboard player Joe Bashorun, but the album's wide-ranging musical reference points, covering the whole spectrum from acoustic traditional music to urban funk, are very much Robinson's own. He himself plays not only African music's staple marimba but also jazz vibes, and his collaborators similarly veer between continents and musical styles. The results are distinctly variable. In general, Bashorun's compositions are better vehicles for good improvisation, being more immediately accessible and tuneful than Robinson's (unsurprising, given the keyboard player's session and tour experience with the Womacks and his stints with electric bands like Desperately Seeking Fusion), but the album suffers from a shortage of sustained improvisational interest to flesh out the occasionally ponderous, fussy compositions. Too often an intriguing rhythm is set up, a strikingly unusual instrumental mix assembled, and then the piece's potential remains unrealized for lack of a biting soloist. The album thus gives the impression of being too long for the number of musical ideas it contains, which is a shame, because those that are there are usually original and striking. Still, it remains better than the follow-up, **The Vibes Decides**.                                                                                  **CP**

## Perry Robinson                                                                              1938

**Call to the Stars** Robinson (cl); **Simon Nabatov** (p); **Ed Schuller** (b); **Ernst Bier** (d). West Wind
  Ⓕ 2052 (64 minutes). Recorded 1990.

⑧  ❽

Although that rarest of breeds, the modern jazz clarinettist, Robinson has never quite received the attention he deserves. From the time of his first, early-sixties LP for Savoy he has straddled the populist folk and experimental traditions à la Jimmy Giuffre, adding an Eastern slant in the seventies by recording with percussionists Badal Roy and Nana Vasconcelos. He brings all of these influences to bear on **Call To The Stars**.

*Farmer Alfalfa*, a Henry Grimes tune from the Savoy days, shows how subtly his style has changed, from a 'cool' Lesterian chromaticism to a harder Coltrane swing. He has always liked to contrast low swoops with high squeals, and there are more slurs, bent pitches, and unorthodox effects today, equal parts mid-Eastern reed technique and Pee Wee Russell. Robinson's chalumeau *sotto voce* entry on bassist Schuller's *Shu Bass Blues* is pure Pee Wee, as are his curious note choices, changes of direction and harmonic curves. Similarly, *Henry's Dance* shows off his circuitous logic to good advantage. Nabatov's Tyneresque heft is an excellent foil and grounding force to Robinson's freer tendencies; he turns Darius Brubeck's *Sindaram Song* from a raga with Eastern European modes to a soulful romp. Like Pee Wee, Sandy Brown, and Ed Chace, Robinson's unconventional playing is still denied acceptance in certain quarters. A pity.                                                                          **AL**

## Reginald R. Robinson                                                                       1973

**Sounds in Silhouette** Robinson (p). Delmark Ⓕ DE670 (61 minutes). Recorded 1994.

⑧  ❽

As the dates above reveal, Reginald Robinson was 21 years old when he made this, his second CD. Jazz musicians nowadays are making their débuts younger every year, so this would not normally be a matter for comment. But Reginald Robinson is not exactly a jazz musician: he is a ragtime pianist and composer. The 19 tracks here are all his compositions, except for one, which is his medley of three pieces by Charles L. Johnson, a contemporary of Joplin. They include rags, cakewalks and one charming tango, *Dream Natasha*, and all have that dignified but jaunty air which is unique to ragtime. Both composition and playing sound meticulously authentic. How an African-American child growing up in Chicago in the eighties came to be obsessed with ragtime, to the extent of setting out to teach himself the piano with the aid of library books and eventually going on to study at the American Conservatory, is one of those mysteries which occur from time to time. They bring with them the cheering message that there is no such thing as a completely dead musical language, that youth and fashion do not necessarily go together, and that everybody is not the same as everybody else.                                                                               **DG**

## Spike Robinson                                                                             1930

**Henry B. Meets Alvin G. / Once in a Wild** Robinson, Al Cohn (ts); **Richard Wyands** (p); **Steve LaSpina** (b); **Akira Tana** (d). Capri Ⓕ 1061787 (67 minutes). Recorded 1987.

⑦  ❻

Like Buck Hill, another 'recent' tenor saxophone discovery, Robinson worked full-time at another career and only turned to music as a vocation in 1985 when he retired as an engineer. He's been written about in some circles as an extension of the Cool West Coast fifties sound, but this album is quite a heated affair. All he really shares with a number of the Cool saxists is an affinity for Lester

Young – witness his relaxed phrasing on the laidback *Sweets Blues* as well as his breathy, elaborate ballad playing on a favourite of Pres's, *These Foolish Things*. Rhythmically, both he and Cohn inhabit that grey area between swing and bop, leaning towards the former. More complementary than combative, they mesh well together on Bob Brookmeyer's bouncy *Rustic Hop* and the evergreen *Once in a While*, taken at a slightly brighter tempo than usual. But they are capable of high-spirited blowing too, primarily on *Sippin' at Bells*, and they put an old war-horse like *Bye Bye Blues* through some lively paces, concluding with a contrapuntal chorus *sans* rhythm section. Richard Wyands is an underrated journeyman accompanist with a light touch: he introduces *Sweets' Blues* with a casual insouciance worthy of Count Basie. Steve LaSpina and Akira Tana combine as a solid, unobtrusive rhythm team (audio note: the slightly lower rating for the digital sound was due to a tad too much echo on the horns, though it's still quite easy to distinguish Robinson's burnished tone from Cohn's bristling tenor). **AL**

# Joe Roccisano                                                              1939

New review
**The Shape I'm In** Roccisano, Lou Marini (as); Tim Ries, Ken Hitchcock (ts, ss); Jack Stuckey (bs, bcl); Bob Millikan, Bud Burridge, Tom Harrell (t); Jim Pugh, Matt Finders, Paul Faulise (tb); Bill Charlap (p); Scott Lee, Paul Adamy (b); John Basile (g); Terry Clarke (d). Landmark
Ⓕ LCD1535-2 (61 minutes). Recorded 1992.
⑥ ❾

In an impressive début, the New York City-based Joe Roccisano Orchestra sizzle, soar and swing with a postmodern panache that is lean, mean and muscular. Roccisano, a gifted reedman/arranger with a truckload of playing/writing credits including Bill Holman, Don Ellis, Toshiko Akiyoshi, Woody Herman, Supersax, Ray Charles and Walter Becker, is an original. Indeed, in scorchers like the leader's *Prism*, Bill Charlap's piano, Tom Harrell's trumpet and Roccisano's Yamaha WX11 meld laser-light refractions embracing both the big band's 'inside' and 'outside' traditions.

The guts of the band's persona are to be found in Roccisano's charts. And while functioning as sinewy soloistic slingshots, Roccisano's maps are freestanding and forceful fusings where form and content resonate with dramatic dash and structural *élan*. Indeed, Roccisano's capacity to combine the red-blooded with the coolly thoughtful gives him a Clint Eastwood-like aura that can't help but make one's day. At the same time, and in the best of the Ellington and Herman traditions, this is also a players' band where Marini, Ries, Harrell, Hitchcock, Pugh, Scott, Charlap and Clarke paint boldly between and beyond the lines. **CB**

# Betty Roché                                                               1920

New review
**Singin' and Swingin'** Roché (v); Jimmy Forrest (ts); Jack McDuff (org); Bill Jennings (g); Wendell Marshall (b); Roy Haynes (d). Prestige Ⓜ OJCCD1718-2 (31 minutes). Recorded 1960.
⑦ ❽

Roché was a band singer with Ellington for some years before embarking on an off-on free-lance career. This all-too-short set is one of the solo albums from the middle of her free-lance period, a ballad-dominated anthology underpinned by McDuff's long notes on the organ and some low-key backing from Marshall and Haynes. Roché does well when she sticks to the lyrics, but her scat singing and improvisations round the words include the kinds of vowel sounds that would have made the late Kingsley Amis apoplectic. The backing band comes into its own on the faster tempos, *A Foggy Day* receiving the cliché corner treatment from Jennings, who manages a vast chunk of quotation from *An English Country Garden* in his solo, but otherwise redeemed by Forrest tearing into a wild and woolly solo. At least Roché is stylistically indebted to no other singer and remains her own woman throughout. Her most characteristic piece is a nonchalant *Blue Moon*, placing her in Sarah Vaughan/Carmen McRea territory but with a distinct grid reference of her own. **AS**

# Claudio Roditi                                                            1946

New review
**Milestones** Roditi (t, flh); Paquito D'Rivera (as, cl); Kenny Barron (p); Ray Drummond (b); Ben Riley (d). Candid Ⓕ CCD79515 (70 minutes). Recorded 1990.
⑦ ❽

Born in Brazil, Roditi was introduced to jazz by listening to the American giants on record. He came through the Berklee School in Boston in the early sixties and moved to New York in 1976. At first active in the loft scene, he later joined Dizzy Gillespie's United Nations Orchestra and is now a regular on the world festival circuit. This CD provides a good example of his work as musician and combo leader; he is in the company of another fine horn player and with one of the most powerful rhythm sections available. He demonstrates himself to be a gifted and flamboyant trumpeter, a player with a bristling attack and a natural ability to swing. He also shows himself to be as comfortable on a modal base as he is with a ballad's story-telling potential and his choice of material is examplary. His own shortcoming is in the area of précis; there are times when his detailed and flowing line would have benefited from a degree of selective abbreviation, still retaining the salient points in his excellent improvisations but excluding some of the decorative rhetoric. *But Not For Me* and *Brussels in the Rain* come near to this ideal and perhaps suggest that allowance must be made for the fact that this is a live album, made in New York's Birdland and that, with an audience present, a degree of showboating is inevitable. **BMcR**

# Red Rodney

1927-94

**Then and Now**  Rodney (flh); **Chris Potter** (as, ts); **Garry Dial** (p); **Jay Anderson** (b); **Jimmy Madison** (d); **Bob Belden** (arr). Chesky Ⓕ JD79 (75 minutes). Recorded 1992.

⑧ ❽

A great deal of care and preparation went into the making of this album and the title says it all. Here are nearly a dozen bebop tunes played with equal ackowledgement of the time of their original creation and of contemporary 1992 music. Rodney and arranger Bob Belden have made adjustments, updating the pieces without losing the character of the compositions. Tadd Dameron's *The Scene Is Clean*, for example, is played as a waltz (and very attractively too) and an adjustment has been made to the middle-eight of *Confirmation*. But none of these changes is likely to upset even the most ardent bebop enthusiast, for the music must be judged in its totality and this is a very successful album, far better than yet another attempt to produce note-for-note versions of music first recorded over four decades ago. Rodney is fluent on flügelhorn and Potter fits in well on both saxes (although he is not at heart a bopper). The rhythm section plays with a smooth, efficient continuity and does not attempt to emulate the often harsh and jagged backings of a 1947-vintage team. The final ten minutes of playing time is devoted to an interesting interview with Rodney, although it is not the kind of thing one would want to hear as frequently as the music itself. **AM**

# Shorty Rogers

1924-94

**The Big Shorty Rogers Express**  Rogers (t, arr) with a collective personnel of **Conrad Gozzo, Maynard Ferguson, Pete Candoli, John Howell, Conte Candoli, Harry Edison** (t); **Milt Bernhart, John Halliburton, Harry Betts, Frank Rosolino** (tb); **Bob Enevoldsen** (vtb); **John Graas** (frh); **George Roberts** (btb); **Gene Englund, Paul Sarmento** (tba); **Charlie Mariano** (as); **Art Pepper** (as, ts, bs); **Bud Shank** (as, bs); **Bill Holman, Jack Montrose** (ts); **Jimmy Giuffre** (cl,ts, bs); **Bob Cooper** (ts, bs); **Marty Paich, Lou Levy** (p); **Curtis Counce, Ralph Pena** (b); **Shelly Manne, Stan Levey** (d). RCA Living Stereo Ⓜ 18519-2 (43 minutes). Recorded 1953/6.

⑩ ❽

This was where West Coast Jazz began. Rogers had been using his small group, The Giants, on club dates and featured it in front of what was virtually the Stan Kenton orchestra on those first eight big band tracks made for RCA. Issued originally as a ten-inch LP called **Cool and Crazy**, four additional tracks were recorded in 1956 to make it into a 12-inch with a new title, **The Big Shorty Rogers Express** and this CD is the exact equivalent of that LP complete with the picture of Shorty sitting on the front of the Sante Fé engine. All the big and important West Coast names are here, Pepper, Shank, Cooper, Giuffre, Manne, Paich, the Candolis, and the like, and the music still packs that tremendous punch, like an even more powerful Basie band using the same kind of contrast between the incredible brass passages (with Ferguson doubling Gozzo's lead an octave higher) and the economic piano work from 'Count' Paich and 'Count' Levy. In this context Rogers's own somewhat limited powers as an improvising soloist are masked by the aptness and sheer unbridled excitement of the ensemble work. Pepper and Cooper sound marvellous, Manne is perfect and the dynamics on *Infinity Promenade*, logically building to a splendid climax in just over three minutes, is still a thing to wonder at. The playing time is short because this is an obvious facsimile of an LP; in fact RCA could easily have added the eight titles by Shorty's Giants which they recorded a couple of months before the **Cool and Crazy** album. Despite this shortcoming the CD is highly recommended, because of the lasting quality of this superb big band's music. **AM**

# Adrian Rollini

1904-56

New review

**Bouncin' in Rhythm**  Rollini (bss, hfp, gfs, p, vb, xyl, d); **Chelsea Quealey, Manny Klein, Wingy Manone, Freddy Jenkins** (t); **Bix Beiderbecke, Red Nichols** (c); **Jimmy Dorsey** (t, cl, as); **Tommy Dorsey, Jack Teagarden** (tb); **Don Murray** (cl, bs); **Frankie Trumbauer** (c-ms); **Pee Wee Russell, Benny Goodman, Albert Nicholas** (cl); **Joe Marsala** (cl, as); **Arthur Rollini** (ts); **Fud Livingston** (cl, ts); **Joe Venuti** (vn); **Arthur Schutt, Itzy Riskin, Frank Signorelli, Putney Dandridge, Joe Turner** (p); **Eddie Lang, Dick McDonough, George Van Eps, Carmen Mastren, Bernard Addison**

(g); **Sid Weiss**, **Joe Watts** (b); **Chauncey Morehouse**, **Vic Berton**, **Stan King**, **Sam Weiss** (d). Topaz Ⓕ TPZ1027 (70 minutes). Recorded 1926-35.

⑨ ❼

A child prodigy, Rollini was doubling piano and xylophone and leading his own band in New York when he was only 14 years old. It was not until joining the California Ramblers in the early twenties that he bought his first bass saxophone and so became the instrument's finest exponent. Without any serious precedent, he provided it with an acceptable jazz language and showed how it could simultaneously be both rhythm-section prop and melody-playing horn. The fumbling efforts of Billy Fowler and Coleman Hawkins in the Fletcher Henderson band of the early twenties were never a reference; if anything, Rollini derived as much from the Emmett Hardy/Bix Beiderbecke cornet school as it did from the brass bass men or from players of the other saxophones.

This CD presents his finest work and also encapsulates his entire career. Two California Ramblers tracks from 1926 display his highly personal timing and his ability to lift an ensemble. *Beatin' the Dog* offers an early introduction to chamber jazz and shows how he could match the dashing Venuti in the swing department. There are fine examples of his work with the Beiderbecke and Trumbauer partnership and he is never better than on *Jazz Band Ball* and *Royal Garden Blues* with Bix and His Gang. He swings prodigiously on *Feelin' No Pain* with Miff Mile's Little Molers and brings the same mobility to his Red Norvo-ish vibraphone work on *Vibraphonia*. His 1935 Tap Room Gang had his bass sax leading the ensemble on *Honeysuckle Rose*, while on the Harlem Seven's *Toledo Shuffle* he plays uncomplicated but swinging drums. Rollini was a genuine all-rounder, and despite the Art Ensemble of Chicago's revival of the large instrument in more recent years, there is little to challenge his status as its most outstanding player. **BMcR**

# Sonny Rollins

1930

**The Complete Prestige Recordings** Rollins (ts); with a collective personnel of **Miles Davis**, **Kenny Dorham**, **Art Farmer**, **Clifford Brown** (t); **J.J. Johnson**, **Bennie Green** (tb); **Julius Watkins** (frh); **Jackie McLean** (as); **Charlie Parker**, **John Coltrane** (ts); **John Lewis**, **Miles Davis**, **Walter Bishop Jr**, **Kenny Drew**, **Thelonious Monk**, **Horace Silver**, **Elmo Hope**, **Ray Bryant**, **Tommy Flanagan**, **Richie Powell**, **Red Garland**, **Wade Legge** (p); **Milt Jackson** (vb); **Leonard Gaskin**, **Percy Heath**, **Tommy Potter**, **George Morrow**, **Paul Chambers**, **Doug Watkins** (b); **Max Roach**, **Roy Haynes**, **Art Blakey**, **Philly Joe Jones**, **Willie Jones**, **Kenny Clarke**, **Art Taylor** (d); **Earl Coleman** (v). Prestige Ⓕ 7PCD4407-2 (seven discs: 496 minutes). Recorded 1949-56.

⑨ ❽

Rollins grew up as an artist while he was under contract to Prestige. His first session as a leader occurred in 1951: previous to that, from 1949 onwards he had been a sideman on J.J. Johnson and Miles Davis dates for Prestige (and a Johnson date for Savoy), and had also recorded for Bud Powell over at Blue Note.

There are efficacious things amongst the earlier tracks, but life gets serious in late 1953 with the Rollins/Milt Jackson session, followed one month later by the four tracks with Monk. By this time, Rollins had made great stylistic strides and was an instantly recognizable player, both for the sound he created and for the personal way he negotiated the harmonic structures of the repertoire being recorded. Yet within a year the tenor player had taken himself off the scene, unhappy with both himself and his playing. A 12-month silence was broken by the spectacular success of the quartet album, **Worktime**, contained on disc four here, recorded in December 1955. Its mastery was only overshadowed by the towering achievements, just six months later, on **Saxophone Colossus** (which takes up the first half of disc six). By the end of 1956 Rollins was moving on to other record companies and other ideas, but one wonders whether anything he did later was *better* than what he did in that *annus mirabilis*, or whether it was simply *different*. Different peaks, different troughs. All equally fascinating.

This boxed set is a superb presentation, neatly encapsulating early Rollins in a way the similar Prestige box of early Coltrane (1955-8), with its sprawling 16 CDs and multitude of sideman dates for the saxophonist, cannot hope to. The 48-page booklet contains an erudite commentary by Bob Blumenthal, a full Prestige Rollins discography and plenty of first-class photographs. The playing times are exemplary. Prestige got this one right. **KS**

**Saxophone Colossus** **Sonny Rollins** (ts); **Tommy Flanagan** (p); **Doug Watkins** (b); **Max Roach** (d). Prestige Ⓜ OJCCD291-2 (40 minutes). Recorded 1956.

❶ ⑩ ❽

**Saxophone Colossus** is one of the undisputed masterpieces of jazz. In form it is very simple – tenor saxophone and rhythm section playing a set of five tunes; two standards, an original, a West Indian folk-song and a blues. Like all great works, it operates at many levels. It is swinging, optimistic and entirely understandable music; the balance of the instruments and the subtlety of their interplay represent perfection in the post-bop idiom; Rollins's sound is massive yet flexible and intimate, with none of the slightly hectoring tone which it later assumed.

At a deeper level, Rollins builds his improvisations with a cogency that is little short of miraculous. Gunther Schuller produced a famous thematic analysis of one of the album's pieces, *Blue Seven*, demonstrating that Rollins's entire long solo is constructed from motifs based on the intervals of the third and flattened fifth. Just as remarkable is his rhythmic freedom within the gridlines of the beat and the chord sequence, creating endless patterns of tension and release. In short, **Saxophone Colossus** is a record with which you can happily spend a lifetime. **DG**

**Way Out West** Rollins (ts); **Ray Brown** (b); **Shelly Manne** (d). Contemporary Ⓜ OJCCD337-2
(71 minutes). Recorded 1957.

⑧ ⑧

**Way Out West** was recorded during Rollins's first visit to the West Coast. His sense of humour was evident in the famous cover-photo of him with stetson, holster and horn and immediately confirmed by the opening *I'm an Old Cow Hand*, with its tongue-in-cheek clip-clop beat ("I want that cat out on the range all the way," Rollins told drummer Manne) and droll tenor dissections of the tune.

Such comic guying was a gift Rollins had honed in his stint with Thelonious Monk, and this album also shows him following Monk's advice to "use the melody" (not just the chord changes) when improvising. He had, moreover, been keen to try working without piano; **Way Out West** was his first trio record and he revels in the extra space. He ranges all over his horn, from high peals to gruff interjections, and rhythmically is both buoyant and assured. He devours the up-tempo *Come, Gone* (to the initial discomfiture of Manne) and elsewhere rides the beat with authority as he delivers his jaunty dabs and flourishes, turning to smoother lines and a more imploring tone for the ballads, *Solitude* and *There is No Greater Love*. It all makes for an exhilarating display of saxophone virtuosity. The CD contains three alternative (longer) takes that were not on the original **Way Out West** LP, but which did appear on Contemporary's **Alternate Takes** LP. **GL**

**A Night at the Village Vanguard, Volumes 1 and 2** Rollins (ts); **Wilbur Ware** (b); **Elvin Jones** (d); **Donald Bailey** (b); **Pete LaRoca** (d). Blue Note Ⓜ CDP7 46517/8-2 (two discs, oas: 58 and 69 minutes). Recorded 1957.

✓ ⑩ ⑥

In 1957, Sonny Rollins began a decade of superior recordings bracketed by **Way Out West** and 1966's **East Broadway Rundown**. The absence of piano on many of them gave Rollins freedom to ignore or transcend the disciplines of harmony and time-keeping the instrument imposed and linked him implicitly with piano-averse Ornette Coleman.

The Vanguard sessions were recorded at afternoon and evening shows one Sunday. Sonny's harsh tone complements his booting rhythmic energy and embodies Monk's concept of 'ugly beauty'. A flood of ideas pours from his tenor, as on *Striver's Row* (Volume 2). *Old Devil Moon* (Volume 1) demonstrates how much his celebrated penchant for thematic improvisation involves careful attention to the melody (in that sense, this modernist is decidedly conservative). He brings radical rhythmic displacements to *Get Happy* (Volume 2), and tosses in typically outlandish quotes, tagging *Woody 'n' You* (Volume 1) with *March of the Siamese Children*.

Elvin's loose accents goad Rollins on; the harmonic simplicity of Ware's plump, propulsive bass further liberates rather than restricts him. The less-noted Bailey and LaRoca, heard at the matinée, are similarly progressive, never a hindrance. These separately-available volumes are evenly matched; the first features both rhythm sections, the second contains perhaps a few more peaks. A good collection deserves both. **KW**

New review

**Freedom Suite** Rollins (ts), **Oscar Pettiford** (b), **Max Roach** (d). Riverside Ⓜ OJCCD067-2
(41 minutes). Recorded 1958.

✓ ⑩ ⑧

An early, lean form of free music (maybe), **The Freedom Suite** is full of bracing space; the musicians, to an alarming extent, lay out at length or go where they want to go. Balance between composition and improvisation, brought home by Rollins's constant returning to the theme during his solos in the 19-minute piece, is as much the subject here as any socio-political notion obliquely conjured up by Orrin Keepnews's booklet-essay. The dry note-bending we call 'humour' in Rollins's playing stays front and centre; shorn back to the basics in every way, the record displays the spartan, ascetic Rollins, not the champagne-sweet or quicksilver one. It's also some of the greatest hard-driving music of post-bop, which seems like a contradiction; the point is, the ideas are diamond-hard. Completed with some romantic old waltzes and show tunes, the record has personality; it's short, but more organic than any other early Rollins record except for **Way Out West** and **Saxophone Colossus**, and certainly one of the two or three most consistently listenable. **BR**

**The Bridge** Rollins (ts); **Jim Hall** (g); **Bob Cranshaw** (b); **Ben Riley** (d). RCA Victor Ⓜ 68518-2
(41 minutes). Recorded 1962.

✓ ⑧ ⑧

It seemed strange that the passionate and urgent series of improvisations Rollins recorded for Prestige should come forth from such a reticent and modest man. Hindsight tells us that this was a time of great turbulence in Rollins's life. At the beginning of the sixties, he chose to drop from the public eye to re-evaluate his musical resources. Famously he was heard practicing on his tenor at night on New York's Williamsburg Bridge, and when, in late 1961, he returned to the jazz scene, a legend had built up around the incident and considerable hype resulted in the music press about what was to all intents a non-event. On his return Rollins was found to be dispensing the potent mixture much as before and this, his first post-Williamsburg Bridge album, found his dry and pithy embellishments not radically different. What did make a difference was the presence of Jim Hall on guitar instead of a pianist. Hall's chording gave Rollins much more freedom – this was a variation on the piano-less quartet theory operated by Gerry Mulligan and the guitarist proved to be a match for Rollins in his creative soloing. The long and impressive improvisation on *John S.* has a free atmosphere about it and has pre-echoes of the later and much longer *East Broadway Rundown*. The title track consists of two choruses, one alternating 6/8 with 4/4 whilst the other chorus is straight fours. In contrast to the overall idea that Rollins was a 'hard' player, *Where Are You?* and *God Bless the Child* are ballad performances of great sensitivity and again Hall's chording is vital. Typically of Rollins's work, the music has not dated at all, and indeed the comparatively concise nature of the playing makes this one more attractive than many of his later albums. **SV**

New review

**Sonny Rollins & Co. 1964** Rollins (ts); **Jim Hall** (g – three tracks); **Herbie Hancock** (p – five tracks); **Ron Carter**, **Bob Cranshaw** (b); **Roy McCurdy**, **Mickey Roker** (d). Bluebird Ⓜ 66530-2 (66 minutes). Recorded 1964.

⑦ ❼

Seven of these tracks originally appeared either on **Now's the Time** or **The Standard Sonny Rollins**, albums thought somewhat disappointing when first released (especially the second), while the remaining six are from **The Alternative Rollins**, a French RCA-originated collection of out-takes disowned by the saxophonist but greeted with considerable interest by *aficionados*. One of the latter group lasts almost 16 minutes, but half of the tracks are around the three-minute mark (a couple ending with a premature fade), whereas the version of *Django* is missing its opening phrase and has an awkward edit near the end. Such finds from the cutting-room floor have their disconcerting side, but also some very fine moments, precisely because they show Rollins's invention and indecision working hand in hand. As Bob Blumenthal astutely implies in the notes, this is an example of the saxist's live experimentation becoming evident in the studio. Sadly, the live documentation of this phase is sparse, consisting of 1963's **Our Man in Jazz**, 1965's **There Will Never Be Another You** (MCA/Impulse!) – another unauthorized major-label issue – and various European bootlegs. Since what emerged from studio sessions henceforth rarely showed the same cliff-hanging audacity as the live work, the value of the present album is ensured. Remaining unreissued so far on CD are the long alternative take of *Trav'lin' Light* and the fragment of *I'll Be Seeing You*, both of which could have been squeezed in here. **BP**

**Alfie** Rollins (ts); **Jimmy Cleveland**, **J.J. Johnson** (tb); **Phil Woods** (as); **Bob Ashton** (ts); **Danny Bank** (bs); **Roger Kellaway** (p); **Kenny Burrell** (g); **Walter Booker** (b); **Frankie Dunlop** (d); **Oliver Nelson** (arr, cond). Impulse! Ⓜ IMP12242 (33 minutes). Recorded 1966.

✓ ⑩ ❽

Although this is advertised as containing "original music from the score" of Lewis Gilbert's 1966 film starring Michael Caine as the eponymous cockney Casanova, that is not quite true. The themes are those written by Rollins for the movie, where he plays them with just a rhythm section. On disc, those themes are re-recorded, with orchestrations by Nelson. *Alfie's Theme*, the jukeing Rollins blues heard under the titles, expanded to ten glorious minutes here, has latterly become a rival to *St Thomas* as Rollins's signature tune. Meant to signal the title character's raffishness, the tune also signals the saxophonist's. It features a solo that, if transcribed, might appear to be one by any hucklebucking r&b saxophonist of the fifties or sixties. What identifies it as Rollins on actual hearing is his elliptical note placement and the sardonic vehemence of his honks and growls. The other five tracks, all of which have something going for them, include a lovely waltz in *On Impulse!* and one of Rollins's most affecting ballad performances on *He's Younger Than You Are*. Burrell and Kellway spell Rollins nicely, and although Nelson falls short of being Sonny's Gil Evans, his arrangements are serviceable: he does not blunt the rough edges, as he later would Pee Wee Russell's and Thelonious Monk's. This is from a period when Rollins, although working steadily and placing high in the polls, was somewhat taken for granted in some quarters because his music lacked the political and spiritual connotations of Coltrane's. The evidence here, and on the RCA albums which preceded his Impulse! deal, suggests that he was then at the top of his game, regardless of whether or not he was still in fashion. **FD**

New review

**Silver City** Rollins (ts); **Jon Faddis**, **Byron Stripling** (flh); **Clifton Anderson** (tb); **Alex Brofsky** (frh); **Bob Stewart** (tba); **George Cables**, **Stanley Cowell**, **Tommy Flanagan**, **Stephen Scott** (p); **Mark Soskin** (p, kbds); **Bobby Broom**, **Yoshiaki Masuo**, **Aurell Ray** (g); **Jerome Harris** (g, elb); **Russell Blake** (elb); **Bob Cranshaw** (b, elb); **Tommy Campbell**, **Jack DeJohnette**, **Al Foster**, **Steve Jordan**, **David Lee**, **Marvin 'Smitty' Smith**, **Tony Williams** (d); **Jimmy Heath** (arr); **Mtume**, **Lucille Rollins**, **Bill Summers** (perc). Milestone Ⓜ 2MCD2501/2 (two discs: 139 minutes). Recorded 1972-95.

⑨ ❽

Compiling a 'Best-of' two-CD set from Rollins's quarter-century as a Milestone recording artist does not exactly refute the notion that he has failed to make great albums, or that the quality of his supporting ensembles is a clear cut below his studio heyday of the fifties. Yet Rollins has delivered several great recorded moments since emerging from his last prolonged sabbatical in 1972, and **Silver**

**City** includes the best of the unaccompanied cadenzas (*Skylark*, *Autumn Nocturne*), up-tempo blowouts (*G-Man* and the title track) and calypso/funk confections (*Duke of Iron*, *Harlem Boys*). The programme also reminds us that Rollins continues to write catchy, memorable lines (*Biji* from 1995 should enjoy a long life) and plumb the depths of pop-music arcana for such unlikely material as (*This is My*) *Lucky Day* and *To a Wild Rose*. If there is less flexibility in Rollins's tone and the rhythm section's beat than in the past, the extensive interview indicates that this is at least a matter of choice rather than necessity. Non-completist Rollins fans will want this anthology as an economic alternative to picking from among the uneven Milestone discography. **BB**

**Sonny Rollins in Japan** Rollins (ts); **Yoshiaki Masuo** (g); **Bob Cranshaw** (el b); **David Lee** (d); James Mtume (cga). JVC Ⓜ VICJ23001 (47 minutes). Recorded 1973.

Ⓑ **⑦** **❻**

For Rollins, the seventies, on record at least, was hardly a memorable decade. Many of his albums were disappointing displays of self-indulgent filibustering, bolstered by an overdose of electronics and occasional forays on the soprano saxophone. This CD stands out from many surrounding it and sounds like a return to the days of the Impulse!, even the Prestige, sessions. Recorded at a Tokyo concert, it opens with a lengthy work-out on one of those Rollins compositions based on a repeated, and largely rhythmic, figure which, when spread over 18 minutes, becomes hypnotic. *Powaii* has comparatively short solo passages by the leader, but Sonny's massive presence is felt throughout and Masuo plays with logic and conviction. The other three tracks will appeal immediately to long-term Rollins enthusiasts for they comprise welcome reworkings of *St Thomas*, *Alfie's Theme* and *Moritat*, all of which receive careful examination from Sonny and are not merely thrown into the programme to satisfy the groundlings. After his initial impact on the Prestige, Riverside, Blue Note and RCA labels, Rollins appeared often to be in danger of losing his artistic direction, but this Tokyo concert shows that, in 1973, he was still playing living, vital music when the occasion demanded it. **AM**

New review
**Sonny Rollins +3** Rollins (ts); **Tommy Flanagan, Stephen Scott** (p); **Bob Cranshaw** (b); **Jack DeJohnette, Al Foster** (d). Milestone Ⓕ MCD9250-2 (56 minutes). Recorded 1995.

**⑨** **❽**

This recent snap-shot of Sonny Rollins puts the tenor titan back in the familiar horn-and-rhythm section format. It is a happy return. There are handsome standards such as *What a Diff'rence a Day Made* and *I've Never Been in Love Before*. Rollins also spins gold from such improbable material as *Mona Lisa* and *Cabin in the Sky*. There are two new originals. *Biji*, an abridged version of Rollins's 'ancestral' name Brungbigi, is a rollicking ride reminiscent of the tenorist's indelible *Alfie*. *H.S.*, dedicated to pianist Horace Silver, is another cooker, but cast with a funky blues-tinged edge. Graced with puckish melodic twists and gritty chordal maps, both tunes promise to become standards of the rank of Rollins's *St Thomas* and *Tenor Madness*. Urged on by two terrific trios, one featuring pianist Tommy Flanagan, the other with newcomer Stephen Scott, Rollins is on tip-top form, teasing the pulse here, flirting with the melody there. By returning to roots, Rollins seems to have rediscovered his fountain of youth. **CB**

# Aldo Romano
1941

**Ten Tales** Romano (d); **Joe Lovano** (ts). Owl Ⓕ 053CD (47 minutes). Recorded 1989.

**⑧** **❽**

Putting two musicians in a studio and expecting an album to emerge from their creative interplay could be a somewhat risky strategy, but the odds are considerably shortened if the musicians in question have track records like Romano's and Lovano's. The drummer, after learning his trade in Paris backing locals like Barney Wilen and Michel Portal and visiting Americans like Jackie McLean, became immersed in free jazz in the mid sixties, collaborating with Steve Lacy, Don Cherry and Joachim Kühn in the medium before becoming a leader in the late seventies. Joe Lovano was sitting in with his father's rhythm section when he was 13, studying at Berklee at 20 and recording with Lonnie Smith at 22. Since then he has become one of the most prodigious and sought-after talents on the scene, collaborating tellingly with guitarists Bill Frisell and John Scofield, but he is equally at home playing free music. On **Ten Tales** he himself describes as "completely free, but an attempt to put together the harmony and rhythm I felt within that free form to create structure and form without playing a re-creation of it." A particular pitfall in wait for unwary players of such music is repetition, throwing off stock phrases by rote, but both participants combine to mould a rewarding, varied and imaginative set, impeccably performed. **Ten Tales** is, as one of its track titles suggests, a *Monologue For Two*, an object lesson in intense, sustained duo improvisation. **CP**

# Dom Um Romao
1925

**Dom Um Romao** Romao (d, perc); **William Campbell** (t); **Jimmy Bossey** (tb); **Lloyd McNeil** (f); **Jerry Dodgion** (as, f); **Mauricio Smith** (ss, ts, f); **Sivuca** (org, p, g); **Dom Salvador** (p); **Richard**

**Kimball** (syn); **Amauri Tristao** (g); **Stanley Clarke**, **Frank Tusa** (b); **Eric Gravatt**, **Portintio** (perc). Muse Ⓕ MCD6012 (64 Minutes). Recorded 1973.

⑧ ❽

Brazilian drummer/percussionist Dom Um Romao first came to prominence in Rio de Janeiro with Sergio Mendes's Bossa Rio. Moving to the US in the mid sixties, he worked with Oscar Brown Jr and with Mendes's Brazil 66 and Antonio Carlos Jobim. In 1971, he took over the percussion chair with Weather Report from former student Airto Moreira. In the sixties, Brazil had become associated with the breezy and wistful bossa nova. While Romao benefited from its popularity, his first love was the street music of the people, particularly the working black underclass, rather than the Spanish and Portuguese gentry. That commitment is reflected in these uniquely appealing sessions from 1973, recorded in the midst of Romao's highly successful tenure with Weather Report. Indeed, on tracks like *Shake* (*Ginga Gingou*) we catch the spirit of the samba de rua or street samba. And though the mood and density are lighter in lines like *Highway*, where Lloyd McNeil's quicksilver flute dances freely, even in these there is a gritty edge.

Throughout, Romao's infectious rhythmic currents seethe and swirl. In sum, these are well-produced and well-rehearsed sessions where the Afro-Brazilian impulse is paraded with brio and carnivalesque high spirits. **CB**

# Antoine Roney

1963

**The Traveler** Roney (ts); **Wallace Roney** (t); **James Spaulding** (ss, as, f); **Jacky Terrasson** (p); **Dwayne Burno** (b); **Louis Hayes** (d). Muse Ⓕ MCD5469 (52 minutes). Recorded 1992.

⑦ ❽

Antoine Roney, Wallace's younger brother by three years, has taken a little longer to come to his first recording session than his brother. A thinker, he has done much reappraisal of his music as an ongoing commitment and this has probably slowed his journey into the spotlight. Judging by the fact that he bought a copy of Wayne Shorter's **The All-Seeing Eye** at the age of just eight, it may not be too surprising to find that the music on this record often sounds like the more imaginative and progressive efforts to come out of the Blue Note stable between, say, 1963 and 1966 (James Spaulding, present on four tracks here, was actually on some of those records).

Roney has chosen a very capable rhythm section, with Louis Hayes being a truly great – and greatly undervalued – drummer who once formed a vital part of one of the classic modern jazz rhythm sections: Timmons, Jones and himself with Cannonball. Jacky Terrasson has gone on to make his own record as a leader, and here shows hundreds of felicitous touches, both behind others and in solos of his own. Which leaves the two Roneys. Wallace here is concise, fiery and controlled, while Antoine sounds more diffuse, as if searching for the optimum way of expressing his musical thoughts. In a sense, Antoine, certainly the less consistently successful improviser and still clearly indebted to Shorter, is the more exciting, precisely because of that sense of the unknown, being on the edge of possibility. The date is nicely paced and the compositions thoughtful. A good start for a promising career, and one which has been kept up by his second Muse album, **Whirling**, a quartet date featuring Ronnie Mathews on piano. **KS**

# Wallace Roney

1960

**New review**

**Crunchin'** Roney (t); **Antonio Hart** (as); **Geri Allen** (p); **Ron Carter** (b); **Kenny Washington** (d). Muse Ⓕ MCD5518 (54 minutes). Recorded 1993.

⑨ ❿

Of all the superb young trumpeters to come along in the eighties in the wake of Wynton Marsalis, Wallace Roney is the most impressive. Technique and resourcefulness are taken for granted these days, but there is about Roney a poise, a stillness, a sense of ease that none of the others can quite command. The format of this set is simple: a conventional quintet playing a mixture of standards and themes by Monk and Miles Davis. The outcome, however, is anything but run-of-the-mill, with Roney, Hart and Allen all playing at their considerable best and the rhythm team of Carter and Washington providing matchless support. **DG**

**Mistérios** Roney (t, arr) with: **Antoine Roney**, **Ravi Coltrane** (ts); **Geri Allen** (p, arr); **Gil Goldstein** (kbds, arr); **Clarence Seay** (b); **Eric Allen** (d); **Steve Barrios**, **Steve Thornton**, **Valtinho Anastacio** (perc); and string/woodwind orchestra cond. by **Gil Goldstein** (**Geri Allen**, one track). Warner Bros Ⓕ 245641-2 (59 minutes). Recorded 1993.

The tradition which this album continues is clear, from Dizzy to Clifford Brown to Miles to Hubbard to Marsalis and on up to now. A solo trumpeter supported by orchestra and rhythm section. Roney has possessed the technical chops for such a venture for a number of years now, but this album shows that the timing was pretty much right: he is neither cowed by the situation into playing falsely, nor is he merely exhibitionistic. He uses the skilful arrangements as a carefully designed cushion for his melodic statements, and uses the rhythm section as an alert and colourful partner in his controlled and concise improvisational flights. It seems to me that the arrangements are the best I've heard in a context such as this since the Gil Evans/Miles days, and that's not because they imitate those classic sessions, because they don't. This is more like Legrand at his peak.

But Roney is the soloist under the spotlight, and he deserves to be there, playing with poise and intelligence, not going for flash, but winning the listener through his warmth and sincerity. Neither does he play down to the situation: his solos bristle with his usual arsenal of inversions, chromaticisms and rhythmic displacements. Thus the album can be listened to on two levels – as mood music or as something much more substantial. It works well either way. Since this record Roney has returned to the quintet format with an equally recommendable album called, simply, **The Wallace Roney Quintet** (Warner Bros), which includes his brother Antoine in the line-up.                                                    **KS**

# Wally Rose                                                                                          1913

New review

**Ragtime Classics**  Rose (p); **Morty Corb** (b); **Nick Fatool** (d). Good Time Jazz Ⓜ GTJCD
   10034-2 (36 minutes). Recorded 1960.

⑦ ❽

Rose was the pianist with Lu Watters's Yerba Buena Band, his contributions to that band's recordings, or his duets with the idiosyncratic clarinettist Ellis Horne suggesting that his approach to ragtime would be similarly inflexible and robust. In fact Rose was a classical pianist of distinction (he appeared as a solo pianist with Arthur Feidler and the Boston Pops while doubling by night with various jazz bands) and his approach to these rags is a delight. Fatool and Corb add an unobtrusive backdrop, but Rose surges through up-tempo pieces like Henry Lodge's *Red Pepper Rag* with a jazzy momentum all his own (those who only know Fatool from his work with Goodman may be impressed by his mastery of old-style New Orleans press-rolls and hand stopped cymbals on *Frog Legs Rag.*). Rose creates the right kind of nostalgic breathing space in his reading of Joplin's *Euphonic Rag* and pays reverential tribute to Jelly Roll Morton in a version of *The Pearls* that shows that other pianistic approaches to this material work as well as Jelly's own. Only the meagre playing time makes this anything less than an essential addition to a ragtime collection.                                               **AS**

# Ted Rosenthal

New review

**Rosenthology**  Rosenthal (p); **Mike Formanek** (b); **Billy Drummond** (d). Concord Jazz
   Ⓕ CCD4702 (63 minutes). Recorded 1994.

⑥ ❽

Pianist Ted Rosenthal is a born-and-bred New Yorker whose credits include Phil Woods, Ron Carter, Mel Lewis, Clark Terry and Gerry Mulligan. He's also a successful leader whose trio is a New York fixture when he's not on the road. Armed with several degrees in piano performance from the Manhattan School of Music, Rosenthal is as comfortable with Mozart as he is with Monk. A serious composer, he is also an alumnus of the BMI Jazz Composers Workshop presided over by Bob Brookmeyer and Manny Albam. Rosenthal is an exceptional pianist who is in the lyrical line of Bill Evans. But while there are luminescent takes of standards like *Will You Still Be Mine?*, there are also bracing forays like the aptly tagged *Wow* by the iconoclastic Lennie Tristano with whom Rosenthal studied as a teenager. A Gershwin devotee, Rosenthal includes an extraordinary, reading of *Strike Up the Band* which alternately floats, flies and grooves. Among his originals, *Slippin' and Slidin'* takes inspiration from Paul Bley, Ornette Coleman and Chick Corea. Throughout, the pianist gets hand-in-glove support from the empathic Mike Formanek on bass and Billy Drummond on drums.   **CB**

# Michele Rosewoman

**Harvest**  Rosewoman (p, v, perc); **Steve Wilson** (ss, as); **Gary Thomas** (ts, f); **Kenny Davis** (b, elb);
   **Gene Jackson** (d); **Eddie Bobe** (cgas, cajon, quinto, palitos, v). Enja Ⓕ ENJ7069-2 (71 minutes).
   Recorded 1993.

⑧ ❽

Rosewoman first arrived in New York in 1978, and by 1983 she had impressed observers sufficiently to begin winning critics' polls. A key reason for that quick respect is that she is gifted both as a pianist and as a composer, and has originality to offer in both areas. She is also able to realize her compositions powerfully through the deployment of imaginative arrangements. In all this she at times evokes the angularity and intellectual challenge of Andrew Hill: she shares his clear, firm touch and his liking for fragmented rhythms across a steady tempo; they also both enjoy the investigation of long series of dissonant inversions. Her choice of support on this album is sound, with Steve Wilson in particular having the agility and angularity to play with the structures Rosewoman sets up for each soloist. But she herself remains at the centre of the music throughout, and contributes mightily to the success of the final track, *Warriors*, which sees her unite with Yoruba musician Eddie Bobe for 15 minutes of sustained interaction between two related musical cultures.

**Harvest** is a challenging and fully mature album which nonetheless is immensely approachable for the uninitiated. If you doubt me, then try the heartfelt treatment of Billy Strayhorn's lament on mortality, *Blood Count*. **KS**

# Renée Rosnes
1962

New review

**Ancestors**  Rosnes (p); **Nicholas Payton** (t); **Chris Potter** (ss, ts, f); **Peter Washington** (b); **Al Foster** (d); **Don Alias** (perc). Blue Note Ⓕ CDP8 34634-2 (61 minutes). Recorded 1995.

⑧ ❿

Whether heard as a leader, co-leader or follower, Rosnes has amassed a considerable body of recorded evidence which suggests that she is a top-drawer musician. This, her fourth as a leader for Blue Note, stems from EMI Canada (her previous Blue Note albums came via EMI Toshiba's Somethin' Else label) and marks a significant new level of accomplishment. The album was conceived as a tribute to her own family (the booklet-notes detail the unusual circumstances which brought about this dedication) and Rosnes wrote all the (decidedly superior) material played. She leads this group in the proper way, suggesting ideas here, laying out there, but always choosing the apposite thing to play and never crowding the soloists (in this respect bringing Duke Pearson to mind); this, along with her assured touch, is a clear sign of confidence in her own abilities. Her choice of chord voicings is continually enlivening, the effect on the two frontmen being consistently apparent in what they are then spurred on to play. Her own soloing is beautifully paced and carefully judged to suit the very individual character of each piece: she can be as challengingly dynamic as the best of them, overwhelming the listener with an unstoppable rush of ideas, but for the most part here she eschews this approach in the pursuance of continual structuring through light and shade, making fresh and exciting choices in her improvisatory options. Both horns solo with exceptional aplomb, Payton shining on the ballads and Potter tugging and pulling at the more rugged material from a welter of angles in his solos in a way rarely heard since Wayne Shorter went electric and dropped his tenor. The bass and drums do all the right things and complete a circle of excellence in this programme which is evident in every stage of its conception and execution. That, to me, makes this disc something special. **KS**

# Frank Rosolino
1926-78

**Free for All**  Rosolino (tb); **Harold Land** (ts); **Victor Feldman** (p); **Leroy Vinnegar** (b); **Stan Levey** (d). Speciality Ⓜ OJCCD1763-2 (58 minutes). Recorded 1958.

⑥ ❽

Rosolino had all the right credentials for a major jazz soloist; he was a master of the trombone and had years of experience with the big bands of Gene Krupa and Stan Kenton. He enlivened many a West Coast recording date and it is difficult to say why this album lacks the spark of, say, the two he did for Capitol (not yet transferred to CD). All the right ingredients are here, including a fine rhythm section made up of men who played together often. Harold Land is a most dependable tenor player but somehow the music just lacks the spark which would have pushed it over the dividing line between good and very good. Perhaps the arrangements are over-fussy at times and the inclusion of three alternative takes does little to improve the quality of the record. Although made in 1958, the music was not issued in any form until 1986, a fact which may be its own quality assessment; perhaps the parent company waited until they felt the field was less competitive than at the time of the original session. **AM**

# Billy Ross

New review

**Woody**  Ross (ts, as, ss, cl, f); **Tony Concepcion, Jeff Kievit, Ira Sullivan, Barry Ries, Pete Minger** (t); **Dana Teboe, John Allred, Joe Barodi** (tb); **Turk Mauro, Ed Calle, Frank Tiberi, Flip Phillips** (ts); **Mike Birignola, Whit Sidener** (bs); **Nester Torres** (f); **Mike Levine** (p); **Dan Warner Dennis Marks** (b); **James Martin, Lee Levin, Richard Bravo Ed Metz Archie Pena** (d); **Wendy Pederson** (v). Contemporary Ⓕ CCD14079 (66 minutes). Recorded 1996.

⑧ ❽

Here's a brave idea, well carried through. Normally 'graveyard' bands are, to coin a phrase, fatally flawed. Ross, a very junior Herman sideman, has put together 13 tracks by a variety of combinations, large and small, designed to capture the fire and spirit of the old Woody Herman bands. He has succeeded so well by not copying Herman's original versions, and he has indeed revived the Herman spirit. He is a capable player on all his horns and he gets good support from trumpeters Minger and Sullivan. Ross's tenor duels with that of Turk Mauro on *Apple Honey,* duets with himself on *Northwest Passage.* He plays Getz-like tenor and is Woody to the life on clarinet for *Woody*, his imaginative composition which opens the album. The closing *For the First Herd*, a spanking medium-tempo blues original, includes a brief and not particularly distinguished appearance by Flip Phillips in its string of solos (at the age of 80 Phillips, still a potent player, could have been better used), as well as some tasty flute from Ross and a declamation from Allred which seems to wander between Rosolino and Harris and back. It all swings manfully. **SV**

# Ronnie Ross                                                                1933-91

**Messages from Munich**  Ross (bs) with the following collective personnel: **Rick Kiefer** (t); **Rudy Friesen** (tb); **Rudi Risavy** (f); **Dick Spencer** (f, as); **Olaf Kubler** (ss, ts); **Don Menza** (as, ts); **Hans Koller, Rudi Fierl** (ts); **Pepsi Auer, Joe Haider, Bill Le Sage** (p); **Peter Trunk, Hans Rätenbacher, Jiri Mraz** (b); **Cees See, Meinrad Geppert, Pierre Favre** (d). Hot House Ⓕ HH0CD1017 (57 minutes). Recorded 1963-7

⑥ ❽

No less a jazz authority than John Lewis recognized Ross's importance and individuality as a baritone soloist as far back as 1958 when he employed him as the featured voice on **European Windows** (RCA LP – nla). The following year Ronnie toured the UK with the Modern Jazz Quartet. This CD comprises previously unissued material recorded in Munich studios, and although the multi-national groups included Americans Don Menza, Rick Kiefer and Dick Spencer, Ronnie's is the most commanding solo voice. Virtually all of the music was composed by Ross and is played by varying combinations, most of which produce the tight, clean ensemble sound associated with West Coast jazz. *Since Yesterday* has a relaxed, Basie-like feeling while *Sub-Basement Blues*, done at the same session, is arguably one of Ronnie's finest solos on record, a beautiful performance by just baritone, bass and drums. The 1963 date has some splendid playing by an all-saxophone front line while the 1967 session has the youthful Jiri Mraz on bass (soloing on two tracks). At the time of these sessions most of the musicians were working in the German studios, an almost exact parallel with the circumstances which gave rise to West Coast jazz in the previous decade. The result is musicianship of the highest order sparked by fine solo playing by Spencer, Koller, Menza and especially Ross. **AM**

# Charlie Rouse                                                              1924-88

**Takin' Care of Business**  Rouse (ts); **Blue Mitchell** (t); **Walter Bishop** (p); **Earl May** (b); **Art Taylor** (d). Jazzland Ⓜ OJCCD491 (38 minutes). Recorded 1960.

⑥ ❻

Charlie Rouse is usually remembered as the tenor saxophonist in Thelonious Monk's quartet. It is true that he spent more than a decade with Monk, but he was nobody's sidekick. Prior to Monk, for example, he co-led with Julius Watkins a most imaginative small group, Les Jazz Modes. Rouse's playing provides perfect evidence for the proposition that it is quite possible for an artist to exercise individuality while remaining entirely within a convention. Stylistically he was a hard bopper of the Hank Mobley/Junior Cook school, but you could never mistake him for anyone else. His tone is thick and furry and his phrasing has an energetic, perky gait. The effect is amiable and never strident.

This album is in the convention of its time – a blowing session for two horns and rhythm. Nobody could call it revolutionary, mind-searing, mould-breaking or whatever, but you can have too much of that sort of thing. All goes smoothly and everybody plays well. Rouse, in particular, shines in this relaxed setting: fast-thinking and eloquent. **DG**

# Rova Saxophone Quartet

New review
**From the Bureau of Both**  Bruce Ackley (ss); **Steve Adams** (as, snino s); **Larry Ochs** (ts); **Jon Raskin** (bs). Black Saint Ⓕ 120135-2 (55 minutes). Recorded 1992.

⑦ ❽

Formed in 1977, this West Coast group has taken its own individual place in the now well-populated world of saxophone quartets. They show little awareness of the World Saxophone Quartet, formed a year earlier but, rather, take their inspiration from the likes of Anthony Braxton, Roscoe Mitchell and various Chicago ensembles. Their orchestral mix is distinctive but, as with their fellow runners, it embraces unisons, solos, duets and full counterpoint. In the main, their riff supports are built up as 'heads'. Tempo changes are handled adroitly and the responsibility for time-keeping is to some extent passed to the listener. The advantage of a constant personnel and extensive touring was favourably reflected in several successful albums made throughout the eighties and it was not until the start of the next decade that the first change came, with Adams replacing Andrew Voigt. As this CD shows, there was no adverse affect on group cohesion, with the newcomer sensitive to the sound of the group, the execution of the arrangements and his own solo parts. *Swapmeet* has particularly impressive work by him, while *The Floater* offers the new quartet at its contrapuntal best, playing off the cuff and imaginatively using all of the space available. **BMcR**

# Jimmy Rowles

1918-96

**The Peacocks**  Rowles (p); **Stan Getz** (ts); **Buster Williams** (b); **Elvin Jones** (d). Columbia
Ⓜ CK52975 (59 minutes). Recorded 1975.

⑧ ❽

This album was originally conceived to display Rowles solo and accompanied by rhythm. It was the
idea of Stan Getz, who had agreed to record 'commercial' albums for CBS provided they let him
produce more committed albums featuring artists of his own choice. This was to be his first. But the
producer was so carried away by the music that he went home for his tenor sax and joined in.

The result is a jazz classic. Rowles was a superb all-round player who, as Getz knew, has made
ridiculously few albums under his own name. Since this one he has made more. A modest man, he
easily fell into the accompanying role that he played so well and yet he ranks with Hank Jones, Mel
Powell and Oscar Peterson in terms of musical stature. Like Powell he swung hard without ever being
heavy-handed. He sings on several of these tracks and has a gentle, world-weary voice, ideal for the
kind of music he plays. *I'll Never Be the Same* and *My Buddy* have particularly appealing
combinations of voice and piano and solo tenor. It is one of those sets where new delights come
tumbling out at each hearing.                                                                **SV**

# Gonzalo Rubalcaba

1963

**Suite 4 y 20**  Rubalcaba (p); **Reynaldo Melian** (t); **Charlie Haden** (b); **Felipe Cabrera** (elb); **Julio
Barreto** (d). Blue Note Ⓕ CDP7 80054-2 (69 minutes: ). Recorded 1992.

⑥ ❽

Cuban-born Rubalcaba's earlier Blue Note albums contained some performances on which his
technique seemed to take the upper hand. On this very attractive release, recorded in Madrid, he plays
with such poise, such careful attention to detail, that there are times when it might almost be a
different pianist. As on his previous Blue Notes, Charlie Haden is present on bass (although this time
on only five of the 13 tracks), while Melian plays trumpet on nine, occasionally multi-tracking his
efforts. The most impressive titles are those on which the thematic material is strongest; songs such as
the Lennon/McCartney ballad *Here, There and Everywhere*, *Love Letters* and *Perfidia*. The delicacy
of Gonzalo's playing is at its most marked here, for his style is based on the careful delineation of
melody. Some of the tracks are too self-indulgent for repeated listening, as when the quartet hits
relentlessly on a repeated phrase of no great importance. But overall Rubalcaba is a most interesting
performer who has successfully united the musics of North and Central America without relying
simply on what has gone before. Rubalcaba continues to make albums for Blue Note (his **Diz**, a
tribute to one of his mentors, is notable), but none outstrip the playing here.                **AM**

# Vanessa Rubin

**I'm Glad There Is You**  Rubin (v) with: **Cecil Bridgewater** (t); **Grover Washington Jr** (ss, ts);
**Antonio Hart** (as); **Frank Foster** (ts); **Aaron Graves**, **Carlos McKinney**, **Monty Alexander** (p);
**Kenny Burrell** (g); **Charles Fambrough** (b); **Yoron Israel** (d); **Michael Rubin** (perc); and string
section led by **Akua Dixon**. RCA Novus Ⓕ 163170-2 (57 minutes). Recorded 1993.

⑤ ❽

Rubin is a young American singer whose admiration for Carmen McRae has led her to dedicate this
album to the older musician. Rubin's homage to McRae extends to the treatment she gives her
material as well as the edge she projects into her voice. At this stage of her career she seems more
inclined to concentrate on musicality and swing than on interpretation, and it would be mistaken of
a listener to approach this disc with too much hope of an emotional experience. On the technical side,
she is promising but has much to develop. Her intonation, generally accurate, can go worryingly
wrong at times, especially on sustained notes, while her rhythm can be leaden (the even notes of
*Midnight Sun*'s chromatic theme defeat her to the point where the listener is longing for the melody
to end, so as to escape the foursquare singing). Yet her personality comes across quite pleasantly, the
arrangements are serviceable, and the vocal colour is attractive. Let us hope for subsequent recorded
development.                                                                                **KS**

# Roswell Rudd

1935

**Regeneration**  Rudd (tb); **Steve Lacy** (ss); **Misha Mengelberg** (p); **Kent Carter** (b); **Han Bennink**
(d). Soul Note Ⓕ 121054-2 (41 minutes). Recorded 1982.

⑧ ❽

Though this is actually a co-operative group with roots that separate and intertwine back some 20
years, the neglected trombonist/arranger Roswell Rudd gets pride of place due to his fervency behind
this project, his closeness to and advocacy of Herbie Nichols, and his invigorating presence in the
proceedings. And it is an important disc, for the first time fleshing out with horns Nichols's at-one-

time impenetrable piano pieces, proving that they were possible to play and reminding musicians weaned on freedom that Monk continues to be a source of strength and stimulation. Lacy's own experience with Monk, and his previous collaboration with Rudd in a sixties quartet that played nothing but Monk, assures integrity and illumination. Monk's influence on Mengelberg is reflected in his splashes of Dada wit and frequent harmonic curves. The Nichols tunes, meanwhile, are loaded with irony, whether the ricky-tick rhythm (goaded by Rudd's juicy slides) of *Twelve Bars* or the humorous, deceptively simple (even Monk-like) *2300 Skidoo*, where Lacy's logic is simultaneously formal and elusive, Rudd bursts with almost scatological humour and Mengelberg accents with aplomb. Throughout, Bennink reminds us of his ability to swing a small band eloquently. By suggesting that the jazz repertory could be expanded, both faithfully and creatively, this disc was a breakthrough.                                                                                    **AL**

## Hilton Ruiz                                                                                    1952

**A Moment's Notice**  Ruiz (p); **Kenny Garrett** (as); **George Coleman** (ts); **Dave Valentin** (f); **Andy Gonzales**, **Joe Santiago** (b); **Steve Berrios** (d); **Daniel Ponce**, **Endel Dweno** (perc). RCA Novus Ⓔ 83123-2 (54 minutes). Recorded 1991.

⑦ ❽

Pianist Hilton Ruiz is an outstanding young player with roots in both Latin and mainstream jazz. His credits include Frank Foster, Freddie Hubbard, Joe Henderson, Rahsaan Roland Kirk and a host of Latin bands. In his own groups the emphasis, though Latin tinged, has been on achieving a synergetic balance between the two stylistic tendencies. Instead of setting (and leaving) the fire at the boiling point as most Latin bands tend to do, Ruiz keeps varying the temperature through frequent shifts in texture and dynamics. Typically, as in *Cuchi Chuchi* and *Mambo Inn*, the flame smoulders rather than sears. Things bubble over here and there, but even in these instances there's a breeze that suddenly appears to provide contrast and perspective.

Ruiz's decision to use acoustic rather than electric piano also helps in constantly reinvoking the bop-based mainstream. So, too, does his choice of standards like Coltrane's *Moment's Notice* and *Naima*, and Van Heusen's *Like Someone in Love*. With soloists the calibre of saxophonist George Coleman and flutist Dave Valentin, it is clear that Ruiz is a jazzman, through and through. He is a spare but effective pianist; classically trained and influenced by the bop piano heritage of Bud Powell, his effectively understated solos – and compositions – are compellingly taut and structurally sound. But then, seeing him live is another matter altogether.                                            **CB**

## Howard Rumsey                                                                                    1917

**Sunday Jazz à la Lighthouse**  Rumsey (b); **Shorty Rogers**, **Maynard Ferguson** (t); **Milt Berhart** (tb); **Jimmy Giuffre**, **Bob Cooper** (ts); **Frank Patchen**, **Hampton Hawes** (p); **Shelly Manne** (d); **Carlos Vidal** (cga). Contemporary Ⓜ OJCCD151-2 (50 minutes). Recorded 1953.

❽ ❻

There was always a strong Stan Kenton connection with the Lighthouse Club at California's Hermosa Beach. Rumsey, the ex-Kenton bass player, formed the jazz policy there in 1949 and it was, in many ways, the birthplace of West Coast jazz. The album here was actually recorded at the club by the resident band which featured many of the principal figures in the movement, including Rogers, Giuffre and Manne. With the brittle, driving piano of Hampton Hawes on two tracks, including the superb Hawes-Rogers duet version of *All the Things You Are*, this is a CD of both musical and historic importance. Later Rumsey-led groups presented a variety of tone colours including the most attractive chamber jazz set featuring the flute and oboe of Bud Shank and Bob Cooper. The music is exquisite and some tracks have a timeless quality which not even Rumsey's sometimes leaden bass can destroy. Essential West Coast history for even the most casual listener.                    **AM**

## Jimmy Rushing                                                                                    1902-72

**The You and Me That Used to Be**  Rushing (v); **Ray Nance** (c, vn); **Budd Johnson** (ss); **Al Cohn**, **Zoot Sims** (ts); **Dave Frishberg** (p, arr); **Milt Hinton** (b); **Mel Lewis** (d). RCA Novus Ⓜ 6460-2 (44 minutes). Recorded 1971.

✔                                                                                    ⑩ ❻

This was deleted almost immediately after its initial LP release, despite being voted Album of the Year in a Down Beat critics' poll. Its reissue on CD in 1988 was cause for jubilation, even though its muffled transfer left something to be desired. Rushing died little more than a year after these sessions. Nicknamed Mister Five by Five, he was revered for the impudent cheer he brought to his blues performances with Count Basie in the thirties and forties, and to a series of classic albums produced by John Hammond for Vanguard and Columbia in the fifties. It was sometimes forgotten, though, that the blues was not all that Rushing could sing. His swan song turned out to be the finest album he ever recorded, thanks in large part to its uncharacteristic material – torch songs such as *I Surrender*,

*Dear* and lightly swinging vintage pop tunes such as *Bei Mir Bist Du Schoen* and *When I Grow too Old To Dream*, with nary a blues among them except for *Fine and Mellow*. All four of the featured horn soloists shine here, as do Frishberg's piano accompaniments and captivating small group arrangements. **FD**

# George Russell 1923

**Ezz-Thetics** Russell (p); **Don Ellis** (t); **Dave Baker** (tb); **Eric Dolphy** (as, bcl); **Steve Swallow** (b); **Joe Hunt** (d). Riverside Ⓜ OJCCD070-2 (43 minutes). Recorded 1961.
✓ ⑨ ❽
In the early fifties Russell developed his Lydian Concept of Tonal Organization. A theory based on the ancient Lydian mode, it transformed chords into scales and took his music into the field of pan-tonality. In practice, the music was still accessible to laymen: it shunned the discipline of bebop and its adherence to the chord sequence and introduced scalar relationships that were uniquely his. In a manner far removed from that of Ornette Coleman, it proffered melodic expression and left it in the hands of his band members,

This CD is particularly blessed in this direction. Three startlingly different horn stylists accept the Russell brief and present their own excellent reactions to it. To the facile Baker, triple tonguing is no empty gimmick and the bombast of his *Ezz-Thetics* reading is in contrast to his more studied manipulations of tempo changes on *Thoughts*. Ellis combines lyrical delivery with attacking conviction and he excels on *Ezz-Thetics* and *Lydiot*. Dolphy is outstanding throughout, but very special indeed on Monk's *'Round Midnight*; spare during his theme statement, he grows richly rhetorical during a solo that makes this title the climax of a session with an important place in jazz history. **BMcR**

**The Outer View** Russell (p, arr); **Don Ellis** (t); **Garnett Brown** (tb); **Paul Plummer** (ts); **Steve Swallow** (b); **Pete LaRoca** (d); **Sheila Jordan**. Riverside Ⓜ OJCCD616-2 (51 minutes). Recorded 1962.
✓ ⑧ ❼
For such an important creative and theoretical force in the music, Russell is woefully under-represented on recordings, and of those recordings, dotted over a 50-year career, only a handful are presently on CD (this handful was recently reduced by the deletion of his 1956 album for RCA, **Jazz Workshop**). Thankfully, two of his brilliant small-group Riverside dates are still with us. This, the second of them (see above for **Ezz-Thetics**), is the less celebrated, perhaps due to the absence of the galvanic Dolphy. However, it contains piquant and highly original arrangements of material originally written by, among others, Charlie Parker, Carla Bley and Russell himself. The group interplay is even more developed than on the 1961 album, Ellis in particular distinguishing himself with a series of finely-wrought solos, bringing an intensely personal vision and expressive range to the material. Ellis also adds mightily to the character of the ensemble sections.

The standout track here – and the abum's perennial talking point since its original release – is the old thirties hit, *You Are My Sunshine*. Russell's treatment is radical but observant of the song's core meaning, allowing the melody to rise untrammelled from his new setting. Sheila Jordan contributes an arresting delivery of the lyrics. **KS**

New review
**The Essence of George Russell** Russell (comp, cond, p); Collective personnel: **Jan Allan, Palle Boldtvig, Stanton Davis, Maffy Falay, Bertil Lovgren, Palle Mikkelborg, Lars Samuelsson** (tp); **Runo Ericksson, Ole Lind, Gunnar Medberg, Georg Vernon** (tb); **Christer Boustedt, Arne Domnerus, Claes Rosendahl, Lennart Aberg, Jan Garbarek, Bernt Rosengren, Erik Nilsson** (reeds); **Bengt Hallberg** (p); **Berndt Egerbladh** (vb, xyl); **Rune Gustafsson, Terje Rypdahl** (g); **Arild Andersen, Roman Dylag, Georg Riedel** (g); **Jon Christensen, Egil Johnasen** (d); **Rupert Clemendore, Sabu Martinez** (cga). Soul Note Ⓕ 121044-2 (75 minutes). Recorded 1966-70.
⑦ ❼
Like many another American jazz musician in the sixties, Russell headed for Europe and ended up making his home in Scandinavia for five years. Here he not only enjoyed exceptional support from the jazz section of Swedish Radio, but he made an enormous impact on the young generation of Norwegian musicians such as Garbarek, Rypdal and Christensen. These three plus members of the Swedish Radio big band are essential to the success of the album's one-hour centrepiece, *Electronic Sonata for Souls Loved by Nature*. This performance, apparently from October 6th, 1970 (or perhaps broadcast then, for the cover attributes it to 1967), differs from the 1969 small-group version also with the three Norwegians, and from the disappointing 1980 version with an almost all-American sextet. With a recorded background tape containing a collage of electronic and ethnic music (common to all the versions), Russell is heard coming to terms with both funk and free jazz, as represented by Garbarek's Shepp-like tone, and yet retaining the exciting big-band riffs which link his early work with the recent **It's About Time**. The 1966 *Now and Then* dispenses with electronics and with the double rhythm section for a more openly avant-garde *mélange*, completing a reissue of the previous double LP which omits only the 1968 *Concerto for Self-Accompanied Guitar*. **BP**

# Hal Russell

**The Hal Russell Story** Russell (t, ss, ts, vb, d, v); **Mars Williams** (as, ts, bss, f, bells, perc, v);
**Brian Sandstrom** (b, t, g, perc, v); **Kent Kessler** (b, tb, perc, v); **Steve Hunt** (d, vb, perc, v). ECM
Ⓕ 517 364-2 (67 minutes). Recorded 1992.

⑧ ❽

Hal Russell, for over two decades the *paterfamilias* and Puck of Chicago's free-jazz scene, was a
remarkable man and musician. Originally a drummer, his career in the forties and fifties was
typical of the times – swinging big bands or ones offering saccharine charts, theatre-pit bands,
vaudeville and burlesque house bands, and those occasional magical gigs where he would back a
visiting Miles or Billie, Rollins or Sarah. Come the sixties, he was a member of possibly Chicago's
first 'free' trio, simultaneous with Ornette, and shortly thereafter, inspired by Albert Ayler, learning
the saxophone at age 50 and picking up the trumpet again after 30 years, and starting the polystylistic
NRG Ensemble. He cut a fistful of freer, more volatile recordings than this one, but **The Hal Russell
Story**, recorded just a few weeks before his untimely death, is not only a celebratory, hallucinogenic
overview of his career, but a cornucopia of delights – from the priceless spoken/poetic interludes
between tunes to Russell's own striking multi-instrumentalism and the versatility and devotion of
the supporting NRG cast. The music essays mock fanfares, pseudo-swing, hard-edge blowing,
and free fantasies, each reflecting the humour which was so much a part of Russell's vision. Flowing
together as a near-cinematic suite, the 21 pieces include all-but-unrecognizable, tongue-in-
cheek reconstitutions of standards like *You're Blasé*, *My Little Grass Shack*, and a haunting *Gloomy
Sunday*; pun-filled transformations of fondly-remembered tunes like *Air Mail Special* (*Hair Mail*);
*Woodchopper's Ball* (*Wood Chips*), and *Rockin' Chair* (*Mildred*); and his own volcanic, post-Ayler
conflagrations.
**AL**

# Luis Russell

**Luis Russell 1929-30** Russell (p, arr); **Louis Metcalf, Henry Allen, Bill Coleman, Otis Johnson**
(t); **J.C. Higginbotham, Henry Hicks** (tb); **Charlie Holmes, Albert Nicholas** (cl, ss, as); **Teddy Hill,
Charlie Grimes, Greely Walton** (ts); **Will Johnson** (bj, g); **William 'Bass' Moore** (tba); **Paul
Barbarin** (d, vb); **Elmer Snowden** (bj); **Henry Edwards** (tba, perc); **Pops Foster** (b); **Walter Pichon,
Jesse Cryor, Andy Razaf** (v); also on two tracks: **J.C.Higginbotham and His Six Hicks** (Henry
Allen, t; Higginbotham, tb; Charlie Holmes, as; Will Johnson, g; Pops Foster, b; Paul Barbarin,
d). JSP Ⓕ CD308 (71 minutes). Recorded 1929/30.

⑧ ❽

This CD catches the Russell band at the peak of its powers. Some of the undoubted elation may be
due to the fact that, during late 1929 and early 1930, Louis Armstrong used the band for both public
and record appearances (in fact Louis plays and sings on *Song of The Islands* from the January 1930
session, a fact which the insert-card fails to mention). From the performances here it is easy to
understand why the Russell band was such a sensation; it had a fine sax team, an outstanding
trombone soloist in J.C. Higginbotham and, of course, Red Allen taking most of the trumpet solos.
But the lightness of the ensemble was due in large part to Pops Foster who came into the band to play
string bass in place of Henry Edwards and his tuba. The music still sounds fresh, notably tunes such
as *New Call of the Freaks, Jersey Lightning* and the two takes of *Louisiana Swing* with Foster playing
*arco* rhythm bass. The two tracks under Higginbotham's name are by a 'band-within-a-band'
featuring soloists including the underrated Charlie Holmes on alto. The remastering has been done to
perfection by John R.T. Davies, who allows us to hear Foster's bass notes in their correct spatial
relationship to the ensemble.
**AM**

# Pee Wee Russell

**Jack Teagarden's Big Eight/Pee Wee Russell's Rhythmakers** Russell (cl); with **Max
Kaminsky** (t); **Dicky Wells** (tb); **Al Gold** (ts); **James P. Johnson, Billy Kyle** (p); **Freddie Green** (g);
**Wellman Braud, Billy Taylor** (b); **Zutty Singleton** (d, v); **Teagarden** (tb, v) with **Rex Stewart** (c);
**Barney Bigard** (cl); **Ben Webster** (ts); **Brick Fleagle** (g); **Dave Tough** (d). Riverside
Ⓜ OJCCD1708-2 (32 minutes). Recorded 1938/40.

⑧ ❻

Pee Wee Russell was unique, even in the company of the individuals who have made up the jazz world.
His strangulated tone, glottal effects and unpredictable turns of phrase are well represented on these
six tracks made by a strange grouping of players (Wells and Green from the Basie band, Johnson from
the Harlem stride school and Singleton from Sidney Bechet's group). But there is homogeneity here
thanks to the powerful lead playing of Kaminsky and the all-pervading swing of the rhythm section.
Russell always finds a place for himself in the ensembles and comes into his own as a soloist on *I've
Found A New Baby* and *Everybody Loves My Baby,* the two trio numbers. A special mention must be
made of Dicky Wells whose blues playing both solo and in obbligato to the vocal on *Zutty's Hootie
Blues* is in the same class as the records he made in Paris with Django Reinhardt a year before. The

Teagarden tracks feature three fugitives from the Duke Ellington band and another good rhythm section. All ten titles come from the old HRS catalogue (Hot Record Society) and have been dubbed from, we assume, the best available 78s. The sound is not perfect but is certainly superior to the original Riverside LP. Russell's superb sides for Commodore have recently become available once more, on the album **Jazz Original** (Commodore CMD14042), which has seven late-thirties tracks from Condon-led groups, the four 1941 sides from the Three Deuces, single forties sides from Condon, Spanier and Wild Bill Davison and eight cuts from 1944 by Pee Wee Russell's Hot Four (three of these being alternative takes). Something of a smorgasbord, then, but fine music all the way. **AM**

---

**Jazz Reunion** Russell (cl); **Emmett Berry** (t); **Bob Brookmeyer** (tb); **Coleman Hawkins** (ts); **Nat Pierce** (p); **Milt Hinton** (b); **Jo Jones** (d). Candid Ⓜ CCD79020 (46 minutes). Recorded 1961.
⑨ ❼

"For 30 years I've been listening to him play those funny notes", Coleman Hawkins remarked at the end of this session. "He's always been way out, but they didn't have a word for it then." By the early sixties Pee Wee Russell's wheezy, waif-like tone, his slurs and flutters of notes, had been given a context by newer forms of jazz that helped people to appreciate his eccentricity as 'way out' rather than simply wayward. Encounters with modernists such as Jimmy Giuffre and Thelonious Monk left him unfazed, though it was the more forward looking of his various mainstream dates on which he seemed to thrive best. A 1960 Prestige date with Tommy Flanagan and Buck Clayton found him on fine form, as did this **Jazz Reunion** with the ever-versatile Hawkins.

Russell and Hawkins had last played together in the Mound City Blue Blowers in 1929, when they made a famous recording of James P. Johnson's *If I Could be with You One Hour Tonight*. **Jazz Reunion** opens with a new version of the tune, Russell's diffident, skewed lines a riveting contrast to Hawkins's forceful bustle. The dichotomy is maintained throughout this enjoyable set, which also boasts two Ellington tunes, a slinky *Tin Tin Deo* and Russell's own *Mariooch*, a ballad feature that calls forth a marvellous display of breathy, sidling, squeaky poetry from his singular clarinet. **GL**

# Paul Rutherford

1940

---

**1989 – and All That** Rutherford (tb); **George Haslam** (bs). Slam Ⓕ CD301 (77 minutes). Recorded 1989.
⑧ ❼

A founder member of the Spontaneous Music Ensemble, Rutherford is a major voice in Europe's free music scene. He was comfortable performing in the more orthodox atmosphere of the Mike West-brook Concert Band, but in 1970 he formed Iskra 1903 with guitarist Derek Bailey and bassist Barry Guy. This challenging group's commitment to free improvisation was total and Rutherford emerged as an extremely influential figure, inspiring fellow European trombonists with the possibilities of his horn and voice overlay. With solo albums **Gentle Harm Of The Bourgeoisie** and **Old Moer's Almanac** unavailable, this CD with the admirable Haslam represents the best opportunity to hear Rutherford's superbly rustic free playing. The session includes duets but it is the solos that best display his talents. His *Sigma* solo makes use of his daunting range while the outstanding *Orion*, with its mixture of throaty growls and declamatory statements, acknowledges his links with the music's past. It introduces breaks with the alacrity of the Dixielander and delivers his *glissandos* with the delicious slur of the tail-gate primitives. As with the trio he led in the eighties, this CD has him setting himself high creative standards but it still leaves one of jazz's most daringly inventive players struggling for work because 'free improvisation', his chosen method of self expression, is not 'nice'. **BMcR**

# Ali Ryerson

---

New review

**In Her Own Sweet Way** Ryerson (f); **Harold Danko** (p); **Jeff Fuller** (b); **Terry Clarke** (d). Concord Jazz Ⓕ CCD4687 (60 minutes). Recorded 1995.
⑦ ❿

This is Ryerson's second album for Concord and her fourth as a leader. On it she plays the best and most confident music of her recorded career, so it is fair to say that there has been distinct progress, although in other respects there is little to choose between this and the previous Concord disc, **Portraits in Silver**, which featured Kenny Werner on sparkling form on piano. However, no one could describe Harold Danko as second-best, and he certainly provides apt support and imaginative soloing to bolster the flautist at every turn in the music. As before, Ryerson is mostly at centre stage, her full tone and lithe rhythm being the core of her appeal as a musician. Danko's ballad, *Martina,* shows she can carry a graceful melody with full effect without lapsing into cliché or sentimentality, while the Latin-inflected numbers give her a chance to dance her lines in and out of the rhythmic matrix. This is exceptionally pleasant, modern mainstream music which, while in no way world shaking or even challenging to the average listener, will make them feel pretty good. The recording quality, by the way, is exemplary. **KS**

# Terje Rypdal

**EOS**  Rypdal (g, Casio MT-30); **David Darling** (vc). ECM Ⓕ 1263 (815 333-2) (46 minutes). Recorded 1983.

⑧  ⑩

Norwegian guitarist/composer Rypdal joined the ECM stable early on, along with his partner from George Russell days, Jan Garbarek. His early albums helped define the ECM sound, where broad washes of music could hang in space for minutes on end (his partly-orchestral album **Whenever I Seem To Be Far Away** is an apt illustration of this side to his work). Yet his subsequent career on records has shown him to be greatly more diversified a talent than this, and he has made trio albums with Vitous and DeJohnette, quasi-heavy metal albums with his own band, and fascinating collaborations such as this disc with cellist David Darling. His latest album on ECM, **QED**, returns to orchestral realizations of some of his most recent compositions. **EOS** has a lot going for it in the sheer diversity of the music to be found therein. The first track, a solo venture by Rypdal, verges on an all-out heavy metal power-chord assault worthy of AC/DC, but subverts it in the way Rypdal distorts the textures and contexts he plays the chords within. The sombre tones of the cello dominate the album's eponymous longest track, but Rypdal also contributes an impassioned solo which again is unthinkable without the absorbed legacy of rock and fusion guitarists such as Hendrix, Beck and McLaughlin. The rest of the album is taken up with smaller-scale realizations of different sonic combinations. On this album, Rypdal gets the balance between passion and beauty just right.  **KS**

# Sergio Salvatore

New review

**Always a Beginning**  Salvatore (p); **John Patitucci** (b); **Peter Erskine** (d). Concord Jazz Ⓕ CCD4704 (63 minutes). Recorded 1996.

⑨⑩

This is Sergio Salvatore's third album. When it was recorded, in January 1996, he was 14 years old. These two facts together would be noteworthy, even if the work he produced were run-of-the-mill. But the maturity and technical fluency of his playing suggest that he may be a child prodigy of the Menuhin class. Just to complicate matters, the CD insert-note is decorated with his own drawings, including one of Henry Mancini, which looks simply brilliant to me. One of the most impressive aspects of his playing is its restraint. There are times, as in the opening chorus of *Darn That Dream*, when he picks out the tune in single notes, departing only slightly from the written melody yet suggesting a world of possibilities. The extreme youth of the performer is a phenomenon that can't be ignored, but by any standards this is a fine piano trio record.  **DG**

# Perico Sambeat

New review

**Dual Force**  Sambeat (as); **Steve Melling** (p); **Dave Green** (b); **Steven Keogh** (d). Ronnie Scott's Jazz House Ⓕ JHCD031 (59 minutes). Recorded 1993.

⑥  ⑦

Alto saxophonist Perico Sambeat is an Iberian whirlwind whose impassioned playing recalls the bluesy intensity of Cannonball Adderley and boppish grit of Jackie McLean. Born in Valencia, Spain in 1962, Sambeat took to jazz after hearing Catalonian pianist Tete Montoliu. Switching to alto, and honing his jazz skills first in Barcelona and then in New York where he studied with Joe Lovano, Ralph Moore and Lew Tabackin, Sambeat has become a national treasure of Spain and a reminder of jazzdom's universality. In a high energy date recorded at Ronnie Scott's Jazz Club in London, Sambeat sails with edgy originals such as the boppish *Body*. In his exhilarating take on the standard, *Wonderful Wonderful*, one hears echoes of tenor giants John Coltrane and Charles Lloyd. And when he swings, there's a pulsing throb reminiscent of Phil Woods. A truly spontaneous player, Sambeat's turn-on-a-dime shifts are shadowed and embellished by the limber and responsive rhythms of pianist Steve Melling, bassist Dave Green and drummer Steven Keogh. Although a 'work in progress', Sambeat possesses an excitment that promises to burn even brighter.  **CB**

# Joe Sample

New review

**Old Places, Old Faces**  Sample (p, elp); **Charles Lloyd** (ts); **Dean Parks** (g); **Jay Anderson** (b); **Ralph Penland** (d); **Lenny Castro** (perc, d). Warner Ⓕ 9362-46182-2 (54 minutes). Recorded 1995.

⑦  ⑧

Sample's last album, the dynamic and powerful *Did You Feel That?* (WB45729) explored the soul side of his career, during which he was from time to time teamed with the giants of the genre from Diana Ross to the Jackson Five. This is a more consciously retrospective exploration of his jazz career, with compositions actively designed to investigate moments from his past. His long-term associate, percussionist Castro, is joined by the other regular member of Sample's gigging trio, Anderson, and these three form the core of the disc. The star guest is saxophonist Charles Lloyd, and his presence on three of the ten tracks is masterly, crying out for a full album of similar collaborations. Lloyd's bleak and individual saxophone tone paradoxically enlivens one of two new compositions exploring the connections between jazz and Creole Cajun music, as well as being a perfect complement to Sample on a tribute to Ben Webster and the touching *First Love*. The best moments on this disc (mainly the interaction with Lloyd) outdo anything Sample has recorded in recent years, but the dangers of such a boldly self-exploratory album make it slightly more uneven than its soul-tinged predecessor, albeit far more satisfying when Sample gets it right. The other considerable bonus on this disc is that it represents a real chance to hear just what an original and interesting pianist Sample is, with a very individual touch, particularly on high-register solo lines.                    **AS**

# David Sanborn                                                                1945

**Close Up**  Sanborn (as, v); **Hiram Bullock, Nile Rodgers, G.E. Smith, Paul Jackson Jr** (g); **Jeff Mironov** (g); **Richard Tee** (p); **Ricky Peterson** (elp, kbds); **Marcus Miller** (elb, kbds, p, perc, g, v); **Steve Jordan, Andy Newmark, Vinnie Colaiuta, William Ju Ju House** (d); **Paulinho da Costa** (perc); **Vocal Chorus**. Reprise Ⓜ 925715-2 (51 minutes). Recorded 1988.

⓿                                                                        ⑧ ❽

Not withstanding the interest excited among the arts pages by **Another Hand**, David Sanborn's 1991 excursion into post-modernism, there is little doubt that history will remember Sanborn for the work he least intended for serious consumption – the polished but impassioned funk which reached a hi-tech peak on **Close Up**. Although the session has its slack moments – the rock routines of *J.T. and Lesley Ann* and the maudlin sentiment of *You Are Everything* can be safely passed over – the more muscular funk tracks – *Slam, Pyramid*, and, in particular, *Tough* – have a steely, combative quality which is infectiously exciting. Much of the credit for this is due to Marcus Miller's ingenious arrangements, but anyone still puzzled by Gil Evan's glowing endorsement of Sanborn's 'cry' should examine the extraordinary note with which Sanborn leaves the bridge of *Pyramid*. His vocabulary may lack harmonic depth, but this searing, penetrating sound, and the simple but urgent variations which constitute his solo on *Touch*, have been enough to make him one of the most imitated altoists of his generation. He has regretted any part he may have played in inspiring 'a certain blandness' in instrumental pop music, but at moments like these, he plays as if his life depended on it.  **MG**

# David Sanchez                                                             1969

**New review**
**Street Scene**  Sanchez (ts, as, perc); **Kenny Garrett** (as); **Danilo Perez** (p); **Larry Grenadier, John Benitez, Charnett Moffett** (b); **Clarence Penn, Horacio Hernandez** (d); **Milton Cardona, Richie Flores** (perc); **Cassandra Wilson** (v). Columbia Ⓕ 485137-2 (51 minutes). Recorded 1996.

⑦ ❿

As is becoming *de rigeur* in recording circles these days, not all the above play on every track; indeed, vocalist Wilson appears just once, saxophonist Garrett twice. As with the Puerto Rican Sanchez's earlier efforts there is a duality to his music which is both engaging and at times suggestive of a few unresolved musical issues for the young player. He can play, as on *Caras Negras* or Monk's *Four in One*, the most straight-ahead post-bop tenor sax you could desire, or mix it with Central American rhythms (*Los Cronopios*) to the manner born. Be that as it may, he is impressive in his confidence and assertiveness as a player, sometimes switching the rhythms around like Rollins from an earlier era, sometimes burning straight ahead like a Stitt, sometimes suggesting Mike Brecker. As on **Sketches of Dreams** (Columbia, 1994) Sanchez is not over-generous with solo space for others, though Garrett gets a foot in the door on *Cronopios* and proceeds to run away with the track, while Perez solos tastily on Monk's theme. Sanchez's plaintive soprano balladry on *Carmina* rounds out the self-portrait. **KS**

# Pharoah Sanders                                                           1940

**New review**
**Karma**  Sanders (ts); **James Spaulding** (f); **Julius Watkins** (frh); **Lonnie Liston Smith** (p); **Richard Davis, Reggie Workman, Ron Carter** (b); **Billy Hart, Freddie Waits** (d); **Nat Bettis** (perc); **Leon Thomas** (v, perc). Impulse! Ⓜ IMP11532 (38 minutes). Recorded 1969.

⑦ ❽

Although Archie Shepp made some appearances as an added starter with the Coltrane Quartet, it was Sanders who became a regular member of Trane's group from the second half of 1965 onwards. Coltrane's addition of African percussion and other more exotic instruments during his last period fed Sanders's late sixties recordings, which sold faster than his mentor's ever had. Pharoah's Southern origins may have encouraged his development of a tenor style simpler than either Trane and Ayler, which was then easy for Gato Barbieri to reduce to its commercial essentials. Later in the seventies Lonnie Liston Smith, who worked for both Sanders and Barbieri, took the formula further into definitive blandness. It's possible to see that Sanders thought he was achieving something new with his nearly 33-minute *The Creator Has a Master Plan* by alternating sections of quasi-free out-of-tempo improvisation with the supremely laid-back vamp underpinning Thomas's idiosyncratic vocal. It works equally as accompaniment to the favourite substances of the peace-and-love generation, and to those of today's dance-club freaks. The remaining track, *Colors*, is similar without the ethereal Spaulding but still with the great Watkins in the background, and if nothing else is a great period piece. **BP**

**Journey to the One** Sanders (ts); **Eddie Henderson** (flh); **John Hicks**, **Joe Bonner** (p); **Mark Isham** (synth); **Carl Lockett**, **Chris Hayes** (g); **Ray Drummond** (b); **Idris Muhammad** (d); **Yoko Ito Gates** (koto); **James Pomcrantz** (sitar); **Bedria Sanders**, **Paul Arslanian** (harmonium); **Vicki Randle**, **Ngoh Spencer**, **Bobby McFerrin**, **Donna Dickerson** (v). Evidence ℗ ECD22016-2 (73 minutes). Recorded 1980.

⑦ ❽

Now more than a decade old, this album still accurately reflects the type of music Sanders is playing today. It was recorded for the now-defunct Theresa label, its first issue on CD by Evidence. This was originally a gatefold double-album vinyl release, and the transfer to CD sees no dropping of tracks.

Sanders has travelled a long way since his brain-scorching solos in the last John Coltrane group. He has developed a larger, more majestic tone than of old, has picked up a handy line in ballad interpretation, and has revisited many of Coltrane's compositions. This date has the beautiful *After The Rain*, and Sanders does his reputation no harm at all with a reverential interpretation. Elsewhere, the album is clearly set up to show the tenor player to his best advantage in a variety of musical groupings. He plays good lean tenor solos on a string of quartet and quintet tracks, all but *Easy To Remember* being Sanders originals. On what was originally side two of the first vinyl disc, his sole accompanists on the majority of the side are koto, sitar and harmonium players, and the music is very peaceful. Elsewhere, as on the street-cred *You've Got To Have Freedom*, there is a small group of backing vocalists urging the group on.

Taken in tandem with 1981's **Rejoice** (Evidence 22020-2: another single-CD reissue of a double-vinyl set), which details his continuing involvement in African rhythms and melodies and also features a ravishing version of *Central Park West*, this shows conclusively where Sanders now rests his case. **KS**

# Randy Sandke 1949

**New review**

**The Chase** Sandke (t); **Ray Anderson** (tb); **Chris Potter**, **Michael Brecker**, **Scott Robinson** (reeds); **Ted Rosenthal** (p); **John Goldsby** (b); **Marvin 'Smitty' Smith** (d). Concord Jazz ℗ CCD4642 (61 minutes). Recorded 1994.

⑨ ❽

The curtains of Sandke's vision have opened wide from the initial mainstream that he played as Buck Clayton's protégé to let in advanced bebop. His abilities have increased with the new view and his playing here is very impressive. The bebop trumpet on *Jordu* has all the eloquence and confidence of the young Lee Morgan and Sandke plays with great fire. His companions include young musicians from the very top of the tree, notably pianist Rosenthal, who made his name with Gerry Mulligan and who has, since Mulligan's final illness, forged a potent partnership with Chris Potter, who plays alto and soprano saxes on these tracks and is a welcome member of the Phil Woods school of jazz. Potter, 23 at the time of this recording, is at his peak in a partnership with Sandke on the trumpeter's tune, *The Chase*. Rosenthal's solo playing and accompanying are exemplary. Michael Brecker, already established and slightly older than his confrères, partners Sandke in a two-piece front line on *Lullaby Of Birdland* and two Sandke originals. He is phenomenally fast and mobile throughout the registers, but Sandke's calmer albeit still declamatory trumpet on *Booker* keeps up the pace. By comparison trombonist Anderson is similarly agile, but lacks profundity in his playing, which is at its most spectacular on *Ill Wind*. **SV**

# Arturo Sandoval 1949

**New review**

**Swingin'** Sandoval (t, flh, p); **Clark Terry** (t, flh); **Dana Teboe** (tb); **Ed Calle** (ts, bs, f); **Michael Brecker** (ts); **Eddie Daniels** (cl); **Mike Stern** (g); **Joey Calderazzo** (p); **John Patitucci** (b); **Greg Hutchinson** (d). GRP ℗ 98462 (72 minutes). Recorded 1996.

⑦ ❽

When Dizzy Gillespie's reign as trumpet playing ambassador, bon vivant and band leader ended, the crown was shared by his protégé Jon Faddis and his compadré Sandoval. The Cuban had been a founder member of Cubana De Musica Moderna in the early seventies and, when it changed its name to Irakere, he remained with them until 1981. Gillespie was an initial influence and, when Sandoval found life in his homeland intolerable, it was logical that he should move to the US. As a virtuoso trumpeter, he rapidly became established in America and, ten years later, added his prodigious fire power to Gillespie's United Nations Orchestra. Bebop remained Sandoval's core inspiration but, as this CD illustrates, his outlook has become more expansive. His original roots are clearly evident on *Dizzy Atmosphere*, his bristling hard-bop attack addresses *Moontrane* and *Woody*, while *Reflections* suggests a constructive attention to Miles Davis. *It Never Gets Old* suggests a more mainstream stance and his nonchalant jousting with Terry on *Mack the Knife* endorses the fact. Calderazzo's solos swing impressively and he leads a rhythm section that suits each stylistic circumstance. Brecker, Daniels and Stern fit seamlessly into their feature spots but it is the leader who makes the greatest impact.                                                         **BMcR**

## Mongo Santamaria                                                                    1920

**Mongo Explodes/Watermelon Man** Santamaria (cgas, bgs); with: **Marty Sheller** (t); **Nat Adderley** (c); **Bobby Capers** (f, as); **Mauricio Smith** (f); **Hubert Laws** (f, pic, ts); **Rodgers Grant** (p); **Victor Venegas** (b); **Ray Lucas**, **Jimmy Cobb** (d); **Frank Hernandez** (d, perc); **Carmelo Garcia**, **Joseph Gorgas**, **Osvaldo Marinez**, **'Kako'**, **Wito Kortwright** (perc); **Chihuahua Martinez** (perc, v). Ace/Fantasy Ⓜ CDBGPD062 (78 minutes). Recorded 1962-4.

⑦ ❻

Cuban-born Santamaria moved to America in his late twenties. He paid his dues in the commercial bands of Tito Puente and Perez Prado, then in 1957 was confronted with jazz when he joined Cal Tjader. In the years since he has played an important part in spreading the Cuban/jazz doctrine. In 1958 he began his own recording career as a leader and his band, rich in rhythmic complexity, was populated by timbales, guiro, cow bells and sundry noise-creating equipment. By 1962 he had become increasingly committed to jazz, with men such as Paul Serano, Pat Patrick, Chick Corea and Al McKibbon appearing in his ranks. He had also begun to work in New York jazz nighteries, and the first half of this CD was recorded live at the Village Gate. The basis of his music remained Cuban, but jazz solos became an increasingly important part of his music, as if he was aware of spicing up a Latin dance band. Adderley's three guest spots at the Gate offer very little, but Sheller, his regular trumpeter, shows himself as a more than capable alternative. Since the palmy days of the sixties, Santamaria has to some extent fallen from commercial grace, but recordings for Concord and jazz tour performances have maintained the public's awareness of him.                               **BMcR**

## Akio Sasajima                                                                        1952

**Humpty Dumpty** Sasajima (g); **Joe Henderson** (ts); **Renée Rosnes** (p); **Kelly Sill** (b); **Joel Spencer** (d). Enja Ⓕ ENJ8032 2 (47 minutes). Recorded 1988.

⑦ ❽

Sasjima has made albums subsequent for this (the 1991 duet with Ron Carter, **Acoustically Sound** on Muse, for example), but **Humpty Dumpty** remains his most immediate and enjoyable. He is a fine musician in the Wes Montgomery tradition, and someone who has a superb group with him on this album playing the heck out of a selection of originals and what can safely be called 'jazz standards'; that is, songs which jazzmen other than the composers often play. Sasajima came to the US from his native Japan in 1977 and quickly made himself known to local musicians in the Chicago area. By the mid eighties he had formed a particularly close musical understanding with Joe Henderson – this is, in fact, their second album together under Sasajima's name – and the fruits of that friendship can be heard here. Henderson himself is on burning form on this disc, playing with the type of *élan* and occasional abandon which has rarely surfaced since his early Blue Note records. This may be to do with the impressively energetic rhythm section where Rosnes and Spencer, in particular, shine (Rosnes also takes some fine solos). Sasajima himself has a burnished tone, an individual way of phrasing and a natural sense of play. He sounds happy in the music and it is a thoroughly enjoyable modern jazz date, the type of which Blue Note used to make about three a month in its sixties heyday.                                                           **KS**

## Stefan Scaggiari                                                                     1948

New review
**Stefan Out** Scaggiari (p); **Jim Hughart** (b); **Colin Bailey** (d). Concord Jazz Ⓕ CCD4659 (62 minutes). Recorded 1994.

⑦ ❾

Having heard the first of the dozen pieces in the programme, *Love Walked In*, you might conclude that Stefan Scaggiari was of the hard-swinging Oscar Peterson persuasion. Later comes *Willow Weep For Me*, with overtones of Gene Harris, and shortly after that a version of *Ill Wind* reminiscent of Bill Evans. He handles this multiplicity of styles with conviction and aplomb and never descends to mere pastiche. Some, no doubt, would view such versatility with a jaundiced eye and ask where his 'true style' was, but originality is not the only virtue in this world. Technical accomplishment and natural flair are valuable, too – especially when they come in such large quantities as this.                   **DG**

# Mario Schiano

**Tracks** Schiano (as, ss); **Joëlle Léandre, Peter Kowald** (b, v). LeParc ⓕ 512-2 (50 minutes). Recorded 1993.

⑦ ⑧

So far, Italian saxophonist Mario Schiano's international reputation has not reached a level corresponding to his unique talents and historical significance in his native land's turbulent free-jazz movement (during the sixties and seventies, Italian free jazz was an active and often volatile commentary on the changing political climate). Hopefully this situation will improve now that Schiano is receiving additional European visibility thanks in part to his participation in the all-star Italian Instabile Orchestra, and to the greater availability of his recordings on labels like Splasc(h), Le Parc, and Victo (Canada). At least one measure of his stature may be taken from the quality of non-local musicians with whom he's worked. On disc, Schiano's inescapable lyricism and impish wit has tempered the highly-focused improvising of an Evan Parker or an Alex von Schlippenbach, he's discovered a common language with Russian and Estonian players from the (former) Ganelin Trio, and met Dutch eccentrics Misha Mengelberg and Han Bennink on equal footing.

Often a voice of moderation in otherwise open, explosive ensembles (for example, alongside Evan Parker, Barry Guy, *et al* on **Social Security** [Victo]), **Tracks** finds him in an unusually intimate setting, where he fits neatly in between two of the most imaginative bassists in modern jazz. Léandre and Kowald are an especially compatible pair; both are capable of a huge range of colours and textures in addition to a fluid melodicism, and they create vivid tactile episodes often throughout these four lengthy free pieces. Schiano responds with typically (and deceptively) low-key, conversational phrasing; linking short motives that can be tender, biting, or humorous by turns. He finds a way to caress the most brittle bass passages, and at one point his piping bird-song inspires Léandre to vocalize in an impromptu twittering duet. Though this is a good sample of his warm and witty approach to improvisation, interested listeners are advised to keep up the search – Schiano blossoms in the most unexpected places. **AL**

# Lalo Schifrin

1932

**More Jazz Meets the Symphony** Schifrin (p); **James Morrison** (flh); **Paquito D'Rivera** (as, cl); **Ray Brown** (b); **Grady Tate** (d); **Jon Faddis** (t); **The London Philharmonic**. Atlantic ⓕ 82653-2 (61 minutes). Recorded 1993.

⑧ ⑨

Argentinian pianist/composer Lalo Schifrin came to jazz prominence with Dizzy Gillespie in the early sixties. From 1962 on Schifrin has focused his energies on establishing a successful career in Los Angeles as one of Hollywood's most resourceful and respected composers of film and television scores. Here, we meet both sides of the Schifrin persona, the master painter of vividly coloured soundscapes and the encyclopaedic jazz *aficionado* whose musical passions range from Satchmo to Miles as well as to Tin Pan Alley.

The first of the set pieces, *Sketches of Miles*, is an artful melding of eight Davis-associated lines including *All Blues*, *So What* and *Four*. Buoyed by the lush strings of the London Philharmonic and the boppish flights of Faddis, Morrison, D'Rivera and the strong rhythmic currents let loose by the leader's piano, bassist Brown and drummer Tate, Schifrin's iridescent chart sparkles. So, too, does his evocative *Portrait of Louis Armstrong*, a Gershwinized pastiche seamlessly stitching together such Armstrong classics as *Nobody Knows the Trouble I've Seen*, *When It's Sleepytime Down South* and *Struttin' with Some Barbeque*. In these lovingly-crafted Hollywood Bowl-esque tributes as well as in the poignant takes on standards such as *Begin the Beguine* and *Django*, Schifrin offers an engaging and musically substantive jazz-pops stroll with broad appeal. **CB**

# Rolf Schimmermann

**Suru** Schimmermann (kbds, p); **Stuart Brookes** (t); **Tony Roberts** (ss, ts, f); **Ray Russell** (g, g-syn); **Dill Katz, Fredy Studer** (d); **Miriam Stockley** (v). B&W ⓕ 009 (49 minutes). Recorded 1991.

⑥ ⑧

Schimmermann and company deliver a lovingly-constructed and finely recorded set of originals which, by and large, reinvestigate territory originally mapped out by various members of Weather Report, and by Miles in his last decade. Nothing wrong with that – not all bands have to deliver something new to make it good. In fact, there is much tasteful playing, especially from Russell and Brookes, and the group by and large manage to avoid the sort of pomp-fusion which tends to send the jazz end of the instrumental electric audience screaming from the room. Most of the material consists of vamps upon which to lay suggestive harmonic inversions through which a solo will snake in a generally satisfying fashion. Schimmermann opens the album with a solo piano piece which is atypical of the rest of the album, so do not be put off by it. The vocals are of a piece with the instruments, and mostly there to add atmosphere, apart from on the penultimate track, *Endless*

*Longing*, where Stockley sings some lyrics, and her voice shows itself to be lacking in individuality but still a pleasant experience. This is the modern-day electric equivalent of fifties West Coast.    **KS**

# Alexander Von Schlippenbach                    1938

**Berlin Contemporary Jazz Orchestra** Von Schlippenbach (cond, arr); **Benny Bailey**, **Thomas Heberer**, **Henry Lowther** (t); **Kenny Wheeler** (t, flh); **Paul Van Kemenade**, **Felix Wahnschaffe** (as); **Gerd Dudek** (ss, ts, cl, f); **Walter Gauchel** (ts); **E.L. Petrowsky** (bs); **Willem Breuker** (bs, bcl); **Henning Berg**, **Herman Breuer**, **Hubert Katzenbeier** (tb); **Utz Zimmermann** (btb); **Aki Takase** (p); **Gunter Lenz** (b); **Ed Thigpen** (d); **Misha Mengelberg** (p). ECM Ⓔ 841 777-2 (50 minutes). Recorded 1989.

⑧ ❽

This band, founded by Von Schlippenbach in 1988, is the chart-playing equivalent of his explosively free unit, Globe Unity. No attempt is made to match that orchestra's unbridled fire, although the BCJO is not without its own slow burn. It fits its soloists into arranged pieces without inhibiting them and it achieves a genuine depth of ensemble sound commensurate with the size of the line-up. Significantly, its three-man rhythm team answers every question asked of them and when the need is for attack they show themselves well able to generate the old-style 'American' drive. Von Schlippenbach has recruited many players from outside the city of Berlin and the quality of the solos on this CD is impressive. The score for Wheeler's *Ana* presents an almost stately face, yet it also boasts a string of formidable solos. Mengelberg's compositions, *Salz*, and *Reef Und Kneebus*, a suite in three parts, have a constrastingly zany quality and perhaps tax the orchestra in a somewhat different manner. In one sense they accommodate Thigpen's rhythmic aspirations rather more but the former still elicits strong individual contributions. The album's best counterpoint is heard in the minuet movement of *Reef Und Kneebus*, but the whole is such a good group effort that it seems invidious to select isolated high spots from a performance that must establish the BCJO as one of the most outstanding big bands in the world.    **BMcR**

New review

**Elf Bagatellen** Von Schlippenbach (p); **Evan Parker** (ss, ts); **Paul Lovens** (d, perc). FMP Ⓔ 27 (72 minutes). Recorded 1990.

⑨ ❽

A key figure from the burgeoning late sixties, European free-jazz movement up to the present day, Von Schlippenbach's leadership and organizational talents in such groups as Globe Unity, the more recent Berlin Contemporary Jazz Orchestra and this long-standing trio may be equally as important as his playing. The Von Schlippenbach Trio has been together since the early seventies and has made many fine recordings; if this one is special it is due to the care and consideration that went into its production. The programme looks to the past fondly; *Resurrection of Yarak*, *Yarak: Reforged* and *The Forge: Rebellowed* refer to Von Schlippenbach compositions which he's recorded solo and/or with Globe Unity, likewise *Sun-Luck: Revisited* with an Evan Parker piece which appeared on the trio's 1972 FMP début. Since then they have refined their distinctive approach – a redefining of roles (often it's impossible to tell who is outlining the primary theme and who is commenting on or accompanying it) and an intense investigation of colours and degrees of energy within the trio format. The timbral palette and rhythmic caesurae of Paul Lovens should not be underestimated, as it demands each member affect their own accented phrasing, creating a precarious balance of polyrhythms. Von Schlippenbach brings a European quality to the group; what little he adapts from the jazz canon (specifically Jelly Roll Morton, Monk, and Cecil Taylor) is viewed from a distant perspective and funnelled through his classical background. Alternating brief sound paintings with longer motivic improvisations – the episodes of shifting narrative and splashy colour make *Analogue: Scaled* seem like a nine-minute Chinese opera – these 11 'bagatelles' (titled with tongue-in-cheek) display the magnetic interaction, varied expression and insistent risk-taking that typifies this ensemble.    **AL**

# Maria Schneider                    1951

New review

**Coming About** Schneider (comp, arr, dir); **Mark Vinci**, **Tim Ries** (as, ss, cl, f); **Rich Perry**, **Rick Margitza** (ts); **Scott Robinson** (bs, bcl, cl, theremin, bari); **Charles Pillow** (ehn, cl); **Tony Dadleck**, **Greg Gisbert**, **Laurie Frink**, **Tim Hagans** (t, frh); **Keith O'Quinn**, **Rock Ciccarone**, **Larry Farrell**, **George Flynn** (tb); **Ben Monder** (g); **Frank Kimbrough** (p); **Tony Scherr** (b, elb); **Tim Horner** (d). Enja Ⓔ ENJ9069-2 (68 minutes). Recorded 1995.

⑨ ❾

Though born and raised in Minnesota, composer/arranger Maria Schneider has made her mark in the tumultuous take-no-prisoners jazz scene of New York City. While one hears echoes of mentors Bob Brookmeyer and Gil Evans, Schneider is an original in both conception and design. It is an originality based on a willingness to bear her soul, her emotions, and, indeed, her own unique 'story'. In the three-part *Scenes from Childhood*, for instance, we share her youthful *Angst* over the atomic threat in a section called *Bombshelter Beast*, a seething soundscape made sci-fi eerie by Schneider's eddying whirlpools, Ben Monder's laser-powered guitar, and Scott Robinson's lava-searing bari and other-worldy theremin. Like Ellington, Schneider uses her players' unique personas to flesh out compositions. In *El Viento*, guitarist Monder and trombonist Larry Farrell add 'sketches of Spain' which enlarge the 11-minute work to a scale comparable to that of Picasso's *Guernica*. Indeed, one of her hallmarks is a keen visual sense. The result is an almost kinesthetic response in which we not only 'hear' but also 'see'. Even in her treatment of Coltrane's *Giant Steps*, the lasting impression is that of the arranger, a talent which is already hugely impressive but still has room to grow.     **CB**

# Rob Schneiderman                    1957

**Radio Waves**  Schneiderman (p); **Brian Lynch** (t); **Ralph Moore** (ts); **Gary Smulyan** (bs); **Todd Coolman** (b); **Jeff Hirschfield** (d). Reservoir Ⓕ RSRCD120 (71 minutes). Recorded 1991.

⑥ ❾

Born in Boston, raised in San Diego, Schneiderman's mother was a piano teacher, yet it was not until he heard jazz at high school that he took advantage of that fact. Nevertheless, by the time he was 16, he was already playing semi-professionally. He moved to New York in 1982, has since worked with Art Farmer, Eddie Harris and Slide Hampton and has already made three albums as a leader. This CD presents Schneiderman the writer as well as pianist. Seven of the nine titles are by him and none are mere outlines for a mainstream, hard-bop, blowing session. Themes like the blues waltz, *The Juggler*, and the dance-inspired *Slapdance-Tapstick* demonstrate the range of his composing brief, and all boast arrangements that are similarly imaginative. With quality horn men like Lynch and Moore it would have been easy to take the soft option, but the leader ensures that soloists are correctly framed and that textural depths are cleverly regulated. The listener becomes increasingly aware that Schneiderman has provided a serious up-dating of the late-fifties message and has done so in a very colourful way. As a pianist, he shines because his impressive technique is put to real work and not just paraded. He works the full length of the keyboard and there is conviction in all he plays.     **BMcR**

# Lauren Schoenberg

**Time Waits For No One**  Laurie Frink, John Eckert, Dick Sudhalter, Burt Collins (t); **Matt Finders**, **Eddie Bert**, **Bobby Pring** (tb); **Chuck Wilson** (as, f, cl); **Jack Stuckey** (as, cl, ss); **Schoenberg**, **Doug Lawrence** (ts); **Ken Peplowski** (ts, cl); **Danny Bank** (bs, bcl); **Dick Katz** (p); **Chris Flory** (g); **Phil Flanigan** (b); **Mel Lewis** (d). MusicMasters Ⓕ 5032-2 (54 minutes). Recorded 1987.

⑥ ❻

Time did wait for Schoenberg, a highly gifted musicologist and musician whose association with Buck Clayton and some of the veteran jazz musicians has given him a sharp ear for period music. The range of his re-creations spreads from Henderson's *Queer Notions* to Gil Evans's *Buster's Last Stand*, by way of charts from Benny Carter, Buck Clayton, Ellington, Rugolo, Brookmeyer and McFarland. The soloists are imaginative and sympathetic and the drumming of Mel Lewis, appearing on one of his last recordings, is responsible for a most successful rhythm section. Every track is invigorating – the brass ensembles on Buck Clayton's *Smoothie*, the transcription of Artie Shaw's solo on *Lady Day* for an ensemble of clarinets, and a similar job on Duke's *Harmony In Harlem* succeed completely. Schoenberg must be congratulated on his ability to rehouse these classics of the past in a way which preserves their qualities without making his band sound old-fashioned or arch.     **SV**

# Matthias Schubert                    1960

New review
**Blue and Grey Suite**  Schubert (ts); **Simon Nabatov** (p); **Lindsay Horner** (b); **Tom Rainey** (d). Enja Ⓕ ENJ9045-2 (62 minutes). Recorded 1994.

⑦ ❽

Schubert's playing is renowned for its intensity and physicality. This album, and the quartet assembled for the record, display several aspects of Schubert's work, from the structured tribute to Herbie Nichols called *Nichols' Dime* to the alternating free improvising and passages of head arrangement in the title track (which runs to 34 minutes, with a useful chart of how the sections fit together in the booklet-note). The influence of Steve Lacy is present in some of Schubert's work, notably in an intriguing out-of-tempo tribute to Messiaen called *Le Maître*. Nabatov is a wilder, more random improviser than Rainey's usual rhythm section partner, Fred Hersch, and Horner's role is generally as understated as in his work with the New York Composers' Orchestra, so the the rhythm section dynamics are largely built on the balance between Rainey and Nabatov, stimulated by the power of Schubert's playing and composition. Ironically, despite his credentials as a free player, Schubert's playing here suggests that his ideas flow better in the more thoroughly composed material, and this communicates to his fellow musicians. There are several impressive passages in the *Blue and Grey Suite*, but it tends to fall apart in some of the free sections, whilst *Nichols' Dime* is a thoroughly watertight piece of construction and soloing, and benefits the listener accordingly.                **AS**

# Ed Schuller

New review
**To Know Where One Is**  Ed Schuller (b); Joe Lovano (ts, ss); Gary Valente (tb); Billy Hart (d); Bill Bickford (g). GM Ⓕ GM3019 (63 minutes). Recorded 1994.

⑦ ❻

A versatile musician of the New York scene who oscillates between the mainstream and quite far-out, Schuller's bass tone is thick and his style declarative; he lumbers with a kind of heavyweight grace through tunes. His rhythms aren't sleek but he has a great groove and he keeps resorting to ostinato vamps to ride the pulse. He's all about accessibility; he wants to give you something to hang on to, and this set of originals has a touch of souled-out Ornette (*Sooner Than Before*) and avant-gutbucket (*Big Daddy's Magic Row Blues*). This is an especially good showcase for Lovano: he sounds hungry. But so do they all, except for glassy-toned Bickford, more of a prog-rocker; Valente wails, and Hart drives the band. Muffled, cheap production sound (and a clunky jazz-rock call for world peace at the end of the album, with Schuller intoning his own poem) mars an otherwise impressive album.     **BR**

# Diane Schuur

New review
**Love Walked In**  Schuur (v); Jack Sheldon, Wayne Bergeron (t); Richard Todd (frh); Andrew Martin (tb); John T. Johnson (tba); Pete Christlieb, Gary Foster (saxes); Michael Wofford (p); Phil Upchurch (g); John Patitucci (b); John Guerin (d) plus unidentified string section. GRP Ⓕ 98412 (36 minutes). Recorded 1995.

⑥ ❾

There are many who would question Schuur's inclusion in this Guide, and to be truthful there are a number of tracks on this album which would lend support to their opinions, including a *Say It Isn't So* replete with meaningless 1,001 strings and tinkling piano backdrop which takes the whole thing way beyond pastiche and into kitsch. Yet Schuur redeems herself with a swinging *Love Walked In* which features nice solos from Pete Christlieb and Jack Sheldon and casts the shadow of mid-sixties Nancy Wilson from Schuur's vocal style, a shadow at its deepest when the singer is enmeshed in the soft mattress of strings to be found on half of the ten tracks here. The arrangements on the five tracks featuring the horns sound Marty Paich-ish, and it is no surprise to find arranger Al Schmitt dedicating the album to the recently departed master (Schuur dedicates the album to Les Crocket 'Rocket', so I hope she and her arranger didn't come to blows over this). Schuur's singing style isn't big on subtlety or nuance, but she is a confident singer with a big voice and secure technique, and the music she makes leaves few uncommitted. If you like your music big, bright and breezy, with a considerable jazz aura, then half this album will be just for you. What you do with the other half I leave to your imagination, but a glance at the recording length means half of 36 minutes makes it a considerable financial investment.     **KS**

# Louis Sclavis

**Ellington On the Air**  Sclavis (cl, bcl, ss); Yves Robert (tb); Dominique Pifarely (vn); François Raulin (p, kbds, melodica); Bruno Chevillon (b); Francis Lassus (d, fedounon, keles). Ida Ⓕ 032CD (68 minutes). Recorded 1991-2.

❼                                                                                ⑧ ❿

This is certainly one of the most unusual Ellington invocations on record. Sclavis has, of course, established himself as a man with strong ties to both the regional French music he still plays and to jazz. Here he moulds the two traditions together in a most extraordinary way. For the most part, Ellington themes appear either as a prologue or an epilogue to what is probably best described as a fantasy on that theme or its harmonic structure, composed by one of the band members. The use of clarinet, harmonium and violin adds to the distancing of the familiar melodies from their normal environment, and increases the excitement of discovery, both in the sense of what can be found in Ellington and what these men can reveal about themselves and their own talents, brought into sharp relief by the Duke. As Sclavis writes in the booklet-notes, "Duke Ellington is the link between the American jazz tradition and its contemporary European expression ... Duke Ellington is the origin, the point of reference and the inspiration. He is ... in the air."

At times, these musicians wander very far from that source, but the way they always dovetail their explorations back into Ellington territory is fascinating. The trombone of Robert, wah-wah mutes and all, very clearly evokes the Ducal spirit: his solo in *Harlem Pancake/A Tone Parallel* to *Harlem/West Indian Pancake* is one to treasure, as are the steel drums. A masterful and wide-ranging album which confirms Sclavis's increasing importance in contemporary music, although his latest album, **Les Violences de Rameau** (ECM), is something of a tangential step. **KS**

# Bob Scobey
1916-63

New review

**Direct from San Francisco** Scobey (t); **Jack Buck** (tb); **Bob Short** (tba); **Bill Napier** (cl); **Jesse (Tiny) Crump** (p); **Clancy Hayes** (bj, v); **Hal McCormack** (b); **Fred Higuera** (d). Good Time Jazz Ⓜ GTJCD12023-2 (38 minutes). Recorded 1956.

⑥ ❽

Poor Bob Scobey was always something of a second fiddle, first to Lu Watters in the elephantine Yerba Buena Jazz Band, later to Mutt Carey, Alvin Alcorn and Teddy Buckner, for whom he deputized in Kid Ory's band when any of them was indisposed. This view does him a disservice. He led one of the West Coast's most consistent Dixieland bands for many years, occasionally enlarged to a big band, and he provided first-rate backings for many visitors to the Bay Area including Bing Crosby, who cut rather a good album with Scobey. The Watters pachyderm tendency reappears here with the odd decision to include both string bass and tuba. Otherwise, for a West Coast band this is a light and swinging set of unexceptional Dixieland, featuring good-time vocals by the banjo-playing George Melly of the San Francisco revival, Clancy Hayes. Scobey's Louis-tinged trumpet and Napier's edge-toned clarinet take the outstanding solos, with the exception of the band's most remarkable member, pianist Jesse Crump, who was Ida Cox's husband and accompanist in the twenties, a genuine ragtime innovator (shown by his private-label discs from 1923) and tutor to many a jazz pianist, including Sammy Price. Crump's idiosyncratic piano is a delight whenever it emerges from the Dixie mêlée (notably shedding the Morton legacy on *Dr Jazz*) and makes this album far more than hokum. **AS**

# John Scofield
1951

**Still Warm** Scofield (g); **Don Grolnick** (kbds); **Darryl Jones** (elb); **Omar Hakim** (d, perc). Gramavision Ⓕ 18-8508-2 (43 minutes). Recorded 1985.

✓ ⑧ ❽

**Still Warm** is perhaps one of the records which critics have in mind when they put forward the risible suggestion that Scofield's playing acquired a new impetus under the tutelage of Miles Davis. Miles was no doubt happy to give the impression of hiring Scofield for his potential, but when Miles discovered him, Scofield was already one of the most distinctive, dues-paid guitar stylists of his generation, and the arrival of **Still Warm**, his most dynamic funk record, was the culmination of a development which had begun in the mid seventies. There are references to the past – *Rule Of Thumb*, for example, operates rather like Scofield's 1981 recording *Holidays* – but two tracks – *Techno* and, in particular, *Protocol* – suggest a quite new perspective. Both are brisk funk stomps, based, unremarkably, on two-bar bass pockets. However, in *Protocol*'s quasi-atonal riff and the wide intervallic leaps of both themes (*Protocol*'s arching hysterically from end to end of a diminished arpeggio), Scofield contrived a new, darker angle on the funky verities. Unsurprisingly, the discovery prompted solos of fearsome intensity. Other tracks are less unusual, some previewing the spongy bluesy vamps of later albums in the Gramavision series, but on the pieces mentioned, fusion was jolted into a new dimension. **MG**

**Hand Jive** Scofield (g); **Eddie Harris** (ts); **Larry Goldberg** (p, org); **Dennis Irwin** (b); **Bill Stewart** (d); **Don Alias** (perc). Blue Note Ⓕ CDP8 27327-2 (64 minutes). Recorded 1993.

⑧ ❿

Scofield has always displayed deep blues roots, even at his most reserved and discreet. It's there in his phrasing, in his approach to the placement of a bent tone, in his conversationalism. No matter how extended the harmonic sequence may be, that blues power is one of the prime sources of his momentum. On **Hand Jive** he makes no bones about it. After a sequence of fine but rather subdued albums featuring tenorist Joe Lovano, he has dirtied up his tone again, gone for a more biting angularity, and brought in one of the founders of funky tenor playing, Eddie Harris. The saxophonist's role seems in part to be a staff of formal stylistic identification around which Scofield can strut his more unorthodox patterns. If so, the juxtaposition works a keen magic, giving Harris a reflected lustre not always present on his own albums, however sophisticated his playing occasionally became.

The presence of pianist Goldings also releases Scofield from the dilemma of being the eternal harmonic provider to all and sundry, so he can go along with the flow in his own chosen way rather than have to steer the vessel of each tune. Harris is not present on every track, although variations of the funky beats most closely associated with him are. But Scofield rightly commands our closest attention, and on a piece like *Do Like Eddie*, where Harris is present, Scofield takes a quite extraordinary solo over a single pedal note, twisting and turning, sliding and diving around the tonic, using distantly related scales which suddenly dovetail back into the simple riff, taking chances at every turn. It's a bench-mark solo and one worth returning to repeatedly. As is the album. **KS**

**New review**

**Quiet** Scofield (g); **Wayne Shorter** (ts); **Steve Swallow** (elb); **Bill Stewart** (d); **Duduka Da Fonseca** (perc); **Randy Brecker** (t, flh); **John Clark**, **Fred Griffen** (frh); **Charles Pillow** (f, ehn, ts); **Lawrence Feldman** (af, f, ts); **Howard Johnson** (tba, bs); **Roger Rosenberg** (bcl). Verve Ⓕ 533 185-2 (51 minutes). Recorded 1996.

🔟 🔟

It's called **Quiet**, on the cover it has a picture of Scofield with his finger to his lips and it is an example of the guitarist taking time away from his previously favoured electric guitar, and picking out subtle, intricate solos on the acoustic instrument instead. It's brilliant, too.

Scofield's guitar style, though stirring and bluesy and rarely shy of a bit of distortion, has always held up as the pinnacle of its art a tricky, off-beat articulation. Like Joe Henderson's tenor saxophone work, or Joe Lovano's, it swings hard even when you're not sure how. On the classical guitar, his lines are breathtakingly beautiful, and tense in their off-beat logic. Scofield makes clever use of the range of timbres, moving around the sound hole to produce warm chords and trebly lines, weaving in and out of the arrangements. The compositions are beautiful as well. Bassist Steve Swallow (always an immaculate player) and drummer Bill Stewart swing hard without raising the volume, there are inspired contributions by Wayne Shorter on tenor, and the whole thing is packed with some of the loveliest contemporary jazz arrangements this side of 1990. **LC**

# Hazel Scott
1920-81

**New review**

**Relaxed Piano Moods** Scott (p); **Charles Mingus** (b); **Max Roach** (d). Début Ⓜ OJCCD1702-2 (41 minutes). Recorded 1955.

⑥ ❽

Backed by the two co-proprietors of Début records, who originally issued six of the nine tracks in this set of material by West-Indian born pianist Scott as an LP, this is a dream trio. However, the three opening ballads are almost too much of a relaxed, dreamy good thing and it is not until the fourth track, a robust, compelling *Jeep Is Jumpin'*, that the trio really starts to show what it can do. Scott's up-tempo playing is electrifying – locked hands, dazzling runs and harmonic invention jostling for the attention and showing why she was the star attraction at New York's Cafe Society clubs for many years. A raunchy *Git Up from There* (with an alternative take) has some fine playing from Mingus and even more dazzling playing from Scott as she yells encouragement to herself. In contrast to her more introspective playing, she also chooses to take *A Foggy Day* at a sprightly lick and this shows some of her most interesting playing, stabbing left-hand figures contrasting with rapid-fire ornamental patterns in the right that show just how stride piano might have evolved into the bop era. Here, too, there is a long solo from Mingus showing the full power of his melodic imagination at work on standard source material. For these central tracks alone the album is worth checking out, and overall it is an interesting addition to any collection of piano jazz by a relatively less-known figure. **AS**

# Jimmy Scott

**Lost and Found** Jimmy Scott (v); **Frank Wess** (ts); **David 'Fathead' Newman** (ts, f); **Ray Bryant**, **Junior Mance** (p); **David Spinoza, Eric Gale, Billy Butler** (g); **Richard Davis, Ron Carter** (b); **Billy Cobham, Bruno Carr** (d); strings arranged and conducted by **Eumir Deodate, Gene Orloff, Selwart Clarke, William Fischer, Arif Mardin**. Sequel Ⓜ RSACD804 (49 minutes). Recorded 1969/72.

② ❻

Jimmy Scott could have been one of the great oddball voices of popular music, like Johnnie Ray or Eartha Kitt. His sound, as producer Joel Dorn observes in the notes to this release, "defines androgyny". It is high, almost falsetto, with a little sobbing catch in it, and projected with quite alarming force. He often takes songs at tempos so slow that you could, as the saying goes, eat lunch between the beats. Ray Charles loved Scott's style, and so did Atlantic Records boss, Nesuhi Ertegun, but their efforts to help him came to little because he was tied hand and foot by a youthful contract with Savoy. This CD consists partly of material recorded by Ertegun in 1969 but not issued until now. The 1972 tracks came out that year on an Atlantic album entitled **The Source**. A glance at the personnel above suggests that Ertegun was quite sincere in his admiration and ensured that the very best players and arrangers were hired to accompany Jimmy Scott. I can only say that, after puzzling long and hard, I cannot for the life of me understand his enthusiasm. **DG**

# Ronnie Scott
1927-96

**Never Pat A Burning Dog** Ronnie Scott, **Mornington Lockett** (ts); **Dick Pearce** (t); **John Critchinson** (p); **Ron Mathewson** (b); **Martin Drew** (d). Jazz House Ⓕ JHCD012 (74 minutes). Recorded 1990.

Given his long career and the admiration which his playing always attracted, Ronnie Scott recorded remarkably little. When this CD was issued in 1991 it arrived after a gap of almost 14 years, during which time the Ronnie Scott Quintet had been working regularly, both at his own club and around the world. It is perhaps the best he has ever made, displaying his formidable musicianship and grasp of the jazz idiom (Jazz House have recently compiled **When I Want Your Opinion, I'll Ask For It**, a selection of mid-sixties tapes from the original Ronnie Scott's site which, despite the poor recording quality, features Scott himself in good shape, although this latter-day effort remains much more approachable).Whether it is a modal piece such as McCoy Tyner's *Contemplation* or a ballad like *This Love Of Mine*, Scott's playing has that effortlessly authoritative feel to it which is a mark of rare distinction. He also possessed a beautiful tone, warm and fibrous, with a delightful, lazy vibrato creeping in at slow tempos. This is much more readily appreciated on record than it was in person. Recording also reveals what a superb band the quintet was, with its supple rhythm section and mellow front-line blend. Pearce is a world-class trumpeter who has been sadly undervalued by the critics. On one track Pearce is replaced by the tenor saxophone of Lockett. The CD title is the punchline of a Ronnie Scott joke, the full import of which could be adequately conveyed only by its creator in person. Hopefully the reader of these lines was able to take advantage of Ronnie's presence at the club over the years to hear this and other examples of the unique Scott humour before his sad demise.   **DG**

## Shirley Scott

1934

**Queen Of The Organ** Scott (org); **Stanley Turrentine** (ts); **Bob Cranshaw** (b), **Otis 'Candy' Finch** (d). Impulse! Ⓜ GRP11232 (72 minutes). Recorded 1964.

⑧ ❽

Initially a pianist and trumpeter, Scott was encouraged to change to the organ by hearing Jimmy Smith (her 1992 trio CD **Skylark** on Candid shows how effectively she still works on occasion as a pianist). Nevertheless her first choice instrument remains the organ. She came to prominence in the tenor and organ trios of the fifties and sixties. In this field her finest work was with Lockjaw Davis and one-time husband Turrentine. This CD represents that latter partnership and, although she worked well with Jimmy Forrest and Dexter Gordon during the eighties, it remains a high watermark and confirms her status as one of the finest of all jazz organists. Her streetwise bebop is delivered with a stinging attack, her solo lines are well marshalled and titles like *Cute*, *Rapid Shave* and *That's For Me* demonstrate her skill at solo conjugation. Her latent power on *Like Blue* and *Mean, Angry, Nasty And Lowdown* is a reminder of the organ's role in blues since Fred Longshaw. Turrentine plays well and Cranshaw and Finch show that they know how to accept the special responsibilities of a rhythm team in an organ group. When the roles are reversed, however, it is the sparse and superbly buoyant backgrounds that Scott supplies that confirm she is also a master of understatement. Her series of fine latter-day piano albums for Candid should be sought out for a balanced view of her career to date.   **BMcR**

## Stephen Scott

New review

**The Beautiful Thing** Scott (p); **Jesse Davis, Kenny Garrett** (as); **Ron Blake, Branford Marsalis** (ts); **Russell Malone** (g); **Dwayne Burno** (b); **Victor Lewis, Dion Parson, Steve Kroon** (d). Verve Ⓔ 533 186-2 (68 minutes). Recorded 1996.

⑥ ❿

Scott, who came to notice when accompanying Betty Carter in the late eighties, has made two other albums for Verve, each one with a different personnel. One glance at the people on board this time and the prospective listener will more or less know what's coming. As has become essential recording practice these days (almost as *de rigeur* as long jams on *I Got Rhythm* and blues changes in front of a studio microphone were back in the fifties), each track features a different permutation of the string of people listed on the back cover. Everyone plays immaculately, no one even thinks of hitting clinker, and the whole thing is brilliantly recorded: it is all in the best possible taste. They play very fast, they play slow, they play with tricky rhytmic patterns. But this album is a little like a careful re-enactment of a crime or an old love-affair: the feelin' ain't so warm the second time around, even if the interest is still there, in theory at least.   **KS**

## Tom Scott

1948

**Born Again** Scott (ts, as, ss); **Randy Brecker** (t, flh); **George Bohanon** (tb); **Pete Christlieb** (ts); **Kenny Kirkland** (p); **John Patitucci** (b); **William Kennedy** (d); **Mike Fisher** (perc). GRP Ⓔ 96752 (46 minutes). Recorded 1992.

⑥ ❽

While still a teenager, Scott had worked with Don Ellis and Oliver Nelson. He later studied Indian music under Ravi Shankar, but his reputation was really made in the studios, backing singers like Joni

Mitchell and Carole King and with his main interest centred on the commercial end of jazz-rock fusion. On this CD he goes back to his alleged roots and in his booklet-notes he claims that he wanted to record something more mainstream. In the event he has had a fair stab at it. The three-man rhythm section, with Kirkland assertively at its head, conjures up just the right box of tricks while Scott's own solos, most particularly on *Back Burner* and *Song No. 1*, have a degree more content than his output over the last 15 years has led us to expect. He has wisely included Brecker on four tracks and the two men work well together, but it is the loose-jointed quartets like *Close View* and *Silhouettes* that will come as a shock to listeners who have come to regard Scott's work as the most perfect sleeping draught yet devised. Patitucci and Kennedy certainly stir up the rhythmic activity on the former, but it is the alto of the leader that captures the interest on the latter.                **BMcR**

# Tony Scott                                                                     1921

New review

**The Clarinet Album**  Scott (cl); **Massimo Farao** (p); **Aldo Zunino** (b); **Giulio Capiozzo** (d).
   Philology Ⓕ W113-2 (75 minutes). Recorded 1993.

⑨  ⑧

Scott's eloquent clarinet combines the breathy sensuality of Ben Webster with Charlie Parker's mercurial ingenuity. In the fifties he worked with Billie Holiday and Sarah Vaughan (as performer and arranger), recorded some of the earliest free improvisation and brought together Bill Evans, Scott LeFaro and Paul Motian to play on his fine **Dedications** set. In 1959 he left America and spent six years travelling, mostly in the Far East. On his return to New York he began to blend his jazz with elements from the indigenous musics he had studied, a pioneering attempt to create 'world music'. In the early seventies he settled in Italy and has since recorded only infrequently. **The Clarinet Album** is a bravura display of clarinet virtuosity, all the more remarkable from a man of 72. The backing trio swing neatly through this set of standards, but Scott plays as if possessed, blowing the loudest, softest, sexiest, wildest, most astonishing clarinet. Once or twice he sounds as if he's (metaphorically) banging his head against the wall, but more often the results are transfixing – as with the chalumeau arabesques of *Do Nothin' Till You Hear From Me* or a refigured *My Funny Valentine*, where the clarinet flutters around the melody like a candle-flame's hypnotic dance on the wick.                **GL**

# Terry Seabrook

New review

**Can't Stop Now**  Seabrook (p); **Raoul D'Olivera**, **Matt Holland** (t); **Joe Robinson** (ts, ss); **Bobby
   Wellins** (ts); **Dave Barnard** (b); **Tristan Banks**, **Satin Singh**, **Gareth Stevens**, **Sewanu TJ James**,
   **Adekoye Williams** (perc). TSM Ⓕ CBCD1 (72 minutes). Recorded 1995.

⑨  ⑨

Seabrook's Cubana Bop is an exciting and highly original Latin band. The rhythms are as nifty as one could hope for but, in place of the customary endless montuno, Seabrook and his musicians have devised a marvellous variety of harmonic and textural effects. He was lucky in being able to call upon Bobby Wellins as guest soloist, who contributes some memorable solos in his inimitable, plaintive tone. It says a great deal for the strength of the band that he fits happily into the proceedings rather than dominating them. Raoul D'Olivera, formerly of Wham! and other pop extravaganzas, is without doubt one of the finest lead trumpeters in Europe, especially in a Latin context, and the ensemble crackles under his leadership. The growth of Latin music in Britain over the past decade has been quite remarkable. From pedestrian beginnings it has increased in skill and confidence to the point where a band like Cubana Bop is contributing something new and exciting to the idiom.                **DG**

# Al Sears                                                                       1910-90

New review

**Swing's the Thing**  Sears (ts); **Don Abney** (p); **Wally Richardson** (g); **Wendell Marshall** (b); **Joe
   Marshall** (d). Prestige Swingville Ⓜ OJCCD838-2 (37 minutes). Recorded 1960.

⑧  ⑩

As mentioned in the previous Guide, Sears had the misfortune to follow Ben Webster into the greatest edition of Duke Ellington's Famous Orchestra, thereby incurring the wrath of a generation or more of critics with his simpler, more jump-jazz style of playing. The comparison between Sears and Webster was, as comparisons go, particularly invidious to a fine, wholehearted player who moreover is one of a very few tenor players of his generation to have an instantly recognizable tone and style. After leaving Ellington in 1949 Sears spent most of his professional life playing music closer to the r&b fashions of those times; even his most famous solo away from Ellington, on Johnny Hodges's *Castle Rock*, derives from that style of playing. By the end of the fifties he was concentrating largely on the management, publishing and promotion side of the music business, making this return to the recording studio unique in being his first and last jazz album as a leader. That such a fine and wholly individualistic mainstream player could have fallen so completely from view in the jazz fraternity speaks volumes for the state of the music in the fifties, for on this record Sears combines a large, sensual tone with a sinuous, off-centre delivery, unfailing good taste and a mightily relaxed approach, thereby belying those who said he could only deliver the goods on medium-tempo screamers. He knows the value of space in music and makes his excellently integrated group swing so hard on the head of *In a Mellotone* by what he *doesn't* play that it would be perverse for the listener not to tap their feet as the band (with drummer Marshall on brushes) gets deep into one of the most gloriously relaxed swing grooves you could hear outside of the Basie band at *its* mellowest. This is slow-burn *par excellence*, and a spot of Astaire-type dancing around the room in response would not go astray – a reaction not lost on Sears, who in the booklet-notes says "I think that anyone who can make contemporary jazz that can be danced to will be doing a very important thing." Amen to that. **KS**

# Bernie Senensky

New review

**Homeland** Senensky (p); **Gary Bartz** (as, ss); **Harvie Swartz** (b); **Akira Tana** (d). Timeless CDSJP426 (75 minutes). Recorded 1994.

⑧ ❾

This is Senensky's second Timeless release and demonstrates at length his talents as both pianist and composer. He has a very characteristic style of theme writing, spiky and unpredictable, which makes soloists think instead of simply whizzing through the changes. Gary Bartz, who plays on six of the nine tracks, falls into the Senensky way of thinking as to the manner born. At the keyboard Senensky has brilliantly crisp articulation and delights in full-voiced chords. There is tremendous tonal variety in his playing. Given all this, it may seem surprising that Bernie Senensky's name is virtually unknown to the jazz public at large; it does not even appear in *Grove*. The reason must be that he lives and works in Toronto, which might as well be the dark side of the moon as far as the jazz media are concerned. **DG**

# Boyd Senter

New review

**Jazzologist Supreme** Senter (cl, as, ts); **Mickey Bloom, Phil Napoleon, James Miglione** (t); **Bill Haukenheiser** (cl); **Tommy Dorsey, Charlie Butterfield, Herb Winfield** (tb); **Ray Stilwell** (tb, v); **Jimmy Dorsey** (cl, as); **Fud Livingston** (cl, ts); **Jack Russell, Frank Signorelli** (p); **Eddie Lang, Carl Kress** (g); **Dan Calker** (bj, g); **Ward Lay** (b); **Stan King** (d, kz); **Walter Meyer** (d); **Paul Small** (v). Timeless Ⓕ CBC1-032 (74 minutes). Recorded 1928-30.

⑤ ❻

Senter was billed as 'The Jazzologist Supreme' and, at the height of his career, played a jewel-studded clarinet. Not a promising start for a player who also showed a propensity for jumping over the taste barrier with some room to spare. Born in Nebraska, he became interested in jazz as a result of hearing records by the Original Dixieland Jazz Band. He became something of a multi-instrumentalist, playing clarinet, trumpet, banjo and all of the saxophone family. He was with the Marie Hart Saxophone Quartet in 1920 and in the following year led his own band. He worked with the Chicago De Luxe Orchestra in 1923 and in 1924 made his recording début for the Autograph label. This CD presents the bulk of his recorded work and shows that he surrounded himself with good musicians. Bloom, Napoleon and the Dorseys acquit themselves well but regrettably it is Senter who takes centre stage. In truth, titles such as *Original Stacko'Lee Blues, Goin' Back to Tennessee* and *Doin' You Good* show him more than capable of leading the ensemble on clarinet but it is his corny solos, with the bolted on 'laughing policeman' parts, that remain his most lasting legacy. *Mobile Blues* and *No More* show that he could play without the worst excesses and, to his credit, he admitted that his trick effects were meant as audience pleasers. He continued to play until the early sixties but will best be remembered for eccentric clarinet work during the period represented here. **BMcR**

# Shakti

**Shakti With John McLaughlin** John McLaughlin (g); L. Shankar (v); R. Raghavan, T.S. Vinayakaram, Zakir Hussain (perc). Columbia Ⓜ CK46868 (52 minutes). Recorded 1976.

⑧ ❽

A record that effectively launched two jazz careers and took a third, already established, in an altogether unexpected direction, Shakti remains one of the most delightful statements of art-as-culture-clash, a truly genuine, unembarrassed missive from the global village. By 1975 McLaughlin had blown his brains out for several years, transporting his blistering, take-no-prisoners guitar playing from Tony Williams's Lifetime to Miles's seminal Bitches' Brew band and on to his own personal jazz-rock apocalypse with the Mahavishnu Orchestra. Shakti brought McLaughlin together with an otherwise all-Indian group: violin prodigy L. Shankar (nephew of the famed sitarist Ravi and now a star of sessions with artists as diverse as Jan Garbarek, Peter Gabriel and Frank Zappa, not to mention the creator of a series of highly acclaimed albums for ECM), percussionists Vikayakaram and Raghavan, and tabla master Zakir Hussain, recently reunited with McLaughlin for two or three sold-out world tours and a live album. The music on this, the first of three albums by the group, is primarily raga-based, and its resulting modal nature allows the guitarist more space for extended improvising than practically anywhere else in his *oeuvre*, and amply demonstrates that many critics' dismissal of this intensely lyrical musician's playing as purely that of a technique fetishist is hugely unfair.                                                                                    **SH**

# Bud Shank                                                                                          1926

**New review**
**New Gold!**  Shank (as); **Conte Candoli** (t); **Bill Perkins** (ts, ss); **Jack Nimitz** (bs); **John Clayton** (b); **Sherman Ferguson** (d). Candid Ⓕ CCD79707 (62 minutes). Recorded 1993.

⑧ **9**

Shank's alto playing has always sounded young, fresh and notably propulsive. He's now 70 but all these qualities are enhanced in his contemporary playing and his work with this piano-less sextet is totally lacking in the dignities of old age. His playing never seems to vary from excellent and he has the cream of the West Coast veterans around him in this new (or it was when this was recorded) band. The writing by the leader and a variety of composers including Monk and Golson provides some good charts for the men to get their chops around, and it's surprising to hear right at the start of Shank's *Port Townsend* a sudden foray by him into the nearest Parker sound-alike he'll ever produce. Candoli has always been too easily taken for granted. He is one of the giants of the horn and his power and sensitive imagination are another attraction. The writing exploits the interesting front line in ensemble and the rhythm players respond well to the added flexibility given by the absence of a keyboard. The freshness generated by the original Mulligan Quartet permeates these tracks but with the extra horns there is a much wider musical spectrum.                                              **SV**

# Kendra Shank

**Afterglow**  Shank (v, g); **Larry Willis** (p); **Steve Novosel** (b); **Steve Williams**, **Paul Murphy** (d); **Steve Berrios** (d, perc); **Gary Bartz** (as) on two tracks. Mapleshade Ⓕ 02132 (49 minutes). Recorded 1992.

⑥ **8**

Shank is a young singer from California who has spent a number of years in Paris and so has a slowly burgeoning reputation on both sides of the Atlantic. Her full-toned, vibrato-less singing recalls Helen Merrill and Shirley Horn at their early peak, and while she tends to go for the slow tempos once favoured by another influence, Billie Holiday, the material is varied enough in style to stave off listener *ennui*. She also has the priceless advantage of having Larry Willis at the piano to support her every musical move (although the Holiday dedication here, *Left Alone*, is a stark and convincing duet between voice and bass).

Shank has some way to go before she matches the expressive levels of her models, but she has made an impressive start here, and her honesty and sincerity is evident in every performance. Her approach eschews the glitz which often substitutes for real feeling in this type of singing, and the album is an enjoyable experience for the listener from beginning to end. Bartz appears on two tracks and plays sensitively, but the main focus lies elsewhere. There is a decided bossa cast to a number of the tracks, and within this style Shank is entirely at home.                                              **KS**

# L. Shankar                                                                                         1950

**Vision**  Shankar (dbl vn, perc); **Palle Mikkelborg** (t, flh); **Jan Garbarek** (ss, ts, bss, perc). ECM Ⓕ 1261 (811 969-2) (45 minutes). Recorded 1983.

⑥ **8**

Shankar (or to give him his formal name, Lakshminarayana Shankar) first came to international attention as one of the more vital components in John McLaughlin's Shakti, the generally rather misunderstood group McLaughlin formed after the dissolution of the Mahavishnu Orchestra. Shankar came to ECM therefore with solid credentials in both Indian classical music and modern Western styles. Both avenues have been explored on the label: this record is the most rewarding from a more orthodox jazz point of view, although it is by no means a trip down swingsville lane, or even a *Blues March*.

This album benefits greatly from the energy and cutting edge Garbarek brings to the ensemble passages and his own solos: his work carries great conviction and generates a lot of power. Shankar, left to his own devices, can get worryingly disparate at times, losing all sense of forward movement, but his two colleagues help him generate momentum again. This is not to deny the considerable grace and beauty of his playing and of the compositions he has presented here: they all have their moments, and flesh-and-blood emotions always finally win through. Worth sticking with to the end. Excellent

sound quality.                                                                                   **KS**

# Sonny Sharrock
1940

**Ask the Ages**  Sharrock (g); **Pharoah Sanders** (ts); **Charnett Moffett** (b); **Elvin Jones** (d). Axiom
Ⓕ 848 957-2 (45 minutes). Recorded c1991.

⑩ Ⓘⓞ

Sharrock's small cult following probably includes more metalheads (cerebral metalheads, to be sure) than hard boppers, who tend either to shrink in horror from him or to ignore him altogether. Like most on-edge black guitarists, regardless of genre, he's often stereotyped as Jimi Hendrix's progeny, but some of us are old enough to remember him playing more or less the way he does now as early as 1966, a full year before Hendrix's *Are You Experienced?* was released in the US. **Ask the Ages**, which reunites Sharrock with Sanders, with whom he made his recording début on **Tauhid** in 1967, burns from beginning to end in a way that conjures up a sixties 'chitlin circuit combo', despite deliberate echoes of the same decade's jazz avant-garde. Elvin Jones's thunderous rolls lend authenticity as well as urgency to *As We Used To Sing*, a see-saw modal waltz à la Coltrane (Sharrock's chief influence, rather than any jazz or blues guitarist). He doesn't comp behind Sanders, but their unison heads and overlapping freak-outs illustrate that their rapport is as complete now as it was 25 years ago, with one important difference – Sharrock no longer sounds at a disadvantage for only phrasing like a horn, not actually playing one. **FD**

# Charlie Shavers
1917-71

New review
**And the Blues Singers**  Shavers (t) with a collective personnel of **Sidney Bechet, Buster Bailey** (cl); **Sammy Price, Lil Hardin-Armstrong** (p); **Teddy Bunn, Ulysses Livingston** (g); **Richard Fullbright, Wellman Braud** (b); **O'Neil Spencer** (d); **Trixie Smith, Coot Grant, Kid Wesley Wilson, Lether McGraw, Rosetta Howard, Alberta Hunter** (v). Timeless Historical Ⓜ CBC1-025 (70 minutes). Recorded 1938/9.

⑤ ⑦

Shavers, an exact contemporary of Dizzy Gillespie, but a man who on more than one occasion said for the record that his prime source of inspiration in jazz was Louis Armstrong, was a player possessed of phenomenal bravura technique and a beautiful brass tone. Yet he quickly fell out of the front line in jazz when his favoured style – swing – was superseded by bop and its fellow-travellers. Not an innovator on the level of Eldridge or Gillespie, Shavers was for the main content to carve a successful career in the chamber-music-like atmosphere of bassist John Kirby's small group. This and the composer credits for the oft-played song, *Undecided,* seemed likely to be his lot in jazz until he appeared during the fifties with Norman Granz's Jazz At The Philharmonic touring troupe. Wildly exciting trumpet battles with the likes of Roy Eldridge proved beyond dispute that, when the blood rushed to the head, Shavers could emote with the best of them, but this sort of bad behaviour only led him into further disrepute with the music's moral guardians.

His role on this collection is exclusively supportive, and in all honesty there are times when the listener is apt to forget that Shavers is supposed to be the focal point of the album, so remorselessly is the spotlight on the featured vocalists. When given the chance he swings cleanly, bends his notes and does the occasional growl or exquisite technical high-wire twist which identifies him amongst any company, but this is not the best representation of his talent (although at least on *Toot It, Brother Armstrong*, a rather lame attempt by Grant and Wilson to cash in on Louis Armstrong's fame and glamour, Shavers is allowed to open up his big tone and let rip in between the vocals). Sadly, this is the only CD currently under his name (although the five Rosetta Howard tracks here are dubious entries in his discography), so there is little choice. For those seeking a larger dose, he can be heard at greater length on the French Columbia two-CD set of the John Kirby band reviewed elsewhere in this book. The JATP sides featuring him are currently not available on CD. **KS**

# Artie Shaw
1910

**Begin the Beguine**  Artie Shaw (cl); with big band including: **Billy Butterfield** (t); **Al Hendrickson** (g); **Johnny Guarnieri** (h); **Jud DeNaut** (b); **Nick Fatool** (d). RCA Bluebird Ⓜ ND86274 (67 minutes). Recorded 1938-41.

✓ ⑧ ⑧

Essentially, this is a '20 Greatest Hits' compilation and some of the pieces, including the title tune, feature no full-blown jazz at all. Yet in any consideration of the swing era Artie Shaw is a large and unignorable fact, and this CD represents his work very adequately.

The sound of Shaw's clarinet, in tone and especially in articulation, is quite different from Goodman's. Whereas Goodman cultivated a limpid, legato flow, Shaw fired out staccato volleys of sharp-edged notes. He made much of the extreme top of the clarinet's range and in the middle register had a most remarkable and unorthodox sound – dark, woody and fibrous. You hear this quality to perfection in the opening theme statement to *Begin The Beguine* (set in the key of D in order to exploit it) and in *Frenesi*. At its best, Shaw's playing is full of character and it can sound marvellously exciting, riding high above the band in full cry on a number like *Traffic Jam*.

Apart from a couple of tunes by the Gramercy Five, there are no notable solos by anyone else, but there is one vocal by Billie Holiday (*Any Old Time*) and several by Helen Forrest. **DG**

---

**The Complete Gramercy Five Sessions** Shaw (cl); **Billy Butterfield**, **Roy Eldridge** (t); **Johnny Guarnieri** (h); **Al Hendrickson**, **Barney Kessel** (g); **Jud DeNaut**, **Morris Rayman** (b); **Dodo Marmarosa** (p); **Lou Fromm**, **Nick Fatool** (d). RCA Bluebird Ⓜ ND87637 (46 minutes). Recorded 1940-5.

⑧ ❽

The Gramercy Five held a very special place in Shaw's on-off love affair with music. It came about in 1940 after one of his anti-music sabbaticals, and was far from being the first band-within-a-band. Duke Ellington, Benny Goodman, Bob Crosby and Tommy Dorsey had already ploughed that field, but Shaw sowed it in his own inimitable way. For some, the use of the harpsichord in the 1940 unit was seen as a gimmick, but Guarnieri was an articulate soloist and it is difficult to imagine his famous *Summit Ridge Drive* solo on piano. Butterfield's well-designed solos, with their adroit use of mutes, gave the group genuine impetus but it was Shaw's suave, cleverly improvised solos that gave the Five its urbane appeal. In terms of technique, the 1945 was the better of the two units. In Eldridge and Kessel it had superior soloists and, together with Marmarosa, they helped the clarinettist stay abreast of the bebop revolution. Shaw's solos were never actually conceived in the Minton language but, as his excellent excursions on *The Sad Sack* and *Scuttlebutt* show, Shaw's timeless artistry could be accommodated by groups of any size and of most stylistic persuasions. The Gramercy Five gave notice of being neoteric in aspirations but had, in fact, only dressed an excellent establishment style in new clothes. **BMcR**

# Ian Shaw

**The Echo of a Song** Shaw (v) with the following collective personnel: **Mornington Lockett** (cl, ss, ts); **Simon Wallace** (p); **Geoff Gascoyne** (b); **Mark Fletcher** (d); **Claire Martin** (v). Ronnie Scott's Jazz House Ⓕ JHCD048 (59 minutes). Recorded 1996.

⑧ ❽

Shaw's previous CD for the same label (**Taking it to Hart**, JHCD036) was made up of songs written by Richard Rodgers and Lorenz Hart, an indication that the singer was familiarizing himself with the standard repertoire of jazz and the American song form. The new CD takes matters a step further and consists of tunes taken from a list prepared by Ronnie Scott, "tunes he'd grown up with and whispered suggestions for songs I'd never heard before". Although this takes Ian into the realm of Sinatra, Bennett, Tormé and the like, there is no attempt to copy, just to enjoy with them such marvellous songs as *It Could Happen to You*, *Time After Time* and *Taking a Chance On Love*. And these are not easy songs; *You Stepped Out of a Dream*, for example, is not for beginners. Having a reliable, flexible rhythm section allows Shaw to take occasional liberties with the melody lines, just like a jazz soloist, and the loving care of Mornington Lockett's tenor in solo or obbligato will make many ask why this musician appears on so few records. Scott's memory served him well, for he was able to recall a Jerome Kern song, *Just Let Me Look At You*, from the 1938 film *Joy of Living*. Hopefully Shaw will dip into the list for his next CD. Claire Martin joins in for just one song, *Taking a Chance On Love*, presumably played in Claire's key as it sounds fractionally too high for Ian. **AM**

# Woody Shaw

1944-89

**The Moontrane** Shaw (t); **Azar Lawrence** (ss, ts); **Steve Turre** (tb); **Onaje Allen Gumbs** (p, elp); **Buster Williams**, **Cecil McBee** (b); **Victor Lewis** (d); **Tony Waters** (cga); **Guilherme Franco** (perc). Muse Ⓜ CD5472 (59 minutes). Recorded 1974.

⑧ ❼

It's no small measure of Shaw's genius that it shone through a short career beset by tragic circumstances and played out in a period with little sympathy for straight-ahead jazz. Despite the inhospitable environment of the seventies, there were enough discerning individuals, among them the Muse label and Michael Cuscuna, producer of this record, to ensure that Shaw's strikingly individual jazz trumpet playing was disseminated and preserved. By 1974 Shaw's helter-skelter adaptation of the pentatonic and intervallic qualities of the Coltrane quartet was well established, his superbly sculpted inside-outside lines liberally strewn throughout this record. His writing displays a similarly rich harmonic ingenuity and, without undermining his commitment to bop, ranges from the straight swing of *The Moontrane* to *Sanyas*, an exotic Eastern reading of *Impressions*-like changes. The sound, rather boxy and lacking in ballast, leaves something to be desired, and the playing, especially on *Sanyas,* is a little loose – due apparently to shortage of rehearsal time – but Shaw's trumpet was never better and there's no hint of the occasionally bland soul-inflected work which followed on Columbia. This CD reissue also adds alternative takes of *Tapscott's Blues* and *Katrina Ballerina* to the LP issue and restores 70 seconds originally faded from the end of *Sanyas*. **MG**

# George Shearing 1919

**Jazz Masters** Shearing (p) with the following collective personnel: **Marjorie Hyams**, **Joe Roland**, **Cal Tjader** (vb); **Chuck Wayne**, **Dick Garcia**, **Toots Thielemans** (g); **John Levy**, **Al McKibbon** (b); **Denzil Best**, **Marquis Foster**, **Bill Clark**, **Teddi King** (v). Verve Jazz Masters Ⓜ 529 900-2 (47 minutes). Recorded 1949/54.

⑧ ❻

This is where the Shearing Sound began. Admittedly a session for the small Discovery label predated the first MGM recordings by a week, back in 1949, but it was the MGM material which captured the public's imagination, and it was that sound which was to manifest itself in all kinds of contexts for years to come. Brian Priestley has selected 16 of the most important representative performances from the period including the style-setting *September in the Rain* and *I'll Remember April*. These were, of course, 78rpm discs originally, so solos are short (apart from George's) but this discipline makes those eight-or-16-bar statements highly concentrated in terms of invention. Shearing's playing is consistently remarkable with long, flowing runs and occasional Tatum-like flourishes. *Summertime*, played as an unaccompanied solo, sounds like an amalgam of Art and Debussy. The late Teddi King sings Ralph Rainger's *I Wished on the Moon* like someone who knew and loved the Billie Holiday version but didn't attempt to copy it. So influential were these early Shearing Quintet recordings that other jazzmen often copied George's arrangements, *vide* Lionel Hampton's 1953 version of *September in the Rain*. Several of the early MGMs suffered from a lack of separation, giving a muffled sound; it sounds as if the Verve engineers have not been wholly successful in correcting the fault. **AM**

**The Best of George Shearing** Shearing (p); **Johnny Rae**, **Emil Richards**, **Warren Chaisson** (vb); **Toots Thielemans**, **Dick Garcia** (g); **Al McKibbon**, **Jimmy Bond**, **Carl Pruitt**, **Wyatt Reuther** (b); **Bill Clark**, **Percy Brice**, **Ray Mosca**, **Roy Haynes**, **Larance Marable** (d); **Cal Massey**, **Lamar Wright** (t); **Bob Northern**, **Julius Watkins** (frh); **Dennis Farnon**, **Billy May** (cond/arr). Capitol Ⓜ CDP8 33750-2 (58 minutes). Recorded 1955-60.

❻ ⑧

The classic MGM sessions (see above) saw the birth of the Shearing 'sound', while this series for Capitol in the late fifties shows the durability of the style. Unfortunately, it only offers a limited number of the new quintet with Richards and Thielemans, although *Midnight in the Air*, *Later* and the remakes of his *September in the Rain* and *East of the Sun* hits are good examples of the sound, with the pianist parading his lock-hand, block chord system and taking a clever improvisational look at inviting material. Latin percussion muddles the issue on items like *Cuban Love Song* and *Sand in my Shoes* and although offered the choice of greater freedom on the solo, *Friendly Persuasion*, Shearing seems disinclined to examine the tune too deeply. The titles with the Farnon and May orchestras are not an unqualified success. Shearing's combo sound is merely grafted on to the orchestral landscape and on the string-dominated titles, the resulting compromise leads him into elevator music. Farnon's and May's arrangement are not without a certain charm, but only on the brass-driven *Cheek to Cheek* is the quintet actually enhanced, making it hard to escape the conclusion that they had an emasculating effect on the principal and his sidemen and fall short of fulfilling the promise of the album's title. **BMcR**

**I Hear a Rhapsody** Shearing (p); **Neil Swainson** (b); **Grady Tate** (d). Telarc Jazz Ⓔ CD83310 (71 minutes). Recorded 1992.

⑧ ❽

Shearing has had to live down success beyond the wildest dreams of most jazz and jazz-associated musicians. For long stretches of his career he played a type of small-group music which at best could only be described as a sort of jazz, and during his peak years as a popular attraction he was making records with banks of strings, voices and the like which were about as jazz-inflected as Eddy Duchin.

However, at either end of his career he has played strong, imaginative piano. At the present moment, his early years, when he first moved to the US from London, are poorly served on CD, so the above is an example of his current form. The most immediately obvious thing is that for this date Shearing abandoned the piano-vibes-guitar unison statements which dominated his sound 30 years ago, and allows his own playing to carry the major load (although a more recent album reconvenes his classic 'sound' instrumentally). This can only be a good thing as far as jazz is concerned, because Shearing is uncommonly gifted when it comes to the inner voicing of chords, paraphrasing melodies, and extracting a beautiful sound from the instrument he is playing. His area of greatest weakness, his rhythm, is occasionally exposed, but this is not such a problem in the overall scheme of things, and his suppleness is extraordinary, bearing in mind his age. Check out Brubeck's *The Duke* on this disc to hear Shearing's current capabilities, or take a dip into his latest for Telarc, the solo effort, **Favorite Things**, where his style is distilled to its pianistic essence. **KS**

# Jack Sheldon

1931

**On My Own** Sheldon (t, v); **Ross Tompkins** (p). Concord Jazz Ⓕ CCD4529 (62 minutes). Recorded 1991.

⑧ ❽

Sheldon, one of the most gifted soloists to emerge from the West Coast era of the fifties, has since gone from strength to strength. His playing and singing is now better than ever, due to his continuing studies with eminent trumpet and voice teachers in Los Angeles.

While the singing is often a lugubrious send-up of itself (Sheldon's humour is both brilliant and irrepressible), his trumpet playing has the sincerity and feeling of a Hackett or a Berigan and there are few more effective jazz soloists playing today.

The trumpeter easily handles the exposed setting of the simple piano accompaniment, and it is obvious that Tompkins and he have worked together regularly, for there is a close affinity between Sheldon and the younger man. Ballad improvsations like that on the Ellington/Strayhorn *Day Dream* and Sondheim's *Losing My Mind* have always been Sheldon's *forte* and his brisk recycling of *Opus One* produces a crackling string of trumpet fireworks. Delightful surprises come tumbling from every track, and at a time when jazz is often po-faced, this is a radiant lesson that humour and easy virtuosity can still complement each other in the great Armstrong tradition. **SV**

# Archie Shepp

1937

New review

**Four for Trane** Shepp (ts, arr); **Alan Shorter** (t); **Roswell Rudd** (tb); **John Tchicai** (as); **Reggie Workman** (b); **Charles Moffett** (d). Impulse! Ⓜ IMP12182 (37 minutes). Recorded 1964.

❼ ⑩ ❿

This was not Shepp's first as a leader (there were two albums for Savoy in tandem with Bill Dixon) but it was his first major statement and remains a masterpiece. The impatience with which he delivers his musical message here is almost palpable as Shepp's fiery, blustering playing is channelled into four Coltrane compositions neatly reinvented by the younger man. The spirit of the band and its sheer joy in playing is captured in one of the most inspired pieces of engineering even Rudy van Gelder has ever managed, with Workman and Moffett particularly well registered. The ensemble playing is neat and full of character, Shepp's soloing is awash with humanity and humour, and then there is the work of both Tchicai and Rudd. Even after over 30 years of listening I still excitedly prepare myself for the jet-propelled take-off that is Rudd's opening gambit on his *Syeeda's Song Flute* solo. Elsewhere Tchicai impresses with his oblique phraseology and elusive sound, a presence which undoubtedly gives the album another dimension altogether, especially on the one piece which is a Shepp original, *Rufus*, where the tumult, drama and hurry of the piece could otherwise make it seem rushed and unfocused (its fate, incidentally, when Shepp re-recorded it as part of his live set at Newport 1965). Shepp later commented that **On This Night** was the first album he felt to be wholly his own, and that **Four for Trane** and **Fire Music**, due to the ensemble approach he took to both albums, were somehow not a personalized enough statement. Coltrane's presence in the studio and on the manuscripts aside, this date is 100 per cent Shepp, and he doesn't get better than this. Quite frankly there's not a lot from any of the sixties moderns that does. **KS**

**Fire Music** Shepp (ts); **Ted Curson** (t); **Joseph Orange** (tb); **Marion Brown** (as); **Reggie Johnson** (b); **Joe Chambers**, **J.C. Moses** (d); **David Izenson** (b). Impulse! Ⓜ GRP39121 (40 minutes). Recorded 1965.

⑧ ❼

**Fire Music** may not be the most strikingly beautiful or convincing of Archie Shepp's early, severely underrated Impulse! discs – my vote would go to **Four for Trane** – but, motivated by his deeply-felt political and social concerns, it is a meaningful one, with an emotional urgency barely under control. Shepp, a poet and playwright in this period as well, pushed the music towards a dramatic, near-theatrical, immediacy; for example, the background riffs behind the soloists on *Hambone* contain strong echoes of r&b, but seem inescapably claustrophobic, like life in a ghetto. Similarly, the episode of rootless tonality in the middle of *Los Olivados* seems to reflect the homeless, the hopeless, the politically disenfranchized. The pop idealization of *The Girl From Ipanema* must be bitterly ironic to a ghetto black. The necessity for beauty is revealed in the reharmonization of *Prelude to a Kiss*, an act of homage to both the master, Ellington, and the saxophonists most inspirational to Shepp's own expressionistic style, Webster and Gonsalves. This is the true basis for David Murray's tenor style a decade later; likewise, the voicings of Shepp's sextet – the open, often gleefully dissonant, clashing harmonies, the way solos emerge or erupt from the jostling interaction of instruments, the dramatic multi-sectional charts – are undoubtedly an outgrowth of Mingus's mid-sized groups, and a direct precedent for Murray's eighties octet. **AL**

**On This Night** Shepp (ts, p, v); **Bobby Hutcherson** (vb); **David Izenzon**, **Henry Grimes** (b); **Rashied Ali**, **J.C. Moses**, **Joe Chambers** (d, perc); **Ed Blackwell** (rhythm logs); **Christine Spencer** (v). Impulse! Ⓜ GRP11252 (72 minutes). Recorded 1965.

**⑧ ❽**

Archie Shepp has always talked a good fight – he describes **On This Night** as "the essence of a people fighting for emancipation" – but his actual performances are frequently a touch disappointing. This CD reissue sensibly replaces the original album's live-at-Newport *Gingerbread, Gingerbread Boy* (now to be found, along with the rest of the Newport set, on **New Thing At Newport**) with hitherto scattered material from a trio session with Izenzon and Moses designed to fill **Fire Music**, plus an alternative take of *The Mac Man*. This new material, however impressive, cannot quite rescue the music from the two sessions from Shepp's besetting sins: an over-reliance on unusual tonal effects and a lack of overall cogency in his soloing. Thus the title track tellingly features Christine Spencer's soprano voice against an interestingly textured backdrop of vibes, bass, drums and timpani, augmented by Shepp's piano, but never sufficiently coheres to fulfil its considerable promise. *The Mac Man* highlights Shepp's trademark bleary tenor, replete with growls, smears and honks, and Bobby Hutcherson's fluent vibes, but the restless shifts between tempos dissipate rather than concentrate the music's impact. The trio sides feature superbly expressive free playing from Izenzon and Moses – especially on *The Chased* (third take) – but Shepp often plays on past the point of inspiration. Nevertheless, **On This Night** remains an exhilarating and important recording, both as an early peak in Shepp's career, and as an archetypal example of mid-sixties radicalism, musical and social.    **CP**

---

**Goin' Home**  Shepp (ts, ss); **Horace Parlan** (p). SteepleChase Ⓕ SCCD31079 (51 minutes). Recorded 1977.

**⑨ ❾**

Although traditional elements had long played a part in Archie Shepp's music, it was his experiences as an educator that convinced him of the need to play what he termed "re-creative music". "If I say 'who's Sidney Bechet?', nobody knows", he reported of his students. In response, his own music has since the mid seventies been largely devoted to upholding and celebrating the black music tradition up to and including John Coltrane.

Goin' Home, a collection of spirituals, was among the first of Shepp's re-creative projects and remains his most striking success. Horace Parlan (his partner on many of these later recordings) provides sensitive accompaniments that ground the performance in respect for the music's fundamental dignity. Shepp's contemporary argot of cracked tones and jagged phrasing is used sparingly, edging the material with a declamatory passion that illuminates but never overwhelms its deeper spirituality. The results have a stark grandeur, the tenor a taut, rasping preacher against the piano's calm. On four tracks Shepp turns to his more poignant soprano, notably for a tender, intense version of Ellington's *Come Sunday* that was not included on the original LP.    **GL**

---

**Soul Song**  Shepp (ts, ss, v); **Kenny Werner** (p); **Santi DeBriano** (b); **Marvin 'Smitty' Smith** (d). Enja Ⓕ ENJ4050-2 (46 minutes). Recorded 1982.

**⑦ ❽**

Although recorded when Shepp was firmly on his retreat from a musical freedom policy, this CD does not fit comfortably into his potted history of the tenor saxophone. He does not set himself up in the didactic driving seat and makes no attempt to remind the jazz world of Coleman Hawkins, Don Byas and Paul Gonsalves through the bell of his own horn. For a start, he has chosen a rhythm section that chops up the rhythmic flow, thereby stopping titles like *Mama Rose*, where he plays soprano in any case, from taking an easy mainstream gait. This is a John Coltrane quartet-type contest with horn forced, at least partially, to free itself from the busy background turmoil cooked up by Werner, De Briano and Smith. The title track follows the *Mama Rose* pattern despite Werner's ostinato piano, while *Geechee*, an excellent tenor foray, keeps Shepp in his investigative rather than educational role and produces a lengthy solo that reminds the listener of nobody save Shepp himself. Only on *My Romance*, which concludes this powerful session, is the listener treated to a rhapsodic, Ben Webster-ish piece of story-telling, but even this performance, built up on roughened terrain, is not prepared to surrender to the excesses of romanticism.    **BMcR**

---

# Andy Sheppard                                                                                      1957

---

**Rhythm Method**  Sheppard (ss, ts); **Claude Deppa** (t); **Kevin Robinson** (t, flh); **Gary Valente** (tb); **Steve Lodder** (kbds); **Sylvan Richardson** (b); **Dave Adams** (d); add on one track only: **Ashley Slater** (tb); **Jerry Underwood** (ts); **Julian Argüelles** (bs). Blue Note Ⓕ CDBLP1007 (62 minutes). Recorded 1993.

**⑧ ❽**

Sheppard's first new album for Blue Note found him in the main sticking to the group of players with which he had grown comfortable, In Co-Motion, with additional players (Gary Valente, Kevin Robinson) appearing to make effective contributions to a couple of the longer and more ambitious tracks. The added depth this brings to even the slightest compositional ideas here certainly justifies their inclusion, and also nicely offsets the quintet line-up of the majority of the album. Sheppard himself plays with great poise and assurance, and his tone on either of the two saxes is full and pleasing: his essential good manners and equable temperament as a soloist preclude him from ever outstaying his welcome. Some of the tracks are very long, and occasionally lapse into shapelessness when one too many player bags some solo space, but then there are pieces such as the opener, *Sofa Safari* and the remarkable slow burn of *So ...* , which exhibit all the signs of careful organization and maximum usage of minimum resources. On *So ...* Sheppard has clearly listened to the work of other fusion players (as well as used the ideas of band members), but then has taken some core ideas – such as encouraging group interplay at all stages, rather than allowing one solo voice to dominate – and expanded them into a musical *raison d'être*. It works beautifully; similarly, parts of *Well Kept Secret* cohere in this fashion, although overall it is a more diffuse construction.

Other pieces fit more comfortably into large group styles which Sheppard has mined successfully in the past, and are therefore a continuation of his musical processes, but there is sufficient which is new and good to merit a recommendation for this as his most completely realized disc yet. Sadly, this and its partner, **Delivery Suite**, are the only products of Sheppard's short period at Blue Note, as he and the label have since parted company. Sheppard has recently arrived at Verve, where his first album has been a co-led effort with Steve Lodder, **Moving Image**, which sounds disappointingly MOR. **KS**

# Bobby Shew                                                                                          1941

**New review**
**Heavyweights** Shew (t); **Carl Fontana** (tb); **George Cables** (p); **Bob Magnusson** (b); **Joe LaBarbera** (d). Mama Ⓕ MMF1013 (72 minutes). Recorded 1995.

⑥ ⑧

Bobby Shew is a flawless neo-mainstream trumpeter capable of playing big band lead or soloing with neo-boppish *élan*. Catching on at the tail of the big band era, Shew got his start with Tommy Dorsey, Woody Herman and Buddy Rich. In 1973, after a nine-year stint working Las Vegas, the trumpeter moved to Los Angeles where he has pursued both studio and jazz work. During the seventies Shew added fire to the LA-based bands of Toshiko Akiyoshi, Don Menza, Frankie Capp and Louie Bellson. Since the eighties Shew has focused on small-group settings including notable stints with Art Pepper and Bud Shank. Here, Shew realizes a long-held dream of collaborating with idol Carl Fontana. The interplay is warm and witty, recalling the ebullient dovetailings of the early-sixties tandem of Clark Terry and Bob Brookmeyer. The spirit of unabashed *joie de vivre* is most palpable in lines like *But Not for Me* and *Just in Time*. But even in darker treks like the brooding *Autumn Serenade*, things sparkle. Blending complementary sonorities both burnished and brassy, Shew and Fontana bubble with aplomb against tasteful rhythms delivered by the nonpareil Cables, Magnusson and LaBarbera. In all, a gem attesting to the timeless qualities of insouciant mainstream swing. **CB**

# Sahib Shihab                                                                                     1925-89

**Jazz Sahib** Shihab (bs); **Phil Woods** (as); **Benny Golson** (ts); **Hank Jones, Bill Evans** (p); **Paul Chambers, Oscar Pettiford** (b); **Art Taylor** (d). Denon/Savoy Ⓜ SV0141 (45 minutes). Recorded 1957.

⑥ ⑥

Shihab (as Edmund Gregory) played alto with Roy Eldridge's big band in the late forties before becoming identified with the boppers, notably the groups of Art Blakey, Thelonious Monk and Tadd Dameron. He switched to baritone and worked with Dizzy Gillespie's small group in 1953, remaining with the larger horn in subsequent years. All the writing on this CD was done by Melba Liston and Shihab; both of them make expert use of the three-sax front line, although the addition of a brass instrument would have made for more varied tone colours. All three saxophonists take good solos but it is Phil Woods who invariably makes the most lasting impression. He erupts from the ensemble on *Jamila* with startling results. The leader's baritone playing is warm toned, as is that of tenor saxist Golson. For the reissue on CD Denon/Savoy have added *Ba-Dut-Du-Dat,* which was not on the original LP, but they have not included *Sugar Dugar,* made at the session with Hank Jones and Chambers and which was released as part of a sampler LP. Logic, anyone? **AM**

# Matthew Shipp                                                                                   1961

**Points** Shipp (p); **Rob Brown** (as); **William Parker** (b); **Whit Dickey** (d). Silkhead Ⓕ SHCD129 (71 minutes). Recorded 1990.

⑦ ⑦

Although one of a younger generation which has drawn upon the jazz past for inspiration, Matthew Shipp does not accept the current orthodox of the neo-conservative gospel. He has instead sought an alternative direction and cites, along with Ellington, Scriabin and Debussy, quixotic artists Andrew Hill and Hasaan Ibn Ali as piano influences. Thus it is easy to see why Shipp's attention to melody proceeds not in a straight line, but is quick to curve, to stop and start in ellipses, to piece together asymmetrical phrases in mosaic fashion or to cluster in percussive gestures. Saxophonist Rob Brown is also quite comfortable with sustaining a melodic line around angular intervals (often punctuated with a spirited alto cry, both reminiscent of the late Jimmy Lyons); considering that Whit Dickey is a light, lyrical drummer and William Parker sharpened his ability to unify discursive counterpoint during a long tenure with Cecil Taylor, it is apparent that this is a quartet capable of transforming emotion into articulate musical detail. The two long versions of *Points* highlight the group's methods of construction. As composer, Shipp's graphic design provides an open architectural shape, allowing solo, duo and trio combinations, continuously shifting textures and dynamics, creating peaks and valleys of intensity. Chameleon-like in nature, the two interpretations are vastly different in mood and detail. *Piano Pyramid* uses the checks and balances of the piano trio format unchanged from that of, say, the classic Bill Evans Trio, but by working outside of the song form they construct a radically shaped new edifice with unexpected edges and angles that reflect light and shadow in fascinating ways. **AL**

# Wayne Shorter                                                                      1933

---

**Speak No Evil**  Shorter (ts); **Freddie Hubbard** (t); **Herbie Hancock** (p); **Ron Carter** (b); **Elvin Jones** (d). Blue Note Ⓜ CDP7 46509-2 (42 minutes). Recorded 1964.

⑧ ❿

The saxophonist who became most widely known for his work with Weather Report in the seventies was in an interesting period of transition here. He had been signed to Blue Note as a solo artist earlier in 1964, when it was becoming obvious that he might end his five-year stint with Art Blakey and give in to the blandishments of Miles Davis.

With Davis a matter of months away by the time of this Christmas Eve session, Shorter's two previous albums, **Night Dreamer** and **Juju**, had created much memorable material and a couple of pieces which are still played around the world, while four out of the six tracks on the present album have since become standards. The 14-bar A-section of the title track and the melodically-related *Witch Hunt* are both disguised blues, while an insinuating *Fe-Fi-Fo-Fum* and the ballad *Infant Eyes* stray just far enough from the Shorter-directed Jazz Messengers to presage his later work for Miles.

Meanwhile, Shorter's astonishing tenor tone and his dramatic use of dynamics are captured in an ostensibly relaxed atmosphere which conceals enormous expertise. While Hancock and Hubbard sound typically excellent for the period, Jones and Carter are understatedly at the service of the compositions. **BP**

---

New review

**Atlantis**  Shorter (ss, ts); **Jim Walker** (f, alto f, pic); **Yaron Gershovsky, Michiko Hill** (p); **J. Vitarelli** (kybd); **Larry Klein** (elb); **Alejandro Acuna** (d, perc); **Ralph Humphry** (d); **Lenny Castro** (pc); **Diana Acuna, Dee Dee Bellson, Nani Brunel, Sanaa Lathan, Kathy Lucien, Troye Davenport, Edgy Lee** (v). Columbia Ⓜ 481617-2 (42 minutes). Recorded 1985.

⑥ ❾

With the passing years, it's seeming less and less likely that we will see a second coming of the Wayne Shorter who produced such flawless gems for Blue Note and recharged the Miles Davis Quintet in the Sixties. News of a deal with the legendary Verve label last year raised high hopes, but these were not sustained by the disappointing **High Life** (see below). However, this 1985 recording, on CD for the first time, evinces a respectable residue of that once spectacular talent. **Atlantis**, like its sister albums from Shorter's Columbia period, is not afraid to use space as a component of its well-developed themes. By subscribing to this approach, the opening piece, *Endangered Species,* is more effective than the whole of **High Life**, which seems to abandon the very quality – dramatic contour – which made the Blue Notes so potent. Because it echoes Weather Report, **Atlantis** is less original than the great sixties records, but it seemed a minor revelation at the time, perhaps because it was the first flowering of Shorter's individuality after the dissolution of Weather Report. Its apparent brilliance has faded with time, but it's still one of his best electric albums. **MG**

---

New review

**High Life**  Shorter (bs, ts, as, ss); **Rachel Z** (p, syn, prog); **David Gilmore** (g); **Marcus Miller** (elb, bcl, prog); **Lenny Castro, Airto Moreira, Munyungo Jackson; Kevin Ricard** (perc); **Will Calhoun** (d); **Terri Lyne Carrington** (d on one track); **David Ward** (prog). Verve Ⓕ 529 224-2 (55 minutes). Recorded 1995.

⑧ ❾

Saxophonist Wayne Shorter hadn't made an outstanding album in a fair while when he followed his former boss Miles Davis and looked to multi-instrumentalist and studio star Marcus Miller for fresh inspiration. Miller sometimes dominates sessions like this, his skill in the complex, hi-tech modern studio leaving little except a squeaky-clean homage to digital sound and electronics. Luckily Shorter, one of contemporary jazz's masters of the melody, retained composer and arranger credits, and it would take more than Miller to quell a musical personality as strong as his. Nevertheless, the result is unashamedly a studio album. Improvised lines have been doubled up later and orchestrations occasionally written around them. The music varies between the mildly funky fusion of *Children of the Night*, kicked along by Miller's trademark metallic bass figures, to the minimal, percussion-based soprano feature. Wayne Shorter is a master of the sustained melodic improvisation. Less climax-orientated than most contemporary saxophone players, he floats across a background with constant invention. *At the Fair*, a clever composition with a slight Spanish tinge (a nod to *Will o' the Wisp* from

Miles Davis's **Sketches of Spain**), and *Midnight in Carlotta's Hair*, with its beautiful tune, creepy atmosphere and lovely tenor saxophone work, are high points on what is essentially an attractive and original album and a good representation of Shorter in the nineties.                                    **LC**

# Michael Shrieve

New review

**Two Doors** Shrieve (d); **Shawn Lane**, **Bill Frisell** (g); **Wayne Horvitz** (org); **Jonas Hellborg** (b). CMP Ⓔ CD74 (two discs: 76 minutes). Recorded 1993-5.

⑥ ❿

The two CDs in this set serve to divide the two trios Shrieve leads here. Subtitled **Deep Umbra** and **Flying Polly**, they represent the two sides to Shrieve's ongoing career. **Deep Umbra**, with Lane and Hellborg, was recorded in 1995 and concentrates on the power-trio fusion style of music Shrieve has often been involved in. The most obvious models include McLaughlin and Holdsworth, with Lane able to machine-gun his notes with the best of them as well as caress an arpeggio in best mystical-fusion tradition. At its best **Deep Umbra** is very exciting, providing the sort of adrenalin rush only to be found in the most extreme fusion forms and heavy metal. Recorded two years earlier but placed second is the **Flying Polly** band with Frisell and Horvitz. A predictably more eclectic set, it is full of the special personal effects that have come to be associated with Frisell (although of late the guitarist has shied away from such free playing) and features some imaginative organ work from Horvitz, largely cast as he is in a supporting role. Several tracks from this group last under a minute: others go on for ten or more. Just why the two bands weren't accommodated on one CD is beyond me.     **KS**

# Ben Sidran                                                                          1943

New review

**Mr P's Shuffle** Sidran (p, v); **Margie Cox** (v); **Rosco Mitchell** (ss); **Frank Morgan** (as); **Howard Levy** (hca); **Ricky Peterson** (org); **Phil Upchurch** (g); **Richard Davis** (b); **Clyde Stubblefield** (d); **Leo Sidran**, **Alejo Poveda** (perc). Go Jazz Ⓔ GoJ6019-2 (57 minutes). Recorded 1996.

⑦ ❾

In his note, Sidran draws a charming word-picture of the club called Mr P's, where he was the resident organist a quarter of a century ago. He doesn't actually say where it is, but internal evidence suggests Madison, Wisconsin. This programme, by ever-changing combinations of the above cast, is intended to re-create the mellow mood which Mr P's continues to foster in its lucky clients. If you want to know what sort of music it is, and you have never heard Ben Sidran before, imagine Georgie Fame, Mose Allison, Lou Donaldson and a few like-minded friends taking turns on the stand for each other's entertainment and you'll be pretty close. It's always better live – especially in a place like Mr P's – but this CD gets pretty close.                                                                 **DG**

# Alan Silva                                                                          1939

**Alan Silva** Silva (vn, p, vc); **Becky Friend** (f); **Karl Berger** (vb); **Mike Ephron** (p, org); **Dave Burrell** (p); **Barry Altschul** (perc); **Lawrence Cooke** (d, perc). ESP-Disk Ⓜ 1091-2 (38 minutes). Recorded 1968.

⑤ ❺

Initially trained on piano, violin and trumpet, Silva took up the bass in 1962. He was a prominent figure in the late-sixties free movement, playing with Cecil Taylor, Sun Ra, Albert Ayler and Archie Shepp. On this rather strange album nothing is heard of his first choice instrument; his composer's piano and Ornette Coleman-like violin are heard on *Skilfulness* and *Solestrial Communications Number One*, but only his cello gives any real satisfaction. Silva delivers his solos with a sawing intensity, full of jangling dissonance and with strangely macabre overtones. Little effort is made to improvise, either in free mode or traditionally, and much of what he plays is mood-provoking rather than musically enquiring. Friend contributes thin-toned flute solos and, together with Berger's hollow-sounding vibes, produces some interesting ensembles. In the main, freedom overtakes them and the music becomes vaguely static. Only Burrell's genuinely exciting piano seems to have any real purpose and the temptation is to see this as a fashion-following session of the time.     **BMcR**

# Horace Silver                                                                      1928

**Horace Silver and the Jazz Messengers** Silver (p); **Kenny Dorham** (t); **Hank Mobley** (ts); **Doug Watkins** (b); **Art Blakey** (d). Blue Note Ⓜ CDP7 46140-2. Recorded 1954/5.

✔                                                                              ❿ ❽

The funk starts here, as far as modern jazz is concerned; and the passage of nearly 40 years has only enhanced the gritty invention of these eight tracks, originally released on two ten-inch LPs. The Jazz

Messengers was a co-operative quintet at the time, and wisely chose to focus on Silver's compositions in their initial studio recordings. The results gave instant popularity to the earthy, percussion-driven brand of bop that had also been forming on contemporary Miles Davis sessions (several of which included Silver and/or Blakey). The busy, brittle comping of both piano and drums gain importance in this music, allowing the horn players to slow down and attend more to phrasing and sound. Dorham and Mobley are masters at this approach, incorporating the heat of Blakey and Silver into their improvisations. The pianist blends bop and church in both his playing and writing, and introduces his fundamental yet elegant approach to harmonizing trumpet and tenor sax. While *The Preacher* and *Doodlin'* were major hits, *Room 608*, *Creepin' In* and the other titles (including Mobley's *Hankerin'*) are also inspired frames for blowing. Everything that Silver would create subsequently stems from these classic performances. **BB**

---

**New review**

**Silver's Blue** Silver (p); **Joe Gordon**, **Donald Byrd** (t); **Hank Mobley** (ts); **Doug Watkins** (b); **Kenny Clarke**, **Art Taylor** (d). Columbia/Epic Ⓜ 476521. Recorded 1956.

⑧ ❽

Silver had already made three or four albums for Blue Note when he turned to Epic for this one. After its completion he returned immediately to Blue Note and stayed there for the next two decades. The change of label made no difference to the quality of the music and the two quintets here, which were recorded within a fortnight of each other, feature crisp hard bop at its best. Silver opens **Silver's Blue** with a long, primeval piano solo which, had you not known otherwise, you could have been forgiven for thinking was by Sammy Price or one of that school. It is classic blues and contrasts nicely with *To Beat or Not to Beat*, a prototype Silver bop line which has beautifully played and unfortunately rare trumpet from Joe Gordon, one of the best players of the time. Standards like *How Long Has This Been Going On?* and *The Night Has a Thousand Eyes* sound a bit routine by comparison with Silver's originals such as *Shoutin' Out*. The leader's accompaniment provides a lesson for any pianist and it's good to hear the undervalued Hank Mobley on such good form. **SV**

---

**Song for My Father** Silver (p); **Carmell Jones**, **Blue Mitchell** (t); **Joe Henderson**, **Junior Cook** (ts); **Teddy Smith**, **Gene Taylor** (b); **Roger Humphries**, **Roy Brooks** (d). Blue Note Ⓜ CDP7 84185-2 (61 minutes). Recorded 1963/4.

✓ ⑧ ❽

Undoubtedly Silver's most famous album, **Song for My Father** marks a turning-point for the specialist jazz record market, since both this and Lee Morgan's **The Sidewinder** were unexpected hits in the popular field. Alfred Lion, who produced them, had (as Michael Cuscuna wrote) "inadvertently proved that you do not have to bury jazz in gimmicks and sweetening to sell records", but Silver's subsequent output was less affected by thoughts of fame and riches than some others'.

Horace had, after all, been creating catchy Latin-jazz material for a decade already, and the title track is matched for modal moodiness by *Que Pasa* (now also included on this CD in a trio version from a year before). The new line-up heard on these and two up-tempo blues brings attacking solos by Henderson and, to a lesser extent, Jones. Whatever affected the earlier Mitchell/Cook band, it is significant that their tracks (two on the original LP, six on CD) have Silver as the only soloist.

It goes unnoticed by most people that tape stretching has caused some wow, especially on the title tune. If anyone has that unlikely object, an unplayed LP copy, Blue Note ought to use it for further remastering. **BP**

---

**The Cape Verdean Blues** Silver (p); **Woody Shaw** (t); **Joe Henderson** (ts); **J.J. Johnson** (tb); **Bob Cranshaw** (b); **Roger Humphries** (d). Blue Note Ⓜ CDP7 84220-2 (44 minutes). Recorded 1965.

⑧ ❽

Coming from a mid-sixties period which also produced the watershed, **Song for My Father** (see above) and the slightly earlier **Tokyo Blues** (recently reissued on CD), this edition of Horace Silver's cookin' unit featured a galvanizing front line with rising stars Henderson on tenor and trumpeter Shaw, plus (on half the tracks – one side of the old LP) veteran trombonist Johnson. Anchored by bassist Cranshaw and drummer Humphries, Silver's sextet was a sizzling exemplar of the pianist-composer's patented hard-bop approach where elements of gospel and r&b fused with a no-nonsense, boppish attack. Silver's most compelling accomplishment has been the ability to combine catchy melodies and intriguing harmonies with simple yet insinuating rhythmic grooves that swing with understated power and panache. On the sextet tracks the recipe is given spicy up-tempo expression in the bubbling, burbling *Nutville*. In contrast, the exotic *Bonita* sways with a mysterious, drums-in-the-distant-jungle pulse set in motion by Humphries mallets.

The title track is a jaunty, calypso-propelled outing with exuberant forays by Silver and Henderson. Here, as in the bulk of Silver's work, we glimpse a music of immediate and mesmerizing appeal, whose subtle complexities percolate beneath seductive surfaces that engage body, soul and brain. Also notable are Silver's spartan pianistics. Indeed, Silver might be thought of as the Basie of Bop, a stylist of unusual economy whose every note (and rest) counts. **CB**

# Edward Simon

1969

**Edward Simon** Simon (p); **Mark Turner** (ts); **Larry Grenadier** (b); **Adam Cruz** (d); **Café, Milton Cardona** (perc). Kokopelli Ⓕ KOKO1305 (61 minutes). Recorded 1995.

⑦ ❾

As evidenced by this, his second album, Simon's is a distinctive and mature pianistic and compositional voice. He naturally seeks out the contemplative, the melodic, but is equally capable of pouring out long lines of notes in the search for adequate expression of what's inside (check his solo on *Caballo Viejo*). His first album, on the AudioQuest label, featured him mainly in a trio setting and exposed more of his Latin background; here, the presence of Turner's Shorteresque tenor pushes the music closer to the jazz mainstream. Some of what Simon reaches for here has faint traces of the exactitude and rhythmic sophistication of Andrew Hill; at other times he is closer to Chick Corea's more Latinate ventures. Whatever, he is consistently engaging, demanding from the listener a considerable commitment to concentration but amply rewarding such intensity. This is not difficult music, though it is modern and quite complex; like a good vintage wine it has many dimensions to reveal on opening. **KS**

# Richard Simon

1949

**Groove Therapy** Simon (b); **Gabe Baltazar** (as); **Buddy Collette** (as, f); **Ronnell Bright, Marty Harris, Art Hillery, Howlett Smith, Gerald Wiggins** (p); **Al Viola** (g); **Sherman Ferguson, Johnny Kirkwood** (d). UFO/Bass Ⓕ 001 (66 minutes). Recorded 1995.

⑥ ❾

Simon, who only began playing bass at the age of 30, was a pupil of the late Red Callender and is now one of the most in-demand bassists in Southern California. The album brings together some of the state's most accomplished mainstreamers, many of whom contribute compositions to the disc. As one might expect there are more bass solos than on the average album, and even as well played as Simon's are, with fluency of both ideas and execution, one can have too much of a good thing. Nevertheless, his overall conception goes some way beyond simply creating a framework for his own playing, and the album is an opportunity to hear a cross-section of current Californian talent: some storming alto from Baltazar, some ballad playing from Bright (notably on his own *Sea Mist*), and the splendid flute playing of Collette (who stars on Bright's *Sweet Pumpkin*). Collette (on alto) and Baltazar trade fours on *Bop Suey*, an original idea of building a number out of an overdose of four-bar bop clichés, which works surprisingly well. Not one of the albums of the year, but a good collection of work by a team of West Coast players who deserve to be heard more. **AS**

# Sonny Simmons

1933

**Staying on the Watch** Simmons (as); **Barbara Donald** (t); **John Hicks** (p); **Teddy Smith** (b); **Marvin Pattillo** (d). ESP-Disk Ⓜ 1030-2 (44 minutes). Recorded 1966.

⑧ ⑥

Simmons had the bad luck to be a sixties avant-gardist based in California. He and Prince Lasha more or less held the fort after Ornette jumped ship in 1959, heading for New York and fame. It was only in the late sixties that Simmons made the move to the East Coast, but there he was an isolated figure, and his talent was consequently overlooked. Judging by this disc and others made under his name, this is a real pity. He plays in a style which has grown out of Coleman's, but is freer than that of his model's. The tremendous fire and energy he develops is not dissipated in typical mid-sixties screechings and brawlings for minutes on end, and it is clear from the care he has shown with his compositions here that he did not regard a performance simply as an event where you stand up, play a minimal theme as an excuse to get started, then blow until you drop. Each track here has a clear structure, often with different solos receiving completely separate tempos and instrumental backing. Much of the album is in metre, with free tempo sections. Pianist Hicks is a complete player even at this early stage, while Barbara Donald is one of a tiny handful of trumpeters to make sense out of the sixties without ignoring them. A very good album indeed. Simmons has in the last year made his major label début with **Ancient Ritual** on Q West/Reprise, but **Staying on the Watch** remains his most significant statement. **KS**

# Nina Simone

1933

**Feeling Good: The Very Best** Simone (p, v) with various unidentified aggregations, including trio, strings, brass sections. Verve Ⓜ 522 669-2 (73 minutes). Recorded 1957-71.

⑦ ⑦

Simone albums with similar titles are not exactly hard to find, but this is the only one of them to come within a half-mile of the truth. Of course, long ago the pop charts claimed Simone as one of their own, so every latter-day compilation tends to keep not one but two eyes firmly fixed on that side of her recording activity. With such matters in mind, if you want to concentrate on her more jazz-based output, you'll have to seek out either CD reissues of the original Bethlehem and RCA albums, or the original vinyl efforts on Colpix, RCA and Philips themselves. In terms of jazz ouput, the current CD unavailability of most of the Colpix material and the RCA effort, **Nina And Piano!**, is the greatest loss, and on this disc only *Don't Smoke In Bed, Strange Fruit, Don't Explain, The Other Woman* and *I Loves You, Porgy* show Simone at her most unadorned and burningly intense. Indeed *Don't Smoke In Bed* is a terrifyingly powerful evocation of loss and regret. Still, if you want the more insouciant side of Simone, then *My Baby Just Cares For Me* is here, as is *Here Comes the Sun, Work Song* and *To Love Somebody*. But there isn't a single Simone treatment of Kurt Weill here – one of her greatest strengths – and the powerful **Wild Is the Wind** album, recorded with just a trio, is not represented at all. Nor, strangely, are a couple of her other RCA hits, *Mr Bojangles* and *I Shall Be Released*, though the dreadful *Mississippi Goddam* crops up yet again. There's still that half-mile to go ... **KS**

## Zoot Sims

1925-85

### Al Cohn and Zoot Sims: Body And Soul  Sims (ts, ss); Cohn (ts); Jaki Byard (p); George
Duvivier (b); Mel Lewis (d). Muse Ⓕ MCD5356 (47 minutes). Recorded 1973.

⑧ ⑧

Both Sims and Cohn based their styles on that of Lester Young, and both came to prominence in Woody Herman's Second Herd of 1947-9. Singly they were powerful and inventive swingers, and when they played together the effect was compounded – theirs was easily the best of any of the fashionable two-tenor teams. The tandem recorded with many different rhythm sections, but few gave them better support than this one, and the ever happy Sims responds with some of his best work, including a notable feature on *Recado Bossa Nova*. Sims had an unstable relationship with the soprano saxophone, which he played very well (he nicknamed his horn Leprosy). His delicate work on another feature, *Jean*, shows him at his best on the instrument. But once Sims and Cohn had locked horns it was not practical to separate their performances for appraisal. This is one of the best of the recordings by that most cheerful of bands and no more needs to be said. **SV**

**New review**
### Zoot Sims Live in Copenhagen  Sims (ts, ss); Kenny Drew (p); Niels-Henning Ørsted Pedersen
(b); Ed Thigpen (d). Storyville Ⓕ STCD8244 (73 minutes). Recorded 1978.

⑨ ⑧

This is Zoot Sims at his mature best – mellow and poised, his blithe, open phrasing and feather-edged tone in full bloom. This set, recorded by the Danish Broadcasting Corporation at Jazzhouse Slukefter in Copenhagen, is typical of his nightly performances in jazz clubs around the world. In this case the house rhythm section was exceptional, a noted trio in its own right, and it swings impeccably throughout. We could have done with a little less bass, but that is a small matter in the circumstances. By this stage in his career Zoot had reached the point where he could simply play the tune and make it sound as though he had just thought of it. A good example here is his version of Sam Coslow's *In the Middle of a Kiss*, in which there is no divide between 'theme' and 'improvisation', merely one long, evolving melody. **DG**

## Frank Sinatra

1915

### Come Dance With Me!  Sinatra (v) Orchestra / Billy May (arr). Capitol Ⓜ CDP7 48470-2
(42 minutes). Recorded 1958.

✔ ⑩ ⑧

There seems little point in arguing that Sinatra, as the greatest popular male singer of his age, does not deserve inclusion in a guide to the best in jazz recordings. Not only did he first come to international attention as a featured singer with the swing bands of Tommy Dorsey and Harry James, but his whole approach to rhythm, phrasing and intonation comes from listening to jazz instrumentalists and to singers who could use their voices almost in the manner of a solo instrument. Certainly his contemporary jazz audiences appreciated him. He not only won *down beat* polls with monotonous regularity, but he also appeared one year at the Newport Jazz Festival when it was still in Newport, Rhode Island.

His jazz heritage has rarely been more evident than on this superb 1958 session, when his voice was still wholly intact and his interpretative artistry had reached its mature peak. The album starts with the title track, and in the second verse Sinatra makes no secret of his intentions when he alters the lyrics to "hey there cutes/put on your Basie boots/come dance with me". Billy May, for years used as the forceful, swinging big-band accompanist for so many of Capitol's jazz-inflected singing stars, continually pushes Sinatra towards some of the most relaxed and open music he ever made. The singer, clearly inspired by the waves of sound behind him and the infectious Basie-type groove of the rhythm section, on *Something's Gotta Give* actually interrupts his closing chorus to shout to the band "c'mon, let's tear it up!". And tear it up they do.

The album is not just a collection of Maynard Ferguson-like scorchers, however. Sinatra shows he has lost none of his patented romantic approach on titles such as *Just In Time* or *The Last Dance*, while the transformation of *I Could Have Danced All Night* from frothy Broadway show-stopper to carefree swinger is little short of miraculous. The CD version adds four extra tracks to the original vinyl, three from the same March 1958 session (including two duets with Keely Smith), plus a previously unissued *It All Depends On You* from September of the same year. For a top-drawer sample of Sinatra in jazz mode from a later decade, **Sinatra at the Sands** (Reprise, 1966), backed by the Count Basie Orchestra, has recently returned on CD at mid price. **KS**

## Hal Singer

1919

New review
**Blue Stompin'** Singer (ts); **Charlie Shavers** (t); **Ray Bryant** (p); **Wendell Marshall** (b); **Osie Johnson** (d). Prestige Swingville Ⓜ OJCCD834-2 (39 minutes). Recorded 1959.

⑥ ⑧

Nicknamed 'Cornbread' after his first hit as a solo artist, made for Savoy in 1948, Singer was a mainstay of many swing bands during the thirties and forties, working with Ellington in 1948 before taking the hint of the public's repsonse to his hit that year and moving over to r&b and rock 'n' roll for the following decade. When this album was recorded he was leader of the house band at the Metropole in New York, hacking away at the rock circuit with diminishing dividends. Within a few years he had returned to jazz and his mainstream tenor style, out of Hawkins and Jacquet, had reasserted itself. That is the style which dominates here, though Singer can't resist the occasional growl more associated with Lionel Hampton's tenor circuses than with Jay McShann and Lucky Millinder, swinging bands with whom he had also worked.

It is precisely because Singer has been infected with the bad taste and raucousness of the r&b scene that he is more exciting than most mainstream players, and this record is definitely worth hunting out. Singer's high spirits and drive infect Shavers, who lets rip at every opportunity with solos and fours straight out of the vocabulary he utilized during his cutting-session nights with JATP in the fifties. Pianist Bryant is perfect for this situation, providing ballast as accompanist as well as solo interest of his own, while Marshall and Johnson pour on the heat in the right places, on the slow blues *Midnight* (lasting 11 minutes) giving it a backbeat shuffle while on *With a Song in My Heart* (taken here as a ballad) providing restrained support. **KS**

## Alan Skidmore

1942

**Tribute to Trane** Skidmore (ts); **Jason Rebello** (p); **Dave Green** (b); **Stephen Keogh** (d). Miles Music Ⓕ MMCD075 (46 minutes). Recorded 1988.

⑦ ⑧

Son of tenor saxophonist Jimmy, Skidmore has worked with big names on both sides of the Atlantic. He once declined a Berkley scholarship but was a member of the widely influential SOS group with Mike Osborne and John Surman. He worked for some time with the George Gruntz Concert Band, the European Jazz Quintet, SOH and Tenor Tonic. On this CD he literally takes on his mentor, John Coltrane, in a programme of the great man's music seen very much through Skidmore's eyes. The Englishman has deliberately chosen powerful Trane themes and has homogenized them in his own image. The raw passion has been replaced by a caring involvement and, on *Resolution* and *Crescent* in particular, he has taken his own improvisational routes. The spirit of the original recording is most retained on *Lonnie's Lament* and *Naima*, where Skidmore shows his emotional commitment as well as his instrumental facility. The rhythm section, built around Rebello's buoyant piano and Green's steadfast bass, provide just the right support. No attempt is made to pressurize the leader and the expressive reins remain with him throughout a recital that could introduce the newcomer to the music of Coltrane without a hint of compromise on Skidmore's part. **BMcR**

## Slickaphonics

**Wow Bag** Ray Anderson (tb, perc, v); **Steve Elson** (ts, kbds, perc, v); **Allan Jaffe** (g, v); **Mark Helias** (b, v); **Jim Payne** (d, perc, v). Enja Ⓕ ENJ4024-2 (42 minutes). Recorded 1982.

⑤ ⑥

This pioneering rock-jazz collective formed in 1980 was the toast of New York clubland when its brand of highly vocal jazz-funk first hit the streets. The horns have a particular tonality, being tenor and trombone, and their riffs and tightly-structured solos are deftly worked into the pulsing texture of the band's predominantly vocal pieces. The first track here, *You Can Do What You Want*, typifies their approach: a repeated vocal line over a mesmeric funk beat, with the horns adding richness after a chorus or two. But ultimately the band suffers from the qualities suggested in its very name. It is too slick by half, and lacks the excitement and experiment of, say, Steve Coleman and the Five Elements, who also avoid Slickaphonics's tendency toward the bland. **AS**

# Carol Sloane

New review
**The Songs Sinatra Sang** Sloane (v); **Byron Stribling**, **Greg Gisbert** (t); **Steve Turre** (tb); **Frank Wess** (ts, f); **Bill Eastley** (ss, as, ts); **Scott Robinson** (bs, bss, bcl); **Bill Charlap** (p); **Ben Brown**, **Sean Smith** (b); **Dennis Mackrel**, **Ron Vincent** (d) Concord Jazz Ⓕ CCD4725 (61 minutes). Recorded 1996.

⑥ ❾

The result, apparently, of a flood of requests from Japanese fans, this set finds Carol Sloane accompanied on six songs by a nine-piece band and on the remaining five by a quartet featuring Wess. I am bound to say that I think the band was a mistake. The arrangements are too busy, in the main, and the parts don't sound quite together. This is not to say that they are poorly played but the effect is muddled. This happens quite often nowadays, and every time it does I lament once more the passing of Al Cohn, who could make three instruments sound like six, and mellow with it. In all other respects this is a vintage Carol Sloane album. Her voice retains its throbbing warmth, she approaches the lyrics with rare delicacy and intelligence, and her timing is immaculate. Pianist Bill Charlap is an accompanist of great sympathy and subtle swing. The choice of songs is perhaps a little obvious, but when people ask for 'Sinatra songs' they mean *I've Got You Under My Skin* and *Young at Heart*, so there's not much room for enterprise. True songhounds will have to get this CD anyway because it contains the almost forgotten introductory verse to *The Night We Called It a Day*. **DG**

# Bessie Smith

**1925-33** Smith (v); **Louis Armstrong**, **Joe Smith**, **Ed Allen** (c); **Tommy Ladnier**, **Demas Dean**, **Frankie Newton** (t); **Charlie Green**, **Jimmy Harrison**, **Jack Teagarden** (tb); **Buster Bailey**, **Benny Goodman** (cl); **Garvin Bushell** (as); **Chu Berry**, **Coleman Hawkins**, **Greely Walton** (ts); **Fletcher Henderson**, **Clarence Williams**, **James P. Johnson**, **Porter Grainger**, **Fred Longshaw**, **Buck Washington** (p); **Eddie Lang**, **Bobby Johnson**, **Lincoln Conaway** (g); **Charlie Dixon** (bj); **Billy Taylor** (b); **June Cole**, **Cyrus St Clair** (bb). Hermcs Ⓜ HRM6003 (64 minutes). Recorded 1925-33.

✔ ⑩ ❽

If history had denied us the opportunity to hear any blues singer but Bessie Smith, we should still think the blues a rich and subtle music. Knowing what we do, we realize that she also conferred on it a quality that most of her peers did not attempt or were unable to attain: a monumental grandeur. It appears in almost all her work, from the marmoreal *Dyin' by the Hour* to the feisty *Lock and Key*; it is not confined to her weightier subjects or slower tempos, but rises equally from the resignation of *Nobody Knows You When You're Down and Out* and the hedonism of *Gimme a Pigfoot*. It is partly the weight and texture of her voice, but its essence is an authority derived from personal experience and an extraordinary command of the musical means of expressing it. This selection is not quite perfect – although it has those mentioned, it lacks *St Louis Blues* and *Young Woman's Blues* – but it admirably conveys her different moods and manners. It also couples her with her aptest associates: Armstrong, her own favourite Joe Smith, and Tommy Ladnier and James P. Johnson. The transfers, made not from 78s but from new vinyl pressings from the original metal parts, are outstandingly clear. **TR**

# Jabbo Smith
1908-91

New review
**Jabbo Smith's Rhythm Aces, 1929-38** Smith (c, v) with, on 20 tracks: **Omer Simeon** (cl, as, ts); **George James** (cl); **Millard Robbins** (bss); **Cassino Simpson** or **Earl Frazier** (p); **Ikey Robinson** (bj); **Hayes Alvis** or **Lawson Buford** (bb); on four tracks: **Leslie Johnakins**, **Ben Smith** (as); **Sam Simmons** (ts); **Jimmy Reynolds** (p); **Connie Wainwright** (g); **Elmer James** (b); **Alfred Taylor** (d). Classics Ⓜ 669 (75 minutes). Recorded 1929/38.

⑧ ❽

Smith was one of a handful of Armstrong contemporaries who had the capacity to upset Louis, such was the fire and imagination of his playing, allied to a big, brassy tone and remarkably advanced rhythmic feel. In his Rhythm Aces he had a fine band which could hold its own with any other working small group of the period and gave him firm ensemble and rhythmic support: the 20 sides cut by the original band have long been regarded as classics in their own right. This compilation contains all 20 of those 1929 recordings, with four tracks cut by the 1938 band more usefully seen as makeweight, and as evidence of Smith's inability to fully adapt to changing jazz fashions. Yet it is impossible to ignore Smith's authority and command on the earlier sides, where his technical assuredness, coupled with his rich rhythmic invention, delight the listener whatever tempo the song is set at. Smith is not an original: most of his conception can be traced quite straightforwardly back to Armstrong (his muted playing has clear echoes of Oliver), but Smith was happy to play hard and high for longer than anyone of his generation – longer even than the indefatigable Armstrong – and built a reputation on that fact until his love of high living eventually proved his undoing. He would only make a full recovery of his career after close to 20 years out of the ranks of professional musicians.

No matter: the music here is a fitting memorial, and will always be ranked among the greatest early jazz small-group sides. It is packed full of the 100 per cent-proof excitement of youthful musical discovery, and can bowl the unwary listener clean over.  **KS**

# Jimmy Smith                                                                                    1925

**Open House** Smith (org); **Blue Mitchell** (t); **Jackie McLean** (as); **Ike Quebec** (ts); **Quentin Warren** (g); **Donald Bailey** (d). Blue Note Ⓜ CDP7 84269-2 (77 minutes). Recorded 1960.

✔                                                                                    ⑧ ❿

Not until Smith arrived on the Blue Note record lists did the organ have a genuine jazz identity. Claims had been made on behalf of Fats Waller, Count Basie and Wild Bill Davis, but there was no traceable jazz language. Smith's switch from piano to organ in the mid fifties changed that and in the process shored up a slightly ailing record label. His bebop on the organ reached New York in 1956 and he was an instant success. Here was a one-man combo; his feet were the bass line, his left hand the pianist's feeds and the right the solo horn improvisations. He used a greater variety of stops than his predecessors and made telling use of the instrumental devices unique to the organ. Initially he worked with a guitar and drum trio, but the advantage of added horns became obvious and this CD has him in fast company and he matches it blow for blow. He caresses the gentle curves of *Old Folks*, drives remorselessly on *Plain Talk* and provides an improvisational investigation of *My One And Only Love* that cannot be bettered, even by the impressive horn soloists present here. By the time of this session he had a legion of copyists and, some time later, Verve records would give him big band recording projects which would make him a worldwide household name by the mid sixties.  **BMcR**

**Further Adventures of Jimmy and Wes** Smith (org); **Wes Montgomery** (g); **Grady Tate** (d); **Ray Barretto** (perc); also 14-piece big band arranged/conducted by **Oliver Nelson**. Verve Ⓜ 519 802-2 (40 minutes). Recorded 1966.

⑥ ❽

'Further' because it was originally a follow-up to their successful album, **Dynamic Duo**, currently unavailable. **Adventures**, however, is pitching it a bit strong. The atmosphere of the whole session is serene and laid-back, with Smith revealing a lightness of touch and a feeling for subdued tone colours which must have surprised those who knew him only from his skirling, funky-bebop records. Montgomery's guitar is at its mellowest and, wrapped around with dark, woody organ tones, it imparts a wan, ethereal beauty even to a jaunty little tune like Roger Miller's *King Of the Road*. Everything is so tastefully and lovingly done that it hardly seems to matter that little is actually going on. Tunes like *Call Me* and *Maybe September* do seem to induce a kind of languor in the participants. The producer, Creed Taylor, made a speciality of turning out records of the highest technical quality by the very best players, which were intended not to be listened to too closely. This is a typical Taylor product – not exactly background music, but not foreground music either – and as such not really typical of either Smith or Montgomery. On the other hand, only musicians of their calibre could have made it.  **DG**

**New review**

**Angel Eyes** Smith (org); **Roy Hargrove** (t, flh); **Nicholas Payton** (t); **Mark Whitfield** (g); **Christian McBride** (b); **Gregory Hutchinson** (d). Verve Ⓕ 527 632-2 (55 minutes). Recorded 1995.

⑧ ❾

When last year Smith released **Damn!**, his first Verve new release in decades, that was precisely my reaction. It represented something of an opportunity lost, for the album while having a reasonable amount of high spots certainly managed to leave a lot of its good feeling on the studio floor. Remarkably, the second culling of tracks from the selfsame sessions has presented us with what in years to come will be held in as much reverence as his best Blue Note and Verve dates of the sixties. This album is subtitled 'ballads and blues jams', and that describes precisely what goes on here, although it would be idle to conclude from this that the album has been thrown together from old favourites remembered in the studio. For a start, few of the tunes here have been recorded before by Smith, including – incredibly, considering their long and successful collaboration in the sixties – Oliver Nelson's *Stolen Moments*. Secondly, each song has been given a specific instrumentation, so that *You Better Go Now* becomes a duet between Smith and Hargrove, while *Bess, Oh Where's My Bess* is a Hammond solo from beginning to end. Neal Hefti's classic Basie chart *L'il Darlin'* becomes a moody late-nighter with the organ trio (Smith playing the bass pedals), while *Slow Freight* adds Roy Hargrove on flügelhorn to create a smooth groove. All in all, then, an intelligent and moody programme which brings to mind similar understated Smith triumphs of years gone by, including **Plays Fats Waller**, yet to make it on to CD 30 years after its creation.  **KS**

# Johnny 'Hammond' Smith                                                              1933

**That Good Feelin'/Talk That Talk** Smith (org); **Thornel Schwartz** (g); **George Tucker** (b); **Leo Stevens, Art Taylor** (d); **Oliver Nelson** (ts); **Ray Barretto** (perc). Prestige New Jazz/Beat Goes On Ⓜ CDBGPD061 (70 minutes). Recorded 1959/60.

⑤ ❽

Smith has become – at least in England – something of a cult figure in recent years, largely as a result of his funkin' it up in the late sixties and early seventies. The vinyl changes hands for silly money. However, there is precious little of his material available on CD, and of that selection, this very generous coupling represents his most jazz-oriented approach to the best advantage. It reveals him to be, at the opening of the sixties, a player still greatly in debt to Wild Bill Davis, Milt Buckner and others, and still in the throes of plumbing the radical new Hammond Organ territory then being opened up by another fellow by the name of Smith. The 1959 session really is pretty turgid stuff, but *Talk That Talk* has a lot more going for it, not least the presence of that superior musician Oliver Nelson. Apart from this, Smith himself has moved up a gear and manages to swing quite convincingly, introducing the Jimmy Smith-patented blue phrases at every meaningful moment. For this reason it is enjoyable, unpretentious stuff, and certainly will not upset a quiet evening at home with the partner of your choice. **KS**

## Keely Smith

1932

**Spotlight on Keely Smith** Smith (v); with orchestras arranged and conducted by **Nelson Riddle**, **Billy May**. Capitol Ⓜ CDP7 80327-2 (61 minutes). Recorded 1957/8.

⑧ ❽

Keely Smith (born Dorothy Keely; her name was changed by her first major employer and future husband, Louis Prima) had only the merest of professional experience when at the age of 16 she joined Prima's band in 1948. By the mid fifties Prima and Smith were both professionally and personally a duo and opening in Las Vegas. Within a short space of time they were the toast of the town and under contract to Capitol. We must be grateful to Prima that his good musical taste and professional ethics allowed his wife to record not only the best songs available, but songs she actually wanted to sing. The results are evident in this fine collection. If the arrangements more than hint at the *Ella Song Books* and the classic Sinatra albums then being recorded, this is no coincidence: Smith admired both singers, and they all shared the talents of Nelson Riddle and Billy May. That Smith has her own style and makes these versions of such standards as *You Go To My Head*, *I Can't Get Started*, *Someone To Watch Over Me* and *Stormy Weather* as distinctive as any others of her era is a tribute not only to her professionalism and talent, but to her integrity as an artist. Her clear, ringing voice, perfect intonation and graceful phrasing is perfectly joined with her expressive ability. This is an acute selection from her best period and a complete delight **KS**

## Leo Smith

1941

New review
**Divine Love** Smith (t flh, perc); **Lester Bowie, Kenny Wheeler** (t); **Dwight Andrews** (f, bcl, ts); **Bobby Naughton** (vb); **Charlie Haden** (b). ECM Ⓕ 529 126-2 (45 minutes). Recorded 1978.

Smith hails from the blues land of Mississippi yet his contribution to jazz and improvised music could hardly have been on a more expansive scale. He was pro-actively involved in the musical investigations of the Association for the Advancement of Creative Musicians and this was matched by the impact he made on the European free jazz scene. Further evidence of his musical imagination was shown in groups such as the Creative Construction Company, with Leroy Jenkins and Anthony Braxton and in his own New Dalta Ahkri. This CD provides an ideal example of the way in which he weighs the value of silence against the projection of sound. *Divine Love* affirms his progression from Miles Davis ideals and is realized conversationally in two and three voice counterpoints. *Tastalum* is the most obviously prepared piece but Smith's method of scoring sets a degree of space evaluation against improvisation, a situation to which Bowie and Wheeler respond superbly. The presence of bassist Haden on *Spirituals* is a mildly restraining arm but it makes the creative path more accessible rather than predictable. The 1983 **Process of the Great Ancestry** (Chief CD6) is an ideal companion album. **BMcR**

## Lonnie Smith

1943

**Drives** Smith (org); **Dave Hubbard** (ts); **Ronnie Cuber** (bs); **Larry McGhee** (g); **Joe Dukes** (d). Blue Note Ⓜ CDP8 28266-2 (36 minutes). Recorded 1970.

⑤ ❽

Smith – not to be confused with the keyboardist Lonnie Liston Smith who played with Pharoah Sanders and then went on to considerable fame in the crossover end of fusion – came to attention first with Lee Morgan, in whose group he played, and who appeared on his first Blue Note album, **Think!** (it was reissued on CD but is now deleted). **Drives** comes from two years later and is unequivocally trailing its r&b and soul credentials across a set of instrumentals which includes a tough version of Blood, Sweat & Tears's big hit, *Spinning Wheel*. However, all is not groove, and there is a racy outing on Victor Feldman's *Seven Steps To Heaven* which demonstrates not only that Lonnie could pedal the bass line at horserace tempo, but could also come up with some tasty improvising at the same time. Cuber and Dave Hubbard eat up the pulse in their solos, and a nice halving of the tempo through a vamp tag gives a bluesy outro, the band strutting off into the wings *à la* James Brown.

Smith is no mere touter of other people's clichés, although he has had no hesitation in using the popular modes of the day. He is still playing professionally, being a member of Lou Donaldson's band, and he recently surfaced on records, playing as strongly as ever. An album on Mike Manieri's NYC label celebrating the Blue Note years called **Chartbusters** finds Smith also rubbing keyboards with John Scofield, Craig Handy and Lennie White. On the recent **Secret Agent Men** he was coupled with Rufus Reid, among others. **KS**

## Louis Smith                                                      1931

**New review**

**Here Comes Louis Smith**  Smith (t); **Bushshot la Funke (Cannonball Adderley)** (as); **Duke Jordan**, **Tommy Flanagan** (p); **Doug Watkins** (b); **Art Taylor** (d). Blue Note Ⓜ CDP8 52438-2 (42 minutes). Recorded 1957.

⑦ ❼

When Smith made this, his first record as a leader, he was 25 years old and the latest Browniephile to burst on to a New York scene full to bursting with young players looking to inherit the tragically deceased trumpeter's crown. He was to complete another record for Blue Note and get as far as joining Horace Silver before switching careers into teaching (he was a music postgraduate by 1954). Since that time he has made occasional forays back into performance, and has resumed a recording career (SteepleChase has latterly made a number of albums with him). As a general rule these albums find him an older and less sprightly figure. On this 1957 outing, however, the music is effervescent (with Taylor contributing some of his most powerful drumming on record) and the song selection fresh. Of the six pieces, just one (*Stardust*, a vehicle for Smith alone) is a standard, with Duke Pearson's *Tribute to Brownie* starting the session and the other four originals coming from Smith's pen. The trumpeter is technically assured and has an attractively full tone as well as an improvisational fluency which hints at the potential to develop a fuller individuality, but the star soloist is Adderley. The altoist at this stage was recording for Mercury (hence the pseudonym) and in the first flush of stylistic maturity, and is simply unstoppable here. A good hard-bop session, then, with an added dimension brought about through Adderley's presence. **KS**

## Mike Smith

**Unit 7**  Smith (as); **Ron Friedman** (t, flh); **Sid Jacobs** (g); **Jodie Christian** (p); **John Whitfield** (b); **Robert Shy** (d); **Alejo Provedo** (perc). Delmark Ⓕ DD444 (51 minutes). Recorded 1989.

⑧ ❽

Like his later album **On a Cool Night**, **Unit 7** showcases an alto style which owes a great deal – especially in its agility and power, its blues roots – to Cannonball Adderley. Here, this debt is made overt, the album dedicated to the late alto player and containing material with which he was associated. It is a tribute to Mike Smith's artistic integrity that he has managed to retain his individuality in this process. As Nat Adderley comments in his booklet-notes, Smith has managed to emulate without slavishly copying his chief influence on a selection of tunes ranging from the Sam Jones title track through Randy Weston's *Hi Fly* to Adderley classics like *Work Song* and Bobby Timmons's celebrated *Dat Dere*. The overall group sound is less harsh and frenetic than Adderley's, particularly when the wonderfully laid-back and mellow-sounding Ron Friedman is compared with Nat Adderley, but the spirit and freshness of the original group imbues Smith's entire album with infectious vitality, enabling it to avoid completely the air of bloodless contrivance that often permeates such projects. Smith and his augmented rhythm section will win no prizes for adventurous innovation, but for gutsy, tight, well-arranged small-group jazz, they are hard to beat. **CP**

## Stuff Smith                                                     1909-67

**Stuff Smith-Dizzy Gillespie-Oscar Peterson**  Smith (vn); with, on 11 tracks: **Carl Perkins** (p); **Red Callender**, **Curtis Counce** (b); **Oscar Bradley**, **Frank Butler** (d); on nine tracks: **Oscar Peterson** (p); **Barney Kessel** (g); **Ray Brown** (b); **Alvin Stoller** (d); on five tracks: **Dizzy Gillespie** (t); **Wynton Kelly** (p); **Paul West** (b); **J.C. Heard** (d); **The Gordon Family** (v, one track). Verve Ⓜ 521 676-2 (two discs: 154 minutes). Recorded 1957.

⑦ ❽

Smith was born in Ohio and was playing professionally by 1924. By the early thirties, after spending half a decade with the Alfonso Trent band, he was ready to set up his own small sextet, a band which played in and around Buffalo, New York. With Jonah Jones on trumpet, this band landed a spot at the Onyx Club and thereafer Smith's reputation was assured, making his first recordings in 1936, one of which, *I'se a-Muggin'*, was a hit. Like many swing stars, by the early fifties Smith had hit hard times, and this string of dates for Norman Granz was an oasis indeed for a somewhat forgotten man.

The first disc starts off with the Carl Perkins session. For a West Coast rhythm team these men accompany the hard-swinging Smith with crisp fire, and Perkins takes a number of typically neat, varied solos. The spotlight is kept firmly on Smith, who responds with the type of playing which made his reputation. His tone is thin and gritty, but this he uses to his advantage, manipulating it to give him attack and great rhythmic drive. It also enables him to avoid the tendency to saccharine or lugubrious expression which jazz violinists find hard to escape. Smith clips his notes and phrases more than, say, Grappelli, giving more forward momentum; he also allows pauses and rests to give pacing and variety to his playing. This all helps keep his solos consistently interesting, and he always swings. The tracks with Gillespie are all quite long, and are considerably more exotic than the rest of the programme, Gillespie quite clearly lending his big-band experience to throw together some head arrangements (*Rio Pakistan, Purple Sounds*) which are unusually provocative for the time. The two main soloists work particularly well together while the Peterson trio in support do nothing wrong. One anomaly to point out: on the Peterson session without Gillespie (from which there are three previously unissued tracks, including a long but engaging *Body and Soul*), there is clearly a guitarist present (Barney Kessel, according to Ruppli) who is nowhere credited in the CD personnel listing, though he is mentioned in the booklet-notes. He takes a fetching blues-drenched solo on *In A Mellotone*. The Gordon Family add a vocal harmony treatment of *Oh Lady, Be Good!* in a style which may have sounded fine in the forties, but was fast growing a cornfield by 1957. **KS**

## Tab Smith                                                           1909-71

**Jump Time**  Smith (ss, as, ts, v); **Sonny Cohn** (t); **Leon Washington** (ts); **Lavern Dillon**, **Teddy Brandon** (p); **Wilfred Middlebrooks** (b); **Walter Johnson** (d); **Louis Blackwell** (v). Delmark Ⓔ DD447 (59 minutes). Recorded 1951/2.

⑥ ❻

Tab Smith is not exactly a name to conjure with these days, but he was a fine altoist who graced both the Count Basie and Lucky Millinder bands in the early forties, and a player who never deserted his original inspirations. On this, the first of a projected series of Delmark CDs covering Smith's 92 sides recorded for the United label from 1951 to 1957, the altoist's indebtedness to Hodges comes across loud and clear on the ballads (*Because of You*, his big hit, is virtual daylight robbery of Hodge's style), but his medium-tempo 'jump' playing is more cosmopolitan in its influences. Smith was someone playing jump music from a strictly jazz background, for there are no hysterics, no grandstanding and little hyperbole on these sides. Smith either sings a melody with a great deal of soul and panàche, or he swings a number against the drummer's back-beat as if he is still sitting in the Basie or Millinder sax sections. This is not front-rank music, but it is tasteful and eminently enjoyable for what it is. **KS**

## Tommy Smith                                                         1967

**Misty Morning and No Time**  Smith (ts, ss); **Julian Argüelles** (as, ss); **Guy Barker** (t, monette); **Steve Hamilton** (p); **Terje Gewelt** (b); **Ian Froman** (d). Linn Records Ⓔ AKD040 (70 minutes). Recorded 1994.

⑧ ❽

Amidst the windy rhetoric of the time, the horn-splitting, Coltrane-inspired tenor of the 17-year-old Tommy Smith on 1984's **The Berklee Tapes** (Hep 2026) was one of the real revelations of the eighties jazz boom. Oddly, its intensity was in inverse proportion to the sponginess of Smith's subsequent first dates for Blue Note, but happily **Standards** (1991) indicated renewed focus, and **Paris** (1992) restated the old virtuosity and announced a striking writing talent. These qualities are sustained and advanced in this outstanding second album for the Scottish label, Linn. While referring often enough to the post-bop touchstones (Miles, Coltrane, Hancock, Tyner) which informed **Paris**, Smith also explores more esoteric, sometimes classical ideas, as on the stark, perhaps serialist, *Rag & Bone* and the bleak, Garbarek-ésque soprano duet, *Two Friends*. Above all, as on **Paris**, welcome attention is paid to the totality of the music. Composition seems to be the watchword at every level, whether Smith is considering the programme sequence or the merest detail of voicing and instrumentation. There is generous space for the superb soloists, but improvisation is part of the means rather than an end in itself, and by sidestepping the blowing session mentality and heeding various non-jazz influences, Smith has considerably freshened the jazz sound-palette. A sequel on Linn, **Beasts of Scotland**, follows a similar route but with less emphasis on jazz, the non-jazz elements taking greater hold. **MG**

## Willie 'The Lion' Smith                                             1897-1973

**Willie 'The Lion' Smith and His Cubs**  Smith (p, v) with: on 12 tracks: **Ed Allen** (c); **Cecil Scott** (as, ts); **Willie Williams** (wbd); on four tracks: **Dave Nelson** (t); **Buster Bailey** (cl); **Robert Carroll**

(ts); **Jimmy McLin** (g); **Ellsworth Reynolds** (b); **Eric Henry** (d); on eight tracks **Frankie Newton** (t); **Buster Bailey** (cl); **Pete Brown** (as); **Jimmy McLin** (g); **John Kirby** (b); **O'Neil Spencer** (d, v). Timeless Ⓜ CBC1-012 (69 minutes). Recorded 1935-7.

✅ ⑧ ❻

The Lion was one of the great Harlem stride pianists, a close friend of keyboard men such as Duke Ellington, Fats Waller and James P. Johnson. This chronologically programmed CD, containing four alternative takes from the two 1935 sessions with cornettist Ed Allen, brings together the products of five sessions. The ones with Allen are driven along in fine fashion by a two-man rhythm section comprising just The Lion (listen to that left hand!) and the impeccable washboard playing of Williams. The music is joyful and effervescent, just the kind of thing to keep the patrons happy at the Harlem speakeasys and after-hours clubs. One interesting discographical point; pianist Pat Hawes has pointed to the fact that there are two piano players on *Breeze (Blow My Baby To Me)* and suggests that it is Clarence Williams sharing the keyboard with Smith. The 1937 sessions have a different musical character and feature such excellent swing musicians as Frankie Newton, Pete Brown and Buster Bailey, but the strength of Smith's playing remains the important pivot. The clarity of the sound has been achieved by John R.T. Davies who was responsible for the remastering. **AM**

---

**New review**
**The Lion and the Lambs** Smith, **Joe Bushkin** (p); **Ed Allen** (c); **Frankie Newton, Dave Nelson, Charlie Shavers, Max Kaminsky** (t); **Frank Orchard** (tb); **Cecil Scott** (cl, ts); **Bud Freeman, Robert Carroll** (ts); **Pete Brown** (as); **Mezz Mezzrow, Buster Bailey, Rod Cless** (cl); **Sidney Bechet** (cl, ss); **Albert Casey, Jimmy McLin, Everett Barksdale** (g); **Wellman Braud, Ellsworth Reynolds, John Kirby, Jack Lesberg** (b); **George Stafford, Eric Henry, O'Neil Spencer, Manzie Johnson, Sid Catlett, Mac McGrath** (d); **Willie Williams** (wbd). Topaz Ⓔ TPZ1057 (74 minutes). Recorded 1935-44.

⑧ ❼

Although six of its first eight titles are duplicated on the excellent Timeless release, this CD makes a fine companion. It boasts 11 solo performances that show not only Smith's talent for writing spicy and impressionistic compositions but also his skill at extending them with hard-driving improvisations. *Finger Buster* is a *tour de force*, yet it's the medium bounce of *Concentration* and *Passionette* that best illustrates the mastery of his stride piano style. The remaining titles find him as an authoritarian band pianist, nurturing his 'cubs' and taking on the daunting talent of certain peers. His bowler hat and large-cigar confidence brings out the best in Allen and Scott. He is the ideal partner for Newton and Brown and he is well up for the exciting bombast of Bechet and Shavers. His partnership with Mezzrow is something of an unfair contest but titles such as *Lost* and *Mutiny in the Parlour* have him providing a rhythmic crutch where it would have been tempting to offer a merciless back-stabbing. Such gestures came naturally, however, and Smith always remains the unspoilt piano tickler. He seems to have that indefinable quality that encourages fellow musicians to match him stride for stride. **BMcR**

# Paul Smoker
1941

**New review**
**Genuine Fables** Smoker (t); **Ron Rohovit** (b); **Phil Haynes** (perc). Hat Hut Ⓔ ARTCD6126 (60 minutes). Recorded 1988.

⑧ ⑧

Smoker's early influences included Harry James, Louis Armstrong and Doc Severinsen, the latter being his teacher in the mid sixties. Despite a growing attraction to more avant-garde musics, he played mostly bebop in the seventies, later explaining that "to keep working, I reined in my 'weirdness' as much as possible". A chance meeting with Anthony Braxton, whose work he'd long admired, proved a turning point. Encouraged by Braxton, Smoker set up his own label and recorded his own music, his début, **QB**, appearing in 1984. He has since recorded with his trio for Sound Aspects (notably **Alone** and **Come Rain or Come Shine**), with the group, Joint Venture, for Enja and occasionally with Braxton (**Charlie Parker Project 1993**). **Genuine Fables** exemplifies Smoker's desire to find new challenges, even in older musics. His array of trumpet effects on *St Louis Blues* recalls Lester Bowie, but whereas Bowie often takes his bravura to humorous extremes, Smoker's use of growls, honks, squeals and so on remains 'straight' (the CD's only hint of parody comes with the breakneck tempo on *Hello Young Lovers*). Smoker's own *Tetra* is the set's most distinctive piece, its tensile spaces and beautifully shaded dynamics a model of group sensitivity. **GL**

# Gary Smulyan

---

**Saxophone Mosaic** Smulyan (bs); **Billy Drewes, Ralph Lalama** (f, cl, ts); **Dick Oatts** (f, ss, as); **Scott Robinson** (bcl, bs); **Richie Perry** (ts); **Mike LeDonne** (p); **Dennis Irwin** (b); **Kenny Washington** (d); **Bob Belden** (arr, cond). Criss Cross Ⓔ 1092CD (55 minutes). Recorded 1993.

⑧ ⑧

Pepper Adams lives, to judge by the playing of Gary Smulyan, who followed Adams into the Mel Lewis Jazz Orchestra. On this, as on his previous two Criss Cross sessions, he puts himself in an environment recalling his model. Jimmy Knepper and Tommy Flanagan were on the earlier volumes, while here the reed section of the Lewis/Vanguard Jazz Orchestra surround Smulyan's featured horn, which still sports a sure attack and honest feeling and comes out a bit from under Adams's shadow. The programme is choice, with a heavy emphasis on neglected jazz tunes from the fifties (Horace Silver's *Speculation*, Russ Freeman's *The Wind* and Quincy Jones's *Stockholm Sweetnin'* among them), placing the session more in the hard-bop orbit the rhythm section has favoured on LeDonne's Criss Cross recordings than the late-middle Coltrane proclivities usually preferred by the saxophonists involved. Belden's arrangements are brisk and well executed, succeeding in their intent to showcase the leader. The above-referenced LeDonne albums, two of which feature Smulyan and Tom Harrell, are also highly recommended. **BB**

## Jim Snidero

**Blue Afternoon** Snidero (as); **Brian Lynch** (t); **Benny Green** (p); **Peter Washington** (b); **Marvin 'Smitty' Smith** (d). Criss Cross Ⓕ 1072CD (59 minutes). Recorded 1989.

⑥ ❽

Jim Snidero's decade as the main alto soloist in Toshiko Akiyoshi's big band has turned him into a robust and eloquent player whose heart is steeped in the Blakey tradition. This was the last of his three recording sessions with trumpeter, Brian Lynch (Snidero now works with the equally imposing Tom Harrell) and the power and range of the partnership gives this wide-ranging session its appeal. The opening fast tempo variation on *Speak Low*, which Snidero calls *Enforcement,* has him at his flag-waving best with a fast and ideas-packed solo, matched by a fiery one from the trumpeter. The ballad treatments of Mal Waldron's *Soul Eyes* and Shorter's *Infant Eyes* show Snidero's maturity and these are both outstanding performances. The Blakey feel is heightened by the drumming of Smith who, while not emulating Art in any way, keeps a similar control of the band by replacing Blakey's thunder with a busier precision which places more emphasis on the top of the drum kit. The piano role of Benny Green is restrained when it needs to be and very buoyant elsewhere, with the expected worthy solos. **SV**

## Elmer Snowden

1900-73

New review

**Harlem Banjo** Snowden (bj); **Cliff Jackson** (p); **Tommy Bryant** (b); **Jimmy Crawford** (d). Riverside Ⓜ OJCCD1752-2 (39 minutes). Recorded 1960.

⑥ ❼

Multi-instrumentalist Snowden's position as a musical catalyst in the early days of jazz has received less than its due. While still a teenager, he had played with Eubie Blake and Duke Ellington. His own band in Washington DC included later Ellingtonians such as Otto Hardwick, Arthur Whetsol and Sonny Greer and he was responsible for encouraging many more aspiring musicians. During his early twenties he began doubling on various saxophones but the banjo-mandolin remained his main instrument. His approach to it was highly personal. His rhythm section work was propulsively strummed, swing like mad and was light years away from the lifeless clanging of the 'trad' man's tenor banjo. As this CD demonstrates he was mainly a melody-carrying front-line player, light of touch and imaginative in the way in which he complemented Jackson. There are occasions when he is momentarily 'thrown' by the 'changes' but solos on *Them There Eyes*, *C Jam Blues* and *Twelfth Street Rag*, in particular, show a sharp musical mind and a flair for melodic improvisation. His versatility can best be judged by the fact that there seems nothing incongruous in his playing with a stride pianist, a drummer who was a Jimmy Lunceford alumnus and a bassist who worked with Dizzy Gillespie and Sonny Rollins. **BMcR**

## Soft Machine

New review

**Fifth** **Elton Dean** (as, saxello, elp); **Mike Ratledge** (org, elp) **Hugh Hopper**, **Roy Babbington** (b); **Phil Howard**, **John Marshall** (d). One Way Records Ⓜ CDA26227 (37 minutes). Recorded 1971-2.

⑧ ❼

The last studio Soft Machine album featuring Elton Dean, **Fifth** – and this is no coincidence – is also the last of the band's albums to feature truly spontaneous-sounding (even, at times, rough) jazz-based improvisation rather than the increasingly formularized jazz-rock of later albums such as **Sixth**, **Seventh** (both on One Way Records) and, particularly, the later guitar-led music featuring Allan Holdsworth and John Etheridge originally released on Harvest and now anthologized as **The Best of Soft Machine** (See For Miles Records). Dean, then as now, is a player more interested in free improvisation than in the more structured approach introduced into the band's music by his replacement, multi-instrumentalist Karl Jenkins, and on this album, he plays with typically abrasive inventiveness, particularly on his trademark instrument, saxello. The brooding, often hypnotically repetitive compositions are mostly Mike Ratledge's and feature both his distinctively querulous, buzzing organ and Dean's cracked but always dignified reeds. The clanky electronic piano, of course, dates the overall group sound to the cheesecloth-and-denims era, but the quality of the group interaction, underpinned for half the album by the smart, vigorous drumming of John Marshall, which was to grace and energize all the Soft Machine's subsequent output, raising this consistently absorbing album way beyond the realms of simple period nostalgia. Dean, Ratledge, Hugh Hopper and Marshall can also be heard performing much of this material to a suitably enthusiastic continental audience on **Live in France**, a One Way Records double CD.                    **CP**

## Martial Solal                                                                  1927

**Live 1959-85: The Best** Solal (p); Roger Guerin (t); Lee Konitz (as); Stephane Grappelli (vn); Paul Rovere, Gilbert Rovere, Niels-Henning Ørsted Pedersen (b); Daniel Humair, Charles Bellonzi (d). Flat & Sharp Ⓔ 239963 (61 minutes). Recorded 1959-85.

⑧ ❻

Few pianists of any persuasion can boast of virtuosity the equal of Martial Solal. He is also a fascinating composer, having written piano concertos, chamber music, big-band scores, extended suites, and solo pieces. Yet outside of France, where he is revered, he is probably better known as a sideman to the likes of Django Reinhardt, Sidney Bechet, Lucky Thompson, Stephane Grappelli or Lee Konitz. Considering the large number of recordings he has made, Solal's unique talents are under-represented on CD, so this pot-pourri of scattered performances from concerts and festivals is a good place to start, despite the uneven sound. NHØP, Konitz and Grappelli appear on only one track each, illustrating Solal's quick reflexes in parrying with the altoist on *Just Friends*, and providing solid support for the fiddler's brilliance on *Fascinating Rhythm*. His roots in Art Tatum and Bud Powell can be heard in his solo fantasias on *Sophisticated Lady* and *Night In Tunisia* – the latter especially becomes a patchwork quilt of quotes, counter-themes, and wildly chromatic episodes. His technique can be dazzling, but not always put to the best use; for example, his *Blue Danube* becomes a frothy Gershwinesque divertissement. For a fuller view of this remarkable artist, though, do try to hear one of his trio recordings and adventurous big-band discs.                    **AL**

## Lew Soloff                                                                     1944

**Little Wing** Soloff (t); Ray Anderson (tb); Gil Goldstein (p, syn, acc); Pete Levin (org, syn, vocoder); Mark Egan (elb); Kenwood Dennard (b); Manolo Badrena (perc). Sweet Basil/Bellaphon Ⓔ 660 55 015 (65 minutes). Recorded 1991.

⑥ ❽

In recent years, Lew Soloff has been most visible as a dynamic hard-bop trumpeter on several Nippon-generated straight-ahead dates. However, his experiences in the New York studios through the seventies and in Blood, Sweat & Tears and the later Gil Evans Orchestras also left him well equipped for the funkier line of work heard here. Soloff has a first-class technique, but he does not fit the studio archetype, all chops and no taste; his virtuosity is married to an impeccable aesthetic sense and a strikingly wide range of expression. Thus he is able to deliver the tightly phrased theme of Kenwood Dennard's *La Toalla* with absolute precision, and follow it with a loose-knit solo rich in perfectly controlled vocal effects. His versatility is also apparent on *Coral Canyon*, where he affects a muted sound reminiscent of Miles Davis before shifting to a rounded flügel-like tone. Trombonist Ray Anderson might have a less formidable technique, but in sharing an interest in the vocal potential of his horn he makes the ideal front-line partner for Soloff. There are also fine solos from Gil Goldstein on Orlando Lopez's *Para Los Papinos* (wrongly credited to Don Alias) and Mark Egan on *Little Wing*, a theme that was virtually a signature tune for the later Gil Evans Orchestra.                    **MG**

## Eddie South                                                                    1904-62

**Eddie South 1923-37** South (vn, v); Walter Wright, Stephane Grappelli, Michel Warlop (vn); Jimmy Wade (c); William Dover (tb); Arnett Nelson (cl, as); Vernon Roulette (cl, ts); Clifford King (cl, bl, as); Sterling Conway, Django Reinhardt, Roger Chaput, Mike McKendrick (g); Everett Barksdale (bj, g, v); Teddy Weatherford, Antonia Spaulding (p); Louis 'Buddy' Gross (bb); Milt Hinton, Wilson Myers, Paul Cordonnier (b); Edwin Jackson (d); Jerome Burke (d, v); Jimmy Bertrand (d, perc); Nino (v). Classics Ⓜ 707 (72 minutes). Recorded 1923-37.

✔                                                                                ⑧ ❻

A child prodigy on violin, South studied under Charles Elgar and at the age of 20 became musical director of Jimmy Wade's Syncopators in his adopted town. As the 1923 *Someday, Sweetheart* shows, he was already a mature soloist, his phrase shapes capturing something of the Armstrong magic and his solos built with genuine musical logic. In 1928 he led his own band to Europe and introduced another continent to his superb brand of jazz violin. The driving solo on *Doin' The Raccoon* is typical, but on his return to America in the early thirties he didn't always fully grasp his recording opportunities. Items like *La Rosita* answered Depression-hit America's call for compensatory schmaltz, even if the jazz hand was kept in shape with the impressive *Nagasaki* and *Gotta Go*. This CD also documents his 1937 European visit and the superb partnership he forged with Reinhardt, especially on *Sweet Georgia Brown* and *Somebody Loves Me*, which are models of creative construction. His throbbing *Eddie's Blues* is proof that his ability to hit the crown of a note was no barrier to emotional projection or the ability to swing. He remains, along with Joe Venuti, Stuff Smith, Leroy Jenkins and Billy Bang, one of the five giants of jazz violin.                **BMcR**

## Jeri Southern                                                                      1926-91

**Southern Breeze**  Southern (v); **Frank Beach, Don Fagerquist** (t); **Bob Enevoldsen** (tb); **Vince DeRosa** (frh); **John Kitzmiller** (tba); **Herb Geller** (as); **Georgie Auld** (ts); **Jack Dulong** (bs); **Bill Pitman** (g); **Bud Clark** (b); **Mel Lewis** (d); **Marty Paich** (arr). Fresh Sounds Ⓟ FSRCD104 (39 minutes). Recorded *c*1959.

⑧ ❽

Miles Davis is supposed to have scouted this stage-shy singer's albums for tunes no less vigilantly than he did Sinatra's and Ahmad Jamal's, and she tied with Annie Ross as a new star in Down Beat's first critics' poll, in 1953. Yet her electronic cameo (singing *Ev'ry Time We Say Goodbye*) on Charlie Haden's **Haunted Heart** in 1992 was probably the first that most contemporary jazz fans had ever heard of her. Southern's lack of jazz recognition has much to do with her withdrawal from performance in the early sixties, but even more to do with the widening of the gap between jazz and pop in the last three decades. Southern was more a pop singer than a jazz singer, which is to say she in no way improvised or riffed on a song. But if there is such a thing as jazz *feeling*, and if it is mostly a question of phrasing, she had it in abundance. She rivalled Davis, Sinatra, and Chet Baker in setting a mood with a ballad. Even her slight lisp worked in her favour, adding to the virginal shiver she could bring to a love song.

The ideal introduction to Southern would be **You Better Go Now**, a reissue of her first LP (named after her first and biggest hit), last available on Official, a label from Denmark. Although lacking the intimacy of those performances on which Southern accompanied herself on piano, and seeming to be singing as much to herself as to the listener, this date with what amounts to a choir of brass and woodwinds is an agreeable substitute.                **FD**

## Muggsy Spanier                                                                      1906-67

**The 'Ragtime Band' Sessions**  Spanier (c); **George Brunies** (tb); **Rod Cless** (cl); **Ray McKinstry, Bernie Billings, Nick Calazza** (ts); **George Zack, Joe Bushkin** (p); **Bob Casey** (g, b); **Pat Pattison** (b); **Marty Greenberg, Don Carter, Al Sidell** (d). RCA Bluebird Ⓜ 366550-2 (67 minutes). Recorded 1939.

✅                ⑧ ❽

Alun Morgan has observed that music contained on this collection "has served as the best introduction to real jazz for several generations of collectors". Reissue producer Orrin Keepnews claims this to be "the first American compilation to include all existing alternative takes. It may even be the first anywhere ... I do know that there is no evidence of metal parts having been requested from the vaults in this country, so this is in any case the first all-original-parts CD". Certainly the sound quality has benefited greatly from having the metal parts to work from. The combination of the CEDAR system of noise suppression and superior originals means that little presence or sparkle has been removed from the upper tonal characteristics. The 24 tracks here make up the complete sessions which created 'the great 16' of 1939, the two sessions of eight tracks apiece which pleased contemporary fans so much.

Of course, the music on this disc bears little resemblance to ragtime. This is New Orleans courtesy of Chicago, no frills, plenty of drive and melody, and none the worse for it. Spanier sticks mostly to the theme, leaving the tricky bits in between mostly to his reeds and piano, but this only helps the flow and variety of these short, powerful swingers. For those unaccustomed to the type of music Spanier played, it is unassuming but driving thirties small-group jazz of the very best kind.                **KS**

## James Spaulding                                                                      1937

**Gotta Be a Better Way**  Spaulding (as, f, pic); **Monte Croft** (vb); **Mulgrew Miller** (p); **Ron Carter** (b); **Ralph Peterson** (d); **Ray Mantilla** (perc). Muse Ⓟ MCD5413 (55 minutes). Recorded 1988.

⑦ ❽

Following early experiences with Sun Ra, Spaulding moved to New York in 1962. Since then he has been something of a perpetual sideman. He has worked with Freddie Hubbard, Art Blakey, Horace Silver and Bobby Hutcherson and has only rarely fronted a recording date. This CD has him leading an impressive line-up and taking full advantage of a fine Miller-led rhythm section, with its Peterson power base. The arrangements are a trifle perfunctory, but Spaulding's fiercely propulsive alto bites hard into *Bold Steps*, *Little Niles* and the title track. His shrill flute lines dance their way through *Ginger Flower Song* and flatter the languid *Remember There's Hope*, while his attacking piccolo adds its spark to *In Flight Out*. Whatever the horn, the language is hard bop and Spaulding ensures that full weight is given to the adjective as well as the noun. His solos do not have gentle contours but they are all well-constructed and there is an excitement about nearly everything he does. The little-known Croft impresses in all of his solo opportunities but it is Spaulding, allowed the driving seat for once, who puts his own brand on a useful showcase for his often undervalued talents. **BMcR**

# Sphere

**Pumpkins Delight** Charlie Rouse (ts); **Kenny Barron** (p); **Buster Williams** (b); **Ben Riley** (d). Red ℗ 123207-2 (55 minutes). Recorded 1986.

⑦ ❽

This group was formed in 1982 by the four musicians involved here. It was dedicated to the memory of Thelonious Sphere Monk and the choice of title was a mere formality. Rouse and Riley had been stalwarts of Monk groups for many years, but Barron's and Williams's commitment to the project was equally steadfast. As this CD shows, no attempt is made merely to play Monk's themes or to simulate the sound of a Monk quartet. Barron is particularly careful to avoid the minefield that has led to the downfall of countless would-be Monks. He plays pure Barron quite brilliantly and is at the heart of a very accomplished quartet. Williams's beautiful tone lights up every track, Riley bristles to order and Rouse shoulders a good share of the solo responsibilities. The tenor saxophonist's strangely stifled tone is well on show and titles like *Tokudo* and *Christina* in their different ways both suggest that there is something of the latter-day Coleman Hawkins in a style reputed to belong to Monk bebop. In the early days of their association, certain critics thought the partnership inappropriate. In practice, however, Rouse's near swing-era-style phrasing and strangulated sound seemed to fit the deliberately sour temper of Thelonious's music ideally. Sphere kept that tradition intact. **BMcR**

# Splatter Trio

New review

**Jump or Die** Keith Hedger (c); **Tom Plsek** (tb); **Steve Norton** (ss, as, bs, bcl); **Dave Barrett** (saxello, as, ts); **Randy McKean** (as, b-flat cl); **Arthor Weinstein** (g, mand, vc, syn, electronics); **Myles Boisen** (g, b); **Gregg Bendian** (vb, gspiel, xyl); **Curt Newton** (d); **Gino Robair** (d, mand, vb, toy p, syn, electronics, cond). Music & Arts ℗ CD843 (77 minutes). Recorded 1992.

⑧ ❽

In 1992 San Francisco's Splatter Trio and Boston-based quartet Debris, two left-field ensembles, joined forces with guests Bendian, McKean and Plsek to record this spirited foray into the similarly left-field sound-world of Anthony Braxton. **Jump or Die** is the first CD not by Braxton himself to be devoted exclusively to his music. Splatter leader Robair has studied and recorded with Braxton, so the group had access to unpublished scores and were well versed in his latest performance practices, notably the collaging procedures he began to use in the eighties. The nine tracks on this disc actually include 21 compositions, several excerpted, some played simultaneously, many previously unrecorded. The players also follow Braxton's lead in employing a variety of unconventional instrumentations: *Composition 74C*, for example, pitches bass clarinet against toy piano, baritone saxophone against mandolin. Better still, they heed his advice to "have fun with this material", creating a sonic kaleidoscope that whisks the listener through stomping marches, rasping bebop and inspired ensemble mayhem. Braxton's *oeuvre* is often perceived as daunting; Splatter and Debris have ventured within and found a musical treasure-house through which they romp with inventive gusto. **GL**

# Spontaneous Music Ensemble

New review

**A New Distance** John Stevens (d, pkt t); **Roger Smith** (g); **John Butcher** (ts, ss) Acta ℗ ACTA8 (54 minutes). Recorded 1994.

⑧ ❼

The SME line-up changed frequently over the years but Smith was one constant. He worked with the group for more than 20 years and, as this CD shows, had an almost telepathic understanding with Stevens. Butcher arrived in the nineties and this edition of the group rates with the finest of the past. As expected with the SME, full use is made of space and, despite the urgency, the trio balances its resources adroitly. Stevens's pocket trumpet remains a resistible part of the music but his drumming in this context is masterful. He shines most on *Stig*, a piece dedicated to a gifted Gambian percussionist, but it would be difficult to imagine another drummer in his chair. Smith's use of the Spanish guitar tells us of his instrument, not his stylistic choice and he demonstrates impressive creative powers throughout. Butcher comes from the Evan Parker stable but has already fashioned his own style. The SME sets certain ground rules, requiring a uniformity of purpose and the saxophonist responds, monitoring the progress of his colleagues and ensuring that the details of his own improvisations have no intrusive effect. **BMcR**

# Jess Stacy

1904-94

New review
**Ec-Stacy** Stacy (p) with the following collective personnel: **Bud Freeman**, **Muggsy Spanier** (c); **Lee Wiley** (v); **Jess Stacy Big Band**; **Benny Goodman Orchestra**; **Bob Crosby Orchestra**; **George Wettling Rhythm Kings**; **Gene Krupa Chicagoans**; **Jam Session At Commodore**. Topaz Ⓕ TPZ1050 (74 minutes). Recorded 1935/45.

⑨ ❻

Stacy was one of the most inspirational of all swing era pianists. His crisp, precise touch and irresistible drive made him an ideal pianist in all manner of contexts, from the powerhouse band of Benny Goodman to Condon-style groups and small, intimate units. All of these aspects are well illustrated here in a good Tony Watts-Colin Brown compilation which suffers only from slightly muffled transfers, notably on the Goodman titles. The set leans heavily on Commodore masters plus some of the titles John Hammond produced for Parlophone, including the pairing of Beiderbecke's impressionist pieces, *In the Dark* and *Flashes*. The strength of Jess's playing at faster tempo may be judged from gems such as the long *Sell Out* (complete with pounding foot) and the broadcast transcription version of *Jumpin' with Jess*. Those ringing tremolos with the right hand were Stacy's unmistakable trademark and it is unfortunate that he failed to make a success of his own big band. One track by the short-lived unit, *Daybreak Serenade*, closes this selection with the Stacy piano the only solo voice set against the precise 13-man ensemble. Considering his status in jazz there are still remarkably few CDs of Jess Stacy available, which makes this Topaz set of even greater value. **AM**

# Jo Stafford

1920

**Jo Plus Jazz** Stafford (v) with the following collective personnel: **Ray Nance**, **Don Fagerquist**, **Conte Candoli** (t); **Lawrence Brown** (tb); **Johnny Hodges** (as); **Ben Webster** (ts); **Harry Carney** (bs); **Russ Freeman** (cel); **Jimmy Rowles** (p); **Bob Gibbons** (g); **Joe Mondragon** (b); **Mel Lewis** (d); **Johnny Mandel** (arr). Corinthian Ⓕ COR108CD (42 minutes). Recorded 1960.

⑥ ❻

Jo Stafford was one of the Pied Pipers with Tommy Dorsey before moving on to become a solo artist and recording under her own name for Capitol and Columbia. She appears to have perfect pitch and her intonation is one of the remarkable aspects of her work, along with her clear diction and keen rhythmic understanding. She is not, in the narrowest sense, a jazz singer but is very content to allow jazz to happen around her, playing her part as the academically correct singer of the lyrics. This is her very successful involvement with high-flying jazzmen, four of them (Nance, Hodges, Brown and Carney) from the Duke Ellington orchestra plus that noted ex-Ellingtonian Ben Webster. It is Ben who gets most of the instrumental solo space here, closely followed by the individual trumpet work of Don Fagerquist. Johnny Hodges takes beautiful solos on *Just Squeeze Me* and, of course, *Day Dream* where his creamy sound adds a truly Ducal atmosphere. Jo's singing is perfect in this context, helped by Rowles's expert accompaniment (and occasionally Russ Freeman's celeste) and a very obvious love for the chosen songs, which include gems such as *Midnight Sun*, *Imagination* and Ellington's neglected *I Didn't Know About You*. Issued originally on Columbia and Philips, this has now reappeared on Stafford's own label. **AM**

# Terrell Stafford

New review
**Time to Let Go** Stafford (t, flh); **Steve Wilson** (as, ss); **Tim Warfield** (ts); **Ed Simon** (p); **Steve Nelson** (vb); **Mike Bowie** (b); **Victor Lewis** (d); **Victor See-Yuen** (perc). Candid Ⓕ CACD79702 (53 minutes). Recorded 1995.

⑧ ❾

A remarkable young man, not unaware of the existence of Miles Davis and under 30 at the time of writing, Stafford combines dazzling virtuosity with a firmly tailored band setting which reveals his expertise both as a soloist and leader. He is on sure ground when he laments, in the insert-notes, the absence of musical apprenticeship in the careers of today's younger players, for he was a member of Bobby Watson's quintet for five years and, since 1992, has been director of bands at Cheyney University. The musicians he works with here are long-time friends and very much see eye to eye. Stafford's choice of line-up is made unusual by the inclusion of vibes, which occasionally give an impression of coldness to the band sound, perhaps compounded by the unusually high academic standards of the musicians. But it is illusory and there is nothing wrong with the emotional levels, whether it be the fine display when the trumpeter breaks into his improvisation on *Send in the Clowns* or in the mainstream warmth of his muted playing on *Soon*. His saxophones are well chosen and Ed Simon is in the Victor Lewis class of rhythm player. **SV**

# Mary Stallings

New review

**Spectrum** Stallings (v) with the following collective personnel: **Harry Edison** (t); **Rickey Woodard** (ts); **Gerry Wiggins** (p); **Ron Eschéte** (g); **Andy Simpkins** (b); **Paul Humphrey** (d). Add woodwind section and **Alan Broadbent** (cond, arr) on two tracks. Concord Jazz Ⓕ CCD4689 (55 minutes). Recorded 1995.

⑨ ❾

Mary Stallings made her recording début with the late Cal Tjader back in 1961 on a Fantasy LP; this is her second CD for Concord and on the strength of it one may well wonder why she is still comparatively unknown. Her voice has all the tonal qualities of a true jazz singer and while insert-note writer Jim Merod mentions Dinah, Billie and Sarah, she seems closest to Carmen McRae. Concord have given her top-class support and although Edison and Woodard play together on only one tune, their presence and solos obviously added a great deal to the marvellously relaxed musical atmosphere. Mary's pitching and diction are excellent; when you add all that to a well-chosen set of a dozen songs including two by Ellington, a couple of jazz standards with lyrics (*Soft Winds* and *Robbins's Nest*, *Black Coffee* and so on) then you have more than the makings of an outstanding vocal album. Alan Broadbent and a six-man woodwind section are added on *Just as Though You Were Here* and *It Had to Be You* while *Solitude* is just Mary and Gerry Wiggins. In every case the singer sounds supremely relaxed. There are apt solos on three tracks by Ron Eschéte, the guitarist who normally works with pianist Gene Harris. He, like Mary Stallings, is obviously someone to watch out for. **AM**

# Marvin Stamm                                                  1939

**Mystery Man** Stamm (t, flh) **Bob Mintzer** (ts); **Bob Malach** (ss, ts); **Bill Charlap** (p); **Mike Richmond** (b); **Terry Clarke** (d). MusicMasters Jazz Ⓕ 65085-2 (66 minutes). Recorded 1992.

⑧ ❽

Stamm's playing will be familiar to followers of the Stan Kenton, Woody Herman, Duke Pearson, Oliver Nelson, Thad Jones-Mel Lewis big bands and countless other studio-formed units. This is the best showcase to date of his talents as small-band leader, trumpeter and flügelhorn soloist. "This is a 'live-in-the-studio' recording, no overdubbing", Stamm writes in the notes and there is certainly a lot to be said for the immediacy of performances which actually took place as we hear them on record. Marvin is not only a most fluent soloist but is also the possessor of a lovely sound on ballads. He additionally knows how to pick suitable tunes; four of the ten tracks are by European-based writers, two apiece by Kenny Wheeler and Sweden's Lars Jansson. A sextet is present on three tracks (the accompanying notes identify the two tenors where necessary) with various groupings on the remaining titles. This is contemporary music which retains strong links with what has gone before; Jansson's thoughtful *Marionette* produces exceptional trumpet and piano playing from Stamm and Bill Charlap. Strongly recommended. **AM**

# Tomasz Stanko                                                1942

New review

**Matka Joanna** Stanko (t); **Bobo Stenson** (p); **Anders Jormin** (b); **Tony Oxley** (d). ECM Ⓕ 1544 (69 minutes). Recorded 1994.

⑧ ❽

This atmospheric album of music dedicated to film director Jerzy Kawalerowicz, inspired by his 1961 *Matka Joanna from the Angels*, veers from the free to the formed. With a conventional quartet instrumentation this offers Stanko more tonal, stylistic and formal variety than some of his piano-less ensembles, such as his 1991 collaboration with Jon Christensen and Arild Andersen on drums and bass (available on Power Bros 00113). Here, Stanko's lyrical but pained trumpet and Stenson's piano produce an intense and consistently exploratory reading of *Maldoror's War Song*, which also has a long bass solo from Jormin. This and the searing, slow, *Tales for a Girl, 12*, are among the album's more obviously thematic and composed material, the preceding programmatic *Monastery in the Dark* and *Green Sky* having more in common with the freer world of drummer Oxley, who plays inventively and sensitively throughout the album. Stanko's own compositions, as opposed to those collectively ascribed to the group, are the core of the album, sinister themes like the opening of *Cain's Brand* finding echoes in the collectively-created pieces, although that particular composition extends from a sinuous theme into a free solo from Stanko before regaining its original direction from

Stenson's piano. Like much of Stanko's music this demands sustained attention from the listener, but repays it amply. **AS**

# State Street Ramblers

New review

**Volume One** Jimmy Blythe (p, ldr); Natty Dominique, Lawrence 'Cicero' Thomas, Johnny Dodds (cl); Joe Walker (as); Baldy McDonald, Angelo 'Alvin' Fernandez (cl, as); Bill Johnson (b); Warren 'Baby' Dodds (wbd); W.E. 'Buddy' Burton (p, d, speech); Clifford 'Snags' Jones (d, kz); Marie Grinter (v). Gannet Ⓕ CJR1003 (72 minutes). Recorded 1927-8.

⑥ ❻

The skiffle music of Chicago's South Side was a blend of blues, jazz and irreverent hokum and one of the style's most eminent champions were the State Street Ramblers. Their recording career extended from 1927 to 1931, their leader was pianist Jimmy Blythe and the high quality of his playing is a constant throughout. Vocal encouragement is frequently shouted, there is a casual air about all of their recordings and this CD covers the better end of the group's output. The Dominique and Dodds team plays with distinction on the first session. Despite the woefully fumbling alto of Walker on the second, Thomas lifts the group with some brassily outspoken cornet and the good-time element is maintained. Fernandez and McDonald, present on the third session, were commonplace reed men but their modest front-line contributions tend to highlight the rhythmic potency of Blythe's ensemble part and the quality of his solos. Although nine titles are not strictly Ramblers items they all feature Blythe, use the same musicians and belong to the same genre. A piano duet teams Blythe and Burton, the Dixie Four concentrate on the same two pianists and there are three titles that find these men behind the acidic blues voice of Marie Grinter. None of the titles here are to be found on the Blythe album reviewed elsewhere in this Guide and a second album to complete the issue of all Ramblers material is planned. **BMcR**

# Jeremy Steig

1942

New review

**Elephant Hump** Steig (f); Jan Hammer (el p); Gene Parla (elb); Don Alias (d, perc). Musidisc Jazz Ⓜ 500812 (36 minutes). Recorded 1970.

⑦ ❼

Hardly a prolific performer since the late seventies, Steig has never fully received the credit for broadening and developing the tonal range and appeal of the flute in contemporary jazz. Steig also played a pivotal role in the earliest murmurs of jazz-rock with Jeremy and the Satyrs, formed in 1967. A stylish virtuoso on the entire flute family, Steig's robust mastery of overblowing, together with his command of other unusual playing techniques, gave him few peers. Yet his restless nature has led to a haphazard recording history, scattered across numerous labels, most of them now long out of print. Surviving as the only CD in the catalogue from the New York sessions in 1970, this is almost identical to the now deleted **Something Else** date on Denon except it loses a few of the tracks but gains a slightly superior sound quality. The ridiculously short playing time, especially considering the missing tracks, is palliated by the chance to catch Steig in a rare, uncompromisingly electric setting, a direction that he should have explored a good deal further.

Most of his compositions here are little more than jazz-rock vamps, somewhat light on depth and character but more than packed with a punishing showcase of his unique flutterings, breathings, groans and startlingly aggressive overblowing. Hammer's ring modulated piano on *Swamp Carol* adds a dark, distinctly nasty edge, while Steig's engaging lyricism on *Slow Blues in G* updates Roland Kirk's legacy. Given more assertive tempos, as on *Energy* and the title track, Alias and Parla produce more than enough raw sparks to convince you that this quintet would have made a red-hot live attraction in the early seventies. **JN**

# Bobo Stenson

1944

New review

**Reflections** Stenson (p); Anders Jormin (b); Jon Christensen (d). ECM Ⓕ 523 160-2 (50 minutes). Recorded 1993.

⑦ ❿

Stenson came up through the contemporary Swedish jazz circles of the sixties and by the opening of the next decade was touring with jazz names such as Stan Getz and Red Mitchell, finally settling into Jan Garbarek's band when the saxophonist was making his first major impact outside his native country. A long interest in Indian classical music manifested itself in the seventies and led to the performance of many Karnatic Indian-influenced pieces, but by the eighties Stenson once again was playing more wholly jazz-based piano, and a series of albums for ECM with Charles Lloyd cemented his still growing reputation. His latest album is cast very much in the Jarrett mould (and, through that, finds its roots in the Bill Evans trio with Motian and LaFaro); the treatment of *My Man's Gone Now*, recorded by Evans with LaFaro, sounds like a Jarrett reworking. The playing is exemplary at every stage and the recording faultless, as one would expect from ECM. This is a beautiful album of piano trio music, but it lies dangerously near other mens' jazz territory.                                                    **KS**

# Steps Ahead

New review

**Vibe**  Mike Mainieri (vb, p); **Tim Hagans** (t); **Donny McCaslin** (ss, ts); **Aaron Heick** (as); **Michael Cain**, **Rachel Z** (p, syn); **Victor Bailey**, **Reggie Washington** (elb); **James Genus** (b, elb); **Clarence Penn** (d); **Adam Holzman** (kbds, d-prog). NYC Ⓕ 6012-2 (61 minutes). Recorded 1995.

⑨ ❾

In the early eighties, after a decade in which the word 'fusion' had been equated (sometimes wrongly) with monolithic textures and bludgeoning volumes, the arrival of Steps Ahead signalled the advent of a cooler aesthetic – an unplugged fusion in which r&b rhythms were moderated by the use of space and unamplified instruments. Simultaneously (though the Brecker Brothers had actually been there before) the harmonic stock of the music was geometrically enriched with sequences which had been heard infrequently or not at all in jazz. This approach was perfectly illustrated by the early Steps Ahead albums, especially **Steps Ahead** (recently reissued on Elektra Musician 7559-60168-2), before a steep decline into accountant-led pop-jazz seemed to signal the end of the band's useful life. However, things have been gradually improving through a series of albums which have been unafraid to venture into more esoteric areas. **Vibe** is a peak in that progress and marks a strong return to non-electric values. Victor Bailey has adopted a non-slap bass style, picking delicately around the end of the fingerboard to get a rounder sound, the piano is acoustic, the sax sound unmodified and when the vibes are underscored by synth, it is only in the most subtle manner. With few exceptions (*Green Dolphin Street* will not bend to that particular funk rhythm) the writing, no doubt inspired by the album's dedicatees Miles Davis and Bill Evans, is superb, and there is yard upon yard of Mainieri's unfailingly hip vibes playing.                                                    **MG**

# Leni Stern

**Secrets**  Stern (g); **Bob Berg** (ts); **Wayne Krantz** (g); **Dave Tronzo** (slide g); **Lincoln Goines** (elb); **Harvie Swartz** (b); **Dennis Chambers** (d); **Don Alias** (perc). Enja Ⓕ ENJ5093-2 (48 minutes). Recorded 1988.

⑦ ❽

Stern plays a Fender Strat with great skill and imagination and is one of very few jazz guitarists to favour this instrument over the Gibsons and Gretschs of this world. She uses the earthy, shallow sound it produces naturally to great effect, generating a tone which is both flexible and highly vocalized without being too derivative of the legions of rock heroes who made the Strat their own. All but one of the tracks on the album are written by her, and she exhibits a flair for melodic composition which makes the album very easy to listen to repeatedly. Like most of the latter-day guitarists, she is not afraid to bend a note (an approach which largely seemed to disappear from jazz guitar for about two decades), so her improvisations over blues or minor chord sequences are especially piquant. Bob Berg's muscular saxophone adds a pleasing contrast to Stern's approach and gives the album a balance which Stern was clearly looking for. An accomplished and spirited record.                                                    **KS**

# Mike Stern                                                                                                    1953

New review

**Between the Lines**  Stern (g); **Bob Malach** (ts); **Jim Beard** (kbds); **Jeff Andrews, Lincoln Goines** (b); **Dave Weckl, Dennis Chambers** (d). Atlantic Ⓕ 782835-2 (70 minutes). Recorded 1995.

⑨ ❿

Mike Stern is a no-holds-barred electric guitarist. Slamming spiralling, melodic strands against massive slaps of sonic noise, the ex-Miles Davis sideman summons up Vesuvian flows at times comparable to Jimi Hendrix. Stern has also absorbed bebop as well as the post-bop modalism of Miles and Trane. It's a striking combination. Along with pounding rhythms and laser-driven bolts melodies, the fusionistic Stern draws on the resources of volume and distortion. In a manner comparable to minimalist Philip Glass, Stern lets loose pile-driving grooves capable of inducing trancelike states. In this gritty session, Stern paints with Jackson Pollock-like boldness. In *Sunnyside* and *The Vine*, the guitarist's neon expressionism is framed by the taut rhythms of keyboardist Jim Beard, bassist Jeff Andrews and drummer Dave Weckl (Goines and Chambers guest on *Wing and a Prayer*, a poignant free-flow ballad, and *With a Twist*, a jaunty funk-strut). Beard, doubling as producer, helps channel Stern's walks on the wild side with dynamic yet lean backdrops. Another plus is the thundering tenor of Bob Malach. Though not for mainstream listeners, this is a landmark album in Stern's impressively heavyweight career.                                                    **CB**

# John Stevens

**Re-Touch and Quartet** Stevens (d); **Trevor Watts** (ss); **Jeff Young** (p); **Allan Holdsworth** (g);
**Barry Guy, Ron Mathewson, Ron Herman** (b); **Julie Tippetts** (v, g). Konnex Ⓕ KCD5027
(66 minutes). Recorded 1971-7.

⑧ ❼

Stevens is an important figure in European jazz, not only for his leadership of the Spontaneous Music
Ensemble and other bands, but also for the inspiration he gave to a generation of European
drummers. Originally inspired by Max Roach, Phil Seaman and Elvin Jones, he fashioned a style of
free drumming very much his own. He was a founder member of the SME in 1965 and this CD
presents two contrasting versions of the group. The 1971 edition has subtle rhythmic accents from
Herman and Stevens scurrying behind Tippetts's anguished voice and Watts's fluent soprano. Stevens
was keen on using the human voice at this time and *One, Two, Albert Ayler* was one of Tippetts's most
expressive contributions. *No Fear* offers one of Stevens's gentle brushes with post-Miles Davis
electronics, with Young and Guy imaginative as the play-makers, and Holdsworth's superbly fleet
improvisations making their own special mark. It was a session with the occasional gentle moment
which also shows that Stevens never surrendered to the throb of rock drums. Whatever the emotional
temper of the music, he remained the dynamo around which all of his groups revolved, even in the
calmest moments. **BMcR**

# Bill Stewart

New review

**Snide Remarks** Stewart (d); **Joe Lovano** (ts); **Eddie Henderson** (t, frh); **Bill Carrothers** (p); **Larry
Grenadier** (b). Blue Note Ⓕ CDP8 32489-2 (57 minutes). Recorded 1995.

⑥ ❽

Born in Des Moines, Iowa to a musical family, drummer Bill Stewart honed his considerable jazz
chops at New Jersey's William Patterson College in the mid eighties. Casual gigs led to a highly visible
stint with r&b altoist Maceo Parker. A modernist whose influences include Bernard Purdie, Jack
DeJohnette, Elvin Jones and Roy Haynes, Stewart has fired up groups helmed by James Moody, Marc
Copland, Ron McClure, Lee Konitz and Richie Beirach. Since the early nineties, Stewart's star has
risen further as a key player in significant projects by guitarist John Scofield, tenor saxophonist Joe
Lovano and organist Larry Goldings.

In this impressive, major label, leader début, Stewart is joined by Lovano, trumpeter Eddie
Henderson, pianist Bill Carrothers and bassist Larry Grenadier in a programme of galvanizing
originals. Representing the best of the contemporary New York scene, the music pops with edgy
sounds of surprise. On *7.5*, Stewart's seven-and-a-half measure blues is a bluesy springboard for a
roundelay of solos that dance with manic glee. For balladic contrast, there's Stewart's starkly poignant
*Shadow of the Spire*, a showcase for Lovano's haunting meditations and Carrother's pointillistic
impressionism. Equally first-rate are crisp, neo-Blakey romps like *Crosstalk*. At centre is Stewart's
subtle and responsive drumming, a uniquely loose-jointed yet fluid affair which has made him one of
improvisation's most musical and sought-after timekeepers. **CB**

# Rex Stewart

New review

**Rexatious** Stewart (c); **Cootie Williams, Freddie Jenkins, Tommy Ladnier, Russell Smith, Joe
Smith** (t); **Lawrence Brown Joe Nanton, Juan Tizol, Benny Morton** (tb); **Don Redman, Buster
Bailey** (as, cl); **Johnny Hodges** (as, ss); **Ben Webster** (ts); **Barney Bigard** (cl); **Harry Carney** (cl, bs);
**Duke Ellington, Billy Kyle, Fats Waller** (p); **Django Reinhardt** (g); **Wellman Braud, Billy Taylor,
Jimmy Blanton** (b); **Sonny Greer, Dave Tough** (d). ASV Living Era Ⓜ CDAJA5200 (75 minutes).
Recorded 1926-41.

⑩ ❼

The one blemish in the album isn't really one at all. *Jackass Blues* by the Fletcher Henderson
Orchestra turns out to be *Henderson Stomp*. It is doubly unfortunate in that Rex had decided that he'd
had it up to here with trying to replace Louis Armstrong in Henderson's band and was away up the
road by the time this wonderful track was recorded. But it's a great track to have, with trumpet by
Smith and Fats Waller on piano. For the rest, this is a most powerful collection, well chosen and taken
from good 78 rpm copies except in the case of *Rex's Big Seven* which has soaring solos by Barney
Bigard, Lawrence Brown and Ben Webster as well as the leader. But the original sound quality of the
recordings of this session was uniformly horrible. Rex returned to the Henderson band in 1928 and
stayed until 1933. These years, reputedly the best of his career, are also represented here by some of
the tracks he made with McKinney's Cotton Pickers. His playing then, typified by the pungent
intensity of his work on *Rocky Road*, showed him to be one of the greatest band trumpeters, much
more natural than the eccentric stylist of the Ellington years which make up the main source of the
music here. The track recorded at a dance, played by Ellington in 1940 from the Crystal Ballroom,

Fargo may seem an oddity, but in fact it is the best available of the many versions of Stewart's half-valve feature, *Boy Meets Horn*. If you haven't acquired this music already then you need to be told to add it to your collection at once. This version is, *pace Henderson Stomp*, outstanding.   **SV**

# Slam Stewart                                                                                     1914-87

**Two Big Mice**  Stewart (b, v); **Major Holley** (b, v); **Hank Jones**, **Gerry Wiggins** (p); **George Duvivier** (b); **Oliver Jackson** (d). Black & Blue Ⓕ 59 124-2 (59 minutes). Recorded 1977.

⑥ ❻

Stewart is usually credited with the popularizing of the singing and playing style of bass work, anathema to many dedicated jazz enthusiasts but undoubtedly a great crowd pleaser. Six of the tracks here have Stewart with another bowing-singing bassist, Major Holley, plus George Duvivier to keep time (he also takes the occasional solo). With such a plethora of 'novelty' bass playing it is best to sit back and enjoy it, for it is all very musical and extremely good fun. Slam sings an octave above the notes he bows, Major in unison (for he has a deeper voice); both men have very good intonation and are adept at inserting amusing quotations into their solos. Added to that there are the occasional, and quite beautiful, solos from Hank Jones. On five tracks Stewart drops out and Wiggins takes over at the keyboard. There is less bowing-singing here; in fact the tender *Lush Life* is virtually a feature for Wiggins, who treats the tune with considerable respect. On both sessions the recording engineer has captured the depth and resonance of the basses with clarity.   **AM**

# Sonny Stitt                                                                                      1924-82

**Prestige First Sessions**  Stitt (as, ts, bs) with various personnel including: **Bill Massey** (t); **Eph Greenlea**, **Al Outcalt**, **Matthew Gee** (tb); **Gene Ammons** (ts, bs); **Kenny Drew**, **Duke Jordan**, **Junior Mance**, **Charles Bateman**, **Clarence Anderson** (p); **Tommy Potter**, **Gene Wright**, **Earl May** (b); **Art Blakey**, **Jo Jones**, **Teddy Stewart** (d); **Teddy Williams**, **Larry Townsend** (v). Prestige Ⓜ PCD24115-2 (69 minutes). Recorded 1950-1.

⑦ ❻

Stitt's closeness of conception to Charlie Parker, and the comment it provoked, got to him so severely that for a number of years around the end of the forties and beginning of the fifties he rarely ventured forth on the alto, so intent was he on showing daylight between himself and Parker. That this plan was only partially successful can be judged by the fact that everyone still comments on how close Stitt's playing on alto was to Bird. *C'est la vie.* I happen to prefer his tenor playing, so the feast of Stitt tenor on this disc sits well with me. For one thing, it stresses his allegiance to Parker's avowed model, Lester Young. The ballad playing on this album such as *Mean to Me* and *Stairway to the Stars* (all initially released as 78s, of course), has even taken over the slightly lost, hesitant quality Young acquired later in his career, as his confidence and health began to fail. On faster tempos Stitt carves out a more individual niche, his muscular and harmonically sophisticated style in clear focus, his solos bristling with ideas which are an individual amalgam of all his initial influences. The extra weight of the tenor gives him more forward thrust and offers the listener more visceral thrills than his alto playing, so this early set of performances, still wholly within the original bebop framework, becomes a record to be listened to for pleasure as well as for being a valuable piece of bop history.   **KS**

**Sits in With the Oscar Peterson Trio**  Stitt (as, ts); **Oscar Peterson** (p); **Ray Brown** (b); **Ed Thigpen**, **Stan Levey** (d); **Herb Ellis** (g). Verve Ⓜ 849 396-2 (51 minutes). Recorded 1957-9.

⑧ ❽

On the basis of his considerable volume of work on record, Sonny Stitt was seldom, if ever, off form, with the performance level heightened by the quality of the rhythm section available, but Sonny could drag even a weak team along with him. Needless to say he is immaculately served here by two different Peterson Trios (with Levey added to the 1957 edition), and it is fascinating to observe the slight changes in style when he switches from alto to tenor. On the smaller saxophone he subdivides the beat like Charlie Parker and takes off like a rocket on the faster tempos. He plays tenor on three tracks from the 1959 date and immediately drops slightly behind the beat, like Lester Young. His tenor playing on a blues and the Trummy Young tune, *Easy Does It,* are highlights here, but all the saxophone playing is exemplary. The original LP has been fleshed out with three previously unissued titles, which might have been limbering up exercises for the **Only The Blues** date (with Roy Eldridge added) which took place a few hours later. Peterson and his cohorts provide faultless and very helpful support throughout, and the remastering gives the music an immediacy which is exhilarating.   **AM**

# Billy Strayhorn                                                                                  1915-67

**... And His Mother Called Him Bill**  Strayhorn (arr); **Cat Anderson**, **Herbie Jones**, **Mercer Ellington**, **Cootie Williams** (t); **Clark Terry** (flh); **Lawrence Brown**; **Chuck Connors**, **Buster Cooper** (tb); **John Sanders** (vtb); **Johnny Hodges** (as); **Russell Procope** (as, cl); **Jimmy Hamilton** (ts, cl);

**Paul Gonsalves** (ts); **Harry Carney** (bs); **Duke Ellington** (p, arr); **Aaron Bell**, **Jeff Castleman** (b); **Steve Little**, **Sam Woodyard** (d). RCA Bluebird Ⓜ ND86287 (61 minutes). Recorded 1967.

⑦ ❻

No conventional X-plays-Y tribute for, although performed by and issued as the Ellington orchestra of the day, this was the organization for which Strayhorn's compositions were first conceived. To enhance the symbiosis, for one session each Duke added Clark Terry and the valve-trombone of Sanders, sounds unavailable since their departure from the band in 1959. Robert Palmer's notes have useful pointers to Strayhorn's elusive musical identity and this is an impressive collection of his shorter pieces. Some of the innovations include the concealment of 32-bar song-forms on *Raincheck* (from 1941) and *Midriff* (1945) – both heard in uncut versions – and the orchestrating of piano stab-chords for trombones in *Rock-Skippin' at the Blue Note* (1951, some years before Gil Evans popular-ized the idea). In addition there are some wonderful solos, including Carney's on *Lotus Blossom* – originally rejected in favour of Duke's informal solo, which is also included – and several vehicles for Hodges, who turns *Blood Count* into a passionate lament for the late composer. Very close miking and/or inexpert mixing on some tracks compares unfavourably to the 'natural' blend of the *Far East Suite*, done mere months before. Nevertheless, the warts-and-all immediacy is part of the album's unique aura. Strayhorn's rather curious piano-plus-strings album for United Artists has recently been reissued on CD, but it hardly competes with the majesty of this Ellingtonian tribute. **BP**

## String Trio of New York

**Time Never Lies** James Emery (g); Charles Burnham (vn); John Lindberg (b). Stash Ⓕ 544 (69 minutes). Recorded 1991.

⑩ ❽

The String Trio of New York's initial reputation was based on extended improvisation and an open compositional format that integrated elements of freedom. They recorded only original material on their first five albums. But in 1986 Burnham replaced violinist Billy Bang, which seemed to provoke a reconsideration of their repertoire. **Time Never Lies** is their second disc to incorporate refreshing takes on jazz standards, exotic (including Asian and Middle Eastern effects) originals, and seldom-encountered items by the likes of Bud Powell and Charles Mingus. Though they may have sacrificed some of the exploratory verve of their early days, they've consolidated their many and varied influences into a satisfying, tunefully accessible identity. The juxtaposition, for example, of the South-Western swing of Ornette Coleman's *Ramblin'* (which reflects the STNY's roots in the small string bands, black and white, of the twenties and thirties, like the Tennessee Chocolate Drops and the Hackberry Ramblers) with the 'sophistication' of W.C. Handy's *St Louis Blues* (performed both bluesily and 'jazzed up') is striking, energized by Burnham's expressive technique and Emery's bent notes and slides. Their links to the Reinhardt/Grappelli Hot Club tradition are displayed on *Honey-suckle Rose*, and bebop is recast in prickly timbres on Bud Powell's *Celia*. A nearly flawless disc. **AL**

## Jan Strinnholm

1937

New review

**Strinnholm 95** Strinnholm (p). Sittel Ⓕ SITCD9224 (66 minutes). Recorded 1995.

⑦ ❽

In its own way this intimate solo piano portrait of a major Swedish talent is a remarkable document. Like most other European pianists Strinnholm discovered jazz via records, grew into the music during adolescence and, in his case, became a confirmed fan of the beboppers. Later waves of American jazz had their effect, however, and Strinnholm readily admits to the influence of Bill Evans, John Coltrane and Keith Jarrett. All these muses can be heard in his playing, but there is a core of identity which is him, and which makes this mostly ruminative set repeatedly stimulating and emotionally involving. Strinnholm here plays mostly his own originals, addressing a number of issues as he does. *Old Age*, for example, is his wry comment on "all that talk about New Age", both musical and otherwise. Strinnholm on this album is more than a pianist: he is a complete musician, able to evoke his own world of music from the keyboard. For that reason alone this is a release to look out for. **KS**

## Dave Stryker

New review

**The Greeting** Stryker (elg); **Bruce Barth** (p); **Scott Colley** (b); **Tony Reedus** (d); **Daniel Sadownick** (perc). SteepleChase Ⓕ SCCD31387 (67 minutes). Recorded 1995.

⑦ ❾

Dave Stryker emerged in the eighties soon after John Scofield had set about revolutionizing jazz guitar, and it was evident in fragments then that he had caught some of Scofield's oblique harmonic sense. Scofield moved on to heavy duty fusion and then Ornette-influenced freedom, but Stryker kept digging deeper into the post-bop bag and here produces something reminiscent of Scofield's Enja quartets from the late seventies. This is essentially a 'classic', pre-modern position, but Stryker does demonstrate an exciting, masterly and above all creative approach to his idiom, building compelling, well-contoured solos. The same creativity infects the whole ensemble, and it's evident that Stryker has a special empathy with the Tynerist pianist, Bruce Barth. They mesh together beautifully well in the trading in Tyner's *The Greeting*, an episode which well demonstrates, around 5'26" into the track, Stryker's similarity to early Scofield. However, Stryker is not all bop and ballads and expands his stylistic palette with a nylon-string Latin piece, a couple of African grooves and a long, often brilliant tribute to Sonny Sharrock. It seems quality is guaranteed every time he touches the instrument. **MG**

## John Stubblefield                                      1946

**Countin' On the Blues** Stubblefield (ts, ss); **Hamiet Bluiett** (bs); **Mulgrew Miller** (p); **Charnett Moffett** (b); **Victor Lewis** (d). Enja Ⓕ ENJ5051-2 (46 minutes). Recorded 1987.

Early in his career Stubblefield was something of a chameleon, as at home in support of the Drifters as he was in the Jones/Lewis reed section. He worked with Charles Mingus and Miles Davis but in neither set-ups did the real man surface. This CD is probably his best. It is pitched in the 'consolidation of free' field, using some of the vernacular of sixties free jazz but tempering it with a large amount of hard-bop know-how. Although capable of playing lines usually associated with high-note trumpeters, he makes sparing use of multiphonics. He teams well with Bluiett and lets the excellent rhythm section get on with its work. The quality of his solos on both horns is impressive. His tenor puts the backbone into a ballad like *Those Who Didn't Know*, hints at the romantic on *My Ideal*, but forges real steel in the blues duel on the title track. *Remembrance* has his soprano dancing elegantly over Miller's brawny chordal calibrations, while on *Montauk* he sets out his own structural patterns. The reason for his successful involvement with the World Saxophone Quartet, George Russell and the underrated McCoy Tyner big band becomes obvious as you become increasingly aware of his improvisational conviction, his genuine emotional commitment and his relaxed rhythmic authority. **BMcR**

## Charles Sullivan                                      1944

New review

**Kamau** Sullivan (t); **Crag Handy** (as, ts); **Kenny Barron** (p); **Rodney Whittaker** (b); **Victor Lewis** (d). Arabesque Jazz Ⓕ AJ0121 (60 minutes). Recorded 1995.

Sullivan, who has worked with Lionel Hampton, Roy Haynes, Abdullah Ibrahim and many others in the past, has been virtually off the jazz scene for 15 years, working in Broadway orchestra pits. This is his impressive way of announcing his return. He is a superb, straightforward player with enormous reserves of invention and technique. All the material on here is his own, much of it dedicated to African and African-American figures. Sullivan and Craig Handy were colleagues in Roy Haynes's band during the late sixties and their styles work well together, Handy's quirky and humorous turn of phrase contrasting well with Sullivan's intensity. The rhythm section, led by the ubiquitous Barron, is a model of its kind. It is worth noting for the future that Charles Sullivan changed his name some time ago to Kamau Muata Adilifu, and will presumably one day be known by that name alone. **DG**

## Ira Sullivan                                      1932

**Nicky's Tune** Sullivan (t); **Nicky Hill** (ts); **Jodie Christian** (p); **Victor Sproles** (b); **Wilbur Campbell** (d). Delmark Ⓕ DD422 (44 minutes). Recorded 1958.

Sullivan was an elusive multi-instrumental marvel on Chicago's modern scene in the fifties, then he became even more elusive by moving to the Miami area in the early sixties. Only when he rejoined an early associate, Red Rodney, in 1980 did Sullivan receive some of the attention he deserved. This session, one of the very few under his name, is indicative of the muscular hard-bop slant of several Chicago regulars, many of whom suffered the same familiar problems that formerly kept Sullivan off the scene and all of whom were competitive with more frequently recorded New York peers. Hill's presence keeps the leader confined to trumpet, however. Too bad Delmark has not made its other Sullivan session of similar vintage, last available on LP as **Blue Stroll** (DL402), available on disc. It has Johnny Griffin with the same rhythm section and features a spirited jam on which the latter plays alto, tenor and baritone saxes while Sullivan is heard on trumpet, peck horn, alto and baritone. **BB**

## Joe Sullivan                                      1906-71

New review

**Joe Sullivan 1933-41** Sullivan (p); **Ed Anderson** (t); **Benny Morton** (tb); **Danny Polo** (cl, ts);

**Edmond Hall**, **Pee Wee Russell** (cl); **Freddy Green** (g); **Henry Turner**, **Billy Taylor** (b); **Johnny Wells**, **Yank Porter**, **Zutty Singleton** (d); **Joe Turner**, **Helen Ward** (v). Classics Ⓜ 821 (72 minutes). Recorded 1933-41.

⑦ ❼

Sullivan played his own brand of orderly stride piano with unruffled ease and with a propulsive rhythmic momentum. He was a stalwart of the Chicago jazz scene of the late twenties, acted as Bing Crosby's accompanist and later worked with brother Bob Crosby's band. A talented soloist, two versions of *Little Rock Getaway* confirm his improvisational range, while others highlight an attack that rendered rhythm sections superfluous. He was also a talented composer, happy to introduce apt tempo changes for colour and equally skilled at arranging for medium-sized groups. This he did in style with the racially integrated band he led at the Café Society in New York during the early forties. Its eight titles here display its warm ensemble sound and the articulate solo talents of Anderson, Morton and Hall. It had Sullivan as a solo bonus and occasionally enjoyed the presence of talented but vastly contrasting vocalists Turner and Ward. Sullivan's more *ad lib* organizational skills are evident on four trio tracks that show him cushioning the eccentricities of Russell. Sullivan made the West Coast his base for much of his later life and, although he worked sporadically in the late sixties, the era portrayed on this disc represents the high point of his career. **BMcR**

# Maxine Sullivan
1911-87

**Swingin' Sweet**  Sullivan (v); **Scott Hamilton** (ts); **Chris Flory** (g); **John Bunch** (p); **Phil Flanagan** (b); **Chuck Riggs** (d). Concord Jazz Ⓕ CCD4351 (50 minutes). Recorded 1986.

✔️ ⑧ ❽

It may seem perverse to recommend the last recording of a 75-year-old singer, but Maxine Sullivan was a most remarkable woman. In 1937 her record of *Loch Lomond* made her as popular as Ella Fitzgerald was later to become (there has been a recent CD of her 1944-8 recordings with Ellis Larkins directing, but these are more often than not supper-club style). Her speciality was gentle swinging versions of folk-songs and old ballads like *Nellie Gray*, charming but very lightweight. From those early records it is obvious that she was capable of much more. Supremely level-headed and well-adjusted, she gave up show business when it stopped being either profitable or enjoyable and trained as a school health counsellor. She finally returned to full-time performing when she was nearly 60 and it was this second career that brought out the real artistry in Sullivan. Changing musical fashion had completely passed her by and she simply took up where she had left off. She was born four years before Billie Holiday, but far from deteriorating with age her voice had matured and warmed, and her natural sense of swing responded wonderfully to the relaxed rhythms of modern mainstream jazz. Her accompanists on this 1986 concert recording, made in Japan, are the Scott Hamilton Quintet, and she sings with a relaxed grace that has rarely been heard since the swing era. The vital link between jazz and American song was rarely more conclusively or delightfully demonstrated. **DG**

# Stan Sulzmann
1948

**New review**

**Treasure Trove**  Sulzmann (f, cl, af, ss, ts); **Nikki Iles** (p); **Martin Pyne** (perc). ASC Ⓕ CD7 (61 minutes). Recorded 1995.

⑦ ❾

For nine of its ten tracks this gentle, absorbing album consists of duos between Sulzmann and Iles, with Pyne only joining them for the spectral landscape of Sulzmann's *Midnight*. The spirit of Bill Evans (always a strong influence over Iles's introspective piano work) lingers over the disc and the first track is the Evans composition *Since We Met*. There's one piece by Paul Simon and all the remainder are by one or other member of the duo, suggesting a sympathetic and similar approach to composition. Reviewing Sulzmann's previous album, **Feudal Rabbits** (Ah Um 011), I felt his quartet showcased only one aspect of a musician who consistently worked with and flourished in a big band environment, but ironically this disc, with its minimalist backdrops for his velvety tenor tone, agile flute lines and seam of lyrical ideas is a far more effective example of his work. For the most part the tempos are slow to medium, but the fluidity of the duo allows time to ebb and flow creatively, and Iles proves herself both an ideal accompanist for Sulzmann and a burgeoning talent as both composer and soloist. **AS**

# Sun Ra
1914-93

**Jazz in Silhouette**  Sun Ra (p); **Hobart Dotson** (t); **Julian Priester** (tb); **Marshall Allen**, **James Spaulding** (as, f); **John Gilmore** (ts); **Pat Patrick** (bs, f); **Charles Davis** (bs); **Ronnie Boykins** (b); **William Cochran** (d). Evidence Ⓕ ECD22012-2 (45 minutes). Recorded 1958.

⑨ ❽

In 1992 Evidence reissued 13 early Sun Ra recordings, first released on his own Saturn label, that had been virtually impossible to find for almost 30 years. Beautifully repackaged and with the original sound quality much improved, these albums confirmed Sun Ra's reputation as the most brilliant big band leader of the post-bebop era. The batch of 13 LPs (accommodated on ten CDs) included 1963's weirdly wonderful **Cosmic Tones for Mental Therapy** and 1961's **Interstellar Low Ways**, arguably the first masterpieces of Ra's embryonic space-age jazz. The real surprise, however, was **Jazz in Silhouette**, which showed just how adept Ra could be in more traditional areas, though already enhancing the music with his distinctive touches and colours.

His swing roots are evident (*Hours After*), as is his assimilation of bebop (*Saturn, Horoscope*), but more fascinating is his ability to create the uncategorizable *frisson* of, say, *Enlightenment*, with its sumptuous baritone sax lines, brass/reed counterpoints and darting excursion into Latin bop. Another captivating hybrid is *Ancient Aiethiopia*, which does point to the future with its percussive polyrhythms and free passages, though no less striking is the elegant trumpet solo by the underrated Hobart Dotson. There are strong solos too by John Gilmore (*Saturn, Blues at Midnight*) but the emphasis, characteristic of Ra, is on a highly-disciplined group-playing to match those early big bands which, like the Ancient Egyptian civilization to which his music so often makes reference, represented for him a pinnacle of black achievement. **GL**

---

**The Heliocentric Worlds Of Sun Ra, Volumes 1 and 2** Sun Ra (p, cel, clavioline, bass mba, timp, perc); **Chris Capers**, **Walter Miller** (t); **Teddy Nance**, **Bernard Pettaway** (tb); **Marshall Allen** (pic, f, as, perc); **Danny Davis** (f, as); **John Gilmore** (ts, perc); **Pat Patrick** (bs, perc); **Robert Cummings** (bcl, perc); **Ronnie Boykins** (b); **Jimhmi Johnson**, **Roger Blank** (d, perc). ESP-Disk Ⓜ 1014/17-2 (two discs, oas: 35 and 37 minutes). Recorded 1965.

✓ ⑩ ❼

These two discs, although recorded seven months apart, fit together like the halves of a Chinese painted screen, and the picture we see when they are combined is a view of the future. Although he had broken with song form to explore new organizations of sound a year or two earlier (on hard to find Saturn LPs **Cosmic Tones for Mental Therapy** and **Other Planes of There**, now reissued on Evidence), these ESP discs reveal him experimenting with a new approach to arranging based on disciplined freedom. The shorter performances on Volume 1 plot a drastic change in the relation between instruments, distinct from recognizable jazz interaction. These are tone-poems with a chamber music approach to dynamics, colours and textures, the material organized by spontaneous cues. The search for new sonorities led him to a particularly mysterious, dark sound (with bass marimba, bass clarinet, bass trombone, timpani and acoustic bass prominent – Ronnie Boykins is the unsung hero here). The result is largely arhythmic, with atonal lines, harmonic clusters and starkly dramatic contrasts of timbres. On Volume 2 Ra puts this concept into the framework of the full band, extending the music longer (with the exception of *Other Planes of There*) than he had ever previously recorded. On *The Sun Myth* and *Cosmic Chaos* the full band plays fractured rhythms; their individual lines do not coalesce but intersect in free polyphony. This seems the precedent not only for larger ensembles like Globe Unity, but also the spontaneous 'conduction' of Butch Morris. (The personnel listed above is compiled from both discs; actual personnel differs slightly, but not significantly, between the two. The refurbished sound quality is quite good, considering the originals.) **AL**

---

**Sunrise in Different Dimensions** Sun Ra (p); **Michael Ray** (t); **Marshall Allen** (as, ob, f); **Noel Scott** (as, bs, f); **John Gilmore** (ts, cl, f); **Kenneth Williams** (ts, bs, f); **Danny Thompson** (bs, f); **Chris Henderson**, **Eric Walker** (d). hatART Ⓕ 6099 (71 minutes). Recorded 1980.

⑧ ❻

In the seventies, Sun Ra added something new to his Arkestra's psychedelic mix of antic spectacle and free jazz: a brace of thirties swing tunes – five from Fletcher Henderson's book here, two from Ellington's – which fit right in, being pitched on the same riotous energy level. Sun Ra, like Ellington and other smart leaders, let key soloists set much of the band's style. Standouts include trumpeter Ray, a solid lead player with an arsenal of special effects at his command, and *glissando*-master Allen, whose note-bending skills unite his abrasive tea-kettle squeals and affectionate re-creations of Johnny Hodges's soothing blues.

The raucous swing and bop covers illuminate the leader's piano style, with its hot flashes of early jazz devices and Hinesian chaos. Despite his deft stride and penchant for close-interval dissonances, on *'Round Midnight* he owes little to composer Monk.

This concert recording is atypical in two ways. The touring band is roughly half the size of the full Arkestra, although with five saxes it can summon appropriate bluster. More critically, in reducing two LPs to one CD, hatART regrettably dropped the chant, *On Jupiter*, featuring vocalist June Tyson, one of the Arkestra's signature stylists. There was room for it. **KW**

---

**Live at the Hackney Empire** Sun Ra (p, kbds, v); **Michael Ray** (t, v); **Jothan Callins** (t); **Tyrone Hill** (tb); **Marshall Allen** (as, f, pic, ob); **Noel Scott** (as, bcl); **John Gilmore** (ts, cl perc, v); **Charles Davis** (bs); **James Jackson** (bn, perc); **India Cooke** (vn); **Kash Killion** (vc); **John Ore** (b); **Earl 'Buster' Smith**, **Clifford Barbaro** (d); **Talvin Singh** (tab, v); **Elson Nascimento** (perc); **June Tyson** (v). Leo Double CD Ⓕ LR214/15 (two discs: 149 minutes). Recorded 1990.

⑦ ❻

Too much of Sun Ra's discography is taken up by indifferent live concert recordings in the Arkestra's final years. There was suspicion of pirate label activities in certain cases and some issues were inferior both in terms of musical performance and sound quality. This CD is found wanting on neither count and presents the Year 2000 Myth Science Arkestra playing near to the top of its game.

The leader's piano is prominent throughout, producing his own unique brand of stride and, on *Blue Lou*, actually sounding like Basie. His arrangements offer an 'over-view', ranging from the blues band sound of *Skimming and Loping* to the exotic and almost Ellingtonian *Sunset on the Nile*. Riffs are used judiciously on *Planet Earth Day* and *Frisco Fog*, a string trio plus tabla suggest a contemporary spasm band on *Astro Black* and *String Singhs*, while the rattling percussion and permutation of vocal chants make their customary appearance. The trumpet division apart, the quality of the solos is high. The strings of Cooke and Killion are used sensitively and, although the extrovert sax parts are left mainly to Allen, all of the reeds play well. Cognisance is taken of individual needs and despite failing health, Sun Ra ensures that each musician is showcased appropriately. **BMcR**

## Monty Sunshine

1928

New review

**New Orleans Hula** Sunshine (cl); **Alan Gresty** (t); **John Beecham** (tb); **Barry Dew** (bj); **Tony Bagot** (b); **Geoff Downs** (d). Lake Ⓕ LACD47 (56 minutes). Recorded 1985.

⑥ ❼

Less famous than the 'three B's' of British traditional jazz, (although responsible as a sideman for Chris Barber's biggest early hits), Sunshine has kept a good career going for well over three decades since leaving Barber. For most of the time his line-up has been very similar to this one and his mid-nineties band is almost unaltered. Like any regular working band, Sunshine has produced a stream of records to sell at concerts. His more recent efforts for Timeless lack something of the vitality of this mid-eighties effort, originally issued in the US on Stomp Off and now reissued by Lake with extra tracks. For long-term fans, there's a glance over the shoulder to Barber days with a solo clarinet version of *Wild Cat Blues*, but the rest of the tracks are standard New Orleans fare, with a decidedly authentic two-beat from Downs. Since he left the Kinks brass section, and after a few years with Ken Colyer's latter-day groups, John Beecham has been a regular member of Sunshine's groups. His is the hidden talent here, a gutsy, authentic New Orleans sound that excels on the slow blues and street parade marches like *Bugle Boy*. Sunshine re-creates his cross-bred George Lewis/Sidney Bechet style made famous during his Crane River/Chris Barber days and, like fellow Barber alumnus Ian Wheeler, manages within fairly narrow stylistic confines to sound completely unlike anyone else. **AS**

## John Surman

1944

**Such Winters of Memory** Surman (ss, bs, bcl, rec, p, synth, v); **Karin Krog** (v); **Pierre Favre** (d). ECM Ⓕ 810 621-2 (46 minutes). Recorded 1983.

✔

⑩ ❿

Odd that this, one of Surman's most complete efforts, has taken the longest to appear on CD from his back catalogue, arriving only in the summer of 1993, almost ten years after its recording date. It may be that the tack Surman takes on each of his fascinating albums for ECM determines one's reaction to them and that, independent of subjective viewpoints, they are all as good as each other. However, I hold a torch for this one. Surman seems to have been on outstanding solo form and also seems to be happy to give us plenty of himself as a soloist, which is not invariably the case on his own albums. His compositions are perhaps better described as frameworks, but they are uncommonly evocative frameworks at that, and set him enough problems and points of stimulus for the listener to be grateful that his compositional mind works in that way. He has a sure gift for memorable and oddly dignified melody, often built on whole-tone steps much in the way that Coltrane's were, and it seems therefore appropriate that there is a compelling solo piano rendering of the initial theme of Coltrane's tune *Expression*.

Surman has pursued a mostly solitary creative path for the last couple of decades, and one that has taken him away from Britain a great deal, but he is quite probably Britain's greatest post-Coltrane musician working in an avowedly modern idiom, and it is a triumph for everyone concerned that this album could never in a million listenings be mistaken for New Age music, regardless of instrumentation or the number of synthesizer patterns set up. As Ira Gitler said in a very different context, "This is jazz, Jim." **KS**

**The Brass Project** Surman (acl, bcl, ss, bs, p); **Henry Lowther**, **Steve Waterman**, **Stuart Brooks** (t); **Malcolm Griffiths**, **Chris Pyne** (tb); **David Stewart**, **Richard Edwards**, **Andrew Waddicor** (btb); **Chris Laurence** (b); **John Marshall** (d, perc); **John Warren** (cond). ECM Ⓕ 517 362-2 (62 minutes). Recorded 1992.

⑨ ❾

Surman formed The Brass Project with John Warren in 1981. With the trio of Surman, Laurence and Marshall acting as a focal point, the plan was for Warren to cue in the brass section "when the trio's improvisations needed it". This notion proved unworkable in practice so the tracks here, on the group's début CD, are more carefully arranged. In the event, Warren has deployed his forces with great skill, whether blending them into bright, sumptuous textures or pitting them against each other in thrilling two and three-part rhythmic counterpoint.

One of the chief pleasures of the record is to hear Surman rekindle the excitement of his youthful glory days in the Mike Westbrook big band. He is superb blowing against a large ensemble, his baritone riding the punchy groove of *Wider Vision*, the soprano darting above the racing brass lines of *Tantrum Clangley*. His fondness for pastoral moods reemerges on *Coastline*, but there is an unexpected dabble in more abstract areas on *Spacial Motive* and the multi-tracked *All for a Shadow*. The brass sound magnificent, with notable solo contributions from Henry Lowther and Stephen Waterman. A bold contrast to the private reflections of his solo records, **The Brass Project** stands among Surman's most ambitious and original works to date.                                **GL**

# Ralph Sutton                                                                 1922

**Last of the Whorehouse Piano Players (The Original Sessions)** Sutton, Jay McShann (p); **Milt Hinton** (b); **Gus Johnson** (d). Chiaroscuro Ⓕ CR(D)206 (71 minutes ). Recorded 1979.
✔                                                                            ⑧ ❽

As to the question of its fitness to be in a Basic Jazz Library, "it's a resounding yes," as Philip Larkin might have said. It is difficult to imagine that this is not what the jazz deity who invented the music had in mind when he first thought it up. The combination of melody, good extemporization and perfect, swinging rhythm is completely irresistible. Ignore the sensationalist title, demeaning to both the sensitive and shy Ralph Sutton and to his guest McShann. The music is happy piano which rolls from stride to boogie and deep blues. More importantly, it is as good as you will get in any of these idioms, *pace* James P. Johnson and Fats Waller. *Little Rock Getaway* is only one of several tours de force, the two men distilling beautiful melody in a slow section before racing away in the best Sullivan manner. Sutton came along a little later than Willie The Lion, Fats and James P., but even though he emerged after Jess Stacy, Joe Bushkin and Mel Powell his devotion is to the earlier ticklers and he is a throwback of the most welcome kind.

McShann must not be downgraded in all this, for he matches Sutton in every bar, and probably has not made a better recording. Apart from his fine blues and boogie he also gets a chance to sing (as does Sutton). A perfect jazz partnership in action here, with veterans Hinton and Johnson suitably inspired by the occasion.                                                         **SV**

# Esbjorn Svensson

New review

**Mr and Mrs Handkerchief** Svensson (p); **Dan Berglund** (b); **Magnus Ostrom** (d). Prophone Ⓕ PCD028 (61 minutes). Recorded 1995.
                                                                            ⑦ ❽

The packaging gives little away; EST is obviously a working unit and this CD was recorded at various Swedish (and Danish) locations, some live and a few with Svensson playing upright piano. One or two tracks have a boxy sound which is, apparently, deliberate as the booklet warns that "for your information, yeah, the distortion is supposed to be there!" Having disposed of the lack of information we are left with a very fine trio playing ten of the pianist's pieces of such a varied quality that they might almost be the work of different composers. The opening *Say Hello to Mr D (To Mr S)* is slow and reflective, the kind of thing we associate with Keith Jarrett. But tracks such as *Same as Before* and *The Rube Thing* develop tremendous impetus, although some of the repeated phrases are irritating. It would be interesting to learn more about Svensson and the rest of the trio but for that information the purchaser must look elsewhere. I think we have to blame Miles Davis for decreeing that explanatory sleeve-notes were not necessary. Ridiculous!                          **AM**

# Steve Swallow                                                               1940

**Real Book** Swallow (b); **Tom Harrell** (t, flh); **Joe Lovano** (ts); **Mulgrew Miller** (p); **Jack DeJohnette** (d). Watt Ⓕ XTRAWATT7 (521 637-2) (50 minutes). Recorded 1993.
                                                                            ⑧ ❿

Steve Swallow himself describes this album as an attempt to capture the feeling he associates with the original *Real Book*, "of friends meetings to leaf through the book and work out a few tunes to see where they lead." That there were no rehearsals, and few takes needed, is a tribute both to the professionalism of the band assembled and to the limpid clarity of the tunes – all by Swallow – they were asked to play. They range from bustling themes with bright horn arrangements through to bluesy or Latin-tinged informal readings from Swallow's state-of-the-art studio band. The front-line soloists are in particularly good form; Joe Lovano plays with his customary cultured approach, all bustling querulousness laced with occasional moments of fluting tenderness; Tom Harrell is almost unrivalled in contemporary jazz for purity of tone, precision of intonation and sheer flair and sure-footedness. The rhythm section with Swallow and Mulgrew Miller discreetly alternates between crisp comping and fluent, sparkling solos with unruffled aplomb. Jack DeJohnette is constantly active, alive to every rhythmic nuance. A first-class album by a supremely accomplished band. **CP**

## Gabor Szabo
1936-82

New review

**The Sorcerer** Szabo (g); **Jimmy Stewart** (g); **Louis Kabok** (b); **Marty Morrell** (d); **Hal Gordon** (perc). Impulse! ⓜ IMP12112 (59 minutes). Recorded 1967.

⑤ ❼

This album, recorded live at San Francisco's Jazz Workshop, shows us the best of Szabo's small talent. The guitarist left Hungary in the wake of the Russian invasion of 1956, when the Revolution was crushed. After studying at Berklee he followed a string of idiosyncratic guitarists into the Chico Hamilton Quintet, joining in 1962 and there meeting Charles Lloyd, then operating as the band's arranger and chief composer. Szabo stayed with Hamilton for three years, by which time his peculiar drone-like style and gipsy-like inflections gave him a following which led to his making records under his own name. These proved popular enough for him to launch a solo career and, by the time of this record, he was a consistent presence as performer and recording artist. Around the time of this record Szabo claimed in an interview that "jazz is dead", and that he was more interested in what was going on in other areas of popular music. Within a year or so of **The Sorcerer** Szabo had virtually abandoned any real jazz content in his music, toying with rock and so-called psychedelic elements in an attempt to forge a commercially successful and "contemporary" personality for himself (he was often hooked up with Gary McFarland in these pursuits). Long before his death his ties with the jazz community had withered. **The Sorcerer** (this CD has three extra tracks originally released on **More Sorcery**, a half-live half-studio set of oddments released to cash in on the Szabo vogue of the time) at least has the advantage of presenting him with his working band, improvising manfully and not relying on someone else's charts to fill in the time between his inimitable melodic statements. The band coalesces quite successfully and from time to time the music escapes its contemporary references to appeal to a less time-bound audience. Today's, for example. It could be you, if you're in the mood and especially if you're off down the club for an intellectual rave session with your mates. **KS**

## Lew Tabackin
1940

**What a Little Moonlight Can Do** Tabackin (ts, f, af); **Benny Green** (p); **Peter Washington** (b); **Lewis Nash** (d). Concord Ⓕ CCD4617 (58 minutes). Recorded 1994.

⑧ ❽

Lew Tabackin is a man with considerable big-band and studio experience but his tenor and flute are equally at home in the jazz combo. An inmate of various orchestras over the years, he has in more recent times worked with smaller units. An early influence was Sonny Rollins but (as this CD demonstrates) he now has a style of his own. *Love Letters* and the title track admit to the inspiration but show that Tabackin is creatively driven at any tempo. *Easy Living* squeezes choice tenor saxophone oratory between a challenging cadenza and a dashing coda to confirm his sense of formal presentation, while on *Poinciana* he transforms a straight theme statement into pure jazz with only a modicum of phrase re-emphasis and contour adjustment. *The Dream's on Me* gently simmers with a trace of Ben Websterish romance, whereas *Dig*, cooked from an old style bebop recipe, shows how effortlessly he lends fluency to an angular line. The high standard of his writing is confirmed by *Broken Dreams* and he endorses that theme's inherent quality by developing its melody line into an equally coherent solo. He fully merits the excellent rhythmic support he enjoys here and he remains a player with few rivals in his chosen area of jazz. **BMcR**

## Jamaaladeen Tacuma
1956

**Live in Köln** Tacuma (b); **Walter Wierbos** (tb); **Paul Van Kemenade** (as); **Jan Kuiper** (g); **Cornell Rochester** (d). Timeless Ⓕ CDSJP421 (70 minutes). Recorded 1993.

⑤ ❽

Tacuma fits comfortably into absolutely no stylistic homestead. He sang doo-wop in his youth, played with organ trios and happily embraced soul bands. In 1975, he went harmolodic with Ornette Coleman and his own first album reflected that influence. His relationship with Coleman's Prime Time was an on-off affair but he looked in a similar musical direction with the likes of Blood Ulmer. He is probably most at home in a heavy funk environment but he can be relied upon to confuse the issue by taking propulsive and inventive solos.

On this CD he is joined by Podium 3 and Rochester, a drummer who infallibly makes rock verticalities swing. As *Mo's Mood* emphasizes, the Dutch three are essentially jazzmen but they do know the harmolodic route and, with Tacuma to drive them along, there is a potent alchemy. The funk element puts the power into the other titles but jazz is never neglected and the bassist shows his own solo agility most especially on *Mr Monk*. He does not once spurn his rhythm section responsibilities, however, and it is doubtful if Podium 3 has ever been more rhythmically focused. Tacuma dance-band dates have always remained important to him but, for every one of them, there is probably a more challenging one such as this. **BMcR**

# Masayuki Takayanagi

1932-91

**New review**

**Call in Question** Takayanagi (g); **Mototeru Takagi** (reeds); **Motoharu Yoshizawa** (b); **Yoshisaburo Toyozumi** (d). PSF Records Ⓕ PSFD41 (54 minutes). Recorded 1970.

⑦ ❼

In one important detail, the life of 'JoJo' Takayanagi had a parallel in the career of fellow guitarist Derek Bailey. Both began as orthodox instrumentalists and 'transgressed' into the area of free music. Takayanagi made his professional début at 19 and gained a reputation as an accomplished session man, able to handle any score in any style. Like Bailey, however, he became dissatisfied with his musical lot and, in 1965, abandoned all other groups in order to concentrate on his own music. Four years later, he reformed his own group along freer lines, came to regard their work as his *raison d'être* and his session work as an unwelcome necessity. His new style was very much his own and, as this CD demonstrates, no easy phrase fell to his fingers. He uses chains, bows and metal bars as plectrum substitutes and produces sheets of sound marked out with their own punctuation. It is a style that shows him as a guitar samurai and highlights his control of feedback and volume as part of an improvisational process. It certainly sees Toyozumi's contribution as significant in introducing vertical resistance to an essentially linear freedom. Takayanagi's social persona did leave much to be desired and his outspoken manner alienated many former supporters in Japan. He died just short of 60 and left behind a little-known body of ferocious work that posterity may well judge to be equal to, and different from, guitar mavericks Bailey, Fred Frith, Sonny Sharrock and Blood Ulmer. **BMcR**

# Aki Takase

**Shima Shoka** Takase (p). Enja Ⓕ 6062-2 (60 minutes). Recorded 1990.

⑦ ❽

Aki Takase has recorded a handful of discs in intimate settings – including with string quartet, duos with vocalist Maria João and saxophonist David Murray. Yet the best showcase for her impressive talents is solo, where she exhibits a bright, percussive touch and fluid ideas. She also has good taste in repertoire (Ellington, Mingus, Rollins, Coltrane and Carla Bley) to which she brings surprisingly fresh viewpoints. For example, her harmonic approach to Duke's *Rockin' in Rhythm*, a lively stride romp, may be that of a Modernist, but even the staunchest trad fan would have to admire her strong left hand. Elsewhere she attaches an elegiac prelude to *Goodbye Porkpie Hat* and turns *Giant Steps* into an episodic *tour de force*. Most expressive is her interpretation of Carla Bley's rhapsodic homage to actress and film director *Ida Lupino*, where Takase first plants a thicket of moody, noirish chords, then proceeds on a long chromatic journey, drifting in and out of relation to the theme. Her own compositions have not quite the same bite or substance, and none of them blossoms with the delicacy of detail and adept handling of transparent themes she brings to husband Alex von Schlippenbach's *Point*. Takase's thoughtfulness and willingness to take a risk place her among a select few. **AL**

# Horace Tapscott

1934

**New review**

**Aiee! The Phantom** Tapscott (p); **Marcus Belgrave** (t); **Abraham Burton** (as); **Reggie Workman** (b); **Andrew Cyrille** (d). Arabesque Jazz Ⓕ AJ0119 (59 minutes). Recorded 1995.

⑧ ❽

Tapscott has been a leading figure in the West Coast jazz community for the last 35 years. After early stints with Gerald Wilson and Lionel Hampton, he settled in Los Angeles and in 1961 co-founded the Underground Musicians Association, later renamed the Union of God's Musicians and Artists Ascension (UGMAA), a self-help organization that preceded Chicago's AACM. Also in 1961 he started a local big band, the Pan Afrikan Peoples Arkestra, still going strong today. Unfortunately, little of Tapscott's music has appeared on vinyl or CD, though notable exceptions include a handful of fine solo LPs for the tiny Nimbus label and two live Hat Hut CDs with John Carter. **Aiee! The Phantom** is a valuable chance to hear not only Tapscott but the similarly under-recorded Detroit veteran Marcus Belgrave, a trumpeter of dark-fire tone and rhythmic grace. Tapscott's piano reflects his admiration for Andrew Hill; he's terse, lyrical and dramatic by turns, rapture and eruption spaced by brooding ostinatos. His compositions are marked by elegant tunes and odd metres; witness the skewed charm of *Drunken Mary/Mary on Sunday*. Or the haunting, sinuous figures that make the title track the most seductive item on this excellent set. **GL**

# Buddy Tate

**New review**

**Groovin' with Tate** Tate (ts, cl); **Pat Jenkins** (t); **Eli Robinson** (tb); **Ben Richardson** (as, bs, cl); **Sadik Hakim, Ronnell Bright** (p); **Wally Richardson** (g); **Wendell Marshall, George Tucker** (b); **Osie Johnson, Roy Brooks** (d). Prestige Ⓜ 24152-2 (78 minutes). Recorded 1959-61.

⑧ ❽

The generous playing time of this CD is made up by jazz from two LPs and it offers Tate playing at the peak of what could be called his second coming. The first, as an extrovert tenor saxophonist in the territory bands of Terrence Holder, Andy Kirk and Nat Towles, reached fruition when he replaced Herschel Evans in the Count Basie Orchestra in 1939. Since then he has carried the mainstream banner throughout the world, with the early sixties a particularly fruitful period. On **Groovin' with Tate** he is supported by second division players who have raised their game and Robinson, Hakim and Bright all acquit themselves with distinction. Tate's own pedigree is obvious. *Me 'n' You* has five trenchant blues choruses, while *Blues for Trix* shows that his approach to the 12-bar can be more softly contoured. The loping gait of *Blow Low* contrasts with the latent insistence of *Makin' Whoopee* and his mischievous clarinet tells its own *sotto voce* story as required. His work in the seventies and eighties was rarely without interest and releases such as the 1981 **Ballad Artistry** (Sackville) were impressive. Nevertheless his sidemen did not always match his quality and, although there were hardly glaring deficiencies, few sessions matched the conviction found on **Groovin' with Tate**.          **BMcR**

# Art Tatum

**Classic Early Solos (1934-7)** Tatum (p). MCA/Decca Ⓜ GRP16072 (58 minutes). Recorded 1934-7.

⑧ ❻

When Tatum was heard by travelling musicians in his native Ohio, and when he arrived in New York backing Adelaide Hall, he seemed too good to be true. His concentration on musical sound focused by his extremely restricted vision, he had the kind of technical command of an instrument that was unheard of until Parker and Coltrane, both of whom listened to him avidly.

In addition, he had seemingly absorbed everything he needed from the showy stride piano of Johnson and Waller and the rhythmic independence of Hines, as these 1934 tracks demonstrate (only the last four are from 1937). Less noticed immediately except by other musicians, a harmonic sophistication equal to Ellington's was lurking in the background, and what contemporaries made of touches such as the coda to the first *After You've Gone* or the whole-tone passages in the second *Liza* is anyone's guess.

Remastering uses the NoNOISE system, now largely abandoned in favour of CEDAR, and while the piano sound is reasonably consistent, it is quite thin. In addition, several items (not just the few alternate takes) have continuous surface sound, from which the piano is a fortunate distraction. **BP**

**The Complete Capitol Recordings, Volumes 1 and 2** Tatum (p); **Everett Barksdale** (g); **Slam Stewart** (b). Capitol Ⓜ CDP7 92866/7-2 (two discs: 84 minutes). Recorded 1949-52.

✔          ⑩ ❹

Art Tatum signed for Capitol Records in 1949 and from then until 1952 produced the titles to be heard on these two CDs. All were recorded for 78rpm issues and as a result were restricted to little more than three minutes. Despite this, Tatum played at his brilliant best, treating each parent melody to a breathtaking improvisational face-lift. He imbued the rather trite *Dardanella* with stature, turned Rubinstein's *Melody In F* into a swing classic and made any other piano treatment of *Someone to Watch over Me* seem like a travesty. Every aspect of the jazz piano art is on view: there is the ineluctable power of his striding left hand, the brilliantly articulated treble runs and, above all else, the architectural perfection of his re-designs. His command of the instrument is awesome and the listener becomes increasingly aware of a harmonic sophistication matched by an unpredictable rhythmic audacity. Despite the time constraints and the complexity of improvisations, many of these Capitol versions became blueprints for all subsequent Tatum performances of these tunes.          **BMcR**

**The Complete Pablo Solo Masterpieces** Tatum (p). Pablo Ⓜ 7PACD4404-2 (seven discs: 503 minutes ). Recorded 1953-6.

✔          ⑩ ❻

Thanks to impresario Norman Granz, Art Tatum recorded more music in the last three years of his life than in the previous 21. The solo titles, which appeared originally as 13 LPs, are the product of four marathon record sessions at which Art was given complete freedom in terms of choice of material, tempos, lengths of performances, etc. It was Granz's idea to place as much of Tatum's artistry on record before it was too late. This package comprises 119 of the 121 tracks previously issued on the LPs, omitting *Blues in My Heart* and *I Gotta Right to Sing the Blues* but adding the four solo performances from Art's Hollywood Bowl appearance less than three months before his death. (Note: this applies to the copy under review, but a later edition of the **Solo Masterpieces**, with the same catalogue number, contains all 121 solos and the four Hollywood Bowl titles. The reader is advised to check carefully before buying.) It goes without saying that this is an important body of recorded work in which Tatum worked his way through established material such as *Elegie, Tea for Two, Sweet Lorraine* etc. but the set also includes no less than 20 songs which Art never recorded at any other time, tunes such as *The Way You Look Tonight, You're Blasé, I've Got a Crush on You* and *There's a Small Hotel.* Unhampered by other musicians, Art is allowed to change key, tempo and the direction of his extemporizations at will, for it was as a solo performer that he really excelled. The sheer volume of his output here may have a daunting effect on listeners who have not immersed themselves in this man's genius, but the advice is to persevere; you will not hear a finer, more complete and wholly talented jazz pianist than Art Tatum. The remastering, by Danny Kopelson, has resulted in the best sound yet; the Pablo LPs were disappointing and not as good as the old British Columbia Clef albums. There is occasional tape hiss, but the full resonance of the instrument has been preserved.                                                    **AM**

---

**New review**

**The Complete Pablo Group Masterpieces**  Tatum (p); **Buddy DeFranco** (cl); **Benny Carter** (as); **Ben Webster** (ts); **Harry Edison, Roy Eldridge** (tm); **Barney Kessel** (g); **Lionel Hampton** (vb); **Red Callender, John Simmons** (b); **Louis Bellson, Bill Douglass, Jo Jones, Buddy Rich, Alvin Stoller** (d). Pablo Ⓜ 6PACD4401-2 (six discs: 444 minutes). Recorded 1954-6

✅                                                                                          ⑧ ⑧

Though initially released in the seventies as a series of nine LPs, and then in the eighties as a series of eight separate CDs, here we get the complete run of material produced by impresario Norman Granz now compressed into a handsome six-disc boxed set issued under the rubric, **Group Masterpieces**. In the course of its fascinating seven hours and 44 minutes we have an opportunity to re-hear the great virtuoso in tandem with fellow legends Benny Carter, Buddy DeFranco, Harry Edison, Roy Eldridge, Lionel Hampton and Ben Webster. Added to the lofty yet idiosyncratic summits is an hour of previously unreleased material and an informative booklet with complete discographical information, sumptuous photos, and Benny Green's passionate and insightful essay.

In Pablo's impressive **Solo Masterpieces** (reviewed above), also from the early fifties, Tatum's star is displayed in all its uninhibited glory. In the **Group Masterpieces**, the pianist's largely unbridled virtuosity keeps bumping up against the equally loquacious artistry of his peers. Given that tension, collision is probably a more apt way of describing these dates than collaboration. Still, and in spite of Tatum's penchant for filling in each and every space and therefore dictating each track's harmonic contours, there is a curiously compelling audacity at work. Wisely, Tatum's 'collaborators', even the hyperkinetic Hampton, opted for an approach cleaving close to the melody, thus allowing the pianist's rococo filigrees to shine instead of smash. In this climate, of course, some partners were more naturally able to respond to Tatum's presence, and the Webster and Carter sides have long been praised for their extraordinary balance between the torrent of Tatum and the eloquent voice of the soloist. Among the other wondrous exoticisms are the quartets featuring Roy Eldridge or Buddy DeFranco.                              **CB**

# Billy Taylor                                                                                        1921

**My Fair Lady Loves Jazz**  Taylor (p); **Earl May** (b); **Ed Thigpen** (d); **Ernie Royal** (t); **Don Elliott** (t, mph); **Jimmy Cleveland** (tb); **Jimmy Buffington** (frh); **Don Butterfield, Jay McAllister** (bb); **Anthony Artega** (as, ts); **Charles Fowlkes, Gerry Mulligan** (bs). Impulse! Ⓜ GRP11412 (34 minutes). Recorded 1957.

                                                                                                 ⑥ ⑧

For some years house-pianist at Birdland, Taylor was something of a musical chameleon. He was able to sound convincing with swing-era men and boppers alike and he became a player of immense experience. The trio is perhaps his happiest hunting ground but this CD shows that, with the aid of arranger Quincy Jones, he could expand the scope of the three-man unit. This is not a trio with 'bolt-on' horn parts; Jones has integrated them into arrangements that have them as both rhythm section and as a unit within the band. Taylor's cultured piano, with the occasional nod toward George Shearing, is well displayed. His ideas on *Show Me* and *Street Where You Live* are delivered with studied care; the emphasis is on paraphrasing rather than tune dismantling and he does all with a light, easy swing. His strength as a bandsman is shown by his orthodox support for the soloist on most titles but almost more by his adroit linking parts of *Church on Time*. His style has changed little since these 1957 sides. He is now an eminent educator but there is something about his somewhat sanitized style that is as valid today as it was in the Cool era.                                        **BMcR**

# Cecil Taylor                                                                                        1929

**Jumpin' Punkins**  Taylor (p); **Clark Terry** (t); **Roswell Rudd** (tb); **Archie Shepp** (ts); **Steve Lacy** (ss); **Charles Davis** (bs); **Buell Neidinger** (b); **Billy Higgins** (d); **Dennis Charles** (d). Candid Ⓜ CD9013 (34 minutes). Recorded 1961.

✅                                                                                          ⑧ ⑦

The lack of recording opportunities was the bane of Taylor's early musical life (he would make up for it later). Between the time of his first recording in 1955 and the mini series he made for Candid in 1960, he fronted only three studio dates. The well-known Contemporary session **Looking Ahead** introduced Taylor to the international jazz world, but the 'nuts and bolts' of his style are clearer on this CD. *O.P.* shows him trading in pure improvisation, his roaring tone clusters pouring over the urgent punctuation of his left hand while totally ignoring the syntactical rules of earlier jazz forms. The remaining three titles are less iconoclastic and, by their very nature, approach the music in a different manner. The trio, joined by Shepp on *I Forgot*, takes a similarly free route but the reflective mood allows ideas to breathe, illustrating Taylor's structural line of musical thought. The principle is further developed on the Ellington themes as his irreverent piano interjections transform the strengths of the originals into a Taylor-controlled world which is so close as to be an extension of the Thelonious Monk music ethic. **BMcR**

---

**Unit Structures** Taylor (p); **Eddie Gale Stevens** (t); **Jimmy Lyons** (as); **Ken McIntyre** (as, ob, bcl); **Henry Grimes**, **Alan Silva** (b); **Andrew Cyrille** (d). Blue Note Ⓜ CDP7 84237-2 (57 minutes). Recorded 1966.

✅      ⑩ ⑧

For the first 20 years of his professional life, Taylor was a sparsely-recorded artist. This album and its Blue Note stablemate **Conquistador!** (see below) fall roughly in the middle of that period, and for many years it was possible to see them as the culmination of his art. Today, close on 30 years further down the line, the perspective has shifted, and **Unit Structures**, in particular, seems both a summation of all that has gone before in Taylor's career and the first definitive statement of a stylistic position which the pianist/composer has never completely abandoned since.

There are four compositions here, played by a band made up mostly of old sweats, with Stevens and McIntyre being the relative newcomers. *Steps* is a type of work to be found on many a Taylor album, a short opening statement which sets the rhythmic and harmonic patterns to be explored, then every man for himself. *Enter, Evening* is something quite different, and harks back to some of the more formally laid-out compositions Taylor recorded in 1961 on **Into the Hot**. It moves through several phases and at points arrives at a hushed poignancy all the more moving for being so rare in the pianist's music. Bassist Silva is paticularly impressive. **Unit Structures** combines elements of both procedures, having a firm episodic structure which helps to maintain the impression of forward movement in the work and the solos. The final track, *Tales (8 whisps)*, is almost entirely a solo piano piece (the basses and drums enter for a couple of the whisps), and in some ways is the most remarkable performance on the record. Clearly much of it is composed, with Taylor moving between written sections and improvisation at will, but the music is so tightly knit, the themes so cleverly developed and transformed, and the whole performance conceived on such a dense and cryptic level that it repays intense study as well as an immediate emotional reaction. Taylor has often approached but never attained such pregnant concision again. **KS**

---

**Conquistador!** **Taylor** (p); **Bill Dixon** (t); **Jimmy Lyons** (as); **Henry Grimes**, **Alan Silva** (b); **Andrew Cyrille** (d). Blue Note Ⓜ CDP7 84260-2 (55 minutes). Recorded 1966.

✅      ⑩ ⑧

Featuring three extended performances – the stirring *Conquistador!* and two takes (one a CD bonus track) of the slower and more fitful *With (Exit)* – this followed **Unit Structures** and was a transitional album for Taylor, who hindsight suggests was as much influenced by the free jazz of this period as he was influential upon it. The pianist is cracking his containers here; there is little of the mathematical calculation one senses even in his seemingly open-ended Cafe Montmartre recordings with Lyons and Sunny Murray. At the same time, Taylor's performances hadn't yet taken on the air of ritual, or become endurance contests between him and his audiences. One senses him looking for, and finding, organic form in these three performances, and the line between composition and improvisation is bracingly thin on all of them. *Conquistador!*, in particular, with its late-emerging and mordant central theme, pinpoints an irony central to Taylor's music of this period. Although thought of as being the antithesis of hard bop, this music furthers one of hard bop's pet causes in granting the rhythm section parity with the horns. Although there are horn 'solos' here, most of these play out more dialogues, due to Taylor's strategy of testing Dixon and Lyons rather than 'accompanying' them in the conventional sense. Many bands of this period experimented with the use of two bassists, and not always successfully. In the case of Grimes and Silva, the concept works because each adheres to his well-defined role: Silva is the floater and Grimes the one who digs in and probes the chords (or the absence of them). Lyons is as penetrating as always and Cyrille again shows that he has few equals in supplying an insistent pulse without shifting into predictable metre. But the man who makes the biggest difference here is Dixon. An important if insufficiently recognized figure in his own right, he takes his time and refuses to be rushed, even with Taylor eddying around him. His lyricism wounds, as does Taylor's. **FD**

---

**For Olim** Taylor (p). Soul Note Ⓕ SN121150-2 (45 minutes). Recorded 1986.

     ⑩ ⑨

Cecil Taylor's solo piano work did not appear on record until the mid seventies. Since then, however, solo albums have been released at regular intervals, with **Indent, Silent Tongues, Garden** and **Erzulie Maketh Scent** among the recitals that explore this particular facet of his art.

Listeners deterred by the intensity and textural density of Taylor's group performances may find his solo music less daunting, although the phenomenal technique can seem even more awesome heard in its naked glory. In fact the speed, power and relentless energy of Taylor's playing long disguised his music's formal principles. These were analyzed, however, in an important 1988 essay by Ekkehard Jost, *Instant Composing as Body Language*. Jost identifies both recurring elements in Taylor's solo music – *staccato* runs, clusters, brief bass figures, parallel chords – and its main structural procedures, such as call-and-response, layering and motivic development. He also makes the point that for all its torrential attack, Taylor's music is always precisely articulated and often shows great delicacy of touch.

All of these qualities are evident on **For Olim**, recorded live at Berlin's annual Free Music Workshop and probably the most diverse of Taylor's solo recordings. Its atypical mixture of one long track and several short pieces means there is a rich variety of moods, textures, forms. *Mirror and Water Gazing* and *The Question* are darkly ruminative; *Glossalalia – part four* rocks like a train; *For the Rabbit* is a collage of spectacular right-hand runs and crashing bass clusters. The long *Olim* – "an Aztec hieroglyph meaning movement, motion, earthquake" – exemplifies the breadth of Taylor's resources.                                                                                      **GL**

---

**New review**

**The Hearth** Taylor (p); **Tristan Honsinger** (vc); **Evan Parker** (ts). FMP Ⓕ 11 (62 minutes). Recorded 1988.

⑩ ❽

After three decades of unrelenting creativity, Cecil Taylor's reputation seems set in granite. Descriptions of his music most frequently derive from metaphors for forces of nature – torrents of notes, a whirlwind of rhythms, volcanic explosions of energy. And we've all heard countless times where the urgency of Taylor's playing overwhelms everything in its path. That's precisely why this live performance stands out from the great mass of Taylor recordings. Instead of the free jazz catharsis one might have expected, this hour-long spontaneous composition exploits chamber music textures, acute dynamics, and mosaic-like thematic references. The results are stunning. Honsinger and Parker set the tone with carefully dovetailed invention, and when Taylor enters he matches their rhythmic orientation and area of pitch investigation. As their playing slowly expands outward into abstract counterpoint they retain complementary phrasing, passing through shifting tonal centres, rhythmic consensus, phrase length and accentuation. The fragile thread that binds them together is never broken. Parker's tenor playing repays its debt to Sonny Rollins here, sustaining great labyrinths of melody with elongated curlicues and jagged phrase twists. When he drops out, Honsinger and Taylor develop sparse, captivating interludes. There is no percussive hammering or cascades of notes from Taylor; instead, referring back to the precedents of his earliest recordings, his concise, short motifs preserve the tight, tense momentum of the ongoing thematic line and imply myriad directions for it to follow. With such inventive, concentrated, generous playing from all three participants, **The Hearth** is, following Taylor's punning titles, music of both the heart and the earth, in equal measure.   **AL**

# Eva Taylor
1895-1977

---

**New review**

**In Chronological Order, Volume 1** Taylor (v); **Johnny Dunn, Tom Morris** (c); **Charlie Irvis, John Mayfield** (tb); **Garvin Bushell, Clarence Robinson, Ernest Elliott, Sidney Bechet** (cl); **Clarence Williams** (p); **Buddy Christian** (bj). Document Ⓕ DOCD5408 (72 minutes). Recorded 1922-3.

⑤ ❺

Born Irene Gibson in St Louis, Taylor was a genuine child prodigy. She was a three-year-old 'Pick' with Josephine Gassman and her Pickaninnies and, before the age of 11, had toured world-wide. She married pianist Clarence Williams in 1921 and enjoyed an extensive recording career that spanned from 1922 to shortly before her death in 1977. At the height of her career, in the twenties, she enjoyed considerable commercial success. Her records, mainly with husband Williams, sold well and she was a first-class cabaret singer. Her acute sense of pitch and her warm contralto voice made her highly adaptable, capable of essaying all types of jazz and blues material and perfectly equipped for the promotional work that she also undertook in department and music stores. Perhaps because of her precise diction, early recordings such as *Blue Moon* or *You Can Have My Man* boast slender jazz virtues. More obviously, jazz material like *Sister Kate, Da Da Strain* and *Farewell Blues* find her more flexible in timing and showing more obvious rapport with accompanying musicians. Williams's own solo backings were occasionally a trace perfunctory, but in their better moments they made a formidable partnership. The jazz credentials of the other backing groups are not in question, even if their identities are. The presence of Dunn is open to question but the preaching cornet work of Morris, the slurringly emotional trombone by Irvis and briefly exposed clarinet by Bechet (on two titles) all put an indelible jazz stamp on the proceedings.   **BMcR**

# John Taylor
1942

---

**Ambleside Days** Taylor (p); **John Surman** (ss, bs, cl, bcl). Ah Um Ⓕ 013 (46 minutes). Recorded 1992.

⑧ ❽

Like John Surman's highly successful **Road To St Ives** and Ian Carr's **Old Heartland**, John Taylor's **Ambleside Days** is a selection of connected pieces inspired by countryside familiar from childhood. All Taylor's pianistic and compositional strengths are represented; an ability to sustain vigorously rhythmic tempos without sacrificing either fluency or lyricism; a sensitivity and delicacy of touch, never lapsing into sentimentality; an imaginative improvisational skill which enables him to sustain ideas without contrivance over lines of unusual length. Surman is the perfect partner; not only does he have a special rapport with Taylor, having played with him for nearly three decades – since the 1964 Surman octet – but he has also amassed considerable experience playing this sort of intensely personal, impressionistic music on his series of ECM solo albums. Unsurprisingly, given these ingredients, **Ambleside Days** is a memorable album, gentle and beguiling, airy, tuneful and hauntingly atmospheric. Taylor's virtuosity and Surman's robustness – and the range of sound available from his selection of reeds – militate entirely successfully against any suggestion that the music could be merely a pretty soundtrack to Lake District scenery, and the recording confirms both men's position in the very front rank of UK jazz players.                                                                         **CP**

## Martin Taylor                                                                                                    1956

**Don't Fret** Taylor (g); **David Newton** (p, syn); **Dave Green** (b); **Allan Ganley** (d). Linn Ⓟ AKD014
(48 minutes). Recorded 1990.

⑧ ❽

Equally effective as a solo performer or fronting a small group, and celebrated for his regular collaborations with Stephane Grappelli, Martin Taylor is the UK's most accomplished mainstream guitarist. **Don't Fret** is the perfect showcase for his many gifts; a peerless, pure tone, producing a mellow, warm but always penetrative sound; an apparently unquenchable flow of improvisational ideas, which imparts a relaxed informality (not unlike Grappelli's) to everything he plays; a discreetly propulsive power which imbues all his music with a gentle but powerful swing. All these gifts are set off here by the Rolls-Royce of UK rhythm sections; bassist Dave Green is justly ubiquitous on the British jazz scene, demonstrating his assured technical prowess with everyone from Stan Tracey to Humphrey Lyttelton; Allan Ganley is his drumming equivalent, winner of mainstream awards year after year. David Newton too is an excellent foil, luminous yet cogent. Indeed, if **Don't Fret** has a fault, it is in the undemanding nature of its standard material; the two originals on the album, especially Taylor's own title track, stretch the participants more than the war-horses by the likes of Cole Porter and Oscar Pettiford, and are high points of an excellent mainstream album.                              **CP**

## John Tchicai                                                                                                     1936

**Timo's Message** Tchicai (as, ts); **Thomas Dürst**, **Christian Kuntner** (b); **Timo Fleig** (d, perc).
Black Saint Ⓟ 20094-2 (42 minutes). Recorded 1984.

⑦ ❽

Born in Copenhagen to a Danish mother and a Congolese father, after meeting Bill Dixon and Archie Shepp in Warsaw in 1962 John Tchicai moved to the US and became a leading figure in the avant-garde jazz of the mid sixties. He recorded with both the New York Contemporary Five and the New York Art Quartet and also played on John Coltrane's **Ascension**. On returning to Europe, Tchicai was less in the international limelight, concentrating for a considerable time on teaching, but continued to record through the seventies and eighties, notably with Johnny Dyani and Pierre Dørge. **Timo's Message** is the only album he made with a young Swiss group whose drummer, Timo Fleig, died before the record was released. **Timo's Message** finds Tchicai switching from alto to tenor saxophone. He plays the latter on the disc's six quartet tracks but retains his alto for three brief solo improvisations (inspired by the surrealist painter Yves Tanguy) that are heavily indebted to AACM saxophonists such as Anthony Braxton and Roscoe Mitchell. The quartet tracks are more striking, with the tenor's gravitas lending new authority and interest to Tchicai's agile phrasing. The wide range of material includes Marilyn Mazur's funky *Frisk Baglaens*, the tersely lyrical *Stella by Starlight* and a dark, grieving tribute to Albert Ayler on *Mothers*.            **GL**

## Jack Teagarden                                                                                                1905-64

**The Indispensable Jack Teagarden** Teagarden (tb, v); featuring: **Leonard Davis**, **Charlie Teagarden**, **Max Kaminsky**, **Billy Butterfield** (t); **Benny Goodman**, **Peanuts Hucko** (cl); **Happy Caldwell**, **Bud Freeman** (ts); **Joe Sullivan**, **Roy Bargy**, **Gene Schroeder** (p); **Ramona Davies** (p,v); **Nappy Lamare** (g, v); **Eddie Lang** (g); **Eddie Condon** (bj); **Joe Venuti** (vn); **Art Miller** (b); **George Stafford**, **Ray Bauduc**, **George Wettling** (d); **Red McKenzie** (comb); **Gene Austin**, **Red McKenzie**, **Johnny Mercer**, **Ben Pollack**, **Charles Roberts** (v). RCA Jazz Tribune Ⓜ 89613-2 (two discs: 105 minutes). Recorded 1928-57.

⑥ ❻

Born not far from the Red River, raised in Texas and Oklahoma, Jack Teagarden is often called the first great white jazzman – a claim usually accompanied by testimony to his authentic trombone blues, which stem from early exposure to black music. But Teagarden brought his own roots to jazz, conspicuously in his singing; he never lost the offhand manner or lazy drawl of a cowpoke. Singing *I Cover the Waterfront* he sounds like he is sitting by the campfire. It is one of three late pieces here from 1957, but there are cowboy echoes even on a 1935 *Ain't Misbehavin'*. In jazz, where biography often has a mythological cast, Teagarden the singer and *legato* trombonist updated an American stock figure: the slow-drawling cowpuncher who nonchalantly does virtuoso rope tricks. Teagarden was among the first to show by example that jazz could cross-pollinate with almost any strain of ethnic music.

There are several blues in this anthology, culled from RCA's vaults, which mostly find Teagarden as sideman – with early employers Ben Pollack, Paul Whiteman and the Mound City Blue Blowers, and various permutations of the Condon/Freeman Chicagoans which sometimes include Jack's brother Charlie. The set's desultory nature matches the haphazard spirit of Teagarden's career; like some other great soloists, he was an indifferent leader. **KW**

---

**A Hundred Years from Today** Jack Teagarden (tb, v); Charlie Teagarden, Sterling Bose, Manny Klein, Shirley Clay (t); Benny Goodman, Pee Wee Russell, Rod Cless (cl); Frank Trumbauer (c-ms); Jimmy Dorsey (as); Bud Freeman, Art Karle, (ts); Adrian Rollini (bss); Joe Venuti (v); Casper Reardon (hp); Fats Waller (p, v); Joe Sullivan, Charlie LaVere, Terry Shand, Frank Froeba (p); Nappy Lamare, Dick McDonough (g); Artie Bernstein (b); Gene Krupa, Stan King (d). Conifer Ⓜ CDHD153 (74 minutes ). Recorded 1931-4.

⑧ ⑧

These classic tracks have Teagarden and his friends playing with the fire and spirit of comparative youth. They show clearly what a daunting example the Texan's playing must have been to younger trombonists of the period. Within the limited range of material he chose, Teagarden's melodic sense and timing were superb and his vocals and solos in this generous collection are as good as any that could have been collected.

The riotous collaborations with Fats Waller on *You Rascal You* and *That's What I Like About You* rank amongst the most infectiously cheerful jazz records on CD and there is always the chance that Bose, Charlie Teagarden or Goodman will pop up with a good solo when Jack is not holding the floor.

Tucked away amongst this well-chosen accumulation of Teagarden's best tracks is the charming *Junk Man*, an unusual feature for the harp of Casper Reardon, which also has good solos from the two Teagardens and Goodman. If, as seems likely, these recordings were originally intended for the mass market, then it says much for the state of pop music of the day. As so often, the crisp and clear transfers are the work of engineer John R.T. Davies.. **SV**

## Joe Temperley
1929

---

**Concerto for Joe** Temperley (bs); Steve Sidwell, Gerard Presencer (t); Eddie Severn (t, flh); Gordon Campbell, Nichol Thomson (tb); Peter King (as); Duncan Lamont (ts); Brian Lemon, Brian Kellock (p); Alec Dankworth, Dave Green (b); Martin Drew, Jack Parnell (d). Hep Ⓔ CD2062 (70 minutes). Recorded 1993/4.

⑥ ⑧

Born in Scotland, Temperley was playing with top-flight British leaders by the age of 20. He joined Humphrey Lyttelton's first mainstream band in 1958 and, on leaving it in 1965, settled in New York. There he established a reputation with Woody Herman, Buddy Rich and actually took Harry Carney's place in the Duke Ellington Orchestra.

Latterly he has been something of a festival traveller and this CD, recorded in Britain, offers two sides of the Temperley persona. The first, a programme of jazz standards with a well-knit, professional trio behind him; the second, as ensemble backbone, soloist and dedicatee in a suite played by an 11 piece. On the combo dates he shows that his baritone line flows as comfortably over Monk's angularities on *Hackensack*, Ellington's soft contours on *Snibor* or over a driving blues of his own. His ensemble presence is pronounced on *Concerto for Joe* and, although his improvisational skills have less room to flourish, his attention seems more focused and solos on *Slow for Joe* and *Sixes and Sevens* have much to say. The nineties Temperley is a consummate artist at home in the baritone chair of a big band or swinging lightly with his own combo. **BMcR**

## Tempo King

---

**1936/7** King (v); Marty Marsala (t); Joe Marsala (cl); Queenie Ada Rubin (p); Eddie Condon (g); Mort Stuhlmaker, George Yorke (b); Stan King (d). Timeless Ⓜ CBC1-002 (68 minutes) Recorded 1936/7.

⑦ ⑥

First things first: nobody seems to know or remember much about Tempo King. Such basic biographical facts as his real name seem to have eluded even the record company he made these old 78s for. Someone with a long memory recollects him as a thirties bandleader down in Florida, and- well, that's about it. So much for personal profiles. Whoever he was, he had enough clout to assemble an excellent studio band to make these sides, and a casual dip into any of the 23 titles on this collection will reveal his intentions. He is a Fats Waller imitator (even down to the vocal interjections), which is another strange twist, because Tempo King's entire output was made for RCA Victor's Bluebird label at a time when Waller himself was constantly in the studios for RCA Victor. Why have an imitation (who doesn't even play the piano and isn't particularly witty) when you've got the real thing? The clue is the personnel playing with him: they're all white, and it's just conceivable that RCA wanted to create a white version of Waller.

Whatever their intentions, the true interest in these sides today is not Tempo King but the well-recorded group supporting him. They have a fierce and natural swing (the equally obscure Queenie Ada Rubin is a very acceptable Waller substitute on piano and Condon, of course, is impeccable), with the two Marsala brothers playing biting section work and solos. It is fine small-group music, and if Lee Wiley or Mildred Bailey had been the vocalist, these would long ago have been pronounced classics of the genre. As it is, Tempo King landed on his feet when he fell in with this tidy group.                                                                                **KS**

## Jacky Terrasson                                                                   1966

**New review**
**Reach** Terrasson (p); **Ugonna Ukegwo** (b); **Leon Parker** (d). Blue Note Ⓔ CDP8 37570-2
(57 minutes). Recorded 1995.

⑧ ❽

Terrasson's 1994 début album (**Jacky Terrasson** – Blue Note CDP8 29351-2) was rightly hailed as a remarkable first effort by the Berlin-born French/American pianist. His second album is the assured work of a pianist confident in his direction and taking the daring risks possible from such a sure footing. **Reach** was recorded in a domestic setting with two overhead microphones, and just as that system of recording has affinities with Rudy Van Gelder's fifties Blue Note sessions, Terrasson's playing develops ideas rooted in the work of Bud Powell and Monk. The opening *I Should Care* has obvious affinities with Powell's versions of the song, but from the gentle Erroll Garner-ish swing of the first chorus to the breathtaking sweep of his subsequent choruses Terrasson extends the song in his own way, worrying phrases like a terrier, stabbing chords with his left hand and managing to pull everything together with runs that have all the smoothness of Tatum. Much as altoist Frank Morgan has revisited Charlie Parker's playing and turned it in a direction subtly different from the historic legacy of the last 40 years, Terrasson has taken the basis of bebop piano playing and developed a style that starts again from where Powell and Monk left off. His classical technique, formidable improvisatory imagination and lack of musical fear all make this one of the most assured and mature examples of jazz piano from anyone currently playing.                             **AS**

## Clark Terry                                                                      1920

**Color Changes** Terry (t, flh); **Jimmy Knepper** (tb); **Julius Watkins** (frh); **Yusef Lateef** (ts, f, ehn, ob); **Seldon Powell** (ts, f); **Tommy Flanagan**, **Budd Johnson** (p); **Joe Benjamin** (b); **Ed Shaughnessy** (d). Candid Ⓜ CD9009 (43 minutes). Recorded 1960.

⑧ ❽

At the time of this recording, Terry was regarded as a virtuoso trumpet player on the strength of his work with Duke Ellington. His earliest recordings under his own name, the best of which included sessions with Thelonious Monk and Johnny Griffin, tended to concentrate on athletic displays of bebop improvisation. As well as using a powerful and versatile array of soloists, this album is notable for the six finely-crafted arrangements by Bob Wilber, Yusef Lateef, Al Cohn and Budd Johnson. The result is an album in which the arrangers are given the upper hand. The depth and originality of the writing gives the set an unusual strength of character and guides the soloists into channels where they are able to solo with a freshness and enthusiasm absent from the less organized 'blowing sessions' so popular at the time. *Flutin' and Fluglin'* has an early example of Terry duetting with himself on trumpet and flügelhorn and, although some of the musicians are prompted to play above themselves, the outstanding trombonist Jimmy Knepper has a field day, and is heard at his best on Cohn's delicate arrangement of Terry's *La Rive Gauche*. The subtle use of flute and oboe in the ensembles recalls some of the best of Rod Levitt's writing for his octet. This remains Terry's masterpiece, but two quality CDs have been reissued of late: **The Happy Horns of Clark Terry** (Impulse!, 1964) and **Clark After Dark** (MPS), the latter featuring him in small and large group settings.                                                                        **SV**

## Frank Teschemacher                                                              1906-32

**Muggsy, Tesch and the Chicagoans** Teschemacher (cl, as); **Muggsy Spanier, Jimmy McPartland, Dick Fiege, Charley Altier, Red Nichols** (c); **Jack Reid, Miff Mole** (tb); **Charles Pierce** (as); **Bud Freeman, Ralph Rudder** (ts); **Maurie Bercov** (cl, as); **Mezz Mezzrow** (ts, cl);

**Rod Cless** (as); **Joe Sullivan**, **Dan Lipscomb** (p); **Jim Lanigan** (b, bb); **Johnny Mueller** (b); **Stuart Branch** (bj); **Eddie Condon** (bj, v); **Gene Krupa**, **Paul Kettler** (d); **Red McKenzie** (v). Village Ⓕ VILCD001-2 (60 minutes ). Recorded 1927/8.

✔️                                                                                                    ⑦ ❹

A member of the Austin High School gang in Chicago, Teschemacher played tenor, alto, violin and banjo as well as his beloved clarinet. He worked with the bands of Charlie Straight and Floyd Towne but came to the notice of jazz followers world-wide due to his involvement in the 1927 McKenzie/Condon Chicagoan recordings found on this CD. Teschemacher was an enigmatic figure; his ensemble playing often encroached on the trumpet's part, although the presence of a good tailgate trombonist like Mole returns him to a more orthodox role on *Windy City Stomp*. He was essentially an inspirational musician, capable of the stunning melodic inventiveness that made his fluent *Darktown Stutters Ball* solo a virtual test piece for subsequent performances. There were, however, also moments of pedestrian mediocrity and *Baby Won't You Please Come Home* has him at his most stiff and unyielding. Titles such as *Jazz Me Blues*, *I've Found a New Baby* and *Nobody's Sweetheart* display a mobility of purpose that runs in parallel with the uniquely agitated aspect of his playing. His consciously sour tone is ideal for his style and his use of dissonance adds colour to items such as *There'll Be Some Changes Made*. Although dead at 26, Teschemacher was a strong influence on early white clarinettists. **BMcR**

# Toots Thielemans                                                                                    1922

`New review`

**Jazz Masters 59** Thielemans (hca, elg, whistle); with personnel including: **George Shearing**, **Quincy Jones**, **Georges Arvanitas**, **Cees Schrama**, **Ruud Bos**, **Niels-Henning Ørsted Pedersen**, **Sivuca**, **Marc Johnson**, **Pierre Michelot**, **Mulgrew Miller** and **Shirley Horn**. Verve Ⓜ 535 271-2 (73 minutes). Recorded 1953-91.

                                                                                                      ⑧ ❾

Like his fellow Belgian Django Reinhardt, Toots Thielemans has introduced a particularly European romanticism into jazz. Reinhardt's contribution was a florid, rococo guitar style, but Thielemans has taken the Europeanization of jazz even further. His chromatic harmonica instantly evokes French musette music and Bohemian lifestyles, but he adds whistling and then introduces these sounds into a far wider variety of idioms than Django attempted. This compilation's 16 tracks feature Thielemans in almost every popular idiom of the past 50 years – swing (*Undecided* with Shearing's quintet) orchestral and big band (*Soldier in the Rain* and *Brown Ballad* with Quincy Jones, *Big Bossa* with Ruud Bos), bebop (*Tenor Madness* with NHØP and *C to G Jam Blues* with Mulgrew Miller), ballad (*The Peacocks* with Pierre Michelot), delta blues (*You're My Blues Machine*), r&b (*Hummin'* with Quincy Jones) and bossa nova (an excellent version of *Bluesette* with Quincy Jones). Thielemans's openness to idiom can be a two-edged sword, as the easy-listening schmaltz of *Nocturne* shows, but it's a small price to pay for a generally entertaining collection. The packaging is exemplary in the usual Verve way, and I spotted only one mistake in the discography – Toots plays harmonica, not guitar, on *You're My Blues Machine*. **MG**

# Big Charlie Thomas

`New review`

**Big Charlie Thomas** Thomas (c); with various personnel and bands, many under the direction of **Clarence Williams** (p, v) and including: **Thomas Morris** (c); **Jimmy Harrison**, **Charlie Irvis**, **Geechie Fields** (tb); **Buster Bailey**, **Happy Caldwell**, **Bennie Moten** (cl); **Bob Fuller**, **Ernest Elliott** (cl, as); **Mike Jackson**, **Fats Waller** (p); **Buddy Christian** (bj); **Eva Taylor**, **Margaret Johnson**, **Clarence Todd**, **Bessie Brown**, **Rosa Henderson**, **Joe Sims** (v). Timeless Historical Ⓕ CBC1030 (73 minutes). Recorded 1925-7.

                                                                                                      ⑦ ❼

Although this constitutes an entire disc dedicated to the brass player Charlie Thomas, even the producer of the album, John R.T. Davies, confesses defeat when it comes to any biographical details on the man, and even admits that as basic thing as his name is by no means fixed in stone, or anything else for that matter. Charlie Thomas is a name as re-constituted as the superior CD transfers Davies has effected, for it is deduced through Eva Taylor recalling some 50 years later that the cornettist was called Thomas-something, or maybe something-Thomas, and through Margaret Johnson at one point on *Come and Get Me Papa Before I Faint* exhorting her cornettist to "play that thing, Big Charlie". This serendipity, plus Davies's admonition in his booklet-notes for researchers to avoid hearing only what they want to hear on old records (mostly previously unidentified gems by the already-acknowledged greats), rather than admitting that many of these musicians remain not only unidentified and obscure, but nameless as well, gives much pause for thought. In the case of Charlie Thomas there is an identifiable sound, style and personality, clearly much taken with the young Louis Armstrong but also exhibiting defining traces of a more antique cornet tradition traceable to Keppard

and beyond, displaying shorter phrase lengths, a more fragile and rapid vibrato, a tidier, less expansive way of stating a melody and a cautious approach to obbligatos. Thomas is best at medium and slow-medium tempos, running out of both ideas and puff on racetrack-speed novelty numbers such as *The Skunk*, which also carries a lame vocal, probably by Williams. It is important to point out that on none of these sides is he a leader, acting normally as accompanist to a parade of mostly excellent blues singers, but his playing is unusually blessed in both technique and invention, the bands he plays within are mostly well drilled and never less than competent, and the sound quality is good enough to make the listening experience pleasurable rather than painful. All in all, a salutary historical lesson.    **KS**

## Gary Thomas                                            1961

**By Any Means Necessary**  Thomas (ts, f, syn); **Greg Osby** (as, syn); **Tim Murphy, Geri Allen** (p, syn); **John Scofield, Mick Goodrick** (g); **Anthony Cox** (b); **Dennis Chambers** (d); **Nana Vasconcelos** (perc). JMT Ⓔ 834 432-2 (55 minutes). Recorded 1989.

⑧ ❽

Gary Thomas made clear his distaste for funk licks in 1987, when he quit the Miles Davis band rather than play "pentatonic scales and big loud blues-scale things over funk grooves". Nevertheless, this record, presenting his band Seventh Quadrant at its peak, might be thought pretty funky: most tracks are punched along by the thundering backbeats of former Funkadelic juggernaut Dennis Chambers, most feature synthesizers, and John Scofield's *You're Under Arrest*, here more fully realized than on its first appearance on the Miles Davis album of the same name, boasts an unequivocally funky bass line. However, funky or not, Thomas's music with menaces is a million miles from Davis's candied readings of *The Perfect Way*, *Human Nature* and the like. As Davis became more diatonic, Thomas became more diabolical, using remorselessly atonal harmony, a complex rhythmic conception and Gothic synthesizer textures to create a chilling, apocalyptic soundscape. He rejects suggestions that his austere harmonic vocabulary is modelled on Coltrane, but it may be, indirectly, through his major influence Woody Shaw. There are excellent guest spots by Scofield and Goodrick, two guitarists much in sympathy with their host's stylistic objectives.    **MG**

## René Thomas                                           1927-75

**Guitar Genius**  Thomas (g); **Jacques Pelzer** (f); **Robert Jeanne** (ts); **Leo Flechet, Rein de Graaff** (p); **Henk Haverhoek, Benoit Quersin, Jean Lerusse** (b); **Eric Ineke, Jacques Thollot, Felix Simtaine** (d). Prestige Record Co Ltd Ⓜ 009 (69 minutes). Recorded 1964-74.

⑧ ❹

The title overstates the case, but Thomas was one fine guitarist. A Belgian who spent significant periods working in Paris, Montreal and New York, and who recorded with Chet Baker, Stan Getz and others, Thomas plays peek-a-boo with his ethnic roots on these seven tracks, drawn from four live gigs with various small bands. Thomas's basic approach is post-Charlie Christian linear swing, but every so often (as on *All the Things You Are* and *Just Friends*) he will end a thought with stinging, vibrato-laden flurries or chords that echo his countryman and early idol Django Reinhardt. Perhaps due to Django's influence, Thomas's tone has more edge and bite than that of the many jazz guitarists who keep their treble controls turned down low. Thomas is not the only soloist, but it is his show; the sidemen – like Pelzer, whose thin-sounding flute dominates *Deep Purple* – are not always up to his level. An exception is drummer Ineke, who swings *All the Things You Are* with a minimum of effort, sometimes cantering quietly on rims.

Also noteworthy is Thomas's 1960 New York date **Guitar Groove** (on the American Prestige OJC label, no relation to this English one). But **Guitar Genius** offers more generous helpings of his smartly swinging guitar.    **KW**

## Barbara Thompson                                       1944

**Breathless**  Thompson (ss, as, af); **Malcolm Macfarlane** (g, gsyn); **Peter Lemer** (kbds); **Phil Mulford** (b); **Jon Hiseman** (d); **Noel Langley** (t); **Ashley Slater** (tb); **Hossam Ramzy, Frank Holder** (perc). veraBra Ⓔ CDM13-2 (62 minutes). Recorded 1990/1.

⑧ ❿

Along with Ian Carr's Nucleus, Barbara Thompson's various versions of her band Paraphernalia can arguably lay claim to having established jazz-rock in the UK. Her music is always highly accessible yet surprisingly subtle, full of delicate embellishments and dynamic contrast, propelled and ornamented by her husband Jon Hiseman's excellent drumming. **Breathless** is a sound collage of the moods engendered by city life, embracing the self-explanatory *Jaunty, Cheeky, Squiffy* and *Gracey* through the dark, faintly sinister *Bad Blues* with its breathy flute, to the abrasive *You Must Be Joking* and the extrovert back-slapping beat of *Sax Rap*, featuring Thompson's conversational saxophone – usually vocal – rapper's part. Like a number of her previous albums, particularly the excellent live set **A Cry from the Heart**, **Breathless** is anthemic without being ponderous, infectiously perky without sliding into cuteness or banality, and impeccably and enthusiastically performed. It is also faultlessly produced and cleverly presented, with three of its most commercial tracks thoughtfully edited and added at the end for the convenience of radio plays.                                                    **CP**

## Sir Charles Thompson                                                                      1918

**Takin' Off** Thompson (p, ldr); with, on four tracks: **Buck Clayton** (t); **Charlie Parker** (as); **Dexter Gordon** (ts); **Danny Barker** (g); **Jimmy Butts** (b); **J.C. Heard** (d); on four tracks: **Joe Newman** (t); **Bob Dorsey** (ts); **Leo Parker** (bs); **Freddy Green** (g); **John Simmons** (b); **Shadow Wilson** (d); on eight tracks: **Joe Newman, Taft Jordan** (t); **H.B. Mitchell** (tb); **Bob Dorsey** (ts); **Pete Brown** (as); **Tate Houston** (bs); **Hank Morton** (g); **John Simmons** (b); **Shadow Wilson** (d). Delmark Apollo Series Ⓕ DD450 (50 minutes) Recorded 1945-7.

Ⓑ ❼

Thompson, given his nickname 'Sir Charles' by Lester Young, was from Springfield, Ohio, and initially learned violin before making the switch to piano. By the early forties he was working in small groups up and down New York's 52nd Street, including that led by Young and his drummer brother, Lee. By the end of that decade he had worked with Charlie Barnet and also toured overseas as a solo, gradually reaching the point where he was consistently making albums as a leader. That he has always had a gift for leadership can be heard on this collation of mid-forties performances, and those on the Vanguard reissue below. The four tracks with Parker and Gordon are not the usual mid-forties frantic jams: they have written arrangements and a proper order of performance. Unsurprisingly, then, they hang together very well indeed, in a sort of late blooming of the swing style. Even *The Street Beat*, a typically brisk bop line although it was written by Thompson, has humorous – and identifying – breaks and pauses in it. All three soloists respond with hard-hitting work, with Clayton clearly pointing the way for Howard McGhee's later style.

Thompson, of course, wrote *Robbins' Nest*, a hit in the forties with a number of bands. Naturally he wrote a number of medium-tempo swingers along the same lines, and one of the more distinguished of these is *Strange Hours*, recorded in the summer of 1947, which has a varied arrangement and fetching work from Joe Newman and Bob Dorsey. In a sense, this music points to a direction Basie could have taken up, had he wanted to update at this time. The final session, from the winter of the same year, has an expanded ensemble and seven previously unissued alternative takes. Pete Brown in this context is an interesting choice, and although the arrangements hue a little closer to the Basie-cum-Hampton model, the playing is disciplined and the sound quality good.      **KS**

**His Personal Vanguard Recordings** Thompson (p); with, on four tracks: **Joe Newman** (t); **Benny Powell** (tb); **Pete Brown** (as); **Gene Ramey** (b); **Osie Johnson** (d); on four tracks **Freddie Green** (g); **Walter Page** (b); **Jo Jones** (d); on five tracks: **Emmett Berry** (t); **Benny Morton** (tb); **Earl Warren** (as); **Coleman Hawkins** (ts); **Steve Jordan** (g); **Aaron Bell** (b); **Osie Johnson** (d); on six tracks: **Skeeter Best** (g); **Aaron Bell** (b). Vanguard (Fr) Ⓕ 662143 (two discs: 99 minutes). Recorded 1953-5.

❿ Ⓑ

John Hammond conceived the idea of recording the near-forgotten middle period jazz soloists under optimum studio conditions and this fine release comprises reissues of the original four 10-inch Vanguard LPs under Thompson's name, complete with readable reprints of the original sleeve-notes by Hammond. 'Sir Charles' was a key figure on many of those important mainstream recording dates from the fifties, including some of the Buck Clayton Jam Sessions and the Vic Dickenson Septets on Vanguard. Possessed of a light touch and an ability to swing at any tempo, the value of his work can be judged from the second session here, the one on which he took Basie's place with the "All American Rhythm Section" (Green, Page, Jones). He retains the springiness and economy of notes associated with the Count and turns in four deft performances of tunes such as *Honeysuckle Rose*. The first date pairs a couple of Basie men with the quirky, piping alto sound of Pete Brown to produce splendid swing-cum-bebop. But the jewel in the crown is the third date and particularly the magnificent solo features for Coleman Hawkins, the majestic *Talk of the Town* and Thompson's own *Sweetheart Tree*. Berry and Morton are also superb and having Jordan on rhythm guitar is an asset. The sound is the best yet for these sessions and the two CDs are housed in an ingenious 'gate-fold' case.                                                            **AM**

## Eddie Thompson

**New review**
**Memories of You** Thompson (p); **Len Skeat** (b); **Jim Hall** (d). HEP Ⓕ CD2021 (63 minutes). Recorded 1983.

❼ Ⓑ

British pianist Eddie Thompson was a genial stylist who adapted his persuasive swing-based style to meet the varied circumstances arising in the wee small hours in posh after-hours watering holes like New York's Hickory House, which Thompson worked during its post-war heyday. He was capable of no-nonsense cooking as demonstrated in a sparkling version of Earl Garner's *Paris Mambo*. Still, as in his rococo take of *Misty*, Thompson had no qualms about piling on cocktailish flourishes. Although dismissed by self-anointed purists, the craft of lounge pianists like Thompson is something to ponder. In his salute to pianistic peers – Ellington, Hines, Blake, Garner and Monk, all of whom he knew – there is something special which emerges in the 'art' of a saloon pianist who spent his life cheek-to-jowl with his public. Tasteful support is provided by bassist Len Skeat and drummer Jim Hall. **CB**

## Lucky Thompson                                                    1924

---

**Tricotism** Thompson (ts); **Jimmy Cleveland** (tb); **Hank Jones, Don Abney** (p); **Skeeter Best** (g); **Oscar Pettiford** (b); **Osie Johnson** (d). Impulse! Ⓜ GRP11352 (66 minutes). Recorded 1956.

⑧ ❽

The alarmingly high rate of attrition among leading jazz musicians has usually been the result of self-abuse or mental illness, with sometimes little separation between the two. But there have been a considerable number of performers who, from dissatisfaction and disillusionment, have merely given up playing. For example the querulous Lawrence Brown, leaving the Ellington band in his early sixties, vowed never to touch his instrument again and Lucky Thompson, still living in Seattle, has done likewise since he turned 50. The promise he displayed on his 1946 sessions, with Gillespie and especially Parker, flowered briefly and spectacularly in the mid fifties, when these sessions (as well as work with Miles Davis, Milt Jackson and Quincy Jones) found his Byas-derived sinuosity at its most ingratiating. The combined contents of two LPs include seven quintet tracks featuring Cleveland, here more creative than on many occasions, but the jewels are the nine drum-less trios with Pettiford as the other main soloist. *Deep Passion* (not the Thompson original that gives its name to the Pettiford album reviewed elsewhere) takes off explicitly from Hawkins's *Body and Soul* and is not disgraced by the comparison, while *Dancing Sunbeam*'s chord-sequence (*I Remember You*) should be an injunction to every reader not to overlook Thompson. **BP**

---

**Lucky Strikes** Thompson (ts, ss); **Hank Jones** (p); **Richard Davis** (b); **Connie Kay** (d). Prestige Ⓜ OJCCD194-2 (40 minutes). Recorded 1964.

⑨ ❼

A very underrated saxophonist, Lucky Thompson is a superbly inventive and melodic player. Although his early style bore a resemblance to Don Byas, he absorbed the harmonic and rhythmic subtleties of Charlie Parker and Lester Young, then continued to evolve, his playing becoming simultaneously more forceful yet more sensitive. *Just One More Chance* (one of the great tenor solos of the forties) appears and disappears on various CD compilations with alarming rapidity, but his exquisite mid-fifties work with Milt Jackson, Oscar Pettiford (see previous entry) and Martial Solal (on several fine Paris recordings) is now being reissued in full.

**Lucky Strikes** is an elegant example of his sixties music for Prestige. Thompson himself is in disarming form and the rhythm section complement him with the discretion of true class. Thompson features soprano saxophone on several tracks, his sleek phrasing and pure tone very different from either Coltrane or Steve Lacy (the other leading straight horn players at the time). He is an able composer too, his charts here encompassing the spry *Prey-Loot*, the lightly swinging *Reminiscent* and the intimate balladry of *I Forgot to Remember*. Top honours, however, go to Duke Ellington's *In a Sentimental Mood*, fashioned by Lucky into a wafted soprano reverie. **GL**

## Malachi Thompson

---

New review
**Buddy Bolden's Rag (100 Years of Jazz)** Thompson (t, steer horn, conch, sekulu, ldr), **David Spencer, Kenny Anderson, Phillip Perkins, Lester Bowie** (t); **Edwin Williams, Bill McFarland, Ray Riperton, Steve Berry** (tb); **Ari Brown, Zane Massey** (ts); **Harrison Bankhead** (b); **Darryl Ervin** (d); **Dr Cuz, Richard Lawrence** (perc). Delmark Ⓕ DE481 (72 minutes). Recorded 1995.

⑥ ❽

Thompson has long shared with his mentor Lester Bowie a fascination with large brass ensembles and a view that using the jazz heritage as a departure point for new ideas is more rewarding than the jazz repertory movement. Here he takes the concept of the New Orleans brass band, but with none of the preconceptions that beset native New Orleanians like The Dirty Dozen or Rebirth. By adding string bass to produce walking bass lines and disciplined section playing that would grace any big band, then mixing this with world music rhythms, Thompson has conjured a stimulatingly original album. Chicagoan colleagues like saxophonist Zane Massey appear as guests alongside the powerhouse eight-piece brass line-up (Bowie only appearing on three tracks). There are Mingus-like parodies of traditional songs (*Mouse in the House* has exemplary muted playing from Thompson and a wild solo from McFarland), bop section work reminiscent of Gillespie's big band (*We Bop*) and some exotically rhythmic tracks (*The Chaser in Brazil* or *Kojo Time*). Thompson's solo horn would be welcome on any Crescent City parade, but his band's playing is far above that city's present-day average in power, accuracy and creativity. **AS**

# Claude Thornhill
1909-65

**Best of the Big Bands** Thornhill (ldr, p, arr); with the following collective personnel: **Rusty Dedrick, Conrad Gozzo, Bob Spretall, Randy Brooks, Steve Steck, Jake Koven, Louis Mucci, Clarence Willard, Emil Terry, Ed Zandy, Red Rodney** (t); **Tasso Harris, Bob Jenney, Bud Smith, Ray Schmidt, Jerry Rosa, Tak Takvorian, Allan Langstaff** (tb); **John Graas, Vincent Jacobs, Mike Glas, Fred Schmidt, Sandy Siegelstein, Al Antoucci** (frh); **Harold Wekel, Bill Barber** (tba); **Irving Fazola, Dale Brown, George Paulson, John Nelson, Hammond Russum, Ted Goddard, Buddy Dean, Conn Humphries, Carl Swift, Chet Pardee, Joe Aglora, Jack Dulong, James Gemus, Vic Harris, Bob Glover, Ed Stang, Mickey Folus, Mario Rolo, Bill Bushey, Les Clark, Lee Konitz** (reeds); **Chuck Robinson, Barry Galbraith, Zeb Julian** (g); **Harvey Cell, Marty Blitz, Barnet Spieler, Iggy Shevack, Joe Shulman** (b); **Gene Leman, Irv Cottler, Billy Exiner** (d); **Gil Evans, Bill Borden, Charles Naylor** (arr); **Fran Warren, Buddy Hughes, Snow Flakes** (v). Columbia Ⓜ CK46152 (62 minutes). Recorded 1941-7.

⑧ ❻

Miles Davis's 1948-vintage Birth of the Cool band and its subsequent Capitol recordings (q.v. Davis) Mulligan and the rest never denied the influence of the band on their work and while Thornhill's recordings have been dusted off by the critics to illustrate the earlier work of Gil Evans, Lee Konitz, Red Rodney, etc., it must not be forgotten that Thornhill's orchestra had a highly individual personality of its own. Although this release contains the expected Evans scores such as *Robbin's Nest*, *Yardbird Suite* and *Anthropology,* it also presents some of Claude's own quite masterly work both at the keyboard and the composer's desk. Thornhill flourished (the term is entirely relative) during the big dance band era when orchestras invariably comprised six or seven brass, four or five saxes and a rhythm section. Claude changed that; some of his writing called for six clarinets and two French horns (and this was before Gil Evans joined his staff). The ensemble sound of Thornhill's band "hung like a cloud", as someone once remarked. This is a well-compiled CD opening with Thornhill's signature-tune, the lovely *Snowfall*, and containing Fran Warren's features, *Sunday Kind of Love* and *Early Autumn* (not the Ralph Burns composition). Both are arranged by Charles Naylor and each is a minor classic in the vocalist-with-band division. Although now deleted it is worth trawling through the second-hand catalogues for Thornhill's **Tapestries** (Affinity CD CHARLY 82), which contains ten of the tracks on the present CD plus 13 more from the same period. **AM**

# Henry Threadgill
1944

**Carry the Day** Threadgill (as, f); **Mark Taylor** (flh); **Brandon Ross, Masujaa** (g); **Edwin Rodriguez, Marcus Rojas** (tba); **Gene Lake** (d); **Wu Man** (pipa); **Jason Hwang** (vn); **Tony Cedras** (acc); add, on two tracks: **Johnny Rudas, Miguel Urbina** (perc, v); **Sentienla Toy, Mossa Bildner** (v). Columbia Ⓕ CK66995 (37 minutes). Recorded 1994

⑧ ❽

It is difficult, if not impossible, to rate this music: by what standards? under what category? Threadgill would no doubt be pleased at such indecision; after all, throughout his impressively varied career he has made a point of frustrating expectations and erasing stylistic boundaries. It is a shame that none of his excellent Sextett records from the eighties are currently available on CD – they at least build upon more explicit jazz references. Threadgill's most recent work, exhibited on the brief and at times bewildering **Carry the Day**, incorporates so many of his compositional interests that his septet Very Very Circus resembles no other 'jazz' band of my acquaintance. The opening piece alone, *Come Carry the Day*, mixes Tex-Mex accordion, African Highlife, Latin/Caribbean percussion, a Spanish vocal chant and the unconventional instrumentation of the core band into a dense, swirling, multicultural stew. The guests bring additional spice, and the simultaneous layers of activity do approximate the colourful near-chaos of a three-ring circus. But even on those selections where the unadulterated Circus performs – like the patchwork quilt of tubas, guitars and flute on *Growing a Big Banana* and the spikier *Jenkins Boys Again, Wish Somebody Die, It's Hot* – Threadgill's off-kilter rhythmic accents, labyrinthine harmonic progressions and polyphonic interplay can be as dazzlingly enigmatic as his song titles. **AL**

# Bobby Timmons
1935-74

**This Here Is** Timmons (p); **Sam Jones** (b); **Jimmy Cobb** (d). Riverside Ⓜ OJCCD104-2 (38 minutes). Recorded 1960.

⑦ ❻

It is important to remember that Timmons was an outstanding song-writer as well as a fine pianist. It was his compositions, more than anyone else's (Horace Silver included), which really got the soul-jazz craze out of the clubs and beyond the clutches of the hipsters and established groups like the Jazz Messengers and Cannonball Adderley's quintet on a popular basis which went beyond the usual jazz audience. This was his first album as a leader, and it is somewhat schizophrenic, containing trio versions of his three big hits, *This Here*, *Moanin'* and *Dat Dere*, but also having its fair share of evergreens and jazz standards (*Lush Life*, *My Funny Valentine*, etc.) which are given a pretty much straightforward interpretation and are certainly not souled-out. Timmons was a considerable and sophisticated talent at the keyboard, not given to ostentation or the trotting out of clichés, and this is why his own albums always deliver a lot more than they promise on the cover. Like many others, he became trapped by the public's demands for him just to stick to the hits, but it is to his credit that he always went beyond just doing that.                                                                           **KS**

# Keith Tippett                                                                                                      1947

**New review**

**Frames** Tippett (p, hmn); **Mark Charig** (t, thn, thumb p); **Henry Lowther** (t); **Dave Amis**, **Nick Evans** (tb); **Elton Dean** (as, saxello); **Trevor Watts** (as, ss); **Brian Smith** (ts, ss, f); **Larry Stabbins** (ts, ss, f); **Stan Tracey** (p); **Phil Wachsmann** (vn, elvn); **Geoffrey Wharton**, **Steve Levine**, **Rod Skeaping** (vn); **Alexandra Robinson**, **Tim Kramer** (vc); **Peter Kowald** (b, bb); **Harry Miller** (b); **Lewis Moholo** (d); **Frank Perry** (perc); **Maggie Nicols**, **Julie Tippett** (v). Ogun Ⓕ OGCD010/1 (two discs: 84 minutes). Recorded 1978.

⑧ ❽

Jazz is a music that has never bothered with numerical issues. Good enough is big enough and Tippett has made very good music alone. Born in Bristol, England, he graduated through trad and bop circles in his home town and moved to London in 1967. He played an important part in the free movement in the early seventies, recorded with his 50-piece group, Centipede, and distinguished himself in many of the music's working combos. This CD continues the larger unit tradition and presents his 22-piece Ark. **Frames** is divided into four sections and is the music for an imaginary film. Its themes are used as frames; solos and minor contrapuntal interludes carry the thematic guide-lines into free areas and, as organic parts of the composition, progress the entire work. In so doing, they provide their own sequential logic and introduce shading and melodic contrasts that still manage to sound Tippett-like. There are fine solo contributions from Stabbins, Dean and Watts in the reeds, Amis, Lowther and Kowald in the brass, Wachsmann on electric violin and from pianists Tracey and Tippett. It provides an ideal introduction to Tippett's work in other guises.                                                    **BMcR**

**New review**

**Une Croix dans l'Océan** Tippett (p, perc). Victo Ⓕ 031 (46 minutes). Recorded 1994.

⑧ ❽

A key figure on the British jazz (and progressive rock) scene for decades, Tippett's work is remarkably ill-served on CD. Neither his intimate small bands (including duos with partners ranging from Stan Tracey to Louis Moholo) nor one of his two leviathan large ensembles (the 50-piece Centipede) are currently represented, so the focus turns to his expansive solo piano. Similar in design to other recorded concerts (**Mujician III** on FMP and **The Dartington Concert** on Editions EG/Virgin among them), this performance consists of a single unbroken flow of music, beginning with tiny bells and whispery inside-the-piano work and gradually building to a firestorm of sound. The progress of the music is inseparable from the process of its creation; the mood is of undetermined forces being called forth and finding a way to make them cohere. Tippett's note-to-note concentration never disrupts the music's spontaneity. The most energizing passages are fed by rapid arpeggiations and filigree from which themes emerge, but do not linger, as atmosphere and textural considerations overtake them. There is one notable passage where he juxtaposes a cloudy pedalled effect in the low register with a glistening inside-the-piano at the top. Tippett seeks an escape into an ecstatic state of inspiration, and for some listeners the full experience may prove exhausting, but unlike any other.                     **AL**

# Cal Tjader                                                                                                       1925-82

**Cal Tjader-Stan Getz Sextet** Tjader (vb); **Getz** (ts); **Vince Guaraldi** (p); **Eddie Duran** (g); **Scott LaFaro** (b); **Billy Higgins** (d). Fantasy Ⓜ OJCCD275-2 (43 minutes). Recorded 1958.

⑧ ❼

Tjader first came to the wider jazz audience in the George Shearing Quintet which patented the Shearing Sound – the unison piano-vibes-guitar theme statements and the touch of Latin rhythm. Some of this clearly rubbed off on Tjader, who continually looked to Latin music of all kinds to recharge his creative batteries when they were running low. It worked for him in the same way as it did for Shearing, and for a number of years Tjader was very big commercial news indeed.

This date, made when Tjader was rapidly coming to the attention of the record-buying public, uses Latin elements but is mostly a straightforward blowing session, albeit with consummate blowers. The rhythm section of Guaraldi, Duran, LaFaro and Higgins is very strong indeed, having an admirable combination of imagination and drive. At this time, both LaFaro and Higgins were West Coast unknowns, but both make big contributions here. Tjader and Getz fit together beautifully, and while the saxophonist has the emotional depth to tear you to pieces on *I've Grown Accustomed to Her Face*, Tjader always plays with great sensitivity and economy. His straight jazz style is inextricably bound up in Milt Jackson's, but then there wasn't a post-war vibes player who escaped Bags's groove until the following decade.

As a rather bizarre footnote, the CD sleeve and booklet both claim that this record was made in 1963, while the booklet-notes mention 1958. The later date is of course a nonsense, as LaFaro died in 1961. **KS**

## Charles Tolliver

1942

**Grand Max** Tolliver (t, flh); **John Hicks** (p); **Reggie Workman** (b); **Alvin Queen** (d). Black Lion Ⓜ BLCD760145 (67 minutes). Recorded 1972.

In November 1993, Tolliver opened to enthusiastic audiences at a New York residency, and the critical reaction to his playing centred around his ability to respond to and manipulate the mood of an audience. Twenty-one years before, he demonstrated just how much this has always been an essential part of his art in this tight performance, recorded at Loosdrecht in Holland, by his Music Inc. quartet. The title track is dedicated to Tolliver's former mentor, Max Roach, but the most impressive playing here is on the central performance of *Prayer for Peace* which swells from a gentle bass and drums duo to an impassioned piece of preaching trumpet. Tolliver's hallmark is long, flowing solos that turn ideas inside out and upside down over many choruses, and his co-operative quartets of the early seventies were an ideal vehicle for him to do this within. The Loosdrecht concert was clearly a happy affair for all concerned, and the Dutch radio engineers who recorded it caught much of the live atmosphere, especially in the rousing encore based on Neal Hefti's *Repetition*. **AS**

## Sumi Tonooka

1956

New review

**Here Comes Kai** Tonooka (p); **Rufus Reid** (b); **Lewis Nash** (d). Candid Ⓔ CCD79516 (57 minutes). Recorded 1991.

This is Tonooka's second album for Candid, and before you think "oh no, not another piano trio album", may I reassure you that this one shows a lot more imagination and panache than most. OK, it does start with *Giant Steps*, but instead of trying to play it three times faster and five times harder than anyone else, Philadelphia-born Tonooka prefaces it with an attractive *a cappella* solo and during the trio improvisation goes for content, not speed. This sets the tone for the whole album, where a sense of unhurried invention pervades each track. In this the pianist is aided by the vastly experienced team of Reid and Nash. Five of the eight tracks are Tonooka originals, and all of them show a talent for elegant but unlikely melodies moving through interesting chord patterns. Her Ellington/Strayhorn leanings come through on distinctive performances of *Warm Valley* and *U.M.M.G.* **KS**

## Mel Tormé

1925

**The Duke Ellington and Count Basie Songbooks** Tormé (v); **Jack Sheldon** (t); **Stu Williamson** (vtb); **Frank Rosolino** (tb); **Joe Maini** (as); **Teddy Edwards** (ts); **Bill Perkins** (ts, bs); **Jimmy Rowles** (p); **Al Hendrickson** (g); **Joe Mondragon** (b); **Shelly Manne** (d); **Johnny Mandel** (arr, cond). Verve Ⓜ 823 248-2 (37 minutes). Recorded 1961.

It is difficult to understand the rejection some jazz fans feel towards Mel Tormé. He is probably the most technically gifted male singer of all and this combined with his good taste, well-controlled histrionics and fundamental knowledge of jazz, give him the standing of one of the better horn players. He works most often with consummate bands of West Coast musicians and his music is subtle as well as dexterous. He is unique in the potential of his appeal to both popular and jazz audiences. Latterly his recordings with George Shearing have been his most rewarding, but it would be hard to improve on the combination on this disc. The material is the best, Mandel's arrangements are perfect and the soloists in the band, with Rosolino, Sheldon, Edwards and Maini outstanding, all on good form. The choice of obscure material like Ellington's *Reminiscing in Tempo* (lyrics by Tormé) and *I Like the Sunrise* was inspired, and Mandel's orchestrations, particularly of the latter, are very fulfilling. Switch straight from those to *In the Evening* and you find Tormé treading Joe Williams/Joe Turner country in his own most effective way. Jimmy Rowles's piano is most effective here, as it is throughout the album. The 'mountain jack' climax is powerful and Tormé's held high note beautifully judged. **SV**

## Jean Toussaint

1957

New review

**Life I Want** Toussaint (ss, ts); with various line-ups including: **Dennis Rollins** (tb); **Jason Rebello**, **Jean-Michel Pilc** (p, kbds); **Clyo Brown**, (g); **Tony Remy** (g, kbds) **Wayne Batchelor** (b); **Darren**

**Abraham**, **Mark Mondesir**, **Winston Clifford** (d); **Nana Tsiboe**, **Carl Vanden Bossche** (perc); **Cleveland Watkiss** (v). New Note Ⓕ NNCD1001 (73 minutes). Recorded 1995.

⑥ ❾

Toussaint emerged into the international spotlight with Art Blakey's Jazz Messengers between 1982 and 1986, after which he opted for life in London rather than America. His first album, **What Goes Around** (World Circuit), was dedicated to the great drummer; this new one is jointly dedicated to Toussaint's mother and father. A short note from the saxophonist in the CD insert explains the title: observing during his time with Blakey a number of talented young musicians succumbing to drugs and worse, he asked one player why he did it. The predictable reply was "If I knew better I never would have done it. Then I could have lived the life I want, not the one it wants me to."

The music here is as at peace with itself as the man Toussaint appears to be with himself. There is a pleasant mix of various contemporary styles, including a generous slice of Jamaican rhythms and colours (Toussaint's background is centred in that part of the world), plus more straightforward American funk and fusion tinges. Toussaint tends to use his companions as suppliers of musical canvases rather than as people to challenge him to greater heights, and though Jason Rebello is capable of doing both with ease, he sticks mostly to the former here. Each track has a varied line-up depending on the music genre it is cast in. Toussaint plays confidently on tenor and lyrically on soprano, but struggles with intonation problems on the higher-pitched instrument. That aside, this is a competent album compiled by a talented player, no more and no less. **KS**

# Ralph Towner

1940

**Solstice** Towner (g, p); **Jan Garbarek** (ss, ts, f); **Eberhard Weber** (vc, b); **Jon Christensen** (d, perc). ECM Ⓕ 825 458-2 (41 minutes). Recorded 1974.

✔

⑧ ❽

Unsurprisingly, given Ralph Towner's membership of folk/jazz/classical fusionists Oregon, **Solstice** occupies territory abutting on all three genres, but leans most closely towards jazz, courtesy of his distinguished sidemen. The music itself incorporates both free and more structured material, ranging from contemplative, impressionistic sound-collages with titles like *Drifting Petals* and *Nimbus* (featuring Jan Garbarek on flute) to hectic, swirling guitar-saxophone duels set against Eberhard Weber's supple, sonorous bass and Jon Christensen's vigorous but sensitive drumming and percussion work. The following year, Garbarek and Christensen were to collaborate unforgettably with Keith Jarrett on the masterpiece **Belonging**, and Weber was to set out on tour as – unusually for a bassist – featured soloist with Gary Burton, so **Solstice** catches these sidemen at a pivotal period in their careers, all poised to capture world attention. Towner himself employs his much-praised 'pianistic' acoustic guitar style to great effect throughout, although the slightly unfocused, loose nature of the material militates against the album as a whole reaching the summit of four-way improvised interaction achieved by Jarrett's **Belonging**. Nevertheless, **Solstice** neatly epitomizes the seventies ECM sound, one which has maintained its appeal over the intervening years a great deal better than some of the electronic fusion then being played in contemporary US studios. **CP**

**Blue Sun** Towner (g, p, syn, frh, c, perc). ECM Ⓕ 829 162-2 (45 minutes). Recorded 1982.

⑩ ❿

Towner is best known for his work in the widely acclaimed group Oregon (see above); but he has made a distinctive series of records under his own name on the ECM label, some of them solo, some of them with small groupings of people. **Blue Sun** is a perfect example of his work as a solo artist. Towner was trained as both pianist and guitarist, so there is no drop in quality when he turns from plucked to hammered strings. His musical thinking is clearly orchestral and he arranges the different instruments here so astutely that one always has the sense that a tight-knit group of like-minded souls are recording the music live in the studio. Considering that it is all just multi-tracked Towner, the spark and presence which comes across is no mean feat in itself.

The different tracks here cover a considerable emotional range, although they are stylistically homogeneous. Towner uses his synthesizer tracks as discreet and beautifully voiced backdrops for the melodies of his improvisations and compositions. On *The Prince and the Sage* they glow, they are so luminescent behind the solo classical guitar. On other tracks, such as *C.T. Kangaroo*, there is a great deal more bounce, humour and rhythmic lift. Like Gil Evans, Towner has the ability to create exciting as well as beautiful and languid things. **KS**

# Colin Towns

New review

**Nowhere and Heaven** Towns (p, comp, arr, dir) and **The Mask Orchestra: John Barclay**, **Graham Russell**, **Henry Lowther**, **Guy Barker**, **Gerard Presencer** (t); **Mark Nightingale**, **Richard Edwards**, **Peter Beachill**, **Phil Hartley**, **Roger Williams** (tb); **Phil Todd** (bcl); **Peter King** (as); **Jamie Talbot**

(cl, ss, as); **Alan Skidmore**, **Nigel Hitchcock** (ss, ts); **Julian Argüelles** (ss, bs); **Alan Barnes** (bs); **Andrea Hess** (vc); **Dudley Phillips** (b); **Clark Tracey** (d); **Maria Pia de Vito** (v). PVC Ⓟ 1013 (two discs: 149 minutes). Recorded 1995.

⑧ ❾

Best known for his composing for films and television as well as for his song-writing and work on keyboards for Ian Gillan's rock band, Colin Towns nurtured the idea of launching a jazz big band for many years. The Mask Orchestra is the result, and this second CD, partly arising out of a 1995 UK tour, demonstrates that a formidable new talent has arrived in British jazz. Towns's writing is uncompromising, some of the section work is extraordinarily difficult, and the results, given his judicious choice of soloists and band musicians, are outstanding. There's a programmatic quality to his work, and pieces like the title track (which illustrates Oliver Sachs's book *Awakening*) retain a strong narrative line. Others are delicate (yet robust) settings of poetry – Carol Ann Duffy's *Standing Female Nude* is a vehicle for the singing of Maria Pia de Vito. Her electric stage presence galvanizes the band's live concerts and this is remarkably effectively conveyed to CD, along with some first-rate solos from Peter King and Jamie Talbot. Towns himself revels in interjecting some stimulating chordal playing into the dense textures of the band. His writing ranges from the strongly structured to the looser *Short Stories Suite*, which occupies most of the second CD and gives his soloists ample space to tell their own stories. By putting together such a distinguished band and feeding it with such a collection of original composition, Towns is doing for the nineties what Mike Westbrook and Stan Tracey achieved in the sixties, and his efforts are to be welcomed wholeheartedly. **AS**

## Stan Tracey
1926

**Portraits Plus** Tracey (p); **Guy Barker** (t); **Malcolm Griffiths** (tb); **Peter King** (as); **Don Weller** (ts); **Art Themen** (ss, ts); **Dave Green** (b); **Clark Tracey** (d). Blue Note Ⓟ CDP7 80696-2 (59 minutes ). Recorded 1992.

⑥ ❻

Quite a mellow Stan Tracey on this recent Blue Note issue, which note-writer John Fordham says is (at the age of 65) his first appearance on a major international label. A faintly nostalgic feel about it too, as Tracey sketches some portraits of musicians who have meant a lot to him in the past – Rollins, Monk, Gil Evans, Duke – although frankly the portraits are rough sketches rather than recognizable likenesses. The scoring is fluid but not startling, and everyone solos in their accustomed manner. Hard to find anything bad about this session, or anything very outstanding either, although it does occur to me listening to Malcolm Griffiths's roaring trombone that he was doing things with the instrument in Britain 20 years ago for which Gary Valente and Ray Anderson got a lot of credit a lot later. **MK**

New review

**For Heaven's Sake** Tracey (p); **Gerard Presencer** (t, flh), **Andy Cleyndert** (b); **Clark Tracey** (d). Cadillac Ⓟ SGCCD04 (61 minutes). Recorded 1995.

⑧ ❽

Can anyone remember when Stan Tracey last made a bad record? Did he ever make a recording that was less than remarkable? If so, this is certainly not one. Tracey has the ability to wrap his quartets in a meniscus of his energized improvisation which never flags. This quality in his playing is the one of his which most resembles Thelonious Monk. Unusually there is only one composition of his own, *H.J.C.* and so we are able to hear what he does with a number of compositions by Monk (three), Bill Evans and, in *Blah de Blah de Blah*, Gerard Presencer. On the latter Tracey rattles the keyboard to good effect. Although the days at Ronnie Scott's club when "the bit of the piano from here to here doesn't work" are long gone, from his firm and considered touch one feels that Tracey is somehow expecting the current instrument to let him down. The piano dominates the quartet and Presencer, who has apparently hitched his career to Tracey from an early age, is provided with a challenging rostrum from which to launch his rapid and finely constructed inventions. He is at his best on the ballad *For Heaven's Sake*, a beautiful performance by anyone's standards, and his fount of ideas reminds one of a young Lee Morgan. Clark Tracey is an old hand at his father's side and Cleyndert confirms his emergence as one of the London scene's better players. **SV**

## Theo Travis

New review

**Secret Island** Travis (ts); **David Gordon** (p); **John Etheridge** (g); **Rob Statham**, **Dave Sturt** (b); **Marc Parnell**, **Andrew Small** (d); **Gary Hammond** (perc). 33 Jazz Records Ⓟ 033CD (61 minutes). Recorded 1996.

⑥ ❽

Theo Travis is a promising young saxophonist from Britain. In moody soundscapes like *Lulworth Night* there are North Sea echoes of Norwegian tenorman Jan Garbarek. For the freewheeling *The Crow Road*, Travis's cascading horn suggests the jazz-rock whirlwinds of Michael Brecker. Though favouring tenor, Travis switches to soprano for effective mood changes in tracks like *After the Storm*. Guitarist John Etheridge, whose wired-up sounds suggest Metheny and Frisell, is the most impressive of Travis's colleagues. In the gently swinging *Waterlily Boogie* Travis puts on yet another mask, this time affecting a Getz-like ethereality. The saxophonist, however, is still seeking a voice to call his own. **CB**

# Tribal Tech

New review
**Reality Check** Scott Henderson (elg); Scott Kinsey (kbds); Gary Willis (b); Kirk Covington (d). Blue Moon Ⓕ 2-92549 (69 minutes). Recorded 1994.

⑧ ❾

Like Weather Report, Tribal Tech is built around a two-man core, and it parallels that band in stylistic terms too. Scott Henderson was able to indulge his love of Weather Report in The Zawinul Syndicate of the late eighties and much of **Reality Check** hews close to the Zawinul-Shorter model. Bassist Gary Willis is thoroughly convincing in the Pastorius mode – notably on *Speak,* a brisk Latin funk vamp complete with the steel pan sound which was a defining element of the Pastorius edition of Weather Report – and *Worlds Waiting* is strongly evocative of such Zawinul pieces as *Dream Clock.* However, Henderson's penchant for bebop, heavy metal and blues ensures that Tribal Tech is more than a Weather Report tribute band. *Nite Club,* for example, is a roaring slice of altered r&b, *Susie's Dingsbums* an alternately swinging and funky paraphrase of *I Got Rhythm* and *Stella by Starlight* inspires two treatments, one a relatively conventional ballad reading, the other – titled *Stella by Infra-red High Particle Neutron Beam* – a Goth-metal thrash. The playing throughout is exemplary, but Henderson is an outstanding demonstration of the breadth of expression possible in the absurdly maligned fusion of jazz and rock. The two genres were never that far apart anyway and Henderson's interpretation of both styles is far and away more original and pertinent than those of the modish straight-ahead players of recent years. **MG**

# Trio Con X

New review
**Trio Con X and Friends** Anders Bromander (kbds); Per Johansson (b); Joakim Ekberg (d); with Joakim Milder (ss), Tomas Arnesen (g), Rafael Sida (perc) and Anders Astrand (perc, vb, mba). Phono Suecia Ⓕ PSCD90 (56 minutes). Recorded 1995.

⑧ ❾

Trio Con X was the victim of a Swedish government financial cut-back when funds for Regional Music Foundations were reduced. The trio had been the resident rhythm section for all manner of musical activities in Uppland since 1987 and still exists as an independent unit. In this capacity they decided to make this CD, adding some of the soloists they had worked with in the past. Although attention will almost inevitably focus on the two performances by Joakim Milder, who plays warm-toned soprano on both, the actual competence of the trio is manifest throughout. All but one of the nine compositions come from Trio Con X itself and two of them, *Signe* and *African Samba*, are by the trio with no added voices. There is a pleasing, pastoral quality to their music which is apt and obviously to the satisfaction of Milder. Three tracks have additional percussion with Astrand's vibes and marimba playing quite outstanding. A CD of attractive, beautifully played music which should not be overlooked. **AM**

# The Trio

New review
**The Trio** John Surman (ss, bs, bcl); Barre Phillips (b); Stu Martin (d). Beat Goes On Records Ⓜ BGOCD231 (two discs: 99 minutes). Recorded 1970.

⑧ ⑧

Just the title alone laid bare the ambitions of this short-lived but influential unit. The cover made it even plainer: just **The Trio**, in black type on a pure white background. This was a power trio with no connections to electric kilowatts, with musical responsibilities finely balanced between all three members. With just their instruments and their own physical frames they intended to make the world sit up and take notice. Americans Phillips and Martin found in Surman a quixotic and deeply original reed instrumentalist who could both lead and follow in ways not being investigated by contemporary New Yorkers and perhaps only found in the less well-known members of Chicago's AACM. Surman's virtuosity was an established fact by the time this band was formed; what was surprising was the extreme degree of cohesion and form these musicians discovered when playing through their shared themes and compositions. What remains unique about the combinations of sound these three men created together was the unfailing lyricism to be found in their counterpoint: these musicians quite clearly believed in the strength of song, even if the songs they were spontaneously evolving were of the wild, scarcely containable variety from time to time. This was not music of pain and surrender: it was a celebration of what could be achieved in the coming together of imagination and refined technique. In that sense the band's own demise was inbuilt from the first: once a level of perfection had been obtained in the created dialogues, it would be time to move on. In Surman's case in particular, that would lead to an ever-fascinating (and still evolving) musical odyssey. **KS**

## Lennie Tristano
1919-78

**Lennie Tristano/The New Tristano** Tristano (p); Lee Konitz (as); Peter Ind, Gene Ramey (b); Jeff Morton, Art Taylor (d). Rhino/Atlantic Ⓜ 271595-2 (78 minutes). Recorded 1955-62.
✔ ⑧ ❼

Tristano didn't make that many records, and what there are never stays in catalogue that long because he's not an easy listen and people shy away from the effort needed. Fair enough, but when the pianist/theorist/teacher is functioning at peak power, as on much of this generous doubling of two classic Atlantic LPs on one disc, then the music becomes compelling, because the theories are delivered in such an exciting way that what can often sound meretricious suddenly becomes revelatory.

The influence of Tristano on one whole stream of jazz musicians is well documented, and his anticipations of many later developments in jazz have also been widely commented on, but his influence on the mainstream is largely unexplored. A striking example is neatly encapsulated on the first four tracks here, recorded privately by Tristano and using multi-tracking techniques at that time mostly used for novelty records. *Requiem*, a solo blues for Charlie Parker, is a clear antecedent for Bill Evans's *NYC's No Lark*, his lament for Sonny Clark. Tristano here provides a jazz framework within which he uses musical thinking derived from twentieth-century classical music, and thus points the way for the personal synthesis Evans was soon to make. That synthesis remains to this day the basis of the modern jazz piano mainstream. The second album here, **The New Tristano**, finds the pianist for the most part utilizing walking bass figures which root him in an earlier jazz tradition, while his right-hand figures rarely wander far from swing and Tatumesque rhythmic concepts, no matter where the harmony goes. **KS**

## Gianluigi Trovesi
1944

**From G to G** Trovesi (as, cl, bcl); Pina Minafra (tp, flh, didjeridu, v); Rodolfo Migliardi (tb, tba); Marco Remondini (vc); Roberto Bonati, Marco Micheli (b); Vittorio Marinoni (d); Fulvio Maras (perc). Soul Note Ⓕ 121 231-2 (59 minutes). Recorded 1992.
⑧ ⑧

Trovesi is an excellent example of the European jazz musician who is not content to merely solo over the traditional song forms of American jazz; instead, he finds aspects of his native music which can support improvisational manoeuvres and are compatible with jazz inflections and arrangements. Trovesi goes a step or two beyond most Europeans, however, in his familiarity with Mediterranean dance rhythms plus Italian mediaeval and renaissance music. He recorded an LP in 1978 which featured his improvisations on a thirteenth-century saltarello as well as a 12-tone series. Later trio albums reinforced his connections with folk and dance musics; the recent **From G to G** is no exception, but places Trovesi's ideas in a larger ensemble. The results are very attractive, thanks in part due to the unusual instrumentation – two drummers, two bassists, and a cellist among the eight players – and the unexpected ways Trovesi uses them. He makes ingenious use of the two basses, alternating between rhythmic ostinatos and contrapuntal lines, and the drummers not only keep time but add splashes of percussive colour. He is also able to integrate his influences into the eclectic, memorable compositions, from the loose-limbed Ornette Coleman flavour of *Herbop* to the twenties two-beat, slap bass parodies (along with 'mumbled' vocals in the manner of Clark Terry) of *Now I Can* and *Hercab*, the Australian didjeridu (reminiscent of the drone of Sardinian reed instruments) and pungent bite of Pina Minafra's trumpet in *Dedalo* to the title tune, in the style of a classical chaconne, with solo variations of a melody of touching simplicity over an unchanging bass line. As **From G to G** shows, Trovesi is one of Europe's best talents, and deserves wider recognition. **AL**

## Gust William Tsilis

**Sequestered Days** Tsilis (vb, mba); Joe Lovano (ts, f); Peter Madsen (p); Anthony Cox (b); Billy Hart (d). Enja Ⓕ 6094-2 (70 minutes). Recorded 1991.
⑧ ⑧

Tsilis's jazz philosophy leads him to tight, coherent writing from which long solos develop naturally. His band, obviously used to playing together regularly, is endowed with superior soloists who, while asserting their individuality, all play with the group sound in mind. The leader, who to judge by the skills shown here should be better known, plays eloquent and original vibes in the territory which lies between Milt Jackson and Gary Burton.

Joe Lovano's tenor playing is happily derivative of the great men of the forties – Ammons and Byas come to mind – and, as he has shown elsewhere, he plays with great passion and technique. He is one of the more rewarding saxophone players of the day, who has burgeoned through the Woody Herman, Thad Jones-Mel Lewis and Charlie Haden orchestras and is now a vital component in guitarist John Scofield's quartet, Lovano is able to concoct a direct mixture of traditional and modern elements which give him a unique sound in the jazz of the day. He is perhaps less palpably influenced by John Coltrane than is the fashion and, oddly for such an outstanding player, little has been written about him in the reference books.

Peter Madsen is one of the crop of inventive young pianists who have arrived in the last few years, and as ever Billy Hart franks the character of the session with his crisp and intelligent drumming. The quintet swings with great fire and it would be nice to think that jazz will follow the directions suggested here by Tsilis and Lovano.                                                                **SV**

## Jimi Tunnell

New review

**Trilateral Commission**  Tunnell (elg, kbds, v); **Bendik Hofseth** (s, v); **Rachel Z** (kbds); **Jeff Andrews** (elb); **Arto Tuncboyaciyan** (perc). 101 South Ⓟ 87 7083 (51 minutes). Recorded 1991-2.

⑦ ⑨

It's unusual to find a fusion guitar player who can double as a convincing pop singer, but on Bob Belden's Prince tribute **When Doves Cry** Jimi Tunnell atomized the mould not only by offering stunning vocal renditions of Prince's *Kiss* and *Baby I'm a Star*, but by improving both with hip Scofield-type guitar lines and, on the latter, also playing fluent bass and keyboard. Perhaps we shouldn't be surprised to learn that Tunnell began the jazz life as a trumpet student before doing backing vocals for The Bee Gees. In many ways, Tunnell's pan-stylistic, multi-skilled approach follows the Joe Zawinul musical ethos. He may never have played with the Zawinul Syndicate, but Zawinul would surely take a shine to him: like Jaco Pastorius he is a jazzman with attitude, a consummate instrumentalist, a singer and, on *Zalimo* and *Big Pig,* he paraphrases such Zawinul pieces as *The Harvest* and *March of the Lost Children*. The palette is broader though, encompassing a Scofesque rock ballad in *Not 4* and a Methenyish mood on the rather overworked country lament of *True West*. The latter becomes mawkish and the record as a whole rarely approaches the intensity of its leader's contributions to the Belden album, but it is nevertheless impressive notice of another fine talent, as well as reassurance that the central tradition of jazz – innovation – is in safe hands.                                                          **MG**

## Bruce Turner                                                                  1922-93

New review

**The Controversial Bruce Turner – "That's the Blues, Dad!"**  Turner (cl, as); **Kenny Baker, Terry Brown** (t); **Keith Christie** (tb); **Wally Fawkes** (cl); **Jimmy Skidmore** (ts); **Harry Klein** (bs); **Dill Jones, Lennie Felix** (p); **Ike Isaacs, Cedric West, Fitzroy Coleman** (g); **Frank Clarke, Jim Bray, Major Holley, Danny Haggerty** (b); **Benny Goodman, Eric Delaney, Stan Greig, Don Lawson, Phil Seamen, Billy Loch** (d). Lake Ⓟ LACD49 (70 minutes). Recorded 1955-8.

⑥ ⑥

The late Bruce Turner was one of the most original British talents on alto saxophone and clarinet. Although all but one of the 20 tracks here (*On Treasure Island*) were issued in the fifties, this is the first CD cross-section from Turner's EPs and LPs of that era. Four basic configurations are included (with minor alterations here and there): the groups Turner co-led with clarinettist Wally Fawkes, Turner's own quartet, his Jump Band, and a larger mainsteam ensemble called the Jazz Today Unit. The Fawkes/Turner sides have always been a high point in the British jazz of the fifties, owing a debt to the Mezzrow/Bechet two-reed approach, but having individuality as well. With either Lennie Felix or Dill Jones on piano, the balance between Turner's breathy alto or delicate clarinet and Fawkes's broader-toned clarinet is always maintained, although the best results are with Jones, US expatriate Major Holley and Phil Seamen, notably on *Blues Gone Away*. When Turner goes it alone with a rhythm section, his solo on Jimmy Van Heusen's *Imagination* (accompanied by Jones) is his best ballad playing on the disc. In the larger ensemble, Turner's ability stands out, even in the company of Kenny Baker, Keith Christie and Jimmy Skidmore, but the ideal setting for his playing is the Jump Band, where his clarinet illuminates the eccentric *Stop, Look and Listen* and his alto brings both ensemble depth and startling solos to *Jumpin' at the Woodside*.                                                          **AS**

## Joe Turner                                                                    1907-90

**Sweet and Lovely**  Turner (p). Vogue Ⓜ 111507-2 (42 minutes). Recorded 1952.

⑦ ⑥

There is a moment, in the opening statement of the first take of *Sweet and Lovely*, when the figure of Thelonious Monk looms suddenly over this music. Turner has used such an odd harmonization, bottom-heavy and lurching toward the off-beat, that the only parallels which make sense are either the Kurt Weill of *Surabaya Johnny* or of solo Monk. Later in the same performance the harmonic course of the song is normalized, but then Turner breaks up his usually metronomic left-hand patterns to interpolate a whole swathe of rhythms usually associated exclusively with Erroll Garner. All this is the more remarkable when the recording date is taken into account: Garner may have been a popular figure, but Monk was still on the road to Damascus as far as the jazz public was concerned, and was nearing the lowest point of his career. As if admonished from the control room, Turner delivers a second take suitably toned-down from the first, but with small vestiges of the daring which overcame him the previous time round.

This is an important moment on an otherwise typical Turner stride-dominated date, because during it you can glimpse the true range of this great but neglected figure. His roots may well be in the soil of Jelly Roll Morton-inspired ragtime, as transmuted by the next generation of New York stride players such as Waller and Johnson (this is clearly signalled on *Between the Devil and the Deep Blue Sea*), but he continued to listen to each new wave of pianists, and certainly absorbed a great deal of Tatum. This last point is evidenced by his approach to the arrangement of *I Cover the Waterfront* (out-of-tempo intro, delicate stride for the theme and variations; end with a dinky little chord progression).

As with all the best solo pianists, Turner demands close listening while simultaneously evincing a cast-iron *joie de vivre* which would make him the life and soul of any party he played at. Stick to close listening in front of your speakers and you will be amply rewarded.                    **KS**

# 'Big' Joe Turner                                           1911-85

**The Boss of the Blues**  Turner (v); **Joe Newman, Jimmy Nottingham** (t); **Lawrence Brown** (tb); **Pete Brown** (as); **Frank Wess, Seldon Powell** (ts); **Pete Johnson** (p); **Freddie Green** (g); **Walter Page** (b); **Cliff Leeman** (d); **Ernie Wilkins** (arr). Atlantic Ⓜ 781459-2 (45 minutes). Recorded 1956.

✔                                                               ⑧ ❽

At his best Turner was an unequalled handler of band blues in the Kansas City idiom; a big man with a big, wide-open-space voice, plain in his delivery, little given to ornamentation, but with a wonderful rhythmic insistence. As Whitney Balliert remarked, "it is as if he were driving his voice into your mind". He kept a good part of his voice until near the end of a long life, and consequently was much recorded. Too much, and sometimes in wretchedly inappropriate company, as on the sixties tracks on **Every Day in the Week** (MCA/Decca). But that album is not to be ignored; most of it dates from two decades earlier, and it includes the stately small-group recordings with pianists Freddie Slack (*Rocks in My Bed*) and Pete Johnson (*Rebecca*).

It has been generally agreed for more than 30 years that Turner's finest studio hours were spent making **The Boss of the Blues**. The album was subtitled *Joe Turner Sings Kansas City Jazz* and the local connections of several of the musicians need no spelling out. Possibly no finer band was ever assembled for such a purpose, and the producers were rewarded with a programme of majestic, authoritative, yet fluid and mutually responsive blues singing and playing. Many of the songs were or would become the singer's personal standards – *Cherry Red, I Want a Little Girl, Wee Baby Blues, Morning Glories* – but these recordings had an integrity of conception and rightness of execution that were seldom matched.                    **TR**

# Steve Turré                                                   1948

**Right There**  Turré (tb, shells); **John Blake** (vn); **Akua Dixon Turré** (vc, v); **Benny Green, Willie Rodriguez** (p); **Buster Williams, Andy Gonzalez** (b); **Billy Higgins** (d); **Wynton Marsalis** (t); **Benny Golson** (ts); **Dave Valentin** (f); **George Delgado, Manny Oquendo** (perc); **Herman Olivera** (v, perc). Antilles Ⓕ 510 040-2 (58 minutes). Recorded 1991.

⑦ ❽

A graduate of North Texas State University and a former Jazz Messenger, Turré and his trombone skills are at home in most musical situations. He is as comfortable in the big bands of Thad Jones/Mel Lewis or Dizzy Gillespie's United Nations Orchestra as he is in a hard-bop combo or in a jazz environment such as that found on this CD. Here the basic line-up teams trombone, violin and cello to provide a pleasing, yet unusual, textural base and he is joined on three titles by Wynton Marsalis, with one further piece featuring Benny Golson. Most of the arrangements are by Turré, but it is as a soloist that he stands out. The up-tempo *Ginseng People* tests his prodigious technique, the changing time signatures of *Sanyas* check out his assured sense of timing, while his outstanding plunger mute playing on *Echoes of Harlem* and *Duke's Mountain* confirms his emotional commitment. His adroit conch shell blowing is no mere novelty effect and, with the aid of Manny Oquendo's rhythm section, he treats *Descarga de Turré* to a full two-shell attack. As this release demonstrates, Turré occupies the middle ground between the occasionally incontinent outpourings of the European trombones and the didactic insistence of J.J. Johnson and his many

disciples.                    **BMcR**

# Stanley Turrentine

**New review**

**Blue Flames** Turrentine (ts); **Shirley Scott** (org); **Bob Cranshaw** (b); **Otis Finch** (d). Prestige
Ⓜ OJCCD328-2 (34 minutes). Recorded 1964.

⑥ ❽

Turrentine, like Gene Ammons before him, occupies the borderland between r&b and jazz, with early experience alongside Ray Charles and Max Roach defining and refining his strengths. Though some of his later albums sold extremely well, it would be a mistake to dismiss him as a mere popularizer. Whereas many earnest tenor players of a later generation convey less than they aim for, Turrentine's work appears undemanding and unambitious while frequently achieving considerable depth. Strolling through this straight-ahead 1964 session jointly credited to his then-wife Shirley Scott, who receives top billing, the saxophonist makes nuances count and simple ideas speak volumes. Some of his best work with organ backing having disappeared, **Blue Flames** shows him on entirely typical form and features a typical programme of material. The two blues are the slow *Hips Knees an' Legs* (in G, *pace* the insert-note) and Golson's *Five Spot After Dark* (here transposed to C minor), while the two groovy medium-tempo 16-bar tunes include Rollins's *Grand Street*. All that remains to complete the short playing time is a long ballad performance of *Flamingo*, pleasantly astringent despite the temptations of the tenor-and-organ format. It will be interesting to see what emerges from Turrentine's new contract with Impulse!, but meanwhile this is a satisfactory representation of its period. **BP**

**New review**

**More Than a Mood** Turrentine (ts); **Freddie Hubbard** (t, flh); **Cedar Walton** (p); **Ron Carter** (b); **Billy Higgins** (d). MusicMasters Ⓕ 65079-2 (55 minutes). Recorded 1992.

⑧ ❽

In the booklet-notes to this album Turrentine is quoted as saying that, early in his career, he used to play clubs where "you couldn't just play the songs, you had to get the *sound*, capture the feeling, express the *emotion*." There have been times on recent records when Turrentine has done little more than hint at his feelings through a stack of funky personal clichés, but on this one he's going for broke. Even the song selection (Gershwin, Ellington and Roland Kirk, among others) suggests that he's attempting something a little more ambitious than the usual rambling run-through, and the very first number, a Hubbard original called *Thomasville*, has Turrentine sweating it out in a convincing solo which has shape, creativity, excitement and a barrowload of jazz sensibility. His fellow-soloist Hubbard gets so excited that he fluffs a couple of high note runs and exhibits a surprisingly thin tone in the upper register (much as he did on the disappointing **Live at Fat Tuesday's** CD set from 1991), suggesting that the once impossibly clean execution and tireless embouchure has had time knocking at its door. However, any sense of let-down is banished by the easy, graceful medium-tempo swing of *They Can't Take That Away From Me* and the intimacy of *In a Sentimental Mood*, both of which are quartet tracks (on which the other band members are consistently outstanding). Hubbard takes only one further bow during the programme, on Kirk's contribution *Spirits up Above*, where his flügelhorn initially takes the melody, and his own solo, against a sweetly executed waltz metre, is for the most part lyrical and poised but hardly special by his standards. Not to worry; Turrentine gets to the meat of every song played here, and his work on the title track ("always something I've wanted to do", according to the CD sleeve) is sheer late-night, blissful intimacy as only a caressing tenor sax can be. Turrentine has been making records now for over 35 years, but this is one of the special ones. **KS**

# Alvin 'Red' Tyler

**Graciously** Tyler (ts); **Clyde Kerr Jr** (t, flh, perc); **David Torkanowsky** (p); **Steve Masakowski** (g); **James Singleton** (b); **Johnny Vidacovich** (d). Rounder Ⓕ 2061 (45 minutes). Recorded 1986.

⑧ ⑥

New Orleans, like other American cities, has its share of musicians who prefer the rootedness of home to the hot house of New York. Tyler, veteran of numerous Fats Domino sessions and the Crescent City's sixties hard-bop scene, was still a hometown fixture when he made two albums for Rounder in the mid eighties.

Tyler at this stage had a dark, pleasing tone, highlighted by varied, nimble phrasing. Decidedly a swinger, he tends to lean into the beat rather than lagging behind. A medium-grooving *Here's That Rainy Day*, for quartet with guitar, shows off his deft balladry, alert and relaxed at once. Elsewhere, Kerr's tart, hot trumpet nicely offsets Tyler's smoke-laced tenor.

The compatible rhythm players are among the city's most sought after, but explicit regionalisms are seldom apparent. Vidacovich lets parade beats emerge, closing Tyler's fetching jazz waltz *Greystoke*, and *My Shoes Hold Out* mambos in good second-line fashion. But usually the local accent comes out more subtly. The way tunes and improvisers drift between 2/4 and 4/4 (*Cutie Pie*), or duple and triple metre (*Greystoke*, *Count 'Em*) reflects a musical environment where Afro-Latin polyrhythms are second nature. **KW**

# Charles Tyler

1941-92

**Charles Tyler Ensemble** Tyler (as); **Joel Friedman** (vc); **Henry Grimes** (b); **Ronald Jackson** (d); **Charles Moffett** (d). ESP-Disk ⓕ 1029-2 (44 minutes). Recorded 1966.

⑥ ❺

Tyler made two albums for ESP-Disk, the second called **Eastern Man Alone**. This first album is the more coherent. Tyler came to prominence when he joined Albert Ayler's ensemble in the mid sixties for a brief time, and recorded on the tenor player's epochal **Bells** (also on ESP-Disk). Tyler clearly learned a lot from Ayler (they had known each other back in Cleveland, before either had any general reputation), mimicking his tone and delivery on the higher-pitched alto, and using many of the noise-effects from fierce overblowing of the instrument that Ayler was then specializing in. It is quite possible that Tyler also borrowed the idea of playing with cello and bass, but then it could just as easily have been the other way around. Whatever the true story, Tyler plays with great passion and commitment on every track, and although his music is a little limited in range, it is very effectively delivered here, with each instrument very clear on its role within the music (quite a rarity on ESP Disks in general at this time). We even come across common time on more than one occasion. Ayler's pioneering approach may have ultimately produced a series of dead-ends as far as development goes, but Tyler here suggests that there were other ways out which perhaps were not followed all the way by those following on behind. **KS**

# McCoy Tyner

1938

**New review**

**Plays Ellington** Tyner (p); **Jimmy Garrison** (b); **Elvin Jones** (d); on four tracks add **Willie Rodriguez**, **Johnny Pacheco** (perc). Impulse! Ⓜ IMP12162 (48 minutes). Recorded 1964.

⑦ ❿

It's interesting that, during the two days before the Coltrane Quartet entered Rudy van Gelder's New Jersey studios to record one of the most influential of all jazz records, **A Love Supreme**, McCoy Tyner had borrowed Coltrane's bassist and drummer to make this low-key but in its own way quite charming little tribute to Duke Ellington, groovy latin percussion and all. Far from being the type of turbulent, soul-bearing music one would associate with Coltrane at the time and Tyner later in his career, this could well have been produced by a piano trio led by someone like Red Garland, such is the insouciance and general even-temperedness. Tyner foxes with the tunes at times, taking *Solitude*, for example, at a sprightly tempo (much as Coltrane had done when he'd come to record *Body and Soul*), and making *It Don't Mean a Thing* into something of a latter-day roller-coaster (Elvin raises a sweat on this one), which may explain its exclusion from the original quite laid-back LP (it is one of three extra tracks included here). Early Tyner is well represented on this album, in style and content: certainly better than in the mean-minded parallel Impulse! reissues of **Nights of Ballads and Blues** and **Inception** as separate CDs, neither of which have any extra music on them, both of which used to fit on a single CD which was included in the previous Guide as a recommended disc. **SV**

**New review**

**Quartets 4x4** Tyner (p); **Cecil McBee** (b); **Al Foster** (d); with four separate guests: **Freddie Hubbard** (t, flh); **John Abercrombie** (g); **Bobby Hutcherson** (vb); **Arthur Blythe** (as). Milestone Ⓜ MCD55007-2 (76 minutes). Recorded 1980.

⑧ ❾

Originally released as a gatefold double vinyl album, this was a follow-up project from the excellent **Supertrios** double of 1977, also now on a Milestone CD, where he made separate sets with a Ron Carter/Tony Williams and a Eddie Gomez/Jack DeJohnette rhythm team. On this one the rhythm section remains constant and the soloists change. Hubbard is on first, and displays his usual crackling inventiveness and brilliant technique. The opener, the Tyner original, *Inner Glimpse*, comes close to Coltrane quartet-like intensity in places, with the rhythm team mounting a remorseless tidal wave of rhythm for Hubbard to surf, and while *Manhã de Carnaval* cools things out, the fast 4/4 *Paradox* has everyone stretching once again. Abercrombie's pellucid tone and more measured style keeps the two tracks he appears on more sedate affairs, but as the pair of them near ten minutes each, there is plenty of blowing space for Tyner in typically forthright mode. The three selections featuring Bobby Hutcherson have an outstanding level of simpatico between all four musicians, with a characterful and touchingly moody reading of Monk's *Pannonica* as perhaps the pick of the bunch. Hutcherson in particular gets everything just *so*, while Tyner revels in the slow tempo's easy lope and gives a wonderfully measured statement in his own solo spot. The three final tunes are with Arthur Blythe; the altoist is in fiery form on *Blues in the Minor*, sings the melody of the old standard *Stay as Sweet as You Are* in a manner worthy of Willie Smith, then burns up the changes on Jule Styne's *It's You or No One*. Tyner gives him plenty of room, laying out from time to time as he did with Coltrane and giving the rhythm team the space to cook. The varied attack and imaginative programme displayed in this set, on top of the uniformly excellent playing from all concerned, makes this an inclusion in this year's Guide in advance of the 1970 Blue Note session **Extensions**, reissued this year and featuring Wayne Shorter and Elvin Jones, where the programme occasionally gets in the way of the often excellent music and there are a few too many intonation problems amongst the front line. **KS**

---

**The Turning Point** Tyner (p, arr); **Kamau Adilifu, Earl Gardner, Virgil Jones** (t); **Steve Turré, Frank Lacy** (tb); **John Clark** (frh); **Howard Johnson** (tba); **Doug Harris** (ss, f); **Joe Ford** (as); **John Stubblefield, Junior Cook** (ts); **Avery Sharpe** (b); **Aaron Scott** (d); **Jerry Gonzales** (perc); **Dennis Mackrel**, Turré, Johnson, **Slide Hampton** (arr); **Bob Belden**, Hampton (cond). Birdology Ⓕ 513 163-2 (55 minutes ). Recorded 1991.

⑧ ⑧

Tyner has been extremely prolific on record during the last few years, producing trios and quartets, several solo albums and a couple of big band sessions. Although initially McCoy's piano style might seem just too dense to do other than compete with a large ensemble, some of his seventies Milestone recordings showed the assumption to be too simplistic and this album in particular vindicates the format completely.

At times the section writing doubles the piano theme-statements, but by and large they bounce off each other to great effect, thanks to the work of the five arrangers. And what a band it is! Recorded with just a sufficient halo of reverberation, the brass pack a terrific punch and the soloists (mostly uncredited, unlike the writers) include all the saxes, Clark and one of the trumpeters.

The remakes of *Passion Dance* (originally a quartet track featuring Joe Henderson) and *Fly with the Wind* come up brand new, while Tyner's *Update* (an *I Got Rhythm* variant) and the Monk-dedicated *High Priest* create straight-ahead contrasts. Of the ballads, *Angel Eyes* is a Hampton score influenced by early Gil Evans that would be too lush without Tyner's pianistics, while *In a Sentimental Mood* is his unaccompanied coda. **BP**

---

New review
**Prelude and Sonata** Tyner (p); **Joshua Redman** (ts); **Antonio Hart** (as); **Christian McBride** (b); **Marvin 'Smitty' Smith** (d). Milestone Ⓕ MCD9244-2 (64 Minutes). Recorded 1995.
✓

⑨ ⑩

A worthy successor to **Manhattan Moods**, Tyner's splendid 1993 collaboration with Bobby Hutcherson, this CD finds him in peak form and bringing out exceptional performances from the two young saxophonists. Something of Tyner's contemplative calm communicates itself to Hart, in particular, who plays with a warmth and simple passion that he has not displayed before – on record at any rate. Redman continues to bear out his early promise with unfailingly imaginative solos in his three numbers. The word 'magisterial' might have been coined to describe Tyner's own performance. There are moments when the rhythm section, even one as good as this, seems almost redundant as he strides purposefully forward. His solos, with their subtle, shifting densities and dark harmonic colours, are among the great achievements of contemporary jazz. Without doubt, these are vintage years for McCoy Tyner. **DG**

---

New review
**Infinity** Tyner (p); **Michael Brecker** (ts); **Avery Sharpe** (b); **Aaron Scott** (d); **Valtinho Anastacio** (cga, perc). Impulse! Ⓕ IMP11712 (72 minutes). Recorded 1995.

⑧ ⑨

Like it or not (and the man in question, with characteristic modesty, emphatically does not like it), Michael Brecker has often been regarded as Coltrane's successor – not a clone, but someone who has expanded the vocabulary which Coltrane pioneered. The sound of Brecker stepping into Coltrane's shoes is the chief fascination of **Infinity**, a session which has further historical resonance in bringing Tyner back to Impulse!, the label for which he and Coltrane made so many momentous recordings in the sixties. In recent years, while standing well back from the cutting edge of jazz, Tyner has added other dimensions to the tense quartal style which was his trade mark in the Coltrane quartet. The inclusion here of the Senegal-inspired 'Afro-Gospel' of *Happy Days,* the old-time stride of *Blues Stride* and *Good Morning, Heartache* and Tyner's frequent adoption of an upbeat harmonic style (though one still realized through a dancing, glittering straight-eighth delivery) all contribute to a relatively bright emotional climate. The mood stays dark, however, for Brecker's encounter with Coltrane. As he has in so many other similar settings, Brecker passes the modern tenor test of *Impressions* with distinction, developing a five-minute solo which further pummels the boundaries first challenged by his mentor. **MG**

# James Blood Ulmer

1942

---

New review
**Tales of Captain Black** Ulmer (g); **Ornette Coleman** (as); **Jamaaladeen Tacuma** (elb); **Denardo Coleman** (d). DIW Records Ⓕ DIW403 (33 minutes). Recorded 1978.

⑧ ⑧

Ulmer's early playing experience encompassed blues, soul and organ-based jazz with Hank Marr and Big John Patton. In 1971 he moved to New York, later working with Rashied Ali, Art Blakey, Joe Henderson and Larry Young; he also began to study harmolodics with Ornette Coleman, with whom he continued to play and record throughout the decade. In the eighties Ulmer led his groups Music Revelation Ensemble and Phalanx (which often featured saxophonists David Murray and George Adams respectively) and made a number of unexceptional blues-cum-funk discs. The best recordings under his own name tend to be the earlier ones, in particular his remarkable début, **Tales of Captain Black**. The first fruits of his harmolodic studies, **Tales** shows Ulmer somewhat upstaged by his teacher. In fact, the Coleman family virtually hijack the set, with Ornette's banshee alto and Denardo's clunk-thunder drums the dominant voices. Yet Ulmer's crabbed, stinging guitar fights back hard, and if his tunes lack the barbed melodic charm that characterizes Coleman's music, **Tales** may still be the most brutally streamlined example of harmolodics on record. Regrettably, with a playing time of just 33 minutes, it may also be the shortest.                                    **GL**

## Urbanator

New review

**Urbanator II** **Michal Urbaniak** (arr, orch, vn, saxes, kbds, prog); **Jon Dryden** (p, elp); **Al MacDowell** (b, kbds, arr); **Rodney Holmes** (d); with guests **Tom Browne**, **Issei Igarachi** (t); **Ed Hamilton** (g); **Denzil Miller** (kbd); **Solid**, **Six**, **Sharaye White** (v). Hip Bop Ⓕ HIBD8012 (64 minutes). Recorded 1996.

⑥ ❾

Urbanator is the brainchild of Michal Urbaniak, the Polish violinist who has always had a dual fascination with all things electronic and with improvisation. Urbanator is a studio group which allows him to be as street-credible as is possible or desirable, delivering him the full array of sampling, programming and rapping techniques as currently practised in the pop world. Thus you would not expect to come across much more than swingbeat and funk rhythms here, and those expectations are not disappointed. **Urbanator I** had guests such as Herbie Hancock, Michael Brecker and Tom Browne. This new one still has Tom Browne, and not much more, but the quality is not noticeably less, the melodies being hip and hummable, the occasional raps being identical to raps you hear everywhere else (same tone of voice, same avoidance of pitch and so on). But the improvisation remains, and it is what lifts this album out of the pop arena and into jazz, however funky it be.                                    **KS**

## Michal Urbaniak                                    1943

**Songbird** Urbaniak (vn); **Kenny Barron** (p); **Peter Washington** (b); **Kenny Washington** (d). SteepleChase Ⓕ SCCD31278 (64 minutes). Recorded 1990.

⑦ ❽

A versatile man, Urbaniak began his musical career in Poland as a Dixielander. He progressed firstly to bop and then came under the musical spell of John Coltrane. While still playing saxophone, he worked as a classical violinist before switching to that instrument as his first choice in both musical codes. His imaginative electronic group of the seventies featured his vocalist wife Ursula Dudziak, while in the eighties he worked with Larry Coryell and Archie Shepp. During that time, his playing deliberately retreated from the idea of either fusion or experimentation and he increasingly coloured his music with idiosyncratic Polish elements. This CD nails his colours to the mast most effectively. He has chosen one of jazz's best rhythm sections, the commitment is to his own brand of refined violin jazz and he has written excellent themes to accommodate both contingencies. The quizzical *Doubts*, the impelling *Deadline* and the jaunty *Aladdin's Lamp* stand out, but all are good vehicles for improvisation. Urbaniak's solos in 1990 have returned him to the harmonic approach; no attempt is made to desert the parent structure and it is perhaps significant that his most ingenious solos are on *Beautiful Love* and *Songbird*, the two tunes he did not write.                                    **BMcR**

## René Urtreger                                    1934

**Jazzman** Urtreger (p). Carlyne Music Ⓕ CARC10CD (53 minutes). Recorded 1985.

⑧ ❽

Urtreger has been a major part of the French jazz scene since the late fifties (he recorded with Miles Davis on the famous *Elevator to the Scaffold* soundtrack for Louis Malle), but like saxophonist Barney Wilen he had a long period away from the music. His return to jazz in the late seventies found him just as complete a player as before, but one with more confidence in his own abilities. This album has the authoritative ease in execution which only comes through complete mastery, and the opening track, *Budomania*, is a reworking of Bud Powell's *Parisian Thoroughfare* which is the best recording of the piece since the composer's own in 1951. Urtreger, a classically trained player (he studied with Marguérite Long, thereby becoming one of that very rare breed of jazz pianists, those whose training involved a direct link with Debussy, Ravel and Poulenc), never wanders greatly from his bop roots, but at the same time he is not limited by them into regurgitating familiar licks. He takes the harmonic and rhythmic disciplines of the music on board and forges fresh, inspiring music from them. Most of the compositions are his own, although J.J. Johnson's *Lament* and Monk's *Ruby, My Dear* and *'Round Midnight* are revealed in new and enticing ways here.                                        **KS**

# Warren Vaché                                                                                    1951

**Warm Evenings** Vaché (c); **Ben Aranov** (p); **Lincoln Millman** (b); **Giampaolo Biagi** (d); **The Beaux-Arts String Quartet**. Concord Ⓕ CCD4392 (52 minutes). Recorded 1989.

⑧ ❽

Like Ruby Braff before him, Vaché became a gap-filler. He came to be noticed as a child virtuoso and by his late teens it was obvious that he was to be a creative soloist of some stature. At the time of Vaché's birth Braff had been the only new mainstream player for some years and after Vaché established himself in his own particular gap it was to be some years before the next wave of great players (Alden, Peplowski *et al*) grew up to join him. Like Billy Butterfield before him he has suffered from neglect as the establishment fixates on the black players. It is only in the nineties that his eloquent, poised and yet fiery improvisations have made his footing secure. He is probably valued more in Europe than in his homeland. His many albums are consistently good, but this one with a string quartet places him in an unusual and very appropriate setting. His playing is so delicate that his melody statements stand on their own as works of art that Butterfield and Hackett would have been proud to own. *That Old Feeling* is one of four tracks where the strings lay out to leave an improviser's crucible for the cornet. All the tunes are well chosen with *This Is All I Ask* confirming once again that Gordon Jenkins was one of the great song composers.                                          **SV**

# Jesus 'Chucho' Valdes

**Solo Piano** Valdes (p); on two tracks, add: **Dave Green** (b); **Enrique Pla** (d); **Miguel 'Angar' Diaz** (perc). Blue Note Ⓕ CDP7 80597-2 (63 minutes). Recorded 1991.

⑧ ❽

Valdes hails from a village near Havana and received a formal musical education. In 1967 the Cuban band Irakere was formed, with Valdes as its leader, pianist and principal composer/arranger. Since 1985 Irakere has been a popular attraction at Ronnie Scott's in London with its annual appearances there. This CD was recorded at the club after the night's audience had left. Away from Irakere, Valdes is revealed as a most astonishing soloist with infallible technique and a great understanding of jazz. The note production alone is remarkable, but this is not technique for its own sake. Like Art Tatum, 'Chucho' clearly has no other way of playing, but remains always the master of his enormous instrumental command, never the other way around. Eight of the tracks are Valdes compositions, and one, *Bill (Evans)*, is a sincere tribute to one of his idols. Although some of the tunes hark back to a Cuban background, most of the music is firmly implanted in North American jazz (a fact reinforced by the final *Blues (Untitled)*, with bass and drums added). Although sub-titled **The Music of Cuba**, this is very definitely an outstanding example of pure jazz piano.                                 **AM**

# Kid Thomas Valentine                                                                      1896-1987

**Kid Thomas and his Algiers Stompers** Valentine (t, slapstick); **Louis Nelson** (tb); **Albert Burbank**, **Emil Barnes** (cl); **Joe James** (p); **Homer Eugene** (bj); **Joseph Butler** (b); **Sammy Penn** (d). Riverside Ⓜ OJCCD1833-2 (50 minutes.). Recorded 1960/1.

⑧ ❽

Thomas was leading a band in his native Reserve, Louisiana, and later in Algiers, across the Mississippi from New Orleans, before Louis Armstrong left the waif's home. His aggressive, punchy phrases, stabbing at the melodies rather than playing them, are the product of a musical imagination that never felt the influence of Armstrong or Oliver and which led one of New Orleans's most popular functional dance bands for over half a century. This vibrant, hard-swinging set is the epitome of Thomas's dancehall style: crude, rugged and uncompromising. Those weaned on Armstrong's *Mack The Knife* might find the Algiers Stompers version barely recognizable, but even with its altered chords, trombone/trumpet duet and a piano solo carried forward on the tide of Penn's offbeat, it shows Thomas's unique ability to stamp his personality on everything the band played. His is the image on the thousands of postcards sold over the years by Preservation Hall and his is the style that survived longest there, from around the time of this record into the eighties, by which time even the Humphrey brothers had diluted their style to something more befitting very old men. This is one of his very best discs; only his party-piece on *Milk Cow Blues* is missing from what was otherwise the core of his standard repertoire. Penn's drum punctuations have their roots in the marching bands, Nelson's trombone croons the ballads before punching out tailgate choruses in his trade mark style and for all but one track the filigree Creole clarinet of Albert Burbank wails its blue inflections over the ensemble. This band was not part of the New Orleans revival – it was there all along.    **AS**

# George Van Eps

1913

**Keepin' Time**  Van Eps, Howard Alden (g); Michael Moore (b); Jake Hanna (d). Concord
Ⓕ CCD4713 (59 minutes). Recorded 1994.

⑥ ⑧

Confronted with the easy-listening guitar moods on this CD, it is difficult to visualize Van Eps as an innovator. In fact, his earlier years saw him adopting an empirical attitude toward his trade. In order to provide his own bass line he experimented with his tuning; his investigations led him to the use of a seven string instrument and, in the late thirties, he wrote a paper that prompted its use by other guitarists. His own harmonic awareness directed his style and, as spells with Benny Goodman and Ray Noble suggest, he was very much a band player. The relaxed atmosphere on **Keepin' Time** exploits this fact. The technically accomplished Alden also plays a seven string and, on most titles, they enjoy support from the estimable Moore and Hanna. This is the guitarists' fourth Concord release and they make a natural team. *Honeysuckle Rose* is Van Eps's only unaccompanied performance but all show the harmonic depth of his style. Each of his solos is a tasteful amalgam of single note oratory and rich chordal support and he contrasts his softly contoured patterns with Alden's more incisive work in perfect style. Van Eps is only missing from *The Chant* and *Kay's Fantasy* but they are his compositions and, in a rather comforting way, show that his seemingly dated musical concept can still intrigue younger players.                                                                                     **BMcR**

# Ken Vandermark

**International Front**  Vandermark (ts, cl, bcl); Kent Kessler (b); Curt Newton (d). Okka Disk
Ⓕ OD12005 (74 minutes). Recorded 1994.

⑧ ⑨

In just a few short years the independent Okka Disk has become Chicago's most important record label, documenting criminally neglected players like local tenor sax legend Fred Anderson, selected free jazz guests like Sweden's Mats Gustafsson and, most crucially, the city's younger, vibrant, post-AACM generation, of whom multi-reedman Ken Vandermark is the most notable. Though originally from Boston, Vandermark settled in Chicago several years back and quickly became the hardest working man on the scene – fronting at least a half-dozen different groups, ranging from the open-ended improvisational trio Caffeine to the rock-influenced Vandermark Quartet. If any measure of his stylistic versatility, technical proficiency, and indefatigable energy were needed, the fact that Vandermark was invited to join the NRG Ensemble following the passing of their leader, the irrepressible Hal Russell, speaks volumes. Of his consistently increasing catalogue to date, the Steelwool Trio on this disc is a good introduction to Vandermark's multiple personalities. Each of the nine original tunes has a dedication, from Sun Ra to Jimmy Blanton, and vary from *noir*-ish escapades to unsentimental motivic ballads to high-octane relay races. Bass clarinet is his most Dolphyesque horn, which he plays in a skittering, flamboyant fashion, and it's always nice to hear him on clarinet, though in moments of extreme excitement he's liable to resort to a pinched, shrill urgency. Tenor sax is his main axe, and in moments of greatest intensity he sometimes inhales the beat in the manner of r&b honkers like Big Jay McNeely and Willis 'Gator' Jackson, in between the brawny sensibility of a Booker Ervin and the abandon of Albert Ayler – balancing on the precipice of sound and fury. Sometimes sheer exuberance overwhelms details in his improvising, and at moments like that it's essential to have a bassist like Kent Kessler on hand. Curt Newton, from Boston, is a light, colourful drummer with notable empathy for this set-up. Strong stuff.                                                                                          **AL**

# Jasper Van't Hof

1947

**Face to Face**  Van't Hof (p); Ernie Watts (ts); Bo Stief (b); Aldo Romano (d). veraBra
Ⓕ vBr2063-2 (53 minutes). Recorded 1994.

⑥ ⑧

Dutch pianist Van't Hof's wide-ranging involvements have stretched from work with Archie Shepp to his commercially successful 1984 world-music album, **Pili-Pili**, in which he employed African percussion and computer. **Face to Face** represents a largely uncompromising return to first principles. The spirit of Coltrane looms large throughout the date, the lead role played with admirable conviction and virtuosity by Ernie Watts, a player who in recent years has done more than enough to shake off the reputation he garnered in the seventies as a West Coast studio smoothie. Unsurprisingly, Van't Hof sounds not unlike McCoy Tyner and (when essaying later Trane styles) Alice Coltrane.

However, while the quartet adheres firmly to Trane's approach in several respects (most notably in the rolling, elegiac hymn, *Il Piacere*, and the unreconstructed hard bop of *As Well*) it follows the principle rather than the letter of Trane's pioneering world-music explorations, drawing its 'world' influences from such diverse contemporary sources as African High-Life music (*Zaïre*) and what sounds like Bulgarian gipsy music (*Three Doors*).                                                **MG**

# Tom Varner

**The Mystery of Compassion**  Varner (frh, arr); **Ed Jackson** (as); **Rich Rothenberg** (ts); **Mike Richmond** (b); **Tom Rainey** (d). **Mark Feldman** (vn) on one track; **Matt Derriau** (as); **Ellery Eskelin** (ts); **Jim Hartog** (bs)on one track; **Steve Swell** (tb); **Dave Taylor** (btb) on two tracks. Soul Note 121217-2 (75 minutes). Recorded 1992.

⑥ ❽

Varner is a well-travelled if little-known french-horn player who works with such different leaders as John Zorn, avant-garde 'composer' LaMonte Young and big-band specialist George Gruntz. He benefits from a ripe tone and an adventurous ear, and has made several previous albums on Soul Note. Half of the ten tracks here find him leading a quintet including Ed Jackson and Rich Rothenberg of the 29th Street Saxophone Quartet, and he sounds as mobile and forthright as most trombonists. This set, produced by drummer Joey Baron, is impressive for Varner's composition and organization skills. Some of the items have a subliminal Mingus feel in their mixture of written and improvised material in which the horn playing is more catalytic than cataclysmic. Featuring himself on three short tracks without rhythm, he has elsewhere stimulated some excellent collective playing, with the added attractions of the five extra brassmen on *Death at the Right Time*. The long *The Well*, on the other hand, features violinist Mark Feldman (who has played with Tim Berne and Anthony Davis) on an episodic piece that nods to both Philip Glass and 12-tone composition, while retaining an improvised content.                                                **BP**

# Nana Vasconcelos                                                1944

**Saludades**  Vasconcelos (perc, v); **Egberto Gismonti** (g, arr); **Stuttgart Radio Symphony Orchestra**. ECM Ⓕ 829 380-2 (44 minutes). Recorded 1979.

⑧ ❾

Brazilian drummer Vasconcelos is a percussive painter of exotically shimmering colours derived from South American, African and Asian sources. Having gained prominence in the mid sixties with countryman Milton Nascimento, he migrated to the US as a member of Argentinian saxophonist Gato Barbieri's group in 1971. In Europe he worked extensively with Brazilian guitarist Egberto Gismonti, and in 1978 co-founded the exploratory trio Codena with Don Cherry and Collin Walcott. Vasconcelos also had a prominent tenure with guitarist Pat Metheny's high-profile fusion group in the early eighties.

On **Saludades**, Vasconcelos conjures up intense percussion-based soundscapes whose *tramontane* other-world ambience is transmitted through Gismonti's ethereal string arrangements and Vasconcelos's inspired percussion and vocal gestures. His use of the berimbau, a bowed single-string affair connected to a resonating gourd, provides a distinctly melodic as well as percussive voice in the extended *O Berimbau* and elsewhere. Similarly impressive is Gismonti's *Cego Aderaldo* which also features Vasconcelos's long-standing colleague on eight-string guitar. A key element in the project's success is the sublime string playing of the Stuttgart aggregation.                                                **CB**

# Sarah Vaughan                                                1924-90

**Sarah Vaughan with Clifford Brown**  Vaughan (v); **Brown** (t); **Herbie Mann** (f); **Paul Quinichette** (ts); **Jimmy Jones** (p); **Joe Benjamin** (b); **Roy Haynes** (d); **Ernie Wilkins** (arr, cond). EmArcy Ⓜ 814 641-2 (50 minutes ). Recorded 1954.

✔                                                ❾ ❼

Although she began as a bebopper, trading choruses with Charlie Parker and Dizzy Gillespie, it took Sarah Vaughan nearly ten years to escape the pop market long enough to record her first classic set of jazz vocals. The occasion was her meeting with the young Clifford Brown, already on the verge of greatness, who contributes a handful of excellent solos. Quinichette and Mann add pleasant obbligatos, but they are really just icing on the cake. The two leaders apart, the musical honours go to the rhythm trio, Vaughan's regular group at the time, who accompany with peerless tact.

The session was a relaxed affair, the musicians filling out the arrangements in the studio and leaving plenty of room for improvisation. Vaughan seizes the chance gleefully, scatting duets with the horns on *Lullaby of Birdland*, skating around the melody of *Embraceable You*, signing-off *You're Not the Kind* with a surprise cascade of notes. Blessed with an extraordinary voice (her range was four octaves), she uses it, with great finesse, like an instrument, letting the long notes shimmer (*September Song*), swooping down to lean on a syllable (*Jim*), or darkening the timbre for a rueful *April in Paris*.

With her sensuous sound wedded to her impeccable timing (honed too on the whetstone of bebop), **With Clifford Brown** offers glorious Vaughan – hence glorious jazz – singing throughout.     **GL**   597

**Swingin' Easy** Vaughan (v); **John Malachi**, **Jimmy Jones** (p); **Joe Benjamin**, **Richard Davis** (b); **Roy Haynes** (d). EmArcy Ⓜ 514 072-2 (37 minutes). Recorded 1954-7.

✓ ⑩ ⑧

This CD would be worth buying for the version it contains of Ellington's *Prelude to a Kiss* alone – just one simple delicate, unerring chorus. It is very un-songlike song, with intervals that might have been specially devised as traps for a singer with an insecure sense of pitch, which is exactly the kind of song that Sarah Vaughan relished. She had a miraculous ear and the vocal equipment to follow it wherever it led, a combination of which she was justly proud. Much of the enjoyment of listening to the young Sarah comes from the delight she takes in making tunes turn somersaults and jump through hoops. She seems, quite frankly, to take little interest in the words at this stage. The last piece here, a breakneck two choruses of *Linger Awhile*, would have been quite outrageous coming from anyone else, but who can object to a bit of showing off when the result is as spectacular as this? It puts one in mind of the completely unjustified but breathtaking swoop of almost an octave in the middle of her famous *Just Friends* – she just could not resist it. These two sessions were recorded when Sarah was aged 30 and 33 respectively, right at the end of her first flush of youthful exuberance, and they are magnificent. Well worth having, despite the short playing time. **DG**

New review
**Count Basie and Sarah Vaughan** Vaughan, Joe Williams (v); Sonny Cohn, Thad Jones, Joe Newman, **Snooky Young** (t); **Henry Coker**, **Al Grey**, **Benny Powell** (tb); **Marshall Royal** (as); **Frank Wess** (as, ts, f); **Frank Foster**, **Billy Mitchell** (ts); **Charlie Fowlkes** (bs); **Kirk Stuart** (p); **Freddie Green** (g); **Eddie Jones** (b); **Sonny Payne** (d). Roulette Ⓜ CDP8 37241-2 (47 minutes). Recorded 1960-1.

⑨ ⑧

As one of the top three or four jazz singers, Vaughan should have made more consistently good recordings than she did. Too often she was not quite on form or compromised by stodgy accompaniment. Albums which were designed to be popular achieved the lowest common denominator. Her best recordings were for Mercury and her **In the Land of Hi-Fi** with Ernie Wilkins and Cannonball Adderley remains the yardstick by which her other big band albums should be judged. The best small-group set was **Swingin' Easy**. Another outstanding set was done for Columbia with the Basie band minus its leader. The current album tucks in somewhere behind that with the singing not at her most inspired but good enough of course to frighten off any emulators. Care must be taken not to damn her with faint praise, for this is a very desirable album with immaculate performances and imaginative and beautifully recorded arrangements written by Thad Jones – the writing is understandably conventional Basie rather than experimental Jones! There is little in the way of instrumental solos, but Joe Newman has a nice one on *Mean to Me* and Vaughan's unique and oblique variation of the melody at the beginning of the piece is as ear-grabbing as her gymnastic coda. The band were sight-reading the charts – they did it brilliantly – and maybe this and Vaughan's natural exuberance are responsible for the spontaneity of sound which is such an attractive quality of the session. Basie does not play, by the way, and Williams sings on two tracks. **SV**

**Crazy and Mixed Up** Vaughan (v); **Roland Hanna** (p); **Joe Pass** (g); **Andy Simpkins** (b); **Harold Jones** (d). Pablo Ⓜ PACD2312 137-2 (33 minutes). Recorded 1982.

✓ ⑨ ⑨

This is simply one of the finest jazz vocal albums ever produced. Sarah Vaughan, at the height of her extraordinary powers in 1982, swings with a god-like combination of authority and abandon. Indeed, if anyone ever sounded like she was born to be a jazz singer, Sarah Vaughan, at least here, is it. The ballads are impeccable. And when she limns *That's All* or *Love Dance*, that dark rich voice cannot help but envelop all in its powerfully seductive wake. Then, when she jumps from a musical cliff as she does on the free-fall flight of *Autumn Leaves*, one is left simply breathless. Vaughan's trade mark vibrato quavers in the rubato intro of *The Island* before shifting gears into a hauntingly languid bossa nova. And though pronunciations are typically diffuse, she somehow makes the lyrics lucid and alive.

What makes this album a special case, even for Sarah Vaughan, is the singer's overall control of herself and the project. Pablo chief Norman Granz gave the production reins to Vaughan, who selected the repertoire as well as the musicians. And what a supporting cast! Pianist Hanna, guitarist Pass, bassist Simpkins and drummer Jones weave magic carpets on which Vaughan soars, sails and dips with delight. This was an obvious labour of love in which Vaughan's concentration was totally focused and inspired. **CB**

# Charlie Ventura

1916

New review
**Live at the Three Deuces** Ventura (ts); **Bill Harris** (tb); **Ralph Burns** (p); **Bob Leininger** (b); **Dave Tough** (d). Jazz Band Ⓔ EBCD2122-2 (72 minutes). Recorded 1947.

⑥ ⑤

At the time of these small-group airshot recordings from a small 52nd Street club in New York Ventura was a poll-winning saxophonist with featured roles in both Gene Krupa's and Teddy Powell's big bands behind him. His smooth technique, big tone and showmanship had earned him a loyal following, and though his 1946 big band was a failure (the economics of the immediate post-war years put paid to virtually every big band apart from Ellington and Hampton) he ran popular small groups culminating in 1948's "Bop to the People" campaign, which combined bop phraseology with vocals. He also appeared regularly in Norman Granz's Jazz-at-the-Philharmonic troupes. By the fifties Ventura had resumed his role as a sideman, winning particular notice for his often tongue-in-cheek work with Gene Krupa's small groups of this era. By this time he had been largely discounted as an influence in the wider world of jazz and his reputation has never really recovered. However, as the fair-to-middling sound quality of this radio broadcast reveals, Ventura was a superior stylist with his roots in the swing era, his tone and rhythmic drive owing much to Ben Webster and Illinois Jacquet. He was capable of generating considerable excitement with his playing while retaining full control of his instrument and the music around him, and he always swung. His companions on this disc are all (apart from bassist Leininger) straight from the recently disbanded Woody Herman First Herd, with Tough, Burns and Leininger bringing the same light, driving swing to this group that is to be found in the Herd's music. Bill Harris is the greatest trombone stylist outside of the Ellington bands between Teagarden and J.J. Johnson; here he gets plenty of solo space to demonstrate his highly vocalized, dynamic approach. By the time of this group's residency at the Three Deuces in April 1947 the style they were using had been superseded by bop, but this cannot invalidate the meaning of this finely played, committed set of improvisations by a group of men serious about enjoying themselves.   **KS**

## Joe Venuti                                                                    1903-78

**Violin Jazz**  Venuti (vn); **Jimmy Dorsey** (t, cl, as, bs); **Benny Goodman** (cl); **Don Murray** (cl, bs); **Frankie Trumbauer** (c-ms); **Adrian Rollini** (bss, gfs, hfp, vb, p); **Arthur Schutt, Frank Signorelli, Phil Wall, Rube Bloom** (p); **Eddie Lang, Dick McDonough** (g). Yazoo Ⓔ 1062 (43 minutes). Recorded 1927-34.

✅                                                                               ⑧ 🎱

Venuti's "blend of solid musicianship and hokum," as the notes observe, "remains exhilarating to this day ... confound[ing] conventional distinctions between highbrow and lowbrow art". The hokum character stems in part from the use of novelty instruments like Adrian Rollini's goofus and hot fountain pen, though some listeners may apply the description to the unremitting gaiety of the material, which preserves in a tangy aspic the Charleston-and-cocktail euphoria of its time. To be sure, there is no darkness in this music, and next to nothing of the blues, but to dismiss it as lightweight not only maligns the stupendous virtuosity of the principals Venuit and Lang but proscribes an optimism that is a legitimate part of the expressive vocabulary of jazz.

Louis Armstrong had revealed in his Hot Five and Seven recordings a few years earlier the dominant role a soloist could claim, yet these small-group performances, although nominally led by a forceful musical personality, are essentially collaborative. Instrumental roles constantly alter as the basic musical material is cut up and re-stitched into independent themes or elaborations. The product is not, as sometimes with Armstrong, monologue but the shifting textures of an animated and clever conversation.                                                                **TR**

## Billy Ver Planck                                                             1930

**Jazz for Playgirls**  Ver Planck (tb, arr); **Clyde Reasinger, Joe Wilder, Bernie Glow, Phil Sunkel** (t); **Bill Harris** (tb); **Phil Woods** (cl, as); **Seldon Powell** (ts); **Gene Allen, Sol Schlinger** (bs); **Eddie Costa** (p, vb); **George Duvivier, Wendell Marshall** (b); **Bobby Donaldson, Gus Johnson** (d). Denon/Savoy Ⓜ SV0209 (37 minutes). Recorded 1957.

⑧ 🎱

This is a fine mainstream album which might be in danger of being overlooked by collectors unfamiliar with Ver Planck's name and credentials. He is a splendid writer whose scores have enlivened the books of dance bands such as those of Claude Thornhill, Jimmy Dorsey and Ralph Marterie. Savoy gave him a free hand on three or four albums in the fifties and this is a supreme example of his skills at combining orchestral efficiency with deep-rooted jazz feeling. Bill Harris, surely one of the most individual of all jazz trombonists, is one of the main soloists; he is clearly one of Ver Planck's idols. This is shown in another way on *Du-Udah-Udah*, where Ver Planck takes the trombone solo himself, only to reveal a style deeply indebted to Harris. Another heavily featured soloist is Phil Woods (he has *Aw C'mon Sugah!* to himself), caught here at his most joyfully uninhibited. Rudy Van Gelder's engineering (in mono) captures the music with a sense of immediacy that is most attractive. An additional asset on this rather brief reissue is the playing of the late Eddie Costa on both piano and vibraphone. Recommended.                             **AM**

## Edward Vesala                                                                1945

**Ode to the Death of Jazz**  Vesala (d); **Matti Riikonen** (t); **Jorma Tapio** (as, bcl, f); **Jouni Kannisto** (ts, f); **Pepa Paivinen** (ss, ts, bs, f, cl, bcl); **Tim Ferchen** (mba, bells); **Taito Vainio**

(accordion); **Iro Haarla** (p, hp, syn); **Jimi Sumen** (g); **Uffe Krokfors** (b). ECM Ⓕ 843 196-2 (56 minutes). Recorded 1989.

⑩ ❽

Vesala's vision is among the most unsettling, exotic, and unique in all of jazz – if you call what he does jazz. Given the (tongue-in-cheek?) title of this magnificent programme, I am not sure he does. Architect of several previous albums of atmospheric design, Vesala composes for contrast and mood rather than cohesiveness. As a percussionist, he has brought knowledge of ethnic musics, rock and a determined rejection of glib virtuosity and convention to bear on a highly personal style, and the same could be said for his scoring. These are magically evocative pieces, manipulating instrumental colour and texture to evoke fascinating soundscapes of light and dark, water and ice, shadow and substance. *Sylvan Swizzle* (suggesting a tour through other-worldly caverns), the hauntingly spare *Time to Think*, and the shimmering *Watching for the Signal* are carefully constructed ensemble works, full of unexpected details and emotional curves. But there are surprises everywhere – the forceful blend of folkish melody, industrial noise and machine-gun drumming of *Winds of Sahara*, the wispy, disembodied electronics behind the tribal percussion and horn eruptions of *Infinite Express* and the incongruous tango *A Glimmer of Sepal*. Absolutely original music, totally engaging. **AL**

## Andrea Vicari                                          1966

**Suburban Gorillas** Vicari (p, kbds, perc): **Simon Da Silva** (t, flh); **Malcolm Earle Smith** (tb); **Martin Dunsdon** (f); **Leigh Etherington** (f, ss, ts); **Mornington Lockett** (ts, perc); **Hilary Cameron** (kbds, v); **Mark Ridout** (g); **Dorian Lockett** (b, elb); **Simon Pearson** (d, perc); **Rony Barrak** (tabla). 33 Records Ⓕ 33Jazz016 (78 minutes). Recorded 1994.

⑥ ❽

Vicari, born in Florida but based in Birmingham since 1972, studied at Cardiff University, with a postgrad course at the Guildhall to round out her musical background, before beginning a professional career in London in the early nineties. She appeared with David Jean Baptiste, both live and on CD, during the course of 1993, and formed Suburban Gorillas, her own big-band, when the opportunity for a UK tour came about. That tour brought about this record, her début as a leader. As with many débuts it tends occasionally to be over-ambitious in scope, but there is nothing wrong with that, and there is nothing truly bad on this album, although some of the infrequent lyrics come close on occasion.

The playing, from a band of notable talents, is sharp enough without being soulless, and although the improvisations occasionally veer too close to competent rather than inspired or individualistic, the writing is unfussy, melodic and consistently upbeat. Vicari takes the Duke Ellington approach to leading this band, rather than the Cecil Taylor: her presence is discerned through the directions the band takes rather than her own piano work suborning all else to its needs. A good example of this is *Southern Comfort*, which opens with a three-minute unaccompanied piano solo, but then vamps into a piece for the whole ensemble to unfold. Ellington's method in a nutshell, even if the style is unrelated. An enjoyable album which suggests more and better things to come. Vicari's subsequent album for 33, **Lunar Spell** (1996), continues the good work of her début. **KS**

## Harold Vick                                          1936-87

New review
**Steppin' Out** Vick (ts); **Blue Mitchell** (t); **John Patton** (org); **Grant Green** (g); **Ben Dixon** (d). Blue Note Ⓜ CDP8 52433-2 (36 minutes). Recorded 1963.

⑤ ❼

This was Vick's first record as a leader and his only one in that role for Blue Note. He went on to make three good LPs for RCA in the mid sixties, **Caribbean Suite**, **Straight Up** and **Watch What Happens**, and a mid-seventies album for Muse which brought him full circle back to the type of music made on this disc. He came to attention initially playing with organists such as Patton, Jimmy McGriff and Jack McDuff, but the RCA records showed him as a more rounded player capable of bringing a much more cosmopolitan outlook to his music. This is currently the only Harold Vick-led session on CD. Unfortunately it is not very good, rarely rising above the routine. Vick has intonation trouble from time to time, his solo style often sounds an uneasy cross between Dexter Gordon and the raunchier, more r&b-derived punch of Willis Jackson and Gene Ammons, and his ideas are unvaryingly routine. Given this as his only exposure on record, a listener fresh to his talents would conclude that Vick was just another saxophonist scuffling in New York in the sixties. There is one standard here, *Laura*, which is generally handled adequately; the rest are Vick originals, some of which have interesting constructions in a hard-bop framework. What there is of musical interest in the improvisations tends to stem from Patton or Mitchell, both of whom conjure nice things from time to time, while Green sounds uninterested and Ben Dixon is quietly competent. Until Vick's true ability is more fully exposed by the CD re-issue of the RCA discs, this mediocre set will have to do. **KS**

# Vienna Art Orchestra

**The Minimalism of Erik Satie** Lauren Newton (v); **Karl 'Bumi' Fian** (t, flh); **Hannes Kottek** (t, flh); **Christian Radovan** (tb); **John Sass** (bb); **Harry Sokal** (ss, ts, f); **Wolfgang Puschnig** (as, bcl, f, snino s); **Roman Schwaller** (ts, cl); **Woody Schabata** (vb); **Wolfgang Reisinger** (perc); **Mathias Rüegg** (ldr, cond, arr); **Ima** (tbra). hatART Ⓔ CD6024 (76 minutes ). Recorded 1983/4.

⑥ ❽

Formed by pianist and arranger Mathias Rüegg in 1977, the Vienna Art Orchestra has enjoyed a colourful career. It has worked the jazz festival circuit and has not been deterred from drawing musical inspiration from sources as wide as Scott Joplin, Lennie Tristano and Anthony Braxton. This lengthy CD dedicates itself to the spirit of Erik Satie and introduces the listener to the surrealistic music of the enigmatic Frenchman. It is significant that only one Satie composition is played, but his *Gnossiennes* from 1890 was an important avant-garde work. It was Satie's first experimentation with barless notation, it had no key signature and it dispensed with normal thematic construction. This mood of perambulating free melodic interaction is well-captured by Rüegg in his own arrangements. Throughout the whole album he successfully interprets the spirit of Satie's music in modern guise. He has used the vocal (jazz) talents of Lauren Newton, the present-day vibraphone figures of Woody Schabata and the saxophone playing of Harry Sokal and Roman Schwaller in a way that fits effortlessly into the contemporary jazz world but continues to champion the Satie dictum of "music without sauerkraut". **BMcR**

# Leroy Vinnegar

1928

**Leroy Walks!** Vinnegar (b); **Gerald Wilson** (t); **Teddy Edwards** (ts); **Carl Perkins** (p); **Victor Feldman** (vb); **Tony Bazley** (d). Contemporary Ⓜ OJCCD160-2 (42 minutes). Recorded 1957.

⑧ ❽

From the time of his arrival in Los Angeles in 1954 Vinnegar has been the rock on which many outstanding rhythm sections have been founded. Perhaps 'reliable' does not sound an over-complimentary term, but it is the highest praise for Leroy, whose faultless time-keeping, full tone and ability to mark the passage of time through the most stimulating choice of notes from the chords make him still one of the most in-demand of all West Coast bass players. He has always 'walked' (i.e. played a steady four-in-a-bar) behind others as well as in his own solos and choosing a programme of seven tunes, six of which had the word 'walk' in their titles, was an inevitable A&R man's ploy. Wilson (muted throughout) and Edwards both solo to good effect, but the chief interest lies in the work of the rhythm section and Feldman (the horns are absent on *Would You Like to Take a Walk* and *I'll Walk Alone,* probably the most impressive tracks). Perkins and Vinnegar were actually at school together and the way their work interlocks is masterly, but then so too are the solos of London-born Feldman. This remains Vinnegar's best album as a leader. **KS**

# Miroslav Vitous

1947

**Journey's End** Vitous (b); **John Surman** (ss, bs, bcl); **John Taylor** (p); **Jon Christensen** (d). ECM Ⓕ 843 171-2 (41 minutes). Recorded 1982.

⑧ ❿

Vitous came bursting onto the New York jazz scene from his native Prague in the late sixties, then garnered even greater fame as a charter member of Weather Report. His tenure there was brief, however, and for most the seventies he pursued other interests away from the bass. At the close of the decade, he came back to the instrument and began teaching, finally becoming head of the Jazz Department at New England Conservatory in the early eighties. His return to the recording studio found his faculties unimpaired: he still had one of the most beautiful tones and fecund melodic imaginations in the music, as well as stupendous technique, whether plucking or bowing.

This album illustrates more than just his instrumental facility, however. Two of the album's more evocative songs are his, and the way he has structured the group to play them means that there is nothing conventional or dull in the way they are performed. Surman is generally in an assertive mood on this date, though his two compositions are both marked by a bittersweet tenderness. Vitous grabs the attention at every turn either with his arresting ideas or, more subtly, by the beautiful support he gives the group. Like Mingus, he is a real leader from the bass, and the music is all the stronger for it. **KS**

# Allen Vizzutti

New review

**Skyrocket** Vizzutti (t, flh, pic t, frh); **Harold Garrett** (tb); **Joe Farrell** (ts); **Mike Miller, Grant Geisman** (g); **Chick Corea** (p, elp, Moog, clavinet); **Ken Shima** (p); **Bunny Brunel, Leon Gaer** (b); **Tom Brechtlein** (d). Summit Records Ⓕ DCD179 (63 minutes). Recorded *c*1980.

⑥ ❼

A re-release of Woody Herman/Chick Corea sideman Allen Vizzutti's eponymous septet album, its tracks interspersed with three quintet pieces for CD, **Skyrocket** showcases a prodigious trumpet talent equally proficient at producing stratospheric fusion-based surefootedness and a bell-like, classical purity of tone. In both these areas Vizzutti is particularly well matched with Corea, whose ability to choose the exact shade of synthesized sound to showcase the trumpeter's skill is based on a similar range of aptitude. A welcome touch of querulousness is brought to the proceedings by Joe Farrell, and Bunny Brunel's fretless bass imparts a particularly effective plaintive singing sound to the ensemble, but overall the brightness of the album's mix of bubbling fusion, tender flügelhorn ballads and the odd baroque-influenced piccolo trumpet feature is dimmed by the occasional blandness of the basic material. Vizzutti's themes range from sub-Zappa bustles through loose funk to anthemic flag-wavers, and the textural variety achieved courtesy of his band's virtuosity is the album's most attractive feature, but the writing is not quite biting enough, and the basic group sound too studio-bound to enable this recording to stand out from the bulk of contemporary fusion products.          **CP**

# V.S.O.P.

**Live under the Sky**  Freddie Hubbard (t, flh); **Wayne Shorter** (ts, ss); **Herbie Hancock** (p); **Ron Carter** (b); **Tony Williams** (d). Columbia ⓜ 471063-2 (77 minutes). Recorded 1979.

⑦ ❼

Formed in 1976, V.S.O.P. were hailed as representing a retreat from fusion excesses. In fact, all five musicians had made their mark on jazz long before the arrival of Miles Davis's **In a Silent Way**, and in most cases had continued with fusion music while still working V.S.O.P. As this CD shows, there was no problem with their return to Jazz Messenger territory. As is perhaps inevitable in a unit boasting five virtuoso musicians, the collective effect is never quite as good as the individual contributions. They were a semi-permanent band, but there were times when a jam session mood prevailed.

The most co-ordinated pieces are *Teardrop* and *Para Orients*, but Hubbard is at his best when the jousting gets serious. Shorter's tenor blossoms on titles such as *Pee Wee*, where he can journey over the consciously uneven terrain laid by a rhythm section roughed up by Williams's brilliant drumming. Carter is wonderfully coherent in all he does and Hancock leaves the listener wondering why he did not always play in the V.S.O.P.-way.          **BMcR**

# Chad Wackerman                                                    1960

**Forty Reasons**  Wackerman (d, ldr); **Allan Holdsworth** (g); **Jim Cox** (kbds, org); **Jimmy Johnson** (b). CMP ⓕ CD48 (45 minutes ). Recorded 1991.

⑥ ❽

The very aptly named Chad Wackerman is perhaps best known as a drummer with Frank Zappa but, like bassist Jimmy Johnson, he has also served for several years in Allan Holdsworth's Californian bands. Holdsworth – the album's star attraction – here becomes the sideman, and the role reversal exposes often submerged aspects of his style. His own hi-tech fusion records have frequently foundered under a welter of complexity, but the modal settings, airy textures and regular pulses heard here provide an uncluttered platform for his virtuoso flights. Wackerman, bravura fusion drummer that he is, could easily have dominated the session, but this is very much an ensemble effort. The composed pieces, mostly his, demonstrate a surprising lyricism and restraint, and almost half the tracks appear to be freely improvised. As far as the present writer knows, Holdsworth has not been publicly involved in free collective improvisation since the days of John Stevens's group Plough, and these short pieces, by adding a wide range of natural and electronic tone colours to Plough's fairly orthodox range of instrumental and stylistic resources, add a fresh idiom to the Holdsworth catalogue.          **MG**

# Collin Walcott                                                    1945-84

**Cloud Dance**  Walcott (sitar, tabla); **John Abercrombie** (g); **Dave Holland** (b); **Jack DeJohnette** (d). ECM ⓕ 825 469-2 (39 minutes). Recorded 1975.

⑧ ❾

Collin Walcott was a true internationalist in terms of philosophy and choice of instruments. After graduating as a percussion major at Indiana University, Walcott studied sitar with Ravi Shankar and tabla with Alla Rakha. In the late sixties he worked with clarinettist Tony Scott, a pioneer in the serious investigation of melding modern jazz with Eastern music. In 1970, Walcott joined Paul Winter's Consort and explored various combinations of ethnic music and jazz. Out of Winter's group came Oregon (with Ralph Towner, Paul McCandless and Glen Moore). Before his tragic death in an auto accident in East Germany, Walcott worked with Codona, the co-operative trio with Don Cherry and Nana Vasconcelos.

Here, in an exceptional date from 1975, Walcott engages guitarist Abercrombie, bassist Holland and drummer DeJohnette in eight varied settings that, in toto, constitute a virtual suite. There are duos such as *Prancing* for tablas and bass, and trios such as *Vedanas* for sitar, bass and guitar, whereas the concluding *Cloud Dance* involves all four musicians. The sonic textures, given the prominence of

Walcott's tablas and sitar, ripple with exotic colours and swirling rhythmic currents, but often there is also a driving pulse. Due to the vision of Walcott and his estimable colleagues, this singular meeting of Eastern and Western musics continues to refresh and inspire as it also opens doors. **CB**

## Myron Walden

New review
**Hypnosis** Walden (as); **Mulgrew Miller**, **Kevin Hayes** (p); **Dwayne Burno** (b); **Eric McPherson**, **Eric Harland** (d). NYC Ⓕ 6025-2 (55 minutes). Recorded 1995.

⑥ ❻

Walden is a young hard-playing neo-classicist with a big tone and a penchant for strangulated long screams from the upper harmonics of his instrument that recalls Coltrane in the early sixties. Walden's basic musical conception is not particularly beholden to the great tenor man; his style seems closer to the ideas pursued by people like Gary Bartz, Greg Osby and others of the present generation. He has a persuasive edge to his playing and exploits an emotionalism which is not often present in neo-classicists and which is all the more attractive for its presence. He is supported ably by the two rhythm teams, arising from two separate sessions. (At least both drummers were called Eric, thereby avoiding confusion in the studio when the engineer asked Eric to play quieter.) The recording balance, by the way, is not ideal, with Walden too far forward and the drummer (both Erics) much too far back in the mix, thereby giving an oddly top-heavy sound-image to the whole thing. Not the musicians' fault, I know, but it impinges on the overall success of the album. **KS**

## Mal Waldron

1926

New review
**Mal/3 Sounds** Waldron (p); **Art Farmer** (t); **Eric Dixon** (f); **Calo Scott** (vc); **Julian Euell** (b); **Elvin Jones** (d); **Elaine Waldron** (v). Prestige Ⓜ OJCCD1814-2 (39 minutes). Recorded 1958.

⑧ ❽

Apart from recording as part of various Charles Mingus groups at the start of his career, Mal Waldron also associated himself with Mingus's Composers' Workshop and was clearly much involved with formal composition. The opening *Tension* has affiliations with *Vibrations* that he recorded a couple of years earlier with Teddy Charles, even down to tempo changes and the bustling finale. Farmer takes the first of several solos in his best conversational manner, muted here over the bracing beat and making every note count. Two of the five tracks include settings for the deep contralto of Elaine Waldron. *Portrait of a Young Mother* could almost be a Duke Ellington homage, beginning with wordless voice as in *Creole Love Call* before edging into a stately blues theme, Farmer taking the Arthur Whetsol role alongside bowed cello. The leader solos in his most typical fashion on the up-tempo *The Cattin' Toddler* – one of his dog-worrying-bone efforts, filled with odd rhythmic accents that go round engagingly in circles. **RA**

**The Quest** Waldron (p); **Eric Dolphy** (as, cl); **Booker Ervin** (ts); **Ron Carter** (vc); **Joe Benjamin** (b); **Charles Persip** (d). New Jazz Ⓜ OJC082-2 (42 minutes). Recorded 1961.
✓

⑩ ❽

Previous LP reissues of this music under Dolphy's more marketable name did Mal Waldron a disservice, as it was his date and all the compositions his own. As a composer Waldron has been given short shrift; he not only contributed many more or less memorable blowing vehicles to countless Prestige sessions, but also penned a few standards and more formal successes. The seven tunes here are wonderful, ranging from the soulful r&b of *Warp and Woof* to the buoyant *Fire Waltz*, which Waldron and Dolphy would revisit in a celebrated live date a mere three weeks later, in the company of another Booker, Little. Carter's cello is a curious touch, although reminiscent of the chamber music textures of Chico Hamilton's group and Mingus's early experiments. Despite occasionally questionable intonation, he brings a plaintive quality to the melody of *Duquility*, and a secure *pizzicato* to the haunting *Warm Canto* – the latter with Dolphy especially sensitive on clarinet, Persip's exquisite brushwork on cymbals, and Waldron's motivic insistence that would soon be his trade mark. Elsewhere, Booker Ervin's barnstorming tenor seems frequently inspired by Dolphy's careening chromaticism, in solos that are concise and still exciting. All told, a marvellous, fully realized programme. **AL**

## Bennie Wallace

1946

**The Fourteen Bar Blues** Wallace (ts); **Eddie Gomez** (b); **Eddie Moore** (d). Enja Ⓕ 3029-2. Recorded 1978 (47 minutes).

⑧ ❽

The last few years have seen Bennie Wallace find success scoring films, often ones with a Southern atmosphere, and celebrating his Tennessee roadhouse roots with the likes of Dr John and the late Stevie Ray Vaughan. It would have been hard to anticipate his current direction from this smashing début album. The hard-edged, volatile improvising found here pushed the limits of song form and jazz convention, rather than indulging in the entertaining avenues of popular culture. It is obvious that the early Wallace had listened hard to Sonny Rollins; although the wild chromaticism owes a debt to Dolphy, his intense thematic construction, long unaccompanied cadenza on *Flamingo*, and the neo-calypso *Green and Yellow* are all Sonny's terrain. At this stage Wallace is feeling out various approaches – Hawkins's finesse and relentless drive, Bird's rhythmic impetus, even a near-parody of Ayler's huge vibrato (on *Vicissitudes*), and breathy Ben Websterism (*Chelsea Bridge*). All stops out, the rhythm section creates eddys of counter-currents, and Gomez is an especially fine foil. His own horn-like lines parry Wallace's, and they exchange roles and later chase each other's tails on the title tune. As soon as Wallace's album with the equally incandescent Jimmy Knepper, **...Plays Monk**, is released on CD, it is unreservedly recommended. In the meantime, this one sizzles.　　**AL**

## Beulah 'Sippie' Wallace　　1898-1986

**New review**

**Complete Recorded Works 1923-5, Volume 1** Wallace (v) with: **Louis Armstrong, Tom Morris, Joe 'King' Oliver** (c); **Charlie Irvis, Aaron Thompson** (tb); **Ernest Elliott, Buster Bailey, Rudolph Jackson** (cl); **Sidney Bechet** (ss, cl); **Eddie Heywood, Clarence Williams, Hersal Thomas, Perry Bradford** (p); **Buddy Christian** (bj). Document Ⓟ DOCD5399 (72 minutes). Recorded 1923-5.
　　　⑥ ❻

Beulah 'Sippie' Wallace began her public singing in church, toured on the famous TOBA circuit and recorded quite prolifically in a career that spanned from 1923 to 1984. At her best she was a vaudeville blues singer, with a natural resonance in her voice's lower register and a strength of delivery throughout her range. She knew how to add drama by graduation of tone and, as the Texas Nightingale, learned the tricks of audience manipulation in tent shows and theatres throughout the South. The quality of her singing attracted the OKeh company and her earliest recordings were with the simple piano backing of Heywood and Williams. Their success earned for her high-quality support teams and shifted her work more firmly into the jazz category. On this CD, the Clarence Williams's Harmonizers line-up includes the estimable Morris and Irvis, while two Blue Five titles feature the superbly throbbing soprano of Bechet as well as the assured, if slightly off-microphone, cornet of Armstrong. Bechet's soprano makes an even more telling contribution to *I'm So Glad I'm Brownskin*, while his work on *Off and On Blues* is a model of clarinet blues playing. Oliver was still in good instrumental voice in 1925 and his preaching cornet teams up with Thomas's accomplished piano to form a timeless jazz duo. Wallace was still touring into the eighties and remained a singer who surrounded herself with jazz musicians of note.　　**BMcR**

## Fats Waller　　1904-43

**Fats and His Buddies** Waller (p); with, on two tracks: **Charlie Gaines** (t); **Charlie Irvis** (tb); **Arville Harris** (reeds); **Eddie Condon** (bj); on two tracks **Red Allen** (t); **Jack Teagarden** (tb, vb) ; **Albert Nicholas, Otto Hardwick** (as); **Larry Binyon** (ts); **Eddie Condon** (bj); **Al Morgan** (b); **Gene Krupa** (d); **Four Wanderers** (v); on four tracks: **Red Allen, Leonard Davis** (t); **Jack Teagarden, J.C. Higginbotham** (tb); **Albert Nicholas, Charlie Holmes** (cl, as); **Larry Binyon** (ts); **Will Johnson** (bj); **Pops Foster** (b); **Kaiser Marshall** (d); **Orlando Robertson** (v); on six tracks: **Waller** (org); **Jabbo Smith** (c); **Garvin Bushell** (cl, as); **James P Johnson** (p); on three tracks: **Waller** (p, org); **Tom Morris** (c); **Charlie Irvis** (tb); **Eddie King** (d); on four tracks: **Waller** (p, org); **Tom Morris** (c); **Jimmy Archey** (tb); **Bobbie Leecan** (g); **Eddie King** (d). RCA Bluebird Ⓜ ND90649 (65 minutes). Recorded 1927-9.
　　　⑧ ❻

These tracks date from the late twenties, before Waller's international success with his small band. The opening *Minor Drag* and *Harlem Fuss* have been written about since Eddie Condon told the story of the session in his autobiography. They are good small-band sides in which the massive power of Waller's left hand makes it clear why no bass player or drummer was necessary. The six tracks by a bigger band are noteworthy for the solo work of Red Allen, Jack Teagarden (he is the trombone soloist on *Ridin' but Walkin'*), Albert Nicholas and Charlie Holmes as well as Fats. There is just one Waller vocal on the 21 tracks which comprise this CD, but he does play organ on the six titles by the Louisiana Sugar Babies and the seven by Thomas Waller with Morris's Hot Babies. On the former, the organ tends to get in the way and things only improve when Waller keeps quiet, allowing Johnson to add his support to the wonderful muted trumpet playing of Jabbo Smith. The titles with cornettist Tom Morris come off better, with Fats occasionally switching smoothly from organ to piano. There is merely a hint of the jollity which was to come later with the formation of Fats Waller and His Rhythm in the thirties. The transfers have been achieved using the CEDAR system and are generally successful.　　**AM**

**Turn on the Heat** Waller (p); with, on two tracks: **Benny Payne** (p). Bluebird Ⓜ ND82482-2 (two discs: 122 minutes). Recorded 1927-41.
　　　⑧ ❻

This is the Waller who was the star pupil of James P. Johnson, rather than the 'family favourite' who savaged fifth-rate songs and turned some of them into standards despite himself. Although the later persona largely buried the dynamic stride player, the humour implicit in the piano style was the basis of his whole approach to entertaining the public.

The 1929 material which takes up more than half of this set contains a few contemporary pops such as the title track and *Love Me or Leave Me*, as well as Waller's current production including *Ain't Misbehavin'* and the influential chord-sequence of *I've Got a Feeling I'm Falling*. But the meat of this part of the programme, casually tossed off at the same period as his 'Buddies' sessions, consists of his take-on of the Johnson tradition with such as *Handful of Keys* and *Valentine Stomp*.

A key 1934 date, when the 'Rhythm' series was just taking off, has more sophisticated originals in *Viper's Drag* and *Clothes Line Ballet*, while the remaining numbers are revisited standards. Two are his own, three Hoagy Carmichael's, and all receive thoughtful, varied interpretations, while the set comes full circle with two versions of Johnson's *Carolina Shout*.                                    **BP**

**New review**
### Fats Waller and his Rhythm: The Middle Years Part 1 Waller (p, v); with various
personnel, mainly **Herman Autrey** (t); **Gene Sedric** (ts, cl); **Al Casey** (g); **Cedric Wallace** (b); **Slick Jones** (d). Bluebird Ⓜ 66083-2 (three discs: 207 minutes). Recorded 1936-8.

The band known as Fats Waller and His Rhythm was one of the finest small combos of the swing era – versatile, flexible and infinitely responsive. It acted as an extension of Fats's musical personality and could switch from tea-shop gentility to gin-mill anarchy in the blink of an eye. Among these 69 numbers are famous set-pieces, such as *Smarty* and the high-spirited *The Joint is Jumpin'*, unjustly neglected songs like the beautiful *Don't You Know or Don't You Care?*, demolition jobs on old parlour-favourites, sentimental pot-boilers, piano solos, instrumentals. They were all recorded quickly, usually after just one run-through, and although loose ends and ragged edges are not uncommon, the spirited freshness of these performances is worth more than days of preparation. Quite apart from his other talents, the man was a wonder of productivity. Just how prolific his output was can be judged from the fact that this is Volume 1 of the **Middle Years**. There is a **Middle Years, Volume 2** (66552-2), a **Last Years** (ND90411) and at least one **Early Years** collection (66618-2) currently released in this same series – all of them three-CD sets - and there are yet more to come.                          **DG**

### The Last Years (1940-3) Fats Waller and His Rhythm Waller (p, org, v); June 'Bugs' Hamilton,
**Herman Autrey, Bob Williams, Joe Thomas, Nat Williams** (t); **Eugene 'Honeybear' Sedric, Bob Carroll** (ts); **John Smith, Al Casey** (g); **Sedric Wallace** (b); **Slick Jones, Arthur Trappier** (d); **Kathryn Perry** (v); **Fats Waller, His Rhythm and His Orchestra: George Wilson, Ray Hogan, Bugs Hamilton, Herb Flemming** (tb); **Jimmy Powell, Dave McRae, George Jones, Lawrence Fields** (as). RCA Bluebird Ⓜ ND90411 (three discs: 194 minutes). Recorded 1940-3.

RCA's reissue programme played around with Waller on CD for a few years, making tentative stabs at what is an enormous archive (over 400 sides). In the last 12 months or so, there have been signs that their nerve has been steadying. First this three-CD set appeared, and more recently there have been two three-CD volumes of **The Middle Years (1936-40)** launched onto the market. While there are more hits on the thirties collections, many of them turn up on single CD releases, and it is the forties collection which contains the CD rarities and the pleasant surprises. The reason for their rarity has nothing to do with poor playing; it is much more humdrum than that. As reissue overseer Orrin Keepnews explains in his notes to the box, most large reissue programmes falter and fold before they reach the end (RCA France in the vinyl era excepted), and so the early Waller, being the logical place to start, has been oft-revisited, while the later work has remained undisturbed (he didn't point out that the later material had until 1993 also still lain in copyright so no one but RCA could mount a legitimate reissue of it).

This collection contains the original studio versions of *Little Curly Hair in a High Chair*, *Everybody Loves My Baby*, *Mamacita*, *Shortnin' Bread*, *Rump Steak Serenade*, *Buck Jumpin'* (a vehicle for guitarist Casey), *Fat and Greasy* and the beautiful *Jitterbug Waltz*. Waller's humorous asides are not so apparent here as in the late thirties, although he certainly has not dispensed with them, and there is a more mellow atmosphere across the three sides. One wonders whether the approach of middle age was giving him a new light on his material. If so, it did not lead to any shifts in style or content. Waller's career is remarkable for the lack of any real stylistic change once maturity had been reached at the dawn of the thirties. Yet it seems unlikely that *Jitterbug Waltz* would have been countenanced six years before, and although all speculation is futile, I can't help wondering where Waller would have placed himself in the post-war entertainment world, had he survived that long.                  **KS**

## Per Henrik Wallin                                                              1946

### Dolphins, Dolphins, Dolphins Wallin (p); Mats Gustafsson (ss, ts, bs); Kjell Nordeson (d).
Dragon Ⓕ DRCD215 (64 minutes). Recorded 1991.

Although an important, if idiosyncratic, figure on the Swedish jazz scene for over two decades, Wallin has yet to make a deep mark internationally. It may be that his music is an acquired taste, difficult to grasp on first hearing. A pianist of great facility, his lines seem to follow a personal logic; occasionally he will strip a theme down to its essence – or to silence – then ornament it with staggered phrasing or a florid abundance of notes. For example, the pensive solo, *J.W.*, dedicated to a painter friend, alternates rhapsodic cascades of melody with stark Monkish chords that threaten to turn violent. Even when explosions erupt, Wallin avoids sounding like Cecil Taylor or any other contemporary pianist for that matter. In fact, one wonders if **Dolphins, Dolphins, Dolphins** may not be an unacknowledged homage to Monk; he picks apart *I Should Care*, a standard to which Monk also turned his scalpel, to end the programme, and at various points injects elliptical hints or echoes of Monk lines or a bit of offbeat stride. The younger saxist Gustafsson is an especially good foil for Wallin, chewing up and spitting out notes or relaxing into a loose, limber phrasing to match the pianist's demeanour. Nordeson is an aggressive drummer. The three fit together like pieces of a puzzle, but the music will not behave, there is always an unexpected jolt of emotion, rhythm or colour eager to break into the consensus. At all times, Wallin's peculiar impulses of nonchalance and bravado give the music its contradictory tension – and its curious charm. **AL**

## George Wallington 1924-93

**The George Wallington Trios** **Wallington** (p); with, on four tracks: **Charles Mingus** (b); **Max Roach** (d); and on one track **Chuck Wayne** (mandola); on four tracks: **Oscar Pettiford** (b); **Max Roach** (d); on eight tracks: **Curley Russell** (b); **Max Roach** (d). Prestige Ⓜ OJCCD1754 (42 minutes). Recorded 1952-3.

**⑧ ❻**

Wallington was the pianist in the first bebop group to play on 52nd Street in 1944, the one co-led by Dizzy Gillespie and Oscar Pettiford with Max Roach on drums. He was probably the first white musician to work in the bop idiom, cropping up on many record dates as a sideman. But it was as a trio leader and soloist that Wallington opened many eyes, for his keyboard technique was phenomenal. He was also an important composer, best known for his tunes *Godchild* and *Lemon Drop*. Of the 15 titles here, ten are Wallington compositions, one of them a multi-tempoed reworking of his earlier *Polka Dot*. He moves accurately all over the keyboard on the fast tempos (*Escalating*, for example, is a furious attack on the chords of *Cherokee*) and the comparison with Bud Powell must be made, but Wallington's actual extemporizations were always more melodic, almost as if he was writing fresh tunes along the way. His command of harmony gave his ballad work a richness seldom found in any other pianist of the period. He is superbly served by Max Roach on all tracks, and the three bassists would sound more impressive if the balance did not result in occasional muddiness. These dates were never well reproduced as 10-inch or 12-inch LPs and it sounds as if the remastering has been done from discs rather than original masters or tapes, so not much improvement there. **AM**

## Jack Walrath 1946

**New review**
**Journey, Man!** **Walrath** (t); **Craig Handy** (ts, ss); **Bobby Watson** (as); **Kenny Drew Jr** (p); **Ray Drummond** (b); **Victor Lewis** (d). Evidence Ⓕ ECD22150-2 (61 minutes). Recorded 1995.

**⑦ ❾**

Very clearly, the title of this album is made up of two words. It shows that the imaginative Walrath is anything but a journeyman. A graduate of Berklee, he had experience with minor r&b groups before transferring to California. In the seventies he did sterling service with Ray Charles and Charles Mingus and is currently leading his own groups world-wide. This CD delivers the complete package, composer, arranger, trumpeter and leader, it shows him at ease with waltz-time, reggae and modal routes and demonstrates the way in which he uses diverse arranging traditions to put substance onto his compositional frames. Certainly, the Walrath brand is on all of them and the sustained creativity of his solos adds a further dimension. As a leader he has chosen well. The contrast between Handy's fierce chromatics and Watson's cultured Messengerisms is exploited well and Drew swings prodigiously in every solo outing. Together with Drummond and Lewis, he upgrades an already potent duo into a brilliantly effective rhythm section. **BMcR**

## Cedar Walton 1939

**Among Friends** **Walton** (p); **Buster Williams** (b); **Billy Higgins** (d); **Bobby Hutcherson** (vb). Evidence Ⓕ ECD22023-2 (62 minutes). Recorded 1992.

**⑦ ❽**

For more than three years Walton was a member of one of the finest of all Jazz Messengers line-ups. He was also house pianist for Prestige for a similar period, and he chanced his arm with fusion in his Soundscapes unit in the seventies. This CD returns him to what he does best, re-uniting a trio that enjoyed a short residency at San Francisco's Keystone Korner in 1982. The superbly inventive Hutcherson makes a guest appearance on *My Foolish Heart* but the remaining titles, with Buster in the place of Dave Williams from Walton's eighties trio, produce hard, driving bop in the pianist's distinctive manner. His treble investigations on *Midnight Waltz* show his skill as a 'single note' improviser, but like most band pianists, Walton thinks orchestrally. He is equally happy to inhabit the centre of the keyboard and his chord patterns on *For All We Know* and *Off Minor* are powerful and coercive. It is perhaps this assertiveness that makes it easy for the trio to come over as an integrated unit and not as three individuals. Unfortunately, too little is heard here of Walton the writer, but his one composition, *Midnight Waltz*, is up to his own highest standards. **BMcR**

# Carlos Ward                                                                    1940

**Lito**  Ward (as, f); **Woody Shaw** (t); **Walter Schmocker** (b); **Alex Deutsch** (d). Leo Ⓕ 166 (59 minutes). Recorded 1988.

⑥ ❻

The Panama-born altoist's singing, searing lead-alto sound and turbulent improvising have served him well in contexts both tuneful (Abdullah Ibrahim, Carla Bley) and outward-bound (Cecil Taylor, Edward Blackwell). This Dutch concert showcases both sides of his personality. Ward's tunes, notably *Pettiford Bridge*, can be quite catchy, but the blowing is open-ended and adventurous. *Lito* should be of special interest to Shaw fans, as the trumpeter was rarely captured in so loose a context. His bugling tone here is perfect for the setting. Shaw's inflections make you hear Ward's *Lee* as a blues although it is not in standard blues form. Ward has a knack for writing bass lines that stand up on their own. Two movements of the three-part *Lito* suite are anchored to simple, propulsive bass figures – one of them a descending broken chord – which linger in the ear, but do not inhibit soloists. In this open frame, Deutsch provides colour as well as drive. The leader plays a little leafy flute on *Lito*, but mostly concentrates on emphatic, biting alto, played with a big, broad, distinctive sound. Even so, he does not dominate these stretched-out jams; the set has a real band feel. **KW**

# David S. Ware                                                                  1949

**Third Ear Recitation**  Ware (ts); **Matthew Shipp** (p); **William Parker** (b); **Whit Dickey** (d). DIW Ⓕ DIW870 (60 minutes). Recorded 1992.

⑧ ❽

A Berklee graduate, Ware has always been associated with his own uncompromising brand of free jazz. In the seventies he worked with Andrew Cyrille and Cecil Taylor but was not widely recorded. One good solo album and a couple of tenor and percussion duels gave notice of his talent, but not until the eighties was there more available evidence. This CD is a good representative example as he takes his own multi-phonic route to detailed and frequently dense improvisational conclusions. He is not without a flexibility of approach, however, and *Autumn Leaves* shows the way in which he can loosely relate his free flights to Shipp's clearly defined structures. *Angel Eyes* is somewhat more orthodox, with convoluted runs used to bridge the space between theme affirmations, while *Mystic* takes on an Albert Ayler-like march quality. His respectful approach to *East Broadway Run Down* is faster than the Sonny Rollins original, *Free Flow* is a more open-ended piece and *Sentient Compassion* displays the degree of intensity he can bring to a dirge. The presence of a pianist means that there are harmonic frames available but, with Parker and Dickey more contrapuntally inclined and deliberately non-supportive in the normal sense, Ware remains loyal to his free-form principles. **BMcR**

# Wilbur Ware                                                                 1932-79

**New review**

**The Chicago Sound**  Ware (b); **Johnny Griffin** (ts); **John Jenkins** (as); **Junior Mance** (p); **Wilbur Campbell**, **Frank Dunlop** (d). Riverside Ⓜ OJCCD1737-2 (40 minutes). Recorded 1957.

⑦ ❼

Although recorded in New York, this CD provides an excellent cameo of the largely unsung Chicago hard-bop scene of the late fifties. Its leader, Ware, was a fine bassist, his tone full, his attack almost forbiddingly urgent and his interaction with his fellow players setting his bass on an equal footing with them. His fleet-fingered dexterity did not disguise his astute musical mind and at times he had an almost horn-like approach. His 'training' as house bassist at the Beehive and Flame Lounge in his hometown set him up to later become a Jazz Messenger and to work with Thelonious Monk, John Coltrane, Sonny Rollins and Archie Shepp. He even had a spell with Sun Ra but, whatever the company, he listened as he played. This 'session' confirms him as a useful composer with *Mamma-Daddy* and *31st and State* but it is in his imaginative reading of *Lullaby of the Leaves* and *The Man I Love* that the young man shines most. Even at this stage he showed why he was so willingly accepted by forward-looking players. His rhythmic suppleness was astylistic but, more significantly, he was already freeing his support figures from orthodox harmonic guide-lines. Although not similarly motivated, Griffin, Jenkins and Mance sound comfortable. For an accurate view of Chicago jazz of 1957, look no further. **BMcR**

## Washboard Rhythm Kings

**Washboard Rhythm Kings Collection, Volume 1: 1931**  Jake Fenderson, Buck Franklin, **The Melody Four** (v); **Dave Page**, **Dave Riddick** (t); **Ben Smith** (as); **Jimmy Shine** (as, v); **Carl Wade** (ts); **Eddie Miles** (p, v); **Teddy Bunn** (g); **Steve Washington** (bj); **Jimmy Spencer** (d, wshbd, v). Collector's Classics Ⓜ COCD17 (73 minutes). Recorded 1931-2.

⑤ ❻

For many observers, it is rather difficult to give credence to the art of rubbing metal thimbles on the ridges of a washboard. Yet, since before the turn of the century, spasm bands were using the likes of kazoos, jugs and, most especially, washboards as part of the 'orchestral' armoury. Men like 'Washboard' Sam ratified its use in the blues world and recordings by washboard bands found a limited market well into the thirties.

The Washboard Rhythm Kings were stalwarts of the style; they had an ever changing line-up and this CD presents all aspects of their music. They were least appealing in comedy numbers with Fenderson's maudlin singing, but more impressive on blues such as *Crooked World* or when their reasonably proficient horns had their say. Early titles were blighted by 'period' alto and, in 1931, Bunn was some way short of his peak. The Kings last recorded in 1933 but the final two sessions here offer what is a fine example of their work. Titles like *Shoot 'Em*, *Pepper Steak* and *Wake 'Em Up* are driven by Spencer's genuinely flexible and swinging washboard patterns and, with Riddick's Armstrong-inspired lead, they make good music. It was not for the academic but in 1931 the Kings were for fun. **BMcR**

## Dinah Washington                                       1924-62

**Mellow Mama**  Washington (v); **Karl George** (t); **Lucky Thompson** (ts); **Jewel Grant** (as); **Gene Thompson** (as, cl); **Milt Jackson** (vb); **Wilbert Baranco** (p); **Charles Mingus** (b); **Lee Young** (d). Delmark Ⓔ DD451 (34 minutes). Recorded 1945.

⑧ ❽

Dinah Washington, the name given to 18-year-old Ruth Jones by Lionel Hampton when he discovered the young washroom girl at Chicago's Regal Theatre and put her on the road to stardom with his band, was a natural. Nurtured in the rich gospel tradition of the southern Baptist Church, Washington was gifted with an overall vibrancy marked by pinpoint intonation, precise articulation and a penetratingly melismatic bluesiness which she successfully adapted to a variety of settings, including her pop classic, *What a Diff'rence a Day Makes* (1959).

Here, at the threshold of her solo career in 1945, we catch the saucy 21-year-old belting out a repertoire of blues-based lines including *Rich Man's Blues*, *Blues for a Day* and *Wise Woman Blues*. While lacking the wrenching poignancy of a Billie Holiday, Washington displays a compelling bravado not unlike that displayed by such silver screen heroines as Bette Davis and Barbara Stanwyck. Another of the date's great attractions is the sinewy and smooth tenor saxophone of the under-valued Lucky Thompson. Milt Jackson's bluesy vibes are also featured, and the rhythm tandem of pianist Wilbert Baranco, bassist Charles Mingus and drummer Lee Young is perfect in its supporting role. The CEDAR restoration process brings the music to life. **CB**

**The Complete Dinah Washington on Mercury, Volume 3 (1952-4)**  Washington (v); featuring **Clark Terry**, **Clifford Brown**, **Maynard Ferguson** (t); **Russell Procope** (as, cl); **Herb Geller** (as); **Paul Gonsalves**, **Paul Quinichette**, **Eddie Chamblee**, **Eddie 'Lockjaw' Davis**, **Harold Land** (ts); **Junior Mance**, **Richie Powell** (p); **Jackie Davis** (org); **Keeter Betts**, **George Morrow** (b); **Jimmy Cobb**, **Ed Thigpen**, **Max Roach** (d). Mercury Ⓜ 834 675-2 (three discs: 198 minutes). Recorded 1942-54.

⑧ ❽

Like Fats Waller, Washington could sing anything, so producers often made her do just that. These 53 selections include such things as Hank Williams's hit *Half as Much*; double-entendre songs (like the wonderful *TV is the Thing This Year*, with washing-machine organ); Ellington evergreens; forgettable tearjerkers; doo-wop; a homeless woman's calypso; hardcore blues (her *Gambler's Blues* features Procope's Hodges-like alto obbligatos); blues with leaden lyrics and melodies the band riffs through unperturbed; even *Silent Night*. She is also heard in two studio jams, one with Terry and 'Lockjaw', where she sings *A Foggy Day* with the introductory verse, the other (with demonstrative audience) powered by Max Roach. That one produced a hard-bop mambo on *I've Got You under My Skin*, recorded at the dawn of hard bop, and a *You Go to My Head* where her phrases swing hard even as she sings the pitches as written.

Few singers have ever sounded so comfortable on such disparate material but Dinah was not really a cross-over artist. For her, a song was a song; a heart-render from Nashville got the same treatment as one from Broadway. Her wine-rich voice always had a maturity beyond her years. When the last of these sides was cut, she was two weeks shy of 30. **KW**

**For Those in Love** Washington (v); **Clark Terry** (t); **Jimmy Cleveland** (tb); **Paul Quinichette** (ts); **Cecil Payne** (bs); **Wynton Kelly** (p); **Barry Galbraith** (g); **Keeter Betts** (b); **Jimmy Cobb** (d); **Quincy Jones** (arr). EmArcy Ⓜ 514 073-2 (49 minutes). Recorded 1955.

✔  ⑧ ❽

The jazz establishment has always been grudging about Washington's status as a jazz vocalist. And yet it seems she was incapable of singing anything but good jazz, and many of her 'pop' recordings for EmArcy and Mercury are redolent with fine jazz singing.

This is a much better session for Washington than the sloppy jam sessions which Mercury recorded using her with some of the same musicians who play here. Washington's own form varied little; she is easily able to handle unlikely material like *Blue Gardenia* and *You Don't Know What Love Is* and she imposes her climactic blues feelings into numbers like *This Can't Be Love*, *I Could Write a Book* and *Make the Man Love Me*.

Jones's arrangements are ideal and leave plenty of solo space. The band includes a host of under-rated musicians who were or are exceptional jazz soloists – Jimmy Cleveland, Paul Quinichette, Cecil Payne, Wynton Kelly and Barry Galbraith. They all respond tastefully to the opportunities given them by Jones. Terry's effervescent personality comes through in his fine solos, but he is a disciplined and expert contributor to the scored ensembles. This album shows what could have been. But then what actually was must have made a lot more money. **SV**

# Grover Washington Jr.
1943

New review
**All My Tomorrows** Washington (ss, as, ts); **Eddie Henderson**, **Earl Gardner** (t, flh); **Robin Eubanks** (tb); **Bobby Watson** (as); **Bobby LaVell** (ts); **Jimmy Cozier** (bs); **Hank Jones** (p); **Romero Lubambo** (g); **George Mraz** (b); **Billy Hart**, **Lewis Nash** (d); **Freddy Cole**, **Jeanie Bryson** (v). Columbia Ⓕ CK64319 (75 minutes). Recorded 1994.

⑧ ❿

"The most popular saxophonist in jazz" pronounces the publicity blurb for Washington, whose lightweight jazz-rock recordings and tours, plus a tendency for critics to overlook him because of his very success, should not disguise the fact that he is a jazz saxophonist of substance, power and originality. This mellow, well-planned album is a showcase for Grover on all his saxophones, but also a team effort that involves some excellent charts from Larry Willis and Slide Hampton, plus some outstanding solos from Henderson. Among musicians, Grover is perhaps most admired for his unique and beautiful sound on soprano, which gets several opportunities to be heard here, notably on the opening *E Preciso Perdoar*. At the keyboard throughout is Hank Jones, providing perfect backing, though perhaps underexposed here as a soloist. When given the chance to show his paces Jones keeps within the understated and gentle tone of the whole session, but packs small surprises into his windows of opportunity. Nat King Cole's brother Freddy puts in a couple of cameo appearances plus a duet with Bryson, but the show belongs to Grover, with the two central large-band arrangements, *Please Send Me Someone to Love* and the title track being the core of the album. The luscious soprano sound wallows in the feather-bed of Hampton's chart for *Tomorrows*, while the more muscular tenor, helped by a slow-but-solid backbeat, shows Grover at his best on *Please Send Me Someone*. This is a first-rate album by a cast of excellent musicians. **AS**

# Kazumi Watanabe

**Dogatana** Watanabe (g); with various personnels including: **Mike Mainieri** (vb); **B.J. Yamagishi**, **David Liebman** (f); **Warren Bernhardt** (p); **Nobuyoshi Ino** (b); **Hideo Yamahi** (d). Denon Ⓕ CY72374 (42 minutes). Recorded 1981.

⑥ ❽

Essentially a guitarist's guitarist, for over ten years Japanese fusioneer Watanabe has been turning in the sort of virtuosic jazz-rock that has hoards of impressionable young men at music trade fairs gasping in delight and envy. Drawing as it does on most non-jazz aspects of American pop music – country, funk, r&b – Watanabe's electric playing often over-resembles the jack-of-all-trades approach of seasoned session musicians, a feeling obviously helped by a tendency to use improvised solos as a forum for technical display. But back in 1981, despite an already highly developed technical facility, Watanabe turned in an all-acoustic (or very nearly so) album that has sufficient grace to convince even the most sceptical jazz-rockophobe. A series of duets and trios with some of his own, equally gifted, if largely unknown, countrymen and with a series of American stars, **Dogatana** is a delight. With the exception of Wayne Shorter's pretty ballad *Diana*, all the pieces are Watanabe's own, and all provide ample room for his cohorts' contributions. Steps Ahead leader Mike Mainieri's vibes solo on the opening *Nuevo Espresso*, a laid-back affair to be sure, sets the affable tone of the set, and a later duet with fusion guitar progenitor Coryell shows the Japanese at ease in such celebrated company. **SH**

# Sadao Watanabe 1933

**Bird of Paradise** **Watanabe** (as); **The Great Jazz Trio** (Hank Jones, p, Ron Carter, b, Tony Williams, d). JVC Ⓕ VIJC23021 (38 minutes). Recorded 1977.

⑦ ❾

Watanabe has become known outside his native Japan mostly through his fusion and soul efforts, but he is a much more complete musician than those records would have us believe. This album, dedicated to Charlie Parker and full of tunes closely identified with him, is a handy illustration of what Watanabe can do when he picks up some momentum in bebop territory. Watanabe has been playing bop and its descendents since the fifties, when he took over Toshiko Akiyoshi's Tokyo group after the pianist's departure for New York, and he has also spent a great deal of his time as a teacher, taking up a post of director at the Yamaha Institute of Popular Music. This record is one of over 50 Watanabe has made during his career, and comes right in the middle of a swathe of fusion albums recorded in New York for the same label. On this disc, Watanabe's style and tone is not far removed from that of Phil Woods, and he is not at a loss for ideas at any point on the date. Having said that, it would be a poor player who got into difficulties in this repertoire with the backing group provided here. The Great Jazz Trio (something of a fixture on JVC at this time) provides both thoughtful (Jones), swinging (Carter) and immensely stimulating (Williams) support to the main soloist, and help greatly to lift this release out of the mundane and into the worth-looking-out-for category. **KS**

# Steve Waterman 1960

**New review**
**Destination Unknown** **Waterman** (t, flh); **Liam Noble** (p); **Jeff Clyne** (b); **Paul Clarvis** (d). ASC Records Ⓕ ASCCD4 (62 minutes). Recorded 1995.

⑥ ❽

Trumpter Steve Waterman makes a promising début with **Destination Unknown**. Among his credentials are the Carla Bley Very Big Band, the John Surman Brass Project and Andy Shephard's Big Co-Motion. He also is a trumpet tutor at the Royal Academy of Music and co-author of *The Jazz Method for Trumpet*. Stylistically, Waterman is a post-bop modernist with an agile technique and a warm, burnished sound. In terms of conception, one is reminded of such provocatively lyrical players as Kenny Wheeler and Mike Mantler. Still, Waterman, although a work-in-progress, is his own man. His emotive range is broad. *Long Forgotten Dreams*, for example, displays a haunting and pensive melodism. Also impressive is Waterman's up-tempo work in tracks like *Mute Retrieval* where swirling lines and dramatic stop-start splatters recall the time-shifting bravado of cutting edge players like Randy Brecker. On occasion, however, his upper register sounds pinched. Still, Waterman possesses an admirable spirit of adventure, a spirit effectively elaborated on by pianist Liam Noble, bassist Jeff Clyne and drummer Paul Clarvis. **CB**

# Benny Waters 1902

**From Paradise (Small's) to Shangri-La** **Waters** (as, ts, cl, v); **Don Coates** (p); **Earl May** (b); **Ronnie Cole** (d). Muse Ⓕ MCD5340 (51 minutes ). Recorded 1987.

⑥ ❻

Traditionally, pianists last the longest in jazz. They sit down to play and they do not have to strain their lungs. For a long time Eubie Blake was the oldest survivor in jazz (when Peter Boizot rang up New York to inquire about Eubie Blake's availability next year at his Pizza Express, Mrs Blake said "Honey, we ain't planning that far ahead!"). But now that he has gone, Benny Waters seems to be the oldest and one of the toughest men in jazz. Born in 1902, he gigged happily round New York for many years until he decided to settle in Paris, where he became the senior member of the American jazz community. There is an ageless enthusiasm about Waters's presence and about his music which comes over best in his presence but which is well captured on this record, made in America with an American rhythm section which clicks along together very nicely. I am told that Benny Waters has gone back to the USA now he is over 90. Lucky old USA. **MK**

# Ethel Waters 1896-1977

**Ethel Waters 1929-39** **Waters** (v); with, amongst others: **Manny Klein, Arthur Whetsol, Cootie Williams, Freddy Jenkins, Sterling Bose, Bunny Berigan, Charlie Teagarden, Shirley Clay, Taft Jordan** (t); **Tommy Dorsey, Joe Nanton, Lawrence Brown, Jack Teagarden, Sandy Williams** (tb); **Tyree Glenn** (tb, vb); **Jimmy Dorsey** (cl, as); **Benny Goodman** (cl); **Johnny Hodges** (as, ss); **Harry Carney** (bs); **Edgar Sampson** (as, vn); **Benny Carter** (as); **Frank Signorelli, Duke Ellington** (p); **John Trueheart, Danny Barker** (g); **Joe Venuti** (vn); **Joe Tarto, Wellman Braud, Artie Bernstein, John Kirby** (b); **Stan King, Sonny Greer, Gene Krupa** (d). Timeless Ⓜ CBC1-007 (70 minutes). Recorded 1929-39.

⑦ ❽

First recorded in 1921, Waters was hardly a jazz singer. She was, however, highly successful with popular tunes and was often supported by jazz musicians of real quality. She was disliked by classic blues singers like Ma Rainey and Bessie Smith for being, one suspects, too beautiful and too 'white' sounding as a singer. Certainly there was very little of the blues in her style and, although she did swing at times, she was usually governed by the material she used. In that sense only, this CD does give a slightly false impression. *Shoo Shoo Boogie Boo* and *You Can't Stop Me from Loving Me* are just a couple of duds in a programme that otherwise provides her with consistently good tunes. She is least successful when she tries to be a jazz singer as on *Please Don't Talk about Me* and at her best when she merely 'puts over' the likes of *Am I Blue?*, *Black and Blue* or *Stormy Weather*. The backings are excellent but they are designed purely to showcase Waters and only rarely do the soloists get to make a contribution. For the last 15 years of her performing career she sang with evangelist Billy Graham but she remains an important figure in the world of films, vaudeville and popular song. **BMcR**

# Patty Waters

1943

**New review**

**Patty Waters Sings** Waters (v, p); **Burton Greene** (p); **Steve Tintweiss** (b); **Tom Price** (b). ESP-Disk Ⓜ 1025-2 (28 minutes). Recorded 1965.

⑤ ❼

Waters made two discs in quick succession for ESP after being introduced to that label by Albert Ayler, made a cameo appearance with Marzette Watts for the Savoy label, then vanished. Recently she has been coaxed back into the studio to produce a third album. Of the two ESP-Disk records, **On Tour**, made with a rag-bag bunch of avant-gardists, starts weird and stays weird. If the recorded applause at the beginning and end of a couple of tracks didn't prove the contrary, I would have thought her groups' collective efforts had cleared each auditorium they played in, which tends to beg the question as to what college audiences were on at that time. The earlier studio album is a deal more coherent and less febrile. As a vinyl release, side one had seven short ballads, sung and accompanied (with Waters alone at the piano) in largely conventional manner. The songs (all hers) are good examples of the late-night torch-song tradition, Water's attractive alto voice given a nicely expressive edge by her sincere and sometimes wry interpretation of her own lyrics. Side two was wholly taken up by 13 minutes of weirdness as the old folk-song *Black is the Colour (of my true love's hair)* was put to the sword and given a treatment by Waters and the Burton Greene Group not unlike a Black Mass, screams and erotic overtones included gratis. Waters demonstrates, apart from a truly spectacular line in hysterics and an obsession with the word 'black', a considerable vocal range and an impressive technical control. It's still weird, though. Don't tell the neighbours you've got it. **KS**

# Matt Wates

1951

**New review**

**Two Matt** Wates (as); **Martin Shaw** (t); **Andy Panayi** (ts, f); **John Pearce** (p); **Malcolm Creese** (b); **Mark Fletcher** (d). AB Ⓔ CD5 (59 minutes). Recorded 1995.

⑨ ❽

The remarkable flow of young giants from the ranks of the National Youth Jazz Orchestra continues with these young men who play with maturity beyond their years both as soloists and as a group. This is quite simply the best new British band in years and its music is amazing for being totally effective and completely original (one of the problems with the parent orchestra is the determined originality and continuous obscurity of its material). All but one of the titles are compositions by Wates and they shout with jubilation and ear-catching invention. The band manages to be without period and this is neither hard nor soft bop, achieving a relevance and individuality which obviates any need for pigeon-holing. Wates's mates are a fine bunch, most of them thus far better known than their leader, but this album means that all that is about to change. Perhaps the nearest thing to bop is in the comping of Pearce and the soloing of Shaw but Wates and Panayi stand out as giants with the latter playing tenor with great authority and flute with lissom agility. This album should please an unusually wide spectrum of listeners. **SV**

# Doug Watkins

1934-62

**New review**

**Soulnik** Watkins (vc); **Yusef Lateef** (f, ob); **Hugh Lawson** (p); **Herman Wright** (b); **Lex Humphries** (d). Prestige Ⓜ OJCCD1848-2 (38 minutes). Recorded 1960.

⑥ ❼

This was recorded a couple of years before Doug Watkins was killed in a car crash and, judging by what one knows of his career, could hardly be less typical. With the Jazz Messengers and similar groups, he was admired as a bass-playing pillar of the rhythm section, not often to be found taking a solo. The original sleeve-notes by Ira Gitler tell us he picked up a cello for the first time three days before this session. Whether one event led to the other is not clear, but a front-line of flute and cello, even if plucked throughout, hardly fits the hard-bop stereotype. Surrounded here by fellow-Detroiters, Watkins may have been helped organizationally by Yusef Lateef, who wrote two of the three originals. Lateef is a class act on both flute and oboe, eliciting from both a full and reedy sound, and Watkins plays with commendable authority, especially on the up-tempo *I Remember You*. Beyond that, there is nothing really distinctive about his solos, and the session probably needed a livener or two from Lateef's tenor to get things moving. **RA**

# Bill Watrous 1939

**In London** Watrous (tb); **Brian Dee** (p); **Len Skeat** (b); **Martin Drew** (d). Mole Ⓕ CDMOLE7 (79 minutes). Recorded 1982.

⑥ ❻

On the evidence of this CD alone Watrous must be the most technically gifted trombonist jazz has ever seen. There seems to be no limit to his range, the semi-quavers he can produce at the fastest tempos and the swaggering sense of swing. With such qualities apparently on tap (there is no hint of a missed note or even a semi-tentative approach to a phrase) it is hardly surprising that Watrous has worked with a number of prestigious big bands as well as serving as a studio musician for a time. If his playing has a fault it is that sometimes his solos lack light and shade, although his slow ballad version of *When Your Lover Has Gone* is a clear indication that he can scale down his massive technique and attack when required. The opening of *Straight, No Chaser* is the kind of thing that must cause acute depression amongst other trombone players; for over three minutes he produces a breathtaking cadenza which almost becomes a composition in itself. Recorded at London's Pizza Express, the sound of the trombone is occasionally foggy, probably due to Watrous shifting his position relative to his microphone. Trombonists can safely add one more star to the rating and the Brian Dee-led rhythm section deserves a special mention. **AM**

# Bobby Watson 1953

New review
**Midwest Shuffle** Watson (as); **Terell Stafford** (t); **Edward Simon** (p); **Essiet Essiet** (b); **Victor Lewis** (d). Columbia Ⓕ 475925 2 (64 minutes). Recorded 1993.

⑧ ❼

Recorded variously in Pittsburgh, Louisville, St Paul and St Louis, this is Watson's most impressive record so far. The altoist was known during his time as Musical Director of the Jazz Messengers for his dynamic playing and for several original tunes which virtually became standards such as *E.T.A.* (based on Coltrane's *Lazy Bird*) and *Wheel Within a Wheel*. He is certainly on form with his original material here, including the 6/4 title track, the fast 7/4 *Mabel is Able* and the beautiful ballad *Mirrors*, the last two both distantly reminiscent of specific pop songs. Co-leader Lewis wrote two tracks with slightly different premises, but the post-bop, post-modal feel of the whole album stimulates some very consistent playing. The less well-known trumpeter and pianist both display individual touches in their performance and prove that this apparently conservative style is a long way from being synonymous with repertory work. This last Watson album for Columbia is lively, well mixed but not desiccated, and the production is rather nineties. Just as Arthur Taylor's **Wailin' at the Vanguard** began with a 'documentary' approach, this has examples of the band rehearsing and relaxing and of verbal audience reaction, but fortunately this doesn't distract from the musical quality. **BP**

# Eric Watson

**The Memory of Water** Watson (p); **John Lindberg** (b). Label Bleu Ⓕ LBLC6535 (52 minutes.). Recorded 1990.

⑧ ❽

Watson is a pianist who works primarily in Europe. He has recorded frequently, on his own in solo and group formats and with Lindberg on several occasions as well as with John Carter, Steve Lacy and Linda Sharrock, although little of his work has reached the US and his reputation is consequently limited in his native country. A thoroughly schooled musician with an impressive technique, Watson has acquired notice as an interpreter of Charles Ives as well as for his improvisational efforts. This fairly recent example of his longstanding partnership with String Trio of New York bassist Lindberg gives one of the better samplings of Watson's writing (seven of the ten compositions are his), as well as the gently brooding perspective he brings to most musical situations. More recent Soul Note volumes under Lindberg's name, where the pair are joined by trombonist Albert Mangelsdorff, present the more rhythmically intense side of the pianist's playing; but the focus here is more directly on him, and the session builds a stealthy tension that Watson and Lindberg manage to sustain throughout. **BB**

## Lu Watters

1911-89

**The Complete Good Time Jazz Recordings** Watters, Bob Scobey, Benny Strickler (c, t); Turk Murphy, Bill Bardin (tb); Ellis Horne, Bob Helm (cl); Wally Rose, Burt Bales (p); Clancy Hayes, Russ Bennett, Harry Mordecai (bj); Squire Girsback, Dick Lammi (bb); Bill Dart (d). Good Time Jazz Ⓜ 4GTJCD4409-2 (four discs: 290 minutes). Recorded 1941-7.

⑥ ❽

Originally a big-band leader, Watters became a leading figure in the New Orleans revival. In 1940, he formed a band using some of his former sidemen and specialized in the music of the Crescent City – most especially, King Oliver. The band was distinguished by a rather leaden-footed rhythmic movement. It had a tuba and heavy banjo emphasis but the front line, with Scobey, Murphy and latterly Helm, produced a righteous noise and no little drive. The Yerba Buena Jazz Band kept solo comment to a minimum and relied strongly on its well-crafted trumpet unisons.

As this four-CD set demonstrates, the band was most comfortable with the strutting medium tempo of tunes like *Georgia Camp Meeting*, *Milenberg Joys* and *Ostrich Walk*. The subtleties required by compositions like *New Orleans Blues* or *Creole Belles* seemed to elude them but, when the band did get up a full head of steam on items like *That's a Plenty* and *Chattanooga Stomp*, the horns seemed able to detach themselves from the restrictive practices of Lammi's lugubrious tuba and Mordecai's jangling banjo. The demise of the Yerba Buenas came in 1951 but, as leaders in their own right, Scobey and Murphy kept the tradition alive for some years. **BMcR**

## Ernie Watts

1945

New review

**The Long Road Home** Watts (ts); Kenny Barron (p); Reggie Workman (b); Mark Whitfield (g); Carmen Lundy (v). JVC Ⓕ 2059-2 (57 minutes). Recorded 1996.

✔ ⑩ ⑩

One of the most gratifying events of the nineties has been the growing recognition of Ernie Watts as one of the unqualified greats of the tenor saxophone. Buried for decades beneath a busy studio schedule, Watts was a largely forgotten figure among hard-core jazz fans. Ten years ago, with his inclusion at the onset of Charlie Haden's Quartet West, Watts's fortunes began to brighten. In 1994 Watt's credentials were further enhanced by **Unity** (JVC), an inspired and no-nonsense jazz date. With **The Long Road Home**, Watts's stock continues to soar.

As with Haden's often brooding Quartet West, Watts gives us evocative moodscapes replete with shadowy intrigues of *film-noir* intensity. In his after-hours colouring of Mingus's *Nostalgia in Times Square*, Watts's roiling tenor emits vaporous jetties which speak to both past and present. For *River of Light*, with its modal swirls *à la All Blues*, Watts's voyage is reflective as well as turbulent. Watts, of course, is a virtuoso. Here, however, the tension derives as much from his plangent sound and dramatic use of space. Still, when the tempo flies as it does in *Bird's Idea*, so, too, does Watts. Abetting at every turn is the bedrock tandem of the *non-pareil* Kenny Barron and Reggie Workman, and on four of the nine tracks, guitarist Mark Whitfield. Carmen Lundy's two cameos, especially her heartfelt and restrained take on *Willow Weep for Me*, are additional assets. The apogee of the noirish approach comes in the final track, the absolutely haunting *Moonlight and Shadows*. **CB**

## Marzette Watts

**Marzette Watts** Watts (ss, ts, bcl); Clifford Thornton (c, tb); Byard Lancaster (f, as, bcl); Karl Berger (vb); Sonny Sharrock (g); Henry Grimes, Juney Booth (b); J.C. Moses (d). ESP-Disk Ⓕ 1044-2 (37 minutes). Recorded 1966.

③ ❹

This is a pretty horrible album, but then it is not as horrible as the record for Savoy Watts made two years later, with Bill Dixon joining in on trumpet. At least all the musicians are in tune on this one. The date suffers from that quandary which bedevilled most mid-sixties free-jazz blow-outs: how do you give coherence and meaning to music which arrives by the happenstance of a band arriving in a studio, setting up their instruments and more or less blowing chaotically until they stop? The answer is not to be found here. Despite the impressive line-up of names, no one grabs the album by the scruff of the neck and makes it work through the sheer force of his personality, and the leader is too busy approximating the free-jazz licks he has picked up from other, better players to apply himself in that direction. The wasted opportunity is all the more a shame considering the lack of recording chances sent Byard Lancaster's way and the remarkable work he came up with when presented with a musical equation which worked (the Bill Dixon RCA LP of the same period, for example). **KS**

# Trevor Watts

1939

**Moiré** Watts (as, ss); **Colin McKenzie** (elb); **Paapa J. Mensah** (d, p, bells, djembe, v). Intakt
ⓕ CD039/1995. (56 minutes). Recorded 1995.

⑥ ❼

Considering that he was a prominent figure at London's free-jazz Minton's, The Little Theatre Club
and a founder member of the Spontaneous Music Ensemble in 1965, there is a disappointingly small
amount of Watts's recorded material available. His group Amalgam was an important free-jazz voice
and he did significant work with Don Cherry, Steve Lacy, Bobby Bradford, John Stevens and the
London Jazz Composers' Orchestra. He formed Moiré Music in 1982 and, since that date, has edged
somewhat away from free jazz; concerning himself more with the rhythmic aspects of his music. He
has led his Drum Orchestra and Moiré units of various sizes but the trio on this CD presents the bare
bones of the style. *Moiré Patterns* has a shimmering, watered appearance and the word well describes
this group's music. As Watts superimposes his flowing alto and soprano lines over percussion and
vocal effects, he creates a tapestry of sound that continually varies in density. It reflects few free-jazz
aspirations; it may lack the intensity of his earlier work but it does accommodate several ethnic
inspirations. *Yantra Groove*, with its pleasureground exoticism, would be an ideal sampler but none of
the titles are without their own special colour. **BMcR**

# Chuck Wayne

1923-93

**Jazz Guitarist** Wayne (g); **Zoot Sims, Brew Moore** (ts); **Harvey Leonard, John Mehegan** (p);
**George Duvivier, Vinne Burke** (b); **Ed Shaughnessy, Joe Morello** (d). Denon/Savoy Ⓜ SV-0189
(35 minutes). Recorded 1951-3.

⑧ ❽

The post-bop white musician may now seem lacking in emotion to some but, as these tracks show,
many of them were highly skilled musicians who swung hard, even if they did not shout about it.
Wayne made the transition from being a swing musician via a strong influence from Charlie
Christian, and at the end of it he emerged in the period under consideration as an eloquent
craftsman much in the manner of Jimmy Raney, Billy Bauer and Tal Farlow. He chose his
musicians well, and the presence of Sims and Moore guarantees the impact of both the ballads and
the swingers.
   Interestingly, four of the dozen tracks were actually recorded under the leadership of pianist
Mehegan, then the progressive leader of a whole school of students and a man who we can now see
as having been a prophet with considerable foresight. The interplay between his piano and Wayne's
guitar on *Stella by Starlight* makes one wonder if Wayne was indeed one of his students. *Sidewalks of
Cuba* is a number Wayne played with Herman, and here his handful of a Herd spikes it with some fine
tenor from both men. While Mehegan's music is the more rewarding long-term, *Sidewalks* was
certainly the biggest swinger within the album's desperately short number of minutes. **SV**

# Weather Report

**I Sing the Body Electric** Wayne Shorter (reeds); **Josef Zawinul** (p, kbds); **Miroslav Vitous** (b);
**Eric Gravatt** (d); **Dom Um Romao** (p); **Andrew White** (ehn); **Hubert Laws Jr** (f); **Wilmer Wise**
(pic); **Yolande Bavan, Joshie Armstrong, Chapman Roberts** (v); **Ralph Towner** (g). Columbia
Ⓜ 468207 2 (47 minutes). Recorded 1971/2.

✔ ⑨ ❽

Formed in 1971, Weather Report was the finest of all the fusion bands. This CD acts as a progress
report in that it documents the integration of two newcomers. Gravatt and Romao had replaced the
powerful Alphonze Mouzon and Airto Moreiro team just months before the band embarked on a
Far Eastern tour. This release allows the listener to compare the rather disorganized *The Moors,*
made in a studio with guest Towner, to the cohesion of the ferocious *Directions,* made live in Tokyo.
Weather Report had needed to re-muster after these important changes and had done so with
aplomb. The core design of the band had not changed, however, and was still built around the
instrumental and compositional talents of Zawinul and Shorter. Zawinul's pyramid of keyboards
distilled an internationally musical brew and provided the entire unit with its inner direction.
Shorter remained the jazzer, his intricate lines on tenor and soprano always chastizing the odd,
vertically slanted, rhythmic passage with a linear reprimand. More than any of his colleagues, it was
Shorter who put the creativity of the jazz ideal highest on Weather Report's list of priorities; no
mean distinction. **BMcR**

**This Is Jazz** Josef Zawinul (p, elp, syn, melodica, v); **Wayne Shorter** (ss, ts, lyricon); **Ralph Towner**
(g); **Alphonso Johnson** (elb); **Jaco Pastorius** (elb, d, v); **Miroslav Vitous** (b, elb); **Eric Gravatt**,
**Narada Michael Walden, Alex Acuna, Ndugu (Leon Chancler), Steve Gadd, Ishmael Wilburn,**

**Skip Hadden, Alphonse Mouzon** (d); **Airto Moreira, Dom Um Romao, Don Alias, Alyrio Lima, Manolo Badrena** (perc). Columbia Ⓜ CK64627 (57 minutes). Recorded 1971-8.

✓      ⑧ ❾

Although it ignores the excellent 1980 album **Night Passage**, the Weather Report issue in Sony's This Is Jazz series provides a useful introduction to the greatest of the jazz-rock bands. Covering the years 1971-8 (though not in chronological order), it traces Zawinul's and Shorter's progression from virtually avant-garde extemporists to carefully controlled commercially aware jazz-rockers. The ethereal *Orange Lady* (1971) and the more abrasive *The Moors* (1972) mark out the raw early period before *Mysterious Traveller* (1974), *Man in the Green Shirt* (1975) and *Black Market* (1976) point the way to the massively successful 1977 album, **Heavy Weather**, the significance of which is marked by the inclusion of three of its tracks – Zawinul's ubiquitous riff masterpiece *Birdland*, the Jaco Pastorius bass showcase *Teen Town* and the ballad *A Remark You Made*. *Young and Fine* (1978) fleshes out the collection. As far as it goes, the music is fine, but once again the Sony packaging department was on a tea-break, resulting in a superficial booklet-note, abstruse typography and the feeble plea "Recording Date Not Available" on seven of nine tracks from their own archives.    **MG**

# Chick Webb

1909-39

**Rhythm Man** Webb (d, ldr): with on three tracks: **Shelton Hemphill, Louis Hunt, Louis Bacon** (t); **Jimmy Harrison** (tb); **Benny Carter, Hilton Jefferson** (as); **Elmer Williams** (ts); **Don Kirkpatrick** (p); **John Truehart** (bj); **Elmer James** (tba); **Louis Bacon** (v); on 20 tracks: **Mario Bauzá, Reunald Jones, Bobby Stark, Taft Jordan** (t); **Sandy Williams, Fernando Arbello, Claude Jones** (tb); **Pete Clark, Edgar Sampson** (as); **Elmer Williams** (ts); **Wayman Carver** (ts, f); **Joe Steele** (p); **John Truehart** (g); **Elmer James, Delevan Thomas, John Kirby** (b, tba); **Taft Jordan, Chuck Richards, Charles Linton** (v). Hep Ⓜ HEPCD1023 (70 minutes). Recorded 1931-4.

✓      ⑧ ⑧

Despite his physical handicap (an early attack of tuberculosis resulted in a height of only four feet), Chick Webb formed and led what was probably the best of all the pre-war Harlem swing bands. During his long residencies at the Savoy he invariably won band 'battles' with all competitors; on the strength of this essential CD it is not difficult to understand why. Although Webb takes no solos, the thrust and power of his drumming makes itself felt throughout the 23 tracks, underpinning the soloists and cueing in the ensemble figures. No less than 17 of the tracks were arranged by Chick's alto soloist Edgar Sampson, while another alto man present on the earlier tracks, Benny Carter, contributed four more. Taft Jordan, who went on to play with Duke Ellington, is the principal trumpet soloist and vocalist, modelling himself on the playing and singing style of Louis Armstrong. Jimmy Harrison takes his last solos on the tracks from 1933 (he died soon afterwards) while Sandy and Elmer Williams are well featured on the 1933-4 titles. The performances are programmed in chronological order and the sound has never been better. John R.T. Davies is responsible for the magnificent remastering from best-available 78s and the result is an object lesson in the business of jazz reissues.    **AM**

# Eberhard Weber

1940

**The Colours of Chloë** Weber (b, vc, ocarina); **Ack Van Rooyen** (flh); **Rainer Brüninghaus** (p, syn); **Peter Giger** (d, perc); **Ralf Hübner** (d); **Cellos of the Stuttgart Südfunk Orchestra**. ECM Ⓕ 833 331-2 (40 minutes). Recorded 1973.

✓      ⑦ ⑧

German-born Weber switched from cello to bass in his teens. He met Wolfgang Dauner in the early sixties and they worked together for almost ten years. This CD from the emerging ECM label was his first as a leader and it ideally fitted that company's musical policy. It employs the cellos of the Stuttgart Südfunk Symphony but makes no attempt at a synthesis of 'classical' and jazz forms. The concept is nearer to *musique concrète* with the background strata set to contrast with the foreground rather than to interact with it. The cello section does all that is asked of it but, apart from the leader, the jazz soloists are not strong enough to make this a totally successful project. The exception is Weber, whose work on the title track is especially strong, as well as challengingly inventive. All of the themes are by him and they are both varied and stimulating. The arrangements are less convincing, the human voice additions add very little but the whole does have a certain charm. The original release received international acclaim and several European awards but must finally be considered a superior piece of music making which is more concerned with effect than content.    **BMcR**

**Pendulum** Weber (b). ECM Ⓕ 519 707-2 (54 minutes). Recorded 1993.

⑨ ❿

This solo album is an extraordinary achievement. Presaged somewhat by a previous album, **Orchestra** (ECM 1374), it takes the basic idea of that set – the use of echo machines and various delay and sampling equipment – one step further by using studio edits of Weber's performances. Previously, the bassist had not allowed himself the luxury of such techniques, preferring to release only those tracks made entirely at one time, in one take.

This new freedom enables Weber to be much more structured in his approach, and to build each piece in a more deliberate way. None of the freshness is lost because he is still using musical material derived from spontaneous creation, but some of the longueurs of an unedited performance are avoided. The result is a compelling sequence of tracks, none of them short, yet none of them of any great length (the average is around five minutes), and each very much containing its own character. Weber's resourcefulness on his instrument is awesome, while his addiction to the sheer beauty of the sound he creates and also his basically lyrical approach make this a delightful aural experience. There are so many layers, and such a texture, created – often by melodies and patterns over deep ostinatos – that one is constantly tempted to luxuriate in its richness. The stunning sound quality here (this is some of the best-recorded music I have ever come across) enhances every such sensation. **KS**

# Ben Webster
1909-73

**King of the Tenors** Webster (ts) with: **Oscar Peterson** (p); **Barney Kessel** or **Herb Ellis** (g); **Ray Brown** (b); **J.C. Heard** or **Alvin Stoller** (d); on six tracks add: **Harry Edison** (t); **Benny Carter** (as). Verve Ⓜ 519 806-2 (39 minutes). Recorded 1953.

⑧ ❼

The years Webster spent with Norman Granz's Verve label saw the production of some of his best American-made recordings. He was united in the studios with men of near-equal stature who provided him with the competition which was often lacking in the recordings he was to make in Europe later. This CD comprises his first two sessions for Verve and includes a previously unissued *Poutin'* (a Webster blues in minor key), plus two takes of *That's All* and *Bounce Blues*. The quality and reliability of the support from the Oscar Peterson Trio (plus drums) makes one appreciate what a fine unit this was and how fortunate Granz was to be able to call on it to accompany so many outstanding artistes. There are some gorgeous ballads here, including a superb *Tenderly* and a fine *That's All*, with the notes dying away, leaving just an expressive vibrating column of air. As was usually the case with Webster there are reminders of Ellington, this time in the form of *Cottontail* and *Don't Get Around Much Anymore*. Tom Ruff's remastering remains faithful to what was a good set of mono recordings and the only complaint centres around the miserly playing time. **AM**

**Soulville** Webster (ts, p); **Oscar Peterson** (p); **Herb Ellis** (g); **Ray Brown** (b); **Stan Levy** (d). Verve Ⓜ 833 551-2 (49 minutes). Recorded 1957.

✔ ⑩ ❽

The two sides of Ben Webster – the urgent, gritty side and the blowsy, sentimental one – were never captured better than on this album. It was a curious juxtaposition, but Webster expressed himself with such candid simplicity that what emerged was a portrait of himself, a man of complicated and unquiet personality.

*Where Are You?* is the archetypal Webster ballad, silky and insinuating, with a great deal of breath around the notes and an almost desperately pleading air. This is achieved partly by pitching the piece in the almost unheard-of jazz key of E major, which causes the melody to climb repeatedly to a high, keening B natural. In a matter such as this Webster was the most meticulous of artists.

For mid-tempo swing it would be hard to find a better example than *Makin' Whoopee* (key of A flat, right in the middle of the range), with the impeccable Ray Brown laying down one of his vintage bass lines and Peterson proving yet again what a magnificent accompanist he could be.

This CD reissue contains a further attraction in the shape of hitherto-unknown Ben Webster piano solos. Ben began his musical career as a pianist, playing for silent movies and the patrons of sundry bars and dives, and was always ready to sit down and rattle off a tune. On this evidence he posed no threat to Fats Waller or Willie The Lion. **DG**

**Ben Webster Meets Oscar Peterson** Webster (ts); **Peterson** (p); **Ray Brown** (b); **Ed Thigpen** (d). Verve Ⓜ 829 167-2 (37 minutes). Recorded 1959.

✔ ⑩ ❽

Webster is the obvious exception to the rule that says that no Ellington sideman ever continued to progress after leaving Ellington. His innovative riffing and chord busting on the orchestra's 1941 recording of *Cottontail* notwithstanding, he turned in the work for which he is now most remembered almost two decades later, by which time he had ripened into one of the most economical and seductive slow-and-medium-tempo players jazz has ever known. This date with Peterson catches Webster at a peak, playing what it is tempting to describe as Irish tenor. The prolix Peterson, although more compatible with Webster than he was with Lester Young, tends to approach every number as a medium-tempo bounce, even *In the Wee Small Hours of the Morning* and *When Your Lover Has Gone*. But this hardly deters Webster, who was no less mindful than Young was of a song's lyric, and who succeeds in transforming the seven numbers here into melted tallow and low-burning wick; early-morning recollections of amorous nights. **FD**

**See You at the Fair** Webster (ts); **Hank Jones** (p); **Roger Kellaway** (p, h); **Richard Davis** (b); **Osie Johnson**, **Grady Tate** (d); **Thad Jones** (t); **Phil Woods** (as); **Phil Bodner** (ts, ehn); **Pepper Adams** (bs); **Oliver Nelson** (arr, cond) on two tracks only. Impulse! Ⓜ GRP11212 (49 minutes). Recorded 1964.

⑧ ⑩

After his return from California in the early sixties and the ending of his Verve contract, Webster's appearances on disc were few. An unlikely album shared with Joe Zawinul was followed by the above quartet-based set and a few guest shots for Impulse! (including two tracks appended here from Oliver Nelson's **More Blues and the Abstract Truth**). The splendid quartet sessions certainly made a fitting conclusion to Webster's American career, with an appropriate exhibition of his various strengths. Nothing exceeds a bouncing, fast-medium tempo, at which speed the title track is outstanding for its simplicity and vitality, while medium-medium tempos such as *In a Mellow Tone* allow the leader to play fewer notes and express more by mere nuance. But, partly thanks to sensitive accompaniment by either Jones or Kellaway, Ben really shines on the ballads, of which Ellington's *Single Petal of a Rose* (originally a piano solo) was previously only available on a compilation LP while Dmitri Tiomkin's *Fall of Love* reflects the jazz vogue for film themes initiated by Eddie Harris's *Exodus*.

The two added octet tracks necessarily diffuse the effect somewhat but, on Hefti's *Midnight Blue*, Webster is featured in a slow blues from **The Atomic Mr Basie**. **BP**

# Susan Weinert
1965

---

**Crunch Time** Weinert (elg, gsyn); **Martin Weinert** (elb); **Hardy Fischotter** (d); **Oliver Heuss** (kbds). veraBra Ⓕ vBr2144-2 (47 minutes). Recorded 1994.

⑧ ❽

Despite talk of equality, the number of prominent female jazz guitarists – Mary Osborne, Emily Remler, Leni Stern – can almost be counted on the fully functioning fingers of Django Reinhardt's crippled hand. At a time when jazz prodigies are spilling from the music schools, the advent of the extraordinarily capable Susan Weinert is a double phenomenon – such comprehensively virtuosic guitar-playing and writing is a rarity in either sex.

Less can be said about the originality of Weinert's style. Her début album, **Mysterious Stories** (vBr 2111 2), inclined towards John Scofield's lyrical, country-inflected early Gramavision approach. Her second, **Crunch Time**, adopts a heavier attitude, fusing funky, harmonically hip mid-eighties Scofield (cf. **Still Warm**) and Scott Henderson's (cf. Tribal Tech's **Reality Check**). By half-time, the unrelenting heavy metal guitar textures and the stylistically unvarying writing cloy somewhat, but all reservations evaporate in the heat of such moments as the superbly controlled stop-time interlude of *Don't Try That Again, M.F.,* the beautifully developed solo which follows, the clever metric metamorphosis of *Hopeless Case* and the incisively funky guitar riffing which opens *Don't You Guys Know Any Nice Songs?*. Weinert's marginally quieter third album for veraBra, **The Bottom Line**, adds acoustic textures to the mix as well as some fine keyboard work by Rachel Z. **MG**

# Bobby Wellins
1926

---

**Nomad** Wellins (ts); **Jonathan Gee** (p); **Thad Kelly** (b); **Spike Wells** (d); on three tracks: **Claire Martin** (v). Hot House Ⓕ HHCD1008 (65 minutes). Recorded 1992.

⑥ ❼

Wellins, born in the same year as John Coltrane, has been an admirable fixture on the British jazz scene since the early fifties. He served an apprenticeship in the big bands of the time, and also had fruitful stints with creative talents such as Stan Tracey and Tubby Hayes. Of the albums recorded under his own name, this is certainly the most recent, and seems to be the only one currently available on CD. However, this is nothing to worry about unduly, because what is to be found here is excellently crafted and satisfying jazz of the variety spawned by various saxophone giants of the post-war years, including Sonny Rollins, Al Cohn and Wardell Gray. By this stage in his career, however, Wellins is his own man and utterly at home both on his instrument and in his style. He plays with a relaxed power here which is engaging, and he also generously gives a great deal of solo space to the members of his quartet. In fact, I would suggest that he has been a little too generous with space for others and occasionally a trifle mean in the time he has allotted for himself. That said, it is always a pleasure to hear him negotiate effortless lines through such terrain as *Little Rootie Tootie* or *Love for Sale* (which segues seamlessly into an impressive *Willow Weep for Me*).

Claire Martin appears on three Wellins originals, and her usual impeccable control and good taste are well in evidence. To sum up, a highly enjoyable album by one of Britain's unsung greats. **KS**

# Dicky Wells
1907-85

---

**Swingin' in Paris** Wells (tb); **Bill Coleman, Bill Dillard, Shad Collins** (t); **Howard Johnson** (as); **Django Reinhardt** (g); **Sam Allen** (p); **Dick Fullbright** (b); **Bill Beason** (d). Charly LeJazz Ⓑ CD20 (59 minutes). Recorded 1937/8.

❿ ❽

The two 1937 Paris sessions by sidemen of the visiting Teddy Hill Orchestra, under the leadership of Dicky Wells, produced some of the finest swing chamber music ever recorded. All 12 numbers are included here, plus a further eight by Bill Coleman from around the same period.

Wells, who was shortly to become a star soloist with Count Basie, was just reaching his musical maturity in 1937. His style, a combination of lyrical melancholy and a kind of grave jocularity, which marked him out as one of the great individual voices of jazz, is in full bloom here. In the three blues pieces he plays with the simple eloquence that only a master could achieve, while *Lady Be Good* makes a worthy companion-piece to Lester Young's version of the previous year. Perhaps the most exciting passage of all, though, is the first chorus of *Between the Devil and the Deep Blue Sea*, in which the trombone skips and prances around the melody before launching into an inspired paraphrase of the middle-eight strain. The presence of Django Reinhardt on five of these pieces is a further reason for recommending this fine reissue.                                                          **DG**

# Alex Welsh                                                                    1929-82

**Classic Concert** Welsh (t, v); **Roy Williams** (tb, v); **Johnny Barnes** (cl, as, bs, f, v); **Fred Hunt** (p);
    **Jim Douglas** (g, bj); **Harvey Weston** (bs, bg); **Lennie Hastings** (d). Black Lion Ⓜ BLCD760503
    (75 minutes). Recorded 1971.

⑥ ❻

"To their many admirers Alex Welsh and his band made up the best and best-loved jazz ensemble in Britain, or perhaps anywhere," says Digby Fairweather in his notes, with typical over-statement. (Better than Duke? Better-loved than Louis?) Elsewhere he calls the group "probably Britain's greatest-ever Dixieland band," which again is odd, as there was a lot about the Welsh unit which was not Dixieland at all. Roy Williams's duets with guitar, or his unaccompanied choruses; Barnes's baritone and flute solos – nothing very Dixieland there. In fact Williams's trombone playing – the single finest thing in the group – is pretty modern in its sweep; he is just as nimble and liberated as J.J. Johnson in his prime, and a lot warmer. Yet when you listen to a concert like this, recorded in East Germany in Dresden's intriguingly named Hygiene-Halle, you can see, and remember, what Digby means. He first heard the band in 1969. I first heard it in 1959. Over the years Welsh, with his American visitors, has given me more pleasure than any other British band, and on this date he was giving a lot of Germans a great deal of pleasure too. You know when the Germans are enjoying it: because their clapping slowly coagulates into a gigantic unison clapping, quite often at the right tempo, so that Welsh can go straight into a reprise ...

The good numbers – *Oh! Baby*, *9.20 Special*, *Dippermouth Blues* – are terrific. The not-so-good numbers are usually the flashy features for Fred Hunt, or the ones with vocals. British trad/Dixieland players have a fatal urge to open their mouths and sing the words to such dreary songs as *If I Had a Talking Picture of You*, *Little Girl*, and *Dapper Dan* as if a) they were any good, and b) they could remember them. I didn't realize until I heard this record just how bad the words to *Tangerine* were. How can a man like Roy Williams sing so shoddily and play so beautifully on the same number? **MK**

# Kenny Werner

New review
**Live at Visiones/Standards** Werner (p); **Ratzo Harris** (b); **Tom Rainey** (d). Concord
    Ⓕ CCD4675 (59 minutes). Recorded 1995.

⑧ ❾

In his determination to avoid the obvious and find new routes through old territory, Kenny Werner is a jazzman to the core. **Gu-Ru**, his representation in the first edition of this book, contained only two standards by which to measure his invention, but this record is full of them, ranging from such pre-war fare as *Stella by Starlight* to Wayne Shorter's still modern *Fall*. It's easy to appreciate Werner's method when he's playing such familiar pieces as *All the Things You Are*. Indeed, this track works as a comprehensive introduction to his lunacy, clearly revealing the means by which he reawakens old tunes and his listeners' ears. First he forces the comfortable old melody to grow up by hanging an unsettling dissonance beneath it, and then, as if impatient with the pedantic regularity of the original tune, he pushes its phrasing way out of kilter to the point where the trio is about to trip over itself. Of course such feats wouldn't be possible without a sympathetic rhythm section and, significantly, Werner, Harris and Rainey have been partners in crime for years. This is where 'straight-ahead' should be today, and it's further welcome evidence of Concord's willingness to step outside the safe modern-mainstream limits which used to define its output. It certainly isn't an indication that Werner has gone over to the other side.     **MG**

# Fred Wesley

**Swing and Be Funky** Wesley (tb, v); **Hugh Ragin** (t, flh, v); **Karl Denson** (ts, v); **Peter Madsen** (p,
    v); **Dwayne Dolphin** (b, v); **Bruce Cox** (d, v). Minor Music Ⓕ MM801027 (77 minutes).
    Recorded 1992.

⑥ ❽

Fred Wesley has played in the backing bands for countless funk and soul stars, and has also stacked
up useful jazz credentials. This album stresses the jazz side but does not entirely abandon backbeats

and the odd spot of funk (Maceo Parker's *Just Like That* is something The Crusaders would have had fun with). The opening track, written by Prince, is called *For the Elders* and is a graceful tribute to the jazz players who have now gone on before. Each solo horn gets plenty of room and the track runs for over 14 minutes. Even longer is a Latinized version of *On Green Dolphin Street*, which finally exhausts itself at 21 minutes. The music, recorded live in Germany, is generally cast in a happy frame and is relatively conservative in style. Each player acquits himself handsomely, and the band sounds commendably relaxed – in fact, the lengths of the tracks (the shortest is over eight minutes) tends to suggest that they occasionally get too relaxed – so, if it is fun you are looking for, you won't go wrong here. **KS**

# Frank Wess                                                           1922

**Entre Nous**  Wess (ts, f); Snooky Young, Ron Tooley (t); Pete Minger (t, flh); Joe Newman (t, v); Art Baron, Grover Mitchell, Dennis Wilson, Doug Purviance (tb); Curtis Peagler, Bill Ramsey (as); Billy Mitchell (ts); Arthur 'Babe' Clarke (bs); Ted Dunbar (g); Tee Carson (p); Eddie Jones (b); Dennis Mackrell (d). Concord Ⓕ CCD4456 (57 minutes). Recorded 1990.

⑦ ❿

Wess worked in the big bands of Blanche Calloway, Eddie Heywood and Lucky Millinder, but it was his spell with Count Basie from 1953 to 1964 that brought him international attention. This CD features him on tenor and flute and shows him as an accomplished arranger – on *Order in the Court*, *Lover* and *Shiny Stockings* in particular. This Basie-style, 17-piece orchestra is a good one, if lacking a fraction of the model band's rhythmic elasticity. The reeds flow pleasingly and there is real bite in the brass section. The leader gives *Entre Nous* some delicately creative flute treatment, while his tenor on *Rink Rat* is smoothly assertive. There are also polished solos from Young, Baron, Minger, Dunbar and Carson to give further substance. In the eighties Wess worked with Dameronia and New York Jazz Quartet, as well as in a quintet with former Basie colleague, Frank Foster. He is perhaps most at home, as here, with 17 men swinging. **BMcR**

# Kate Westbrook                                                      1939

New review
**Stage Set**  Westbrook (v); Mike Westbrook (p). ASC Records Ⓕ ASCCD9 (62 minutes). Recorded 1995.

⑧ ❽

On this rich and varied album, a fair representation of the live act the husband and wife duo has performed all over Europe in recent years, Kate Westbrook once again demonstrates just how subtle yet dramatic an interpreter she is of an astonishingly wide range of material, embracing everything from settings of European poets – Goethe, Eluard, Blake – through classic jazz and blues – Ellington, Bessie Smith – to the odd original. Her approach has always privileged the skilfully affecting projection of lyric nuances over jazz-vocal virtuosity, so Brecht/Weill songs provide her with near-perfect vehicles for her talent. The album thus starts on a high with a breathlessly tender rendition of the Maxwell Anderson/Kurt Weill classic *September Song*, immediately followed by a rollickingly intense, almost stagy version of *Pirate Jenny* in which music hall collides imaginatively but entirely appositely with jazz cabaret – a fertile sub-genre the Westbrooks have been exploiting for nearly two decades now. Rossini and Theodorakis compositions are sung in their original languages, standards such as *Don't Explain* and *As Times Goes By* – this last given extra resonance by being juxtaposed with a setting of Jean-Luc Lagarce's *Casablanca* – are tellingly re-examined, but it is an utterly compelling multi-language setting of Abdulah Sidran's poignant homage to Sarajevo, *The Blind Man Sings to His Home Town*, that provides the album's centrepiece, encapsulating as it does all the duo's strengths: sensitivity, keen musical intelligence, and above all a willingness to express a refreshingly pan-European sensibility. **CP**

# Mike Westbrook                                                      1936

**Bright as Fire – The Westbrook Blake**  Westbrook (p, v); Kate Westbrook (h, perc, v); Phil Minton (t, v); Mike Davies, Dave Hancock, Henry Lowther (t); Malcolm Griffiths (tb); Alan Sinclair, Nick Patrick (tba) Alan Wakeman (ss, ts, f); Chris Biscoe (ss, as, cl); Georgie Born (vc); Chris Laurence (b); Dave Barry (d, perc); Gospel Oak Primary School Children's Choir (v). Impetus Ⓕ IMPCD18013 (43 minutes). Recorded 1980.

⑨ ❽

The UK's premier jazz composer, Mike Westbrook is known both for his ambitious big-band projects and for his links with poetry, cabaret and theatre, pursued chiefly through various small groups such as his Brass Band and his trio, A Little Westbrook Music. His most successful large-scale piece to date is **The Cortège**, a sprawling three-album *tour de force* that recently appeared on CD on the Enja label. **Bright as Fire**, although smaller in scale, matches it for quality: passionate, incisive settings of seven

William Blake poems that Westbrook first composed in 1971 (for Adrian Mitchell's play *Tyger*), performed here by an augmented Brass Band line-up.

Although he makes full use of his two striking vocalists and coaxes a rare fervour from the saxophonists, it is Westbrook's brilliant writing that ultimately illuminates Blake's verse. He finds music to match the ecstatic vision of *I See Thy Form* and the bleakness of *London Song*, turns *A Poison Tree* into a macabre tango and extends *Holy Thursday* into a searing howl of protest. The finale – Minton singing *Let the Slave*, Westbrook himself declaiming *The Price of Experience* – makes a magnificent anthem of Blake's paeans to freedom and compassion. **Bright as Fire** may not offer the most comprehensive view of Westbrook's manifold talents but its power and stark intensity have yet to be surpassed. **GL**

# Randy Weston
1926

**Monterey '66** Weston (p); **Ray Copeland** (t, flh); **Booker Ervin** (ts); **Cecil Payne** (bs); **Bill Wood** (b); **Lenny McBrowne** (d); **Big Black** (perc). Verve Ⓕ 519 698-2 (74 minutes). Recorded 1966.

⑧ ⑧

There are many reasons for this album (made from a private tape in Randy Weston's possession) being both historically significant and intrinsically worthwhile. It catches a lively and innovative working band at a peak of creativity, having been together three years and shortly to disband; it documents the live sound of one of the music's most underrated saxophonists, Booker Ervin, just four years before his death; it demonstrates the depth and strength of Weston's commitment to the dissemination of African culture years before such concerns became widespread in the popular-musical world. The music itself – rousing, loosely informal and spontaneous yet tightly organized where necessary – bears all the hallmarks of longstanding intimate association between group members; Weston himself refers to it simply as "the best band I've ever had". In a lengthy set made up entirely of Weston compositions, his septet provide a heady mix of uninhibited front-line blowing over hypnotic, rumbustious percussion and more restrained, contemplative moments, such as Ervin's affecting contribution to *Portrait of Vivian*, dedicated to Weston's mother. What lingers in the mind, however, are the two long, heavily percussive pieces, *Afro Black* and *African Cookbook*, which form the musical and philosophical heart of an unusually fine live recording. **CP**

**The Spirit of Our Ancestors** Weston (p); **Idrees Sulieman** (t); **Benny Powell** (tb); **Talib Kibwe** (f, as); **Billy Harper, Pharoah Sanders, Dewey Redman** (ts); **Alex Blake, Jamil Nasser** (b); **Idris Muhammad** (d); **Big Black, Azzedin Weston** (perc); add on one track each: **Yassir Chadly** (v, genbri, karkaba), **Dizzy Gillespie** (t). Antilles Ⓕ 511 896-2 (two discs, oas: 44 and 62 minutes). Recorded 1991.

✓ ⑩ ⑧

There are many memorable recordings from various high points in the career of Randy Weston – solo piano sessions emphasizing his unique link to the blues tradition or acknowledging influences Ellington and Monk; quintet dates with partners like tenor legend Coleman Hawkins or young firebrand Billy Harper; colourful orchestral arrangements, usually by the talented Melba Liston, of Weston's exotic, expansive tunes. Over the years he has been an exciting and consistent performer with a dark, haunting piano tone, percussive touch, and a wealth of rhythms from Caribbean, American jazz and North African sources. **The Spirits of Our Ancestors** combines these sources brilliantly. Liston's charts on tunes like *African Cookbook*, *The Call* and *Blue Moses* sing with unconventional voicings and subtle use of polyrhythms and polytonalities. Fine contributions from trombonist Powell and saxists Sanders and Harper add spice, and Dizzy Gillespie is special guest soloist on the extended *African Sunrise*, composed by Weston for him and Machito's orchestra. The drummers deserve special mention for providing the intense rhythmic impetus, from the riffing refrains of *African Village Bedford-Stuyvesant* to the evocative Arabic modal *The Healers*. But Weston's superb piano is the glue that holds it all together. **AL**

# Kenny Wheeler
1930

**New review**

**Around 6** Wheeler (t, flh): **Evan Parker** (ss, ts); **Eje Thelin** (tb); **Tom Van Der Geld** (vb); **J.F. Jenny-Clark** (b); **Edward Vesala** (d). ECM Ⓕ 529 124-2 (47 minutes). Recorded 1979.

⑧ ⑨

Wheeler is a musical chameleon, comfortable in any stylistic company. Born in Toronto, Canada, he moved to London in 1952 and since that time has shown himself to be a trumpeter of prodigious talent. He was on the first Spontaneous Music Ensemble record date, he worked in a bop environment with Johnny Dankworth and Tubby Hayes and had spells with Anthony Braxton. Often in the Globe Unity and Mike Gibbs Orchestras, he also played in the trio Azimuth. This CD presents six of his imaginative compositions and is performed by six sympathetic artists. With Jenny-Clark as the cultured map reader, and Vesala, the wayward traveller, the pianoless rhythm section is perfect. It is certainly an ideal environment for Wheeler's ringing trumpet tone and fertile imagination. His bonding of composition and arrangement is natural and he combines form, both genteel and wild solos elements, as well as ferocious contrapuntal contrasts. His band here is very much an All Star unit. It was a productive period for Parker and, with Thelin's virtuoso trombone and Van Der Geld's tasteful vibes, Wheeler has a support team to do justice to his deeper musical aspirations. **BMcR**

**Music for Large and Small Ensembles** Wheeler (t, flh); Derek Watkins, Henry Lowther, Alan Downey, Ian Hamer (t); Dave Horler, Chris Pyne, Paul Rutherford, Hugh Fraser (tb); Ray Warleigh, Duncan Lamont, Evan Parker, Stan Sulzmann, Julian Argüelles (reeds); John Abercrombie (g); John Taylor (p); Dave Holland (b); Peter Erskine (d); Norma Winstone (v). ECM Ⓕ 843 152-2 (two discs: 105 minutes). Recorded 1990.

⑨ ❾

Although famously diffident, Canadian trumpeter Kenny Wheeler has long been recognized as a world-class instrumentalist and composer. Based in the UK since 1952, he has participated in many varieties of modern jazz, a valued contributor to groups as diverse as Azimuth and the Globe Unity Orchestra. His earlier ECM recordings present him in a selection of small-group settings but on **Music for Large and Small Ensembles** the emphasis is on his writing for a large big band of the kind he's been leading, albeit on a very occasional basis, for some 25 years.

The eight-part *Sweet Time Suite* takes up the first of the two discs. Its deft timbral shadings and well-framed solos (all excellent) affirm Wheeler's arranging skills, while *Freddy C*'s jaunty swing and the desolate balladry of *Consolation* point to his range as a composer. His tunes are often pastoral in mood, their frequent tinges of melancholia offset by a rich harmonic world that is given extra colouring here by Norma Winstone's wordless vocals. The second CD mixes tracks for big band and small groups, the latter including duos, trios and a sparkling quintet version of *By Myself*. If the three further orchestra works substantiate Wheeler's claim that "I'm always trying to write a beautiful tune", his two trio tracks (with Holland and Erskine) demonstrate that his melodic gift can also flourish in the context of free improvisation. **GL**

# Carla White

New review

**Listen Here** White (v); Lew Tabackin (ts, f); Peter Madsen (p); Dean Johnson (b); Lewis Nash (d). Evidence Ⓕ ECD22109-2 (62 minutes). Recorded 1991.

⑦ ❾

Carla White is an exceptionally good scat singer. There is a unison voice-and-piano line here on *It's You or No-One* that sounds as good as Jackie Cain, which means as good as there is. She is a former pupil of Lennie Tristano, which is interesting and perhaps contributed to the purity of her tone and precision of her pitch. I do not find her work with lyrics as convincing, perhaps because there are just a few too many hip notes and sliding tones, but this is well within the boundaries of personal preference. Lew Tabackin contributes some beautifully understated tenor on *Lotus Blossom*, pure-toned flute on *Dreamsville*, and Dean Johnson has one of the finest bass sounds to be heard these days. Fortunately, it is the bass that is recorded, not the bass speaker, which is often the case. **DG**

# Lenny White                                                        1949

New review

**Renderers of Spirit** White (d, kbds, prog); Mark Ledford (t); Danny Walsh (as); Bennie Maupin, Javon Jackson, Michael Brecker (ts); Geri Allen, Patrice Rushen (p); George Duke (moog); Donald Blackman (org, kbds); Bernard Wright (syn); Vince Evans (kbds); Dean Brown, Dechown Jenkens (g); Victor Bailey, Darryl Jones, Jerry Brooks (b); Stanley Clarke (elb); Audrey Northington, Nicki Richards (v). Hip Bop Essence Ⓕ HIBD8014 (62 minutes). Recorded 1996.

⑤ ❾

There is a strange old-timey sense to this record. It uses all the currently fashionable grooves, sounds and samples and is intelligently programmed to be as contemporary as one could wish, but its soul is stuck in the early seventies, when funk and fusion were proposing marriage and the honeymoon was about to begin in terms of sales potential. Shaft, James Brown and other juicy stylistic clichés are fleetingly referred to here from track to track, and we even get a soul-stirred version of Bacharach's *Walk on By*, vocals and all. Over everything is the beat, that back-beat metronome which governs this music as much as rinky-tink did swing. In terms of the upper layers, the interest waxes and wanes, depending who is soloing. Danny Walsh is profoundly forgettable on his four tracks but Brecker fashions something more interesting. Geri Allen is left decorating Nicki Richards's slow soul vocals on *Sailing* before getting a brief solo. And so it goes. White is an intelligent and accomplished musician who has played with, among others, Stan Getz and Joe Henderson before hitting fame with Return to Forever. This new effort leans towards Return's electric dreams, and then some. **KS**

# Annie Whitehead

1955

**Naked** Whitehead (tb); **Jasper van't Hof** (kbds); **Ian Maidman** (g, perc, moog); **Dudley Philips** (b); **Liam Genockey** (d). EFZ Ⓕ 1019 (72 minutes). Recorded 1995.

⑥ ❿

Whitehead started to make a more than local impression on moving to London in the early eighties and working with Chris McGregor. By the latter part of that decade her most regular sessions were with John Stevens, and by the nineties she was working regularly with Carla Bley, among others. Having begun her musical career playing ska and reggae with various bands, she has continued to interpolate many elements of these genres into her current music. This album showcases many facets of her style, from ska to Ellington to latin to funk and soul. Through it all is the very beautiful open sound of her instrument (her favourites include Knepper and Rudd, two players with outstandingly human, full trombone sounds). Her contexts remain unremittingly modern here, the compositions almost entirely her own (there are a couple of collaborative efforts which sound like they evolved from group jams), and while the thematic and harmonic bases are usually simple and open, her talent is sufficient to continually inject colour and interest at appropriate points to lift things out of the ordinary. **KS**

# Paul Whiteman

1890-1967

**The King of Jazz** Whiteman (dir); **Henry Busse, Bix Beiderbecke** (c); **Charles Margulis, Manny Klein, Charlie Teagarden** (t); **Tommy Dorsey, Bill Rank, Jack Teagarden** (tb); **Charles Strickfaden** (as, bs); **Jimmy Dorsey** (cl, as); **Izzy Friedman** (cl, as, ts); **Frankie Trumbauer** (c-ms, ss); **Roy Bargy** (p); **Min Leibrook** (bb, bss); **Joe Venuti** (vn); **Mark Pingitore** (bj); **Art Miller, Steve Brown** (b); **Harold McDonald** (d, vb); **Bing Crosby, Mildred Bailey, Paul Robeson, Red McKenzie** (v). ASV Ⓜ CDAJA5170 (76 minutes). Recorded 1920-36.

⑥ ❼

During his career Whiteman made more than 600 recordings, he commissioned Gershwin to write *Rhapsody in Blue* and, as the 'King of Jazz', presented 'symphonic jazz' to the world. His orchestra often included jazz musicians of stature but his normal programme contained sham, classical elements, popular tunes of the day, a smattering of trivial novelty numbers and little real jazz. The standard of musicianship was high and in men like Bill Challis and Tommy Satterfield, he had arrangers who produced a quality product. Even before their time there were Whiteman band charts worthy of some examination. Certainly *Wang Wang Blues* on this CD, with Busse sounding almost King Oliver-like, is an arrangement that compares favourably with those used by early Johnny Dunn or Fletcher Henderson. Later there is genuine merit in *Whiteman Stomp* and *Darktown Strutters Ball*, although dreadful dirges such as *Three O'Clock in the Morning* and the pretentious *Rhapsody in Blue* rendition do balance the scales. The famed Beiderbeck contributions are covered elsewhere, but on this disc there are fine solo offerings from Trumbauer, Klein, Venuti and Teagarden. These are isolated moments of pure jazz, however, and for most of the time the 'King of Jazz' produces music typified by the cod-drama of *Slaughter on Tenth Avenue*. Too often it lacked the vital ingredient that would have made Whiteman's trade mark title acceptable. **BMcR**

# Mark Whitfield

1966

**7th Avenue Stroll** Whitfield (g); **Tommy Flanagan, Stephen Scott** (p); **Dave Holland, Christian McBride** (b); **Al Foster, Greg Hutchinson** (d). Verve Ⓕ 529 223-2 (66 minutes). Recorded 1995.

⑦ ❾

This young player was drawn to jazz on hearing George Benson and became his disciple, even to the extent of letting Benson arrange his career. The list, in the booklet, of people he has played with includes Art Blakey, Kenny Barron and the Marsalis Brothers, but it doesn't say for how long. However, Whitfield worked (on Benson's recommendation) in the trio of organist Jack McDuff for two years. He is the latest manifestation of the line from Charlie Christian and his work is adept, amiable, vigorous and pretty, if not impelled by deep emotion. He has a great respect for the jazz tradition, swings well and uses a lightness of touch here which would probably not have been possible in McDuff's group. His improvisations are well thought through and his lines flow with conviction. His is the lion's share but there are plenty of other solos, notably from Flanagan, at his most fetching on *Businessman's Bounce*. There can be no questioning Whitfield's talent, and he reaches his peak on this album with a taut performance on his own *Headin' to the Wes' Side*. A subsequent album, **Forever Love** (Verve), matches him with an orchestra arranged and conducted by Dale Ochler on a set of tried and true ballads but finds him no nearer the deeper waters of expressivity. **SV**

# Weslia Whitfield

1947

**Nice Work ...** Whitfield (v); **Mike Greensill** (p); **Gene Bertoncini** (g); **Michael Moore** (b).
Landmark Ⓕ LCD1544-2 (56 minutes). Recorded 1994.

⑦ ❽

Weslia Whitfield is a wonder, a vocalist gifted with flawless intonation, an impressive range and, most significantly, an intimate dramatic sensibility perfectly attuned to the lyrics and melodies of the classic American popular song. Thanks to gilt-edged engagements at venues such as the Oak Room in New York's fabled Algonquin Hotel, Westfield has at last found her audience. With a straight-away delivery successfully tapping the emotive and musical depths of a stellar repertoire, Westfield has won the hearts of jazz and cabaret fans alike. That she has done so without undue fuss or hyperbolic theatrics is another plus. Whitfield's charms emanate from a keen intelligence. When she gives voice to *Where's the Rainbow?*, the tune's wistful melancholy rings authentic. Confined to a wheelchair due to a drive-by shooting in her hometown of San Francisco, it is clear that Westfield is a person who has meditated upon life's vicissitudes. Also significant is her heart-on-sleeve vulnerability. When she intones *I Concentrate on You*, the directness of her confession is compelling. Indeed, when Whitfield sings, it is an invitation to share worlds both personal and public. She also swings, an aspect most evident in her ebullient take on Nat Cole's *I'm an Errand Girl (Boy) for Rhythm*. The insouciant title track, *Nice Work if You Can Get It*, sums up the intensity of Whitfield's engagement with her muse. **CB**

# Putte Wickman

1924

**Bewitched** Wickman (cl); **Claes Crona** (p); **Mads Vinding**, **Ove Stenberg** (b); **Bjarne Rostvold**, **Nils-Erik Slorner** (d). Bluebell Ⓕ ABCD051 (67 minutes). Recorded 1980-2.

⑧ ❽

Like his contemporary and fellow-countryman the late Stan Hasselgard, the Swedish clarinettist Putte Wickman grew up under the overwhelming influence of Benny Goodman but succeeded in developing a personal style quite early in his career. Bop and cool jazz have left distinct marks on his playing, and he has also shown a natural affinity for the bossa nova. This collection of 18 short, exquisitely turned versions of standard tunes shows off his delicate tone and fluid phrasing to perfection. Pianist Claes Crona deserves to be far more widely appreciated; as an accompanist he has the firm lightness of a Hank Jones or a Tommy Flanagan. The recording, by engineers of Swedish Radio, is first rate. **DG**

# Gerry Wiggins

1922

**Soulidarity** Wiggins (p); **Andy Simpkins** (b); **Paul Humphrey** (d). Concord Ⓕ CCD4706
(64 minutes). Recorded 1995.

⑥ ❾

Wiggins has spent much of his long career in Los Angeles, and has been accompanist to a range of first-rate singers, including Lena Horne, Kay Starr and Helen Humes. From time to time he ran his own trio and made the occasional record for a small independent company which would surface for a season and then disappear, to be reissued years later as a collectors' item. Wiggins drew much of his early style from the giants of his youth such as Art Tatum, George Shearing and Teddy Wilson (all of whom are still faintly discernible today), but as the years advanced he moved into a more modern mainstream style which incorporated bop and its rash of superb second-generation pianists (his own contemporaries) such as Hank Jones, Erroll Garner and Tommy Flanagan. Always happy to dig into the blues, Wiggins is today perhaps more forceful than he used to be, which can't be a bad thing in a piano trio. This means that **Soulidarity** is more lively than the previous entry in this Guide, which had been made in 1957 and suffered from excessively low temperatures, as well as poor playing time. **KS**

# Bob Wilber

1928

**Summit Reunion** Wilber (ss); **Kenny Davern** (cl); **Dick Hyman** (p); **Bucky Pizzarelli** (g); **Milt Hinton** (b); **Bobby Rosengarden** (d). Chiaroscuro Ⓕ CR(D)311 (68 minutes). Recorded 1990.

⑧ ❽

Soprano saxophonist/clarinettist Bob Wilber is one of the true champions of traditional jazz, studying for several years as a teenager with no less a legend than Sidney Bechet. As a prime mover in the traditional jazz revival centred in New York during the late forties and fifties, he worked with Bobby Hackett, Benny Goodman and Jack Teagarden. In 1969, he helped found the World's Greatest Jazz Band, and in 1974 he and fellow reedman Keny Davern organized Soprano Summit.

It was a wonderful group that during its five-year run seamlessly fused prime elements from the New Orleans, Chicago and Swing Era heritages, with Wilber and Davern, both virtuoso players, melding their warmly rendered countermelodies with precision and dash. When the group disbanded in 1979, Wilber took on such varied projects as the score for Francis Coppola's film *The Cotton Club* (for which he received a 1986 Grammy) and the directorship of the Smithsonian Jazz Repertory Ensemble.

Here, the 1990 recording reunion of Wilbur and Davern finds Wilber on soprano and Davern on clarinet. It is an upbeat and musically immaculate affair where chestnuts like *Lover Come Back to Me*, *Black and Blue* and *Limehouse Blues* are toasted to perfection. In-the-pocket support by the original rhythm section cements the good feelings and music. There is also an 11-minute dialogue where Wilber and Davern reminisce and opine. **CB**

# Joe Wilder                                                                    1922

**Wilder 'n' Wilder** Wilder (t); **Hank Jones** (p); **Wendell Marshall** (b); **Kenny Clarke** (d).
  Denon/Savoy Ⓜ SV0131 (38 minutes). Recorded 1956.

⑧ ❽

One of the most reliable trumpet sidemen, Wilder worked with Les Hite, Lionel Hampton, Dizzy Gillespie, Jimmie Lunceford and Lucky Millinder in the forties. He worked for six months with Count Basie in 1953, but in 1957 began a career on the musical staff of ABC. It has been contended with some justification that the comfort of studio work somewhat blunted the cutting edge of his jazz performances. The virtuoso trumpeter did not challenge himself enough or bother to put himself into motivating situations. This excellent CD is one of only two recordings issued under his leadership during the 16 years he spent in the studio but it reveals a very fine jazz musician. His masterful interpretations of the testing *Cherokee* or *Darn That Dream* confirm his inherent improvisational skill but throughout he displays his fluency, his unique tone and his highly personal manner of phrasing. On *Six Bit Blues* he adds a little surface grit by growling through a waltzing blues theme ideally suited to this style of treatment. Not all of his output has been of this quality but it does seem that with Jones, Marshall and Clarke to provide the stimulation, Wilder was in the mood to respond. **BMcR**

# Barney Wilen                                                               1937-96

**Wild Dogs of the Ruwenzori** Wilen (ss, as, ts); **Alain Jean-Marie** (p); **Riccardo del Fra** (b);
  **Sangoma Everett** (d); **Henri Guedon** (perc). IDA Ⓔ 020CD (71 minutes). Recorded 1988.

⑤ ❻

Barney Wilen flashed into the jazz consciousness in the late fifties as a young man when he was picked to play with Miles Davis on the sound track for the film *Lift to the Scaffold*, and as far as the British public is concerned has not been heard much of since. Judging by this CD he latterly developed into a capable, warm swinging tenor player, not much touched by the Coltrane, free or fusion eras. The record is pleasant and quite varied, but ... There is no explanation for the title provided, neither what the Ruwenzori is nor why there are wild dogs there, although there is a reproduction of a painting of that name, under which it says (in French) "It is easier to leave no trace behind than to walk without touching the ground." Deep, these French. **MK**

# Lee Wiley                                                                    1915-75

**Night in Manhattan** Wiley (v); **Bobby Hackett** (c); **Joe Bushkin, Stan Freeman, Cy Walter** (p);
  **unknown** (b, d); strings. Columbia Ⓜ SRS75010 (38 minutes). Recorded 1950.

✅                                                                              ⑧ ❽

One has to search nowadays for Lee Wiley's records, of which this is a quite delectable example. It features her breathy-cool voice against the accompaniment of Hackett's cornet, a rhythm section led by Bushkin and the subtlest and most minimal of string backgrounds. She was one of the very first white jazz singers, along with Connee Boswell and Mildred Bailey, and by 1950 had evolved a style of ethereal, but at the same time worldly, charm. This ambivalence lies at the heart of her singing persona and is inherent in the stylistic means which she employs. There is, for instance, a quite deliberate, girlish breathiness about her higher notes, yet at the same time no one ever handled the trembling downward *glissando* (indicative of barely controlled passion) to greater effect. But, these devices aside, Lee Wiley's most captivating quality is her ability to make notes and words swing together, which is – or should be – the definition of a good jazz singer. She produces small miracles in this line here, in songs such as *Manhattan* (a strong rival to Ella's version), *Oh! Look At Me Now* and *Sugar*. On four of the 12 titles the accompaniment changes to the piano-duo of Freeman and Walter, with which she does the best she can. But it is worth buying this disc for the remaining eight. It is also worth searching out the Japanese issue of this album, released on CD in the original mono sound. **DG**

**Duologue** Wiley (v); **Ruby Braff** (t); **Jimmy Jones** (p); **Bill Pemberton** (b); **Jo Jones** (d); on four tracks: **Ellis Larkins** (p). Black Lion Ⓜ BLCD760911 (36 minutes). Recorded 1954.

⑧ ❻

Four out of the dozen tracks are piano solos by Larkins which are very compatible with the tasteful and imaginative performances from Wiley and her group. This CD is a straight transfer of an old 12-inch LP which was cobbled together from an old Storyville 10-inch Wiley LP with the Larkins tracks thrown in to make up the new format's playing-time. Nothing has been added, however, to make up the CD format's rather miserly playing time.

Wiley is a jazz singer to class with Billie Holiday, Mildred Bailey and Peggy Lee. Listening to her warm and delicately phrased singing, it is difficult to reconcile her with Wild Bill Davison's description of a fist fight in a bar in which she was involved with another musician's wife. According to Davison, Wiley and the other woman, a lady called Sea Biscuit, slugged it out toe to toe like men. Despite her most feminine mien Wiley was often able to physically intimidate her male colleagues.

Regrettably, most of Wiley's recordings were marred by oppressive commercial backing or, when she was with jazz small groups, poor recording quality. This makes the album under review doubly valuable for, while George Wein's Storyville recordings hardly count as hi-fi, they are comparatively superior. The backing, with young Braff ideally suited to the singer, is as good as any she ever had and recalls her session with Muggsy Spanier and Jess Stacy of many years earlier. Wiley's choice of material was unerringly good and songs like *My Romance*, *It Never Entered My Mind*, and *My Heart Stood Still* are perfect for her. Larkins's unaccompanied tracks are similarly tasteful and his accomplished solos are the next best thing to four more songs from Wiley. **SV**

# Ernie Wilkins

1922

**Suite for Jazz Band** Wilkins (ldr, arr); with **Danish Radio Big Band**: **Benny Rosenfeld**, **Palle Bolvig**, **Henrik Bolberg**, **Lars Togeby**, **Perry Knudsen** (t); **Vincent Nilsson**, **Ture Larsen**, **Steen Hansen**, **Jens Engels** (tb); **Axel Windfeld** (btb); **Jan Zum Vohrde**, **Michael Hove** (as); **Tomas Franck**, **Uffe Marcussen** (ts); **Flemming Madsen** (bs); **Nikolaj Bentzon** (p); **Anders Lindvall** (g); **Jesper Lundgaard** (b); **Jonas Johansen** (d); **Peter Reim** (perc). Hep Ⓕ HEPCD2051 (68 minutes). Recorded 1991.

⑥ ❻

Wilkins became one of the most prolific writers for big bands, starting his career with the Count Basie Orchestra, which he joined as a saxophonist in 1952. He came to live in Denmark in 1980 and, at the time of writing, the fine LPs by his "Almost Big Band" made in that country have not been transferred to the compact disc format. On this well-recorded concert transcription he heads the Danish Radio Big Band on one of its annual tours of Britain (the CD was taped at a Croydon concert). Half of the playing time is devoted to music composed and arranged, with typical efficiency, by Ernie. The major work is his *Suite for Jazz Band*, divided into three sections and lasting for 24 minutes. It is an impressive piece of writing and the band is well up to interpreting it with accuracy and verve. The suite reminds us that Wilkins wrote an extended *From Coast to Coast* for Basie in 1956 which the Count seldom performed, presumably preferring more orthodox Wilkins pieces such as *Peace Pipe* and *The Midgets*. Pianist Bentzon and tenor saxist Marcussen are two outstanding soloists in the Radio Big Band and alto saxist Jan Zum Vohrde takes the featured role on Phil Woods's arrangement of *This is All I Ask* with considerable skill and flair. **AM**

# Jack Wilkins

New review

**Keep in Touch** Wilkins (elg); **Kenny Drew** (p); **Andy McKee** (b); **Akira Tana** (d). Claves Jazz Ⓕ 50-1295 (69 minutes). Recorded 1995.

⑧ ❾

Despite the fact that Akira Tana sports a back-to-front baseball cap on the cover, this is a fairly conventional, straight-ahead session by a co-operatively led band direct from the bebop heartland. However, as Kenny Drew Jr. repeatedly shows here, there are still enormous creative possibilities in that idiom. His spectacular technique is exciting enough, but it is entirely the servant of a quite prodigious imagination. While any given track (*Short Story* and *East Coasting* are two fine examples) can be motoring along decorously within the prescribed bebop guidelines, Drew will pop up like an unruly child and set the place alight. His co-leader Jack Wilkins also has bags of technique, but it seems to be as much a confining as a liberating feature. He is rather good on the bossa *Street of Dreams*, where he produces some considered, compelling lines, but too often elsewhere he seems to be on autopilot, as if he were letting his fingers do the talking. Not helped by his grey, muffled, typical jazz guitar tone, his relentless strings of eighths and sixteenths tend to fuse into an indistinct blur of warm, round sound in which the ideas are submerged. The backroom boys function well, with the occasional solo, but finally this is Drew's date, whatever the credits say. **MG**

## Baby Face Willette 1933

**Stop and Listen** Willette (org); **Grant Green** (g); **Ben Dixon** (d). Blue Note Ⓜ CDP8 28998-2 (50 minutes). Recorded 1961.

⑤ ❽

Willette – nobody seems to have recorded his given first name – made his recording début on Blue Note with **Face to Face**, an album made in the same year and also featuring Grant Green. Currently unavailable, its bonus was the robust tenor of Fred Jackson. Here Baby Face has to lead the line himself, and while he's a capable player who eschews the grosser combinations of sounds of which a Hammond B3 is capable, he struggles to keep the listener's undivided attention for 50 minutes. Perhaps in a Harlem bar in 1961 this would have been ideal, and there is no doubting that his pedal work is nicely grooved with drummer Ben Dixon, but his right hand is sparing in its use of the unexpected. So it is to Green that we must look for that type of aural stimulation, and he obliges on more tracks than not, even if it is merely in the fine art of rhythmic displacement.

The rating indicates that this is a good album, and it is. Within its given genre it is successful, and if organ jazz is your meat, you will not be disappointed here. For those wishing to dip their toes for the first time, there are better places to start. **KS**

## Buster Williams 1942

**Something More** Williams (b, pic b); **Shunzo Ohno** (t); **Wayne Shorter** (ts, ss); **Herbie Hancock** (p, kbds); **Al Foster** (d). In & Out Ⓕ 7004-2 (59 minutes). Recorded 1989.

⑧ ❽

At home with the bop of Jimmy Heath and Sonny Stitt as well as in the company of singers such as Betty Carter or Sarah Vaughan, Williams moved with the times and worked with Miles Davis and Hancock in the sixties and early seventies. More recently found in the comparatively conservative atmosphere of The Timeless All Stars and Sphere, he remains one of music's finest bassists. This CD is, in fact, just what such a player's session should be like. Williams is at the heart of the ensemble, his full tone and faultless intonation a vital factor in the band's overall sound. Apart from a rather bland piccolo bass outing on *Sophisticated Lady*, his solos are richly inventive and are delivered with an ideally dark-brown resonance. Williams has also written five impressive tunes, with two waltzes, *Air Dancing* and *Something More*, being genuinely memorable. He has also provided the listener with the perfect guarantee by picking a line-up at the top of their game. Shorter, close to the theme on *Christina* and *Something More* and raw-edged on *Fortune Dance*, responds splendidly. Ohno excels on *Deception*, while Williams, Hancock and Foster sound as if they have been together for years. The album reflects great credit on its leader. **BMcR**

## Clarence Williams 1898-1965

**1927-34** Williams (p, jug, v); **Ed Allen, Louis Metcalf** (c); **Red Allen** (t); **Charlie Irvis** (tb); **Cecil Scott** (cl); **Buster Bailey** (cl, as); **Arville Harris** (cl, as, ts); **Herman Chittison, Willie 'The Lion' Smith, James P. Johnson** (p); **Leroy Harris, Ikey Robinson** (b); **Cyrus St Clair** (bb); **Floyd Casey** (wshbd); **Eva Taylor** (v). CDS Ⓕ RPCD633 (69 minutes). Recorded 1927-34.

⑦ ❽

Williams was one of the first black musicians to make a success of a multifarious career in the music industry, working as publisher, booker, retailer and record producer. In the mid twenties he organized sessions by his Blue Five with Louis Armstrong and Sidney Bechet which yielded such classics of their period as *Coal Cart Blues* and *Mandy, Make Up Your Mind*. These are being systematically reissued on Hot 'n' Sweet and Classics. The CDS compilation is devoted to his later small groups, which he employed largely on cheerful novelty songs, typically with washboard rather than drums and featuring himself or his wife Eva Taylor as singer. Numbers like *Chizzlin' Sam* and *He Wouldn't Stop Doin' It* are essentially party-blues material in the manner of groups like the Hokum Boys, given musical settings a step or two ahead of the jazzier jugbands but several short of Fats Waller. Scattered amid these effusions are more sober performances like *Log Cabin Blues*, nicely paced by St Clair's brass bass (an important voice in Williams's ensembles), *Trouble* and *Chocolate Avenue,* to which Ed Allen and Cecil Scott supply eloquent blues solos. Williams's track record as a producer enabled him to call on excellent sidemen, and even his more ephemeral pieces have inventive touches, as well as an élan that Robert Parker's transfers reproduce in scrupulous detail. **TR**

## Cootie Williams 1911-85

New review

**Cootie Williams and His Orchestra 1941-4** Williams, Joe Guy, George Treadwell, Harold 'Money' Johnson, E.V. Perry, Lamar Wright (t); **Louis Bacon** (t, v); **Lou McGarity, Robert Horton, Sandy Williams, George Stevenson** (tb); **Charlie Holmes, Frank Powell** (as); **Eddie 'Cleanhead' Vinson** (as, v); **Greely Walton, Eddie 'Lockjaw' Davis, Lee Pope, Sam 'The Man'**

**Taylor** (ts); **Skippy Martin**, **John Williams**, **Eddie De Verteuill** (bar); **Johnny Guarnieri**, **Kenny Kersey**, **Bud Powell** (p); **Artie Bernstein**, **Norman Keenan**, **Carl Pruitt** (b); **Jo Jones**, **Butch Ballard**, **Vess Payne** (d); **Pearl Bailey** (v). Classics Ⓜ 827 (73 minutes). Recorded 1941-4.

⑦ ❼

Williams's early work in the territory band of Alonzo Ross in Florida, brief stays with Chick Webb and Fletcher Henderson and his illustrious career as feature trumpeter with Duke Ellington is well documented. His original inspiration was Louis Armstrong and this is evident in all of his playing. It was not even disguised when he took over the 'growl' chair from Bubber Miley in the Ellington band and it shaped the way in which he soloed throughout his life. This CD covers the period after he left the Duke in 1940, spent time in the Benny Goodman Orchestra and began leading his own band. It also provides an important commentary on the jazz of the Second World War years. It features sophisticated blues figure 'Cleanhead' Vinson and r&b's Sam 'The Man' Taylor; it also has emerging bop pianist Bud Powell as well as including *Fly Right*, later to be Thelonious Monk's *Epistrophy*, as well as his *'Round Midnight*.

Due to the variety of line-ups, it is a mixed bag. There are stately readings of *West End Blues* and *Sweet Lorraine* in the Armstrong manner. *Ain't Misbehavin'* is treated in the riff style of the day, while the ghost of Miley walks with grace on *Echoes of Harlem*. In contrast, there are several pot-boilers, Williams sings unconvincingly on one title and Bailey's input is essentially lightweight. Fortunately, the trumpeter plays with conviction throughout and it is perhaps the case that he was simply unsure of his musical direction. That problem was solved when, in 1962, he returned to his spiritual home in the Ellington Orchestra, a position he retained until his leader's death in 1964.　　**BMcR**

## James Williams　　1951

**Talkin' Trash**　**Williams** (p, org); **Clark Terry** (t, flh, v); **Billy Pierce** (ss, ts); **Steve Nelson** (vb); **Christian McBride** (b); **Tony Reddus** (d). DIW Ⓕ 887 (65 minutes). Recorded 1993.

⑦ ❽

Memphis-born, gospel-inspired and r&b trained, Williams met jazz along with his further education at Memphis State University. He later moved to Boston, taught at Berklee and became a prominent figure on the Massachusetts scene. In the seventies, four productive years with the Jazz Messengers honed up his playing and writing talents so that throughout the eighties he worked as a leader and as an in-demand sideman in New York.

This CD parades his skills effectively. The storefront gospel of *The Orator* is a reminder that he had played church organ in Memphis for six years. In contrast, *Chuckles* offers a pianist with a finely graded touch, flawless execution and a creative bent that makes musical story-telling sound easy. Three choruses of blues piano on *SKJ* show how much he can say with little effort, while *Lotus Blossom* is a gem indicating that he can decorate a thematic line as well as construct a new one. His solos are ever full of confidence, matched only by the support he gives his ebullient colleagues, Terry and Pierce. Even the difficult piano-vibraphone balance is navigated with ease and this is a worthy progress report on a highly professional jazzman.　　**BMcR**

## Jessica Williams　　1948

**The Next Step**　**Williams** (p). Hep Ⓕ HEPCD2054 (75 minutes). Recorded 1993.

⑩ ❽

Jessica Williams has been described as the "best unknown pianist in jazz", and her lack of acceptance as one of the greatest keyboard artistes can only be due to her lack of exposure on record labels with international distribution. She has produced several albums on her own Quanta label, and now has CDs on Timeless, Candid and Concord (Candid in fact has her latest, **Gratitude** [1995]), but her first album for the British Hep label is arguably the very finest showcase for her talents. Not only is she a remarkable pianist, she is also a true composer, not simply a writer of riffs or flimsy lines sketched on top of someone else's chord sequences. There are four of her tunes here, nestling amongst interpretations of works by Mingus, Ellington, Ron Carter and the best Broadway composers. There is also a quite beautiful song by Dave Brubeck, *I Didn't Know Until You Told Me*, which Jessica has taken from the **Real Ambassadors** album which Brubeck made with Louis Armstrong. Her constantly enquiring mind, her knowledge of jazz tradition and her love for the musical philosophy of Thelonious Monk, allied to her ability to extract a beautiful and personal sound from the piano results in music above and beyond the level normally found in a jazz keyboard artist. Her own *Stonewall Blues* is a masterpiece, and sounds like a look back at Leadbelly while simultaneously viewing the future. But there is not a weak track here: this is an essential album of contemporary jazz piano.　　**AM**

## Joe Williams　　1918

**Every Day: The Best of the Verve Years**　**Williams** (v); with various ensembles, including: **The Count Basie Orchestra** (Wendell Culley, Renauld Jones, Thad Jones, Joe Newman, t; Henry Coker, Bill Hughes, Benny Powell, tb; Marshall Royal, cl, as; Bill Graham, as; Frank Foster, f, ts, arr; Charlie Fowlkes, bs; Basie, p; Freddie Green, g; Eddie Jones, b; Sonny Payne, d; Buddy Bregman, Edgar Sampson, Ernie Wilkins, arr); and small groups featuring: **Clark Terry, Joe Wilder** (t); **Al Grey** (tb); **Bobby Watson** (as, arr); **Frank Wess** (ts); **Seldon Powell** (bs); **Norman Simmons** (p, arr); **Shirley Horn** (p, v); **Henry Johnson, Kenny Burrell** (g); **Bob Badgley, Bob Cranshaw, Charles Ables** (b); **Gerryck King, Dennis Mackrel, Steve Williams** (d); **Marlena Shaw** (v); **Johnny Pate** (arr). Verve Ⓜ 519 813-2 (two discs: 127 minutes). Recorded 1955-90.

Ⓖ Ⓖ

Williams has so much going for him as a vocalist – great voice, fine diction, admirably seamless phrasing – it seems odd that for so much of his career he's been perceived as something of an anomaly on the jazz scene. Perhaps the nub of the conundrum lies in that boring and endless argument – what is a jazz singer? It seems to me that if we simply discount Williams as a jazz singer per se, then most of the problems evaporate. One of Williams's favourite latter-day albums of his own (featured on this compilation) is **Ballad and Blues Master**, and this seems a more apt decription of his ambit. If you listen to the powerful impact he makes on the Basie band with his big hit numbers, it's through bringing r&b and popular music techniques to blues structures which have been arranged in a jazz style. Williams skilfully combines traits he's picked up from a multiplicity of artists, including Eckstine, Wynonie Harris, Charles Brown, Memphis Slim, Ella Fitzgerald and even Louis Armstrong, and projects them through his big, gorgeous voice-box to create a sensual and exciting mix. The fact that, with Basie, he invariably sounds like he's smiling, whatever the lyrics are telling us, not only lets us know he's having a good time, but that he's not the greatest interpreter we've ever heard, and that, at times, he's closer to showbiz than to jazz. This aspect of his art is much less evident on the latter-day performances, where tenderness, hurt and sorrowful wisdom can also be successfully projected.

Depending on what you're looking for from a singer, Williams can give you either raw excitement a-plenty (with the Basie material) or an all-round musical display (on CD number two, with his own quartet mainly as backing). The only question mark I would place over this collection as a perfect summing-up of Williams's career is that the second recording of *Every Day*, with the Basie Band and Ella joining in, is missing. **KS**

---

**New review**
## Presenting Joe Williams and the Thad Jones-Mel Lewis Orchestra Joe Williams (v);
**Thad Jones** (flh); **Snooky Young, Jimmy Nottingham, Bill Berry, Richard Williams** (t); **Bob Brookmeyer, Garnett Brown, Tom McIntosh, Cliff Heather** (tb); **Jerome Richardson, Jerry Dodgion** (as); **Eddie Daniels, Joe Farrell** (ts); **Pepper Adams** (bs); **Roland Hanna** (p); **Sam Herman** (g); **Richard Davis** (b); **Mel Lewis** (d). Blue Note Ⓜ CDP8 30454-2 (41 minutes). Recorded 1966.

Ⓗ Ⓗ

At the age of 48 Joe Williams was in fine voice. His rich, oaken tones, his impeccable diction, the easy gravitas of his manner – all had reached a point of perfect balance. Not since Eckstine had there been a full-voiced baritone singer with such exquisite vocal control. His repertoire was actually much more varied than most of these trusty old favourites and then new soul songs might suggest, but to hear him deliver them remains a heartening experience. Williams's interpretation of Ellington's *Come Sunday* is masterly enough to prompt the reflection that his was exactly the type of voice that Duke valued – and that he might have been more creatively employed in the Ellington orchestra than in Basie's. The Jones-Lewis band, a battalion of virtuosos if ever there was one, plays with staggering brio and assurance. The saxophones' solo passage in *It Don't Mean a Thing* is enough on its own to demoralize every rehearsal band on the face of the planet. **DG**

# Mary Lou Williams 1907-81

---

## The Chronological Mary Lou Williams, 1927-40 Williams (p, arr); Henry McCord, Earl
**Thompson, Harold Baker** (t); **Bradley Bullett, Ted Donnelly** (tb); **Edward Inge** (cl) **John Williams** (as, bs); **Earl Miller** (as, cl); **Dick Wilson** (ts); **Ted Robinson, Floyd Smith** (g); **Joe Williams** (bj); **Booker Collins** (b); **Bob Price, Ben Thigpen** (d). Classics Ⓜ 630 (73 minutes). Recorded 1927-40.

Ⓗ Ⓖ

Williams has the distinction of being the most important woman musician of early jazz, and in addition her encouragement was significant for several later generations of players. Consistent with the latter is her contribution to the art of big-band arranging, particularly during her years with the Andy Kirk band, whereas her piano work heard here is more often overlooked these days.

The first six tracks, tolerably reproduced but the least well recorded, find her in the sextet of husband John who later was first to join Kirk, and they afford little scope except for brief, ebullient stride outbursts. The saxophonist is not present on the last six septets led by Mary Lou herself (although Baker, who became her second husband, is on two), where her mature style is matched by the neglected Dick Wilson.

The remaining 13 items, three solo and the rest with the Kirk rhythm secion, are the core of the album. Two 1930 tracks (*Night Life* and *Drag 'Em*) show the stride mixed with a muted Hines influence, while the remainder have a linear approach which is bluesier and meatier than contemporary Teddy Wilson and must have had a considerable effect on the young Nat Cole. **BP**

# Roy Williams

**New review**
**Something Wonderful** Williams (tb); **Eddie Thompson** (p, syn); **Len Skeat** (b); **Jim Hall** (d).
Hep Ⓕ 2015 (50 minutes). Recorded 1980-1.

**⑨ ⑧**

Roy Williams ranks amongst the best trombonists playing today and indeed he has more individuality in his playing than most of them. He should have separate entries in this book for his work in his early and later periods, for they are quite different. This album, from his earlier manifestation, is so good that one suspects divine intervention. There is an exuberance about the trombone here which later modulated into a more sophisticated style. This is the Williams who fired jazz ensembles with his inspiration, climbing over and yet fitting in with the other horns in his exultation. Here that kind of inspiration is applied to his duets with Thompson, whose death in 1986 deprived jazz of an inventor and humorist whose playing was the perfect match for Williams. Williams has truly taken the trombone forwards from the innovations of forebears like Teagarden and Harris and one can only wonder whatever next. The range of material is extraordinary and well chosen and while the word irrepressible comes to one's mind, the ballads have a different inspirational quality which is linked to the voluptuousness of a Getz or Hackett.    **SV**

# Tony Williams

**Emergency!** Williams (d); **John McLaughlin** (g); **Larry Young** (org). Polydor Ⓜ 849 068-2
(71 minutes). Recorded 1969.

**⑧ ⑤**

This flawed, wildly exciting, pretentious, groundbreaking album was the real start of the marriage between rock and the cutting edge of jazz which would ultimately deliver up such bands as Weather Report, The Mahavishnu Orchestra and Return to Forever, not to mention Miles Davis's continuing explorations. Although people like Gary Burton and Larry Coryell had attempted an earlier and more measured joining together, Williams's group Lifetime were leaders, not followers. Their music utilized the volume, instrumentation and soundscapes of rock, but applied jazz techniques and attitudes to the material being played. Unfortunately, Williams also made the occasional foray into 'singing', sounding like a lobotomized Mose Allison at the end of a hard day (the painfully self-conscious lyrics didn't help much). If you are willing to overlook these, however, you will discover music with an energy level and exhilaration factor matched at that time only by Jimi Hendrix. It is my guess that Hendrix would have been quite at home jamming with this band (he had already jammed with Young).

The sound quality on the original double-vinyl release was truly appalling. The CD reissue is a considerable improvement against insuperable odds: the reissue engineer notes in the CD disclaimer that there was "distortion in all eight channels" the worst being in Williams's bass drum mike. The original studio recording machine was also completely out of phase with itself. That the sound is now passable is something of a miracle. In the very near future Polygram will be reissuing a Life-Time CD culled from all three of their albums for the label, and though it contains many tracks from **Emergency!**, the albums previously unavailable on CD such as **Turn It Over** get a look in too.    **KS**

**The Story of Neptune** Williams (d); **Wallace Roney** (t); **Bill Pierce** (ts, ss); **Mulgrew Miller** (p);
**Ira Coleman** (b). Blue Note Ⓕ CDP7 98169-2 (45 minutes). Recorded 1991.

**⑥ ⑧**

Williams started his recording career on Blue Note, appearing with Jackie McLean prior to joining Miles Davis in 1963. His first two records as a leader, **Life Time** and **Spring**, have both been transferred to CD and subsequently deleted, so at the present moment his early career as a leader prior to the fusion years is somewhat under-documented. After leaving Miles Davis in 1969 Williams led an erratic variety of groups culminating in this one, which kept a pretty consistent personnel after 1985 and evolved its own distinct character. Older drummer/leaders Art Blakey and Max Roach were strong influences on Williams, and like theirs, his bands tended to be dominated by his percussion rather than by the horns. Williams was also an arranger of some distinction, and his three-part *Neptune Suite* is a refreshingly robust invention, well taken advantage of by Roney, Pierce and Miller, all three of whom are outstandingly gifted soloists as well as worthy leaders in their own right. The third part of the suite, *Creatures of Conscience*, has a brisk display of drumming both in solo and in conversation with the horns. There is also an unusual interpretation of Paul McCartney's *Blackbird* wherein Pierce displays his mastery of the soprano sax, using a much more gentle and melodic approach than is customary in post-bop jazz. Roney is at his most Davis-like in a melancholy ten-minute version of *Poinciana*, but the group returns to prototype hard bop with a scaring version of Freddie Hubbard's *Birdlike*. The drummer's untimely death robbed jazz of a major and still highly creative voice, as was proved on the newly recorded trio album, **Young At Heart** (Columbia), released within days of the news of his demise arriving.    **SV**

# Willie Williams

**WW3** Williams (ts); **Scott Colley** (b); **Harold Summey Jr.** (d). Enja Ⓕ ENJ8060-2. Recorded 1993 (57 minutes).

⑥ ❻

The album title signifies several layers of meaning: Williams's third album, his own trio and a central apocalyptic composition of the same title. To carry off almost an hour's music in this chordless setting and avoid repetition, deviation and hesitation generally requires a talent of the level of a Sonny Rollins. It would be no exaggeration to say that this album shows Williams moving firmly towards that level, and his tenor playing clearly owes a lot to Rollins, particularly on the opening piece, Odean Pope's *Out for a Walk*, where the saxophone conjures up a Caribbean carnival atmosphere. His soprano playing is less authoritative, but this is not necessarily a disadvantage, and on Summey's excellent composition *You Can If You Try*, Williams injects his playing with delicacy and humour. The title track runs to 12 minutes and ends with the politically-charged *Babylon Falls*. Summey plays consistently well on his début album, while Williams and Colley demonstrate that their work together with T.S. Monk and the early faith placed in Williams by Bobby Watson and Art Taylor has paid dividends. **AS**

# Claude Williamson                                                   1926

**New review**
**Hallucinations** Williamson (p); **Dave Carpenter** (b); **Paul Kreibich** (d). VSOP Ⓕ 95CD (66 minutes). Recorded 1995.

⑩ ❿

Although Williamson became strongly associated with jazz in California during the fifties and sixties his roots are embedded in New York's 52nd Street. He spent all his free time there in the mid-forties when he was studying at the New England Conservatory of Music in Boston, seeking out Bud Powell, Al Haig and Charlie Parker. His admiration for Bud and all-pervading love for his music has remained with him and this superb album is devoted to a dozen tunes composed by, or associated with, Powell. No one plays Bud with more technique or understanding nowadays than Williamson and this production is a triumph for all concerned. This is not merely pastiche Powell; Williamson knows the entire repertoire and gets the correct feeling and tempo for each piece. *Parisian Thoroughfare* and *Polka Dots and Moonbeams* are played as unaccompanied solos and on the remaining performances Carpenter and Kreibich mesh perfectly with Williamson, making this a truly memorable trio. CDs as good as this are rare and it is gratifying to find that Claude Williamson, who first erupted on the recording scene with the Charlie Barnet band in the late forties, is now playing better than ever. **AM**

# Larry Willis                                                       1940

**New review**
**A Tribute to Someone** Willis (p); **Tom Williams** (t); **Curtis Fuller** (tb); **John Stubblefield** (ts, ss); **David Williams** (b); **Ben Riley** (d). AudioQuest Ⓕ AQ-CD1022 (53 minutes). Recorded 1994.

⑧ ❽

There is a substantial ambience of Herbie Hancock about Willis's work which in itself is no mean achievement. This means that by definition he is a skilful and eloquent player who weaves many of his mentor's devices into his playing and his long and eloquent lines place him well ahead of the other soloists in his group. He has had a long association with Hancock but claims he does not have a similar style. He deceives himself, although he does specifically eschew Hancock's ventures into fusion. Three of Hancock's own compositions (including the title track and *Maiden Voyage*) are included, but Willis is a good writer in his own right, with a notable ballad in his composition *Sensei*, played by piano only, and a fine solo on *A Tribute to Someone*. The title track has pleasing gentle trumpet from Williams but less than lustrous solos from Stubblefield and Fuller, although both raise their game elsewhere in the session. Riley works well behind the pianist throughout the album. **SV**

# Cassandra Wilson                                                   1955

**Blue Light 'Til Dawn** Wilson (v); with, amongst others: **Olu Dara** (c); **Don Byron** (cl); **Charlie Burnham** (vn, mandocello); **Brandon Ross, Gib Wharton, Chris Whitley** (g); **Kenny Davis** (b); **Lonnie Plaxico** (b); **Tony Cedras** (acc); **Lance Carter, Kevin Johnson** (d, perc); **Vinx, Bill McCellan, Jeff Haynes, Cyro Baptista** (perc). Blue Note Ⓕ CDP7 81357-2 (57 minutes ). Recorded 1993.

⑦ ❽

Wilson emerged in the eighties as a member of the M-Base movement of New York musicians and she made an immediate impact. Her own compositions complemented her singing style, if they did not always do much to enhance it. There were times when melismatic excess and the desire to surprise led her into improvisational cul-de-sacs. She became too elaborate, a touch overdramatic and seemingly oblivious to the overall meaning of the lyrics. Maturity has seen her address these failings. The 1988 **Blue Skies** (JMT 834419CD) and the 1991 **After the Beginning Again** (JMT 514001-2) documented the elimination of certain extreme characteristics, but this CD completes the process, matching the quality of her contemporary live performances. *You Don't Know What Love Is* and *Tupelo Honey* demonstrate a balance between lyric projection, rhythmic variety and melodic adjustment that is ideal. The rap influence remains a factor in *Black Crow* and *Children of the Night*, but it has become an aid to her timing rather than a *modus operandi*. Her daring stab at material by blues legend Robert Johnson is a success but the significant fact is that she applies the same moaning emotionalism to *Can't Stand The Rain* with no loss of credibility. Her jazz standing can never have been higher, and indeed this is no bad thing, for her subsequent albums for Blue Note have moved progessively further away once again from a jazz programme. **BMcR**

# Gerald Wilson
1918

**Portraits** Wilson (arr, ldr); with the following collective personnel: **Al Porcino**, **Ray Triscari**, **Carmell Jones**, **Nathaniel Meeks**, **Freddie Hill**, **Julius Chaikin** (t); **Bob Edmondson**, **John Ewing**, **Don Switzer**, **Lester Robinson**, **Lew McCreary** (tb); **Bud Shank** (f); **Joe Maini**, **Jimmy Woods** (as); **Teddy Edwards**, **Harold Land** (ts); **Jack Nimitz** (bs); **Jack Wilson** (p); **Joe Pass** (g); **Leroy Vinnegar**, **Dave Dyson** (b); **Chuck Carter** (d); **Modesto Duran** (bongos). Pacific Jazz Ⓜ CDP7 93414 2 (38 minutes). Recorded 1963.

⑧ ⑥

Gerald Wilson replaced Sy Oliver in the Jimmie Lunceford trumpet section and also contributed compositions and arrangements to the Lunceford library. In later years he wrote for Basie, Gillespie's big band, Duke Ellington, etc. and also retired temporarily from the music business. This is probably the best of the albums he recorded under his own name for Pacific Jazz. The seven tracks are dedications to various people as diverse as a Spanish bull fighter, the Armenian composer Khachaturian and the late Eric Dolphy. Wilson is a master of ensemble writing and achieving section perfection (something he probably learned in his days with Lunceford). A glance at the personnel reveals the presence of some outstanding Hollywood section men, including trumpeters Al Porcino and Ray Triscari. Solos are taken by Carmell Jones, Jack Wilson, Jimmy Woods, Harold Land and Teddy Edwards, but the most impressive performance is by Joe Pass's acoustic guitar on Wilson's brooding arrangement of *'Round Midnight*. The CD is the exact equivalent of the original LP, hence the meagre playing time. It would have been possible to present all three LPs Wilson did for Pacific Jazz as two CDs without any loss of original LP tracks. **AM**

# Glenn Wilson

**Bittersweet** Wilson (bs, bcl, f); **Rory Stuart** (g). Sunnyside Ⓕ SSC1057D (69 minutes). Recorded 1990.

⑧ ⑧

Both ex-Cadence recording artists who have been part of the Cadence All-Stars, Glenn Wilson and Rory Stuart developed the repertoire for this album on a duo tour of the Midwest in 1986. Like their thoughtful, careful playing, their taste is impeccable, encompassing tunes by Oliver Nelson, Sam Jones, Duke Pearson, Ron Carter and Wayne Shorter, leavened with a trio of Stuart originals and a couple of reworked standards. The album's chief appeal lies in the way the pair negotiate their way through the problems inherent in the duo format, intuitively swapping leading and accompanying roles and occasionally attaining what Stuart himself refers to as "a sort of loose but energetic two-part counterpoint." Particularly skilful is the way Wilson comps on baritone, functioning (as he points out) "at various times as a pianist, bassist, drummer and horn section." Overdubbing occasionally allows the music to avail itself of a brass-chorale effect, but otherwise the attractive textural contrast between the two instruments, baritone saxophone and guitar – reminiscent of the Surman-McLaughlin masterpiece **Extrapolation** – makes this a consistently enjoyable, if unusual, album. **CP**

# Jack Wilson
1936

**In New York** Wilson (p); **James Chirillo** (g); **Leon Maleson** (b); **Jimmy Cobb** (d). DIW Ⓕ DIW615 (53 minutes). Recorded 1993.

⑥ ⑨

Wilson has been moving in heavyweight circles since the early fifties, when he was a member of James Moody's group. Since then he has been a consistent supporter of other people's causes, only occasionally turning up at a recording session which he himself led. This is his latest foray as a leader, and it neatly encapsulates his style. Wilson has the tidiness and elegance of Teddy Wilson or George

Shearing, and occasionally sounds a little like Shearing in his blocked-hands approach, but his heart is deeply in a post-bop piano style perhaps most poignantly perfected by Hank Jones. To that he also adds an occasional spice of sanctification, Horace Silver or Oscar Peterson style.

The set of tunes negotiated here are all standards, and the most relaxed approach imaginable is taken to gently swinging each number. That is not to say that the session is somnambulent: Wilson contantly catches the attention with his ear for harmonic detail and his willingness to spin a line further than usual, or land it in an uncommon place. But most of all he has a great time, and could easily sustain a solo recital. For openers, try the perfectly-paced version of *Moon Mist*. **KS**

# Joe Lee Wilson                                                                                    1935

**New review**
**Acid Rain** **Wilson** (v); **Kirk Lightsey** (p); **Jack Gregg** (b); **Sangoma Everett** (d).
   Bloomdido Ⓕ BL012CD (66 minutes). Recorded 1992.

Ⓖ ❺

Wilson took formal studies in both classical and jazz singing in Los Angeles before moving to New York at the turn of the sixties. In the early part of that decade he worked with a cavalcade of top jazzers, including Sonny Rollins, Lee Morgan and Miles Davis, before moving left of centre and appearing with the likes of Pharoah Sanders and Archie Shepp when those masters were still in their *avant* phases. By the early seventies he had appeared on a couple of Shepp records documenting the saxophonist's deepening interest in more populist musics, but the rest of that decade was spent working solo, singing with Mtume or running his own projects. By the eighties Wilson had relocated to Europe, his big baritone voice more appreciated there than in the US. This record was made 'live' at Au Duc des Lombards in Paris with a top-drawer trio, and the playing indicates that everyone (including the audience) was happy with what was going down in this mixed set of originals, standards and blues. Unfortunately the recording is unkind to Wilson's voice, which sounds distant and rather hollow, thus robbing him of one of his most potent musical weapons. If the listener can put up with that (the piano trio sounds just fine), then this is an enjoyable live set. **KS**

# Nancy Wilson                                                                                    1937

**New review**
**Lush Life** **Wilson** (v); **John Collins** (elg); **Donn Trenner** (p); **Buster Williams** (b); **Shelly Manne** (d);
   **Larry Bunker**, **Victor Feldman** (perc); 25-piece orchestra arr and cond by **Billy May**, **Oliver**
   **Nelson**, **Sid Feller**. Capitol Jazz Ⓜ CDP7 32745-2 (40 minutes). Recorded 1967.

❺ ❾

Nancy Wilson's singing today amounts not to a style so much as a collection of mannerisms. Back in 1967 things had only just begun to deteriorate and many of these dozen pieces are restrained and effective – notably a phenomenally slow version of *When the World Was Young*. She has always been good at semi-recitative, partly because of her very clear diction, and her introductory verses are often the best thing about her interpretations. There's a real beauty here at the beginning of *Over the Weekend*, although the song soon degenerates into Shirley Bassey-style gasps and Eartha Kittish melodrama. The arrangements are everything that a singer could ask for, particularly Billy May's. His reputation as the master of beefy, brassy swingers has obscured his talent for pastel-shaded string writing, which is considerable. For those who, heartened by this album, want to look further for jazz-based Wilson, **The Best of Nancy Wilson (The Jazz and Blues Sessions)** on Capitol will probably fit the bill, especially as it duplicates not a single track from **Lush Life**. Hardly a surprise, considering the title and normal record company logic. **DG**

# Phil Wilson                                                                                     1937

**New review**
**Ac-Cent-Tchu-Ate the Positive** **Wilson** (tb); **Paul Schmeling** (p). Seaside Recordings
   Ⓕ SSWS136 (71 minutes). Recorded 1995.

❾ ❾

Wilson was one of the virtuoso trombonists of the sixties whose style evolved from the Harris, Johnson and Winding cartel. He was one of the most spine-tingling soloists of the day, as he proved as one of the sparks of the Woody Herman band from 1962 to 1965. He left Herman to take a teaching job at Berklee and he has been there ever since, making regular forays to tour the world or visit the recording studios. He is one of a long line of distinguished jazz musicians to teach at the college and played there with the many jazz combinations of tutors and students, including the ex-Art Blakey tenor player Billy Pierce and Wilson's own protégé pianist Makoto Ozone. The current album, made in the midst of a series of tributes and concerts promoted in his honour at Berklee, is his first in some time, and it is less radical than earlier recordings. It is measured and quietly wailing mainstream jazz. On these 17 Harold Arlen tunes (Arlen is one of his favourite writers) Wilson gives a gentle and eloquent display of his magnificent technique and wondrous tone, elegantly supported by a piano exposition from Schmeling (a college colleague) which can only be described as matchless. A solo album from Schmeling on the lines of the Maybeck series would be most satisfying.　　**SV**

# Reuben Wilson

**New review**

**Love Bug** Wilson (org); **Lee Morgan** (t); **George Coleman** (ts); **Grant Green** (g); **Jimmy Lewis** (elb); **Idris Muhammad** (d). Blue Note Ⓜ CDP8 29905-2 (50 minutes). Recorded 1969.

④ ❾

I know that Blue Note is the hippest label in the history of the universe and that Reid Miles designed beautiful covers and that Alfred Lion always got his musicians to rehearse and so on, but there was a reason why the label slowly went down the pan as the sixties segued into the seventies, and records like this tell a large part of the story. Since discovering Jimmy Smith, Blue Note had always had more than a few organists on the label, many of them genuinely talented (John Patton and Larry Young, for example) but by the time Reuben Wilson joined, a cast-iron formula had overtaken much of the label's output, led by the chillingly uninspired populist music Lou Donaldson was making (soon to be followed by Grant Green) as the lowest common denominators got chased long and hard for a few dollars more. Wilson was a good technician, but in the taste department he often left a lot to be desired. Here, corny arrangements of such chart fodder as *I'm Gonna Make You Love Me*, *I Say a Little Prayer* (where the soloists don't even follow the unusual chord progression, but just doodle over a one-chord vamp) and *Hold On, I'm Comin'*, plus that relentless boogaloo beat which all Blue Note executives by this stage equated with 'hip', make for deeply depressing listening. I know that the young'n'hip would argue that, in these heady acid jazz days, you're supposed to be out there on the club floor, ingesting large amounts of something good for you, dancing the night away to this stuff, but when I hear Lee Morgan and George Coleman sleepwalking through this glutinous mess, I feel genuine despair. No wonder the label was closed down by the mid-seventies. In spite of the enormous talents still signed to Blue Note at the time, there was nowhere else to go.　　**KS**

# Steve Wilson

1961

**Step Lively** Wilson (ss, as); **Cyrus Chestnut** (p); **Freddie Bryant** (g); **Dennis Irwin** (b); **Gregory Hutchinson** (d); **Daniel Sadownick** (perc). Criss Cross Ⓕ 1096CD (62 minutes). Recorded 1993.

⑥ ❽

Wilson has been making his way in the jazz world since the mid-eighties and this new Criss Cross CD is his third as a leader for the label. Gerry Teekens must be congratulated for moving the altoist along in sympathetic surroundings and surrounded by genuine talent: his previous release, **Blues for Marcus**, had Steve Nelson along to help, while here we can enjoy the entirely simpatico piano of Cyrus Chestnut (listen to his comping on *For Stan* to demonstrate this quality) as well as the rawer edge of Freddie Bryant's guitar. Wilson's style sits nicely in the modern mainstream approach, and his tone is bright, full and bell-like. He has great rhythmic dexterity and a quick musical imagination. His soprano work is a little more derivative than his alto, but both horns sustain the listener's interest. This is good, honest music from the middle of the modern jazz road, well played and excellently recorded. If that attracts you, then purchase both this and its follow-up CD with confidence.　　**KS**

# Teddy Wilson

1912-86

**The Complete Piano Solos, 1934-41** Wilson (p). Columbia Ⓜ 467690-2 (two discs: 133 minutes). Recorded 1934-41.

⑧ ❺

Wilson's importance as a piano stylist is often obscured by the role he played in the careers of people such as Benny Goodman (as a sideman) and Billie Holiday (as a session organizer and leader). Yet he led a variety of excellent bands from the mid thirties on, both in the studios and in person, and was also prolific as a solo pianist, as this collection attests.

Wilson's style combines the relative freedom given to the right hand by Earl Hines in the years immediately preceding these sessions with the metronome-like precision of the stride left hand as practised by all the best New York jazz pianists, from James P. Johnson to Fats Waller. What Wilson brought to this synthesis was a very high order of technical accuracy, a neat and logical turn of improvisatory phrase, and (unlike Tatum) a very correct interpretation of each tune's harmonic path. He also (again unlike Tatum) generally avoided rubato, preferring to keep things moving along at a steady clip. Wilson was a musical conservative, and was sometimes severely restricted in the emotional range he brought to his performances. Yet he had a flawless technique, as these sides attest, and a sufficiently orchestral conception of solo piano work to vary his interpretations of each piece and keep a performance alive. This set, rather indigestible at one sitting (Wilson never intended these solos to be played end-to-end), is very rewarding taken in small doses.　　　**KS**

---

**Teddy Wilson and His Orchestra 1939-41** Wilson (p); with various personnel, including: **Bill Coleman, Doc Cheatham, Harold Baker, Emmett Berry** (t); **Floyd Brady, Benny Morton** (tb); **Jimmy Hamilton** (cl); **Rudy Powell** (as, cl); **Ben Webster, George Irish** (ts); **George James** (bs); **Al Casey, Eddie Gibbs** (g); **Al Hall, Johnny Williams** (b); **J.C. Heard, Yank Porter** (d, v); **Jean Eldridge, Helen Ward, Lena Horne** (v). Classics Ⓜ 620 (70 minutes). Recorded 1939-41.

✅　　　　　　　　　　　　　　　　　　　　　　　　　　　　　　　⑧ ❽

Starting with the short-lived big band led by Teddy Wilson in 1939-40, this excellent compilation of 23 numbers follows his recording career for almost two years. In doing so, it illustrates in microcosm all the musical settings in which he shone. After the big band pieces (including, incidentally, a fascinating alternative arrangement to the then-current Glenn Miller hit *In the Mood)* we come to the chamber music of swing, that delightful genre of which Teddy Wilson was the undoubted master. It involved three or four front-line instruments and rhythm section, often with a vocalist, playing simple head arrangements of standard tunes with short solos all round. The most famous of these are, of course, the sessions built around Billie Holiday, but here the featured vocalists are the young Lena Horne, Benny Goodman's vocalist Helen Ward and the now forgotten Jean Eldridge.

The rest of the disc is taken up with piano solos, both with and without rhythm section, demonstrating yet again what a faultless swing pianist Wilson was. It is astounding to realize that music of this quality was regarded as almost run-of-the-mill stuff at the time, because the general level was so high.　　　**DG**

# Lem Winchester　　　　　　　　　　　　　　　　　　　　　1928-61

---

New review

**Lem's Beat** Winchester (vb); **Oliver Nelson** (ts); **Curtis Peagler** (as); **Billy Brown, Roy Johnson** (p); **Wendell Marshall** (b); **Arthur Taylor** (d). Prestige/New Jazz Ⓜ OJCCD1785-2 (39 minutes). Recorded 1960.

　　　　　　　　　　　　　　　　　　　　　　　　　　　　　　⑦ ❼

In high school, Winchester was something of a multi-instrumentalist, but it was not until the age of 19 that he graduated to vibes. His first inspiration was Lionel Hampton, although only three years after taking up the instrument he put his musical career on hold. Whether becoming a beat policeman can be considered a sabbatical, this is what he did for nearly ten years. Fortunately, he continued to play and formed his own group in 1957. A series of recordings from 1958 to 1961 show that his tastes had changed. He had discovered Milt Jackson. His now mature style was sharply defined, boasted a percussive tone and was equipped with an appealing undertow that directed his levels of tension. He had acquired the ability to breathe warmth into the instrument's cold persona and Friendly Persuasion on this CD is an ideal track by which to judge him. He remains close to the melody line in an improvisation of genuine grace, exploiting his rubato skills and showing how well he swings, in real terms, at any tempo. His blues credentials are presented on an excellent *Eddy's Dilemma* while *Just Friends* is a model of driving, mid-tempo, ballad reading. His death, a Russian Roulette victim at 33, robbed jazz of a distinctive instrumental voice.　　　**BMcR**

# Kai Winding　　　　　　　　　　　　　　　　　　　　　　1922-83

---

New review

**Jay and Kai Plus Six** Winding, **J.J. Johnson** (tb, tromboniums); **Urbie Green, Bob Alexander, Eddie Bert, Jimmy Cleveland, Bart Varsalona, Tom Mitchell** (tb); **Hank Jones** (p); **Milt Hinton, Ray Brown** (b); **Osie Johnson** (d); **Candido Camero** (perc). Columbia Ⓜ 480 990-2 (35 minutes). Recorded 1956.

　　　　　　　　　　　　　　　　　　　　　　　　　　　　　　⑧ ❽

Kai Winding has often suffered when he has been compared to Johnson, who is the acknowledged master of be-bop trombone. Johnson had no rough edges and his sublime technique meant that what were really pyrotechnical solos were delivered by him with aplomb. Winding on the other hand sounded much more as though he was striving and there was a joyousness that came through in his playing when he triumphed that was most infectious. The truth was that nobody could stand comparison with Johnson, whether it was Urbie Green or Jimmy Cleveland, two giants here reduced to accompanying the protagonists. This album goes far beyond the usual pairing of Jay and Kai. Although their duets were always immaculately tailored, the backing trombone choir here plays some propulsive arrangements and becomes in effect a third voice. Needless to say at this level the well-written charts are perfectly played over top-class rhythm. In their time Jay and Kai disproved the record producers' code which said that trombone albums don't sell – goodness knows how many great recordings that tenet has deprived us of. This album succeeds at every level. It is inventive, it is packed with craftsmanship and it is also great fun.　　　**SV**

# Louis Winsberg

**Appassionata** Winsberg (g, bouzouki); **Jean Rene Dalerci** (b); **Tony Rabeson** (d). Kid Records
Ⓕ KR002-2 (44 minutes). Recorded 1989.

⑦ ❻

Winsberg has played in the French fusion group Nexus and has over the years branched out to make some interesting albums on his own. He is a guitarist with bags of technique and imagination, but more importantly, he is blessed with 'feel'. He is a natural, able to caress, bludgeon, stroke and force his guitar into divulging the essential information about each selection he plays. In this he is perhaps closer to Bireli Lagrene than to John McLaughlin, but he has elements of both players within him. For one thing, he is as completely at home on acoustic as on electric guitars, and again he is utterly at ease both on a blues and a non-blues original. His electric tone has the burnt-ochre timbre of the latter-day John Scofield, but his style owes little to the American. The backing bass and drums are discreet and sympathetic, but this is very much Winsberg's album. It is worth a close listen.    **KS**

# Norma Winstone                                        1941

**Somewhere Called Home** Winstone (v); **Tony Coe** (cl, ts); **John Taylor** (p). ECM Ⓕ 831 107-2
(49 minutes). Recorded 1986.

⑧ ❾

Inspired by Miles Davis and John Coltrane – "I wanted to incorporate that instrumental freedom in a vocal way" – Norma Winstone first made her mark in 1968, singing wordless vocals in the Michael Garrick groups. She later worked with many leading UK musicians (notably Joe Harriott and Mike Westbrook) and in 1972 released her own **Edge of Time** LP. In the seventies she co-founded the trio Azimuth (husband John Taylor on piano, Kenny Wheeler on trumpet), where she honed her art of wordless improvisation, her 'choirboy's voice' blending with the other instruments to create beautiful, ethereal textures.

**Somewhere Called Home**, only her second recording as leader, reminds us that she is also a magnificent interpreter of lyrics. Her intimate vocal style relies on subtle phrasing and a faultless sense of time. The songs here are taken at a gentle pace, their lyrics tending to a rueful romanticism underscored by Tony Coe's reeds. Winstone has the gift of turning unlikely material into great art: here she turns *Hi Lili, Hi Lo* into a meditation on love, then strips the jauntiness from *Tea for Two*, making it a forlorn reverie. Such gripping transformations show why she is Europe's premier jazz vocalist. The 1995 **Well Kept Secret** (Hat House) on which Winstone sings standards accompanied by the estimable Jimmy Rowles, is also highly recommended.    **GL**

# Stefan F. Winter

New review

**The Little Trumpet** Herb Robertson (pic t, flh, c); **Tim Berne** (as); **Robin Eubanks** (tb); **Bob Stewart** (bb); **Warren Smith** (vb); **Bill Frisell** (g, elg); **Anthony Cox** (b); **Reggie Nicholson** (d).
JMT Ⓕ 514027-2 (45 minutes). Recorded 1995.

⑦ ❽

Jazz and Music Today (JMT records) is run by Winter. Here he has extended his brief and written a ten-movement folk work regarding the planet Panacoustica, home of musical instruments. He has selected an outstanding octet for its realization and has been careful to employ players with a broad brush approach. Robertson worked out the arrangements and, although some pieces are little more than melodic motifs, soloists are encouraged to tell their tale in their own manner. The *Overture* nudges Eubanks gently toward Vic Dickenson, *Wild Disputes* conducts its altercations with heavy percussion inputs, while *Harmony* is ideally titled. *Friendship* is established with a brief duo by Robertson and Berne, *The Night* escorts Smith on a stealthy walk, while *The Marvelous Event* takes them all to the finale. There is a natural continuity in the development of the total work and descriptive music of the cinema soundtrack variety is absent. Whether the outcome is most influenced by the compositions, or by the men involved, is not obviously apparent, but it is doubtful if any of the musicans involved would resent a jazz evaluation of their work based on this CD.    **BMcR**

# Jimmy Witherspoon                                    1923

**Rockin' With Spoon** Witherspoon (v); **Roy Eldridge** (t); **Urbie Green** (tb); **Woody Herman** (cl);
**Ben Webster**, **Coleman Hawkins** (ts); **Gerry Mulligan** (bs); **Earl Hines, Jimmy Rowles** (p); **Vernon Alley, Leroy Vinnegar** (b); **Mel Lewis** (d). Charly Ⓑ CDBM25 (62 minutes). Recorded 1959.

✅  ⑧ ❽

Witherspoon is conventionally grouped with Joe Turner and Walter Brown under the description of 'blues shouters'. While some of his early work with Jay McShann (collected on Black Lion BLCD

760173) does find him exuberantly riding big-band blues riffs, he is more telling at medium and slow tempos, where he can display his handsome voice and superb sense of pace and dynamics. This collection catches him on two days in late 1959. A set at the Renaissance Club in Los Angeles boasts the odd but satisfying combination of Webster's furry, loquacious tenor and Mulligan's dry, pithy baritone on a programme of blues standards like *How Long* and *Outskirts of Town*. The remaining tracks are from the Monterey Jazz Festival, where the all-star line-up is self-effacingly discreet, allowing 'Spoon to give a performance he has never surpassed. It is all blues, pleading, caressing, sensuous but unsentimental, and on *Ain't Nobody's Business* Webster joins in with a solo of such feeling that the world seems to stand still until he has completed it.

The Monterey and Renaissance sessions have always been highly thought of as LPs; gathered on a single inexpensive CD they make a programme of astonishing value. **TR**

## Piotr Wojtasik 1964

New review
**Lonely Town** Wojtasik (t, flh); **Leszek Mozdzer** (p); **Jacek Niedziela** (b, arr); **Marcin Jahr** (d); 12-piece string section: **Jerzy Jarosik** (cond, arr); **Piotr Lobos** (arr); on two tracks **Zbigniew Nayslowski** (as) and **Jaroslaw Smietana** (g); on two tracks **Krzysztof Popek** (f); on one track **Maciej Sikala** (ts). Power Bros Ⓕ PB00137 (44 minutes). Recorded 1994.

⑥ ❼

Wojtasik is a fine Polish trumpeter whose first album under his own name this is, as far as I know. That it should be a programme dominated by the use of a string-section is perhaps a pity for, although he fits the context admirably, there are signs that he is capable of more forthright playing. The other adverse comments – while we're about it – concern a couple of separate misreadings of Johnny Mandel's melody *Emilly* (sic) and a very unsatisfactory chord-sequence for Leonard Bernstein's title track from *On the Town* – check Mel Tormé's or even Maynard Ferguson's versions.

The whole session sounds strongly reminiscent of a couple of Art Farmer's Japanese albums arranged by Masahiko Satoh, the string writing being alternately portentous and bland. But the comparison of Wojtasik with Farmer is also just, for his combination of poise and enterprise, melancholy and energy is consistently engaging. Finally in the album's favour is the fact that, unlike the other guest artists, the veteran Namyslowski turns up the heat on his two appearances. **BP**

## Anthony Wonsey 1971

New review
**Anthology** Wonsey (p); **Christian McBride** (b); **Carl Allen** (d). Alfa Jazz Ⓕ ALCB3901 (57 minutes). Recorded 1995.

⑦ ❽

There is every sign that Wonsey is going to be one of the major jazz piano soloists of the decade. Still only 24 when this was recorded, he shows remarkable maturity and poise, both on his own compositions and working his way through a pile of standards. That this album is no one-off flash in the pan is confirmed by his presence on Eddie Allen's **R'n'B** album (Enja 9033-2; q.v. Allen), in which he is just as confident and assured in a band context as he is here leading his own trio. The headlong rush of his version of Clifford Brown's *Daahoud* compares interestingly with Ahmad Jamal's more theatrical reading of it on **Chicago Revisited** (Telarc), Wonsey using the piece as a vehicle for some dynamic right-hand set-piece phrases which he pulls off magnificently. That Wonsey is in a league worthy of comparison to the currently on-form Jamal is praise indeed, and when he turns his hand to ballads he shows an investigative imagination unusual in jazz pianists of any generation. Clearly Wonsey is immersed in the jazz tradition, this rich and satisfying album's final unaccompanied *Sweet Lorraine* paying homage to the classic Tatum recording, but daring to go its own way. **AS**

## Rickey Woodard 1956

New review
**The Silver Strut** Woodard (ts); **Oscar Brashear** (t); **Cedar Walton** (p); **John Clayton** (b); **Jeff Hamilton** (d). Concord Ⓕ CCD4716 (65 minutes). Recorded 1995.

⑧ ❾

Concord has a valuable property in Woodard; apart from his own albums he has made significant contributions to CDs by Jeannie & Jimmy Cheatham, Mary Stallings and the Clayton-Hamilton Jazz Orchestra. This quintet is virtually a small group from the Clayton-Hamilton band; it plays a brisk, virile form of music reminiscent of a classic Horace Silver quintet, hence the dedicatory album title. Although Woodard names John Coltrane amongst his favourite tenor players he doesn't attempt to sound like him; instead he manifests the bold approach of men such as Stanley Turrentine, Gene Ammons and Coleman Hawkins. He also names Hank Mobley amongst his favourites and pays tribute to Mobley by including Hank's *Take Your Pick* in this nine-track programme. This is refreshing, exuberant music with the beat always prominent and all the solos relying on healthy regard for melodic invention. *Stardust*, played by Rickey and the rhythm section, is in the best tradition of ballad tenor using a huge, cavernous tone and lavishing Carmichael's tune with multi-layered passion. *Loverman* is taken at medium tempo over a Latin rhythm, proving there are still plenty of surprises to be found in familiar material. A fine example of modern-mainstream jazz. **AM**

## Phil Woods
1931

**Flash** Woods (as, cl); **Tom Harrell** (t, flh); **Hal Crook** (tb); **Hal Galper** (p); **Steve Gilmore** (b); **Bill Goodwin** (d). Concord Ⓕ CCD4408 (63 minutes). Recorded 1989.

⑧ ❾

Initially better known for his work in the big bands of Dizzy Gillespie, Buddy Rich and Quincy Jones, Woods established his combo skills in the quintet Phil And Quill with Gene Quill. He lived for some time in Europe but one of his finest groups is the American one heard on this CD. It came into being in its present form when Harrell joined in 1983, and this was the trumpeter's final date with the group. Between those dates, the Woods/Harrell team played some very impressive music. Woods, for all his previous triumphs, relished the group interaction and his enthusiasm is projected into all of his solos here. He has always tended to allow his phrases to be somewhat disconnected from the pulse and, particularly at the blistering pace of *Flash,* he relies for success on the linear qualities of his note choices rather than on the ideas they carry. Very different in concept is Harrell, a lucid musical thinker who brings grace to his solos without emasculating them. The contrast works well and, although the presence of a trombonist makes the classic Woods ensemble more Messengers-like, this remains one of the best of a fine series of albums made by an otherwise consistently unchanged personnel. **BMcR**

## Reggie Workman
1937

**New review**

**Summit Conference** Workman (b); **Julian Priester** (tb); **Sam Rivers** (f, ss, ts); **Andrew Hill** (p); **Pheeroan akLaff** (d). Postcards Ⓕ POST1003 (57 minutes). Recorded 1993.

⑩ ⑩

One of the premier bassists in post-war jazz, Reggie Workman played with John Coltrane, the Jazz Messengers and the New York Art Quartet in the sixties, proving himself equally adept at hard bop, modal and freeform idioms. Later he devoted much of his time to education, but continued to play in a variety of contexts. In the eighties he made notable contributions to David Murray's **Morning Song** and Marilyn Crispell's **Gaia** and also recorded with his own ensemble, which included Crispell, Don Byron and Jeanne Lee. **Summit Conference** taps a different facet of his creativity. These Workman-led 'all stars' confound all expectations with the power and intensity of their playing. If the music recalls the more adventurous Blue Note dates of the sixties – such as those led by Hill and Rivers – it also shows the players' post-sixties perspective, the new possibilities offered by freeform assessed and assimilated to create (to quote Workman) "sounds deeply rooted in our history and evolution and yet also truly futuristic". Priester and Rivers lock horns with relish, Hill stabs out terse, implacable rejoinders, Workman and akLaff stoke the firestorm. The climax of an excellent set is *Hill's Gone*, a flute/piano ballad of rare gravitas; elsewhere the group's ferocious interplay raises the benchmark for passionate engagement. A contemporary classic. **GL**

## World Saxophone Quartet

**Revue** Hamiet Bluiett (cl, bs); **Julius Hemphill** (f, ss, as); **Oliver Lake** (f, ss, as, ts); **David Murray** (bcl, ts). Black Saint Ⓕ 120056-2 (45 minutes). Recorded 1980.

⑧ ❽

The WSQ came together for a concert in New Orleans in 1976 and later developed into one of the benchmark groups of the eighties. Their showmanship, instrumental bravura and comprehensive grasp of the jazz tradition fitted in well with the decade's ethos of smartly-dressed conservatism. But – especially on their earlier albums – there was also a thrilling sense of discovery, a willingness to push back limits. Whether drawing on Ellington big band charts or the new solo languages developed by the ΛACM, the WSQ created a group feeling that transcended the sum of its parts (even though all four members continued to pursue parallel careers as leaders).

Revue was their fourth record and remains one of the best: the first time perhaps that the different elements the WSQ were juggling (especially the core dialogue between solo and ensemble) were held in balance. It is also the album that affirmed Hemphill as the group's most original composer. His four tunes spark a variety of ensemble interplays, from the disparate flute and clarinet ribbons that wind through *Affairs of the Heart* to the stabbing unison lines of *Slide*. Other tracks turn the spotlight more on individual players. Bluiett's *I Heard That* sets a melismatic alto solo (by Hemphill) amidst a pack of coursing r&b riffs, while both Lake's *Hymn for the Old Year* and Murray's *Ming* begin with *a cappella* solos that are later cradled in a web of harmonies. The playing is fierce, tender, impeccable.     However, with Hemphill's departure in 1990 (to form his excellent saxophone sextet), the group seemed to lose much of their cohesion, and their recent releases have, for the most part, been disappointing.     **GL**

## Frank Wright
1935-90

**New review**

**Trio**  Wright (ts); **Henry Grimes** (b); **Tom Price** (d). ESP-Disk Ⓜ 1023-2 (34 minutes). Recorded 1965.
⑦ ❻

Wright made two albums for ESP (the second, 1967's **Your Prayer**, featured some of the players he took up with after moving to Paris at the end of the sixties, including Arthur Jones and Jacques Coursil). This exuberant trio outing gives the curious listener a clear enough idea of Wright's musical philosophy. Coming from Mississippi, Wright grew up playing electric bass in r&b bands but was converted to musical expressionism when he struck up a friendship with Albert Ayler. He worked with many in the New York avant-garde scene, including live sessions with Cecil Taylor and John Coltrane, and the ESP albums made his name internationally. Economics and the search for a better life drove him to Europe, where he remained, giving concerts (including one in 1984 with Cecil Taylor) and recording albums until his untimely death in Germany in 1990. This first album reveals him to be practicing the scorched-earth approach to saxophone playing espoused at the time by Ayler and Pharoah Sanders (in fact he adopts many more of Sanders's licks than Ayler's), but although the proceedings are suitably wild and woolly, the music comes across as high-spirited and expansive, rather than neurotic or blazingly angry. Though no virtuoso, he is also a good deal more technically secure than many mid-sixties *avant* saxophonists. Grimes plays well in support but is not greatly helped by an unkind recording mix, while Price (also at this time playing with Burton Greene) is neat and attentive in a Rashied Ali-type way. All three tracks are quite long.     **KS**

## John Wright

**New review**

**Mr Soul**   Wright (p); **Wendell Marshall** (b); **Walter Perkins Jr.** (d). Prestige Ⓜ OJCCD1876-2 (35 minutes). Recorded 1962.
⑥ ❼

When John Wright made his handful of albums at the beginning of the sixties there was a market for gospel-styled performers that attracted pianists as different as Junior Mance and Les McCann. Wright might have been aiming for this market, even if one suspects he did so with less than total enthusiasm. Though very much of his time (the routine he uses on *Blue Prelude*, from dynamic contrast to choppy rhythms, derives from Ahmad Jamal and he throws in plenty of blocked chords) and at least as good a jazz pianist as McCann, he doesn't appear to be enough of an extrovert.

Tunes on the latter part of the album run the gamut of backbeats and bluesy effects, yet it all seems rather tasteful. Such titles as *Shake*, *Strut*, *Now Hang in There* and *Mr Soul* itself were obviously part of the marketing strategy, the last actually composed by the man who supervised the session. By contrast, *Our Waltz* starts off rather like Bill Evans and ends with a chunk of Sonny Rollins's *Valse Hot* while *What's New* gets a ballad performance totally devoid of frills.     **RA**

## Richard Wyands
1928

**New review**

**Reunited**   Wyands (p); **Peter Washington** (b); **Kenny Washington** (d). Criss Cross Ⓕ 1105CD (61 minutes). Recorded 1995.
⑦ ❽

Californian Wyands graduated as a BA from San Francisco State College. He first recorded in the fifties and, after a brief sojourn in Canada, settled in New York. He recorded on important dates with Charles Mingus and Oliver Nelson and, for more than ten years, worked with Kenny Burrell. More recently, he has occupied the piano chair with Illinois Jacquet, Benny Carter and Don Sickler with a style that could be described as resembling that of Wynton Kelly, with minor stride overtones. Its strong chordal base provides its own calibration and it allows him to employ his mischievious melodic variations without losing track of the narrative. He deliberately chooses strong themes but, despite excelling in an accompanist's disciplines with Ella Fitzgerald, Carmen McRae and Etta Jones, is never the pianist for the predictable route. On this CD it is instructive to observe the way in which he molests the gently-paced *Easy Living*, adds a little *Old Man River* jive to *How Long Has This Been Going On?* and kicks against Washington's fiery drum barrage on *Moon and Sand*. He romps unashamedly on *Blues for Pepper* and strips *Yesterdays* of its dangerous romanticisms to show that nothing in Wyands' piano world is cosmetically enhanced.     **BMcR**

# Albert Wynn

**New review**

**And His Gutbucket Seven** Wynn (tb); **Bill Martin** (t, v); **Darnell Howard** (cl); **Bus Moten, Blind John Davis** (p); **Mike Mckendrick** (g, bj); **Robert Wilson** (b); **Booker Washington** (d). Riverside Ⓜ OJCCD1826-2 (47 minutes). Recorded 1961.

⑦ ❽

In the twenties Wynn was a pioneer of jazz and blues, working with Ma Rainey and touring Europe with Sam Wooding. Like many New Orleans *émigrés* to have settled in Chicago, he kept alive the style of his home town, fronting this traditional-style band for Chris Albertson's Riverside field recordings in the sixties. The band has more dash and verve than many a New Orleans group of the same period, with Wynn clearly showing that he comes out of the same heritage as Kid Ory. The Ory parallels extend to the stiff two-beat rhythm section, anchored by Booker Washington's drums and Robert Wilson's uninspired bass, as well as the neat arranged riffs for brass that punctuate Howard's solos. Moten's Kansas City piano pushes against the rigidity of Washington on some of the up-tempo numbers but comes into its own on Leroy Carr's blues, *In the Evening*. The discovery, apart from Wynn himself, is Alabama-born trumpeter Bill Martin (a veteran of Zach White's territory band), who sings a mean blues and takes off on *Bourbon Street* like a New Orleans native. **AS**

# Yosuke Yamashita

**Crescendo: Live at Sweet Basil** Yamashita (p); **Cecil McBee** (b); **Pheeroan akLaff** (d). Kitty H32U20011 (53 minutes). Recorded 1988.

⑧ ❽

When he was playing an extraordinarily intense brand of 'free' jazz in the seventies, Yosuke Yamashita was often compared to Cecil Taylor due to his strength, stamina and concentration. As he has evolved into interpreting standards and more traditionally structured material, the results are not so easily stereotyped. There is a reminiscence of Don Pullen in the percussive chording and slashing leaps of register, often followed by the florid melodic invention of a Tete Montoliu or Martial Solal. So *Take the 'A' Train* becomes a roller-coaster of arpeggios and *Autumn Leaves* is reharmonized and recontextualized into *Autumn Changes*. Nor does this trio fall into the established piano trio guidelines. McBee is an anchor, especially when Yamashita threatens to explode out of the confines of bar lines. AkLaff is the wild card; his individual approach, less timekeeper than rhythmic instigator, opens up the arrangements ever more. *First Bridge* shows how together they stretch song form to the breaking point, creating enormous tension between freer phrasing impulses and the artificial restrictions that song form imposes. When Yamashita's exhilarating Enja recordings with Akira Sakata are issued on CD they are highly recommended; in the meantime **Crescendo** should prove exciting and ear-opening for mainstream and more adventurous listeners alike. Yamahita continues to release new albums on Verve (his latest, a solo excursion called **Canvas in Quiet**, is worth hearing), but this is probably stll the best point at which to dip into his music. **AL**

# Jimmy Yancey

**Barrelhouse Boogie** Yancey (p, v); **Albert Ammons, Pete Johnson, Meade Lux Lewis** (p). RCA Bluebird Ⓜ ND88334 (58 minutes). Recorded 1939-40.

⑦ ❽

Yancey's ten performances here are probably the best-recorded, and certainly among the best, of all his work. Despite the album's title, approaching Yancey as a boogie-woogie pianist is to come at him from the wrong direction (it is suggestive that the word 'Boogie' almost never occurs in his tunes' titles). Although older than Albert Ammons, Pete Johnson and Meade Lux Lewis he was active about the same time and admired by the same sort of people, but the character of his music was very different. Not for him their driving abandon, relentlessly hammering left hands and capering tempos; Yancey's style was all sparseness, an affair of considered inflections and suble timing, Monk rather than Hines. Yet it is not technically inferior playing; the interplay of left and right-hand lines is the more gripping for being less obvious, less (one might almost say) mechanical.

Given all that, Yancey's music inevitably seems more introspective and melancholic than, say, Pete Johnson's. There is no denying these properties in the sober and moving vocal numbers *Crying In My Sleep* and *Death Letter Blues*, but *Yancey Stomp* and *Tell 'Em About Me*, on the other hand, jauntily evoke Chicago ambiences of street and bar. The rest of the CD contains nine duets by Johnson and Ammons and two items by Lewis: a very fine compilation. **TR**

# Yellowjackets

**Collection** Bob Mintzer (ss, as, ts, bcl); **Russell Ferrante** (kbds); **Jimmy Haslip** (b); **William Kennedy** (d) with **Steve Croes, Judd Miller** (syn); **Paulinho Da Costa, Alex Acuna, Nana**

**Vasconcelos** (perc); **Bill Gable**, **Michael Franks**, **Brenda Russell**, **Marylin Scott** (v). GRP Ⓕ 98092 (63 minutes). Recorded 1988-92.

⑥ ❿

Yellowjackets albums tend to meander in and out of the jazz framework, so this sampler is the ideal way for jazz-minded interested bodies to get a whiff of what they're on about, because the vast majority of this disc exhibits healthy jazz tendencies. One of the most pleasing aspects of their albums is the exact synthesis of the four players into the overall musical balance and landscape. No one instrument dominates, although some play more than others. No-one sticks out like a sore thumb, and it is an unusual and pleasant experience to hear in Mintzer a saxophonist who not only blends seamlessly with his cohorts, but avoids the normal warmed-over stylistic trappings of a post-Tom Scott/ post-David Sanborn clone. He can both carry a melody and improvise dexterously. He also has a tone which blends with the electrics and electronics alongside him.

The rhythm section is uniformly hot and precise, with Jimmy Haslip's fluid bass patterns a particular plus. The compositions on this compilation avoid pomp and posture and are sufficiently open for the players to really come to grips with the underlying structures. There is plenty of soloing. But one of the most surprising and satisfying aspects of this disc is the production and the instrumental balance, or 'mix'. The instruments have been superbly recorded across a number of dates and years, each sounding true and full. Everything can be heard but nothing pushes too far to the fore. A special cheer, then, for the engineer on all these sessions, Mick Guzauski.                    **KS**

## Nora York

**To Dream the World**  York (v); **Rich Perry** (ts); **Mark Feldman** (vn); **Rob Schwimmer** (org); **Richie Bierach** (p); **Jack Wilkins** (g); **Michael Formanek** (b); **Terry Clarke** (d). TCOB Ⓕ 94602 (68 minutes). Recorded 1992.

European Nora York has been singing on the New York scene for a while (and, as this album demonstrates, has got to know some interesting accompanying musicians); this first album represents her both as a singer and as an songwriter/arranger. Like may young musicians today, she exhibits an eclectic taste, with her own songs covering stylistic ground which includes old-fashioned mainstream swing and what for lack of a better phrase could be called sub-New Age. Her cover versions include pieces by Cole Porter, The Beatles and Jimi Hendrix.

I get the feeling that her musicality often exceeds her small voice's natural limits. Her range is not great; neither is it greatly expressive. But the musical settings are often evocative and the playing quite engaging. Lennon/McCartney's *If I Fell* is a perfect example of this dichotomy. Always one of their better early ballads, this Beatles song is given a very slow tempo and a steamy, emotive setting which, with the right voice, would provide revelatory listening. But York has yet to learn how to work her delivery to give the listener the full emotional load. Still, an interesting effort.                    **KS**

## Hajime Yoshizawa                    1963

**Hajime**  Yoshizawa (p); **Bob Mintzer** (ts); **John Abercrombie** (g); **Marc Johnson** (b); **Peter Erskine** (d). Ah Um 008 Ⓕ (65 minutes). Recorded 1990.

⑥ ❻

This is a promising and absorbing début album by a Japanese pianist who has worked with a variety of musicians in jazz and theatre. Above all, it is introspective, even the bravura moments at the keyboard being somehow understated. In *Beyond Twilight*, for instance, the piano is strangely detached, lacking the immediacy of his contemporaries Michel Petrucciani and Benny Green. This works to Hajime's advantage, especially on ballads like *Stardust*, where he seems to dissect the music from inside in a compelling way. It also makes him a more than usually sensitive accompanist, and he plays a willing and perfect second fiddle to Abercrombie on *Bless Me with Your Breath*, the extended opener that was written in tribute to Yoshizawa's father.

*Tropic of Cancer* is a platform for Mintzer and Erskine, while Marc Johnson opens *Voyage* with a deeply felt solo. Overall, an album of reflection and poetic self-absorption, yet with generous space allotted to his fellow musicians.                    **AS**

## Dave Young

**New review**

**Two by Two, Volume Two**  Young (b); duets with the following pianists: **Ellis Marsalis**, **Cyrus Chestnut**, **Oliver Jones**, **Kenny Barron**, **Barry Harris**, **Renee Rosnes**. Justin Time Ⓕ JUST81-2 (70 minutes). Recorded 1995.

⑦ ❽

Dave Young played with Oscar Peterson in 1986 and Volume 1 in this **Two by Two** series paired him off with another collection of pianists including Peterson (and Tommy Flanagan, Cedar Walton, John

Hicks and Mulgrew Miller). He produces a deep, satisfying sound and 'walks' with authority, rather like Leroy Vinnegar. Each piano-bass duo plays two tunes and to some extent the quality of the music is dependent on how well the two musicians find they can interlock. The easy way out is for the pianist to play and simply allow Young to supply a rhythm. Alternatively Young could take the leading role, which is what happens on **Loverman**, with Kenny Barron providing the keyboard support. The best duo tracks, in which bass and piano assume equal roles, are those with Barry Harris (*Nascimento* is a gem) and, most successful of all, the two titles with fellow Canadian Oliver Jones. Young and Jones have worked together frequently, which almost certainly accounts for the perfectly natural way the two instruments fuse together. The Justin Time catalogue has two Oliver Jones CDs with Dave Young on bass. The closing title, by Young and Renee Rosnes, has a special charm of its own, pairing the richness of the bass and Renee's delicate treble. *I'm All Smiles* (shades of the memorable version of the song by Hampton Hawes) is a very intimate piece of music making.                                                   **AM**

## John Young                                                                                          1922

**Serenata** Young (p); **Victor Sproles** (b); **Phil Thomas** (d). Delmark Ⓕ DD403 (42 minutes).
   Recorded 1959.

⑧ ⑧

When it comes to rhythm – where musicians place the beat to achieve maximum swing – Chicago has more in common with laid-back Kansas City than hyperactive New York. That mid-continent sense of relaxation is a hallmark of Chicago's John Young, a pianist of uncommon charm. On *I Don't Wanna Be Kissed*, he combines an infectious fingerpop groove with a light touch at the keyboard. In the mid sixties, Young cited Memphis pianist Phineas Newborn as a favourite. You can hear Newborn's influence in the dancing locked-octaves John plays with his right hand, exploring the piano's brighter sonorities (Young was born in Little Rock, not far from Memphis). There is a subtle Latin influence here too, something many Chicagoans are sensitive to; Windy City bluesmen love to mambo.

   Young's rhythm section makes a crucial contribution. Drummer Thomas often plays strong backbeats surrounded by generous amounts of space, letting the music breathe. He eases the trio into hypnotic grooves not unlike what Sun Ra's Chicago band of that time might play (Sproles, who has enviably springy time, had recorded with Ra). Thomas's pet tactics do threaten to wear themselves out, but 41 minutes worth is about right.                                                                   **KW**

## Larry Young                                                                                       1940-78

**The Art of Larry Young** Young (org); **Grant Green** (g); **Sam Rivers, Joe Henderson, Herbert Morgan** (ts); **James Spaulding** (as); **Woody Shaw, Eddie Gale, Lee Morgan** (t); **Elvin Jones, Wilson Moorman III, Jerry Thomas, Eddie Gladen** (d). Blue Note Ⓜ CDP7 99177-2 (55 minutes). Recorded 1964-9.

⑧ ⑧

Organist Larry Young was an original. Although incorporating the Hammond B-3's gospel, rock and soul traditions, this native of Newark, New Jersey, took the instrument into new territory by adapting harmonic and rhythmic concepts associated with John Coltrane. Although primarily known for his contributions to the fusion of Tony Williams's Lifetime and Miles Davis's **Bitches Brew** bands, Young's best work for Blue Note most effectively encapsulates the organist's cutting-edge jazz approach.

   The anthology's intimate duo and trio tracks are especially compelling. Indeed, the combination of Young, guitarist Grant Green and drummer Elvis Jones (momentarily on leave from Coltrane) is a dream team whose interplay on the organist's *Talkin' About J.C.* pushes neo-bop assumptions to the mainstream's margins. Young's bluesy jazz waltz, the poignant *Tyrone* with Sam Rivers's probing tenor, juxtaposes modal lines against a gospel groove simmering with a barely muted volatility that was the quintessence of Blue Note 'hip'. Also definitive is the Young-Jones analysis of the provocative yet happily inscrutable *Monk's Dream*. The hydro-plane ride across *Seven Steps to Heaven* most clearly reflects the influence of Coltrane's mid-sixties free-jazz experiments. Here, waters are set roiling by the combined drums of Wilson Moorman III and Jerry Thomas, Eddie Gale's *outré* trumpet and the saxes of James Spaulding and Herbert Morgan.

   For those interested in the early phase of Young's career, Prestige have reissued a couple of chitlin'-time albums from the dawn of the sixties, **Testifyin'** and **Groove Street**, both of which have their strictly down-here-on-the-ground charms.                                                                **CB**

## Lester Young                                                                                     1909 59

**A Lester Young Story** Young (ts, cl) with various bands including **Jones-Smith Incorporated, Count Basie Orchestra, Kansas City Six** and **Seven, Teddy Wilson, Billie Holiday**. Jazz Archives Ⓑ 157342 (67 minutes). Recorded 1936-40.

✓                                                                                                   ⑩ ④

As a single-volume anthology of Lester Young's best period this would be hard to beat. Opening with the twin masterpieces that marked his recording début in 1936 (*Shoe Shine Boy* and *Lady Be Good*), the selection includes 11 numbers by the Count Basie Band, featuring celebrated Lester Young solos (*Every Tub*, *Taxi War Dance*, *Tickle Toe*, etc.), a few pieces from the Billie Holiday sessions (*Me, Myself and I*, *If Dreams Come True*, etc.), two by the Kansas City Six (*Way Down Yonder* and *Countless Blues*) and two by the K.C. Seven (*Dickie's Dream* and *Lester Leaps In*). All these contain the most superb playing, by both Lester and his contemporaries, such as Buck Clayton, Dickie Wells, Herschel Evans and Benny Morton – not to mention Billie Holiday.

For this reason I place this CD in the 'essential' category, but it is as well to realize that most of these 22 pieces also appear on 'essential' CDs by Basie and Billie. The sound quality is also slightly odd at times, although nothing like as odd as some of the earlier vinyl editions. A few pieces seem to have been cleaned up rather zealously, with added 'presence', while others retain a generous measure of 78rpm surface noise. Nevertheless if you want an uninterrupted hour of the choicest Lester, this is the edition for you. Young fans may also want to note the very recent reissue, in the latest revival of the Commodore catalogue, of the **Lester Young/Kansas City Six/Five** sides from 1938/44 which have long been regarded as essential items in the canon of his greatest work. The catalogue number is CMD14022. **DG**

---

**Lester–Amadeus!** Young (ts, cl); with, on two tracks: **Carl 'Tatti' Smith** (t); **Count Basie** (p); **Walter Page** (b); **Jo Jones** (d); on ten tracks with the **Count Basie Orchestra** with the following collective personnel: **Buck Clayton, Ed Lewis, Bobby Moore, Harry Edison** (t); **George Hunt, Dan Minor, Dickie Wells, Benny Morton** (tb); **Earl Warren** (as, bs); **Hershel Evans** (ts); **Jack Washington** (bs); **Count Basie** (p); **Freddie Green** (g); **Walter Page** (b); **Jo Jones** (d); **Jimmy Rushing** (v); on eight tracks with the following collective personnel: **Buck Clayton** (t); **Count Basie** (p); **Freddie Green, Eddie Durham** (g); **Walter Page** (b); **Jo Jones** (d); **Helen Humes** (v). Phontastic Ⓜ CD7639 (65 minutes). Recorded 1936-8.

✓ ⑩ ❻

Some of the finest Lester Young solos will be found on this attractive CD of Swedish origin. Opening with the classic *Lady Be Good* and *Shoe Shine Boy,* from the first record date on which Young was heard solo, the mood is set for music of quite remarkable quality. Nine titles featuring Young come from a June 1937 radio broadcast from Harlem's Savoy Ballroom with the Basie band in exceptional form. The drive from the rhythm section can almost be felt as shock waves from the speakers, and through it all sails the clear-toned beauty of Lester. A further Basie title, *John's Idea,* dates from 1938 and the Famous Door; this time Young shares the solo choruses with Harry Edison. In between are eight tracks from two small group dates, the first in a studio (but later given added applause to simulate a "Spirituals to Swing" concert held in Carnegie Hall) and the final two, never previously released until the appearance of this CD, from the actual Carnegie Hall concert of December, 1938. The magic, to say nothing of the rarity value, of these tracks brushes aside any quibbles about recording quality (it must be pointed out there is some distortion from Durham's electric guitar on the Carnegie Hall tracks), and Gert Palmcrantz deserves credit for his work on transferring the music from, in some cases, badly worn acetates. **AM**

---

**The Complete Lester Young** Young (ts); **Buck Clayton** (t); **Dicky Wells** (tb); **Johnny Guarnieri, Count Basie** (p); **Freddie Green** (g); **Slam Stewart, Rodney Richardson** (b); **Big Sid Catlett, Jo Jones** (d). Mercury Ⓜ 830 920-2 (55 minutes). Recorded 1943-4.

✓ ⑨ ❽

These landmark sessions, originally produced by Harry Lim for the Keynote label, conclusively demonstrate why Young became one of jazzdom's most influential stylists. First was his then unique sound which, in comparison to his stylistic opposite Coleman Hawkins was lighter in weight, at times almost transparent; he also used far less vibrato than Hawkins. Second was his gift for creating long lyrical lines whose logic and natural swingingness were the envy of his peers. In 1944, catapulted by intermittent tenures with Count Basie and by his own recordings, Young took top honours in the tenor category of Down Beat's Readers Poll, the first of many such honours.

The initial 1943 session in this superb reissue puts Lester together with an exceptionally compatible rhythm section, Johnny Guarnieri, Slam Stewart and Big Sid Catlett. It's a simpatico-plus date as Lester employs relaxed yet inspired poignancy on standards such as *Just You, Just Me* and *Sometimes I'm Happy*. The 1944 tracks find Young at a bright, happy get-together with the cream of the Basie band heating up such riff-based lines as *Lester Leaps Again* and *Destination K.C.* Working under the title of the Kansas City Seven, with Basie appearing under the pseudonym of Prince Charming, it's a loose, swinging date with a lithe Lester only months away from his traumatic incarceration in the US Army. Here, though, all is sunshine and smiles. **CB**

---

**Blue Lester/The Immortal Lester Young** Young (ts); with a collective personnel of: **Billy Butterfield, Jesse Drakes** (t); **Jerry Elliott** (tb); **Hank D'Amico** (cl); **Johnny Guarnieri, Count Basie, Junior Mance** (p); **Dexter Hall, Freddie Green** (g); **Billy Taylor, Rodney Richardson, Leroy Jackson** (b); **Cozy Cole, Shadow Wilson, Roy Haynes** (d); on three tracks only: **Earl Warren and his Orchestra**, including: **Harry Edison** (t); **Dickie Wells** (tb); **Clyde Hart** (p). Denon/Savoy Ⓜ SV0112 (45 minutes). Recorded 1944-9.

⑥ ❻

Before these 1944 recordings, Young's post-Basie style had undergone a sea-change, possibly reflecting his initial lack of success as a free-lance. His tone became darker and the phrasing, especially at slower tempos not favoured by Basie, began to hint at the tragic depths beneath the casual exterior.

The four tracks each led by Guarnieri and with a moonlighting Count on piano reveal the incipient transformation, particularly on the ballads *Ghost of a Chance* and *These Foolish Things* (not to be confused with the superior 1945 version). But the distinction is subtle, like Lester's entire approach, and on the slow-medium *Blue Lester* and *Salute to Fats* the graceful lines disguise the undertow. Four items by his 1949 bop-oriented sextet with Mance and Haynes seem more laboured, presaging his fifties output.

Although all described as "Take 1", these are not necessarily the first recorded or first issued versions. Unusually for Denon's Savoy reissues, three tracks are appended from a mid-seventies LP with Warren fronting the full Basie band (no personnel given) in material not otherwise recorded for commercial release. Though not as notable as the currently unavailable Commodore or the Keynote sides of the period, the tracks named should be heard.                                              **BP**

---

**Lester Young Trio** Young (ts); Nat Cole (p); Buddy Rich (d); on four tracks, the following
   personnel only: **Dexter Gordon** (ts). **Harry Edison** (t); **Nat Cole** (p); probably **Red Callender** or
   **Johnny Miller** (b); **Clifford 'Juicy' Owens** (d). Verve Ⓜ 521 650-2 (61 minutes). Recorded 1943-6.

✅                                                                                        ⑧ ❽

The records Young made as a member of the Basic orchestra had more sway on saxophone players than on any body of music since the profound Coleman Hawkins influence which had guided tenor players after 1929. Young's method was the opposite of Hawk's. Whereas Hawk bustled and played with a rich romanticism, Young managed, while playing with fleet dexterity, to sound poised and dry. Even though he was capable of playing as fast as any other saxophonist, his mind moved so quickly that his solos always sounded considered and phrased like the building of Rome. His lightness of touch began to evaporate at the beginning of the forties and his work here is from the second phase of his career. His punch was not quite so feathery and world-weariness had already begun to replace the gaiety of his earlier solos.

Despite a step off the pinnacle of his earlier greatness, most of his work from 1944 to 1947, including the magnificent tracks here, was classic in every respect. The work of the trio with Cole and Rich is exquisite and in particular Young's exploration of ballads offered new signposts to players brought up under the Hawkins spell. The CD is worth acquiring for the delicious piano of Nat Cole alone, to say nothing of the lesson to be learned from Rich's restrained drumming. Every track is good and the stomping *I Want to Be Happy* shows Young to be every bit as effective on an up-tempo as on a ballad. The addition of four tracks by Young's disciple Gordon is an apparent irrelevance in the face of Young's magnificence. But, even given a particularly on-form Gordon, Nat Cole's piano playing is so good that he steals the limelight.                                                      **SV**

---

**The President Plays with the Oscar Peterson Trio** Young (ts, v); Oscar Peterson (p);
   Barney Kessel (g); Ray Brown (b); J.C. Heard (d). Verve Ⓜ 831 670-2 (63 minutes). Recorded
   1952.

✅                                                                                       ⑩ ❽

Young has by now been the subject of so much mythologizing that sometimes the actual music he created gets buried in the rush to articulate a response to the image rather than the substance. His career has been analysed from every conceivable angle and virtually every judgement has been turned on its head. Perhaps there is no overall career trajectory to follow, and we should just take every date as it comes.

That said, this 1952 session finds Mr Young in high spirits and playing with unusual clarity and firmness for the period. That he is fully engaged is evident from the first number, *Ad Lib Blues*, where he is not merely joining up his own personal clichés into a string until the solo ends, but fashioning a complete musical statement. On *Tea for Two* his sly humour surfaces in the way he reduces the already bare theme to complete nakedness, then bursts in with a powerful solo at what can confidently be called a fast tempo. On the previously unissued *These Foolish Things* he avoids comparisons with his mid-forties masterpiece for Aladdin and fashions a hauntingly simple statement where he stays close to the melody most of the way. On *I Can't Get Started* he is even better, toying with the combination of nonchalance and pain inherent in the song's lyrics. By the time the CD gets to *Stardust* the listener could be forgiven for thinking they have made it to heaven, because what Young does here is heavenly. In all this, the Peterson group do everything absolutely right.

The CD reissue contains four previously unreleased tracks, including a Young vocal on two takes of *Two to Tango*. Contrary to the rather hysterical assertions in the booklet-notes, the latter are a good jape, but nothing more. Pearl Bailey certainly didn't have to worry about the competition.             **KS**

---

**Pres and Teddy** Young (ts); Teddy Wilson (p); Gene Ramey (b); Jo Jones (d). Verve Ⓜ 831 270-2
   (43 minutes). Recorded 1956.

                                                                                         ⑨ ❽

1956 was arguably the last year that Lester Young made consistently good records. There were still outstanding moments to come, but little to match the quality of his performances on the live **In Washington** albums or the two studio sessions he recorded on consecutive days in January, **Jazz Giants** and **Pres and Teddy**. The former LP reunited him with several old friends – Roy Eldridge, Vic

Dickenson and Freddie Green as well as Wilson, Ramey and Jones – and producer Norman Granz was so delighted by Young's playing he decided to record him again the following day in a quartet setting. It was a more testing format but one which Lester Young liked and, with Wilson in vibrant form and Jones showing his customary sensitivity, the results are a joy.

There is no doubt that Young's health deteriorated in the fifties, but the changes in his playing are as much due to his stated desire to play modern. There is a harsher edge to his tone here, the phrasing can seem brusque, but the ideas are still fluent, the timing good. Listen to his attacking flair on *All of Me*, the delicacy with which he caresses the tune on *Prisoner of Love*, the surprise twists of his solo on *Taking a Chance on Love*. These are the hallmarks of a man who is not only in control of his art but still seeking to develop it. **GL**

## Webster Young

**New review**

**For Lady**  Young (c); **Paul Quinichette** (ts); **Mal Waldron** (p); **Joe Puma** (g). **Earl May** (b);
  **Ed Thigpen** (d). Prestige Ⓜ OJCCD1716-2 (43 minutes). Recorded 1957.

⑥ ❼

Webster Young appeared on a few Prestige albums around this time. He based his style very much on early fifties Miles Davis and aimed seemingly to produce a kind of wistful tenderness – there is no hint of the more aggressive musical side of Davis that by now was well documented. As the title implies, this session was intended as a tribute to Billie Holiday. All tunes were associated with her except for *The Lady*, an attractive minor-keyed original by Young himself. Songs such as *Good Morning Heartache* and even *God Bless the Child* demand that jazz soloists work hard to get much out of them. Young doesn't have quite enough going for him. Easily his best solo comes on *The Lady*. He also devises an effective arrangement for *Strange Fruit*, on which his cornet playing projects a confidence not always apparent elsewhere. Paul Quinichette usually starts well but overdoes the Lester Young mannerisms, while Puma and Waldron easily hold their own. **RA**

## Rachel Z (Nicolazzo)

**New review**

**Room of One's Own**  Nicolazzo (p, arr); **George Garzone** (ss, ts); **Regina Carter** (vn); **Tracy Wormworth**, **Charnett Moffett** (b); **Cindy Blackman**, **Terri Lyne Carrington** (d); **Mino Cinelu** (perc); wind ensemble; **Melena Herrup** (v). NYC Ⓕ 6023-2 (57 minutes). Recorded 1995.

⑧ ❾

The reason for the rather strange entry regarding Rachel Z's name is that she apparently despaired of anyone ever spelling her given name correctly so opted for something a little more zappy. Hence the Z. Leaving identity crises aside for the moment, it is pleasing to say that the music itself effortlessly transcends such mundane issues and settles into a modern groove which perhaps is most easily summed up as music written in the shade of Herbie Hancock's **Speak Like a Child**, although the string writing moves some pieces into another dimension entirely. Nicolazzo is a pianist with superb touch and lithe rhythm and a distinguished song-writer as well. Her own arrangements for the 8-strong wind ensemble are expert and evocative, supplementing each tune's own story successfully and helping the listener sink into the music's fabric (Maria Schneider is responsible for some orchestrations). All the soloing is tailored to fit the overall musical design, and each piece is very specifically written, usually to illustrate a dedicatee or illustrative story. Coleridge once mentioned the twin ideas of entertaining while instructing. Nicolazzo is perhaps attempting to adapt that tradition to her own concerns. **KS**

## Aziza Mustafa Zadeh                                            1970

**Always**  Zadeh (p, v); **John Patitucci** (b); **Dave Weckl** (d). Columbia Ⓕ 473885-2 (64 minutes).
  Recorded 1992.

⑥ ❽

Before anyone gets the wrong idea, this is not a conventional piano-and-vocals record. Zadeh is a young Azerbaijani who comes from a family of jazz musicians and who packs a significant level of intensity into her piano playing. She also tends to perform original material. Her singing, mostly a vocalese of considerable dexterity, most clearly signals the folk roots of her own country, with its long, swooping lines and use of Middle-Eastern scales. But the singing is not the centrepiece here: the piano playing is. Zadeh has a formidable technique. She hits the keyboard very hard indeed, and she is not afraid of taking the listener on extended musical flights. Her influences occasionally float very close to the surface, be they classical, folk or jazz, and in this there is the hint of a parallel with Dave Brubeck, who also wrested an original rhythmic and harmonic approach from such a combination, although the specific elements may have differed

considerably.

This is her second album (the first was a solo effort, the third a rather curious collaboration with Al DiMeola, Stanley Clarke and Bill Evans, among others) and it is currently the most fully realized expression of her talents. She could do with finding more subtlety and contrast in her attack (her rhythmic patterns are often complex but oddly static through excessive repetition) and perhaps a more varied harmonic development (there are a few too many Tyneresque vamps for my liking here), but there is no doubting her talent. She has already made a significant impact in Germany, and there is little reason why this success should not be repeated elsewhere.                **KS**

## Joe Zawinul                                                                          1932

**Zawinul**  Zawinul (kbds); **Woody Shaw, Jimmy Owens** (t); **George Davis, Hubert Laws** (f); **Earl Turbington, Wayne Shorter** (ss); **Herbie Hancock** (p); **Miroslav Vitous, Walter Booker** (b); **Joe Chambers, Billy Hart, David Lee, Jack DeJohnette** (d, perc). Atlantic Ⓜ 781579-2 (37 minutes). Recorded 1970.

✅                                                                                    ⑧ ❽

Austrian pianist Joe Zawinul, who studied at the Viennese Conservatory, brought a highly developed technique and classical background to his varied jazz endeavours. When he emigrated to the US in 1959, stints with Maynard Ferguson and Dinah Washington led to an important nine-year association with Cannonball Adderley, for whom he composed such hits as *Mercy, Mercy, Mercy*. He also participated in Miles Davis's move from straight-ahead to fusion.

In this evocative 1970 "music for two electric pianos, jazz flute, trumpet, soprano saxophone, two contrabasses and percussion," which followed on from two less certain albums for Atlantic under his own name, **The Rise & Fall of the Third Stream** and **Money in the Pocket** (recently reissued on one CD by Rhino/Atlantic) we catch a glimpse of the acoustic-electronic blends and rock rhythms that, while reflecting the experiments with Davis, would also become central to the stylistics of Weather Report, the explosive fusion unit formed by Zawinul and Wayne Shorter in the same year. Prominent among the tracks is a haunting version of the title track Zawinul penned for Davis's pivotal jazz-rock breakthrough, **In a Silent Way** (1969). There is also the stirring yet contemplative *Doctor Honoris Causa*, dedicated to Hancock on the occasion of the awarding of an honorary doctorate from Grinnell University, Hancock's alma mater. The autobiographical dimension emerges as well in *Arrival in New York*, a brief, pithy sound collage resonant with the sounds of gulls, steamship whistles and clattering subway trains.                **CB**

**New review**

**My People**  The Zawinul Syndicate: **Zawinul** (kbds, v) **Gary Poulson** (elg); **Matthew Garrison** (elb); **Paco Sery** (d); **Arto Tunboyaciyan** (v, perc). Guests: **Salif Keita, Thania Sanchez, Richard Bona, Burhan Ocal** (v); **Bolot** (v, topshur); **Cheik Tidiane Seck** (kbds); **Bob Malach** (ts); **Mike Mossman** (t, tb); **Trilok Gurtu** (perc); **Amit Chatterjee** (elg); plus others. Escapade Ⓕ ESC03651-2 (52 minutes). Recorded 1992-6.

                                                                                      ⑧ ❾

There have been more than a few routine moments in the work of the Zawinul Syndicate in recent years, but here, in his finest record since Weather Report's **Night Passage** (1980), one of the leading grandads of fusion shows that he has not become just another ordinary Joe. World music is once again the matter in hand, but this time Zawinul's range of inspirations is wider and each source is focused upon closely rather than being absorbed into a generalized ethnic sound. Zawinul has some specialized help in this, engaging the expertise of Salif Keita to portray the African branch of "my people" in *Waraya*, inviting throat-singer Bolot to represent the Eurasian brotherhood in *Ochy-Balal Pazyryk* and letting Thania Sanchez do the Latin American thing in (what else?) *Mi Gente*. Despite the guest appearances, Zawinul actually writes most of the music himself and where he hasn't, he has orchestrated. Indeed, this has been chiefly an arranging job, executed with even more flair than usual. Inevitably in a record where ensemble and lead vocals dominate there are few solo breaks, but the spirit of jazz pervades the whole project and the sampled voice of Duke Ellington, doyenne of twentieth-century musical free-thinkers, in the first track does not seem at all incongruous.                **MG**

## Denny Zeitlin

**Time Remembers One Time Once**  Zeitlin (p); **Charlie Haden** (b). ECM Ⓕ 837 020-2 (54 minutes). Recorded 1981.

                                                                                      ⑧ ❽

Zeitlin is something of a stylistic halfway-house between Bill Evans and Paul Bley. More adventurous in virtually every way than Evans, he nonetheless has a considerable amount of the clarity and corresponding angularity of the avant-garde pianist without sacrificing his natural warmth and expressivity. Since his first recordings in the early sixties, Zeitlin has pursued an independent course, and although he has combined his musical career with another career in psychiatry, he has never fallen below a very high level of performing excellence.

This album is his only one for ECM and benefits from the towering presence of bassist Haden, who contributes two eloquent compositions to the proceedings as well as his persuasive bass playing. For a great deal of the time, Zeitlin is happy to provide a backdrop for Haden to strike out strongly over, and it is one of the great pleasures of this album to hear Haden be so much to the fore on a date. The obvious comparison is with Haden's duets with Hampton Hawes, and there is a version of *As Long as There's Music* here which provides a fascinating contrast to the earlier one with Hawes. This is an absorbing and beautiful album from two highly intelligent and talented musicians.　　　**KS**

## Attila Zoller　　　1927

**Overcome**　Zoller (g); Kirk Lightsey (p); Michael Formanek (b); Daniel Humair (d). Enja Ⓕ 5053-2 (45 minutes). Recorded 1986.

⑥ ❻

Zoller, a Hungarian guitarist who has been in the vanguard of the European scene since the fifties (he played with Jutta Hipp, for example, before she went off to New York), has spent the last decade making records for the German label, Enja. This is one of the few to make it onto CD so far (the new and rather disappointing **When It's Time**, featuring Lee Konitz and Larry Willis, is another), so although it is arguable that this is not his best Enja album, it will have to do for now.

The album was recorded live at the Leverkusen Jazz Festival, and that fact points to its deficiencies as well as to its strengths. The recorded sound, for one thing, is rather hollow and lacking in presence, which does not help Zoller to cut through in the comfort of your living room. The tracks are without exception over ten minutes long, so there are the occasional boring bits upon which to practice one's stoicism. All that aside, Zoller and Lightsey were very much in touch musically on this occasion, and careful listening will bring much of interest and pleasure to your ear. Zoller manages to combine both European and American guitar traditions in his approach, thereby avoiding falling into the stereotyped phrases many guitarists find it impossible to refrain from. Drummer Humair is his usual strong, flexible self.　　　**KS**

## John Zorn　　　1953

**Cobra**　Zorn (prompter); Jim Staley, J.A. Deane (tb); Anthony Coleman, Wayne Horvitz, David Weinstein (kbds); Guy Klucevsek (acc); Carol Emanuel, Zeena Parkins (hp); Bill Frisell (g); Arto Lindsay (g, v); Elliott Sharp (g, b, v); Bob James (tapes); Christian Marclay (tt); Bobby Previte (perc). hatART Ⓕ 2-6040 (two discs: 113 minutes). Recorded 1985/6.

⑧ ❽

Zorn has said he is more interested in how things work than how they sound. His composition *Cobra* makes the point. It is a non-competitive 'game' for improvisers, the object of which is to create a piece of music, using rules which encourage abrupt and frequent change – the deliberate discontinuity of the forties cartoon music he loves. There is no score, but a set of instructions. *Cobra* is designed so each musician periodically directs the flow of the entire unit, using various 'calls' to determine who plays when, or the tactics improvisers might use: for instance, one call requires the music to change but the players to stay the same; another demands the opposite. Players use hand signals to communicate their desires to a prompter, who uses cue cards to direct the band. Typically, change is instant and abrupt – most calls make a clean break with what went before.

These live and studio versions are pretty good, achieving their own choppy flow. But *Cobra* is a spectator sport as well as a musical event; the visual element makes it easier to follow. Since January 1992 there have been monthly performances at New York's Knitting Factory, making *Cobra* the first piece of music from New York's downtown scene to become genuinely shared repertoire. There has been a recent release on Avant of a Japanese performance from 1994 whch has a decidedly novel angle on the piece.　　　**KW**

**Spy vs. Spy**　Zorn, Tim Berne (as); Mark Dresser (b); Joey Baron, Michael Vatchér (d). Elektra/Musician Ⓕ 960844-2 (41 minutes). Recorded 1988.

✓　　　⑩ ❽

The cover of this disc says the musicians listed above "play the music of Ornette Coleman". Do they? They attack 17 of his themes, in versions ranging in length from barely a minute to nearly five, subjected to a rhythmic context unrecognizable to that of the composer's. There are audible debts to Ornette: the instrumental configuration is a kind of double trio balancing on the fulcrum of Dresser's heroic bass (a reference to **Free Jazz** and classic **Prime Time**?); Berne and Zorn's sparring benefits from the lessons of Coleman and Cherry; there are echoes of Ornette's wail everywhere. Ultimately, the warmth, wit and passion of the originals are replaced by the regimen of hard-core rock speed, brevity, intensity, noise. Although not an intentional distortion (they are faithful to the themes), the rearrangements are drastic. But they are arranged; you can hear it in the consistent theme/simultaneous solos/theme format; the alto's careful articulation; how the drums phrase within the themes of *Enfant* and *Peace Warrior*; how the altos hold the theme of *Space Church* in strict tempo while the background explodes; the fragments of *Blues Connotation* within the solos. It is sometimes painful, and other times exhilarating, to hear the buoyant, basically optimistic themes fight to retain their character within such a barrage. Yet what Zorn does is not all that far, conceptually at least, from bebop's break with swing, or Ornette's break with bebop.            **AL**

---

**New review**
**Masada Two** Zorn (as); **Dave Douglas** (t); **Greg Cohen** (b); **Joey Baron** (d). DIW Ⓕ 889
(60 minutes). Recorded 1994.

⑨  ❽

It is perhaps significant that the nearest Zorn has come to the spirit of Ornette Coleman's music is with material of his own. A series of recordings made under the Masada banner in the mid nineties use Zorn's own compositions, deliver them with Colemanesque cadence and offer a trenchant examination of the material in a manner that recalls the Atlantic quartets of 35 years earlier. More than any previous recordings, the Masadas show Zorn to be as concerned with the finished product as he is with the act of building it. Earlier works had seemed to parody the foibles and mannerisms of free jazz, whereas the music on this series elicits a response from the four musicians that speaks of an awareness of the outcome. Zorn has been selective in his choice of sidemen and Douglas's response is ideal. Both horns enjoy a bass player sensitive to open space and a drummer careful to contain the more extrovert elements. Personally, Zorn plays his full hand throughout; at times restlessly lyrical, at others dabbling in minor explosions and sometimes playing with almost Ellingtonian grace. He does not mince musical words and **Masada Two** is almost an arbitrary choice in a large ongoing series that could be considered another major turning point in his career.            **BMcR**

# Bojan Zulfikarpasic

---

**New review**
**Yopla!** Zulfikarpasic (p, bgo); **Julien Lourau** (ts, ss, bs); **Marc Buronfosse** (b); **Francois Merville** (d);
**Kudsi Erguner** (ney). Label Bleu Ⓕ LBLC6590 HM83 (50 minutes). Recorded 1995.

⑦  ❿

Blindfolded, you might identify Lourau's composition *Un Demi-Porc et Deux Caisses de Bière* as John Zorn's group Masada with a pianist sitting in: it has the same Eastern European dance inside it, a similar frisky saxophone and hand-drumming energy over appropriate scales. Unlike Masada, those aren't the only scales to be heard on the record. Bojan Z (as the cover calls him), a Macedonian musician, goes in many different directions: he has a pop sensibility (*Zajdi, Zajdi*, a traditional song of his home country, gets a pastel bridge and a Herbie Hancock funk touch), as well as an affinity for the galloping, broken-metre style in which Myra Melford works. There are a few soprano saxophone features using a tired soft-jazz mood, but the group – all members contribute compositions – possesses real sensitivity, and the excellent rhythm section (Buronfosse's bass is well miked, and he plays it hard) usually breaks through what saccharine there is.            **BR**

Information

# Manufacturers and distributors

Entries are listed as follows: **Manufacturer** or **Label** – UK Distributor

**33 Records** New Note
**A&M** PolyGram Record Operations
**Ace** Complete Record Company
**ACT** New Note
**Affinity** Charly
**Ahum** New Note
**Amadeo** PolyGram Record Operations
**Antilles** PolyGram Record Operations
**Arabesque** New Note
**ASV** Koch
**Atlantic** Warner Music
**Avant** Harmonia Mundi
**Azure** Chris Wellard
**B&W** New Note
**Babel** Harmonia Mundi
**Bellaphon** New Note
**Biograph** Direct
**Black & Blue** Discovery Imports
**Black Lion** Koch
**Black Saint** Harmonia Mundi
**Blue Moon** New Note
**Blue Note** EMI
**Bluebell** Complete Record Company
**Bluebird** BMG
**Calligraph** New Note
**Candid** Direct
**Capitol** EMI
**Caprice** Complete Record Company
**Castle** BMG
**CBS** Sony Music Operations
**Challenge** Direct
**Charly** Charly
**Chesky** Complete Record Company
**Chess** New Note
**Chief** Cadillac
**Chronoscope** Harmonia Mundi
**Classics** Discovery
**Claves** Complete Record Company
**CMP** BMG
**Columbia** Sony Music Operations
**Commodore** New Note
**Concord** New Note
**Conifer** BMG
**Contemporary** Complete Record Company
**Cream** New Note
**Criss Cross** Vital
**CTI** Sony Music Operations
**Delmark** Direct
**Delos** BMG
**Denon** Denon
**DGG** PolyGram Record Operations
**Discovery** Warner Music
**DIW** Harmonia Mundi
**Dormouse** BMG
**Dreyfus** New Note
**DRG** New Note
**East West** Warner Music
**ECM** New Note
**Elektra** Warner Music
**EmArcy** PolyGram Record Operations
**EMI** EMI

**Enja** New Note
**Epic** Sony Music Operations
**Epicure** Sony Music Operations
**ESP** New Note
**Europe 1** Discovery Imports
**Evidence** Harmonia Mundi
**Fantasy** Complete Record Company
**Flapper** Pinnacle
**FMP** Cadillac
**Four Leaf Clover** Cadillac
**Freelance** Harmonia Mundi
**Fresh Sounds** Charly
**Fret** New Note
**Future Music** Harmonia Mundi
**Geffen** BMG
**Go Jazz** New Note
**Good Time Jazz** Complete Record Company
**Gramavision** Vital
**GRP** New Note
**hatART** Harmonia Mundi
**Hep** New Note
**Horatio Nelson** New Note
**Hot House** Harmonia Mundi
**Impulse!** New Note
**In & Out** Vital
**Intuition** New Note
**Island** Polygram Record Services
**ITM** Koch
**Jass** Direct
**Jazz City** New Note
**Jazz House** New Note
**JMS** New Note
**JMT** PolyGram Record Operations
**JSP** Direct
**Jukebox Lil** Chris Wellard
**Justice** Koch
**Justin Time** Harmonia Mundi
**JVC** New Note
**King** Koch
**Konnex** New Note
**Label Bleu** New Note
**Lake** Jazz Music
**Landmark** New Note
**Largo** Complete Record Company
**Laserlight** Target
**leJazz** Charly
**Leo** Cadillac
**Limelight** PolyGram Record Operations
**Linn** PolyGram Record Operations
**Living Era** Koch
**Living Music** New Note
**LRC** New Note
**Mastermix** New Note
**MCA** BMG
**Memoir** Target
**Mercury** PolyGram Record Operations
**Messidor** Koch
**Milan** BMG
**Milestone** Complete Record Company
**Minor Music** Charly
**Mode** Harmonia Mundi
**MoJazz** PolyGram Record Operations

**Mole Jazz** Harmonia Mundi
**MRC** PolyGram Record Operations
**Muse** New Note
**Music & Arts** Harmonia Mundi
**Musidisc** Harmonia Mundi
**MusicMasters** Nimbus
**Natasha Imports** Direct
**New World** Harmonia Mundi
**Novus** BMG
**OJC** Complete Record Company
**Pablo** Complete Record Company
**Pacific** EMI
**Paddlewheel** New Note
**Philips** PolyGram Record Operations
**Phontastic** Chris Wellard
**Polydor** PolyGram Record Operations
**PolyGram** PolyGram Record Operations
**Prestige** Complete Record Company
**QWest** Warner Music
**RCA Victor** BMG
**Red** Harmonia Mundi
**Reservoir** Cadillac
**Retrieval** Direct
**Riverside** Complete Record Company
**Roulette** EMI
**Rounder** Direct
**Rykodisc** Vital
**Sackville** Spotlite
**Savoy** Conifer
**Sonet** PolyGram Record Operations
**Soul Note** Harmonia Mundi
**Stash** Direct
**SteepleChase** Discovery Imports
**Strata East** New Note
**Sunnyside** New Note
**Tall Poppies** Complete Record Company
**TCB** New Note
**Telarc Jazz** BMG
**Three Line Whip** New Note
**Timeless** New Note
**Totem** New Note
**Triloka** New Note
**Vanguard** Complete Record Company
**VeraBra** New Note
**Verve** PolyGram Record Operations
**Virgin** EMI
**Vintage Jazz Classics** Direct
**Viper's Nest** Direct
**Vogue** BMG
**Warner Bros** Warner Music
**Watt** New Note
**World Circuit** New Note
**World Pacific** EMI
**Yazoo** Koch

For additional information on Manufacturers and distributors, refer to the Label distribution directory published in *Gramophone*.

# UK distributors' names and addresses

**BMG UK**
Lyng Lane, West Bromwich,
West Midlands B70 7ST
Telephone 0121-500 5545 Fax 0121-553 6880

**Cadillac Distribution**
61-71 Collier Street, London N1 9DF
Telephone 0171-278 7391 Fax 0171-278 7394

**Charly Records**
156-166 Ilderton Road, London SE15 1NT
Telephone 0171-639 8603 Fax 0171-639 2532

**The Complete Record Company**
12 Pepys Court, 84 The Chase,
London SW4 0NF
Telephone 0171-498 9666 Fax 0171- 498 1828

**Direct Distribution**
50 Stroud Green Road, London N4 3EF
Telephone 0171-281 3465 Fax 0171-281 5671

**Discovery Imports**
The Old Church Mission Room, King's Corner,
Pewsey, Wiltshire SN9 5BS
Telephone 01672 63931 Fax 01672 63934

**EMI Sales and Distribution Centre**
Hermes Close, Tachbrook Park,
Leamington Spa, Warwickshire CV34 6RP
Telephone 01926 888888 Fax 0181-479 5992

**Harmonia Mundi**
19-21 Nile Street, London N1 7LL
Telephone 0171-253 0863 Fax 0171-253 3237

**Koch International**
24 Concord Road, London W3 0TH
Telephone 0181-992 7177 Fax 0181-896 0817

**New Note**
Unit 2, Orpington Trading Estate, Sevenoaks Way,
St Mary Cray, Orpington, Kent BR5 3SR
Telephone 01689 877884 Fax 01689 877891

**Nimbus Records**
Wyastone Leys, Monmouth, Gwent NP5 3SR
Telephone 01600 890682 Fax 01600 890779

**Pinnacle Records**
Electron House, Cray Avenue, St Mary Cray,
Orpington, Kent BR5 3RJ
Telephone 016898 70622 Fax 016898 78269

**PolyGram Record Operations**
PO Box 36, Clyde Works, Grove Road, Romford,
Essex RM6 4QR
Telephone 0181-590 6044 Fax 0181-597 1011

**Select Music and Video Distribution**
34a Holmethorpe Avenue, Holmethorpe Estate,
Redhill, Surrey RH1 2NN
Telephone 01737 760020 Fax 01737 766316

**Sony Music Operations**
Rabans Lane, Aylesbury, Buckinghamshire
HP19 3RT Telephone 01296 395151 Fax 01296 81009

**Target Records**
23 Gardner Industrial Estate, Kent House Lane,
Beckenham Lane, Kent BR3 1QZ
Telephone 0181-778 4040 Fax 0181-676 9949

**Vital Distribution**
Portland House, 22-24 Portland Square, Bristol,
Avon BS2 8RZ
Telephone 0117-944 6777 Fax 0117-944 6888

**Warner Music (UK) Distribution**
PO Box 59, Alperton Lane, Alperton, Middlesex
HA0 1FJ
Telephone 0181-998 8844 Fax 0181-998 3429

**Chris Wellard, Independent Record Sales**
110 Eltham Hill, London SE9 5EF
Telephone 0181-850 3161 Fax 0181-294 2129

# Specialist dealers and Mail order services

**Acorn Music**
PO Box 17, Sidmouth, Devon EX10 9EH
Telephone 01395 578 145

**ACTA**
28 Aylmer Road, London W12 9LQ
Telephone 0181-740 1349 (Mail order only)

**Arcade Music**
13-14 Grand Arcade, Tally-Ho Corner, Finchley,
London N12 0EH Telephone 0181-445 6369

**Coda**
Unit 15, Waverley Shopping Centre, Princes Street,
Edinburgh EH2 2EH Telephone 0131-557 4694

**Collectors Items**
121 Hersham Road, Walton on Thames, Surrey
KT12 3BX Telephone 01932 242862

**Crazy Jazz**
5 Prospect Road, Cheshunt, Hertfordshire EN8
9QX Telephone 01992 625436

**Decoy Records**
30 Deansgate, Manchester, Lancashire M3 1RH
Telephone 0161-832 0183

**Farringdons Records**
64-72 Leadenhall Market, London EC3V 1LT
Telephone 0171-623 9605

**Farringdons Records**
Royal Festival Hall, South Bank Centre, London
SE1 8XX Telephone 0171-620 0198

**Fopp**
13 McCombies Court, Aberdeen AB1 1AW
Telephone 01224 625052

**Fopp**
55 Cockburn Street, Edinburgh EH1 1BS
Telephone 0131-220 0133

**Fopp**
358 Byres Road, Hillhead, Glasgow G12 4EQ
Telephone 0141-357 0774

**Fopp**
110 Regent Street, Leamington Spa CV32 4NR
Telephone 01926 425443

**Fopp**
40 Division Street, Sheffield S1 4GS
Telephone 01224 757585

**Garon Records**
70 King Street, Cambridge,
CB1 1LN
Telephone 01223 62086

**Good Price Jazz**
1 St James Close, Littleworth, Norton, Worcester,
WR5 2QF Telephone 01905 619649

**Harveys**
5 Church Street, Chatham ME4 4BS
Telephone 01634 827694

**HMV**
129 Princes Street, Edinburgh EH2 4AH
Telephone 0131-226 3466

**HMV**
150 Oxford Street, London W1N 0DJ
Telephone 0171-631 3423

**HMV**
363 Oxford Street, London W1R 2BJ
Telephone 0171-629 1240

**HMV**
90-110 Market Street, Manchester M1 1PD
Telephone 0161-834 8550

**Honest Jon's**
276 Portobello Road, London W19 5TE
Telephone 0181-969 9822

**James Asman**
23a New Row, St Martins Lane, London WC2
Telephone 0171-240 1380

**Jazz 'n' Blues Records**
7 Conesford Drive, Norwich NR1 2BB
Telephone 01603 467777

**Jazz FM Music Store**
Freepost TK1833, PO Box 123, Brentford, Essex
TW8 OBR
Telephone 0181-232 1212 (Mail order only)

**Jazz Music**
Glenview, Moylegrove, Cardigan, Dyfed
SA43 3BW
Telephone 01239 881278

**Jazzwise Publications**
2b Gleneagle Mews, London SW16 6AE
Telephone 0181- 769 7725

**Jelly Roll Records**
Pentwyn House, South View, Blackwood, Gwent
NP2 1HW Telephone 01495 225530

**Jumbo Records**
5/6 St John's Centre, Leeds LS2 8LQ
Telephone 0113 245 5570

**Just Jazz**
271 Peterborough Road, Farcett, Peterborough
PE7 3BW Telephone 01733 347905

**Mainly Big Bands**
21b Kings Road, Sutton Coldfield, West Midlands
B73 5AB Telephone 0121-355 0426

**Mole Jazz**
311 Grays Inn Road, London WC1X 8PX
Telephone 0171-278 8623

**Montpellier Records**
7 The Courtyard, Montpellier Street, Cheltenham,
Gloucestershire Telephone 01242 222009

**Mr Bongo**
Latin Record Centre, 9 Berwick Street, London W1
Telephone 0171-287 1887

**Music Box**
5 Kings Walk, Guildhall Street, Grantham,
Lincolnshire NG31 6NL Telephone 01476 72151

**Music Matters**
11 Broad Street, Bath, Avon BA1 5LJ
Telephone 01225 427494

**Presto Music**
23 Portland Street, Leamington Spa, Warwickshire
CV32 5EZ Telephone 01926 334834

**RAD Jazz**
Unit 3d, New Exchange Buildings, Queen's Square,
Middlesborough, Cleveland TS2 1AA
Telephone 01642 231352

**Rays Jazz Shop Ltd**
180 Shaftesbury Avenue, London WC2
Telephone 0171-240 3969

**Recommended Records**
387 Wandsworth Road, London SW8 2JL
Telephone 0171-622 8834

**The Record Centre**
45/46 Loveday Street, Birmingham B4 6NR
Telephone 0121-359 7399

**Record House**
84 Sycamore Road, Amersham, Buckinghamshire
HP6 5DR Telephone 01494 433311

**Red Lick Records**
PO Box 3, Porthmadog, Gwynedd LL48 6AQ
Telephone 01766 770990

**Ron's Jazz Services**
PO Box 818, Oxford
Telephone 01865 724880 (Mail order only)

**Sound Barrier**
24 Tunsgate, Guildford, Surrey GU1 3QS
Telephone 01483 300947

**Spiller's Records**
36 The Hayes, Cardiff CF1 2AJ
Telephone 01222 224905

**Station Street Jazz**
119 Station Street, Burton on Trent DE14 1BC
Telephone 01283 516020

**Teleskill Ltd**
3-4 Market Street, St Peter Port, Guernsey, Channel
Islands Telephone 01481 722323

**Tower Records**
217-221 Argyle Street, Glasgow G2 8DL
Telephone 0141-204 2500

**Tower Records**
1 Piccadilly Circus, London W1R 8TR
Telephone 0171-439 2500

**Tower Records**
62-64 Kensington High Street, London NW4 3FB
Telephone 0171-938 3511

**Trax Music**
59 High Street, Christchurch, Dorset BH23 1AS
Telephone 01202 499629

**Virgin Megastore**
527 Oxford Street, London W1R 1DD
Telephone 0171-491 8582

**Virgin Megastore**
14-16 Oxford Street, London W1R 7DD
Telephone 0171-580 5822/0171-631 1234

**Way Ahead**
47 Sadlergate, Derby DE1 3NQ
Telephone 01332 346 808

**J G Windows Ltd**
1-7 Central Arcade, Newcastle-upon-Tyne, Tyne &
Wear NE1 5BP Telephone 0191-232 1356

**The Woods**
12 The Arcade, Bognor Regis, West Sussex
PO21 1LH Telephone 01243 827712

**X Records**
44 Bridge Street, Bolton BL1 2EG
Telephone 01204 524 018

## Second hand specialists

**Ben's Collectors Records**
101 West Street, Farnham, Surrey GU9 7NS
Telephone 01252 734409

**Mole Jazz**
311 Grays Inn Road, London, WC1X 8PX
Telephone 0171-278 8623

**Blake Head Record Shop**
89 Micklegate, York, North Yorkshire YO1 1NA
Telephone 01904 625482

**Garon Records**
65-66 The Covered Market, Oxford, Oxfordshire
OX1 3DX Telephone 01865 246887

**Rays Jazz Shop Ltd**
180 Shaftesbury Avenue, London WC2
Telephone 0171-240 3969

**The Record Centre**
45/46 Loveday Street, Birmingham B4 6NR
Telephone 0121-359 7399

**Station Street Jazz**
119 Station Street, Burton on Trent DE14 1BC
Telephone 01283 516020

**The 78 Record Exchange**
9 Lower Hillgate, Stockport, Cheshire SK1 1JQ

Further information on local retailers who stock Jazz
recordings is available in the *Gramophone Blue Riband*
guide, published annually. For the location of your
nearest local branch of the major retailers contact the
following:
Andy's Records Telephone 01284 756600
HMV Telephone 0171-439 2112
Music and Video Club Telephone 0181-424 0101
Tower Records Telephone 0171-938 3625
Virgin/Our Price Telephone 0181-400 4000
WH Smith Telephone 01793 616161

# Index

656

663

664

668

669